W. H. AUDEN

PROSE

VOLUME IV: 1956–1962

THE COMPLETE
WORKS OF

W. H. AUDEN

POEMS

PLAYS (WITH CHRISTOPHER ISHERWOOD)

LIBRETTI (WITH CHESTER KALLMAN)

PROSE

W. H. AUDEN

PROSE

VOLUME IV

□

1956–1962

EDITED BY

Edward Mendelson

PRINCETON UNIVERSITY
PRESS

Published by Princeton University Press, 41 William Street,
Princeton, New Jersey, 08540

Library of Congress Catalog Card Number 2007920515
ISBN-13: 978-0-691-14755-0
This book has been composed in New Baskerville

Printed on acid-free paper. ∞
press.princeton.edu

Printed in the United States of America

2 4 6 8 10 9 7 5 3 1

CONTENTS

THE DYER'S HAND

APPENDICES

TEXTUAL NOTES

PREFACE

THIS volume, the sixth to be published in a complete edition of Auden's works, includes the essays, reviews, and other prose that he published or prepared for publication from 1956, when he was elected Professor of Poetry at Oxford, through the end of 1962, shortly after the publication of *The Dyer's Hand*. The remaining volumes in the edition will include Auden's prose through 1973 and his complete poems. The five volumes in the edition already published contain his complete plays, libretti, and other dramatic writings, and his prose works and travel books written from 1926 through 1955. The texts throughout this edition are, wherever possible, newly edited from Auden's manuscripts, and the notes report variant readings from all published editions.

ACKNOWLEDGEMENTS

THE TEXT and notes in this volume have benefitted from the learning and intelligence of John Fuller, Nicholas Jenkins, J. D. McClatchy, Barbara Thimm, and many other friends and colleagues. The entire edition continues to be based ultimately on years of research by B. C. Bloomfield, followed by many more years of his advice. The Hellen Plummer Foundation gave generous support for the preparation of this volume.

For help with major and minor problems I am grateful to the late Alan Ansen, Jacques Barzun, George Bradley, John Bodley, Katherine Bucknell, Thekla Clark, Kathy Eden, Valerie Eliot, the late Orlan Fox, the late J. G. Griffith, Alan Jacobs, Samuel Hynes, Sir Frank Kermode, Arthur Krystal, Alexander McCall Smith, and Gareth Williams.

Much of my work on this volume was conducted in the generous company of librarians and curators. I am indebted above all to Isaac Gewirtz, Stephen Crook, and Philip Milito at the Henry W. and Albert A. Berg Collection of the New York Public Library; the curators and staff of all the many departments of the Columbia University Library; Stephen Enniss, David Faulds, and Kevin Young at the Emory University Library; and the expert staff of the BBC Written Archives Centre. I am grateful for courtesies received from librarians and curators at the American Academy of Arts and Letters, the Library of Congress, the Museum of Television and Radio, the New York Public Library Manuscripts and Archives Division, the Bodleian Library, Edinburgh University Library, Exeter College Library, Harvard College Library, the Library of the University of Massachusetts at Amherst, the University of Michigan Library, the University of Minnesota Library, New York University Library, Northwestern University Library, Princeton University Library, Syracuse University Library, the Harry Ransom Center at the University of Texas at Austin, the University of Virginia Library, and the Yale University Library. I am grateful also to the Vice-Chancellor's Office at the University of Oxford and to archivists of the Columbia Broadcasting System, the National Broadcasting Company, and the Metropolitan Opera.

Auden's readers will share my continuing gratitude to Tracy Baldwin and Jan Lilly for the clarity and elegance of the design of this edition and to Princeton University Press for the intelligence and care with which it has published this and all previous volumes.

INTRODUCTION

In 1956 Auden began his five-year term as Professor of Poetry at Oxford. His duties were minimal—three lectures each year and a public oration every second year—but his highly publicized return to the university where he had been an undergraduate in the 1920s had an effect on him that unsettled his whole sense of himself and his career. He lived and worked during these five years with a profound new sense of menace and dread, as if he were subject to judgement by a censorious and unforgiving eye. Though he knew his mood had been provoked by inner psychological causes, not external and objective ones, his sense of dread at an imaginary threat was stronger than any he had felt at any real one. His mood lightened over the years of his professorship, but he was unable to escape it until after his term of appointment ended in 1961. The essays and lectures he wrote during these years were more urbane and accessible than anything in his earlier prose, yet they contain, hidden beneath their polished surfaces, some of his darkest explorations of responsibility and guilt. His poems from this same period include some of his deepest meditations on the deceptive powers of poetic language.

The Professor of Poetry at Oxford is the world's only academic chair chosen by an election. Every Oxford M.A. is eligible to vote but must vote in person in Oxford. (The Master of Arts degree is granted on application to any Oxford Bachelor of Arts, seven years after he or she first entered the university.) In the summer of 1955 Enid Starkie, Reader in French at Somerville College and a tireless academic politician, asked Auden to stand for election as successor to his friend Cecil Day-Lewis, who was nearing the end of his five-year term. Auden at first refused. "I am an American citizen," he wrote to Starkie. "Even if the statutes do not automatically exclude me, this would be a fatal handicap to any election." The professorship had always required three annual lectures, one each term; Auden assumed he would be expected to live in England during the months when he normally lived in New York, and this was financially impossible for him. "The winter months are those in which I earn enough dollars to allow me to live here [Ischia] in the summer and devote myself to the unprofitable occupation of writing poetry. I do not see any way in which I could earn the equivalent if I had to reside in England during that period."

When Starkie persisted, Auden answered that "the fit person for the Chair is Robert Graves", but he added that Starkie's "continued interest on my behalf is weakening my reluctance." In November 1955 he agreed to stand for election, and Starkie began to gather support from her colleagues. Auden wrote only half-jokingly to his friend Professor E. R. Dodds: "I must frankly admit that I should like the honor . . . and, should it come to an election, please vote for me, and remind all the elderly clergy from Magdalen you meet that I'm a good little American Anglican." By tradition, however, the candidates left electioneering to their supporters, who campaigned mostly in junior and senior common rooms.

Auden's rivals were the Shakespearean scholar G. Wilson Knight and the diplomat Sir Harold Nicolson, a literary amateur who had written biographies of Byron, Tennyson, and Swinburne. Wilson Knight's visionary approach to Shakespeare was too eccentric to win him wide support, so Nicolson became the favorite of those who disliked the prospect of an American citizen in the chair, and especially of those who despised Auden for having decamped to America in 1939. The undergraduates had no vote but vocally favored Auden in what they regarded as a contest between cosmopolitan intelligence and insular tradition. One day before the election *The Times* reported: "An unprecedented campaign on behalf of the three candidates . . . has been conducted by their supporters, and Mr Auden is now regarded as a firm favourite." At Convocation on 9 February 1956 Auden won with 216 votes against Nicolson's 192 and Wilson Knight's 91. Auden wrote to Starkie: "*Entre nous*, I'm surprised that the anti-Americans didn't have the political sense to put up a really distinguished academic scholar, for, if they had, I should immediately have withdrawn."

His earlier reluctance now re-emerged as something close to terror. He was returning to Oxford as Professor Auden, but he knew he would be facing learned dons who had voted against him, who remembered that he had finished with a third-class degree, and who had never forgiven him for having left England. His inaugural was scheduled for 11 June 1956. On 8 May he wrote to Stephen Spender:

> I have been discovering surprising things about myself in relation to England and Oxford in particular while working on my inaugural lecture. Fits of real blind sweating panic during which a printed sentence makes no sense and I do not take in what people say to me. Ça passe, I hope. Why are the English so terrifying?

When he arrived in Oxford at the end of May he said to an interviewer: "It is the fear you feel when you go back to a place where you spent some of your youth, and all sorts of things from your youth come up at you."

He devised his lecture, titled "Making, Knowing and Judging", as a spell to ward off enmity. It was the most effective rhetorical performance of his career. Addressing the packed Sheldonian Theatre, he began by declaring his inadequacy for his task:

> Even the greatest of that long line of scholars and poets who have held this chair before me—when I recall the names of some, I am filled with

fear and trembling—must have asked themselves: "What *is* a Professor of Poetry? How can Poetry be *professed*?"

I can imagine one possible answer, though unfortunately it is not the right one. I should be feeling less uneasy at this moment than I do, if the duties of the Professor of Poetry were to produce, as occasion should demand, an epithalamium for the nuptials of a Reader in Romance Languages, an elegy on a deceased Canon of Christ Church, a May-day Masque for Somerville or an election ballad for his successor. I should at least be working in the medium to which I am accustomed.

But these are not his duties. His primary duty is to give lectures— which presupposes that he knows something which his audience does not. You have chosen for your new Professor someone who has no more right to the learned garb he is wearing than he would have to a clerical collar. One of his secondary duties is to deliver every other year an oration in Latin. You have chosen a barbarian who cannot write in that tongue and does not know how to pronounce it. . . .

But it is my primary duty which I must attempt to do this afternoon. If I am in any way to deserve your extraordinary choice for what one of the noblest and most learned of my predecessors [W. P. Ker] so aptly called *The Siege Perilous*, then I must find some topic about which I cannot help knowing something simply because I have written some poems, and, for an inaugural lecture, this topic should be of general and, if possible, central concern to the verbal Art of Numbers.

The topic he had found, he continued, was the critic within the mind of every poet whose sole task is to judge the poet's own work. Auden's unspoken purpose in reporting the judgements of this critic from within was to disarm the judgements of the critics from without.

Anyone who writes poetry ought to have something to say about this critic who is only interested in one author and only concerned with works that do not yet exist. To distinguish him from the critic who is concerned with the already existing works of others, let us call him the Censor.

How does the Censor get his education? How does his attitude towards the literature of the past differ from that of the scholarly critic? If a poet should take to writing criticism, what help to him in that activity are the experiences of his Censor? Is there any truth in Dryden's statement: "Poets themselves are the most proper, though not, I conclude, the only critics"?

In trying to answer these questions, I shall be compelled, from time to time, to give autobiographical illustrations. This is regrettable but unavoidable. I have no other guinea pig.

The lecture then described the growth of a poet's mind through examples from his adolescence and observations about poets in general. He makes no excuses for the errors and absurdities of his younger self, but presents them as the inevitable missteps of youth:

> Presently the curtain rises on a scene rather like the finale to Act II of *Die Meistersinger*. Let us call it The Gathering of the Apprentices. The apprentices gather together from all over and discover that they are a new generation; somebody shouts the word "modern" and the riot is on.

This scene prompts the lecturer to pay homage to his audience: "Really, how do the dons stand it, for I'm sure this scene repeats itself year after year. When I recall the kindness of my tutors, the patience with which they listened, the courtesy with which they hid their boredom, I am overwhelmed by their sheer goodness." Shortly afterward, Auden defends his listeners against Yeats's poem "The Scholars", in which the poems that young poets "Rhymed out in love's despair" are soberly edited by "Old, learned, respectable bald heads":

> Ignoring the obvious libel—that all dons are bald and respectable—the sentiments are still nonsense. Edit indeed! Thank God they do. If it had not been for scholars working themselves blind copying and collating manuscripts, how many poems would be unavailable, including those of Catullus, and how many others full of lines that made no sense? . . . Even a young poet knows or very soon will realize that, but for scholars, he would be at the mercy of the literary taste of a past generation, since, once a book has gone out of print and been forgotten, only the scholar with his unselfish courage to read the unreadable will retrieve the rare prize. How much Donne, even, would he have read, had it not been for Professor Grierson? What would he know of Clare or Barnes or Christopher Smart but for Messrs Blunden, Grigson, Force Stead and Bond?

Auden waited until halfway through his lecture before he claimed any merit for poets and critics, and when he did so, he claimed mostly the virtues of modesty. "Whatever his defects, a poet at least thinks a poem more important than anything which can be said about it"; furthermore, when reading a poem by another poet, "he would rather it were good than bad", and "the last thing he wants is that it should be like one of his own". A poet's general statements about poetry are less likely to be valuable than his appreciations of individual poems, but they may be illuminating about the poet who makes them:

> I am always interested in hearing what a poet has to say about the nature of poetry, though I do not take it too seriously. As objective statements his definitions are never accurate, never complete and always one-sided. Not one would stand up under a rigorous analysis. In unkind moments one is almost tempted to think that all they are really saying is: "Read

me. Don't read the other fellows." But, taken as critical admonitions addressed by his Censor to the poet himself, there is generally something to be learned from them.

He then offered "some general statements of my own", adding, "I hope they are not nonsense, but I cannot be sure." He began by borrowing from Coleridge's *Biographia Literaria* the terms Primary and Secondary Imagination while ignoring Coleridge's meanings for them. The Primary Imagination, as Auden described it, is concerned only "with sacred beings and sacred events". It cannot choose what is sacred, nor whether or not to respond to it. "The sacred is that to which it is obliged to respond; the profane is that to which it cannot respond and therefore does not know." The Primary Imagination responds to sacred beings with awe:

> This awe may vary greatly in intensity and range in tone from joyous wonder to panic dread. A sacred being may be attractive or repulsive—a swan or an octopus—beautiful or ugly—a toothless hag or a fair young child—good or evil—a Beatrice or a Belle Dame Sans Merci—historical fact or fiction—a person met on the road or an image encountered in a story or a dream—it may be noble or something unmentionable in a drawing room, it may be anything it likes on condition, but this condition is absolute, that it arouse awe. The realm of the Primary Imagination is without freedom, sense of time or humor.

In contrast, the Secondary Imagination is concerned not with awe but with beauty:

> It does not worship the beautiful; it approves of it and can give reasons for its approval. The Secondary Imagination has, one might say, a bourgeois nature. It approves of regularity, of spatial symmetry and temporal repetition, of law and order: it disapproves of loose ends, irrelevance and mess.
>
> Lastly, the Secondary Imagination is social and craves agreement with other minds.

An artist creates a work of art when the awe felt by the Primary Imagination "is transformed into a desire to express that awe in a rite of worship or homage, and to be fit homage, this rite must be beautiful." This rite is neither magical—"nothing is expected in return"—nor an act of devotion in the Christian sense, in that it never praises the Creator, only His creatures. "With God as Redeemer, it has, so far as I can see, little if anything to do."

A poem is a rite performed by a poet. While this rite "involves his whole past", in that, for example, his childhood love for obsolete machinery may inform his adult love for another person, it is always "rooted in imaginative awe." Whatever else any individual poem may do—"delight, sadden, disturb, amuse, instruct"—whatever emotion it may express or event it may describe, "there is only one thing that all poetry must do; it must praise all it can for being and for happening."

This all-affirming peroration concludes the text of the lecture that Auden included in *The Dyer's Hand*, the massive book of critical notes and essays that he published in 1962. In 1956, when he delivered his lecture in Oxford, he continued with a few more words. He would now read, he said, a poem by Thomas Hardy "as an epilogue to this lecture", both because it illustrated what he had to say and because, "but for the man who wrote it, I should not now be here." He ended by reciting Hardy's "Afterwards". When he finished, any of his old antagonists who refused to applaud for W. H. Auden would be obliged also to refuse to applaud for Thomas Hardy.

"I had a triumph and won over my enemies", Auden wrote to Chester Kallman a few weeks later. But he also reported: "Never in my life have I been so terrified." He said in his lecture that imaginative awe can "range in tone from joyous wonder to panic dread", and panic dread was precisely his awed response to that terrifying sacred being, his Oxford audience.

Auden made his triumph possible by omitting from his lecture anything he had said in earlier essays about the limits and ambiguities of an imaginative awe that, with no freedom of its own, responds immediately to sacred beings. Auden insisted repeatedly that imaginative awe, no matter how much it may pride itself on its mythical intensity, is ultimately one of the means by which human beings worship impersonal force. A poem he wrote around 1951 begins:

> Appearing unannounced, the moon
> Avoids a mountain's jagged prongs
> And sweeps into the open sky
> Like one who knows where she belongs.
>
> To me, immediately, my heart:
> "Adore Her, Mother, Virgin, Muse,
> A Face worth watching Who can make
> Or break you as Her fancy choose."

To the heart's involuntary impulse of awe, the mind responds with an equally involuntary "reflex" of doubt:

> At which the reflex of my mind:
> "You will not tell me, I presume,
> That bunch of barren craters care
> Who sleeps with or who tortures whom."

(The verb "care" is plural because the mind recognizes the moon as a plural cluster of objects, not a singular goddess.) The mind is tougher than the heart, but no wiser about the psychological significance of its response:

Tonight, like umpteen other nights,
The baser frankness wins of course,
My tougher mind which dares admit
That both are worshipers of force.

Granted what both of them believe,
The Goddess clearly, has to go,
Whose majesty is but a mask
That hides a faceless dynamo;

And neither of my natures can
Complain if I should be reduced
To a small functionary whose dreams
Are vast, unscrupulous, confused.

He glossed these stanzas in an aphoristic paragraph first published in *The Dyer's Hand*, but first written in the early 1950s, around the same time as the poem:

> Henry Adams thought that Venus and the Virgin of Chartres were the same persons. Actually, Venus is the Dynamo in disguise, a symbol for an impersonal natural force, and Adams' nostalgic preference for Chartres to Chicago was nothing but aestheticism; he thought the disguise was prettier than the reality, but it was the Dynamo he worshiped, not the Virgin.

Auden believed everything that "Making, Knowing and Judging" said about the poet, but his lecture said nothing about the complementary and opposing figure of the historian whom he had described a year earlier, in the first of a series of three broadcasts titled "The Dyer's Hand". (These broadcasts have almost no connection with the book of the same title published in 1962.) The broadcast begins with two character sketches, one of the Poet, who closely resembled the poet in his inaugural lecture, the other of the Historian, a figure who is interested only in human beings and the choices that shape their lives, not in the sacred beings that concern the Poet. In the Historian's world, unlike the Poet's, persons are always making or facing choices: "They are always being tested or tempted, often without their being aware of it." The Poet's stories often include verbal riddles that can be solved; the Historian's stories are full of contradictions and paradoxes that defy solution. To the Poet, comic characters are inferior to sacred beings; to the Historian "it is often the comic character who is superior to other characters."

The Poet feels sacred awe at beings that can never be other than what they are. The Historian makes historical judgements about persons who could have chosen to be otherwise. The world of the Poet corresponds to the pagan classical tradition. "It would be incorrect, however, to say that the historical element in our literature comes solely through the Judaic-Christian tradition. *The Aeneid*, for example, already exhibits traces of it."

"Making, Knowing and Judging" consciously and deliberately omits the whole moral and historical world that Auden always believed was more important than the world of art. In *The Dyer's Hand* in 1962—a year after the end of his professorship—he immediately followed "Making, Knowing and Judging" with a set of aphorisms titled "The Virgin & The Dynamo" which contained his observations on Henry Adams as a worshiper of force and ended with a paragraph (borrowed from a 1950 essay, "Nature, History and Poetry") on the moral effects of the kind of praise that he had celebrated so grandly at the end of "Making, Knowing and Judging":

> The effect of beauty, therefore, is good to the degree that, through its analogies, the goodness of created existence, the historical fall into unfreedom and disorder, and the possibility of regaining paradise through repentance and forgiveness are recognized. Its effect is evil to the degree that beauty is taken, not as analogous to, but as identical with goodness, so that the artist regards himself or is regarded by others as God, the pleasure of beauty taken for the joy of Paradise, and the conclusion drawn that, since all is well in the work of art, all is well in history. But all is not well there.

Auden had told Enid Starkie that he wintered in America in order to make enough money to let him write poetry while summering in Ischia. Much of his income came from lectures and readings at American colleges, but he gave this up to spend the winter of 1956–57 in Ischia, so that he could fulfill his obligation to lecture once each term in Oxford without crossing the Atlantic each time. After he had settled in Ischia and sublet his flat in New York, Oxford changed its rules so that he could deliver all three lectures during a single three-week period, and he resumed wintering in New York the following year.

The terrors provoked by his return to Oxford stayed with him in Ischia. Later that summer he wrote a poem, "There Will Be No Peace", which he later said "was an attempt to describe a very unpleasant dark-night-of-the-soul sort of experience which for several months in 1956 attacked me". The attack has ended but the threat remains: "You will not forget, ever, / The darkness blotting out hope, the gale / Prophesying your downfall." The vague demonic forces that had attacked him—identified in grammatical terms as "Beings of unknown number and gender"—are still out there, "And they do not like you."

Another poem, apparently written soon afterward, signals his gradual recovery from the attack. In "There Will Be No Peace" a gale had prophesied his downfall. Now, in "First Things First", his ear construes a storm's uproar as "a love-speech indicative of a Proper Name", praising a long-lost lover as a sacred being: "Kenning you a god-child of the Moon and the West Wind." The poem ends in a tone of gratitude for having been able to translate the

storm as a speech of praise, and also in a tone of sober realism that understands what the storm had accomplished in the real, physical world: "So
many cubic metres the more in my cistern / Against a leonine summer—putting first things first: / Thousands have lived without love, not one without
water."

Auden's winter in Ischia in 1956–57, a friend reported, "was the only time
I heard him express any doubts about his work, not a single piece, but the
whole thing". The tone and content of his poems and prose during the next
few years, until the end of his professorship, tended to be less assertive and
idiosyncratic than before or after. In his annual month-long visit to Oxford
he took on responsibilities that no one had asked of him, making himself
available in a coffee shop every day to students who might want to talk with
him, and donating a refrigerator to the senior common room in Christ
Church, his old college. His other formal obligation, beside his lectures, included writing and delivering the Creweian Oration, a speech in Latin that
recorded the significant events of the past year in the university. (The Professor of Poetry and the Public Orator delivered the address in alternate years.)
Auden drafted the English text of his orations (reprinted in Appendix I) in
playfully Baroque formal diction, as if dressing for a costume party; a classics
don translated them into Latin, and Auden delivered them in Church Latin
pronunciation, claiming not to understand a word he said. In preparing his
lectures on poetry, he put all his craft and energy into making them as useful
and entertaining as he knew how. (One was enlivened by tape recordings he
had made of Marianne Moore reading her poems.) "I know my lectures were
full of faults," he told his old tutor Nevill Coghill after his professorship was
over, "but I *slaved* at them—each one took me at least a month to write." He
had remade himself as a fifty-year-old smiling public man.

Auden's central theme during these years was the troubled relations in
literature, language, and society between the Poet and the Historian. He had
said in his "The Dyer's Hand" broadcasts in 1955: "Though nearly all poems
written in the past nineteen hundred years are the joint product of the Poet
and the Historian, the collaboration is one of uneasy tension." In the collaboration between Poet and Historian that produced his own poems, he
evidently believed he had made himself into a better poet by encouraging
the Historian—and by restraining the Poet who had dazzled his early readers. For the subject of his first lecture after his inaugural he chose Robert
Frost, in whose work the Historian almost totally dominated the Poet, and
who scarcely resembled the kind of writer Auden had described in "Making,
Knowing and Judging". But in arguing the case for the Historian, he was
recommending a future for himself, not prescribing a set of rules for other
writers. In the next few years he wrote three essays and three broadcasts in
praise of Robert Graves, whose poems were almost entirely the work of the
Poet, not the Historian, and who had written an extravagant manifesto for

the Poet's point of view in *The White Goddess: A Historical Grammar of Poetic Myth*. In the same way, Auden paid homage to another Poet-dominated writer, Walter de la Mare, in reviews, memorial essays, and a volume that he edited of de la Mare's selected poems.

Auden earned most of his living in these years by writing workmanlike reviews of biographies, anthologies, and novels for the *New Yorker*, *Encounter*, other English and American magazines and newspapers, and the monthly bulletins of two book clubs in which he shared editorial responsibilities with Jacques Barzun and Lionel Trilling, first The Readers' Subscription (1951–59), then The Mid-Century Book Society (1959–62). The thread that connected these reviews was the interplay between the voluntary choices that interest the Historian and the instinctive or social forces that interest the Poet. In a review of Erik Erikson's biography of Martin Luther, he distinguished between behavior and deeds: "A deed is an act by which the doer voluntarily discloses himself to others: behavior is involuntary and discloses, not a unique self, but either those natural needs common to all men or those diagnosable complexes which the patient shares with other sufferers of the same kind." In a review of James Pope-Hennessy's biography of Queen Mary, the consort of George V, he began by pointing out that the special interest of a royal life lies in its exceptionally limited range of voluntary choices:

> The biographer of a statesman or a scientist or an artist or a courtesan traces the steps by which a person realizes his latent possibilities and finally succeeds in becoming what from the beginning he desired or was meant to be. In such a history, though many lucky or unlucky events occur outside the hero's control, the main interest lies in the decisions taken by himself, in watching how he surmounts obstacles and seizes opportunities and thus makes his own history.
>
> Royalty, on the other hand, can play very little part in determining its destiny. A certain heredity is essential, but in a formal sense only; it is not genetic constitution that decides who shall wear the Crown but the chance order of births and deaths in a particular family. Royal princes and princesses have some degree of personal choice in their marriages, but much less than other folk. . . .

Around the same time, Auden began thinking about politics as an arena in which the Poet and the Historian continued their perennial argument by other means. In 1956, in his introduction to a selection of Sydney Smith's writings, he defended the Whig tradition of English liberalism that Smith exemplified and which was the political work of the Historian. In an earlier version of this essay ("Portrait of a Whig", 1952), he had listed the tenets of English liberalism, and the list appeared again, slightly revised, in the 1956 version: all people differ in character and temperament, but social life requires certain common beliefs (which should be formulated vaguely enough to avoid dissension) and common ways of outward behaving (which should be formulated more precisely); because the method of a reform is as important as the reform itself, "violent change is as injurious to freedom as inertia", and "utopians are a public menace". In rewriting the essay in 1956 he added an explicit defense of the modern version of liberalism, which was widely "under attack for being aesthetically unappealing and psychologically or metaphysically shallow":

> Yet, unattractive and shallow as one may feel so many liberals to be, how rarely on any concrete social issue does one find the liberal position the wrong one. Again, how often, alas, do those very philosophers and writers who have most astounded us by their profound insights into the human heart and human existence, dismay us by the folly and worse of their judgments on the issues of everyday life.

The sociable, bourgeois Secondary Imagination perceives some things better than the Promethean Primary one can ever do.

In 1957, in his Oxford lecture on Robert Frost, Auden restated his distinction between Poet and Historian as a somewhat different contrast between two kinds of poetic imagination: "One might say that every poem shows some sign of a rivalry between Ariel and Prospero; in every good poem their relation is more or less happy, but it is never without its tensions." A poem dominated by Ariel evokes "a timeless world of pure play," a world "from which the evils and problems of this life . . . are deliberately excluded." A poem dominated by Prospero is interested more in historical truth than in aesthetic beauty, "and a poet cannot bring us any truth without introducing into his poetry the problematic, the painful, the disorderly, the ugly." An Ariel-dominated poem may be more beautiful, but Ariel "has no passions", so his poetry can never be profound. "The earthly paradise is a beautiful place but nothing of serious importance can occur in it." This is close to the distinction Auden made a few years later in the title of a section of *The Dyer's Hand*: "The Frivolous & The Earnest". In his lecture on Frost he observed that "Ariel's other name is Narcissus."

A novel by William Faulkner prompted him to distinguish between three different kinds of prose fiction. One is the Feigned History (e.g. *Anna Karenina*), effectively the work of Auden's character-type the Historian who values the problems and contradictions of personal choice. Another is the Fairy Tale, effectively the work of the character-type of the Poet, who prefers the simple intensities of myth:

> The Fairy Tale is unabashedly fiction; it presents us with a world of beings and events more extraordinary, more surprising than the world in which we live, and at the same time less problematic, less obscure. What in the historical world is internal and known by introspection and intu-

ition is, in the fairy tale, externalized and made manifest to the senses. Thus the fairy tale tends to represent the conflict between good and evil impulses which goes on inside all of us as an external battle between good and bad beings; it tends to isolate the various passions, for love, for power, for understanding, etc., which compete for the attention of our hearts and minds, and embody them one by one in monomaniac beings, whose physical appearance, behavior and conversation are caricatures in the sense that they reveal the life within immediately and exactly; there are no psycho-somatic contradictions.

Auden's examples of Fairy-Tale writers were Dickens, Ronald Firbank, Ivy Compton-Burnett, and Faulkner; he was probably the one critic who could name Firbank and Faulkner in the same sentence. Auden's other category of novel, the Prose Poem (e.g. *The Waves* and *Ulysses*), seems to be the work of a different kind of writer from either the essentially pagan Poet or the essentially Judeo-Christian Historian, a more recent kind of writer who is interested more in language itself than in sacred beings or human personalities.

During the first years of his Oxford professorship Auden explored all these questions in poems that confronted the powers and contradictions of literary language, explicitly in "First Things First", implicitly in "Objects", "Words", and "The Song", three brief, gnomic poems that seem to be footnotes to it. These three poems present a triad not unlike that of the Fairy Tale, the Feigned History, and the Prose Poem. In "Objects" the separate existence of "wordless creatures"—everything that is not human, everything "outside our sort of why"—gives comfort in the same way that unchangeable sacred beings give comfort to the Poet. When death reduces someone else to an object, heartless Ariel, rejoicing in a new wordless creature to sing about, "Extols the silence of how soon a loss." In "Words" language is the medium in which real persons live and choose their lives; "fact" for us is "fiction at its best"; "our fate" is "by verbal chance expressed". And in "The Song", sung speech hopes to redeem shabby mortality and "make amends / For whiteness drabbed"; but by rising above the world of guilt into the realm of pure song, it forgets the suffering that provoked it, and "ends / Denying what it started up to say."

Auden's longest and most thoughtful reviews in these years were mostly devoted to the question of how the Historian's point of view evolved from the Poet's, and he answered this question through a series of reflections on ancient Greece. As an editor of The Readers' Subscription book club, which offered its subscribers worthy older books in addition to new ones, he was able to assign himself the task of reviewing books that had been published decades earlier and that he now wanted to write about. He ended one such review, on Werner Jaeger's *Paideia: The Ideals of Greek Culture*, by insisting on the Historian's superiority:

Our *paideia* is superior to that of the Greeks in one thing, at least, and we have the study of the Classics to thank for it; it includes the study of history. Plato would probably disapprove of historical studies even more than he disapproved of poetry, for "what really happened" is even more crowded with bad examples, with the triumph of injustice and unrighteousness, than the feigned history of the poets. But he would be wrong.

A few months later he wrote at length about Bruno Snell's *The Discovery of Mind*, then about Hannah Arendt's *The Human Condition* ("a book which gives me the impression of having been especially written for me"), and both these reviews emphasized the effect of words upon thought and the ways in which changes in language affect the realms of politics, psychology, and morals.

Some of Auden's Oxford lectures were newly written from the start; others were partly adapted from lectures he had given in America since the early 1950s. His three lectures in May 1957—delivered, like all except his inaugural, in one of the lecture halls in the Examinations Schools—were entirely new. After opening the series with his lecture on Robert Frost, he lectured next on D. H. Lawrence, Frost's dialectical opposite and an embodiment of the myth-making Poet. He seems to have chosen both subjects partly to avoid treading on his hosts' toes, because neither of these two writers was included in the Oxford curriculum. In his third lecture in 1957, "The Dramatic Use of Music in Shakespeare's Plays", he did not pretend to academic expertise, but approached his subject from the special perspective of a poet who had written for music in his collaborations with Benjamin Britten and Igor Stravinsky.

A few weeks after he gave these lectures he was awarded the Feltrinelli Prize for Literature, and for the first time could afford to buy a summer house in Europe. He thought of buying the villa he had been renting in Ischia, but he had already persuaded himself that ten summers in Italy were enough. He had first stayed in Italy in 1947, partly in order to find in a shared Catholic culture of the flesh a possible alternative to his inward Protestant culture of the mind. With the help of a friend in Vienna he now began to look for a house in rural Austria, and in September 1957 he bought an old farmhouse in Kirchstetten, an hour by train from Vienna. He later explained that he wanted to live in a wine-drinking, Catholic culture, close to an opera house. Another motive, perhaps too deep to have been conscious, seems to have been his wish to live in a culture that, having collaborated with the Nazis, could not escape from its awareness of its own guilt. As he wrote a few years later in "The Cave of Making": "we shan't, not since Stalin and Hitler, / trust ourselves ever again".

In 1958 he was preoccupied with his move to Kirchstetten and with the practical difficulties of installing a modern kitchen into an eighteenth-century farmhouse. (While anticipating his new kitchen, he wrote "The Kitchen of

Life", a long review of M.F.K. Fisher's *The Art of Eating*, a book published four years earlier; he had already described it to friends as "the best American prose-book of this century".) Perhaps because of the pressure on his time, he adapted all three of his May 1958 Oxford lectures partly from older talks and essays. A review he had written about Byron a few months earlier provided some material for the first, "Byron's *Don Juan*". The second, "The Quest Hero", seems to have been based on his many earlier essays on the quests in folk tales and *The Magic Flute*, and on his reviews of Tolkien's *Lord of the Rings*. The third, "Dingley Dell and the Fleet: Reflections on *Pickwick Papers*", derives from a lecture he first gave in 1950. Later that summer he read typescript submissions for the Yale Series of Younger Poets, which he had edited since 1946. After writing his preface to the volume he had chosen, he resigned from the editorship. "Twelve years is a long time", he told an editor at the Yale University Press.

Auden moved into his Austrian farmhouse with its "miraculous kitchen" at the end of August 1958. A few weeks later he wrote his reflections on his Ischian interlude, "Good-Bye to the Mezzogiorno", a poem in which he identified himself as a Historian, a product of the guilt-culture of "the gothic North," unlike the Poet, who was most at home in the sunburnt south:

> between those who mean by a life a
> *Bildungsroman* and those to whom living
> Means to-be-visible-now, there yawns a gulf
> Embraces cannot bridge.

In 1959 Auden wrote three lectures for Oxford that seem to have been mostly new. The first, in praise of Marianne Moore, another poet outside the Oxford curriculum, made the point that provincial British tastes in poetry, and his own tastes in earlier years, excluded much that he had learned to value; this point may have been only implicit in his lecture, but a review-essay about Marianne Moore a few months later made it explicit. The second lecture, "Translating Opera Libretti", was another product of his professional expertise. It was the work of a new convert to the lecture's theme. In an essay on music seven years earlier he had written, "I am violently hostile to the performances of operas in translation". Then, in 1955, NBC Television invited him and Chester Kallman to translate *The Magic Flute* for broadcasting. Auden explained in his lecture that the television screen was different enough from the opera house to justify translations. He added, with characteristic attention to bourgeois reality: "And then, of course, the big broadcasting companies are willing to pay handsomely for translations and we saw no reason why, if a translation *was* going to be made, we shouldn't get the money." When he reprinted his earlier essay on music in *The Dyer's Hand* he replaced "violently hostile to" with "not generally in favor of".

His third lecture in 1959, on Shakespeare's *Henry IV*, was the first venture he made into a field already occupied by academic Oxford. The printed text—and probably the lost spoken version—opens with a rhetorical gesture of inadequacy like those that opened his inaugural lecture in 1956. What he was about to say, he suggested, would largely be about himself: "It has been observed that critics who write about Shakespeare reveal more about themselves than about Shakespeare, but perhaps that is the great value of drama of the Shakespearian kind, namely, that whatever he may see taking place on stage, its final effect upon each spectator is a self-revelation." Much of what the lecture said about Falstaff was partly a concealed caricature of those parts of Auden himself that he had condemned in his many poems and essays on the theme of the artist's inherent frivolity; his account of Falstaff's infant-like obesity alludes to his own passage through what he had called (in his poem "Under Which Lyre") "The fattening forties". But as the lecture proceeded, it gradually turned into a defense of Falstaff despite all his faults and limits, much in the same way that Auden had praised the backward, provincial landscape of his poem "In Praise of Limestone", for having "a worldly duty which in spite of itself / It does not neglect, but calls into question / All the Great Powers assume":

> The drunk is unlovely to look at, intolerable to listen to, and his self-pity is contemptible. Nevertheless, as not merely a worldly failure but also a willful failure, he is a disturbing image for the sober citizen. His refusal to accept the realities of this world, babyish as it may be, compels us to take another look at this world and reflect upon our motives for accepting it. The drunkard's suffering may be self-inflicted, but it is real suffering and reminds us of all the suffering in this world which we prefer not to think about because, from the moment we accepted this world, we acquired our share of responsibility for everything that happens in it.

At the close of the lecture, citing one of the Hasidic parables that he often used to illustrate his Christian arguments about grace and love, Auden compared Falstaff to the Sinner of Lublin who overwhelmed the rabbi with "the radiance of his happiness." Falstaff, Auden said, "is never tired, never bored, and until he is rejected he radiates happiness as Hal radiates power, and this happiness without apparent cause, this untiring devotion to making others laugh becomes a comic image for a love which is absolutely self-giving." The comic image of a state of grace was one of Auden's recurring themes, and he made it the subject of one of the eight parts of *The Dyer's Hand*. He wrote of P. G. Wodehouse's Jeeves: "So speaks comically—and in what other mode than the comic could it on earth truthfully speak?—the voice of Agape, of Holy Love."

Later in the summer of 1959 Auden wrote two large-scale works about poetic language in its relation to the moral realms of love and power. The first was "Dichtung und Wahrheit" (also the title of Goethe's autobiography), which he subtitled "An Unwritten Poem". The second was *Elegy for Young Lovers*, a libretto written in collaboration with Chester Kallman for an opera by the young German composer Hans Werner Henze, whom Auden had met a few years earlier in Ischia.

"Dichtung und Wahrheit" is a meditation in fifty sections of heightened, aphoristic prose, prompted by the wish to write a love poem that could satisfy the ambition of the Poet to praise and of the Historian to be truthful:

> Expecting your arrival tomorrow, I find myself thinking I love You: then comes the thought—I should like to write a poem which would express exactly what I mean when I think those words.

The poem he wishes to write must be a good one; it must also be a "genuine" one in the sense that it is recognizably his own and doesn't sound as if it had been written by someone else; and "if it is to satisfy me, it must also be true." These three attributes prove to be impossible to achieve, partly for reasons that Auden spelled out in earlier essays about poetry and language and in poems such as "The Song", where verbal art "ends / Denying what it started up to say". These were themes he would explore again throughout *The Dyer's Hand.*

Elegy for Young Lovers, set in Austria in 1910, is a portrait of "the artist-genius of the nineteenth and early twentieth century", and also a study of the aesthetic doctrine that regarded the artist-genius as "the highest, most authentic, mode of human existence". In aesthetics the artist's production is what matters, not his personality or character, and the artist-hero was heroic because he sacrificed everything to his artistic production. He was not merely obliged to sacrifice his personal happiness for art, but also "morally bound as a sacred duty to exploit others whenever such exploitation will benefit his work and to sacrifice them whenever their existence is a hindrance to his production". Gregor von Mittenhofer, the artist-genius in the libretto, "(morally) murders two people and breaks the spirit of a third", in order to write the great poem that he has finished by the end of the opera. Mittenhofer is an exaggerated portrait of two believers in this aesthetic doctrine, W. B. Yeats and Stefan George, but some of the events in Mittenhofer's life echo some minor incidents in Auden's personal history that were known mostly to himself and a few friends. Auden was filling in all the dark shadings of artistic life that he had omitted from his shining image of the all-praising poet in "Making, Knowing and Judging".

Since the start of his career, Auden had compiled a new volume of poems every five years (occasionally varying this schedule by one year more or less). In 1959 he gathered his shorter poems of 1955–59, together with "Dichtung und Wahrheit", and gave this book a title that evoked the Historian's muse: *Homage to Clio.* The book appeared in 1960. During that year he wrote only one new poem, "You", a riddling address to his own body, while he worked to finish his Oxford lectures. He wrote a series of three for the academic year 1959–60, which he delivered in May 1960, and the two required for the academic year 1960–61, which he delivered in October 1960. (The full set of fifteen lectures included his inaugural, the four sets of three lectures that he delivered in May, and these final two.)

The first of his three lectures in May 1960 was "The Hero in Modern Poetry"—a title he had used for earlier lectures in America—in which he identified the modern hero as anyone who can speak in the first person and resist the pervasive depersonalization of the age. The lecture probably included a new variation on this theme, which briefly appeared in his work around the end of 1959 and early 1960—the "Intellectual Dandy" who was an unpredictable member of a class of one, neither highbrow nor lowbrow; the Intellectual Dandy was "neither a conformist nor a rebel, for both these terms imply a concern for Public Opinion and the Dandy has none: on one occasion his views may coincide with those of the majority, on another with those of the minority, but in both cases the coincidence is accidental". (Auden wrote this description in a review of a book by Edmund Wilson.) In a review-essay about Yeats around the same time, Auden offered a variation on this theme as an imperative addressed to himself: "A writer can neither love nor hate the public; either he must be obsessed by it, as a speculator is obsessed by the stock market, or he must not think about it at all." He was reminding himself, after years of attending to his Oxford audience, to follow the second of these two ways of thinking.

The modern hero was a reassuring subject, one from which almost anyone in his Oxford audience could take self-flattering comfort. Auden's next two lectures were less comfortable. Each was about a Shakespearian outsider, first Shylock, then Othello. His lecture on *The Merchant of Venice* pointed to Shakespeare's insistence that Shylock, no matter how unjust he may be, is unjustly an outsider: in Venice, "a Jew is not regarded, even in law, as a brother". And Antonio, although he accepts the likelihood that he must die for the sake of his friend, is excluded at the end from the happiness his friend enjoys. The scenes set in Belmont almost portray it as "a community in a state of grace", but the scenes set in Venice are a reminder that Belmont's happiness is limited to a frivolous, parasitic leisure class. Belmont holds the mediterranean, mythical view of life held by Auden's Poet; Venice holds the problematic, contradictory views of his Historian. "Belmont would like to believe that men and women are either good or bad by nature, but Shylock and Antonio remind us that this is an illusion: in the real world, no hatred is totally without justification, no love totally innocent."

Auden's lecture on *Othello* began by considering the ways in which Venice relies on the services of a general who can never fully belong to its society. Auden then proposed that "Iago is a portrait of a practical joker of a particularly appalling kind", and proceeded to a general consideration of the

Practical Joker as someone who can accurately guess his victims' weaknesses, desires, and social reflexes, not because he wants anything from them, but because he wants to demonstrate to them and to himself his own superiority over them. He has no other wish; and, having "a self lacking in authentic feelings" ("I am not what I am", he says), he envies his victims, "because their desires, however childish and mistaken, are real to them, whereas he has no desire which he can call his own." Iago's ultimate goal is nothingness: "he must not only destroy others, but himself as well."

Auden's lecture on *Henry IV* a year earlier had begun with the modest suggestion that anything he would say about Shakespeare would be a revelation of himself. As he approached the end of his lecture on *Othello*, the last of his Oxford lectures on Shakespeare, he described Shakespeare as a different kind of mirror, one who held up a disturbing picture of our contemporary culture.

A play, as Shakespeare said, is a mirror held up to nature. This particular mirror bears the date 1604, but, when we look into it, the face that confronts us is our own in the middle of the twentieth century. We hear Iago say the same words and see him do the same things as an Elizabethan audience heard and saw, but what they mean to us cannot be exactly the same. To his first audience and even, maybe, to his creator, Iago appeared to be just another Machiavellian villain who might exist in real life but with whom one would never dream of identifying oneself. To us, I think, he is a much more alarming figure; we cannot hiss at him when he appears as we can hiss at the villain in a Western movie because none of us can honestly say that he does not understand how such a wicked person can exist. For is not Iago, the practical joker, a parabolic figure for the autonomous pursuit of scientific knowledge through experiment which we all, whether we are scientists or not, take for granted as natural and right?

Auden then distinguished two kinds of knowledge, impersonal scientific knowledge which "means, ultimately, to-have-power-over", and the very different mutual knowledge "implied in the Biblical phrase, 'Then Adam knew Eve, his wife,'", the kind still meant "when I say, 'I know John Smith very well.'" This mutual knowledge is not in service to power: "If I know John Smith well, he must also know me well." Iago has acquired scientific knowledge and reduced Othello to a thing. "What makes it impossible for us to condemn him self-righteously is that, in our culture, we have all accepted the notion that the right to know is absolute and unlimited. The gossip column is one side of the medal; the cobalt bomb the other."

After a summer in Italy Auden returned to Oxford in October 1960 for his two final lectures. The first was "The Genius and the Apostle: A Problem of Poetic Presentation", probably the first explicit statement in his Oxford lectures of the theme that he later said was the subject of the whole of *The Dyer's Hand*, Christianity and art. The problem described in the lecture was the literary presentation of two kinds of extraordinary person, the artist-genius, exemplified by Peer in Ibsen's *Peer Gynt*, and the apostle, who exists not for himself but "only as a mouthpiece and a witness to the Truth", exemplified by the title character of Ibsen's *Brand*. These two plays inadvertently demonstrate that these two figures cannot be represented directly. (Auden had explored this same theme in *Elegy for Young Lovers*, where the poem written by the artist-genius Mittenhofer is represented indirectly by wordless musical sounds; a variation on this theme is the "unwritten poem" of "Dichtung und Wahrheit".) "Though a direct portrayal of an apostle is not possible in art," Auden continued, "there exists . . . one great example of a successful indirect portrayal, Cervantes' *Don Quixote*." He concluded with a brief reworking of his 1947 lecture "The Ironic Hero", which interpreted Quixote as a knight of faith whose sainthood could be represented only indirectly:

> For, in the last analysis, the saint cannot be presented aesthetically. The ironic vision gives us a Don Quixote who is innocent of every sin but one; and that one sin he can put off only by ceasing to exist as a character in a book, for all such characters are condemned to it, namely, the sin of being at all times and under all circumstances interesting.

This was Auden's oblique hidden allusion, as he neared the end of his professorship, to his deep sense that his public status was morally damaging to himself and to others. In 1956, a few days after his election, he had quietly given $250 to Dorothy Day so that she could pay a fine imposed on a charitable shelter she maintained on the Bowery in New York. Dorothy Day displayed the check to reporters, and the *New York Times* reported his gift on the front page; a few days later he appeared on a television game show to appeal for funds for the shelter. He said to a friend later about the publicity he received for charitable acts, "theologically it was all wrong".

Auden's final lecture, "Mainly Valedictory", seems to have returned to the lighter tone of his inaugural. It probably included his daydream curriculum for a College for Bards, which he incorporated in "The Poet as Professor", a newspaper piece published shortly before the election of his successor, and, in revised form, in "The Poet & The City" in *The Dyer's Hand*. Probably in this final lecture he made his "savage remarks about the lack of a microphone in the Examination Schools" which (as he said in a letter) made it "almost impossible to be heard properly, however one bellows". He said nothing in public of his other complaints about the professorship, although he later mentioned them to friends: forty-two percent of his stipend had been deducted for taxes at the source; he paid all his expenses; he calculated that each lecture had cost him fifty pounds to deliver.

As Auden had hoped five years earlier, Robert Graves was elected Professor of Poetry on 16 February 1961. A few months later, Auden wrote to Nevill Coghill:

> Have just read RG's Inaugural. Between you and me—ssshhh!—the Old Boy didn't work very hard. . . . I observe that he, too, referred as I did to the Siege Perilous, but without giving credit to W.P.K[er]. Naughty! If you know your *White Goddess*, I hope you will appreciate my good wishes telegram to him which I am rather proud of as being admiring and, as a Queen's admiration should be, a little salty:
>
> "Hals-und-Beinbruch seinem Zwillingsbruder wünscht die fischgeborene Schlange."

The telegram may be translated: "The serpent born under Pisces [Auden was born on 21 February 1907] wishes his twin brother, 'Break a leg.'" This alludes to a passage in *The White Goddess* about the Star-Son and Serpent, mythical twin brothers who continually destroy and succeed each other. (As for Graves's use of a phrase from W. P. Ker, Auden had credited Ker in a footnote to the 1956 pamphlet edition of his inaugural lecture, but in *The Dyer's Hand* the footnote was dropped, perhaps inadvertently, and the book credited only "one of the noblest and most learned of my predecessors".)

A poem that Auden wrote in the summer of 1961, "A Change of Air", was his elliptical thanksgiving hymn for his release from Oxford. The poem presents itself as a fantasia on the theme of a renewing journey—a theme he had explored at length in the introduction he had written a few months earlier to a translation that he and his friend Elizabeth Mayer had made of Goethe's *Italian Journey*. The poem begins:

> Corns, heartburn, sinus headaches, such minor ailments
> Tell of an estrangement between your name and you,
> Advise a change of air: heed them, but let
> The modesty of their discomfort warn you
> Against the flashy errands of your dream.

Auden addresses himself as "you", as he did in "There Will Be No Peace", but with far less urgency. The estrangement between "your name and you" is the conflict between his publicly visible self, robed and celebrated at Oxford, and his invisible inner self. The cure for this estrangement is a change of air, but the estrangement is too mild to call for the kind of visible journey that Auden had made to Iceland, China, or America as cures for earlier estrangements. Now, all that is needed "To go Elsewhere is to withdraw from movement, / A side step, a short one, will convey you thither." The change of air that he has in mind is an entirely internal one, a step back to the concerns of nonpublic life.

The poem predicts that when he returns to the visible world ("for you will") his inner change will have left no visible effect:

No study of your public reappearance
Will show, as judgement on a cure demands,
A sudden change in love, ideas, or diet:
Your sojourn Elsewhere will remain a wordless
Hiatus in your voluble biography.

Only two traces of his journey may someday be detected by "Fanatic scholarship": "That you resigned from some Committee", which is somewhat like
having finished a professorship, and

A letter from the Grand Duke to his cousin,
Remarking, among more important gossip,
That you seem less amusing than you were.

This is a direct allusion to the aftermath of Goethe's return from Italy to
Weimar. It is also an indirect allusion to the way in which Auden hoped, by
withdrawing from the public eye, to achieve something analogous to what
Don Quixote achieved when he put off the "sin of being . . . interesting" by
ceasing to be a character in a book.

For more than a decade Auden had intended to put together a book of his
essays and reviews, but had never got beyond the stage of sketching lists of
possible contents. He now had a thick sheaf of lectures to work from, and
could put together a substantial book of old and new material, using the
same title he had used for his 1955 broadcasts, *The Dyer's Hand*. In the autumn of 1961 he set to work revising essays from the past fifteen years, reworking his Oxford lectures, and writing some new material. The result was
a vast book of almost 170,000 words. Random House, Auden's American publisher, issued the book in 1962 with only minimal editorial changes to the
original typescript. Faber & Faber, his British publisher, worried over the size
of the book and devised a plan to remove some of the contents and split the
rest into two volumes but finally agreed to publish it whole. (Faber reported
to him that the trade magazine *The Dyer* had asked for a review copy; Auden
hoped one had been provided.)

He wrote in his foreword to *The Dyer's Hand*:

A poem must be a closed system, but there is something, in my opinion,
lifeless, even false, about systematic criticism. In going over my critical
pieces, I have reduced them, when possible, to sets of notes because, as a
reader, I prefer a critic's notebooks to his treatises. The order of the chapters, however, is deliberate, and I would like them to be read in sequence.

The book is divided into eight parts, each with two or more sections. Some
of the sections are gatherings of aphorisms and reflections ranging from a
single sentence to a few paragraphs. Others, including those based largely
on Auden's Oxford lectures, are in the form of discursive arguments; a few

of these discursive sections are followed by a brief "Postscript" made up of further aphorisms and reflections. Auden had been writing aphoristic prose since the start of his career; in 1961, a few months before he began *The Dyer's Hand*, he had immersed himself in the form by compiling, together with his friend Louis Kronenberger, an anthology of European and American examples, *The Viking Book of Aphorisms*.

Auden never explained in detail the deliberate "order of the chapters" in *The Dyer's Hand*. He wrote to Stephen Spender, who had evidently mentioned the section titled "Postscript: Christianity & Art": "Re Xtianity and Art, that is what the *whole* book is really about, the theme which dictated my selection of pieces and their order." The sequence of pieces within some of the separate parts seems to move from the pagan world of the Poet to the Christian world of the Historian, as "Making, Knowing and Judging" is followed by "The Virgin & The Dynamo". The sequence of eight parts in the whole book seems to move, with some interruptions, through a spectrum of moral experience that gradually becomes more complex and problematic before shifting toward a vision of forgiveness in time and an eternity beyond it.

This sequence starts with the building blocks of language in the "Prologue", followed by the working life of the poet in the part titled "The Dyer's Hand". These are followed by the world of the inward-focused self in "The Well of Narcissus", then by the contrasting social world of "The Shakespearean City." The next two parts, "Two Bestiaries" and "Americana", seem to concern the relations between spirit and flesh, first in Marianne Moore's and D. H. Lawrence's poetry about animals, then through the special relation of American writers to a wild, dangerous nature unlike the maternal nature of Europe. "The Shield of Perseus" concerns the indirect comic representation of sanctity and grace; the title refers to the indirect representation that Perseus put to use when slaying the monstrous evil of Medusa.

The final part, "Homage to Igor Stravinsky", treats music as a distant analogue of unknowable universal harmonies. The final section in this last part is "Music in Shakespeare", and it concludes with the same doubleness of faith and doubt that marked all of Auden's writings on religious meaning. In the closing paragraph of the book Auden quotes Prospero's final speech, and observes: "The tone is not that of a man who, putting behind him the vanities of mundane music, would meditate like Queen Katharine 'upon that celestial harmony I go to,' but rather of one who longs for a place where silence shall be all."

REFERENCES

Page xiii

> *I am an American Citizen*   Letter to Enid Starkie, 5 August 1955 (St Anne's College, Oxford, quoted in Joanna Richardson, Enid *Starkie* [1973], p. 196)

the fit person   Letter to Starkie, 23 August 1955 (Richardson, p. 197)

Page xiv

I must frankly admit   Letter to E. R. Dodds, 7 November 1955 (Bodleian Library)

Entre nous   Letter to Starkie, 10 February 1956 (Richardson, p. 198)

I have been discovering   Letter to Stephen Spender, 8 May 1956 (Berg Collection)

It is the fear   *Oxford Mail*, 1 June 1956, p. 8

Page xviii

I had a triumph   Letter to Chester Kallman, 25 June 1956 (Berg Collection)

Page xix

They are always   *Prose III*, p. 540

Page xx

was an attempt   BBC Third Programme, 24 December 1962; transcript in the BBC Written Archives Centre

Page xxi

was the only time   Thekla Clark, *Wystan and Chester* (1995), p. 26

I know my lectures   Letter to Nevill Coghill, 6 December 1961 (Berg Collection)

Page xxvi

the best American   Letter to Nevill Coghill, 31 January 1956 (University of Edinburgh Library)

miraculous kitchen   Letter to his American agent Alan Collins, 1 September 1958 (Columbia University Library)

I am violently   *Prose III*, p. 302

Page xxviii

the artist-genius   *Libretti*, pp. 246–47

Page xxxi

theologically it was   V. S. Yanovsky, "W. H. Auden", *Antaeus* (Autumn 1975), p. 119

savage remarks   Letter to Robert Graves, 17 February 1961

Page xxxii

Have just read   Letter to Nevill Coghill, 6 December 1961 (Berg Collection); Auden sent the telegram on 19 October 1961

Page xxxiv

Re Xtianity and art   Letter to Stephen Spender, early 1963 (Berg Collection)

THE TEXT OF THIS EDITION

THIS VOLUME includes the prose that Auden wrote for publication from 1956 through 1962, including the complete text of *The Dyer's Hand*. Some essays in *The Dyer's Hand* had also been published separately during the period covered by this volume; the titles and publication details of these essays are included among the other essays and reviews with a note indicating where the text of the essay may be found in *The Dyer's Hand*, and the textual notes describe the differences between these separately published versions and the versions he prepared for the book. An appendix includes the English texts of the three Creweian Orations that Auden wrote as Professor of Poetry at Oxford, which he delivered in Latin versions that were translated for him by an Oxford classicist, J. G. Griffith.

A few prose pieces written by Auden and Chester Kallman during these years for the programmes and printed editions of their opera libretti and translations may be found in this edition in the volume titled *Libretti*. These pieces include the preface and endnotes to their translation of *The Magic Flute* and their response to a review of the printed text; the afterword to their libretto for Hans Werner Henze's opera *Elegy for Young Lovers*; and the synopsis of *Elegy for Young Lovers* that they wrote for the programme booklet.

A few essays that appeared in 1956 were written earlier and may be found in *Prose III*. These include Auden's untitled contribution to *Modern Canterbury Pilgrims*, edited by James A. Pike; his foreword to *Some Trees*, by John Ashbery; and "Putting It in English".

Some of Auden's prose pieces were originally printed exactly as he wrote them; others were cut and reshaped by editors; and it is often impossible to say how closely a printed text represents what Auden wrote. In the few instances where a manuscript exists, and where the printed version closely resembles it, the text in this edition has been newly edited from the manuscript. In all other cases, the printed text has been reprinted with a minimum of regularization, and I have not tried to impose consistency on spelling or punctuation, nor have I regularized names that occur in more than one form, such as Campian and Campion.

With the exception of one footnote indicating that the text in this edition has been retranslated from a German translation of a lost original, all footnotes and square brackets in the main text and Appendix I are Auden's own. Auden's manuscripts generally indicate footnotes with asterisks, and these have been used in place of the numbers added by some editors and publishers.

Many of the reviews and some of the essays in this volume were almost certainly given their titles by the editors of the magazines and books in which they appeared. Subtitles and breaks that were obviously inserted by newspaper and magazine subeditors in order to break up long columns of type have been omitted; such subtitles and breaks appeared in almost all of Auden's work that first appeared in newspapers or in *Encounter* and some other magazines.

At the head of each book review is a listing in a consistent format of the title, author, publisher, and price of the book reviewed. The format of these headings in the original publications varied according to the style sheets of the magazines and newspapers where the reviews appeared; some magazines used footnotes instead of headings.

The essays and reviews are arranged as closely as possible in chronological order of composition. In most cases, however, no direct evidence of the date of composition survives, and chronological order of publication has been used instead. The original date and place of publication is printed at the end of each work, together with the date of composition when this is known to have been much earlier than the publication date. The dates in the running heads are dates of composition, if known.

Auden almost invariably made minor errors when copying extracts from other authors. The text in this volume corrects the obvious misspellings that the original editors could reasonably be expected to have caught, but in all other instances I have preferred to print the text that Auden wrote instead of the text that he perhaps ought to have written. I have, however, corrected errors that are clearly the work of a typist or compositor working from Auden's hand. The textual notes indicate all significant deviations from the originals.

Auden subdivided many of his essays by using headings and outline levels. The indents and spacing in this edition have been very slightly regularized. In some instances, the punctuation of outline numbers has been changed from a style evidently introduced by a publisher to a style that more closely represents the typical punctuation in Auden's prose manuscripts. Auden generally circled the numbers and letters of his outline headings; these circles are represented here by pairs of parentheses, thus: (1). Where a surviving typescript has only a closing parenthesis after a number in a heading, an opening parenthesis has been added.

Some of the daily newspapers and weekly magazines to which Auden contributed were edited hurriedly, and I have in rare instances silently supplied a comma where the original has an incomplete pair of commas around a subordinate clause, and have made other similarly trivial corrections. Auden's erroneous "*acte gratuite*" has been altered to "*acte gratuit*". In some of his manuscripts Auden inconsistently used double quotation marks to set off quoted extracts and single quotation marks to set off concepts and abstractions; every competent editor normalized the inconsistency by using the same style of quotation marks for both extracts and concepts. I have normalized the rare instances where Auden's practice slipped through to the printed text, but have indicated these instances in the notes.

The textual notes also explain some references that would have been familiar to Auden's contemporaries but are now obscure, and provide brief accounts of the magazines to which Auden contributed; more detail is provided for lesser-known publications than for familiar ones, and little or no description is provided for magazines described in notes to earlier volumes.

ESSAYS AND REVIEWS

1956–1962

At the End of the Quest, Victory

The Return of the King. Being the Third Part of "The Lord of the Rings."
By J. R. R. Tolkien. Houghton Mifflin. $5.

In *The Return of the King*, Frodo Baggins fulfills his Quest, the realm of Sauron is ended forever, the Third Age is over and J. R. R. Tolkien's trilogy *The Lord of the Rings* complete. I rarely remember a book about which I have had such violent arguments. Nobody *seems* to have a moderate opinion: either, like myself, people find it a masterpiece of its genre or they cannot abide it, and among the hostile there are some, I must confess, for whose literary judgment I have great respect. A few of these may have been put off by the first forty pages of the first chapter of the first volume in which the daily life of the hobbits is described; this is light comedy and light comedy is not Mr Tolkien's forte. In most cases, however, the objection must go far deeper. I can only suppose that some people object to Heroic Quests and Imaginary Worlds on principle; such, they feel, cannot be anything but light "escapist" reading. That a man like Mr Tolkien, the English philologist who teaches at Oxford, should lavish such incredible pains upon a genre which is, for them, trifling by definition, is, therefore, very shocking.

The difficulty of presenting a complete picture of reality lies in the gulf between the subjectively real, a man's experience of his own existence, and the objectively real, his experience of the lives of others and the world about him. Life, as I experience it in my own person, is primarily a continuous succession of choices between alternatives, made for a short-term or long-term purpose; the actions I take, that is to say, are less significant to me than the conflicts of motives, temptations, doubts in which they originate. Further, my subjective experience of time is not of a cyclical motion outside myself but of an irreversible history of unique moments which are made by my decisions.

For objectifying this experience, the natural image is that of a journey with a purpose, beset by dangerous hazards and obstacles, some merely difficult, others actively hostile. But when I observe my fellow-men, such an image seems false. I can see, for example, that only the rich and those on vacation can take journeys; most men, most of the time must work in one place.

I cannot observe them making choices, only the actions they take and, if I know someone well, I can usually predict correctly how he will act in a given situation. I observe, all too often, men in conflict with each other, wars and hatreds, but seldom, if ever, a clear-cut issue between Good on the one side and Evil on the other, though I also observe that both sides usually describe it as such. If, then, I try to describe what I see as if I were an impersonal camera, I shall produce, not a Quest, but a "naturalistic" document.

Both extremes, of course, falsify life. There are medieval Quests which deserve the criticism made by Erich Auerbach in his book *Mimesis*:

The world of knightly proving is a world of adventure. It not only contains a practically uninterrupted series of adventures; more specifically, it contains nothing but the requisites of adventure. . . . Except feats of arms and love, nothing occurs in the courtly world—and even these two are of a special sort: they are not occurrences or emotions which can be absent for a time; they are permanently connected with the person of the perfect knight, they are part of his definition, so that he cannot for one moment be without adventure in arms nor for one moment without amorous entanglement. . . . His exploits are feats of arms, not "war," for they are feats accomplished at random which do not fit into any politically purposive pattern.

And there are contemporary "thrillers" in which the identification of hero and villain with contemporary politics is depressingly obvious. On the other hand, there are naturalistic novels in which the characters are the mere puppets of Fate, or rather, of the author who, from some mysterious point of freedom, contemplates the workings of Fate.

If, as I believe, Mr Tolkien has succeeded more completely than any previous writer in this genre in using the traditional properties of the Quest, the heroic journey, the Numinous Object, the conflict between Good and Evil while at the same time satisfying our sense of historical and social reality, it should be possible to show how he has succeeded. To begin with, no previous writer has, to my knowledge, created an imaginary world and a feigned history in such detail. By the time the reader has finished the trilogy, including the appendices to this last volume, he knows as much about Mr Tolkien's Middle Earth, its landscape, its fauna and flora, its peoples, their languages, their history, their cultural habits, as, outside his special field, he knows about the actual world.

Mr Tolkien's world may not be the same as our own: it includes, for example, elves, beings who know good and evil but have not fallen, and, though not physically indestructible, do not suffer natural death. It is afflicted by Sauron, an incarnation of absolute evil, and creatures like Shelob, the monster spider, or the orcs who are corrupt past hope of redemption. But it is a world of intelligible law, not mere wish; the reader's sense of the credible is never violated.

Even the One Ring, the absolute physical and psychological weapon which must corrupt any who dares to use it, is a perfectly plausible hypothesis from which the political duty to destroy it which motivates Frodo's quest logically follows. To present the conflict between Good and Evil as a war in which the good side is ultimately victorious is a ticklish business. Our historical experience tells us that physical power and, to a large extent, mental power are morally neutral and effectively real: wars are won by the stronger side, just or unjust. At the same time most of us believe that the essence of the Good is love and freedom so that Good cannot impose itself by force without ceasing to be good.

The battles in the Apocalypse and *Paradise Lost*, for example, are hard to stomach because of the conjunction of two incompatible notions of Deity, of a God of Love who creates free beings who can reject his love and of a God of absolute Power whom none can withstand. Mr Tolkien is not as great a writer as Milton, but in this matter he has succeeded where Milton failed. As readers of the preceding volumes will remember, the situation in the War of the Ring is as follows: Chance, or Providence, has put the Ring in the hands of the representatives of Good, Elrond, Gandalf, Aragorn. By using it they could destroy Sauron, the incarnation of Evil, but at the cost of becoming his successor. If Sauron recovers the Ring, his victory will be immediate and complete, but even without it his power is greater than any his enemies can bring against him, so that, unless Frodo succeeds in destroying the Ring, Sauron must win.

Evil, that is, has every advantage but one—it is inferior in imagination. Good can imagine the possibility of becoming evil—hence the refusal of Gandalf and Aragorn to use the Ring—but Evil, defiantly chosen, can no longer imagine anything but itself. Sauron cannot imagine any motives except lust for dominion and fear so that, when he has learned that his enemies have the Ring, the thought that they might try to destroy it never enters his head, and his eye is kept turned toward Gondor and away from Mordor and the Mount of Doom.

Further, his worship of power is accompanied, as it must be, by anger and a lust for cruelty: learning of Saruman's attempt to steal the Ring for himself, Sauron is so preoccupied with wrath that for two crucial days he pays no attention to a report of spies on the stairs of Cirith Ungol, and when Pippin is foolish enough to look in the palantir of Orthanc, Sauron could have learned all about Frodo's Quest. His wish to capture Pippin and torture the truth from him makes him miss his precious opportunity.

Sauron is not overthrown, however, before many brave men have died and much damage has been done and even his defeat involves loss—the three Elven Rings lose their power and the Elves must leave Middle Earth. Nor is the victory of Good over Evil final: there was Morgoth before Sauron and no one knows what dread successor may afflict the world in ages to come.

The demands made on the writer's powers in an epic as long as *The Lord of the Rings* are enormous and increase as the tale proceeds—the battles have to get more spectacular, the situations more critical, the adventures more thrilling—but I can only say that Mr Tolkien has proved equal to them. Readers of the previous volumes may be interested to know that Gandalf's hunch about Gollum was right—but for Gollum the Quest would have failed at the last moment.

From the appendices they will get tantalizing glimpses of the First and

Second Ages. The legends of these are, I understand, already written and I hope that, as soon as the publishers have seen *The Lord of the Rings* into a paper-back edition, they will not keep Mr Tolkien's growing army of fans waiting too long.

The New York Times Book Review, 22 January 1956

An Appreciation of the Lyric Verse of Walter de la Mare

O Lovely England, and Other Poems. By Walter de la Mare. Viking. $3.

If Walter de la Mare had never written a line of verse himself, many readers of poetry would owe him a debt which they can never repay, as I can personally testify. When, at the age of fifteen, I first began to take an interest in the art, Providence inspired a relative to give me his anthology *Come Hither*. This volume proved to be not merely a convenient collection of good poems but a many-sided demonstration of the nature of poetry from which I learned more than I have learned from most works of overt literary criticism, and the vision it gave me then has since been confirmed and extended by Mr de la Mare's subsequent creations, *Behold This Dreamer, Desert Islands* and *Love*.

It is, surely, an atrocious irony that the treatment by other anthologists of the poet who has done more than anyone else to justify this curious genre should be one of the strongest arguments against it. Open one anthology of modern poetry after another and what do you find?—the same three or four old warhorses, like "The Listeners," all written before 1920, as if Mr de la Mare—who today is 83—had stopped writing poetry at that time. No critics come to blows over him at cocktail parties, no discussions of his use of metaphor appear in the Little Magazines, no graduate, desperate for a thesis subject, snaps him up. Reviewers have not been unkind, but their words of praise have generally been of the sort which is deadlier than any attack.

Looking at his dust-jackets, I find such phrases as "Should we be bothering over the question, What is Poetry? The answer is just This is"; or "He is a poet to the bone"; or "Well-nigh flawless lyrics which will enthrall lovers of poetry." Now these statements are, I believe, perfectly true, but, if I did not know Mr de la Mare's work previously, they would effectively deter me from ever reading him.

O Lovely England is a collection of sixty-nine poems, some of them written years ago, selected by the poet's son, Richard de la Mare. In a few instances filial piety may have outweighed critical rigor but it doesn't matter—a poem which a reader does not care for can be skipped, but one good line excluded is a pure loss.

"What a writer may say *about* his poems and their subterranean waters," says Mr de la Mare in his preface, "is often dangerous and may be even scientifically inaccurate—metrical craftsmanship is another matter"—advice which a critic, too, would do well to heed. A glib attribution of literary influences is also dangerous, but I shall hazard the guess that the immediate influences on Mr de la Mare as a young man were Christina Rossetti and Mary Coleridge, later, perhaps, Thomas Hardy, and always in the background there have been the sixteenth and seventeenth century lyric poets like Campion and Herrick. When Mr de la Mare "does" a conceit, which he can very beautifully, it is nearer to Marvell than to Donne.

It was from Christina Rossetti, I suspect, that he learned much of his metrical skill, in particular his masterful use of the spondee in lines with an iambic base.

> This is not the place for thee;
> Never doubt it, thou hast come
> By some dark catastrophe
> Far, far from home.
>
> ("Astray")

One of the hardest tests of a poet's prosodic gift is the anapaest (or dactyl: I have never been able to make up my own mind in this old prosodic controversy). It takes the most delicate ear to write English verse in this rhythm for other than comic purposes without sounding jejune. Any poet who has tried will admire and envy the subtle fingering in a stanza such as this:

> There were no clouds in the arch of the evening,
> Mute were the heavens in transient gold;
> Not a leaf stirring, not a bird twittering,
> Dreamed the dark woodland, fold within fold.
>
> ("Intruder")

The fourth line exhibits one characteristic of Mr de la Mare's verse, the inversion of subject and verb, about which I feel less happy. In this particular case I think it works, but sometimes the tension between natural speech and musical demands (which should be felt in every good lyric) is lost and sense is sacrificed to sound. For example:

> Not such for its Master would then I crave.

or

> Keeps she for me, then, safe-enshrined—
> Cold of the North—those bleached grey streets.

Mr de la Mare's concerns in poetry are limited, but whose are not? One of his many excellences has always been his refusal to persuade himself that he was excited by subjects, however important, which as a poet left him cold. As Randall Jarrell said of him in the only good American article about de la Mare's recent work that I have come across: "He is genuinely unassuming, a mouse in a corner, and never thinks to tell you, as better but vainer poets do: 'Now I am going to be humble.'"

His muse has always been like the Moon in "Second Childhood"—

> She who no night-bird ever taught
> To sing, not what it must, but ought.

I mentioned earlier the disgraceful treatment of Mr de la Mare by anthologists. Here are a few titles from his later books (I omit, because of its length, what I believe to be his finest poem, "Winged Chariot") which I commend to their attention: "Good-bye," "The Quiet Enemy," "The Last Coachload," "The Fat Woman," "The Bottle," "The Railway Junction," "A Robin," "She Said," "Lost World," "Forests," "Outcasts."

Finally, in trying to correct the popular impression of Mr de la Mare as a writer of verses for children and beauty-lovers, one should not forget how excellent his poems for children are. Since there is no example in the present volume, I shall quote from an earlier:

> Hi! handsome hunting man,
> Fire your little gun.
> Bang! Now the animal
> Is dead and dumb and done.
> Nevermore to peep again, creep again, leap again,
> Eat or sleep or drink again, Oh, what fun!

A child brought up on such verses may break his mother's heart or die on the gallows but he will never suffer from a tin ear.

The New York Times Book Review, 26 February 1956

Stimulating Scholarship

English Literature in the Sixteenth Century. By C. S. Lewis.
Oxford University Press. $6.50.

When the Press of a great university announces its intention of producing a twelve-volume History of English Literature from its Anglo-Saxon beginnings up to the present day, one can be assured that, when complete, it will be indispensable to all school and college libraries, to the offices of higher class newspapers and to the reading rooms of the more intellectual clubs as a standard work of reference which contains a great many facts and has these facts right; but one does not expect, because one has no right to demand it, that it will at the same time be a work which the non-specialist who reads primarily for pleasure will be eager to buy for his private library. Yet this is just what Professor C. S. Lewis, in his volume on the non-dramatic literature of the Sixteenth Century has managed to produce. He satisfies the most stringent demands of scholarship; he has read everything, good, bad, exciting, dreary, so that if for some curious reason you need to find out about some obscure figure like George Gifford, you can get the information from his pages; at the same time he always has something fresh and valuable to say about the greatest and most commented-upon authors.

Campian, for example, is one of my favorite poets, one about whom I would have prided myself that no one could now point out anything in his poems which I had not already seen; the five pages which Professor Lewis devotes to Campian have cured me of that delusion.

The business of the literary historian, he writes,

> is not with the past as it "really" was (whatever "really" may mean in such a context) but with the past as it seemed to those who lived in it: for of course men felt and thought and wrote about what seemed to be happening to them. The economic or social historian's "appearances" may be the literary historian's "facts." . . . We are to consider what men wrote, and our judgment on it must, of course, attempt to be literary, not theological. This does not mean that we are to confine ourselves rigidly to questions of style. Though we must not judge our authors' doctrine as doctrine, we must certainly attempt to disengage the spirit and temper of their writings to see what particular insights or insensibilities went with their varying beliefs, what kinds of sentiment and imagination they unwittingly encouraged.

Professor Lewis is here talking, of course, about the writers on theological and political subjects who form the background to his main concern, the "Pure" literature of the period. The historian of the latter is in a unique position, firstly because his "past" facts, works of art, are still "present" as experienced by readers or spectators now, and, secondly, because, unlike economic or social facts, they did not have to be. One can imagine a certain political event, the Battle of Actium, let us say, as not occurring or as occurring in a different manner (as a victory for Anthony) but one cannot imagine no event occurring in its place because every man at every instant of his life is a social being. But only some men and only at certain moments in their lives write poems. The alternative to the *Iliad* was not necessarily another epic; it could equally well have been nothing literary at all. The "unnecessary" nature of works of art has the curious consequence of allowing their historian to make more "sense" of them than the political historian can make of his facts. A subsequent political event can cancel the effect of a previous one, but works of art continue to exert their effects side by side and in conjunction with each other for the rest of time. Thus, while no one can be certain that the world would be any different today if Anthony had won the battle of Actium, one can confidently assert that, if the *Iliad* had not been written, we should possess neither the *Aeneid* nor *The Rape of the Lock*.

The literary historian, therefore, has a double task. Like all historians, he has to try to see a given work through the eyes of its maker and his contemporaries, to ask: "What is he trying to do? How far does he succeed or fail in realising his intention?", but then, unlike the social historian, he cannot avoid passing judgment upon it as a work he is now reading: he is obliged to risk making an ass of himself by trying to answer the questions: "What are the criteria by which all works, irrespective of their date or style are to be judged? Given these, is this work good or bad?"

As an example of how well Professor Lewis measures up to both tasks, let us take his treatment of Wyatt's prosody.

> We have seen that Wyatt is often on a level with Barclay. We have seen that, at the other end of the scale, in his poulter's, he ticks out regular metre with the ruthless accuracy of a metronome. Both phases are what we should expect in a man who was escaping from the late medieval swamp; first, his floundering, and then, after conversion, a painful regularity. . . . It is immensely improbable *a priori* that the same man at one period of his career should have gone on, beyond the regularity, to the subtlest departures from it. It is immensely improbable that such departures could have had for him or for his contemporaries the beauty they have for a modern. To us the variation is beautiful because we hear it against the background of the imagined norm: when the norm itself was a novelty to Wyatt (and a mystery to most of his hearers) the particular beauty which we feel could hardly have existed. Nothing, it seems, could incline us to the modern view except our reluctance to believe that melody can come by chance; and I am not sure whether it is a rational reluctance.

No critic will ever amount to much who does not start with strong personal preferences and end by transcending them so that he can see the good in works which are not really his "dish." A narrow taste is a bad taste, but a catholic taste which is not arrived at through a process of self-conquest is no taste at all.

Professor Lewis, thank goodness, makes no bones about his preferences. He divides the post-medieval and pre-metaphysical poetry of the century into two overlapping periods, the earlier, running, roughly, from 1540–1588, which he calls Drab, and the later, beginning to emerge in the work of Spenser, which he calls Golden. His insistence that these terms are purely descriptive will deceive no one; the choice of two words with such strong everyday emotional associations makes it quite obvious that he prefers the

Golden and, from hints dropped here and there, one gathers that he would class nearly all modern poetry, even the best, as Drab and therefore not really to his taste.

However, his terms do describe as well as judge; they point out a stylistic difference which is real and important, the difference, for instance, between:

> The pillar perish'd is whereto I leante
> The strongest stay of mine unquiet minde;
> The like of it no man agayne can finde,
> From east to west stil seekynge though he went.

and

> You Gote-heard Gods that love the grassie mountaines,
> You Nimphes that haunt the springs in pleasant vallies,
> You Satyrs joyde with free and quiet forrests . . .

Moreover, whatever his preferences, Professor Lewis never makes the mistake of treating drab poetry as if it were an unsuccessful attempt at golden, nor pretend that when golden poetry fails, its faults are the drab faults.

> Farewell O Sunn, *Arcadias* clearest light;
> Farewell O pearl, the poore mans plenteous treasure:
> Farewell O golden staffe, the weake mans might:
> Farewell O Joy, the joyfulls onely pleasure.

The bad fourth line reveals the temper of Golden poetry as clearly as the others; where it lacks riches it will still pretend to have them.

Professor Lewis is also blessed with a gift which has been denied to some very great scholars, a sense of the way in which the minds of poets work.

It is not obvious that when poets repeat themselves they must be repeating their recent works: they are surely at least as likely to repeat lines written so long ago that they do not recognise the repetition.

Returning to work on an interrupted story is not like returning to work on a scholarly article. Facts, however long the scholar has left them untouched in his notebook, will still prove the same conclusions; he has only to start the engine running again. But the story is an organism; it goes on surreptitiously growing or decaying while your back is turned. If it decays, the resumption of work is like trying to coax back to life an almost extinguished fire . . . But if (as is far more probable) it grows, then you will come back to find it "Changed like a garden in the heat of spring / After an eight-days' absence." Fertile chaos has obliterated the paths.

> I can hardly conceive a poet moving from the style of the best sonnets to that of *Venus and Adonis,* but can easily conceive one who had achieved Shakespeare's mature dramatic technique still writing the sonnets we have. For in all ages, and especially in that, form affects style. If Shakespeare had taken an hour off from the composition of *Lear* to write a sonnet, the sonnet might not have been in the style of *Lear.*

And then, for good measure, he can make us laugh.

> In the lady the lover sees his potential and more beautiful self. But Spenser sadly bungles the idea by likening the two lovers to two mirrors which face one another. Surely the results would be very uninteresting.

Naturally every reader will find some points over which he disagrees with Professor Lewis; a critical book would be unreadable were this not so. He tries very hard to be just to Wyatt, but I find it remiss in such a felicitous quoter that he does not mention Wyatt's best poem "Stond who so list upon the slypper Toppe." I think Chapman's "*Hymnus in Noctem*" is not quite as bad as he says and Daniel infinitely inferior to Drayton. And on one little matter Professor Lewis almost makes me cross. Why does he object to accented/unaccented rhymes which, as he admits, are too common in the maturest Golden poets to be, like Wyatt's rhythms, unintentional? And why call a form of rhyme which not only has a long literary history but in some verse, Welsh, for example, can be obligatory, after the late Percy Simpson, as if he were the first to discover its existence?

But such objections are trivial indeed. Test him on what you will, a literary question like the rhythmical differences between Shakespeare's sonnets and the Poetry of Donne on the one side and Milton on the other, or questions concerning the history of ideas, like the difference and relation between the Magician and the Astrologer, the temper of the Humanists or the first Puritans, and Professor Lewis passes them all with flying colors, disabusing the reader of conventional pre-conceptions but never tempting him to swallow eccentric novelties in their place.

In this book he exhibits not only great scholarship and excellent aesthetic judgment but also a quality which in any age is rare and in none rarer than in ours, wisdom.

The Griffin, March 1956

Hic et Ille

[See *The Dyer's Hand,* p. 519, and textual notes, p. 954.]

Encounter, April 1956

Introduction to *Selected Writings* of *Sydney Smith*

I

Sydney Smith was born in 1771, two years after the invention of Watt's steam-engine and one year after Goldsmith's *Deserted Village*, that vivid description of the effects of land enclosure. It was still dangerous to walk through the streets of London after dark, there were no waterproof hats, no braces, no calomel, no quinine, no clubs, no savings banks, the government was completely in the hands of great landowners, and, in the best society, one third of the gentlemen were always drunk. He died in 1845, which was also the year in which Engels' *State of the Working Classes in England* was published and Newman was received into the Roman Catholic Church. The American Revolution, the French Revolution, the Napoleonic wars, the Romantic Movement had all occurred, there was gaslight in houses, there were railways through the country, the Victorian proprieties were firmly established (Bowdler's *Shakespeare* appeared in 1818) and public opinion had forced Parliament to soften the rigors of pure laisser-faire (the first Factory Act was passed in 1833).

Sydney Smith's mother, Maria Olier, came of French Huguenot stock; his father, Robert Smith, was an eccentric unstable character who left his bride at the church door and departed to America for several years, spent the rest of his life in travel and unsuccessful speculations, and insisted on his family sitting over the dinner table in the half-dark for hours. His children, however, did better for themselves: three of his sons went to India (the only daughter stayed, of course, at home), where one died young and the other two made fortunes; Sydney, his second son, ended up as a Canon of St Paul's and the most famous wit of his generation.

Physically, he was swarthy, sturdy tending to stoutness and suffering in later life from gout. Mentally, like so many funny men, he had to struggle constantly against melancholia: he found it difficult to get up in the morning, he could not bear dimly lit rooms—"Better," he wrote, "to eat dry bread by the splendour of gas than to dine on wild beef with wax-candles"—and music in a minor key upset him. Writing to a friend who was similarly afflicted, he gave his own recipe for combating low spirits.

(1) Go into the shower-bath with a small quantity of water at a temperature low enough to give you a slight sensation of cold, 75° or 80°.
(2) Short views of human life—not further than dinner or tea.
(3) Be as busy as you can.
(4) See as much as you can of those friends who respect and like you, and of those acquaintances who amuse you.

(5) Attend to the effects tea and coffee produce upon you.
(6) Avoid poetry, dramatic representations (except comedy), music, serious novels, sentimental people, and everything likely to excite feeling and emotion, not ending in active benevolence.
(7) Keep good blazing fires.
(8) Be firm and constant in the exercise of rational religion.

This illustrates well enough both the virtues of his mind and its limitations. Such a man will always have an excellent grasp of the concrete and the immediately possible, but one must not expect from him profound speculative insights. Sydney Smith was perfectly sincere in his religious faith, but one is not surprised to find that, as a young man, his ambition was to read for the Bar and that it was only lack of money which compelled him instead to take Holy Orders. In his admirable attacks on religious intolerance the reader cannot but be conscious of a distrust of all theological dogma until he wonders whether Sydney Smith could have explained just why he was an Anglican and not, say, a Unitarian. His criticisms of the Methodists and the Puseyites are acute enough but one cannot help feeling that it was religious "enthusiasm" as such, not merely the follies to which it is liable, which aroused his scorn and distrust.

II

The Finances of the Church Visible are always a fascinating subject. As a State Church, the revenues of the Church of England are derived, partly from property which it owns, partly from taxation but comparatively little from the alms of the faithful. Patronage is not solely in the hands of the Crown; some livings are bestowed by bishops, some by cathedral chapters and many by private patrons. With its money it has to pay for the upkeep of churches and parsonages and to secure for every parish, if it can, a vicar of good manners and education. Moreover, since most Anglican clergymen are married men, they will need enough money to support and educate their families.

In Sydney Smith's time, by his own calculations, the total revenues of the Church would, if equally divided, have been sufficient to give every minister excluding curates, an annual income of £250—"about the same as that enjoyed by the upper domestic of a nobleman." Needless to say, its revenues were not so divided, but ranged from rich sees like Canterbury, worth £25,000, to country livings worth no more than £150. In the competition for preferment, those who had sufficient private means to endure the rigors of their early clerical years and those with good social connections who could gain the ears of the disposers of patronage had, naturally, a great advantage. It was not, however, impossible for a person of humble birth to succeed.

Sydney Smith paints the following picture of the ecclesiastical career of a baker's son:

> Young Crumpet is sent to school—takes to his books—spends the best years of his life, as all eminent Englishmen do, in making Latin verses—knows that the *crum* in crum-pet is long, and the *pet* short—goes to the University—gets a prize for an Essay on the Dispersion of the Jews—takes orders—becomes a Bishop's chaplain—has a young nobleman for his pupil—publishes an useless classic, and a serious call to the unconverted—and then goes through the Elysian transitions of Prebendary, Dean, Prelate, and the long train of purple, profit and power.

It is not hard to deduce from this description the personal qualities best fitted for a rise from obscurity to a mitre: an unoriginal brightness of intellect which is good at passing exams but not at thinking for itself, a proper respect for titles, a talent for flattery, a solemn mien and, above all, Tory political opinions.

Sydney Smith possessed none of these; intellectual ability he had in abundance but of a dangerously lively kind; though he came to number many titled and rich people among his friends, he was utterly without snobbery and incapable of flattery; he was continually making jokes and, worst of all, he was a convinced Whig. Yet, starting from the bottom—with an income of £100 a year and no influential friends—he rose, if not to a bishopric, to a residential canon of St Paul's at a salary of £2,000 a year. It may be not without interest to consider how he did it. His career began with a stroke of good luck: the local squire of the Wiltshire village where he was a young curate took a shine to him and asked him to accompany his son as a tutor on the Grand Tour. Sydney Smith recommended Weimar but the outbreak of war made it impossible and they went to Edinburgh instead. There he met Jeffrey, Brougham, and Francis Horner and started with them *The Edinburgh Review*, devoted to the criticism of contemporary literature and the furthering of Whig policies. The review was an instantaneous success and Smith began to be talked about. In 1800 he married for love and the marriage seems to have remained a singularly happy one. The only gift he had for his bride was six worn silver teaspoons and she, though she possessed some small means of her own, had presently to sell her mother's jewelry to meet expenses. In 1803 the couple moved to London, where he managed to live by preaching at the Foundling Hospital and lecturing on Moral Philosophy at The Royal Institution. Through his elder brother he was introduced into the Holland House circle, the center of Whig society, of which he quickly became a popular and admired member. He was still, however, too poor to afford an umbrella, far less a carriage; moreover, his new friends, while cultivated and rich, belonged to the party which was out of power and likely to remain so. Again, he had a stroke of luck for, after Pitt's death, the Whigs came into power for a few months, just long enough to appoint him to the living of Foston in Yorkshire, worth £500 a year. Foston had not had a resident vicar since the reign of Charles II and Smith had no intention of leaving the social amenities of London which he loved for the country which he regarded as "a healthy grave" and where it seemed to him as if "the whole creation were going to expire at tea-time." In 1808, however, a Tory government passed the Clergy Residence Bill and he was banished, at the age of thirty-eight, to a village "twelve miles from a lemon," its existing parsonage a brick-floored kitchen with one room above it, there to do duty for the next twenty years.

Any man might have quailed at the prospect but for an intellectual and man-about-town like Smith, anonymous author of *The Peter Plymley Letters* which had electrified the public and enraged the government, accustomed to the best tables, the best conversation, the most elegant ladies and gentlemen, it must have seemed the end, and a stranger might well have expected him to lapse into despondency and drink. He did nothing of the kind. He kept up his reading, his reviewing, and his large correspondence; he designed a new parsonage for himself and got the local carpenter to furnish it; he devised all sorts of ingenious gadgets—devices for added draft to the fires, devices to prevent smoky chimneys, lamps burning mutton-fat to save the expense of candles, a special scratcher pole for all his animals etc., and, far from neglecting his parish duties, became one of the best county vicars of whom there is record, and the idol of his parishioners. Church services were only a small part of his ministrations: he started small vegetable gardens, let out to the laborers at very low rents, to help them augment their food supply; he experimented with diets to discover which were both cheap and nourishing; he acted as their doctor and, as a local magistrate, saved many of them from going unjustly to jail.

During the first half of his residence at Foston, he was never free from financial anxiety—during the bad harvest year of 1816, for instance, he could no more afford to buy white flour than could his parishioners—but in 1820 an unexpected legacy from an aunt lightened his burden and in 1828, as in 1808, a brief Coalition Ministry including Whigs remembered him and procured him a canonry at Bristol and the living of Combe Florey in Somerset which, though it did not increase his income, was a step up in the Ecclesiastical Hierarchy.

From then on his life was smooth sailing: two causes in which he was a leader triumphed—the Catholic Emancipation Act was passed in 1829 and the Reform Bill in 1832,—his services were rewarded in his sixty-first year by a canonry at St Paul's, and then his unmarried younger brother died, leaving him a third of his very large fortune. He was now rich, popular, and famous. A letter he wrote shortly before his death aptly describes the last fourteen years of his life:

Being Canon of St Paul's in London, and a rector of a parish in the country, my time is divided equally between town and country. I am living among the best society in the Metropolis, and at ease in my circumstances; in tolerable health, a mild Whig, a tolerating Churchman, and much given to talking, laughing and noise. I dine with the rich in London, and physic the poor in the country; passing from the sauces of Dives to the sores of Lazarus. I am, upon the whole, a happy man, have found the world an entertaining place, and am thankful to Providence for the part allotted to me in it.

III

Many of Sydney Smith's wisecracks are widely known. Nowell Smith's definitive edition of his letters (Oxford Press, 1953) must already have convinced many readers that he is among the supreme masters of the epistolary art, but his published writings still seem to be little known. This is understandable because Smith was not a poet or a novelist but from first to last a writer of polemics, as pure an example as we have in English of *l'écrivain engagé*.

As a general rule it is the fate of the polemical writer to be forgotten when the cause for which he fought has been won or is no longer a live issue, and it will always be difficult to persuade a later generation that there can be exceptions, polemical writers, journalists if you will, of such brilliance and charm that they can be read with delight and admiration by those to whom their subject matter is in itself of little interest.

Literary criticism, too, is apt to avoid the polemical writer because there is little to say about him. Unlike the creator of "pure" literature, the poet, the novelist, the dramatist etc., he rarely shows "development," stylistic or ideological. His cast of mind, his way of expressing himself are generally established early and any variety that his work may show will come mostly from a variety in the topics upon which he writes.

Nevertheless there are a few such authors who must be ranked very high by any literary standard and first among such I would place Hooker, Swift, Sydney Smith and Bernard Shaw. Milton in his polemical works is too bad-mannered and abusive, and Junius, for all his brilliance, too biased.

Of them all, Sydney Smith has, perhaps, the most exact sense of the particular audience he is addressing on any given occasion, and the widest variation of tone. He can equally well speak to the average educated man—

Is it necessary that the Archbishop of Canterbury should give feasts to Aristocratic London; and that the domestics of the Prelacy should stand with swords and bag-wigs round pig and turkey, and venison, to defend, as it were, the Orthodox gastronome from the fierce Unitarian, the fell Baptist, and all the famished children of Dissent.

(*Letters to Archdeacon Singleton*)

to the unlettered rustic—

> I don't like that red nose, and those blear eyes, and that stupid, down-cast look. You are a drunkard. Another pint, and one pint more; a glass of gin and water, rum and milk, cider and pepper, a glass of peppermint, and all the beastly fluids which drunkards pour down their throats. . . . It is all nonsense about not being able to work without ale, and gin, and cider, and fermented liquors. Do lions and cart-horses drink ale? It is mere habit. . . . I have no objection, you will observe, to a moderate use of ale, or any other liquor you can *afford* to purchase. My objection is, that you cannot afford it; that every penny you spend at the alehouse comes out of the stomachs of the poor children, and strips off the clothes of the wife—
>
> ("Advice to Parishioners")

and a child—

> Lucy, dear child, mind your arithmetic. You know, in the first sum of yours I ever saw, there was a mistake. You had carried two (as a cab is li-censed to do) and you ought, dear Lucy, to have carried but one. Is this a trifle? What would life be without arithmetic but a scene of hor-rors? . . . I now give you my parting advice. Don't marry any body who has not a tolerable understanding and a thousand a year, and God bless you, dear child.

Always lucid, well-informed and fair to his opponents, he is equally at home with the long period and the short, the ornate vocabulary and the plain, and is a master of every rhetorical effect, the satirical inversion—

> Their object is to preserve game; they have no objection to preserve the lives of their fellow creatures also, if both can exist at the same time; if not, the least worthy of God's creatures must fall—the rustic without a soul—not the Christian partridge—not the immortal pheasant—not the rational woodcock, or the accountable hare.

the ironic description of shocking facts in tea-table terms—

> One summer's whipping, only one: the thumb-screw for a short season; a little light easy torturing between Lady-day and Michaelmas.

the homely simile—

> You may not be aware of it yourself, most reverend Abraham, but you deny their freedom to the Catholics upon the same principle that Sarah your wife refuses to give the receipt for a ham or a gooseberry dump-ling: she refuses her receipts, not because they secure to her a certain flavour, but because they remind her that her neighbours want it: a feel-

ing laughable in a priestess, shameful in a priest; venial when it withholds the blessings of a ham, tyrannical and execrable when it narrows the boon of religious freedom.

and the ringing peroration of righteous anger—

If I lived at Hampstead upon stewed meats and claret; if I walked to church every Sunday before eleven young gentlemen of my own begetting with their faces washed, and their hair pleasingly combed; if the Almighty had blessed me with every earthly comfort—how awfully would I pause before I sent forth the flame and the sword over the cabins of the poor, brave, generous, open-hearted peasants of Ireland. . . . The vigour I love consists in finding out wherein subjects are aggrieved, in relieving them, in studying the temper and genius of a people, in consulting their prejudices, in selecting proper persons to lead and manage them, in the laborious, watchful, and difficult task of increasing public happiness by allaying each particular discontent. . . . But this, in the eyes of Mr Percival, is imbecility and meanness: houses are not broken open—women are not insulted—the people seem all to be happy; they are not rode over by horses, and cut by whips. Do you call this vigour? Is this government?

His command of comic effects is equally extensive and masterly. Many of his impromptu puns are still remembered, such as his remark on hearing two women screaming insults at each other from upper stories on opposite sides of a narrow street in Edinburgh:

Those two women will never agree: they are arguing from different premises.

His particular forte, perhaps, is the treatment of analogical situations as identical; during the period of the Luddite riots he wrote to a friend:

What do you think of all these burnings? and have you heard of the new sort of burnings? Ladies' maids have taken to setting their mistresses on fire. Two dowagers were burned last week, and large rewards are offered! They are inventing little fire-engines for the toilet table, worked with lavender water!

Lastly, he can create pictures in what might be called the ludicrous baroque style, as surely as Pope:

Frequently did Lord John meet the destroying Bishops; much did he commend their daily heap of ruins; sweetly did they smile on each other, and much charming talk was there of meteorology and catarrh, and the particular cathedral they were pulling down at the time; till one fine morning the Home Secretary, with a voice more bland, and a look more

ardently affectionate, than that which the masculine mouse bestows on
his nibbling female, informed them that the Government meant to take
all the Church property into their own hands, to pay the rates out of it,
and deliver the residue to the rightful possessors. Such an effect, they
say, was never before produced by a *coup de théâtre.* The Commission was
separated in an instant: London clenched his fist; Canterbury was hurried out by his chaplains, and put into a warm bed; a solemn vacancy
spread itself over the face of Gloucester; Lincoln was taken out in strong
hysterics.

IV

Sydney Smith is a perfect expression of the Whig mentality, of that English
form of Liberalism which has always perplexed and sometimes enraged Continental observers both on the political Right and on the political Left. European liberalism, which has normally been anti-clerical, republican, and materialist, finds it bewildering that social reform in England should owe so much
to religion—that the British Labour Party, for example, should be so closely
associated with the Evangelical movement, and the increasing concern over
juvenile delinquency and other cultural problems of urbanization with Anglo-
Catholicism—and that the English Liberal who desires the abolition of the
Crown or the House of Lords should be so rare a bird. Liberals like Godwin
and H. G. Wells are a-typical, and much closer to the European mind.

For the European who knows a little history, it is all the more puzzling,
since he is aware that Voltaire and the French Encyclopaedists of the Enlightenment who were the founders of continental Liberalism were inspired
by and took many of their ideas from Locke, the Deists, and the Whig authors of the Glorious Revolution of 1688. If he is a pro-clerical monarchist,
he is apt to conclude that the English Liberal is a materialist at heart who is
only using religious sentiments as a smoke-screen, and to point to the ambiguities of the Thirty-Nine Articles as proof that an Anglican does not know
what he believes; if he is an anti-clerical rationalist, he is apt to come to similar doubts about the Englishman's Liberal convictions, citing in evidence his
devotion to irrational political institutions.

The clue to the difference is to be found in the difference in meaning of
the word *Revolution* as applied to the events which took place in France in
1789 and as applied to the events which took place in England in 1688. In
the former case it means a radical transformation, the birth of a new kind of
society, in the latter it is an astronomical metaphor, meaning a restoration of
balance. The radical transformation of English society which corresponds to
the French Revolution was the work of the Tudors. The execution of Charles
I was not, like the execution of Louis XVI, a revolutionary breach with the

past but the restoration of a conservative, even medieval, idea, namely, that the ruler is not above but subject to Natural Law. Then, from their experiences under the Protectorate, Englishmen learned that the dangers of arbitrary power were not necessarily removed simply by the abolition of the Crown, for the claims of self-appointed saints to know by divine inspiration what the good life should be and to have the right to impose their notions on the ungodly could be as great a threat as the divine right of kings. The historical experience with which the Whigs of 1688 and their successors had to cope was a century and a half of bitter quarrels and drastic changes imposed upon the public by individuals or minorities. The most fundamental notion in English Liberalism, therefore, is the notion of limited sovereignty and its characteristic way of thinking goes something like this:

(1) All people differ from each other in character and temperament so that any attempt to impose an absolute uniformity is a tyranny. On the other hand there can be no social life unless the members of a society hold certain beliefs in common, and behave in certain commonly accepted ways.

(2) The beliefs which it is necessary to hold in common must therefore be so defined that differences of emphasis are possible and the laws which regulate social conduct must be such that they command common consent. In so far as conformity has to be enforced, this should be in matters of outward behavior not of private belief, firstly because there can be no doubt whether an individual does or does not conform, and secondly because men find behaving in a way with which they are not in complete sympathy more tolerable than being told to believe something they consider false. Thus, in the English Prayer Book the rules for conducting the Liturgy are precise, while the meaning of the Thirty-Nine Articles is purposely left vague.

(3) The way in which a reform is effected is just as important as the reform itself. Violent change is as injurious to freedom as inertia.

(4) Utopians are a public menace. Reformers must concern themselves with the concrete and the possible.

The authors of the French Enlightenment were confronted with a very different situation, a static society in which nothing had changed. To the French Liberal, therefore, nothing could seem to matter except that a radical change should occur and the threat to freedom was not absolute sovereignty as such but the imprisonment of the majority in an arbitrary social status. A Jacobin like St Just could accept the notion of absolute sovereignty without question so long as it was taken from the Crown and given to the people. Materialism was a natural philosophy for French Liberalism to adopt since its enemy was the aristocrat who claimed privilege on biological grounds (few of the English peerages in the eighteenth century were more than two hundred years old), and it was no less natural that this materialism should be militantly dogmatic since the philosophy European Liberalism associated with the *ancien régime*, the theology of the Roman Catholic Church, was itself rigid and uncompromising.

Sydney Smith is an example of English Liberalism at its best. He is never Utopian or given to large generalizations but always attacks a specific abuse, and the reform he proposes is equally specific and always possible to realize. Further, he assumes that, though most people are selfish and many people are stupid, few are either lunatics or deliberate scoundrels impervious to rational argument.

Thus, in attacking the Game Laws, he avoids raising ultimate questions about the justice or injustice of private property and its unequal distribution, and sticks to the immediate issue of man-traps, spring-guns and the like. Assuming that no sane man will deny that they are cruel, he points out that they are unnecessary for the purpose for which they are intended; the prevention of poaching can be achieved by humane means, namely by giving every landlord, great or small, the right to kill game, by making game private property like geese or ducks and by allowing the owner to sell game to whom he chooses since, as long as the sale of game is forbidden and there are rich men who want it, a black market supplied by poachers is inevitable.

Knowing both the world of the rich and the world of the poor and an enemy of neither, he is aware that many injustices to the poor exist, not because the rich are intentionally unjust but because their own world has never felt them. In attacking the law which denied defense counsel to prisoners accused of a felony, a leftover from feudal times when a defense of prisoners accused by the Crown was felt to imply disloyalty, he explains very simply why, though this feeling no longer existed, the law still remained on the statute books.

> To ask why there are not petitions—why the evil is not more noticed, is mere parliamentary froth and ministerial juggling. Gentlemen are rarely hung. If they were so, there would be petitions without end for counsel.

There is a certain type of professional Liberal who assumes that in every issue the liberal position must be on the Left. Sydney Smith was never fooled in this way, as a comparison of his two principal set of pamphlets, the *Peter Plymley Letters* and the *Letters to Archdeacon Singleton*, clearly demonstrates. In the former his opponent is the conservative. Laws prohibiting Roman Catholics from voting or holding public offices, which when they were originally passed may have had some justification—an attempt to bring back the Stuarts might have met with their support—were still in effect, long after any such danger had passed. Sydney Smith assumes that the vast majority of those who opposed their repeal were capable of seeing that they were unjust, if he can demonstrate that there was no danger incurred by removing them. With the inveterately stupid or demagogic minority, his argument is different; he warns them of the unpleasant material consequences to themselves which will follow if they refuse to listen to their conscience.

In the case of the Singleton letters, his enemies are not those who refuse to make a needed reform but those who would impose a necessary reform from above in a hasty and unjust manner. What right, he asks, have the bishops to make changes without consulting the lower clergy who will be most affected by them and whose experience of parochial life make them better equipped to make concrete judgements about abuses instead of generalisations. Further he complains that much of the plan for reform was Utopian, since to do what it was intended to do would require a sum of money which the Church did not possess.

In his opposition to secret ballot, later experience has shown us that he was mistaken, because he did not foresee—neither, for that matter, did his opponents—a day when there would arise one-party governments prepared to use all the instruments of coercion at their disposal to ensure an overwhelming vote in their favour. Even so, he makes two points in his pamphlet which no liberal democracy should forget; firstly, that the free voter must hold himself responsible for the consequence of his vote:

> Who brought that mischievous profligate villain into Parliament? Let us see the names of his real supporters. Who stood out against the strong and uplifted arm of power? Who discovered this excellent and hitherto unknown person? . . . Is it not a dark and demoralising system to draw this veil over human actions, to say to the mass, be base, and you will not be despised; be victorious and you will not be honored—

and secondly that the free voter is the voter whose choice is determined by what he believes to be in the best interest of his country and by nothing else.

> The Radicals are quite satisfied if a rich man of popular manners gains the votes and affections of his dependents; but why is not this as bad as intimidation? The real object is to vote for the good politician, not for the kind-hearted or agreeable man: the mischief is just the same to the country whether I am smiled into a corrupt choice, or frowned into a corrupt choice.

V

Today the Whig tradition which Sydney Smith represented is under a cloud. It is under attack for being aesthetically unappealing and psychologically or metaphysically shallow.

> . . . what is Whiggery?
> A levelling, rancorous, rational sort of mind
> That never looked out of the eye of a saint
> Or out of a drunkard's eye.

Yet, unattractive and shallow as one may feel so many liberals to be, how rarely on any concrete social issue does one find the liberal position the wrong one. Again, how often, alas, do those very philosophers and writers who have most astounded us by their profound insights into the human heart and human existence, dismay us by the folly and worse of their judgments on the issues of everyday life.

Liberalism is also under criticism for being ineffective and in so far as we have to combat enemies with whom rational discussion is impossible because the absolute presuppositions on both sides are radically different, the criticism has some justification. Some of us, however, seem in danger of forgetting that rational discussion is desirable and that liberty is not just a value of which one approves in the abstract but, to be real, must be embodied in one's own person and daily acts. Indeed, the more critical a situation, the less the opinions a man expresses matter in comparison with his behavior. On this, if nothing else, the sober Whig and the wild Existentialist will agree. What a challenge to a second Landor it would be to compose an Imaginary Conversation between the shades of the author of the *Letters to Archdeacon Singleton* and the author of *Attack on Christendom*.

I should not be surprised if they understood each other much better than one would naturally expect. They both disliked abstract systems, they were both strikingly original personalities and they could both be very funny. Kierkegaard, whose chief complaint against the bourgeois was that they were a parody of the Knight of Faith, would have appreciated, I think, Sydney Smith's use of bourgeois terms to define *A Nice Person*:

> A nice person is neither too tall nor too short, looks clean and cheerful, has no prominent features, makes no difficulties, is never displaced, sits bodkin, is never foolishly affronted, and is void of affectations. . . . A nice person is clear of trumpery little passions, acknowledges superiority, delights in talent, shelters humility, pardons adversity, forgives deficiency, respects all men's rights, never stops the bottle, is never long and never wrong, always knows the day of the month, the name of everybody at table, and never gives pain to any human being. . . . A nice person never knocks over wine or melted butter, does not tread upon the dog's foot, or molest the family cat, eats soup without noise, laughs in the right place, and has a watchful and attentive eye.

> *Selected Writings of Sydney Smith,* edited and with an
> introduction by W. H. Auden, 1956

Introduction to *The Descent of the Dove,* by Charles Williams

As a rule, personal reminiscences are out of place in a literary discussion, but Charles Williams is an exception. As T. S. Eliot wrote in an introduction to *All Hallows' Eve*: "Some men are less than their works, some are more. Charles Williams cannot be placed in either class. To have known the man would have been enough; to know his books is enough; but no one who has known both the man and his works would have willingly foregone either experience. I can think of no writer who was more wholly the same man in his life and in his writings."

When I met Charles Williams I had read none of his books; our meetings were few and on business, yet I count them among my most unforgettable and precious experiences. I have met great and good men in whose presence one was conscious of one's own littleness; Charles Williams' effect on me and on others with whom I have spoken was quite different: in his company one felt twice as intelligent and infinitely nicer than, out of it, one knew oneself to be. It wasn't simply that he was a sympathetic listener—he talked a lot and he talked well—but, more than anyone else I have ever known, he gave himself completely to the company that he was in. So many conversations, even good ones, are really several monologues which only now and then and by accident relate to each other, for the talkers are more concerned with their own thoughts than with a living exchange of ideas, but any conversation with Charles Williams, no matter how trivial or impersonal the topic, was a genuine dialogue.

When, later, I began to read his books, I realized why this was so; the basic theme which runs through all of them is a doctrine of exchange and substitution, a way of life by which, it was clear, he himself lived.

> The Company's second mode bore farther
> the labour and fruition; it exchanged the proper self
> and wherever need was drew breath daily
> in another's place, according to the grace of the Spirit
> "dying each other's life, living each other's death."
>
> Terrible and lovely is the general substitution of souls
> the Flesh-taking ordained for its mortal images
> in its first creation, and now in its sublime self
> shows, since It deigned to be dead in the stead of each man.

The doctrine might be briefly summarized as follows: the first law of the spiritual universe, the Real City, is that nobody can carry his own burden; he only can, and therefore he must, carry someone else's. Whose burden in particular he should carry is up to him to decide: usually, this choice is dictated by his character and his social circumstances—in *All Hallows' Eve* the dead girl Lester takes upon herself the suffering of her old school acquaintance Betty to whom, in life, she had been distantly and superiorly kind; however, a few—Taliessin, the poet in Mr Williams' poetic cycle on the Arthurian legend, is one—can become so adept in this practice that they can do it for anybody.

This has nothing to do with the self-righteous attitude I once heard expressed in a parody of a sermon: "We are all here on earth to help others: what on earth the others are here for I don't know." One-sided exchange is a contradiction. Choosing to bear another's burden involves at the same time permitting another to carry one's own, and this may well be the harder choice, just as it is usually easier to forgive than be forgiven. The motto of the City is: "Your life and death are with your neighbor," and this co-inherence is not limited to contemporaries, for it includes the already dead and the as yet unborn. Thus Taliessin describes the rescue of Virgil from the Second Death.

> Unborn pieties lived.
> Out of the infinity of time to that moment's infinity
> they lived, they rushed, they dived below him, they rose
> to close with his fall; all, while man is, that could
> live, and would, by his hexameters, found
> there the ground of their power, and their power's use.
> Others he saved; himself he could not save.
> In that hour, they came; more and faster, they sped
> To their dead master; they sought him to save
> from the spectral grave and the endless falling,
> who had heard, for their own instruction, the sound of his calling.
> There was intervention, suspension, the net of their loves,
> all their throng's songs:
> *Virgil, master and friend,*
> *holy poet, priest, president of priests,*
> *priest long since of all our energies' end,*
> *deign to accept adoration, and what salvation*
> *may reign here by us, deign of goodwill to endure . . .*

I believe that Charles Williams would have gone even further and said that, in fact, there is no such thing as one's own cross; the troubles that one thinks of and too often resents as one's own may well be really another's, and once this is realised they become tolerable. Thus Pauline in *Descent into Hell* suffers from a recurrent nightmare of meeting her own double and discovers that its origin lies in the terrors of an ancestor who was burned as a heretic.

It is a pity, I think, that Charles Williams' best known works should be his fiction, for, extraordinary as the novels are, I find them the least satisfactory of his books. To begin with, he is interested, like Blake, in states of being rather than in individuals, and fiction is not an ideal medium for describing such. Secondly, it is virtually impossible, I believe, to describe the state of grace artistically, because to this state the capacity of the individual soul for expression is irrelevant; a commonplace person who can only utter banalities is just as capable of redemption as a genius; indeed, the chances of his redemption are probably greater: "It is easier for a camel to pass through the eye of a needle than for a rich man to enter into the Kingdom of Heaven" is a warning not only to the wealthy but to the gifted of all kinds. If a writer pick a genius to represent the state of grace, he is almost bound to suggest that salvation is the consequence of genius, that the redeemed are a superior elite; but if, on the other hand, he chooses a commonplace person, banalities remain artistically, banalities, whatever glories they may conceal. The saved characters in Mr Williams' novels, like Lester, are unsatisfactory from a literary point of view because of the unbridgeable gulf between their experiences and their power of describing them.

In describing the state of damnation this problem does not arise, and I know of no other writer, living or dead, who has given us so convincing and terrifying portraits of damned souls as Charles Williams. The popular notion of Hell is morally revolting and intellectually incredible because it is conceived of in terms of human criminal law, as a torture imposed upon the sinner against his will by an all-powerful God. Charles Williams succeeds, where even Dante, I think, fails, in showing us that nobody is ever *sent* to hell; he, or she, insists on going there. If, as Christians believe, God is love, then in one sense He is not omnipotent, for He cannot compel His creatures to accept His Love without ceasing to be Himself. The wrath of God is not *His* wrath but the way in which those feel His Love who refuse it, and the right of refusal is a privilege which not even their Creator can take from them.

> . . . in an overpowering ordinariness, they stood, as any three young women might, deciding occupation, exchanging chat. It was Evelyn who spoke. Her eyes darting from Betty to Lester and back, she said, "Don't you interfere with me. I won't let you. I won't. Don't try."
>
> Lester said, "Look, Evelyn, we've often gone out together; let's do it again. Come with me today and we'll think what there is to do . . . let's go and see what we can find."
>
> Evelyn said, "I suppose you think that's kind. You think it's clever to be kind, don't you? I always hated being with you, and I daresay sooner or later I can find someone else there, thank you."
>
> "Yes," said Lester, "I'm afraid you may."
>
> The words, to all but Evelyn, brought a sinister thought of that other strange world. But Evelyn was past noting even that. . . . Lester and Betty were trying to catch her, to keep her, to pain her; they had always hated

her. But she would beat them. She made a rush; she ran between them; she dodged the hands that were not flung out; she cried, "Let me go" to those who had not held her. She ran to the window; the yard outside was very lonely and spectral. She almost hesitated. But she looked back over her shoulder and saw Lester move. She cried out, "You thought you'd got me, didn't you?" They saw the immortal fixity of her constricted face, gleeful in her supposed triumph, lunatic in her escape, as it had once a subdued lunatic glee in its cruel indulgence; and then she broke through the window again and was gone into that other City, there to wait and wander and mutter till she found what companions she could.

Judging by my own experience, I should advise readers to postpone reading Charles Williams' poetry until, through reading his prose works, they have become thoroughly familiar with his ideas and his sensibility. I must confess that, when I first tried to read his poetry, though as a fellow verse writer I could see its great technical interest, I could not make head or tail of it. Like the Blake of the Prophetic Books, Charles Williams has his own mythology which a reader must master, and previous geographical associations can make this difficult. To me, for example, the word *Caucasia* has certain geographical and ethnic associations which I had first to dismiss in order to accept it as the poet's term for the unfallen order of Nature. I can only say, however, that the more I read *Taliessin Through Logres* and *The Region of the Summer Stars*, the more rewarding I find them. (For an excellent, if perhaps excessively enthusiastic, introduction to these works, the reader should consult the exposition by C. S. Lewis in the posthumous volume *Arthurian Torso*.)

Charles Williams wrote many books in many different genres and I have no space to discuss them all. Among his studies in literary criticism, I would particularly recommend *Reason and Beauty in the Poetic Mind* and his magnificent book on Dante, *The Figure of Beatrice*; of his theological essays, *He Came Down from Heaven* and *The Forgiveness of Sins. The Descent of the Dove* is not only the best of his historical writings (though *James the First* is very fine), but, in my opinion, his masterpiece.

Charles Williams was a devout member of that "odd (but not, for that, necessarily less sacred)" body the Anglican Church and as far removed as possible from that point of view which would cure the disunity of Christendom by denying the importance of Christian dogma.

"The intellect," said Luther, "is the Devil's whore." She may be, at least, the mistress of a passionate emotion, or she may indulge her own sensuality. But, to be fair to her, it is not only self-indulgence which drives her into controversies. Something has, in this world, to be *said*. It was all very well for the Incarnate Glory to refrain from defining his gospel, but he left the task to his disciples, and all the infallibilities have not yet succeeded in making it very much plainer. . . . Jewels and words are but images, but then so are grass and sparrows. And jewels and words are no less and no more necessary than cotton and silence.

Thus Williams in *The Descent of the Dove.* I have never read, however, a history of the church so completely imbued with ecumenical passion. Never was there a historian more courteous to all alike. Whatever the issue, Faith against Works, Pelagian versus Jansenist, whoever the party leader, Calvin, St Ignatius Loyola, Montaigne, Pascal, Voltaire, Williams never fails to be just to both sides. Of the Marxist-materialist revolt against the Church, for example, he writes:

Christendom was largely identified by the revolutionaries with the owners of property, as well as with the abstract defence of property. This view was not so incorrect as it ought to have been. The theologians might accurately define, and the saints might labour on behalf of the poor, but all this was hampered by three things. The first was the undoubted fact that the co-inherence of sensuality in substance, however true, however just, was of no great interest to those whose sensuality was only a continual despair. An anguish of need and more need can only be used as the Way by those already advanced in sanctity; the authorities of the Church were never intended to impose (or even too much seem to impose) such a terrible Rejection of Images upon their co-inheritors of glory. No doubt there were some few who followed that Way even so, but of those to whom it was a mockery and an obscene parody of grace there were millions. The second difficulty was that the mass of professing Christians were definitely not in need of food, nor did they show any signs of selling much of what they had and giving it to the poor. Morally perhaps they were not required to do so, but their retention of their possessions under the patronage of the Cross made the Cross too much a sign of their possessions. "Having nothing," wrote St Paul, "and yet possessing all things." The second clause was obvious; the first was hidden with God. A few priests, a few laymen, surrendered their lives to the needs of the destitute; the rest consoled them only with ritual prayers. The third difficulty was (briefly) philanthropy, using the word in its less bearable sense. Even those who wished to help wished also to direct.

Perhaps the most remarkable thing about Charles Williams, in this book and all the others, is what one might call the orthodoxy of his imagination, as distinct from his beliefs, for this is very rare in our technological culture. In describing the life of the body and its finite existence in time, most contemporary writers, whatever their beliefs, show a manichean bias, an emphasis on the drab and the sordid. If they are materialists they place the beautiful and the exciting in some temporal future; if they are professing Christians the only road to salvation they can imagine is the Negative Way of ascetic renunciation. Even the few who, like D. H. Lawrence, do not suffer from this bias, cannot find anything in the contemporary world to their relish and turn for sustenance to pre-industrial societies.

Chesterton, a writer by whom, I think, Charles Williams was influenced, did try to keep his balance and his nerve, but in his praise of wonder and wine there is a shrillness of tone, an exaggerated heartiness which betrays an inner strain. In the work of Charles Williams I can detect no strain whatever; he can imagine Beatrice in the Finchley Road as easily as in Thirteenth Century Florence.

I have been reading and rereading *The Descent of the Dove* for some sixteen years now and I find it a source of intellectual delight and spiritual nourishment which remains inexhaustible.

The Christian Century, 2 May 1956;
The Descent of the Dove, by Charles Williams, 1956

Wisdom, Wit, Music

Evenings with the Orchestra. By Hector Berlioz.
Translated by Jacques Barzun. Knopf. $6.

Evenings with the Orchestra belongs to that literary genre which is the most difficult of all for a reviewer, "the artful hodge-podge."

To succeed in it, as Berlioz most brilliantly does, requires a combination of qualities which is very rare, the many-faceted curiosity of the dramatist with the aggressively personal vision of the lyric poet. Without the former, the result will be a monotony unmitigated by formal charm; without the latter an arbitrary heap of fragments which, however interesting when taken separately, fail to relate into any coherent pattern. It is almost impossible for a reviewer to prove to a prospective reader that such a success has been achieved because, to do equal justice to the variety and the unity, he would have to quote the greater part of the book.

The structural idea of the book is based on the critical presupposition that bad art is boring. Night after night the orchestra of an opera house in northern Europe assemble to perform the opera appointed for that evening: when the opera is a bad one, and it usually is, the members of the orchestra, with the exception of the bass-drum player who is kept too busy, chatter among themselves, exchanging gossip and anecdotes. Occasionally, however, the opera is good—Berlioz mentions six, *Der Freischütz, Fidelio, Il Barbiere di Siviglia, Don Giovanni, Iphigenia in Tauris, Les Huguenots*—then, the orchestra keep silent and do their conscientious best. Berlioz himself appears in two roles, sometimes in his actual role of music critic (I'm not quite certain how he is able to talk to the orchestra in this capacity, but he does) and some-times as the concertmaster and composer Corsino. The imaginative centre of the book, though we do not hear about it until the last, or twenty-fifth evening, is Berlioz' vision of Euphonia, the musical Utopia. From the view-point of this imaginary perfection, he surveys the realities of musical life in his time, the arrogance of patrons and the commercialism of managers, the snobbery of the fashionable and the vulgarity of the mob, the lack of profes-sional pride among performers and the lack of artistic taste, alas, in the Fair Sex, the anatomy of claques and the psychology of tenors.

What strikes me most on re-reading *Evenings with the Orchestra* after an in-terval of several years is Berlioz' common sense and willingness to see what is good in the actual state of affairs, however far from perfection that may be. Most descriptions of Utopia are humorless, but Berlioz exhibits his Eupho-nia as a comic day-dream which he knows neither can nor should become actual.

> The singers and players of instruments are grouped by categories in the several quarters of the town. Each type of voice and instrument has a street bearing its name, which is inhabited only by the section of the population which practices that particular voice or instrument. There are streets of sopranos, of basses, of tenors, of contraltos; of violins, of horns, of flutes, of harps, and so on.
>
> Needless to say, Euphonia is governed in military fashion and sub-jected to a despotic regime.
>
> They are also trained to silence, a silence so absolute and profound that if three thousand Euphonian choristers were assembled in the amphi-theatre or in any other resonant place, one could still hear the buzzing of an insect, and a blind man in their midst might think he was quite alone.
>
> A minute later, each one recovering breath and voice—and in this you see again our Euphonian's musical sense—without either the prefect of the choruses or myself making the slightest signs to suggest the har-mony, ten thousand voices burst out spontaneously on the chord of the diminished seventh followed by a magnificent cadence in C major.

From passages such as these, it is quite clear Berlioz knew that Euphonia was not a New Jerusalem to be realised if possible but an Eden which it is fun to imagine but madness to believe one can enter.

It would have been excusable in a musician who was a perfectionist and temperamentally passionate in his likes and dislikes had he written of the realities of musical life with a kind of Swiftian disgust but, amazingly enough, Berlioz, however savagely satirical he may be, rarely loses compassion and understanding; note, for instance, the adjective *sincere* in the following:

I have never yet attended a first night at the Opera without finding among the judges in the lobby a large majority hostile to the new work, however beautiful and great it may have been. Nor is there a single score, however flat and empty, null and void, that does not gather a few votes of approval or that fails to number sincere admirers, as if to justify the proverb that says there is no pot without a lid.

Popular tenors may be a pain in the neck, but Berlioz does not allow us to forget that their voices are great god-given gifts or that their end is usually disgrace and oblivion.

One of the most famous stories in the book is the tale of Adolphe, the Spontini fan, and Hortense, the brainless and vain singer, at the end of which Adolphe commits suicide after hearing a perfect performance of *La Vestale*, and Hortense, passing by at that moment, thinks he has done it out of hopeless love for her: as Berlioz tells it, the hero is made to look quite as ridiculous as the heroine. (My reading of this story may, I must admit, be influenced by my inability to appreciate *La Vestale* which I find almost as boring as works by another of Berlioz' great heroes, Gluck.)

Again, he exhibits a healthy realism and self-knowledge when he allows Berlioz-Corsini to say to Berlioz-author:

The woman singer of whom you wrote: "we thought she was in labor," retorted sourly: "At any rate, he'll never be the father of my children." Here I cannot congratulate you, for she is an enchanting little fool.

Nor is the book all fun and games; interspersed at intervals come serious and interesting studies of Spontini, Paganini and Beethoven.

Still, it is, of course, the fun and games that one remembers, the despiser of Weber whose skull was used in *Freischütz*, the claque in church:

"How do you mean? You can't applaud in church."

"I know. But you can cough, blow your nose, shift your chair, scrape your feet, hum and haw, lift your eyes to heaven—the whole bag of tricks, don't you know. We could have done a sweet job for you and given you a real success, just as we do for a fashionable preacher."

the arrival of Jenny Lind in the United States:

the dolphins and whales that had for more than twenty-five hundred miles shared in the triumphal progress of this new Galatea, convoying her ship while spouting scented jets, were twisting and turning outside the port, in despair at their inability to accompany her ashore. Sea-lions shedding salt tears could be heard bellowing their lamentations . . . gulls, frigate birds, loons, and other wild inhabitants of the solitary ocean wastes, luckier than the seals, circled fearlessly about the adorable creature, perched on her pure shoulders, and hovered over her

Olympian head, bearing in their bills abnormally large pearls, which they presented to her most courteously, cooing gently the while.

the political quarrel of the stage hands under the artificial storm during a performance of Adolphe Adam's *Le Fanal*, which created such a tempestuous effect, or best of all, perhaps, and certainly the most frightening, his encounter in the beautiful countryside with the crippled little girl who tried to keep a crippled swallow.

"I did what grandmother told me; I cleaned her leg all up, and tied it together with matchsticks . . . And I gave her nice flies all the time, and I only pulled their heads off so's they wouldn't fly away. And grandmother kept on saying: 'That's right, you must be good to animals if you want them to get well. Only a few days more and you'll be well yourself.' And just now she hears that flock of other swallows squalling up there in the steeple, and the mean thing pushes up the lid of her basket, and while I'm busy getting more flies ready for her, she—hee-hee! she—hoo-hoo! she hooked it."

"I know how you feel, my child; you loved your swallow very much."

"Me? What an idea! But she wasn't quite well yet, and now I won't be well myself at all. The others she's gone off with are going to break her leg for her again, I know they will."

"What makes you think the others will do that?"

"Because they're wicked, o'course, like all the birds are. I saw it all right this winter, when it was so cold; I plucked the feathers off a sparrow somebody gave me; I left only his wing and tail feathers; then I let him loose in front of some others. He flew to them, and they all pounced and pecked him to death. I saw it I tell you" (crying) "I never laughed so—hee-hee! And now you see my leg will never get well. Oh, if I'd known—boo-hoo! I'd have wrung her neck proper the minute I found her."

Mozart's letters are evidence of great potential literary gifts which he had no time and, perhaps, no inclination to develop; there are prose works of Wagner's which are much more readable and interesting than is generally supposed, but the *Autobiography* and *Evenings with the Orchestra* are literary achievements which would have made Berlioz famous if he had never written a note, and he and his English-speaking audience are now lucky in having found in Jacques Barzun a translator who really knows his business. Not only is he accurate as regards the meaning of individual words, including technical terms (which should be easy but is not always, apparently, found to be so) but also his sentences never betray, either in their syntax or their cadence, a foreign origin and anybody who has ever tried to translate even the simplest passage from another tongue knows what constant vigilance this requires.

A frank and humorous picture of the conditions under which music is composed, performed, judged and paid for is a job which needs re-doing every twenty-five years or so. Some things, of course, never change.

A composer-pianist to-day who is foolish enough to give a concert in a fishing port on the day that the herring have come in, will be as disappointed as his nineteenth century forebear, and have no more right to complain. Food must always take precedence over art. Arrangers, alas, are still with us. Smarting under the tyranny of divas and tenors, Berlioz day-dreamed of an Eden where the conductor would be absolute master: it came to pass, and the new tyranny proved just as insufferable as the old. But now the conductor is becoming a poor old back number, slave to a new master, the evils of whose reign deserve a description by Berlioz in his most blood-thirsty mood, that sworn enemy of music and insolent corrupter of our ears, the Sound-Engineer.

The Griffin, May 1956

Making, Knowing and Judging

[See *The Dyer's Hand*, p. 477, and textual notes, p. 948.]

Making, Knowing and Judging, 1956

Walter de la Mare

In America during the last thirty years—I hope it was otherwise here, though I fear it was not—Mr de la Mare had to endure the most painful fate that a poet can suffer. Everyone knew his name, each new volume of poems that appeared was praised by the reviewers, and nobody read him. The man who in *Come Hither, Behold This Dreamer, Love* and *Desert Islands* proved that the anthology could be a genuine artistic genre was himself worse treated by anthologists than any other poet I can think of.

Open almost any anthology of modern poetry and what will you find? The same old war-horses—"The Listeners," "All That's Past," "The Scribe," "Farewell," etc.—all of them published before 1920. Look at the quotations from reviews on the dust jackets of his books and you will read the kind of praise which is more deadly than any attack—"sheer loveliness," "What is Poetry? This is" and so forth, which immediately relegates him to that schoolmistress category of poets who write about Beauty as contrasted with those who write about Life.

I cannot see any explanation for this except human laziness. Mallarmé did not write about Life in that sense, yet he is taken seriously; if de la Mare is a traditional poet in that he never found it necessary to make a radical break with the metrical tradition of the nineteenth century or with conventional syntax, is not Yeats equally traditional? Yet, in their handling of these matters, are not both equally unique? There is an essay to be written upon de la Mare's metrical fingering, in particular his use of the spondee, yet, so far as I know, nobody has attempted one.

Consider, for example, the masterly variety of the following:—

> Wicket out into the dark
>   That swings but one way;
> Infinite hush in an ocean of silence
>   Aeons away—
> Thou forsaken! even thou!—
>   The dread good-bye;
> The abandoned, the thronged, the watched, the unshared—
>   Awaiting me—I!
>
>   ("The Bottle")

> No; they are only birds—swifts, in the loft of the morning,
> Coursing, disporting, courting, in the pale-blue arc of the sky.
> There is no venom for kin or for kind in their wild-winged archery,
> Nor death in their innocent droppings as fleet in their mansions they fly;
> Swooping with flicker of pinions to couple, the loved one with the loved one,
> Never with malice or hate, in their vehement sallies through space.
>
>   ("Swifts")

> . . . There will be company, but they will not heed you:
>   Yours will be a journey only of two paces
>   Into view of the stars again; but you will not make it.
>   There will be no recognition;
>   No one, who should see you, will say—
>   Throughout the uncountable hours—
> "Why . . . the last time we met. I brought you some flowers."
>
>   ("De Profundis")

Critics to-day are always discussing metaphysical conceits, but I have not seen them quote from de la Mare's most ambitious poem, "Winged Chariot":—

> More silent yet; pure solace to the sight—
> The dwindling candle with her pensive light
> Metes out the leaden watches of the night,
> And, in that service, from herself takes flight.

or

> Fate was appalled. Her See-Saw would not stir.
> Man sat dead-centre and grimaced at her.
> Her prizes? None could shine where none could err;
> So every artless dunce was a philosopher.

One of the surest tests of the stature of a poet is one's reaction to his "selected" poems. In the case of a minor poet—we need not mention names—most readers will agree in their choices of his best poems, but in the case of a really important one, each reader will see a certain aspect of his work which is his personal preference. Reading through Mr Green-Armytage's selection from de la Mare, for example, I get mad. I look to see what he has taken from *The Veil* and *The Fleeting*: "Yes," I think, "he's got 'Good-Bye,' 'The Quiet Enemy,' 'The Railway-Junction,' 'Thus Her Tale,' and that extraordinary verse tale 'The Owl,' but where is 'The Fat Woman,' 'The Feckless Dinner-Party,' 'The Bottle,' 'The Robin'?" Or again, "How *could* he possibly have omitted from his *Inward Companion* selection 'She Said,' 'The Forest,' and, above all, my favourite de la Mare poem, 'Lost World'?" This is, of course, no criticism of Mr Green-Armytage, but a witness to the many-sidedness of a poet who is often regarded as narrow in his poetic concerns.

I should like to conclude by quoting "Lost World," not only for its excellence but also because the only other poet of whom it reminds me is one not generally associated with Mr de la Mare, namely, Baudelaire:—

> Why, inward companion, are you so dark with anguish?
> A trickle of rancid water that oozes and veers,
> Picking its sluggish course through slag and refuse,
> Down at length to the all-oblivious ocean—
> What else were apt comparison for your tears?
>
> But no: not of me are you grieving, not for me either;
> Though I, it seems, am the dungeon in which you dwell,
> Derelict, drear, with skeleton arms to heaven,
> Wheels broken, abandoned, greenless, vacant, silent;
>   Nought living that eye can tell.
>
> Blame any man might the world in which he harbours,
> Washing his hands, like Pilate, of all its woes;
> And yet in deadly revolt at its evil and horror,
> That has brought pure life to this pass, smit through with sorrow,
> Since he was its infamous wrecker full well he knows.
>
> Not yours the blame. Why trouble me with your presence?
> Linger no instant, most Beautiful, in this hell.
> No touch of time has marred your immutable visage;

> Eros himself less radiant was in his dayspring!—
> Or nearer draw to your heartsick infidel!

Even as we mourn the dead, let us rejoice at what he has left us and posterity to read.

The Observer, 24 June 1956

An Eye for Mystery

In his brilliant comic novel *Cards of Identity*, Mr Nigel Dennis has, I believe, put his finger on the great spiritual defect of our modern and Western kind of society: its divorce of the sense of necessity from the sense of possibility. In earlier times, when Nature was still stronger than Man and societies were governed by rigid and hierarchical traditions, much that did not really have to be was accepted as inevitable and man's possibilities, as an individual or as a group, were unduly limited. But men had the psychological security of knowing who they were, and if they wished to become something else, while the obstacles might be insurmountable, at least they were concrete, identifiable and external to the individual.

Today, when the machine has seized the power from both Nature and any recognizable social group and transferred it to the collective, to society as a whole, men do not suffer from a too limited future—its possibilities, indeed, seem infinite—but from an imaginary or fantastic present. Men no longer ask themselves or seem able to answer truthfully the question "Who am I?—not by my own choice but in virtue of the nature I have been given," and in consequence are at the mercy of any suggestion put to them by whoever happens to control the mass media. Revolt against traditional injustice could and often did take a political form; the revolt of the imaginary against the imaginary—that is, the revolt of man lacking a sure sense of identity against ambiguous and shifting forces—tends to take the form of mania, individual or collective: rebellion with no other aim than rebellion.

One may smile at the eagerness with which the public read the psychological columnists and consult the latest book on child rearing, but they are right to be worried, for the years of childhood have never been so crucial as they are today. If, by the age of fourteen, a boy or a girl has not acquired a certainty of his or her identity, modern society is not going to help them find it.

As everybody knows, most learning is imitation. If, therefore, a person's problem is "Who am I?" (rather than "What do I want to become?") what he needs first is the companionship of beings that are unquestionably themselves. At the same time that the urbanization of life is cutting us off from an instinctive, unself-conscious relation to Nature, a relation to the Natural, or non-Historical, Order has become more important to our sanity than ever before, since much that was formerly given us by society can no longer be found there.

As never before it is the duty of parents to train their children to behold the creatures of Nature which can never lose their identities because they can only be what they already are: the flowers "fresh and laughing as on the days of great battles," the beasts who "walk the earth, ignorant, while their splendor lasts, of any weakness" and, most of all, perhaps, the heavenly bodies—the Sun, the Moon, the stars of the night sky, in all their unchanging majesty and stateliness of movement.

Train them to behold, not to observe. The world of beholding is a world of faces and proper names, not of numbers and algebraic signs, and in it no distinction is made between animate and inanimate, for *to live* is a synonym for *to exist*. As an adult refinement of the sense of wonder, detached observation is a blessed activity; when it thinks of itself as autonomous it is deadly. Just as a child must begin by thinking of God as a bigger and nicer Papa before he can grasp the theological definitions of a personal God, so, before he can appreciate the facts of astronomy, he must see the sky as inhabited by noble creatures—a Hunter and his Dog, a Scorpion, a Water-Carrier, a Lion, a Bull and so forth. To begin by telling him about light-years and the lack of life on the other planets is as ridiculous and wrong as to speak to him about some such theological concept as the Absolute Ground of Being.

The first truth for him to learn, which no later knowledge can contradict, is that the stars are there to delight him, that he is there to express delight in them and that both their existence and his are infinitely precious. Their far universe belongs to him, and he to theirs. If he develops an eye for that mystery, he will grow to recognize something of the mystery that is himself.

Teach him, then, the names of these creatures; tell him the traditional stories of what they did and how they came to be in the heavens; train him to watch their behavior through the seasons. For the names, there is an excellent mnemonic rhyme by Walter de la Mare of which I quote the first half:

> If to the heavens thou lift thine eyes
> When Winter rules o'er our northern skies,
> And snow-cloud none the zenith mars,
> At Yule-tide midnight these thy stars:
>
> Low in the south see bleak-blazing Sirius.
> O'er him stand Betelgeuse, Procyon wan.
> Wild-eyed to west of him, Rigel and Bellatrix,
> And rudd-eyed Aldebaran journeying on.
> High in night's roof-tree beams twinkling Capella,

Vega and Deneb prowl low in the north,
Far to the east roves the Lion-heart, Regulus;
While the twin sons of Zeus toward the zenith gleam forth. . . .

And let him learn from their motions what every generation has learned: the notion of Law and Duty. Later on, of course, he will discover that it is an anthropomorphic metaphor to talk of natural objects as "obeying" laws; that, to use a metaphor of Ibsen's, the difference between man and the other creatures of Nature is that the latter's motto is "To thyself be enough" while the former's is "To thyself be true." But where else can he acquire a notion of the imperative of personal duty than through a contemplation of the celestial bodies, with their indicative of impersonal necessity? Besides, as a physical being, a body, he, too, is their kin in being subject to necessity.

Amid all the temptations to collective arrogance and individual despair to which modern technology exposes us, it is both a sobering and consoling reflection that, whatever may happen to our desires, our needs—for food, for sleep, for physical equilibrium—will remain what they have always been, since the first man gazed at the same stars which we still see.

Let us all train our children to gaze at them and pray that, when their time comes to die, whatever knowledge of good and evil they may have acquired in the meantime, whatever personal and social vicissitudes they may have had to endure, they will still be able to ask, like Thomas Hardy,

If, when hearing that I have been stilled at last, they stand at the door,
    Watching the full-starred heavens that winter sees,
Will this thought rise in those who will meet my face no more,
    "He was one who had an eye for such mysteries"?

Harper's Bazaar, July 1956

Foreword to *The Green Wall*, by James Wright

Consciously or unconsciously, every poet draws a frontier between the poetical and the nonpoetical; certain objects, persons, events seem to him capable of embodiment in a poem, even if he has not yet discovered how, while there are others which it would never occur to him to consider himself, whatever other poets may have done with them. Further, among the various moods of feeling of which he is capable, he has preferences as a poet which may have little to do with his preferences as a man; a feeling which he enjoys may make little appeal to his imagination; a state of unpleasure may excite it.

Some of these distinctions are peculiar to himself, but most he shares with his contemporaries. From time to time a poet or a group of poets proclaim that the existing frontier is unjust and should be redrawn; when this happens, a new "period" of poetry begins.

One of the problems for a poet living in a culture with a well developed technology is that the history of technology is one of perpetual revolution, whereas genuine revolutions in the history of art (or society) are few and far between. He is tempted to imagine that, unless he produces something completely novel, he will be unoriginal. The reading public, too, may be similarly misled and attach undue importance to the individual differences between one poet and another, which, of course, exist and matter, ignoring that which is characteristic of them all, though this may really be of greater interest.

For example, Mr Wright uses as an epigraph to this volume the well known medieval carol "Adam Lay Ibounden." It is as impossible to imagine a poet of the twentieth-century writing this as to imagine a fifteenth-century poet writing these lines by Mr Wright:

> She was aware of scavengers in holes
> Of stone, she knew the loosened stones that fell
> Indifferently as pebbles plunging down a well
> And broke for the sake of nothing human souls.

A modern poet might perfectly well be a Catholic, believing in the Divine plan for human redemption of which the medieval carol sings, but his consciousness of historical earthly time is so different that he could never strike the same note of naïve joy in the present; should he attempt it, the note struck would almost certainly be false, expressing not Christian hope but a sort of Rotarian optimism.

A medieval poet, on the other hand, might have written an elegy on the death of a friend, though he would be more likely to choose a public figure, but it would never have occurred to him to celebrate the melancholia of the deceased; he would have described her beauty, her actions, he might even have portrayed her as a mourner, provided that the reason was some objective suffering, but a subjective illness like melancholia would have seemed to him unpoetic.

One way of perceiving the characteristics of an age is to raise certain fundamental questions which human beings have always asked and then see how the poets of that age answer them, such questions, for example as:

What is the essential difference between man and all the other creatures, animal, vegetable, and mineral?

What is the nature and human significance of time?

What qualities are proper to the hero or sacred person who can inspire poets to celebrate him and what is lacking in the churl or profane person whom poetry ignores?

A man in the Middle Ages would have said that the difference between man and other creatures is that only man has an immortal soul eternally related to God. He has, therefore, a goal, salvation or damnation, but this goal is not in time nor is reaching it a matter of time. A baby who has been baptized and an old man who repents after a lifetime of crime die and both are saved; their ages are irrelevant.

On the other hand, so far as his temporal existence, individual or social was concerned, like anyone who lives in a predominantly rural culture without machinery, he would be conscious of little difference between himself and other creatures, that is to say, he would be mainly aware of their common subjection to biological time, the endless cycle of birth, growth, and decay. Of man as creating irreversible historical time so that the next generation is never a repetition of the last, he would be scarcely, if at all, conscious. But to a modern man, whether or not he believes in an immortal soul, this is the great difference, that he and his society have a self-made history while the rest of nature does not. He is anxious by necessity because at every moment he has to choose to become himself. His typical feelings about nature, therefore are feelings of estrangement and nostalgia. In "A Fit against the Country" Mr Wright sees nature as a temptation to try and escape human responsibility by imitating her ways, in "The Seasonless" he contrasts the rotation of the seasons with a human figure to whom no season can ever return, in "The Horse" and "On the Skeleton of a Hound" he contrasts the "poetical" animal and its unchanging identity with the "unpoetical" man who can never say who he is.

Poets have always reflected on the passage of time, comparing the present and the past, but before the modern period this usually meant expressing a sorrow because the present was less valuable than the past, what was once strong is now weak, what was beautiful has faded, and so forth, but past and present were felt to be equally real. But in Mr Wright's poems, as in nearly all modern poetry, the present is not unhappy but unreal, and it is memories, pleasant or unpleasant, which are celebrated for their own sake as the real past. The present can only be celebrated, as in "A Girl in a Window" or "To a Hostess Saying Good Night," by showing it as pure chance; what makes the present moment poetical is an awareness that it is related to nothing so that nothing can come of it.

Two of Mr Wright's poems, "The Assignation" and "My Grandmother's Ghost," are about the dead coming back to haunt the living.

In earlier times the motive for doing this would have been malignant and ghosts were regarded as evil. The good dead were thought to be much too happy in their present state to wish to return to their earthly life; in their thoughts about those on earth whom they had loved they looked not backward but forward to the future when their loved ones would join them. On earth past and present had seemed equally real; in eternity both seem equally unreal.

Given the circumstances of modern life, the feeling that only memories are real is to be expected. When a man usually lived in the house where his father and grandfather had lived before him, the past still existed in the present, not just as his memories but objectively about him. Today when men change not only their house but their part of the world every few years, their present circumstances become more and more impersonal, subjective memories more and more important.

Even more striking than its attitude toward nature and time is the kind of person whom modern poetry chooses to speak of. Aside from love poems and poems addressed to relatives, the persons who have stimulated Mr Wright's imagination include a lunatic, a man who has failed to rescue a boy from drowning, a murderer, a lesbian, a prostitute, a police informer, and some children, one of them deaf. Common to them all is the characteristic of being social outsiders. They play no part in ruling the City nor is its history made by them, nor, even, are they romantic rebels against its injustices; either, like the children (and the ghosts), they are not citizens or they are the City's passive victims.

His one poem to a successful citizen is, significantly, to a singer, that is to say, to someone whose social function is concerned with the play of the City, not with its work.

Mr Wright is not alone in his imaginative preferences. It is difficult to find a modern poem, unless it be a satire, which celebrates a contemporary equivalent of Hector or Aeneas or King Arthur or the Renaissance Prince. To the poetic imagination of our time, it would seem that the authentically human, the truly strong, is someone who to the outward eye is weak or a failure, the only exception being the artist or the intellectual discoverer, the value of whose achievements is independent of his contemporary fame.

There are many reasons for this change, and everyone will be able to think of some for himself. One, obviously, is the impersonal character of modern public life which has become so complex that the personal contribution of any one individual is impossible to identify and even the greatest statesman seems more an official than a man. Another, I think, is the change effected by modern methods of publicity in the nature of fame. Formerly a man was famous *for* something, for this great deed or that which he had done; that is to say, the deed was the important thing and the name of the doer was, in a sense, an accident. Today a famous man is a man whose name is on everybody's lips. Their knowledge of what he has done may be very vague and its value, whether it was noble or shameful, matters very little. So long as he is in the news, he is a famous man; the moment he ceases to have news value, he becomes nobody.

We should not be surprised, then, if modern poets should be drawn to celebrate persons of whom nobody has heard or whom, at least, everybody has forgotten.

I have not said anything about the quality of Mr Wright's poems because assertions have no point without proofs, and the only proof in this case is reading. I will content myself with one or two quotations to illustrate his handling of imagery and rhythm and the variety of his concerns.

> Behind us, where we sit by trees,
> Blundering autos lurch and swerve
> On gravel, crawling on their knees
> Around the unfamiliar curve . . .

★　★　★

> . . . The flop of wings, the jerk of the red comb
> Were a dumb agony,
> Stupid and meaningless. It was no joy
> To leave the body beaten underfoot;
> Life was a flick of corn, a steady roost.
> Chicken. The sound is plain.

★　★　★

> And through the windows, washing hands,
> The patients have the mattress made,
> Their trousers felt for colored stones,
> The pleasures of the noon recalled:
>
> For some were caught and held for hours
> By spiders skating over a pond,
> Some parted veils of hollyhocks
> And looked for rabbit holes beyond.
>
> But now the trousers lie in rows,
> She sees the undressed shadows creep
> Through half-illuminated minds
> And chase the hare and flower to sleep.

★　★　★

> But now I fumble at the single joy
> Of dawn. On the pale ruffle of the lake
> The ripples weave a color I can bear.
> Under a hill I see the city sleep
> And fade. The perfect pleasure of the eyes:
> A tiny bird bathed in a bowl of air,
> Carving a yellow ripple down the bines,
> Posing no storm to blow my wings aside
> As I drift upward dropping a white feather.

The Green Wall, by James Wright, 1957

The Great Captains

The Great Captains. By Henry Treece. Bodley Head. 13s. 6d.

Mr Treece is not the only novelist who has recently been attracted by the Roman breakdown; Bryher, for instance, has dealt with it in a Swiss setting. The attraction is not surprising. If one were to classify literary epochs according to the kind of landscape by which each is obsessed, ours might well be called the Age of the Utter Ruin. Ruins have made an imaginative appeal before—in the eighteenth century, for example—but hitherto as a picturesque element. The relic of the past, crumbling tower or fragment of aqueduct, stood in the midst of a prosperous and civilised present as if to congratulate it upon being so superior in its peace and common sense to the bad old days. But our ruins are not at all like this. They must occupy the whole scene—overgrown roads, washed-out bridges, rusting machinery, a solitary chimney stack and, encroaching upon them, the wilderness. The virgin wilderness by itself will not do, but the returning wilderness, burying some human enterprise that has failed, some civilisation gone to pot—Ah, how our imaginations respond to that! And almost as fascinating to us is the image of the Threatened City. At the moment it is a going concern, people are happy, there is love, comfort, entertainment, money, but, just beyond the horizon, some "rough beast" is already slouching to be born. My, how delicious that is!

Whatever this may indicate about our psychological and social health, this is what we enjoy and we must be grateful to writers like Mr Treece whose historical novel about Arthur, or Artos as he calls him, is generously crammed with such images.

His choice of hero was felicitous for two reasons. Firstly, because, while there almost certainly was such a person, the demonstrable historical facts are very scanty and his imaginative invention has a free hand. He can with good conscience have Aelle slain at the battle of Dubglass and Cerdic besieged on Mount Badon. Secondly, though little can be known about the historical Artos, everybody knows a great deal about the King Arthur of the Medieval romances culminating in the work of Malory.

This gives Mr Treece an extra command upon the interest of his readers who at every moment can contrast what he suggests may have actually occurred with the story told by Malory who never claimed to be writing about anything but an imaginary world. *The Great Captains* is a polemic as well as an exciting narrative; indirectly, by implication, Mr Treece attacks, not Malory's historical veracity, but the *ethos* of his imaginary world, the code of Knightly Chivalry and Courtly Love which (with suitable bowdlerisation) was held up by schoolmasters as an ideal of conduct as late as my own childhood.

Mr Treece, for example, retains the theme of unwitting incest, but he makes Gwynhwyfer instead of Morgause the sister of Artos. Instead of a Queen he gives Artos a "hand-fast wife," a beautiful dancer called Lystra (from Byzantium, natch), who, for political reasons, is about to have an affair with Medrawt when they are both surprised by Artos who takes a terrible revenge.

The entire elimination of the Launcelot-Guinevere theme is significant for, after removing the medieval trappings of the Noble Adultery, there was no historical reason which could forbid Mr Treece, had he wished, to describe a passionate infidelity. That the avoidance was deliberate is borne out by his version of the other great myth of Passion.

Artos sat in his hide tent with Bedwyr and a young lieutenant named Drostan, a relative of Marcus of Cornwall. He was a foolishly gay youngster, who invented dreams which he said he had dreamt, just to cause amusement. . . . Drostan told of a lovely golden-haired girl from Ireland, Yslod, he called her. He said that his Uncle Marcus, in his dream, of course, asked him to sail across to Ireland and fetch this lovely creature back for him to marry.

"But, alas, you know how it is," said Drostan, raising his auburn eyebrows nonchalantly, "she just couldn't resist me! Before we had got back in sight of the cliffs of Cornwall, the job was done! I felt very bad about betraying old uncle Marcus, but who could have disappointed a lady as beautiful, and as insistent, as she was?"

Again, in his portrait of Artos himself, it was not, I think, merely a gloss in Nennius but also a wish to contradict Malory at every point which led Mr Treece to reject the possibility of his having been a fairly educated Romano-Briton from the lowland zone, and choose instead to make him a savage Celt.

The ploughman stopped once more and stood still to wait for Medrodus. He was tall and barrel-chested; so heavily developed were the muscles of his shoulders that he looked at first sight almost hunchbacked. His broad face glistened in the sunlight with sweat, which he wiped away from time to time with the back of a large and calloused hand. His sandy hair was chopped off at the nape of the neck, in the old barbarian style, but hung in two small plaits, one from each temple, almost hiding the heavy gold rings which dangled from his ears. . . . The man's face showed no emotion, no recognition. It was as impassive as a rough-hewn block of sandstone—and rough-hewn it was indeed, for below the unblinking pale blue eyes, the cheekbones were raised by thick horizontal ridges, the result of some ritual surgery into which blue dyes had been rubbed, giving the broad face an inexpressibly savage look.

Lastly, one would gather from reading *The Great Captains* that by the last decade of the fifth century, Christianity had ceased to be an organised cult.

A few might remember a Christian prayer or even try out the Holy Cross as a battle-cry, but the only rites one hears of as being practised are all pagan ones. From a novelist's point of view, pagan rites are, of course, much more fun and Merddin, "the lost one, the maker of dreams," more exciting than a holy hermit, but it is strange that Mr Treece's description of Medrawt's encounter with Merddin is the only passage in his book where the reader cannot tell whether the author is saying what he thinks happened or saying what he thinks one of his characters thinks happened. This is all the stranger because his normal attitude to the romantically odd is as no-nonsense as possible; witness his account of the founding of the Round Table.

> Artos sat and smiled at them strangely. He watched Aurelius spurring on to gain the gap before Bedwyr, and Cei anxious not to be the last.
>
> Then Artos gave a great shout and said, "Between God and myself, but this is more like a maiden's corn-dance than a meeting of great Captains! Each one anxious to be first, afraid to be last!" . . . He reached down at his side and unhooked the great round bronze buckler that swung from his pommel-horn. He took it firmly by its embossed edge and flung it away from him, so that it lay, its round boss uppermost, in the heather. The horsemen looked at him, wondering.
>
> He beckoned to them then. "Come," he said gently, as though to backward children. "Sit on your chargers round this shield."
>
> The men obeyed him, for his voice was one of command. And when they were disposed about the great buckler, he turned to them and said, "Now, at this table, who holds the place of honour?"
>
> They looked down at the shield and then up at the *dux bellorum.* "Why," said Votiporix, "there is no place of honour. All places are the same, round a shield."
>
> Artos smiled at him and said, "Exactly so, King of the Demetae." Then, with a swift movement, he leaned low out of the saddle, took up his buckler, and without another word, rode through the gap.

In a novel which only claims to present one out of many possible re-creations of the past, a bias of sensibility, so long as it is kept, as Mr Treece keeps his, in bounds, is all to the good.

If I say that *The Great Captains* reminds me of a movie script, I mean this as high praise. Whatever scene Mr Treece puts before us—a battle, a hunt, a journey, a council, a ritual dance—we are made to see it in all its concrete, visual details of forms and movements; the contrast of scene against scene, their timing, and the management of tension and relaxation are so expert, that the reader's attention is never lost for a second. As in a good movie, too, the characters are, most of them, archetypal figures—The Wise Ancient, the blue-eyed Noble Savage from the country versus his brown-eyed Brother and Rival from the slums, the Blonde Virgin versus the Brunette Harlot, etc., which in a narrative where the main interest is epic action, is right and proper.

The only character whom Mr Treece presents subjectively is Medrawt. I find it a little odd, I must say, that he should tell us in his preface, "Looking at the problem from a number of directions, I sympathise with Medrawt, who has had a poor defence in the Court of History," for the Medrawt he gives us is one of the most detestable characters in fiction, a really horrid little toad. Dreadful as is his fate, one cannot feel it is undeserved.

As one might expect, in this rip-roaring melodrama everyone, but everyone, comes to a sticky end.

Ambrosius: Stabbed in his bath by Medrawt, his ward.

Artos: Stabbed by Medrawt, his blood-brother, in a fit of madness.

Medrawt: Castrated by Cissa. Killed by Bedwyr.

Bedwyr: Clubbed to death by the London mob.

Cei: Poisoned by a Caerwent innkeeper.

Uther Pendragon: Poisoned by Gwynhwyfer, his daughter, on order from Artos, his son.

Gwynhwyfer: Accidentally trampled to death by Artos, her brother and lover.

Anir, their son: Accidentally trampled to death by Artos.

Troynt, her dog: Killed by Artos.

Lystra: Gored to death by a bull in the arena at Caerleon.

Having first read *The Great Captains* in the American edition, I am surprised and shocked to discover that the whole penultimate chapter has been omitted from the English edition.

This chapter tells how, after escaping half-dead from the fight in the amphitheatre, Medrawt is found by a woman belonging to a primitive tribe of shore scavengers. He does not die but his wits are gone and he is now subject to fits in which he speaks in a strange tongue which the tribe take to be the voice of Merddin, so that they adopt him as a sort of shaman.

Incapable of recognising others, he wanders one night into a hut where is sitting Cissa, the Saxon whose kinsfolk he had blinded after the battle of Bassas.

They recognise him and castrate him. In the morning he is found by Cerdic who takes charge of him for the reasons given in the last chapter.

I can only suppose that the British publisher objected to the castration and can only say that Mr Treece's description seemed perfectly discreet to me. The omission of the chapter spoils the pace—without it we are hurried on to the last years of Artos too quickly—and the account of Medrawt's "voices" which it gives prepares us for his sudden turning upon Artos, which is hard to understand without such a preparation.

The Great Captains is one of those books which one cannot put down until one has finished it. It is also a book that one is glad to re-read. These two qualities are not always found in the same book and Mr Treece is greatly to be congratulated.

Encounter, September 1956

D. H. Lawrence as a Critic

D. H. Lawrence: Selected Literary Criticism. Edited by
Anthony Beale. Viking. $5.

D. H. Lawrence: Novelist. By F. R. Leavis. Knopf. $4.75.

Is D. H. Lawrence a neglected writer? Yes, says Professor F. R. Leavis, and not only neglected but the victim of a critical conspiracy with Mr T. S. Eliot as its ring-leader, to ignore, disparage or misrepresent his work.

I do not know if Mr Leavis is right—I should like to know what Lawrence's publishers have to say—but since he sees a significant and sinister coincidence between this neglect and my appearance on the literary scene, I must say that Lawrence has been and remains one of my literary heroes, one of the few modern writers whom I constantly reread.

Eliot's willful unfairness towards Lawrence is as well-known as his jibes against Goethe and Milton, but Mr Leavis is mistaken if he imagines that even Eliot's most devout admirers grant him a papal infallibility any more than, I hope, an admirer of Lawrence is obliged to follow him in his utter rejection of Joyce. One would hardly expect Lawrence and Joyce to be soul-mates and, for my part, Lawrence is more my dish, but the world of letters is a big place. Mr Leavis is also mistaken if he thinks that the writers of my generation were so silly as, on the grounds of a few passages in *Kangaroo* and *The Plumed Serpent*, to dismiss Lawrence as a fascist: we continued to read and admire him just as we continued to read Yeats, some of whose statements were much more questionable. I am somewhat bewildered, too, to learn that the official literary world backs Norman Douglas against Lawrence. It would seem to me that, whoever behaved badly to whom, Norman Douglas is under the hopeless disadvantage of not having written the introduction to *Memoirs of the Foreign Legion.*

Be all this as it may, Mr Leavis' study of Lawrence as a novelist is very welcome. He cares passionately about Lawrence and about him as a great artist rather than as a man with a gospel, and he likes the right books, that is to say, the ones I like.

As if in timely rebuttal of the charge of neglect, Mr Anthony Beale has had the happy idea of collecting into one volume the bulk of Lawrence's own literary criticism. He includes most of the one book of criticism which Lawrence published in his lifetime, *Studies in Classical American Literature*, most of the long study of Thomas Hardy, the essay on Galsworthy, the two pieces on Verga, the *Pornography and Obscenity* pamphlet, a number of scattered articles and reviews and relevant extracts from letters.

Lawrence had better things to do with his time than spend much of it on criticism but, if he had been going to live to Shaw's age, one would find oneself wishing, for our sakes if not for his, that, like Shaw, he had done a stint as a regular reviewer, for the few reviews he did write are wonderful. His nose for the genuine and the spurious is unerring—he can see the reality in writers as poles apart as Baron Corvo and Ernest Hemingway—and he is so lively and on occasions extremely funny.

> You may know a new utterance by the element of danger in it. "My heart aches," says Keats, and you bet it's no joke.
>
> > Why do I think of stairways
> > With a rush of hurt surprise?
>
> Heaven knows, my dear, unless you once fell down.

The style of the American studies is like nothing else one ever read. Lawrence accomplishes the extraordinary feat of taking what was his worst literary vice, a certain repetitiousness and transforming it into a virtue so that the repetitions seem like an acrobatic dance. One thinks: "Surely, at any moment now, he is going to come a cropper," but he doesn't.

> *Moby Dick, or the White Whale.*
>
> A hunt. The last great hunt.
>
> For what?
>
> For Moby Dick, the huge white sperm whale: who is old, hoary, monstrous, and swims alone; who is unspeakably terrible in his wrath, having so often been attacked; and snow-white.
>
> Of course he is a symbol.
>
> Of what?
>
> I doubt if even Melville knew exactly. That's the best of it.
>
> He is warm-blooded, he is lovable. He is lonely Leviathan, not a Hobbes sort. Or is he?
>
> But he is warm-blooded and lovable. The South Sea Islanders, and Polynesians and Malays, who worship shark, or crocodile, or weave endless frigate-bird distortions, why did they never worship the whales? So big!
>
> Because the whale is not wicked. He doesn't bite. And their gods had to bite.
>
> He's not a dragon. He is Leviathan. He never coils like the Chinese dragon of the sun. He's not a serpent of the waters. He is warm-blooded, a mammal. And hunted, hunted down.
>
> It is a great book.

To read one of Lawrence's critical essays is to be made a witness to a dramatic encounter between two persons, Lawrence and a book. What we are given, that is, is not so much a description of the book as a description of Lawrence reading it. To call this subjective would be misleading since it suggests that Lawrence is doing everything and the poor book is merely a passive victim. No, Lawrence is really reading, reading with such absorption, indeed, that he is quite unaware of us—we may overhear him but we are hardly addressed; matters may come up which seem far afield from the book itself but they are prompted by it. We learn about Lawrence and the book he is reading in equal measure. There may be many things in it which he does not mention but that is all the more reason why we should read it for ourselves, and Lawrence's approach has the enormous advantage of making the reader wish to read for themselves. Any book, we feel, that can get Lawrence so excited, even if to anger, must be worth reading.

Lawrence is never an intellectual show-off who drags in the names of obscure authors or quotes in foreign languages, but when he does make a historical point it is obvious that he knows what he is talking about.

> ... whereas in Shakespeare or Sophocles the greater, uncomprehended morality, or fate, is actively transgressed and gives active punishment, in Hardy and Tolstoi the lesser, human morality, is actively transgressed, and holds, and punishes the protagonist, while the greater morality is only passively, negatively, transgressed. It is represented merely as being present in background, in scenery, not taking any active part, having no direct connexion with the protagonist.
>
> Had Oedipus, Hamlet, Macbeth been weaker, less full of real potent life they would have made no tragedy. But, being, as they are, men to the fullest capacity, when they find themselves, daggers drawn, with the very forces of life itself, they can only fight till they themselves are killed, since the morality of life, the greater morality is eternally unalterable and invincible. It can be dodged for some time, but not opposed. On the other hand, Anna, Eustacia, Tess or Sue—what was there in their position that was necessarily tragic? Necessarily painful it was, but they were not at war with God, only with Society. Yet they were all cowed by the mere judgment of man upon them, and all the while by their own souls they were right. And the judgment of men killed them, not the judgment of their own souls or the judgment of Eternal God.
>
> Which is the weakness of modern tragedy, where transgression against the social code is made to bring destruction, as though the social code worked our irrevocable fate.

No man who had not read widely and thought long about his reading could have written such a passage.

If Lawrence is sometimes unfair, he never pretends to be an impartial judge; he writes as a practicing novelist of the first half of the twentieth century whose main concern with novels of the past is to find what hints and warnings they can give to the living.

His dislike of Dostoevsky, for example, is at the same time a tribute to his genius for what he detests is the Dostoevsky hero, the fallen angel whom he finds so common in our civilisation, but whose existence nobody before Dostoevsky had perceived. So, too, with the typical heroes of the *verismo* school. At present they are a danger because the particular emotional and moral bias they show—no age can have a completely undistorted vision—is one from which we must get away so that, at least our distortion shall be our own.

If *I Malavoglia* dates, so does *Madame Bovary*. They belong to the emotional-democratic, treasure-of-the-humble period of the nineteen century. When the emotion will have quite gone out of us, we can accept *Madame Bovary* and *I Malavoglia* in the same free spirit with the same detachment as that in which we accept Dickens or Richardson.

The great problem for the contemporary novelist, as Lawrence saw so clearly, is to find people whom it is worth writing about. All art is concerned with celebrating the heroic, the authentically human and in fighting the churlish and life-destructive, but most of the arts, and none more than the novel, are bound to historical reality; the novelist must make us believe that his heroes and heroines could exist, that we might be able to meet one at dinner. As a prose writer he cannot translate a character by endowing him with magnificent poetry as Shakespeare could, and in the twentieth century he cannot avail himself of any class of person, like a Renaissance Prince who is socially recognised as numinous. The problem is easier to state than to solve.

In Lawrence's work, no less than in that of other modern novelists, his "churlish" characters are more believable than his "heroic" who tend either to preach the heroic gospel or to be inarticulate so that we have to depend upon Lawrence telling us that they are heroes.

Unlike many other modern novelists, however, Lawrence tried and never stopped trying to create a contemporary character that one could admire; what makes him a greater novelist than some whose work has more finish is that he never shirked the issue; he never pretended that perfection of style and form, admirable as they are, can make up for the lack of the "kingly and the saintly."

Lawrence believed that all novels that are worth anything give us some kind of new vision; by making us conscious of feelings which we have not been able to recognise for ourselves, they release us from the torture of inarticulate nervousness. He also had a definite idea of the kind of novel he himself wished to write.

> You mustn't look in my novel for the old stable *ego* of the character. There is another *ego*, according to whose action the individual is unrecognisable, and passes through, as it were, allotropic states which it needs a deeper sense than any we've been used to exercise, to discover are states of the same radically unchanged element. (Like as diamond and coal are the same pure element of carbon. The ordinary novel would trace the history of the diamond—but I say, "Diamond, what! This is carbon.")

But he had no theory of the novel in general. About modern poetry, on the other hand, he does, in his introductions of *New Poems* and *Pansies*, expound a theory which, if I have not misunderstood it, seems to be unsound and, moreover contradicted by all of Lawrence's best poems.

As against what he calls the poetry of the beginning and the end with its formal perfection and completeness of utterance, he would have modern poetry be the poetry of the immediate present.

> In the immediate present there is no perfection, no consummation, nothing finished. . . . The seething poetry of the incarnate now is supreme, beyond even the everlasting gems of the before and after. . . . It is obvious that the poetry of the instant present cannot have the same body or the same motion as the poetry of the before and after. It can never submit to the same conditions. It is never finished. . . . Free verse is, or should be, direct utterance from the instant, whole man. It is the soul and the mind and the body surging at once, nothing left out. The utterance is like a spasm, naked contact with all influences at once. It does not want to get anywhere. It just takes place.

My objection to this is not an objection to free verse as such, but to the notion that any poem, any work of art, any living creature, for that matter, can be unfinished: each one is a world in itself and obedient to the laws of its being. A poem that is like a pansy is a welcome gift, but who would be grateful for a torn fragment of a pansy petal? In his Hardy essay Lawrence discusses the tension in all artists between what he calls Law and Love, the Flesh and the spirit, the Father and the Son, which principles he finds represented by Woman and Man respectively, and with sure insight he notices the reflection of this in the work of art.

> The very adherence of rhyme and regular rhythm is a concession to the law, a concession to the body, to the being and requirements of the body. They are an admission of the living, positive inertia which is the other half of life, other than the pure will to motion.

Exactly. That is why poetry, however free, is nearer to the world of the Father and his eternal cycles than prose which is more concerned with the Open Road of the Son.

There is of course no absolute line of division, both media belong to both worlds, but in verse, even in the freest we are more conscious of the obedience of the words to some law which is not of the writer's making.

One curious consequence of this is that the shorter a poem, the stricter must be the form if it is to satisfy us. A longish poem which contains a host of images, feelings, notions can be organised into a world in a host of ways, but a poem consisting of a single sentence can only be verbally organised, that is, its laws are the laws of metre and rhyme.

Lawrence's own poetry bears this out. Nearly all his best "free" poems, like those in *Birds, Beasts and Flowers* are of some length, while the best of short *Pansies* are rhymed.

> I can't stand Willy wet-leg,
> Can't stand him at any price.
> He's resigned and when you hit him
> he lets you hit him twice.

is a whole pansy, but

> When I hear a man spouting about humility to-day
> I know he is either a bed-bug, battening on sleeping people
> or a hyena, eating corpses

is only a fragment of a petal.

But Lawrence's poetic theory is a small matter. A man who can write as beautiful and extraordinary a poem as "Tortoise Family Connections" can hold any theory he pleases.

The Griffin, September 1956

Dostoevsky in Siberia

F. M. Dostoyevsky. *Memoirs from the House of the Dead.*
Translated by Jessie Coulson. Oxford University Press. $3.50.

The House of the Dead is not Dostoevsky's greatest work but it is, perhaps, his least irritating. The Slavophil and west-hating Dostoevsky has not yet appeared and there is very little of the Creeping Jesus. What is disturbing and, in the end, unpleasant about the novels is Dostoevsky's inability, despite all the talk about Love, to create a single character whom the reader can *like*. As D. H. Lawrence said of them:—"All the people are *fallen angels*—even the dirtiest scrubs. This I cannot stomach. People are not fallen angels, they are merely people. But Dostoevsky used them all as theological or religious units. . . ." Dostoevsky may have made up some of the incidents in *The House of the Dead,* but it does not read like fiction; it reads like straight factual reportage upon life in a Siberian convict prison of which we know Dostoevsky had personal experience. One does not feel that the facts have been tailored to suit a particular kind of imagination but that any man in Dostoevsky's position would have had the same experiences, though he might not be able to express them.

The memoirs purport to be written by a member of the minor gentry, Alexander Petrovich Goryanchikov, who had murdered his wife in a fit of jealousy and then given himself up. Having been released from prison he remains in the small Siberian town and lives by giving lessons to children whom he loves; adults he hates and avoids.

It is interesting that Dostoevsky should have made his *alter ego* not a political offender like himself but a murderer who, one presumes from his giving himself up, must have repented of his act and wished to atone for it. A political offender cannot be guilty in his own eyes for it is his own conscience, or so he must think, that has made him commit his offence, and he must wish that everyone else should do likewise. Dostoevsky himself must have been doubly estranged from the majority of his fellow prisoners, first, like Goryanchikov, because he was gentry and they were peasants, and, secondly, because in his eyes they were criminals and he was not. On the other hand, Goryanchikov has his special kind of isolation. Though he never, thank goodness, refers to his own crime, he is presented as the one prisoner who, in contrast to the rest, recognizes that he has committed a crime which deserves punishment.

> I never once saw among these men the slightest sign of remorse, the least gnawing at conscience, and that the majority of them believed themselves to have done nothing wrong. . . . I heard tales of the most terrible, the most unnatural actions, the most monstrous murders, told with absolutely irrepressible, childishly merry laughter.

One is never allowed to forget—and in this lies the greatness and terror of the book—that prisons, with all their senseless horrors, are populated mostly by horrid people. Even if we could eliminate from criminal law all notion of retribution, the necessity to segregate the criminal would remain and criminals, however humanely treated, are unlikely to reform in each other's company.

Here are some of Dostoevsky's observations about his fellow inmates.

> Generally speaking, the whole tribe with the exception of a few unquenchably cheerful souls, who for that reason enjoyed universal contempt, was sullen, envious, terribly conceited, boastful, touchy, and preoccupied in the highest degree with forms . . . they were all vitally concerned about one thing: what sort of figure they cut. . . . All the prisoners robbed one

another shamelessly. . . . As for informing in general, it commonly flourishes in prison. The informer is not subjected to any infamy; nobody so
much as thinks of being indignant with him. He is not shunned, his
friendship is acceptable, and anybody who tried to demonstrate the full
vileness of informing would be quite incomprehensible. . . .

After dinner we learned that the fugitives had been captured in such-
and-such a village seventy versts away. It is difficult to convey the impression produced on the prisoners by this news. At first they all seemed to
fly into a temper, then gloom overwhelmed them. Later an inclination
to jeer showed itself. They began to laugh, no longer at the pursuers but
at the recaptured men; at first it was only a few who laughed, but afterwards almost everybody except a few strong and serious characters. . . .
In a word, Kukilov and Aristov were now just as much decried, and even
decried with pleasure, as they had before been extolled. It was as if they
had somehow done everybody an injury.

Such disagreeable characteristics may be aggravated by life in prison, but
the prisoners already possessed them when they came.

Dostoevsky was the first novelist to make a serious study of the criminal
personality and our present knowledge has not advanced very far beyond
the point to which his insights brought us.

He shows us that what distinguishes the typical criminal from the average
man whose criminal wishes are not realized in action is that the former's
conception of himself is fantastic; quite literally he does not know who he is.
The average man can distinguish between wishes which he knows are fantastic and his real desires which are possible to fulfill because they are grounded
in his actual nature; the criminal cannot. Thus, while all men desire to be
valued by others, the "normal" man recognizes that if this desire is to be
gratified he must do or make something valuable, and that what he himself
can do depends upon his capacities and his circumstances; the criminal, on
the other hand, does not want to be valued for this or that concrete reason,
he simply wants to be important and, since this desire is without relation to
anything concrete, he desires to be infinitely important and other people,
except in so far as they minister to this have no reality for him.

There exists, for example, and in very large numbers, the following type
of murderer. This man lives quietly and meekly. His lot is bitter but he
endures it. Let us suppose that he is a peasant farmer, a house-serf, a
tradesman or a soldier. Suddenly something snaps inside him: he can
stand it no longer and sticks a knife into his enemy and persecutor. Now
begins the strange part: the man runs temporarily amock. His first killing was of his enemy, his persecutor; that was criminal but understandable; there was a motive; but afterwards he kills not enemies but chance

passers-by, kills for amusement, because of a harsh word or look, for a string of beads, or simply: "Get out of the way and don't let me catch you; I'm coming!"

The fact that the first murder was not enough is evidence that what seemed to be its motive, a concrete revenge, was not its real motive.

Over against the fantastic existence of the criminal, however, stands something equally fantastic, the Penal System, based on the impossible notion of impersonal retribution or punishment. The replacement of the blood-feud by the Law of the State is no doubt an advance in civilization, but if it is made, then the notion that the criminal should be punished must be abandoned because punishment cannot be inflicted by the State but only by individuals acting on its behalf. A man who kills another in a blood-feud may be cruel but he remains human; he has a personal motive for his action and he accepts it as his own. The Public Executioner who tortures and kills, not for any personal grievance but because torturing and killing are his legal "mystery" is a monster.

> Although the flogging may give him satisfaction, he hardly ever feels any personal hatred for his victim. The skill of his hand, his knowledge of his art, the desire to impress his fellows and the public, all stimulate his vanity. . . . It is strange that all the many executioners I have come across have been fairly highly developed people with common sense, intelligence, and unusual vanity or even pride . . . Before the beginning of the punishment the executioner is in a state of great exaltation, conscious of his strength and knowing himself to be supreme; at that moment he is an actor; his audience is filled with wonder and dismay and it is certainly not without some pleasure that he cries out to his victim, before the first stroke, the familiar and ominous words: "Hold tight, I'm going to flay you!"

Of the other prison officials whom Dostoevsky describes, some, like Lieutenant Zherebyatnikov were simple sadists, some, like the major Commandant, tyrannical because afraid, and some, like the house surgeon, kind and good. How a man will behave towards others is determined partly by his character and partly by his occupation. Generally these are related. The one who chooses a profession the function of which is the relief of suffering is likely to be someone who, consciously at least, does not desire to inflict it, and the habit of relieving suffering will develop his compassion. Vice versa it is impossible to conceive of a kind-hearted man choosing the profession of executioner, or even a job in which he would exercise absolute power over others. But it has been made only too clear in recent years that occupational habit is a stronger force in most cases than character. Put an averagely decent man, who would never have chosen the job for himself, in charge of a concentration camp and he will presently come to enjoy cruelty.

In Utopia there would be no executions because nobody would consent to be the executioner: in the world we know, we can only abolish the death penalty by law and deprive the would-be executioner of his fun. We cannot do very much, for, so long as there are criminals and lunatics whom for our safety we must deprive of their freedom, dreadful things will always occur, however "advanced" our methods of treatment: a psychologist can be as cruel as a warder.

Many books have been written about prison life since *The House of The Dead*, some about worse prisons, some about better, but they have found little to add to Dostoevsky's account and nothing to contradict. The best and the worst prisons are more like each other than they resemble any sane and civil community.

The Griffin, November 1956

Concrete and Fastidious

Njál's Saga. Translated by Carl Bayerschmidt and Lee Hollander.
Allen & Unwin. 30s.

Disinfected of all polemical associations, "social realism" could be a useful descriptive term for a certain kind of literature. To call a writer a social realist would mean that, whether writing real or feigned history, he deliberately confined his portrayal of human nature to those aspects which individuals reveal to each other through their deeds, their words and their looks. There is, of course, a great deal more to human nature than this. There is much which a man is unwilling or unable to reveal about himself to others, though others, through their own subjective experiences, can imagine some of it, but all this the social realist deliberately excludes.

He also, so far as it is possible, deliberately excludes himself from his narrative. He may possess, or believe that he does, a truer grasp of the real significance of their actions than his characters themselves, he may see them, for instance, as the unwitting agents of Divine Providence or the forces of History but, if so, he keeps his opinions to himself. In his narrative, cause, motive, effect, are what his characters think they are. Similarly, his own moral values may be very different from those of the society he is describing, but the only overt moral judgments he will express are those which his characters pass on each other.

This combination of impersonal narration plus the exclusion of all subjective elements of dream and fancy gives all social realist works certain literary qualities in common. In all of them, the variation in character lies within the human range and is consistent with the society to which the character belongs: the best are not demigods, the worst are not devils. Secondly, individuals will be presented in their social context which influences their character but never wholly commands it: kings are always distinguishable from peasants, but all kings are not serious-minded, nor all peasants comic clowns. Lastly, their speech, from its most elevated to its lowest, lies within the range of credible conversation. It follows from this that, though it is possible to write social realist works in verse, provided that the poet uses a mixed or middle style, prose is the natural and proper medium, and a prose, moreover, which is as free as possible from all rhetorical schematisation and metaphorical elaboration. Social realism is not, of course, the only or necessarily the best kind of literature. It seems, however, to be the latest kind to evolve and in some ways, perhaps, it is the most grown-up.

The Icelandic Sagas are one of the most extraordinary phenomena in cultural history, not because they are so good but because of the kind of goodness which they exhibit. Had the Icelanders of the Middle Ages gone on writing verse epics like *The Battle of Maldon* or turned to ballads, we might admire them as much but we should not be so astonished. What they actually did, however, was to produce a socially realist literature centuries before any other part of Europe even attempted such a thing, and of a quality which, within its limited scale, has never been surpassed.

So long as one does not claim that, given their circumstances, the Icelanders were bound to write as they did, there is some point in considering the ways in which, compared with their contemporaries in the rest of Europe, their life was peculiar. The majority of the settlers were of aristocratic origin who had left Scandinavia because they wished neither to be ruled nor to rule but to be independent. They had inherited the warrior *ethos* of their class, but their profession was no longer fighting or conquering subject peoples. They might from time to time go on pirate raids but such expeditions were interludes in their daily life of farming and fishing. Some might own larger and better farms than others, but there were no great feudal landowners with their private armies. We hear of the existence of slaves but not of a leisure class which considers work beneath its dignity. Living on a small, not very fertile, island, far from the main centres of political, religious and intellectual activity, their interests were bound to be parochial. Everyone, to some degree, knew everyone else, and world events aroused less interest than the doings of the neighbours.

Granted the wish to write in a socially realistic way, it is clearly easier for a writer to succeed in such a society than in a larger and less homogeneous one, for the social realist is necessarily confined to a kind of life of which he has first-hand intimate knowledge. If he attempts to deal with people and societies which he does not really know, he will either conventionalise or produce a lifeless and ponderous documentation. Throughout the Sagas one is conscious of first-hand experience. In the literature of societies with a slave-servant class, members of the lower orders generally appear either as faithful retainers who only exist in and for their masters, or as comic rogues, or, as in the Courtly Romances, they are ignored. But the slave Melkof in *Njál's Saga* is as real an individual as his mistress Hallgerd.

> When Gunnar had gone Hallgerd came to speak with the slave Melkof. [*We have previously been told that he was "Irish and a man very much disliked."*]
> "I have thought of an errand for you," she said. "I want you to ride to Kirkby."
> "What am I to do there?" he asked.
> "You are to steal enough food to load two horses, and be sure to take butter and cheese and then set fire to the storehouse. They will all believe it happened through carelessness and no one will be thinking of a theft."
> The slave said: "I have done bad things, but never was I a thief."
> "You don't say!" answered Hallgerd. "You act as though you were an honourable man and yet you have been both a thief and a murderer. And don't you dare refuse or I shall have you killed."
> He believed he knew her well enough to know that she would do so: so he took two horses, placed packsaddles on them, and rode to Kirkby.

An even more remarkable example of emancipation from literary convention is the portrait of Bjorn the White. He is introduced as a henpecked husband and a braggart of the Parolles type and the reader naturally expects a comic denouement in which his cowardice is exposed. But something quite different happens.

> Kári then went and took his stand under a projecting crag and Bjorn asked: "Where shall I stand now?"
> Kári answered: "You can choose one of two things: either stand behind me and use your shield to protect yourself, if necessary, or else mount your horse and ride away as fast as you can."
> "That I don't want to do," said Bjorn, "and for a number of reasons. In the first place, if I ride away, malicious tongues might say that I left you in the lurch out of cowardice, and, in the second place, I know what a catch they think they have in me, so two or three would pursue me. No! I prefer to stand by you and defend myself with you."

And he does. Nobody without first-hand experience would have dared, when describing events in a culture to which physical courage was the supreme virtue, to present a character who is neither absolutely brave nor absolutely a coward but brave—and cowardly—to a certain degree.

First-hand knowledge of a small homogeneous society is not enough by itself to produce social realism; if it were, it would be one of the most primitive *genres*. It also requires a humanist attitude of mind which has rid itself of superstition, that is to say, of the notion that God intervenes directly in events so that their only significance and importance lies in their providential meaning. It is the development of this mentality, centuries before the rest of Europe, that remains so inexplicable about the Icelanders. Thus, in *Njál's Saga*, which was almost certainly put into its present shape by a cleric, there is an account of the conversion of Iceland to Christianity. One would expect to find, and anywhere else in the same age one would find, an account in black and white. All the Christians would be heroes, all pagans villains. In the struggle between them all the miracles would be on the Christian side and victory for the Faith would be a foregone conclusion. But we are given nothing of this sort. Thangbrand, the missionary sent by King Olaf, may, it is true, carry a crucifix instead of a shield when he defeats his pagan challenger, but his victory does not seem particularly miraculous because we have already been shown that he is a great warrior. Nor does such magical assistance as he gets make him a superman: he is nearly destroyed by the counter-magic of a heathen sorcerer and withdraws before he has completed his job.

> Thangbrand discussed with Gest the advisability of travelling to the firths further west, but Gest advised against it, saying that there lived men who were very hard and difficult to deal with—"But if it is ordained that this faith is to gain strength, then it is likely to be accepted at the Althing. . . . You are the one who has done most to promote it, even though it may be granted to others to introduce it into the laws."

Not long after the Althing meets.

> Both sides went to the Law-Mount, and Christians as well as heathens named witnesses and declared their former community of laws dissolved. . . . The Christians chose as their law-speaker Hall of Sida, but he went to Thorgeir, the *godi* of Ljosovatn, and gave him three marks of silver in order that he proclaim what the law should be. This, however, was a very risky step, because Thorgeir was still a heathen.
>
> That entire day Thorgeir lay with a cloak spread over his head so that no one might speak to him. The following day all assembled before the Law-Mount.
>
> Then Thorgeir asked to be heard and spoke: "It seems to me that our affairs have come to a dangerous pass if we do not all have one and the same law. If the laws are torn asunder, then security can no longer prevail, and we cannot afford to incur that danger. Now, therefore, I shall ask both heathens and Christians whether they will abide by the laws I shall proclaim." All agreed to that.
>
> "This is the foundation of our laws," he said, "that all men in this land are to be Christians and that they are no longer to worship idols, nor

expose children, nor eat horse-meat. If any man is found guilty of these practices, he shall be condemned to outlawry, but if he carries them on in secret, there shall be no punishment involved."

Though the Christian party includes some bad-hats like Mord Valgardsson and killers like Skarphedin Njalsson, it is supported by most of the wisest and most level-headed members of the community like Njál himself, Hall of Sida and Flosi, and the unbiased reader can see good secular reasons why they should.

The pagan culture of Iceland had been a shame culture in which it was a matter of personal honour and duty to avenge injuries and insults to oneself or to one's kin. The attempt to replace the private blood-feud by public law and arbitration had been only partially successful because there was in Iceland no single authority powerful enough to enforce the acceptance of a legal decision by anyone who, out of pride or passion, chose to reject it.

I have met people who dislike the Sagas and, though I do not share their dislike, I can understand why. I know of no other literature in which the characters seem, by our standards, so sane and their actions so lunatic. The code by which they live puts the society at the mercy of its most violent members and the havoc wrought by the malicious and the hot-headed is out of all proportion to their numbers. One row between two housewives—one of the curious things about Icelandic society seems to have been the complete inability of the husbands to keep their wives in order—can result in a whole chain of murders. With what a surprise and relief one reads of someone, like Snorri, ignoring an insult.

Under the circumstances a religion like Christianity which replaced shame by guilt and valued love of one's neighbour above courage would, apart from any theological or spiritual considerations, make an appeal to common sense.

Any work of art is the joint product of a sensibility and a medium of expression, and one reason, at least, why social realism did not appear outside of Iceland until much later was the lack, elsewhere, of an adequate prose instrument. The Saga writers were fortunate in two respects. Poetry in Scandinavia had become a highly specialised esoteric art of immense technical virtuosity, highly allusive and rhetorical, and, consequently, very limited in its subject-matter. A northern writer who wished to tell an intelligible story was bound to tell it in prose because it would have been impossible to tell it in skaldic verse. Secondly, thanks to the geographical remoteness of Scandinavia, classical Latin and the whole rhetorical tradition that went with it had had little influence upon the northern languages. The speeches of the lawyers at the Althing would have seemed childishly naive to Cicero; on the other hand, a piece of concrete narrative like the story of Gunnar's death could not have been written in Ciceronian Latin.

In the rest of Europe verse had remained a much looser medium, the formal demands of which were not severe enough to prevent its narrative use, but sufficient to prevent a thorough-going realism. At the same time, particularly in those countries which had been part of the Roman Empire, the Roman notion of what prose should be like persisted despite the changes that had taken place in the Latin tongue. Gregory of Tours, for example, seems to have been after the same kind of historical storytelling as the Icelandic historians but the Latin at his disposal was always getting in his way.

The prose of the Sagas, especially the dialogue, is not easy to translate. It is not a high style like that of epic; on the other hand, it is not an unbuttoned go-as-you-please style but the language of an aristocratic society with a great respect for forms and its own dignity. In their new translation of *Njál's Saga*, Messrs Bayerschmidt and Hollander have been able to profit from modern textual scholarship and a reading public which can tolerate an unbowdlerised version. I am inclined to feel, however, that Dasent's translation, despite some archaisms, may be closer in spirit to the original. In their laudable wish not to be quaint, the present translators sometimes fall into colloquialisms which are equally anachronistic because their associations are irrevocably modern and local, phrases, for example, like "You're a brick" or "That's mighty good of you." (Once, very oddly, they allow themselves the impossible archaism "caitiff wretch.") More seriously, they write what may be called standard American English. An American, when he is not being consciously hard-boiled and slangy, writes sentences which are slower in rhythm and more latinate in diction than an Englishman. Thus the translators write "Father has retired" where an Englishman would have written "Father has gone to bed"; where Dasent has "Such words of comfort had he for them all, and others still more strong," they have "With such exhortations and with other words even more indomitable he encouraged them."

Needless to say, I am not trying to suggest that American English is in any way inferior to British English as a language: I do believe, however, that in attempting to reproduce the terseness of Icelandic, a British translator has a certain innate advantage. But this may be prejudice and, in any case, it is as easy to criticise a translation, however good, as it is hard to make one, however bad.

I wish the translators had supplied genealogical maps and trees. I do not agree with their opinion, given in the introduction, that genealogies are boring, but for a modern reader they are easier to follow in a visual form, and, boring or not, it is impossible to follow a tale of blood-feuds without a clear knowledge of the kin relationships. The canvas in *Njál's Saga* is unusually large and I would advise anyone reading it for the first time to construct his own genealogical diagrams as he goes along.

The New Statesman and Nation, 3 November 1956

Squares and Oblongs

> There is a square; there is an oblong. The players take the square and place it upon the oblong. They place it very accurately; they make a perfect dwelling-place. Very little is left outside. The structure is now visible; what is inchoate is here stated; we are not so various or so mean; we have made oblongs and stood them upon squares. This is our consolation.—*The Waves*, Virginia Woolf

Man belongs to two orders of being, the natural and the historical, the first of which may be subdivided into the inorganic and the organic. As a being composed of matter he is subject to the laws of physics and chemistry; as a biological organism he is involved in the cyclical organic process of birth, reproduction, and decay; as a conscious being who makes choices he is responsible for his history, social and personal. Consequently he is concerned with two classes of events, natural events and historical events, which form the subject matter of the sciences and the arts respectively.

Considered as a verbal system, the poem is a natural not a historical object. The laws of prosody and syntax are to it what the laws of physics and chemistry are to the physical universe. When he writes, the poet has to presuppose that the history of language is at an end, that the meaning and metrical value of the words he employs will not alter so that his poem becomes unintelligible or unmusical.

There is only one physical universe, but, in every language, a very large number of verbal universes are possible. The nature of any language, however, imposes certain limitations and preferences. Thus, in English, unrhymed five-foot iambics please the ear, unrhymed four-foot iambics do not.

The final poetic order of a poem is the outcome of a dialectical struggle between the feelings and the verbal system. As a society, the verbal system is actively coercive upon the feelings it is attempting to embody; what it cannot embody truthfully, it excludes. As a potential community, the feelings are passively resistant to all claims of the system to embody them which they do not recognize as just; they decline all unjust persuasions. As members of crowds, every feeling competes with every other, demanding inclusion and a dominant position to which it is not necessarily entitled, and every word demands that the system shall modify itself for its sake, that a special exception shall be made in its case.

To the degree that a poem is successful, society and community form one common order, and the system may justly love itself because the feelings which it embodies form a true community loving each other and it.

In a poem, as distinct from many other verbal societies, meaning and being are identical. Like an image in a mirror, a poem is a pseudo-person, i.e. it has uniqueness and addresses the reader face to face or person to person, but, like all natural beings and unlike historical beings, it cannot lie. One cannot say of a poem that it is true or false, for one does not have to consider anything but itself to discover whether or no it is a true order. If unfreedom or disorder are present, the poem itself reveals this on inspection. We may be, and frequently are, mistaken about a poem, but the cause is our own self-deception, not the poem.

In writing a poem, the poet can work in two ways. Starting with an intuitive idea of the kind of community he desires to call into being, he may work backwards in search of the system which will embody it most justly, or, starting with a certain system, he may work forward in search of the community which that system can most truthfully embody. In practice, he nearly always works simultaneously in both directions, modifying his conception of the ultimate nature of the community at the immediate suggestions of the system and modifying the system in response to his idea, as it becomes increasingly clear, of the future needs of the community.

Classical and Romantic are misleading terms for the two poetic parties, the Aristocratic and the Democratic, which have always existed, and to either of which every poet belongs, though he may switch his party allegiance during his poetic career or, on some specific issue, refuse to obey his Party Whip.

The Aristocratic Principle as regards the poetic subject: No material shall be made the subject of a poem which poetry cannot transform into its own universe. It defends poetry against didacticism and journalism.

The Democratic Principle as regards the poetic subject: No material shall be excluded from becoming the subject of a poem which can be poetically transformed. It defends poetry against limited or false notions of what is "poetic."

The Aristocratic Principle as regards poetic treatment: No irrelevant aspects of a given subject shall be expressed in the poem which treats it. It defends poetry against formlessness and diffuseness.

The Democratic Principle as regards poetic treatment: No relevant aspects of a given subject shall remain unexpressed in the poem which treats it. It defends poetry against academic aridity.

Any chosen metrical scheme is a law—for the poet and of the poem. Once he has chosen it, the poet is on his honor to find such words as can conform to its demands. He cannot scan "river" as an iamb or make it a three-syllable word.

A verbal system cannot be selected completely arbitrarily, nor can one say that any given system is absolutely necessary. The poet searches for the one which seems to him to impose the most just obligations on the feelings. Ought always implies Can, so that a system whose claims cannot be met must be scrapped, but the poet has to beware of accusing the system of injustice when the real fault is his incompetence and laziness.

As a natural object, the verbal system of a poem belongs to the organic rather than the inorganic order, i.e. instead of the mathematically exact symmetry of the inorganic, it is rhythmical, its symmetries are perceptible but unmeasurable. Seen from a certain distance, the features of the human face appear to be symmetrically arranged and constant in size and position, so that a face with a nose a foot long or a left eye only would appear monstrous. But, seen at close quarters, this regularity disappears, and the size and position of the features is different in every case. If a face could exist in which the symmetry was mathematically exact, it, too, would appear monstrous.

So with the metrical structure of a poem. If blank verse could be written so that every foot in every line was identical, all accented syllables carrying identically the same weight of accent and all unaccented syllables of exactly the same lightness, the poem would sound intolerable to the ear.

The process of poetic composition is a work of civilizing. A barbaric horde of emotions which cannot rule themselves are transformed into a just, loving, and self-ruling polis. Unless, however, there is already present in the initial horde a nucleus of self-rule, an idea, a phrase, the poet has no point from which to start. The degree of justice and self-rule possible in a poem is very much higher than in any historical political society. Every good poem is very nearly a Utopia.

In the earlier stages of composition, the poet has to act like a Greek tyrant; the decision to write this phrase rather than that must be largely his, for the demands of the poem are as yet inarticulate or contradictory. As composition proceeds, the poem begins to take over the job of ruling itself; the transient rule of the poet gets weaker and weaker until, in the final stages, he is like the elected representative of a democracy whose duty it is to listen to and execute the demands of the poem, which now knows exactly what it wishes to be. On completion, the poem rules itself immanently, and the poet is dismissed into private life.

The writing of a short poem is a more democratic process than the writing of a long one. As in a small political society, the demands of the material make themselves more directly heard and are more easily reconciled with each other. In a long poem, as in a large political society, direct rule by the material is impossible, and the poet is, at best, a wise and responsible representative who plans and legislates on its bewildered and grumbling behalf and, at worst, a dictator who establishes his empire by force.

All works of art are commissioned, in that the idea which stimulates an artist to create a given work "comes" to him. Among those works which are failures because uninspired, the number of self-commissioned works is probably greater than the number commissioned by patrons.

If works of art could be created by "inspiration" alone, i.e. automatically in a trance, artistic creation would be so boring or so unpleasant that only substantial rewards in money or social prestige could induce a man to become an artist.

The poet has to wrestle with the Muse as Jacob had to wrestle with the Angel at the ford, before She will bless him with truth. For those who are willing to believe everything She says, She has nothing but contempt, which She shows by telling them lies.

Artistic judgment is the capacity to distinguish between blind chance and providence.

> When I was writing the chorus in G minor, I suddenly dipped my pen into the medicine bottle instead of the ink; I made a blot, and when I dried it with sand [blotting paper was not invented then], it took the form of a natural, which instantly gave me the idea of the effect which the change from G minor to G major would make, and to this blot all the effect—if any—is due. (Rossini to Louis Engel)

All those whose success in life depends, neither upon a job which satisfies some specific and constant natural need like a farmer, nor upon inborn skill and acquired knowledge like a surgeon, but upon "inspiration," the lucky hazard of ideas, live "by their wits." Every "original" scientist or artist has something slightly shady about him like a gambler or a medium.

A poet is, before everything else, a person who is passionately in love with language. Whether this love is a sign of his poetic gift or the gift itself—falling in love is something which happens to a person, not something he chooses—it is impossible to say.

Language: An Enquiry Into Its Meaning and Function,
planned and edited by Ruth Nanda Anshen, 1957

The Wish Game

[See *The Dyer's Hand,* p. 599, and textual notes, p. 961.]

The New Yorker, 16 March 1957

Guy Burgess

Letter to the Editor of the *Sunday Times*

Sir,—Mr Stephen Spender has sent me a copy of his letter to *The Sunday Times* concerning Mr Driberg's book *Guy Burgess, a Portrait With a Background*.

In it he states, correctly, that his wife did tell me that Guy Burgess had called. He goes on to say, however, that my reply was that "I did not wish to speak to Burgess or to see him." Since this suggests that I had quarrelled with Mr Burgess or did not regard him as a friend I must say that, had I been in when the call was made and had Mr Burgess really proposed visiting me in Ischia, I should have invited him.

I was not in. I was busy and thought as one often does in such cases: "Oh bother! I can't call now. If it's important, he'll call again." Of course, I knew nothing about any "goings-on" and I find it difficult to believe that so momentous a decision as going or not going to Russia can have turned upon such an accident.

But, in any case, it would be dishonourable of me to deny a friendship because the party in question has become publicly notorious.

W. H. Auden

Forio d'Ischia.

Sunday Times, 20 January 1957

The Voltaire of Music

Life of Rossini. By Stendhal. Translated by Richard Coe.
John Calder. 30s.

Stendhal was never tired of speculating about the relation between the way in which a people lives, its climatic, social and political condition, and the kind of art which it produces and values. Were he alive today, he would certainly come up with some explanation, more or less plausible, for the interest in opera taken during the past twenty years by the *dilettanti* of the English-speaking countries. When I was a boy Covent Garden and the Metropolitan were social institutions, not places to which those who considered themselves "musical" would think of going. Real serious music meant the three B's and the instrumental music of Mozart who was just ceasing to be regarded as a charming rococo composer, incapable of expressing the graver emotions. Wagner was definitely "out" and, as for the Italians, they were little more than Wops who wrote for the hurdy-gurdy. *Lieder* were OK, but Opera was obviously a bastard art-form which anyone with good taste would avoid. Who would have dared prophesy that within half a generation nobody who could not knowledgeably discuss *I Puritani*, or even *Gianni Schicchi*, could hope to be musically One-Up?

Radio broadcasts and long-playing records have encouraged this new interest but they did not, I think, create it. I can imagine a Stendhalian *esquisse* on Opera as an escape from the Egalitarian Welfare State, but, not being Stendhal, I shall refrain from writing it. Historically, at least, it is clear that in England, the change began in the thirties with Glyndebourne and Mozart. Once Mozart became Top Composer, it was impossible to ignore the medium in which he wrote some of his major works. It is interesting to find that Stendhal's feeling about his music was much closer to our own than to our fathers'.

Mozart is like a mistress who is always serious and often sad. He never suspected that love could ever exist without a hint of sadness or fear.

Indeed Stendhal's only criticism of Mozart is the same that was later levelled at Wagner, namely, that his orchestral accompaniments are sometimes too heavy and important, and that he makes too great demands upon the listener's attention. Thus, in comparing the two Figaros, he makes an observation which is as original as, I believe, it is just.

The Figaro of *The Barber* is a great and profoundly comic figure: the Figaro of *Le Nozze* is only a brilliant musician.

After Mozart came Verdi; first, of course, only the later works but presently even *La Traviata* became respectable and now, within the last five years, we have begun to realize that *The Barber* and *William Tell* were not the only operas Rossini wrote. We have still, however, a long way to go. Of the operas which Stendhal singles out for special praise, I find that I only know two: *L'Italiana in Algeri* and *Il Turco in Italia*. I have never heard a note of *Demetrio e Polibio, La Pietra del Paragone, Tancredi* (apart from the overture), *Elizabetta: Regina d'Inghilterra* or *Otello*, all of which Stendhal, rightly or wrongly, preferred to two which have had successful revivals, *La Cenerentola* and *La Gazza Ladra*. Of the operas he does not discuss because they were written after his book, I have heard and loved *Le Siège de Corinthe* and *Le Comte Ory*.

Personally, I should welcome a moratorium for ten years on the operas of Mozart: wonderful as they are, we know them almost by heart, and there are so many operas of Rossini's and Donizetti's which we shall never see until a space in the repertory is cleared for them.

Life of Rossini belongs, with *Soirées d'Orchestre, The Case of Wagner* and Shaw's reviews to that very small list of writings about music which are neither ephemeral nor unreadable.

To begin with, Stendhal never forgets, as too many critics do, that liking music is prior to judging it.

> A race which is dominated by an overmastering passion for bad music would be closer to the reality of good taste than a race of scholars who, by dint of mental application, had learned to appreciate sensibly, rationally, or moderately the most exquisite music which was ever conceived.

and he draws amusing portraits of two types, one a clerk from the War Office with absolute pitch:

> Every sound in nature speaks to him in a language which (technically speaking) is of pellucid clarity, and he can transfer it to paper, but he has not the faintest inkling of its *real* meaning.

The other a Venetian nobleman:

> Not only was this charming young man to all intents and purposes tone-deaf; but he was incapable of singing four notes on end without committing the most excruciating cacophony. But the astonishing fact was, that, in spite of being constitutionally incapable of singing in tune, he adored music with a passionate intensity which is rare to find even in Italy.

And then, because he really enjoys listening to music, Stendhal does not make a religion out of it. He has no patience with what he calls listening academically:

> One *feels it one's duty* not to miss a single note. O what a phrase: *to feel it one's duty!* How unspeakably English! How anti-musical!

and admits that he prefers to sit in a box at the opera because

> The human soul *requires* four or five minutes of whispered conversation to release itself from the tension which may be built up by some sublime duet; only then will it be in any fit state to appreciate the aria which follows next on the programme.

As a critic of Rossini's music, he is just the sort which every artist would like to find; he admires passionately but he does not idolize or pretend that Rossini has no limitations. He calls him the Voltaire of music and means it, that is to say, he values Rossini because he is always amusing and never boring but is well aware that passionate love is not his forte.

> In *The Barber*, whenever the scene requires a note of natural and profound emotion, Rossini offers us instead *preciosity* or elegance, with never a hint of weakening self-control: his lovers seem to speak the language of Fontanelle.

And though he considered Rossini as unique in his creative facility, he did not fail to notice his habit of repeating himself.

> There is a curious thesis still to be written—an analytical survey of all the musical items in Rossini's operas which are *really distinct and independent*; this to be followed by a second survey of all the items based upon *similar musical ideas*, with footnotes indicating in each instance the particular aria or duet which embodies the most satisfactory version.

Some of the most interesting pages in the book are devoted to the revolution in the style of singing which Rossini effected and which Stendhal himself deplored. Stendhal had been brought up on and become a connoisseur of a kind of singing which we have never heard. Then the composer supplied the permanent *structural* frame within which the singer was free to improvise according to his feelings at each performance; the expressive *utterance* was the singer's responsibility.

> At one performance, he may tend towards ornaments redolent of indolence and *morbidezza*; on a different occasion, from the very moment when he sets foot on the stage, he may find himself in a mood for *gorgheggi* instinct with energy and life. Unless he yield to the inspiration of the moment he can never attain to perfection in his singing. A great singer is essentially a creature of nerves; a great violinist, on the other hand, needs a temperament of a radically different quality.

The male soprano, Velluti, Stendhal tells us, always prepared three different sets of ornamentation for every aria from which to select according to his mood and the state of his voice. The dangers of this approach are obvious, for it makes demands upon the singer's taste as well as his technique which were too much, even in Stendhal's time, for all but the greatest.

From his own descriptions, the result in the case of a singer who had learned the tricks but had no genius for improvisation must have been excruciating, while the vanity of the great performer constantly tempted him to distort the composer's original melody out of all recognition. It was after an experience of this kind with Velluti that Rossini decided that in future he would write in the ornamentation himself. Stendhal's objection to this course was twofold: firstly to deprive the singer of his freedom was to transform the most profoundly moving of all the arts into "a trade for mechanicals", and secondly, in writing a kind of ornamentation suited to a particular singer, like Colbran or Davide, Rossini was making his work unperformable by others, and he says, I think with justice:

> Even if a good half of Rossini's *fioriture* were to be omitted in performance (or alternatively, even if all the *fioriture* are used, but in a different order of distribution throughout the scene), the opera will still

manage to be successful. Rossini's operas, in fact, do not require great interpreters.

Neither Stendhal nor Rossini, of course, realized how far the tendency would go, that the increasingly important role played by the orchestra would presently demand a kind of declamatory voice line without any *fioriture* at all.

I have no space in this review to deal with all the wise and amusing reflections which the book contains, and must content myself with one anecdote about a performance of *Demetrio e Polibio.*

> ... the effect upon the audience was so instantaneous, that, not content with calling for one *encore,* they were on the point of reviving an ancient practice, and calling for a second, when a personal friend of the Mombelli family stepped down into the auditorium, and appealed to the enraptured *dilettanti,* explaining that neither of the Mombelli girls was particularly strong in health and that if they insisted upon a second encore for the quartet, there was a very real danger that the singers might not be able to get through the remainder of the opera. "But", protested the *dilettanti,* "is there anything still to come which is worth hearing, compared with *this*?" "Most assuredly there is!" answered the family friend. "There is the duet between the lover and his mistress, and at least two or three others besides." This argument at last took effect upon the pit, and sheer curiosity conquered the wilder manifestation of enthusiasm.

How far from Bayreuth!

Mr Richard Coe, as translator and editor, has done a wonderful job with a wonderful book.

Time and Tide, 9 February 1957

A Great Hater

The Diary Of A Writer. By Fyodor Dostoievsky.
Translated by Boris Brasol. W. H. Allen. 45s.

This review will be both inadequate and unjust. Inadequate because *The Diary of a Writer* runs to over 1,000 closely printed pages and, in the time allowed me, it has been impossible to read them all; unjust because, though Dostoievsky is, of course, a great genius, I cannot bear him.

The diary contains a character sketch of an anonymous letter-writer which is as good as anything Dostoievsky ever wrote, and two short-stories, "The Meek One" and "The Dream of a Strange Man," which are so bad they might be parodies, but there is very little in it about his activities as a writer, and, apart from addresses on Nekrasov and Pushkin, which no one who does not read Russian can judge, and an appreciation of George Sand, almost nothing about literature. Dostoievsky appears in it as what we now call a columnist, as someone, already famous, whose opinions, therefore, on current affairs, religion, the future, attract public interest. A novelist can disclaim responsibility for anything his characters may say; a columnist speaks in his own person, and *The Diary of a Writer* reveals a man quite as peculiar as any character in his novels and, if possible, more disagreeable.

The greater part of the diary covers the years 1876–7, when the Serbians and Bulgarians revolted against the Ottoman Empire and Russia went to war with Turkey on their behalf. Dostoievsky was passionately pro-war and, so long as he is describing Turkish atrocities, he has all our sympathies. Every decent person, when he hears of such things happening anywhere, thinks— "This ought to be stopped. Cannot our Government do something about it?" But when he starts to discuss the significance and aims of the war, he chills the blood, and, if his views were in any way shared by the Russian Government, then the desire of Disraeli and Franz Joseph to preserve the Ottoman Empire, corrupt and cruel as it was, becomes understandable.

What really concerns Dostoievsky is not Turkish cruelty but Russia's historic mission:—

> The Slavophile doctrine, in addition to that assimilation of all the Slavs under the rule of Russia, signifies and comprises a spiritual union of all those who believe that our Great Russia, at the head of the united Slavs, will utter to the world, to the whole of European mankind and to civilisation, her new, sane, and as yet unheard-of word. That word will be uttered for the good and genuine unification of mankind as a whole in a new, brotherly, universal union whose inception is derived from the Slavic genius.

Dostoievsky admits that the liberated Slavs will probably be ungrateful and that

> . . . for a long while Russia will be left with the anguish and task of making peace among them, teaching them and, perhaps, occasionally drawing her sword in their defence.

Was the sword she drew in 1863 in defence of Poland? According to Dostoievsky it apparently was:—

> Come! Reconcile yourselves and submit, but know that there will never be an old Poland. There is a new Poland, a Poland liberated by the Czar, a regenerated Poland, which unquestionably may expect in the future a lot equal with that of any Slavic tribe, when Slavdom is liberated and resurrected in Europe. However there never will be an Old Poland, because she could not live at peace with Russia.

When the Slavs have been liberated, the Eastern problem has to be settled, of course,

> not by means of political violence, not by the sword, but by persuasion, example, love, disinterestedness, by light; to elevate those little ones to our level, so that they shall perceive in Russia her motherly mission.

The first step in this process of elevation is to capture and keep Constantinople. Suppose a little one, like Austria, objects?

> We should suddenly declare: we do not wish to recognise any Austrian seizures in Turkey! And all seizures will instantly vanish, perhaps, together with Austria herself.

Through the sheer power of love, presumably. East of Constantinople lies Asia, waiting to be loved:—

> In Europe we were hangers-on and slaves, whereas we shall go to Asia as masters. In Europe we were Asiatics, whereas in Asia, we, too, are Europeans. Our civilising mission will bribe our spirit, drive us thither.

Naturally, one becomes curious to learn some concrete details about this New Jerusalem which Mother Russia is so unselfishly going to build for us all. What, for example, will be the religion?

> Roman Catholicism—by the Will of Providence—will be replaced with regenerated Eastern Christianity.

So much for the future of the Jesuits. The future of the Jews is best left to the imagination. Dostoievsky's line on them is roughly as follows: We Russians, being Christians, are just longing to be their brothers, but they, being Jews, will never agree to become our brothers, so . . .

What about the legal system? Well, there will be nothing vulgar like a contest between rival counsel before a jury:—

> This, mechanical method of dragging truth to the surface perhaps will be replaced in Russia—simply by truth . . . in some remote future the prosecutor may even be able to plead the cause of the defendant instead of accusing him.

After the prisoner has confessed? What about freedom in general?

> Civil liberty may be established in Russia on an integral scale, more complete than anywhere in the world. . . . It will be based, not upon a written sheet of paper, but upon the children's affection of the people to the Czar as their father, since children may be permitted many a thing which is inconceivable in the case of contractual nations: they may be entrusted with much that has nowhere been encountered, since chil-

dren will not betray their father, and, being children, they will lovingly accept from him any correction of their errors.

That the same man who, in his distinctive criticism of society, is as precise and profound as any writer who ever lived should, when he tries to say something positive, talk such drivel is significant. The real object of Dostoievsky's hatred is not the errors of this or that society, but civilisation as such and, speaking personally, I owe him a debt for making me see what all civilisations, good or bad, have in common.

The aim of any civilisation is to conserve psychic energy by limiting the exercise of reason and moral choice to those occasions when right action is impossible without them; whenever thought and volition can be replaced by habit, they should be for the sake of economy.

For example, let us take the case of the anonymous letter-writer, since Dostoievsky discusses him in this book. Many, perhaps most, people have been tempted at some time or other to write a malicious anonymous letter and, if they are curious to know their motive, Dostoievsky is the man to tell them. But a civilised man does not need to know his motive in order to refrain from writing the letter. Nor does he refrain from fear of being found out or offending God. He simply says to himself: "Nice people do not write anonymous letters." This nice person is not some ideal figure whom he is striving to become and to whom the idea of an anonymous letter would never occur; it is an image of what, by habit, he thinks himself to be.

Again, since civilisation is a process of habit-forming which takes time, civility is to be judged in terms of more-or-less, not the either-or of ethics and religion. A husband who beats his wife only on Saturdays is no better than one who beats his every day of the week, but he is, just a bit, more civilised.

It is just these two characteristics of civilisation, habit and slow improvement, which Dostoievsky cannot stand. In this he claims to be a Christian, but while Christianity declares that the Law, like everything which is Caesar's, is not enough, it does not say they are of no account. In the parable of the Pharisee and the Publican, the former is condemned because he identifies being a nice person with being a good one. In Dostoievsky's version of Christianity, the Publican's prayer would run: "I thank thee, Lord, that I am a miserable sinner and not as this Pharisee who gives tithes of all that he possesses."

The Observer, 17 February 1957

A Grecian Eye

The Stones of Troy. By C. A. Trypanis. Faber & Faber. 10s. 6d.

The title sequence of Mr Trypanis' book consists of thirteen poems, each headed by a phrase or sentence from the *Iliad* upon which it is a comment. The risk of such a procedure is of being unintelligible to those to whom the original means nothing, and the *Iliad* is one of the very few poems which could be used in this way. To Mr Trypanis, as a Greek, it must, of course, have a unique significance, historically and poetically, but to any citizen of the West, however Greekless, the Homeric world is the archetype of his own. Even the proper names, Diomedes, Pedasus, Deiphobos, etc., have a poetic resonance in his ear which the proper names in, say, an Indian epic cannot have.

A poem which is to serve as an image of man and the world and so itself stimulate further poems must have two qualities, historical distance and universality. The reader must be simultaneously aware of how different the world it describes is from his own and yet how analogous. Thus the *Iliad*, like most epics, assumes that war is as normal a human activity as farming and sees it in terms of personal combat. Precisely because, for us, war is neither, the epic conflict can serve as an image of man, as a history-making creature, necessarily at odds with what he is since he has to become something else, and aware that, since no human experience can recur, every moment is death.

Again, epic celebrates the hero, that is, the exceptionally gifted individual, stronger, braver, wiser than the average, and this can serve us as a symbol for the quite unhomeric conception of the uniqueness of every human person, which has nothing whatever to do with his gifts or lack of them.

I am always expecting the Communists to interpret the *Aeneid* as an *ur*-Marxist poem, the first attempt to see history as a dialectical conflict with an inevitable and sense-making conclusion. To those of us who are not Marxists, the *Iliad* is the more sympathetic work precisely because it does not attempt to make sense of the Trojan War. Men fight and die because "hateful Ares bids." This is terrifying but, at least, it lacks that revolting justification for horror which is implied by the expression: "You can't make an omelette without breaking eggs." Mr Trypanis, in my opinion, is over-generous to Virgil when he writes:

> Pious Aeneas does not move, especially
> Since we know, what you did not know, Virgil,
> The Empire after Augustus.

Virgil did know the history of the Roman Republic, he knew about the Punic wars, Marius, Sulla, etc., and that should have been enough.

To show what Mr Trypanis' poems are about, let me give some quotations. The homeric line "And with them eighty black ships followed" makes him think of the anonymous millions who throughout history are involved and perish in causes they do not understand.

> They did not know why they were setting out.
> They did not want to fight the whole damned
> Army of Troy, or to bring Helen back.
> They never cared a jot, they never learnt
> How their eighty ships rowed

> Into the second book of the Iliad. All they knew
> Was Diomedes of the loud war-cry, their lord.

The unexplained absence of Hector's spearman at the moment when Achilles is upon him, he takes as a figure for the solitude of every death.

> There must be a Deiphobos who will not hear.
> And if there isn't one, the urgency of death
> Conjures him up. . . .
> Hoping your heart like steel will break, not bend,
> Call to Deiphobos, although he cannot hear.
> Because Deiphobos is your best friend.
> Break out into angry curses at this raw deal,
> Swearing makes you less alone—and death's dark frown
> Looks less humiliating when you feel
> It was Deiphobos who let you down.

And Achilles' mistreatment of Hector's corpse becomes a parable about genuine passion and shameful habit.

> It can become a habit every morning
> To drag broad Hector's body round the tomb,
> Fling it face downward, and with hollow scorning
> Return to your beaked hut, the hours of gloom.
> It can become a habit, but the heart
> Will soon forget her barren anger-lust.
> Only your hands will act the villain part. . . .

As will be seen from these passages, much of their effect depends upon a contrast between the epic subject-matter and the deliberate avoidance of the high epic style. Diction and rhythm are kept as near as possible to what Professor C. S. Lewis would call the drab. The technical difficulty in writing verse which is conversational in tone and rhythm yet formally rhymed is to make the speech unit and the rhythm-rhyme unit coincide without strain, and occasionally, I think, Mr Trypanis trips up on this.

> And will offer food—Niobe long before
> You tasted food in her stone grief. Back to the city
> You will bring Hector's body untouched, and what is more
> Will make Achilles greater in his pity.

Here the speech unit "Niobe long before you" has been broken for the sake of the rhyme. But Mr Trypanis is rarely guilty of such awkwardness.

As deliberate as the plainness of the diction, is the sparing use of metaphor. It is, indeed, unfair to this kind of poetry to quote lines out of a poem because, in isolation, they sound like commonplace statements. The complexity of feeling and reference lie in the poem as a whole: the poem itself, so to speak, is a metaphor.

I can imagine someone, who read these poems without knowing their authorship, guessing them to be translations of hitherto unknown poems by Cavafy. About this two things may be said. Firstly, that what matters is, not that a poem be original, but that it be genuine. Secondly, though Mr Trypanis writes in English, he and Cavafy are both Greeks.

When an Englishman reads, say, Racine and Mallarmé, they seem much more like each other than they do to a Frenchman, because what the English reader notices first is the difference between all French poetry and all English poetry.

When a poet of entirely English ancestry and background reads the *Iliad*, his feelings, whatever they are, cannot escape being affected by two facts: that England has not been invaded for nine hundred years, and that England has been a great imperial power.

He can imagine himself, for example, in the epic situation of defending the narrow pass against hopeless odds, but he cannot really imagine that his side will not win in the end. A Greek, like Mr Trypanis, can imagine final defeat quite easily.

Again, he may be pro- or anti-imperialist but he can never see history from the point of view of someone bred in a country which has never been a great ruling power. A Greek inherits memories of a time when Greece was great, but as a collection of city states and colonies, not as a centralised military empire.

One of the characteristics of Mr Trypanis' poetry which I find particularly refreshing, because it is rare in English poetry, is that of pessimism without a trace of melancholia.

English poets are excellent at expressing melancholia: when they try to be pessimists, they generally sound too theoretical and theatrical.

The Stones of Troy is a collection of real and beautiful poems. In addition, given the times in which we live, the attitude to life which they embody is one of which we may well stand in moral need.

Encounter, March 1957

Just How I Feel

Chaucer and the Fifteenth Century. By H. S. Bennet.
Oxford University Press. $5.

English Literature at the Close of the Middle Ages. By E. K. Chambers.
Oxford University Press. $5.

whan that the month of May
Is comen, and that I here the joules synge
And that the floures gynnen for to sprynge,
Farwel my bok, and my devocioun.

That's just how I feel. True, it is only March, not May, but this is Southern Italy, not England. The sky is a blazing cloudless blue which may be pleasant, but we need at least a month's continuous rain. The Easter lilies are out, the roses are in bud, and the last thing I feel like doing is an article on *The Oxford History of English Literature, Vol. II, parts 1 & 2*. Besides, what business have I to write about works of scholarship? Such volumes are generally sent to rival scholars who begin with conventional compliments and end, cattily, with a list of misprints or misdates. But if Mr Bennett, who deals with the "artful" poetry and prose from Chaucer to Henryson, or Professor Chambers, who covers the "artless" literature of the same period, the Mystery and Miracle plays, the carols, the ballads, etc., had as a practical joke, invented half the writings to which they refer, I should be taken in. On questions of fact, I must accept their authority as Apostolic.

Perhaps, however, being relieved by ignorance from any obligation to check, I can browse through a history of literature with all the more pleasure.

Such histories, for example, keep reminding one of books which one has read, but not for a long time, and the refreshed memory divides them into the sheep and the goats, that is to say, those which one looks forward to re-reading when one has time, and those which one is determined never to read again.

I have not read Malory since I was a schoolboy, and now, at a quotation by Mr Bennett, suddenly the old magic comes back.

> Allas said Sir Bors that euer Sir Launcelot's kyyne sawe yow for now haue ye lost the best knyght of oure blood / and he that was alle oure leder and oure socour / and I dare saye and make it good that all kynges crysten nor hethen may not fynde suche a knyghte for to speke of his nobylnesse and courtosye with his beaute and heis gentylnesse / Alas said sire Bors what shalle we doo that ben of his blood / Allas said Ector de marys / Allas said Lyonel.

This, for me, was one of the voices in the Garden of Eden. It had nothing to do with real human beings and never pretended to. I enjoyed it all the more because it was so unlike the picture of Arthur and his knights as muscular clean-minded middle-class Protestants presented to us by our schoolmasters. I shall enjoy re-reading the *Morte D'Arthur* still more now that I learn from Professor Chambers that Malory himself was a rapist and a cattle-thief.

On the other hand, I shudder slightly on even seeing the title *The Imitation of Christ*. I was given a copy, bound in limp black leather, when I was confirmed. I know it is a book which has brought spiritual insight and comfort to thousands, but each to his own style of piety. For me, no, never, never again.

A proper literary history not only reminds, but also brings good news. The Official historian is bound to spend most of his space on the well-known because the well-known is usually the best, but his quotations should, whenever possible, come as a pleasant surprise. Professor Chambers does not have to quote *I synge of a mayden* because, lovely as it is, it can be found in all the anthologies. He might, instead, have given us the whole of a "ribald carol," of which he gives only the promising refrain

> *Inducas, inducas*
> *In temptationibus.*

However, I found a lot of pleasant surprises in these two volumes. I certainly want to read more of the excellent prose of Nicholas Love; I don't think I want to read much Peacock, but I am glad to have read him on the syllogism:

> so stronge and so myghti in al kindis of maters, that though al the aungels of hevene wolden seie his conclusions were not trewe, yitt schulde leeve the aungels seiyng, and we schulden truste more to the proof of thilk sillogisme than to the contrarie seiyng of alle the aungels in hevene . . .

and even if I never get round to reading an obscure morality play which may have been called *Anima*, I shall not forget one of its stage directions for the Devil:

> Her he takyt a screwed boy with him, and goeth his wey cryenge.

Then, corresponding to the "goats" of one's past reading, one hears of books which one need never read. What a relief to learn that I may go happily to my grave without having read *The Life of St Katherine*, 8372 lines in rhyme royal by John Capgrove, or Lydgate's translation of de Deguilleville's *The Pilgrimage of the Life of Man*, of which even Professor C. S. Lewis, who has the literary digestion of an ostrich, is compelled to say:

> The poem is unpleasant to read, not only because of its monstrous length and imperfect art, but because of the repellent and suffocating nature of its content.

Poor old Lydgate. Always getting a spanking. "Even the unflagging efforts of F. J. Furnival to found a Lydgate Society to print everything Lydgate wrote was unsuccessful." Every poet, I think,—for who does not fear the same posthumous fate?—will be happy to learn that Lydgate has at last found one friend, Mr Churton Collins, who is convinced that he was a great genius. Mr Collins' claims are, I fear, exaggerated, but it is only the excessive enthusiasms of individuals that prevent the Canon from becoming a dead convention. Accepted Opinion is, more or less, and in the long run, just, but at any moment it is overindulgent with some authors and over-severe to others. Accepted Opinion, which is shared by both Professor Chambers and Mr Bennett, holds that Chaucer's only worthy successors were all Scotch, and that the only valuable poetic contribution of fifteenth century England are anonymous dramas, lyrics, ballads. From this one cannot dissent strongly. Nothing that Lydgate or Hoccleve or Hawes wrote is as good as *The Kingis Quair* or *The Testament of Cresseid*, but all three, particularly Hawes, have written stuff that is well worth reading.

> She commaunded her minstrelles right anone to play
> Mamours, the swete and the gentill daunce;
> With La Bell Pucell that was faire and gaye
> She me recommaunded with all pleasuance
> To dance true mesures without variaunce.
> O Lorde God, how glad than was I
> So for to daunce with my swete lady.
>
> (*The Pastime of Pleasure*)

is not the sort of poetry that can be dismissed, even if the sixth line is an example of what Professor Saintsbury used to call "the Abominable C" after Siever's classification of lines with a syllable missing at the caesura.

Again, Accepted Opinion is more or less justified in its condemnation of literary follies like Euphuism or Classical meters in English but the literary historian, even when he is writing a standard history, might at least admit that follies are fun and that many beautiful things would never have come into existence without them. Without the Classical Meter Craze, for instance, we should not have the choruses of *Samson Agonistes*. In the Fifteenth Century the folly was aureate diction. One can hardly expect Professor Chambers or Mr Bennett to recommend such diction as a good example, but they might have admitted that some beautiful poems have employed it, e.g.

> The twinklling stremowris of the orient
> Sched purpour sprangis with gold and asure ment.
> Persand the sabill barmkyn nocturnall,
> Bet doun the skyis mantill wall.
>
> (Gavin Douglas. Prologue to *Aeneid*, Book XII)

In giving the general historical background, the problem for the literary historian is deciding where to stop. Everything that happens is in some way relevant to what is written, but the degree of relevance depends upon the kind of question to which the reader wants an answer, and readers vary. My first questions, for instance, are technical. I know that Chaucer arrived at his style of poetry through translation and imitation of French and Italian models. Reading his lines I hear a peculiar lilt which is not to be heard in English poetry before him. The first thing, therefore, I want from the historian is a detailed discussion of French and Italian prosody in that period, for I suspect that it has much to do with Chaucer's highly original fingering. So far, I must admit, I have been disappointed. No one even bothers to say where and when the rhyme royal stanza was first used. Another thing that interests me about a poet or a period is rhetorical organisation. When Mr Bennett, speaking of *Troilus and Crisede*, writes:

> *Descriptio; circumlocutio; expolitio; exclamatio*, and the rest are all employed at length, according to the best medieval theory and practice . . . We shall serve Chaucer best by frankly recognising them as matters mainly of medieval and not of permanent interest

I am at once tantalised and annoyed. I want to know all about medieval theories of rhetoric; Mr Bennett could tell me, but he won't.

When it comes to the life and times of a poet, the most interesting aspects are precisely those which find no place in his poetry, but must have been of concern to the man. If a poet, living in a sceptical and politically stable age, shows no concern for theology or politics, it does not tell us much about him, but Chaucer's circumstances were very different. Though the statute *De Heretico Comburendo* was not passed till after his death, heresy was a serious matter; from 1306–76, the Pope had resided in Avignon, a puppet of England's hereditary enemy, France, and there had been a continual conflict between the Pope and the English Crown as evidenced by the Statutes of Provisors and Praemunire. Then, in 1378—Chaucer was actually in Italy on a diplomatic mission at the time,—occurred the Great Schism in which England supported Urban and France followed Clement. It is impossible to believe that such events meant nothing to Chaucer personally: if he does not write about them, the omission was a deliberate personal choice, made partly, no doubt, from prudence and partly, perhaps, from strong feelings about bigotry and persecution, that is to say, his famous humorous "tolerance" may have been as much a cultivated virtue as a temperamental characteristic.

Politically, judging by his career, he must have been rather an old sly boots, to keep in favor at Court through so many upheavals, to survive Richard the Second's downfall and even get a pension from his successor Henry the Fourth.

I should have welcomed a more extensive treatment of both the religious and the political background than Mr Bennett has found room for, but I dare say he himself regrets the lack of room. Anyway, he has done one thing which a good literary historian should, sent me back to reading Chaucer again. How misleading it is to call Chaucer the Father of English Poetry! Different as is his matter, as a "maker" he is more like Milton than any other poet. Both set to work quite consciously to create a poetic style, both owed more to foreign models than to their native predecessors, and the poetry of both proved too idiosyncratic to be of much use to others; they have both had imitators but no sons. We can see the oddity in Milton more easily because the spoken language has changed little since his day, but I suspect that Chaucer's handling of the language sounded more peculiar to his contemporaries than we realize. This much, at least, is clear. If one compares Chaucer's decasyllabics with those of Spencer or Surrey, though single lines may strike the ear as similar, in batches they sound like two different meters.

Professor Chambers sticks pretty closely to purely literary facts which is probably wise when dealing with anonymous writings. On these he seems as omniscient as is possible for a human being. There are only two points on which I wish he had enlightened us. I should like to know more about the theological objection to the theatre, the notion that it is sinful for one person to pretend to be another, as distinct from the objection to the moral character of actors. The other point concerns the relation of words and music and perhaps the information one would like is simply unavailable. Were carols and ballads written for already existing tunes, or were the tunes written for the words? Were both composed by the same person or by two different people?

The contrast between the metrical incompleteness of non-lyrical poetry of the fifteenth century and the metrical ease and skill of the lyrics and ballads inclines me to believe that the virtues of the latter owe much to music. Saintsbury wrote, very justly:

> Chaucer's work was done, did not want doing again, and might have been overdone. . . . It was not his task—and we may even doubt whether it was the bent of his special genius—to develop the irregular side of English prosody, to give us the swing and sway of lyric, to utilize the elasticity and variety, while perfecting the harmony and melody, of trisyllabic equivalence.
>
> Now this in a humble, but all the more effectual way, *was* the task of the anonymous folk-singers. It is very possible—indeed much more than possible—that they could not have written the severer and more regular measures if they would; it is at least possible that they would not if they could; it is certain that we ought to thank God and them for not doing so.

What Saintsbury missed owing to his quarrel with the cranks who would scan poetry by musical notation, was the part played by music, with its completely different rhythmical values, in encouraging that freedom.

The Griffin, April 1957

Sydney Smith: The Kind-Hearted Wit

To say that a writer is neglected is not the same as saying that he is underrated, though the evidence for the assertion is the same in both cases, namely, that he is not read. An underrated writer suffers from current fashions in taste, and the critic who would promote him must first change the fashion; a neglected writer suffers merely from public ignorance, and, to rescue him from neglect, it should be sufficient to make his work available to the public and draw attention to its existence.

I have chosen Sydney Smith because, while everybody has heard of him and can probably quote some of his wisecracks—several books, even, have been written about him as a man—his actual writings are, so far as I know, out of print. In 1953 appeared Mr Nowell Smith's definitive edition of his letters, and those who can afford to buy these two volumes will discover that Smith is one of the supreme masters of the epistolary art, but what he wrote for publication is still unavailable.

This is understandable, for Sydney Smith was neither a poet nor a novelist nor even an essayist, but from first to last a writer of polemics, as pure an example as we have in English of *l'écrivain engagé*. As a general rule it is the just fate of a polemical writer to be forgotten when the causes for which he fought have been won or are no longer a live issue, and it will always be difficult to persuade a later generation that there can be exceptions—polemical writers, journalists if you will, of such brilliance and charm that they can be read with delight and admiration by those to whom their subject matter is, in itself, of little interest.

Literary criticism, too, is apt to avoid the polemical writer because it can find little to say about him. Unlike the poet, the novelist or the dramatist, he rarely shows "development," stylistic or ideological. His cast of mind, his way of expressing his ideas and presenting his arguments, are usually established early in his career, and any variety his work may show will come for the most part from a variety in the topics upon which he writes.

Nevertheless, there are a few such authors who must be ranked high by any literary standard, and I would put Smith in the first class, beside Hooker, Swift and Bernard Shaw. Milton in his polemical writings is too bad-tempered, Junius too unfair.

Sydney Smith's mother came of French Huguenot stock, his father was an eccentric, unstable character who left his bride at the church door and departed to America for several years, spent the rest of his life in travel and unsuccessful speculations, and insisted upon his family sitting over the dinner table in the half-dark for hours. Sydney, the second son, was, physically, swarthy, sturdy, tending to stoutness, and he suffered in later life from gout. Mentally, like so many funny men, he suffered much from melancholia: he found it difficult to get up in the morning, he could not bear dimly-lit rooms—"Better," he wrote, "to eat dry bread by the splendour of gas than to dine upon wild-beef with wax candles"—and music in a minor key upset him.

As a young man his ambition was to read for the Bar, but lack of money compelled him instead to take Holy Orders. There is no reason to doubt the sincerity of his religious faith, but he was certainly neither a theologian nor a mystic. In his admirable attacks upon religious bigotry and intolerance the reader cannot but be conscious of a certain lack of interest in all theological dogma.

A man's faith is his secret, his works are public and about these, in Sydney Smith's case, there can be no doubt whatsoever. When the Clergy Residence Bill was passed in 1808, Sydney Smith was banished at the age of thirty-eight to Foston in Yorkshire, a village "twelve miles from a lemon," which had not had a resident vicar since the reign of Charles II, its existing parsonage a brick-floored kitchen with one room above it. There he did duty for the next twenty years.

Any man might have quailed at the prospect, but for an intellectual and city-lover like Smith, accustomed to the best tables, the most brilliant conversation, the most elegant ladies and gentlemen, it must have seemed the end, and one might well have expected him to lapse into despondency and drink.

He did nothing of the kind. He kept up his reviewing and his large correspondence. Far from neglecting his parish duties, he became one of the most hard-working country vicars of whom we have record, and the idol of his parishioners. Church services were only a small part of his ministrations: he started small vegetable gardens, let out to the labourers at very low rents, to help them augment their food supply; he experimented with diets to discover which were both cheap and nourishing; he acted as their doctor and, as a local magistrate, saved many of them from going to gaol.

This willingness to take an interest in whatever problem or company circumstance might present is reflected in his writings. There are very few writers who can address more than one kind of audience; some are excellent at speaking to one person, some at speaking to a group, some to a crowd, but it is a rare talent to be able to do all three equally well, and this Sydney Smith preeminently possessed. He is equally at home with the educated reader:

> Old wheat and beans blazing for twenty miles around; cart mares shot; sows of Lord Somerville's breed running wild over the country; the minister of the parish wounded sorely in his hinder parts; Mrs Plymley in fits; all these scenes of war an Austrian or a Russian has seen three or four times over; but it is now three centuries since an English pig has fallen in fair battle upon English ground, or a farm-house been rifled, or a clergyman's wife been subjected to any other proposals of love than the connubial endearments of her sleek and orthodox mate.

with the unlettered rustic:

> I don't like that red nose, and those blear eyes, and that stupid downcast look. You are a drunkard. Another pint, and one pint more; a glass of gin and water, rum and milk, elder and peppermint, and all the beastly fluids which drunkards pour down their throats. . . . It is all nonsense about not being able to work without ale, and gin, and cider, and fer-

mented liquors. Do lions and cart-horses drink ale? It is mere habit. . . .
I have no objection, you will observe, to a moderate use of ale, or any
other liquor you can afford to purchase. My objection is, that you cannot afford it; that every penny you spend at the ale-house comes out of
the stomachs of the poor children, and strips off the clothes of the wife.

and with a child:

Lucy, my dear, mind your arithmetic. You know, in the first sum of yours
I ever saw, there was a mistake. You had carried two (as a cab is licensed
to do) and you ought, dear Lucy, to have carried but one. Is this a trifle?
What would life be without arithmetic, but a scene of horrors. . . . I now
give you my parting advice. Don't marry any body who has not a tolerable understanding and a thousand a year, and God bless you, dear child.

About half of his published writings consist of articles written for *The Edinburgh Review*, of which he was one of the four founders. This periodical,
which Stendhal thought the best in Europe, was devoted to the criticism of
contemporary literature and the furtherance of Whig principles in political
and social matters. From the standpoint of the twentieth century it would
appear that its literary judgments were usually wrong, its stand on social issues almost always right.

Apart from one very funny review of a bad tragedy, Sydney Smith dealt
with the social subjects, with the Game Laws, Prisons, Education, Chimney-
sweepers, etc. As a reformer, he possessed two great moral virtues which
many reformers have lacked. He never accuses his opponent of bad motives;
he impugns only what he can demonstrate, their lack of imagination and
their faulty reasoning. He assumes that most people tolerate and even defend abuses because they do not suffer from them personally and have a resistance to the notion of change, and that very few people are either lunatics
or deliberate scoundrels impervious to rational argument.

Thus, in attacking the law which denied defence counsel to prisoners accused of a felony, a left-over from feudal times when a defence of prisoners
accused by the Crown was felt to imply disloyalty, he explains very simply
why, though this feeling no longer existed, the law still remained on the
statute books:

To ask why there are not more petitions—why the evil is not more noticed, is mere parliamentary froth and ministerial juggling. Gentlemen
are rarely hung. If they were so, there would be petitions without end
for counsel.

His other great virtue is that he takes sensibly short views. He is never Utopian or given to large generalisations, but always attacks a specific abuse, and
the reform he proposes is equally specific and possible to realise.

After a vivid description of the appalling sufferings of chimney boys, he admits that what is desirable is not immediately attainable:

> We must own that it was quite right to throw out the bill for prohibiting the sweeping of chimneys by boys—because humanity is a modern invention; and there are many chimneys in old houses which cannot possibly be swept in any other manner. . . . We should have been very glad to have seconded the views of the Climbing Society, and to have pleaded for the complete abolition of climbing boys, if we could conscientiously have done so. But such a measure, we are convinced from the evidence, could not be carried into execution without great injury to property, and great increased risk of fire.

Of the pieces which appeared outside *The Edinburgh Review,* the most important are the ten *Letters to Peter Plymley* (1807–08), pleading the cause of Catholic Emancipation, the three *Letters to Archdeacon Singleton* (1837) concerned with a Bill for reforming the finances of the Church of England, and the pamphlet *Ballot,* attacking Grote's proposal to substitute the ballot box for open voting.

Of these I find the *Letters to Archdeacon Singleton* the most fascinating because the case Sydney Smith has to argue is more complicated. In the *Peter Plymley Letters* he is so obviously in the right that what he argues, as distinct from how, seems obvious, too. The *Ballot* pamphlet dates a little because historical developments which neither he nor Grote foresaw have vitiated his reasoning, though it does contain a paragraph which no democracy should forget:

> The Radicals are quite satisfied if a rich man of popular manners gains the votes and affections of his dependants; but why is not this as bad as intimidation? The real object is to vote for the good politician, not the kind-hearted or agreeable man: the mischief is just the same to the country whether I am smiled into a corrupt choice, or frowned into a corrupt choice.

The subject of the *Singleton Letters* was a scheme proposed by the Ecclesiastical Commissioners for making the value of livings less unequal—which, at first sight, would seem something of which a liberal like Sydney Smith would approve. He did not. The fact that while the cathedral chapters were to make sacrifices, the incomes of the Bishops were to remain untouched did not miss his attention or his sarcasm, but his main argument is that the notion of equal payment was neither practical nor desirable:

> The whole income of the Church, if equally divided, would be about £250 for each minister. Who would go into the Church and spend £1,200 or £1,500 upon his education, if such were the highest remuneration he could ever look to? At present, men are tempted into the

Church by the prizes of the Church, and bring into that Church a great deal of capital, which enables them to live in decency, supporting themselves, not with the money of the public, but with their own money, which, but for this temptation, would have been carried into some retail trade. . . .

We have had sufficient experience in our own day, of reforms imposed by well-intentioned persons who put equality before liberty, to appreciate this.

For the purposes of debate Smith's literary style is a perfect instrument, rapid and colloquial—few writers read aloud better—yet never slovenly. Whatever his audience, it is treated as an equal; he appeals to our common sense and decent feeling and never seeks to inflame our passions. Equally at home with the long period and the short, the ornate vocabulary and the plain, he is a master of every rhetorical effect—the satirical inversion:

> Their object is to preserve game; they have no objection to preserving the lives of their fellow-creatures also, if both can exist at the same time; if not, the least worthy of God's creatures must fall—the rustic without a soul—not the Christian partridge—not the immortal pheasant—not the rational woodcock, or the accountable hare.

the ironic description of shocking facts in tea-table terms:

> One summer's whipping, only one: the thumb-screw for a short season: a little light easy torturing between Lady-day and Michaelmas.

and the ringing peroration of righteous anger:

> If I lived at Hampstead upon stewed meats and claret: If I walked to church every Sunday before eleven young gentlemen of my own begetting with their faces washed, and their hair pleasingly combed; if the Almighty had blessed me with every earthly comfort—how awfully would I pause before I sent forth the flame and sword over the cabins of the poor, brave, generous, open-hearted peasants of Ireland. . . . The vigour I love consists in finding out wherein subjects are aggrieved, in relieving them, in studying the temper and genius of a people, in consulting their prejudices, in selecting proper persons to lend and manage them, in the laborious, watchful and difficult task of increasing public happiness by allaying each particular discontent. . . . But this, in the eyes of Mr Percival, is imbecility and meanness: houses are not broken open—women are not insulted—the people seem all to be happy; they are not rode over by horses, and cut, by whips. Do you call this vigour? Is this government?

Lastly, he can create pictures in what might be called the ludicrous baroque as brilliantly as Pope:

Frequently did Lord John meet the destroying bishops; much did he commend their daily heap of ruins; sweetly did they smile on each other, and much charming talk was there of meteorology and catarrh, and the particular cathedral they were pulling down at the time: till one fine morning the Home Secretary, with a voice more bland, and a look more ardently affectionate, than that which the masculine mouse bestows on his nibbling female, informed them that the Government meant to take all the Church property into their own hands. . . . The Commission was separated in an instant: London clenched his fist; Canterbury was hurried out by his chaplains and put into a warm bed; a solemn vacancy spread itself over the face of Gloucester: Lincoln was taken out in strong hysterics.

Today the Whig mentality, of which Sydney Smith is one of the finest examples, is under a bit of a cloud:

> A levelling, rancorous, rational sort of mind
> That never looked out of the eye of a saint
> Or out of a drunkard's eye.

Liberalism is attacked for being aesthetically colourless and metaphysically shallow, yet how rarely on any concrete social issue does one find the liberal position to be the wrong one. And how often, alas, do these philosophers and writers who have most astounded us by their profound insights into the human heart and the human condition dismay us by the folly and worse of their judgments on the issues of everyday life.

Sunday Times, 21 April 1957

West's Disease

[See *The Dyer's Hand*, p. 619, and textual notes, p. 963.]

The Griffin, May 1957

Straw Without Bricks

A. E. Housman: A Divided Life. By George L. Watson. Hart-Davis. 25s.

In a foreword Mr Watson describes his book as "an undertaking, against his (Housman's) will but in emulation of his own search for truth, to exhume the pattern, half-obliterated like a Roman pavement, of his buried life." The investigation of a man's private life can, perhaps, be justified if the findings enable us to judge and understand better his public acts, which, in Housman's case, mean his poems and his work in Classical Philology. It can also afford the reader a certain guilty enjoyment, like reading the *News of the World*, if the facts revealed are sufficiently spicy, but they must be documented facts, not conjectures.

On neither ground, however, is Housman a suitable victim. There have been few poets in history as incapable as he of "dramatising" their personal experiences, of projecting them into characters and situations which bear no obvious relation to their original source. Whenever Housman tried to disguise himself as somebody else, as a heterosexual rustic or a soldier, the result was, poetically, a failure. Most of his best poems are perfectly straightforward hymns to one or other of his three Muses, The Dead Mother (the topographical poems like "Far in a western brookland" or "Tell me not here, it needs no saying"), The Cruel Friend ("The Merry Guide" and most of the "You" poems), or The Uniformed Stranger ("In valleys green and still"). In these, what Housman "really felt" is stated without any concealment, and the only thing a biographer can tell us is that the Cruel Friend was Moses Jackson. If, like most poetry, they sometimes exhibit ambiguities and ambivalent feelings, it is knowledge of poetry and the ways in which language is used, not biographical information, that is needed to clarify the meaning. If I say, for example, that in the assassinated Satan of "Hell Gate," Housman combines, by a process of condensation so common in dreams, "the household traitor" and the Mrs Grundy who sends him to prison "for the colour of his hair", and that the "finery of fire" in which Ned, the sentry, is dressed and which dies after his revolt signifies, among other things, both the sexual desire of the lover and the sexual charms of the beloved which are the cause of that desire, or if I say that the couplet

> Where you would not, lie you must,
> Lie you must and not with me—

is as much the expression of an aggressive vengeance on "hearts that loved me not again" as it is one of sympathetic regret, my statements are based upon a study of the poems, not upon anything I may know or imagine about Housman as a person.

As for our prurient curiosity, and I fear that most of us have wondered, like E. M. Forster, "whether Professor Housman ever tasted of those stolen waters which he recommends so ardently to others," neither Mr Watson nor any other biographer has yet been able to gratify it. Mr Watson speaks of "missing letters and other unpublished material from which quotation was forbidden" which might provide a definite answer, but on the available evidence, we are left with unprovable conjecture. (The most plausible, to my mind, is that he did not.)

I have always thought that Housman would make an admirable model for a novelist to use for a fictional character, because the essential structure of his personality was so unusually clear. He was one of those rare people whose skeleton, so to speak, was always showing, and this is just what a novelist finds stimulating, a solid ground upon which he can build the body of his imaginary details.

One of the salient differences between the "neurotic" and the "normal" man—and normal means little more than someone who has learned to live on good terms with his neuroses—is that the latter can hide his thoughts and feelings from others if he wants to, while the former cannot. The inner life of the neurotic is always projecting itself into external symptoms which are symbolic but decipherable confessions. The savagery of Housman's scholarly polemics, which included the composition of annihilating rebukes before he had found the occasion and victim to deserve them, his obsession with punctuation beyond the call of duty, are as revealing as if he had written pornographic verse.

But the very traits which make him a good subject for a novelist, who is concerned with creating a possible being, make him a bad subject for a biographer, who is concerned with an actual one. I am not surprised, therefore, that Mr Watson has succumbed again and again to the temptation to employ subjunctives, "he may have," "perhaps he," "it must have been," etc., phrases which a novelist does not need to use and a biographer is forbidden to use. Thus, speaking of Housman's second, and last, creative outburst in April, 1922, he writes:

> . . . the process was a laggard rather than a spontaneous one that must have required, for its climactic phase, some aggressive external prod; and about this time, as it happened, the kind of message that would be sure to cause such an emotional disturbance may have reached Housman from Vancouver. . . . Jackson was being driven to overtax his strength at an age when the sturdiest bodies are liable to collapse; and by 1922, he had already begun to manifest the symptoms of a disorder that was to grant him no reprieve. Thus, overshadowed by the presentiment if not the knowledge of his own impending death, he would have been likely to seek consolation from the friend whose tenderness had come at last to seem not unacceptable; and receiving a signal at once so urgent yet so conclusive, Housman could reply, at a distance of ten thousand miles, with nothing more than a gift of words drawn from his almost, but not quite, exhausted supply.

This, apart from the prose style, would be a perfectly appropriate entry in the note-book of our hypothetical novelist and the result, in his novel, of such cogitations, would be a chapter containing the necessary letters and emotional reactions of his two characters, as interesting and moving as his imagination could make them. But what right has Mr Watson, as a biographer, to make such suggestions for which he can offer no documentary evidence whatsoever?

Oddly enough, when dealing with the first period of "continuous excitement" in the first half of 1895, he mentions the fact of Edward Housman's death in December, 1894, but does not hazard a guess that this is significant—which I should have thought, if a biographer is ever allowed to make guesses, was a legitimate occasion.

Another question of interest is why Housman should have chosen, for his "enduring monument," the study of poets whom he did not like. Even his fellow scholar and friend A. S. Gow seems to have been a little puzzled.

> Lucan and Manilius were certainly not chosen because they were special favourites. For he made no pretence of admiring them, wrote of the first that his vocabulary was as commonplace as his versification, and called the second a facile and frivolous poet, the brightest facet of whose genius was an eminent aptitude for doing sums in verse. Presumably he saw in these two more opportunity than in Propertius of displaying his special gifts, and more hope of approaching finality in the solution of the problems presented, but one cannot help regretting that he abandoned a great and congenial poet on whom so much time had already been lavished.

The last of his published papers on Propertius appeared in 1895. Housman's assertion in his Cambridge Inaugural that the scholar "has no more concern with the merits of the literature with which he deals than Linnaeus or Newton with the beauties of the countryside or of the starry heavens" is a suspiciously over-dramatic way of saying that the scholar's question is "What did this poet actually write here?", not "What ought he to have written?", still less "What would I have written?"

One cannot help feeling that, in addition to whatever opportunities the texts of Lucan and Manilius offered to the scholar, they had the further advantage, unlike Propertius, of arousing no painful emotional associations. On this matter, one would like a biographer to ascertain exactly when Housman made the transcription of Propertius, with apparatus, which was found among his papers after his death. This may be an impossible task, but Mr Watson shows no sign of having tried.

His biography, however, is a work of love, not a hack job, and no book so written can be quite worthless. His account of Housman's family background and childhood is full, convincing and illuminating, and he provides some information which is new, at least to me. I am grateful to him for telling me that, when the first volume of Manilius appeared, Housman hired the services of a press-cutting agency, and for a scene as appalling as anything in *The Last Laugh* or *The Blue Angel*—it makes me want to bellow—

. . . when Jackson did infrequently revisit his native land, at intervals of five years or more, their encounters were confined to those brief holidays, snatched from their normal pursuits, during which the most dignified of men incongruously revert to their antic youth. One such occasion, as Pollard remembered it, was enlivened by that rudimentary practical joke—the apple-pie bed—of which "I think the Professor of Latin was a fellow victim, though I'm not quite sure that he wasn't an aggressor."

I am also grateful to Mr Watson for making me re-read all of Housman's poems, something I had not done for many years. It has often been said that Housman is a poet of adolescence, and this is fair enough as long as this judgment is not meant to imply, as it usually is, that nobody over the age of twenty-one can or should enjoy reading him. To grow up does not mean to outgrow either childhood or adolescence but to make use of them in an adult way. But for the child in us, we should be incapable of intellectual curiosity; but for the adolescent, of serious feeling for other individuals. I can imagine a person who had "outgrown" both, though I have never met one; he would be a completely social official being with no personal identity. All that a mature man can give his child and adolescent in return for what they keep giving him are humility, humour, charity and hope. He will never teach them to despise any strong passion, however strange and limited, or to reject a poet, like Housman, who gives it utterance.

The New Statesman and Nation, 18 May 1957

Seventh Heavens

Mysticism Sacred and Profane. By R. C. Zaehner. Clarendon Press. 42s.

It is impossible in a short review to do justice to this excellent book. Dr Zaehner is a scholar with full command of those eastern languages in which so much of the world's mystical literature has been written. Without the help of linguistic scholarship the average reader is often at a loss to know the meaning of the terminology of alien philosophical and religious traditions, to know, so to speak, whether he is faced with a different fowl, a different method of carving, or both.

Dr Zaehner is also a Roman Catholic who examines his material from a defined theistic position. Even for readers who hold other views, this makes for clarity and interest; it at least ensures that all mystical experiences will not be lumped together either as equally pathological or as visions of the same God. Lastly, he writes with charity. Naturally he believes non-Catholics to be in error, but he treats the non-European religions with the interest and respect they deserve, instead of dismissing them (as, alas, too many have done) as the ridiculous errors of those who are not white folks. Thus of Ramakrishna he writes:—

His case shows that the Grace of God is withheld from no one, whatever his inherited theology, provided he is animated by charity.

Dr Zaehner recognises four main Ways to praeternatural experience. The first is the Way he calls pan-en-henic which seeks a union with Nature. The characteristics of the pan-en-henic experience are a greatly intensified awareness of the phenomenal world, a sense of communion with it so strong that the distinction between object and subject is lost, and a sense of detachment from the everyday world of selves, time, utilitarian notions and moral judgments.

This experience may be "given" without warning, as in the case of Proust:—

But at the very moment when the mouthful mixed with the crumbs of the cake touched my palate I shuddered as I took note of the strange things that were going on inside me. An exquisite pleasure had invaded me—isolated, with no idea of what its cause might be. Immediately it had made the vicissitudes of life indifferent, its disasters inoffensive, its brevity illusory. . . . I had ceased to feel mediocre, contingent or mortal.

This given experience is probably quite common in childhood and I suspect that it plays a part whenever someone, be he an artist or a scientist, feels, as we say, "inspired." The same experience can occur during the manic phase of the manic-depressive psychosis, and it can be induced by drugs like mescalin, psycho-physical exercises of the Rajayoga type, or, as in Rimbaud's case, by a deliberate *dérèglement* of the senses. Unlike the other mystical Ways, however, it does not seem to require either any particular set of beliefs or any moral ascesis, any disciplining of emotion and conduct by the will.

All the instances of this kind of vision which Dr Zaehner gives are experiences of communion by solitary individuals with non-human and predominately inanimate Nature. I should like to know more about such phenomena as Maenadism, Witches' Sabbaths, etc., in which the pan-en-henic communion is established between human beings as a group. Also, since he deals so understandingly with artists, I should like to hear him on poets like Hölderlin and Clare whose visions were schizophrenic rather than manic.

Nature mysticism is often called pantheistic, but I suspect that if the whole range of pan-en-henic experiences were reviewed, the theology they would imply, if accepted as ultimate visions of reality, would be polytheistic. If they are to be regarded, as Dr Zaehner regards them, as morally neutral though dangerous, then the test of validity might be the works of art which they engender; beauty and wisdom might be the test on the natural level which charity is on the spiritual.

The three Ways which seek experience of the supernatural differ both in their metaphysics and their aims. The Way of Samkhya is dualist, the two principles being Nature (*prakṛti*) and the single soul (*puruṣa*) and the goal is isolation (*kaivalyam*):—

> The Yogin's isolation would seem to be the detachment of his spirit, the highest point of the soul of the Christian mystics, from all purely physical and psychic, and therefore temporal, elements. . . . It is the soul contemplating itself in its essence; and in view of the fact that it has, in accomplishing the Yoga discipline, purged itself of all desire, all that can attach it to purely created things, it must necessarily be sinless, and equally it must be devoid of positive virtue, for detachment means a total indifference to all actions, whether they be good or evil.

The Way of the Upaniṣads, on the other hand, is based on a monist doctrine:—

> There is only one reality—Brahman who is identical with the individual soul. The Brahman-soul, quite pointlessly, it seems, imagines both the internal world of ideas and the external world of objective phenomena, and is deceived by his own imaginings.

And the release sought is more akin to dreamless sleep than to anything else:—

> In such a state there is no perception of external objects nor is there any discursive thought, not because one has detached oneself from them . . . but because one realises that they simply do not exist . . . since nothing exists except the One, realised as oneself, all actions, all religious ceremonies are pure illusion.

In contrast to both of these, there is the Way, found both in Islam and Christianity, which presupposes a God who created the world and with whom it is possible for a creature created in His likeness to achieve a communion in love best symbolised by the figure of marriage.

It is understandable that Dr Zaehner should have concentrated on the difference between the kinds of mystical experiences in India, Islam and Christendom, and said little about the difference in attitude taken by them towards the mystic. The chief objection to Christianity of those Western writers who prefer Vedanta or some Perennial Philosophy, is the relative unimportance which Christianity attaches to the mystical experiences of individuals compared with the emphasis it lays on the corporate life of the Church as the Mystical Body of Christ with its focus in the corporate rite of the Mass. The main purpose of even the most austere, enclosed and contemplative Christian orders is a corporate one, to worship God and to pray for the world, and the Church has always been a bit suspicious, often most unjustly, of her mystics, because she has always rejected the notion that there can be a class of Superior Persons in the Kingdom of God.

The Observer, 26 May 1957

Crying Spoils the Appearance

My Dear Dorothea: A practical system of moral education for females.
By Bernard Shaw. Vanguard. $3.

If I had the job, which God forbid, of putting people through psychological tests, one of the first things I should ask them to do would be to compose a letter of advice to a junior, the choice of sex and age being left to the victim. The "You" imagined as the recipient will always be a projected "I" of the writer, and the age at which one sees oneself as in need of advice will be the age at which in fact one felt most in need of it, the time of one's greatest bewilderment and desperation so far.

My Dear Dorothea was written in 1878. The writer, Bernard Shaw, is twenty-one and has recently arrived in London, having thrown up a steady job to embark on a literary career; the recipient is a girl of five. In Shaw's case, in addition to any psychological motives for such a choice, there is, of course, a technical literary problem that he is trying to solve. One of the most striking merits of Shaw's prose is its lucidity; if he sometimes makes a difficult question seem simpler than it is, he never confuses the profound with the obscure, and *My Dear Dorothea* shows how early he formed his ideal of a prose style. "How," one hears him saying to himself, "can I state the theory of the Social Contract in terms that a five-year-old child can understand?"

> You must know that this world in which we live is a very badly arranged one. Some people are born with a great deal more money and clothes than others; some are even born without any at all. Everybody likes money and clothes, and the consequence is, that the people who have none want to take some from the people who have plenty; and the people who have plenty are angry because they have not as much as the Queen. But if they were to steal whatever they wanted, and hurt those with whom they were angry, the world would be so full of thieves and murderers that nobody could live happily in it.
>
> As everybody wishes to be happy, they make an agreement together that each man and woman will keep whatever he or she has. They also agree that they will not strike or kill one another, and if any person breaks the agreement and robs, strikes, or murders another, all the rest shut him up in prison to prevent him from doing so any more. They do this by paying some men to watch for evil-doers and catch them: and the men who are paid are called policemen. I am sure you have seen them in the park talking to your nurse.

If I had been confronted with this anonymously, I think I should have guessed the author, but by the next page I should have had no doubt whatsoever.

Elijah the prophet, a good man who never died, but went straight up to heaven in a horse-and-car, asked God to kill him because he could not bear to live. Jesus Christ was so melancholy that he never smiled, or took any amusement, except some boating occasionally.

Shaw is generally thought of as a late starter, who did not discover his proper métier till he was thirty-five or find his public till he was fifty, but a plausible case could be made out for regarding him as someone whose powers and view of life developed exceptionally early. His attempt to write novels was a mistake, it is true, but his dramatic and musical criticism cannot be thought of as mere steps on the way to becoming a dramatist; they are achievements in their own right, as mature and brilliant as anything he wrote. As for the plays, a reader who tried to date them by internal evidence might be able to identify the later ones by an increased liberty in their construction, but I doubt if either the style or the ideas would demonstrate that *Caesar and Cleopatra*, say, was written much earlier than *Too True to Be Good*. The clarity, the moral passion masquerading as irreverent *opera buffo*, the physical fastidiousness that is almost old-maidish are there from the beginning.

Shaw addresses his Dorothea as if she were an average little girl from an average middle-class home. If this were really the case, one can only say that the world would be an even more appalling vale of tears than it is. Dorothea has no one to play with but her doll. Her experience of human nature is limited to four beings. Papa is "a perverter of truth for gold," presumably a journalist, but he is so remote a figure that Shaw does not feel it necessary to give her any advice about her relations with him. Mama is "a frivolous and selfish woman" who, "having long exhausted the novelty of having a child of her own, thinks of you only as a troublesome and inquisitive little creature, whose dresses are continually torn and dirty, and whose face is too sticky to be kissed with pleasure."

The rules for dealing with Mama are never to let oneself feel affection, never to tell her one's sorrows, and to keep out of her way as much as possible, comforting oneself with the reflection that soon one will be sent to school and thus get rid of her. In the background are Aunt Tabitha, a spinster who presents little girls with religious tracts, and a henpecked godfather, Mr Whenzentoul, who has an affectionate nature but is too timid and too stupid to bear with. A jolly household!

But there is worse to follow. To right and left of Dorothea's Real-Life Mum, Shaw places contrasted exceptions, the Daydream Mum and the Nightmare Mum. D.M. is always kind, though for a reason; N.M. beats. That is to say, the possibility, for good or evil, of parents actually loving their children is ruled out.

The kind-unkind criterion is the one we very properly apply to others with whom relations are superficial on both sides, because we feel that it takes an exceptionally nasty nature to be unkind to strangers. When the temptation to be unkind is slight, it can be resisted by applying the same hedonistic calculation that Shaw's Daydream Mum applies: "She is kind because she remembers how she liked people to be kind to her." But intimate relations, in particular those in which there is any physical warmth, cannot be measured by this scale, for we know only too well that it is precisely toward those for whom we care the most that we are most likely to behave like toads, in defiance of both our reason and our conscience.

Oddly, when speaking of fairy tales, Shaw writes,

> You will find that the men who make the pictures seldom make the princesses pretty enough or the goblins ugly enough. . . .

for is not this just the criticism one is inclined to make of Shaw's own work? One whose primary experience in childhood is of the indifference of adults must find a selfless love inconceivable and at the same time be spared a knowledge of the circle of Hell that is inhabited by Spiritual Vampires. (There is always Candida. To me she is a marvellously realized portrait of a fiend, but I suspect that Shaw rather liked her.)

To return to Dorothea, what does she possess that will enable her to cope with her utter loneliness and prevent her from becoming a helpless neurotic? Not, apparently, either pride of birth or physical beauty:

> You are but too prone to think little of that which you have, and to covet what is beyond your reach. . . . Whatever your birth may be, or whatever your face is like, remember that you cannot alter it: so it is useless to spend a moment in grieving over either the one or the other.

But intelligence, yes, in abundance:

> Even the wise people give wrong advice because they forget their own childhood, and think that children have no sense. But you, my dear Dorothea, know better than that. You often understand what the grownup people are talking about, when they fancy that you are too young to mind them. I know how clever you are, and I advise you just as I would an older person.

And she has her doll—in other words, a talent that is death to hide and that is to be loved more, even, than Daydream Mum:

> You know more about your doll than anyone else. If you are told to dress her in red, instead of going at once to do it, you must first consider whether she likes red; whether it suits her complexion; whether it is the fashion or not; and so on. Then, if you think it the proper thing for her, dress her in it at once. But if not, let her alone; and remember for the future that the person who advised you to dress her in red knows nothing about dressing dolls. . . . You often think that other dolls are prettier than your own. But, in truth, your doll is the prettiest one I ever saw.

In speaking of the vices to which human beings are liable, it is clear, from his tone of voice when he talks of Greed and, by implication, the other Sins of the Flesh, that Shaw does not expect them to bother his Dorothea very much:

Some girls think, for instance, that greedy people are selfish. This is not the case. They are only silly people trying to be selfish without knowing how. They make themselves ill, and are disliked by those who live with them; and the bad opinion of those around them makes them so unhappy, that they never enjoy themselves except when they are eating.

On the other hand, he warns her most seriously against three things: showing when she is unhappy, losing her temper, and telling the truth on inappropriate occasions:

Crying is the worst habit you can possibly form. It spoils your appearance, and only gratifies those who inflict pain upon you. . . . Tears are only useful in exciting the compassion of persons who have something which you wish them to give you. And surely you would not care to receive a gift, as a bone is flung to a troublesome dog, merely to get rid of an annoyance. . . . Those who see you weeping will either despise you or pity you. And pity is akin to contempt.

People only lose their temper when they are angry. Therefore they think that in order to keep their temper, they must not get angry. But this is absurd; for people cannot help being angry when they are offended. It is when your anger makes you forget what you are doing, that your temper is lost. Then you say or do things which you are sorry for or ashamed of afterwards; you look like a savage or a wild cat; and everybody, seeing you in such a state, believes you to be in the wrong.

You must also pretend to think that all your acquaintances' dead friends are in heaven, although you may privately feel quite certain that they are in hell. Indeed, you may lay it down as a rule for practising Hypocrisy, that unpleasant things which you may know about people should never be mentioned.

While warning Dorothea against these temptations, Shaw encourages her to regard as virtues her natural love of independence and her sense of being unlike others:

Nothing is more important to your happiness than the habit, which you must try to form, of never wishing for anything that you cannot either buy or make for yourself. Everybody in this world is expected to take care of himself, and live without asking help from his fellow creatures. . . . Therefore, never ask anything as a favor, but only those things which you are entitled to have, or which you have deserved by your conduct.

I am sure you would not like to be called commonplace. Therefore you must preserve your Individuality by never imitating others, or pretending to be what you are not.

Also remember constantly this rule; the more you think for yourself, the more marked will your Individuality be. The more you allow others to think for you, the more you will resemble others. And just think how shocking the world would be if all people were as much alike as soldiers in a box are.

When she grows up and enters the adult world, she is cautioned, she should mistrust the Authorities:

Remember that the schoolmistress is the natural enemy of all, and never on any account tell tales to her. No matter how badly any girl treats you, never complain of her unless she is much bigger than you and you cannot find any other remedy.

I do not think that Shaw would have made an exception for a Socialist headmistress.

My Dear Dorothea is only twenty-six and a half pages long, scarcely longer than some of the speeches in the plays, and, like them, should be listened to as one listens to an operatic aria. Writing on Shaw several years ago, I called him the Rossini of English Letters, and that is the impression his work still induces in me. Rossini, not his beloved Mozart. The music of the Marble Statue, which one hears at moments in Pirandello, Brecht, and even Cocteau, is beyond him, and his occasional attempts to write an adagio, to be grave and reverent, seem strained. Officially, most of his plays are about problems—social, economic, political—but in fact these problems are as much a useful theatrical convention as romantic love, the rules by which the Shavian *jeu d'esprit* is played, and ideas are to his prose what metaphors are to Shakespeare's verse. That is why his plays continue to hold the stage when the problems discussed are no longer an issue of concern. The headlong rush of the speeches, the dazzling intellectual *fioritura* intoxicate like champagne. A man's art is often a riposte to his nature, and it may well be that the most high-spirited and witty literature is created by melancholic temperaments. The peculiar interest of *My Dear Dorothea* lies in the glimpses it gives of Shaw as a sufferer. Comedy, it seems to say, is the noblest form of Stoicism.

The New Yorker, 7 September 1957

Preface to *Nulla Vogliamo dal Sogno,* by Nino D'Ambra

Since they are not written in my mother tongue, I cannot, of course, speak of Signor D'Ambra's poems with real authority. I can only say how much, personally, I have enjoyed reading them.

Of all kinds of verse, the unrhymed short lyric is, perhaps, the most difficult to write with success, but Signor D'Ambra has, to my mind, succeeded. I find the expression direct without triviality, elegant without affectation, and the emotions, whether of nostalgia, irony, stoic resignation, at once genuine, subtle and significant. I am particularly struck by his ability to write free verse in such a way that the lines do not sound like arbitrarily chopped-up prose, but charm the ear as only living rhythmical creatures can do.

Nulla Vogliamo dal Sogno, by Nino D'Ambra, 1957

Commentary on the Poetry and Tragedy of *Romeo and Juliet*

The Theme

In many of Shakespeare's plays one finds speeches which could be cut without affecting the plot or the characterization and which, printed by themselves in an anthology, read like complete poems. Almost always, however, they are important clues to what the particular play they occur in is about, to the general notions which were preoccupying Shakespeare at the time and influenced his choice of dramatic subject.

In *Romeo and Juliet* there are two such speeches. One is spoken by Friar Laurence.

> The earth that's nature's mother is her tomb;
> What is her burying grave, that is her womb.
> And from her womb children of divers kind
> We sucking on her natural bosom find;
> Many for many virtues excellent,
> None but for some, and yet all different. . . .
> For naught so vile that on the earth doth live,
> But to the earth some special good doth give;
> Nor aught so good, but strained from that fair use,
> Revolts from true birth, stumbling on abuse.
> Virtue itself turns vice being misapplied,
> And vice sometime's by action dignified.
> Within the infant rind of this weak flower
> Poison hath residence, and medicine power;
> For this being smelt with that part cheers each part;
> Being tasted, slays all senses with the heart.
> Two such opposed kings encamp them still
> In man as well as herbs—grace and rude will;

> And where the worser is predominant,
> Full soon the canker death eats up that plant.
>
> (Act II, Scene 3)

The Friar draws an analogy between the natural order and the moral order; what disease is to the physical life, sin is to the spiritual, for both are derangements of the true order. As every species of plant has its proper place and function, so has every human person: men destroy themselves and each other when each insists upon being a law unto himself, irrespective of the common good.

The tragedy of *Romeo and Juliet*, that is to say, is not simply a tragedy of two individuals, but the tragedy of a city. Everybody in the city is in one way or another involved in and responsible for what happens.

Further, it is a play about sympathetic, basically well-meaning people—the only character who could be called bad is Tybalt—who come to disaster because each insists on having his own way irrespective of the common good.

The other set speech is Mercutio's account of Queen Mab (Act I, Scene 4) in which he describes how each type of person, lover, courtier, lawyer, parson, soldier, dreams that he has what he wishes, though on waking he will find that it is not the case.

> True, I talk of dreams;
> Which are the children of an idle brain,
> Begot of nothing but vain fantasy; . . .

Mercutio is a light-hearted young man, not a philosopher like the Friar, and draws no moral, but the moral is there to be drawn. What is harmless in sleep is dangerous in waking life. Much of the evil in the world is caused by the refusal of human beings to accept themselves and the world as it is in favor of some false picture more flattering to their self-esteem. Further, this tendency to illusion is fostered by idleness; he who works soon learns that he cannot succeed unless he accepts reality. The tragedy of *Romeo and Juliet* is the tragedy of a social group which has nothing to do but feud with their neighbors, give parties, cultivate elegance of manner and speech, and indulge their emotions. The fatal weakness which affects them all, even the lovers, is a wish to show off. Instead of asking, "What ought I to do?" or even "What would I really like to do?" they ask "If I do this, what sort of a figure shall I cut in the eyes of others?"

The Language

As is his usual practice, Shakespeare makes the lower orders in *Romeo and Juliet* talk in prose, but he also gives the elegant young gentlemen, Romeo, Benvolio, and Mercutio, prose for their scenes of badinage. The effect of this is to point up the way in which the servants of the great families imitate and

are corrupted by their masters. Not only do they imitate their habit of brawl-
ing but also, so far as their inferior education permits, their habits of talking.
The dialogue between Sampson and Gregory

> SAMPSON. 'Tis all one. I will show myself a tyrant. When I have fought
>   with the men, I will be cruel with the maids—I will cut off their
>   heads.
> GREGORY. The heads of the maids?
> SAMPSON. Ay, the heads of the maids, or their maidenheads—take it in
>   what sense thou wilt.
> GREGORY. They must take it in sense that feel it.
> SAMPSON. Me they shall feel while I am able to stand, . . .

is the understairs version of the kind of word play indulged in by Romeo and
Mercutio.

> ROMEO. Why then is my pump well flowered.
> MERCUTIO. Sure wit. Follow me this jest now, till thou has worn out thy
>   pump, that when the single sole of it is worn, the jest may remain
>   after the wearing solely singular.
> ROMEO. O single-soled jest, solely singular for the singleness.

Unless Shakespeare wrote one version of the play at one time and then revised it some years later—and there is no evidence to suggest that he did—
the variety of styles in the verse is surprising. There is a lot of rhymed verse
which on one occasion is very effective, when, during the Capulets' ball,
Romeo and Juliet talk to each other in sonnet form. There are passages of
end-stopped blank verse typical of his early period, e.g.

> Many a morning hath he there been seen,
> With tears augmenting the fresh morning's dew,
> Adding to clouds more clouds with his deep sighs.
> But all so soon as the all-cheering sun
> Should in the farthest east begin to draw
> The shady curtains from Aurora's bed,
> Away from light steals home my heavy son,
> And private in his chamber pens himself,
> Shuts up his windows, locks fair daylight out,
> And makes himself an artificial night.

But there are also passages which in their capacity to make the rhythm follow
every shade of variation in the sense without losing the basic metrical pattern
foreshadow his most mature verse, e.g.

> When the sun sets, the earth doth drizzle dew;
> But for the sunset of my brother's son

> It rains downright.
> How now, a conduit, girl? What, still in tears?
> Evermore showering? In one little body
> Thou counterfeits a bark, a sea, a wind.
> For still thy eyes, which I may call the sea,
> So ebb and flow with tears; the bark thy body is,
> Sailing in this salt flood; the winds, thy sighs,
> Who, raging with thy tears, and they with them,
> Without a sudden calm, will overset
> Thy tempest-tossed body. How now wife,
> Have you delivered to her our decree?

In general, the imagery is straightforwardly "poetical"—there are no obscure metaphors—and the subtleties are all in play upon words.

In so far as Shakespeare intended to present a highly polished artificial and leisured society, he succeeds admirably. The trouble is that the play is a tragedy not a comedy, and there are occasions upon which the use of such language seems out of place.

For example, when Juliet's body is discovered, it is hard to believe that her parents would keep up this kind of rhetoric.

> LADY CAPULET. Accursed, unhappy, wretched, hateful day,
>   Most miserable hour that e'er time saw
>   In lasting labour of his pilgrimage!
>   But one, poor one, one poor and loving child,
>   But one thing to rejoice and solace in,
>   And cruel Death hath catched it from my sight.
> NURSE. O woe, o woeful, woeful, woeful day,
>   Most lamentable day, most woeful day
>   That ever, ever, I did yet behold!
>   O day, o day, o day, o hateful day,
>   Never was seen so black a day as this.
>   O woeful day, o woeful day! . . .
> CAPULET. Despised, distressed, hated, martyred, killed!
>   Uncomfortable time, why cam'st thou now
>   To murder, murder, our solemnity?
>   O child, o child, my soul and not my child,
>   Dead art thou, alack my child is dead,
>   And with my child my joys are buried.

Nor can one believe that a Juliet who is capable of "Gallop apace, you fiery-footed steeds, . . ." should react to the news that Romeo has killed Tybalt in terms like these:

> O serpent heart, hid with a flow'ring face!
> Did ever dragon keep so fair a cave?
> Beautiful tyrant, fiend angelical,
> Dove-feathered raven, wolvish-ravening lamb,
> Despised substance of divinest show,
> Just opposite of what thou justly seem'st,
> A damned saint, an honourable villain!

In *Romeo and Juliet*, as in many other plays, Shakespeare keys the background of nature to the human drama. The particular aspect which he emphasizes is the alternation of night and day in a hot summer climate. For the lovers, night is the "good" half of time, when they can meet, day the "bad" half when they are separated. For the others, night is the time for feasting and peace, day the time for quarreling. The hot weather corresponds to their hot blood, but the regular impassive alternation of light and dark, the obedience of the heavenly bodies to natural law stands in contrast to the wilful and rebellious nature of the human characters.

Music

Music is only heard once in the play, as a background to the Capulets' party when Romeo and Juliet meet for the first time and all those present, except Tybalt, are in concord. The principal characters in Act IV, Scene 5, are professional musicians who have been hired to play for the Paris-Juliet wedding and arrive to discover that Juliet has, apparently, died and the wedding is off. Their attitude is one of professional disappointment: they fear they will not get paid. With a felicitous irony, Shakespeare makes the clown Peter quote from Richard Edward's poem *In Commendation of Musick*.

PETER.   *When griping grief the heart doth wound,*
                       And doleful dumps the mind oppress,
                       Then music with her silver sound—
    Why silver sound, Why music with her silver sound? What say you Simon Catling?
CATLING. Marry sir, because silver hath a sweet sound.
PETER. Pretty. What say you Hugh Rebeck?
REBECK. I say, silver sound, because musicians sound for silver.

Rather oddly, in so elegant a society, to call someone a musician seems to be an insult.

TYBALT. Mercutio, thou consortest with Romeo.
MERCUTIO. Consort? What, dost thou make us minstrels? An thou make minstrels of us, look to hear nothing but discords. Here's my fiddlestick, here's that shall make you dance. . . .
                                        (Act III, Scene 1)

The Tragedy

Our experiences as historical beings fall into one of three categories, Fate, Choice, and Chance. Under the category of Fate comes all that is already and all that is at all times. Fate can be recognized and must be accepted, for it cannot be changed and, therefore, cannot be judged as good or evil, lucky or unlucky. Under the category of Choice come all the possibilities of action in a certain situation at a certain moment, out of which a human will has the power to select one and exclude the others. Choice only exists in the here and now; once a man has made a choice, it becomes part of his fate. A choice is either correct or mistaken, good or evil. Under the category of Chance come all events which, like a choice, cannot be predicted, but like a fact of Fate, are outside the control of human volition. Whether a chance event is to be judged lucky or unlucky depends not on itself alone but on the final outcome of its interaction with Fate and Choice; what at first seems unlucky may finally turn out to be lucky, and vice versa.

Cultures vary in the relative importance they attach to Fate and Choice in determining human history—Greek Tragedy, for example, assigns a greater significance to Fate, Elizabethan Tragedy to Choice—but there can be no tragic emotion without some element of both. If a man is so situated that he is powerless to make any choice at all, he is pathetic, not tragic; if there is nothing in his situation to tempt him into making a wrong choice, yet he makes one, then he is not tragic, but a fool, a madman, or a devil.

Unlike Comedy, in which it plays the predominant role, Tragedy can dispense with Chance altogether; if Tragedy does introduce it, then the chance events must strike the audience as probable under the circumstances; an extraordinary piece of ill-luck or an exceptional run of misfortune make the hero pathetic rather than tragic.

In *Romeo and Juliet* we find all three elements. The chances and the choices are easy to identify because they are single events, but to say that one understands the fate of a character is the same thing as saying that one understands him, and in our "reading" of a character we often differ.

The Chances

The events which may be called events of Chance are four in number.

1. Capulet's servant happens to show Romeo the list of the guests for the party, which includes his present flame Rosaline, thus providing him with a motive for going to the party uninvited. This is plausible because the servant is illiterate and must ask someone, and Romeo, in appearance and manner, looks the sort of person who could help him.

2. Romeo and Juliet happen to fall in love with each other at first sight. This is plausible because they are physically, mentally, and socially well-matched. But for their feud, both Montague and Capulet would welcome such a marriage.

3. When he intervenes between Mercutio and Tybalt, Romeo happens to be standing in such a way that Tybalt is able to strike at Mercutio under his arm. In any such an intervention, this would be as likely to happen as not.

4. Friar John is detained by the authorities under suspicion of having entered a plague-infected house. Plausible, because visiting the sick is one of the professional duties of a friar and risking infection an occupational hazard.

The Choices

In order to describe the action of a character as a wrong choice, it must be possible to say what, given his character, circumstances, and knowledge, he could have done instead. One cannot say, for example, that Tybalt ever makes a wrong choice because it is impossible to imagine him capable of restraining his aggressive passion. The clear instances of a wrong choice in *Romeo and Juliet* are ten.

Character	Wrong Choice	Consequence	Right Choice
1. Prince Escalus.	Delays in banning the Montague-Capulet feud until the fourth outbreak.	Memories have grown too long and passions too high, so that the feud breaks out again despite his ban.	He should have issued his ban after the first brawl.
2. Mercutio.	Allows himself to be baited by Tybalt.	He gets killed and Romeo is tempted to take personal vengeance.	He should have listened to Benvolio and avoided a quarrel.
3. Romeo.	Takes personal vengeance on Tybalt for Mercutio's death.	He is banished.	He should have left the punishment of Tybalt to the Prince.
4. Capulet.	Insists on a speedy marriage of Juliet to Paris.	She takes the potion to avoid it.	He should have stuck to his original intention of letting Juliet make up her own mind.
5. Friar Laurence.	Gives Juliet the potion.	Believing her dead, Romeo is tempted to suicide.	He should have gone to Capulet or to the Prince and told them that Juliet was already married.

Character	Wrong Choice	Consequence	Right Choice
6. The Nurse.	Advises Juliet to forget Romeo and commit bigamy.	Juliet does not confide in her about the potion scheme.	She should have kept her mouth shut.
7. The Apothecary.	Sells poison to Romeo.	Romeo's temptation to suicide is strengthened by his possession of the means.	He should have obeyed the law and refused to sell Romeo the poison.
8. Romeo.	Kills himself.	He is damned.	Even if Juliet had really been dead, he should, at whatever cost of suffering, have remained alive and true to her memory.
9. Friar Laurence.	Leaves Juliet alone when he hears the watch coming.	Juliet's temptation to commit suicide is strengthened by being given the opportunity.	At whatever cost to himself, he should have stayed with Juliet to prevent her killing herself.
10. Juliet.	Kills herself.	She is damned.	She should have remained alive and true to Romeo's memory.

The Characters

1. *Prince Escalus.* Like the Duke in *Measure for Measure*, he is God's secular representative on earth whose function is to see that the order of Justice is observed by the City. Since men are sinners, the maintenance of Justice requires the coercion of the Law, which the Prince must administer impartially without fear or favor. Prince Escalus' error is one of partiality to the great families of Verona to whom he is related, so that he is too lenient at first with the Montagues and Capulets, and for this he is appropriately punished.

> And I for winking at your discords too
> Have lost a brace of kinsmen. . . .

2. *Benvolio. Tybalt. Mercutio.* Benvolio and Tybalt are not, strictly speaking, characters at all, but embodiments of contrasted states; that is to say, one

cannot imagine any circumstances in which either would be different from what he is. Benvolio would always speak with the voice of reason and good-nature; Tybalt would always play the truculent bully. Their dramatic function is to show what is wrong with the city of Verona. In a truly just city Benvolio would be listened to instead of being ignored, and Tybalt would be in jail instead of being socially honored.

In another kind of society, however, Mercutio's behavior would be different. Sanguine, elegant, popular, a wit, he is inclined by temperament and his youth to look on life as an amusing game. He has not committed himself to love—

> . . . this drivelling love is like a great natural that runs lolling up and down to hide his bauble in a hole.

If he ever were to fall in love, he would be like Biron or Benedict, not Romeo, and his choice of girl would be like theirs. To him, the Montague-Capulet feud is a sport like mountain-climbing or racing automobiles; he cannot imagine that anybody on either side means serious mischief, so that he sees no difference between a Benvolio who falls out with his tailor and a killer like Tybalt. Too late he discovers that the feud is not just a game and that a duel can be more than a display of dexterity and high spirits, and his dying words express his shocked surprise.

> . . . A plague a both your houses! Zounds, a dog, a rat, a mouse, a cat, to scratch a man to death! A braggart, a rogue, a villain, that fights by the book of arithmetic!

3. *The Slaying of Tybalt.* In a society which lacks a strong central authority to enforce a legal justice, the only protection against tyranny by the strongest and most ruthless is clan loyalty. Such loyalty regards a wrong done against one of its members as a wrong against all which it is a matter of honor to avenge. But Verona is no longer such a society; it has a Prince and a State. There is no possibility that Mercutio's death will go unavenged if Romeo does not take action. Tybalt was clearly the aggressor and, moreover, Mercutio is a relative of the Prince. The fact that the Prince waives his death decree and only banishes Romeo suggests the short shrift which Tybalt would have gotten at his hands.

Further, Romeo has every personal reason for wishing the feud at an end. Unfortunately Mercutio was killed while Romeo was trying to intervene, and Romeo knows that many people will say, perhaps rightly, that, if he had not intervened, Mercutio would have been the victor and Tybalt the corpse. This is too much for his self-esteem.

4. *Capulet.* Take away his money, his grand family, and he becomes Justice Shallow. Dominated by his wife and suffering from the melancholy of old age, he likes to have light, music, and youth about him. Whatever he may have been in his youth, he is not now a choleric nature—

> ... 'tis not hard, I think,
> For men so old as we to keep the peace.

and when Tybalt recognizes Romeo at his party, Capulet is pleased, not angry.

> 'A bears him like a portly gentleman;
> And to say truth, Verona brags of him
> To be a virtuous and well governed youth.

When Tybalt is killed, it is Capulet's wife, not he, who demands vengeance. The event only reminds him of his own approaching end.

> Look you, she loved her kinsman Tybalt dearly,
> And so did I. Well, we were born to die.
> 'Tis very late. . . .

His attempt to escape from this thought, from the fear that nobody needs him any more, undoes him and the daughter he loves. The father who had recently spoken thus—

> CAPULET. My child is yet a stranger to the world,
>   She hath not seen the change of fourteen years.
>   Let two more summers wither in their pride
>   Ere we may think her ripe to be a bride.
> PARIS. Younger than she are happy mothers made.
> CAPULET. And too soon marred are those so early made. . . .
>   But woo her gentle Paris, get her heart,
>   My will to her consent is but a part.
>   An she agree, within her scope of choice
>   Lies my consent and fair according voice.

suddenly orders her to marry Paris at once and, when she is not immediately enthusiastic, flies into a King Lear rage which shocks both his wife and the nurse. His behavior is the desperate attempt of an old man to assert an authority which, in his heart of hearts, he knows he no longer possesses. How revealing and pathetic are the following passages.

> LADY CAPULET. We shall be short in our provision;
>   'TIS now near night.
> CAPULET. Tush, I will stir about,
>   And all things shall be well, I warrant thee wife.
>   Go thou to Juliet, help to deck up her;
>   I'll not to bed to-night, let me alone.
>   I'll play the housewife for this once.

> (Act IV, Scene 2)

NURSE. Get you to bed, faith you'll be sick to-morrow
    For this night's watching.
CAPULET. No, not a whit; what, I have watched ere now
    All night for lesser cause, and ne'er been sick.
LADY CAPULET. Ay you have been a mouse-hunt in your time,
    But I will watch you from such watching now.

(Act IV, Scene 4)

5 & 9. *Friar Laurence.* A priest, he is the representative on earth of the spiritual order of charity, as the Prince is of the temporal order of justice. Whenever he acts in his proper role as a spiritual adviser, he shows himself charitable and wise, but when he takes it upon himself to interfere in temporal and practical matters, there is something not quite wholesome, even something Machiavellian, about him. He knows that a marriage between Romeo and Juliet cannot be kept secret for long, and that, when the families hear of it, there is likely to be a row. He could have said to Romeo: "The marriage is an excellent idea and I wish you both well, but I dare not do it." But, once he has agreed to marry them, he makes himself responsible. Then the unforeseen happens: Romeo is banished and Capulet is insisting on a speedy marriage to Paris. As a priest committed to a sacramental view of marriage, Friar Laurence knows that this cannot be allowed to take place since Juliet is already married.

Yet instead of doing his obvious duty and informing either the parents or the Prince, he thinks up the devious and highly dangerous scheme of the potion. His failure to do his duty is due partly to self-conceit—he prides himself on being able to fix things—but chiefly to plain cowardice. He dare not face the parents. And it is cowardice again which makes him desert Juliet when he hears the watch approaching the tomb, when he should have stayed to give her ghostly counsel.

6. *The Nurse.* A type who turns up often in Shakespeare, at her noblest as Paulina (*A Winter's Tale*), at her most corrupt as Mistress Overdone (*Measure for Measure*), at her most formidable as Dame Quickly (*The Merry Wives of Windsor*).

She is the sworn champion of her own sex in a world dominated by men whom she considers the inferior sex. To her Romeo and Paris are merely two young men and she does not believe that it will make any difference to Juliet's happiness in the end which she marries. Passion will pass and she will find out that all men are pretty much alike; the important thing is to survive and be one's own mistress. One cannot blame her for thinking that, after what had happened, it would be best for Juliet to forget Romeo and marry Paris, for, given her nature, she could not think otherwise. She can be blamed, however, for telling Juliet what she thinks. To speak out at such a moment shows a lack of imaginative sympathy with Juliet's feelings which is blameworthy because, having brought her up, she must know Juliet very well. Juliet's reaction is the thought "Thou and my bosom henceforth shall be twain," so that she says nothing to her about the potion. Had she known, one feels sure that, brave and resourceful woman that she is, she would have found a way of keeping watch on the tomb.

7. *The Apothecary.* A just city does not imply an absolutely egalitarian society but one in which every citizen, whatever his station, feels that he has an interest in the common good. It is a lack of justice if there are some who are so rich and powerful that they can consider themselves above the law and with no duties, and it is a lack of justice if there are some who are so poor and defenseless that they feel themselves outside the law and with no rights.

The Montagues and Capulets exemplify the former, the apothecary the latter. As they are tempted into breaking the Prince's law by pride, the apothecary is tempted by poverty.

> . . . Famine is in thy cheeks,
> Need and oppression starveth in thy eyes,
> Contempt and beggary hangs upon thy back.
> The world is not thy friend, nor the world's law,
> The world affords no law to make thee rich;
> Then be not poor, but break it, and take this. . . .
> Farewell, buy food, and get thyself in flesh.

8 & 10. *The deaths of Romeo and Juliet.* Many, perhaps the majority, who attend a performance of *Romeo and Juliet* today, regard suicide more or less as the Greeks and Romans regarded it.

> . . . the pagan was not conscious of himself before God as spirit. Hence it came about that the pagans judged self-slaughter so lightly, yea, even praised it, notwithstanding that for the spirit it is the most decisive sin, that to break out of existence in this way is a rebellion against God. The pagan lacked the spirit's definition of the self, therefore, he expressed such a judgment of *self*-slaughter—and this the same pagan did who condemned with moral severity theft, unchastity, etc. . . . From a purely pagan point of view self-slaughter is a thing indifferent, a thing every man may do if he likes because it concerns nobody else. If from a pagan point of view one were to warn against self-slaughter, it must be by a long detour, by showing that it was a breach of duty toward one's fellow man. The point in self-slaughter, that it is a crime against God, entirely escapes the pagan.
>
> (Kierkegaard. *Fear and Trembling*)

From such a point of view Romeo's death is not tragic but a Hardyesque irony—he should not have killed himself, it is true, but only because Juliet was not really dead—and Juliet's death is not tragic either but noble or pathetic.

It is impossible to feel the full tragic import of the play unless one can entertain, at least in imagination, the Christian belief held by everyone in an Elizabethan audience that suicide is a mortal sin, and that suicides go to Hell for all eternity. In real life, when a sane person commits suicide, it is always possible for a Christian to hope that, in the last split second, he or she made an act of contrition, but a character in a play is transparent; there is no more to him than the dramatist tells us. If the dramatist makes a suicide utter words of repentance before death, then he repents; if the dramatist does not, then he dies unrepentant and goes to Hell.

The tragedy of Romeo and Juliet is one that could only occur to two people who loved each other very much. Yet the fact that they kill themselves is, in the profoundest sense, a failure to love, a proof of selfishness.

That most people will never become guilty of this particular failure is to their discredit; they do not care enough about another person to be tempted. When circumstances prevent their love being gratified, they have a good cry and take up with someone else. Romeo and Juliet are tragic figures because both are absolutely committed and can truthfully say "Either you or no one," but when fate answers "no one," the love they bear each other is not perfect enough to support them and they destroy themselves.

From the beginning there are warnings of danger. In their first interview, Friar Laurence cross-examines Romeo.

> FRIAR. Thou and these woes were all for Rosaline.
>   And art thou changed? Pronounce this sentence then,
>   Women may fall, when there's no strength in men.
> ROMEO. Thou chid'st me oft for loving Rosaline.
> FRIAR. For doting, not for loving, pupil mine.
> ROMEO. And bad'st me bury love.
> FRIAR.   Not in a grave
>   To lay one in another out to have.
> ROMEO. I pray thee chide me not, her I love now
>   Both grace for grace, and love for love allow.
>   The other did not so.
> FRIAR.   O she knew well
>   Thy love did read by rote, that could not spell.

The proof Romeo offers for the genuineness of his love this time, namely, that it is returned, is proximately valid—Rosaline could not return an imaginary and literary passion—but ultimately it is no proof: The true lover hopes, of course, that his love will be returned, but he cannot make his absolute commitment conditional upon this.

Then, when he is only banished and Juliet is certainly alive, he threatens suicide and it is only with difficulty that the Friar argues him out of it.

> Thou hast amazed me. By my holy order,
> I thought thy disposition better tempered.
> Hast thou slain Tybalt? Wilt thou slay thyself,
> And slay thy lady that in thy life lives,
> By doing damned hate upon thyself? . . .
> Thou pouts upon thy fortune and thy love.
> Take heed, take heed, for such die miserable.

In the end, alas, that is what they both do. To kill oneself for love is, perhaps, the noblest act of vanity, but vanity it is, death for the sake of making *una bella figura.*

Romeo and Juliet, by William Shakespeare (The Laurel Shakespeare, Francis Fergusson, General Editor), 1958

Foreword to *A Crackling of Thorns,* by John Hollander

Every poem, be it big or small, simple or complex, is recognizably a world. What we call *the* world we infer to be a world, but no individual can perceive it as such; for each of us it is broken into fragments, some of which he knows quite well, some a little, some not at all, and even of those he knows best he can never truthfully say "I know what it is" but only "I know what it was."

In a poetic world, however, these obstacles to knowledge are eliminated: in a poem there are no strangers—every inhabitant is related to every other and the relationship is known; there are no secrets—a reader may notice something on a second reading which he missed on the first, but it was never concealed; there is no chance—the series of cause and effect is without any hiatus; and there is no time but the present—nothing can grow, die, or change.

There is among poetic worlds, however, an element of physical diversity which is lacking in the worlds, for instance, of painting and music; though the inhabitants of all poetic worlds are made of a verbal substance, this has developed into different linguistic strains which rarely permit of intermarriage. English is a more mongrel tongue than most and, for this reason, is perhaps the least prejudiced against words of another color; but even in English successful assimilation is rare and cannot be hurried.

So far as the practical and political life of the world is concerned, what happened at the Tower of Babel must, no doubt, be regarded as a curse but

for poetry I can imagine no greater blessing. Indeed, at a time when so many
of the forces making for world unity are so dangerous and disagreeable, the
defiantly parochial character of poetry may even have an extra-artistic moral
value. One can imagine a future world in which everybody on earth believes
the same dogmas, obeys the same authorities, and is nourished on the same
diet; but one cannot imagine a world in which Hungarian poetry, let us say,
would be indistinguishable from Finnish.

It is just and proper that literary criticism should concern itself primarily
with those problems and values which are common to all poetry, the nature
of image and metaphor, the boundaries between the poetic and the nonpo-
etic, etc.; but it should also keep a place for the consideration of that which
is peculiar to the poetry of a particular tongue, of those elements in a poem
which are a priori untranslatable. Thus, while metaphors are usually, at least
in theory, translatable, it is obvious that puns are not.

When Mr Hollander writes:

> The question was whether to live like trees or towers,
> Evolving from the bare hills like conifers,
> Pretending ignorance of the changes of winter,
> Or standing bare as sorrow in the snow,
> Striped red and green to show one's parentage
> In the colored rocks of the hills he's quarried from.
> Was memory to be the philogeny of towers
> Or the languages of trees? A Past, that honors
> Bright spears and perils held surely to the canter,
> Or a History, with garlands at the brow
> Of verdure and all her silent heritage?
> The branch, or the eternal stone to come?

for all the complexity of this passage, one can imagine a translation of it into
another tongue which would be intelligible so long as, in the culture which
spoke that tongue, towers, trees, and time had the same kind of significance
that they have in our English-speaking culture. But when he writes:

> Europe, Europe is over, but they lie here still,
> While the wind, increasing,
> Sands teeth, sands eyes, sands taste, sands everything.

one cannot imagine any translation which would at once give the overt meaning and recall the line from Jaques' speech. (The operative word in this case
reminds me of a line by Humbert Wolfe which I cannot resist quoting. "'Sugar,'
he said, and pointed to the sand.")

Puns are, of course, a minor matter, but the linguistic idiosyncrasy of which
they are an extreme case is exhibited in every aspect of poetry that is concerned with forms.

Many of Mr Hollander's most successful poems are songs or, at least, "words for music perhaps." The song—the lyric is not quite the same thing—is, of all kinds of poetry, the one in which the formal verbal elements play the greatest role and are, indeed, the main source of interest. In the world of the song, one might say, the important relationship between the inhabitants is not any community of concern or action so much as family kinship. The satisfaction I get from reading a poem by Campion, for example, is similar to the satisfaction I get from studying a well worked out genealogical tree. (A wet afternoon could be pleasantly spent developing this analogy. Starting with the notion that masculine rhymes represent brothers, feminine rhymes sisters, refrains identical twins, one could ask what verbal relationship would be equivalent to a second cousin once removed. From there one could go on to consider what discords correspond to marriage within the prohibited degrees, e.g. to marrying one's deceased wife's sister.)

English is a language to which the most natural measured rhythm is accentual iambic; it has many common monosyllables, the metrical value of which depends not upon their intrinsic quantity but upon their position in the line; and it has, relatively, few rhymes, in particular few noncomic feminine rhymes. The criteria, therefore, by which one judges a song writer are firstly, his ability, by the use of equivalence and substitution of feet, to avoid rhythmical monotony without falling into rhythmical anarchy; secondly, his ability to vary the line length within a stanza in a way that sounds natural to what is said; and lastly, his skill in the finding of rhymes which sound neither forced nor cliché and in the placing of them so that the stanza is made an indivisible whole.

To my ear Mr Hollander passes all these tests with ease.

> Advocate the cause of cloth,
> Though it's absurd;
> And tender a suit against the moth;
> Question him, and watch his sloth
> To speak a word.
> The furry silence that he keeps
> Can be shown to be
> Like the one that creeps
> From quiet Roseblush as she sleeps
> As silent as the moth, but not with me;
> Softly in a bush, but not with me.

The use of masculine rhymes throughout preserves the iambic ground, but the omission of the first syllable in lines one, four, and eleven suggests a trochaic counterpoint; in lines seven and eight there is a felicitous hint of the anapaest, which is, however, kept within bounds since it is possible to scan these lines either as three feet or as two. The lines vary in length from five

feet to two, and it will be noticed how Mr Hollander keeps his stanza together by his placing of the rhymes in relation to this variation; sometimes
rhyme and line length coincide, sometimes they run in contrast.

He is particularly skillful in his handling of feminine rhymes. The following two examples show what a difference the placing of such rhymes can
make to the whole movement of a stanza.

> Save one who, with a pair
> Of emeralds at her ear,
>   Felt for her shining toys
>   And nestled to their nearness,
>   Making a tiny noise,
>   Idolatrous and bald.
>   This was unenvying queerness.
>   The boys were quite enthralled.

> Living with men has made me
> A dialectical cat;
> Ergo, I argued that
> Her course was to upbraid me:
> She refused and she spat
> (She claimed no punishment
> But held that I'd repent).
>   All this was repaid me
> When, at the end of the quarrel,
> I had her over a barrel.

They also show how, in a song, the thought and emotion, what the words
mean, are inseparable from the form, the way in which the words move. It is
impossible to imagine the one without the other: both are two aspects of a
single imaginative act which, like all acts of the imagination, is a marriage of
the given to the calculated.

In longer, nonlyrical, discursive poems, the element of conscious calculation is likely to be greater, and greater the danger, therefore, of a form which
seems arbitrarily imposed upon the subject matter.

The test in such cases is, I believe, the opposite of what it is in a song. In a
song the reader should be immediately aware of the formal structure, but in
a discursive poem the latter should be unobtrusive so that he does not perceive it unless he deliberately looks for it.

In several poems Mr Hollander has set himself the formidable task of constructing a fourteen-line stanza.

> Feeling that it is vaguely undignified
> To win someone else's bet for him by choosing
> The quiet girl in the corner, not refusing
> But simply not preferring the other one;

Abashed by having it known that we decide
To save the icing on the chocolate bun
Until the last, that we prefer to ride
Next to the window always; more than afraid
Of knowing that They know what sends us screaming
Out of the movie; even shocked by the dreaming
Our friends do about us, we vainly hope
That certain predictions never can be made,
That the mind can never spin the Golden Rope
By which we feel bound, determined, and betrayed.

Beyond noticing that all the lines are five-foot iambic and that there are rhymes, one's attention at first reading is concentrated upon what is being said, and one will never be obliged to see the structure unless one is curious about such matters. But if one investigates one will see that, in its rhyme structure, the stanza divides into two symmetrical halves rhymed abbcaca, the b's being feminine.

To prevent the stanza simply breaking in two Mr Hollander allows no pause in sense at the end of the seventh line and generally, indeed, allows such pauses only in the middle of lines; thus the main pause comes in the middle of line eleven with subsidiary pauses in the middle of lines three, seven, eight, and ten. Further, there is no full stop until the end of the final line.

If in "The Fear of Trembling" and "The Great Bear," which are also written in fourteen-line stanzas, though differently constructed, the form seems more obtrusive than it ought to be, one of the reasons is that Mr Hollander runs the sentences on from one stanza to the next so that the choice of fourteen lines seems a bit arbitrary.

In the pleasure he takes in begetting closely knit verbal clans, Mr Hollander is a traditionalist, but he also shows a desire, characteristic of our own time, for the maximum amount of physical diversity. Like many modern poets, one of the questions he puts to himself is: "How many oddities, dwarfs, giants, albinos and the like can I credibly make my family breed? What variety of costume and haircut can I make socially tolerable?" This search for diversity is apt to breed a family of Bohemian eccentrics; that is to say, it is usually more successful when the poem is intended to be comic or seriocomic.

I should rather
Not involve her father,
Nor did some bumbling fool
    Push her into the pool
Without design;
And we are all far subtler
Than to accuse The Butler.
    Waly O how rotten
    That she was never mine.

In a serious poem there is a greater risk.

> For then, with the sun upon us, we remember
> That old prayers were extrapolations, fears
> Held in the cold were no mere casual guesses . . .

It was sporting of Mr Hollander to try to get in "extrapolations," but the result, I'm afraid, is a miscarriage.

I suppose Mr Hollander must be called a "literary" poet in the sense that the inhabitants of his poems know more about poetry, particularly poetry of the seventeenth century, than they know about, say, gardening or cooking; and one has the impression that, on returning from a walk, they could tell one more of what they had worried about than of what they had seen. But, after all, why shouldn't they? Parnassus is a free country. Besides, when the worrier does manage to look at something, he may see what the naturalist would miss.

> No wind we know can stir
> This olive blackness that surrounds us when
> It becomes the boundary of what we know
> By limiting the edge of what we see.
> When sunlight shows several spruces in a row,
> To know the green of a particular tree
>   Means disbelief in darkness; and the lack
>   Of a singular green is what we mean by black.

A Crackling of Thorns, by John Hollander, 1958

Talent, Genius, and Unhappiness

Sainte-Beuve. By Sir Harold Nicolson. Doubleday. $5.

Gogol: A Life. By David Magarshack. Grove. $6.50.

Sir Harold Nicolson's life of Sainte-Beuve and Mr David Magarshack's life of Gogol are excellent examples of the two ways in which biography, like history, can be written. One says, as it were, "There was a man called Sainte-Beuve in whom I am interested. Let me tell you about him in the hope that you will find him as interesting as I do." The other says, "If you are curious about Gogol, the documented facts about his life are these." Each approach has, of course, its dangers. The impersonal biographer is at the mercy of his subject; there are very few people in whose lives there are no dull patches, so when his hero strikes one, his biography must become dull, for he is forbidden to enliven it with amusing digressions of his own. On the other hand, provided his sentences are clear and grammatical, he can be criticized only on points of scholarship; as long as he has not overlooked a significant document or mistranslated one, he is immune. The personal-portrait painter is much more exposed. He must be continually entertaining about his hero, and both his style and his judgments are always open to criticism. Moreover, while he must never be caught out on a point of scholarship, he must not parade his learning; it is for him, not for his reader, to select from his mass of material what is essential and revealing.

Sir Harold Nicolson's forte has always been the comic and slightly malicious, whether it be asides:

If he succeed [in becoming an Academician], he may withdraw into self-satisfaction, becoming obese, unproductive and proud.

quoted remarks:

"She had a great soul," he wrote of her in his notebook, "and a perfectly enormous bottom."

or grotesque anecdotes:

His material circumstances also underwent a change. In June of that year Louise Colet, the exacting, irrational, and most pathetic mistress of Victor Cousin and Flaubert, had been libelled in the *Guêpes* by Alphonse Karr. She decided to take revenge. She called at Karr's flat; when he opened the door to her and turned to lead the way to the sitting room, she stabbed him in the back with a kitchen knife. Victor Cousin, who was at the time Minister of Education, feared a scandal would result and appealed to Sainte-Beuve to persuade Alphonse Karr to take the assault quietly. Sainte-Beuve's mission was successful and Karr contented himself by having the knife enclosed in a glass case with the inscription "Received from Louise Colet—in the back." As a reward for this service, as Karr maliciously contended, Victor Cousin appointed Sainte-Beuve Assistant Librarian at the Mazarine Library with a flat in the Institute Building and a salary of 4,000 francs a year.

In the end her [Jenny Delval's] infidelity became intolerable and he turned her out of his house. . . . She was succeeded for a while by Céline Debauve, known as "La Manchotte," since she had lost one of her hands. She was so rude to his visitors that she was kept downstairs. In the end, she also was sent back to the streets.

Sir Harold is less at his ease when he attempts the "beautiful" or the serious. I agree with him that *Port-Royal* is a wonderful book, but his concluding sentence on this work would never make me think so:

When they read Sainte-Beuve's *Port-Royal*, they will enter upon a new world, become intimate with strange dissimilar minds and characters, discover that the irrational may be rendered a fascinating rather than an irritating mystery, linger in cool white corridors, or observe how in the grey hour before the dawn the sound of bells tolling will hush the chatter of the frogs.

His writing "I" is the tolerant, slightly cynical man of the world whom nothing shocks; when, therefore, he is morally shocked, as he is by Sainte-Beuve's sexual habits, he has no language of his own; a phrase like "his dark indulgence" is pure journalese.

In describing Sainte-Beuve's relation to the political life of his time, Sir Harold has the advantage of having, unlike most English men of letters, enjoyed a wide experience of public and political life. As one of them, he knows that

> It has always been a characteristic of intellectuals that, while they dislike authority, they like order. What they enjoy is being able to exercise their wits and discharge their grievances from a firm basis of established liberty. . . . If he [Sainte-Beuve] possessed any political convictions it was the conviction that under any system the intellectual must have the right, and be accorded the opportunity, to proclaim that the authorities are invariably evil, stupid, and wrong.

As a man who has held authority, Nicolson knows how emotional, uninformed, and oversimplified the criticism of intellectuals is apt to be. In consequence, he can show an understanding compassion for Sainte-Beuve's support of Napoleon III, not because he thinks Sainte-Beuve was right in his advocacy of the Second Empire and Victor Cousin wrong in opposing it, but because he knows that the political opinions and behavior of intellectuals are seldom to be taken seriously.

Neither by temperament nor by upbringing is Nicolson well equipped to understand theological and ecclesiastical matters. He admits that the doctrine of Grace bores him, and his chapter on Sainte-Beuve's *Port-Royal* and the contest between the Jansenists and the Jesuits over the monastery from which the book takes its name reads like an essay written by an intelligent undergraduate for his tutor. He has dutifully read up on his material, but it has not become alive for him. Thus Pascal, who in his *Lettres Provinciales* bitterly assailed the Jesuits, would be surprised, surely, to hear that, according to Nicolson, he "had broken the harsh tyranny of scholasticism" and demonstrated "that ethics fundamentally derive, not from doctrinal prohibitions, but from the natural promptings of the mind and heart." The remark of the religious historian Abbé Bremond, quoted by Sir Harold, that the story of *Port-Royal* is "the story of a conversion that failed" seems to me just; that is to say, Sainte-Beuve, who was on the side of the Jansenists, may well have begun

his studies of Jansenism with the hope that he would find a faith in the process, but Sir Harold's contention that Sainte-Beuve did not finally lose his
faith until 1848, some years before the completion of *Port-Royal*, seems to me
highly doubtful; I can find no evidence in anything we are told about him to
suggest that he ever had any. To see the losing struggle of the Jansenists
against the Jesuits, as both Sainte-Beuve and his biographer see it, in terms
only of human character and political interests makes the story of *Port-Royal*
merely pathetic—the defeat of the unworldly by the worldly. If they are to be
considered solely as human beings, there can be no comparison between the
saintly Dr Hamon, who spent the last thirty-seven years of his life in the monastery, and the horrible Père Tellier, the Jesuit who, as a confessor of Louis
XIV, helped persuade him to order the destruction of Port-Royal—a situation so unforgettably described by the Duc de Saint-Simon in his memoirs.
But the tragedy of Port-Royal is that, despite the personal characters, the motives, and the methods of the Jesuits, their victory was in the long run a victory for Christian charity and humility. It was the Jansenists, not their opponents, who believed that salvation outside the Church was impossible, and
the consequences of Pascal's views on sin have been admirably summed up
in *The Descent of the Dove*, by Mr Charles Williams:

> He gibed at the Fathers of the Society [the Jesuits] for having said that
> a servant did not sin if he made his wages up to the market value of his
> services by stealing from his master. It is indeed a scandalous doctrine;
> it seems to permit theft. Only by chance does it occur to one that Pascal
> is coming near to damning, on his own showing, any underpaid servant
> girl who pockets a penny her mistress has left about. Perhaps he did not
> intend it. but here at least one can follow him to a single rule: if the
> servant girl is excusable, then the Jesuits were technically right; if Pascal
> is right, then she is (except by repentance) damned. The Apostolic
> Church, by and large, and despite the saints, has always known better.

In writing his book, Sir Harold has been prompted by two aims—to paint
the portrait of a complicated, talented, unhappy, and not very pleasant man,
and to defend a certain kind of literary criticism that in recent years has
fallen into disrepute. It is not Sainte-Beuve's literary reputation alone that he
wishes to save; it is also the reputations of such English critics as Edmund
Gosse and George Saintsbury.

> If we allow ourselves to despise Sainte-Beuve as a person, we shall end by
> despising him as a writer. This would be an unrewarding approach.

If this were true, then his attempt to vindicate the writer would fail, for
nothing he tells about the man can convince either us or himself that he
deserves more than pity.

To begin with, he was exceptionally physically repulsive:

His school-fellows at the Institut Blériot at Boulogne had called him "*le matou*" signifying thereby a ginger cat of rather unpleasant character. The malformation of his urethra . . . rendered his appearance epicene and his manner propitiatory. His skull was pear shaped, prematurely bald, and so shiny in his middle age that Nicolardot likened it to a third knee. It was too large for his body and sunk into his shoulders. He was only five feet two inches in height and became corpulent very soon. His nose was far too long for his face; his lower lip protruded; his ears were enormous. He was incapable of looking a person in the face, and when walking in the street would keep his eyes fixed on the gutter in fear lest he might encounter an enemy. He would seldom gesticulate, but rub his little hands together continuously.

In a fairy tale, such an unprepossessing exterior might have hidden a beautiful soul, kind to all and cherishing a lifelong and never disclosed devotion to a beautiful princess. In real life, there was no such paradox. Sainte-Beuve was as lecherous as a monkey and, as a friend, envious and disloyal. One would like to hear what a woman would have to say about his affair with Mme Hugo, for to any man it is incomprehensible. Dissatisfied wives have often been unfaithful with friends of their husbands, but when the husband is Victor Hugo, who, whatever his faults, was a magnificent male animal and a genius, and the friend is Sainte-Beuve, the masculine imagination boggles. Yet the liaison lasted for a full five years and Mme Hugo seems to have been genuinely in love with him. This did not prevent his printing and distributing copies of compromising poems about her or writing in his notebook, "I loathe her! No longer has she any heart and she never had any brains." One is not surprised to learn that when he was asked if he had ever truly loved a woman, his reply was "That is a box which I never open." As for men, though he was never without friends, he rarely managed to keep one for long. In all fairness, one must add that the situation of a critic and reviewer is not easy. Many of those he knows best are writers, and whether they consciously cultivate his friendship for that purpose or are truly fond of him, all of them expect him to give favorable notices of their books. Sainte-Beuve was not the first or the last critic to say one thing about an author in a signed review and another, his true opinion, in an anonymous article or in private; it is not very brave, but it is very understandable. Also, many critics are, like Sainte-Beuve, men who started out with the ambition to become novelists or poets themselves, and took to criticism only because they found that their hope was denied them. To conquer envy of their more fortunate contemporaries, to master the desire to find their faults rather than their virtues, calls for a humility and a strength of character that are too uncommon to justify those who are not so tempted in throwing stones.

Besides, every writer has faults, and it is one of the critic's duties to expose them. It is easy today to forget that Sainte-Beuve's adverse opinion of Chateaubriand or the plays of Hugo was once a minority verdict, and if we can all sneer at him for having failed to recognize the greatness of Stendhal, our admiration of that author should not blind us to the defect in *La Chartreuse de Parme* that Sainte-Beuve was clearsighted enough to see—the dullness of its juvenile hero, Fabrice.

In any case, Sainte-Beuve never pretended to be an expert on contemporary literature; his real interests, as evidenced by his collection of essays called *Les Lundis*, were the past and the historical circumstances, the social milieu and personalities, attendant on literature rather than the texts themselves. Sir Harold gives an amusing list of subjects (more amusing, it is true, to British readers than to Americans) about which he might have written had he been English instead of French:

> Beattie's Minstrel, the Blickling Homilies, Mrs Vesey, Tottel's Miscellany, the Army Manual on Sanitation, Jack of Newbury, Green's coney-catching, Wycliffe and scholasticism, Adelaide Anne Procter, Drummond of Hawthornden, Lady Melbourne, Rifleman Harris, the Paston Letters, the Warwickshire coterie, Caroline Norton, Barclay's Eclogues, Jacob Tonson and the Two Angry Women of Abington.

From such a transliteration, everyone can decide whether *Les Lundis* is likely to appeal to him. Personally, I must say no; I lack that particular kind of curiosity. I can admire Sainte-Beuve's industry and scrupulous accuracy:

> He would begin by "cutting out" the material and during the days that followed he would fit, and sew and shape . . . he would constantly send his secretary off to the Bibliothèque Nationale, or the Mazarine or the Sorbonne, to verify dates, references and quotations, or to borrow books. . . . If he were discussing the work of some still living author he would not hesitate to approach him directly, demanding details of his life and character, or asking him to elucidate obscure passages in his works. This preparatory labor would occupy his whole time from Tuesday to Friday. When once the blocking out had been completed, he would dictate the article to his secretary and get him to read it aloud. He would contend that the ear was a more sensitive organ than the eye; it was only when he could listen to his articles as read aloud that he could detect repetitions, assonances or obscurity of language. On Saturday mornings his secretary would go round early to the printer and return with the proof. The whole of Saturday and often of Sunday also would be devoted to correcting, verifying and adding to the proof. . . . By late Sunday afternoon the final version would be delivered. This was Sainte-Beuve's moment of relaxation. He would have an excellent dinner at Pinson's restaurant and thereafter go to the theatre or circus,

which he much enjoyed, and walk up and down the boulevards inquisitive and often gay. Then on Tuesday the whole dreary round would
begin all over again.

The final impression, however, that he makes on me is the one (in *Twilight
of the Gods*) he made on Nietzsche:

> As a psychologist a genius for *médisance*, inexhaustibly rich in expedients
> for the purpose; nobody understands better how to mix poison with
> praise. . . . Ill at ease in the presence of everything possessing strength
> (public opinion, the Academy, the Court, and even Port-Royal). Embit-
> tered against all greatness in men and things, against all that believes in
> itself. Poet enough and half-woman enough to be sensible of greatness
> as a power; continually turning like the celebrated worm, because he
> continually feels himself trodden upon. As a critic, without a standard,
> without firmness, and without backbone, with the tongue of the cosmo-
> politan *libertin* in favor of variety, but even without sufficient courage to
> confess the *libertinage*. As a historian, without a philosophy, without the
> power of philosophic vision—on that account declining the task of pass-
> ing judgment in all great questions, holding up "objectivity" as a mask.
> He behaves otherwise, however, with regard to all matters where a deli-
> cate worn-out taste is the highest tribunal; there he really has the cour-
> age of himself, pleasure in himself—there he is a master.

Gogol's verdict would probably have been even more severe, for though
he was not officially a Slavophile, he shared the Slavs' dislike and fear of all
the liberal and rationalistic ideas they associated with the French Enlightenment and Revolution. Nor would he have approved of Sainte-Beuve's personal life, for Gogol seems to have been as nearly sexless as it is possible for
a man to be. His physical appearance may not have repelled others like
Sainte-Beuve's, but it did not charm them. The critic Sergey Aksakov, who
knew him intimately, said:

> I don't know a single person who loved Gogol as a friend irrespective of
> his talent. People laughed at me when I used to say that Gogol did not
> exist for me as a personality, that I looked with veneration and love
> upon this precious vessel in which the great gift of creative art was en-
> closed, though I disliked the form of this vessel. . . . To such an extent
> was Gogol not a man to me, that I, who in my youth was terribly afraid
> of corpses, could not arouse in myself this feeling of natural dread in
> the presence of his dead body.

"Every time," writes Mr Magarshack, "Gogol depicts a beautiful and sexually desirable young woman, he either makes her into an insipid 'chocolate-

box beauty,' as in his *Evenings on a Farm Near Dikanka*, or endows her with demonic powers which lead to the utter ruin of her lover, as, for example, in *Viy*, *Nevsky Avenue*, *Taras Bulba*, or even in *Dead Souls*." The sudden and violent crush on his childhood friend Danilevsky that he developed in 1838 suggests a homosexual tendency, but it cannot have become conscious; if it had, the following "Freudian" incident could not have occurred:

> His desire to possess some part of Danilevsky made him wish to have at least his stick. "You made me a present of it," he wrote three weeks later on the 7th of March 1839, "and I don't know why I didn't take it with me." On April the 2nd he got it. "I went into my room," he wrote to Danilevsky on that date, "and saw your stick lying on the table. That was a wonderful surprise. It seemed to me as though I saw a part of you."

Gogol is one of those authors who have become the subject of a legend— Gogol was a satirical genius, the first Russian writer to expose the rottenness of the social structure of his country, until he had the tragic misfortune to encounter a fanatic priest, Father Matthew, who sent him mad, so that he suddenly renounced everything he had stood for, became violently reactionary, and ended by burning the second part of his masterpiece, *Dead Souls*. Legends are seldom baseless, but they are equally seldom quite right, and one of the great merits of Mr Magarshack's biography is that it corrects this legend with facts. Thus, while it is a fact that the bulk of his writing up till 1842 is, in effect, satirical and critical of Russia, Gogol was never a revolutionary who wished to change the regime under which he lived. The truth is that most writers, whatever they may say, are at heart conservative, for the material out of which they create their art, even when it is satire, is life as it actually is. Moreover, the kind of life they understand best is the kind of life they experienced during their formative years; that is to say, their first twenty years. If they do show revolutionary enthusiasms, the motive behind them is usually the romantic and poetic pleasure of seeing things go pop, or a hope that a change of regime will give them an importance and an audience that are at present denied them.

Under any autocratic regime in which all overtly political opposition is impossible, novelists and poets are in an unfortunate position, for everything they write assumes a political importance that they are far from desiring. In a democratic society, *Selected Passages* could never have caused such an uproar. People would have said, "Poor old Gogol! He is a genius but in political matters a baby," and gone back to reading *The Government Inspector* or *Dead Souls*. But in Russia such a lighthearted dismissal was impossible; the sense of outrage expressed in the famous letter from the critic Belinsky to Gogol is an indication of the kind of political inspiration Gogol's earlier work had given him.

On the question of religious mania, it is clear that Gogol, who had always been a manic-depressive, began to suffer from it long before he met those two fanatics, Father Matthew and Count Alexander Tolstoy, for as early as 1841 he is writing such sentences as this:

> You must do as I tell you, for henceforth my words are invested with divine power, and woe to him who does not listen to them.

As for the burning of the second part of *Dead Souls*, this may well have been both a sadder and less tragic event than legend makes it. In the first place, it was not the first time Gogol had burned manuscripts. In 1829, he bought up all the copies he could find of his poem *Hans Kuechelgarten* and burned them; in 1841, he threw the manuscript of his historical play "The Shaven Mustache" into the fire because a friend didn't like it. In the second place, such evidence as exists suggests that the real reason Gogol succumbed to Father Matthew's bullying and destroyed the *Dead Souls* manuscript was that his artistic conscience told him that his continuation of the novel was not very good.

It is always suspicious when an author keeps writing to his friends about how wonderful his book is going to be, while at the same time little of it gets written, and the chapters from an early draft that were found after Gogol's death do not allay this suspicion. Of them, Mr Magarshack has this to say:

> Like his *Selected Passages*, they are devoid of humor. Secondly, their positive characters, such as the idealized landowner Kostanjoglo and the idealized tax-farmer Murazov, are not living men at all, but merely pegs on which Gogol hangs the naïve ideas on the complex problems of his time he had already expressed in his *Selected Passages*. Chichikov appears in them as a pale reflection of what he was in the first part of the novel, and the Governor-General, who forgives Chichikov as well as his corrupt officials because injustice cannot be rooted out by punishment and the only way of restoring justice in Russia is to appeal to the inbred sense of honor in every Russian heart, is so fantastic a character that he could only have been created by a man who had lost all sense of reality. Even the gormandizer Petukh, the only solid character in the second part, lacks that vitalizing humor of Gogol's which would have brought him to life.

Even Gogol's own comment after he had done the deed is enigmatic:

> Some of it ought to have been burnt. As for the rest, they [Tolstoy and Father Matthew] ought to have prayed for me. But when I recover from my illness I'll put it right again.

He did not recover, nor does it seem that he wished to. The doctors could diagnose nothing specific, but nine days later he died screaming.

If it is silly to imagine the might-have-beens in the life of an individual or a nation, it is a silliness none can resist. It would seem that Gogol was one of those writers—there have been many others—whose creative period began and ended early. *Shponka*, written when he was only twenty-two, is a completely mature and typical work, and there is little one wishes to read after *The Overcoat*, completed when he was thirty-three. Given his temperament, one cannot help feeling that the best solution for him, when his well dried up, would have been the cloister. He would have been happier, that is, if, instead of trying to write a more "moral" kind of work and tell the secular world what it should do, he had simply renounced that world and literature for the contemplative life. This would have involved, of course, renouncing the desire to cut a figure in the world, and for a man who had always thought that great poets should be summoned "to important councils of State as experts on the human heart," such humility would have been difficult. There was more truth than there should have been in Belinsky's accusation:

> The humility you preach is, in the first place, not new, and secondly, smacks of terrible pride. . . . Your book does not convey true Christian teaching, but a morbid fear of death, hell, and the devil.

Also, Father Matthew is scarcely the spiritual adviser one would have chosen for him. Had there been a Russian equivalent of Port-Royal, his end might have been happier.

Some of the most interesting passages in Mr Magarshack's book, as in Sir Harold Nicolson's, are concerned with habits of work. Unlike Sainte-Beuve, Gogol oscillated between periods of intense activity and periods when he was unable to write a word. The early part of the summer of 1838, for example, was a bad period, and we find him writing to Danilevsky in Paris to buy him a wig, in the hope that "it would help to open up the pores of my scalp and thus release my inspiration which is getting clogged." But in July, while he was journeying in Italy from Genzano to Albano, release came:

> Halfway between those towns is a miserable inn standing on a little hill, with a billiard table in its main saloon, where people are constantly talking in different languages and the billiard balls never cease clicking. I stopped there. I was writing the first volume of *Dead Souls* at the time and never parted from my manuscript. I don't know why, but I felt like writing as soon as I entered the inn. I ordered a small table to be brought and sat down in a corner of the saloon. I took out my manuscript and, in spite of the noise made by the rolling balls, the indescribable din, the rushing about of the pot boys, the smoke, the close atmosphere, I became completely lost to the world and wrote a whole chapter without stirring from my seat. I consider that chapter one of the most inspired in the whole novel.

Like many artists, Gogol had his private magical rites for invoking the Muse:

"He waved his arms about," his friend, who watched him through the keyhole of his room, records, "planted his fists on his hips, went through all sorts of contortions and clutched at his hair, ruffling it wildly and pulling most extraordinary faces."

Rather surprisingly for one who wrote in bursts, he was as great a perfectionist in matters of style as Flaubert. One finds him saying:

At first you ought to jot down in a notebook everything as it occurs to you, however bad and watery it may be, but absolutely everything, and then forget all about it. After a month or two or even longer (you'll know when yourself), take your notebook out and read it over again: you will see that a great deal in it isn't as it should be, that a great deal of it is superfluous and that something is missing. Make your corrections and observations in the margin and put it away again. When you come to read it again, make new notes in the margin, and if there's no room left there, take a piece of paper and paste it in at the side. When the page is all covered, copy it out in your own hand. While doing this, new ideas, cuts, additions and emendations of style will occur to you by themselves. Among the words you have already written new words will suddenly appear, words which simply have to be there, but which for some reason did not come to you at once. Then, again, put it away. Go on a journey, enjoy yourself, do nothing or write something else. When the right time comes, you will remember your notebook: take it out, read it over again, correct it in the same way, and when it is all filled again, copy it out in your own hand. You will notice as you do so that, together with the improvement in your style and the greater polish of your sentences, your hand seems to have become stronger; you write the letters more firmly and more resolutely. This, in my opinion, must be done at least eight times. Someone may find that he could do it in fewer times, and someone else in more times. I do it eight times. Only after being copied out for the eighth time, and always in my own hand, is my work completely and artistically finished. Any further corrections and revisions are quite likely to spoil it.

The life paths of Sainte-Beuve and Gogol crossed once, in June of 1839, on a boat between Civitavecchia and Marseille. Although he was the elder, Sainte-Beuve's successes—*Port-Royal, Les Lundis*, the Academy, the Senate— were all to come, while Gogol's life as a writer was already nearly over. Gogol recommended to Sainte-Beuve the poet Belli, whose sonnets in Roman dialect have only recently been published. The meeting was without significance to either.

The New Yorker, 30 November 1957

The Great Divide

The Disinherited Mind. By Erich Heller. Dufour & Saifer. $3.75.

Of the seven German writers whom Mr Heller discusses, only two, Rilke and Kafka, are, I believe, really well known to English and American readers. Goethe and Nietzsche are, of course, extremely famous names, but how much of their work is read by those who are not specialists in German litera- ture? Most people of my generation read Spengler's *Decline of the West* in the Twenties but he seems now to be completely forgotten. Burckhardt is known to historians but to few others and, as for Karl Kraus, I have never met any- body who had not spent some time in Germany who has even heard his name. (I myself have only read *Die letzten Tage der Menschheit* and a few numbers of *Die Fackel,* but this is enough to convince me that he was one of the most important writers of this century.)

Some readers of *The Disinherited Mind* may be well advised, therefore, to read the chapters on Rilke and Kafka first, where they can check Mr Heller's observations against their own knowledge. The excellence of these two es- says—the one on Kafka seems to me the best thing written about that most enigmatic of writers—will convince them that the judgments Mr Heller passes on, say *Iphigenie,* have authority.

His principal concern is the relation between thought and feeling and the catastrophic effect of their increasing estrangement from each other during the last century and a half, as "thinking" and, consequently, "truth" have more and more become identified with the scientific concern for the pro- cesses and relations of the phenomenal world so that only answers to the question "How do things happen?" are to be taken seriously. Any answers to the ontological question "What are things and what do they mean?" and, indeed, the question itself are dismissed as emotive noises.

To such questions the modern intelligence is prone to respond with that mixture of shame, embarrassment, revulsion and arrogance which is the characteristic reaction of impotence to unfortunately unmanage- able demands. This invalid has been left in the nursing care of unhappy poets, dreamers or religious eccentrics if he was not satisfied with the treatment he received as an outpatient of the Church.

It is Mr Heller's contention that, as we believe, so we shall make a world that conforms to our belief. A society that refuses to ask what things mean presently becomes meaningless.

The totems and taboos of savages, the pyramids of Egypt, the acropolis of Athens, the Cathedral of Chartres *pragmatically* prove as much, or as little, of the ultimate nature of reality as any modern scientific experiment. It is indeed amazing how malleable the world is and how easily it models and remodels itself according to the inner vision of man, how readily it responds to his "theorizing". Thus the most important advice which an educator can give to his pupils, may easily be: Be careful how you interpret the world; it *is* like that.

So long as man's thinking and feeling are integrated his search for knowledge is conditioned by the question "What ought I, what am I meant to know?" He is aware, like Goethe, that knowledge can only be true as long as it is not in excess of his feelings or, as Nietzsche put it, that "man ought not to know more of a thing than he can creatively live up to." In the present epoch man has almost lost all sense of this categorical imperative and he asks instead "What would I like to know?" and truth becomes for him either that which it is amusing to know or that which increases his power to do as he likes. The Gossip Column and the Hydrogen Bomb are two sides of one coin.

In such a society, artists of any sort must find themselves not critical but totally at odds, for all art presupposes both the existence of the numinous (be it good or evil) and its manifestation in the world of concrete particulars or, as Goethe would put it, that what is is only real in so far as it is symbolic, and it is precisely this presupposition which modern society as a society denies.

The artist is left, therefore, at the mercy of his own subjectivity. What the modern mind perceives as order is established through the tidy relationship between things themselves. In one word: the only conceivable order is positivist-scientific . . . in the sphere of art the symbolic substance, dismissed from its disciplined commitments to "reality" dissolves into incoherence, ready to attach itself to any fragment of experience, invading it with irresistible power, so that a pair of boots, or a chair in the painter's attic, or a single tree on a slope which the poet passes, or an obscure inscription in a Venetian church, may suddenly become the precariously unstable center of an otherwise unfocussed universe.

Goethe spent his life trying to keep together "the life of poetry and the poetry of life." His scientific works are of immense importance, not because of any discoveries he made, but because they suggest that there may be ways of investigating Nature which are just as scientific as the positivist procedure of putting her on the rack. Yet the best that Goethe could do was live a double life; the lyric genius-magician, beloved of the Earth Spirit and The Mothers, and the Geheimrat doing his social duty in the Prosaic City could never really become friends. To those who came after him, even the double life ceased to be possible. As can be seen from such examples as Nietzsche, Wagner and Rilke, the greater the talent of an artist or thinker in this epoch, the more he is tempted to think of himself as God, that is to say, not as one who manifests to others a pre-existing reality, but as one who creates it himself out of nothing. The world outside the artist is nothing until he transforms it by magic. The awkward question arises: "For whom, then, does he transform the world?" If the question sent Nietzsche clinically insane while Wagner succeeded in making kings bow down and worship him, it was because Nietzsche felt a Christian love for his neighbor and Wagner felt none. It may well be that Wagner was the crazier. And Rilke, too. "The earth," he wrote, "has no refuge but to become invisible in us—only in us can the intimate and enduring transformation of the visible into the invisible be accomplished."

This belief may be true or false, but, if it is true, then the writing of poetry is either impossible or undesirable, for poetry, like any art is a form of manifestation and communication between real persons in the real world.

Despite passages which I find magnificent precisely because they make visible something hitherto unseen, the general impression which the later poems of Rilke make on me is of a lot of humourless and unmanly fuss about *les splendeurs et misères* of being St Rilke.

"God is dead!" cried Nietzsche, and there is a sense in which a Christian like Mr Heller can agree with him. Up until the middle of the nineteenth century, it was possible and, despite the theologians, probably inevitable that most people should imagine God as The Top Being to whom the predicates omnipotent, omniscient, omnipresent, apply literally, because there were still vast areas of human experience in which man's will was powerless, and it was still possible to speak of plague or lightning as "an act of God." Nietzsche saw prophetically what has already come to pass, that man's control over nature would reach a point at which an unbeliever can say—"God does not exist because he is impotent and an impotent God is a contradiction"—and a Christian is forced to realize that there are no limits to God's love, that is to say, there is no point at which God will ever say to man—"No, your rebellion has gone far enough; beyond this point I shall compel you to obey me. Even if you choose to make your world the world of Kafka's novels, I shall let you."

It is, as Mr Heller says, very odd that sensitive and intelligent critics should have described *The Castle* as a sort of modern *Pilgrim's Progress* when it is "as much a religious allegory as a photographic likeness of the Devil could be said to be an allegory of Evil, or that they should have interpreted the castle itself as the residence of divine law and divine grace when its officers are totally indifferent to good if they are not positively wicked. Neither in their decrees nor in their activities is there discernible any trace of love, mercy, charity or majesty. In their icy detachment they inspire certainly no awe, but fear and revulsion. . . . The castle of Kafka's novel is, as it were, the heavily fortified garrison of a company of Gnostic demons, successfully holding an advanced position against the maneuvers of an impatient soul."

One of the proofs of Kafka's genius is that the more one admires him, the more one is inclined to think that his request that his works be destroyed should have been honored. On the one hand every sentence convinces one that the author is a person of extraordinary nobility and integrity; on the other one finds oneself asking the same question one asks about the work of some really wicked talent like the Marquis de Sade: "Have I sufficient spiritual strength and health to read this without doing serious damage to my soul?" The world he presents is so appallingly like our experiences that we are tempted to believe that this is what is ultimately real and become, like Spengler, worshippers of the Prince of this world, for few of us have Kafka's strength.

> No comfort can be found *within* this world. Yet the power, not only to experience, but poetically to create this world, must have its source *outside*. Only a mind keeping alive in at least one of its recesses the memory of a place where the soul is truly at home, is able to contemplate with such creative vigor the struggles of a soul lost in a hostile land; and only an immensity of goodness can be so helplessly overcome by the vision of the worst of all possible worlds.

The Griffin, October 1957

"A Mental Prince"

There is Blake the designer and engraver; of him I have no authority to speak. There is Blake the author, the best English aphorist whether in verse or in prose, a great lyric poet, who also produced, at what he believed to be Divine Dictation, a number of long "unfettered" works which are, alas, totally unreadable; I could say something about him, though there are others who could say more. But on the bicentenary of his birth, this month, it seems most fitting to remember Blake the prophet, as he himself defined one:—

> Every honest man is a Prophet; he utters his opinion both of private & public matters. Thus: If you go on So, the result is So. He never says, such a thing shall happen let you do what you will. A Prophet is a Seer, not an Arbitrary Dictator.

There are many people, even among readers of *The Observer*, who do not care particularly for pictures or poems, but there is no one who does not care about his (or her) happiness nor wish for help when he lacks it.

When Privates Schofield and Cock, being too drunk and ignorant to know the difference between a miniature painter and a military painter, suggested that Blake's house be searched, it is just as well, perhaps, that the authorities never acted on the suggestion, for, though the infamous pair perjured themselves when they swore that Blake had said "God damn the King," they were nearer the truth than they suspected. A search would not have discovered plans of fortifications, but it would have come upon drawings and writings in plenty which, from an official point of view, deserved either Bedlam or the Old Bailey for their author. For the magistrate there were such remarks as:—

> King James was Bacon's primum mobile. A tyrant is the worst disease, and the cause of all others. Everybody hates a king!

for the bishop:—

> This angel who is now become a Devil, is my particular friend; we often read the Bible together in its infernal or diabolical sense, which the world shall have if it behaves well.

for the gentleman of culture:—

> It is the Classics, & not Goths nor Monks, that Desolate Europe with wars.

and for the ordinary decent citizen:—

> In a wife I would desire
> What in whores is always found—
> The lineaments of Gratified desire.

All this, of course, was in the Dark Ages of 1803, when there was no Freedom of the Press, no Progressive Education, no Manuals of Sexual Hygiene, and nearly everybody still went to Church.

But we have only to choose a little differently to find statements equally shocking in 1957:—

> Man is born a spectre or Satan & is altogether an Evil, & requires a New Self continually, and must continually be changed into his direct contrary. But your Greek Philosophy teaches that Man is righteous in his Vegetated spectre: an opinion of fatal and accursed consequence to Man. . . . There is no such thing as natural piety, because the natural man is at enmity with God.

What is the decent liberal to make of this? "Grecian Form is Mathematic form: Gothic is Living Form." "Art cannot exist without naked beauty displayed," and "Mechanical Excellence is the only Vehicle of Genius" manage, between them, to condemn the greater part of modern painting and architecture; and "Science is the tree of death," if taken seriously, is asking us to believe that all the comforts of life from refrigerators to cheap books are fruits of death.

Worse still, the statement, "Nothing is displeasing to God but Unbelief & Eating of the Tree of Knowledge of Good & Evil," challenges one of our most sacred presuppositions, that it is our duty to know as much truth as possible. The notion that something might be true but worthless or evil for us to know, that there could be anything which we are capable of knowing but should refrain from discovering, has become inconceivable. We may, of course, and we often do think that some piece of knowledge should be withheld from other people, but there is no knowledge which we do not think would be safe with us.

The most fascinating thing about Blake's polemics is their unity: his attack, for instance, upon Bacon, Locke and Newton is not to be separated from his attack on the "Classical" poets, Homer, Virgil, Dante and even Shakespeare. For Blake, the poetry of the one and the science of the other were both symptoms of the same disease, the worship of the Lord of Power who is the Prince of this world.

By their choice of heroes, the poets had made people believe that the only kind of man worth talking about, the only one whose joys and sorrows deserve serious treatment—all the rest can only be treated comically—is the warrior-conqueror, the man who holds or seeks dominion over other men. The "Experimental" scientist who puts Nature to the torture, was, in his turn, leading people to believe that the only kind of truth worth knowing is the kind that gives man dominion over nature. Blake feared that people would come to the point of believing: "only when I can make someone do exactly what I wish can I say that I 'really' know him." After two hundred years of triumphantly successful science, is that not just what, in our heart of hearts, we do believe?

No man, however strongly he revolts against the beliefs and attitudes which dominate his age, can escape being infected by them. "Natural objects always did & now do weaken, deaden & obliterate Imagination in me" is not a remark which Blake's hero, Raphael, would have made, because in Raphael's time the validity of sacramental symbols was still taken for granted; the sensory and temporal was felt to be the outward sign of the invisible and eternal and therefore valuable.

Though on one occasion Blake calls the creation "an act of mercy," he often comes very near to denying matter any value whatsoever; that is to say, he accepts the "Newtonian" picture of the material universe as "a mill with complicated wheels," soulless and profane, as the true picture, but since the affections and the imagination cannot live in such a world, they must live in another world of Vision which has no relation whatever to matter. Blake is the first English example of a dotty artist (Smart's *Jubilate Agno* is insane, not dotty), a term which applies to many artists in Europe since his time, including many of the best, such as Mallarmé, Rimbaud and Rilke, all of whom attempted to create their own "real" world out of nothing. It is better to be dotty than dead, but a lively sanity would be better still. It may be that in this age we can only choose between an art of "the Land of Dreams" and a "Land of unbelief & fear" in which there can be no art at all, but such subjectivity remains a defect.

When I think of any writer whom I really like, I find myself imagining works which I wish they had written. In Blake's case, for instance, I would like to read a sequel to *An Island in the Moon* written when he was fifty; I would give anything to possess a Blake-annotated copy of Goethe's *Theory of Colours.* Another sign of real affection is remembering any dates which are connected with them. I can always recall that on Tuesday, January 20, 1807, between the hours of two and seven, Blake was in despair, and that on May 23, 1810, he found the word *Golden.*

The Observer, 17 November 1957

Music in Shakespeare
Its Dramatic Use in His Plays

[See *The Dyer's Hand,* p. 807, and textual notes, p. 914.]

Encounter, December 1957

Preface to *Jean Sans Terre,* by Yvan Goll

To pass judgment on poetry written in another tongue than one's own is impudent and I shall not attempt to evaluate Yvan Goll as a poet. The translation of poetry is so difficult and thankless a task that no one, unless he greatly loves and admires a poem, will think of attempting it: the distinguished list of translators of *Jean Sans Terre* testifies to the esteem in which the author is held by his Anglo-American colleagues.

Judgment is impossible, but even literary placement is dangerous. I can safely say, I think, that one of M. Goll's poetic ancestors is the Rimbaud of *Bateau Ivre* and *Une Saison en Enfer* because there is almost no contemporary French poetry, and little modern poetry anywhere, which Rimbaud has not influenced, but should I try to be more specific to decide for example whether Yvan Goll is or is not a surrealist, I should find myself in the position of a historian who would discuss fourth-century Christianity without knowing the difference between *homo-ousios* and *homoi-ousios.*

One is left, therefore, with what can only, though most inadequately, be called subject matter. Whatever language they may write in, all poets living in the same historical period and more or less the same kind of society answer such questions as "What experiences are important and authentic? What is a good, what is a bad man? What is man's relation to Nature, his neighbors, the past and the future?" in ways which, despite all differences, are more like each other's than like the answers of their predecessors.

Thus the hero of M. Goll's cycle of poems, *Jean Sans Terre*, or John Landless, is an Everyman figure, but a very different Everyman from the hero of the medieval morality play. Like the Quest Hero of fairy tales he takes journeys, but these journeys are of another kind. Spenser and Goll both make use of dreams and dream imagery, but there the resemblance ends.

It would be interesting some time to make a historical study of the notion of Everyman and of his literary treatment. The Classical world, for example, lacked him; it knew only the exceptional man, the epic or tragic hero, and the chorus of citizens who keep the Golden Mean.

Everyman first appears in Christendom as an expression of the belief that every soul is equally the child of God, and his true end, even if he refuse it, to become a citizen of the Heavenly city. During the Renaissance we hear very little about him, but he returns in the age of the Enlightenment as the Man of Common Sense, a citizen of the universal city of Reason.

During the early period, at least, of Romanticism, he disappears again in favor of the heroic Faustian explorer of new experiences, of the Byronic rebel against unjust and outworn conventions. With the full development of technology he has reappeared as the Collective Man and grown so big that he now elbows almost every other figure off the scene. There have been few more revolutionary changes in human sensibility than that which, after the first World War, made all countries, victors and vanquished alike, erect monuments, not to great commanders, but to the Unknown Soldier or, as Yvan Goll would call him, Landless John.

To own land signifies membership in some particular *polis*, with its particular memories, traditions, beliefs, ways of living. But the Machine has destroyed every such *polis*; it has made all lands its land, reduced all ways of living to its single way. Worse still, having deprived us of personal experience, it submerges us in a flood of arbitrary unfelt facts. Think of the amount of information contained in one issue of a Sunday newspaper; think of the radio—five minutes of Old Dutch music, five minutes of recipes followed by a talk on Buddhism or some primitive tribe in New Guinea, etc.

Surrealism seems a very natural response to a world in which our daily life comes more and more to resemble a dream, in which we must passively submit to a succession of incongruous and discontinuous experiences.

Jean Sans Terre is equally at home on the Ponte Vecchio and Brooklyn Bridge because neither is really his: he must sleep on "the mattress of the thousand truths" because he is personally committed to none. Cut off from a personal past ("The King is dead, I'm not his heir"), estranged from Nature ("The sea-gulls all their patience gone / Head for another universe"), and confined to suburbs where "The insane trees drink petrol," no longer anyone in particular ("Wifeless with nothing"), he has become, fantastically, everybody and everything:

> He crosses the bridges of all the ages
> The bridges of all contradictions
> From the left bank to the right bank
> From yes to no from just to unjust

He is the Wandering Jew, forced to be forever on the move without any hope of finding hidden treasure or a Sleeping Beauty, without even the Whitman-esque exhilaration of the novelty of the Open Road, forever anxious about a future which he cannot imagine:

> He asks the mirror if he will arrive on time
> On time no matter where nowhere

Of course, with the loss of his past, certain evils are buried, such as the intol-erance of his forefathers who "used the oaks to hang a man with thoughts," but neither he nor, I fancy, Yvan Goll, take much comfort from that. One would not say that Jean Sans Terre, any more than the rest of us, was a strik-ingly happy man.

Jean Sans Terre, by Yvan Goll, preface by W. H. Auden, 1958

A Jolly Magpie

Aubrey's Brief Lives. Edited by Oliver Lawson Dick.
University of Michigan Press. $5.95.

It has taken eight years for Mr Oliver Lawson Dick's edition of John Aubrey's *Brief Lives* to find an American publisher, the University of Michigan Press. The delay surprises me because, aside from its individual excellence, Au-brey's kind of writing is very much to the modern taste. This is not altogether to our credit. That we should so much prefer the anecdotal, the casual, the unfinished sketch to the planned, constructed, perfected work would seem to indicate that the only experience we trust and consider "real" is the expe-rience of the immediate moment. The notion of endurance has become so foreign to our thinking that a work of art which is clearly intended to endure strikes us as arrogant and boring. One notes, too, with alarm, that Aubrey is advertised to the public as a retailer of spicy backstairs gossip who might have written for *Confidential.*

One of our most contemptible traits is our belief that bad news is more real than good news. The Greeks found it odd that the beautiful soul of

Socrates should be incarnate in an ugly body, but to them his beautiful soul was the real and important fact and his body the perplexing accident. With us this order has become reversed; knowing what a man is "really" like has come to mean knowing his defects and weaknesses, and it is his virtues that seem to us the mysterious accident.

In fact, however, a reader who opens the *Brief Lives* expecting to find the sort of juicy passages that occur in Suetonius is going to be very disappointed. Though Aubrey himself describes his work thus:

> I here lay-downe to you (out of the conjunct friendship between us) the Trueth, and, as neer as I can and that religiously as a Poenitent to his Confessor, nothing but the trueth: the naked and plaine trueth, which is here exposed so bare that the very pudenda are not covered

the proportion of scandalous anecdotes to the whole is small, and most of them are Merry Tales rather than scandals. Even when he is writing the life of a famous whore, Elizabeth Broughton, who died of the pox, he shows no prurient curiosity. He tells us that "she lost her Mayden-head to a poor young fellow, then I beleeve handsome, but, in 1660, a pittifull poor old weaver, Clarke of the Parish. He had fine curled haire, but gray," and records that her father "was the first that used the Improvement of Land by Soape-ashes."

Aubrey wrote these lives not for publication but as notes that his Oxford friend Anthony Wood or he himself might use as a basis for a polished work, so it is by accident rather than by design that, stylistically, he is the first "modern" English prose writer, in the sense that he is the first educated Englishman in whose prose one can detect no influence of the classical humanistic, rhetorical training that was the standard education until this century. Indeed, he would probably be very surprised to learn how thankful we are that, instead of composing carefully balanced and syntactically articulated sentences, he jotted things down anyhow, as they came into his head:

> Elizabeth Danvers, his mother, an Italian, prodigious parts for a Woman. I have heard my father's mother say that she had Chaucer at her fingers' ends. A great Politician; great Witt and spirit, but revengefull: knew how to manage her estate as well as any man; understood Jewels as well as any Jeweller. Very Beautifull, but only short-sighted.

> Scobberlotchers (these did no hurt, were sober but went idleing about the Grove with their hands in their pockets, and telling the number of the trees There, or so).

There are in this book a hundred and thirty-four of Aubrey's lives, ranging in length from thirteen pages (Hobbes) to five lines (Everard Digby); a few of his subjects—like Erasmus, Colet, Wolsey, Sir Thomas More—had been dead for some time, but the majority were his contemporaries, most of whom he had known or at least met. None of the lives is or claims to be exhaustive, and some contain errors of fact—unless there was another poet of the same name, Ben Jonson did not kill Marlowe—but every one of them provides material for a serious biographer that cannot be found anywhere else. Moreover, read all together, they give the general reader a better sense of what it must have been like to live in the seventeenth century than he can get from any textbook history.

Mr Dick's introduction gives such a thorough account of Aubrey's own life and background that a reviewer of the *Brief Lives* is left with little to do but quote from them. One or two statements of Mr Dick's seem to me nonsense; e.g. "The destruction of the Church of Rome brought with it a release from the burden of sin which had weighed down the English spirit in the past" and "Since the fires of Smithfield had died out on Queen Mary's death eighty-four years before, the country of England had been at quiet within itself," but this is not the place to argue them.

When one writes the history of a past period of religious or political revolution, the general issues loom so important that it is difficult for the historian to see the individuals involved in them. Aubrey's great value to us is, firstly, that he was an eyewitness of the events, and, secondly, that by temperament he was an addict of the particular, were it a person or a fact, and incapable of taking general issues seriously. His attitude to religion, for example, was aesthetic rather than doctrinal. He hated the Puritans, as he hated drunken young noblemen, because they wantonly smashed things, and because they wanted to stop other people from having a good time, but provided a man was gentle and amusing to talk to, he did not care what he believed; his friends included Catholics, Anglicans, Baptists, Quakers, and Deists, and one of his closest friends, Hobbes, was suspected, probably rightly, of being an atheist. When, desperate for money, Aubrey considered taking holy orders, his reflections were like those of the Vicar of Bray:

> I am stormed by my chiefest freinds afresh, viz. Baron Bertie, Sir William Petty, Sir John Hoskyns, Bishop of Sarum, etc. to turne Ecclesiastique but the King of France growes stronger and stronger, and what if the Roman Religion should come-in againe? Why then, say they, cannot you turne too? You, I say, know well that I am no puritan, nor an enimy to the old Gentleman on the other side of the Alps. Truly, if I had a good Parsonage of 2 or 300 pounds per annum (as you told me) it would be a shrewd temptation.

Politically, he was prepared to accept any system that did not boss people about. Hence his interest in James Harrington's ballot theory:

> . . . this Modell upon Rotation was that the third part of the Senate should rote out by ballot every yeare, so that every ninth yeare the

House would be wholly alterd; no Magistrate to continue above 3 yeares, and all to be chosen by Ballot. The Doctrine was very taking, and the more because, as to human foresight, there was no possibility of the King's returne. But the greatest part of the Parliament-men perfectly hated this design . . . for they were cursed Tyrants, and in love with their Power, and 'twas death to them, except 8 or 10, to admitt of this way.

If mildly a Royalist, he shows no disapproval of men like Thomas Chaloner and Henry Martin, who, having been injured and insulted personally by the King, became regicides:

King Charles I had a complaint against him [Martin] for his Wenching. It happened that Henry was in Hyde parke one time when his Majestie was there, goeing to see a race. The King espied him, and sayd aloud, Let that ugly Rascall be gonne out of the Parke, that whoremaster, or els I will not see the sport. So Henry went away patiently . . . (but it lay stored up deep in his heart). That Sarcasme raysed the whole Countie of Berks against him. He was as far from a Puritane as light from darknesse . . .

A godly member made a Motion to have all profane and unsanctified persons expelled the Houses. H. M. [Martin] stood up and moved that all Fooles might be putt out likewise, and then there would be a thin House . . .

The Lord Falkland saved his life [at the Restoration] by Witt, saying, Gentlemen, yee talke here of makeing a Sacrifice; it was the old Lawe, all Sacrifices were to be without spott or blemish; and now you are going to make an old Rotten Rascall a Sacrifice. This Witt tooke in the House, and saved his life.

Elsewhere, Aubrey records how Martin had previously saved the life of the Royalist judge David Jenkins by a similar argument:

In his Circuit in Wales at the beginning of the Warres, he caused to be Indicted severall men of those parts (that were Parliament etc. engaged against the King) for highe Treason; and the grand jury indicted them. Afterwards, when he was prisoner in Newgate, some of these Grandees came to him to triumph over him, and told him that if they had been thus in his power, he would have hanged them. *God forbid els!* replied he: which undaunted returne they much admired.

The Parliament intended to have hanged him; and he expected no less, but resolved to be hangd with the Bible under one arme and Magna Charta under the other. And hangd he had been, had not Harry Martyn [*sic*] told them in the House that the blood of martyrs is the seed of the Church and that that way would doe them more mischiefe.

If choice of sides in the civil war was sometimes more a matter of personal feeling than political conviction, there were also some whose motives were purely mercenary:

Captain Carlo Fantom, a Croatian, spake 13 languages; was a Captain under the Earle of Essex. He was very quarrelsome and a great Ravisher. He left the Parliament Party, and went to the King Ch. the first at Oxford, where he was hanged for Ravishing.

Sd. he, I care not for your Cause: I come to fight for your half-crowne, and your handsome woemen: my father was a R. Catholiq; and so was my grandfather. I have fought for the Christians, against the Turkes, and for the Turkes against the Christians.

Again, thanks to Aubrey's presence in London at the time and his lack of political passion, we have an account of the Restoration that no official historian would have dared write:

Col. Massey (Sir Edward afterwards) and T. Mariett every day were tampering with G.M. as also Col. Robinson (afterwards Liewtenant of the Tower) whom I remember they counted not so wise as King Salomon and they could not find any inclination or propensity in G.M. for their purpose, *scil.* to be instrumentall to bring in the King. Every night late, I had an account of all these Transactions in bed, which like a Sott as I was, I did not, while freshe in Memorie, committ to writing, as neither has T.M., but I remember in the maine, that they were satisfied he no more intended the King's restauration, when he came into England, or first came to London, then his Horse did. But shortly after, finding himselfe at a Losse; and that he was purposely made Odious to the Citie, as aforsayd—and that he was a lost man—by the Parliament; and that the generality of the Citie and countrey were for the restoring the King, having long groaned under the Tyranny of other Governments; he had no way to save himselfe but to close with the citie, etc., again.

Thredneedle Street was all day long, and late at night, crammed with multitudes, crying out, *A free Parliament, a free Parliament,* that the aire rang with their clamours. One evening, he comeing out on horseback, they were so violent that he was almost afrayd of himselfe, and so, to satisfie them (as they used to doe to importunate children) *Pray be quiet, yee shall have a free Parliament.* This about 7, or rather 8, as I remember, at night, Immediately a Loud Holla and shout was given, all the Bells in Citie ringing and the whole Citie looked as if it had been in a flame by the Bonfires. . . . So that the return of his most gracious Majestie was by the hand of God, but as by this person meerly accidental, whatever the pompous history in 8vo. sayes.

In one of his common cantankerous moods, Anthony Wood, who was, apparently, the only friend who ever quarrelled with him, wrote of Aubrey, "He was a shiftless person, roving and maggotie-headed, and sometimes little better than crazed . . . exceedingly credulous . . ." Shiftless he was, perhaps, in that he had no head for business, and lost every penny he inherited by the age of forty-five, and spent the last twenty-seven years of his life in constant danger of arrest for debt and largely dependent upon the charity of friends. But it does not seem to have bothered him much or, which is more surprising, annoyed his friends, who were always glad to see him and help him out. He was also one of those temperaments to whom the present moment means so much that they can never concentrate upon one subject long enough to finish anything, and he had the mind of a magpie, collecting isolated facts that attracted his attention yet incapable of any general principle of selection. But it is impossible to believe that the many distinguished and intelligent men who were his friends would have put up with him if he had been stupid. His reputation for foolish credulity is particularly unjust. As an amateur folklorist in an age when there were no professionals, he collected superstitions and ghost stories because he liked them, not because he believed them. Indeed, as Mr Dick points out, he often makes skeptical comments. After describing the mysterious knockings at Tydworth House, he notes that when Sir Christopher Wren stayed there, "he observed that this drumming was not, but onely, when a certain Maid-servant was in the next Room: But all these remarqued that the Devill kept no very unseasonable houres, sc. it seldom knock't after twelve at night: or before 6 in the morning," and even when he is speaking of such a commonly accepted belief as touching for the King's Evil, he adds:

> Dr Ralph Bathurst, Dean of Wells and one of the Chaplains to King Charles, who is no Superstitious Man, protested to me that the curing of the King's Evill by the Touch of the King does puzzle his Philosophie: for whether they were of the House of Yorke, or Lancaster, it did.

If his curiosity is undisciplined, it is also unlimited. As an observer of an age of great social, economic, and intellectual change, Aubrey possessed the rare virtue of being equally interested in the old and the new. A regret at the passing away of something ancient is always balanced by a welcome of the arrival of something new, and the final impression he leaves is of being very happy that he is living when he is, neither earlier nor later.

When he was a child, women were unlettered and his nurse "had the History from the Conquest down to Carl I in Ballad," "every Gentleman almost kept a Harper in his house: and some of them could versifie," "all Gentlemen of a thousand pounds per annum kept a Horse or Horses for a Man at Arms," Tom o' Bedlams still travelled about the country begging, belief in fairies was common, and sin-eaters could still be found:

When the Corps was brought out of the house and layd on a Biere: a Loafe of bread was brought out, and delivered to the sinne-eater over the Corps, as also a Mazar-bowle of maple (Gossips bowle) full of beer; which he was to drinke up, and sixpence in money, in consideration whereof he tooke upon him (ipso facto) all the Sinnes of the Defuncte, and freed him (or her) from Walking after they were dead.

By the time he was middle-aged, "the divine art of Printing and Gunpowder have frightened away Robin-good fellow and the Fayries . . . no Suffimen is a greater fugator of Phantasmoes than gunpowder." Aubrey remembered such things nostalgically, but there were other aspects of the Good Old Days of which he disapproved:

Gentlemen of 30 or 40 years old, fitt for any employment in the common wealth, were to stand like great mutes and fools bare headed before their Parents; and the Daughters (grown woemen) were to stand at the Cupboards side during the whole time of the proud mothers visitt . . . fathers and mothers slash't their daughters . . . when they were perfect woemen.

'Twas held . . . not to be good Manners, to be more knowing than his Neighbours and Forefathers; even to attempt an improvement in Husbandry (though it succeeded with profit) was look'd upon with an ill Eie.

. . . the Mathematicall Sciences were lock't up in the Greeke and Latin tongues and there lay untoucht, kept safe in some libraries.

Nothing, too, pleases Aubrey more than being able to record "firsts":

The first Coffe howse in London was in St Michael's Alley in Cornehill, opposite to the church, which was sett up by one Bowman (Coachman to Mr Hodges, a Turkey merchant, who putt him upon it) in or about the yeare 1652.

. . . because Playes . . . were in those Presbyterian times scandalous, he [William Davenant] contrived to set up an Opera *stylo recitativo* . . . It began at Rutland howse in Charter-house-yard . . . This first brought Scenes in fashion in England; before at playes, was only a Hanging.

He [James Bovey, after his retirement from business in 1654] wrote *Active Philosophy* (a thing not donne before) wherein are enumerated all the Arts and Tricks practised in Negotiation, and how they were to be ballanced by counter-prudentiall Rules.

The Pleasure and Use of Gardens were unknown to our Great Grandfathers: They were contented with Pot-herbs: and did mind chiefly their Stables. But in the time of King Charles IId Gardening was much im-

proved, and became common. 'Twas Sir John Danvers of Chelsey . . .
who first taught us the way of Italian Gardens.

The Penny-Post was sett up anno Domini 1680, Our Lady day, being
Fryday, a most ingeniose and usefull Project. Invented by Mr Murray
first, and then Mr Dockery joined with him.

Above all, Aubrey is a modern in his choice of biographical subjects. Traditionally, the only people whose lives as historical individuals were considered worth recording were kings, conquerors, saints, and a few divines and
poets. The rest were material out of which poets and dramatists might create
their humors, but no one would have thought of writing their biographies.
Yet no less than twenty of Aubrey's lives are devoted to mathematicians, as
compared to fifteen devoted to poets, and his list includes practical engineers who drain fens and cut canals, inventors who make stocking machines
or Venetian glass, and even Company Promotors:

Mr Bushell was the greatest Master of the Art of running in Debt (perhaps) in the whole world: and lived so long that his depts were forgott,
so that they were the great-grandchildren of the creditors. He died one
hundred and twenty thousand pounds in debt. He had so delicate a way
of making his Projects alluring and feazible, profitable, that he drewe to
his Baits not only rich men of no designe, but also the craftiest Knaves
in the countrey, such who had cosened and undon others; e.g. Mr
Goodyeere who undid Mr Nicholas Mees' father, etc.

He is modern, too, in his sense of the credit that is owed to originality. He
scolds Isaac Newton for not acknowledging that he owed to Robert Hooke
the theory that the force of gravity is in inverse proportion to the square of
the distance, and uses his life of Sir Hugh Middleton as an opportunity to
redress an injustice:

Mr Ingelbert was the first Inventor or Projector of bringing the water
from *Ware* to London called *Middleton's water*. He was a poore-man but
Sir Hugh Middleton, Alderman of London, moneyed the businesse. . . .
This Sir Hugh Middleton had his Picture in Goldsmyth's hall with a
Waterpott by him, as if he had been the Sole Inventor. . . . Fabian Philips sawe Ingolbert afterwards, in a poore Rug-gowne like an Almes-man,
sitting by an apple-woman at the Parliament-stayres.

It is a similar feeling that leads him to exclude from his *Lives* any facts already published by someone else and to confine himself to details forgotten
or theretofore unknown or unnoticed. The kinds of thing he likes to record
about a man are his psycho-physical habitus, his habits of work, the amount
of money he made or lost, what he died of, where he was buried, and any
odd anecdote that is revealing either about the man himself or about the

times in which he lived. He may quote someone else's opinion on the man's achievements, but he hardly ever makes a judgment of his own. Scrappy he is, but his feeling for the significant scrap is so unerring that he can tell us more about a person in a sentence than most writers can tell in a page. His few lines about the minor poetess Katherine Philips in childhood and then in middle age give one the illusion of knowing everything about her:

> She was when a Child much against the Bishops, and prayd to God to take them to him, but afterwards was reconciled to them. Prayed aloud, as the hypocriticall fashion then was, and was overheard.
>
> Very good-natured; not at all high-minded; pretty fatt; not tall; read pumpled face; wrote out Verses in Innes, or Mottos in windowes in her table-booke.

What a nice man he must have been!

The New Yorker, 15 February 1958

Reflections upon Reading
Werner Jaeger's *Paideia*

Paideia: The Ideals of Greek Culture. By Werner Jaeger. Translated by
Gilbert Highet. Oxford University Press. Three volumes. $19.50.

Professor Jaeger's book is by now too famous to need a review, and, in any case I lack the scholarship to write one.

The three aspects of *paideia*, education of the mind, education of the body and education of the soul, are excellently defined in the advice of the Red Queen to Alice: "Speak in French when you can't think of the English for a thing—turn out your toes as you walk—and remember who you are!" The first two of these are matters of *techne*, of knowledge and skills which the pupil can in large measure acquire from others, but the third and most important, which is concerned with the development of *aretè* or virtue, cannot be directly acquired from others who can only inspire the pupil with the desire to educate himself.

In societies more primitive than the earliest Greek societies of which we have record, there is no sharp distinction between techniques and virtues—to sow seed at the wrong season or on an unlucky day and to commit incest are errors of the same kind and incur the same penalty of a bad harvest. The drawing of the distinction depends upon the realization that fortune and misfortune can befall individuals or a class within a society while the rest are unaffected, in particular an individual or a class which does not work but rules.

It is impossible for a group to be in a superior social position without be-lieving that it is superior by nature and therefore to ask what superiority means so as to train its children in the qualities proper to their status. The first aristocracies were military and success in primitive types of warfare de-pends less on the technique of handling weapons, though this is, of course, important, than on the spiritual virtues of courage and loyalty, and the latter cannot be taught in the same way as the former. The young warrior-to-be must acquire the art of swordsmanship. For this he goes to someone who is already proficient in that art. At the end of his period of instruction the boy is, as a character, unchanged; the difference is that now he can do what he could not do before, handle a sword properly. But the military virtues of courage and loyalty cannot be acquired in this way. All the teacher, be he an individual or a group, can do is try to arouse in the pupil the desire to be brave and loyal. To succeed in this, the teacher must possess such personal author-ity over the pupil that the latter desires his praise and dreads his contempt more than he desires to run away from danger or fears physical pain. Such authority the teacher will never have unless he exemplifies in his person the virtues he preaches—it is not sufficient that he be able to define courage; he must himself be brave. All character training must begin by being training by example, the example of ancestors, parents, exceptional heroes, and rely on the motives of love of public honor and fear of public shame. Before a man can say to himself "Remember who you are!", he must have learned to say "Remember who *we* are!" An aristocratic *paideia* stops at this first stage, that is to say, its culture is what the anthropologists call a shame culture, not a guilt culture. For as long as the aristocracy is in fact an aristocracy that dom-inates, it has no need to go further. So long as there is common social agree-ment as to which acts are honorable and which dishonorable, the sense of honor and shame are effective in determining the conduct of individuals— the Trojans may be defeated by the Achaeans, but their values are the same, so that defeat in battle is not the defeat of a system of values. But in the last analysis an honor-shame ethic is a success ethic. If, through social or eco-nomic change, an aristocracy should cease to be the ruling class, it loses the ground upon which it has made its moral demands. Transfer an aristocrat, for example, to a mercantile culture where honor and shame are attached, not to physical courage and cowardice, but to wealth and poverty, and his corruption is only too likely, for social approval is the only standard by which he has been taught to distinguish right action. The history of Greek *paideia*, from the Tragedians on, is the history of their attempts to find a remedy for the inadequacies of a shame culture in a changing society.

When I read *The Iliad*, I cannot escape suspecting that it contains a large measure of satire, that is to say, that the theological beliefs and moral values of the poet or poets who wrote it, were different from those of the world which they describe. The Homeric Gods are so humanized that they cannot arouse the reverent awe which worships without question; it is impossible not to compare their moral behavior with that of men, and by comparison they come off very badly. The Trojans and the Greeks may, overcome by their passions, behave unjustly or cruelly but they at least suffer. The Gods of Olympus are equally the slaves of passion, but no serious consequences can ensue. They are frivolous in the bad sense for, while they are well aware of the sufferings of mortals, they refuse to take them seriously: they meddle with their lives, not for the good of man or even for their own advantage but out of sheer whim:

> When Zeus had brought the Trojans and Hector close to the ships, he left them beside the ships to bear the toil and woe unceasingly, and he himself turned his shining eyes away, gazing afar at the land of the horse-rearing Thracians and the Mysians, who fight in close order, and the noble Hippemolgoi, who live on milk, and the Abioi, most righteous of men.
>
> *(Iliad*, Book XIII)

Similarly, I find it hard to believe that, if Homer had intended his readers to regard Achilles as an heroic example, worthy of imitation, he would have portrayed him as a brainless and brutal lout. Plato's condemnation of the poets as educators would seem to indicate that the Greeks of his day reacted to *The Iliad* more or less as we do. Whether his condemnation was justified or not depends upon something we do not know, the conclusions which a Greek of the Fourth Century would draw from his reaction. If his conclusion was either "So that is what the Gods are like! In that case, let me imitate them and be as immoral and frivolous as I wish," or "So that is what people who believe in the gods think they are like: in that case, it is clear that the gods do not exist," Plato was right. He was wrong however, if the reaction was "Goodness me, I never realized till Homer showed me, how ridiculous and immoral some of my notions of the gods have been: I must seek a true notion of what the gods are really like." In so far as poetry is "a mirror held up to Nature" the moral effect it has depends upon the conscience of the beholder; it passes no judgments, but each reader is judged by how he reacts.

The notion of guilt, as distinct from shame, begins to emerge in the Greek Tragedians. Thus, in its plot, *Oedipus Rex* still conforms to the shame pattern. The crimes of parricide and incest which Oedipus commits, he commits unwittingly, without desire and without guilt, for his motives in slaying Laius and marrying Jocasta are, both in his own eyes and in the eyes of his society, innocent: then the truth about their identity comes out and he is brought to public shame. But the shameful acts which he commits are a heaven-sent punishment for a state of soul, a hybris for which he is responsible in the eyes of the gods. The primitive notion that Fortune is a proof of goodness and Misfortune a proof of error is called into question. Misfortune is still the proof of error, but since hybris is a sin into which only the fortunate can be tempted, the success ethic is already in doubt. It is a mark of a transition in moral ideas that it should be so impossible to say what Oedipus should and could have done to avoid catastrophe. In a purely shame culture the dramatist would have told us exactly what Oedipus had done to offend the gods or, more probably, one of them, and the offense might well have been, not what we should call a moral offense, but rather some kind of social error, an affront, perhaps accidental, to the dignity of a more powerful being. In a fully developed guilt culture on the other hand, the dramatist would have to show us why the hybris of Oedipus should create in him the desire to commit parricide and incest rather than some other crimes. Euripides seems to us the most modern of the tragedians in that he is the first to describe the experience we call "yielding to temptation," that is to say, a situation in which a human being is neither so dominated by a passion that he can only conceive of one course of action, which is the wrong one, nor, like Orestes or Antigone, confronted by two alternative courses of action both of which are, to some degree wrong, but one in which, knowing that of two courses of action one is right and the other wrong, he nevertheless chooses the wrong.

In a shame culture the question "Who am I," is answered in terms of past fact—"I am the child of such and such a family and I have done this or that." A person's own conception of who he is and the conception of others are, therefore, identical. The characters in Greek Tragedy are members of a shame culture in that their nature is defined completely by what they do and suffer, so that it would be impossible for a critic to write a controversial article about the characters in Aeschylus or Sophocles, as he can about the characters in Shakespeare. Their speeches, too, are transparent; there is never a distinction between what they actually say and their private motives for saying it.

In a guilt culture, which is the only viable kind of morality for an open and changing society, the conscience of the adult individual has become internalized so that his judgment of his thoughts and actions is independent of the approval or disapproval of others and even of whether or not others are aware of them. His answer to the question "Who am I?" is given, not in terms of his past history but in terms of what he believes and loves, and these verbs, since they apply to states of mind, only exist in the singular; fifty people may love the same thing but they remain fifty different people. Before a person can make the transition from a shame culture to a guilt culture, instead of asking "Is this act good or bad, just or unjust?", he must ask "What is goodness? What is Justice?" This makes the task of *paideia* immensely more difficult. The internal *aretè* it aims at imparting can neither be taught like a craft nor acquired by direct imitation of a model example, for no human being can be an embodiment of goodness or justice. The kind of teacher required is neither someone who knows all the answers nor someone who does all that should be done, but someone whose passion to learn what he does not yet know and to become what he is not yet, is contagious. What he can preach is not a doctrine or a code but a way.

Both in his life and death, Socrates is the first Greek whose conduct is regulated by what we mean by conscience. As a teacher, he refuses to "teach" his pupils in the traditional sense of telling them what to think and do, insisting rather that they educate themselves, intervening only to point out errors which they must admit once their attention is drawn to them. He is the first Greek of whom one feels that he is more than what we are told he said and did: by comparison even Plato seems not a personality but a great writer who composed philosophic dialogues. Socrates is the only Greek one can imagine talking to himself.

The education of the young cannot, however, be conducted on Socratic lines. So long as an individual has not reached the point of being conscious of himself as a unique entity, a person, he is not a free man and must to some degree be treated as a slave. Before he can take over the moral responsibility for himself, he has to pass through the shame culture stage. Children have to be told that this is right or wrong because Father says so and acquire the habit of obedience out of desire for approval and fear of disapproval and punishment. Modern permissive methods of education attempt to by-pass the shame culture stage in order to arrive directly at a guilt culture. What they produce is that disastrous kind of character which David Riesman has called "other-directed." Such a character has a personal conscience and personal feelings of guilt, but what arouses such feelings is not any act or desire of his own, but the experience of being unpopular. In a traditional shame society, there is a direct relation between social approval and a code of behavior; a man who incurs social disgrace knows exactly what he has done to incur it, and, since the values of that society are for him absolute, he acknowledges his disgrace to be just. But in an other-directed society, everything is blurred and a man can feel guilty at not being liked by people whom he does not himself admire.

Poetry as paideia. Poetry is the mother of Science in that the necessary presupposition of Science, that nature is a world in which events occur according to laws which it is possible to discover, could scarcely have occurred to men unless they were previously acquainted with worlds in which law and order are immediately manifest. On the direct evidence of our senses, there are some natural phenomena like the alternation of night and day and the movements of some of the heavenly bodies which exhibit an orderly behaviour and some properties of certain things which are constant—e.g. flames rise, streams run downhill—but these traces of order are few and far between: to naive observation the vast majority of natural phenomena seem quite arbitrary. To believe that this arbitrariness was apparent not real, men had first to learn that order can exist. By taking as their material the disorder of sen-

sory experience and creating out of it imaginary worlds in which that disorder was transformed into something far more orderly than either nature or
human society exhibited, the poets proved that it could. But if the example
of poetry was a stimulus, it was also misleading. A poet imposes laws upon his
passive or recalcitrant material and with varying degrees of success; some
poems are better than others. This led the first scientists to think of natural
laws as laws-for nature, imperatives imposed upon bodies which some of
them might refuse to obey, not as laws-of, which define not what events
ought to occur but how in fact they do occur. Thus the use of mathematics
as a language for scientific description was initially hampered by an aesthetic
attitude towards number which thought of some numbers as being better or
more beautiful than others, so that we find St Augustine making the, to us,
surprising statement that Six is not a perfect number because God created
the world in six days, but God created the world in six days because Six is the
perfect Number.

In our age when the practical applications of experimental science have
caused such amazing transformations in the conditions of human life that
the kind of truth sought by science seems to many the only kind, the most
important educational role of poetry and the other arts is to assert that the
verb "to know" can be used in another sense than that in which the experimental scientist uses it. The kind of knowledge which the arts seek for is
symbolized by the expression—"Then Adam knew his wife, Eve." It is only
possible to know persons in this kind of way but it is the only possible way in
which they can be known. To know in the experimental scientific sense means,
ultimately, to have power over; when the scientist can predict what event will
occur under certain conditions and can arrange the conditions so as to cause
some event to occur or prevent it from occurring, he knows the scientific
truth about it. It is a highly valuable form of knowledge but is only fully valid
for things. In respect of any living organism it is only partially valid—an organism is more than a cluster of physico-chemical events—and for persons it
is not only invalid but also immoral to seek for it. To the degree that it is possible to know a person in the scientific sense, he is not a person, that is to say,
a freeman, but a slave, and our moral duty is to try to educate him to the point
where such knowledge is no longer possible. Propaganda, commercial or
political, and much that passes under the name of scientific psychology and
education are immoral because they deliberately try to keep human beings
on or reduce them to a sub-personal level at which they can be scientifically
controlled, and it is no longer possible to know them in the poetic sense.

Poetry and Politics. If the example of the ordered world of a poem was an encouragement to the first scientist, it was a danger to the political theorist. A
beautiful poem, certainly, presents, analogically, a picture of the Just City, in
which every member is happy to be in its place and obey the law and every

part serves the interests of every other and of the whole. But the poet is able to achieve this beautiful result because words are innocent—they cannot wish to be or imagine they are, either in sound and meaning, other than they are—and because he is able to select the right words to be citizens of this particular poem and leave the rest waiting in the dictionary for another occasion. But a ruler has not only to deal with persons whose notions, true or false, of who they are may differ from his, but also with all who happen to live in his City; he can only imitate the poet's selection of the right words by killing or deporting the citizens who are unfitted to his purpose. The ideal community described by Plato in *The Laws* would be pleasant enough if its inhabitants were words—it would be as reasonable, for example, that it should be limited to 5040 families, neither more nor less, as it is that a sonnet should consist of fourteen lines—but, if it were, there would be no need of a Night Council. For human beings, it would be a nightmare of tyranny.

Medicine and Politics. The Hippocratic writings and Thucydides who applied the Hippocratic way of thinking to the study of history seem to me both wiser and more sympathetic than either Plato or Aristotle. They show a sense for the concrete and particular, be it a patient or a state, where the philosophers are preoccupied with the universal or the typical. The medical analogy of the body in sickness and in health is much apter to the political life than the poetic analogy, and it becomes even apter if we extend it to include the sickness and health of the mind as the medical psychologist studies it. The purely biological analogy holds to the degree that a society is healthy when the various interests of its members are satisfied, and sick when the behaviour of some members or even of the society as a whole are endangering its survival so that the momentary advantage sought by such behaviour is, in the long run, doomed to be lost. And in so far as it is in the power of the State, by legislation or coercion, to remedy the disharmony, the role of the political adviser is truly analogous to that of the physician. But the Body Politic analogy can be and has been misused. A biological organism undergoes cyclical change, birth, growth, maturity, age, death, but no historical change. A new species may evolve, by mutation, but then there are two species where previously there was only one. The terms sickness and health can only be defined in terms of the welfare of a particular organism. What is health for a tapeworm is sickness for its dog host. But a political society can undergo historical change. Of any such change it is usually possible to say that it is to the advantage of members or classes of that society and to the disadvantage of others, but is often impossible to say whether this is to the general advantage or disadvantage: a change may mean that a tape-worm society, so to speak, is evolving into a dog society. Those who employ the body-politic analogy are, only too often, party politicians, usually conservative. Again, the human body, as defined in political terms, is a tyranny, just or unjust, of the volitional Ego over the rest. I am physically in good health when I am unaware of my body except as efficiently obeying the demands I make upon it. If it intrudes itself upon my consciousness as pain or refuses to move when and as I wish, then I am sick, and consult a physician. He may decide that the fault is not mine— I have caught some infection—or he may tell me that the cause is my own injustice to myself—I am eating or drinking or working too much. But the State, be it a tyranny, an oligarchy or a democracy, has an interest in maintaining its own power which is never completely identical with the interests of the Society it rules, so that the State is not always the best judge of social health. Political ill-health is more akin to neurosis than it is to physical sickness. My judgment of my mental and moral health cannot be based upon what I desire because my desires may themselves be a sign of sickness; indeed, the sicker I am in this sense, the more likely I am to be convinced that I am in perfect health. If the body-politic analogy really held, then a tyranny would not only be the best kind of government, it would be the only possible kind; those political theorists who have been fondest of the analogy have almost all been in favor of one-man government.

One of our difficulties in understanding both the dialecticians and the sophists of Athens is that they make no distinction between the politician and what we should call the man in public life, that is to say, a man who sits on a jury or a hospital committee, or is a civil servant of some kind; to them he is as political as a Senator or a Member of Congress and requires the same kind of education, whatever that may be. Rhetorical power, with all its dangers, is essential to the politician in the strict sense, but a rhetorical education is unnecessary and may even be a drawback to those in public life whose activities do not depend upon debate.

If Plato or Isocrates had visited any school or university in Europe during the nineteenth century, they would have been pleased to find the pupils studying Grammar, Rhetoric, Arithmetic and Geometry. (What, they might have asked, had happened to Music and Astronomy?) But they would have been very startled to learn that grammar and rhetoric were being taught through the study, not of the pupil's native tongue, but of Latin and Greek. No Greek conception of *paideia* ever included the study of a foreign language—they would probably have despised such study as fit only for metic merchants. The Romans included in their education the study of Greek because, for them, it was the contemporary language of culture, much as French used to be the language of diplomacy. Men in the Middle Ages learned Latin but in order to use it themselves in speaking and writing. But by the nineteenth century, Latin and Greek were completely dead languages; even scholars had taken to writing their works in their vernacular. Now that the study of Latin and Greek as an essential element in our *paideia* has been abandoned, we can see from what we have lost, whatever we may have gained in return, what its great virtue was. Through the constant exercise of translating from English into languages as syntactically and rhythmically different as Latin and Greek, and back again, schoolboys acquired a respect for language, a sense of the importance of the accurate use of words which, it would seem, cannot be acquired so well in any other way. Those who benefited most were not the literary artists—on some of them, indeed, classical studies had a harmful effect—but those, like lawyers, scientists, journalists, scholars of all kinds, who need to use language for expressing ideas or for practical purposes of communication. It is among these sort of people that the deterioration that has occurred since the classical curriculum was abandoned is so marked. A hundred years ago the politician or scholar who spoke or wrote badly was the exception; today it is hard to hear or read a sentence of most of them without wincing.

Our *paideia* is superior to that of the Greeks in one thing, at least, and we have the study of the Classics to thank for it; it includes the study of history. Plato would probably disapprove of historical studies even more than he disapproved of poetry, for "what really happened" is even more crowded with bad examples, with the triumph of injustice and unrighteousness, than the feigned history of the poets. But he would be wrong.

The Griffin, March 1958

The Life of a That-There Poet

Byron: A Biography. By Leslie A. Marchand. Knopf. $20.

During the last thirty years, American scholarship has inherited the unenviable reputation, formerly held by the Germans, for overindulgence in "the sensual ease of pedantry," of producing works prodigious in their accumulation of singular facts but totally and defiantly devoid of imagination, judgment, grace, or humor.

I must confess that, when I first heard of Mr Leslie A. Marchand's Byronic enterprise, of his travels, of the thousands of microfilms he had examined, my heart sank. Alas, I thought, since I am particularly interested in Byron, I suppose I shall have to look at it, but shall I ever be able to wade through it? I am happy to say that my fears were misplaced; the meticulous, detailed scholarship is there, all right, but Mr Marchand has digested it, and despite an occasional ponderous phrase like "his natatorial skill," his three volumes (*Byron: A Biography*, a twenty-dollar venture by Knopf) are as fascinating to read as they are informative and, as a biography of the poet, as nearly definitive as any such book can be. I have three minor criticisms, which I will make at once and have done with. It is, I know, common practice in a multi-volume work to put the only index at the end of the last volume, but it is nonetheless deplorable; any reader who wishes to consult such a biography about some special point requires an index at the end of every volume. Secondly, the opening chapters, in which Mr Marchand deals with the history of Byron's family, would be very much easier to follow if he had drawn a genealogical table—a simple and pleasant task. Lastly, though I am sure the facts are well known to scholars in the field, my layman's curiosity would like to know why the family Lovelace Papers, which were available to Miss Ethel Mayne when she did her biography of Annabella, Lady Byron, have been withdrawn from scrutiny.

The new material unearthed by Mr Marchand does not alter our conception of Byron in any essential way, but it does help us to see him more in the round, both as a physical and as a social being. Everybody knows, for example, that Byron had a tendency to put on weight and went on a diet from time to time to get it down. I always imagined that the tendency was the normal result of an appetite for good living, but the following figures, quoted by Mr Marchand from a ledger of the Messrs Berry, St James's Street, tell another story:

Date	Weight
Jan. 1806	194 lbs
Autumn 1806	202
July 1807	153
May 1808	155
June 1809	159¾
July 1811	137½

When a young man of eighteen years of age and five feet eight and a half inches in height weighs two hundred and two pounds, it is an indication not of overeating but of some glandular dysfunction. Since medicine in his time knew nothing of such matters, Byron was forced, if he did not wish to look grotesque, to take heroic but dangerous steps. Thus, in 1811 he was trying to live on hard biscuits and soda water; in 1816:

A thin slice of bread, with tea, at breakfast—a light, vegetable dinner, with a bottle or two of Seltzer water, tinged with vin de Grave, and in the evening, a cup of green tea, without milk or sugar, formed the whole of his sustenance. The pangs of hunger he appeased by privately chewing tobacco and smoking cigars.

And in 1823 he was not only avoiding nourishing food but also

had recourse almost daily to strong drastic pills, of which extract of colocynth, gamboge, scammony. &c. were the chief ingredients; and if he observed the slightest increase in the size of his wrists or waist, which he measured with scrupulous exactness every morning, he immediately sought to reduce it by taking a large dose of Epsom salts, besides the usual pills.

There is no reason to suppose that in Venice in 1818 he was eating more than the average person—he was certainly taking regular exercise—but the consequences of not dieting were alarming:

Lord Byron [his friend Newton Hanson observed] could not have been more than 30, but he looked 40. His face had become pale, bloated, and sallow. He had grown very fat, his shoulders broad and round, and the knuckles of his hands were lost in fat.

It may well be that his early death was largely due not to any riotous excesses but to prolonged undernourishment.

Again, it is well known that Byron was a dandy about his clothes, but the details supplied by Mr Marchand are surprising:

On June 20 [1812] he bought "12 Fine white Quilting Waistcoats;" on July 1 "A spfine [superfine] Olive Court dress Coat lined Completely thro wh White Silk, 20 Elegantly Cut & Highly polished Steele buttons, A very rich Embroidered Court dress Waistcoat [and] A pair rich black Silk Breeches." In August and September he added dozens of other items, bringing the total bill on September 18 to £243.10s.

And his military wardrobe for Greece must have taken some packing:

Two Braided Plaid Jackets, 4 pair of Trowsers, Red Cloth Jacket braided with Black, Red Cloth Jacket trimmed with Gold Lace, Four Full Dress Uniform Coats trimmed with Gold Lace, Two Pair blue Trowsers trimmed with Gold Lace . . . 2 Helmets with Gilt Ornaments (Homeric helmets, gilt with an overtowering plume, under which . . . were his coat of arms and the motto "*Crede Byron*"), Six Pair of Gold Lace Epaulets, One Pair of Silver Lace Epaulets, 5 Gold Lace Sword Knots, and various guns and equipment including ten swords and a sword stick.

It is curious, and sympathetic, to learn that this dandyism was intermittent, for when Lady Blessington met Byron in Genoa, she noted that his clothes were outmoded in cut and no longer fitted him because of his reduction in weight, for he didn't want to spend money on new clothes till the old ones were worn out.

Until I read Mr Marchand, I had never realized that one of Byron's most marked characteristics was a very "un-Byronic" obsession with a clock routine. If his hours were bohemian—rising at two in the afternoon and retiring at three in the morning—their regulation was bourgeois, as, indeed, is essential to any writer who hopes to leave a substantial body of work. He got up, breakfasted, dawdled over his toilet, took a horseback ride, spent the early evening in social life, but then, at midnight, back to work or letters.

Acute psychologist though he was, Stendhal misunderstood Byron when he wrote:

His vanity, however, frequently induced him to lose sight of the end, in his attention to the means. Love was sacrificed; an affair of the heart would have interfered with his daily exercise on horseback.

Routine, in an intelligent man, is a sign not of vanity but of ambition.

Unless some surreptitious copy of the burnt "Memoirs" should miraculously turn up, it is unlikely that we shall ever know more about Byron's private life than we know now. On the ground that "the circumstantial evidence in Byron's letters can not be ignored, and . . . certain aspects of his life and correspondence can not be explained sensibly in any other terms," Mr Marchand believes that he actually committed incest with his half sister Augusta.

About the nature of his feelings, there can, I think, be no doubt, but the assumption of incestuous acts raises as many problems as it solves. Admittedly, Byron was unreticent about himself, but if he was guilty, is it credible that his correspondence with even so broadminded a person as Lady Melbourne and his poems openly addressed to Augusta should have been so frank? Is it credible that he should have risked his marriage by deliberately encouraging a friendship between Augusta and Annabella? It is to be remarked that in the case of the poems he wrote to boys—though here again it is impossible to know the exact nature of his relation with them—he always tried, rather clumsily, to cover his tracks.

Moreover, what we do know about his sexual relations with women and his own comments on the subject make it clear that he belonged to that not uncommon type of male for whom sexual passion is incompatible with equality in friendship or understanding. He hated to see a woman eat, he hated to share a bed with one, and the following reflections are typical:

> . . . a true voluptuary will never abandon his mind to the grossness of reality. It is by exalting the earthly, the material, the physique of our pleasures, by veiling these ideas, by forgetting them altogether, or, at least, never naming them hardly to one's self, that we alone can prevent them from disgusting.

> . . . a man and woman can make far better friendships than can exist between two of the same sex, but then with this condition that they never have made or are to make love with each other. . . . Indeed I rather look on love as a sort of hostile transaction, very necessary to make or to break in order to keep the world a-going, but by no means a sinecure to the parties concerned.

In a man of such a temperament, I find the relaxed intimacy of the letters to Augusta, to whom he writes as if she were the only woman who really understood him, difficult to reconcile with an overtly sexual relationship. But, of course, there is no telling. In any case, Augusta was not the immediate cause of Lady Byron's sudden demand for a separation. Though I cannot put as much faith in the pertinence of the anonymous "Don Leon" poems as Professor Wilson Knight does, I am pretty sure that he is correct in his assertion that Annabella's revelation to her solicitor, Dr Lushington, in her quarters in Mivart's Hotel, on February 22, 1816, after she had separated from her husband, concerned not intercourse within a prohibited degree but intercourse in a prohibited mode, an act that, even between a man and a woman, was still a capital offense. Given the violently aggressive feelings toward her that Byron displayed from the day of their marriage, it seems psychologically only too likely that he would do such a thing in order to humiliate her, just as it appears probable that Teresa Guiccioli's husband inflicted a similar indignity upon her when she returned to him after Byron's death.

The real mystery in Byron's life is not scandalous; the inexplicable fact is that he married Annabella at all. His motive was certainly not money; whatever his faults, Byron was not, like his father, a sponger on women, and had he been fortune-hunting, he could have done much better. To escape Caroline Lamb, Lady Oxford, and the life of a literary lion, he had only to leave England on a tour. In many of his affairs, Byron was, like his hero Don Juan, the passive partner who took what was offered, but it cannot be said that Annabella ran after him. Even if he thought it was time that he overcame his horror of marriage and settled down, why choose the very type of woman with whom he knew he had least sympathy, a bluestocking with no light conversation?

One can only suppose that Byron was tempted into such an insane act by sheer pride, the wish to prove that he, like God, could do the impossible. Needless to say, he couldn't. The nearer the wedding drew, the "less impatient" he became; on the wedding morning, he did not put on his wedding suit when he got up; for a wedding ring he used his mother's, which had been dug up in the garden and was too big for the bride's finger; in the coach on the way to the estate at Halnaby, he talked of a separation; on arrival, he had her on the sofa before dinner; when they retired, he couldn't stand it and left their bed in the middle of the night; and during the three hundred and seventy-eight days they lived together, his behavior toward her, after making all allowances for exaggeration in her accounts, was clearly outrageous to the point of insanity. And yet, badly treated as she was, it is impossible in the end to feel very much sympathy for her. Her intention to reform her future husband, which she confided to her diary, may be excused as adolescent vanity, but one cannot pardon her subtle and prolonged spiritual bullying of Augusta after the separation; cruelty and prurient curiosity masquerading as the desire to do moral good are signs of a thoroughly nasty nature.

Teresa Guiccioli was in many ways a silly woman, yet how nice and how much wiser in her understanding of a human relationship she seems by comparison. But then Teresa had one tremendous advantage; since she was a Catholic with a husband still living, Byron knew he could not be trapped into marrying her.

Mr Marchand's account of Byron's treatment of Claire Clairmont and their daughter Allegra is detailed and impartial. Once he had made his initial, disastrous mistake of having an affair with Claire at all—but when was Byron ever capable of saying no to an insistent female?—it is difficult to see how he could have acted otherwise. A modern psychologist might argue that it is always better to give the custody of a child to its mother, however neurotic, than to a bachelor father, but neither Byron nor anyone who knew both him and Claire saw it that way. Even Shelley, who felt the greatest pity for Claire and did not share Byron's conventional views about education, never advised entrusting Allegra to her. What was Byron to do? He knew that his own household was no home for a child. At the same time, he wanted to do the best he could for her, which meant that he did not intend her "to perish of Starvation, and green fruit, or be taught to believe that there is no Deity." He did not put her in a convent simply to be rid of her; given her circumstances, his plans for her future seem very sensible:

I by no means intended, nor intend, to give a *natural* child an *English* education, because with the disadvantages of her birth, her after settlement would be doubly difficult. Abroad, with a fair foreign education and a portion of five or six thousand pounds, she might and may marry very respectably. In England such a dowry would be a pittance, while elsewhere it is a fortune. It is, besides, my wish that she should be a Roman Catholic, which I look upon as the best religion, as it is assuredly the oldest of the various branches of Christianity.

Unless one has a strong predilection for another faith, which Byron did not, it is obviously best that someone who is destined to live in a Catholic country should be brought up a Catholic. As it happened, Allegra died when she was five; poor thing, perhaps it was just as well.

In keeping with Byron's attitude to women was the need to be top, to come first, that is so apparent in his social life. "To be the first man," he wrote when he was twenty-five, "not the Dictator—not the Sylla, but the Washington or the Aristides—the leader in talent and truth—is next to the Divinity." The natural ambition of a talented man was complicated and reinforced by a number of factors. He was (like his father's first wife, his wife, his daughter, his half sister, his half sister's mother, and his natural daughter) an only child, he had a clubfoot, and he became a peer by accident. It is difficult for us today to imagine the religious awe inspired by a lord in Byron's time, or the vast difference between being a lord and being the relative of one. If the grandson of the fifth Lord Byron (the Wicked Lord) had not been killed at the siege of Calvi, Byron would have been regarded as a member of the middle classes, and a poor one at that. Suddenly, he became a semidivine being, whom schoolmasters and college tutors would hardly dare to discipline, the absolute master of an estate, for whom, when he was financially embarrassed, credit would always be forthcoming. Even though he was only ten when this happened, and enjoyed the education at Harrow and Cambridge proper to his station, the memory of the squalor of his early childhood prevented him from ever really feeling at ease with those whose social equal he had become.

When, after the publication of the first two cantos of *Childe Harold*, Byron was the social lion of London, Lord Holland observed:

> It was *not* from his birth that Lord Byron had taken the station he held in society, for till his talents became known, he was, in spite of his birth, in any thing but good society, and *but* for his talents would never, perhaps, have been in any better.

None of his close men friends, such as John Hobhouse and Thomas Moore, was a member of the aristocracy, but at the same time he was very conscious of his rank. When he was invited to join in an official procession in Constantinople and found that he was to walk behind the First Secretary of the British Embassy, he left the party in a huff, and near the end of his life he made a revealing comment on himself to Lady Blessington:

> I am so little fastidious in the selection, or rather want of selection, of associates, that the most stupid men satisfy me quite as well, nay, perhaps better than the most brilliant. . . . The effort of letting myself down to them costs me nothing, though my pride is hurt that they do not seem more sensible of the condescension.

For such a character, the life of an expatriate must always have a strong appeal. In England he could only be one lord among many, most of them richer and grander than he; in Venice he could be *milord inglese*, who owned the only live horses in the city and could afford a *palazzo* on the Grand Canal. And, according to his friends, he much exaggerated the scandal caused by his separation from Lady Byron. He was not, as he said, hissed in the House of Lords or insulted in the streets, nor was the *Examiner* the only newspaper to defend him. He was even reëlected, after the event, to a grand club. But if the scandal did not make departure from England necessary, it provided a convenient excuse, which he never regretted and but for which he would probably never have written *Don Juan*. In his excursions into politics, his defense of the rebellious Luddite mill-workers, his involvement with the Italian revolutionaries, his expedition to Greece, he displayed the same desire to be conspicuous, to be at once the isolated rebel and the leader of noble birth. When Hobhouse was sent to jail for writing a pamphlet in favor of political reform, Byron took fright at the political company he had been keeping:

> Mr H[obhouse], I hear, will stand for Westminster: I shall be glad to hear of his standing any where except in the pillory, which, from the company he must have lately kept (I always except Burdett, and Douglas K.,

and the genteel part of the reformers), was perhaps to be appre-
hended. . . . I am out of all patience to see my friends sacrifice themselves for a pack of blackguards, who disgust one with their Cause, although I have always been a friend to and a Voter for reform. . . . If we
must have a tyrant, let him at least be a gentleman who has been bred to
the business, and let us fall by the axe and not by the butcher's cleaver.

The report of the police spy Torelli, assigned to watch Byron because of
his association with the Italian revolutionaries, was, if malicious, not without
its grain of truth:

Lord Byron has finally decided to leave for Genoa. It is said that he is
already sated or tired of his Favorite, the Guiccioli. He has, however,
expressed his intention of not remaining in Genoa, but of going on to
Athens in order to make himself adored by the Greeks.

But if, as Colonel Stanhope, of the London Greek Committee, told Hobhouse, Byron did little in Greece but shoot pistols and ride and drink punch
with one of the artillerymen, he really did manage to help the cause of Greek
independence, firstly by dying there, and secondly by his support of Mavrokordatos, the president of the first Greek National Assembly, in the internal
struggle in Greece during the war with Turkey. In Mr Marchand's judgment:

The Legislative gradually won the ascendancy [over Mavrokordatos' opponent, Kolokotrones, and the Executive] largely because of the expectation of the English loan, the first installments of which arrived after
Byron's death. But during the whole period of his stay at Missolonghi
the government was stalemated in all its activities by these factional
quarrels, half military and half political, complicated by personal enmi-
ties and intrigues. It may be said, however, that Byron's part in getting
the deputies started for England, as well as his efforts to get the loan
launched and his aid to the fleet and to Mavrokordatos, who was favored by the constitutional party, did in the long run have a far-reaching
effect on the progress of the Revolution. Certainly he judged rightly in
not going to Eastern Greece in 1823. He would only have lost the personal prestige which eventually made his name a unifying force in Greece.

Moreover, if his political activities were largely theatre, his feelings were
human and genuine. He shocked some of his Italian revolutionary friends
by taking into his house a mortally wounded soldier of the Papal Legate in
Ravenna, and he made great efforts, with some success, to secure decent
treatment for both Greek and Turkish prisoners of war.

Mr Marchand deliberately—and, I think, rightly—abstains from passing
any judgment on Byron's poetry. He records all the known facts of date and
circumstance of composition; he tells us what Byron thought about his own
poetry and that of others; and he stops there, assuming that since his poems

are easily available, we can read and judge them for ourselves. Incidentally, I think Mr Marchand might have devoted a few pages to the historical and political backgrounds of Italy and Greece in the early nineteenth century, because they are unfamiliar to the average reader. It is clear, however, that though he writes as a biographer, not as a literary critic, he knows Byron's poetry very well. For example, I am grateful to him for drawing my attention to an early poem I had overlooked, "To a Lady Who . . . Appointed a Night in December to Meet Him in the Garden":

> Why should you weep like Lydia Languish
> And fret with self-created anguish?
> Or doom the lover you have chosen.
> On winter nights to sigh half frozen;
> In leafless shades to sue for pardon,
> Only because the scene's a garden?
> For gardens seem, by one consent
> (Since Shakespeare set the precedent,
> Since Juliet first declared her passion),
> To form the place of assignation.
> Oh! would some modern muse inspire,
> And seat her by a sea-coal fire;
> Or had the bard at Christmas written.
> And laid the scene of love in Britain,
> He surely, in commiseration,
> Had changed the place of declaration.
> In Italy I've no objection;
> Warm nights are proper for reflection;
> But here our climate is so rigid,
> That love itself is rather frigid:
> Think on our chilly situation,
> And curb this rage for imitation.

This, as Mr Marchand observes, anticipates in a startling way the style of Byron's mature and important works. One notices that the octosyllabics give him the opportunity for speed and feminine rhymes, his particular forte, which the end-stopped heroic couplets of *English Bards* and *Hints from Horace* deny him. The tune of the Dryden and Pope couplet is too much in his ear to allow him to find his own. (There are only three couplets with feminine rhymes in the first, and only one in the second.)

If Byron's genuine poems—*Beppo, Don Juan, The Vision of Judgment*—are all satirical, it is not the satire of Dryden and Pope; in spirit (I am not speaking of literary influences) it is akin, rather, to the poetry of Skelton and D. H. Lawrence. In currently fashionable terms, one is the work of an insider, the other of an outsider. Neo-classical satire presupposes that the City of Man owes allegiance to certain eternal laws that are known to human reason and conscience; its purpose is to demonstrate that the individual or institution attacked violates these laws out of presumption, malice, or stupidity. Satire of the Byronic kind presupposes no such fixed laws. It is the weapon of the rebel who refuses to accept conventional laws and pieties as binding or worthy of respect. Instead of speaking in the name of all well-educated and sensible people, it speaks in the name of the individual whose innocence of vision has not been corrupted by education and social convention. Where Pope, so to speak, says, "The Emperor is wearing a celluloid collar," Byron says, "The Emperor has no clothes." The strict and regular formality of the couplet, therefore, will never do for this variety of satire; the sort of verse it needs is what may be termed, though not pejoratively, doggerel—verse, that is to say, in which the element of chance in language seems to predominate over the element of fate and choice.

If William Stewart Rose had arrived in Venice in September, 1817, with nothing but the magnesia and the red tooth powder Byron's publisher, John Murray, had sent him, Byron would probably be considered today a very minor poet. It is true that since he could read Italian well, he might have discovered the latent possibilities of the mock-heroic *ottava rima* for himself, but the fact is that he did not realize the importance of Berni or Pulci as exponents of the *ottava rima* till Rose had given him John Frere's *The Monks and the Giants*. If he had never realized it and therefore never written *Don Juan*, *Beppo*, and *The Vision of Judgment*, what would be left? A few charming lyrics, though none of them quite as good as the best of Moore; "Darkness," a fine piece of blank verse, marred by some false sentiment; one or two amusing occasional pieces, like "Lines to Mr Hodgson" and the "Epistles" to and from Mr Murray; half a dozen stanzas from *Childe Harold*; half a dozen lines from *Cain*—and that's about all. I can think of no other poet in the world whose work demonstrates so clearly the creative role played by form.

Thus the failure of *Childe Harold* is due, first and foremost, to Byron's disastrous choice of the Spenserian stanza. The only poet, in my opinion, who has ever succeeded in using it since Spenser was Tennyson, in "The Lotos-Eaters," and nothing could be further from Byron's cast of mind than its slow, visionary quality. One is not surprised to learn that when Leigh Hunt lent him *The Faerie Queene*, he hated it. As long as he tried to write Poetry with a capital "P," to express deep emotion and profound thoughts, his work deserves that epithet he most dreaded, *una seccatura*, for he possessed neither the imaginative vision nor the sensitivity for language that "serious" poetry demands. Lady Byron, of all people, put her finger on his great defect as a poet:

He is the absolute monarch of words, and uses them, as Bonaparte did lives, for conquest, without more regard to their intrinsic value.

Given his production up till that time, he showed better judgment than his public when he wrote to Moore, in 1817:

If I live ten years longer, you will see, however, that it is not over with me—I don't mean in literature, for that is nothing; and it may seem odd enough to say, I do not think it my vocation.

Soon after this letter, he discovered *ottava rima*; as he foretold, it was not all over with him, but, as he had not foreseen, his vocation was to be literature. The authentic poet in him, the master of detached irreverence, was released. An authentic and original work nearly always shocks its first readers, and it is fascinating to notice the reactions of Byron's contemporaries to his new manner:

Beppo is just imported but not perused. The greater the levity of Lord Byron's Compositions, the more I imagine him to suffer from the turbid state of his mind. (*Lady Byron*)

Frere particularly observed that the world had now given up the foolish notion that you were to be identified with your sombre heroes, and had acknowledged with what great success and good keeping you had portrayed a grand imaginary being. But the same admiration cannot be bestowed upon, and will not be due to the Rake Juan. . . . All the idle stories about your Venetian life will be more than confirmed. (*Hobhouse*)

Dear *Adorable* Lord Byron, *don't* make a mere *coarse* old libertine of yourself. . . . When you don't feel quite up to a spirit of benevolence . . . throw away your pen, my love, and take a little *calomel*. (*Harriette Wilson, who soon offered to come and pimp for him*)

I would rather have the fame of Childe Harold for THREE YEARS than an IMMORTALITY of Don Juan. (*Teresa Guiccioli*)

Some of his friends, among them Hobhouse, admired parts of *Don Juan*, but the only person who seems to have realized how utterly different in kind it was from all Byron's previous work was John Lockhart:

Stick to Don Juan; it is the only sincere thing you have ever written . . . out of all sight the best of your works; it is by far the most spirited, the most straightforward, the most interesting, and the most poetical . . . the great charm of its style is, that it is not much like the style of any other poem in the world.

And Byron himself knew it. Normally, he was not given to praising his own work, but of *Don Juan* he was openly proud:

Of the fate of the "pome" I am quite uncertain, and do not anticipate much brilliancy from your silence. But I do not care. I am as sure as the Archbishop of Granada that I never wrote better, and I wish you all better taste.

As to "Don Juan," confess, confess—you dog and be candid—that it is the sublime of *that there* sort of writing—it may be bawdy but is it not good English? It may be profligate, but is it not *life*, is it not *the thing*? Could any man have written it who has not lived in the world?—and tooled in a post-chaise?—in a hackney coach?—in a gondola?—against a wall?—in a court carriage?—in a vis-à-vis?—on a table?—and under it?

There is an element of swank in this description, for the poem is far less bawdy than he makes it sound. Only a small part of the experience upon which Byron drew in writing it was amorous. As a libertine, his Don Juan, who sleeps with only four women, and then either because they take the initiative or because they happen to be around, makes a poor showing beside the Don Giovanni of the opera's "Catalogue Aria" or even Byron himself, with his two hundred Venetian girls. In fact, Don Juan, who never behaves badly or loses his social savoir-faire, is a dummy, not a hero, a peg upon which Byron can hang his reflections about the world. For this reason, the poem was never finished, and could not ever be finished except by the author's death. Byron might have gone on with the poem as he intended, showing Don Juan as a *cavalier servente* in Italy, a cause for divorce in England, and a sentimental "Werther-faced man" in Germany, but since he is a purely passive object of experience with no history of his own, any end devised for him would have been arbitrary.

What Byron means by "life"—which explains why he could never appreciate Wordsworth or Keats—is the motion of life, the *passage* of events and thoughts. His visual descriptions of scenery or architecture are not particularly vivid, nor are his portrayals of states of mind particularly profound, but at the description of things in motion and the way in which the mind wanders from one thought to another he is a great master.

Unlike most poets, he must be read very rapidly, as if the words were single frames in a movie film; stop on a word or a line and the poetry vanishes—the feeling seems superficial, the rhyme forced, the grammar all over the place— but read at the proper pace, it gives a conviction of watching the real thing, which many profounder writers fail to inspire, for though motion is not the only characteristic of life, it is an essential one.

If Byron was sometimes slipshod in his handling of the language, he was a stickler for factual accuracy: "I don't care one lump of sugar," he once wrote, "for my poetry; but for my *costume*, and my *correctness* . . . I will combat lustily," and, on another occasion, "I hate things *all fiction*. . . . There should always be some foundation of fact for the most airy fabric, and pure invention is but the talent of a liar." He was furious when the poem "Pilgrimage to Jerusalem" was attributed to him: "How the devil should I write about *Jerusalem*, never having been yet there?" And he pounced, with justice, on Wordsworth's lines about Greece:

> Rivers, fertile plains, and sounding shores,
> Under a cope of variegated sky.

The rivers, he said, are dry half the year, the plains are barren, and the shores as "still" and "tideless" as the Mediterranean can make them; the sky is anything but variegated, being for months and months "darkly, deeply, beautifully blue." The material of his poems is always drawn from events that actually happened, either to himself or to people he knew, and he took great trouble to get his technical facts, such as sea terms, correct.

When he stopped work on *Don Juan*, he had by no means exhausted his experience. Reading through Mr Marchand's biography, one comes across story after story that seems a natural for the poem: Caroline Lamb, for example, surrounded by little girls in white, burning effigies of Byron's picture and casting into the flames copies of his letters because she could not bear to part with the originals; Byron himself, at Shelley's cremation, getting acutely sunburned, and Teresa preserving a piece of skin when he peeled; Teresa forbidding an amateur performance of *Othello* because she couldn't speak English and wasn't going to have anybody else play Desdemona. And if Byron's shade is still interested in writing, there are plenty of posthumous incidents to make use of. The Greeks got his lungs as a relique and then lost them; at his funeral, noble carriage after noble carriage lumbered by empty, because the aristocracy felt they must show some respect to a fellow-peer but did not dare seem to show approval of his politics or his private life; Fletcher, his valet, started a macaroni factory and failed; Teresa married a French marquis, who used to introduce her as "*La Marquise de Boissy, ma femme, ancienne maîtresse de Bryon*," and, after his death, devoted herself to spiritualism, talking with the spirits of both Byron and her first husband. What stanzas they could all provide! How suitable, too, for a *that-there* poet that the room in which his "Memoirs" were burned should now be called the Byron Room, and how perfect the scene John Buchan sets in *Memory Hold-the-Door* as he and Henry James examine the archives of Lady Lovelace:

> . . . during a summer weekend, Henry James and I waded through masses of ancient indecency, and duly wrote an opinion. . . . My colleague never turned a hair. His only words for some special vileness were "singular"—"most curious"—"nauseating, perhaps, but how quite inexpressibly significant."

The New Yorker, 26 April 1958

The Kitchen of Life

The Art of Eating. By M. F. K. Fisher. World Publishing
Company. $6.50.

Though it contains a number of recipes, *The Art of Eating* is a book for the
library, not for the kitchen shelf. If it were a manual of culinary technique I
could not discuss it because, much as I enjoy reading recipes, like most
people who rarely cook themselves, I cannot combine the various ingredients in my imagination so as to guess what the dish will taste like. When I
read Mrs Fisher's recipe for *Prune Roast,* though I expect it must be delicious,
I can only taste the prunes in isolation and shudder.

Her book, or rather her collection of four books, is about Food and
People. For such a theme she is singularly well qualified. Firstly, because
cooking is her avocation not her profession. Several famous chefs have published their reminiscences but, in discussing their clients, they are at the
disadvantage of only knowing them as diners. But Mrs Fisher has known her
guests, not as eaters only, but also as friends, lovers, husbands, so that she has
been able to see their gastronomical habits in relation to the rest of their
personalities. Again, since she is not a professional chef she is not tied to one
palace or hotel kitchen, but is free to dine at the tables of others or in restau-
rants and is immune from professional jealousy.

Secondly, though an amateur, she is a real cook, not a member of some
Food and Wine Society. The average gourmet who writes on gastronomy
gives the impression of a selfish reactionary snob who thinks that other
human beings were created for the sole purpose of feeding him exquisitely
and amusing him with brilliant conversation; he talks about food in the same
way that another kind of elderly roué talks about sex and the effect on me is
the same—he makes pleasure sound disgusting so that, after listening to him
holding forth, I feel like living on capsules for the rest of my life.

The difference between a cook like Mrs Fisher and a professional gourmet
is the difference between the artist and the connoisseur. Because he does not
work for his pleasure but only pays for it, the connoisseur can and only too
often does divorce pleasure from love; Mrs Fisher, like any practicing artist,
enjoys doing her job well but she knows that this pleasure always involves real
and sometimes painful effort.

Last but not least, Mrs Fisher is as talented a writer as she is a cook and one
is happy to observe that the excellence of her writing increases as she goes
on; *An Alphabet For Gourmets,* the last book of the four, is the best.

It is extraordinary to me how little attention has been paid both by historians and by novelists to the eating habits of nations, generations and indi-

viduals. Nobody, so far as I know, has seriously tackled the history of cooking, which is full of fascinating problems. For instance, neither the potato nor pasta were native to Europe and must, when first introduced, have been exotic foods. By what steps did they become staple diets? Why did the northern peoples take to the potato and the Italians to pasta? The more people travel, the more politically important cultural tastes and prejudices in food become. The average man is more conservative in his gastronomical habits than in any other; at the same time the greatest insult one can offer anybody is to refuse his food.

Americans intending to travel abroad now receive with their passport a letter from the President reminding them that even as tourists they are emissaries of their country. I am sorry to see that food is not mentioned. They ought to be warned that an American who refuses to eat the typical food of a country he is visiting is doing more to create ill-will than if he stole it.

I don't say that this necessary adaptation is always easy. Having grown up in England, I belong to a class of persons for whom Mrs Fisher feels an exasperated pity, those who desire potatoes at least twice a day. When I started to read her description of The Perfect Dinner, my mouth began to water but presently I came to the main meat course with which she would serve noodles and I salivated no more. Of course, I can eat noodles or spaghetti or rice but, alas, they don't *say* anything to me, whereas I can hear a song in any overboiled potato.

One grows older, one travels, one's taste in food gets wider and, let us hope, more discriminating, but there are certain early joys (vices?) which those who have not known them in childhood can ever understand or cure. Who but an Englishman can know the delights of stone-cold leathery toast for breakfast, or the wonders of Dead Man's Leg? I fully agree with Mrs Fisher's principle that one *ought* to try every taste in the world at least once, but could even she face that Bedouin delicacy, a sheep's eye? I have so far been spared that ordeal but I was confronted once in China with large boiled waterbeetles and I failed miserably.

More interesting than such cultural differences are the differences in eating tastes and habits of individuals and I cannot understand why so few novelists have explored them. It is not an accident that the central rite of the Christian religion, its symbol for agape, freely given love untainted by selfish desire or self-projection, should be the act of eating bread and drinking wine. For such a symbol, a sexual rite would never do. In the first place it divides as well as unites since it presupposes two sexes which are different, and, in the second, it is not intrinsically selfish enough for, though it is necessary to the survival of the race, it is not necessary to the survival of the individual so that, even at its crudest, the sexual act contains an element of giving, while eating is an act of pure taking. Only the absolutely necessary and selfish can stand as a symbol for its opposite, the absolutely voluntary and self-sacrificing.

From watching the way in which a person eats, one can learn a great deal about the way in which he loves himself and, in consequence, of the way in which he will probably love or hate his neighbor. The behavior towards others of the gobbler will be different from that of the pecker, of the person who eats his tidbit first from the person who leaves his to the last.

Mrs Fisher gives us a whole gallery of portraits. Here, for example, is Madame Biarnet.

> She ate like a madwoman, crumbs falling from her mouth, her cheeks bulging, her eyes glistening and darting about the plates and cups and her hands tearing at chunks of meat and crusts of bread. Occasionally she stopped long enough to put a tiny bite between the wet delicate lips of her little terrier Tango, who sat silently on her knees through every meal. . . . She drank only in Lent, for some deeply hidden reason. Then she grew uproarious and affectionate and finally tearful on hot spiced *Moulin à Vent* in which she sopped fried pastries called *Friandises de Carême*. They immediately became very limp and noisy to eat, and she loved them; a way to make long soughings which irritated her husband and satisfied her bitter insistence that we are all beasts.

And here is a horrible young American Blonde.

> She smoked all through the meal, which none of us was doing, and once when she let her pretty arm fall towards Chexbres and the fingers unfold commandingly, I saw him pick up the cigarette box and offer it to her, so that she had to lift her hand again and choose one for herself, and I knew that he was deeply angry with her, in spite of his wisdom and tolerance.
>
> The rest of us were disjointing our little brown birds and eating them in our fingers, as is only proper on a summer night among friends in a friendly room. But the girl cut one little piece off one side of the breast, one little piece off the other, and then pushed the plump carcase almost fretfully away. She picked a few late summer peas from the vegetables on her plate, and ate a little bread, and then asked Chexbres for coffee.

Though nutrition and reproduction are distinct biological activities and though eating does not demand a partner, among mammals food and sex are necessarily related and, in man, eating is felt to be a social act. There can, as Mrs Fisher says, be times when there is a special pleasure in cooking and eating a meal by oneself, but the pleasure depends upon the occasion being unusual; no sane person could enjoy solitary eating for very long. As for sex, it is clear that the relations of a child to its father and mother affect its attitude towards food and continue to affect it in adult life.

The portrait which Mrs Fisher draws of herself interests me very much. On her own showing, she believes in and practices equality of the sexes; there is nothing of the Little Woman about her. The male wolf neither shocks nor frightens her—she sounds capable of playing the wolf herself—she knows how to handle waiters and can dine alone in a restaurant with perfect composure.

If this self-portrait is accurate, it confirms a theory of mine that, in most women who develop a passion for cooking, their *animus*, their unconscious masculine side, is unusually strong, while in men who show the same passion, it is their *anima* which is stronger than normal. One might put it like this. The male who loves cooking as an art owes his love to the fact that he has no breasts; in his female colleague the origin of such a love is the wish that her status as a human being shall not depend upon her possessing them. (Needless to say, all this has nothing to do with sexual abnormality.)

By social custom, in all households except those rich enough to afford a professional chef, it is the woman not the man who does the cooking, but there is no reason to suppose that an avocation for cooking is any commoner among women than it is among men. One can generally spot the woman who does not love cooking for its own sake by two symptoms. If she is cooking for someone she likes, she may cook very well but she almost always serves too much; if, on the other hand, she dislikes or is angry with the person she is obliged to feed, no matter how conscientious she is or how good a cook she can be, she almost always cooks badly. Men are not obliged socially to cook so that a man for whom cooking is not a passion rarely serves a meal except to a girl he is out to make. His characteristic culinary defect is due to the self-centredness of the masculine imagination; he tends to plan his meal in terms of what he imagines would seduce him if he were a woman.

Mrs Fisher has attended a number of Bachelor Dinners and has some shrewd observations to make.

> I have found that most bachelors like the exotic, at least culinarily speaking: they would rather fuss around with a complex recipe for Le Hochepot de Queue de Boeuf than with a simple one called Stewed Oxtail, even if both come from André Simon's *Concise Encyclopedia of Gastronomy*. . . . The drink is good. He pops discreetly in and out of his gastronomical workshop, where he brews his sly receipts, his digestive attacks upon the fortress of her virtue. She represses her natural curiosity, and if she is at all experienced in such wars, she knows fairly well that she will have a patterned meal which has already been indicated by his ordering in restaurants. More often than not it will be some kind of chicken, elaborately disguised with everything from Australian pine-nuts to herbs grown by the landlady's daughter.

In the reverse situation when it is the Spinster or, shall we say, the Merry Widow who is giving the dinner, men are so transparent that she can hardly go wrong. If he is shy, the right kind and right amount of alcohol may be important, but the food is unlikely to affect his intentions. The only mistake she can make is to serve her Desirable Guest with some dish to which he happens to have a profound aversion, rooted in childhood. No matter how charming the server, I should have to be very much in love indeed to survive Cold Shape or tapioca. But, being a woman, this is a mistake the Merry Widow hardly ever makes. Her problem is more likely to be one of how to avoid having to say No, thus spoiling a pleasant evening. If she can cook, she has only to follow Mrs Fisher's recipe.

> I would serve one too many Martinis, that is, about three. Then while his appetite raged, thus whipped with alcohol, I would serve generous, rich, salty Italian hors d'oeuvres: prosciutto, little chilled marinated shrimps, olives stuffed with anchovy, spiced and pickled tomatoes—things that would lead him on. Next would come something he no longer wanted but couldn't resist, something like a ragout of venison, or squabs stuffed with mushrooms and wild rice, and plenty of red wine, sure danger after the cocktails and the highly salted appetizers. I would waste no time on a salad, unless perhaps a freakish rich one, treacherously containing truffles and new potatoes. The dessert would be cold, superficially refreshing and tempting, but venomous; a chilled bowl of figs soaked in kirsch with heavy cream. There would be a small bottle of Sauterne, sly and icy, or a judicious bit of champagne, and then a small cup of coffee so black and bitter that my victim could not down it, even therapeutically.

On every social aspect of the eating, whether it be the gastronomic education of children or the place and size for the perfect dinner—one person dining alone, usually upon a couch or a hill-side; two people, of no matter what sex or age, dining in a good restaurant; six people (two beautiful, one intelligent, three of correlated professions such as architecture, music and photography)—Mrs Fisher shows wisdom and common sense. Only on the subject of the Family Dinner do I find her shocking; however psychologically beneficial it may prove to shift Father's position at table or to serve untraditional food, it still seems to me blasphemous. What is the use pretending that one can treat members of one's family as if they were ordinary human beings?

As an observer of the human condition, Mrs Fisher has had a varied life. She has lived in many places, Alsace, Dijon, Switzerland, Italy, Mexico, and met all kinds of persons from peasants to Hollywood stars. She has lived in boarding houses, rented apartments and houses of her own. She has known poverty and relative affluence. She has had several husbands, with one of whom she had to live in the knowledge that he was doomed to die from an incurable disease. She came from what must have been a happy family and she has children of her own.

Of the many stories and anecdotes scattered through her books, some are hilarious, some macabre, some tragic. If most of them are bitter-sweet, she is never saccharine or acid. The following anecdote illustrates, I think, both the acuteness of her observation and the charity of her heart and there are not many writers who possess both in equal measure.

I know a large, greedy, and basically unthinking man who spent all the middle years of his life working hard in a small town and eating in waffle shops and now and then gorging himself at friends' houses on Christmas Day. Quite late he married a large, greedy, and unthinking woman who introduced him to the dubious joys of whatever she heard about on the radio: Miracle Sponge Delight, Aunt Martha's Whipped Cream Surprise, and all the homogenized, pasteurized, vitalized, dehydratized products intrinsic to the preparation of the Delights and the Surprises. My friend was happy.

He worked hard in the shop and his wife worked hard at the stove, her sink-side portable going full blast in order not to miss a single culinary hint. Each night they wedged themselves into their breakfast-bar-dinette and ate and ate and ate. They always meant to take up Canfield, but somehow they felt too sleepy. About a year ago he brought home a little set of dominoes, thinking it would be fun to shove the pieces around in a couple of games of Fives before she cleared the table. But she looked hard at him, gave a great belch, and died.

He was desperately lonely. We all thought he would go back to living in the rooming house near the shop, or take up straight rye whiskey, or at least start raising tropical fish.

Instead he stayed home more and more, sitting across from the inadequate little chromium chair his wife had died in, eating an almost ceaseless meal. He cooked it himself very carefully. He listened without pause to her radio, which had literally not been turned off since her death. He wrote down every cooking tip he heard, and "enclosed twenty-five cents in stamps" for countless packages of Whipperoo, Jellerino, and Vita-Glugg. He wore her tent-like aprons as he bent over the stove and the sink and the solitary table, and friends told me never, never, *never* to let him invite me to a meal.

But I liked him. And one day when I met him in the Pep Brothers' Shopping Basket, he asked me so nicely and straightforwardly to come to supper with him that I said I'd love to. He lumbered off, a look of happy purpose wiping the misery from his big face; it was like sunlight breaking through smog.

The night came, and I did something I very seldom do when I am to

be a guest: I drank a sturdy shot of dry vermouth and gin, which I fig-
ured from long experience could give me an appetite immune to almost any gastronomical shocks. I was agreeably mellow and uncaring by
the time I sat down in the chair across from my great, wallowing, bewildered friend and heard him subside with a fat man's alarming *puff*! into
his own seat.

I noticed that he was larger than ever. You like your own cooking, I
teased. He said gravely to me that gastronomy had saved his life and
reason, and before I could recover from the shock of such fancy words
on his strictly one-to-two syllable tongue, he had jumped up lightly, as
only a fat man can do, and started opening oven doors.

We had a tinned "fruit cup," predominantly gooseberries and obviously a sop to current health hints on station JWRB. Once having disposed of this bit of medical hugger-muggery, we surged on happily
through one of the ghastliest meals I ever ate in my life. On second
thought I can safely say *the* ghastliest. There is no point in describing it,
and to tell the truth a merciful mist has blurred its high points. There was
too much spice where there should have been none; there was sogginess
where crispness was all-important; there was an artificially whipped and
heavily sweetened canned-milk dessert where nothing at all was wanted.

And all through the dinner, in the small, hot, crowded room, we drank
luke-warm Muscatel, a fortified dessert wine sold locally in gallon jugs,
mixed in cheese-spread glasses with equal parts of a popular bottled
lemon soda. It is incredible, but it happened.

I am glad it did. I know now what I may only have surmised theoretically before: there is indeed a gastronomic innocence, more admirable
and more enviable than any cunning cognizance of menus and vintages
and kitchen subtleties. My gross friend, untroubled by affectations of
knowledge, served forth to me a meal that I was proud to partake of. If
I felt myself at times a kind of sacrificial lamb, stretched on the altar of
devotion, I was glad to be that lamb, for never was nectar poured for any
goddess with more innocent and trusting enjoyment than was my hideous glass filled with a mixture of citric acid, carbon dioxide, and pure
vinous hell for me. . . .

He had not pretended with me nor tried to impress me. He knew that
I liked to eat, so he cooked for me what he himself enjoyed the most. He
remembered hearing somewhere that I liked wine with my meals, so he
had bought "the mixings" as he knew them, because he wanted me to
feel gay and relaxed and well thought of, there in his dear woman's
chair, with her radio still blasting and her stove still hot. I felt truly grateful, and I too felt innocent.

The Griffin, June 1958

The Sacred Cold

From the Ends of the Earth: An Anthology of Polar Writings, found
by Augustine Courtauld. Oxford University Press. 21s.

By purely literary standards, an anthology of extracts from the writings of
polar explorers must, I suppose, be unsatisfactory in the same way as an anthology of passages from plays. A journey, like a drama, is an indivisible action; the significance of any one instant in its course depends, not only upon
every instant that preceded it and their order of succession, but also upon
every instant that is to follow. What the actor experiences in the present can
only be comprehended by him and become *his* when the whole action is
completed. To isolate, as an anthology is bound to do, the most exciting or
poignant incidents in a journey is to falsify their meaning because the elements of anticipation and recollection which are essential for grasping them
fully have been cut out.

But, of course, the real purpose of *From the Ends of the Earth* is not literary.
First and foremost, it is intended for those of us to whom, though we have
never seen them, the Polar Regions are numinous places which our imaginations worship with religious awe so that any scrap of information about them
fascinates us. In this matter every reader has his own idiosyncracies. To me,
for example, the Arctic, and anywhere that lies to my north, is sacred, but the
Antarctic is not (though Cape Horn, somehow, is). I may rationalise this
preference by telling myself that a land inhabited by Eskimos must be more
interesting than a land inhabited by penguins, but I know quite well this is
not my real reason which lies hidden from me in my subconscious like my
reason for being fascinated by the Gobi desert but bored by the Sahara.

For Polar addicts a review of Mr Courtauld's book is superfluous; once we
know what it is about, we shall buy it and enjoy it whatever anybody says. A
reviewer, therefore, must ask himself what it contains which might interest
those for whom, odd though it may seem to him, the Poles are places just
like any other places. Though it was not compiled with him in mind, a student of the historical development of English prose may find it highly instructive because it allows him to compare sentences in which the subject-
matter and even the sensibility are similar, and which only differ widely in
the dates of their composition.

For example, here are three passages, one written in the seventeenth century, one in the nineteenth, and the last in our own.

> And albeit, by reason of the fleeting yce, which was dispersed here al-
> most the whole sea over, they were brought many times to the extreme
> point of perill, mountaines of yce tenne thousand times scraping them

scarce one ynch, which to have striken had been their present destruction, considering the swift course and way of the ships, and the unwield-
inesse of them to stay and turn as a man would wish . . . (*One of Frobisher's
officers*)

After some alternation of commotion and pauses, and when all was still
and apparently ended, suddenly the vast bodies in contact with, and immediately surrounding the ship, were in fearful agitation, rising up in
grinding conflict, piece thrown over piece until the ponderous walls
tumbled over, and the whole accompanied by a screeching and howling
and whining which was absolutely hideous. (*George Back*)

The pressure-ridges, massive and threatening, testified to the overwhelming nature of the forces that were at work. Huge blocks of ice,
weighing many tons, were lifted into the air and tossed aside as other
masses rose beneath them. We were helpless intruders in a strange
world, our lives dependent upon the play of grim elementary forces that
made a mock of our puny efforts. (*Ernest Shackleton*)

To the anthropologist Mr Courtauld has much to offer. In getting for their
first missionaries men as unbigoted and observant as Hans Egede, David
Crantz and Hans Saabye, the Eskimos seem to have been unusually fortunate,
or, perhaps it was the missionaries who were fortunate in being called to
preach the Gospel to pagans as lovable as the Eskimos. In this dialogue between a bigamous Eskimo and Saabye, it is hard to say which comes out better.

"Will the good God reject me, because I cannot reject her? You know
that I wish to become a believer. You know, too, that I know him, and
that I live like a believer." "Yes," I answered, "I know all this, and I wished
to baptize you; but, besides what I have already said to you, my masters
in our country have forbidden me." I unwillingly said this, and he heard
it with some displeasure. "Do you not think, Priest," continued he, "that
the great Master of Heaven is more benevolent than those in your country?" "Certainly, he is," continued I: "he is all goodness: he judges differently from man, because he knows the heart better." "I wish to be a believer, and I dare not!" said he, affected: "but I will continue to obey
God, and to avoid evil; and I hope that he will not reject me when I die."

The same missionary tells us how he and his colleagues successfully "chris-
tianised" the Eskimo custom of marriage by capture.

The Clergyman sends for the girl; she comes, and after some indifferent
questions, he begins his suit as follows: "It will soon be time that you
should marry." "I will not marry."—"That is a pity: I have a suitor for
you."—"Whom?" The Clergyman names him. "He is a good for nothing;
I will not have him." Then the Clergyman enumerates all his good qual-

ities: "he is young, a good and successful fisherman, sits upright in his Kajak, throws his dart with skill and strength, and what is most important, he has a good disposition, and he loves you." She listens very attentively; her looks betray her approbation; yet she still answers, "I will not marry; I will not have him."—"Well, I will not constrain you; I shall easily find a wife for this active young fellow." The Clergyman now says no more, as if he considered her "No" as coming from the heart. At last she says softly, with a sigh, or with tears in her eyes, "As you will, Priest."—"No, as you will: I will not persuade you any farther." Now comes a profound sigh, "Yes"; and the affair is settled.

From the beginning, travellers had noted the extraordinarily permissive attitude of Eskimo parents to their children, but Stefansson was the first to discover the reason.

When a child is born, it comes into the world with a soul of its own (*nappan*) but this soul is as inexperienced, foolish and feeble as a child is and looks. It is evident, therefore, that the child needs a more experienced and wiser soul than its own to do the thinking for it and take care of it. Accordingly the mother, so soon as she can after the birth of the child, pronounces a magic formula to summon from the grave a guardian soul for the child, or its *atka* . . . Let us suppose that the dead person was an old wise man by the name of John. . . . The spirit of John not only teaches the child to talk, but after the child learns to talk it is really the soul of John which talks to you and not the inborn soul of the child. The child, therefore, speaks with all the acquired wisdom which John accumulated in a long lifetime, plus the higher wisdom which only comes after death. Evidently, therefore, the child is the wisest person in the family or in the community, and its opinions should be listened to accordingly.

No one who has lived with Eskimos ever seems to have disliked them. Even their shamans seem relatively benevolent. Of the many stories about them here, the most moving, perhaps, is a tale of cannibalism, told to Knud Rasmussen.

Entering into the shelter, we found the woman seated on the floor. Her face was turned towards us and we saw that blood was trickling from the corners of her eyes; so greatly had she wept.

"Kikaq," she said, "I have eaten my husband and my children!" She was but skin and bone herself, and seemed to have no life in her. And she was almost naked, having eaten most of her clothing. My husband bent down over her, and she said:

"I have eaten him who was your comrade when he lived." And my husband answered: "You had the will to live, and so you are still alive".

Those who are more interested in their own people than in primitive cultures can also learn much from Mr Courtauld's selections about the behaviour of Europeans in situations of crisis. Behaviour as atrocious as that of the mutineers who cast Hudson and eight other men adrift in a shallop seems to be rare. John Franklin is illuminating about the effect of hunger and immobility upon men who are snowed up.

Each of us thought the other weaker in intellect than himself, and more in need of advice and assistance. So trifling a circumstance as a change of place, recommended by one as being warmer and more comfortable, and refused by the other from a dread of motion, frequently called forth fretful expressions which were no sooner uttered than atoned for, to be repeated perhaps in the course of a few minutes. The same thing often occurred when we endeavoured to assist each other in carrying wood to the fire; none of us were willing to receive assistance, although the task was disproportionate to our strength.

Frank Debenham points out the difference, when pulling sledges over miles of snow, between the leader of the expedition and being one of the followers. The thoughts of the latter naturally run rather to the affairs of the day and

. . . the break for meals or even the hourly halt becomes a milestone in this process of thought. Thus, should the leader not call a halt until long after the established mealtime he may set his companions' thoughts "fussing" until they build up a minor grievance. The leader himself is very much better off, for he knows exactly what he proposes to do, he has the choice of route to occupy his mind, and altogether he is much more mentally free and alert than his companions.

Explorers themselves are the last people to be able to tell us what particular combination of motives urges them to choose their particular path to glory and, often enough, the grave. If they knew they would probably not be explorers. What they can say is the kind of man who is most likely to stand up to the physical and psychological hardships of their vocation.

Other things being equal, the men with the greatest store of nervous energy came best through this expedition. Having more imagination, they have a worse time than their more phlegmatic companions; but they get things done. . . . If you want a good polar traveller, get a man without too much muscle, with good physical tone, and let his mind be on wires—of steel. And if you can't get both, sacrifice physique and bank on will. (*Cherry-Garrard*)

Mr Courtauld divides the history of polar exploration into five epochs, the Ages of Conjecture, the Vikings, the Merchant Adventurers, the Navy and, lastly, the Age of Attainment. With the establishment of permanent air-bases, a Sixth Age, the Age of Exploitation, has already begun. The prospect, even if we assume that all the political problems are peacefully and justly solved, is unalluring. *The Northern Lights Hotel, The Igloo Snack-Bar, The Southern Cross Night-Club*; aeroplanes named *The William Barents, The Edgar Christian, The Gino Watkins*; organised bear-hunting expeditions. For the Polar addict the only consolation is the hope that, at our present rate of progress, in fifty years time we shall be ruining the moon and both Poles will have become madly unfashionable.

New Statesman, 19 July 1958

A Song of Life's Power to Renew

Seamarks. By St-John Perse. Bilingual edition, translated by
Wallace Fowlie from the French *Amers*. Bollingen Series.
Pantheon Books. $6.

The first test of any poet is his ability to create a world which is unique but credible to a reader because he finds he can inhabit it. It may be a very small world, like A. E. Housman's, or a very peculiar one, like Constantine Cavafy's; its laws may be quite different from the laws—natural, social or grammatical—of the public world so long as the beings which compose it and the events that occur in it are consistent with each other. The distinction between the minor and the major poet is largely a matter of size; the greater the poet, the bigger his world, the greater the number and variety of its inhabitants, the wider the range of possible events.

If one reads through all of the poems of St-John Perse, one is immediately aware that each is, as it were, an installment of one great oeuvre. He is one of those fortunate poets who discovered both his vision and the proper linguistic means to express it quite early. Both in its properties and in its style, *Eloges*, published in 1911 (in America in 1956), already contains in germ everything that was to flower so magnificently in its grander successors, *Anabase* (translated into English in 1930), *Exil, Suivi de Poème à l'Etrangère, Pluies, Neiges* and *Vents* (published in America, respectively, as *Exile and Other Poems* and *Winds*). Now comes *Amers*, just published in a bilingual version as *Seamarks*. St-John Perse, to my knowledge, is the only French poet the whole of whose output is available in English translation.

Only the poet himself has the authority to say what his literary influences have been, but a reader may legitimately say, "To me the poems of A seem to have a certain kinship with the poems of B but are totally alien to the poems of C." Thus, St-John Perse's imagery seems to me to have an affinity with the imagery of Arthur Rimbaud's *Les Illuminations*. Then, not only his fondness

for catalogues but also the way in which he organizes his longer poems recall
Whitman, particularly a poem like "Passage to India." But in spirit his work
makes me think first and foremost of Pindar. His psalms of praise share with
Pindar's odes an aristocratic poise and a personal anonymity which is foreign
to Whitman, and his metaphors are generally more elaborately developed
than Rimbaud's.

The world in which Pindar lived and which he celebrated was a small locality in which the significant individuals, their family histories and their deeds
were known to all his audience. The only modern poet who grew up in anything like the same sort of world was W. B. Yeats, but in our time Ireland is,
or was, the exception while in Pindar's time history on the parochial scale
was the norm. But St-John Perse has quite deliberately set out to sing of the
whole globe and of Man the Maker of World History. For this formidable
task his own history has made him unusually well qualified. He was born in
the Antilles, christened Alexis St Léger Léger; he has traveled all over the
world; as a very important civil servant indeed, he has had firsthand experience of international politics; and if exile to America was originally forced
upon him (the Vichy Government revoked his French citizenship), he has
chosen to remain here, although it is impossible to imagine two cultures less
like each other than that of the United States and of France.

It is as if he had said to himself: "to feel and therefore to be able to sing of
the modern world as it really is, one must, at whatever cost to one's happiness, sever all ties with a particular place and live as a wanderer upon the face
of the earth. The aristocrat of the present age is a *déraciné*." Thus, one of the
first characteristics of his world is the complete absence of proper names.
Landscapes are vividly described but no indication is given of where they are
situated. As befits a modern world in which historical knowledge has made
all the past present, the events which occur in St-John Perse's poem could be
taking place in any historical epoch. Its inhabitants have neither names nor
genealogies; they have functions.

There is suffering and death in this world, but not tragedy. What the poet
celebrates, that is to say, is not the refusal of the noble individual to live at
any price, but the inexhaustible power of life to renew itself and triumph
over every disaster, natural or human. What he looks for and tries to express
in every one of his poems is the sacredness of being.

The sacred being which is the central theme of *Amers* is the sea. The mere
title gives some faint indication of the problems facing a translator. *Seamarks*
is only one of its meanings; it also means a gall with all its bitter associations,
and in medieval French it can mean love.

The poem opens with an Invocation in which the poet announces his subject: "the Sea . . . on its confines, under its falconry of white clouds, like a
tax-free domain and like entailed land, like a province of rank weeds that
was wagered on the dice"; and his intention: "the fair land of birth has to be

reconquered, the fair land of the King that has not been seen since child-hood, and its defense is my song."

The main body of the poem consists of nine strophes. First we are shown the harbor cities, then we hear the male voice of the master of stars and navigation. Next come two female choruses. "The Tragédiennes," servants of the Muses, speak of decline of the arts of the past, "the whole decaying ap-paratus of drama and fable, we lay down!" and pray for a new song—"May a larger breath rise up in us which will be to us like the sea itself and its great breath of a stranger"—and a new singer—"a man new in his bearing, indif-ferent to his power and unconcerned with his birth: his eyes still burning from the scarlet flies of the night. May he gather under his reins this very large scattered course of wandering things in our age!"

They are followed by the Patrician Women who pray to accept the new society: "We remembered the natal place where we were not born, we re-membered the royal palace where we have no seat." A prophetess appears, then a hero explorer. The ninth strophe and the climax of the poem is a love duet which lasts from nightfall till dawn. "Narrow," sings the man, "are the vessels, narrow the alliance, and narrower still your measure, O faithful body of the beloved . . . and what is this body itself save image and form of the ship?" "Who then in you," sings the woman, "always becomes estranged with the daylight? Will you go tomorrow on the alien sea without me? Who then is your host, far from me? Or what silent Pilot mounts alone to your deck, from that seaward side whence no one boards?"

The poem concludes with a Chorus and Dedication, similar in mood to the opening, speaking of the Sea as "the One of the last evening, who makes us ashamed of our works, and will also release us from our shame."

As with Whitman, a reader may be tempted at first to think *Amers* prolix and repetitious until he tries to see where he could cut it and discovers that he cannot; the recurrence of certain ideas in ever new forms of expression is an essential part of the poetic effect.

St-John Perse speaks of this poem as "my last song." Let us hope that this is only a poetic fiction. In any case, if he does not win the Nobel Prize very soon, he certainly deserves to.

The New York Times Book Review, 27 July 1958

Foreword to *Of the Festivity,* by William Dickey

Since this is the last year in which I shall be editing the Yale Series of Younger Poets, I hope Mr Dickey will forgive me for taking this foreword to his book as an opportunity to make a few valedictory observations.

Who should edit a series of this kind? The answer is easy. He should be someone with such a passionate desire to discover new talent that he spends his days reading every Little Magazine, every pamphlet published by tiny presses which he can lay his hands on; he should be gifted with an infallible nose for detecting the difference between the genuine and the spurious novelty; *and* he should be without the slightest desire to write a line of poetry himself.

A practicing poet is never a perfect editor: if he is young, he will be intolerant of any kinds of poetry other than the kind he is trying to write himself; if he is middle aged, the greater tolerance of his judgment is offset by the decline of his interest in contemporary poetry. The books which interest him most are unlikely to be books of poetry, and when he does read poems for pleasure, they are likely to be of a date and style as far removed from the contemporary as possible. As an editor, therefore, however conscientious he may try to be in appraising the manuscripts submitted to him, he will not and cannot, as an ideal editor should, go on the hunt for more and better manuscripts because he does not know where to look. Since, alas, the ideal editor does not exist, a practicing poet over the age of thirty-five is perhaps the best second-best, but he should be changed fairly frequently.

Whatever his virtues or defects, any editor of the Yale Series of Younger Poets will face problems which are not of his making and which he is powerless to solve.

He can only select the best manuscript from those submitted to him, yet he knows that there are probably a number of poets around without a published book whose work may well be better. Perhaps they have never heard of the Yale Press or perhaps, having seen some of its previous publications, they have no wish to be seen in such company.

Then, he can only choose one manuscript a year to publish. This can be most unfair. During my period as editor, there have been years when there were several volumes I should have been glad to publish, and there was one year when not a single one seemed good enough.

Few people, on retiring from a position, can resist offering advice to their successors, who probably do not want it and will not heed it. Accordingly, I shall pass on to mine, for his imaginary benefit, a description of my procedure upon receiving in the spring a heavy parcel of manuscripts by names unknown to me.

First Reading

The first time I go through them, I try to exclude from my mind any such considerations as originality, style, taste, or even sense, while I look for one thing only, *lines* of poetry. By this I mean a line which speaks itself, which, as it were, no longer needs its author's help to exist.

Thus, in my first reading of Mr Dickey, I came upon lines like

> Spinning and smiling as the world diminished
>
> . . .
>
> That showed him whole, when we had gone away
>
> . . .
>
> Their husbands carve the dressing and the bird,
> The day, the napkin, and the carving plate
> To bits that are too little to be heard.

whereupon he went onto the pile of potential winners. It is possible to show evidence of great intelligence and sensibility but to be lacking in the first power essential to poetry, the power to *speak*. Mr Dickey's lines have both.

Second Reading

By now the number of manuscripts is considerably reduced. Again I read through them, looking for only one thing, the power to notice, the possession of what one might call uncommon common sense. This may appear either as an accurate and vivid description of some creature or object which we have all seen or as a truthful and illuminating comment upon some experience with which we are all familiar. For example, everyone carries some scar or other upon his body, but it is Mr Dickey and not everyone who makes this observation:

> Like hasty marks on an explorer's chart:
> This white stream bed, this blue lake on my knee
> Are an angry doctor at midnight, or a girl
> Looking at the blood and trying not to see
> What we both have seen. Most of my body lives,
> But the scars are dead like the grooving of a frown,
> Cannot be changed, and ceaselessly record
> How much of me is already written down.

The capacity to notice is not, like the power to speak, essential to all poetry—there are beautiful lyrics in which it plays no part at all—but I value it very highly in this age as a *moral* virtue.

Almost every aspect of modern life tends to alienate us, poets and nonpoets alike, from a common world and shut us up with our subjective selves, a tendency which is aggravated, not cured, by the writer who likes to think of himself as *engagé*. The only proper resistance is the cultivation of a dispassionate passion to see things as they are and to remember what really happened. We all need each other's help in this matter and whenever a poet makes me recognize something in our common world which I could have recognized for myself but did not, I am grateful.

Third Reading

Having satisfied myself that the author of a manuscript can make words speak and is interested in something more than his precious little self, I now read it poem by poem, looking to see if he has learned to write a whole poem and has written enough of them to be ready to publish a book. How many is enough? Remembering that, when reading a volume by the greatest and most famous names, one almost always says of some of the poems "Why did he include that?" but that one never says this about a volume of one's own, I regard a manuscript as meriting publication if I like a third of its contents.

Like any work of art, a successful poem is a complete world with which, though it is a thing, the reader can make personal contact. But poetry is peculiar in that it is made of words; the medium of this art is the same as that of guidebooks, treatises on plumbing, business correspondence, and the *Congressional Record.* A poem therefore is, necessarily, what a painting need not be and a piece of music cannot be, a double world of things (words) and meanings. "Pure" poetry, poetry, that is to say, in which word and meaning are identical, is an impossibility; even a lyric like "Full Fathom Five" is "representational." Further, since the meaning of words depends upon common social agreement, poetry is the most "traditional" of all the arts. No poet can invent a language of his own; even the puns in *Finnegans Wake* presuppose an unchanging traditional language. Assuming that he had learned to speak French, the shade of Homer would have little difficulty, I believe, in reading the poetry of Rimbaud; he might not like it but he would know why. But a Greek musician confronted with a piece by Webern, let us say, would be unable to pass any judgment whatsoever, because he would hear no musical sounds, only noises.

Thus while in the other arts an original vision may often seem to be the result of a change of style or method, in poetry an original and in itself nonverbal vision seems the necessary precondition for a change in the handling of the language.

Most arguments about *how* poetry should be written seem to me futile because they conceal the real difference between the parties, which is their respective notions of the proper poetical subject, what poetry should be *about.*

As an example of one of Mr Dickey's poems, let me cite "Part Song, with Concert of Recorders." I choose it because it is a song, and of all kinds of poetry songs are the least personal and most verbal.

This poem is a little ballad, a melodramatic dialogue between a lady and her doctor-lover, who has just murdered her husband. In each of the seven five-line stanzas, the first line ends with the word *there* or *where*, the fourth and fifth lines with the word *care.*

SHE And he lies dead—

HE   His blood is seeping there—

SHE Where we have kissed—
HE   Where we have done much more—
SHE I liked it best the way it was before.
HE You like it now.
SHE   I like it, but I care.
HE No longer care.
. . .
SHE Come, Doctor, we must fly someotherwhere.
HE I have my bag full of essential things,
    False passports, currency, and diamond rings—
SHE True pledge of love for those who truly care.
HE Who live and care.

A lucky chance of the English language gave Mr Dickey two rhyme words which can be used in a number of different senses, but his use of them, and of a simple, melodramatic situation which might all too easily have been ridiculous, to compose a poignant and resonant parable comes from his personal vision, not the English language.

At present, to judge from this volume, Mr Dickey's speciality is nightmare worlds described in the simplest possible diction.

> Both of these women are fat. Anchovy paste
> Is the staple of their helter-skelter meals,
> And other things rich or alien to the taste,
> Cheap salmon roe, cream, the meat of eels.
>
> Moon-disks, they smile at each other over the dishes
> Vast buttery smiles of appetite and love;
> In a hazy light they swim like cannibal fishes,
> Each waits for each to make the precipitate move.

This satisfies the three demands I have made in my readings: the lines speak, something has been noticed, and speech and observation have become the servants of a personal vision.

In conclusion, one more teaser for my editorial successor. Suppose that one year he is confronted with two manuscripts which seem to him of equal merit. He can publish only one. How, then, is he to make his choice? The only criterion in such a case, so far as I can see, is the variety of the Series. I would choose whichever of the two was, stylistically, the least like the winning manuscripts of the previous three years. But could one dare tell the author of the rejected manuscript this? No, let him attribute his rejection to the editor's bad taste.

Of the Festivity, by William Dickey, 1959

Thinking What We Are Doing

The Human Condition. By Hannah Arendt.
University of Chicago Press. $4.75.

The normal consequence of having read a book with admiration and enjoyment is a desire that others should share one's feelings. There are, however,
if I can judge from myself, occasional exceptions to this rule. Every now and
then, I come across a book which gives me the impression of having been
especially written for me. In the case of a work of art, the author seems to
have created a world for which I have been waiting all my life; in the case of
a "think" book, it seems to answer precisely those questions which I have
been putting to myself. My attitude toward such a book, therefore, is one of
jealous possessiveness. I don't want anybody else to read it; I want to keep it
all to myself. Miss Hannah Arendt's *The Human Condition* belongs to this
small and select class; the only other member which, like hers, is concerned
with historical-political matters, is Rosenstock-Huessey's *Out of Revolution.*

Possessiveness is, of course, an immoral emotion and, if the following remarks misrepresent or fail to do justice to Miss Arendt, at least they have
been a moral discipline for me.

Nobody, I fancy, feels "happy" about the age in which we live or the future
which even the living may know before they die. At all times in history men
have felt anxious about their own fate or the fate of their class or community,
but there has seldom been a time, I believe, when the present and future of
the whole human endeavor on this earth has seemed questionable to so
many people.

Miss Arendt is not, of course, so foolish or presumptuous as to offer saving
solutions. She merely asks us to think what we are doing, which we can never
manage unless we can first agree about the meaning of the words we think
with, which, in its turn, requires that we become aware of what these words
have meant in the past.

It would not be inaccurate, I believe, to call *The Human Condition* an essay
in Etymology, a re-examination of what we think we mean, what we actually
mean and what we ought to mean when we use such words as nature, world,
labor, work, action, private, public, social, political, etc.

Consequently, the best way to approach it might be by discussing some of
its definitions as if it were a dictionary.

Nature

Man is part of nature in that he is a biological organism subject, like all
other creatures, to the laws of nature and the temporal cycle of generation.
From the point of view of nature, man has no history, only the protohistory
of the evolutionary processes by which the human species came into being.

For nature, every man is an anonymous member of his species, identical with every other, or, at most, divisible into male and female. For nature, therefore, so long as the human species exists, there is no such thing as death, only life, and terms like growth and decay have no meaning, for these are only relevant to individuals of whom nature knows nothing. This natural biological man is, like some but not all animals, *social*—the survival of this species requires that its members associate constantly with each other—and he is a *laborer*. Miss Arendt defines as *labor*, any behaviour which is imposed by the need to survive. Thus, a tiger hunting its prey, can be said to be laboring. Man, however, is the laboring animal par excellence—the bee runs him pretty close—firstly because his particular needs and his numbers require that he spend a much greater part of his time in acquiring or producing what he needs to survive, and secondly, because he seems to be endowed with both the capacity and the instinct to produce a surplus over and above his immediate needs of consumption.

Man, the laboring animal, does not act; he exhibits human behaviour, the goal of which is not a matter of personal decision, dictated by the natural instinct to survive and propagate life. His motive, if the word can properly be used at all, is pleasure, or rather the avoidance of pain. Though he is social, the experiences of the laboring animal are essentially *private* and subjective. What he experiences are the unshareable experiences of the body. He needs the presence of his fellows not as persons but as bodies, another set of muscles, a fertile member of the opposite sex.

To man the laboring animal, past and future have no meaning. All that is temporally real to him is the present point on the biological cycle. For this reason he has no need of *speech*. If he uses words, he uses them as bees use dance-movements, as a code for conveying necessary information.

Lastly, man the laboring animal does not and cannot ask what his behaviour means for life as life is something given, not made. It is like asking whether we live to eat or eat to live.

World

In addition to being a member of the human species, every man is, what no other animal is, a mortal individual, aware that, though the race may be immortal, he and every other human individual must die.

At the same time he is aware—or was aware until modern science has made him doubt the evidence of his senses—that the realm of nature is made up not only of mortal creatures, but also of things, the earth, the ocean, the sun, moon and stars, which are always there.

Out of this double awareness, of human mortality and the ever-lastingness of things, arises the desire and hope of transcending the cycle of natural birth and death by *making* a *world* of things which endure and in which, therefore, man can always be at home.

As Miss Arendt says:

Birth and death presuppose a world which is not in constant movement, but where durability and relative permanence make appearance and disappearance possible, which existed before any one individual appeared in it and will survive his eventual departure. Without a world into which men are born and from which they die, there would be nothing but eternal recurrence, the deathless everlastingless of the human as of any other animal species.

The mortal individual who is man the maker is not social, that is, for the process of fabrication he requires the presence, not of human beings, but of the various materials out of which he fashions a world. The objects, he makes, on the other hand require the existence of a public community of human beings to use them and enjoy them. The fabricated world has an objective reality which is lacking in both human behaviour and human action.

Against the subjectivity of men stands the objectivity of the man-made world rather than the sublime indifference of an untouched nature. Only we who have erected the objectivity of a world of our own from what nature gives us, who have built it into the environment of nature so that we are protected from her, can look upon nature as something "objective." Without a world between man and nature, there is eternal movement but no objectivity.

What distinguishes working from laboring is that the results of labor are immediately consumed by the laborer while the products of work, whether use-objects like tools or enjoyment-objects like works of art, once they are completed, persist as they are unchanged and, ideally, for ever. A tool may wear out or be replaced by a better one, but this is an accident, while the notion of a loaf of bread that lasts for ever is absurd; if it is not consumed, it is worthless.

The attitude of the worker or maker towards time, therefore, is quite different from that of the laborer. The past and future have a meaning for him but in a special way. What he assumes is that the future will be like the past; time for the maker, that is, has neither the cyclical motion of nature, nor the unilinear irreversible flow of history—like space it does not move but is there. All he knows about time is that it takes time to make an object so that he can only define it to himself as that which must not be wasted.

While the laborer always remains the servant of nature upon whose fertility his survival ultimately depends, the worker regards nature as raw material which has no value until he confers value upon it by transforming it into a world of objects.

To the degree that these objects have enjoyment value as well as use value, they may be said to be forms of speech. A beautiful temple "addresses" us no less than a beautiful poem. But it is the thing that speaks not its maker. While the laborer cannot even ask the question "what does life mean", the worker can say "life itself is meaningless but it provides the opportunity for making a meaningful world. He does not desire glory for himself but immortality for the things made with his hands.

Action

In addition to being a member of the human species, subject to natural necessity, and a mortal individual who can transform mortal life into immortal objects, every man is a unique person. Though all must die, the birth of every human being marks the beginning of the existence of a being the like of whom never existed before and will never exist again. To be a person is to be able to say "I" and to have a biography of one's own, and the sum of all human biographies constitutes what we call history. While the laborer may require the society of other members of his kind and the worker the existence of others to use or enjoy his works, only the person requires a *public* realm of other persons to whom through his *actions* he discloses who he is. For human action is unintelligible without speech whereby the agent identifies who he is, what he is doing, and intends to do.

Labor is recurrent, work comes to an end when it has completed its task (which can be undone), but action is unpredictable, unrepeatable and irretrievable. The name of the actor, even the act itself, may be forgotten, but it will affect the actions of others till the end of time. Action tends to be as boundless as the freedom in which it is grounded and would destroy us if we did not voluntarily set limits to what we do. The three principal limitations are law, forgiveness and promises. By laws we establish a common agreement to prohibit certain actions and to punish offenders rather than take unlimited vengeance. By forgiveness we dismiss an error for the sake of the person who committed it. In an admirable sentence, Miss Arendt indicates the relation between law and forgiveness.

> Men are unable to forgive what they cannot punish, and they are unable to punish what has turned out to be unforgivable.

By promises we set a bound to our actions in the unknown future. Promises are always specific, valid for an agreed purpose; a general promise like saying "I promise to be good" is meaningless.

In her historical review of these notions, Miss Arendt starts with the Greeks.

It is hard to say which is the most astonishing, the Greek pride which identified the human with the human person who acts out of freedom not necessity and relegated all that men do with their bodies or their hands, all that is necessary or useful to a sub-human status, or the Greek clearsightedness which saw exactly what, in their age, such a premise must involve. The truly human person can only exist if there are semi- or sub-human beings who will supply his necessities and build his world for him. But no human beings exist who will do this of their own free will; they must be compelled. The necessary pre-political condition for the free community of persons is violence and slavery. It is to their credit that the Greeks never pretended, as some later upholders of slavery have done, that certain kinds of human beings are happier as slaves than they would be as free men; on the contrary, they argued that a slave must be a base fellow because he did not kill himself rather than be enslaved.

Life in the Greek City state was divided, therefore, into two realms, the private realm of the household, which its master ruled by force, and in which not only the business of rearing a family but also all the activities we call economic were carried on, and the public realm of politics in which the free citizen disclosed himself to his peers by speech and action and strove to win glory.

Miss Arendt is more reticent than, perhaps, she should be, about what actually went on in this public realm of the Greeks. My knowledge of Greek History is very limited, but the picture given by Thucydides is not, to my mind, very alluring. Miss Arendt may be right when she deplores Plato's attempt to eliminate the freedom of the public realm and turn politics into a form of craftsmanship, but the way in which the Greeks had used their freedom makes it understandable. They realized that the great political virtue was moderation and the great political vice *hubris*, but how their ideal man who, thanks to the labor of others, was freed from all natural necessity could escape the temptation to *hubris*, it is hard to imagine, for he was not a god but a mortal man leading something very like the life of a god. As Miss Arendt says:

> The price of absolute freedom from necessity is, in a sense, life itself, or rather the substitution of vicarious life for real life . . . for mortals the easy life of the gods would be a lifeless life.

To make a vicarious life real, to prevent it being meaningless and boring, the free Greek citizen had to seek to make it as extraordinary and daring as possible, and politics conducted thus are apt to end in disaster.

Miss Arendt's definition of political power, as distinct from violence or strength, is admirable, but I do not think the Greeks possessed it.

> Power is actualised only where word and deed have not parted company, where words are not empty and deeds not brutal, when words are not used to veil intentions but to disclose realities, and deeds are not used to violate and destroy, but to establish relations and create new realities.

If the Greeks made the mistake of attempting to split up the threefold nature of man, to assign his laboring body to one class of men, his working hands to another, and his active personality to a third, they were perfectly correct to value action so highly. While someone who neither labors nor works ceases to be human, it is in personal action, not in laboring to live or working to make a world, that a man becomes himself and gives meaning to his existence. A society dominated by the modes of thought proper to work, as was the mercantile society at the beginning of the nineteenth century, loses its *raison d'être*.

> While only fabrication with its instrumentality is capable of building a world, this same world becomes as worthless as the employed materials, a mere means to further ends, if the standards which governed its coming into being are permitted to rule after its establishment.

Our own modern technological society, whether it call itself capitalist or communist, is dominated by the modes of thought proper to labor; its members consider whatever they do primarily as a way to sustain their own lives and those of their families—the artist is virtually the only worker left—and their value to society is conceived in terms, not of what each produces but of his function in the collective productive process. So long as these standards prevail, the more successful our society becomes in achieving its goal—a mastery over natural necessity which will abolish the necessity for labor—the more meaningless it will get. Technology has already advanced to the point where it is possible to conceive of a society in which production has become automatic and the only necessity left to men is consumption. The land of Cockaigne, so charming as a wish-dream, would be less charming in reality.

> The danger is that such a society, dazzled by the abundance of its growing fertility and caught in the smooth functioning of a never-ending process would no longer be able to recognise its own futility—the futility of a life which does not fix or realise itself in any permanent object which endures after its labor is past. . . . What we are confronted with is the prospect of a society of laborers without labor, that is, without the only activity left to them. Surely, nothing could be worse . . . The spare time of the *animal laborans* is never spent in anything but consumption, and the more time left to him, the greedier and more craving his appetites.

The significance of the words *private* and *public* in the life of the modern nation state are almost the reverse of their significance in the Greek *polis*.

Politically, even in a democracy, we are divided, like the Greek household, into rulers and the ruled. The rulers, it is true, are not persons, but officials and the obedience of the ruled is secured less by naked violence than by the anonymous pressure of social conformity, but "the rule by nobody is not necessarily no rule: it may indeed, under certain circumstances, turn out to be one of the cruellest and most tyrannical versions."

Public Life, in the Greek sense, has been replaced by social life, that is to say, the private activity of earning one's bread is now carried on in public.

What a modern man thinks of as the realm where he is free to be himself and to disclose himself to others, is what he calls his private or personal life, that is to say, the nearest modern equivalent to the public realm of the

Greeks is the intimate realm, and we have a noun, unknown to the Greeks, *the Public*, that curious body made up, as Kierkegaard said, of people at moments when they are not themselves.

The modern equivalent to the Greek man of action is the scientist who can say, like Werner Von Braun—"Basic research is when I am doing what I don't know what I'm doing," and the historical consequence of their deeds has been the alienation of man, not from himself, but from his world.

> What is new is not that things exist of which we cannot form an image . . . but that the material things we see and represent and against which we had measured immaterial things for which we can form no images should likewise be "unimaginable for however we think it is wrong; not perhaps quite as meaningless as a triangular circle, but much more so than a winged lion."
>
> What men now have in common is not the world but the structure of their minds, and this they cannot have in common, strictly speaking; their faculty of reasoning can only happen to be the same in everybody.

At first sight it might seem logical to hand over the government of society to the scientists, but the only kind of action they understand is action into nature; with the human being they can only deal in so far as he is natural and impersonal.

> The reason why it may be wise to distrust the political judgment of scientists qua scientists is that they move in a world where speech has lost its power.

I hope that these remarks and quotations give a faint idea of the richness and fascination of *The Human Condition*. Let me end with one final epigram by Miss Arendt which we may, if we are unlucky, have cause to remember.

> It is far easier to act under conditions of tyranny than it is to think.

The Griffin, September 1958; *Encounter*, June 1959

The Creation of Music and Poetry

Conversations with Igor Stravinsky. By Igor Stravinsky
and Robert Craft. Doubleday. $4.

The Art of Poetry. By Paul Valéry. Translated by Denise Folliot.
Bollingen Series. Pantheon. $3.50.

After the première of *Persephone* in 1934, Valéry wrote Stravinsky this congratulatory note:

I am only a "profane" listener, but the divine detachment of your work touched me. It seems to me that what I have sometimes searched for in the ways of poetry, you pursue and join in your art. The point is to attain purity through the will.

Though the poet was some ten years older than the composer, both belong to that extraordinary generation of revolutionaries who, in every medium, created what is known as "modern" art. When they talk about their experiences, therefore, they must be listened to with the utmost attention and reverence. At the same time, their statements must be viewed in the light of the polemical situation with which they were faced but which for us, their juniors, thanks to their achievements, has altered.

Furthermore, in assessing the critical remarks of any practicing artist, we must remember that his primary concern is, very properly, with the works which he is making himself, and that the works of others are important to him mainly as examples to follow or avoid. What he says about his art is never false, but it may only be true of the kind of work he desires and is able to produce.

No one can appreciate an art who is not a proto-artist, who has not, that is to say, had certain experiences which, were he creative, he would be able to objectify in some artistic medium. There are proto-poetic, proto-graphic, and proto-musical experiences which are quite distinct from each other, though they may overlap. Valéry gives us an account of a proto-musical experience of his own.

As I went along my street, which mounted steeply, I was gripped by a rhythm which took possession of me and soon gave me the impression of some force outside myself. Another rhythm overtook and combined with the first, and certain strange transverse relations were set up between them. . . . in my case walking is often conducive to a quickened flow of ideas, but this time my movements assailed my consciousness through a subtle arrangement of rhythms, instead of provoking that amalgam of images, inner words, and virtual acts that one calls an Idea. . . . This grace had descended on the wrong head, since I could make no use of a gift which, in a musician, would doubtless have assumed a lasting shape, and it was in vain that these two themes offered me a composition whose sequence and complexity amazed my ignorance and reduced it to despair.

It is revealing to compare this story with Valéry's description of the genesis of *Le Cimetière Marin*:

My intention was at first no more than a rhythmic figure, empty and filled with meaningless syllables, which obsessed me for some time. I noticed that this figure was decasyllabic, and I pondered on that model which is very little used in modern French poetry; it struck me as poor and monotonous, of little worth compared with the alexandrine.... The demon of generalization prompted me to try raising this Ten to the power of Twelve. It suggested a certain stanza of six lines, and the idea of a composition founded on the number of these stanzas and strengthened by a diversity of tones and functions to be assigned to them. Between the stanzas contrasts and correspondences would be set up. This last condition soon required the potential poem to be a monologue of "self" in which the simplest and most enduring themes of my affective and intellectual life, as they had imposed themselves upon my adolescence, associated with the sea and the light of a particular spot on the Mediterranean coast were called up.... All this led to the theme of death and suggested the theme of pure thought. (The chosen line of ten syllables bears some relation to the Dantesque line.) My line had to be solid and strongly rhythmical. I knew I was tending towards a monologue as personal, but also as universal, as I could make it.

Just as in the case of the "musical" experience which baffled him, Valéry's initial impulse is a rhythm, but this time he recognizes it as decasyllabics—that is, a *verbal* rhythm—which draws to it images and ideas which can be formulated and only formulated in words.

So few composers have given us accounts of the process of musical composition that Stravinsky's remarks are particularly valuable. It would seem that what a word is to a poet, an interval is to a composer.

When I compose an interval, I am aware of it as an object, as something outside me, the contrary of an impression.

Like words in poetry, intervals do not begin to become music until they are associated with a rhythm.

I recognize musical ideas when they start to exercise a certain kind of auditive sense. But long before ideas take shape I begin to work by relating intervals rhythmically. This exploration of possibilities is always conducted at the piano. Only after I have established my melodic or harmonic relationships do I pass to composition. When my main theme has been decided on, I know in general lines what kind of musical material it will require. I start to look for my material, sometimes playing old masters (to put myself in motion), sometimes starting directly to improvise rhythmic units on a provisional row of notes (which can become a final row).

This second stage seems to be analogous to the stage at which a poet becomes conscious in a general sort of way of what his poem is to be "about." But for the poet, so far as I can see, there is no problem analogous to the composer's search for the right pitch and timbre since, in the case of words, these qualities are decided by the normal speech habits of those who speak the poet's mother tongue, whereas the composer is free and therefore obliged to choose them for himself.

> The sound (timbre) will not always be present. But if the musical idea is a group of notes, a motive coming suddenly to your mind, it very often comes together with its sound. . . . It is very important to me to remember the pitch of the music at its first appearance: if I transpose it for some reason, I am in danger of losing the freshness of first contact and I will have difficulty in recapturing its attractiveness.

Although nearly all poets think of their poems as heard speech, most of them also attach importance to how they look on the page; they associate the sound of the words with a certain length of line and shape of stanza. It had not occurred to me, I must confess, that composers can feel the same way.

> As a composer I associate a certain kind of music, a certain tempo of music, with a certain kind of note unit . . . the unit of the note and the tempo appear in my imagination at the same time as the interval itself. . . . It is difficult for me to judge whether a work of mine, translated into larger or smaller note units, but played at the same tempo, would make an aural difference. However I know that I could not look at the music in its translated shape, for the shape of the notes as one writes them is the shape of the original conception itself. . . . I do believe in a relation between the character of my music and the kind of note unit of the pulsation, and I do not care that this is undemonstrable.

Valéry and Stravinsky have many likes and dislikes in common. Both prefer the formal to the happy-go-lucky, an art which disintoxicates to an art which would bewitch, both have a horror of the pseudo-grandiloquent. But, as practising artists, their careers have been very different. Valéry's poetic output was small, most of it produced during a few years between the ages of forty-five and fifty, and stylistically uniform. Having found his voice in *La Jeune Parque*, he never felt a need to change it, and the themes which excited his imagination were unusually limited in range. Stravinsky, on the other hand, has composed steadily from youth till now, and is one of the most striking examples in musical history of continuous growth.

Growth does not mean, of course, that each new work is necessarily better than its predecessors or that it supersedes them, only that each work is a fresh departure. Musical journalism usually divides Stravinsky's works into periods—the Russian period, the Neo-Classical period and now, in his seventies, the Serial period—but, like all journalistic labels, this is misleading: every important composition of Stravinsky's has a style, a musical language all its own.

Lastly, while Valéry was obsessed all his life with the question of *La Poésie pure*, Stravinsky seems never to have worried about "pure" music. More than half his compositions so far have been ballet scores or settings of words, about which one can say, not only that they are good to listen to, but also that they are good to choreograph and dance to, or good settings of their text. Beautiful, for example, as *Agon* sounds on the phonograph, it requires to be seen with Balanchine's choreography to make its full effect; nor, whatever Stravinsky may have said at times about treating words as syllables, has he ever really thought of language as a mere pretext for singing. Few composers have shown better *literary* taste in their choice of texts to set, and his feelings about this can be gauged from his criticism of Schönberg:

> . . . nearly all of his texts are appallingly bad, some of them so bad as to discourage performance of the music.

Poetry is in a unique position among the arts in that its medium, language, is neither the creation and private property of poets, as musical sounds are of composers, nor passive matter upon which they can impose any significance they choose, like the stone of architects and the colors of painters.

The poet can only write his poetry after the linguistic group to which he belongs has created both the words themselves and their meanings, and these are needed for a great many other purposes than simply providing building materials for poetry. Even so peculiar a language as that of *Finnegans Wake* would be meaningless without the pre-existence of the conventional languages which it breaks up and recombines.

Poets, therefore, unlike composers, are faced with the perplexing question: "How is the poetic use of language to be distinguished from all the other uses to which language is put?" The formal distinction between metrical verse and prose is obvious enough but tells us very little.

Valéry, who was both a practicing poet and a highly intelligent man, devoted more time than most to this problem, and the inadequacy of the solutions he offers—no one has suggested better and most have suggested worse—convinces me that a clear and definite answer is impossible.

The French *Symbolistes* among whom Valéry grew up and by whom he was greatly influenced, tried to assimilate poetry to music.

> What was baptized Symbolism can be very simply described as the common intention of several groups of poets (otherwise mutually inimical) to reclaim their own from Music—our literary minds dreamed of extracting from language the same effects as were produced upon our nervous systems by sound alone. Some cherished Wagner, others Schumann. I could as well say that they hated them. In the heart of passionate interest these two states are undistinguishable.

But language can never become pure sound and tonal relations without ceasing to be language; when we listen to someone speaking a tongue we do not know, we do indeed hear it as if it were music, but as a music without any artistic significance. It is unfortunate, too, for their argument, that these French poets made statements about music, for what they said about that art makes it clear that they valued music for its capacity to induce vague daydreams in the listener; in the structural side of music they showed no interest whatsoever.

Abandoning this theory, Valéry tried to make a division between the poetic and the prosaic based on an analogy between action with a practical purpose and play. The example which, following Malherbe, he uses as an illustration is the difference between walking and dancing.

> Walking, like prose, has a definite aim. It is an act directed at something we wish to reach. Actual circumstances, such as the need for some object, the state of my body, my sight, the terrain, etc., which order the manner of walking, prescribe its direction and speed. . . . There are no movements in walking which are not special adaptations, but, each time they are abolished and, as it were, absorbed by the accomplishment of the act, by the attainment of the goal.
>
> The dance is quite another matter. It is, of course, a system of actions; but of actions whose end is in themselves. It goes nowhere. It is therefore not a question of carrying out a limited operation whose end is situated somewhere in our surroundings, but rather of creating, maintaining and exalting a certain state, by a periodic movement that can be executed on the spot.

But is the distinction as sharp as Valéry says? A commuter may walk to the railroad station every morning, but at the same time he may enjoy the motion of walking for its own sake; the fact that his walk is necessary does not exclude the possibility of its also being a form of play. Conversely, the ritual play of dancing can be and frequently has been associated with practical ends, like securing a good harvest, without thereby ceasing to have artistic merit as a dance.

And the same is true of different modes of speech. If I call at the house of a sick peer to inquire after his health, and the butler tells me: "His Lordship is up but not down," the butler's intention may be merely the practical one of satisfying my curiosity by giving me correct information, yet I can and do relish his answer as poetry.

On the other hand, though there are certain lyrics the appeal of which lies almost entirely in their beautiful verbal play, most of the poetry we call great possesses a quality, call it vision, wisdom, what you will, which transcends the actual verbal expression. It is impossible to read a prose translation of *The Iliad* or *The Divine Comedy* without being made to feel that these are works of great value, although their "music" has been abolished.

Music, of course, has no such problem: the formal conventions of music are not, like those of verse, conventions applied *to* a language; they are more like the rules of syntax which are essential properties *of* a language. To change them, to shift, for example, from a horizontal polyphonic system of composition to a vertical harmonic system, or from a triadic to a twelve-tone, is like changing from Greek to English, or Hebrew to Russian.

The counterpart among composers to the quarrel between poets as to what use of language is and is not poetic, seems to be a quarrel over the question whether a certain musical language has or has not exhausted its possibilities. Here again, I think, every composer has to answer for himself and must beware of making a dogma out of his personal needs. Stravinsky has lately taken to a serial system of composition and is therefore quite properly in its favor, but when asked if he thinks the masterpieces of the next decade will be composed in serial technique, he is sensibly cautious.

> Nothing is likely about masterpieces, least of all whether there will be any. Nevertheless, a masterpiece is more likely to happen to the composer with the most highly developed language. This language is serial at present, and though our contemporary development of it could be tangential to an evolution we do not yet see, for us this doesn't matter. Developments in language are not easily abandoned, and the composer who fails to take account of them may lose the mainstream. Masterpieces aside, it seems to me that the new music will be serial.

Practicing artists, like Valéry and Stravinsky, usually prefer, when they speak of their art, to talk about technique and conscious judgment and to avoid words like *inspiration*. They know that to be inspired and to make a good work are one and the same thing; what they will not do is disclaim responsibility for what they offer to the public, or claim immunity from criticism on the grounds that messages from the Muses must be accepted on faith. They also know that technique is not, as the public is apt to believe, something that anyone can acquire, but is itself a gift of the Muses, and the one about which it is hardest for an artist to deceive others.

So Valéry says:

> The spirit blows where it will: one sees it blow on fools, and it whispers to them what they are able to hear.

And Stravinsky:

> Most artists are sincere anyway and most art is bad, though, of course, some insincere art (sincerely insincere) is quite good.

It is a pity that nobody, so far as I know, ever noted down Valéry's table talk for he, like Stravinsky, was not only an artist but also a man of the world who got around. As Stravinsky's Boswell, Mr Robert Craft has an excellent sense of the right questions to ask the maestro but he does not—perhaps deliberately—put down the answers with the accuracy of a tape recorder. The substance is obviously *correct*, but the cadences and sentence structure are not always those of a speaking voice. I also suspect that Mr Craft has at times played the tactful censor. Every genius, from time to time, talks nonsense— only minor artists are never foolish—and I suspect that Stravinsky's comments are not always as sensible as those we are permitted to hear. I would also welcome more catty remarks like the one on Pergolesi—

Pergolesi? *Pulcinella* is the only work of "his" I like.

or this one about the French—

They will do absolutely anything to get theatre tickets except buy them.

We are snobbish enough to enjoy anecdotes about famous people. How fascinating it is to learn that Diaghilev died singing Puccini, and how much more convincing than Cocteau is Stravinsky's account of the evening after the scandalous première of *Sacre du Printemps*.

I went with Diaghilev and Nijinsky to a restaurant. So far from weeping and reciting Pushkin in the Bois de Boulogne, Diaghilev's only comment was "Exactly what I wanted."

Such pleasures are of course minor compared with the privilege of hearing a great composer talk about the theoretical and practical problems of his art. And who except Stravinsky could say at the age of seventy-seven without sounding shy-making:

I don't mind my music going on trial for, if I'm to keep my position as a promising young composer, I must accept that.

Written late 1958 for *The Griffin*; published in
The Mid-Century, August 1959

The Co-Inherence

The Image of the City and Other Essays. By Charles Williams.
Selected by Anne Ridler. Oxford University Press. $6.

Perhaps one should warn readers unacquainted with Charles Williams that his *The Image of the City and Other Essays* is not about Town Planning. Williams uses the word *City* in its original sense, which the French *Cité* retains, of the human community in all its aspects, our family, political and economic life.

It is a collection, made by a friend and one-time pupil, of what are called, often unjustly, "fugitive" pieces, essays, reviews, editorial introductions which Williams would probably not have written if somebody hadn't asked him to or he had been blessed with a private income. But, as every writer knows, being given a subject to write on can often stimulate thought and imagination so that what at first seemed a purely hack job can turn out to be much more interesting than the writer anticipated.

Mrs Ridler has grouped them under six headings: Literary Subjects, The

Incarnation, The City, Pardon and Justice, Exchange and the Affirmative
Way, and On the Arthurian Myth, the last being concerned with Williams'
own cycle of poems on that subject. The literary essays are, perhaps, the
slightest, but there is something interesting to be found in all of them.
Though a very different kind of person with a very different prose style, as a
critic Charles Williams reminds me in more ways than one of Dr Johnson; he
has the same interest in those aspects of literature in which aesthetics and
morality are inseparable, his judgments show the same refreshing common
sense and, in his own way, he has the same gift for epigrammatic statement.

> Landor was himself [as his first biographer, Forster, remarked] apt
> when he had power to become tyrannical—with the highest motives.
> The motives of other tyrants did not seem nearly so high.

> They [religious dramatists] might, in fact, take up the business of defin-
> ing, with intense excitement, the nature, habits and mode of operation
> of Almighty Love, infusing into their excitement a proper scepticism as
> to its existence at all. It is not dogma that creates narrowness; it is the
> inability to ask an infinite number of questions about dogma.

Charles Williams was a prolific writer and tried his hand at nearly every
form—poetry, drama, fiction, history, essay—but it may be said that he had
only two themes, which are summed up in two of his favorite quotations, one
from Juliana of Norwich: "I saw full assuredly that our Substance is in God,
and also I saw that in our sensualitie God is"; the other from St Anthony of
Egypt: "Your life and your death are with your neighbor."
A devout and orthodox Anglican, he directed a lifelong polemic against
the heresy of Manichaeism into which, consciously or unconsciously, Christians who cannot or do not wish to take the other "natural" alternative, atheistic humanism, always have been and always will be tempted to fall.
For to think of spirit and matter as irreconcilably hostile, to attribute the
evil we do and suffer to the weakness of matter, to think that a good God
could not have created matter (either it must be coeternal with Him and He
can only do the best He can with such rotten material, or it has been created
by an evil God), must, after all, seem to both our common sense and our
moral conscience alike very plausible. To begin with, our immediate consciousness of our own existence is dualistic; everyone feels that his or her *I* is
different from and very often at odds with his body and its demands. Further,
if God did not create the world, then the intolerable question is avoided:
"How can God be good when He permits such appalling evil and suffering,
including the suffering of the innocent?"
The orthodox Christian view is, of course, what Charles Williams says it is.

> Matter, certainly, is by definition the opposite of spirit. It is apparently as
> far the opposite of God (leaving will and morals out of the question) as

God chose to create. But it did not therefore become less significant of Him than that less technical opposite which is called spirit. We have, in fact, only lost proper comprehension of matter by an apostasy in spirit. Matter and "nature" have not, in themselves, sinned; what has sinned is spirit, if spirit and matter are to be regarded as divided. That they so easily can be is due perhaps to that lack of intellectual clarity produced by the Fall.

But it is one of Charles Williams' greatest virtues as an apologist that he never pretends that the orthodox view is easy to believe. . . . In fact, I think he would almost go so far as to say that, but for the Crucifixion, it would be *morally* impossible for us to believe either in the Incarnation or in the Divine origin of the world.

This then has seemed to me now for long perhaps the most flagrant significance of the Cross; it does enable us to use the word "justice" without shame—which otherwise we could not. God therefore becomes tolerable as well as credible. Our justice condemned the innocent, but the innocent it condemned was one who was fundamentally responsible for the existence of all injustice—its existence in the mere, but necessary, sense of time, which His will created and prolonged. . . . We can hardly be in a state of guilt toward something which is not in bearable relations with us. The Crucifixion, restoring these relations, restores very much more. It permits repentance because it enables us to mean something by sin. Without that act, the infliction on us of something terribly like injustice would have made nonsense of any injustice on our side.

Williams would also argue, I think, that the fact that Christ suffered in the flesh as we do, is the proof that the joys of the flesh have a validity of their own and that the soul ought not to be allowed, far less encouraged, "to reduce the body to its own shadow."

This enables him to be equally understanding of that other kind of heretic who, like D. H. Lawrence, would exalt the flesh and the unconscious at the expense of conscious spirit. A vocabulary of four-letter words may be inadequate but no more so than a vocabulary of uplift words. In an essay on Wordsworth's lines, "the human form / To me became an index of delight," Williams, in a way that Lawrence, surely, would have appreciated, points out that it is not only what we are pleased to call the "noble" members of the body which figure in that index.

So even with those poor despised things, the buttocks. There is no seated figure, no image of any seated figure, which does not rely on them for its strength and balance. They are at the bottom of the sober dignity of judges; the grace of a throned woman; the hierarchical session of the Pope himself reposes on them.

As in the relations of the individual to himself, so in the City, in his relations with others, the co-inherence of sensuality and substance is a given fact, not a matter of choice. To be embodied is to be dependent upon others and to have others dependent upon oneself, willy-nilly. If the choice were ours, we should no doubt co-inhere only with those we like or rather with the pleasing images we make of our friends and lovers and so often mistake for their real selves. In her notebooks, Simone Weil defines love as "The belief in the existence of other human beings." Nothing is harder. If we love another very much, we may allow him or her some right to say "I," but never quite as much right as we assume for ourselves, and when it comes to those who, justly or unjustly, we feel to be our enemies, to admit their equal reality is outrageous. Yet the Infamy with which the City cannot compromise is born precisely in the thought that we can choose by whom we shall be nourished.

> There is but one dichotomy: that between those who acknowledge that they live from the life of others, including their "enemies," and those who do not. It is in this sense, that we must "forgive" our enemies. And the moment the dichotomy is admitted, it immediately becomes a temptation. Whoever does not admit it is regarded as an "enemy" and we deny that we can possibly live and be nourished by *him*. *He* at least is alien? No. Terrible humility! We derive from those we denounce; "though they slay me, yet will I trust in them."

And, whenever we start thinking about forgiveness or unselfishness or tolerance, there is the temptation, as Williams reiterates time and time again, that we shall think of the actions they imply only in the active voice. As he wrote in another book: "Many promising reconciliations have broken down because, while both parties came prepared to forgive, neither came prepared to be forgiven."

In a piece written in 1938, Williams says:

> It is comparatively easy to be kind; unfortunately kindness is not enough. Nothing is enough which leaves the lover in a condition of conscious superiority over—Hitler.

Twenty years later the proper names for our fear and disapproval have changed; our obligation has not.

To end this review on a lighter, though related, note, I cannot resist requoting a remark by Charles Williams which Mrs Ridler quotes in her excellent introduction. Talking of the "quiet affection" between man and wife which is supposed to replace their first romantic rapture, he said: "It isn't affection and it is not at all quiet, but the description has to serve."

National Review, 31 January 1959

The Greek Self

The Discovery of the Mind. By Bruno Snell. Translated by
T. G. Rosenmeyer. Harvard University Press. $5.50.

A few years ago I was invited to attend a series of seminars on a very German
topic:—"Was ist der Mensch?" I accepted with some trepidation at the prospect of being surrounded for a week by German Professors. The German
Professor has a high reputation, generally deserved, for industry and accurate scholarship, but also a less enviable reputation for being a prima donna
without humor or common sense. As it turned out, I was very glad that I
went; prima donnas there were in plenty, but there was also Professor Bruno
Snell, who is as good company as he is a good scholar, and someone for
whom, as this book clearly demonstrates, erudition is not an end in itself but
a road towards the Palace of Wisdom.

The Discovery of the Mind is a collection of papers, written between 1929 and
1947, and is concerned with two inter-related questions. Firstly, "What did
the Greeks at any time know about themselves, and what did they not (or not
yet) know?" Secondly, "By what steps did the Greeks, in their conception of
the natural world, make the transition from a mythological conception, in
which the causes of all events are analogous to human motivation, to a logical and scientific conception, in which events happen of themselves according to universal laws?"

The questions are inter-related because as a man learns what his unique
self is, he simultaneously begins to recognize what is not a self, the abstract
and universal.

Professor Snell is a philologist. I am always puzzled when students who
claim to be interested in literature are bored by philology. What, for a would-
be writer in particular, could be a more fascinating discipline than the study
of a language as language, the history of its vocabulary and the peculiarities
of its syntax?

Reading Professor Snell's account of Homeric Greek, for example, is of
the greatest interest to any twentieth century poet. His first thought, I fancy,
will be: "How much easier it must have been to write poetry in Homer's time
than in mine. Then the language itself was so poetic that it was difficult to
write anything in it that was not poetry."

One possible definition of poetry is the art of giving Proper Names to experience; that is why poetry is, strictly speaking, untranslatable from one
language into another. A modern poet achieves his end by a personal manipulation of his language so that, the elements of experience which the
language itself separates and generalizes are re-united and made concrete.
But in Homeric Greek, as in all so-called "primitive" tongues, the words for

thoughts, feelings and actions are much nearer to what we call Proper than to what we call Common or Abstract.

Homer, Professor Snell tells us, has no verb meaning simply "to see," but it has many verbs for specific ways of seeing. Thus, *derkesthai* means "to have a particular look in one's eyes, to look with a specific expression." The snake is called *drakon*, the seeing one, not because his sight functions particularly well, but because his stare commands attention. Of the eagle it may be said that *oxutaton derktai*—he looks very sharply. But whereas in English the adjective would characterize the function and capacity of seeing, Homer has in mind the beams of the eagle's eye which are as penetrating as the rays of the sun. *Paptainein* denotes another mode of looking, namely, a looking about carefully, inquisitively, or with fear.

Neither of these two verbs are found in the First Person. A man would notice such attitudes in others rather than ascribe them to himself.

But the verb *leusso* behaves quite differently. Etymologically related to *leukos*, "gleaming," "white," it means—to see something bright. Feelings of joy and freedom are implied. *Leusso* frequently is found in the first person but never in situations of care or anxiety.

The Verbal Metaphor

Professor Snell approaches his theme of the transition from myth to logic through a study of the development of Greek metaphor and simile.

Metaphors and similes are based upon either adjectives or verbs: those which appear substantival in form always imply one or the other, e.g. the *foot* of the lamp, implies the verb *to support*, the *head* of the nail implies the adjective *round* or *at the top of*.

As one might expect in an epic poet, narrating an action, the typical Homeric simile is verbal, and has the form:

As an *a* behaves so behaved *N*

where *a* is one example of many of its kind, very often a non-human creature or thing, and its behavior a frequent occurrence, while *N* is the proper name of a hero or a god and his action a unique historical event.

For example:

As a huntsman sets dogs on a wild boar, so Hector set the Trojans on the Achaeans.

or

As a rock endures the storm, so the warriors endured Hector's attack.

The function of such similes is to convey the intensity and reality of the action, to make Homer's audience "see" it. For the future of mental development, the simile has two important characteristics. A specific unique event is compared to a recurrent more general event, a distinction which contains in embryo the logical distinction between the particular and the universal. Secondly, the simile would be meaningless, if it were not reversible, if a hunting dog did not suggest a brave warrior or a rock in a storm the notion of human endurance. As Professor Snell says:

> Human behavior is only made clear through reference to something else which in turn is explained by analogy with human behavior. Man must listen to an echo of himself before he may hear or know himself.

Once the habit of comparison is formed, it is possible to move from the poetic comparison in which *like* means similar in some respects to the scientific comparison in which it means identically the same. Wishing to explain the structure of the eye, Empedocles says that, as the horn windows of a lantern keep out the wind but let out the light because the light is subtle enough to pass through the pores of the windows, so, for the same reason, the pupil of the eye keeps in the water but lets out the fire (of seeing). Epic description has become scientific illustration.

The Moral Paradigm

This is found in the Homeric speeches and takes the form:

As N^1 behaved, so N^2 should/should not behave

where N^1 is a mythical personage or distant ancestor and N^2 a living man, whose situation is analogous. Thus: Meleager was angry once as Achilles is now; his wrath brought misfortune; therefore, Achilles should not imitate Meleager but curb his anger.

This again has possibilities for the future. It can lead, for example, to the paradigm of necessity, the form

As a always causes x^1, so n always causes x^2

where a is a natural impersonal cause and n a human morally responsible agent. Thus, Solon says: Lightning causes thunder; tyrants cause the destruction of their city. The novelty here is the assertion of a universal law. All N's are n: there can be no tyrant who does not destroy his city.

The Adjectival Metaphor

Rare in Homer but common in archaic Greek lyric, it takes the form

The p of N is equal to/greater than/less than the p of an a

where p is a specific attribute, say, whiteness, N human, say, the face of the beloved, and a is a member of a class of objects, say, eggs. An adjectival metaphor is essential when the property is a mixed one like color, taste, size, or any moral attribute, which objects and persons possess to a certain degree.

It occurs also in the more complicated form of the proportional metaphor—

in respect of p, N is to n as A to a

as when Sappho declares that Arignota shines among the Lydian ladies as the moon shines among the stars.

The immense importance of such qualitative comparisons for the future of thought is obvious; substitute quantitative comparisons, i.e. exact measurement, and the first principle of the scientific method appears.

The Parabolic Image

Fragment 55 of Heraclitus runs thus: Time is a child playing a game of draughts; the kingship is in the hands of a child.

Heraclitus defines a spiritual or non-sensory experience by comparison with a sensory one, but he leaves it to the reader to decide in what the likeness consists. Presumably, he means that there is no law, the discovery of which would enable man to predict the future. Unlike a Homeric simile which is self-evident, the statement is hypothetical; either the reader believes it or he disbelieves it.

The value of such images, true or false, is that they enable us to think indirectly about things of which we can have no direct cognition. It has only recently been realized that most scientific descriptions of the universe are more like images than like statements of objective fact.

The Discovery of the Self

Our notion of the body as a corporeal entity and the soul as an incorporeal entity, the distinctions we make between involuntary physical movements and sensations and the voluntary, morally responsible, life of the conscious mind, we have learned from the Greeks, but they did not always have them.

Homer, for example, Professor Snell tells us, could speak of the limbs, the joints, the frame, the skin that marks the limit or outline of the human figure, but had no word for the body as a whole. The Homeric soul is equally fragmented and its fragments are conceived of as if they were as distinct and specific as physical organs. By the time of Heraclitus, the word *psyche* has come to mean more or less what we mean by *soul*, but in Homer it means the force which keeps the human being alive and is closely associated with the act of breathing so that, when a man dies, his *psyche* leaves him by the mouth. In addition to his *psyche*, Homeric man possesses a *thymos*, the source of movement and emotional agitation and the seat of physical pleasure and pain, which resides in his limbs, and a *noos*, a word derived from *noien*—to see something in its true colors—which is the source of ideas and mental images.

Since he conceives of mental life in quasi-physical terms, Homer cannot say that two people are of the same mind any more that we could say they were of the same brain; nor can he grasp the uniqueness of every human being, for our physical organs are individual but not unique. Further, since he lacks the notion of the mind as a unified entity, he can only conceive of mental conflict as a conflict between separate entities; where we would say, "He was half-willing, half unwilling," Homer must say, "He was willing but his *thymos* was not."

Nor can he make our distinction between physical force or strength and psychical force or will-power; instead, he distinguishes between *sthenos*, which can mean both the muscular force of the body as a whole and the forceful sway of a ruler, *menos*, the offensive force in the limbs of a man eager to undertake a task, and *alke*, the defensive force which helps him ward off an enemy.

It is difficult to know where, exactly, Homer draws the line between those actions which a man does on his own and those which he does as the result of inspiration by a god, but it seems to correspond to our equally inexact distinction between normal and abnormal. When a man is surprised by a violent emotion or acts in a way which neither he nor others would have expected, Homer ascribes this to the intervention of a god. In consequence, the significant personal decision is unknown to Homer for, whenever the decision is a crucial one, a god is responsible.

The unique personal soul first appears in the lyric poetry of Ionia. When Sappho writes:

Some say an army of horsemen is the fairest thing on the black earth, others an army of footsoldiers, and others a navy of ships—but I say the fairest is one I love.

she not only recognizes clearly what Homer is only vaguely aware of, that different individuals have different values, but also distinguishes between the conventional and the genuine; she knows what is *really* valuable for her, that, were everyone else to call her mad or wicked, she must never deny it. She does not yet conceive of love as arising out of herself and still, like Homer, calls it a visitation from Aphrodite, but she writes of something which Homer does not mention, an unhappy love.

The primary desire may be the Goddess' but when, because the beloved either is absent or loves another, this desire is thwarted, the feeling of helplessness that ensues is her own. Though the feeling is painful, she values it, for to wish it away like a physical pain would be to deny the love which gives value to her existence. She speaks, therefore of "bitter-sweet Eros," a phrase which can only apply to a personal emotion, not to a physical sensation.

The lyric poets were concerned with personal feeling: the discovery of personal action was undertaken by the Greek Tragic Dramatists. The action of a Greek Tragic Hero is his own deed, for which he, not any god, is accountable. He finds himself in a situation in which he is compelled to choose how he will act, and his choice has serious consequences. What, from our modern point of view, is peculiar and archaic about Greek Tragedy, is that the choice is not apparent to the hero himself, only to others. It is impossible to imagine Orestes, Oedipus, Antigone or Hippolytus acting in any other way than they do.

Other characters may advise him to think twice or act differently, but the hero himself has no doubts. The situation as perceived by the audience is one of conflict, but the hero does not see it as such; for him there is only action to take. Euripides, perhaps, recognizes the experiences of temptation and moral conflict within the self. He was the first dramatist to employ the soliloquy, the monologue in which a character does not address others but debates with himself, and he allows Medea to say that one can be aware that an action is wrong and yet do it. Socrates certainly recognizes them, but he makes ignorance responsible. Once, he argues, a man really knows what The Good is, then he can no more refuse its authority and act wrongly than he can refuse assent to logical and mathematical truths. It was, perhaps, inevitable, that, once they had succeeded in distinguishing between the soul and the body, the Greeks should have come to regard them, not as complementary aspects of human existence, but as hostile opposites, to hold the body responsible for whatever is evil in human feeling and behavior, and to think of goodness as a property of the intellect not the will.

That the Greek philosophers, of all people, should have come to this conclusion makes it look as if dualism was a necessary stage in the evolution of human thought, for by culture and temperament the Greeks attached the highest value to physical beauty, athletic prowess and the most this-worldly of all activities, politics.

Art and Science

It has been said that primitive people, like children, are poets, with the implication, of course, that poetry is childish and that maturity must put it away and become a scientist. It would, however, be equally true to say that primitive people and children do not yet know what poetry is. They sing, they dance, they tell stories, they make images, but their primary purpose in so doing is not to enjoy what we call an aesthetic experience but to survive, to make the crops grow, to secure divine favor and ward off divine malignancy, to transmit from one generation to the next the necessary beliefs, social duties and practical techniques.

Homer is, of course, long past this primitive stage; he is consciously making a work of art that shall endure because it is beautiful, not performing a magical rite, but it is of the first importance to him that the story he tells is, he believes, a true story, that the characters in his poem were historical personages and that the events he describes really happened. To Homer the Muses are, in the most literal sense, the daughters of memory; to imagine means to recall. The recognition that the "truth" which art can reveal about human existence can be conveyed quite as well (or better) by "made-up" characters and events, feigned history, as by historical fact, that artistic reality can be fiction, was a discovery of the Greek dramatists. In making it, they owed much to the Pre-Socratic philosophers whose contemplation of nature had led them to question the validity of the mythical cosmology as an explanation of physical events, and to doubt the historical accuracy of some of the statements made by the old poets. Once poetry was seen to have characteristics which distinguish it from theology or philosophy or science, it was inevitable to ask what its precise function and value was. Some two thousand years have passed since Greek culture was merged with Roman and ceased to be a separate entity, yet no one has produced a theory of art which is more than an elaboration of a theory already proposed by some Greek, moreover, so far as poetry is concerned—music is another matter—I do not think that there has been any written since, so different that a poet like Callimachus, who was acquainted with the whole corpus of Greek poetry, would be completely bewildered by it; confronted with a poem, for example, by Rimbaud or Mallarmé (assuming, of course, that his shade had learned French in the meantime), he might approve or disapprove, but he would understand what they were up to.

Readers concerned with modern poetry will find Professor Snell's two final chapters on Callimachus and Vergil's Arcadia of particular interest because the conditions with which these poets had to cope were in many respects similar to our own. The cheap printed book has made even the least intellectual modern poet a literary scholar by comparison with his predecessors. Whether he like it or not, he cannot help being aware, when he writes, of what other writers in the past have written; he cannot separate the question "What do I want to write?" from the question "What can and needs to be written because no one has yet done it?" Even if he, personally, has strong religious or political convictions, he lives in a social climate of scepticism which makes naive belief impossible; he cannot close his imagination to the possibility of believing something else. Callimachus was the first "high-brow" poet who wrote to be read and judged by the few who could appreciate recondite literary references and subtleties of technique. "Judge my poetry," he writes, "by its art not by the Persian cubit." He was the first to disclaim any serious moral purpose for poetry, to call it "childish play," the first to assert, as Poe did later, the aesthetic superiority of the short poem—"A sacrificial victim should be fat, but a poem slender"—and the first to assign great value to originality—Apollo, he says, had warned him at the beginning of his career not to take the broad, much-travelled roads, but to hew out his own path, however narrow.

Dry, ironic comment on the world and one's own self can be found here and there in earlier Greek poets, but Callimachus is the first in whom irony is the dominant characteristic. He is the ancestor, as Professor Snell points out, of such varied works as Ariosto's *Orlando Furioso*, Pope's *Rape of the Lock*, Wieland's verse tales, and Byron's *Don Juan*.

Vergil's kinship to ourselves is of another kind. I cannot think of a single modern poet who is not "against" the age in which he lives. He may find happiness in his personal life or in his contemplation of nature, but public life, what he reads about in the newspapers or sees when he walks down the street, fills him with disgust and foreboding; the only literary treatment it merits is blasphemy and invective. It would seem from Vergil's poetry, even the *Aeneid*, that he felt likewise. His *Eclogues* are the first poems in which a purely imaginary dream world is created as a refuge from the harsh realities of this one. To condemn them as "escapist" is unjust: there is a kind of writing which is pernicious because it pretends to be describing the real world when in fact it is not, so that the credulous reader acquires a false picture of life, but the *Eclogues* make no such pretence. No reader believes for a moment that Arcadia has existed or ever could. Artificial as they are, Vergil's model, the *Idylls* of Theocritus, are social comedies; the landscape and the action are recognizably those of Sicilian shepherds, and the diction is recognizably a parody of the speech of urban Greek literary intellectuals. But in Arcadia the landscape has no geographical location and the figures in it no social position; Vergil's shepherds are poets and nothing else; they only exist as the states of tender and nostalgic feelings which they express. Descriptions of the Earthly Paradise occur before Vergil, but it is conceived as what the actual world would be like if death, suffering and care were banished from it, a jolly place where all human desires are satisfied. Vergil's Arcadia is inhabited by only one kind of person, the sensitive and rather melancholic lover: no one ever laughs there or gets tipsy. Vergil was the begetter of two notions with which we are now very familiar, the conception of the poet as a weaver of dreams and as a superior being.

> . . . in his portrait of Gallus in the tenth eclogue he gives us a general idea of his views on the special function of the poet. The reasons, he hints, why the poet takes his stand among the gods, and why he receives the sympathy of nature, is because his feelings are more profound than those of other men, and because, therefore, he suffers more grievously under the cruelties of the world.

For several centuries after the fall of the Roman Empire, Greek culture was unknown to the West except through the Latin culture it had permeated. When the humanists of the Renaissance made contact with its literature at first hand, their admiration led them to believe that, by imitation, they could turn themselves into Greeks. This belief was fantastic, but the intense study of a past culture which it inspired initiated a new process of intellectual discovery. It is not really his technology which distinguishes "modern" man from his predecessors, but his historical consciousness. The discovery of the mind by itself is discovery in a unique sense. To discover something normally means to become aware or to understand the nature of something which was already there waiting to be discovered, but the discovery of the intellect is an act of creation: "The self does not come into being except through our comprehension of it." The most significant intellectual advance of the last two hundred years has been the discovery that by reliving the stages through which we have come to be what we are, we change what we are.

The Discovery of the Mind has a historical significance aside from its contents. Professor Snell was a professor at Hamburg University throughout the Hitler years. He survived, but only just. There are passages in these essays which take on a special meaning when one notices the date and place of their first publication. Here, for example, is one written for a German learned journal in 1937: its ostensible topic is Schlegel's attack on Euripides as a decadent writer.

> The whole romantic age was oppressed with the notion that thinking blocks the current of life, that man is cut off from the happiness of a naive existence by an undue vigilance of the mind. . . . Some think that the wound can only be cured by the weapon that has struck it, by knowledge itself. . . . Others who feel that their productivity is thwarted by their knowledge allow themselves to conceive a violent hatred of the intellect, of enlightenment and non-conformism.

The Griffin, February 1959

Calm Even in the Catastrophe

The Complete Letters of Vincent van Gogh. Thames & Hudson.
3 vols. 15 guineas.

The publishers, printers, translators, editors, and everyone else responsible for *The Complete Letters of Vincent van Gogh* are to be congratulated upon as beautiful a book as has appeared for some time. But when so much trouble and money have been spent to secure perfection in every detail, I find it extraordinary that two obvious needs of the reader should have been overlooked. A collection of letters is not like a novel which can only be read chapter by chapter from the beginning to end; it is more like an anthology of lyrics to which one returns now for this poem and now for that. On opening it at any page, therefore, the reader wants to know the date and place of the letter before him, but in this edition he is left ignorant. Then—this seems to be a universal oversight of editors—when a book is published in three heavy volumes, nothing is more annoying and time-wasting than to find, when one wishes to look up a particular reference, that the only index is at the end of the last volume. Surely, in an undertaking as luxurious as this, to provide an index to each volume would have added very little to the cost and contributed enormously to the reader's comfort.

The greater part of the collection is taken up, of course, with Van Gogh's letters to his brother between 1872, when Vincent was nineteen and Theo fifteen, and 1890, when he died. The editors have very sensibly interspersed this correspondence with personal reminiscences of Van Gogh by people who knew him in the various places from which he was writing.

The Theo letters are followed by letters to Amice Rappard, a few to his youngest sister Wilhelmina, a batch to the poet-painter Emile Bernard, and, at the end, come the few letters of Theo to Vincent which have survived.

The great masters of letter-writing as an art have probably been more concerned with entertaining their friends than disclosing their innermost thoughts and feelings; their epistolary style is characterised by speed, high spirits, wit, and fantasy. Van Gogh's letters are not art in this sense, but human documents; what makes them great letters is the absolute self-honesty and nobility of the writer.

The nineteenth century created the myth of the Artist as Hero, the man who sacrifices his health and happiness to his art and in compensation claims exemption from all social responsibilities and norms of behaviour.

At first sight Van Gogh seems to fit the myth exactly. He dresses and lives like a tramp, he expects to be supported by others, he works at his painting like a fiend, he goes mad. Yet the more one reads these letters, the less like the myth he becomes.

He knows he is neurotic and difficult but he does not regard this as a sign of superiority, but as an illness like heart disease, and hopes that the great painters of the future will be as healthy as the Old Masters.

> But this painter who is to come—I can't imagine him living in little cafés, working away with a lot of false teeth, and going to the Zouaves' brothels, as I do.

He sees the age in which he is living as one of transition rather than fulfilment, and is extremely modest about his own achievements.

> Giotto and Cimabue, as well as Holbein and Van Dyck, lived in an obelical solidly-framed society, architecturally constructed, in which each individual was a stone and all the stones clung together, forming a monumental society. . . . But, you know, we are in the midst of downright *laisser-aller* and anarchy. We artists who love order and symmetry isolate ourselves and are working to define *only one thing*. . . . We *can* paint an atom of the chaos, a horse, a portrait, your grandmother, apples, a landscape. . . .
>
> We do not feel that we are dying, but we do feel the truth that we are of small account, and that we are paying a hard price to be a link in the chain of artists, in health, in youth, in liberty, none of which we enjoy,

any more than the cab-horse that hauls a coachful of people out to enjoy the spring.

Furthermore, though he never wavers in his belief that painting is his vocation, he does not claim that painters are superior to other folk.

It was Richepin who said somewhere,

L'amour de l'art fait perdre l'amour vrai.

I think that is terribly true, but on the other hand real love makes you disgusted with art. . . .

The rather superstitious ideas they have here about painting sometimes depress me more than I can tell you, because basically it is really fairly true that a painter as a man is too absorbed in what his eyes see, and is not sufficiently master of the rest of his life.

It is true that Van Gogh did not earn his living but was supported all his life by his brother who was by no means a rich man. But when one compares his attitude towards money with that of say, Wagner, or Baudelaire, how immeasurably more decent and self-respecting Van Gogh appears.

No artist ever asked less of a patron—a labourer's standard of living and enough over to buy paints and canvases. He even worries about his right to the paints and wonders whether he ought not to stick to the cheaper medium of drawing. When, occasionally, he gets angry with his brother, his complaint is not that Theo is stingy but that he is cold; it is more intimacy he craves for, not more cash.

. . . against my person, my manners, clothes, world, you, like so many others, seem to think it necessary to raise so many objections—weighty enough and at the same time obviously without redress—that they have caused our personal brotherly intercourse to wither and die off gradually in the course of the years.

This is the dark side of your character—I think you are mean in this respect—but the bright side is your reliability in money matters.

Ergo conclusion—I acknowledge being under an obligation to you with the greatest pleasure. Only—lacking relations with you, with Teersteg, and with whomever I knew in the past—I want *something else.* . . .

There are people, as you know, who support painters during the time when they do not yet earn anything. But how often doesn't it happen that it ends miserably, wretchedly for both parties, partly because the protector is annoyed about the money, which is or at least seems quite thrown away, whereas, on the other hand, the painter feels entitled to more confidence, more patience and interest than is given him? But in most cases the misunderstandings arise from carelessness on both sides.

Few painters read books and fewer can express in words what they are up to. Van Gogh is a notable exception: he read voraciously and with understanding, he had considerable literary talent of his own, and he loved to talk about what he was doing and why. If I understand the meaning of the word *literary* as a pejorative adjective when applied to painting, those who use it are asserting that the world of pictures and the world of phenomenal nature are totally distinct so that one must never be judged by reference to the other. To ask if a picture is "like" any natural object—it makes no difference whether one means a "photographic" or a platonically "real" likeness—or to ask if one "subject" for a picture is humanly more important than another, is irrelevant. The painter creates his own pictorial world and the value of a painting can only be assessed by comparison with other paintings. If that is indeed what critics mean, then Van Gogh must be classified as a literary painter. Like Millet, whom all his life he acknowledged as his master, and like some of his contemporary French novelists, Flaubert, the Goncourts, Zola, he believed that the truly human subject for art in his day was the life of the poor. Hence his quarrel with the art-schools.

> As far as I know there isn't a single academy where one learns to draw and paint a digger, a sower, a woman putting the kettle over the fire or a seamstress. But in every city of some importance there is an academy with a choice of models for historical, Arabic, Louis XV, in short, *all really* non-existent figures. . . . All academic figures are put together in the same way and, let's say, *on ne peut mieux*. Irreproachable, *faultless*. You will guess what I am driving at, they do not reveal anything new. I think that, however correctly academic a figure may be, it will be superfluous, though it were by Ingres himself, when it lacks the essential modern note, the intimate character, the real *action*. Perhaps you will ask: When will a figure not be superfluous? . . . When the digger digs, when the peasant is a peasant and the peasant woman a peasant woman. . . . I ask you, do you know a single digger, a single sower in the old Dutch school? Did they ever try to paint "a labourer"? Did Velasquez try it in his water-carrier or types from the people? No. The figures in the pictures of the old master do not *work*.

It was this same moral preference for the naturally real to the ideally beautiful which led him, during his brief stay at an art-school in Antwerp, when he was set to copy a cast of the Venus de Milo, to make alterations in her figure and roar at the shocked professor: "So you don't know what a young woman is like, God damn you! A woman must have hips and buttocks and a pelvis in which she can hold a child."

Where he differs from most of his French contemporaries is that he never shared their belief that the artist should suppress his own emotions and view his material with clinical detachment. On the contrary, he writes:

. . . whoever wants to do figures must first have what is printed on the Christmas number of *Punch*: "Good Will to all"—and this to a high degree. One must have a warm sympathy with human beings, and go on having it, or the drawings will remain cold and insipid. I consider it very necessary for us to watch ourselves and to take care that we do not become disenchanted in this respect.

and how opposed to any doctrine of "pure" art is this remark written only two months before his death.

Instead of grandiose exhibitions, it would have been better to address oneself to the people and work so that each could have in his home some pictures or reproductions which would be lessons, like the work of Millet.

Here he sounds like Tolstoy, just as he sounds like Dostoievsky when he says:

It always strikes me, and it is very peculiar, that whenever we see the image of indescribable and unutterable desolation—of loneliness, poverty and misery, the end and extreme of all things, the thought of God comes into one's mind.

When he talks of the poor, indeed, Van Gogh sounds more honest and natural than either Tolstoy or Dostoievsky. As a physical and intellectual human being Tolstoy was a king, a superior person; in addition he was a count, a socially superior person. However hard he tried, he could never think of a peasant as an equal; he could only, partly out of a sense of guilt at his own moral shortcomings, admire him as his superior. Dostoievsky was not an aristocrat and he was ugly, but it was with the criminal poor rather than the poor as such that he felt in sympathy. But Van Gogh preferred the life and company of the poor, not in theory but in fact. Tolstoy and Dostoievsky were, as writers, successful in their lifetime with the educated; what the peasants thought of them as men we do not know. Van Gogh was not recognised as an artist in his lifetime; on the other hand, we have records of the personal impression he made upon the coal-miners of the Borinage.

People still talk of the miner whom he went to see after the accident in the Marcasse mine. The man was a habitual drinker, "an unbeliever and blasphemer," according to the people who told me the story. When Vincent entered his house to help and comfort him, he was received with a volley of abuse. He was called especially a *mâcheux d'capelets* (rosary chewer) as if he had been a Roman Catholic priest. But Van Gogh's evangelical tenderness converted the man. . . . People still tell how, at the time of the *tirage au sort*, the drawing of lots for conscription, women begged the holy man to show them a passage in the Holy Scripture which would serve as a talisman for their sons and ensure their drawing a good number and being exempted from service in the barracks. . . . A strike broke out; the mutinous miners would no longer listen to anyone except "*l'pasteur Vincent*" whom they trusted.

Both as a man and as a painter Van Gogh was passionately Christian in feeling though, no doubt, a bit heterodox in doctrine. "Resignation," he declared, "is only for those who *can* be resigned, and religious belief is for those who *can* believe. My friends, let us love what we love. The man who damn well refuses to love what he loves dooms himself." Perhaps the best label for him as a painter would be Religious Realist. A realist because he attached supreme importance to the incessant study of nature and never composed pictures "out of his head"; religious because he regarded nature as the sacramental visible sign of a spiritual grace which it was his aim as a painter to reveal to others. "I want," he said once, "to paint men and women with that something of the eternal which the halo used to symbolise, and which we seek to convey by the actual radiance and vibration of our colouring." He is the first painter, so far as I know, to have consciously attempted to produce a painting which should be religious and yet contain no traditional religious iconography, something which one might call "A Parable for the Eye."

Here is a description of a canvas which is in front of me at the moment. A view of the park of the asylum where I am staying; on the right a grey terrace and a side wall of a house. Some deflowered rose bushes, on the left a stretch of the park—red ochre—the soil scorched by the sun, covered with fallen pine needles. This edge of the park is planted with large pine trees, whose trunks and branches are red-ochre, the foliage green gloomed over by an admixture of black. These high trees stand out against the evening sky with violet stripes on a yellow ground, which higher up turns into pink, into green. A wall—also red-ochre—shuts off the view, and is topped only by a violet and yellow-ochre hill. Now the nearest tree is an enormous trunk, struck by lightning and sawed off. But one side branch shoots up very high and lets fall an avalanche of dark green pine needles. This sombre giant—like a defeated proud man—contrasts, when considered in the nature of a living creature, with the pale smile of a last rose on the fading bush in front of him. Underneath the trees, empty stone benches, sullen box trees; the sky is mirrored—yellow—in a puddle left by the rain. A sunbeam, the last ray of daylight, raises the sombre ochre almost to orange. Here and there small black figures wander among the tree trunks.

You will realise that this combination of red-ochre, of green gloomed over by grey, the black streaks surrounding the contours, produces something of the sensation of anguish, called "rouge-noir," from which certain of my companions in misfortune frequently suffer. Moreover, the motif of the great tree struck by lightning, the sickly green-pink smile of the last flower of autumn serve to confirm this impression.

I am telling you (about this canvas) to remind you that one can try to give an impression of anguish without aiming straight at the historic Garden of Gethsemane.

Evidently, what Van Gogh is trying to do is to substitute for a historic iconography, which has to be learned before it can be recognised, an iconography of colour and form relations which reveals itself instantaneously to the senses, and is therefore impossible to misinterpret. The possibility of such an iconography depends upon whether or not colour-form relations and their impact upon the human mind are governed by universal laws. Van Gogh certainly believed that they were and that, by study, any painter could discover these laws.

The *laws* of the colours are unutterably beautiful, just because they are not *accidental.* In the same way that people nowadays no longer believe in a God who capriciously and despotically flies from one thing to another, but begin to feel more respect and admiration for faith in nature—in the same way, and for the same reasons, I think that in art, the old-fashioned idea of innate genius, inspiration, etc., I do not say must be put aside, but thoroughly reconsidered, verified—and greatly modified.

In another letter he gives Fatality as another name for God, and defines Him by the image—"Who is the White Ray of Light, He in Whose eyes even the Black Ray will have no plausible meaning."

Van Gogh had very little fun, he never knew the satisfactions of good food, glory, or the love of women, and he ended in the bin, but, after reading his correspondence, it is impossible to think of him as the romantic *artiste maudit,* or even as tragic hero; in spite of everything, the final impression is one of triumph. In his last letter to Theo, found on him after his death, he says, with a grateful satisfaction in which there is no trace of vanity:

I tell you again that I shall always consider you to be something more than a simple dealer in Corots, that through my mediation you have your part in the actual production of some canvases, which will retain their calm even in the catastrophe.

What we mean when we speak of a work of art as "great" has, surely, never been better defined than by the concluding relative clause.

Encounter, April 1959; *The Mid-Century,* September 1959

John Betjeman's Poetic Universe

Collected Poems. By John Betjeman. Compiled with an introduction
by the Earl of Birkenhead. Houghton Mifflin. $4.

The Golden Treasury of John Betjeman. Spoken Arts. $5.95.

Thirty-three years ago, when undergraduates wore double-breasted waist-coats and flannel trousers that flapped around their ankles like skirts and—believe it or not—could give extravagant luncheon parties in their rooms lasting till five o'clock, I first met John Betjeman, and the mixture of admiration and envy he aroused in me then has never altered. I felt exactly the same last year when he asked me to meet him at the buffet in Marylebone Station, "the only railway terminus in London", as he informed me, "where you can hear birds singing." (It was true. You could.)

For most young men, particularly if they are intellectual and ambitious, the years between eighteen and twenty-one are, subjectively, rather awful. One has become aware of such questions as "Who am I? What do I like and dislike? What manners of conversation and behavior, eccentric or conventional, are proper to me?" But one cannot answer them. So one alternates between gaucheness and affectation.

But occasionally one runs across the exception. John Betjeman stood out among his fellow freshmen in the mid-nineteen-twenties as Max Beerbohm seems to have done among those of the eighteen-eighties; he was the extraordinary phenomenon, the boy who, because he knows exactly who he is, is already mature.

In a little essay on "Topographical Verse," written in 1945, he states his tastes in poetry; they were already his taste in 1925.

> I find hardly any pleasure in the Elizabethans, less in the seventeenth century (but this may be due to an excessive reverence for those ages from unsympathetic "tutors") and almost the only early poet I can enjoy is Chaucer. In the eighteenth century Dr Watts, Swift, Robert Lloyd, Thomson, Dyer, Shenstone, Mickle, Cowper and Burns are easily among my favorites, not for their finer flights, but for their topographical atmosphere. In the nineteenth century Crabbe, Praed, Hood, Clare, Ebenezer Eliot, Capt. Kennish, Neale, Tennyson, Charles Tennyson Turner, Clough, William Barnes, Meredith, William Morris and a score or so more. I find great pleasure in what is termed minor poetry, in long epics which never get into anthologies; topographical descriptions in verse published locally at Plymouth, Barnstaple, Ipswich or Northampton, Mullingar, Cork, Dublin, Galway.

As one could guess from such a list, his poetry has very little in common with what is generally thought of as "Modern Poetry", the ancestors of which are the English metaphysicals and the French *symbolistes*. (I do not know if Mr Betjeman has ever read any poetry written in a foreign tongue, but I should doubt it.) There is complexity of feeling in his verse, but no ambiguity of image or metaphor; he has an exceptionally sensitive ear and great metrical virtuosity, but he has never felt the slightest need or desire to write free verse or experiment with unconventional prosodies.

At the same time, let me hasten to add that he has never been a prig who makes a dogma out of his personal taste and talent. Now that he has had such a tremendous success in England, his name will undoubtedly be taken in vain as a stick with which to beat his "difficult" contemporaries. Indeed, it already has been; as a life-long admirer, I hope Mr Betjeman regrets as much as I do, having himself described by the Earl of Birkenhead as

> one who has always stood aloof and alien among the modern poets upon many of whom the autumnal blight of obscurity seems finally to have settled.

Since I have struck a slightly sour note, let me make the few criticisms I have to make of Mr Betjeman's poetry straightaway so that I can get on as soon as possible to the more important and pleasant task of appreciation. From time to time, he tries his hand at satire, but in my opinion, whenever he does, he is unsuccessful. His failure as a satirist is to his credit as a human being. Mr Betjeman's universe is made up of a number of sacred objects, most of them dating from the Age of Gaslight and Steam Locomotives (as do my own) to which he is passionately devoted. Upon this universe, a number of profane objects, glass-and-steel architecture, progressive education, electronic industries, etc., keep imposing themselves from the present outside world. Naturally, he dislikes these intrusions upon his devotions, but he does not hate them; he only wishes they were not there. Hatred, like love, can only be felt for what is, to the hater, a sacred object and therefore demands the same concentration of attention as a sacred object which is loved. Mr Betjeman fails as a satirist because since they are to him merely profane, the objects of his satire do not fascinate him sufficiently. When he is writing about one of his loved sacred objects, suburban Surrey, for example, his eye for detail is unerring:

> Her father's euonymus shines as we walk,
> And swing past the summer-house, buried in talk,
> And cool the verandah that welcomes us in
> To the six-o'clock news and a lime-juice and gin.
>
> The scent of the conifers, sound of the bath,
> The view from my bedroom of moss-dappled path,
> As I struggle with double-end evening tie,
> For we dance at the Golf Club, my victor and I.

But when he would satirize Progressive Education, the particulars he mentions are commonplace generalities and even inaccurate. For example:

> The children have a motor-bus instead,
> And in a town eleven miles away
> We train them to be "Citizens of To-day."
> And many a cultivated hour they pass
> In a fine school with walls of vita-glass.
> Civics, eurhythmics, economics, Marx,
> How-to-respect-wild-life-in-National-Parks.

I will bet Mr Betjeman five pounds that he cannot find a high school in England where the pupils study either eurhythmics or *Das Kapital*.

There is one, only one, object in his world which is at once sacred and hated, but it is far too formidable to be satirizable; namely, Death, and it has been the inspiration for many of his best poems. I am glad to learn from his phonograph record that "Remorse" is one of his own favorites, as it is one of mine.

> The lungs draw in the air and rattle it out again;
>   The eyes revolve in their sockets and upwards stare;
> No more worry and waiting and troublesome doubt again—
>   She whom I loved and left is no longer there.
>
> The nurse puts down her knitting and walks across to her;
>   With quick professional eye she surveys the dead.
> Just one patient the less and little the loss to her,
>   Distantly tender she settles the shrunken head.
>
> Protestant claims and Catholic, the wrong and the right of them,
>   Unimportant they seem in the face of death—
> But my neglect and unkindness—to lose the sight of them
>   I would listen even again to that labouring breath.

Hardy is the only other English poet I know who can so employ triple rhymes in a serious poem with triumphant success. Equally moving and metrically interesting is his elegy on an Oxford don:

> Dr Ramsden cannot read *The Times* obituary to-day
> He's dead.
> Let monographs on silk worms by other people be
> Thrown away
> Unread
> For he who best could understand and criticise them, he
> Lies clay
> In bed . . .

> . . . They remember, as the coffin to its final obsequations
> Leaves the gates,
> Buzz of bees in window-boxes on their summer ministrations,
> Kitchen din,
> Cups and plates,
> And the getting of bump suppers for the long-dead generations
> Coming in,
> From Eights.

A great many of Mr Betjeman's poems are expressions of topophilia. As an emotion, topophilia differs both from the peasant's possessive passion for his home soil and the regional novelist's self-conscious limitation of attention to a chosen area; though he generally has some places which he adores above all others—in Mr Betjeman's case, Cornwall, East Anglia, and North London, because he spent his childhood in these places—the practised topophile can find objects to worship in a district he is visiting for the first time.

He is not, however, what is usually meant by a lover of nature; that is to say, wild nature lacking in human history has little charm for him, unless he is a geological topophile, fascinated by the history of the earth itself. Though he may often, like Mr Betjeman, know a lot about architecture, the genuine topophile can always be distinguished from an educated tourist or an art historian by the uniquely personal character of his predilections; a branch railroad can be as precious to him as a Roman Camp, a neo-Tudor tea-shop as interesting as a Gothic cathedral. As for Proper Names, whether of people or of things, he ignores completely that poetic convention, starting with Vergil, according to which certain names are "beautiful" and certain others are "ugly" or comic and therefore unusable in a serious poem; if he loves a person or thing he loves their actual name and would not change it.

Most readers of poetry are so under the spell of this convention that they may be tempted to think that Mr Betjeman is poking fun or being ironic when he is simply speaking the truth. A poem like Burns's "The Cottar's Saturday Night" seems serious poetry to them because the social life of the peasantry is unreal and romantically distant—most readers of poetry are middle class—but when they read "North Coast Recollections," in which Mr Betjeman describes English middle-class life in about 1922, they have difficulty in taking him seriously.

> Within the bungalow of Mrs Hanks
> Her daughter Phoebe now French-chalks the floor.
> Norman and Gordon in their dancing pumps
> Slide up and down, but can't make concrete smooth.
> "My Sweet Hortense . . ."
> Sings louder down the garden than the sea.
> "A practice record, Phoebe. Mummykins,

Gordon and I will do the washing up."
"We picnic here; we scrounge and help ourselves,"
Says Mrs Hanks, and visitors will smile
To see them all turn to it. Boys and girls
Weed in the sterile garden, mostly sand
And dead tomato plants and chicken-runs.
To-day they cleaned the dulled Benares ware
(Dulled by the sea-mist), early made the beds,
And Phoebe twirled the icing round the cake
And Gordon tinkered with the gramophone
While into an immense enamel jug
Norman poured "Eiffel Tower" for lemonade.

The odd thing about the reaction to lines like these of many people who call themselves lovers of poetry is that if Mr Betjeman had said the same things in a prose novel, they would have no difficulty in accepting them; it must be such people, whether as relatives or schoolteachers, who are responsible for the low esteem in which poetry is held by the average man.

I myself have some difficulty, I must confess, with a feminine figure who keeps turning up in Mr Betjeman's poems.

Pam, I adore you, Pam, you great big mountainous sports girl,
    Whizzing them over the net, full of the strength of five;
That Old Malvernian brother, you zephyr and khaki shorts girl,
    Although he's playing for Woking,
Can't stand up to your wonderful backhand drive.

Such a type of beauty is so remote from my personal critical taste that I find it hard to believe that there are men who admire it, and I get no help from conventional love poetry or fashion magazines. But I am as sure that the poets and fashion editors have concealed the attractions of this type as I am certain that it holds none for me, and that Mr Betjeman is not trying to be funny except insofar as, like all people who are capable of serious emotions, he knows that their objects can seem funny to others.

Mr Betjeman's poetic universe, verbally, architecturally, and ecclesiastically, is so British that when I first began introducing his poems to American friends, I was afraid that they might not be able to make head or tail of them. To my surprise and delight, even those who had never visited England in their lives seemed to "get" them quite easily. It proved to me that the human capacity to translate alien experience, provided it is genuinely and truthfully expressed, into its own terms is much greater than one sometimes fears.

In the Spoken Arts recording, Mr Betjeman reads fifteen of his poems and prefaces each of them with a few remarks explaining the background and genesis.

Among records of poets reading their own work, this is one of the best I have ever heard, and certainly *the* most enjoyable. Listeners to his comments will understand why Mr Betjeman has become a T.V. star in England, for he is a born performer. His choice of poems gives a just idea of his poetic range and styles, and his diction and tempi could not be bettered. Recording excellent.

P.S. I should like to complain that The Earl of Birkenhead, who compiled the collection of Mr Betjeman's poems in the book, has omitted several poems which I like very much, in particular, "South London Sketch, 1944." I have therefore asked The Mid-Century Book Society to secure the rights for the publication of the poem, and it appears on the next page.

The Mid-Century, July 1959

The Private Life of a Public Man

Mythologies. By W. B. Yeats. Macmillan. $5.

All myth-making is "anthropomorphic" in that it is based upon the notion of personal responsibility, which cannot be arrived at through observation of the outer world but only through introspection. It is a way of thinking which presupposes that all events are caused by the volition of some being, human or superhuman, so that any event could have been otherwise. Whenever the notion of Fate appears, even though conceived as a personal image, it is a sign that the mythological imagination has realized its limitations.

Roughly speaking, there are two kinds of myth: those which attempt to account for natural events and phenomena which are either unchanging or recurrent, and those that are legendary human history, that is to say, they give an account of human actions in the past which produced revolutionary cultural changes, and their intention is often propagandist—what the victor willed to do is translated into the will of the gods.

It makes little sense to ask if a myth be true or false; one should ask, rather, if it is alive, moribund, or dead, and the test, as a general rule, is whether or not the mythical story is associated with a cult, with ritual actions. A man can be said to believe in Aphrodite or Ares, for example, if, when he desires success in love or war, he performs specific acts of worship and sacrifice in their honor; if he does not, then his use of their names is metaphorical not mythical. Conversely, a cult is only alive so long as it is intimately associated with a myth. When, in certain parts of Ireland, the village boys hunt the wren on St Stephen's day, they are not practising a cult but obeying a traditional custom, for the myth which gave the hunt its meaning has been forgotten.

The Celtic Twilight, one of the seven books included in *Mythologies,* is a collection of anecdotes collected by Yeats while talking to the peasants of Western Ireland, and most of them are concerned with fairies or ghosts. The fairies, the Sidhe, the Untiring Ones, are not spirits, for they have human-like bodies and human appetites; but, unlike human beings they are immortal and know neither pain nor sorrow; morally, they must be classed with the innocent animals, for they are neither good like angels, evil like devils, nor subject to guilt and remorse like man.

Their lives impinge upon ours only occasionally. When a person disappears from his community, it is sometimes held that the fairies have kidnapped him, but the same description can be used when someone dies, particularly if he or she is young, gifted, or beautiful. The fairies are held responsible for mental deficiency but not, apparently, for madness. They can appear to people if they wish and give advice or they can remain invisible.

Judging from Yeats' accounts, his belief in the existence of fairies does not involve the Irish peasant in many ritual acts. The only one he mentions is in connection with a little girl who got lost one night, and it was rumored that the fairies had taken her:

> . . . the local constable instituted a house to house search, and at the same time, advised the people to burn all the *bucalauns* (ragweed) on the field she vanished from, because *bucalauns* are sacred to the fairies. They spent the night burning them, the constable repeating spells all the while.

Similarly, though most of the peasants believe in ghosts, believe, that is to say, that the souls of the dead can take up residence in particular places and can appear to the living in a human or animal shape, the peasants appear to do little to placate or exorcise them, and they have nothing remotely resembling a cult devoted to the dead. Indeed, one of the curious things about the Irish, in contrast, according to Yeats, with the Scotch, is that they have little fear of ghosts and take them for granted. A timid man may talk to himself in this way.

> By the Cross of Jesus! How shall I go? If I pass by the Hill of Dunboy old Captain Burney may look out on me. If I go round by the water, and up by the steps, there is the headless one and another at the quays, and a new one under the old churchyard wall. If I go right round the other way, Mrs Stewart is appearing at Hillside Gate, and the Devil himself is in the Hospital Lane.

But this is hardly the language of terror.

To call such beliefs mythologies seems to me misleading. Some anthropologists have described the peasant culture of Western Europe as if the peasants only pretended to be Christians and were secretly believers in some form or other of a fertility religion. But no one has the right to claim that he knows the peasants better than the peasants know themselves, and the latter are, most of them, quite convinced of their Christian orthodoxy. Whatever may have been the original myths and cults in which the relations of men to fairies and ghosts were elements in a coherent system of beliefs and practices, these have disappeared and what is left is fragmentary and inconsistent, or else has become cultural entertainment like the folk tale and folk song.

The circle of magicians with whom Yeats associated as a young man, and Yeats himself in his later esoteric poems and such prose works as *Per Amica Silentia Lunae* and *The Vision*, can properly be said to have their mythologies and their cults, because, for better or worse, they aim at consistency and completeness.

Speaking for myself, I must confess that I find most of Yeats' later writings about his beliefs hard to take. In *Anima Mundi*, for example, so long as he is telling anecdotes about himself and his friends, I am fascinated, even if I sometimes laugh at what he seems to intend to be taken seriously, but the moment he begins formulating his visionary system, I yawn, not because I find the sentences overwritten but because I cannot attach any meaning, true or false, to the words.

This may be a blind spot on my part but, for those readers who also suffer from it, I would say that they will thoroughly enjoy *The Celtic Twilight*, *Red Hanrahan* and most of *The Secret Rose* for their own sakes, but that they will value *Rosa Alchemica* and *Per Amica Silentia Lunae* mainly for the light they throw on Yeats himself and on a number of his poems.

The relation between folk culture and the sophisticated individual artist, writer, painter, or composer, who is attracted to it, is sad because the cultural benefit is one-sided. The sophisticated artist can find in folk art a stimulus to invention which is new and peculiar to himself, but the folk, anonymous and traditional, can learn nothing from him.

Thus Yeats could never have written his stories about Red Hanrahan if he had known no Irish folk tales. All the properties he employs, the card-playing magician, the Sidhe, the old mad crone, etc., are taken from them, but the purpose to which he puts these properties is one which no folk story teller could have conceived of. Yeats' tales are parables about the nature of the poet as a dedicated being whose vocation dooms him to isolation and the sacrifice of domestic happiness. The kind of poet he has in mind is no folk bard but a quite modern figure, the *poète maudit* of late romanticism, someone like Lionel Johnson or Ernest Dowson, of whom he writes elsewhere:

. . . no fine poet, no matter how disordered his life, has ever, even in his mere life, had pleasure for his end. Johnson and Dowson, friends of my youth, were dissipated men, the one a drunkard, the other a drunkard and mad about women, and yet they had the gravity of men who had found life out and were awakening from the dream; and both, one in life and art and one in art and less in life, had a continual preoccupation with religion.

Similarly, the poet who in "All Souls' Night" summons up by name the ghosts of his dead friends may owe something to the peasant for whom the dead are as real members of his village as the living. But it is quite impossible to imagine a peasant reading Yeats' poem with enjoyment, let alone understanding.

The life of any human being can be pictured as a series of concentric circles: At the center is the unique person, an *I* who has no ancestors and no descendants; surrounding this *I* are the experiences which he has in common with others because he and they live in the same place or time, or belong to the same cultural group, or simply because all are human. It is the unity in tension between the unique and the general that makes art possible; without the unique response to experience art would be utterly banal; without some generality of experience, art would be incomprehensible. One can imagine Yeats' work, for example, first as the work of an Irishman with a Protestant background, secondly as the work of someone writing in English who came of age in 1886, and lastly as the work of a certain Mr W. B. Yeats.

To the outsider, most Irishmen, both in the flesh and in their writings, seem to exhibit certain common characteristics—an extraordinary gift for vivid and musical speech, a greater concern for the charm, humor, beauty of what they say than for its truth, and a temperament to which hating comes easier than loving. Yeats called Ireland a place of "much hatred, little room," and said of himself, "I think the common condition of our life is hatred—I know that this is so with me—irritation with public or private events or persons." In reading him I frequently come upon statements of thought or feeling which seem to me untrue; if he were not Irish, this would not bother me because I should assume that he believed what he was saying or else was telling a deliberate lie but, as it is, I sometimes feel that the question "Is this statement true or false?" has never occurred to him, and this, I must admit, irritates me, however splendid his diction and rhythm.

On the Yeats whose literary milieu was that of the eighties and nineties, people of my generation must be extremely wary of passing judgment, for there is no other period of literary history which is more alien to our own; even the Victorians are much nearer to us. There are typical works of the period, like *The Importance of Being Earnest*, which we can greatly enjoy, but the only writers of the time whom we can understand as human beings are the very untypical figures of Rimbaud and Bernard Shaw. The eighties and nineties were the heyday of the rentier, the middle-class person living on the interest from capital accumulated by his father and grandfather. Unlike them, he no longer had to earn his living, but unlike the aristocracy, he had no responsibilities, either to his estates or to his social position. Many features of the art of the time, its aestheticism, its hatred of the general public, its interest in esoteric religions, seem to me to be characteristic of the rentier mentality.

A young writer might be, as Yeats was, without independent means, but the atmosphere by which he was surrounded was created by those whose cultivation of their sensibility was unhampered either by social convention or economic necessity.

We, on the other hand, live in an age in which the rentier is a rare social fossil and only the very rich can afford a servant. The mental atmosphere which surrounds us and affects all of us, even the most highbrow poet, is that of the wage earner. When an aesthete of the nineties spoke with contempt of the public, he had a clear image in his mind of how it looked, how it behaved, how it felt, but today the public has no specific traits, for these are changed by every change in fashion.

A writer can neither love nor hate the public; either he must be obsessed by it, as a speculator is obsessed by the stock market, or he must not think about it at all. It is significant, I think, that when we seek unusual experience, we do not take up the practice of magic, which requires a long discipline and, even then, may prove beyond our powers; we go to mescaline or marihuana, which produce their effects in any Tom, Dick, or Harry.

There remains that unusual and endlessly fascinating creature, Yeats himself. Unlike his fellow Irishmen, Shaw and Joyce, he was not conspicuously intelligent nor was he nearly so passionate, I think, as he liked to pretend; in all his love poems, whether "Petrarchan" like the earlier or "earthy" like the later, there is a good deal of purely literary passion. But, like both Shaw and Joyce, he was immensely ambitious, iron-willed, a tireless worker, as worldly, in a good sense, as any man is who has made up his mind to be successful in the line he has chosen.

Compared with most of his contemporary poets, his life as a young man was almost as chaste and sober as Milton's. What kind of poetry he would be writing by the time he was sixty, he cannot, of course, have known, but it is clear that, from the first, he promised himself a long poetic career, he would never be satisfied with repeating himself, and ever be on the lookout for people, ideas, events that would aid his development. And *how* he worked! To compare the first drafts of his poems with their final version is a salutary lesson for any young poet who believes inspiration means putting down whatever first comes into his head. In his official farewell poem, "Under Ben Bulben," he bequeaths this advice to future Irish poets:

> Sing the peasantry, and then
> Hard-riding country gentlemen,
> The holiness of monks, and after
> Porter-drinkers' randy laughter;
> Sing the lords and ladies gay

> That were beaten into clay
> Through seven heroic centuries . . .

So, indeed, Yeats began by singing, but the poems of his which we now most admire are about none of these; they are concerned with quite contemporary events, like the Irish Civil War, with his personal friends and, above all, with himself and the problems of being a poet. One is tempted to say that Yeats had to spend the first half of his life as a minor poet in order, in the second half, to write major poetry about his past as a minor poet. All the various interests of his lifetime—Celtic folklore, magic, women—were subordinate to his ambition to write great poetry. All that matters to us is that, in this ambition, he succeeded.

The Mid-Century, October 1959

Miss Marianne Moore, Bless Her!

O to Be a Dragon. By Marianne Moore. Viking. $2.75.

I once read a review of Miss Moore in a British magazine, where the reviewer objected to her "neglect of the sonorities of English poetry." If I understand him correctly, the critic meant that those who expect the diction, rhetorical style, and tone of poetry to be as far removed as possible from those of prose and conversation will be disappointed.

A stranger who enters a drawing room and hears someone saying such lines as

> Come, fix upon me that accusing eye.
> I thirst for accusation. All that was sung,
> All that was said in Ireland is a lie
> Bred out of the contagion of the throng,
> Saving the rhyme rats hear before they die . . .

will know at once that the speaker is either recalling or improvising a poem. But if, instead, the lines were to be

> Saint Nicholas,
>   might I, if you can find it, be given
> a chameleon with tail
> that curls like a watch spring; and vertical
> on the body—including the face—pale
>   tiger-stripes, about seven;
>   (the melanin in the skin
>   having been shaded from the sun by thin

bars; the spinal dome
beaded along the ridge
as if it were platinum. . . .

he might easily think at first that the speaker was merely talking, though, if he has any sensitivity to language, he would add, I think: "But what an extraordinary way to talk!"

Our stranger's first difficulty is, of course, prosodic. Yeats' lines, however personal his fingering, are written in what, since Spenser, has been the traditional prosody of English poetry, so that the ear immediately recognizes their formal structure. The syllabic verse employed by Miss Moore, which disregards accents and permits rhyming on unaccented syllables, is far harder to grasp at a first hearing. But there is a second, perhaps even greater, difficulty for those who are not well acquainted with Miss Moore's poetry. The Yeats can and should be almost chanted, with strong pauses at the ends of the lines, so that the difference between an elevated style of poetic speech and the norm of conversational speech is emphasized. The Moore cannot be read in this way; it must be uttered in a conversational tone with only the slightest line-end pauses. What distinguishes it from conversation is not so much rhythm or tone as the articulation of the thoughts expressed, the sequence of ideas, and it takes time and frequent re-reading to appreciate these as fully as they deserve. For what it is worth, I can only say that Miss Moore is one of the very few modern poets whom I can read on any day and in any mood.

There are few more pleasant ways of spending a wet afternoon than inventing categories by which to classify things or people. Some years ago, on a hint from Lewis Carroll, I began dividing human beings into Alices and Mabels. The best way to explain the difference is to give a few examples.

Alice	*Mabel*
Montaigne	Pascal
Marvell	Donne
Lovelace	Rochester
Jane Austen	Dickens
Turgenev	Dostoievsky
Colette	Gide
E. M. Forster	Joyce
De la Mare	Yeats
Webern	Berg
G. E. Moore	Heidegger

The difference, as these names show, is not in artistic merit, but in character. The Alices never make a fuss. Like all human beings they suffer, but they are stoics who do not weep or lose their temper or undress in public. Though they are generally people with strict moral standards, they are neither preachers nor reformers. They can be sharp, usually in an ironical manner, and tender, but the passionate outburst is not for them. As a general rule, also, while perfectly well aware of evil and ugliness in the world, they prefer to dwell on what is good and beautiful. Alices are always in danger of over-fastidiousness, as Mabels are of vulgarity.

One has only to read a page or two of Miss Moore to recognize that she is a pure Alice.

> . . . A thing yet more rare,
>   though, and different,
>   would be this: Hans von Marees'
>   St Hubert, kneeling with head bent,
>   form erect—in velvet, tense with restraint—
> hand hanging down: the horse, free.
> Not the original, of course. Give me
> a postcard of the scene . . .

> . . . The musk ox
>   has no musk and it is not an ox—
> illiterate epithet.
> Bury your nose in one when wet.

> It smells of water, nothing else,
> and browses goatlike on
>   hind legs. Its great distinction
> is not egocentric scent
> but that it is intelligent. . . .

The initial stimulus for many of Miss Moore's poems lies in her observation of some animal towards which she feels a sympathetic attraction. (The one exception, so far as I remember, is the cobra in "Snakes, Mongooses, Snake-Charmers and the Like," and even in that poem the point is that, though she feels fear and distaste, she knows that the cobra is a wonder of creation with a divine right to exist.) As an animal lover who feels that animals are worth beholding for their own sake, she does her best to make the reader see what she sees by the use of metaphorical comparisons. These may be drawn from other animals or from plants or from human artifacts or from human beings themselves. This procedure is the reverse of the Homeric animal simile which describes a particular human act in terms of the typical behavior of some species. But Miss Moore is a humanist as well as a naturalist. Sometimes, as in the medieval bestiaries, she sees an animal as a symbolic emblem: the devil-fish as an emblem of charity, the camel-sparrow as an emblem of justice, the jerboa rat as an emblem of true freedom, etc. And sometimes, as in animal fables, she presents the conduct of an animal, an elephant, for example, as a paradigm. In consequence, her poems are generally more subtle than they seem at first reading. It took me some time, for instance, to realize that "The Pangolin" is a war poem. The poem is full of praise and joyous wonder—the pangolin is a charming beast and it is a great honor to be created a human being—but behind this lies grief and pity. Men only resemble pangolins when they are wearing armor but this is precisely what should never happen. The pangolin's armor is a natural adaptation which secures his survival, since he is an ant-eater, but man only wears armor when he turns unnatural and starts fighting and slaying his own kind.

O to Be a Dragon contains fourteen new poems. A poet as idiosyncratic as Miss Moore is always in danger of becoming a prisoner of her established manner, so that one is particularly pleased to find in this book several poems in which she does things she has never done before. Who would have foreseen a day when Miss Moore would write ballads in couplet stanzas? Her new book contains two: one, "Hometown Piece for Messrs Alston and Reese," about the Dodgers, the other, "Enough," a historical ballad about Jamestown. The first, alas, remains opaque to me because, having been born in a land where cricket is the sacred game, words like *double-header* or *homer* are profane technical terms without emotional resonance. So, for a quotation to illustrate Miss Moore's handling of the couplet, I had better go to "Enough."

> Marriage, tobacco, and slavery
> initiated liberty
>
> when the Deliverance brought seed
> of that now controversial weed—
>
> a blameless plant Red-Ridinghood.
> Who, after all, knows what is good!
>
> A museum of the mind "presents";
> one can be stronger than events.
>
> The victims of a search for gold
> cast yellow soil into the hold.
>
> With nothing but the feeble tower
> to mark the site that did not flower,
>
> could the most ardent have been sure
> that they had done what would endure?
>
> It was enough; it is enough
> if present faith mend partial proof.

Those who believe as I do that what any poem says should be true and that, in our noisy, overcrowded age, a quiet and intimate poetic speech is the only genuine way of saying it, will find in *O to Be a Dragon* exactly what they are looking for.

The Mid-Century, Fall 1959

The Fallen City

Some Reflections on Shakespeare's Henry IV

[See "The Prince's Dog" in *The Dyer's Hand*, p. 580,
and textual notes, p. 960.]

Encounter, November 1959

Foreword: Brand *versus* Peer

Brand was written in 1865, when Ibsen was thirty-seven. Two years later he completed *Peer Gynt*. Speaking of the influence upon creation of place and atmosphere—both were written in Italy—Ibsen wrote: "May I not, like Christoff in *Jacob von Tyboe*, point to *Brand* and *Peer Gynt* and say: 'See, the wine cup has done this.'"

Both are dramatic poems written in rhymed verse and dominated by a single character; even Brand's wife, Agnes, seems to exist less for her own sake than for what she reveals about him.

That Ibsen should have created, one after the other, two such completely different heroes suggests an underground relation between them, as if each were the complement and critic of the other. (It is interesting to note that the incident of the peasant youth who cuts off his finger to avoid military service, which occurs in *Peer Gynt*, was originally intended for *Brand*.)

Every poet knows that a poem can turn out to be very different when he finishes it from what he thought it was going to be when he began it; it can also happen that he and his readers only realize what a poem really "says" years after its first appearance.

Both poems were written at a time when Ibsen was enraged with and ashamed of his countrymen for their refusal to go to the aid of Denmark when she was attacked by Prussia. When they first appeared, the critics took them to be polemical works. The Brand to whom Compromise is the Devil, and whose motto is "All or Nothing," seemed a portrait of the hero a Norwegian ought to be but was not; the Peer whose Devil is "a dangerous viper" who tempts man to do the "irretrievable" and defines daring as the art of keeping open a bridge to retreat by, seemed a satiric portrait of what a typical Norwegian was but should not be. It is conceivable that this had been Ibsen's conscious intention, but if it was, his Muse knew better.

In real life, moral approval or disapproval and personal liking or disliking are two different judgments; in art they are synonymous: the personally lovable stands for the good, the personally detestable for the bad. If the two poems were really polemical, then the reader would find Brand sympathetic and Peer unsympathetic, but I don't think he does. On the contrary, though Brand is a tragic figure whose courage one admires and whose fate one pities, it is impossible to like him, so that one feels that there is something profoundly wrong with him, even if one cannot understand what it is; Peer is a selfish scoundrel, yet it is impossible not to love him, so that one feels that, in some way or other, he is "in the truth."

I do not know if Ibsen ever read it, but there is an essay by Kierkegaard on the difference between a Genius and an Apostle which, to me, exactly defines the difference between Peer Gynt and Brand. Ibsen told Georg Brandes that he might just as well have made Brand a sculptor or a politician as a priest, but, had he done so, he would have written a completely different play, for the vocation of a priest—which, ideally conceived, is the vocation of an Apostle—is unique and of a totally different order from all other vocations. If the feelings which Brand arouses in the reader are ambivalent, one reason, I believe, is that a genuine Apostle resists direct poetic or dramatic manifestation; Ibsen was attempting the impossible.

In the case of any vocation of Genius, a man is called to it by a natural gift with which he is already endowed. A young man, for example, who tells his parents, "I am going to be a sculptor, cost what it may," bases his statement on the conviction that he has been born with a talent for making beautiful, three-dimensional objects. It makes no difference to his decision whether he is a Christian who believes that this talent is a gift of God or an atheist who attributes it to blind Nature or Chance, for, even if he is a believer, he knows that he is called by his gift, not by God directly. Since the gift is *his*, to say "I must" become a sculptor and "I want" to become one mean the same thing. He may sacrifice many things and other people for the sake of his calling, but such sacrifices are ultimately selfish, in that he suffers for the sake of what gives him the greatest satisfaction: it is impossible to imagine anyone's saying, "A sculptor is the last thing on earth I want to be, but I feel it is my duty to become one."

An Apostle, on the other hand, is called by God directly. Jehovah says to Abraham: "Go get thee up out of the land"; Christ says to Matthew, the tax-collector: "Follow me!" If one asks, "Why Abraham or Matthew and not two other people?" there is no human answer; one cannot speak of a talent for being an Apostle or of the apostolic temperament. Whatever ultimate spiritual rewards there may be for an Apostle, they are unknowable and unimaginable; all he knows is that he is called upon to forsake everything he has been, to venture into an unknown and probably unpleasant future. Hence it is impossible to imagine the apostolic calling's being echoed by a man's natural desire. Any genuine Apostle must, surely, say, "I would not but, alas, I must." The prospective sculptor can correctly be said to *will* to become a sculptor—that is to say, to submit himself to the study, toil and discipline which becoming a sculptor involves—but an Apostle cannot correctly be said to will anything; he can only say, "Not as I will, but as Thou wilt." It is possible for a man to be deceived about a secular calling—he imagines he has a talent when in fact he has none—but there is an objective test to prove whether his calling is genuine or imaginary: either he produces valuable works or he does not. A great sculptor may die with his works totally unrecognized by the public but, in the long run, the test of his greatness is worldly recognition of his work. But in the case of an Apostle, there is no such objective test: he may make a million converts or he may make none, and we are still no nearer knowing whether his vocation was genuine or not. He may give his body to be burned, and still we do not know. There is, at most, a negative test: we are, perhaps, entitled to say that a man who claims apostolic authority is not an Apostle or is false to his calling if his own life and deeds contradict his words. A poet may write poems of great nobility while himself leading an ignoble life, without ceasing to be a noble poet, but an Apostle who preaches that men should give their lives for the truth if necessary and then, when faced with such a necessity, runs away, condemns himself as an Apostle.

Drama, like any art, can only deal with what is or can be made interesting, with things or persons that call attention to themselves; a dramatist, therefore, who attempts to portray an Apostle on the stage is faced with an insoluble problem, for in making his character—as, artistically, he must—interesting, he makes what in an Apostle is an irrelevant accident seem essential.

In *Peer Gynt*, Ibsen faced a problem which, for other reasons, is equally difficult: the dramatic presentation of a Poetic Genius. This time he was completely successful, so that a study of his method of solution in *Peer Gynt* may illuminate the difficulties which he failed to overcome completely in *Brand*.

A poet—or any artist—is a maker, not a man of deeds. A deed takes place at a certain time—Achilles can only kill Hector once—but a work of art persists—the *Iliad* can always be re-read. A work of art, however, is unlike a purely craft-object such as a table, and like a deed in that it is a unique object—no two poems are the same, and no poem written by one poet could have been written by another. Yet a work of art does not reveal its maker as a deed reveals its doer: *King Lear* tells us nothing about Shakespeare except that he was a great poet. One may say, therefore, that, unlike the man of deeds and, for different reasons, the Apostle, the poet has no need of other people as *others*, only as a source of *his* experiences. His poems may require the existence of others to read them, but he is self-sufficient.

Attempts have been made—by Shaw, for example—to portray a poet directly, but they are unconvincing and must necessarily be so. What the audience sees is a man performing various actions like falling in love or dying of consumption who says he is a poet, but there is nothing he can do to convince us that he is a good poet and not a bad one, for there is no kind of behaviour peculiar to poets except the writing of verses.

For this very reason there is a psychological and moral problem which is peculiar to poets (or artists) in that their personal life, which is just as precious to them as to any other human being, is accidental to their essential activity of making. As Yeats wrote:

> The intellect of man is forced to choose
> Perfection of the life or of the work.

That is to say, a person is what he does, but a poet is not what he makes. Keats wrote in a letter that a poet is the most unpoetical thing in the universe because he has no Identity, an observation which Ibsen might well have used as an epigraph for *Peer Gynt*. A poet is a man with a peculiar genius for handling language, but what makes poetry possible is the human capacity to imagine that anything which is the case could be otherwise. We can imagine committing a murder or laying down our lives for our friends without having to do it. In other words, we can both act and "act." Ibsen solves the problem of presenting a poet dramatically by showing us a man who treats nearly everything he does as a rôle, whether it be dealing in slaves and idols or being an Eastern Prophet. A poet in real life would have written a drama about slave trading, then another drama about a prophet, but on the stage, play-acting stands for making.

The kinship of the poet to the dreamer on the one hand and the madman on the other and his difference from them both is shown by Peer's experiences, first in the kingdom of the trolls and then in the asylum. Ibsen forestalled Freud in the notion that dreams are wish-fulfillments. The kingdom of dreams is ruled by wish or desire; the dreaming ego sees as being the case whatever the self desires to be the case. The ego, that is to say, is the helpless victim of the self: it cannot say, "I'm dreaming." In madness it is the self which is the helpless victim of the ego: a madman says "I am Napoleon," and his self cannot tell him "You're a liar." (One of the great difficulties in translating *Peer Gynt* is, I understand, that Norwegian has two words, one for the I which *is* conscious and another for the self *of which* it is conscious, where English has only one. Myself can mean either.)

Both the dreamer and the madman are in earnest; neither is capable of play-acting. The dreamer is like the movie-goer who writes abusive letters to the actor he has seen playing a villain; the madman is the actor who believes the same thing about himself, namely that he is identical with his rôle.

But the poet pretends for fun; he asserts his freedom by lying—that is to say, by creating worlds which he knows are imaginary. When the troll king offers to turn Peer into a real troll by a little eye-operation, Peer indignantly refuses. He is perfectly willing, he says, to swear that a cow is a beautiful maiden, but to be reduced to a condition in which he could not tell one from the other—that he will never submit to.

The difference between trolls and men, says the king, is that the Troll

Motto is *To Thyself be Enough*, while the Human Motto is *To Thyself be True*. The Button-Moulder and The Lean One both have something to say about the latter.

> To be oneself is: to slay oneself.
> But on you that answer is doubtless lost;
> And therefore we'll say: to stand forth everywhere
> With Master's intention displayed like a sign-board.
>
> Remember, in two ways a man can be
> Himself—there's a right and wrong side to the jacket.
> You know they have lately discovered in Paris
> A way to take portraits by help of the sun.
>
> One can either produce a straightforward picture,
> Or else what is known as a negative one.
> In the latter the lights and the shades are reversed.

But suppose there is such a thing as a poetic vocation or, in terms of Ibsen's play, a theatrical vocation; how do their words apply? If a man can be called to be an actor, then the only way he can be "true" to himself is by "acting," that is to say, pretending to be what he is not. The dreamer and the madman are "enough" to themselves because they are unaware that anything exists except their own desires and hallucinations; the poet is "enough" to himself in the sense that, while knowing that others exist, as a poet he does without them. As poet, Peer has no serious relations with others, male or female. But every poet is also a human being, distinguishable from what he makes, and through Peer's relations to Ase and Solveig, Ibsen is trying to show us, I believe, what kind of person is likely to become a poet—assuming, of course, he has the necessary talent. According to Ibsen, the predisposing factors in childhood are first, an isolation from the social group—owing to his father's drunkenness and spendthrift habits, he is looked down on by the neighbours—and secondly, a playmate who stimulates and shares his imaginative life—a role played by his mother.

> Ay, you must know that my husband, he drank,
> Wasted and trampled our gear under foot.
> And meanwhile at home there sat Peerkin and I—
> The best we could do was to try to forget. . . .
> Some take to brandy, and others to lies:
> And we—why, we took to fairy-tales.

In their play together it is the son who takes the initiative and the mother who seems the younger, adoring child. Ase dies and bequeaths to Solveig, the young virgin, the role of being Peer's Muse. If the play were a straight realistic drama, Peer's treatment of Solveig would bear the obvious psychoanalytic explanation—namely, that he suffers from a mother-fixation which forbids any serious sexual relation: he cannot love any woman with whom he sleeps. But the play is a parable and, parabolically, the mother-child relationship has, I believe, another significance: it stands for the kind of love that is unaffected by time and remains unchanged by any act of the partners. If Ase's devotion gives Peer his initial courage to be a poet and live without an identity of his own, Solveig gives him the courage to continue to the end. When at the end of the play he asks her, "Where is the real Peer?"—the human being as distinct from his poetic function—she answers, "In my faith, in my hope, in my love." This is an echo of his own belief. Ibsen leaves in doubt the question whether this faith is justified or not. It may be that, after all, the poet must pay for his vocation by ending in the casting-ladle. But Peer has so far been lucky: "He had women behind him."

Had Ibsen sought a similar indirect or parabolic method of portraying an Apostle, he might have solved his problem in writing *Brand*. (The example of *Don Quixote* comes to mind.) Instead he attempted a direct portrait. He begins, therefore, with giving us a picture of Brand's childhood. Unlike Peer, poor Brand did not have women behind him—later he was to drag Agnes after him. His mother had renounced marriage to the man she loved in order to marry one who was expected to make money. He failed and died, and she had denied all love and happiness both to herself and her son and devoted herself with absolute passion to the acquisition and hoarding of wealth. The relation between mother and son is one of defiant hostility mingled with respect for the other's strength of will and contempt for sentimentality masquerading as love. In preferring damnation to the surrender of all her goods, she shows herself every bit as much a believer in All-or-Nothing as Brand does in refusing to give her the Sacrament unless she renounces her idol. Psychologically, mother and son are alike; the only difference between them is in the God whom each worships.

Such a situation is dramatically interesting and psychologically plausible, but it inevitably makes us suspect Brand's claim to have been called by the True God, since we perceive a personal or hereditary motivation in his thought and conduct.

It is very difficult to conceive of a successful drama without important personal relations, and of such the most intense is naturally the relation between a man and a woman. The scenes between Brand and Agnes are the most exciting and moving parts of the poem, but their effect is to turn Brand into a self-torturing monster, for whose sufferings we can feel pity but no sympathy. Whether one agrees or disagrees with the insistence of the Roman Church that its priests be celibate—The Church Visible, after all, requires administrators, theologians, diplomats, etc., as well as apostles—the apostolic calling, ideally considered, is incompatible with marriage. An Apostle exists for the sake of others but not as a person, only as a mouthpiece and a witness to the Truth; once they have received the Truth and he has borne his witness, his existence is of no account to others. But a husband and wife are bound by a personal tie, and the demands they make upon each other are based on this. If a husband asks his wife to make this or that sacrifice, he asks her to make it for his sake, and his right to ask comes from their mutual personal love. But when an Apostle demands that another make a sacrifice, it cannot be for his sake; he cannot say, "If you love me, please do this," but can only say, "Thus saith the Lord. Your salvation depends upon your doing this."

When Brand first meets Agnes, he is already convinced of his calling and aware that suffering certainly and possibly a martyr's death will be required of him. His words and his risking of his life to bring consolation to a dying man reveal to her the falseness of her relation to Ejnar. At this point I do not think she is in love with Brand, but she is overwhelmed with admiration for him as a witness to the truth and prepared to fall in love with him if he should show any personal interest in her. He does show a personal interest— he is lonely and longing for personal love—they marry, they are mutually happy and they have a son, Ulf. Then comes disaster. Either they must leave the fjord and his work as the village priest—an act which Brand believes would be a betrayal of his calling—or their child must die. Brand decides that they shall remain, and Ulf does die. One would have thought that the obvious solution was to send his wife and child away to a sunnier climate and remain himself (since he inherited his mother's money, he has the means) but this solution does not seem to have occurred to him. (Of course if it had, the big dramatic scenes which follow could not have been written.) Later, he accuses Agnes of idolatry in not accepting Ulf's death as the will of God, and makes her give away all his clothes to a gipsy child. Possibly she is guilty of idolatry and should give the clothes away for the sake of her own soul and, were Brand a stranger, he could tell her so. But he is both the husband whom she loves and the father of her child who took the decision which caused the child's death and so led her into the temptation of idolatry, so that when he tells her:

> You are my wife, and I have the right to demand
> That you shall devote yourself wholly to our calling

the audience feels that he has no such right. This is only the most obvious manifestation of a problem which besets Ibsen throughout the play, namely, the problem of how to make an Apostle dramatically interesting. To be dramatically viable, a character must not only act but talk about his actions and his feelings, and talk a great deal: he must address others as a person—a messenger cannot be a major character on the stage. For dramatic reasons, therefore, Ibsen has to allow Brand to speak in the first person and appear the author of his acts, to say, "I will this." But an Apostle is a messenger, and he acts not by willing but by submitting to the will of God, who cannot appear on the stage. It is inevitable, therefore, that our final impression of Brand is of an idolater who worships not God, but his God. It makes no difference if the God he calls his happens to be the true God; so long as he thinks of Him as his, he is as much an idolater as the savage who bows down to a fetish. To me, one of the most fascinating scenes in the play is Brand's final encounter with Ejnar. Ejnar has had some sort of evangelical conversion, believes that he is saved, and is going off to be a missionary in Africa. Brand tells him of Agnes' death, but he shows no sorrow, though he had once loved her.

EJNAR. How was her faith?
BRAND. Unshakable.
EJNAR. In whom?
BRAND. In her God.
EJNAR. Her God cannot save her. She is damned. . . .
BRAND. You dare to pronounce judgment on her and me,
  Poor, sinning fool?
EJNAR. My faith has washed me clean.
BRAND. Hold your tongue.
EJNAR. Hold yours.

Ejnar is, as it were, a caricature of Brand, but the likeness is cruel.

"Poor Brand!" one says, as one might say "Poor Lear!" or "Poor Captain Ahab!" If the nature of drama prevents him from being a portrait of an Apostle as, I suspect, Ibsen meant him to be, nevertheless Ibsen wrote a grand poem. The Brand we see is a tragic hero, a great, exceptional individual who is fated to choose his suffering and death, and whose passion arouses in the audience tragic pity. (Martyrdom is not a tragic event, because it lacks the elements of both Fate and human choice. Nothing in a man's past can make martyrdom either inevitable or out of the question, and if martyrdom should be demanded of him, the choice is God's, not his.) If there is in Brand, as in all tragic heroes, a flaw, yet he is a great man who towers as an individual over all the other characters. The strength of the others lies not in themselves but in their collective number. The Mayor and the Provost are nobodies, but they can appeal to the cowardice, envy and greed of all men simultaneously, while Brand can only appeal to the conscience of each individual, one by one.

One minor character, the Doctor, is a good man, but his goodness comes not from within but from without—that is to say, from the natural goodness of his professional function. The function of a doctor is to relieve physical suffering, and there are no circumstances under which such relief is not a moral good: a "good doctor" does good, whatever his personal character. In the interchange between the Doctor and Brand concerning Brand's dying mother, some of the Doctor's criticisms may be actually true, but they are true, so to speak, by accident.

DOCTOR. . . . I've got to visit a patient.

BRAND. My mother?

DOCTOR. Yes . . . You've been to see her already, perhaps?

BRAND. No.

DOCTOR. You're a hard man. I've struggled all the way
    Across the moor, through mist and sleet,
    Although I know she pays like a pauper.

BRAND. May God bless your energy and skill.
    Ease her suffering, if you can. . . .

DOCTOR. Don't wait for her to send for you.
    Come now, with me.

BRAND. Until she sends for me, I know no duty there.

DOCTOR.   . . . your credit account
    For strength of will is full, but, priest,
    Your love account is a white virgin page.

The Doctor cannot understand Brand's refusal, because he can only think about the cure of sick souls in terms of the cure of sick bodies. In his world of experience a patient is either in pain or not in pain, and every patient desires to be well. He cannot grasp, because it is outside his professional experience, that in the soul a desire may be the sickness itself. Brand's mother clings to her possessions with passionate desire, and to relinquish them will cause her great suffering, but unless she suffers she can never know true joy. (The analogy to surgery does not hold. The patient must suffer now at the hands of the surgeon in order that he may be free from pain in the future, but he already knows what it means to be free from pain. The sinner does not know what it means to be spiritually happy; he only knows that to give up his sin will be a great suffering.)

Neither *Brand* nor *Peer Gynt* was originally written for stage performance. (I cannot understand why neither, so far as I know, has been made into a movie: I should have thought they were wonderful scripts.) Of the two, *Brand* seems the better suited to the stage, because its hero is emotionally related to all the other characters, while Peer is, for the most part, self-sufficient. In consequence, while *Peer Gynt* is a string of separate episodes—there could be more or fewer of them and their order could be different—*Brand* has a real plot in which each incident follows logically and emotionally from what preceded it. Further, from the director's point of view there are few sets needed and few effects which require elaborate stage-machinery. The only scene which seems to me almost impossible to bring off is the near-final one in which Brand leads the villagers up into the mountains on an expedition to reform the world, until they rebel against the hardships and stone him. Up to this point in the play Ibsen may have made use of symbols, but the visible objects and actions have had a historical reality of their own whatever inner significance may also be attached to them. The sunless fjord with its starving fishermen may symbolize the human condition without spiritual illumination, but it is a real Norwegian fjord and the fishermen catch real fish; the little old church and the new big church may stand for "The Church," but they are perfectly solid pieces of architecture. But in this near-final scene Ibsen starts to write pure allegory: the action has no historical credibility and is only intelligible to those who know the Bible story of Exodus, of Moses leading the Children of Israel through the wilderness. An allegorical play is dramatically perfectly possible, as the example of *Everyman* shows, but it must be allegorical throughout—the dramatist must not begin by making us accept the historical reality of his characters, and then deprive them of it.

In his translation of the play for stage performance Mr Meyer has not attempted to reproduce the rhymed octosyllabics of the original, and in my opinion this was a wise decision. No two languages can have the same rhythmical properties or match rhyme for rhyme. An exact formal copy, even if made by a great poet, is bound sometimes to add to, sometimes to cut and sometimes to change the original meaning.

C. H. Herford, whose verse translation has hitherto been regarded as the standard one—it is sometimes erroneously spoken of as William Archer's, because Archer included it in his collected English edition of Ibsen's plays— would never have claimed he was a great poet, so that it is a little unfair, perhaps, to compare a passage from his rhymed version with the same passage as rendered by Mr Meyer, but for the speed and directness of impact which a stage performance must have there is no doubt, I think, as to the wisdom of Mr Meyer's choice of a loose blank verse.

BRAND.   Do you see?
MAYOR. Yonder.
BRAND.   Yes.
MAYOR.   That great ugly stall?—
    Why, that's the Parsonage granary.
BRAND. No, not that; but the ugly, small—
MAYOR. The Church?
BRAND.   I mean to build it great.
MAYOR. That, by the devil! you shall not!
    No man shall alter it one jot!
    My plan 'twould utterly frustrate.
    Mine's urgent, only waits the word,
    By yours I'm absolutely floored;
    Two weapons can't at once be wielded,
    Yield therefore—
BRAND.   I have never yielded. . . .
MAYOR. And why condemn it now to fall?

'Twas well enough a while ago.
BRAND. Possibly; now it is too small.
MAYOR. *I* never saw it full, I know.
BRAND. Even a single soul is scanted,
 And has not room therein to soar.

(Herford)

BRAND.   Look. Can you see that?
MAYOR. What? That great ugly building? That's your cowshed,
 Isn't it?
BRAND.   Not that. The little ugly one.
MAYOR. What? The church?
BRAND. I shall rebuild it.
MAYOR. Rebuild the church?
BRAND. Make it great.
MAYOR. The devil you don't! That'd ruin my plan.
 We'd never get the people to subscribe to both.
BRAND. That church must come down.
MAYOR. It's always been acceptable to the people,
 At least, in the old days.
BRAND. Possibly. But now that time is past.
 It is too small.
MAYOR. Too small? Well, I've never seen it full.
BRAND. That is because there is not space enough
 For a single soul to rise.

(Meyer)

I have deliberately chosen a passage of low emotional temperature which
makes little demand upon a translator's poetic talent.

Brand is not only a moving tragedy about individuals but also a work full of
a wisdom to which it behoves us to listen. Whatever defects as a human being
Brand may seem to us to have, much of what he says is unpalatable but salutary truth. Conventional Christianity is pretty much the same today as it was
in the middle of the nineteenth century. We still need to be constantly reminded that God's love and the mixture of sex, sentimentality and mutual
back-scratching which most human beings think of when they use the word
love have nothing in common. We may call ourselves Christians, but our
natural impulse on encountering the real Christ is to crucify Him because
we find His love intolerable. A suitable epigraph for *Brand* would be this
entry in Kierkegaard's *Journal.*

The Christianity of the majority consists roughly of what may be called
the two most doubtful extremities of Christianity (or, as the parson says,
the two things which must be clung to in life and death), first of all the

saying about the little child, that one becomes a Christian as a little child and that of such is the Kingdom of Heaven; the second is the thief on the cross. People live by virtue of the former—in death they reckon upon consoling themselves with the example of the thief.

This is the sum of their Christianity; and, correctly defined, it is a mixture of childishness and crime.

Brand, by Henrik Ibsen, newly translated from the
Norwegian by Michael Meyer, 1960

Foreword to *Times Three*, by Phyllis McGinley

If I had Phyllis McGinley's talent I would write a poem with the refrain line *Why can't I ever say No?*, and the subject of one of the stanzas would be requests from publishers to write forewords. How *could* I have been such a fool as to let myself in for writing this one? Phyllis McGinley needs no puff. Her poems are known and loved by tens of thousands. They call for no learned exegesis. If a Ph.D. thesis is ever written about her work, it will be in an alien tongue and an alien alphabet.

I start a sentence: "The poetry of Phyllis McGinley is . . . ," and there I stick, for all I wish to say is ". . . is the poetry of Phyllis McGinley," a statement which I can prove to be true by quoting at random.

> . . . By day the chattering mowers cope
> With grass decreed a final winner.
> Darkness delays. The skipping rope
> Twirls in the driveway after dinner.
>
> Through lupine-lighted borders now
> For winter bones Dalmatians forage.
> Costly the spray on apple bough.
> The canvas chair comes out of storage;
>
> And rose-red golfers dream of par,
> And class-bound children loathe their labors,
> While pilgrims, touring gardens, are
> Cold to petunias of their neighbors. . . .

Without knowing their author, I can recognize the genre of English poetry to which such lines belong, and name some of the masters in it—Hood, Praed, Calverley, Belloc, Chesterton. But when, instead of looking at their style and technique, I think of writers with a comparable kind of sensibility, a similar cast of imagination, the names that come to mind have either, like

Jane Austen, Colette, and Virginia Woolf, written in prose, or, like Laura Riding and Marianne Moore, written poetry in a totally different style. What, in
fact, distinguishes Phyllis McGinley's poems from those of most light-verse
poets is that no man could have written them. The masculine and feminine
imagination are not mutually exclusive—the hundred-per-cent male and the
hundred-per-cent female are equally insufferable—but they can, I believe,
be differentiated. There are two questions about which it seems to me fascinating to speculate: firstly, "What does the poetry men write owe to the influence of women, whether as mothers, sisters, and wives, or as women authors
whom they admire?" and secondly, "What can women who write learn from
men and what should they beware of imitating in masculine literature?"

Naturally, I first look to see what Phyllis McGinley has to say on these matters. She speaks up bravely for her own sex.

> *For the female of the species may be deadlier than the male*
> *But she can make herself a cup of coffee without reducing*
> *The entire kitchen to a shambles.*

> Perverse though their taste in cravats
>   Is deemed by their lords and their betters,
> They know the importance of hats
>   And they write you the news in their letters.
> Their minds may be lighter than foam,
>   Or altered in haste and in hurry,
> But they seldom bring company home
>   When you're warming up yesterday's curry.

> *And when lovely woman stoops to folly,*
> *She does not invariably come in at four A.M.,*
> *Singing "Sweet Adeline."*

On the other hand, she is no ferocious feminist; she is willing to admit that
we have a few small virtues.

> For invitations you decry
> He furnisheth an alibi.
> He jousts with taxi-men in tourney,
> He guards your luggage when you journey,
> And brings you news and quotes you facts
> And figures out your income tax
> And slaughters spiders when you daren't
> And makes a very handy parent.

But, of course, from the beginning, little boys can never hope to be as smart
as little girls. Compare their reactions when they can no longer believe in
Santa Claus.

> *For little boys are rancorous*
> *When robbed of any myth,*
> *And spiteful and cantankerous*
> *To all their kin and kith.*
> *But little girls can draw conclusions*
> *And profit from their lost illusions.*

The masculine imagination lives in a state of perpetual revolt against the limitations of human life. In theological terms, one might say that all men, left to themselves, become gnostics. They may swagger like peacocks, but in their heart of hearts they all think sex an indignity and wish they could beget themselves on themselves. Hence the aggressive hostility toward women so manifest in most club-car stories.

Hence also their attitude toward matter: they love chopping and sawing and drilling and hammering, and it gives them as much pleasure, perhaps even more, to knock a building down as to put one up. And when matter rebels against their injustice, when collar studs roll away and umbrellas go into hiding, they are helpless and have to cry for rescue to their wives.

Left to itself the masculine imagination has very little appreciation for the here and now; it prefers to dwell on what is absent, on what has been or may be. If men are more punctual than women, it is because they know that, without the external discipline of clock time, they would never get anything done.

Above all, the masculine imagination is essentially theatrical. In comparison with women, men are poor liars because their sense of the difference between fact and fiction is so much vaguer: even in domestic life a man expects to be admired, not for telling the truth, but for telling a good story well. Among the poets, the purest examples of the masculine imagination that I know are Victor Hugo and W. B. Yeats. Who could possibly conceive of either of them as a woman?

In contrast, the feminine imagination accepts facts and is coolly realistic. There are certain resemblances between the lines from "June in the Suburbs" which I quoted above and the poetry of John Betjeman, but what makes it impossible that Mr Betjeman could have written them is their total lack of nostalgia. A striking illustration of this is a "sad" poem, "Blues for a Melodion." The theme of this, the passing of youth and the oncome of middle-age, has frequently been treated by men. As a rule, they devote their words to their memories of themselves—once I could run very fast, once I was much admired by the girls, once I was very bright, etc., but now . . . In Phyllis McGinley's poem, the "I" does not appear until the last two lines and the past is hardly mentioned.

> A castor's loose on the buttoned chair—
> The one upholstered in shabby coral.
> I never noticed, before, that tear
> In the dining-room paper.

When did the rocker cease to rock,
    The fringe sag down on the corner sofa?
All of a sudden the Meissen clock
    Has a cherub missing.

All of a sudden the plaster chips,
    The carpet frays by the morning windows;
Careless, a rod from the curtain slips,
    And the gilt is tarnished.

This is the house that I knew by heart.
    Everything here seemed sound, immortal.
When did this delicate ruin start?
    How did the moth come?

Naked by daylight, the paint is airing
    Its rags and tatters. There's dust on the mantel.
And who is that gray-haired stranger staring
    Out of my mirror?

So, too, in her satirical pieces. Confronted with things and people who do not please her, she does not, like many male satirists, lose her temper or even show shocked surprise; she merely observes what is the case with deadly accuracy.

"Evening Musicale"

Candles. Red tulips, ninety cents the bunch.
    Two lions, Grade B. A newly tuned piano.
No cocktails, but a dubious kind of punch,
    Lukewarm and weak. A harp and a soprano.
The "Lullaby" of Brahms. Somebody's cousin
    From Forest Hills, addicted to the pun.
Two dozen gentlemen; ladies, three dozen,
    Earringed and powdered. Sandwiches at one.

The ash trays few, the ventilation meager.
    Shushes to greet the late-arriving guest
Or quell the punch-bowl group. A young man eager
    To render "Danny Deever" by request.
And sixty people trying to relax
On little rented chairs with gilded backs.

After reading this, anyone who, like myself, has had the honor of entertaining Phyllis McGinley, will think twice about inviting her again.

Women do not, I think, excel at what is conventionally called Love Poetry. Indeed, when they try, the results can be embarrassingly awful—think of poor Mrs Browning. Perhaps the feminine imagination is too serious. Men can write good love poems because they are always aware that the girl they happen to be in love with might be someone else (and often one suspects that they are thinking of several girls at the same time). But women write better than men about marriage. When a husband does write about his wife, which is rare, he is apt to become weepy. Not so a wife writing about a husband.

> In garden-colored boots he goes
>> Ardent around perennial borders
> To spray the pink, celestial rose
>> Or give a weed its marching orders.
>
> Draining at dawn his hasty cup,
>> He takes a train to urban places;
> By lamplight, cheerful, figures up
>> The cost of camps and dental braces.
>
> And warm upon my shoulders lays
>> Impetuous at dinner table
> The mantle of familiar praise
>> That's better than a coat of sable.

In order to write well about children, it would seem that a man must be, like Lewis Carroll or Hans Andersen, a bachelor, but a woman a mother. When fathers write about their offspring, their chief concern is not the child as child but the future adult they hope or fear it will grow into. Bachelors, with their masculine nostalgia for their own childhood, are better than women, perhaps, at understanding the fantasy life of children, but only a mother can convey a sense of their physical presence.

> Oh, the peace like heaven
>> That wraps me around,
> Say, at eight-thirty-seven,
>> When they're schoolroom-bound
> With the last glove mated
>> And the last scarf tied,
> With the pig-tail plaited,
>> With the pincurl dried,
> And the egg disparaged
>> And the porridge sneered at,
> And last night's comics furtively peered at,
> The coat apprehended
>> On its ultimate hook,
> And the cover mended
>> On the history book!

There is, perhaps, one thing which women can profitably learn from men, a sense of play. Left to itself, the feminine imagination would get so serious that it would look down on the arts as unworthy frivolities. Phyllis McGinley has her fair element of masculine imagination, to which she owes, among other things, her dexterity in rhyming. But she does not go in for ostentatiously farcical rhymes like

> Among the anthropophagi
> One's friends are one's sarcophagi
> > (Ogden Nash)

or puns like

> The bar-maid of the Crown he lov'd,
> > From whom he never ranged,
> For though he changed his horses there,
> > His love he never changed.
>
> He thought her fairest of all fares,
> > So fondly love prefers;
> And often, among twelve outsides,
> > Deem'd no outside like hers.
> > > (Thomas Hood)

I think she is wise to avoid such things. A gift for standing on one's head and pulling faces seems to be a masculine gift. There have been wonderful comediennes, but who has heard of a woman clown?

Clowns are enchanting in their proper place, the stage, but in real life, private or public, they can be boring and a menace. Ten minutes with a newspaper leave me with the conviction that the human race has little chance of survival unless men are disenfranchised and debarred from political life: in a technological age, only women have the sense to know which toys are dangerous.

> Let them on Archimedes dote
> > Who like to hear the planet rattling.
> I cannot cast a hearty vote
> > For Galileo or for Gatling,
> Preferring, of the Freaks of science,
> The pygmies rather than the giants—
>
> *(And from experience being wary of*
> *Greek geniuses bearing gifts)*—
>
> Deciding on reflection calm,
> > Mankind is better off with trifles:
> With Band-Aid rather than the bomb,
> > With safety match than safety rifles.

Let the earth fall or the earth spin!
A brave new world might well begin
With no invention
Worth the mention
Save paper towels and aspirin.

As for the arts, it may be true that up till now the greatest artists have been men, but from whom did they get the notion of making anything in the first place? Their motive is implied in Dr Johnson's reply to the lady who asked him to define the difference between men and women: "I can't conceive, Madam, can you?"

Times Three: Selected Verse from Three Decades with Seventy
New Poems, by Phyllis McGinley, 1960

The Magician from Mississippi

The Mansion. By William Faulkner. Random House. $4.75.

I think I can recognize three species of novel: the Prose Poem, the Feigned History, and what, for lack of a better term, I must call the Fairy Tale. Most novels are, of course, hybrids but, as in the case of plants and animals, one set of characteristics is usually dominant and the others recessive, so that the classification may still be useful.

By the Prose Poem I mean a novel in which, as in Poetry, Form and Content are inseparable: it would be impossible to translate into another tongue without loss, and impossible to imagine it a page longer or shorter. Examples that occur to me are Virginia Woolf's *The Waves*, Joyce's *Ulysses* and, I think, the later fiction of Henry James. (What equivalent in a foreign tongue could there be for those extraordinary sentences of his?)

By the Feigned History I mean a piece of fiction which attempts to give the reader the illusion that he is reading about real historical characters in a real historical society *as seen from the inside.* (I will try and explain what I mean by this in a moment.) An obvious example is *Anna Karenina.* A great many novelists try to write feigned histories and very few succeed, for any feigned history is a failure unless it convinces an intelligent and sensitive reader that it provides him with a deeper insight into human beings and their history than he could obtain from observing himself and his friends and reading historical documents.

Faulkner's novels—like those of Scott, Dickens, Ronald Firbank, and Ivy Compton-Burnett—are, to me, examples of the Fairy Tale.

The Fairy Tale is unabashedly fiction; it presents us with a world of beings and events more extraordinary, more surprising than the world in which we live, and at the same time less problematic, less obscure. What in the historical world is internal and known by introspection and intuition is, in the fairy tale, externalized and made manifest to the senses. Thus the fairy tale tends to represent the conflict between good and evil impulses which goes on inside all of us as an external battle between good and bad beings; it tends to isolate the various passions, for love, for power, for understanding, etc., which compete for the attention of our hearts and minds, and embody them one by one in monomaniac beings, whose physical appearance, behavior and conversation are caricatures in the sense that they reveal the life within immediately and exactly; there are no psycho-somatic contradictions.

In real life we encounter, of course, extraordinary and grotesque individuals and events, but the true Feigned Historian, like Tolstoi, makes little or no use of them. To ourselves, we each feel unique, but none of us feels himself to be extraordinary, and the better we know someone (that is to say, the more we see him, like ourselves, from the inside), the less significance we attach to any external oddities he may possess. Our friends seem to us "normal" like the characters in Tolstoi; it is the stranger we meet for a moment in a railroad train or a cafeteria who seems to have come out of Dickens or Faulkner.

An author is not a God who can create a world out of nothing; any imaginary world he creates, however fantastic, is fashioned out of experiences taken from the real historical world and is the creation of a certain person born in a certain time and place and living in a certain culture. In reading a fairy tale, therefore, a problem arises which does not arise when reading a feigned history, that of distinguishing, so to speak, between the "real" stones and the "dream" architecture. Yoknapatawpha County is one world for a Southerner, another for a Yankee, and yet another for a European. By birth and upbringing, for instance, I am a native of the fairy tale world of Barchester County. In Barchester we had no Negroes, so when I visit Yoknapatawpha where they are common, they are a fantastic element, as dwarves or elves would be. In Barchester we had our feuds—the Archdeacon and the Cathedral Organist were not on speaking terms for years; the Squire and the Vicar of Horninglow kept exchanging abusive letters—but, aside from the chastisement of children, physical violence was unknown. In *The Mansion*, which is one of Faulkner's gentlest novels, I find reference to three murders, two attempted murders, two suicides, two beatings-up, and one tarring-and-feathering. I accept these as a dreamer accepts odd events in a dream; but, just as sometimes something happens in a dream which is so extraordinary that the dreamer cries—"Wake up! You must be dreaming!"—there is one feature of Yoknapatawpha which completely bewilders me, namely, the social status of Baptists. Sure enough, we had Baptists in Barchester, but they delivered things at the back door and one never met them. Occasionally some unstable relative might become a Catholic "pervert" or a British Israelite or a freethinker; this was deplorable but to be accepted as one of those misfortunes which occur in every family. But the notion of anyone who "mattered" socially becoming a Baptist would have been unthinkable.

However, after discounting all that may only seem strange to me, but to a Southerner is real and natural, I still have no doubt as to the kind of novelist Faulkner essentially is. For example, in real life one can certainly come across, in various places and at different times, persons who strike one as being totally devoid of human affection and caring only for money or power. One might invent a word-label for such people, so that one could say to a friend: "O, I met a perfect Snopes this morning." But only in a fairy tale could the word-label become a family name; only there could such a set of monsters as Flem, Wesley, Byron, Clarence, Vergil, Montgomery Ward, and Orestes not only all be blood relatives but also collected in the same small town of Frenchman's Bend. Again, in real life, we are frequently aware of a struggle between what reason or conscience tells us we ought to do and what some passion would try to make us do: we may have behaved like Gavin Stevens yesterday but that is no guarantee that we shall not behave like Flem Snopes tomorrow. It is only in a fairy tale that persons are good or bad by nature, that it should be as impossible to imagine Gavin Stevens committing a base act as to imagine Flem doing a decent one.

In real life we make two kinds of decision, the strategic or practical, and the personal. My nature and circumstances "give" me a certain goal as desirable and, in my efforts to attain it, I have frequently to decide whether this course of action or that would be the best; the course I take may turn out to be right or wrong but neither I nor others will wonder why I took it. But occasionally I make a decision which is not based upon any calculation of its future consequences (which may turn out to be grave) but upon my immediate conviction that, whatever the consequences, I must do this, or refrain from doing it, *now*. However well I know myself, I cannot explain completely why I take this kind of decision, and to others it will always be mysterious.

The personal decision is one of the main concerns of the Feigned Historian; a great one, like Tolstoi, succeeds in making the reader understand his characters better than they could ever understand themselves. In the pure fairy tale novel, there are no personal decisions, only strategic ones. The characters may be extraordinary and do extraordinary things, the accidents of chance may be extraordinary, but, given their characters and their situations, there is nothing mysterious about why they act in the way they do. In *The Mansion*, I find several examples of a personal decision and in each case I find Faulkner's attempt to explain the mystery unconvincing. For example, the future lives of many people would have been very different if Eula Varner had married Hoake McCarron, by whom she was pregnant with Linda, instead of Flem Snopes. Why didn't she? This is the explanation Faulkner puts into Ratliff's mouth:

> It was Eula herself that done it. . . . That simple natural phenomenon that maybe didn't expect to meet another phenomenon, even a natural one, but at least expected or maybe jest hoped for something at least

tough enough to crash back without losing a arm or a leg the first time they struck. . . . I ain't talking about love. Natural phenomenons ain't got no more concept of love than they have of the alarm and uncertainty and impotence you got to be capable of to know what waiting means. When she said to herself, and likely she did: "The next one of them creek-bridge episodes might destroy him completely," it wasn't that McCarron boy's comfort she had in mind.

Again, in 1923, when Mink's prison sentence is nearly up, Flem, who knows Mink means to kill him, is prepared to play a complicated and very dirty trick so as to keep Mink in prison for another twenty years, but refuses to have him bumped off which, as Montgomery Ward points out, would be the obvious way to ensure Flem's safety. All the explanation Faulkner gives us is this:

> So there's something that even a Snopes won't do. No, that's wrong; Uncle Mink never seemed to have any trouble reconciling Jack Houston up in front of that shotgun when the cheese begun to bind. Maybe what I mean is, every Snopes has one thing he won't do to you—provided you can find out what it is before he has ruined and wrecked you.

I cannot help feeling that what is presented as the personal decisions of Eula and Flem is really the strategic decisions of their author; that is to say, they have to act as they do for the sake of his story, just as, out of the many kinds of injury which Linda might have suffered in the Spanish Civil War, only deafness would make possible the extraordinary platonic love scenes between her and Gavin which Faulkner wished to write.

> "But you can **** me," she said. That's right. She used the explicit word, speaking the hard brutal guttural in the quacking duck's voice. That had been our problem as soon as we undertook the voice lessons: the tone, to soften the voice which she herself couldn't hear. "It's exactly backward," she told me. "When you say I'm whispering, it feels like thunder inside my head. But when I say it this way, I can't even feel it." And this time it would be almost a shout. Which is the way it was now, since she probably believed she had lowered her voice, I standing there while what seemed to me reverberations of thunder died away.

A scene like this, and there are dozens of others, comic and pitiable, as good, makes me grateful for the limitations in Faulkner but for which they would not have got written.

The Mansion is a collection of tales, major and minor. The two major tales concern Mink and Linda. The first covers only a few days in 1946, between a Thursday morning when Mink is released from Parchman Penitentiary and the following Tuesday evening when he fulfills his vow of 1908 to shoot Flem. The second covers ten years of Linda's life, between her marriage to the sculptor Barton Kohl in 1936 and her participation in the murder of her official father, for she, too, though no one else knew this, had vowed vengeance upon Flem since her mother's suicide in (I think) 1928. In addition there are a number of subsidiary comic tales, the tale of Montgomery Ward Snopes and Reba Rivers, the Memphis Madam, the tale of Meadowfill, Orestes Snopes and the Hog, the tale of the political rise and fall of Clarence Snopes the Unspeakable. I shall not spoil a reader's pleasure by giving away what happens in any of these stories, but, no doubt, he will be glad to hear that Virtue is victorious, Vice gets its deserts, and Justice is finally done.

Judged by the standards of the Prose Poem, a novel like *The Mansion* is formless: as regards the tales of Mink and Linda, there is nothing inevitable about the order in which the incidents are related, or even about their number—the stories could have been told in greater detail or in less; as regards the subsidiary tales, there is no compelling reason why just *this* tale should be told and not another one. But the Jamesian formal standard is irrelevant to novels of this genre. Faulkner is not concerned with constructing a perfect verbal object, but with keeping us enchanted, with making us laugh, cry, gape, shudder, hold our breath. Form here is a sort of conjuring trick; it is right if we are kept so fascinated that we never ask how it is done. The story of Mink is a fast-moving "thriller" of action; by frequently breaking off at an exciting moment to tell the story of Linda, which is slow-moving and more concerned with feelings than acts, Faulkner excites in the reader the maximum amount of suspense, and he heightens the pathos and grimness of both their histories by relieving us at the point where sadness might become monotonous, and our attention about to wander, with scenes of farcical comedy.

Faulkner is no thinker—his occasional reflections on politics or the race question do not illuminate their subjects; he is no poet—his purple passages are embarrassingly bad; he is not even, in my opinion, a profound psychologist, but he is a very great magician who can make twenty years in Yoknapatawpha seem to the reader like twenty minutes and make him want to stay there forever. Furthermore, he employs white magic, that is to say, his charms have a moral purpose: he would teach and, I believe, succeeds in teaching us both to love the Good and to realize the price which must be paid for that love.

The Mid-Century, January 1960

A Children's Anthology

A Treasure Chest of Tales: A Collection of Great Stories for Children.
McDowell, Obolensky. $4.95.

The three qualities one looks for in any anthology are Good Taste, Original Taste, and Variety of Taste; and, so far as their prose selections are concerned, which means nine tenths of the book, the anonymous editors of *A Treasure Chest of Tales* have done pretty well.

There is good literature for adults which is not for children, but there is no good literature for children which is not for adults; a story or a poem which one cannot read to a child with pleasure is bad; if the child seems to enjoy it, this is because an inadequate or unauthentic stimulus to his imagination is better than none at all. Of the ten stories in this collection, there is not one which I do not admire and enjoy now. In these days of digests, I should also add that the only condensation and "adaptations" are in *The Travels of Baron Munchausen, Aesop's Fables*, and a story from *The Arabian Nights*, and that none are serious.

Another term for Originality of Taste is Industry: anthologists are notoriously lazy, content to copy some predecessor in the field rather than go to the trouble of reading for themselves. As a rough-and-ready rule one might say that, of two pieces of equal merit, the less well-known should always be chosen. I am glad to see that the editors have avoided, in their selection from *The Arabian Nights*, the obvious choice of *Sinbad*, and Frances Browne's *Granny's Wonderful Chair* will be, if I am not mistaken, an unfamiliar pleasure to many.

On Variety they deserve high marks; in a single volume a child will find *Black Beauty, The Rose and The Ring, The Snow Queen* and *Alice's Adventures in Wonderland*. The only kind of fantasy that seems uncatered for is fantasy about machinery, railroad trains, airplanes, etc.

When it comes to poetry, their choices, I am sorry to say, are not so happy, and it is clear that their heart was not in their work. They make errors in taste—the two Taylor pieces, "John Gilpin," Allingham's "The Fairies" and Goldsmith's "An Elegy on Madam Blaize" are without merit—they are unoriginal—anyone who knows his *Ingoldsby Legends* well could have picked a better example than "The Jackdaw of Rheims"—and their notion of the poetry which appeals to children between the ages of eight and thirteen is far too limited. It may be true that the majority of children in this age-group are embarrassed by poetical expressions of strong feelings, whether about people or nature, but it is certainly not true that the only poetry they can stomach is narrative or comic verse: from my own memories and my experiences as a teacher, I know that a great many children take enormous pleasure in what the French call *poésie pure*, that is to say, in poems of incantatory magic like "Full Fathom Five." Should there be a second edition of *A Treasure Chest of Tales*, I hope the editors will omit the poetry entirely and substitute another story: my candidates for this would be one of the Nesbit tales or Ruskin's *The King of the Golden River*.

The Mid-Century, January 1960

Apologies to the Iroquois

Apologies to the Iroquois. By Edmund Wilson. Farrar, Straus & Cudahy. $4.95.

Mr Edmund Wilson is a specimen of that always rare and now almost extinct creature, the Intellectual Dandy. The generic name is paradoxical for, by definition, no dandy is like another; what they have in common is their un-likeness to anybody else. The Dandy is neither a conformist nor a rebel, for both these terms imply a concern for Public Opinion and the Dandy has none: on one occasion his views may coincide with those of the majority, on another with those of the minority, but in both cases the coincidence is ac-cidental. The same is true of his interests. One of the ways in which an Intel-lectual Dandy can be recognized is by the unpredictability of his work; no knowledge of his previous books offers any clue as to what he will write next. Who, knowing Mr Wilson as the author of *To the Finland Station, Classics and Commercials, Memoirs of Hecate County*, and a study of *The Dead Sea Scrolls*, could have predicted that he would become the author of *Apologies to the Iroquois?* By definition, a Dandy can have no followers: the only influence he can have on others is as an example of what it means to be oneself. It is impossible to imagine a "Wilson School" of writers.

A digression. Mr Wilson is a bit of an anglophobe. Though, naturally, I do not share his feelings, I can understand them. It may take greater moral courage to become a Dandy in the United States than in England; neverthe-less, I believe it is easier. British intellectual society is less boring, more intel-ligent and infinitely more charming than its American counterpart, which makes its collective influence much more dangerous to the individual—to resist seems rather piggy. Further, thanks to the physical size of this country, it is much easier here, if one wishes to be alone, to be left alone (in England, all one's intellectual relatives live within calling distance, and they keep dropping in).

Though the credit for making it financially possible for Mr Wilson to write *Apologies to the Iroquois* belongs to *The New Yorker*—this magazine also printed Mr Joseph Mitchell's 1949 study, *The Mohawks in High Steel*, which Mr Wilson reprints as a prelude to his own—the conception and execution of the book are, clearly, the author's. For the word *apologies* in his title, Mr Wilson has, I believe, two meanings in mind. First, he feels that he owes the Iroquois a personal apology for not having heard of their existence before June 1957, despite the fact that a house which had belonged to his family since the eigh-teenth century stood on the borders of their main reservation. To this per-sonal apology, I am sure the Iroquois would reply: "We prefer White people who ignore us to those, like the tourists in New Mexico, who regard us as zoological curiosities to photograph and buy fake souvenirs from. As for those Whites who 'take us up' and deny their own race and culture because they hate themselves, we despise them and do not trust them. We welcome your interest because we can see that you are proud of being what you are, a Yankee from a long established Presbyterian stock."

Secondly, as a member of the white race, Mr Wilson wishes to apologize for its behavior to the Indians from the time it first arrived on this continent down to the present day. What has been, and still is, unforgivable about us is not our criminal record, the brutalities and treacheries by which we stole

their land—every invader in history has done likewise—but our cultural conceit, our conviction that any individual or society that does not share our
cultural habits is morally and mentally deficient—it makes no difference if
the habit in question is monogamy or a liking for ice cream.

The period of unabashed white exploitation of the Indian is over: what the
Ogden Land Company could do in 1838 could not be done today.

> It was possible for the agents of the land company—resorting, if neces-
> sary, to liquor . . . to get the signature of some of the chiefs by bribery;
> others, who were ill, were induced to sign without knowing what they
> were signing; in other more difficult cases, the victim was made drunk
> in a tavern and engaged in conversation while, without his being aware
> of it, his hand was guided to make its mark. They also set up bogus
> chiefs. "The Company," according to Arthur Parker, "was reduced to the
> necessity of taking debauched Indians to Buffalo and penning them in
> an inn, where they were 'elected and declared chiefs' by company
> agents, and then for pay forced to sign the treaty." As a last resort, the
> agents forged signatures.

But the cultural conceit still remains, the feeling that an Indian ought to
become a "good" American who loves private property, money, and gracious living, American style. The Indians seem to have resisted "integra-
tion" remarkably well but not, alas, completely. According to Mr Mitchell,
the Mohawks, while they can reject our dependence upon running water
and plumbing, have become hopelessly addicted to the radio. I find it immensely depressing that when unmechanized societies, whether Indians or
Greek peasants, come into contact with ours, the one aspect of ours which
none of them, but *none*, can resist is that which, to me, is the most intolerable: its hatred of silence—noise-makers have replaced liquor as our most
potent agent of corruption.

In *Apologies to the Iroquois*, Mr Wilson plays two roles. Part of the time he is
the *engagé* journalist, intent upon arousing public conscience against a kind
of tyranny which, today, threatens not only the Indians but every private citizen, the tyranny of the Big Executive; the rest of the time he writes as a historian and anthropologist, the friendly but detached observer of the Iroquois in a time of ferment and change.

The particular examples of executive tyranny to which he draws our attention are two: the Kinzua Dam Project, a Federal baby, and the Niagara Power
Project, a pet infant of Mr Robert Moses. Both involve Indian reservations;
the first would flood four-fifths of a reservation belonging to the Senecas,
the second a quarter of one belonging to the Tuscaroras. Of the two, the
Federal project is the more disgraceful because, according to two of the best
hydraulic engineers in the country, there is a more efficient and cheaper way

of controlling flood in the Allegheny basin, which is the ostensible purpose
of the dam. In fact, the Project

> has merely served as a pretext for putting through at the public expense
> a particularly costly contrivance intended to serve the interests of a
> group of industrialists in Pittsburgh, who now appear as its principal
> advocates. Though Pittsburgh itself is not seriously in danger from the
> flooding of the upper Allegheny, certain Pittsburgh manufacturers have
> their reasons for wanting the river diluted at the seasons when it is run-
> ning low. The sulphurous drainage from the coal mines is from their
> point of view deleterious because it ruins their boilers by rusting
> them. . . . Mr O'Neill, on behalf of the Indians, contends that industrial
> pollution could be reduced by the industrialists themselves at a cost of
> three or four hundred thousand dollars. (The dam will cost one hun-
> dred and fifty million.)

In resisting disappropriation, the Iroquois, ironically enough, are in a legally
stronger position than they would have been had they been Whites, for they
can appeal to two treaties made with them by the U. S. Government, the
Treaty of Fort Stanwix (1784) and the Pickering Treaty (1794). By the terms
of these treaties, the Iroquois were granted their land in perpetuity and in
common ownership; that is to say, none of the land could be bought from an
Indian individually without the consent of his legal chief and the consent of
the Federal Government. (As one might expect, the question of who is or
was his *legal* chief is a lawyer's paradise.)

In the case of the Kinzua Dam, the future of the Senecas looks dark for,
though President Eisenhower vetoed the Appropriation Bill last September,
his veto was overridden both in the House and in the Senate.

In their battle with Mr Moses over the Niagara Power Project, however,
they have triumphed for, last February, the Federal Power Commission, by a
3–2 vote, decided in their favor, saying: "We regret that we have not been
able to reach any other solution, but we cannot permit our personal views of
what is desirable but must administer the laws as passed by Congress and as
interpreted by the courts." This decision will delight everyone except Mr
Moses and those like him who know so much better than we do what is good
for us. Indian or White, we can all recognize our common enemy by his tone
of voice during negotiation:

> While we understand your reluctance to part with the land, we cannot
> delay longer. We are carrying out an urgent project of vital public im-
> portance under double mandate of State and Federal law, and in accor-
> dance with a Federal license. . . . It is high time for expeditious negotia-
> tion if you are in a mood to negotiate. The advantages to your Nation of

prompt, friendly agreement on the generous terms the authority offers cannot be overstated. We hope you will decide to proceed in this spirit, but we must go ahead in any event;

and by his tantrums when his will is crossed:

We have been jackassed from court to court and judge to judge, and are faced with the prospect of more litigation and further delays, postponement of permanent financing and perhaps stoppage of work. . . . How our democratic system can survive such stultifying domestic weakness, incompetence and ineptitude in the ruthless, world-wide competition with other systems of government more incisive and less tolerant of obstruction, is more than I can figure out.

Mr Wilson's first encounter with the Iroquois was in June of 1957. Events have been moving so rapidly since then that, had he written his book in 1958, it would already, he says, be out of date.

The Iroquois is the name of a confederation of six Indian nations, the Mohawks, the Senecas, the Onondagas, the Oneidas, the Cayugas and the Tuscaroras. The first five of these formed their alliance in 1570; the Tuscaroras applied for membership after they had been driven out of South Carolina in 1722. It is possible that Benjamin Franklin was influenced by their political structure in framing the Constitution with its balance of Federal and States rights. Though no action can be taken without the unanimous consent of all six nations, the Onondagas rank first. The Senecas seem to be the most intelligent, the least hostile to Whites, and the most drunken. Each nation was divided into clans named after totem animals, and marriage within a clan was forbidden. The children of a marriage belonged to the wife's clan, and the wife's brother was responsible for them. Each clan had a clan mother who chose its chief. With the passage of time, however, other kinds of chiefs have appeared. Those Iroquois who lived in French Canada adopted the system of hereditary chiefs. Some of the Senecas formed a republic with a governing Council elected by universal manhood suffrage, and both the American and Canadian governments have tried to install elective chiefs who, in practice, seem to have been government stooges.

During the War of Independence most of the Iroquois sided with the British, but, after it was over, the American government forgave them and their reservations lie in both Canada and the United States along or near the St Lawrence. Of the eighteen million acres originally allotted to them in this country, only seventy-eight thousand remain: the rest were stolen from them during the nineteenth century.

Recent years have seen the birth of a nationalist movement among the Iroquois. From the point of view of the American and Canadian governments— at their most benevolent—the Indians have been regarded as wards, i.e. children who have not yet reached the age of consent. From their own point of view, the Iroquois regard themselves as an independent people who are not living in the United States but in their own country and, therefore, cannot be liable to any duties which the United States government may demand of its own citizens.

So long as they remained on their reservations and the demands made by the State were small, this difference of opinion caused little trouble. But today, it does. Thanks to their extraordinary sense of balance and fearlessness of high places, the Iroquois have found an important place for themselves in our technological society: as steel construction workers on bridges and skyscrapers, the Indians are superior to the Whites. These jobs are highly paid, and it is not unnatural, perhaps, that the government should question their claim to be exempt from income tax because, by the original treaties, they were exempted from property taxes. Again, it is only recently that military service has been made compulsory. In the First World War, the Iroquois made their own declaration of war on Germany; in the Second they did not and many of them went to jail rather than obey an authority which they did not recognize. (Though given the vote in 1924, very few of them exercise their right.) During the last few years their feeling of national identity has grown much more intense and has already led to violence in Canada. As in the case of most nationalist movements, it is difficult to tell how much popular support the politically active minority command. It is a little disquieting to learn that one of their leaders, Mad Bear, had a schoolteacher arrested for criticizing the notion of hereditary chiefs, on the ground that all criticism was treason.

Nor does one feel quite happy about certain eschatological aspects of the movement which prophesy the mutual destruction of America and Russia to be followed by the day of the Red Man. Such prophecies are always accompanied by the expectation of the advent of the Messiah, and messianic hopes are not a healthy symptom in political life.

Mr Wilson makes no prophecies about the future of Iroquois nationalism nor passes judgment; he is only concerned that we should recognize its existence as an historical fact which can no more be ignored than Arab or African nationalism.

The religious beliefs of the Iroquois vary: most of the Mohawks, for example, are Roman Catholics, most of the Tuscaroras, Protestants. Recently there has been some spread, particularly among the more ardent nationalists, of a curious cult called the Handsome Lake Religion. Handsome Lake (1735–1815) was for much of his life a drunkard and a ne'er-do-well. In 1799 he fell ill, began to see visions and presently delivered himself of The Good Message. The ethical side of this was sensible though not very original: treat children with kindness, don't be malicious, don't boast, don't get drunk, be hospitable, etc. More interesting was his conviction that the Indian can only be destroyed if he tries to imitate the white man. Among his visions was one of Paradise, a place of absolute happiness and unlimited berries. No white man could ever enter it, though George Washington was permitted to live in a fort just outside the gates. One of the reasons given for the white men's exclusion was that they had been responsible for the death of Jesus, of which the Indians were innocent.

Some of Mr Wilson's most fascinating pages are devoted to describing tribal dances he attended. I hope it is not mere denseness on my part, but I cannot discover from his account whether these dance-oratorios have become mere social customs or dramas which imply no religious belief in those who sing and dance them, or whether they are genuine rites, so that no Indian who is a Christian, for example, or a freethinker, could conscientiously take part in them.

But from Mr Wilson's descriptions, there seems to be no doubt about their aesthetic beauty and emotional impact.

> The switch in the wall was turned off, and the ceremony proper began. The room with its Corn Flakes had vanished: you were at once in a different world. The single beat of a rattle is heard in the sudden blackness like the striking of a gigantic match, and it is answered by other such flashes that make rippings of sound as startling as a large-scale electric spark. The first of the two chief singers cries "Wee yoh!" and the second "Yoh wee!" and the first of them now sets the rhythm for the rattles, which is picked up by the rest of the company. In this section the tempo is uniform, and it reminds one of the rapid jogging that is heard by the passengers on an express train. . . . In the second section, the rhythms of the rattles are different. While the first and second singers are introducing the couplets, the rattles are going so fast that they seem to weave a kind of veil or screen—a scratching almost visible on the darkness—that hangs before the lyric voices; but when the chorus takes up the theme, this changes to a slow heavy beat that has something of the pound of a march. The shift is extremely effective. When it occurs, this accompaniment of the rattles—contrary to our convention—does not quite coincide with the song and the chorus but always overlaps a little. The big shimmer of the solo begins before the pound of the chorus has ended; in a moment, you are given notice, a fresh song will be springing up. . . . In this section the animals assemble . . . and presently these creatures begin to speak, as they are mentioned pair by pair in the couplets. They are mimicked by one or more singers—who have had their parts assigned them—as the arrival of each pair is announced.

Though, as I said at the beginning of this article, I cannot imagine a Wilson "school" of writers, I would recommend any young prose writer to go to school with Mr Wilson's prose. Plain prose is the opposite of Pure poetry: in poetry language calls attention to itself as an end, in prose language is a self-effacing means. The test of good prose is that the reader does not notice it any more than a man looking through a window at the landscape outside notices the glass; if he does, it means that the window is dirty.

The most famous of all dandies, Beau Brummell, made inconspicuous dress the height of elegance; by the same standard, Mr Wilson is, in my opinion, one of the most elegant prose writers alive.

The Mid-Century, February 1960

An Unclassical Classic

The Anger of Achilles: Homer's Iliad. Translated by Robert Graves.
Doubleday. $4.95.

A poem, like any work of art, is a material object which, from the time of its making, remains permanently on hand in the world while successive generations of readers come into being and pass away. It is, as it were, an immortal face which time cannot change; every individual and generation sees the same features. But no two individuals or generations "read" these features in exactly the same way; what we read remains the same, but how we read is always changing.

In reading a face, I must read it as a whole—if I look only at the mouth and ignore the eyes completely, my reading will certainly be false—but I have the right to do what, in any case, I cannot help doing: decide upon the order of significance in the features I see—in this face, I say, the mouth is more revealing than the eyes.

When we are confronted by a poem in a foreign language, we must distinguish, as Mr Robert Graves says, between a crib and a translation. A crib is like a pair of spectacles to a short-sighted man; a person who knows only a little Greek and is anxious to learn more requires a crib as an aid to spelling out the *Iliad* in the original so that he may then make his own "reading" of that poem. A translation, on the other hand, is like a seeing eye dog to a blind man; a person who knows no Greek nor Greek history must depend upon a translator to read the Iliad for him.

A maker of a crib and a translator must both, of course, have a mastery of Homeric Greek, its syntax, prosody, rhetorical conventions. But, for the translator, this is only the necessary preliminary to his real task, which is to make Homer write the *Iliad* in English.

For example, Homer wrote his epic in unrhymed quantitative hexameters, a meter into which the Greek language naturally and harmoniously composes itself. Attempts have been made to translate it into some form of English hexameter.

He who receives them kindly, who gives God's daughters a welcome,
They never fail to bless him, they hear him calling upon them.
Woe to the man that drives them away and roughly derides them!
Calling upon Cronides they pray their Father to send down
Sin to him and punish him for Sin's sake and to avenge them.

(George Ernle)

But no Homer writing in English could possibly have subjected the language
to such rhythmical tortures.

Most verse translators have asked themselves: "Into what meter does English fall as naturally as Greek falls into hexameters?"

As one might expect, the answer is generally conditioned by the English
verse being written by the translator's contemporaries.

Thus, Chapman chose rhymed fourteeners:

All that Apollo's marble fane in stony Pythos holds,
I value equal with the life that my free breast enfolds.
Sheep, oxen, tripods, crest-deck'd horse, though lost, may come again,
But when the white guard of our teeth no longer can contain
Our human soul . . .

Pope chose the heroic couplet:

There shone the image of the master mind:
There earth, there heaven, there ocean he designed;
Th' unwearied sun, the moon completely round;
The starry lights that heaven's high convex crowned.

Cowper chose a miltonic blank verse:

Thus pondering he stood; meantime appeared
Achilles, terrible as fiery Mars,
Crest-tossing God, and brandished as he came
O'er his right shoulder high the Pelian spear.

while most recent verse translators, since accentual and free verse became
acceptable to our ears, have used an unrhymed five- or six-beat line.

Mr Graves has come to the conclusion that, when Homer is writing historic narrative which is nine tenths of the time, the proper equivalent is a
staid and simple English prose. He says:

Modern audiences are sharp-witted and more easily bored than Homer's; and since the printing press has almost abolished illiteracy in the
West, novels or histories need no longer be clothed in regular meter to
make them easily memorized; nor do English versions of the *Iliad*. Broken meter, which some recent translators adopt, seems to me an unfortunate compromise between verse and prose.

Prose versions have, of course, been made before. Here is a passage from Book XXII, as rendered by Lang, Leaf, and Myers in the last century:

> Thus dying spake unto him Hector of the glancing helm: "Verily I know thee and behold thee as thou art, nor was I destined to persuade thee; truly thy heart is iron in thy breast. Take heed now lest I draw upon thee wrath of gods, in the day when Paris and Phoebus Apollo slay thee, for all thy valour, at the Skaian gate."
>
> He ended, and the shadow of death came down upon him, and his soul fled forth of his limbs and was gone to the house of Hades, wailing her fate, leaving her vigor and youth. Then to the dead man spake noble Achilles: "Die: for my death, I will accept it, whensoever Zeus and the other immortal gods are minded to accomplish it."

In 1950 Chase and Perry rendered the same passage thus:

> Then as he died, Hector of the glancing helmet said to him: "Well do I know you as I look upon you; there was no hope that I could move you, for surely your heart is iron in your breast. Take care now lest I be cause of anger of the gods against you on that day when Paris and Phoebus Apollo shall slay you, for all your valor, at the Scaean gates."
>
> As he said this, the end of death enwrapped him. His soul fled from his limbs and passed into the House of Death, bewailing its fate and forsaking manliness and youth. Even when he had died, godlike Achilles said to him: "Die, and my fate I will accept whenever Zeus and the other immortal gods desire to fulfill it."

There is a stylistic difference between these two versions: Lang, Leaf, and Myers obviously felt that the closest prose equivalent to Homer's verse was the prose of the King James Bible, while Chase and Perry felt that the associations which we have with such a style were out of place, but otherwise, they agree pretty much as to what is actually said in the original.

Graves is more radical:

> Hector spoke his dying words: "Now I know you; now I see you clearly! Fate forbids me to melt a heart of iron, yet beware: my ghost will draw down the wrath of Heaven on your head—when Paris, aided by Phoebus Apollo, destroys you at yonder gate."
>
> The shadow of Death touched Hector, life left him, and a ghost fled to the kingdom of Hades, bewailing his lost youth and vigor. "Die, then!", Achilles stormed. "And I am ready to meet my own doom as soon as Zeus and his fellow-Immortals give the order."

Here as elsewhere Graves omits the conventional descriptive epithet: Hector of-the-glancing-helmet, god-like Achilles become plain Hector and Achilles. For this he gives his reason in his introduction. The *Iliad* was originally composed for oral recitation at banquets but today it is no longer recited but read. The listening ear tolerates and indeed welcomes repetitions which the reading eye finds wearisome and unnecessary.

Where the others have Hector tell Achilles to beware lest "I draw on you the wrath of the gods," Graves changes the *I* to *my ghost*, a word he also uses to translate *psyche*, which the others translate as *soul*. For the average modern reader who knows nothing about Homeric psychology and Homeric beliefs concerning death and the after-life, the word *soul* inevitably carries its Christian meaning of being the immortal essence of a person, his real *I*: to a Homeric Greek, what went down to Hades was a much less important and more pitiable creature. Again, Paris and Phoebus Apollo becomes Paris *aided* by Phoebus Apollo, to prevent the reader from imagining that Achilles was killed by two people when, in fact, he was killed by one person, Paris, acting under the inspiration of a god, Apollo. *Scaean* gate becomes *yonder* gate because it is more important that the reader should realize that this gate was one of the gates of Troy than that he should know its name without being able to locate it. Lastly, it will be observed that where the other translators introduce Achilles' speech with the simple "Achilles *said*," Graves alters this to "Achilles *stormed*." This is a result of Graves' personal and controversial "reading" of the poem which he explains in his introduction and to which I shall return later.

The most original and, indeed, eccentric feature of his translation is the little lyrics which he intersperses throughout the prose narrative.

Mr Graves believes—I do not know with what justification—that the original source material which Homer took and worked up into an epic poem in hexameters was such a mixture of prose and snatches of verse.

> Other professional story-tellers must have been active in Homer's day, but since not a line of their original work, nor any tradition of it, has survived, we are justified in assuming that, like their ancient Irish, Welsh and Gaelic counterparts, they used prose; reserving verse for incidental passages of religious or dramatic importance only, when they took up their lyres and sang. . . . Many of the pastoral, agricultural and hunting similes which strew the later books [of the *Iliad*] and seldom quite suit their contexts, seem authentic festival songs. . . . A solemn prayer, a divine message, a dirge or a country song disguised as a simile—they sound all wrong when turned into English prose; just as wrong as when muster rolls and long detailed accounts of cooking a meal or harnessing a mule are kept in verse.

Using Chase and Perry as a good crib for comparison, here are two examples of Mr Graves' practice.

> Then the god-like Epeius sprang upon the other and struck him on the cheek while he was looking for an opening, and not for long after did

Euryalus stand up, for his glorious limbs collapsed upon the ground. As when from a sea ruffled by Boreas a fish leaps up, just off the weedy shore, and then the dark wave covers him, so had he leaped up when hit. But great-hearted Epeius seized him with his hands and drew him up.

(Chase and Perry)

At last, Epeius rushed in decisively. Euryalus, crouching to block his lead, caught a powerful uppercut on the cheek-bone.

> This beach so virginal and bare
>   Dark piles of weed now stain;
> The brutal north wind brought it there—
> But look, a fish leaps in the air,
>   And then flops back again.

Up went Euryalus, and then down, just like that fish. Epeius amicably heaved him upright.

(Graves)

So they fought about the well-benched ships. But Patroclus stood beside Achilles, shepherd of the people, shedding warm tears like a dark-watered spring which pours its dusky waters over some sheer cliff. Seeing him, swift-footed god-like Achilles pitied him and spoke to him winged words: "Why do you weep, Patroclus, like some little girl who runs beside her mother and bids her take her up, clinging to her robe and hindering her as she would hurry on, and looking tearfully up at her until she takes her up? Like her, Patroclus do you shed soft tears. Are you trying to tell something to the Myrmidons, or to me myself, or have you alone had news from Phthia?

(Chase and Perry)

While this struggle beside the ships was in progress, noble Patroclus visited the hut of Achilles the swift-footed [*Graves wishes to remind the reader that Achilles is not fighting by the ships but sulking in his tent*] and:

> His tears ran down as mournfully as if
> They were some dark stream oozing from a cliff.

Achilles rallied him: "Why come weeping to me, Patroclus, like a heart-broken little girl to her mother?

> "Mother," sobs the pretty creature,
>   Clutching at her gown,
> "Take me with you, pick me up,
>   Carry me to town!"

> And the mother, though molested,
> > Has no other choice.
> She obeys that tearful, shrill,
> > Too insistent voice.

"Have you bad news for the Myrmidons, or for me—some private message from Phthia?"

For these songs and snatches, Graves uses a variety of meters, but all are written in the unadorned, unelevated, easy-going style of folk songs, weather saws, and nursery rhymes. This is true even for the prayers. Thus Achilles invokes Zeus in the measure of *The Groves of Blarney*:

> O Zeus Almighty,
> Quick to show mercy,
> Will no God pity
> > King Peleus' son?
> This cruel river,
> Divine Scamander,
> Pursues me ever,
> > Though swift I run . . .

Those who are acquainted with Mr Graves' theory of Poetry, with its contrast between the True Muse (The White Goddess) and the False Muse (Apollo) are aware that, among the poets of the official canon, he has certain *bêtes noires*, in particular, Virgil and Milton. To him their work at its best is but grandiloquent rhetoric, the product of will, self-admiration, and social and intellectual snobbery rather than humble devotion to the Goddess of Life. His "reading" of the *Iliad* is a conscious polemic against what might be called the Virgilian conception of Homer. His enemies are, first, the sophists and grammarians of classical Greece and Rome, who treated the *Iliad* as a Sacred Book, and, secondly, the humanists and schoolmasters of Europe, who since the Renaissance have made study of the poem part of the curriculum for a genteel education.

Mr Graves would probably be the first to admit that the Greek is a little more ceremonious and elevated in style than his English—after all, it was written to be recited on festival occasions—but, by comparison with the stiff solemnity of Virgil, it is humorous and indecorous: one always feels that, had it not been for Virgil, the humanists of the sixteenth century would have dismissed Homer as a barbaric writer.

Homer's portrayal of the Olympian Gods has always bewildered or shocked readers. Xenophanes complained in 500 B.C. and it was, primarily, the example of the *Iliad* which led Plato to ban poets from his Republic.

What is most shocking about the behavior of the gods is not their immorality and cruelty, but their total lack of dignity; no human being could possibly respect them. One could advance various hypotheses to account for Homer having presented them thus:

(1) Homer and his audience both believed in the existence of the Olympians and that they had the character he describes, but never noticed that they were contemptible.

(2) His audience believed in them, but Homer did not. With a poker face he made fun of the religion of his audience who were too dumb or drunk to notice.

(3) Neither Homer nor his audience believed any longer in the Olympian Gods and treated them as a joke. In that case, the audience must have been either free-thinking or believers in other Gods. I may be quite wrong, but Mr Graves' suggestion that Homer's audiences were "no more and no less religiously sincere than most cradle-Catholics and cradle-Protestants" seems to me psychologically implausible. Surely, it is the conventional social believer who is the most shocked by levity and humor in religious matters; a serious believer always enjoys apparent irreverence.

(4) His audience believed in nothing much, but Homer himself was secretly a member of a non-official religious cult. This is Mr Graves' view. That Demeter and Persephone and Iacchus, the main figures in these (Eleusinian, Samothracian, Orphic) Mysteries, are kept out of Homer's Divine Harlequinade, suggests that he, and his sons after him, were adepts—hence their poor view of official religion.

As regards Homer's human characters, most readers of the *Iliad* have felt much more sympathy for Hector and Priam than for Achilles and Agamemnon. Mr Graves contends that this was intentional on Homer's part.

> . . . By Homer's time the religious High Kingship had perished, all the great cities had fallen, and the semi-barbarous princelings who camped on the ruins were ennobled by no spark of divinity. It is clearly these iron-age princes—descendants of the Dorian invaders who drove his own ancestors overseas—whom Homer satirizes in Mycenaean disguise as Agamemnon, Nestor, Achilles and Odysseus.

By satire, Mr Graves means ironic concealed satire, not direct attack as, for example, the satire of Aristophanes. I have always admired Mr Ronald Searle's satiric drawings in *Punch*, but I think it was a mistake to employ him to illustrate Mr Graves' version of the *Iliad*. By little touches here and there Mr Graves has tried to emphasize the irony, but Mr Searle's drawings make savage ridicule of both Gods and Heroes. If Homer had written as Mr Searle draws, he would not have lived long.

No definitive once-for-all translation of any poem is possible and in the case of a poem as great as the *Iliad*, the reader who knows no Greek should not be content with a single translation, but should read a number, compare them, and see what he can get out of one which he cannot get out of another. Speaking for myself, I can only say that, of all the cribs and translations of the *Iliad* which I know, Mr Graves' is by a long way the most enjoyable. If I were allowed to buy only one version, I would buy his.

The Mid-Century, March 1960

The Queen Is Never Bored

Queen Mary. By James Pope-Hennessy. Knopf. $10.

The biographer of a Royal Personage has a peculiar task. Normally, it may be said of a life which deserves recording that "character is destiny." The biographer of a statesman or a scientist or an artist or a courtesan traces the steps by which a person realizes his latent possibilities and finally succeeds in becoming what from the beginning he desired or was meant to be. In such a history, though many lucky or unlucky events occur outside the hero's control, the main interest lies in the decisions taken by himself, in watching how he surmounts obstacles and seizes opportunities and thus makes his own history.

Royalty, on the other hand, can play very little part in determining its destiny. A certain heredity is essential, but in a formal sense only; it is not genetic constitution that decides who shall wear the Crown but the chance order of births and deaths in a particular family. Royal princes and princesses have some degree of personal choice in their marriages, but much less than other folk. It is easy to say what qualities are desirable in a constitutional monarch who reigns but does not govern: He (and his consort) need not be intelligent or artistic or beautiful or amusing, but he must be dignified, tactful, punctual, and selfless, prepared to be politically impartial, whatever his personal views, and to work like a horse at fulfilling his duties whether he enjoys them or not, and no human being could enjoy many of them. The qualities required, in fact, are all *moral* qualities; that is to say, qualities that nobody is born with or has a peculiar aptitude for but that can be acquired only by training and self-discipline. The interest in reading a royal biography is partly that of watching the mysterious workings of Chance, or Providence, through which *this* person becomes King or Queen, not *that* person, and partly that of watching how a human being, comparable to other human beings, succeeds or fails in training himself or herself and adapting to the incomparable position, imposed by Fate, of a Sacred Being.

What, despite many trials and sorrows, was to turn out a happy story, both for Princess May (the subject of *Queen Mary*, by James Pope-Hennessy, published in this country by Knopf) and for England, began with a comic misfortune—the unusual size of Her Royal Highness Princess Mary Adelaide, daughter of the Duke of Cambridge and a first cousin of Queen Victoria. In 1857, when she was twenty-four, the American Minister to the Court of St James's estimated her weight at two hundred and fifty pounds. The aristocracy referred to her as "our domestic Embonpoint." Once, while dancing with the Comte de Paris, she collided with another girl and knocked her flat down on her back. She herself was quite jolly about it. "She would allow," says Mr Pope-Hennessy, "small relatives to test [her weight] on her velvet-covered scales or spontaneously demonstrate a tarantella to the dancing-class to which her daughter went." Except for her mother's lady in-waiting, Lady Geraldine Somerset, who conceived a pathological jealousy for both her and her daughter and never ceased trying to make mischief, everyone liked her, but how was she to secure a husband? "Alas!" wrote Lord Clarendon. "No German Prince will venture on *so vast an undertaking*."

In 1865, however, the Prince of Wales struck up a friendship with a young gentleman in Vienna whom he invited over to England, and within a month of their meeting he and the Princess Adelaide were engaged. *Der schöne Uhlan*, Francis, Duke of Teck, was four years younger than his bride, he was the child of a morganatic marriage, and he was penniless, but he was extremely handsome. Queen Victoria, who had no patience with the snobbish attitude of her German relatives toward morganatic blood, but possessed a feminine eye for masculine good looks, was delighted, and she wrote to her eldest daughter, the Crown Princess of Prussia:

> I do *wish* one cld find some more black-eyed Pces and Pcesses for *our* children!—I can't help thinking what dear Papa said—that it was in fact a blessing when there was some little *imperfection* in the *pure Royal* descent & that some fresh blood was infused. . . . For that constant fair hair & blue eyes makes the blood so lymphatic. . . it is *not* as *trivial* as you may think for darling Papa—*often* with vehemence said: "We *must have some strong dark blood*."

After their marriage, the Tecks settled down in Kensington Palace and produced a family of one girl—the Princess May of this narrative—and three boys. Nearby, at Marlborough House, lived the Prince and Princess of Wales with their two sons and three daughters, of more or less the same age as the Teck children. The Duchess of Teck had boundless energy, a warm heart, a social conscience—she took her charities very seriously—but she was incapable of keeping anything in order. She had no sense of time—a failing she shared, curiously, with Alexandra, Princess of Wales, who once disorganized the whole railroad system of northern Europe by keeping her special train waiting for hours.

"We dine—that is we ought to dine at 8 o'C . . . it is by now 7:15 but no Mama back from Town yet," the Duke of Teck wrote to his daughter of some evening when they were dining with a Richmond neighbour, "what a Life dear Mama leads me! . . . It is 7:30 now, no Mama yet, but I must dress and if necessary go on foot." It was said in Princess May's family that she had read all three volumes of Motley's *Dutch Republic* while waiting for her mother before meals.

The Duchess also had no sense of money. She would try to economize by saving paper from parcels, hoarding pieces of string, snipping away blank sheets at the end of a letter, but though enjoying the not inconsiderable income, for those days, of eight thousand pounds a year, the Tecks managed to spend about fifteen thousand. The Duke was overly aware of his morganatic blood, and this made him absurdly touchy about social precedent; further, no one would give him a real job. He saw to the interior decoration of the house, he arranged the flowers, he advised his wife upon how to wear her jewelry—tasks for which he had great taste and talent—but they were hardly enough for a full life; he brooded about his social position, he worried about the financial future, and his temper got worse and worse. At the age of forty-four, he had a stroke, and from then on he was a sick man who finally had to be confined.

We reveal the influence of others upon us when we imitate their behavior and when we do exactly the opposite. From her mother, Princess May inherited her robust constitution and energy, and acquired by imitation her sense of social duty and distaste for idleness, and by reaction, maybe, her love of order and her preference for reading and observation to writing and talking.

Mama never has time [to read]. She pumps Dolly and she pumps me as to what we have been reading lately. Then some clever man comes to dine, and Mama talks brilliantly about the books she hasn't read and they say: "It is remarkable how Your Royal Highness can find the time to keep up with the literature of the day!" Now I *have* read the book, but I can't talk about it.

From her father, she acquired his interest in interior decoration and art objects, which, alas, he could never afford to buy, and perhaps his temper tantrums taught her the value of emotional control. She was to carry the reputation through her life of being shy, but "untalkative" would be a better word. As the eldest child and the only girl, she developed a sense of maternal responsibility early and was, even in nursery and school days, referred to as the Peacemaker. Yet she seems to have possessed a capacity for high spirits, which she seldom showed. "I always have to be so careful never to laugh," Princess May remarked on one occasion, "because you see I have such a *vulgar* laugh."

Though the Tecks were patriotically English, they were also proud of being members of that enormous Royal Family descended from George III (ten of whose fifteen children married) and Queen Victoria (all of whose nine children married), which dwelt in palaces and *Schlösser* dotted about all over Protestant and Greek Orthodox Europe. The late King George VI is reputed to have remarked, "Abroad is bloody." Such a sentiment would have been incomprehensible to his mother's generation. The English members might grumble about the dullness of this small German court or the bad food at that, but they all spoke fluent French and German, and the round of family visits by yacht and special train was a normal part of their social routine. The idea of visiting countries in the British Empire had not yet occurred either to them or to their Ministers. As late as 1891, when Edward, the Prince of Wales, proposed sending his eldest son on a tour of the colonies, Queen Victoria was against the idea.

> Eddy's good, & above all, his aptness for his position *must* be *the one thing* to be looked at. He ought to be able to take his place amongst all the European Princes & *how can he*, if he knows nothing of European Courts & Countries? He & Georgie are charming dear good boys, but very *exclusively* English which you & your brothers are not, & this is a great misfortune in these days. . . . They have, especially Eddy, gone nowhere (excepting India) but to *English speaking* Colonies. These Colonies offer no opportunities for the cultivation of art or of any historical interest whatever. . . . This is *not* what is wanted for dear Eddy, who has been nowhere but to Denmark & once or twice, Berlin & Darmstadt. But of Italy, Spain, Austria, Hungary, Russia, Turkey & Holland (very interesting) he knows nothing. . . . You know yourself, who are so fond of going abroad how it enlarges one's views & rubs off that angular insular view of things which is not good for a Prince.

Aside from any cultural benefits to be derived from their European visits, the English Royal Family enjoyed, up till 1914, the advantage of having their private political intelligence service, and were not entirely dependent, as they now are, upon the documents submitted to them by the Government—an advantage that far outweighed any possible danger that they might engage in a royal diplomacy that was contrary to the policy of their Ministers.

Even as a child, Princess May spent many happy days at Schloss Rumpenheim, near Frankfurt; at Schloss Reinthal, near Graz; and at the Court of Mecklenburg-Strelitz, the home of her aunt the Grand Duchess Augusta, whose lifelong friendship contributed greatly to her intellectual development. Short and plump, the Duchess had something of the look of a complacent partridge. Kindhearted and sharp-tongued, she had a passion for politics—her own views were comically reactionary—and Italian opera. She did a great deal for her niece; she was the first person to recognize her qualities and encourage her to have confidence in herself; she imbued her with a sense of the sacred nature of monarchy, and then—unintentionally, perhaps—she aroused her interest in what was happening in the world, for though the Duchess regarded all changes as changes for the worse, her curiosity was much stronger than her distaste, and if one of her niece's most outstanding characteristics in later life was her open-minded attitude toward new experiences, she owed this in large measure to her arch-Tory aunt, who was to die in Germany during the First World War, surrounded by English newspapers.

The Duchess of Teck's obliviousness of her financial position (once, when opening a church hall to which one of her chief creditors among the tradesmen had contributed, she startled the company by turning to him with a smile and saying, "And now I must propose a special vote of thanks to Mr Barker, to whom we all owe so much") was not shared by others, and by 1883, when Princess May was not quite seventeen, the Tecks faced bankruptcy. Their relatives met, the Queen was consulted, and finally, after an exceedingly public auction of the contents of Kensington Palace, they were packed off to Florence, travelling incognito under the name of Hohenstein. These unfortunate events had their profitable side for the Princess. She was introduced to the architecture, landscape, and painting of Italy, she began to study foreign literature, and she got a glimpse, vouchsafed to few Royal Princesses, of upper bohemia.

> The recognized head [of the English society] was old Lady Orford. who kept a weekly *salon* from ten at night till four in the morning, during which she chain-smoked black cigars.
>
> Both in the English and the Italian society of Florence, the tone was, by London standards, unusually free. The *ménage à trois* was accepted, quite naturally, as the only civilized solution to the problems of marriage, and at Lady Orford's *salon* there was even the spectacle of a Florentine lady playing whist with her husband, her ex-husband, and her lover.

In those days, no English girl could "come out" or be presented at Court until she had been confirmed, and when Princess May had celebrated her seventeenth birthday, a battle Royal began. The Queen wished the ceremony performed at once, the Bishop of Gibraltar was ready to come to Florence to perform it, but the Duchess stalled; if her daughter could not be confirmed in the Chapel Royal, she shouldn't be confirmed at all, so it was not until August, 1885, after the family had relented and allowed the Tecks to return to England, that this necessary precondition to becoming a deb was fulfilled, so that Princess May could appear at her first drawing room in the following year.

For the next six years, she acted as her mother's secretary, assisting her in her multifarious charities.

Princess Mary Adelaide gave her patronage to any charity, bazaar, or organization which seemed to her genuine and efficiently run. This patronage was never of a merely nominal character. . . . She would herself open all letters addressed to her, decide which were worthy of immediate attention, draft replies and, with her daughter's aid, classify each case in one of her charity ledgers. . . . [But] owing to her habitual unpunctuality and procrastination she was always behind with her business correspondence. The letters she received were methodically stacked in her davenport . . . but these trim piles of papers tended to accumulate there unanswered. Here, again, Princess May stepped into the breach, acting from that sense of daughterly duty then expected by parents of unmarried girls. It was tiring work.

Often tired and sometimes bored, Princess May nevertheless acquired in this way first-hand acquaintance with poverty and suffering, and a concern for social evils that she never lost. At this time, too, she was given a French governess, Mme Bricka, who became a lifelong friend and one of the very few people to whom she could talk without reserve. Mme Bricka not only widened her intellectual horizon by making her read George Eliot, modern history, and Blue Books on industrial and social conditions but also taught her that it is unbecoming for a Princess to be a snob. "It does not," her governess said, "make people more Loyal to be snubbed."

Princess May had now reached the marriageable age, but her situation was a peculiar one.

Her morganatic blood and her own inclinations prevented Princess May's being absorbed into a minor German royal family. . . . The Duke of Teck had no fortune and his daughter would be virtually dowerless. . . . Only a very rich member of the peerage, like Lord Hopetoun, or the Marquess of Bath's heir, Lord Weymouth, would be in a position to marry Princess May and provide her with an appropriate social position. . . . From the point of view of any marriage Princess May thus had the worst of two worlds: she was too Royal to marry an ordinary English gentleman, and not Royal enough to marry a Royalty.

Meantime, her Wales cousins were also growing up. Family life, both at Marlborough House and at Sandringham, was rather odd. There was a passion for practical jokes. The Prince, a middle-aged man, would himself supervise the construction of apple-pie beds or stuff the pockets of some guest's evening clothes with sticky sweets; parents and children would fill bicycle pumps with water and squirt each other and their guests. As a wife and a Princess, Alexandra, or Motherdear, as she was called, suffered from the notorious infidelities of her husband and her own hereditary deafness, so that, not unnaturally, she lavished all her devotion upon her children.

Though Queen Victoria may have been wrong in thinking that all five were puny and sickly, they showed, as often happens with the overmothered, a marked tendency to hypochondria and an unwillingness to grow up. On her nineteenth birthday, Princess Louise sent invitations for "a children's party."

By the time he had reached his early twenties, the character of Prince Eddy, who stood in the direct line of succession, began to cause his parents alarm. As fond of dissipation as his father, he completely lacked his father's energy, self-confidence, and—despite all his love of pleasure—sense of royal duty. Like many parents before and since, Prince Eddy's decided that what their boy needed was a good, sensible wife. Eddy's first choice had been Princess Alix of Hesse, a prospect of which Queen Victoria approved, but Alix turned him down. (Later, she was to accept Nicholas of Russia and die in the cellars of Ekaterinburg.) Within a month of this refusal, he was greatly taken with Princess Hélène of Orléans, a daughter of the Comte de Paris. This time, his prospective choice was genuinely in love with him, and his mother and sisters were romantically enthusiastic; the Queen was not.

> I have heard it rumoured that *you* had been thinking and talking of Princesse Hélène d'Orléans! I cant believe this for you know that I told you . . . that such a marriage is utterly *impossible.* None of our family can marry a catholic without losing all their rights and I am sure that she would never change her religion and to change her religion merely to marry is a thing much to be deprecated and which would have the very worst effect possible and be most unpopular, besides which *you* could not marry the daughter of the Pretender to the French Throne. Politically in this way it would also be impossible.

The Princess was sufficiently enamored to promise to change her religion, but when her father got to hear of it, he put his foot down. She went to Rome to plead in person with the Pope. The Pope said no. So that was that. The Queen, who was not generally given to self-deception, persuaded herself that Prince Eddy was broken-hearted, but, as Mr Pope-Hennessy remarks of him, "Prince Albert Victor's part in this romantic story would be more touching were it not for documentary evidence that he was simultaneously in love with someone else," Lady Sybil St Clair Erskine. It was only now that Motherdear began to think of Princess May as a possibility. She communicated her thoughts to the Queen, and the Tecks were summoned to Balmoral. The visit was a triumphal success. Queen Victoria took a fancy to May, and Prince Eddy was more or less ordered to propose. The Duchess of Teck's old enemy, Lady Somerset, was wild with rage, as witness her diary:

> Presently the rest of the party came, Princess Mary Adelaide, Prince Teck and Dolly just returned (this morning only) from Balmoral!—Evidently that is to be!!! Princess Mary Adelaide informed me "the Queen

has fallen in love with my children! *specially May*!! she thinks her so well brought up! *so amusing*" (the very last thing in the world I should say she is!!) etc. . . . in short Princess Mary Adelaide at all counts is satisfied it is to be! The Duke talking of May's prospects!! enchanted at them!!

On the evening of December 3, 1891, a county ball was held in the county mansion of Luton Hoo, at which both Prince Eddy and Princess May were present. While the house guests and the country neighbors were frolicking in the ballroom, the Prince led her into an overheated and overfurnished boudoir. Princess May recorded the evening as follows:

> To my great surprise Eddy proposed to me during the evening in Mme de Falbe's boudoir—Of course I said yes—

Within six weeks, her fiancé was dead of pneumonia. Sixteen months passed. On May 3, 1893, Princess May had arranged to go to tea at Sheen Lodge, another country house, belonging to the Duchess of Fife. There, among other guests, was the younger brother to her dead fiancé, Prince George, the Duke of York.

> "Now, Georgie," said the hostess, "don't you think you ought to take May into the garden to look at the frogs in the pond?"

And Princess May's diary recorded that expedition thus:

> We walked together afterwards in the garden and he proposed to me, & I accepted him.

It would be easy for anti-monarchist propaganda to manipulate this story so as to draw a picture of Princess May as either a calculating opportunist, determined at all costs to become Queen of England, or a poor victim heartlessly sacrificed to dynastic necessity, but both pictures would be false. Even if Queen Victoria was right in thinking that the Princess was never in love with Eddy, she had known him since childhood and, had she positively disliked him, could have and would have refused him, just as Princess Alix had; the Royal Family might have been disappointed, but nobody would have tried to force her. There are girls to whom wealth and social prestige are more powerful motives for marriage than love, but they try to marry millionaires or dukes, not the heir to a constitutional throne. The present Queen Mother hesitated for two years to marry George VI, even though, at the time, the chances of his ever becoming more than the Duke of York seemed negligible.

"Of course I said yes" is the phrase not of someone who has realized her worldly ambition but of one who has been called by Providence to a sacred task it is her duty to perform. Whether it was true, as many people at the time believed, that Princess May had always preferred Prince George to his elder brother cannot be proved; what is indubitable is that the marriage turned out an exceptionally happy one. A few months after their honeymoon, her husband wrote to her:

> When I asked you to marry me, I was very fond of you, but not very much in love with you, but I saw in *you* the person I was capable of loving most deeply, if you only returned that love. . . . I have tried to understand you & to know you, & with the happy result that I know now that I do *love* you darling girl with all my *heart*, & am simply *devoted* to you. . . . *I adore you sweet May*, I can't say more than that. . . .

and this devotion to and dependence upon his wife grew deeper year by year.

Painful as Prince Eddy's death and all the gossip must have been, it is impossible, after reading Mr Pope-Hennessy, not to feel that both Princess May and the country had a providential escape, that her first fiancé would have made neither a good husband nor a good king. Prince George, for that matter, was equally fortunate when his first marriage proposal, to the daughter of the Duke of Edinburgh, was refused; as Queen of England, the future Queen Marie of Rumania would not have done.

The newlyweds made their home in York Cottage, which lay on the grounds of Sandringham, the country home of the Prince of Wales, a fact that, wrote Queen Victoria with her usual sagacity, "I regret and think rather *unlucky* and sad." To begin with, the house itself was unattractive. "It resembled those improbable houses which children can concoct with a box of Swiss or German toy bricks," as Mr Pope-Hennessy remarks. There was too little space, the rooms were dark, the whole house reeked, before each meal, of food, and there was an insufficient number of baths. For a bride who had a natural talent for interior decoration, it was disconcerting to find that the whole place had already been done up and furnished by Prince George without any reference to her taste. Nor was it easy for her to be living within stone's throw of a possessive mother-in-law. (When they were living in their town home, York House, it was Prince George's turn to suffer from *his* mother-in-law, the Duchess of Teck.) Only thirteen days after their marriage, a large party arrived at Sandringham.

> The Princess of Wales would drop in at teatime, her many dogs cavorting at her heels, or send a note asking the young couple up to the "Big House" for dinner, followed by a game of *Kegelspiel*. . . . On one occasion the Princess and her two daughters even came and sat with the Duke and Duchess of York while they were having their breakfast.

Nor was it long before family jealousy began to show itself. She who before her marriage had been referred to as "sweet May" now became "poor May," and her sisters-in-law spread it about that she was "deadly dull." Indeed, during all her early married life she had to endure being looked down on by the smart society with which, both as Prince of Wales and as Edward VII, her father-in-law surrounded himself. But she stood her ground.

> *Il n'y a pas de doute* [she wrote to Mme Bricka] *que je ne suis pas populaire parmi de certains gens, pourquoi je ne sais pas, puisque je me donne un mal infini pour plaire, on me trouve trop* "good," *trop* "particular"—*Certes je n'aime pas leurs* "goings on". . . . *C'est égal j'irai mon chemin, et j'ai plus de diablerie en moi, qu'on ne crois!*

Prince George had three passions—shooting, yachting, and philately—at all of which he excelled, and no interest whatever in art objects, sightseeing, and family history, all of which fascinated his wife. They had, however, two temperamental traits in common—a love of order, tidiness, and punctuality, and a preference for a quiet private life, with a few close friends, to the glamour of "Society." As Duke and Duchess of York, for eight years, and then as Prince and Princess of Wales, for another eight, they had public duties that were not very onerous; they paid official visits to Australia in 1901 and to India in 1905, they attended coronations and royal funerals in Europe, but most of their time was their own. Sir Harold Nicolson has described, in *King George the Fifth, His Life and Reign*, the routine of their early married life:

> He was not at that date accorded access to official documents or Cabinet papers. Had it not been for his frequent and intimate conversations with his father, for his occasional meetings with leading politicians, his knowledge of public affairs would have been neither wider nor deeper than that acquired by any other landowner or sportsman from a daily perusal of the *Times* newspaper. At Sandringham, when he was not out shooting, he would play with his children, read aloud to his wife, visit the farms, dairy and pheasantries, go round the kennels and stables, bicycle in the surrounding country with Sir Charles Cust or Mr Derek Keppel, skate on the lake, take his dog "Heather" for a walk and arrange his stamps. When in London he would give dinner parties at York House, to which members of his family were invited, together with a few Ministers and diplomatists; often in the evenings he would go to the theatre or play billiards at the Marlborough Club. From time to time he and the Duchess would be invited to stay in the houses of the old and new aristocracy.

As Duchess of York, Princess May was now well off, and, encouraged by her brother Dolly and her friend Lady Mount Stephen, she began making her collections of art objects, a hobby she kept up for the rest of her life. Handicapped at the start by lack of training and scholarship, but blessed with an excellent memory, she read studiously and cross-examined every expert she met. Her primary interest was in antiques connected with the history of the

Royal Family, her secondary one was in small objects of all kinds—miniature elephants, miniature tea sets, tiny water colors, and so on. She enjoyed herself immensely, and in time acquired an expert's knowledge of English royal iconography of the eighteenth and nineteenth centuries, but an art connoisseur she was not and never pretended to be. "She never bought a good painting in her life," says Mr Pope-Hennessy baldly.

Happy marriages are not as interesting to read about as unhappy ones, and the very virtues of his heroine presented Mr Pope-Hennessy with a problem. Had she, as a wife, attempted to dominate her husband, or, as Queen Consort, tried to play a political role, his task in recounting her forty-two years of married life would have been much easier. Sadly but inevitably, the reader's interest during this period is most held by Mr Pope-Hennessy's account of Mary and George as parents, a role in which neither was perfect. Temperaments aside, it is unusually difficult for royal parents to be ideal parents. Between them and their children stands a royal household of equerries, ladies-in-waiting, secretaries, nurses, tutors, servants, and so on, which makes it hard to know what is really going on in the nursery or the schoolroom.

> It took [George and Mary] three years, for instance, to discover that Prince Edward's first nurse was trying to turn her charge against his parents, and that she always pinched him before bringing him into the drawing-room, so that he would cry and be sent upstairs again in disgrace. Equally, they were astonished when this unusual nurse had a nervous breakdown and when they thereupon learned that she had not had one single day's holiday for three years.

Then, as the children begin to grow up, in addition to the normal parental anxieties about their characters and futures there is the anxiety of knowing that one, possibly more, of them will inherit a position in which a defect in character can be a national misfortune.

As a child, Princess May had been serious and responsible beyond her years, so as a mother she had no instinctive understanding of juvenility. Having been rather overindulged by his mother, George might have been expected to understand the children better, but he didn't. Queen Victoria once confessed to a friend, "I find no especial pleasure in the company of the elder children. . . . Only very occasionally do I find intimate conversation with them either agreeable or easy," and maybe her grandson inherited this trait. His devotion to his mother had the effect of making him regard the social manners, even the fashions in dress, of his youth as the only possible ones. (I am fascinated to learn that Queen Mary's famous paramecium-like headgear was, initially, more the King's choice than hers.) A man who liked each year to be exactly like the last and hated the novel and the unforeseen was fated to live in a period of revolutionary change. As a king, he was heroic in his self-discipline, his subordination of his personal feelings to the desires of his people, but as a father, which is, after all, a personal, not an official, office, he could not and would not conceal his disapproval and dismay.

> With the best possible intentions. King George V frightened and subdued his children. When they were very young he embarrassed them by chaffing questions, and as they grew up he alienated them by continual criticisms, interspersed with fits of impatient anger.

Their mother did what she could to shield and defend them, but she never succeeded in becoming intimate with them, and the older they grew the more oppressive they found the home atmosphere. After the marriage of the Princess Royal, the future George VI, who was still unmarried and living at home, wrote hopefully to his elder brother:

> Papa & Mama will miss her too terribly, I fear, but it may have a good effect in bringing them out again into public. I feel that they can't possibly stay in & dine together every night of their lives. . . . I don't see what they are going to do otherwise, except ask people here or go out themselves.

"She will indeed be a Queen!" the Grand Duchess Augusta had prophesied of Princess May upon receiving news of Edward VII's death, and she was right. Scarcely known to the public at the time of her coronation, in 1911, by the time of her death, in 1953, Queen Mary had become an even more royal, more numinous figure than her husband or her two sons who succeeded him on the throne.

A Queen Consort has no official duties except the negative duty of not indulging in political intrigue: if she chooses to stay home and meet nobody, she can. On the other hand, in addition to the aid and comfort she can give the King as his wife, there is much that, in an unobtrusive way, she can do for the Crown. The Crown is the sacred symbol of social unity. In any society, inequalities of social power threaten the sense of unity; there are always groups who feel that their social contribution is not receiving the reward and recognition it deserves, and others, like the sick and the unemployed, who, through no fault of their own, are unable to contribute and feel unwanted. The sovereign's primary relation is necessarily with the Government; that is to say, with the representatives of the socially powerful. It is possible that, in an unmilitaristic but male-dominated society, a sovereign queen has greater numinous power than a sovereign king, for she can command the loyalty of her male subjects as a mother and of her female subjects as a woman, whereas a king-father may arouse feelings of rebellion in his sons and of resentment in his daughters, as a symbol of male dominance. By showing a simple human concern for the domestic problems of her own sex, by visiting hospitals and slums, a Queen Consort can make the less fortunate subjects of the Crown feel that the Crown has not forgotten them. All this Queen Mary did.

Blessed by nature with a strong constitution, endowed by nature and by art with a presence at once august and gentle, hating to be idle (when she "rested" she would be read to, and she would answer letters while her hair was being done), open-minded and devoted to her country, she made herself universally loved and respected. As proof of her open-mindedness one example will suffice—the friendship she formed at the beginning of the First World War with Mary Macarthur. Mary Macarthur was a radical feminist who had organized the Sweated Industries Exhibition in 1906, headed strikes by chainmakers and jam-makers, established a Women's Trades Union League, and, in addition, married a man who soon became the chairman of the Labour Party. Unlikely company, in fact, for a queen. But when the war broke out, Queen Mary, ignoring any advice to the contrary, insisted upon meeting her to ask her help and advice in organizing the women's war effort, and each immediately recognized the other's quality. It is sad to learn that when, at the end of the war, Queen Mary wanted Mary Macarthur to be rewarded in the Honours List, the King was advised, presumably by Lloyd George, that it would not be suitable.

The outbreak of war, with its special obligations, so early in their reign, coupled with the conscientiousness of both King George V and Queen Mary, set a precedent that was not, perhaps, altogether fortunate. In wartime, when the national existence is in danger, it is desirable that Royalty should appear in public as much as possible, but demands that are just in a situation of crisis should not be made the norm. The continual public appearances that are now expected from the Royal Family are unfair to them and psychologically unwise. The sovereign today is overworked to a degree that is a danger to physical and nervous health. Royal Persons are either Sacred Beings or nonentities, and every public appearance on a trivial occasion tends to weaken their numinous aura. Even more dangerous is the publicity given by the press to everything they do. Sacred Beings cannot be treated as if they were film stars. When Lord Altrincham criticized Queen Elizabeth's style of public speaking, he was acting, whether his criticisms were just or unjust, as a loyal subject concerned with what he believed to be a defect in her as his sovereign. But when the newspapers publish every rumor, true or false, about the private lives of the Royal Family, they are doing their best, whatever loyalty they may profess, to turn the United Kingdom into a republic.

The psychologist Groddeck observed that one can gauge the happiness of a marriage by what happens to the survivor after the death of the other partner. If a marriage has been really happy, the death of his wife has a catastrophic effect upon the husband; the deprivation of the company and affection upon which he has come to depend destroys him. The widow of a happy marriage, on the other hand, grows in character and wisdom; the memory of having been really loved gives her the psychological strength, now that she is on her own, to become herself. If Groddeck's observation is correct, then Queen Mary's seventeen years as a widow prove her marriage to have been happy indeed. Her husband had not been dead a year before she had to endure the shock of her eldest son's abdication. About this unhappy story two things may be said: It was greatly to his honor that Edward VIII did not dodge the issue in the way that almost any sovereign before him would have done, by marrying a suitable lady and keeping the woman he loved as the royal mistress; secondly, those who, like his mother and the vast majority of his subjects, were unwilling to accept Mrs Simpson as Queen Consort were not moral hypocrites, condemning in her what they condoned in themselves; their rejection implied no moral judgment of her as a person like themselves; they simply felt that her history disqualified her from what most people are never called upon to become, a Sacred Being.

The public affection for the Queen Mother did more than anything else to make the transition from the reign of Edward VIII to the reign of George VI a smooth one. It had thitherto been the convention that no crowned head attend the coronation of a European sovereign, but now, with shrewd insight, Queen Mary decided to make an innovation and asked George VI for permission to attend his coronation and take part in the procession through London.

Two and a half years later, the Second World War broke out. Queen Mary, who was now seventy-two, wished to remain in London, but the King persuaded her to accept the hospitality of the Duke of Beaufort and withdraw to Badminton House, in Gloucestershire, which was to be her home for the next six years. She knew nothing about country life, for country sports and animals had never interested her. Now she found herself in a milieu in which the conversation was mainly about crops, livestock, and hunting. At the beginning, she was somewhat bewildered.

> In those first September days she startled the Duchess of Beaufort, who was pointing out to her aunt a remarkable field of hay, by enquiring: "So *that's* what hay looks like?"

But she soon began to learn. She had always detested ivy, which she considered destructive to stonework, brickwork, and trees, and at Badminton House there was plenty of her enemy around. Presently her equerry, her lady-in-waiting, her private secretary, and anyone who happened to be staying in the house were enrolled in the Ivy Squad. By September, 1940, this had become a Wooding Squad, for clearing out undergrowth and cutting down superfluous timber, and enlarged in numbers by the soldiers attached to Badminton House to defend Queen Mary in the event of invasion. The work was arduous, her household were less than enthusiastic, but she kept them at it. The Salvage Campaign also naturally appealed to her love of collecting and tidying.

> Her enthusiasm for salvaging scrap iron, combined with her ignorance of country habits, occasionally carried Queen Mary away: several times the green Daimler returned loaded with field harrows and other imple-

ments which farmers usually leave out in their fields in all weathers, and which Queen Mary had concluded to be discards ready for the scrap dump. In these cases the objects were quietly returned to their owners without the Queen's knowledge.

Badminton House was not far from Bristol and Bath, so air-raid alarms were frequent. Very soon, Queen Mary gave up descending to the shelter, and siren-awakened members of the household, dishevelled and bleary-eyed, would find her "perfectly dressed and sitting bolt upright, solving a crossword puzzle." As soon as she realized that soldiers on foot like to be given lifts, she ordered her chauffeur always to stop and invite into her car any soldier, sailor, or airman he saw. These random and unofficial encounters gave Queen Mary an opportunity, thitherto denied her by royal protocol, of learning about the lives and opinions of the young; she had never been a snob, but she now became more democratic than ever. Despite all the discomforts and anxieties of wartime and her grief at the death, in an air crash, of the Duke of Kent, these six years of country seclusion seem to have been among the happiest years of her life.

Before leaving, Queen Mary gave separate audiences to the nine Heads of Departments on the Duke of Beaufort's estate. Tears streaming down her face, she handed to each a valuable and carefully chosen present. "Oh. I have been happy here!" she said to one of them. "Here I've been anybody to everybody, and back in London I shall have to begin being Queen Mary all over again."

Back again in Marlborough House, though she entertained little, Queen Mary was still very active; she visited galleries and art dealers, she went to the theatre, and she read. After a party at Buckingham Palace to celebrate the wedding of Princess Elizabeth and Prince Philip, she could write in her diary, "I stood from 9:30 till 12:15 A.M.!!! not bad for 80." Sciatica began to bother her, yet she insisted on attending the opening of the Festival of Britain, in a wheelchair. She read Tolstoy and Dostoevski for the first time. On February 6, 1952, she received news of the death of George VI. From this shock she did not recover, and she began to age rapidly, but she refused to give in. "I suppose," she said one day to an old friend, Lady Shaftesbury, "one must force oneself to go on until the end?" "I am sure," replied Lady Shaftesbury, "that Your Majesty will." Aware that she might die before the coronation of Elizabeth II, she gave instructions that this ceremony should on no account be postponed if she did. And she retained her interests until the very end. Her last letter expressed appreciation of a Goya painting, and on the night before she died, she asked for a book about India to be read aloud to her. "As a matter of fact," she had once written, "The Queen is never bored." There are few people who could dare say this, and still fewer expect to be believed. Queen Mary could, and she is.

When one considers the difference between the England of 1867 and the

England of 1953, Queen Mary's extraordinary success in her role provides a lesson in what is likely to be expected of royalty in the future. In a world where tomorrow has so little in common with yesterday, the symbolic value of a hereditary monarch who is a living contemporary, not an ancient monument, yet—like a monument—a visible reminder of the past, is likely to increase. Though royalty must, as Queen Mary saw, "move with the times," it must not try to set the fashion; it is as dangerous for royalty to be too "modern" in its taste and behavior as for it to be too out-of-date. It is probable, too, that the more permissive society becomes about manners and morals, the stricter will be the demands it makes upon the conduct of its Sacred Beings. The sovereign is always one for whom an exception is made. In the past, this was an exception of license; the King could openly keep mistresses, while his subjects could commit adultery only in secret. In the future, it would seem that the sovereign must be the exception whose fidelity in marriage is notorious; in a licentious democracy a King Farouk is impossible.

Though by baptism and conviction I am an Episcopalian—that is to say, a Protestant—and by choice and adoption an American—that is to say, a citizen of a republic—I must confess that 1620 and 1776 are not dates that fill me with rejoicing. On Sunday mornings, when I am requested to pray for the spiritual and temporal rulers "under whom we may be godly and quietly governed," my roster of names includes Pope John XXIII as well as New Ebor and Cantuar, Queen Elizabeth II as well as the thirty-fourth President. God bless them all! (It's a shame that, owing to their Hanoverian origin, the Royal Family are so "Low.") And Prince Charles, now. In twelve years or so, he will have to start thinking of marriage. Who can She, who will She be? A Princess, Royal or Serene? There aren't any. An English girl? Didn't his great-great-grandmother say that a Prince should not be too insular? A Russian? Rather diffy. An American? Why not? Surely, there will be a number who are beautiful, well bred, and neither divorced nor Catholic. The *Daily Express*, the *New Statesman*, the *Chicago Tribune* will probably be cross, but so much the better.

The New Yorker, 21 May 1960

Foreword to *Van Gogh: A Self-Portrait*

In most cases, to go through a man's correspondence and make the proper selection for publication would be easy. One would merely have to pick out the few letters which were interesting and discard the many which were dull or unintelligible to the general reader without elaborate editorial notes. But there is scarcely one letter by Van Gogh which I, who am certainly no expert, do not find fascinating. Anyone who can afford them will want to possess and ought to buy the magnificent three volumes edited by Vincent W. van Gogh.

"What," I asked myself, "is the single most important fact about Van Gogh?" To that there seemed only one answer—"That he painted pictures."

I have, therefore, confined my selection to those of his letters which contain reflections upon the art of painting and the problems of being a painter, and have only included letters concerned with his personal relations, to his father and his brother, for example, in so far as these throw direct light upon his career as a painter.

Van Gogh was such an extraordinary character, however, that I have also generously selected from the descriptions given of him by acquaintances at various times in his life, which are printed in the complete edition.

Van Gogh: A Self-Portrait. Letters revealing his life as a painter,
selected by W. H. Auden, 1961

Statement by W. H. Auden on Cultural Freedom Written on Occasion of Congress Anniversary

Cultural Freedom, as I understand the words, is to Culture what Oecumenicity is to Religion.

A genuine cultural oecumenicity cannot be achieved, either by the imposition of the values of one culture upon all the others, nor by boiling them all together into a tasteless soup of generalities.

Differences exist—it is highly desirable, probably, that they should—and honest discourse requires that all parties be frank about them. But true discourse demands certain rules of debate, of which the most essential seem to me to be as follows.

(1) Differences must be discussed in a dialectical spirit, not an eristic. We must be prepared to believe that our opponents are as concerned with a common truth as ourselves. Debate between parties who regard each other as malevolent or lunatic is not possible.

(2) We must always remember that the verb "to tolerate" is transitive. Too often we come to a debate prepared to tolerate but with no intention of being tolerated.

(3) One of the principal purposes of debate is to discover what the parties to it really mean by the words they use. As a general rule, our opponents do not believe exactly what we imagine they believe, and vice versa.

(4) A Conference on Cultural Freedom or any other topic cannot be organised without public meetings and public speeches. These have, of

course, a value in themselves, but their main purpose should be that of bringing a number of individual persons together in the same place at the same time, and so providing them with the physical opportunity for impromptu private discourse.

Congress for Cultural Freedom News, June 1960

Greatness Finding Itself

Young Man Luther. By Erik Erikson. W. W. Norton. $4.50.

Dr Erikson is that happy exception, a psychoanalyst who knows the difference between a biography and a case history. As a therapy, the goal of psychoanalysis is to free the patient from the slavery of impersonal behavior so that he may become capable of personal deeds. A deed is an act by which the doer voluntarily discloses himself to others: behavior is involuntary and discloses, not a unique self, but either those natural needs common to all men or those diagnosable complexes which the patient shares with other sufferers of the same kind. Thanks to psychoanalysis, it is now a matter of public knowledge that, frequently, when we imagine we are acting as ourselves, we are really only exhibiting behavior, and it is one of the analyst's tasks to unmask this illusion in his patients.

Professionally, that is to say, what the analyst is concerned with and confronted by every day in his consulting room is behavior, not deeds. But a biographer is concerned with deeds, with those events in the life of his subject which distinguish it from the lives of all other human beings. Biographical studies of great men by psychoanalysts only too often leave the reader with the feeling: "Well, if that was really all there was to this life, where was the greatness?" Most great men who do deeds which influence the course of history or make works which outlive their own death have exhibited, at critical points in their lives, extremely neurotic behavior, but their greatness cannot be explained away in terms of their neurosis. Had Hölderlin, for example, not suffered from schizophrenia, his poetry would have been different—he might even not have written any—but his schizophrenia does not explain why his poetry is good and recognizable as written by Hölderlin and nobody else.

In his investigation of the psychological crises in Luther's life up to the age of forty-three, Dr Erikson never allows his professional knowledge of neurotic behavior to obscure his awareness that Luther the historical person transcends Luther the patient. At the same time, quite rightly for him, he approaches Luther's history as a psychoanalyst, not as a theologian, a political economist, or a literary critic.

This being a historical book, religion will occupy our attention primarily as a source of ideologies for those who seek identities. In depicting the identity struggle of a young great man, I am not concerned with the validity of the dogmas which laid claim to him, or the philosophies which influenced his systematic thought, as I am with the spiritual and intellectual milieu which the isms of his time—these isms had to be religious—offered to his passionate search. . . . In this book, Ideology will mean an unconscious tendency underlying religious and scientific as well as political thought: the tendency at a given time to make facts amenable to ideas, and ideas to facts, in order to create a world image convincing enough to support the collective and the individual sense of identity. . . . In some periods of his history, and in some phases of his life cycle, man needs a new ideological orientation as surely and as sorely as he must have light and air.

In the lives of those persons who merit a biography, there are normally, according to Dr Erikson, three periods of psychological crisis: the crisis of Identity, the crisis of Generativity, and the crisis of Integrity. Roughly speaking, these occur in youth, middle age and old age, respectively, but they usually overlap and the intensity and duration of each varies from individual to individual.

In the Identity crisis, the young man or woman is trying to find the answer to the question "Who am I *really*, as distinct from what others believe or desire me to be?" This is a crisis of consciousness. The Generativity crisis is a crisis of conscience. The question now to be answered is: "I have done this and that; my acts have affected others in this or that way. Have I done well or ill? Can I justify the influence which, intentionally or unintentionally, I have had on others?" Both the Identity and the Generativity crisis are preoccupied with freedom and choice. The Integrity crisis of old age is concerned with fate and necessity. As Dr Erikson puts it, it demands "the acceptance of one's one and only life cycle as something that had to be and that, by necessity, permitted of no substitutions, the knowledge that an individual life is the accidental coincidence of but one life cycle with but one segment of history."

In *Young Man Luther*, Dr Erikson traces Luther's development up to the onset of his Generativity crisis which began to trouble him when he had become a husband, a father, and a world-famous public figure. One or two remarks which he makes suggest that he thinks Luther was less successful at solving this crisis than he had been at solving his Identity crisis, but he has limited his study to the latter.

In later life Luther used to refer to himself as the son of a poor peasant. This, as Dr Erikson shows, was largely a fantasy. Hans Luder, it is true, was born a peasant, but left farming to become a miner.

The life of a miner in those days was hard, but honorable and well-regulated. Roman law had not penetrated to it; far from being slave-labor, it had a self-regulating dignity, with maximum hours, sanitation laws, and minimum wages. By succeeding in it at the time when he did, Hans Luder not only escaped the proletarization of the landless peasant and unskilled laborer, he also made a place for himself in the managerial class of mine shareholders and foundry co-leaders. . . . To call Hans Luder a peasant, therefore, shows either sentimentality or contempt. He was an early small industrialist and capitalist, first working to earn enough to invest, and then guarding his investment with a kind of dignified ferocity. When he died he left a house in town and 1250 Gold-gulden.

Like most fathers who have begun to rise in the world, he was anxious that his son should rise still further. He made Martin go to Latin School and University, and hoped to see him become a jurist and, maybe, even a burgomaster.

Parents who are ambitious for their children are rarely permissive with them, and in a culture where corporal punishment is the normal method of discipline, they do not spare the rod. Hans Luder had a violent temper but there is no evidence that he was more sadistic than the average father. His son's account of his reaction to one paternal beating is revealing. "I fled him and I became sadly resentful towards him, until he gradually got me accustomed to him again." This sentence, Dr Erikson points out, reveals two trends in the relationship between father and son. "Martin, even when mortally afraid, *could not really hate his father*, he could only be sad; and Hans, while he could not let the boy come close, and was murderously angry at times, *could not let him go for long*."

Most modern books on bringing up children warn parents against projecting their own ambitions onto their children and demanding of them a high standard of achievement. It seems to me that this warning is merited only in cases where there is no relation between the parents' ambition and the child's actual endowments. If the child is stupid, it is obviously harmful to show anger or shame because it is not at the top of the class, just as it is wrong for a father to try to force a son with a talent for, say, engineering, into the family grocery business. But there are many cases in which a parent's ambition is quite justified—if his child *is* talented, talented in the way which the parent believes. From my own experience, I would say that, in the majority of cases, the children of parents who were ambitious for them are successful and, whatever the conflicts and mistakes may have been, they recognize in later life how much they owe their success to the high standard of achievement which was demanded from them at home. Hans was mistaken in believing that Martin should take up a secular career, but in all other respects he understood his son's character remarkably well. He knew, when Martin was

convinced to the contrary, that the celibate life of a monk was not his vocation and, sure enough, in due time Martin left the monastery and married.
He hoped to see his son a successful figure in public life, and Martin succeeded beyond his wildest dreams.

The Protestant Era might be called the era of the Rebellious Son, but this
rebellion was against the Fathers rather than a father. Protestantism set out
to replace the collective external voice of tradition by the internal voice of
the individual conscience which, since it is internal to the subject, is his contemporary. In religion, it shifts the emphasis from the human reason, which
is a faculty we share with our neighbors, and the human body, which is capable of partaking with other human bodies in the same liturgical acts, to
the human will which is unique and private to every individual.

Since this interiorization of the paternal conscience is a process that each
person can only do for himself, the character and behavior of his actual father became more significant in deciding his development in the Protestant
era than it had previously been when a man's father was one member among
others of the Father class.

At a less conscious level, Protestantism implies a rejection—rejection is
not the same thing as rebellion—of the Mother. The doctrine of Predestina-
tion which makes the actions of God's will arbitrary from a human point of
view makes the notion of necessity meaningless and thereby denies any spiritual significance to the fact that we are born from the bodies of our mothers
through the necessary processes of nature.

In its attitude towards the flesh, Protestant piety, even at its most puritanical, is less ascetic than Catholic piety precisely because it attributes less spiritual importance to the flesh. Whatever views one may hold for or against
fasting and corporal penance, such practices indicate a belief that the body
is a partner with the soul in the spiritual life.

The doctrine of justification by Faith implicitly denies this partnership, for
the flesh, subject to natural necessity, can neither possess faith nor lack it,
but it is by means of the flesh, and by no other means, that works are done.

Consciously, both during his Identity crisis, and in later life, Luther was
preoccupied with his relation to his father and to an overmasculine God, but
there are many things about him which suggest that his mother played a
much more important role in his life than he himself realized. We know little
about her except that she was imaginatively superstitious and a somewhat
submissive character, who is reported to have sung to her young son a ditty:
"For me and you nobody cares. That is our common fault." But, as Dr Erikson says, it is extremely rare for a person to succeed in discovering his identity unless his relation to his mother in the years of infancy was one of basic
trust. Luther's career suggests that his infancy must have been a happy and
secure one, and that, like most fathers, Hans Luder left the care and training
of Martin's early years to his mother. Later, however, when he took over the
supervision and disciplining of his son, his wife was too passive a character to

be able to stand between them or stand up for her child when Papa was un-reasonable or unjust. If the Cranach portrait is a good likeness, the bond of identity between Luther and his mother must have been extraordinarily close, for in the picture Luther looks like a middle-aged woman. We know, too, that in later life he became obese, and an obese male always looks like a cross between a small child and a pregnant woman. Then, however opinions may differ about Luther's theology and actions, no one has ever denied his supreme mastery of his mother tongue, his ability, as a preacher, to offer "the milk" of the word. (Luther himself said: "You must preach as a mother suck-les her child.") Of the three modes of human activity—labor, fabrication, and action—it may be said that labor is sexless, fabrication feminine, and action masculine. Preaching is an art, that is to say, a mode of fabrication, not a mode of action; and all "making" is imitative of motherhood, not fa-therhood. It is fascinating to speculate about what Luther would have be-come had his father died during his early adolescence. My guess is that, in-stead of becoming a theologian and a religious leader, he would have turned into a great secular writer, probably a comic one, and that he would certainly not have become a Protestant. But Papa did not die, so the Pope became Antichrist, the Madonna a nonentity, and the only feminine ideal Luther could offer was, as Dr Erikson wittily remarks, "women who wanted to be like parsons if they couldn't be parsons' wives."

The onset of Luther's identity crisis can be precisely dated. On June 2, 1505, when he was seventeen, he was caught in a thunderstorm. A lightning bolt struck the ground near him. Terrified, he cried out: "Help me, St Anne! [the patron saint of miners] I want to become a monk." Presently, he told his friends that he felt committed to enter a monastery, but did not inform his father. This decision is a clear example of the adoption of an experimental mask (Dr Erikson compares it to Freud's decision to become a research neu-rologist). In that age, entering a monastery was a quite ordinary thing for a young man to do.

> To become a monk meant merely to find an entrance, on a defined professional level, to the Catholic empire's hierarchy of clerical employ-ees, which included in its duties diplomacy, the administration of social welfare in countries, counties, cities and towns, spiritual ministration, and the more or less ascetic cultivation of personal salvation. . . . When Martin joined the Augustinian order he became part of that clerical middle class which corresponded and overlapped with the class in which his father wanted him to find a foothold.

Nor was such a step irrevocable; it was always possible to leave, if this was done with discretion.

Rationally, his father's anger was unjustified, but intuitively Hans was right in guessing that his son was making a mistake and making it moreover to spite him.

The final vow would imply both that Martin was another Father's servant, and that he would never become the father of Hans's grandsons.
Ordination would bestow on the son the ceremonial functions of a spiritual father, a guardian of souls and a guide to eternity, and relegate the
natural father to a merely physical status.

Once inside the monastery, trouble, of course, began. Consciously, Luther
was determined to prove to himself and his father that he was in the right;
subconsciously he knew that the monastic vocation was not for him. In consequence he tried to outdo all the other monks in piety and became that
bugbear of the confessional, a scrupuland. In his middle twenties an event
occurred which shows how near he came to disaster. One day in the choir of
the monastery he suddenly fell to the ground, roaring with the voice of a
bull: "*Ich bin's nit!*" [It isn't me!] Chance, or Divine Providence, saved him by
transferring him to the monastery of Wittenberg and introducing him to the
vicar-general of that province, Dr Staupitz. Staupitz was not particularly remarkable in himself, but he loved Luther like a son, and for the first time in
his life Luther found himself treated by an older man as someone of importance. Moreover, by encouraging Luther to lecture and preach, Staupitz released Luther's real talents. From whatever internal conflicts he might continue to suffer, henceforth his ego had the satisfaction of knowing that there
was something he could do supremely well. Preaching to an audience also
enabled him to objectify his personal problems, to view them not as peculiar
to himself but as representative of the spiritual problems of his age.

A young man has discovered his true identity when he becomes able to
call his thoughts and actions his own. If he is an exceptional young man,
these thoughts and actions will be exceptional also, publicly recognizable as
new and revolutionary. So Freud became Freud when he hit on the idea of
the Oedipus complex, Darwin Darwin when he perceived that higher species must have evolved from lower, Luther Luther when he heard in St Paul's
phrase *The Just shall live by Faith* the authentic voice of God. That this revelation should have come to him in a privy is fascinating but not, I think, surprising. There must be many people to whom religious, intellectual, or artistic insights have come in the same place, for excretion is both the primal
creative act—every child is the mother of its own faeces—and the primal act
of revolt and repudiation of the past—what was once good food has become
bad dirt and must be got rid of. From then on, Luther's fate became his own.

Dr Erikson's book is so full of wise observations not only about Luther but
also about human life, that no quotations could do it justice: it must be read
all through. To me, it is particularly illuminating and important because I
believe that the Protestant Era, that is to say, an era in which the dominant
ideology was protestant (with a small p) and catholic ideology the restraining and critical opposition, is now over, that we have entered a Catholic Era

in which the relative positions of the two ideologies is reversed because today the nature of the identity crisis, individual and collective has changed, and changed precisely because of the success of protestantism in all its forms. A solution to our difficulties cannot be found by protestant approach because it is protestantism which has caused them.

In terms of religious history, Newman's conversion to the Roman Church in 1845 marks the beginning of our era. The Christian doctrine which Protestantism emphasizes is that every human being, irrespective of family, class, or occupation, is unique before God; the complementary and equally Christian doctrine emphasized by Catholicism is that we are all members, one with another, both in the Earthly and the Heavenly City.

Or one might say that, in conjugating the present tense of the verb *to be*, catholicism concentrates on the plural, protestantism on the singular. But authentic human existence demands that equal meaning and value be given to both singular and plural, all three persons, and all three genders. Thus, protestantism is correct in affirming that the *We are* of society expresses a false identity unless each of its members can say *I am*; catholicism correct in affirming that the individual who will not or cannot join with others in saying *We* does not know the meaning of *I*.

Whether one considers oneself, one's friends and neighbors, or the history of the last hundred years, it seems clear that the principal threat to a sense of identity is our current lack of belief in and acceptance of the existence of others. Hence the grisly success of various totalitarian movements, for the Evil One can only seduce us because he offers bogus solutions to real needs, one of which is the need for personal authority both to obey and to command (force is impersonal and altogether evil). The function of protestantism today is not to solve our problems but to warn against and oppose all solutions that are speciously, not authentically, catholic, to point out that the catholic community can only be realized by the will of each lutheran individual to create it. By catholic community I do not mean the Christendom of the thirteenth century, nor by lutheran individual, a Lutheran of the sixteenth: there is, as Lichtenberg observed, "a great difference between believing something *still* and believing it *again*."

The Mid-Century, June 1960

K

[See "The I Without a Self" in *The Dyer's Hand,* p. 565,
and textual notes, p. 959.]

The Mid-Century, Fall 1960

Introduction to *The Complete Poems of Cavafy*

Ever since I was first introduced to his poetry by the late Professor R. M. Dawkins over thirty years ago, C. P. Cavafy has remained an influence on my own writing; that is to say, I can think of poems which, if Cavafy were unknown to me, I should have written quite differently or perhaps not written at all. Yet I do not know a word of Modern Greek, so that my only access to Cavafy's poetry has been through English and French translations.

This perplexes and a little disturbs me. Like everybody else, I think, who writes poetry, I have always believed the essential difference between prose and poetry to be that prose can be translated into another tongue but poetry cannot.

But if it is possible to be poetically influenced by work which one can read only in translation, this belief must be qualified.

There must be some elements in poetry which are separable from their original verbal expression and some which are inseparable. It is obvious, for example, that any association of ideas created by homophones is restricted to the language in which these homophones occur. Only in German does *Welt* rhyme with *Geld*, and only in English is Hilaire Belloc's pun possible.

> When I am dead, I hope it may be said:
> "His sins were scarlet, but his books were read."

When, as in pure lyric, a poet "sings" rather than "speaks," he is rarely, if ever, translatable. The "meaning" of a song by Campion is inseparable from the sound and the rhythmical values of the actual words he employs. It is conceivable that a genuine bilingual poet might write what, to him, was the same lyric in two languages, but if someone else were then to make a literal translation of each version into the language of the other, no reader would be able to recognize their connection.

On the other hand, the technical conventions and devices of verse can be grasped in abstraction from the verse itself. I do not have to know Welsh to become excited about the possibility of applying to English verse the internal rhymes and alliterations in which Welsh verse is so rich. I may very well find that they cannot be copied exactly in English, yet discover by modifying them new and interesting effects.

Another element in poetry which often survives translation is the imagery of similes and metaphors, for these are derived, not from local verbal habits, but from sensory experiences common to all men.

I do not have to read Pindar in Greek in order to appreciate the beauty and aptness with which he praises the island of Delos.

> ... motionless miracle of the
> wide earth, which mortals call Delos, but the
> blessed on Olympus, the far-shining star of
> dark-blue earth.

When difficulties in translating images do arise, this is usually because the verbal resources of the new language cannot make the meaning clear without using so many words that the force of the original is lost. Thus Shakespeare's line

> The hearts that spanielled me at heels

cannot be translated into French without turning the metaphor into a less effective simile.

None of the translatable elements in poetry which I have mentioned so far applies, however, to Cavafy. With the free relaxed iambic verse he generally uses, we are already familiar. The most original aspect of his style, the mixture, both in his vocabulary and his syntax, of demotic and purist Greek, is untranslatable. In English there is nothing comparable to the rivalry between demotic and purist, a rivalry that has excited high passions, both literary and political. We have only Standard English on the one side and regional dialects on the other, and it is impossible for a translator to reproduce this stylistic effect or for an English poet to profit from it.

Nor can one speak of Cavafy's imagery, for simile and metaphor are devices he never uses; whether he is speaking of a scene, an event, or an emotion, every line of his is plain factual description without any ornamentation whatsoever.

What, then, is it in Cavafy's poems that survives translation and excites? Something I can only call, most inadequately, a tone of voice, a personal speech. I have read translations of Cavafy made by many different hands, but every one of them was immediately recognizable as a poem by Cavafy; nobody else could possibly have written it. Reading any poem of his, I feel: "This reveals a person with a unique perspective on the world." That the speech of self-disclosure should be translatable seems to me very odd, but I am convinced that it is. The conclusion I draw is that the only quality which all human beings without exception possess is uniqueness: any characteristic, on the other hand, which one individual can be recognized as having in common with another, like red hair or the English language, implies the existence of other individual qualities which this classification excludes. To the degree, therefore, that a poem is the product of a certain culture, it is difficult to translate it into the terms of another culture, but to the degree that it is the expression of a unique human being, it is as easy, or as difficult, for a person from an alien culture to appreciate as for one of the cultural group to which the poet happens to belong.

But if the importance of Cavafy's poetry is his unique tone of voice, there is nothing for a critic to say, for criticism can only make comparisons. A unique tone of voice cannot be described; it can only be imitated, that is to say, either parodied or quoted.

To be writing an introduction to Cavafy's poetry, therefore, is to be in the embarrassing position of knowing that what one writes can only be of interest to people who have not yet read him; once they have, they will forget it as completely as, when one makes a new friend at a party, one forgets the person who made the introduction.

Cavafy has three principal concerns: love, art, and politics in the original Greek sense.

Cavafy was a homosexual, and his erotic poems make no attempt to conceal the fact. Poems made by human beings are no more exempt from moral judgment than acts done by human beings, but the moral criterion is not the same. One duty of a poem, among others, is to bear witness to the truth. A moral witness is one who gives true testimony to the best of his ability in order that the court (or the reader) shall be in a better position to judge the case justly; an immoral witness is one who tells half-truths or downright lies: but it is not a witness's business to pass verdict. (In the arts, one must distinguish, of course, between the lie and the tall story that the audience is not expected to believe. The tall-story teller gives himself away, either by a wink or by an exaggerated poker face: the born liar always looks absolutely natural.)

As a witness, Cavafy is exceptionally honest. He neither bowdlerizes nor glamorizes nor giggles. The erotic world he depicts is one of casual pickups and short-lived affairs. Love, there, is rarely more than physical passion, and when tenderer emotions do exist, they are almost always one-sided. At the same time, he refuses to pretend that his memories of moments of sensual pleasure are unhappy or spoiled by feelings of guilt. One can feel guilty about one's relation to other persons—one has treated them badly or made them unhappy—but nobody, whatever his moral convictions, can honestly regret a moment of physical pleasure as such. The only criticism that might be made is one that applies to all poets, namely, that Cavafy does not, perhaps, fully appreciate his exceptional good fortune in being someone who can transmute into valuable poetry experiences which, for those who lack this power, may be trivial or even harmful. The sources of poetry lie, as Yeats said, "in the foul rag-and-boneshop of the heart," and Cavafy illustrates this by an anecdote:

> The fulfillment of their deviate, sensual delight
> is done. They rose from the mattress,
> and they dress hurriedly without speaking.
> They leave the house separately, furtively; and as
> they walk somewhat uneasily on the street, it seems

as if they suspect that something about them betrays
into what kind of bed they fell a little while back.

But how the life of the artist has gained.
Tomorrow, the next day, years later, the vigorous verses
will be composed that had their beginning here.

("Their Beginning")

But what, one cannot help wondering, will be the future of the artist's companion?

Cavafy's attitude toward the poetic vocation is an aristocratic one. His poets do not think of themselves as persons of great public importance and entitled to universal homage, but, rather, as citizens of a small republic in which one is judged by one's peers and the standard of judgment is strict. The young poet Eumenes is depressed because, after struggling for two years, he has only managed to write one idyll. Theocritus comforts him thus:

And if you are on the first step,
you ought to be proud and pleased.
Coming as far as this is not little;
what you have achieved is great glory. . . .
To set your foot upon this step
you must rightfully be a citizen
of the city of ideas.
And in that city it is hard
and rare to be naturalized.
In her market place you find Lawmakers
whom no adventurer can dupe. . . .

("The First Step")

His poets write because they enjoy writing and in order to give aesthetic satisfaction, but they never exaggerate the importance of aesthetic satisfaction.

Let the flippant call me flippant.
In serious matters I have always been
most diligent. And I will insist that
no one is more familiar than I
with Fathers or Scriptures, or the Synodical Canons.
In each of his doubts,
in each difficulty concerning church matters,
Botaneiatis consulted me, me first of all.
But exiled here (may the malevolent Irene Doukaina
suffer for it), and dreadfully bored,
it is not at all peculiar that I amuse myself

composing sestets and octets—
that I amuse myself with mythological tales
of Hermes, Apollo, and Dionysus,
or the heroes of Thessaly and the Peloponnese;
and that I compose impeccable iambics,
such as—permit me to say—Constantinople's men of letters
    cannot compose.
This very accuracy, probably, is the cause of their censure.
("A Byzantine Noble in Exile Writing Verses")

Cavafy is intrigued by the comic possibilities created by the indirect relation of poets to the world. While the man of action requires the presence of others here and now, for without a public he cannot act, the poet fabricates his poem in solitude. He desires, it is true, a public for his poem, but he himself need not be personally related to it and, indeed, the public he most hopes for is composed of future generations which will only come into being after he is dead. While he is writing, therefore, he must banish from his mind all thoughts of himself and of others and concentrate on his work. However, he is not a machine for producing verses, but a human being like other human beings, living in a historical society and subject to its cares and vicissitudes. The Cappadocian poet Phernazis is composing an epic on Darius and is trying to imagine the feelings and motives which led Darius to act as he did. Suddenly his servant interrupts him to say that Rome and Cappadocia are at war.

Phernazis is impatient. How unfortunate!
At a time when he was positive that with his "Darius"
he would distinguish himself, and shut forever
the mouths of his critics, the envious ones.
What a delay, what a delay to his plans.

But if it were only a delay, it would still be all right.
But let us see if we have any security at all
in Amisus. It is not a very well-fortified city.
The Romans are the most horrible enemies.
Can we get the best of them, we
Cappadocians? Is that ever possible?
Can we measure ourselves in a time like this against legions?
Mighty Gods, protectors of Asia, help us.—

Yet amid all his agitation and the trouble,
the poetic idea persistently comes and goes.—
The most probable, surely, is arrogance and drunkenness;
Darius must have felt arrogance and drunkenness.
("Darius")

Aside from those dealing with his personal experiences, the settings of Cavafy's poems are seldom contemporary. Some are concerned with the his-

tory of Ancient Greece, one or two with the fall of Rome, but his favorite
historical periods are two: the age of the Greek satellite kingdoms set up by
Rome after the Alexandrian Empire had fallen to pieces, and the period of
Constantine and his successors when Christianity had just triumphed over
paganism and become the official religion.

Of these periods he gives us a number of anecdotes and character vignettes.
His Panhellenic world is politically powerless, and in it, therefore, politics
are regarded with cynical amusement. Officially, the satellite kingdoms are
self-governing, but everyone knows that the rulers are puppets of Rome. Political events that are immensely important to the Romans, like the Battle of
Actium, mean nothing to them. Since they must obey in any case, why should
they care what name their master bears?

> The news of the outcome of the naval battle, at Actium,
> was most certainly unexpected.
> But there is no need to compose a new address.
> Only the name needs to be changed. There, in the last
> lines, instead of "Having liberated the Romans
> from the ruinous Octavius,
> that parody, as it were, of Caesar,"
> now we will put, "Having liberated the Romans
> from the ruinous Antony."
> The whole text fits in beautifully.
>
> > ("In a Township of Asia Minor")

There are some, like the Syrian Demetrius Sôtêr, who dream of restoring
their country to its former greatness, but they are forced to realize that their
dream is vain.

> He suffered, he felt much bitterness in Rome
> as he sensed in the talk of his friends,
> young people of prominent houses,
> amid all the delicacy and politeness
> that they kept showing to him, the son
> of the King Seleucus Philopator—
> as he sensed however that there was always
> a covert indifference to the hellenized dynasties;
> that had declined, that are not for serious works. . .
>
> If only he could find a way to get to the East,
> to succeed in escaping from Italy— . . .
>
> Ah, if only he could find himself in Syria!
> He was so young when he left his country,
> that he can barely remember its face.

> But in his thought he always studied it
> as something sacred you approach with adoration,
> as a vision of a lovely land, as a spectacle
> of Greek cities and harbors.—
>
> And now?
>   Now despair and grief.
> The young men in Rome were right.
> It is not possible for dynasties to survive
> that the Macedonian Conquest gave rise to.
>
> No matter: He himself had tried,
> he had struggled as much as he could.
> And in his dark discouragement,
> one thing alone he reckons
> with pride, that, even in his failure,
> to the world he shows the same indomitable manliness.
>
> The rest—were dreams and vain efforts.
> This Syria—scarcely looks like his own country,
> it is the land of Heracleides and Balas.
>   ("Of Demetrius Sôtêr, 162–150 B.C.")

As this poem illustrates, Cavafy is one of the very few poets who can write a patriotic poem that is not embarrassing. In most poetic expressions of patriotism, it is impossible to distinguish what is one of the greatest human virtues from the worst human vice, collective egoism.

The virtue of patriotism has generally been extolled most loudly and publicly by nations that are in the process of conquering others, by the Romans, for example, in the first century B.C., the French in the 1790's, the English in the nineteenth century, and the Germans in the first half of the twentieth. To such people, love of one's country involves denying the right of others, of the Gauls, the Italians, the Indians, the Poles, to love theirs. Moreover, even when a nation is not actively aggressive, the genuineness of its patriotic feelings remains in doubt so long as it is rich, powerful, and respected. Will the feeling survive if that nation should become poor and of no political account and aware, also, that its decline is final, that there is no hope for the return of its former glory? In this age, no matter to which country we belong, the future is uncertain enough to make this a real question for us all, and Cavafy's poems more topical than, at first reading, they seem.

In Cavafy's Panhellenic world, there is one great object of love and loyalty of which defeat has not deprived them, the Greek language. Even peoples to whom it had not originally been their native tongue have adopted it, and the language has become all the richer for having had to accommodate itself to sensibilities other than Attic.

The inscription, as usual, in Greek;
not exaggerated, not pompous—
lest the proconsul who is always poking about
and reporting to Rome misconstrue it— . . .
Above all I charge you to see to it
(Sithaspes, in God's name, let this not be forgotten)
that after the words King and Savior,
there be engraved in elegant letters, Philhellene.
Now don't try your clever sallies on me,
your "Where are the Greeks?" and "Where is anything Greek
behind Zagros here, beyond Phraata?"
Since so many others more barbarous than we
write it, we too shall write it.
And finally do not forget that at times
sophists from Syria visit us,
and versifiers, and other wiseacres.
So we are not un-Greek, I reckon.

("Philhellene")

In his poems about the relations between Christians and Pagans in the age of Constantine, Cavafy takes no sides. Roman paganism was worldly in the sense that the aim of its ritual practices was to secure prosperity and peace for the state and its citizens. Christianity, while not necessarily despising this world, has always insisted that its principal concern was elsewhere: it has never claimed to guarantee worldly prosperity to believers, and it has always condemned excessive preoccupation with success as a sin.

So long as worship of the Emperor as a god was required by law of all citizens, to become a Christian meant to become a criminal. In consequence, the Christians of the first four centuries A.D., though subject like everybody else to the temptations of the Flesh and the Devil, had been spared the temptation of the World. One could become converted and remain a thorough rascal, but one could not be converted and remain a gentleman.

But after Constantine, it was the Christian who had a better chance than the Pagan of getting on in the world, and the Pagan, even if not persecuted, who became the object of social ridicule.

In one of Cavafy's poems the son of a pagan priest has become a Christian convert.

O Jesus Christ, my daily effort
is to observe the precepts
of Thy most holy church in every act of mine,
in every word, in every single thought.
And all those who renounce Thee,
I shun them.—But now I bewail;

I lament, O Christ, for my father
even though he was—a horrible thing to say—
a priest at the accursed Serapeum.

("Priest at the Serapeum")

In another, the Emperor Julian comes to Antioch and preaches his self-invented neopagan religion. But to the citizens of Antioch, Christianity has become the conventional religion which they hold without letting it interfere in any way with their amusements, and they merely laugh at him as a puritanical old fuddy-duddy.

Was it ever possible that they should renounce
their lovely way of life; the variety of their
daily amusement; their magnificent theater . . .

To renounce all these, to turn to what after all?

To his airy chatter about false gods;
to his tiresome self-centered chatter;
to his childish fear of the theater;
his graceless prudery; his ridiculous beard?

Ah most surely they preferred the CHI,
ah most certainly they preferred the KAPPA; a hundred times.

("Julian and the People of Antioch")

I hope these quotations have given some idea of Cavafy's tone of voice and his perspective on life. If a reader find them unsympathetic, I do not know how one can argue against him. Since language is the creation of a social group, not of an individual, the standards by which it can be judged are relatively objective. Thus, when reading a poem in one's native tongue, one can find the sensibility personally antipathetic and yet be compelled to admire its verbal manifestation. But when one is reading a translation, all one gets is the sensibility, and either one likes it or one does not. I happen to like Cavafy's very much indeed.

The Complete Poems of Cavafy, translated
by Rae Dalven, 1961

Two Ways of Poetry

The Less Deceived. By Philip Larkin. St Martin's. $5.

For the Unfallen. By Geoffrey Hill. André Deutsch. $3.50.

To write about a poet for others who have not yet read him is not criticism but reviewing, and reviewing is not really a respectable occupation. When a critic examines the work of a well-known poet, he may, if he is lucky, succeed in revealing something about it which readers had failed to see for themselves: if, on the other hand, what he says is commonplace or false or half-true, readers have only themselves to blame if they allow themselves to be led astray, since they know the text he is talking about. But a reviewer is responsible for any harm he does, and he can do quite a lot. A "good" review urges the public to buy a book, a "bad" one tells them that it is not worth reading. It does not matter very much if a reviewer praises a bad book—time will correct him—but if he condemns a good one the effect may be serious, for the public can discover his mistake only by reading it and that is precisely what his review has prevented them from doing.

But a reviewer can do worse harm than that. Let us suppose that he has to review four poets in the same article and that they are all of them quite good, which means that the work of each is unique. If he treats them as such, then his article has no focus. But an article must have a focus. So he invents one. He looks for some characteristic which they have in common—it may be something as trivial as their age—and gives this a label—the X School, the Y Generation, the Z Young Men, etc.—and writes his article around it. The Publishers are delighted—it is easier to sell packages—and so is the Public delighted—labels save it from thinking and provide it with party conversation. Everybody, in fact, is pleased except the unfortunate poets. Having suffered from this sort of thing myself, I know that nothing is more insulting to a writer than to have his work lumped together with that of others (particularly if they happen to be his personal friends).

When I read a review of a poet whose work I don't know, I never read what the reviewer says; I only look at his quotations. This is very unsatisfactory. In the first place, there are seldom enough of them and, in the second, it is almost impossible for the reviewer to be just in his selection. If he likes the work, he chooses the best passages; if he dislikes it, the worst. If this were a sensible world, I should now give extensive quotations from Mr Philip Larkin and Mr Geoffrey Hill without any comment whatsoever, but this is not a sensible world.

When I read a poet for the first time, I proceed from the part to the whole. Thus, I begin by skimming through the pages, waiting for my eye to be caught by single lines which, so to speak, say themselves. One could not imagine their length, their arrangement of words, their sound and rhythm being other than they are. Single lines, of course, do not by themselves make a poem, but they are the basic evidence of the poetic gift and, if I cannot find any, I read no further.

Skimming through Mr Larkin, I am stopped by

> But superstition, like belief, must die,
> And what remains when disbelief is gone?

Glancing through Mr Hill, I come across

> A busy vigilance of goose and hound
> Keeps up all guards. Since you are outside, go,
> Closing the doors of the house and the head also.

So I do read further.

   This time, if the poet writes lyrics, I look for single stanzas which seem to me "right," that is to say, the number of lines, their contrasting lengths, their rhyme arrangement and so forth exactly embody the structure of meanings they have to convey. Anybody who has ever written verses has had the experience of beginning a poem and then getting hopelessly stuck until he suddenly realized that his choice of stanza has been wrong—it should have five lines, not four, or the last line should have two feet, not three. Again, I find much in Mr Larkin and Mr Hill to please me.

> The cross staggered him. At the cliff-top
> Thomas, beneath its burden, stood
> While the dulled wood
> Spat on the stones each drop
> Of deliberate blood.

(Hill)

> Since we agreed to let the road between us
> Fall to disuse,
> And bricked our gates up, planted trees to screen us,
> And turned all time's eroding agents loose,
> Silence, and space, and strangers—our neglect
> Has not had much effect.

(Larkin)

Mr Larkin is, I think, the more interesting craftsman; he shows more formal curiosity and variety. For example, the formal structure of his poem "I Remember, I Remember," in which the succession of five-line stanzas is regular but the rhyming is not, being used both within the stanza and as a link across the stanza break, gives me great pleasure as a device, irrespective of the poem's particular contents. I have to remind myself, however, that my fascination with devices of this kind may be excessive, and that there have been many good poets who have not felt it. What always matters is sureness of hand; a good poet always convinces one that his results are exactly what he intended. Here again the critic must beware of his own prejudices. The correct question is: "Has this poet succeeded in writing the poem he set out to write?" All too frequently critics have in their heads some imaginary poem of their own and then condemn the poet for having failed to write it.

   After looking for lines and stanzas, I pick out a poem here and a poem there and read it through to see if its parts are successfully articulated into a whole. If I feel that the number of stanzas and their order could be different or I cannot see a necessary relation between one stanza and the next, then I suspect that there is something wrong with the poem.

There are many possible principles of poetic organization and some of them are much harder to grasp at a first reading than others. The easiest to perceive, though in poetry they are not, perhaps, the most essential, are logical sequences like If-Then, Because-Therefore, and temporal sequences like I-start, I-continue, I-end. If I say that Mr Larkin's poetry is more "traditional" and Mr Hill's more "modern," I am using these detestable adjectives as descriptive, not as value judgements. I mean that Mr Larkin in his organization of a poem makes use of logical and temporal sequences as, until recently, nearly all poets have done, while Mr Hill dispenses with them: his organization is based almost entirely on associations of feeling-states, a way of composing which has only been adopted by poets as a *conscious* principle during the past seventy years or so.

The difference between them in this respect is, in part, a reflection of the difference between their poetic worlds. After satisfying myself that a poet can write a good poem, I read through his whole volume, comparing one poem with another, to discover if he possesses what I value most of all, a world and tone of voice of his own.

In poetry as in religion there is a *via positiva* and a *via negativa*. Poets who follow the first find their inspiration in the temporal and spatial flux of events; poets who follow the second seek for a vision of permanent and universal truth behind the phenomena. As examples of the two types at their most extreme, I think of Praed and Mallarmé. Neither way can entirely ignore the other without becoming trivial or meaningless. The most ascetic of poets must at least use words which have concrete physical properties and a social history; and the most worldly must at least find some beings and events more sacred, more charged with undefinable significance, than others.

One can recognize most easily which way a poet is following on the occasions when he uses the first personal pronoun.

> I detest my room,
> Its specially-chosen junk,
> The good books, the good bed,
> And my life, in perfect order.

Reading this I can visualize the speaker quite easily; he lives in England in the twentieth century, he has had a good education and the name in his passport might very well be Philip Larkin.

> And I renounced on the fourth day,
> This fierce and unregenerate clay,
> Building as a huge myth for man
> The watery Leviathan. . . .

To this I, the fact that there is a living individual called Geoffrey Hill to whom one might be introduced at a party is totally irrelevant.

Another indication can be found in the way each kind of poet titles his poems. I read these lines without looking at their title.

> Caught in the centre of a soundless field
> While hot inexplicable hours go by
> *What trap is this? Where were its teeth concealed?*
> You seem to ask.
> I make a sharp reply,
> Then clean my stick. I'm glad I can't explain
> Just in what jaws you were to suppurate:
> You may have thought things would come right again
> If you could only keep quite still and wait.
>
> (Larkin)

If I now ask myself what would be a suitable title, I think the chances are quite good that I would hit on Mr Larkin's, "Myxomatosis." But when I have read these lines

> They sat. They stood about.
> They were estranged. The air,
> As water curdles from clear,
> Fleshed the silence. They sat.
>
> They were appalled. The bells
> In hollowed Europe spilt
> To the gods of coin and salt.
> The sea creaked with worked vessels
>
> (Hill)

I should have to guess for a very long time indeed before I came up with "The Apostles: Versailles 1919."

One must not judge either kind of poetic world by standards which only apply to the other. To say that a vision is true is not the same thing as saying an observation is true. One cannot, of course, deny one's personal preferences—I myself like my poetry worldly rather than ascetic—but temperament must not masquerade as principle. There is only one question which must be put to all poems without exception: "Is this authentic?" It is required of observer and visionary alike that he shall have seen with his own eyes and not have made it up or looked through someone else's spectacles.

Mr Larkin and Mr Hill look for and see two very different worlds, but both, I believe, have looked and seen for themselves.

The Mid-Century, October 1960

The Problem of Nowness

From Rococo to Cubism in Art and Literature. By Wylie Sypher.
Random House. $7.

I must begin by apologizing to Mr Sypher because I have no business to be writing about his book at all. Nobody can love all the arts with an equal passion and few can feel real affection for more than two. Mr Sypher's first love is, clearly, painting, his second poetry in which the first thing he notices is the presence or absence of visual imagery, but music, I suspect, means little to him. With me poetry, I suppose, comes first but my feelings are complicated by the fact that I try to write it myself, whereas I can love music unselfishly: but when it comes to the visual arts "I know what I like" in the philistine sense of the phrase and what interests me most about a painting is its iconography.

Mr Sypher is, besides being a professor of English, an art historian and the first demand we make of one is the same that we make of any historian, learning: he must tell us, so far as it is possible, *was ist eigentlich geschehen.* Learning Mr Sypher certainly has: if he does not mention some work of the period he is discussing, one feels that the omission is not due to ignorance but is deliberate; he considers it irrelevant to his theme. But in many ways the problems of the art historian are very different from those of the political or social historian. The latter is concerned with human deeds which occur at a moment: though the notion that the political historian should remain morally neutral seems to me nonsense, it is clear that he cannot pass any moral judgment on a political event until he has discovered how the actors themselves regarded their deeds. But a work of art is not an action; though it comes into being at a point in time, it is thenceforth an enduring object existing side by side with all the works produced before and after it. In consequence it is the duty of the art historian to pass his own aesthetic judgment on works of art before he considers the judgments made by their makers or their contemporary public. No art historian worth reading is without a theory of art, but it is most important that his theory should be derived from his taste; first he finds what he likes and dislikes and then he tries to account for the difference. Moreover, while a wicked deed is just as much a deed as a good one, to say that a painting or a poem is bad is to deny its claim to be a work of art at all.

When he writes about painting, Mr Sypher convinces me that he knows exactly his likes and dislikes, and I don't care a button if, at times, I cannot share them. When he writes about poetry I am not so sure. Using the first person plural he says that "Pope is the least sympathetic poet to us moderns." But he follows this statement with one of the best and most sympathetic essays on Pope which I have read and I am convinced that he admires

and loves Pope as much as I do. And at times I suspect him of suppressing his
personal taste for the sake of making a historical point or confirming a theory. I agree with him, for instance, that one of the defects of the romantics
was an insufficient concern for formal problems, but when he singles out the
free verse of Blake's prophetic books as a happy exception, I wonder. Does
Mr Sypher *really* enjoy them? Again, is it his personal bias for the visual that
makes him quote with apparent approval passages from Collins and Shelley
which seem to me atrociously bad? If it is, I have no objection. But I rather
suspect him of merely using them to make points about the *genre pittoresque*
and the use of color by Delacroix and Turner.

It is the business of the art historian as of any other historian to attempt to
trace the causal links both between one work and another and between a
work and the historical circumstances under which it was made, but a good
art historian knows that his conclusions can at best be only half-truths. The
alternative actions possible to a human individual at any given historical moment are so restricted that the political historian can, if his documentation
is adequate, be fairly sure that his account of why X acted as he did is the true
one. But the art historian, though he demonstrate that artist A was influenced by artist B and show what were the intellectual and artistic concerns of
a certain epoch, can do so only in a very general way; it is impossible for him
to say why it was precisely this work which was made and not another of more
or less the same kind. Nor must he ever forget that, whereas the only alternative to one historical event is another historical event, instead of *this* work of
art there could have been no work at all: every work of art is gratuitous. I find
Mr Sypher himself properly modest and undogmatic. I am only sorry that he
seems to take Worringer seriously, for Worringer's notion that when men
feel at home in the world (whatever that means) they produce naturalistic
representational art and abstract art when they feel alienated seems to me
sheer phantasy. (What evidence, for example, is there that the *La Tene* Celts
felt alienated or that the Romans of the late Empire felt at home?)

A critic may have learning, taste, and tact, yet still be unreadable. An important critic is one who asks important questions; that his readers should
agree with his answers matters very little. We have to believe what a political
historian says (till we read another one) because we have neither the talent
nor the time to consult the original sources upon which his account is based.
But the original materials of criticism, the works of art, are always on hand
and the critic who is worth reading is one who sends us back in a new state
of excitement and curiosity to the works themselves.

Mr Sypher is a critic very well worth reading. Though I personally disagree
with most of his conclusions, I am immensely grateful to him for his book,
because it has compelled me to think again about what is one of the most
important and difficult problems which every work of art raises.

To be authentic, a work of art must exhibit two contradictory qualities, the
quality of always-ness and the quality of now-ness. It must remain of perma-

nent significance to later generations, whatever historical changes may
occur, and it must have the uniqueness which comes from being made by a
unique human being at a unique point in time. If it lacks always-ness it is
merely a fashionable entertainment, and let us not forget that the *avant-garde* is as susceptible to fashion as the man in the street; if it lacks now-ness
it lacks life. Faced with the work of his contemporaries it is often possible, I
believe, for a critic to separate the living from the dead, provided that he is
not himself a practicing artist: practicing artists are the worst possible judges
of any contemporary work except their own. But I doubt if anybody can distinguish with certainty between what will prove permanent in contemporary
work and what is merely fashionable. One has only to recall the enthusiasm
aroused at the time of its publication in men of real taste and talent by Ossian: and was any Elizabethan aware of the gulf between Shakespeare and
every other dramatist of the day? This is the problem with which Mr Sypher's
book is concerned and what could be more fascinating? It deals with the
painting and literature of the past two hundred and fifty years, beginning
with the rococo period of Watteau and Pope and ending in our post–Second
World War days with the French a-literate novelists and the tachist painters.
The main tools of his examination are his concepts of style and stylization.

A genuine style, as he defines it is

> an expression of a prevailing, dominant, or authentically contemporary
> view of the world by those artists who have most successfully intuited the
> quality of human experience peculiar to their day and who are able to
> phrase this experience in forms deeply congenial to the thought, sci-
> ence and technology which are part of that experience. . . . The impor-
> tant point is not that a style is entirely new, but that it takes a contempo-
> rary view of past styles. . . . Style is conformity to techniques adequately
> expressing the consciousness of an era and accepted nearly by agree-
> ment among artists who are most sensitive to their contemporary
> world. . . . It may be questioned whether any poetry is successful if it is
> not as contemporary as it can be, intellectually as well as technically.

What he means by stylization is not so clear. If I understand him rightly, a
work exhibits stylization when there is a lack of harmony between the artist's
technique, his means of expression, and the contents he wishes to express; it
can arise from trying to put either new wine into old bottles or old wine into
new bottles. Thus "The Ancient Mariner" is a stylization because, whereas his
symbolic content was new, Coleridge tried to express it in a traditional ballad
verse: impressionist painting was a stylization because, while the impression-
ists had invented a new technique, they still clung to conventional notions of
what a picture should be.

Mr Sypher prefers style to stylization—don't we all?—but his belief that,
after a century and a half of confusion, we have at last in cubism discovered
a style as valid for the twentieth century as rococo was for the eighteenth,

seems to me wishful thinking and belied by many of his own observations, such as the following.

> The pasticheur and virtuoso appear at critical periods in the history of the arts. What would the renaissance be without them? Without Uccello and Leonardo and Michelangelo? . . . Shakespeare did not have a style either. . . . In periods, like the renaissance, changes occur so rapidly that new techniques shift the prevailing view of reality before many artists are able to cope with them. That is one reason why Western art, at least, always needs an *avant-garde* . . . technological revolutions (which are actually the "permanent revolution" always being carried on by the middle class) are always accompanied by a corresponding "permanent revolution" in the arts being carried on by the *avant-garde*.

Precisely. But how can there be a style during a permanent revolution? Style is the product of a culture and a culture cannot exist unless men are more conscious of permanence than of change, of unity than of diversity. For better or worse, we have to live in a cultureless world, a world in which it is very difficult to believe in the reality of other people and therefore very difficult for an artist to distinguish between an authentic impulse and a mere caprice.

Confining myself, as I must, to modern literature, I can think of a number of poets and novelists who seem to me authentic, but I cannot point to a single characteristic common to them all by which their authenticity could be recognized. There are poets like Eliot, William Carlos Williams, St-John Perse, and novelists like Joyce and Virginia Woolf who employ an "advanced" technique; there are others like Yeats, Frost, Valéry, Lawrence (in his prose) who do not, but they all seem good. As for an "authentically contemporary view of the world" who holds it? A who is Catholic, B who worships the Mother Goddess, C who believes in the Dark Gods, or D who is a Marxist?

The relation of the art of an epoch to its science is a tricky business. Art can have only one subject, man as a conscious unique person, so that the only scientific discoveries which can affect it are those which change our conception of what constitutes a person. So far the change has generally been a narrowing—the area of our mental life which is truly singular and free is smaller than we thought—but this trend may be characteristic only of a certain epoch in science, which is drawing to a close. Until recently scientists believed that it would be merely a matter of time before science would know the objective truth about the whole of existence. Already the physicists know their limitations and it is conceivable that in due course even the animal and social psychologists will admit theirs.

The commonest defect of artists during the past two centuries has been, not a refusal to take scientific discoveries into account, but an all too ready willingness to swallow the scientists' assertions as to the conclusions about human or divine nature which must follow from their discoveries. There have been far too few artists who thought enough about science to criticize its fashionable pretensions, as Goethe and Blake criticized Newtonian physics, and Shaw, Darwinian biology. Nothing in the writings of Tennyson or Zola or Hardy has become so dated as their efforts to be scientifically "modern." My own suspicions of tachist painting are confirmed by what Mr Sypher says of it.

> The effect is very similar to a Brownian movement of particles in solution. . . . A modular technique underlies our age of mass observation and human engineering in which the self is treated only by statistical laws like particles in Brownian movements.

A tachist painter may believe this about other people but he cannot believe it about himself because whether he paints a picture or refrains from painting one would then be a matter of statistical probability. And why paint Brownian movements when you can photograph them?

It is quite impossible to do justice in a review to any history. A history is made up of a mass of detailed observations and the wealth and acuteness of Mr Sypher's can only be appreciated by reading his book. One is almost bound to discuss instead what is less important, a historian's conclusions, and I must repeat that only a historian who is worth reading is worth arguing with.

The Mid-Century, November 1960

Three Memoranda on the New
Arden Shakespeare

From W. H. Auden:

Shakespeare, as every schoolboy knows, is Top Bard. In high school the student "does" two or three of his plays and at college two or three more are required reading. He may also be taken to see some performances—he may even act in one.

Every sensible young person has an instinctive antipathy to what is Officially-Approved-Of, and, in Shakespeare's case, this is reinforced by the fact that, of all the major English writers, no one is less a writer for the young, for persons, that is, under the age of thirty.

No young man who cares for poetry reads Shakespeare with the same passion that he reads the Romantics or the Metaphysicals; no young man with an interest in the theatre enjoys Shakespeare's plays as he enjoys those of Congreve, Ibsen, Chekhov, or Shaw.

On the other hand, almost anyone *over* thirty who cares for poetry or drama, will find, if he can once get himself to read him, that the more he reads Shakespeare the more he becomes convinced that Shakespeare really *is* Top Bard, that between him and every other English writer there is an immense gulf.

Shakespeare wrote a lot and each work of his is utterly different from all the others. Dickens is one of my favorite authors and I wouldn't be without a single one of his novels, but it is fair to say, I think, that after you have read three or four of them, you know the Dickensian world: you may not yet have met all its inhabitants, but you already know pretty well what they will be like when you do. But to have read, let us say, one comedy, one tragedy, one chronicle play and one non-dramatic poem of Shakespeare's, will not give you any proper idea of the Shakespearian world: that can only be got by reading everything he wrote.

Shakespeare's work is not only very good and very varied: his enormous vocabulary and extraordinary handling of metaphor and imagery also make him a very difficult writer. So far as his language is concerned, I find Dante easier to follow than an Italian newspaper but, though English is my native tongue, there are many passages in Shakespeare which, despite many readings, still perplex me. It is never sufficient to read a Shakespeare play once.

To be good, an edition of Shakespeare must therefore satisfy the following demands:

(I) It must be designed for reading by the middle-aged and the old. If they like an author, the young will put up with cheap paper, atrocious print, double columns, *anything*. The middle-aged and the old will not. They demand volumes of the right size and the right weight, and a page which is a visual pleasure to behold.

(II) It must be designed for frequent re-reading. It must, that is to say, be sufficiently stoutly made to last a lifetime, but it must not be a de luxe masterpiece of book-making craftsmanship which is much too valuable to be constantly picked up and put down and read with unwashed fingers.

(III) It must be so designed that one play can be read at a time, but in any order. This means one play, one volume.

(IV) It must contain critical notes to assist the reader when either the meaning is difficult to make out or the correct text is in doubt. These must be so placed that (a) when a reader wants to confine himself to the text, his eye is not drawn to the notes willy-nilly and (b) when he does wish to consult a note he can do this immediately and without losing his place. There is only one way of meeting these two demands—to place the critical apparatus at the bottom of the page to which it refers and to set text and notes in unmistakably different type.

How much critical apparatus to supply is debatable. I am inclined to believe that too much is better than too little. The reader can always skip it, and my experience has been that the more familiar I become with the text, the sharper grows my appetite for emendations and explications, not only because some of them are very helpful but also because so many provide superb entertainment as exhibitions of human folly.

I have looked at many editions of Shakespeare and own a number myself, but the only one which completely satisfies me is the Arden. The format is right, the paper is right, the print is right, the notes are in the proper place, the discussions of source material are all I need and the introductions by the various editors, though I may sometimes disagree with them (which is, anyway, as it should be), are neither too elementary nor misbegotten Ph.D. theses.

> Followed by "memoranda" by Jacques Barzun and
> Lionel Trilling; *The Mid-Century,* January 1961

A Public Art

Why do I want to write librettos? Because I have a passion for opera as an artistic genre. Any arguments I may advance to prove the virtues of opera are rationalizations to convince myself that my passion is not a mania.

One of the most striking changes in taste which has occurred during my lifetime has been the change in attitude towards opera among the musical highbrows in England and America. When I was young, it was very difficult for anyone who did not live within reach of Covent Garden or the Metropolitan to hear any operas; they were not, so far as I remember, broadcast, and there were no recordings of complete operas. But these facts do not really explain the change. I was brought up to believe that opera was a bastard art-form. The great Mozart operas might just do because Mozart was Mozart, but Wagner in one way and Verdi in another were considered vulgar; as for Rossini, Bellini and Donizetti, they were simply beyond the pale. (Judging by some articles I have read, this prejudice still survives in certain English quarters.) In addition, we were put off, not entirely without justification, by the kind of public which *did* "go to the opera"; many of them seemed more interested in appearing at the appropriate social event for the London Season than in listening to music.

This attitude had an influence on the composers themselves. Even as late as the thirties, no British or American composer, I fancy, would have entertained the notion of being primarily an operatic composer; he might write an opera as an experiment, but he did not expect it to be taken as one of his major works. All this, thank goodness, is past. The opera houses are packed by an audience in which the socialite element is very small; the broadcasts from Covent Garden, Glyndebourne and the Metropolitan are listened to by tens of thousands; the record companies make a handsome profit from the sale of operatic recordings; almost every living composer of note has written more than one opera with considerable critical and popular success. A writer who shows the slightest talent for making a libretto will find himself in demand.

There are two kinds of stage-work in which a poet can have a hand, verse-drama and opera. If he chooses the first, he is responsible for everything except the interpretation; if he chooses the second, then, though the librettist's contribution is not, I believe, negligible, his role is obviously a subordinate one. Human egoism is such that no poet will prefer the subordinate role unless he prefers opera to any verse-drama, even one he might write himself. He must be convinced, that is to say, that there are things opera can do which verse-drama cannot, and that these are more valuable than anything which could be done in the latter medium. He is thinking, of course, of the present, not the past, of what can and cannot be done *now*.

For what it is worth, my personal conviction is this. Drama is necessarily a public art. To be of public interest a human being must be heroic; his or her actions, sufferings, emotions, must be exceptional and in the grand manner. For a number of reasons the Public Realm is no longer a place where speech can be authentic. Speech, the medium of the poet, is now the expressive medium of the intimate: the singular can address the singular in poetry, but poetry cannot appear in public without becoming false to itself. In our age there are only two public dramatic arts, opera and ballet. Ballet is wordless, but opera requires the singable word. (Let us not presume to call it poetry.) Outside his own proper sphere of the intimate, there is still something a poet, if he is prepared to submit to a librettist's limitations, can contribute to the Public Realm.

Dramatic poetry, to be recognizable as poetry, must raise its voice and be grand. But a poet today cannot raise his voice without sounding false and ridiculous. The modern poetic dramatist seems faced with these alternatives: either he writes the kind of verse which is natural to him, in which case he produces little closet dramas which can only make their effect if the audience is a small intimate one, or, if he wishes to write a public drama, he must so flatten his verse that it sounds to the ear like prose. Neither alternative seems to me satisfactory.

Opera and ballet, it will be noticed, are both virtuoso arts. Without an exceptional physical endowment, vocal cords or a body, granted to very few human beings, no amount of intelligence, taste and training can make a great singer or dancer. It is this, I believe, that, in an age when all the other arts are restricted to the intimate, still allows the opera and the ballet to be public. When we listen to a great singer or watch a great dancer we feel him or her to be a heroic superhuman being even if the music or the choreography is sub-human trash.

Furthermore, there is still a tradition in opera-singing and in classical dancing of how things should be done which is handed on from generation to generation. That is why it is possible to compare the way one singer takes a particular phrase with the way another singer takes it. If there ever were such a tradition governing the speaking of English dramatic verse it has been lost. (The French theatre may be different.) When I attend a performance of a Shakespeare play, most of the cast mangle the verse atrociously; there may be one or two who speak it well, but each has his own style which clashes with the style of the others.

Without going so far as to say that all opera must be *bel canto*, I am prepared to assert that in any satisfactory opera the voices must make as beautiful noises as the orchestra. (*Wozzeck*, in my opinion, fails in this respect.) It is up to the librettist to provide the composer with a set of characters and a kind of verse which make beautiful vocal noises plausible and possible. Before starting work, the librettist needs to know and be in sympathy with, firstly, the kind of sounds the composer is interested in making, and secondly the kind of voices, if possible the actual singers, the composer has in mind.

The suspicion which our modern sensibility has of the heroic, its quickness to detect the least trace of the fake-heroic, makes the discovery of a suitable plot and suitable characters much more difficult than it was in the past. It has, I believe, always been the case that, to be operatic, the principal characters must have a certain mythical significance which transcends their historical and social circumstances. (Violetta in *La Traviata*, for instance, is not merely a *grande cocotte* living in Paris in the early nineteenth century; she is also an archetype which has fascinated our culture for centuries, the Magdalen, the harlot with the loving heart.) Where shall the modern librettist discover mythical figures which have not already been worked to death? That is the problem. But problems are fun.

If I may be excused for daring to make a suggestion to composers, I would hazard the guess that the serious opera possible in our age is *opera buffa*, not *opera seria*.

If it is difficult to get a new opera performed, it is surprising to me, and much to the credit of opera house managers, that any get performed at all. Producing an opera is an extremely expensive business; and an opera cannot, like a musical comedy, have a run. At best, if it is successful, it can become part of the repertory, where it has to compete with acknowledged masterpieces, and however good it is, the chances of it being a masterpiece are bound to be small. Moreover, a new opera has to overcome the unfortunate psycho-physical fact that the musical ear is a conservative organ, which prefers repetition to novelty. While most people would rather see a new play, even an inferior one, than a play they have seen before, most people would rather re-hear a symphony or an opera which they already know well than listen to an unfamiliar work, however good.

Opera, January 1961

Il Faut Payer

Parade's End. By Ford Madox Ford. Knopf. $7.50.

Parade's End is a four-volume study of Retribution and Expiation, retribution upon a society, certain families, and certain individuals.

It opens in the summer of 1912 and ends in the summer of 1928. In 1912 England is, on the surface, still a society governed by a hereditary ruling class with inherited wealth and the social and moral values of such a class. A few quotations may serve to illustrate what these were:

> Gentlemen didn't earn money. Gentlemen, as a matter of fact, didn't do anything. They exist. Perfuming the air like Madonna lilies. Money comes into them as air through petals and foliage. Thus the world is made better and brighter. And, of course, thus political life is kept clean. So you can't make money.

> For social functions you had to have an equal number of men and women or someone got left out of conversations, and so you had to know who, officially, in the social sense, went with whom. Everybody knew that all the children of Lupus at the War Office were really the children of a late Prime Minister. You invited Lord and Lady Lupus together to all functions that would get into the papers, but you took care to have the Lady at any private, weekendish parties or intimate dinners to which the Chief was coming.

> He began to speak an admirable, very old-fashioned French with an atrocious English accent. . . . He would cultivate an English accent to show that he was an English country gentleman. And he would speak correctly to show that an English Tory can do anything in the world if he wants to.

> English people of good class do not dress for dinner on Sundays. This is a politeness to God because, theoretically, you attend evening service and you do not go to church in evening dress. As a matter of fact you never go to evening service, but it is complimentary to suggest by your dress that you might be visited by the impulse.

> He did not imagine that the son of anyone he had ever weekended with would ever walk through standing hay.

But cracks are beginning to open in this surface. It is not only that Welshmen, Scotsmen, and Jews are pushing themselves into politics, or that bounders from the City are beginning to appear in golf clubs; it is also becoming clear that many persons of good family are unfit to rule. Smart young debs dabble in black magic. Some are mad, like the Rev. (Breakfast) Duchemin who suffers from fits in which he spouts obscenities at the table. Others are footlers like Major Wilfrid Fosbrooke Eddicker Perowne.

> His mother was immoderately wealthy, but she received few or no visitors, her cuisine being indifferent and her wine atrocious. She had strong temperance opinions and immediately after the death of her husband she had emptied the contents of his cellar, which were almost as historic as his castle, into the sea. . . . Perowne lived in a great house in Palace Gardens, Kensington, and he lived all alone with rather a large staff of servants who had been selected by his mother, but they did nothing at all, for he ate all his meals, and even took his bath and dressed for dinner at the Bath Club. He was otherwise parsimonious.

And, for a society that claims to be honorable and honest, it is corrupted by its readiness to listen to and believe in scandal. Given their characters and relationship, it is natural that Sylvia, the wife of the hero, Christopher Tietjens, should tell every dirty lie about him she can think up, and that he should do nothing to defend himself, but it is shocking that everybody, including his father, his half-brother, and his godfather should believe them. Nobody who hears that Valentine Wannop is really the daughter of Christopher's father, or that Valentine has had a child by Christopher, or that Christopher lives by selling his wife to other men, or that he is a Socialist, or that his half-brother is dying of syphilis, has any difficulty in swallowing it.

It would be a great mistake to imagine that because his hero is a highly eccentric Tory, Ford is a political reactionary or a social snob. He makes it quite clear that World War I was a retribution visited upon Western Europe for the sins and omissions of its ruling class, for which not only they, but also the innocent conscripted millions on both sides must suffer.

As seen through his hero's eyes, the worst horror of modern warfare is not the bloodshed—people must get killed in wars—but its inefficiency, irresponsibility, and pointlessness. Christopher looks at a twenty-acre field which has been smashed and pulverized by artillery fire, and asks a gunner what the shells to do this must have cost. The gunner's estimate is about three million pounds sterling. Christopher then asks how many men had been killed. "The gunner said he mightn't begin to know. None at all, as like as not. No one was very likely to have been strolling about there for pleasure, and it hadn't contained any trenches." Or again he hears a big gun go off:

> Four coupled railway trains hurtled jovially among the clouds and went a long way away—four in one. They were probably trying to impress the North Sea.

And the consequence of this collective madness is that the power of a hereditary ruling class is broken for good. "Nobody," says Tietjens, "is ever going to be impressed again," or as the girl he loves puts it, "There was to be no more respect. None for constituted Authority and consecrated Experience. No more respect. . . . For the Equator! For the Metric System. For Sir Walter Scott! Or George Washington! Or Abraham Lincoln! Or the Seventh Commandment!"

The protagonists of the personal drama which is played against this background belong to three families, the Tietjens, the Satterthwaites, and the Wannops.

The first Tietjens came over to England with William III in 1688 and cheated the Loundeses, who were Roman Catholics, out of Groby, an estate in Yorkshire. For this act, the family is under a curse. "There has not been a Tietjens since the First Lord Justice but died of a broken neck or a broken heart." Christopher's great-grandfather was scalped by Indians in Canada, his grandfather died in a brothel, his uncle was killed in a hunting accident when drunk. His father, a younger son, has married twice: his eldest son by his first marriage is Mark Tietjens; his youngest, by his second, is Christopher. Unfortunate or not, the family is extremely rich, thanks to coal-mining royalties. In 1912, both Mark and Christopher have jobs in Whitehall; Mark has something to do with Transport, Christopher with Statistics. As the youngest son, Christopher is not very rich in his own right, but still quite comfortably off. He has a little private income under his mother's settlement, a little income from the Civil Service, and for two years he has been married to a woman of means.

It is essential to an understanding of their Tory views to remember that the Tietjens are not, really, of English stock, and owe their position to the Whigs. When, at the end of the last volume, The Great Tree of Groby, the symbol of their family tradition, is cut down, Ford slyly reminds us that it was not an indigenous tree but a cedar imported from Sardinia.

As a family, the Tietjens are exceptionally intelligent, eccentric, and as fantastically proud and obstinate as the characters in an Icelandic saga.

Christopher's father, for example, never spoke to *his* father for forty years because the latter never forgave him for marrying Miss Selby of Biggen, not because he was marrying beneath him but because the father had wanted her for his eldest son.

Christopher's wife, Sylvia, who is to persecute and ruin him, was born a Satterthwaite. Her father is dead and we are told nothing about him except that he was a good man and hated by his wife. Mrs Satterthwaite is a Roman Catholic, very rich, ultra-fashionable, and bored stiff—her only interest in life is befriending handsome, thin, and horribly disreputable young men.

Valentine, the girl with whom, ultimately, Christopher is to find some measure of happiness, is a Wannop. The Wannops were first heard of at Birdlip in Gloucestershire in 1417, probably enriched after Agincourt. Like the Tietjens, they, too, are under a curse. "The real Wannops, they've been executed or attaindered, and falsely accused and killed in carriage accidents or married adventurers or died penniless like father." Professor Wannop had been a famous Latin scholar. When he died, the Liberal Government wouldn't put his wife and family on the Civil List because he had sometimes written for a Tory paper. Mrs Wannop is supporting herself by writing journalism and novels—according to Christopher, she has written the only novel worth reading since the eighteenth century. Valentine, after going into domestic service, is acting as a lady companion and is a militant suffragette.

The family curse began to fall on Christopher in a railway carriage coming down from the Dukeries when he had sexual intercourse with Sylvia Satterthwaite, and felt in honor bound to marry her. The night before the wedding, he discovers that he has been trepanned. She had been brutally seduced by a Mr Drake and feared she was pregnant. A child is born and Christopher does not know whether it is his or Drake's. For the child's sake, he is determined to keep up appearances. Though we are not explicitly told so, it seems probable that he refused to sleep with her any more. He treats her with perfect courtesy, but, in his heart, he does not forgive her. Sylvia, who looks like a Fra Angelico Madonna but is a passionate girl with strong sadistic-masochistic traits, finds this treatment unbearable, and tormenting Christopher becomes her life obsession. When the novel opens, she has left him for Perowne but, after a week, has got bored and is asking to return. Much as she hates Christopher, he has spoilt her for any other man.

> It was the most damnable of his qualities that to hear any other man talk
> of any subject from stable form to the balance of power, from the voice
> of a given opera singer to the recurrence of a comet, hate his ideas how
> you might, was the difference between listening to a grown man and,
> with intense boredom, trying to entertain an inarticulate schoolboy.

Intellectually, Christopher is a cross between Sherlock Holmes and Bernard Shaw. Like the former, he is a specialized polymath. He does not like astronomy because it is not theoretical enough for the pure mathematician and not sufficiently practical for everyday life. Although he detests golf because it is a competitive game, he can enjoy himself while playing by thinking about the mathematics of trajectories. When he gets shell-shocked, he is writing a preface to a book on Arminianism. He knows all about statistics, horses, tying fishing-flies, and old furniture. And like Shaw, he delights in making provocative statements, such as saying that all sick children should be put in lethal chambers but murderers should be set free and encouraged to breed because they are bold fellows. Intellectually and morally, his standards are high and absolutely uncompromising, and he acknowledges no others. He will not fake facts to please a Cabinet Minister; on the other hand, he will not attempt to defend himself against false charges if the truth would do harm to others. "He's so formal he can't do without all the conventions and so truthful he can't use half of them." Sylvia's mind is chaotic:

She delighted most in doing what she called pulling the strings of shower baths. She did extravagant things, mostly of a cruel kind for the fun of seeing what would happen.

In consequence, Christopher is a standing reproach; she must try her utmost to break him down and prove to herself that his superiority is a sham. And then, finally, she is physically, passionately in love with him, the only man she knows who will not yield to her charms.

So all she can do is torment. Father Consett, a saintly priest who is later hanged by the English along with Casement, prophesies what will happen.

> "Her hell on earth will come when her husband goes running, blind, head down, mad after another woman. . . . And then. . . . *Then* she'll tear the house down. The world will echo with her wrongs."
>
> "Do you mean to say," Mrs Satterthwaite said, "that Sylvia would do anything vulgar?"
>
> "Doesn't every woman who's had a man to torture for years when she loses him? The more she's made an occupation of torturing him the less right she thinks she has to lose him."

At moments Sylvia realizes this herself, but she can't stop.

> It's pure sexual passion. God! Can't I get over this? Father! . . . You used to be fond of Christopher. . . . *Get* our Lady to get me over this. . . . It's the ruin of him and the ruin of me. But, oh *damn*, don't! . . . For it's all I have to live for.

The priest's prophesy comes true—she does drive Christopher into the arms of another woman, she does behave vulgarly and in the end the world turns against her—but all this takes a long time.

Christopher first meets Valentine on the golf-links in Rye when she is being pursued by the police as a suffragette. Later they go for a long drive in the fog, discussing politics and Latin poetry. They are both aware of an intellectual rapport—he finds her the most intelligent person to talk to he has ever met—but the thought of serious love does not occur to either, and they see little of each other until 1917 when he is on sick leave. The night before returning to France, he asks her to become his mistress and she accepts, but, actually, nothing happens, and it is only on Armistice night that they at last fall into each other's arms. His health is ruined, and he is bankrupt. His father is dead and Mark is childless, so he has inherited Groby, but he refuses to accept a penny because his father and half-brother had believed the lies told about him. He goes into the Old Furniture business and his partner cheats him. He gives Groby to Sylvia who promptly rents it to an American olive oil king with a wife who walks through standing hay, believes she is descended from Madame de Maintenon, and cuts down the Groby Tree, smashing half the house in the process. Yet, at the end of the tetralogy, one feels that the curse has been lifted. Sylvia can do no more harm, Christopher knows that he is the father of her child, a nice boy who will make a good heir to Groby, and that his father did not, as it had been believed, commit suicide, and Valentine is about to have a child. His honor remains unimpaired, but his sufferings have made him humble; the one real defect in his character as a young man, his arrogance, is gone.

It is impossible in a short article to do justice to a work which is conceived and executed on such a grand scale. I have said nothing about such important characters in the novel as Mark Tietjens, a kind of Phineas Fogg dandy, or Marie Louise, his French mistress, let alone anything about the minor characters. Nor have I the space to discuss Ford's fascinating technique of presentation. But perhaps this is all for the good; to say too much can spoil the reader's pleasure in being surprised.

Parade's End has never yet been a popular success and few critics, I believe, have paid much attention to it. This neglect passes my comprehension. Of the various demands one can make of a novelist, that he show us the way in which a society works, that he show an understanding of the human heart, that he create characters in whose reality we believe and for whose fate we care, that he describe things and people so that we feel their physical presence, that he illuminate our moral consciousness, that he make us laugh and cry, that he delight us by his craftsmanship, there is not one, it seems to me, that Ford does not completely satisfy. There are not many English novels which deserve to be called great: *Parade's End* is one of them.

The Mid-Century, February 1961

The Poet as Professor

The purpose of all educational institutions, public or private, is utilitarian and can never be anything else; their duty is to prepare young persons for that station in life to which it shall please society to call them. My station in life is whatever I can give in my passport as my occupation which passport officials will accept without incredulity or laughter. Would anyone to-day describe himself officially as either "Gentleman" or "Poet"? If not, then to-day these are not stations in life, and the curricula of schools and colleges cannot make provision for them.

At the same time, everybody is preoccupied with his own "self-education" —an unsatisfactory term, but there is no English equivalent for the German word *Bildung*; with cultivating, that is to say, his personal interests, which may be anything from women to numismatics. If he is lucky, these, or some of them, happen to be useful to the recognised needs of the society in which he lives, for in that case there will exist institutions to teach him exactly what he wants to know.

There have been cultures in which poets were considered as useful as dentists and, accordingly, were given a long and arduous professional training. Most living poets, I suspect, have their ideas of what, if a similar attitude existed in our culture, the curriculum of such a Bardic College should be. My own answer, for example, would run something like this.

(1) In addition to English, at least one ancient language, probably Greek or Hebrew, and two modern languages.

(2) Thousands of lines of poetry in these languages to be learnt by heart.

(3) Instruction in prosody, rhetoric and comparative philology.

(4) The only critical exercise required would be the writing of pastiche and parody. All critical writing, other than historical or textual, would be banned from the college library.

(5) Courses in mathematics, natural history, geology, meteorology, archaeology, mythology, liturgies and cooking.

(6) Every student would be required to take personal charge of a domestic animal and a garden plot.

Needless to say, such an institution cannot exist in our civilisation. Who would pay for it? Who would staff it? What jobs would there be for its graduates? In our day, for better or worse, a poet has to educate himself and at the same time obtain some kind of education which will enable him to earn his bread. There are some good poets who are lucky enough to possess a second talent for writing profitable fiction, but they are rare. For the majority, the ideal job would probably be one which was as far removed from literature as possible.

If parents knew in time that one of their offspring was going to be a poet, they could, as the parents of prospective rabbis used to do, apprentice him to some skilled trade like carpentering or plumbing or house-painting which in these days of trade union rates are remunerative enough. They would, of course, probably encounter strenuous opposition from the would-be poet himself, because most would-be poets have a romantic notion of the literary life which only experience can cure. But parents cannot know; and since the kind of boy who, rightly or wrongly, wants to become a poet is usually bright enough to win scholarships, the chances are that he will receive a conventional school and university education, and it is not at all unlikely that, at the university, he will decide to read English.

The function of the Honour School of English Language and Literature is to train future teachers of English for all levels from elementary school to university. It can only be criticised on the grounds that the quality of the teachers it turns out could be improved. I think it is a mistake, for example, to expect a prospective teacher to read through the whole of English literature from Beowulf to Hardy in three years. Would it not be better to demand of him a really thorough knowledge of three or four major writers and of one special period of his own choosing? Would it not be better if he wrote fewer essays and made more translations? If it is probably unwise for a poet to read English, this is not because he will learn nothing thereby which will be of profit to him as a poet. He may very well learn a great deal. It is because the only ways of earning his living for which it will qualify him are teaching or literary journalism, neither of which is a really satisfactory solution to his problem. But, then, there isn't a solution, anyway.

Oxford should feel very proud of herself for having anything so comically absurd as a Chair of Poetry. A professional poet is one who writes poems for money on subjects commissioned by others, but the Oxford Professor of Poetry is not expected to do in English verse what the Public Orator does in Latin prose, though it might be rather fun if he were.

It is proper, as well as amusing, that he should be appointed by an election in which every member of the University from clergymen to biochemists has a vote, for this implies that poetry is not a subject to which normal academic standards apply. Its only drawback is that it makes it difficult to put up a dark horse or a young man as a candidate, and the trouble about the elderly and well known is that, though they may have said some very interesting things about poetry in the past, it is always possible that they have nothing more to say.

Should the Professor be a local or someone from outside Oxford? In view of the fact that tenure is only for five years and the emolument modest, it is better, surely, to elect someone whom Oxford audiences would not otherwise have a chance of hearing than someone whose lectures they can attend anyway.

Should he or she be someone who is primarily known as a poet or someone who is first and foremost a scholar and a critic? Seeing that the principal duty of the Professor is to give lectures, the second is, obviously, the safer bet. People know, as with a poet they never do, more or less what they are going to get. Since, however, the chair is such an oddity, it would be cowardly not to take risks in filling it. If the choice turns out disastrous, the consequences have to be endured for only five years. If a scholar is to be chosen, why not elect a learned crank, a Baconian or a Rosicrucian? But why not a poet? He may mumble, but that can be rectified by a microphone. He may talk nonsense, but it will probably be interesting nonsense. There is only one topic upon which no poet is ever worth listening to, his contemporaries; it is highly unlikely that he has read most of them.

The Observer, 5 February 1961

Two Cultural Monuments

Phaedra and Figaro. Racine's *Phèdre*, translated by Robert Lowell, and
Beaumarchais's *Figaro's Marriage*, translated by Jacques Barzun.
Farrar, Straus & Cudahy. $5.

It is quite impossible to translate *Phèdre* and Mr Robert Lowell has had the
good sense not to try: what he has given us is an English verse drama by Lowell *after* Racine.

Exact translation of any poetry from one language into another is, of
course, impossible, but often a translator can find an equivalent which is sufficiently approximate for it to be possible to criticize a verse translation in
terms of its fidelity to the original, if only to its spirit. In the case of the
French drama of the Seventeenth Century, even this criterion cannot be applied. The French dramatic verse of this period has absolutely nothing in
common with English dramatic verse of any period, either in the way it is
written or in the way that it is spoken on the stage.

Let us take the question of declamation first. In English verse, even in
Shakespeare's grandest rhetorical passages, the ear is always aware of its relation to ordinary everyday speech. A good actor must—alas, today he so seldom does—make the audience hear Shakespeare's lines as verse, not prose,
but if he tries to make verse sound like a different language, he will make
himself ridiculous. But in French drama, verse and prose *are* different languages. One can read Shakespeare to oneself without even mentally *hearing*
the lines and be very moved; indeed one can easily find a performance disappointing, because almost anyone with an understanding of verse could
speak it better than the average actor or actress. But to read Racine to oneself, even if one is a Frenchman, is like reading the score of an opera when
one can neither sing nor play. One can no more get an adequate notion of
Phaedra without having heard a great performance than one can of *Tristan
und Isolde* if one has never heard a great Isolde like Leider or Flagstad.

The "translator" is faced with two problems: firstly, of finding an English
meter which English actors can speak and which seems proper to Racine's
characters, and, secondly, of finding some poetic compensation for the fact
that melody is a far less important element in English poetry than it is in
French.

Mr Lowell has adopted the heroic couplet, but, unlike Dryden, he uses a
great deal of *enjambement*, so that, in some cases, the lines cannot be spoken
as rhymed couplets at all, but must be spoken as prose with internal rhymes.
Since, except after a full stop, he does not capitalize the first letter of his
lines, I take it that this is deliberate. For example:

> I mean to be here
> when he comes. Go, tell her. I will do
> my duty. Wait, I'll see her nurse. What new
> evils torment her?

On first reading, I felt rather doubtful about this—after all, Racine's Alexandrines are almost always end-stopped—but after looking into Dryden again, I understand his reasons. The regular iambic end-stopped couplet in English makes the rhymes come out with an epigrammatic thump which suits argument very well, but is fatal to the expression of passion. Here is an example from Dryden's *Aurengzebe*:

> Kill me not quite with this indifference!
> When you are guiltless, boast not an offence.
> I know you better than yourself you know;
> Your heart was true, but did some frailty show:
> You promised him your love, that I might live;
> But promised what you never meant to give.
> Speak, was't not so? confess; I can forgive.

To compensate for the loss of melody, Mr Lowell has taken the only course possible in English verse, to enrich his lines with concrete images and figures which are not in the French. In almost all French poetry, and particularly in Racine's, if you ignore the sound, the sense seems too abstract and too thin. Here, for comparison, is a passage from Act II, scene V, as Racine wrote it and as Mr Lowell has re-written it.

> *On ne voit point deux fois le rivage des morts,*
> *Seigneur: puisque Thésée a vu les sombres bords,*
> *En vain vous espérez qu'un dieu vous le renvoie;*
> *Et l'avare Achéron ne lâche point sa proie.*
> *Que dis-je? Il n'est point mort, puisqu'il respire en vous.*
> *Toujours devant mes yeux je crois voir mon époux:*
> *Je le vois, je lui parle; et mon coeur. . . . Je m'égare,*
> *Seigneur; ma folle ardeur malgré moi se déclare.*

> That's folly, my lord. Who has twice visited
> Black Hades and the river of the dead
> and returned? No, the poisonous Acheron
> never lets go. Theseus drifts on and on,
> a gutted galley on that clotted waste—
> he woos, he wins Persephone, the chaste. . . .
> What am I saying? Theseus is not dead.
> He lives in you. He speaks, he's taller by a head,

> I see him, touch him, and my heart—a reef. . . .
> Ah, Prince, I wander. Love betrays my grief. . . .

Lines 5 and 6 of Mr Lowell's version are all his own, as is the phrase *he's taller by a head* and Phaedra's comparison of her heart to a *reef.* I think this not only justified, but necessary, for an exact rendering of the original without these additions would lack life. The real test of Mr Lowell's version, of course, will be a performance which I hope we shall see soon, for, though the poetry may be Mr Lowell's, the characters and the world they inhabit is Racine's and that is a very strange world indeed.

When I read the *Hippolytus* of Euripides, upon which *Phaedra* is based, I can recognize, despite all differences, a kinship between the world of Euripides and the world of Shakespeare, but the world of Racine seems to be another planet altogether. Euripides' Aphrodite is as concerned with fish and fowl as she is with human beings; Racine's Venus is not only unconcerned with animals but also she takes no interest in the Lower Orders. It is impossible to imagine any character in Racine sneezing or wanting to go to the bathroom, for in his world there is neither weather nor nature. In consequence, the passions by which his characters are consumed can only exist, as it were, on stage, the creation of the magnificent speech and the grand gestures of the actors and actresses who provide them with their flesh and blood.

Figaro is a very different story. Not only is a faithful translation desirable—and Mr Barzun has demonstrated that it is possible—but also we are back in a world where people do catch cold and want to go to the bathroom. According to the aesthetics of the humanists of the Renaissance, this was permitted in Comedy, but comic characters must be members of the middle or lower classes. What Beaumarchais dared to do—Louis XVI was right when he said it was subversive—was to subject a member of the nobility to comic treatment and, what was worse, to make him a comic victim. Shakespeare wrote comedies in which the aristocracy appear, but it is they who initiate and control the comic intrigue. He would never have dared, for example—he could not have conceived the possibility—to make Don Armado hoodwink Biron, as Figaro hoodwinks the count.

Thanks to Da Ponte and Mozart, those who have not and cannot read Beaumarchais in the original know a good deal about his play, but not all. The play is not, of course, like the opera, one of the great masterpieces of the world; nevertheless, it has qualities which the opera, by the very nature of its medium, lacks.

Mozart's music transports the characters and audience alike into a paradise where suffering cannot exist and thinking is unnecessary. In Beaumarchais' play, for all its comic lightness of tone, the characters both suffer and think and the audience is aware of this. No one can listen, for example, to Figaro's long autobiographical soliloquy—a story obviously related to

Beaumarchais' own life—and not be moved to indignation at social and political injustice. His whole life up till now has been an incessant struggle, not to achieve wealth and success, but merely to keep his head above water; he has known starvation, oppression, and jail.

Again, even if Mozart had set it, the thoughts expressed in Beaumarchais' song finale and their importance in the history of social attitudes would have been lost.

> By the accident of birth,
> One is shepherd, t'other king.
> Chance made lord and underling.
> Only genius threads the maze:
> Twenty kings are fed on praise
> Who in death are common earth,
> While Voltaire immortal stays.

The novelty of this lies in lines 4 and 7. Figaro does not say that all men are or should be equal in the eyes of God or of each other; on the contrary, he stresses the absolute superiority of the exceptional Genius, who is, it will be noted, a writer, an intellectual. It is not really true to say that who my parents are is a matter of chance, unless I am a genius, i.e. it is logical that the eldest son of a Lord should be a Lord, or that the son of a millionaire should be richer than other folks; there is a good statistical probability that the child of parents who both have high I.Q.'s will have a high I.Q., but humanly speaking, the appearance of a Voltaire or a Mozart is completely arbitrary. A genius has no past.

Figaro is not a shepherd—if he were, he would know who his parents are as well as the count does—but a rootless, isolated individual with no home in the world. One of the most interesting points in the play is the twist Beaumarchais gives to that oldest of comic themes, the Stolen Baby Restored. Traditionally, the infant is of royal birth, is brought up as a slave or a peasant, and finally recovers the rights which were his by birth. But when Figaro discovers his parents, no change in his fortunes occurs; they are just as rootless as he is and, indeed, he may well end up having to support them.

Beaumarchais anticipates both the Napoleonic notion of the career open to talent and the romantic notion of the artist-genius as superman. Since the French Revolution won its battle against aristocratic privilege, we are in a better position than Beaumarchais to realize the one-sidedness of his view. The truth is that absolute *laisser-faire* in the talent race is only workable in a celibate society like the Roman Catholic Church; it is not possible nor even, I think, desirable in a society where men, women, and children love some people more than others, irrespective of their merits. One observes that the greatest opposition to promotion by merit comes from the working classes. Talent, after all, is a privilege.

The Mid-Century, April 1961

Introduction to *Italian Journey*, by Johann Wolfgang von Goethe

Everybody knows that the thrones of European Literature are occupied by the triumvirate referred to in *Finnegans Wake* as Daunty, Gouty and Shop-keeper, but to most English-speaking readers the second is merely a name. German is a more difficult language to learn to read than Italian, and whereas Shakespeare, apparently, translates very well into German, Goethe is peculiarly resistant to translation into English; Hölderlin and Rilke, for example, come through much better. From a translation of *Faust*, any reader can see that Goethe must have been extraordinarily intelligent, but he will probably get the impression that he was too intellectual, too lacking in pas-sion, because no translation can give a proper idea of Goethe's amazing command of every style of poetry, from the coarse to the witty to the lyrical to the sublime.

The reader, on the other hand, who does know some German and is be-ginning to take an interest in Goethe comes up against a cultural barrier, the humourless idolization of Goethe by German professors and critics who treat every word he ever uttered as Holy Writ. Even if it were in our cultural tradition to revere our great writers in this way, it would be much more dif-ficult for us to idolize Shakespeare the man because we know nothing about him, whereas Goethe was essentially an autobiographical writer, whose life is the most documented of anyone who ever lived; compared with Goethe, even Dr Johnson is a shadowy figure.

For those whose ignorance of German cuts them off from Goethe's poetry and who have an instinctive prejudice against professional sages, *Italian Jour-ney* may well be the best book of his to start on. To begin with, there are hundreds and thousands of Englishmen and Americans who have made an Italian journey of their own and, to many of them, their encounter with Italy, its landscape, its people, its art, has been as important an experience as it was to Goethe, so that the subject-matter of the book will interest them, irrespec-tive of its author, and they will enjoy comparing the post-World War II Italy they know with the pre-French-Revolution Italy which Goethe saw. (Speak-ing for myself, I am amazed at their similarity. Is there any other country in Europe where the character of the people seems to have been so little af-fected by political and technological change?)

Goethe did not go to Italy as a journalist in search of newsworthy stories, but some of the best passages in *Italian Journey* owe as much to journalistic good luck as they do to literary talent. While sketching a ruined fort in Mal-cesine he is nearly arrested as an Austrian spy; Vesuvius obliges with a major eruption during his stay in Naples; sailing back from Sicily, the boat he has taken is kind enough to get itself nearly shipwrecked on Capri; eccentric and comic characters cross his path, like the Neapolitan Princess with the outrageous tongue, the choleric Governor of Messina, or Miss Hart, the future Lady Hamilton, who seems—God forgive her!—to have invented the Modern Dance; a chance remark overheard leads to his meeting with the humble relatives of Cagliostro, the most famous international swindler of the time. Goethe is not usually thought of as a funny man, but his descriptions of such events reveal a real comic gift and, even more surprisingly, perhaps, they show how ready he was to see himself in a comic light.

To write a successful travel book, one must have an observant eye and a gift for description. Goethe held definite views about how things should be described, which are summed up in a letter he wrote in 1826 about a young writer who had consulted him.

> Up till now he has limited himself to subjective modern poetry, so self-concerned and self-absorbed. He does very well with anything confined to inner experience, feeling, disposition and reflections on these; and he will deal successfully with any theme where they are treated. But he has not yet developed his powers in connection with anything really objective. Like all young men, nowadays, he rather fights shy of reality, although everything imaginative must be based on reality, just as every ideal must come back to it. The theme I set this young man was to describe Hamburg as if he had just returned to it. The thread of ideas he followed from the start was the sentimental one of his mother, his friends, their love, patience and help. The Elbe remained a stream of silver, the anchorage and the town counted for nothing, he did not even mention the swarming crowds—one might as easily have been visiting Naumburg or Merseburg. I told him this quite candidly; he could do something really good, if he could give a panorama of a great northern city as well as his feelings for his home and family.

Goethe's own practice is peculiar and reminds me in a strange way of the a-literature of some contemporary French novelists. The traditional method of description tries to unite the sensory perception of objects with the subjective feelings they arouse by means of a simile or a metaphorical image. This Goethe very rarely does. On the contrary, he deliberately keeps the sensory and the emotional apart. He makes enormous efforts, piling qualifying adjective on qualifying adjective, to say exactly what shape and colour an object is, and precisely where it stands in spatial relation to other objects, but, in contrast to this precision, the adjectives he employs to express his emotional reactions are almost always vague and banal—words like *beautiful, important, valuable* occur over and over again.

The difficulty about this procedure is that, by its nature, language is too abstract a medium. No verbal description, however careful, can describe a unique object; at best, it describes objects of a certain class. The only media for showing an object in its concrete uniqueness are the visual arts and photography. Goethe, of course, knew this, and said so.

> We ought to talk less and draw more. I, personally, should like to renounce speech altogether and, like organic nature, communicate everything I have to say in sketches.

He also knew, of course, that this was an exaggeration. There are certain characteristics of things which are every bit as "objective" as their visual appearance and with which only language can deal. A drawing can show what something is at a moment, but it cannot show us how it came to be that way or what will happen to it next; this only language can do. What gives Goethe's descriptions their value is not his "word-painting"—he cannot make us "see" a landscape or a building as D. H. Lawrence, for example, can—but his passionate interest in historical development—more than most writers he makes us aware of *why* things have come to be as they are. He always refused to separate the beautiful from the necessary, for he was convinced that one cannot really appreciate the beauty of anything without understanding what made it possible and how it came into being. To Goethe, a man who looks at a beautiful cloud without knowing, or wishing to know, any meteorology, at a landscape without knowing any geology, at a plant without studying its structure and way of growth, at the human body without studying anatomy, is imprisoning himself in that aesthetic subjectivity which he deplored as the besetting sin of the writers of his time.

Goethe is more successful at describing works of nature than he is at describing works of art. Indeed, the reader sometimes finds himself wishing he had more often practised what he preached when he said: "Art exists to be seen, not to be talked about, except, perhaps, in its presence." One reason for this is, of course, that Goethe knew a lot about natural history and very little about art history. Another may be that the two kinds of history are different. Natural history, like social and political history, is continuous; there is no moment when nothing is happening. But the history of art is discontinuous; the art historian can show the influences and circumstances which made it possible and likely that a certain painter should paint in a certain way, *if he chooses to paint*, but he cannot explain why he paints a picture instead of not painting one. A work of nature and a great work of art both give us, as Goethe said, a sense of necessity, but whereas the necessity of nature is a *must*, that of art is an *ought*.

When, thirty years later, the first part of *Italian Journey* was published, the German artistic colony in Rome was outraged. Those whom he had not mentioned were offended, and the works he had failed to see and the judgments he passed on those he did made them say that he must have gone through Italy with his eyes shut.

This was unfair. Like everybody's, Goethe's taste had its limitations, owing in part to his temperament and in part to the age in which he lived. It seems that the Giotto frescoes in the Arena Chapel were not on view when he was in Padua, and we know that he tried to see them, but he deliberately refused to visit the Two Churches in Assisi. For Goethe there was no painting or sculpture between Classical antiquity and Mantegna.

Yet, when one considers how little painting and sculpture and architecture Goethe had seen before he came to Italy, one is astounded at his open-mindedness. Though Palladio, for example, is his ideal modern architect, he shows far more appreciation of Baroque than one would have expected, more indeed than most of his successors in the nineteenth century. He started out with a strong prejudice against Christian themes as subjects for paintings and overcame it. Though to him the Apollo Belvedere was the finest achievement in Greek art, he learned to admire works of the archaic period like Paestum, and though he professes to be shocked by the grotesque villa of the Prince of Pallagonia, the zest with which he describes it betrays his fascination. And, in any case, Goethe made no claim to be writing a guide to Italian art; he tells us what he looked at and liked, he makes no claim that his judgments are absolute, and though he may, in our view, have overpraised some pictures, I do not think that he condemned any which seem to us really good.

One reason why we enjoy reading travel books is that a journey is one of the archetypal symbols. It is impossible to take a train or an aeroplane without having a fantasy of oneself as a Quest Hero setting off in search of an enchanted princess or the Waters of Life. And then, some journeys—Goethe's was one—really are quests.

Italian Journey is not only a description of places, persons and things, but also a psychological document of the first importance dealing with a life crisis which, in various degrees of intensity, we all experience somewhere between the ages of thirty-five and forty-five.

The first crisis in Goethe's life had occurred in 1775 when he was twenty-six and already famous as the author of *Götz von Berlichingen* and *Werther*. One might say, though it is a gross oversimplification, that the *Sturm und Drang* literary movement of which Goethe was then regarded as the leader stood for spontaneity of emotion as against convention and decorum, Shakespeare and Ossian as against Racine and Corneille, the warm heart as against the cool reason. Such a movement has often arisen in history and the consequences have almost always been the same; those who embrace it produce some remarkable work at an early age but then peter out if they do not, as they often do, take to drink or shoot themselves. An art which pits Nature against Art is bound to be self-defeating. What Kierkegaard called the aesthetic religion which puts all its faith in the mood of the immediate moment leads, first, to the "cultivation of one's hysteria with delight and terror", as Baudelaire put it, and, ultimately, to despair, and it brought Goethe to the brink of disaster. "I am falling", he wrote in April of 1775, "from one confusion into another." His father suggested a trip to Italy, but he did not go. At the beginning of November he was in Heidelberg; the young Duke of Weimar sent his coach and invited Goethe to join him; without a moment's hesitation, Goethe jumped in and was whisked away.

One would not have expected a young poet, who was well enough off to do as he liked, to choose to become a civil servant at a small court when he could have chosen to go to Italy. That Goethe did so is proof of his amazing instinct, which he was to show all through his life, for taking the leap in the right direction. In the state he was in, what could rescue him from a meaningless existence was not freedom but a curtailment of freedom, that is to say, the curb upon his subjective emotions which would come from being responsible for people and things other than himself, and this was precisely what Weimar offered. With the exception of the Grand Duke and Duchess, who were only eighteen, Goethe was the youngest person at court, yet, a year later, he became a Privy Councillor and, in the course of the next ten years, found himself at one time and another responsible for the mines, the War Department, and the Finances of the Duchy. In addition to these duties and as a further defence against subjectivity, he began to study science seriously, and in March 1784 he made an important discovery: he was able to show that the intermaxillary bone existed in man as well as in the other mammals.

Those first eleven years in Weimar were also the period of his platonic affair, conducted largely by notes and letters, with Charlotte von Stein, a rather plain married woman with three children and eleven years older than he. Again it seems strange that a man in his twenties and thirties should have been satisfied with such a "spiritual", uncarnal relationship; yet again, perhaps, it shows the soundness of Goethe's instinct. While, as a Privy Councillor, he was ready to take impersonal responsibility, he was not yet ready to take emotional responsibility for another person; what he needed at the time was emotional security without responsibility, and that is obtainable only in a platonic relationship, as to a mother or an older sister.

To an outsider, Goethe's life in 1786 must have looked enviable. He held an important position; he was admired and loved. Yet, in fact, he was on the verge of a breakdown. The stability which Weimar had given him was threatening to become a prison. Though it had enabled him to put *Werther* behind him, it had failed to give him any hints as to what kind of thing he should be writing instead, for, while he had come to Weimar to get away from *Werther*, it was as its author that Weimar had welcomed and still regarded him. His official life had had its remedial effect, but as public affairs were not his vocation, his duties were becoming senseless tasks which exhausted his energies without stimulating his imagination. His greatest gains had been in his scientific studies, yet here again Goethe was not a scientist by vocation but a poet; scientific knowledge was essential to the kind of poetry he wanted to write,

but, so long as he remained in Weimar, his scientific researches and his poetry remained two separate activities without real influence upon each other.
As for his Weimar friends, he was beginning—this is one of the misfortunes
of genius—to outgrow them. Herder, to whom, since he was a young student
in Strassburg, he had owed so much, had nothing more to teach him and,
probably, Herder's schoolmaster temperament which liked to keep disciples
was beginning to irk him. So far as Charlotte was concerned, Goethe seems
to have been, like Yeats, a man in whom the need for physical sexual relations became imperative only relatively late in life; by 1786 it had.

When the idea of escaping from Weimar to Italy first occurred to him we
shall never know. He tells us that the longing for "classic soil" had become so
great that he dared not read the classics because they upset him too much,
but his actual decision to go may have been taken at the very last moment.
On August 28, he celebrated his thirty-seventh birthday in Carlsbad, where
a number of the court were taking the waters. Two or three days later, all
the party except Goethe and the Grand Duke returned to Weimar under the
impression that Goethe was going on a short geological excursion into the
mountains. After they had gone, Goethe asked the Duke for leave of absence
and, at three in the morning on September 3, jumped into a coach with no
servant and hardly any luggage, assumed the name of Möller, and bolted. He
does not appear to have been very explicit about his plans even to his sovereign, for the Duke cannot have received his letter, dated September 2, until
after he had left.

Forgive me for being rather vague about my travels and absence when I
took leave of you; even now I do not know quite what will happen to me.

You are happy, you are moving towards an aim you wished and chose
for yourself. Your domestic affairs are in good order and in a good way,
and I know you will permit me now to think of myself. In fact, you have
often urged me to do so. I am certainly not indispensable at this moment; and as for the special affairs entrusted to me, I have left them so
that they can run on for a while quite comfortably without me. Indeed,
I might even die without there being any great shock. I say nothing of
how favourable these circumstances are at present and simply ask you
for an indefinite leave of absence. The baths these two years have done
a great deal for my health and I hope the greatest good for the elasticity
of my mind, too, if it can be left to itself for a while to enjoy seeing the
wide world.

My first four volumes are complete at last. Herder has been a tireless
and faithful helper; now I need to be at leisure and in the mood for the
last four. I have undertaken it all rather lightly, and I am only now beginning to see what is to be done if it is not to become a mess. All this and
much else impels me to lose myself in places where I am totally unknown.

I am going to travel quite alone, under another name, and I have great hopes of this venture, odd as it seems. But please don't let anyone notice that I shall be away for some time. Everyone working with or under me, everyone that has to do with me, expects me from one week to the next, and I want to leave it like that and, although absent, to be as effective as someone expected at any moment. . . .

The only person Goethe knew in Rome, and by correspondence only, was the German painter Tischbein. Through him Goethe was introduced to the German artistic colony, and, though he keeps telling Weimar how lonely he is, it is clear that he was soon leading quite an active social life. But in Rome he was free, as in Weimar he had not been, to choose his own company, and his anonymity, though it did not remain a secret for long, seems to have been respected. Whether by his own choice or because Italians were difficult to get to know, he stuck pretty closely to his fellow countrymen. Whereas in Weimar most of his friends had been older than he was, those of whom he saw most in Rome, with the exception of Angelica Kauffmann, were all younger. When Goethe was thirty-seven, Tischbein was thirty-five, Kayser, Kniep, and Schütz thirty-one, Moritz twenty-nine, Lipps twenty-eight, Meyer twenty-six and Bury twenty-three. Only one of them, Moritz, was a writer and an intellectual, not one of them was a poet or a clergyman, and, again with the exception of Angelica, they were all poorer than he. For Goethe at this period in his life, such a company had many advantages. Before he came to Italy he had seen very little original architecture, sculpture and painting, Classical or Renaissance, and he had the common sense to realize that before he could understand and appreciate it properly, his eye would have to be educated. He also wanted to learn to draw, not so much for its own sake— he never fancied that he might become a serious artist—as for the discipline; drawing was the best way to train his mind to pay attention to the external world. To train his eye, to learn to draw, he needed the help of professional artists, which most of his Roman friends were. Secondly, if he were to develop as a poet, the best companionship for him at this point, failing a real literary equal like Schiller, was an unliterary one or, at least, a company whose literary judgments he did not have to take seriously. They all knew, of course, that he was a famous poet and Angelica was a sympathetic feminine audience, but they did not pretend to be expert judges of poetry, and if they objected to anything, he could disregard their criticisms in a way that he still found it difficult to ignore the criticisms which came from Weimar. He acknowledged a debt to Moritz's prosodical theories, but otherwise the fresh stimuli to his imagination came, not from conversations or reading, but from watching the behaviour of Italians and living in the midst of Italian nature, the climate, shapes and colours of which were so utterly different from the northern nature he had known hitherto. How necessary it was for

Goethe to remove himself from the literary atmosphere of Weimar can be guessed from his letters about his new versions of *Iphigenie* and *Egmont*, for it is clear that Weimar preferred the old versions and did not care for his new classical manner.

Lastly, an artistic, somewhat bohemian, foreign colony in a great city gave him a freedom in his personal life which would have been out of the question at a provincial German court. As he gives us only his side of the correspondence, we have to infer what the reactions of Weimar were to his whole Italian venture. It seems fairly clear that they were hurt, suspicious, disapproving and jealous. If the reader sometimes becomes impatient with Goethe's endless reiterations of how hard he is working, what a lot of good Italy is doing him, he must remember that Goethe is trying to placate his friends for being obviously so radiantly happy without them. One of the reasons why his account of his time in Rome, particularly of his second stay, is less interesting than the rest of *Italian Journey* is that one feels much is happening to Goethe which is of great importance to him, but which he declines to tell. There is no reason to suppose that Goethe's life in Rome was anything like Byron's in Venice, but it is impossible to believe that it was quite so respectable, or so exclusively devoted to higher things as, in his letters home, for obvious reasons, he makes it sound. The difference between the over-refined, delicate, almost neurasthenic face of the pre-Italian portraits and the masculine, self-assured face in the portraits executed after his return is very striking; the latter is that of a man who has known sexual satisfaction.

If Goethe did not tell everything, what he did tell was true enough. He did work very hard and Italy did do him a lot of good. Any writer will find *Italian Journey* fascinating for what Goethe says about his own methods of working. He would compose with extraordinary rapidity and in his head—if he did not write it down at once, he often forgot it—and under any circumstances: there cannot be many poets who have been able to write while suffering from seasickness. His chief difficulty, partly out of a temperamental impatience and partly because he kept having so many ideas and was interested in so many things, was in finishing a work. He starts rewriting *Iphigenie auf Tauris* and becomes distracted by the thought of another play, *Iphigenie in Delphi*; he is walking in the Public Gardens of Palermo, planning a new play about Nausicaa, when suddenly he is struck by an idea about the Primal Plant, and Botany chases away the Muse.

And he has so many unfinished pieces. When at last he finishes *Iphigenie*, begun in 1779, there is *Egmont* waiting, begun in 1775. He finishes *Egmont*, and there are two old *Singspiele* to rewrite. These done with, he takes out the yellowed manuscript of *Faust*, which is eighteen years old, and adds a scene or two, and he departs from Rome with the nine-year-old *Tasso* to rework while travelling. And he does all this in the midst of social life, sightseeing, collecting coins, gems, minerals, plaster casts, taking drawing lessons, attending lectures on perspective and making botanical experiments. If to read about such energy is rather exhausting, to read about a man who is so enjoying himself is enormous fun.

We have tried to produce a translation, not a crib. A crib is like a pair of spectacles for the weak-sighted; a translation is like a book in Braille for the blind. A translator, that is to say, has to assume that his readers cannot and never will be able to read the original. This, in its turn, implies that they are not specialists in his author. On the one hand, they probably know very little about him; on the other, their appetite for scholarly footnotes is probably small.

The translator's most difficult problem is not *what* his author says but his tone of voice. How is a man who thought and wrote in German to think and write in English and yet remain a unique personality called Goethe? To offer a translation to the public is to claim that one does know how Goethe would have written had English been his native tongue, to claim, in fact, that one has mediumistic gifts, and, as we all know, mediums are often rather shady characters.

The circumstances under which *Italian Journey* was written, put together and published present a special problem. Most of its contents are based upon letters and a journal written at the time, but it was not until twenty-five years later that Goethe set to work to make a book out of them, and the third part was not published until he was almost eighty. A compilation of this kind involves editing, and it must be admitted that, as an editor, Goethe did not do a very good job. If a man writes two letters at the same time to two different people, it is only to be expected that he will repeat himself a little, and if at the end of an exciting and exhausting day he hurriedly jots down the events in his journal, it is natural enough if there is some disorder in his narrative—what should have come first comes as an afterthought, etc.—but if he decides to make a book out of such material, one has a right to expect him to cut out what is repetitious, to rearrange what is chaotic and clarify what is obscure.

Even in the first two parts of *Italian Journey*, there are places where Goethe has been careless. For instance, he presents his visit to Cagliostro's relatives as a passage from his journal, dated April 13 and 14, 1787. But suddenly, without warning, the reader finds him referring to events which did not take place until 1789. What Goethe has actually done is to print, not his original journal, but a talk about Cagliostro based on it which he gave in Weimar in 1792. As for Part Three, one can only conclude that Goethe handed the material over to his secretary without rereading it and that the secretary was too overawed by the great man to suggest any corrections.

We have seen fit to do some editing ourselves. One previous English translator, an Anglican clergyman, omitted all favourable references made by

Goethe to the Roman Catholic Church; we have confined ourselves to stylistic matters. We have cut some passages which seemed to us unduly repetitious and some allusions to things which were known to his correspondents but would be unintelligible to a reader without a lengthy note, and, here and there, we have transposed sentences to a more logical position. We have also omitted the whole article *Concerning the Pictorial Imitation of the Beautiful.* Our official excuse is that the ideas in it are not Goethe's but Moritz's; our real reason is that it is verbose rubbish and sounds like a parody of "deep" German prose.

To those who regard such tinkering as sacrilege, we can only cite the authority of the Master himself.

If the translator has really understood his author, he will be able to evoke in his own mind not only what the author has done, but also what he wanted and ought to have done. That at least is the line I have always taken in translation, though I make no claim that it is justifiable. (To Streckfuss, 1827)

> *Encounter,* November 1962; *Italian Journey (1786–1788),*
> by J. W. Goethe, translated by W. H. Auden
> and Elizabeth Mayer, 1962

The Case Is Curious

The Delights of Detection. Edited with an introduction
by Jacques Barzun. Criterion Books. $5.95.

To ask one detective story addict to review an anthology of detective stories compiled by another addict is asking for trouble, for we are as bigoted as psychologists and prosodists. For instance, I have only read a few pages of Mr Barzun's introduction before I find him dismissing all theories which attribute a mythical significance to the detective story as "pretentious rubbish." Alas, I must plead guilty, for I not only hold such a theory but have had the temerity to commit it to print. I shall not repeat it here. Though I agree completely with Mr Barzun that the primary conscious interest in detective fiction is that of following the reasoning—character interest is always secondary, and the less love interest the better—I should like him to answer a few questions.

(1) Is there not an essential difference between the intellectual fascination of the crime problem and the problems of, say, chess (which I don't play), or *The London Times* crossword (of which I am also an addict)?

(2) Why is it that the crime must be murder? Theft offers just as good opportunities for deduction, yet who really finds it as exciting to discover who stole the Vermeer as to discover who strangled the Vicar?

(3) In real life I disapprove of capital punishment, but in detective fiction I want my murderers to be hanged and am disappointed if they commit suicide or go mad. Is this merely my personal idiosyncrasy or do other readers feel the same?

Aside from this, however, there are no disagreements between us. I prefer my tales long and leisurely, with many suspects and lots of copy about the rituals of some special kind of life, and I dare say that Mr Barzun does too, but obviously an anthology of full-length detective novels would be too heavy to lift.

Like him, I exclude both the thriller, which deals with the war between Good (Us) and Evil (Them), and tales, like those of Raymond Chandler, which are really studies of criminal life. Like him, I define the detective story as a Whodunit, and, judging by his selection, he seems to agree with me that, for the reader's desire to find a solution to reach its maximum, the murder must occur in a kind of society where murder is an extraordinary event.

The editor of an anthology of stories has a tough assignment. Like any other kind of anthologist, his choices must be as good as possible to his prospective readers, for very few detective stories can be read twice. As a fellow addict I must congratulate Mr Barzun, for out of the seventeen stories he has selected, I had read only two, and I object to only one, Austin Freeman's "A Case of Premeditation," because it is out of line with one of my dogmas, which is: "The Murderer shall not be sympathetic."

Those who read detective stories must be prepared to accept the sad fact that often the very writers who can invent the best detective puzzles are those who invent the most intolerable detective heroes. In this anthology, for instance, there are excellent tales by H. C. Bailey and Rex Stout, but the reader has to stomach Reggie Fortune and Nero Wolfe. Yet in the detective literature they are only a couple in an appalling crew—think of Lord Peter Wimsey, Sir Henry Merivale, and all those Scotland Yard policemen who are related to the landed aristocracy or married to lady artists! (I must confess to a weakness for Mr Day Lewis' Nigel Strangeways because some of his habits were taken from mine.)

It is really all Conan Doyle's fault. By an extraordinary flash of inspiration he created an eccentric whose eccentricities determine his profession: when he has no problem to solve, he lapses into melancholia and takes cocaine, and his mind is so specialized that he knows nothing about the solar system. One of his satisfactory successors is the Eccentric Don, like Gervase Fen, for dons by profession are interested in intellectual inquiry, so it is reasonable, should a murder occur in their college, for them to become amateur sleuths. The Village Spinster, like Miss Marple, will also do because spinsters do not have jobs, and curiosity about their neighbors becomes them. But in too many cases, the eccentricities of the detective seem *voulu* and his inquiries a repellent minding of other people's business. Aside from Sherlock Holmes, the only absolutely satisfactory detectives I know of are Inspector French, the professional policeman whose job is to protect society, and Father Brown, the priest who is professionally concerned with the soul of the criminal.

Mr Barzun's third section, "Historic Tales," is a novel and happy idea. It includes a piece by Beaumarchais (1776), a story by an American, William Leggett (1828), and a sketch by Dumas (1848), which demonstrate that, though it may be true to say that Poe invented the detective story proper, there were authors before him who had glimpses of the dramatic excitement to be found in pure ratiocination.

The Mid-Century, June 1961

Ronald Firbank and an Amateur World

I hope the shade of Ronald Firbank will forgive me for beginning with what is going to bore him stiff—some abstract ideas.

One of the crucial differences between human beings and all other creatures is that we can distinguish between amateur and professional activities, and they cannot. Or rather, all their activities are professional. Animals play, it is true, but their play is, so to speak, professional education. A kitten playing with a ball of string is anticipating what later it will do with a mouse; and the undirected play of a small baby is probably of the same kind. But a seven-year-old girl pretending to be the mother of her doll is engaged in another kind of activity; for nothing she does will be of any use to her when she grows up and becomes the real mother of a real child.

Schoolmasters may tell us that cricket and football are preparation for life, but we all know this is bosh, except in the exceptional case of someone who is going to become a professional cricketer or footballer. And when two married couples play a game of bridge in the evening they are engaged in an absolutely amateur—that is to say, gratuitous—activity. Suppose they play for two hours: during this period their history as persons is suspended and replaced by their temporary history as players. The beginning of the game is not related to their personal past, nor its conclusion to their personal future.

What characterizes a game, or any amateur activity, is the absence of necessity. There is no obligation, natural or moral, to play, and there is an absence of care: although all the players try to win, the losers do not suffer any serious pain. A professional activity, on the other hand, is dedicated action. The dedication may be passive; like other creatures we are dedicated by nature to keep ourselves alive and, to a slightly lesser degree, to mate and reproduce our kind. And our dedication may be active, as when a man chooses to devote his life to medicine or politics or art: and even then, if the choice is a right one, it is largely dictated by inherited talent and social circumstances which are not chosen by him.

Professional activity, that is, is characterized by necessity, be it the "must" of nature and society, or the "must" and "ought" of ambition and conscience; and by care. Failure causes physical and mental suffering. However, unless we are exceptionally unlucky there is an amateur element even in our most professional activities. Few of us—at least I hope so—derive no enjoyment from the things we are obliged to do. If this were not so, I do not see how man would ever have invented games, in which necessity—the rules of the game— is mock necessity, and the pleasures of winning and pains of losing are mock pleasures and pains. Nor could man have imagined a prehistoric condition called The Earthly Paradise, or Eden, or the Golden Age, in which what, in the world we now live in, are professional activities were amateur games.

But enough of this. Let us play a parlour game. Take a pencil and a sheet of paper, write your name at the top and try to describe your private vision of Eden. Since it will be your creation you don't have to consider your own role in it. Sit at its centre, open your eyes and ears and try to answer as honestly as possible such questions as: "What is the landscape like?" "What is the weather like?" "What sorts of people inhabit it?" "What sorts of houses and furniture do they have?" "What do they wear?" "How do they talk and behave?" "How do they spend their time?"

I cannot see what you are writing, and I have no intention of telling you what I have written. But I possess several sheets written by people who have played this game during the last 150 years. I am surprised, and rather perplexed, to find that the names at the top all seem to be English. I cannot find a single French or German or Italian one. I come on a sheet labelled *Pickwick Papers*, Chapters 1–40, by Charles Dickens; then *Alice Through the Looking-Glass*, by Lewis Carroll; then *The Importance of Being Earnest*, by Oscar Wilde; then a huge pile of sheets by P. G. Wodehouse; and here is a smaller sheaf by someone called Ronald Firbank.

Let us sit down in the middle of his earthly paradise and note what we see and hear. Somewhere a band is playing the inevitable waltz from *The Blue Banana*. Overhead tame doves, looking like plump little pearls, are cooing capriciously as they plume themselves and drop down feathers and platitudes on the passers-by. In the distance, to our left, the landscape seems to be English, for through a belt of osiers and alder we can see a great stone church with the scheming look of an ex-cathedral. And a few stars slip suddenly down behind a country house. In the distance to our right, however, an opera house, uplifting a big naked man, all gilt, who is being mauled by a pack of wild animals carved in stone, soars out of tropical vegetation; while the centre background is occupied by baroque palaces and churches from Europe. In the crowd who pass our bench the females outnumber the males, and there seem to be more old ones than young ones. Most of them wear enormous hats. By the way, on the bench next to us an untidy baroness is watching us through a narrow Gothic window she has cut in the pages of her Court Gazette. A queen flashes past in her motor-car, wearing her crown. Here comes the princess, frightening bats with a rope of pearls, a countess, with the deftness of a virtuoso, seizes and crushes a pale-winged passing gnat with her muff, several nuns, a Negro masseuse. Among the men one observes a Pope with a head like an elderly lady's maid, an extraordinarily large number of priests, a king with the air of a tired pastry-cook, a choir-boy with the vaguely distraught air of a kitten that has seen visions, a musician with a voice like cheap scent, diplomats, courtiers, and several young gentlemen of great and insolent beauty. There are a number of blacks, and evidently in this place there is no racial inequality, for when a Negress says of a duchess, in a tone loud enough for her to hear, "From de complexion dat female hab, she look as doh she bin boiling bananas", the duchess can only glare.

Strange snatches of conversation reach us.

"I think I'm going in."

"Oh, why?"

"Because, dear, I feel armchairish."

"I date my old age from the day I took the lift first at the Uffizi."

"It's not often I see the Cosmos looks so special."

"I'm trying, it's true, to coax the dear archbishop to give the first Act of *La Tosca* in the Blue Jesus."

"Oh, I want to spank the white walls of his cottage."

"Fleas have been found at the Ritz."

"I feel his books are all written in hotels, with the bed unmade at the back of a chair."

Consulting the Firbank telephone directory we find such names as: St Automona Meris, Lilian Bloater, Father Damien Forment, Lady Parvula de Panzoust, Lady Lucy Saunter, Eva Schnerb, Mrs Shamefoot, Monseigneur Silex, Sir Somebody Something, Guy Thin, Canon Wertnose, Madame Wetme, Mrs Yajñavalkya.

As we might expect, their houses are full of pictures. In one we come across a brilliant *croquis* signed Carmontelle, of a duchess trifling with a strawberry; in another a Crucifixion by a pupil of Félicien Rops, showing a pale woman stretched upon a silver cross, in a silver teagown with a pink rose in her powdered hair. And there's lots of ornate furniture. One palace is famous for its cast-off thrones; whenever a throne began to look worn out, or the silk got shrill, it was hurried off to a spare bedroom in the visitors' wing and used as a chair. When a grand-duchess came to stay she was sure to be late for dinner; leaning back on her seat in a regal pose before her dressing-table, her combs arranged *en couronne*, forgetful of time, the queen's temper, and the cold soup.

Talking of soup, Firbank himself was a very delicate feeder. And when I visit his earthly paradise I must confess I feel famished, for the principle of the cuisine seems to be the visual appearance and names of the dishes rather than their flavour or caloric value. A made dish of sugared violets served in aspic, "*points d'asperge à la Laura Leslie*", a cup of cold pear consommé, containing hearts, coronets, and most of the alphabet in vermicelli. One begins to long for the loaded table of Mr Wardle in Dingley Dell.

A few anthropological notes. Politics, none, except for royal match-making. Sports, paddling and a little mild fishing. Public entertainments, opera, ballet. Social discontent, none. Only a few people have any ambition at all: one, for example, wants to get herself into a stained-glass window; another wants to get a saint to come to her party; another wants a villa with a water closet. But most are completely content with their lot. Prominent interests: religion and sex, in that order. For instance,

> invitations to meet Monseigneur This or Father That, who constantly were being coaxed from their musty sacristies and wan-faced acolytes into the capital in order that they might officiate at masses, confessions, and breakfast parties *à la fourchette*, were lavished daily upon the bewildered girl. Messages and hasty informal lightly-pencilled notes, too, would frequently reach her. Such as "I shall be pouring out cocoa after dinner in bed. Bring your biscuits and join me." Or a rat-tat-tat from a round-eyed page and: "The Countess's compliments and she'd take it as a favour if you can make a station with her in chapel later on"; or "The Marchioness will be birched tomorrow and not today."

Only those who think religion is nonsense will be shocked at having it treated as an amateur game. Believers and church-goers will see that just because a church is unnecessary in the earthly paradise, religious activities there will seem more an expression of perfect freedom than any other, because a spectator cannot deduce from what is done the purpose for which it is done: I can watch huntsmen and hounds and know what they are trying to do because the fox is visible; but God is not.

The problem of amateur sex is much more difficult, because sex is in part a natural necessity to which, like all the other animals, we are subjected willynilly. If sexual acts are introduced into the earthly paradise at all then Firbank's procedure is, I think, the only possible one—to make them infantile and polymorphously perverse. The improprieties in Firbank are those of children playing Doctor behind the rhododendron bushes. Serious love is out of the question, for it is inseparable from personal dedication, and the possibility of suffering, if it is unrequited or the beloved dies, is always there. In fact, it is a general axiom of any earthly paradise that if a character in it becomes serious it means that he or she has eaten of the Tree of Knowledge of Good and Evil and must go.

From the moment Mr Pickwick, for example, goes to prison and becomes personally acquainted with real suffering, *Pickwick Papers* becomes a different kind of book, and the kind which Ronald Firbank had neither the talent nor the wish to write. So long as the feelings of his lovers are only theatrical they can stay in his world. Thus, Olga Blumenghast belongs there.

> "He's such a gold-fish, Rara . . . any finger that would throw him bread . . ."
> "And there's no doubt, I'm afraid, that lots do!", Mademoiselle de Nazianzi answered lucidly, sinking down by her side.
> "I would give all my soul to him, Rara . . . my chances of heaven."
> "Your chances, Olga," Mademoiselle de Nazianzi murmured, avoiding some bird-droppings with her skirt.
> "How I envy *the men*, Rara, in his platoon!"
> "Take away his uniform, Olga, and what does he become?"
> "Ah *what*—!"
> Mademoiselle Blumenghast clasped her hands brilliantly across the nape of her neck.
> "I want to possess him at dawn, at dawn." she broke out; "beneath a sky striped with green. . . ."
> "Oh, Olga! And I never shall rest" she declared, turning away on a languid heel, "until I *do*."

Even the jilted Miss Thetis Tooke, though she has tried to commit suicide, belongs:

> "I would have done it yesterday," she moaned, "only the sea was as smooth as a plate!"
> Yet now that the night was slashed with little phantom horses it affrighted her. To be enveloped utterly by that cold stampede! . . .
> "Everything's useless now. For very soon, Dick, I'll be dead. . . . Dead. . . . I suppose they'll put out the Stella Maris and dredge the Bay. But the tide will bear me beyond the Point; fortunately; I'm so lightsome. Seven stone. . . . When Nellie Nackman did the same she never left the rocks. It's a matter of build purely. . . . I shall remove my hat, I think," she cogitated. "It would be a sin indeed to spoil such expensive plumes. . . . It's not perhaps a headpiece that would become every one;—and I can't say I'm sorry!"

On the other hand, though, at the beginning of *The Flower beneath the Foot* Mademoiselle de Nazianzi seems perfectly at home. She can say of the prince "He has such strength! One could niche an idol in his dear, dented chin";

and leave the room warbling *Depuis le jour*; and pray "Heaven help me to be decorative and to do right!", by the end of the book, it turns out she really is in love—and the prince has to marry another.

> Oblivious of what she did, she began to beat her hands, until they streamed with blood, against the broken glass ends on the wall: "Yousef, Yousef, Yousef . . ."

Blood can only be shed outside the gates of Eden and once it flows there's no return. But though blood cannot be shed, death is possible as an amateur event, provided that there is no pain, no bereaved survivor, and life ends with a dramatic gesture. The daughter of a dean is killed by a mousetrap, a cardinal dies of a heart attack while chasing a choir boy round a cathedral wearing nothing but his mitre. The son of Lord Intriguer died of shock on being surprised by a jackal while composing a sonnet. And here is a death-bed scene. The dying woman is the Archduchess Elizabeth whose passions in life have been paddling and erecting public lavatories.

> In the Archduchess's bedchamber, watching the antics of priests and doctors [the Angel of Death] sat there unmoved. Propped high by many bolsters, in a vast blue canopied bed, the Archduchess lay staring laconically at a diminutive model of a flight of steps, leading to what appeared to be intended, perhaps, as a hall of Attent, off which opened quite a lot of little doors, most of which bore the word: "Engaged." A doll, with a ruddy face, in charge, smiled indolently as she sat feigning knitting, suggesting vague "fleshly thoughts," whenever he looked up, in the Archduchess's spiritual advisor.
>
> And the mind of the sinking woman, as her thoughts wandered, appeared to be tinged with "matter" too: "I recollect the first time I heard the *Blue Danube* played", she broke out: "it was at Schönbrunn—schönes Schönbrunn.—My cousin the Ludwig of Bavaria came—I wore—the Emperor said—"
>
> "If your imperial highness would swallow this", Dr Cuncliffe Babcock started forward with a glass.
>
> "Trinquons, trinquons et vive l'amour! Schnieder sang that—"
>
> "If your imperial highness—"
>
> "Ah, my dear Vienna. Where's Teddywegs?"
>
> At the Archduchess's little escritoire at the foot of the bed, her Dreaminess [the Queen] was making ready a few private telegrams, breaking without undue harshness the melancholy news, "Poor Lizzie has ceased articulating", she did not think she could improve on that, and indeed had written it several times in her most temperamental hand, when the Archduchess had started suddenly crackling about Vienna.
>
> "*Sssh* Lizzie—I never can write when people talk."

"I want Teddywegs."

"The Countess Yvorra took him for a run round the courtyard."

"I think I must undertake a convenience next for dogs. . . . It is disgraceful they have not got one already, poor creatures," the Archduchess crooned, accepting the proffered glass.

"Yes, yes, dear," the Queen exclaimed, rising and crossing to the window.

The bitter odour of the oleander flowers outside oppressed the breathless air and filled the room as with a faint funereal music. So still a day. Tending the drooping sun-saturated flowers, a gardener with long ivory arms alone seemed animate.

"Pull up your skirt, Marquise. Pull it up. . . . It's dragging, a little, in the water."

"*Judica me, Deus,*" in imperious tones the priest by the bedside besought: "*et discerne causam meam de gente non sancta. Parce, Domine. Parce populo tuo, ne in aeternum irasceris nobis.*"

"A whale! A whale!"

"*Sustinuit anima mea in verbo ejus, speravit anima mea in Domino.*"

"Elsie?" A look of wondrous happiness overspread the Archduchess's face.—She was wading—wading again among the irises and rushes, wading, her hand in Princess Elsie's hand, through a glittering golden sea, towards the wide horizon.

The plangent cry of a peacock rose disquietingly from the garden.

"I'm nothing but nerves, doctor," her Dreaminess lamented, fidgeting with the crucifix that dangled at her neck upon a chain. *Ultra* feminine, she disliked that another, even *in extremis,* should absorb *all* the limelight.

"A change of scene, ma'am, would be probably beneficial", Dr Cuncliffe Babcock replied, eyeing askance the Countess of Tolga who unobtrusively entered.

"The couturiers attend your pleasure, ma'am", in impassive undertones she said, "to fit your mourning".

"Oh, tell them the Queen is too tired to try on now", her Dreaminess answered, repairing in agitation toward a glass.

"They would come here, ma'am," the Countess said, pointing persuasively to the little anteroom of the Archduchess, where two nuns of the Flaming Hood were industriously telling their beads.

"I don't know why, but this glass refuses to flatter me."

"*Benedicamus Domino! Ostende nobis Domine misericordiam tuam. Et salutare tuum da nobis!*"

"Well, just a toque," the Queen sadly assented.

"*Indulgentiam absolutionem et remissionem peccatorum nostrorum tribuat nobis omnipotens et misericors Dominus.*"

"Guess who was at the Ritz, ma'am, this week," the Countess demurely murmured.

"Who is at the Ritz this week, I can't," the Queen replied.

"*Nobody!*"

"Why, how so?"

"The Ambassadress of England, it seems, has alarmed the world away. I gather they mean to prosecute!"

The Archduchess sighed.

"I want mauve sweet-peas," she listlessly said.

"Her spirit soars; her thoughts are in the *Champs-Elysées*," the Countess exclaimed, withdrawing noiselessly to warn the milliners.

"Or in the garden," the Queen reflected, returning to the window. And she was standing there, her eyes fixed half wistfully upon the long ivory arms of the kneeling gardener, when the Angel of Death (who had sat, unmoved throughout the day) arose.

The earthly paradise is no place for literary critics. Either this scene could occur in yours or it could not. If it could not, then I am afraid you and I could never really be friends. Now let me sign off with a conjugatory jingle from the Kingdom of Pisuerga:

> "I am a political hostess
> Thou art a political hostess
> He is a political hostess
> We are . . ."

BBC Third Programme, 29 April 1961;
The Listener, 8 June 1961

A Poet of Honor

The Collected Poems of Robert Graves. Doubleday. $5.95.

I first came across Robert Graves's poems in the volumes of *Georgian Poetry* when I was a schoolboy, and ever since he has been one of the very few poets whose volumes I have always bought the moment they appeared. There were many others, no doubt, who did the same, but, until recently, Mr Graves was not a Public Name in the way that Mr Eliot, for example, was. Individuals who had discovered his poetry for themselves would talk about it to each other, but his name was not bandied about at cocktail parties to show that the speaker was *au courant*, nor was he made the subject of critical articles in little magazines or of Ph.D. theses.

But now the situation has changed.

> ... though the Otherwhereish currency
> Cannot be quoted yet officially,
> I meet less hindrance now with the exchange
> Nor is my garb, even, considered strange;
> And shy enquiries for literature
> Come in by every post, and the side door.

wrote Mr Graves a few years ago, and already the first two lines are out of date. I do not know whether to be glad or sorry about this. One is always glad when a writer one has long admired gains wide recognition—publicity at least means bigger sales—but public fame has its dangers, not so much for the poet himself, particularly if he has Mr Graves's years and strength of character, as for his public. With his consent or without it, he becomes responsible for a fashion and, though some fashions may be better than others, in all there is an element of falsehood. No poet has been more concerned than Mr Graves with poetic integrity, with being true, at all costs, to his real self. The difficulty is that it is precisely the man who is most obviously himself who can be the greatest threat to those who have not yet found themselves, for instead of taking him as an *example*, inspiring them to do in their way what he has done in his, they are all too apt to take him as a *model* whose style of writing and literary tastes they blindly follow.

As an example, nothing could be more admirable than the way in which, at a time when most of his seniors and juniors were looking to the French poets of the post-Baudelaireian period or to the English metaphysicals for their poetic models, Mr Graves had the courage to ignore them and remain faithful to his personal preferences—nursery rhymes, ballads, Skelton, Caroline poets like Lovelace and Rochester, even romantic poets like Blake, Coleridge, and Christina Rosetti—or that, in an age obsessed with experiment and innovation in meter and poetic organization, he should have gone on quietly writing genuine contemporary poetry within the traditional forms. It would not be equally admirable, however, if Pope and free verse, say, were to become taboo because Mr Graves does not like the one or write in the other. But to turn to his poems themselves is enough to make one forget all such gloomy forebodings.

The kind of critic who regards authors as an opportunity for displaying his own brilliance and ingenuity will find Mr Graves a poor subject. A few of his poems, it is true, can benefit from a gloss, but this Mr Graves has provided himself in *The White Goddess*. For the rest, though he happens to be a learned scholar, he demands no scholarship of his readers; his poems are short, their diction simple, their syntax unambiguous and their concerns, love, nature, the personal life, matters with which all are familiar and in which all are interested. About public life, politics, the world situation, etc., he has nothing to say.

This does not mean that he regards public events as of no significance—
he could never have written his excellent historical novels if he did—only
that it is not a realm with which he believes poetry should be concerned. He
also believes, I suspect, that in our age the Public Realm is irredeemable and
that the only thing a sensible man can do is ignore it and live as decently as
he can in spite of it. I can picture Mr Graves, under certain circumstances, as
a guerilla fighter, but I cannot see him writing pamphlets for any cause.

Like nearly all writers worth reading, Mr Graves is a moralist, and the artistic merits of his poems cannot be divorced from the conception of the good
life which they express. Though Horace is not one of his favorite poets—
Horace is unpassionate and easygoing, Graves passionate and puritanical—
they both attach great importance to measure and good sense, and have a
common dislike for willful disorder and theatrical gestures. If Mr Graves is
the more convincing advocate, it is because one feels that measure and good
sense are values he has had to fight to achieve. It is hard to believe that Horace ever suffered from nightmares or some passion so violent that it could
have destroyed him, but he would have approved, I think, of Graves's description of the climate of thought.

> Wind, sometimes, in the evening chimneys; rain
> On the early morning roof, on sleepy sight;
> Snow streaked upon the hilltop, feeding
> The fond brook at the valley-head
> That greens the valley and that parts the lips;
> The sun, simple, like a country neighbor;
> The moon, grand, not fanciful with clouds.

Graves's good man, leaving aside the special case of the good poet, is somebody who leads an orderly, hard-working, independent life, a good husband
and father who keeps his word and pays his debts, outwardly, in fact, a good
bourgeois, but inwardly never losing his sense of his personal identity or his
capacity for love and reverence.

On the subject of love, no poet in our time has written more or better.
Most of Hardy's love poems are elegies, most of Yeats's are concerned with
unrequited love, but Graves's deal with the joys and griefs of mutual passion.
He shares with D. H. Lawrence a contempt for those who would deny the
physical element in love and call

> . . . for a chaste
> Sodality: all dead below the waist.

but that is the only point on which they agree. He has none of Lawrence's
hysterical aversion to conscious understanding between the sexes; on the
contrary, any sexual relationship that does not lead to personal understanding and affection is, for him, base. Nothing could be further from Lawrence

than his priapic poem "Down, Wanton, Down!" In this, as in many others, he shows his distaste for the vulgarity and crudeness of untamed male sexuality. Woman, to Graves, is the superior sex, and only a woman can teach a man the meaning of true love.

For the poet, as the messenger of the Mother Goddess, there is an additional obligation to speak no more and no less than the truth, and each poet, according to his nature and the time in which he lives, has his own kind of temptation to lie. Mr Graves has told us of his. He was born—the term is inaccurate but convenient—with a natural faculty for writing verse. Ask him to improvise a poem on any subject, and in ten minutes he can turn out something competent and mellifluous. This is a very valuable gift, and a poet like Wordsworth who lacks it is deficient, but it is a dangerous one, for the poet who possesses it can all too easily forsake the truth for verbal display.

> But you know, I know, and you know I know
>   My principal curse:
> Shame at the mounting dues I have come to owe
>   A devil of verse,
> Who caught me young, ingenuous and uncouth,
>   Prompting me how
> To evade the patent clumsiness of truth—
>   Which I do now.

It is of this devil and not of another poet, I think that Graves is speaking in "In Broken Images."

> He is quick, thinking in clear images;
> I am slow, thinking in broken images.
>
> He becomes dull, trusting to his clear images;
> I become sharp, mistrusting my broken images. . . .
>
> He in a new confusion of his understanding;
> I in a new understanding of my confusion.

A comparison between his individual volumes and the *Collected Poems* which follow it, and then between the successive *Collected Poems* of 1926, 1938, 1947, 1955 and 1961 reveals how stern with himself Mr Graves has been in discarding any poem that contained a trace of smartness. Among them, I remember a pastiche of *Speke Parrot*, which was an amazing tour de force. Personally, I regret its omission, but I can see why it has been excluded. The only virtuoso pieces he has retained are comic poems like "Welcome to the Caves of Arta" and "Apollo of the Physiologists," for a comic poem must almost necessarily be a virtuoso performance. If I have a greater fondness for bravura in poetry than Mr Graves, I suspect that we only differ in our notion of what is comic or what may be comically treated. To me, for example, *Lycidas* is a "comic" poem which I can learn "by heart not rote" as I can learn a poem by Edward Lear. It seems to me a verbal arcadia in which death, grief, religion, and politics are games which cannot possibly be taken seriously. On the other hand, because I am convinced of the reality of their emotions, there are religious sonnets by Donne and Hopkins in which I feel that the virtuosity of expression comes between them and the truth.

Mr Graves's other temptation has been the tendency of the romantic imagination to regard the extraordinary and remote as more "poetic", more luminous than everyday events.

> The lost, the freakish, the unspelt
> Drew me: for simple sights I had no eye.
> And did I swear allegiance then
> To wildness, not (as I thought) to truth—
> Become a virtuoso, and this also,
> Later, of simple sights, when tiring
> Of unicorn and upas?

Again, a reading of his collected poems will show how successful he has been in disciplining his imagination and his tongue. Occasionally, perhaps, he indulges his subjective feelings at the expense of objective fact. Among his more recent poems is one entitled "Turn of the Moon" which concludes as follows:

> But if one night she brings us, as she turns,
> Soft, steady, even, copious rain
> That harms no leaf or flower, but gently falls
> Hour after hour, sinking to the taproots,
> And the sodden earth exhales at dawn
> A long sigh scented with pure gratitude,
> Such rain—the first rain of our lives, it seems,
> Neither foretold, cajoled, nor counted on—
> Is woman giving as she loves.

The lines are beautiful and, at first reading, I was carried away. But, then, a tiresome doubt obtruded itself: "Are drought and rainfall *really* caused by the moon? What would a meteorologist say?"

In addition to discarding many poems, Mr Graves has revised some, and, to anyone who writes verses himself, nothing is more instructive than a poet's revisions.

In Mr Graves's case, they are particularly important because they prevent his doctrine of the subordination of art to truth from being misunderstood. It is all right for him to say

> And call the man a liar who says I wrote
>   All that I wrote in love, for love of art.

But we all know the kind of poet who, when one points out to him that a certain line is obscure or clumsy and should be rewritten, replies: "But that is how it came to me." Art without love is nothing, but love without art is insufficient. Here for comparison are two versions of "The Sea Horse."

> Tenderly confide your secret love,
> For one who never pledged you less than love,
> To this indomitable hippocamp,
> Child of your element, coiled a-ramp,
> Having ridden out worse tempests than you know of:
> Make much of him in your despair, and shed
> Salt tears to bathe his taciturn dry head.
>
> (1953)

> Since now in every public place
> Lurk phantoms who assume your walk and face,
> You cannot yet have utterly abjured me
> Nor stifled the insistent roar of sea.
>
> Do as I do: confide your unquiet love
> (For one who never owed you less than love)
> To this indomitable hippocamp,
> Child of your elements, coiled a-ramp,
> Having ridden out worse tempests than you know of;
> Under his horny ribs a blood-red stain
> Portends renewal of our pain.
> Sweetheart, make much of him and shed
> Tears on his taciturn dry head.
>
> (1961)

Only a craftsman as meticulous as Mr Graves can afford to speak lightly of his art.

To read his poems is both a joy and a privilege; they are passionate, truthful, and well-bred.

The Mid-Century, July 1961; *Shenandoah,* Winter 1962

The Alienated City
Reflections on Othello

[See "The Joker in the Pack" in *The Dyer's Hand,* p. 624, and textual notes, p. 963.]

Encounter, August 1961

A Marriage of True Minds

The Correspondence between Richard Strauss and Hugo von Hofmannsthal.
Translated by Hanns Hammelmann and Ewald Osers. Collins. £3 3s.

The mating of minds is, surely, quite as fascinating a relationship as the mating of the sexes, yet how little attention novelists have paid to it. Most of us owe our intellectual initiation to an older person as Octavian owes his initiation into love to the Marschallin, and, like her, our master has to endure being left for minds of our own generation. The mind is naturally and, probably, rightly promiscuous, so that its typical affair (which may be with one of the dead) is short-lived, ending "with the necessity for it as it ought" and with no hard feelings.

Sometimes, however, it ends unhappily. One thinks of Fliess and Freud, the one a talented eccentric, the other a genius. It is fortunate for the world that they met, but one is sorry for poor Fliess, his brain picked and then deserted. The normal intellectual marriage produces one child, e.g. Liddell and Scott, North and Hillard, Russell and Whitehead, but occasionally (more commonly, one surmises, among scientists than among artists) a union is formed which begets a succession of works; the collaboration of Hofmannsthal and Strauss is a striking example and the only one of which, thanks to their correspondence, we possess a detailed record.

One rather suspects that we should not have been so fortunate if they had liked each other more as persons or, at least, if Hofmannsthal had liked Strauss more. It seems evident that Hofmannsthal did not care to see Strauss more often than was absolutely necessary, and he made it quite clear on what plane their relationship was to be kept:

> I am always, and each time anew, pleased to see you. But we are spoilt; we have shared the best men can share: being united in creative production. Every hour we have spent together was connected with our joint work; the transition to ordinary social "intercourse" would now be almost impossible.

Even after collaborating for twenty-three years, they were still not on first-name terms—Strauss will write *Lieber Freund* but Hofmannsthal sticks to *Lieber Doktor Strauss*. Perhaps this formality was normal for their period but, surely, it is a little odd that, at the banquet after the premiere of *Ariadne auf Naxos*, Hofmannsthal should demand separate tables: "one for you, Pulitz, Schillings, Reinhardt and whomever else you want, and one table for me and my close personal friends".

The distance they kept between each other as persons is of great benefit to their letters, for, in consequence, these contain no irrelevant chat. Aside from conventional seasonal greetings and conventional condolences on sickness or bereavement, they write of nothing but the work in hand or of matters, like their health, which affect it. The outbreak of the First World War is just mentioned (Strauss was certain of a quick German victory); otherwise the world outside the opera house might not exist.

The first tentative move in their courtship was made by Hofmannsthal in 1900 when he was twenty-six. He sent Strauss, who was ten years older and already internationally famous, the scenario of a ballet *Der Triumph der Zeit*. Strauss replied, in a very friendly letter, that he could not set it. Six years passed, during which Hofmannsthal wrote a play *Elektra* (1903) and Strauss his first successful opera *Salome* (1905). In 1906 Strauss approached Hofmannsthal with the request that they make an opera together out of *Elektra*, though he thought they might do something else first:

> I would ask you urgently to give me first refusal with anything composable that you write. Your manner has so much in common with mine; we were born for one another and are certain to do fine things together if you remain faithful to me. Have you got an entertaining renaissance subject for me? A really wild Cesare Borgia or Savonarola would be the answer to my prayers.

This was almost fatal. Back, in acid tones of displeasure which Strauss was to hear quite often in the future, came Hofmannsthal's answer:

> Allow me, my dear sir, to make you a frank reply. I do not believe there is any epoch in history which I and, like me, every creative poet among our contemporaries would bar from his work with feelings of such definite disinclination, indeed such unavoidable distaste, as this particular one.

Fortunately, Strauss set to work immediately on *Elektra*, the collaboration went well, and a few months later Hofmannsthal was writing:

> I *know* we are destined to create together one, or several, truly beautiful and memorable works. I should like at the same time to explain to you my notions (fairly liberal as they are) of what I consider possible opera subjects and what, on the other hand, I consider absolutely out of the question nowadays.

In their collaboration, that is to say, the choice of dramatic subject and its style of treatment was to be the librettist's business, not the composer's, who must wait patiently till the librettist found a subject which excited his imagination. In practice, Strauss seldom had to wait long. The premiere of *Elektra* took place on January 15, 1909: on February 11, Hofmannsthal sent him his ideas for *Der Rosenkavalier*. This work had its premiere on January 26, 1911; a week before Hofmannsthal is talking of *Frau ohne Schatten* and by May 15 of *Ariadne auf Naxos* which he decides to write first. Despite all difficulties of wartime—he had a war job—he managed during its four years to complete

Frau ohne Schatten, the second version of *Ariadne* and *Der Bürger als Edelman*. Then came a four-year gap, but in February, 1923, he sent Strauss his ideas for *Die Ägyptische Helene*, produced in 1928, and in November, 1927, a sketch for *Arabella*, his final revisions of which he dispatched five days before his death on June 15, 1929.

As in a marriage, for a collaboration to endure and be successful, each partner must have something valuable to give and to receive. Strauss received from Hofmannsthal a succession of libretti which, while being admirably settable, are a pleasure to read by themselves. The poetry is often beautiful, the characters and situations are interesting. Furthermore, each is unique and sets the composer a new musical and stylistic challenge. A composer like Wagner who also possesses a considerable poetic talent is a freak. Since his literary talents are usually underestimated, it is welcome to find Hofmannsthal, whose taste was certainly fastidious enough, praising his libretti:

> Perhaps the careful study of Wagner libretti which I made in May did me more harm than good. What depressed me was not their dramatic structure . . . but the inimitable excellence with which the way is prepared for the music, that consummate quality through which, as the course of a river determines its landscape, so here the poetic landscape is already figured with streams and brooklets of melodies foreseen by the poet.

That Wagners are rare is probably healthy for opera. Every artist, and few more than Strauss, is in danger of repeating himself, so that a composer who writes his own libretti is liable to write what he finds easiest to set: the challenging of dramatic situations, characters and verses which he has not musically foreseen and which at first seem difficult to him can stimulate his imagination to make unexpected and original efforts. Moreover, too smooth a fit between the words and the music is not necessarily desirable: *Don Giovanni*, for example, owes some of its excitement to the tension between Da Ponte's *buffa* text and Mozart's "serious" setting of them. Similarly, the Strauss-Hofmannsthal operas benefit greatly from the contrast between the extroverted masculine sensibility of their composer and the introverted feminine sensibility of their librettist. Only in *Frau ohne Schatten* does one feel that the contrast is too great. Though it may be Hofmannsthal's finest libretto and contains some of Strauss's most original music—that for the falcon, for example—one suspects that another composer might have done better. But who? Mahler? He was dead and Hofmannsthal did not like his music anyway.

Hofmannsthal also did a great deal not only for Strauss but also for the general cause of opera by insisting that, in the production of their works, as much attention be paid to their visual aspects as to their musical. At the time when they began collaborating, the decor, costumes and stage direction of most productions in most opera houses were appallingly bad—heavy, crude, hugger-mugger. Strauss, who was not very visually-minded, was used to this

and expected no better, but Hofmannsthal belonged to a group, led by Reinhardt, who were determined to revolutionize stage production and succeeded.
(Only too well, alas: today most operas suffer from being over-produced.)
Strauss had the good sense to realize that, in such matters. Hofmannsthal
had better judgment than himself and gave him complete authority. If Hofmannsthal was sometimes excessive in his demands and unnecessarily rude
when they were not met—he could not understand why a composer should
prefer a plain singer with a great voice to a beautiful singer with a second-
rate one—it was probably necessary to bully Strauss a bit or he would have let
things slide.

In return, Strauss gave Hofmannsthal much. In the first place, he gave
him the opportunity to write libretti at all, which had always fascinated him.

There pre-existed within me something which enabled me to fulfil—
within the limits of my gifts—your wishes and made this fulfilment in
turn satisfy a most profound need of my own. Much of what I produced
in all the loneliness of youth, entirely for myself, hardly thinking of
readers, were phantastic little operas and Singspiele—without music.
Your wishes, subsequently, supplied a purpose without restricting my
freedom.

And in the second place he taught him a lot about how to write a good one.
As Hofmannsthal himself admitted, Strauss had the better theatrical sense,
at least for opera, in which the action must be much more immediately intelligible than it need be in a spoken play. If the alterations which Strauss suggested sometimes offended Hofmannsthal's artistic conscience and sent him
into fits, there was always some dramatic flaw which prompted them, and
often, as in the second acts of *Der Rosenkavalier* and *Arabella*, they were brilliantly right.

Again like marriage, any artistic collaboration must have its ups and
downs: there are factors, some personal, some external, which cause friction
and even a threat of divorce. If most of the irritation was on Hofmannsthal's
part, there were more reasons for this than his touchy temperament. Before
Wagner and Verdi in his middle years, no composer worried much about the
libretto: he took what he was given and did the best he could with it. This was
possible because a satisfactory convention had been established about how
libretti should be written, the forms for arias and ensembles, the style for
opera buffa, the style for *opera seria*, and so on, which any competent versifier
could master.

This meant, however, that, while a composer could be assured of getting a
settable text, one libretto was remarkably like another; all originality and
interest had to come from the music. Some librettists might be better than
others and enjoy a reputation among composers, but, to the public, all were
anonymous and content to remain so. Aside from Goethe, who never found

a good enough composer, Hofmannsthal was the first poet with an established public literary reputation to write libretti and, in his day, this was a daring thing to do.

In the literary circle to which he belonged opera was not highly regarded as an art-form and it may well have been that Strauss's music was not much admired either. Certainly most of his friends thought that he was wasting his time and talents writing libretti of which few words would be heard in performance, and, of course, the managers of opera houses and his musical friends, accustomed to the conventional libretto, thought Strauss was wasting *his* time and talents trying to set such dense and incomprehensible texts.

A librettist is always at a disadvantage because operas are reviewed not by literary or dramatic critics but by music critics whose taste and understanding of poetry may be very limited. What is worse, a music critic who wishes to attack the music but is afraid to do so directly, can always attack it indirectly by condemning the libretto. Very sensibly Hofmannsthal insisted upon the right to publish his libretti before the operas were performed and, in the case of *Die Äegptische Helene,* he even asked that the houselights be left half on so that the audience could follow the printed text.

A librettist is at a further disadvantage because music is an international language and poetry a local one. Wherever an opera is performed, audiences hear the same music but, outside the country of its origin, they hear either alien words which are meaningless to them or a translation which, however good—and most translations are very bad—is not what the librettist wrote. To know that, however valuable your contribution, your public fame will always be less than that of your collaborator is not an easy position for anyone, and for Hofmannsthal, to whom fame mattered a great deal, it must often have been a torture.

> You have every reason to be grateful to me for bringing you that element which is sure to bewilder people and provoke a certain amount of antagonism, for you already have too many followers, you are already all too obviously the hero of the day, all too universally accepted.

This may be just: it is certainly envious.

While following this correspondence, the reader must bear in mind the difficulty of Hofmannsthal's position if he is not to do him an injustice. Strauss has the reputation of not having been a very nice man, but, in his relation to Hofmannsthal as revealed in these letters, he appears much the more sympathetic of the two.

To begin with, Hofmannsthal suffered from—and Strauss was happily immune to—a common complaint among artists, even great ones: in order to write he needed continually to be told how wonderful his work-in-progress was and, if others failed to tell him, he had to tell himself—at enormous length. Provided that Strauss's immediate reaction to what he sent him was enthusiastic, he was willing later to listen to criticism and act upon it, but if Strauss sounded cool, he immediately took personal umbrage. This kind of vanity is excusable enough, but it makes embarrassing reading.

Secondly, in addition to being extremely touchy, he was incapable of expressing his displeasure in terms of moderation.

But that in this case *you* should find it possible to disregard everything that matters to me, to disregard all that the realisation of this work of my imagination means to me, to force me into a theatre where I could not appear without a sense of debasement, this *does* touch me. . . . How, if you have so little regard for the unusual nature of this work beyond your own share in it—I mean for the poetry-cum-music aspect, which you must after all bring to fusion if our collaboration is to produce anything of value—how in such circumstances am I to devote myself with joy to the task of working out another project of a similar kind? . . . never let me see you, in matters of art, choose the more convenient alternative in preference to the higher, the richer possibilities. . . . I am meant to associate myself with what is best in your character, and not to do convenient business with you.

You go over the entire building with me and you don't find one word of approval, you don't even notice any of the improvements I have made in this old refractory structure: the lofty chambers, the fine perspectives, the comfortable rooms. We enter the state room with its fine view out on to the garden (and you throw a brick at the mirror in passing) and then you, without more ado, request me to put up a party wall and so shut out the view over garden and landscape, or at least put a big dung-heap where the fountain now is.

I am utterly struck dumb by your letter [Strauss had only suggested getting Elisabeth Rethberg to sing Helen]. How am I to reconcile all this? You want me to write something new for you, and yet at the same time you inflict on me what I consider more loathsome than anything else that could happen. It looks as if, although we have known each other for so long and mean well by each other, you had not the least idea what it is in our collaboration that gives me pleasure and what has the opposite effect. I do not think there is anyone who knows me so little.

Really, Strauss must have been exceptionally good-tempered, for never once does he answer back in kind. To their mutual credit, in spite of everything, differences of taste and temperament, the malice of their friends, the stupidities of the critics, they remained loyal collaborators to the end, aware of how much they owed each other.

On Hofmannsthal's fiftieth birthday Strauss wrote to him:

I have deliberately not participated in any literary demonstration in honour of your fiftieth birthday because I cannot escape the feeling that anything I could tell you in words would be banal in comparison with what, as the composer of your wonderful poetry, I have already said to you in music. It was your words which drew from me the finest music that I had to give.

Those who know their joint works will agree. In the first German edition of this correspondence some passages were omitted, most of them at Hofmannsthal's request. He was afraid that the jocular tone in which Strauss would sometimes speak of "Art" might be misunderstood by the public.

As soon as the German Philistines light, as *ipsissima verba magistri*, upon the following amusing sentence: "Flourishes à la Rückert must do the trick where the action leaves me cold", you yourself, the creator of this incomparable opera [*Ariadne*], become the veritable spokesman of this chorus of the Philistines. . . . I must, above all, still ask you for the following: you use repeatedly the metaphor that I ought to spur, or urge on, my Pegasus, etc. Taken out of the context of this intimate, quite unrestrained exchange of letters and printed, I would not care very much for this description of my method of "poetizing".

If Philistia is to be taken into account, he was right; it is always the unbeliever who is most shocked by blasphemy. But should one care what Philistia thinks?

The translators, Mr Hammelmann and Mr Osers, were faced with the formidable task of finding English equivalents for two very different tones of German voice and they have done a beautiful job. Occasionally, they use a word, like "finalize" or "allergic", which seems too out of period, but one must remember that languages and the ways of thinking they engender differ too much for one to be able to say that the equivalent of the German spoken in 1914 must be the English spoken in that year. We ought to be most grateful to them and to the publisher for making available a document so fascinating and so important, important for the light it sheds not only upon the relation of poetry to music but also upon a kind of human relationship about which we know all too little.

TLS, 10 November 1961 (unsigned);
The Mid-Century, March 1962

Dag Hammarskjöld

One does not always have to see very much of another human being to feel certain of mutual affection and understanding. I don't suppose I met Dag Hammarskjöld more than a dozen times and, though we came to be on first-name terms, we never had a particularly intimate or memorable conversation; yet his death is for me a personal loss and not a superficial one. Of course, it is flattering to a poet when somebody in an exalted public position shows a genuine interest in contemporary poetry, including his own and, what is more, a real understanding. An intellectual is, naturally, surprised and impressed when a person concerned with the fate of nations can be bothered with the fate of individuals and spend time and energy trying to get Ezra Pound released from confinement. The memory of one telephone conversation still makes me blush. Hammarskjöld had asked me to make an English translation of St-John Perse's acceptance speech for the Nobel Prize, a job which had to be done in two days. "I don't see how I can manage it," I said, "I'm frightfully busy." To which he replied, without a hint of sarcasm in his voice, "I've done the Swedish translation and I'm rather busy too, you know."

But a common interest in literature, though it was the cause of our meeting, does not account for my feelings about the man. I have heard it said and seen it written that he was a cold fish to whom life was a matter of intellect and will, not heart; it has even been said that he lacked any firm beliefs or principles and was only interested in virtuoso feats of diplomatic technique. To such criticisms I can only say that my instinct tells me they are utterly wrong. If I am not mistaken, Hammarskjöld was by nature a warm-hearted introvert with a great capacity for intimacy who, if the traditions of his family and his own conscience had not called him to a life of public service, could very happily have led a Horatian kind of private existence, delighting in books, mountain-climbing, the company of a few old friends, and letting the world go its boring way. There are many prominent persons, in politics, journalism, industry, whom one cannot imagine in any milieu except public life— without a public audience and the exercise of public power, they would not know what to do with themselves. (This is not, of course, a moral criticism; some of them are noble characters.) But Hammarskjöld was not, I think, one of them. I don't mean that his choice of a public career was an act of spiritual masochism or that the only satisfaction it gave him was the consciousness of having wearily done his duty; on the contrary, I'm sure he enjoyed being Secretary-General very much. Meeting him shortly after Khrushchev's visit to New York, I remarked that I had been following his recent career with great sympathy. "Oh," he said, "you needn't be sorry for me at all. I had a wonderful time." But in his case public life demanded, as for more extrovert natures it might not, considerable sacrifices.

At this point in history, there can be no more solitary position in the world than that of Secretary-General to the United Nations, unless it be that of the Pope. A national politician can have personal friends among his colleagues for he is a confessed representative of party and national interests. A judge can make friends with other judges because he knows they are never likely to appear in court before him. But the head of an international organisation at a time when national passions are as violent and paranoid as they are to-day, dares not show a personal preference for one member of the Assembly, for he will be immediately accused of political bias. Nor can he make close friends with persons outside political life; he has no time to see them. Moreover, the many political enemies he is bound to make will keep close watch on his private life in the hope of finding some weakness or irregularity they can use as a weapon against him. Hammarskjöld accepted personal isolation as a necessary condition of his post, but he needed will-power to maintain it. Though he would never have complained to others—he was completely free from self-pity—he was, I believe, a lonely man, not a self-sufficient one.

While far too proud to talk in resounding phrases about Ideals, and far too intelligent to have any rosy illusions about human nature, diplomacy was for him a technical means, not an end in itself, and, in the various political decisions he had to take, he never, I am convinced, sacrificed principle to expediency. Would he have incurred such a variety of abuse, ranging from Comrade Khrushchev's girlish tantrums to Sir Roy Welensky's manly bellows if he had?

I know nothing about Katanga beyond what I read in the British and American press which I suspect of soft-pedalling certain aspects of the situation, such as the constitution of the Katanga army. I am neither a politician nor an historian and, for all I know, Hammarskjöld's decision to intervene was a grave mistake. But when I read a newspaper article in which it is asserted that Hammarskjöld was behaving according to that old crook's maxim, "You can't make an omelette without breaking eggs," that, in order to gain the support of the African *bloc*, he cold-bloodedly sacrificed Katanga, I feel like knocking the author down. The man I knew was a diplomat, certainly, but not a smart operator. If he decided to intervene, it was because, rightly or wrongly, he believed intervention to be just. He was one of the two most selfless people I have met in my life, and to have known him, even as slightly as I did, was a privilege.

Encounter, November 1961

The Untruth about Beethoven

The Letters of Beethoven. Collected, translated and edited by Emily
Anderson. Three volumes. Macmillan. 10 guineas.

It is always a joy to see any job done perfectly. Miss Anderson set herself the task of collecting, deciphering and translating every scrap of Beethoven's correspondence that is known to exist, down even to such an ort as:

To? (Ms. not traced. Item from sale catalogue of Henrici, no. XVII, item 21.)

P.P.

Kindly inform me whether I can still obtain all the numbers of this year's volume of your review, to which I should like to subscribe.

She has collected them, scattered though they are all over the world; she has deciphered them, and everyone knows what Beethoven's handwriting was like; and she has translated them into decent English, a formidable task because of Beethoven's passion for puns. Her explanatory annotations are all a reader could ask for. I am delighted to discover from her, for example, that the famous story of Beethoven and Goethe meeting the Imperial Family in Teplitz—Goethe bowing and scraping, Beethoven keeping his hat on, crossing his arms and scowling—was a sheer invention of Bettina von Arnim's.

Macmillan, too, have done a perfect job of book production. Well, almost perfect, for I have two small complaints to make about the index. It never seems to occur to publishers, when a book is so big that it has to be published in more than one volume, how inconvenient and irritating it is for the reader who wants to look up a point not to be able to consult the index in the volume he happens to have in his hand. Surely, once the index is made, it would not greatly increase costs to print it in each volume. Secondly, in this particular index no typographical distinction is made between entries which mean a letter to someone and entries which mean a reference to him. For example, there are forty-four entries under the name Goethe, but, if one wants to find either of the two letters which Beethoven wrote to Goethe, one has to go through them all. These, though, are minor matters. The type, the paper, the illustrations are lovely. Miss Anderson and Macmillan have done superbly well.

But. . . .

It would have been very much better if three-quarters of this correspondence had been destroyed by its recipients immediately after reading it.

What follows is not a review but a sermon.

When we say that someone is a "born" letter-writer, we mean that, for him, a letter is as much a literary genre as a novel or a poem; he uses it to describe people and events, to make general reflections upon life, etcetera, and it is almost an accident who receives the letter; it may be his fiancée, but it is more likely to be either a relative, a friend of his own sex, or an older woman. Even if he refers to troubles and sorrows of his own, he maintains artistic detachment; he remains master of the situation and talks about himself as if in the third person. Obvious examples are Horace Walpole, Gray, Byron, Sydney Smith and, aside from his letters to Fanny Brawne, Keats. It is right and proper that their correspondence should be published because of its artistic impartiality; the reader never feels he is intruding on their privacy, and at the same time he is greatly entertained.

Beethoven, unlike Mozart, had nobody to whom he wrote letters simply for the joy of writing them; if he writes one, there is always some reason which made the letter necessary. Moreover, though, of course, many of his letters are "public" enough, he lacked a literary gift; his verbal humour is painfully ponderous, and when he is serious he suffers from the vices of *Sturm und Drang* literature. (He considered Ossian to be as great as Homer.)

> Oh, Wegeler, do not reject this hand which I am offering you in reconciliation, but place your hand in mine—Oh God—But I will say nothing more—I am coming to see you, to throw myself into your arms, and to plead for the prodigal friend; and you will return to me, to your penitent Beethoven who loves you and will never forget you.

In his whole correspondence I have found only one memorable sentence.

> I am inclined to think that a hunt for folksongs is better than a manhunt of the heroes who are so highly extolled.

Beethoven had humour and gaiety enough, but he could only express it in music: by far the most delightful things in his letters are the impromptu canons he sometimes writes for his friends.

In the case of any great artist, we are legitimately interested in any comments he may have to make about his own work, that of others, or technical problems. On such matters Beethoven says surprisingly little. It is interesting to learn about the *pianoforte* of his time—

> So far as the manner of playing it is concerned, the pianoforte is still the least studied and developed of instruments; often one thinks that one is merely listening to a harp

—and to hear that, when the metronome was invented, Beethoven wanted to abandon the conventional Italian tempo words, like *allegro* and *adagio* in favour of metronome numbers.

Again, the economics of art are always interesting. Beethoven is forever grumbling about how hard-up he is, but many composers have had it much worse. By 1800 he was receiving more commissions than he could cope with, music publishers were eagerly competing for rights to his works, and in the last part of his life he was in the receipt of quite a handsome pension. For all his references to himself as a "poor Austrian musical drudge," he has to confess:

> . . . though admittedly, I am not rich, I have yet been enabled by means of my compositions to live for my art.

But what deserves to be read, because it is either entertaining or instructive, represents but a small fraction of his correspondence. A lot is not worth reading because there is nothing significant to be learned from it. Many of his letters to his publishers, for example, are filled with corrections of errors made by the copyist. These would be significant if the errors had actually got into the published scores and hence into performances: otherwise, all they tell us is that copyists make mistakes, a fact we already know.

The publication of letters which the average reader will skip because they bore him may be silly, but raises no moral problems. What, in my opinion, is immoral, is to publish the kind of letters which journalists call "human documents," meaning by this, letters which are to the writer's discredit, which reveal the flaws and weaknesses in his character and his private sufferings. If the decent side of us is bored and embarrassed by having to listen to other people's woes, this is not because we are hard-hearted, but because, usually, we are powerless to help. To be curious about suffering we cannot relieve— and, alas, we all are a bit—is *schadenfreude* and nothing else. Beethoven had the misfortune to suffer from paranoia which, of all neuroses, is perhaps the hardest to feel sympathy for, since its victim combines highly disagreeable behaviour with an intolerable self-righteousness. In many of his letters, Beethoven reminds one of Rolfe Corvo.

> Stupid conceited ass of a fellow.
> And am I to exchange compliments with such a scoundrel who filches my money? Instead of that I ought to pull his ass's ears.
> Slovenly copyist!
> Stupid fellow!
> Correct the mistakes you have made through your ignorance, arrogance, conceit, stupidity. That is more fitting than to want to teach me. For to do so is exactly as if the cow should want to teach Minerva.
> (To Count Moritz Lichnowsky:) I despise what is false—Don't visit me any more—There will be no concert.

One laughs at the first two or three, but after that one begins to be depressed. The servants of whose iniquities he was always complaining may have had their faults, but a man who can write to a friend when looking for a new manservant—"If he is a bit hunchbacked I shouldn't mind, for then I should know at once the weak spot at which to attack him" is not fit to employ anybody. Nor did he deserve to have friends, for he was lacking in any sense of loyalty: he would write in terms of great affection to one and make a sneering remark about him to another. As for the whole ghastly business of his nephew Karl and his sister-in-law, one can only regret that the courts ever made him Karl's guardian.

We have, of course, no right to judge him—if one of us were a great composer afflicted with deafness and chronic indigestion, we might behave much worse—but that does not make his behaviour any better, and what profit is it to us that we should learn ugly little secrets about another human being? One kind of reader will say to himself: "If a great man can have weaknesses, why should I be ashamed of mine?" And another kind, next time he listens to the *Missa Solemnis,* will say: "Oh yes, his music *sounds* very noble, but we all know what he was *really* like." The shamelessness of the popular press in our time is bad enough, but, at least, it does not pretend to be anything else. What is much more alarming is the shamelessness of educated serious persons like you and me who call our brand scholarship.

The Spectator, 10 November 1961

The Quest Hero

To look for a lost collar button is not a true quest: to go in quest means to look for something of which one has, as yet, no experience; one can imagine what it will be like but whether one's picture is true or false will be known only when one has found it.

Animals, therefore, do not go on quests. They hunt for food or drink or a mate, but the object of their search is determined by what they already are and its purpose is to restore a disturbed equilibrium; they have no choice in the matter.

But man is a history-making creature for whom the future is always open; human "nature" is a nature continually in quest of itself, obliged at every moment to transcend what it was a moment before. For man the present is not real but valuable. He can neither repeat the past exactly—every moment is unique—nor leave it behind—at every moment he adds to and thereby modifies all that has previously happened to him.

Hence the impossibility of expressing his kind of existence in a single image. If one concentrates upon his ever open future, the natural image is of a road stretching ahead into unexplored country, but if one concentrates upon his unforgettable past, then the natural image is of a city, which is built in every style of architecture, and in which the physically dead are as active citizens as the living. The only characteristic common to both images is a sense of purpose; a road, even if its destination is invisible, runs in a certain direction; a city is built to endure and be a home.

The animals who really live in the present have neither roads nor cities and do not miss them. They are at home in the wilderness and, at most, if they are social, set up camps for a generation. But man requires both. The image of a city with no roads leading from it suggests a prison; the image of a road that starts from nowhere in particular suggests, not a true road, but an animal spoor.

A similar difficulty arises if one tries to describe simultaneously our experience of our own lives and our experience of the lives of others. Subjectively,

I am a unique ego set over against a self; my body, desires, feelings, and thoughts seem distinct from the *I* that is aware of them. But I cannot know the Ego of another person directly, only his self, which is not unique but comparable with the selves of others, including my own. Thus, if I am a good observer and a good mimic, it is conceivable that I could imitate another so accurately as to deceive his best friends, but it would still be I imitating him; I can never know what it would feel like to be someone else. The social relation of my Ego to my Self is of a fundamentally different kind from all my other social relations to persons or things.

Again, I am conscious of myself as becoming, of every moment being new, whether or not I show any outward sign of change, but in others I can only perceive the passage of time when it manifests itself objectively; So-and-so looks older or fatter or behaves differently from the way he used to behave. Further, though we all know that all men must die, dying is not an experience that we can share; I cannot take part in the deaths of others nor they in mine.

Lastly, my subjective experience of living is one of having continually to make a choice between given alternatives, and it is this experience of doubt and temptation that seems more important and memorable to me than the actions I take when I have made my choice. But when I observe others, I cannot see them making choices; I can only see their actions; compared with myself, others seem at once less free and more stable in character, good or bad.

The Quest is one of the oldest, hardiest, and most popular of all literary genres. In some instances it may be founded on historical fact—the Quest of the Golden Fleece may have its origin in the search of seafaring traders for amber—and certain themes, like the theme of the enchanted cruel Princess whose heart can be melted only by the predestined lover, may be distorted recollections of religious rites, but the persistent appeal of the Quest as a literary form is due, I believe, to its validity as a symbolic description of our subjective personal experience of existence as historical.

As a typical example of the traditional Quest, let us look at the tale in the Grimm collection called "The Waters of Life." A King has fallen sick. Each of his three sons sets out in turn to find and bring back the water of life which will restore him to health. The motive of the two elder sons is not love of their father but the hope of reward; only the youngest really cares about his father as a person. All three encounter a dwarf who asks them where they are going. The first two rudely refuse to answer and are punished by the dwarf, who imprisons them in a ravine. The youngest answers courteously and truthfully, and the dwarf not only directs him to the castle where the Fountain of the Waters of Life is situated but also gives him a magic wand to open the castle gate and two loaves of bread to appease the lions who guard the Fountain. Furthermore, the dwarf warns him that he must leave before the clock strikes twelve or he will find himself imprisoned. Following these instructions and using the magic gifts, the youngest brother obtains the Water of Life, meets a beautiful Princess who promises to marry him if he will return in a year, and carries away with him a magic sword which can slay whole armies and a magic loaf of bread which will never come to an end. However, he almost fails because, forgetting the dwarf's advice, he lies down on a bed and falls asleep, awakening only just in time as the clock is striking twelve; the closing door takes a piece off his heel.

On his way home he meets the dwarf again and learns what has happened to his brothers; at his entreaty the dwarf reluctantly releases them, warning him that they have evil hearts.

The three brothers continue their homeward journey and, thanks to the sword and the loaf, the youngest is able to deliver three kingdoms from war and famine. The last stretch is by sea. While the hero is asleep, his older brothers steal the Water of Life from his bottle and substitute sea water. When they arrive home, their sick father tries the water offered by the youngest and, naturally, is made worse; then the elder brothers offer him the water they have stolen and cure him.

In consequence the King believes their allegation that the youngest was trying to poison him and orders his huntsman to take the hero into the forest and shoot him in secret. When it comes to the point, however, the huntsman cannot bring himself to do this, and the hero remains in hiding in the forest.

Presently wagons of gold and jewels begin arriving at the palace for the hero, gifts from the grateful kings whose lands he had delivered from war and famine, and his father becomes convinced of his innocence. Meanwhile the Princess, in preparation for her wedding, has built a golden road to her castle and given orders that only he who comes riding straight along it shall be admitted.

Again the two elder brothers attempt to cheat the hero by going to woo her themselves, but, when they come to the golden road, they are afraid of spoiling it; one rides to the left of it, one to the right, and both are refused admission to the castle. When the hero comes to the road he is so preoccupied with thinking about the Princess that he does not notice that it is made of gold and rides straight up it. He is admitted, weds the Princess, returns home with her, and is reconciled to his father. The two wicked brothers put to sea, never to be heard of again, and all ends happily.

The essential elements in this typical Quest story are six.

(1) A precious Object and/or Person to be found and possessed or married.

(2) A long journey to find it, for its whereabouts are not originally known to the seekers.

(3) A hero. The precious Object cannot be found by anybody, but only by

the one person who possesses the right qualities of breeding or character.

(4) A Test or series of Tests by which the unworthy are screened out, and
the hero revealed.

(5) The Guardians of the Object who must be overcome before it can be
won. They may be simply a further test of the hero's *arete*, or they may be
malignant in themselves.

(6) The Helpers who with their knowledge and magical powers assist the
hero and but for whom he would never succeed. They may appear in
human or in animal form.

Does not each of these elements correspond to an aspect of our subjective
experience of life?

(1) Many of my actions are purposive; the *telos* towards which they are directed may be a short-term one, like trying to write a sentence which
shall express my present thoughts accurately, or a lifelong one, the
search to find true happiness or authenticity of being, to become what
I wish or God intends me to become. What more natural image for such
a *telos* than a beautiful Princess or the Waters of Life?

(2) I am conscious of time as a continuous irreversible process of change.
Translated into spatial terms, this process becomes, naturally enough, a
journey.

(3) I am conscious of myself as unique—my goal is for me only—and as
confronting an unknown future—I cannot be certain in advance
whether I shall succeed or fail in achieving my goal. The sense of
uniqueness produces the image of the unique hero; the sense of uncertainty, the images of the unsuccessful rivals.

(4) I am conscious of contradictory forces in myself, some of which I judge
to be good and others evil, which are continually trying to sway my will
this way or that. The existence of these forces is given. I can choose
to yield to a desire or to resist it but I cannot by choice desire or not
desire.

Any image of this experience must be dualistic, a contest between two
sides, friends and enemies.

On the other hand, the Quest provides no image of our objective experience of social life. If I exclude my own feelings and try to look at the world
as if I were the lens of a camera, I observe that the vast majority of people
have to earn their living in a fixed place, and that journeys are confined to
people on holiday or with independent means. I observe that, though there
may be some wars which can be called just, there are none in which one side
is absolutely good and the other absolutely evil, though it is all too common
for both sides to persuade themselves that this is so. As for struggles between

man and the forces of nature or wild beasts, I can see that nature is unaware of being destructive and that, though there are animals which attack men out of hunger or fear, no animal does so out of malice.

In many versions of the Quest, both ancient and modern, the winning or recovery of the Precious Object is for the common good of the society to which the hero belongs. Even when the goal of his quest is marriage, it is not any girl he is after but a Princess. Their personal happiness is incidental to the happiness of the City; now the Kingdom will be well governed, and there will soon be an heir.

But there are other versions in which success is of importance only to the individual who achieves it. The Holy Grail, for example, will never again become visible to all men; only the exceptionally noble and chaste can be allowed to see it.

Again, there are two types of Quest Hero. One resembles the hero of Epic; his superior *arete* is manifest to all. Jason, for example, is instantly recognizable as the kind of man who can win the Golden Fleece if anybody can. The other type, so common in fairy tales, is the hero whose *arete* is concealed. The youngest son, the weakest, the least clever, the one whom everybody would judge as least likely to succeed, turns out to be the hero when his manifest betters have failed. He owes his success, not to his own powers, but to the fairies, magicians, and animals who help him, and he is able to enlist their help because, unlike his betters, he is humble enough to take advice, and kind enough to give assistance to strangers who, like himself, appear to be nobody in particular.

Though the subject of this essay is the Quest in its traditional form, it is worthwhile, perhaps, to mention, very briefly, some variants.

(A) The Detective Story. Here the goal is not an object or a person but the answer to a question—Who committed the murder? Consequently, not only is there no journey, but also the more closed the society, the more restricted the locale, the better. There are two sides, but one side has only one member, the murderer, for the division is not between the Evil and the Good but between the Guilty and the Innocent. The hero, the Detective, is a third party who belongs to neither side.

(B) The Adventure Story. Here the journey and the goal are identical, for the Quest is for more and more adventures. A classic example is Poe's *Gordon Pym*. More sophisticated and subtler examples are Goethe's *Faust* and the *Don Juan* legend.

The condition laid down in his pact with Mephisto is that Faust shall never ask that the flow of time be arrested at an ideal moment, that he shall never say, "Now, I have reached the goal of my quest." Don Juan's Quest can never come to an end because there will always remain girls whom he has not yet seduced. His is also one of the rare cases of an Evil Quest which ought not to be undertaken and in which, therefore, the hero is the villain.

(C) *Moby Dick.* Here the Precious Object and the Malevolent Guardian are combined and the object of the Quest is not possession but destruction. Another example of a Quest which should not have been undertaken, but it is tragic rather than evil. Captain Ahab belongs in the company of Othello, not of Iago.

(D) The Kafka novels. In these the hero fails to achieve his goal, in *The Trial* either to prove himself innocent or learn of what he is guilty, in *The Castle* to obtain official recognition as a land surveyor; and he fails, not because he is unworthy, but because success is humanly impossible. The Guardians are too strong and, though Kafka avoids saying so I think one can add, too malevolent. What makes K a hero is that, despite the evidence that Evil is more powerful than Good in the world, he never gives up the struggle to worship the Prince of this world. By all the rules he ought to despair; yet he doesn't.

Any literary mimesis of the subjective experience of becoming is confronted by problems of form and limitations of subject matter. Like a man's life which has a beginning, birth, and an end, death, the Quest story has two fixed points, the starting out and the final achievement, but the number of adventures in the interval cannot but be arbitrary, for, since the flow of time is continuous, it can be infinitely divided and subdivided into moments. One solution is the imposition of a numerical pattern, analogous to the use of metre in poetry. Thus, in "The Waters of Life" there are three brothers, three kingdoms to be delivered from war and famine, and three ways of approaching the Princess's castle. There are two tests, the dwarf and the golden road, but the right and wrong behaviour are symmetrically opposed; it is right to take notice of the dwarf but wrong to take notice of the road.

The hero twice nearly comes to disaster by falling asleep, on the first occasion in direct disobedience of the dwarf's instructions, on the second in neglect of the warning that his brothers are evil men.

To take a man on a journey is to cut him off from his everyday social relations to women, neighbours, and fellow-workers. The only sustained relation which the Quest Hero can enjoy is with those who accompany him on his journey, that is to say, either the democratic relation between equal comrades-in-arms, or the feudal relation between Knight and Squire. Aside from these, his social life is limited to chance and brief encounters. Even when his motive for undertaking the Quest is erotic, the lady has to remain in wait for him either at the start or the end of the road. Partly for this reason and partly because it deals with adventures, that is, situations of crisis in which a man behaves either well or badly, the Quest tale is ill adapted to subtle portrayals of character; its personages are almost bound to be Archetypes rather than idiosyncratic individuals.

So much for general observations. I shall devote the rest of this essay to an examination of a single work, Mr J.R.R. Tolkien's trilogy, *The Lord of the Rings*.

The Setting

Many Quest tales are set in a dreamland, that is to say, in no definite place or time. This has the advantage of allowing the use of all the wealth of dream imagery, monsters, magical transformations and translations, which are absent from our waking life, but at the cost of aggravating the tendency of the genre to divorce itself from social and historical reality. A dream is at most capable of allegorical interpretation, but such interpretations are apt to be mechanical and shallow. There are other Quest tales, a thriller like *The Thirty-Nine Steps*, for example, which are set in places which we can find in the atlas and in times we can read of in history books. This gives the Quest a social significance, but the moral ambiguities of real history clash with the presupposition which is essential to the genre, that one side is good and the other bad.

Even in wartime, the sensitive reader cannot quite believe this of the two sides which the writer of thrillers takes from real life. He cannot help knowing that, at the same time that John Buchan is making the heroes English and American and the enemies German, some German author may be writing an equally convincing thriller in which the roles are reversed.

Mr Tolkien sets his story neither in a dream world nor in the actual world but in an imaginary world. An imaginary world can be so constructed as to make credible any landscape, inhabitants, and events which its maker wishes to introduce, and since he himself has invented its history, there can be only one correct interpretation of events, his own. What takes place and why is, necessarily, what he says it is.

But the construction of a convincing imaginary world makes formidable demands upon the imagination of its creator. There must be no question which, according to our interests, we ask about the real world to which he cannot give a convincing answer, and any writer who, like Mr Tolkien, sets out to create an imaginary world in the twentieth century has to meet a higher standard of concreteness than, say his medieval predecessor, for he has to reckon with readers who have been exposed to the realistic novel and scientific historical research.

A dream world may be full of inexplicable gaps and logical inconsistencies; an imaginary world may not, for it is a world of law, not of wish. Its laws may be different from those which govern our own, but they must be as intelligible and inviolable. Its history may be unusual but it must not contradict our notion of what history is, an interplay of Fate, Choice, and Chance. Lastly, it must not violate our moral experience. If, as the Quest generally requires, Good and Evil are to be incarnated in individuals and societies, we must be convinced that the Evil side is what every sane man, irrespective of his nationality or culture, would acknowledge as evil. The triumph of Good over Evil which the successful achievement of the Quest implies must appear historically possible, not a daydream. Physical and, to a considerable extent, intellectual power must be shown as what we know them to be, morally neutral and effectively real: battles are won by the stronger side, be it good or evil.

To indicate the magnitude of the task Mr Tolkien set himself, let me give a few figures. The area of his world measures some thirteen hundred miles from east (the Gulf of Lune) to west (the Iron Hills) and twelve hundred miles from north (the Bay of Farochel) to south (the mouth of the River Anduin). In our world there is only one species, man, who is capable of speech and has a real history; in Mr Tolkien's there are at least seven. The actual events of the story cover the last twenty years of the Third Historical Epoch of this world. The First Age is treated as legendary so that its duration is unknown, and its history is only vaguely recalled, but for the 3441 years of the Second Age and the 3021 years of the Third, he has to provide a continuous and credible history.

The first task of the maker of an imaginary world is the same as that of Adam in Eden: he has to find names for everyone and everything in it and if, as in Mr Tolkien's world, there is more than one language, he has to invent as many series of names as there are tongues.

In the nominative gift, Mr Tolkien surpasses any writer, living or dead, whom I have ever read; to find the "right" names is hard enough in a comic world; in a serious one success seems almost magical. Moreover, he shows himself capable of inventing not only names but whole languages which reflect the nature of those who speak them. The Ents, for example, are trees which have acquired movement, consciousness, and speech, but continue to live at the tempo of trees. In consequence their language is "slow, sonorous, agglomerated, repetitive, indeed long-winded." Here is only a part of the Entish word for *hill*:

a-lalla-lalla-rumba-kamanda-lind-or-buruma.

The extremes of good and evil in the story are represented by the Elves and Sauron, respectively. Here is a verse from a poem in Elfish:

A Elbereth Gilthoniel,
silivren penna míriel
o menel alglar elenath!
Na-chaered palan díriel.
o galadhremmin ennorath,
Fanuilos, le linnathon
nef aear, sí nef aearon.

And here is an evil spell in the Black Speech invented by Sauron:

> *Ash nazg durbatulûk, ash nazg gimbatul,*
> *ash nazg thrakatalûk, agh burzum-ishi krimpatul.*

An imaginary world must be as real to the senses of the reader as the actual world. For him to find an imaginary journey convincing, he must feel
that he is seeing the landscape through which it passes as, given his mode of
locomotion and the circumstances of his errand, the fictional traveler himself saw it. Fortunately, Mr Tolkien's gift for topographical description is equal
to his gift for naming and his fertility in inventing incidents. His hero, Frodo
Baggins, is on the road, excluding rests, for eighty days and covers over 1800
miles, much of it on foot, and with his senses kept perpetually sharp by fear,
watching every inch of the way for signs of his pursuers, yet Mr Tolkien succeeds in convincing us that there is nothing Frodo noticed which he has
forgotten to describe.

Technologically, his world is preindustrial. The arts of mining, metallurgy,
architecture, road and bridge building, are highly developed, but there are
no firearms and no mechanical means of transport. It is, however, a world
that has seen better days. Lands that were once cultivated and fertile have
gone back to the wilderness, roads have become impassable, once famous
cities are now ruins. (There is one puzzling discrepancy. Both Sauron and
Saruman seem to have installed heavy machinery in their fortresses. Why, in
that case, are they limited to waging untechnological warfare?) Though without machines, some people in this world possess powers which our civilisation would call magical because it lacks them; telepathic communication
and vision are possible, verbal spells are effective, weather can be controlled,
rings confer invisibility, etc.

Politically, the commonest form of society is a benevolent monarchy, but
the Shire of the hobbits is a kind of small-town democracy and Sauron's kingdom of Mordor is, of course, a totalitarian and slave-owning dictatorship.

Though the unstated presuppositions of the whole work are Christian, we
are not told that any of the inhabitants practise a religious cult.

The Elves, the Wizards, and Sauron, certainly, and perhaps some others,
believe in the existence of the One, the Valar to whom He has entrusted the
guardianship of Middle Earth, and a Land in the Uttermost West which I
take to be an image of Paradise.

The Quest Hero

In our subjective experience, of which the Quest is, I have suggested, a
literary mimesis, what we ought to become is usually dependent upon what
we are; it is idle and cowardly of me if I fail to make the fullest use of any talent with which I have been endowed, but it is presumptuous of me to at-

tempt a task for which I lack the talent it requires. That is why, in the traditional Quest story, the hero desires to undertake the quest and, even when to others he appears lacking in power, he is confident of success. This problem of vocation is specifically dealt with in one Quest tale, *The Magic Flute*. Prince Tamino is the typical hero, who must dare the trials by Fire and Water to attain wisdom and win the hand of the Princess Pamina.

But beside him stands Papageno, who is, in his own way, a hero too. He is asked whether he is prepared to endure the trials like his master and he answers, no, such dangers are not for the likes of him. "But," says the priest, "if you don't, you will never win a girl." "In that case," he replies, "I'll remain single." This answer reveals his humility, and he is rewarded with his mirror image, Papagena. In contrast to him stands the villain Monostatos. Like Papageno, he is incapable of enduring the trials but, unlike him, he lacks the humility to forego the rewards of heroism; he is even unwilling to accept an equivalent of Papagena and demands nothing less than the Princess.

But there is another kind of vocation which may be called religious. Not everybody experiences it, and even for those who do, it may concern only moments of their life. What characterises the religious vocation is that it comes from outside the self and, generally to the self's terror and dismay, as when God calls Abraham out of the land of Ur, or when a man, by nature physically timid, is called to enter a burning building to rescue a child because there is no one else around to do it.

Some of the characters in *The Lord of the Rings*, Gandalf and Aragorn, for instance, are expressions of the natural vocation of talent. It is for Gandalf to plan the strategy of the War against Sauron because he is a very wise man; it is for Aragorn to lead the armies of Gondor because he is a great warrior and the rightful heir to the throne. Whatever they may have to risk and suffer, they are, in a sense, doing what they want to do. But the situation of the real hero, Frodo Baggins, is quite different. When the decision has been taken to send the Ring to the Fire, his *feelings* are those of Papageno: "Such dangerous exploits are not for a little hobbit like me. I would much rather stay at home than risk my life on the very slight chance of winning glory." But his conscience tells him: "You may be nobody in particular in yourself, yet, for some inexplicable reasons, through no choice of your own, the Ring has come into your keeping, so that it is on you and not on Gandalf or Aragorn that the task falls of destroying it."

Because the decision has nothing to do with his talents, nobody else can or should try to help him make up his mind. When he stands up at the Council of Elrond and says: "I will take the Ring though I know not the Way," Elrond replies: "It is a heavy burden. So heavy that none could lay it on another. I do not lay it on you. But if you take it freely, I will say that your choice is right."

Once he has chosen, Frodo is absolutely committed; the others who set out with him are not.

> The Ring Bearer is setting out on the Quest of Mount Doom: on him alone is any charge laid—neither to cast away the Ring nor to deliver it to any servant of the Enemy, nor indeed to let any handle it, save members of the Company and the Council, and only then in gravest need. The others go with him as free companions to help him on his way. You may tarry, or come back, or turn aside to other paths as chance allows. The further you go, the less easy it will be to withdraw; yet no oath or bond is laid upon you to go further than you will. For you do not yet know the strength of your hearts and you cannot foresee what each may meet on the road.
>
> "Faithless is he who says farewell when the road darkens," said Gimli.
>
> "Maybe," said Elrond, "but let him not vow to walk in the dark who has not seen the nightfall."
>
> "Yet sworn vow may strengthen quaking heart," said Gimli.
>
> "Or break it," said Elrond. "Look not too far ahead. But go now with good hearts."

The Conflict of Good and Evil

If it is a defect in the usual Quest tale that Good triumphs over Evil simply because Good is more powerful, this is not a defect that can be avoided by giving Good no power at all. Quite rightly, Mr Tolkien makes the elves, dwarfs, wizards, and men who are Sauron's opponents a formidable lot indeed, but in sheer strength, Sauron is, even without his Ring, the stronger. Yet their power has its part to play, as Gandalf points out.

> Victory cannot be achieved by arms. I still hope for victory but not by arms. For into the midst of all these policies comes the Ring of Power, the foundation of Barad-dûr and the hope of Sauron. If he regains it, your valour is vain, and his victory will be swift and complete; so complete that none can foresee the end of it while this world lasts. If it is destroyed, then he will fall; and his fall will be so low that none can foresee his arising ever again. . . . This, then, is my counsel. We have not the Ring. In wisdom or great folly, it has been sent away to be destroyed lest it destroy us. Without it we cannot by force defeat his force. But we must at all costs keep his eye from his true peril. We cannot achieve victory by arms, but by arms we can give the Ring Bearer his only chance, frail though it be.

The Quest is successful and Sauron is overthrown. One of Mr Tolkien's most impressive achievements is that he convinces the reader that the mistakes which Sauron makes to his undoing are the kind of mistakes which Evil, however powerful, cannot help making just because it is Evil. His primary weakness is a lack of imagination, for, while Good can imagine what it would be like to be Evil, Evil cannot imagine what it would be like to be Good. El-rond, Gandalf, Galadriel, Aragorn are able to imagine themselves as Sauron and therefore can resist the temptation to use the Ring themselves, but Sau-ron cannot imagine that anyone who knows what the Ring can accomplish, his own destruction among other things, will not use it, let alone try to de-stroy it. Had he been capable of imagining this, he had only to sit waiting and watching in Mordor for the Ring Bearer to arrive, and he was bound to catch him and recover the Ring. Instead, he assumes that the Ring has been taken to Gondor where the strongest of his enemies are gathered, which is what he would have done had he been in their place, and launches an attack on that city, neglecting the watch on his own borders.

Secondly, the kind of Evil which Sauron embodies, the lust for domina-tion, will always be irrationally cruel since it is not satisfied if another does what it wants; he must be made to do it against his will. When Pippin looked into the Palantír of Orthanc and so revealed himself to Sauron, the latter had only to question him in order to learn who had the Ring and what he intended to do with it. But, as Gandalf says: "He was too eager. He did not want information only: he wanted *you* quickly, so that he could deal with you in the Dark Tower, slowly."

Thirdly, all alliances of Evil with Evil are necessarily unstable and untrust-worthy since, by definition, Evil loves only itself and its alliances are based on fear or hope of profit, not on affection. Sauron's greatest triumph has been his seduction of the great wizard Saruman but, though he has succeeded in making him a traitor to the cause of Good, he has not yet completely en-slaved him, so that Saruman tries to seize the Ring for himself.

Lastly, unforeseeable by either side, is the role played by Sméagol-Gollum. When Frodo first hears about him from Gandalf, he exclaims:

—What a pity Bilbo did not stab that vile creature when he had the chance!

—Pity? It was pity that stayed his hand. Pity and Mercy: not to strike without need. And he has been well rewarded, Frodo. Be sure that he took so little hurt from the evil, and escaped in the end, because he began his ownership of the Ring so. With Pity.

—I cannot understand you. Do you mean to say that you and the Elves have let him live on after all those horrible deeds? He deserves death.

—Deserves it? I daresay he does. But do not be too eager to deal out death in judgment. For even the wise cannot see all ends. I have not much hope that Gollum can be cured before he dies, but there is a chance of it.

And he is bound up with the fate of the Ring. My heart tells me that he has some part to play yet, for good or ill, before the end; and when that comes, the pity of Bilbo may rule the fate of many, yours not least.

Gollum picks up Frodo's trail in the Mines of Moria and follows him. When Frodo manages to catch him, he remembers Gandalf's words and spares his life. This turns out to his immediate advantage for, without Gollum's help, Frodo and Sam would never have found their way through the Dead Marshes or to the pass of Cirith Ungol. Gollum's motives in guiding them are not wholly evil; one part of him, of course, is waiting for an opportunity to steal the Ring, but another part feels gratitude and genuine affection for Frodo.

Gandalf was right, however, in fearing that there was little hope of his being cured; in the end his evil side triumphs. He leads Frodo and Sam into Shelob's lair and, after their escape, pursues them to Mount Doom and attacks them. Once again they spare his life. And then the unexpected happens.

. . . there on the brink of the chasm, at the very Crack of Doom, stood Frodo, black against the glare, tense, erect, but still as if he had been turned to stone.

"Master!" cried Sam.

Then Frodo stirred and spoke with a clear voice . . . it rose above the throb and turmoil of Mount Doom, ringing in the roofs and walls.

"I have come," he said. "But I do not choose now to do what I came to do. I will not do this deed. The Ring is mine!" And suddenly, as he set it on his finger, he vanished from Sam's sight. . . . Something struck Sam violently in the back, his legs were knocked from under him and he was flung aside, striking his head against the stony floor, as a dark shape sprang over him. . . .

Sam got up. He was dazed, and blood streaming from his head dripped in his eyes. He groped forward, and then he saw a strange and terrible thing. Gollum on the edge of the abyss was fighting like a mad thing with an unseen foe. . . . The fires below awoke in anger, the red light blazed, and all the cavern was filled with a great glare and heat. Suddenly Sam saw Gollum's long hands draw upwards to his mouth; his white fangs gleamed, and then snapped as they bit. Frodo gave a cry, and there he was, fallen upon his knees at the chasm's edge. But Gollum, dancing like a mad thing, held aloft the Ring, a finger still thrust within its circle.

"Precious, precious, precious!" Gollum cried. "My Precious! O my Precious!" And with that, even as his eyes were lifted up to gloat on his prize, he stepped too far, toppled, wavered for a moment on the brink, and then with a shriek he fell. . . .

"Well, this is the end, Sam Gamgee," said a voice by his side. And there was Frodo, pale and worn, and yet himself again; and in his eyes there was peace now, neither strain of will, nor madness, nor any fear. His burden was taken away. . . .

"Yes," said Frodo. "Do you remember Gandalf's words: '*Even Gollum may have something yet to do*'? But for him, Sam, I could not have destroyed the Ring. The Quest would have been in vain, even at the bitter end."

The Fruits of Victory

"And so they lived happily ever after" is a conventional formula for concluding a fairy tale. Alas, it is false and we know it, for it suggests that, once Good has triumphed over Evil, man is translated out of his historical existence into eternity. Mr Tolkien is much too honest to end with such a pious fiction. Good has triumphed over Evil so far as the Third Age of Middle Earth is concerned, but there is no certainty that this triumph is final. There was Morgoth before Sauron and, before the Fourth Age ends, who can be sure that no successor to Sauron will appear? Victory does not mean the restoration of the Earthly Paradise or the advent of the New Jerusalem. In our historical existence even the best solution involves loss as well as gain. With the destruction of the Ruling Ring the three Elven Rings lose their power, as Galadriel foresaw.

> Do you not see now wherefore your coming to us is as the footsteps of Doom? For if you fail, we are laid bare to the Enemy. Yet if you succeed, then our power is diminished, and Lothlórien will fade, and the tide of time will sweep it away. We must depart into the West or dwindle to a rustic folk of dell and cave, slowly to forget and be forgotten.

Even Frodo, the Quest Hero, has to pay for his success.

> "But," said Sam, and tears started from his eyes, "I thought you were going to enjoy the Shire for years and years after all you've done."
>
> "I thought so, too, once. But I have been too deeply hurt, Sam. I tried to save the Shire, and it has been saved, but not for me. It must often be so, Sam, when things are in danger: someone has to give them up, lose them, so that others may keep them."

If there is any Quest Tale which, while primarily concerned with the subjective life of the individual person as all such stories must be, manages to do more justice to our experience of social-historical realities than *The Lord of the Rings*, I should be glad to hear of it.

Texas Quarterly, Winter 1961

A Universal Eccentric

The Genius of Leonardo da Vinci: Leonardo da Vinci on Art and the Artist,
the material assembled, edited and introduced by André Chastel.
Translated from the French by Ellen Callmann. Orion Press. $12.50.

The Genius of Leonardo da Vinci is a compilation of that artist's reflections upon painting and the painter's life. Its main source is the *Trattato della Pittura,* but Monsieur Chastel has rearranged and edited the original text to make it more logical and coherent, and supplemented it with selections from other writings such as the Anatomical Notebooks. Leonardo may, like Pascal, have intended one day to work up his notes into a systematic treatise, but I think we are rather glad he never did. A work of art ought to be a closed, self-sufficient system, but there is something lifeless, even false, about any closed system of thought. Notebooks, at least, are more fun to read, because one never knows what will come next, and Leonardo has a word to say about so many things—how to represent the four seasons; how to represent a battle; which is more important in painting, the shadows or the outlines; of the ten functions of the eye; of the three kinds of perspective; of the color of mountains; of the birth of branches on trees; of the lengthening and shortening of muscles; how to represent someone who is speaking to several people; how to obtain clear oil; how to judge your own work; how to train the memory; etc. And then, suddenly, in the middle of all these technical hints and sage pieces of advice by the Master, there come descriptions of imaginary scenes and a very different Leonardo appears, an eccentric, obsessed by visions of dread and destruction, the Leonardo whose doodles are haunted by two mysterious figures, a melancholy old man with a nutcracker jaw and a long-haired androgynous youth.

Looking at his pictures, even though they have been so retouched or are only known to us through copies, one is aware of the same duality. On the one hand, as masterpieces of three-dimensional representation, they are all that any academy could desire; everything that sureness of hand and scientific knowledge of light and shade, perspective, proportions, and composition can contribute to the imitation of nature has been employed; everything has been calculated and nothing left to chance. But, then, how peculiar, disturbing, and uncanny they are. How un-Italian, one might add, with their soft lighting and secretiveness. This is true even of many of the drawings. One of the studies for *The Adoration of the Magi* starts out as a strictly scientific study of perspective, but then Leonardo sets a host of shadowy wild beasts cavorting through the geometry. It is this side of him which has led the surrealists to claim him as a forerunner, but there is an important difference between his work and theirs. A surrealist picture, however startling, has no secrets: what makes it odd is obvious—a metal watch is as limp as a piece of drapery, or a sewing machine is standing on a dissecting table. But in paintings like *The Madonna of the Rocks, Leda,* or *St John the Baptist,* there is nothing one can put one's finger on as being odd in itself; all is normal yet all is magical.

Similarly, some of the drawings from the Deluge series look almost tachist. A critic, trying to prove the authentic todayness of tachism, said of one tachist work that it resembled the Brownian movements of ionized particles as science has discovered them to be. But if the picture had been by Leonardo, this resemblance would not have been an accident, but the result of a visit to a laboratory. Today everybody remembers his remarks about the ideas for subjects and compositions which can be obtained by staring at stains on walls, but not everybody remembers his warning:

> . . . while these stains supply you with compositions, they do not teach you to complete any detail.

Leonardo, I think, would find the work of most non-representational painters narrow and repetitive, and accuse them of the same kind of narcissism which a representational painter betrays when he makes all the faces in his pictures resemble himself.

But then Leonardo lived before the split between art and science had occurred, which led to the devaluation by both of objects as the senses perceive them. For him, vision was still *Anschauung,* not *Beobachtung*—the nearest English equivalents I can think of for these two indispensable terms are *beholding* and *observing*; that is to say, he regarded the act of seeing as one in which it was impossible to separate the seer from the seen. For him, art and science were one because the test of truth was still sensory reality.

> All sciences seem vain and full of error that are not born of experience, mother of all certainty, and do not terminate in an actual experience; or, to put it another way, that of which neither the beginning nor the middle nor yet the end is made known to one of the five senses.

When he says that no human investigation can be called truly scientific if it is not capable of mathematical demonstration, he is not thinking of the logical certainty of pure mathematics, for this has nothing to do with experience.

> The eye is the prince of mathematics. . . . It has measured the distances and sizes of the stars; it has discovered the elements and their location; it has given birth to architecture and to perspective and to the divine art of painting.

In one paragraph he seems to have a premonition of the course philosophy was going to take in the Seventeenth Century when it separated the primary characters of an object which were measurable and therefore objective from its secondary characters which were subjective qualities.

> Geometry and arithmetic are not concerned with anything but the knowledge of continuous and discontinuous quantity and are not concerned with quality which is the beauty of the natural creation and the grace of the world.

Thus, important as theoretical scientific knowledge might be, for Leonardo it was only the necessary preliminary; he did not feel he had really grasped the truth about an object until he had drawn or painted it.

> The scientific first principle of painting establishes what is darkness, light, color, volume, the play of figures. . . distance, proximity, movement or repose. All this takes place in the mind without any manual activity. . . from it issues the execution which is more noble than the theory or science which preceded it.

Paragoni, debating the rival claims of the various arts, were a favorite pastime among Renaissance intellectuals, and Leonardo's must not be taken too seriously as if they were definitive statements of his aesthetic beliefs. Leonardo is defending painting as a lawyer defends a client. Had he been called on to defend music, for example, he would certainly have countered his own argument that painting is superior to music because it does not die as soon as it is created but remains in being, by pointing out that a painting also dies when nobody is looking at it, and that, while music can be heard by many people at the same time, a picture can only be seen by a few. The main interest in his defense of painting is what it tells us about the kind of arguments against the art he found it necessary to rebuff. The neoplatonists of his day had inherited from the Greeks a prejudice which we find difficult to understand. To a Fifth Century Greek, physical labor was beneath the dignity of a free man. Poetry, therefore, was the noblest of the arts, because the poet can compose in his own head; he can then recite it or dictate it to a scribe, but he does not have to use his hands. Painting was inferior to poetry because it involved handicraft, but superior to sculpture because it involved less arduous physical effort. Curiously enough, Leonardo employs this argument in attacking sculpture, but this is so contradictory to everything else he says, that it seems to be merely a malicious personal dig at Michelangelo. Another objection to painting which he had to meet was theological. Though the Church permitted the making of religious images, She was always conscious of the dangers of their idolatrous use, a distrust She had inherited from the Jews, and was less aware, until Protestantism made it obvious, that idolatry of the word can be quite as dangerous. It is easier to guess what Leonardo did not believe than to know what he did. He certainly did not sympathize with that exaltation of Man displayed by Ficino and other Renaissance humanists.

Like Shakespeare he seems to have been fascinated by human vitality and revolted by human greed.

> Creatures shall be seen on the earth who will always be fighting with one another. . . . There will be no bounds to their malice; by their strong limbs a great portion of the trees in the vast forests of the world shall be laid low; and when they are filled with food the gratification of their desire shall be to deal out death, affliction, labor, terror, and banishment to every living thing. . . . Nothing shall remain on the earth, or under the earth, or in the waters that shall not be pursued, disturbed or spoiled.

None of the human figures in his work are heroic and, aside from anatomical drawings, he shows little interest in the nude. His contemporaries remarked on the fascination that grotesque heads and faces had for him. While a "normal" face is full of possibilities—looking at one, we try to guess what it will become in the future—a grotesque face, like a caricature, can never change; like the face of an animal, it has only one expression. An artist who is fascinated by the grotesque is always someone who is more conscious of man's kinship to the rest of nature, of his bondage to natural necessity, than of his uniqueness and free will. Though Leonardo remarks on one occasion that the two chief objects to paint are man and the intention of his soul, his own interests were much wider. He was the first and remains, perhaps, the only artist, to whom all created beings, human, animal, vegetable and mineral, are equally alive, equal in dignity, and equally deserving of a painter's attention.

I should be failing in my duty if I passed over the translation in silence. On the title page it says *Translated from the French* and I'm afraid this really means what it says. The English of Leonardo's text is at two removes from the original. This is inexcusable. Italian, even of the Fifteenth Century, is not some exotic tongue like Eskimo for which translators are almost impossible to find. Given the finest translators in the world, and Ellen Callmann, alas, is not one of them, it is impossible to translate from Italian into French and then from French into English without distortion.

For example, here is a sentence as it appears via Callmann via Chastel.

> O painter of anatomy, beware lest excessive knowledge of bones, tendons, and muscles turn you into a wooden painter when you wish your nudes to be too revealing.

And here is the same sentence as, translating direct from Italian, Sir Kenneth Clark renders it.

> O anatomical painter, beware, lest, in the attempt to make your nudes display all their emotions by a too strong indication of bones, sinews and muscles, you become a wooden painter.

It simply passes my comprehension how a publisher, who in all other respects shows himself to be responsible and painstaking, could do such a thing.

The matter of *The Genius of Leonardo da Vinci* is, like everything that he wrote, endlessly fascinating. Monsieur Chastel's commentary is modest and to the point, and his textual notes scholarly. The format of the book, the typography, the quality of the reproductions, are all excellent. I am very glad to possess it, and I am sure many members of Mid-Century will be too.

The Mid-Century, Christmas 1961

The Conscience of an Artist

The Burning Brand: Diaries 1935–1950. By Cesare Pavese,
translated by A. E. Murch, with Jeanne Molli. Walker. $7.50.

On a first hasty perusal of this diary, I did Signor Pavese a gross injustice. I thought it was going to be what journalists call a "human" document, by which they mean one which reveals a person's secret weaknesses and shame. In the good old days, a dead man's literary executors destroyed or erased passages in his private papers which they thought discreditable to his memory, and there are pages in Pavese's journal—they are but a small fraction of the whole—which, I think, should not have been made public. Twice in his life, once in the Thirties and once at the end of the Forties, he ran into bad girl-trouble, and the second time he killed himself as a result. About such unhappy matters we do not or ought not to want to know. It is our decent side that is bored and embarrassed when another pours out his troubles to us because, in most cases, we know that we are powerless to help. To be curious about suffering which we cannot relieve—and, alas, most of us are a bit curious—is *Schadenfreude* and nothing else. As Pavese himself wrote: "One stops being a child when one realizes that telling one's trouble does not make it better." Precisely. Not even telling it to oneself. Most of us have known (or will know) shameful moments when we blubbered, beat the wall with our fists, cursed the Power that made us and the world, and wished that we were dead or that someone else was. But at such times, if we are in the habit of keeping a diary, it is better to make no entries: the "I" of the sufferer should have the tact and decency to look the other way. Or, at least, if we do put anything down, we should burn it at once before our executors can lay their paws on it. One regrets the publication of a few pages all the more because the rest of this journal is so magnificent.

When he was in control of himself, he had a clear idea of the function of a journal in a writer's life:

The interest of this journal would be the unforeseen profusion of ideas, the periods of inspiration that, of themselves, automatically, indicate the main trends of your inner life. From time to time you try to understand what you are thinking, and only as an afterthought do you go on to link your present ideas with those of days gone by. The originality of these pages is that you leave the construction to work itself out, and set your own spirit in front of you, objectively.

What he gives us is a fascinating and very moving record, by a mind which was both highly sensitive and exceptionally intelligent, of that quest which every artist has to undertake, the quest for authenticity. The questions, that is to say, which he is continually asking himself are: what kind of poetry or fiction can be genuine (1) for a writer whose cultural tradition is European and who was born in the first decade of the twentieth century; (2) for an Italian writer born at this time; (3) for me, Cesare Pavese?

As a child—and this is usually the case, I believe, with an original writer—Pavese was not particularly interested in literature; he was much more excited by geology and astronomy. It is evident, too, that the decisive imaginative experiences of his childhood were not encounters with human beings but, like Wordsworth, encounters with the numinous in nature or, as he calls it, the "savage," which in his case was the landscape of Piedmont. The great problem for a writer with a childhood of this kind is learning to broaden his imaginative sympathies so that he is able to respond to other landscapes and to human relations. One of the earliest entries in the diary is concerned with this problem:

Why cannot I write about these red cliffs? Because they reflect nothing of myself. The place gives me a vague uneasiness, nothing more, and that should never be sufficient justification for a poem. If these rocks were in Piedmont, though, I could very well absorb them into a flight of fancy and give them meaning.

And so is one of the latest:

Your inordinate passion for natural magic . . . is a sign of your timidity, of your urge to escape the duties and obligations of the human world. While you are so absorbed by this mythical need to grasp the reality of things, it takes courage to look with the same eyes at men and their passions. It is difficult, uncongenial—men lack the immobility of nature, her vast scope for interpretation, her silence. Men come up against us, imposing themselves upon us with their agitations and self-expression. You have tried in various ways to petrify them—isolating them in their most natural moments, immersing them in nature, reducing them to their destiny. Yet your men talk and talk—in them the spirit expresses itself, comes to bloom. This is your tension. But you suffer in creating it, you would never wish to find it in real life. You long for the immobility of nature, silence, death.

So far as I know, this kind of feeling for nature is rare in Italian literature. Pavese himself says that Italian "nature poetry" is mostly to be found in practical prose works on agriculture. But, perhaps, the Piedmontese, like the Sicilians, are a special kind of Italian. According to Pavese, neither Piedmont nor Sicily ever became really fascist, so that writers like Vittorini and himself were in a different position in relation to politics than the writers who came from Rome. The Roman humanist intelligence remained what it had been only more so, ironic and cynical. He and Vittorini, coming from more primitive and less sophisticated regions, "discovered barbarian culture across the sea," that is to say, American literature. Pavese began his literary career as a translator of English and American books, among them, *Moby Dick*, *Portrait of the Artist as a Young Man*, *Manhattan Transfer*, *Alice B. Toklas*, *Three Lives*, *Moll Flanders*, Faulkner's *The Hamlet*, and *David Copperfield*.

All these books, one notices, though superficially quite unpolitical, are anarchistic; though he later got tired of it, what seems to have first attracted him in American literature is that most American novels are concerned with pre-political man; the social relations portrayed are so elementary and so tenuous that the question of politics cannot arise. European writers, who can never forget that man is a political animal, Pavese divides into two kinds. One kind and the kind he personally feels in sympathy with, is represented by Dante, Stendhal and Baudelaire. He calls them "creators of stylised situations." Their verbal style is always in good taste; when they fail, they fall into employing stereotyped situations. Petrarch, Verlaine, and Tolstoi represent the other kind, the kind that is always in search of "experience", so that their books tend to be like diaries. So long as their experience does not give out, the situations they describe will always be fresh, but their verbal style is uncertain; they oscillate between clumsy and "fine" writing. Because they are apt to confuse art and life, making and doing, their artistic conscience is apt to be defective. His preference for the Stendhal kind of writer does not mean, however, that Pavese believed in art for Art's sake, that making is an autonomous activity which can ignore reality. "The beginnings of a creation," he writes, "that knows itself to be a product of the imagination are also the beginnings of *Literature*. Great books are not written with the purpose of creating poetry." Hence his dislike of *Madame Bovary*. Its "realism" is specious, for what Flaubert meant by reality was a hypothesis: "All is filth except the conscientious artist." What is so impressive about Pavese's reflections on the writer's vocation is their sane balance. On the one hand, he insists that any authentic work must be original: it is not enough that a writer's work be unlike anyone else's; each book he writes must be unlike any of his others.

One thing seems to me intolerable to an artist: to lose the feeling of starting something fresh. The only joy in the world is to begin.

On the other hand, he knows, that the "modernist" revolt against the past is futile and "absolute" originality a chimera. Great works of art, he believes, are the result "either of the reflowering of the past or the clash between two cultures." Though each new work of a writer should be a new step, it will be a false step unless it is also a further step. The final goal of a writer is to achieve "complete possession of his own experience, body, rhythm and memories."

> The search for a new personality is sterile. What is fruitful is the human interest the old personality can take in new activities.

Pavese started out as a lyric poet and even when he took to writing novels they were short ones. This worried him. It is, he said, as easy to create a momentary work as to live a moment of morality. There is an unpleasant parallel to be drawn between the poet who writes isolated lyrics and the man whose life is given over to voluptuousness. When he is dead, one ought to be able to see a writer's works as together forming an *oeuvre*, just as a man's life should appear as a consistent history.

I have not, I am ashamed to say, read any of Pavese's poems or fiction, but after reading this diary, I am eager to read everything he wrote as soon as possible. Firstly, because I am certain that only a good writer could show the insight into the nature of his art that this diary shows and, secondly, because on the evidence of this diary alone, he is among the masters of the aphorism. Let me whet the reader's appetite by quoting a few.

> Mistakes are always initial.

> You cannot construct a totalitarian love affair. You can build a totalitarian goodness. But don't play the fool: keep sex out of it.

> When writing poetry, it is not inspiration that produces a bright idea, but the bright idea that kindles the fire of inspiration.

> Hate is always a clash between our own spirit and someone else's body.

> It is not that the child lives in a world of imagination, but that the child within us survives and starts into life only at rare moments of recollection, which make us believe, and it is not true, that in their time they were imaginative.

> Characters that are depressed at a mere nothing are the ones best suited to endure heavy blows.

> Lessons are not given, they are taken.

The Mid-Century, December 1961

Books of the Year . . . from W. H. Auden

New York

I can remember what books I remember reading during the past year, but not their date of publication. Thus my most vivid memory is of Goethe's *Italian Journey* because I spent last winter translating it. The most remarkable volume of poetry published was obviously Robert Graves's *Collected Poems* (Cassell), but I cannot count that as I had read them nearly all before, so I must say that the most interesting poetry I've read this year is still in manuscript. I hardly read any novels so my judgment is worth nothing; however, I did read and enjoy Louis Kronenberger's *A Month of Sundays* (not yet published in England, I believe), J. R. Ackerley's *We Think the World of You* and Philip Toynbee's *Pantaloon* (Chatto & Windus). In biography I was enthralled by the Strauss-Hofmannsthal correspondence, both for the light it throws on the relationship between words and music and as a document about an all too little described relationship, the marriage of true minds.

If I ask myself what single piece of literature gave me greatest pleasure in 1961, it was an article in the *Scientific American* called "Cleaning Shrimps." Perhaps I should explain that it's concerned not with preparing shrimps for the table but with shrimps who live from cleaning fish.

Sunday Times, 24 December 1961

The Chemical Life

The Drug Experience: First-Person Accounts of Addicts, Writers, Scientists, and Others. Edited by David Ebin. Orion. $5.95.

A rag-bag of a book, but rightly so, for the subject is itself miscellaneous. Drugs have a literary interest because of the peculiar experiences undergone by those who take them. They are of anthropological interest because there are societies which make a sacred cult of them. Because of the deadly effect of some kinds of drug-addiction and the criminals who trade on this, they are a social-legal problem. Because of the analgesic and therapeutic effects of drugs, they are of interest to science, and, in the case of those drugs which appear to be physically harmless, there is the moral-religious question as to what effect indulgence may have on the character. Drugs, harmless or dangerous, ignore all social, professional, and cultural frontiers. Among the contributors to this anthology, for example, are naive, sophisticated, conservative, and avant-garde writers; jazz musicians, medical students, a Member of Parliament, an Oxford don, jailbirds and invalids, heroes and cowards. As to the judgment of the editor, I only regret one inclusion, Aleister Crowley's piece which seems to me a phoney penny-novelette, and one omission, which perhaps was unobtainable, Robert Graves's fine poem to the Mushroom God. Whatever the editor's intention was in including it, I am grateful for the Symposium on LSD. It is one of the most extraordinary documents I ever read, or rather failed to read, in my life. The distinguished participants, if one met them in private life or even in their consulting rooms, would, no doubt, show themselves capable of human speech, but here, where they have to appear in public as psychologists, they do not talk badly because they do not talk at all; the noises they make are a sort of non-speech, null and void.

As everybody except the Narcotic Bureau now knows, there are two classes of drugs, the Junk Group which, because of the metabolic changes in the body which they effect, enslave those who take them, and the Hallucinogen Group which are not habit-forming and, so far as is known at present, have no lasting physical aftereffects. Of the Junkies, the only one who has a good word to say for them is Cocteau, who was an addict of the least harmful of them, opium, and even he felt obliged to take a cure and to utter this warning: "Opium cannot bear impatient addicts, bunglers. It moves away, leaving them morphine, heroin, suicide and death."

As William Burroughs, in what is probably the best, as it is certainly the most terrifying, article on Junk in this volume, says: "There are no opium cults. Opium is profane and quantitative like money." Quite aside from the humiliations which a junk addict has to endure in order to procure his drug, and the agonizing withdrawal pains if he tries to give it up, the life of a serious addict, as Mr Burroughs describes it, is hardly appetizing.

> I lived in one room in the Native Quarter of Tangier. I had not taken a bath in a year nor changed my clothes or removed them except to stick a needle every hour in the fibrous grey wooden flesh of terminal addiction. I never cleaned or dusted the room. Empty ampule boxes and garbage piled to the ceiling. Light and water long since turned off for non-payment. I did absolutely nothing. I could look at the end of my shoe for eight hours. If a friend came to visit—and they rarely did since who or what was left to visit—I sat there not caring that he had entered my field of vision—a gray screen always blanker and fainter—and not caring when he walked out of it.

He recommends the apomorphine cure, but there seems to be insufficient evidence as to whether apomorphine is a universal and permanent cure for addiction. One of the morphine-addict contributors, Barney Ross, seems to have broken the habit by heroic willpower, but all agree that very few who take a cure, those, for example, who are sent or voluntarily go to Lexington, do not, sooner or later, relapse. Every junky agrees that society should take steps to reduce the opportunities for becoming addicted, and they are unanimous in their belief that the attitude of the U.S. Narcotic Bureau, which regards drug-taking as a crime, increases the opportunities and encourages the illicit drug traffic. Nearly all the "pushers," those who are directly responsible for making new addicts, are addicts themselves who push junk, not to make a living, but because it is the only way in which they can get junk for themselves. Those who run the drug traffic and make fortunes are, of course, very wicked indeed. To quote Mr Burroughs again:

> Junk is the ultimate merchandise. The junk merchant does not sell his product to the consumer, he sells the consumer to the product. He does not improve and simplify his merchandise. He degrades and simplifies the client.

But moralizing is no use: unless and until the world finds a way to prevent the manufacture of junk, anywhere on earth, except under strict supervision, the junk merchant will exist so long as he can find clients. The only way to run him out of business is to deprive him of clients, and the only country which, so far, has taken a sensible step in this direction seems to be England. In England anybody who has become an addict can register himself as one. He incurs no penalty, his name is kept secret, and he is allowed a ration of drug under minimal supervision. At the same time, the illegal importation and sale of drugs is a criminal offense. In this way, it is hoped that when the present generation of addicts has died off, the profits to be made from trafficking in drugs will be insufficient to offset the risks it involves.

As for the way in which the police in the United States treat the drug taker, even if the drug is as harmless as marihuana, no one can read Billie Holiday's piece in this book without feelings of shock and shame.

Ever since Mr Aldous Huxley published *The Doors of Perception* in 1954, the hallucinogenic drugs, mescaline, LSD, the Mexican Mushroom, etc. have become a topic for cocktail-party conversation, and hundreds of most respectable people have eagerly volunteered to be experimental subjects. Some claim that their experiences under these drugs were indescribably beautiful, some found them terrifying, some vaguely disagreeable, and some comic in a silly way. But when one compares their various accounts, one begins to see certain common denominators. Firstly, however extraordinary the experience of an individual, it is not totally novel to him. As Baudelaire observed more than a century ago:

> The dream will always retain the private tonality of the individual. The man wanted the dream, now the dream will govern the man; but this dream will certainly be the son of its father.

Secondly, a person under the influence of one of these drugs loses all interest in other people; he has no desire to share his experience with others and becomes like Aristotle's apathetic God who "has no need of friends, neither, indeed, can he have any." Not only has he no desire to share his experience, he cannot share it. Professor Zaehner, Mr Ginsberg and Daniel Breslaw, more educated and articulate people than the average, have taken drugs under experimental conditions in which everything they said was reported verbatim, and all three of them talked drivel, strongly reminiscent of the drivel uttered by mediums in their trances.

One is inclined to suspect that habitual taking of this type of drug, even if it has no harmful physical effects, would lead to a selfish indifference towards the common world we live in and a withering of love and affection for others. Monsieur Cocteau complains that, without opium, "the world resembles those revolting films in which ministers unveil statues," and Mr Ginsberg cries "I have to find a new world for the universe, I'm tired of the old one." Very true, no doubt: but better the old revolting world than a world, however beautiful, inhabited only by oneself. Some have claimed that their experiences under drugs were mystical visions of religious significance. Well, a tree must be judged by its fruits. In the case of the famous mystics, the effect of their visions, whether true or an illusion, was to increase their desire to do good works and make them capable of heroic deeds of charity. Has this effect been noted in any taker of mescaline or LSD?

As for the practical help which marihuana can be to jazz musicians, and it is widely believed that it can, Mr Alexander King has this to say:

> The greatest jazz people are rarely addicts. The not-quite ace-performers, when they are off the stuff, will freely confess that junk has never helped their playing a bit. It can't make them play high; it just makes them *think* high.

No, on the whole, I think we had better stick to wine: it tastes nicer and it has even been known to improve the conversation.

P.S. If only I were rich, I would buy advertising space in the subway and fill it with these words by Billie Holiday: "I knew I'd really licked the drug-habit one morning when I couldn't stand television any more."

The Mid-Century, January 1962

Anger

Like all the sins except pride, anger is a perversion, caused by pride, of something in our nature which in itself is innocent, necessary to our existence and good. Thus, while everyone is proud in the same way, each of us is angry or lustful or envious in his own way.

Natural, or innocent, anger is the necessary reaction of a creature when its survival is threatened by the attack of another creature and it cannot save itself (or its offspring) by flight. Such anger, accompanied by physiological changes, like increased secretion of adrenalin, inhibits fear so that the attacked creature is able to resist the threat to its extinction. In the case of young creatures that are not yet capable of looking after themselves, anger is a necessary emotion when their needs are neglected: a hungry baby does right to scream. Natural anger is a reflex reaction, not a voluntary one; it is a response to a real situation of threat and danger, and as soon as the threat is removed, the anger subsides. No animal lets the sun go down upon its wrath. Moreover, Lorentz has shown that, in fights between the social animals, when, by adopting a submissive posture, the weaker puts itself at the mercy of the stronger, this inhibits further aggression by the latter.

Anger, even when it is sinful, has one virtue; it overcomes sloth. Anybody, like a schoolmaster, a stage director or an orchestral conductor, whose business it is to teach others to do something, knows that, on occasions, the quickest—perhaps the only—way to get those under him to do their best is to make them angry.

Anger as a sin is either futile (the situation in which one finds oneself cannot or should not be changed, but must be accepted) or unnecessary (the situation could be mastered as well or better without it). Man is potentially capable of the sin of anger because he is endowed with memory—the experience of an event persists—and with the faculty of symbolization (to him, no object or event is simply itself). He becomes actually guilty of anger because he is first of all guilty of the sin of pride, of which anger is one of many possible manifestations.

Because every human being sees the world from a unique perspective, he can, and does, choose to regard himself as its centre. The sin of anger is one of our reactions to any threat, not to our existence, but to our fancy that our existence is more important than the existence of anybody or anything else. None of us wishes to be omnipotent, because the desires of each are limited. We are glad that other things and people exist with their own ways of behaving—life would be very dull if they didn't—so long as they do not thwart our own. Similarly, we do not want others to conform with our wishes because they must—life would be very lonely if they did—but because they choose to; we want *devoted* slaves.

The British middle-class culture in which I grew up strongly discouraged overt physical expression of anger; it was far more permissive, for example, towards gluttony, lust and avarice. In consequence, I cannot now remember "losing" my temper so that I was beside myself and hardly knew what I was doing. Since childhood, at least, I have never physically assaulted anyone, thrown things or chewed the carpet. (I do, now and again, slam doors.) Nor have I often seen other people do these things. In considering anger, therefore, most of my facts are derived from introspection and may not be valid for others, or from literature, in which truth has to be subordinated to dramatic effect. No fits of temper in real life are quite as interesting as those of Lear, Coriolanus or Timon.

In my own case—I must leave the psychological explanation to professionals—my anger is more easily aroused by things and impersonal events than by other people. I don't, I believe, really expect others to do what I wish and am seldom angry when they don't; on the other hand I do expect God or Fate to oblige me. I do not mind losing at cards if the other players are more skilful than I, but, if I cannot help losing because I have been dealt a poor hand, I get furious. If traffic lights fail to change obligingly to red when I wish to cross the road, I am angry; if I enter a restaurant and it is crowded, I am angry. My anger, that is to say, is most easily aroused by a situation which is (a) not to my liking, (b) one I know I cannot change, and (c) one for which I can hold no human individual responsible.

This last condition is the most decisive. I like others to be on time and hate to be kept waiting, but if someone deliberately keeps me waiting because, say, he is annoyed with me or wishes to impress me with his importance, I am far less angry than I am if I know him to be unpunctual by nature. In the first case, I feel I must be partly responsible—if I had behaved otherwise in the past, he would not have kept me waiting; and I feel hopeful—perhaps I can act in the future in such a way that our relationship will change and he will be punctual next time. In the second case, I know that it is in his nature to be late for others, irrespective of their relationship, so that, in order to be on time, he would have to become another person.

My fantastic expectation that fate will do as I wish goes so far that my immediate reaction to an unexpected event, even a pleasant surprise, is anger.

Among the British middle class, repressed physical violence found its permitted substitute in verbal aggression, and the more physically pacific the cultural subgroup (academic and clerical circles, for instance), the more savage the tongue—one thinks of the families in Miss Compton-Burnett's novels, or of Professor Housman jotting down deadly remarks for future use.

Compared with physical aggression, verbal aggression has one virtue; it does not require the presence of its victim. To say nasty things about someone behind his back is at least preferable to saying them to his face. On the other hand, for intelligent and talented persons, it has two great moral dangers. First, verbal malice, if witty, wins the speaker social approval. (Why is it that kind remarks are very seldom as funny as unkind?) Secondly, since, in verbal malice, the ill-will of the heart is associated with the innocent play of the imagination, a malicious person can forget that he feels ill-will in a way that a physically aggressive person cannot. His audience, however, is not so easily deceived. Two people may make almost the same remark; one, we feel immediately, is being only playful, the other has a compulsive wish to denigrate others.

Simone Weil has described how, when she was suffering from acute migraine, she felt a desire to strike others on the same spot where she felt the pain herself. Most acts of cruelty, surely, are of this kind. We wish to make others suffer because we are impotent to relieve our own sufferings (which need not, of course, be physical). Any threat to our self-importance is enough to create a lifelong resentment, and most of us, probably, cherish a great deal more resentment than we are normally aware of. I like to fancy myself as a kind-hearted person who hates cruelty. And why shouldn't I be kind? I was loved as a child, I have never suffered a serious injury either from another individual or from society, and I enjoy good health. Yet, now and again, I meet a man or a woman who arouses in me the desire to ill-treat them. They are always perfectly harmless people, physically unattractive (I can detect no element of sexual sadism in my feelings) and helpless. It is, I realize with shame, their helplessness which excites my ill-will. Here is someone who, whatever I did to him or her, would not fight back, an ideal victim, therefore, upon whom to vent all my resentments, real or imagined, against life.

If it were really possible for suffering to be transferred like a coin from one person to another, there might be circumstances in which it was morally permissible; and if, however mistakenly, we believed that it was possible, acts of cruelty might occasionally be excusable. The proof that we do not believe such a transfer to be possible is that, when we attempt it, we are unsatisfied unless the suffering we inflict upon others is at least a little greater than the suffering that has been inflicted upon ourselves.

The transferability-of-suffering fallacy underlies the doctrine of retributive punishment, and there is so little evidence that the threat of punishment— the threat of public exposure is another matter—is an effective deterrent to crime, or that its infliction—self-inflicted penance is again another matter— has a reformatory effect, that it is impossible to take any other theory of punishment seriously. By punishment, I mean, of course, the deliberate infliction of physical or mental suffering beyond what the safety of others requires. There will probably always be persons who, whether they like it or not, have to be quarantined, some, perhaps, for the rest of their lives.

The anger felt by the authorities which makes them eager to punish is of the same discreditable kind which one can sometimes observe among parents and dog-owners, an anger at the lack of respect for his betters which the criminal has shown by daring to commit his crime. His real offence in the eyes of the authorities is not that he has done something wrong but that he has done something which *they* have forbidden.

"Righteous anger" is a dubious term. Does it mean anything more than that there are occasions when the sin of anger is a lesser evil than cowardice or sloth? I know that a certain state of affairs or the behaviour of a certain person is morally evil and I know what should be done to put an end to it; but, without getting angry, I cannot summon up the energy and the courage to take action.

Righteous anger can effectively resist and destroy evil, but the more one relies upon it as a source of energy, the less energy and attention one can give to the good which is to replace the evil once it has been removed. That is why, though there may have been some just wars, there has been no just peace. Nor is it only the vanquished who suffer; I have known more than one passionate anti-Nazi who went to pieces once Hitler had been destroyed. Without Hitler to hate, their lives had no *raison d'être*.

"One should hate the sin and love the sinner." Is this possible? The evil actions which I might be said to hate are those which I cannot imagine myself committing. When I read of the deeds of a Hoess or an Eichmann, from whom I have not personally suffered, though I certainly do not love them, their minds are too unintelligible to hate. On the other hand, when I do something of which I am ashamed, I hate myself, not what I have done; if I had hated it, I should not have done it.

I wish the clergy today—I am thinking of the Anglican Church because She is the one I know best—would not avoid, as they seem to, explaining to us what the Church means by Hell and the Wrath of God. The public is left with the impression, either that She no longer believes in them or that She holds a doctrine which is a moral monstrosity no decent person could believe.

Theological definitions are necessarily analogical, but it is singularly unfortunate that the analogies for Hell which the Church has used in the past should have been drawn from Criminal Law. Criminal laws are imposed laws—they come into being because some people are not what they should be, and the purpose of the law is to compel them by force and fear to behave. A law can always be broken and it is ineffective unless the authorities have the power to detect and punish, and the resolution to act at once.

To think of God's laws as imposed leads to absurdities. Thus, the popular conception of what the Church means by Hell could not unfairly be described as follows. God is an omniscient policeman who is not only aware of every sin we have committed but also of every sin we are going to commit. But for seventy years or so He does nothing, but lets every human being commit any sin he chooses. Then, suddenly, He makes an arrest and, in the majority of cases, the sinner is sentenced to eternal torture.

Such a picture is not without its appeal; none of us likes to see his enemies, righteous or unrighteous, flourishing on earth like a green bay tree. But it cannot be called Christian. Some tender-minded souls have accepted the analogy but tried to give eternity a time limit: in the end, they say, the Devil and damned will be converted. But this is really no better. God created the world; He was not brought in later to make it a good one. If His love could ever be coercive and affect the human will without its co-operation, then a failure to exercise it from the first moment would make Him directly responsible for all the evil and suffering in the world.

If God created the world, then the laws of the spiritual life are as much laws of our nature as the laws of physics and physiology, which we can defy but not break. If I jump out of the window or drink too much I cannot be said to break the law of gravity or a biochemical law, nor can I speak of my broken leg or my hangover as a punishment inflicted by an angry Nature. As Wittgenstein said: "Ethics does not treat of the world. Ethics must be a condition of the world like logic." To speak of the Wrath of God cannot mean that God is Himself angry. It is the unpleasant experience of a creature, created to love and be happy, when he defies the laws of his spiritual nature. To believe in Hell as a possibility is to believe that God cannot or will not ever compel us to love and be happy. The analogy which occurs to me is with neurosis. (This, of course, is misleading too because, in these days, many people imagine that, if they can call their behaviour neurotic, they have no moral responsibility for it.) A neurotic, an alcoholic, let us say, is not happy; on the contrary, he suffers terribly, yet no one can relieve his suffering without his consent and this he so often withholds. He insists on suffering because his ego cannot bear the pain of facing reality and the diminution of self-importance which a cure would involve.

If there are any souls in Hell, it is not because they have been sent there, but because Hell is where they insist upon being.

Sunday Times, 21 January 1962; *The Seven Deadly Sins*,
introduction by Raymond Mortimer, 1962

Foreword to *The Viking Book of Aphorisms*

This anthology is devoted to aphoristic writing, not to epigrams. An epigram need only be true of a single case, for example, *Coolidge opened his mouth and a moth flew out*; or effective only in a particular polemical context, for example, *Foxhunting is the pursuit of the uneatable by the unspeakable*, which is an admirable remark when made in a country house in the Shires, but a cheap one if addressed to a society of intellectuals who have never known the pleasures of hunting. An aphorism, on the other hand, must convince every reader that it is either universally true or true of every member of the class to which it refers, irrespective of the reader's convictions. To a Christian, for example, *The knowledge of God is very far from the love of Him* is a true statement about a defect in the relation between himself and God; to the unbeliever, it is a true statement about the psychology of religious belief. An aphorism can be polemic in form but not in meaning. *Do not do unto others as you would they should do unto you—their tastes may not be the same*—is not a denial of the Gospel injunction but an explanation of what it really means. *The road of excess leads to the palace of wisdom* is a borderline case. It is a valid aphorism if one can safely assume that every reader knows the importance of self-control; one cannot help feeling that, were Blake our contemporary, he would have written *sometimes leads.*

Again, an epigram must be amusing and brief, but an aphorism, though it should not be boring and must be succinct in style, need not make the reader laugh and can extend itself to several sentences.

Aphorisms are essentially an aristocratic genre of writing. The aphorist does not argue or explain, he asserts; and implicit in his assertion is a conviction that he is wiser or more intelligent than his readers. For this reason the aphorist who adopts a folksy style with "democratic" diction and grammar is a cowardly and insufferable hypocrite.

No anthologist of aphorisms can be impartial, nor should he try to be. Two statements may be equally true, but, in any society at any given point in history, one of them is probably more important than the other; and, human nature being what it is, the most important truths are likely to be those which that society at that time least wants to hear. In making his selection, it is up to the anthologist to guess what bubbles, intellectual, moral, and political, are at the moment most in need of pricking.

Ignorance has imposed on us a further limitation, which we hope will not be mistaken for arrogance. We have limited our choice to writers belonging to what, for lack of a better term, is called Western civilization, not because we consider that civilization superior to any other, but because it would be folly and presumption on our part to claim that our knowledge of, say, Chinese, Japanese, Indian, or Islamic literature could possibly give an adequate representation of their aphorisms. At a time, however, when it seems as if it were precisely the worst aspects of our technological culture—our noise, our vulgarity, our insane waste of natural resources—which are the most exportable (European intellectuals who imagine these vices to be of American origin are willfully deceiving themselves), we are bold to think of this volume as evidence that there are others—such as humor and a capacity for self-criticism—which, though less intrusive than jukeboxes and bombs, are neither negligible nor unworthy of respect.

W.H.A.

L. K.

The Viking Book of Aphorisms, a personal selection by
W. H. Auden and Louis Kronenberger, 1962

A Marianne Moore Reader

A Marianne Moore Reader. By Marianne Moore. Viking. $6.95.

I am not sure that I approve of "Selections" from an author's writings unless they have been chosen by myself. If one admires a writer, one wants to read everything he or she has written, and even a work which in one's highly fallible judgment seems a failure, is illuminating and endearing; *when* but not before, one has read everything, it is, of course, a personal convenience to have all one's favorites assembled between the covers of one volume. It would be deplorable, for instance, if purchasers of *A Marianne Moore Reader* should imagine that Miss Moore has only written fifty-four good poems, even though these have been chosen by Miss Moore herself, and they will be doing La Fontaine as well as his translator a gross injustice if, having read the twenty-four fables presented here, they do not go off and buy the complete volume.

However, even those who know Miss Moore's writings thoroughly will find new things in this Reader to delight them, and pieces which, though they may have read them in some magazine, they have not kept. It would be worth buying for the "Foreword" and the "Interview with Donald Hall" alone, in which, luckily for us, Miss Moore has overcome the natural modesty and reticence of the wellbred and, for the first time, talks about herself and her own work.

Two years ago, in this magazine, I said my say about her poetry, so that I shall not discuss it now, beyond drawing attention to the fact that she has revised, and greatly improved, "The Steeple-Jack," which is now four stanzas longer. No questioning of how she came to write her syllabic verse has yet succeeded in eliciting from Miss Moore an explanation which does not mystify still further. We know, for example, exactly how Robert Bridges arrived, through a study of Milton's prosody and experiments in quantitative English verse, at his duodecasyllabics, but all we know about Miss Moore's much more varied and complicated syllabic stanzas is that they were *not* suggested to her, as Ezra Pound first thought, by reading Laforgue or any other French poet. When Mr Hall asks her the straight question—"What is the rationale behind syllabic verse?"—her answer is no answer.

> It never occurred to me that what I wrote was something to define. I am governed by the pull of the sentence as the pull of a fabric is governed by gravity. I like the end-stopped line and dislike the reversed order of words; like symmetry.

I hope she will not be offended at my explanation. I strongly suspect that she owes her discovery to providential ignorance, that, when as a child she first read traditional English verse, she noticed that metrically equivalent lines contained, normally, the same number of syllables, but did not notice (and was never told) that they also contained the same number and same kind of feet. O blessed mistake!

About her subject matter and her artistic principles, on the other hand, Miss Moore is admirably lucid. Her only rival as a writer of poetic bestiaries is D. H. Lawrence, but how utterly different are their respective attitudes towards "birds, beasts and flowers." Lawrence's is summed up in his epigram—

> If men were as much men as lizards are lizards,
> They'd be worth looking at.

Miss Moore's by these sentences from her Foreword—

> Why an inordinate interest in animals and athletes? They are subjects for art and exemplars of it, are they not? minding their own business. Pangolins, hornbills, pitchers, catchers, do not pry or prey—or prolong the conversation; do not make us self-conscious; look their best when caring least . . .

Lawrence loved animals because he loathed human beings; Marianne Moore loves animals because she sees them as paradigms of human behavior at its nicest. Her moral and artistic standards are strict, much in modern life and modern art dismays and revolts her, but in passing judgment on others, she has always remembered that "distaste which takes no credit to itself is best" and has always exhibited the charity and hopeful curiosity which looks for virtue in even the most unpromising of subjects. An amazing example of this is her review of an anthology of the "Beat" poets, *The New American Poetry*. Anybody who knows anything about her poetry and theirs will be surprised that she reviewed it at all. She is, needless to say, honest about what she dislikes both in their choice of subject matter and their rejection of linguistic and formal conventions.

> Good content, as Samuel Butler said, is usually matched by good treatment, and poets specializing in "organs and feelings"—severed from culture and literature, dogged by redundance and stench—have a stiff task. By comparison with the vocabularies of science, which are creative, in fact enthralling, exhibitionist content—invaded by the diction of drug-vendors and victims, sex addicts and civic parasites—becomes poetically inoperative.

> Mr Olson advocates open form or "composition by field," projective or field composition being offered as an improvement on inherited or "non-projective" form. Inherited non-projective form can be projective, I would say, and projective form may be weedy and colorless like suckers from an un-sunned tuber.

Yet, feeling this way, Miss Moore then does what not one in a hundred reviewers with the same tastes would have done; she reads every poet and every poem in the book and, whenever she can find a line of value, she quotes it, whereas ninety-nine per cent of reviewers would have quoted the worst lines they could find.

Allen Ginsberg's poetry, for example, can hardly be Miss Moore's cup of tea, but that has not prevented her from seeking and finding something to praise.

> [He] can foul the nest in a way to marvel at, but it is an innocent enough picture of himself which he provides when he "sat down under the huge shade of a Southern Pacific locomotive." That he "found minds unable to receive love because not knowing the self as lovely" is a thoughtful statement.

Questions of taste aside, very few poets over the age of thirty are unselfish enough to know or care about what other poets are writing; Miss Moore is and does. Thus, she concluded the same review as follows:

> . . . from the title, *The New American Poetry*, the article should be omitted, since various new poets are not included—Daniel Hoffman, Robert Bagg, George Starbuck; also striking of late as a poet in prose, Jean Garrigue; and it seems literalistic not to include Mr I. A. Richards, technically "new" and of great attraction.

She admits that reading the unsolicited verse, published or typed, which, like all established poets, she keeps receiving, "does interfere with my work. I can't get much done," but her conscience is tenderer than that of most of us: "I would be a monster if I tossed everything away without looking at it."

Her standards concerning her own work are extremely severe, but without a trace of false modesty. Like every poet of real worth, she knows that if it were easy to write a good poem, it would be no fun. Both the poet and the scientist, she says, "are willing to waste effort. To be hard on himself is one of the main strengths of each. Each is attentive to clues, each must narrow the choice, must strive for precision." And she has a clear awareness of where, if one of her poems is defective, the defect is most apt to lie.

> I think the most difficult thing for me is to be satisfactorily lucid, yet have enough implication in it to suit myself. That's a problem. And I don't approve of my "enigmas," or as somebody said, "the not ungreen grass."

Though many people would feel proud at having written "In Distrust of Merits," she is right, I believe, in thinking that it is not good enough for her and right in her reasons for so thinking.

> . . . as form, what has it? It is just a protest—disjointed, exclamatory. Emotion overpowered me. First this thought and then that.

(In my blind folly, I deplore her poems on baseball; it is hard to transcend one's upbringing.)

I am delighted that she has included the correspondence with the Ford Motor Company, which is, surely, the most extraordinary episode in literary history. Where else on earth but in the United States would the idea of asking a poet to name an automobile have occurred to a business executive, and what poet on earth but Miss Moore would not only have taken the task seriously but also refused payment for her labors? It was a noble enterprise, but both parties should have realized that it was bound to fail because of the nature of poetry. A poet is the right person to consult about a Proper Name, the apt name, that is, for a unique object, but you cannot expect him or her to come up with a suitable Brand Name which will apply to all the objects of a certain class; a poet's names will always be, as Miss Moore's were, too special for a general public.

She says, a little wrily, that she will not object to being called a moralist because she considers some matters more important than poetry. "I do not thrust promises and deeds of mercy right and left to write a lyric." Her sanity on this point may have deprived us of some beautiful poems, but it has ensured that the beauty of the poems she has found time to write is of the sane and righteous kind which, in the long run, is the only kind of beauty which endures. It would be difficult to better Miss Moore's own statement about the relation of art and ethics.

> Must a man be good to write good poems? The villains in Shakespeare are not illiterate, are they? But rectitude *has* a ring that is implicative, I would say. And with *no* integrity, a man is not likely to write the kind of book I read.

Miss Moore is herself so meticulous that I know she would like me to draw attention to a serious misquotation on p. 125, where Pope is made to write the curious line—

> a wedged hole ages in a bodkin's eye

In point of fact, *ages* is a noun not a verb and the line should run—

> Or wedged whole ages in a bodkin's eye.

The Mid-Century, February 1962

The Poet and the City

[See *The Dyer's Hand*, p. 505, and textual notes, p. 952)

Massachusetts Review, Spring 1962

Introduction to *A Choice of de la Mare's Verse*

As an introduction to that best of all anthologies for the young, *Come Hither,*
Mr de la Mare wrote a parable. A schoolboy named Simon has heard from his
mother about a wonderful place of "trees, waters, green pastures, rare birds
and flowers" called East Dene. Setting out one morning to look for it, he
comes to an old stone house in a hollow called Thrae, and makes the acquaintance of its owner, Miss Taroone. When he asks her about East Dene, she gives
him a strange look but does not answer. She tells him, however, that Thrae is
not her only house, and speaks of Sure Vine "as a family mansion, very ancient
and magnificent". She also tells him about a great traveller, Mr Nahum.

> I could not at first make head or tail of Mr Nahum. Even now I am un-
> certain whether he was Miss Taroone's brother or her nephew or a
> cousin many times removed; or whether perhaps she was really and truly
> Mrs Taroone and he her only son; or she still Miss Taroone and he an
> adopted one. I am not sure whether she had much love for him, though
> she appeared to speak of him with pride. What I do know is that Miss
> Taroone had nurtured him from his cradle and had taught him all the
> knowledge that was not already his by right of birth. . . . Strangely
> enough, by the looks on her face and the tones of her voice, Miss Ta-
> roone was inclined to mock a little at Mr Nahum because of his restless-
> ness. She didn't seem to approve of his leaving her so much—though
> she herself had come from Sure Vine.

The names are easy to translate and the general drift of the parable is
clear. Because of his peculiar position as a traveller in search of a joy which
he has yet to find and can only imagine in terms of an innocent happiness
which is no longer his, every man, whether as a writer or a reader of poetry,
demands two things which, though not absolutely incompatible with each
other, are not easy to reconcile completely. On the one hand, we want a
poem to be a beautiful object, a verbal Garden of Eden which, by its formal
perfection, keeps alive in us the hope that there exists a state of joy without
evil or suffering which it can and should be our destiny to attain. At the same
time, we look to a poem for some kind of illumination about our present
wandering condition, since, without self-insight and knowledge of the world,
we must err blindly with little chance of realizing our hope. We expect a
poem to tell us some home truth, however minor, and, as we know, most
home truths are neither pretty nor pleasant. One might say that, in every
poet, there dwells an Ariel, who sings, and a Prospero, who comprehends,
but in any particular poem, sometimes even in the whole work of a particular
poet, one of the partners plays a greater role than the other. Thus Campion,

one of de la Mare's favourite poets, is an example of an Ariel-dominated poet in whose work verbal beauty is *almost* everything, and what is said matters very little. In Wordsworth's *The Prelude*, on the other hand, Prospero dominates and Ariel contributes very little; it might *almost* have been written in prose.

Though the role of Prospero in de la Mare's poetry is much greater than one may realize on a first reading, it would not be unfair, I think, to call him an Ariel-dominated poet. Certainly, his most obvious virtues, those which no reader can fail to see immediately, are verbal and formal, the delicacy of his metrical fingering and the graceful architecture of his stanzas. Neither in his technique nor his sensibility, does he show any trace of influences other than English, either continental, like Eliot and Pound, or Classical, like Bridges. The poets from whom he seems to have learned most are the Elizabethan song-writers, Christina Rossetti and, I would rashly guess, Thomas Hardy. Like Christina Rossetti, he is a master of trisyllabic substitution and foot inversion; the reader's ear is continually excited by rhythmical variations without ever losing a sense of the underlying pattern. In the predominantly anapaestic movement of the following stanza, for example, how surprising and yet convincing is the sudden shift to a trochaic movement in the fifth line and to a spondaic in the sixth.

> Wicket out into the dark
> > That swings but one way;
> Infinite hush in an ocean of silence
> > Aeons away—
> *Thou* forsaken!—even thou!—
> > The dread good-bye;
> The abandoned, the thronged, the watched, the unshared—
> > Awaiting me—I!

Like Hardy, he is a great inventor of stanzas and in command of every effect which can be obtained from contrasts between lines of different lengths, lines with masculine endings and lines with feminine endings, rhymed and unrhymed lines.

> 'Tis strange to see young children
> In such a wintry house;
> Like rabbits on the frozen snow
> Their tell-tale foot-prints go;
> Their laughter rings like timbrels
> 'Neath evening ominous.

★　★　★

> He drew each pure heart with his skill;
> With his beauty,

> And his azure,
> And his topaz,
> Gold for pleasure,
> And his locks wet with the dew of April.

★   ★   ★

> Once gay, now sad; remote—and dear;
> Why turn away in doubt and fear?
> I search again your grieved self-pitying face;
> Kindness sits clouded there. But, love? No, not a trace.

Many poets have some idiosyncrasy or tic of style which can madden the reader if he finds their work basically unsympathetic, but which, if he likes it, becomes endearing like the foibles of an old friend. Hardy's fondness for compound and latinate words is one example, de la Mare's habit of subject-verb inversion another

> Leans now the fair willow, dreaming
> Amid her locks of green.

In his later work such inversions become much rarer. One can observe also a change in his diction. Though this continues to come from what one might call the "beautiful" end of the verbal spectrum—he never, like Yeats and Eliot uses a coarse or brutal word, and seldom a slang colloquialism—a chronological study of his poems shows a steady, patient and successful endeavour to eliminate the overly arty diction which was a vice of his Pre-Raphaelite forebears, and to develop a style which, without ceasing to be lyrical, has the directness of ordinary speech. What a distance there is, for example, between these two extracts, one from an early poem, one from a late.

> Slowly, silently, now the moon
> Walks the night in her silver shoon;
> This way, and that, she peers, and sees
> Silver fruit upon silver trees;
> One by one the casements catch
> Her beams beneath the silvery thatch;

★   ★   ★

> What, do you suppose, we're in this world for, sweet heart?
> What—in this haunted, crazy, beautiful cage—
> *Keeps* so many, like ourselves, poor pining human creatures,
> As if from some assured, yet golden heritage?
> Keeps us lamenting beneath all our happy laughter,
> Silence, dreams, hope for what may *not* come after,
> While life wastes and withers, as it has for mortals,
>   Age on to age, on to age.

His late long poem, *Winged Chariot*, is a surprising performance. He still writes as a lyric poet, not as an epic or dramatic, and it is better read, perhaps, like *In Memoriam*, as a series of lyrics with a metre and theme in common, but readers who are only familiar with his early poetry will find something they would never have predicted, a talent for metaphysical wit.

> The dwindling candle with her pensive light
> Metes out the leaden watches of the night.
> And, in that service, from herself takes flight.

★   ★   ★

> Fate was appalled. Her See-Saw would not stir.
> Man sat dead-centre and grimaced at her.
> Her prizes? None could shine where none could err;
> So every dunce was a philosopher.

★   ★   ★

> Cowed by the spectre for which "no man waits",
> Obsequious hirelings of the witless Fates,
> Time pins down ev'n Dictators to their "dates".

De la Mare wrote many poems with an audience of children specifically in mind, and, in his collected works, these have been published in a volume by themselves. This has a practical convenience, but it must never be forgotten that, while there are some good poems which are only for adults, because they pre-suppose adult experience in their readers, there are no good poems which are only for children. Human beings are blessed with the power to remember; consequently, to grow old means for us, not to discard but to accumulate; in every old man, there still lives a child, an adolescent, a young man and a middle-aged one. It is commonly believed that children are, by nature, more imaginative than adults, but this is questionable. It is probably the case only in cultures like our own which put a higher social and economic value upon practical and abstract thinking than upon wonder and images; in a culture which put a high value on imagination and a low one on logic, children might well appear to be more rational than adults, for a child is not, by nature, more *anything*. In all cultures, however, there is one constant difference between children and adults, namely, that, for the former, learning their native tongue is itself one of the most important experiences in their lives, while, for the latter, language has become an instrument for interpreting and communicating experience; to recapture the sense of language as experience, an adult has to visit a foreign country.

What the child, and the child-in-the-adult, most enjoys in poetry, therefore, is the manipulation of language for its own sake, the sound and rhythm of words. There is a deplorable tendency in the United States, which I hope and pray has not spread to the United Kingdom, to think that books for children should use a very limited vocabulary, and that verses for them should be written in the simplest and most obvious metres. This is utter nonsense. The surest sign that a child has a feeling for language is that he talks like an affected adult and always uses a polysyllabic word when a monosyllabic one would do.

As a revelation of the wonders of the English Language, de la Mare's poems for children are unrivalled. (The only ones which do not seem to me quite to come off are those in which he tries to be humorous. A gift, like Hilaire Belloc's for the comic-satiric is not his; he lacks, perhaps, both the worldliness and the cruelty which the genre calls for.) They include what, for the adult, are among his greatest "pure" lyrics, e.g. "Old Shellover" and "The Song of the Mad Prince", and their rhythms are as subtle as they are varied. Like all good poems, of course, they do more than train the ear. They also teach sensory attention and courage. Unlike a lot of second-rate verse for children, de la Mare's descriptions of birds, beasts, and natural phenomena are always sharp and accurate, and he never prettifies experience or attempts to conceal from the young that terror and nightmare are as essential characteristics of human existence as love and sweet dreams. There is another respect in which, as all writers of good books for them know, children differ from grown-ups; they have a far greater tolerance for didactic instruction, whether in facts or morals. As Chesterton observed:

> The child does not know that men are not only bad from good motives, but also often good from bad motives. Therefore the child has a hearty, unspoiled, and insatiable appetite for mere morality, for the mere difference between a good little girl and a bad little girl.

Without ever being tiresome, de la Mare is not afraid to instruct the young. What could be more practically useful than his mnemonic rhyme "Stars", or more educative, morally as well as musically, than "Hi!"?

> Hi! handsome hunting man
> Fire your little gun.
> Bang! Now the animal
> Is dead and dumb and done.
> Nevermore to peep again, creep again, leap again,
> Eat or sleep or drink again, Oh, what fun!

In considering the work of any poet, it is always easier and safer to discuss the role of Ariel than that of Prospero. There is only one Ariel to a language, but there are as many Prosperos as there are poets. We can describe what one poet does with the language and compare it with what another poet has done, but we cannot compare the perspective on life of any poet with that of any other because each is unique. That is why poets themselves hate being asked what their poems "mean" because, in order to answer such a question, they would have to know themselves which, as Thoreau said, is as impossible as seeing oneself from the back without turning one's head. Every poet will second de la Mare's statement in his prefatory note to *O Lovely England.*

> What a writer has to say *about* his "poems" and their subterranean waters, is often dangerous, and may be even scientifically inaccurate. Verbal and metrical craftsmanship is another matter. . . .

But, as readers of poetry, we can no more help asking, "What is it about this poem, aside from its formal beauties or defects, which makes it sympathetic or unsympathetic to me?", than we can help trying to analyse the qualities of a fellow human being to whom, positively or negatively, we respond. What we "see" in a person or a poem may be quite wrong and is certainly only part of the truth but, if we talk about either, we can only say what we see.

Though all poetry is, ultimately, about human nature, many poems do not look at man directly, but at what he is not, the non-human part of creation which, by convention, we call "Nature" (though it may also contain human artefacts). In the work of certain poets, and de la Mare is one of them, the landscape speaks. His personal landscape is derived from two sources. Firstly, there is the countryside of pre-industrial England, so beautiful in an unspectacular way, and so kindly in climate. (Perhaps, having never suffered from bronchitis, I am biased.) The setting of one poem is a railway-junction, in another the lyric "I" rides a bus, there are a few references to water-mills, but otherwise there is no machinery and no modern building.

As the work of some of the Georgian poets bears witness, the danger of the English landscape as a poetic ingredient is that its gentleness can tempt those who love it into writing genteelly. De la Mare was protected from this, firstly by his conviction that what our senses perceive of the world about us is not all there is to know, and, secondly, by his sense of the powers of evil. This does not mean that he is a Buddhist who regards the sensory world as illusion, or that he would call what we normally are blind to *super*-natural. His view, I take it, is that our eyes and ears do not lie to us, but do not, perhaps cannot, tell us the whole truth, and that those who deny this, end up by actually narrowing their vision.

> What is called realism is usually a record of life at a low pitch and ebb viewed in the sunless light of day—so often a drab waste of gray and white, and an east wind blowing.

What we would see, if our senses and imagination were keener, might be more beautiful than anything we have known.

> It seemed to be a house which might at any moment vanish before your eyes, showing itself to be but the outer shell or hiding place of an abode still more enchanting. . . . If you ever sat and watched a Transformation Scene in a pantomime, did you suppose, just before the harlequin slapped with his wand on what looked like a plain brick-and-mortar wall,

that it would instantly after dissolve into a radiant coloured scene of trees and fountains and hidden beings—growing lovelier in their own showing as the splendour spread and their haunts were revealed? Well, so at times I used to feel in Thrae.

On the other hand, the most beautiful object might turn out to be hiding something neither beautiful nor friendly.

> Masked by that brilliant weed's deceitful green,
> No glint of the dark water can be seen
> Which, festering, slumbers, with this scum for screen.
>
> It is as though a face, as false as fair,
> Dared not, by smiling, show the evil there.
>
> ★   ★   ★
>
> Darkness had fallen. I opened the door:
> And lo, a stranger in the empty room—
> A marvel of moonlight upon wall and floor. . . .
> The quiet of mercy? Or the hush of doom?

Nor, whatever it might turn out to be, can we be certain that, were we mortals to be confronted by the truth, we could endure it.

> Might that secret, if divulged, all we value most bewray!
>   Make a dream of our real,
>   A night of our day. . . .

The other element, more romantic and more disturbing, in the de la Mare landscape is partly derived from Grimm's Maerchen and similar folk-tales, and partly from dreams.

> Still and blanched and cold and lone
>   The icy hills far off from me
> With frosty ulys overgrown
>   Stand in their sculptured secrecy.
>
> No path of theirs the chamois fleet
>   Treads with a nostril to the wind;
> O'er their ice-marbled glaciers beat
>   No wings of eagles to my mind.

Again, the overestimation of dreams and the subjective life shown by some of the lesser Romantic poets, can become boring, for most people are even less original in their dreaming than in their waking life; their dreams are more monotonous than their thoughts and, oddly enough, more literary. Fortunately, de la Mare, as those who have read *Behold This Dreamer* will have learned, was one of those uncommon persons whose dreams are really original. Like Blake, he possessed the rare gift of having visions while awake. (Mescaline and lysergic acid can, it now seems, confer it on us dullards.) He tells, for instance, how once, after dreaming that the Flora of Primavera herself was at that moment passing beneath his bedroom window, he woke up, went to the window, and there, sure enough, she was in the street.

> She sat, uplifted, ethereally lovely, surrounded by her attendant nymphs and *amorini*, and crowned and wreathed with flowers. It was with ropes of flowers, also, that her nymphs were drawing slowly on her low flat Car on its wide clumsy wooden wheels, like gigantic cotton-reels.

"Every artist" said Santayana, "is a moralist though he needn't preach," and de la Mare is one who doesn't. His poems are neither satirical nor occasional; indeed, I cannot recall coming across in his work a single Proper Name, whether of a person or a place, which one could identify as a real historical name. Nor, though he is a lyric, not a dramatic, poet, are his poems "personal" in the sense of being self-confessions; the *I* in them is never identical with the Mr de la Mare one might have met at dinner, and none are of the kind which excite the curiosity of a biographer. Nevertheless, implicit in all his poetry are certain notions of what constitutes the Good Life. Goodness, they seem to say, is rooted in wonder, awe, and reverence for the beauty and strangeness of creation. Wonder itself is not goodness—de la Mare is not an aesthete—but it is the only, or the most favourable, soil in which goodness can grow. Those who lose the capacity for wonder may become clever but not intelligent, they may lead moral lives themselves, but they will become insensitive and moralistic towards others. A sense of wonder is not something we have to learn, for we are born with it; unfortunately, we are also born with an aggressive lust for power which finds its satisfaction in the enslavement and destruction of others. We are, or in the course of our history we have become, predatory animals like the mousing cat and the spotted flycatcher. This lust for power, which, if we surrender completely to it, can turn us into monsters like Seaton's Aunt, is immanent in every child.

> Lovely as Eros, and half-naked too,
> He heaped dried beach-drift, kindled it, and, lo!
> A furious furnace roared, the sea-winds blew . . .
> Vengeance divine! And death to every foe!
> Young god! and not ev'n Nature eyed askance
> The fire-doomed Empire of a myriad ants.

It is only with the help of wonder, then, that we can develop a virtue which we are certainly not born with, compassion, not to be confused with its conceit-created counterfeit, pity. Only from wonder, too, can we learn a style of behaviour and speech which is no less precious in art than in life; for want of a better word we call it good-manners or breeding, though it has little to do with ancestry, school or income. To be well-bred means to have respect for the solitude of others, whether they be mere acquaintances or, and this is much more difficult, persons we love; to be ill-bred is to importune attention and intimacy, to come too close, to ask indiscreet questions and make indiscreet revelations, to lecture, to bore.

Making a selection from the work of any poet one admires is a job which cannot be done satisfactorily because one is always conscious that everything he wrote, even the second best, should be read. De la Mare has, in my opinion, been very shabbily treated by anthologists; in their selections, most have been content to copy each other, and few have included poems he wrote after 1920. This is a gross injustice to a poet who continued to mature, both in technique and wisdom, till the day of his death.

> *A Choice of de la Mare's Verse*, selected with an introduction
> by W. H. Auden, 1963

Today's Poet

The poet is perhaps the only kind of person who can truthfully say, and with full knowledge of what he is saying, that he would rather have been born in an earlier age—very much earlier; an age in which neither publishers nor booksellers yet existed, an age when the statement "The real man speaks in poetry" seemed as self-evident as the statement "Men really speak in prose" seems today.

Then, the "real" meant the sacred or numinous. A real man was not a personality but someone enacting a sacred role, aside from which he or she might be nobody in particular. A real act was some sacred rite by the re-enactment of which the universe and human life were sustained in being and reborn. The individual, the particular, the novel, and the secular were of no account. Particularity showed itself only in the particulars of a rite. It was important that Hercules should have neither more nor less than twelve labors; it was a rule that iambic verses should only be used for curses and satire.

In such an age, the poet has no problem of subject matter—the sacred occasions are public, recognized and shared by the whole community—no problem of communication and, in addition, he is a highly honored and well-rewarded social figure.

The concern of the poet in A.D. 1962 is no different from what it was in 1962 B.C.; that is to say, he is *not* interested in personalities or psychology or progress or news—the extreme opposite of poetry is the daily paper. What moves him to write are his encounters with the sacred in nature, in human beings, nothing else.

By the sacred I do not, of course, mean only the good. The sacred can arouse horror and despair as well as awe, wonder, and gratitude. La belle Dame sans merci is no less a sacred figure than Beatrice. Nor is the sacred confined to the romantically mysterious, to "faery lands forlorn." Indeed, every set of verses, whatever their subject matter may be, are by their formal nature a hymn to Natural Law and a gesture of astonishment at the greatest of all mysteries, the order of the universe. Nothing and no one become sacred through their own efforts; it is rather the sacred that chooses them as vehicles through which to manifest itself. Nor can a poet feel the presence of the sacred simply by wishing or trying to. To say that poetry must be inspired does not mean that it is written in a state of trance like automatic writing; it means that the stimulus to a good poem must be given the poet—he cannot simply think one up.

The obstacles that interfere between the poet and his possible readers in this age are many; but two, one of form and one of content, seem to me particularly serious. Verse is rhythmical, that is, it contains an element of repetition, though, of course, it is the constant variations within the repetitive pattern that make it living and not mechanical. Unfortunately, in a technological civilization the notion of repetition is associated with the identical repetition of the machine (e.g. a road drill) and with all that is most boring and soulless in our life, like punching time clocks.

Secondly, though there are no experiences that are peculiar to poets and unknown to others—we are all, readers and nonreaders alike, in the same boat—the experiences of encounters with the sacred that we all have are more and more experienced in solitude and less and less in public. The present-day reader of poetry has to make an effort that was not demanded of readers in earlier times; he has to translate what is actually said in a poem into the terms of his analogous experiences.

But then perhaps this is true not only of poems but also of our everyday conversation. Before people start complaining about the obscurity of modern poetry, they might ask themselves this question: "How often and to what depth have I shared a profound experience with another person?" One might put it this way: Every modern poem, in addition to the various metaphors and allusions it may contain, is itself, as a whole, not just a story, but a parable.

Mademoiselle, April 1962

A Disturbing Novelist

A Muriel Spark Trio: The Comforters, The Ballad of Peckham Rye, Memento Mori. By Muriel Spark. Lippincott. $5.95.

It is all too easy for a reviewer to confuse his job with that of a literary critic. A reviewer must remember that his audience has not read the book which he is discussing; a critic starts with the assumption that his audience is fairly familiar with the work or author he is reexamining. A critic says, as it were, "This work has certain virtues or defects or technical devices which, so far as

I am aware, no reader has perceived except myself. Here they are. Look at the text again and see for yourself if I am right or wrong." The principal duty of a reviewer, on the other hand, is not judging or explaining, but describing. What he ought to say is, "I have just read a book sent me by its publishers. Let me tell you the kind of book it is, so that you can decide if it sounds like the kind of book you would like to read."

Some kinds of book are easier to describe than others. A reviewer can give a fairly just notion of a book concerned with ideas by outlining its general argument and, if he will only give enough quotations, one can tell immediately whether a new lyric poet is one's cup of tea, but describing prose fiction is much more difficult. One of the great pleasures in reading fiction is that of suspense and surprise—What is going to happen next? What new character is going to appear? What secret is about to be revealed? Consequently, if a reviewer describes the plot or the characters too fully, he spoils half the prospective reader's fun; yet, without doing so, how is he to give a fair idea of the novel?

One can read Miss Spark's novels, as one reads most fiction, as feigned histories. Her characters, that is to say, their speech and social milieu, do not belong to some private imaginary world but to twentieth century England; one could meet their like at dinner or on a bus. But presently, particularly if one has read several of them, one becomes aware of another dimension than the simply historical. The principal concern of the writer of feigned histories is the exploration in depth of individual human characters; since he cannot do this without, as we say, "getting inside" them, his novels are usually confined to the same kind of social milieu, the one to which, by birth or circumstances, he himself belongs, for only there can he feel sure of his insights. But the milieu of each of Miss Spark's novels is different from the others and no reader could conceivably guess the setting of the next. *The Comforters* deals with the upper middle class, *The Ballad of Peckham Rye* with the new post-war lower middle and working classes, *Memento Mori* returns to the upper-middle but all the characters are over seventy, and in her latest novel, *The Prime of Miss Jean Brodie*, all but Miss Brodie herself are pre-adolescent girls. Moreover, Miss Spark deliberately refrains from analyzing her characters in depth; on finishing one of her books, one is left with a set of question marks—her characters have become more and not less mysterious from what we have learned about them. In some of her novels, too, events occur for which it is difficult to find a rational explanation. A man writes a letter to a girl and tears it up, yet it appears verbatim in the novel she is writing; a woman becomes invisible when she falls asleep in the back of a car; mysterious phone calls which the police cannot trace remind a number of aged people that they will soon die.

The reader begins to feel that Miss Spark's characters, plots and background have a parabolic significance beyond their historical reality; each has something and something different obliquely to say about the human condition, irrespective of time and place and, as in all parables, what is obliquely meant is, and must be, different for every reader. To me, for example, *The Comforters* is a parable about Imagination and Experience; we cannot ever know either what is "real" or what is "pure imagination." Is it a novel about a world in which and about which a girl is writing a novel, or is it that world as transformed by her into her novel? *Mememto Mori* seems to be concerned with showing how Pride is the mortal sin from which all the other six are derived. Gluttony, lust, anger, envy, avarice seem "natural" in the able-bodied, mentally active and ambitious; that is to say, the concrete temptations of pleasure and worldly satisfaction seem sufficient explanation for indulging in them. In showing us a group of persons who are senile in body and mind who continue to commit these sins long after committing them can bring any pleasure or happiness, Miss Spark seems to be saying that in all such sins there is an ego factor of willfulness and defiance to which considerations of pleasure or happiness or prudence are irrelevant. *The Ballad of Peckham Rye*, as I read it, is about the vulnerability of the inarticulate and semi-educated to manipulation by clearheaded evil; its villain Dougal Douglas is not a politician but, like Hitler, he is a mesmerist who makes those about him behave in a way they would never have thought of for themselves.

Dougal Douglas is only one example of a kind of character who turns up in most of her novels, someone who, judged by the moral norms of society, is thoroughly bad and, in a parabolic sense, is also a human instrument of the Devil whose name is Legion. In *The Comforters*, the Devil acts through a pious "church cat," Mrs Hogg; in *Mememto Mori* through a blackmailing housekeeper, Mrs Pettigrew. With their help he is able to cause a good deal of harm and suffering but, in each case, his power for evil is limited by the particularity of the human being he uses; each of them is a specialised tool, highly effective for certain purposes but useless for all others. Moreover, he can never succeed in making his human instruments sympathetic and lovable even to their victims. In the end everyone gets bored with them and their master has, so to speak, to fire them; Mrs Hogg gets drowned, Douglas ends up writing "cock-eyed books," Mrs Pettigrew retires with her ill-gotten gains to a South Kensington hotel.

I must confess that I opened my first novel by Miss Spark with some misgivings, having heard that she was a Catholic convert. Converts who write novels are apt to become overexcited by the discovery that there is a difference between sin and unethical conduct; they tend to make their Catholic characters, practising or lapsed, behave worse and suffer more than Protestants or unbelievers and, in particular, to take a ghoulish delight in the plight of Catholic lovers who, for one reason or another, must either part or be debarred from the altar. But Miss Spark, I am happy to say, shows none of this theological romanticism. In *The Comforters*, Laurence Manders, a lapsed

Catholic has been living with Caroline Rose, presumably a lapsed Protestant. She, however, has recently been converted to Catholicism and, consequently, has had to give up cohabiting with him. But Miss Spark carefully avoids making this situation melodramatic. Both accept the situation with good humor— if one is a Catholic, one has to put up with the Church's rules—continue to be good friends, and see each other without hysterical scenes. It is clear to the reader that they are made for each other. One supposes that Laurence had not married her earlier because he was uncertain of his feelings; afterwards it is Caroline who hesitates because she feels that, so long as Laurence remains a lapsed Catholic, complete mutual understanding will be impossible. At the end of the novel, their future is uncertain, but one feels that, probably, Laurence will return to the Faith and all end happily.

As I said at the beginning of this piece, it is not for a reviewer to make detailed critical judgements. I will merely say that I find Miss Spark's novels beautifully executed—she seems to know exactly what she is doing—funny, moving and like nobody else's.

The Mid-Century, May 1962

"The Geste Says this and the Man Who Was on the Field . . ."

In Parenthesis. By David Jones. Chilmark. $5.75.

Complicated as it is in detail, the dramatic structure of *In Parenthesis* is as simple as that of a good thriller. There are two acts. The four scenes of Act I take place in December 1915, the three of Act II in late June and early July 1916. For the very unmilitant hero, Private '01 John Ball, lover of poetry and a drill sergeant's despair, each is a rite of initiation. In the first, a natural civilian who has never been out of England or seen a shot fired in anger is initiated into "a folk-life, a people, a culture already developed, already venerable and roofed", the life of the front-line trenches during a period of military stalemate, when neither the Allies nor the Germans feel themselves in a position to launch a major offensive. In this act the excitement mounts steadily as Ball approaches the front line—on disembarking in France he sees his first German P.O.W., at the end of scene two, a shell falls fifty yards away, he hears his first bullets, sees his first corpse being lifted out of a waterlogged trench, and on Christmas Eve, his first night in the trenches, as he does sentry duty, he hears the rat in no-man's-land

> redeem the time of our uncharity, to sap his own amphibious paradise.
>   You can hear his carrying-parties rustle our corruptions through the night-weeds—contest the choicest morsels in his tiny conduits, bead-eyed feast on us; by a rule of his nature, at night-feast on the broken of us.

This is the emotional climax of the first act. Scene four opens at dawn; he sees the enemy front line for the first time and all is quiet. He learns that most of a soldier's life in the trenches is spent, not in combat, but in waiting under conditions of appalling physical discomfort, and that the most obvious fact about military life is its muddle and inefficiency. His company, for example, is marched away with picks and shovels for an engineering fatigue only to find, when it gets there, that there has been a mistake and they must march back again.

When Act II opens, Ball and his companions are already Old Soldiers, enjoying a rest period behind the lines. During the six months they have lost some officers and men on raiding patrols, but they have still not yet really experienced what their whole training has been for; they have not gone into battle. Now, however, the Allies have started an offensive—they can hear the roar of the bombardment. They are marched off to go into battle, but at the last minute there is a change in the orders and they are sent south to another part of the front. Then finally the hours of procrastination are over; they have to make a frontal attack on a strongly defended wood, half of them are killed and the drama ends with Private Ball, wounded in the foot, dragging himself to a position of relative safety to wait for the stretcher bearers.

In his preface, Mr David Jones speaks of the change that took place in the character of World War I shortly after the period with which his epic deals:

> The wholesale slaughter of the later years, the conscripted levies filling the gaps in every file of four, knocked the bottom out of the intimate, continuing, domestic life of small contingents of men, within whose structure Roland could find, and, for a reasonable while, enjoy, his Oliver. In the earlier months there was a certain attractive amateurishness, and elbow-room for idiosyncracy that connected one with a less exacting past.

In World War II, the mechanization, depersonalization and, above all, specialization were much greater, which leads one to wonder if any great work of art will come out of it. "The work of art", wrote Wittgenstein in his *Notebooks*, "is the object seen *sub specie aeternitatis*. The usual way of looking at things sees objects as it were from the midst of them, the view *sub specie aeternitatis* from outside, in such a way that they have the whole world as background. The object is seen *together with* space and time instead of *in* space and time." It was both the glory and the tragedy of the 1914–18 war that it was so recklessly prodigal with its human resources. It seems unlikely that, in the last war, a man with Mr Jones' intelligence, sensibility and learning, with the capacity, that is, to see it *sub specie aeternitatis*, would have been allowed to become one of

> the rifle strength
> the essential foot-mob, the platoon wallahs, the small men who
> permanently are with their sections, who have no qualifications,
> who look out surprisedly from a confusion of gear, who endure
>   all things.

The chances are, surely, that, on the results of psychological and intelligence tests, he would have found himself pounding a typewriter and unable, therefore, to look straight and closely into war's grim visage.

Mr Jones' purpose in writing *In Parenthesis* was not, he tells us to write a "War Book", though it happens to be concerned with war.

> We find ourselves in foot regiments. We search how we may see formal goodness in a life singularly inimical, hateful, to us.

> Two armies face and hold their crumbling *limites* intact. They're worthy of an intelligent song for all the stupidity of their contest. A boast for the dyke keepers, for the march wardens.

His problem, that is, was to present accurately certain historical and geographical events, yet in such a way that they possess a timeless and universal significance, to do for the British and the Germans what Homer did for the Greeks and the Trojans. For a twentieth-century writer, this is infinitely more difficult than it was for Homer. He cannot, for instance, introduce supernatural beings. Mr Jones happens to be a Roman Catholic, but that does not permit him to identify any particular event as an act of God. Then, for Homer, war can still be seen as a series of personal combats between aristocratic heroes whose sacred quality can be demonstrated by giving their family genealogies and the names of the cities they rule. But twentieth-century warfare is mass warfare; the actual fighting is not done by the great ones of this world, the generals or their staff-officers who,

> sometimes in quiet areas when the morning's aired, do appear—
> immaculate, bright-greaved ambassadors, to the spirits in prison;
> who sip their starry nectar from nickel flasks at noon.

but by those whose names are unknown in Society or to the Press,

> we are rash levied
> from Islington and Hackney
> and the purlieus of Walworth
> flashers from Surbiton
> men of the stock of Abraham
> from Bromley-by-Bow
> Anglo-Welsh from Queens Ferry
> rosary-wallahs from Pembrey Dock
> lightermen with a Norway darling
> from Greenland Stairs . . .
> Dynamite Dawes the old 'un and
> Diamond Phelps his batty

> from Santiago del Estero
> and Bulawayo respectively. . . .

Such people have no family trees; on the other hand, a modern poet like Mr Jones knows much more general history, real or legendary, than Homer, and it must be frankly admitted that he makes considerable demands upon the reader. Though his notes are generous and explicit, fully to appreciate his epic calls for a fairly thorough knowledge of Malory, the *Mabinogion, Y Gododdin* and the Offices of the Catholic Church. His physical descriptions and images present no problem:

> People spoke lightly to each other as they do on fine mornings in England, when the prospect pleases them—and they will insist it's such a lovely day—and Evelyn's operation is next Wednesday at eleven; Alex reckons it's not so serious, but old Mrs Pennyfather wags her ex-professional finger—she's seen too much of that sort of thing.

But his use of proper names may at first bewilder. For example:

> No one to care there for Aneiron Lewis spilled there
> who worshipped his ancestors like a Chink
> who sleeps in Arthur's lap
> who saw Olwen-trefoils some moonlighted night
> on precarious slats at Festubert,
> on narrow foothold on le Plantin marsh—
> more shaved he is to the bare bone
> than Yspaddadan Penkawr.
>   Properly organised chemists can let make more riving power
>   than ever Twrch Trwyth;
> more blistered he is than painted Troy Towers
> and unwholer, limb from limb, than any of them fallen at Catraeth
> or on the seaboard-down, by Salisbury,
> and no maker to contrive his funerary song.

I would advise the average reader to do as it is best to do when reading *The Divine Comedy*; read it first straight through without bothering about allusions which he does not "get", then a second time consulting the notes, after which, before a third reading, he might well do some homework on his own.

Q. "But *The Divine Comedy* is a masterpiece."

A. "Precisely. So is *In Parenthesis*."

In Parenthesis was first published in 1937. In 1952 Mr Jones published his second book *Anathemata*. I am glad to hear that we shall not have to wait until 1977 for an American edition of what is, very probably, the finest long poem written in English in this century, as it will be published here in the fall.

The Mid-Century, May 1962

The Justice of Dame Kind

The Senses of Animals and Men. By Lorus and Margery Milne.
Atheneum. $6.95.

I have never read a book or an article by a naturalist without feeling that the author must be a very nice person, an unusually superior specimen of the human race. By a naturalist, I mean someone who studies the ways of creatures in their natural habitat and, if he interferes at all, confines his interference to establishing a personal relation with them. Professors of animal psychology and behavioral scientists are a very different story. By such I mean those who subject animals to abnormal conditions of their own contriving, usually disagreeable, overcrowding them, providing them with mechanical surrogate mothers, giving them electric shocks, removing portions of their brains, etc., etc.—those, in other words, who perform experiments on animals which they would never dream of performing on themselves or their children. Even when the results of their researches are surprising and interesting, and often elementary common sense could have predicted their findings, I rarely read an article by one of them without feeling I should hate to sit next to him at dinner. His work may be necessary or valuable, but I have no more wish to know him socially than I wish to know the public executioner.

Mr and Mrs Milne, thank goodness, are naturalists who are interested in animals for their own sake. They are pleased and grateful, as we all should be, when knowledge gained by the study of animal behavior, anatomy, or physiology, turns out to have practical uses for man; but human appetite and ambition are not the prime motives for their investigations. *The Senses of Animals and Men* offers the reader a variety of pleasures. To begin with, it is full of curious facts. "Quiz" knowledge may not be a very exalted form of learning, but who does not enjoy acquiring some? I am delighted to have learned, for example, that male yellow fever mosquitoes are attracted most strongly by vibrations of 500 to 550 per second, that the song of the winter wren has 130 notes, that a blowfly's front feet are five times as sensitive to some sugars as its mouth, that the "ink" ejected by squids and octopuses is not just a protective visual screen, but also an anesthetic which dulls the senses of possible predators, that the male and female luna moth which to our eyes both look green are, in their own, a brunette and a blonde respectively.

More important, of course, are the general impressions and tentative conclusions which begin to emerge as the facts about individual species accumulate. There is a certain neo-Darwinian nightmare which haunts the minds of writers of science fiction, based on the assumption that any given species of life would, if it could, be the only kind of life in existence. In this science-fiction nightmare, some species, a fungus, say, undergoes a mutation which enormously increases its powers of growth or even endows it with intelligence. At once, absolute catastrophe threatens the earth, for unless the scientific hero can discover how to destroy it in time, it will obliterate every other kind of life on the planet. (What it would live on when it had is not explained.)

Any reader of the Milnes' book will realize that this terror is imaginary. Phrases like "the struggle for survival" and "the survival of the fittest" only have meaning when applied to the competition between members of the same species, and even there their application is limited. A creature is "fit" if it is adequately adapted to its particular world, and there are as many worlds as there are species. Each of these worlds must overlap with at least one other, usually with two—the world of that which it eats, and the world of that by which it is eaten. But with the vast majority of worlds in existence, it never comes into contact at all.

One of the most striking characteristics of Nature, as this book keeps demonstrating, is the extraordinary elaboration of the precautions she takes to ensure to each species its privacy. To many, for example, she allots their own frequency bands on the visual and aural spectrum; only such frequencies have "meaning" for them, and they have no meaning for others. The noise in our ears which to us means "a cricket," means nothing to crickets; what they attend to are the supersonic sounds which are inaudible to us, but which accompany what we hear.

Particularly striking are ways by which she guarantees privacy of sexual response and prevents random mating of different species. Some 700,000 species of insects have been identified, but each is able to breed true because the mating partners can only cooperate when each presses the other at definite spots sensitive to vibration, and the number and pattern of these areas differ from one species to the next. Occasionally mistakes are made:

> The female firefly perched on a leaf-tip can summon a passing mate by flashing at the correct time interval after he has broadcast a luminous message. Occasionally the flash from a leaf-tip invites the flying male to a female that is not of its own kind. She has winked too early or too late. Usually the ardent male pays for her mistake with his life, for a firefly that cannot become a suitor is merely a meal for her.

The question of survival is a mutual one. No species could survive unless its powers in one direction were balanced by a lack of power in another. If hawks, for example, were as prolific as mice, they would perish from starvation after they had exterminated their diet. Again, from time to time, the ecological balance is upset. In origin, the lamprey is a marine creature; in fresh water, which is more turbid and a poorer conductor of electricity than sea, it becomes too efficient at capturing fish. For the fishermen of the Great Lakes this has been a serious matter, the lamprey having ruined their business, but, in the long run, it would destroy the lamprey too.

Man, one might say, is the only creature who will not mind his own business, nor obey Nature's Game Laws. It is a commonplace that man has been able to develop as he has because, physically, he is an unspecialized, childish creature who has learned to master all environments precisely because he is perfectly adapted to none. After reading what Mr and Mrs Milne have to say about the human senses, however, I am surprised to learn how efficient our sensory endowment is. For a creature that is not by nature nocturnal, our night vision is remarkably good, and the sensitivity of our fingers to differences of touch much greater than is practically necessary. Even in the case of smell and taste, where our inferiority to many animals seems most obvious, we have not been prevented from developing an *haute cuisine*, in comparison with which any animal's taste in food seems crude. Our chief trouble, indeed, seems to be our deliberate abuse, either by neglect or overstimulus, of our inborn sensory gifts, and it is difficult to see a remedy without making changes in our life which seem economically impossible. In any modern city, a great deal of our energy has to be expended in *not* seeing, *not* hearing, *not* smelling. An inhabitant of New York who possessed the sensory acuteness of an African Bushman would very soon go mad.

As for the future, Mr and Mrs Milne hope for the best that somehow "every new understanding of the nervous mechanisms in animals is likely to lead to fresh expansion of man's own world." But they are naturalists and, therefore, nice people. I wish I could feel as sanguine, and that certain passing remarks they make did not haunt my mind more than they seem to haunt theirs.

The noises of civilization match progress. If their deafening sounds double again in intensity, as they have in the recent past, we may all need to wear protective ear stopples and give up trying to talk to one another.

Perhaps all these misunderstood senses will prove to operate through a "pleasure center" located recently in the brain, found by exploring the deeper portions with electrical probes. Direct stimulation of the pleasure center seems to substitute for food and sex and companionship, to the point where the scientists who discovered the center fear the consequences for mankind if unscrupulous people should find a way to market a self-stimulator reaching this region of the brain.

From such Huxley-Orwell nightmares may God protect us! At present, if we are not able ourselves to study fiddler-crabs, bats, megapodes, we can still read about such enchanting children of Nature in the books of those who, like Mr and Mrs Milne, have given their lives to it.

The Mid-Century, Midsummer 1962

Today's "Wonder-World" Needs Alice

In the evening of Friday, July 4, 1862, the Rev. Charles Lutwidge Dodgson, lecturer and tutor in mathematics at Christ Church, Oxford, wrote in his diary:

Atkinson brought over to my rooms some friends of his, a Mrs and Miss Peters, of whom I took photographs, and who afterward looked over my album and stayed to lunch. They then went off to the Museum, and Duckworth and I made an expedition *up* the river to Godstow with the three Liddells: we had tea on the bank there, and did not reach Christ Church again till quarter past 8, when we took them on to my rooms to see my collection of micro-photographs, and restored them to the Deanery just before 9.

"The three Liddells" were the daughters of the Dean of Christ Church, one of the authors of the famous Liddell & Scott Greek lexicon. Their names were Lorina Charlotte, Alice and Edith—nicknamed Matilda. Alice was ten years old.

This was by no means their first expedition together. For some years, they had been seeing a lot of one another. In the winter, they would go to Dodgson's rooms and sit on the sofa beside him while he told them stories, which he illustrated by pencil or ink drawings as he went along. Four or five times in the summer term he would take them out on the river, bringing with him a large basket of cakes and a kettle. On such occasions, Dodgson exchanged his clerical suit for white flannel trousers and his black top hat for a hard white straw hat. He always carried himself upright "as if he had swallowed a poker."

Outwardly there was nothing to distinguish the Godstow expedition from any other. And nobody today would remember that it ever took place but for what seems almost a pure accident. He had told the children many stories before, to which they had listened with delight, and they begged him to tell them another. This time, perhaps, he was in better story telling form than usual, for his friend Mr Duckworth was evidently impressed:

> I rowed *stroke* and he rowed *bow* . . . the story was actually composed and spoken *over my shoulder* for the benefit of Alice Liddell, who was acting as "cox" of our gig. I remember turning round and saying "Dodgson, is this an extempore romance of yours?" And he replied: "Yes, I'm inventing as we go along."

Anyway, this time Alice did what she had never done before—she asked him to write the story down. At first he said he would think about it, but she continued to pester him until, eventually, he gave his promise to do so. In his diary for November 13, he notes: "Began writing the fairy-tale for Alice—I hope to finish it by Christmas."

In fact, the text was finished on February 10, 1863, Tenniel's illustrations were not completed until September, 1864, and *Alice in Wonderland* was published by Macmillan in 1865 (which is also, incidentally, the year of the first performance of another masterpiece, Wagner's *Tristan und Isolde*).

These events are memorable because they reveal a kind of human being who is, I believe, extremely rare—a man of genius who, in regard to his genius, is without egoism. In other respects, Dodgson was neither selfless nor without vanity. As a member of Senior Common Room, he was a difficult colleague, forever complaining about some minor negligence or inconvenience. He held strong and conservative views upon almost every question affecting the College or the University, and the savagery of his polemical pamphlets like *The New Belfry of Christ Church* or *Twelve Months in a Curatorship* cannot have endeared him to his opponents.

He was proud of his photography, and justly so, for he was one of the best portrait photographers of the century. He had great hopes for his theory of Symbolic Logic, which is, I understand, more highly regarded today than it was at the time. As his diaries show, he also thought well of his little inventions—and he was always inventing something: a *memoria technica* for the logarithms of all primes under 100; a game of Arithmetical Croquet; a rule for finding the day of the week for any date of the month; a substitute for glue; a system of Proportional Representation; a method of controlling the carriage traffic at Covent Garden; an apparatus for making notes in the dark; an improved steering-gear for a tricycle. And he always sought publication for his light verse. But when it came to the one thing which he did superbly well, where he was without any rival—namely, telling stories to children—the thought of himself, of publication and immortal fame, never seems to have entered his head.

The two Alice books were no freak achievements. There are passages in letters to children where the writing is just as good. For example:

> It's so frightfully hot here that I've been almost too weak to hold a pen, and even if I had been able, there was no ink—it had all evaporated into a cloud of black steam, and in that state it has been floating about the room, inking the walls and ceiling till they're hardly fit to be seen: to-day, it is cooler, and a little has come back into the ink bottle in the form of black snow.

He went on telling impromptu stories to children all his life, which were never written down and, for all we know, may have surpassed the ones that were.

Though no human character can be explained away in terms of his upbringing or environment, it is legitimate to look for influencing factors. In Dodgson's case, one such factor may have been his position as the eldest boy—the son of a clergyman—in a large family: he had seven sisters and three brothers. By the time he was eleven he had made himself the family entertainer. He constructed a train, built out of a wheelbarrow, a barrel and a small truck, which conveyed passengers from one station in the rectory garden to another, and in the rules he drew up for this game, the Lewis Carroll imagination is already evident:

All passengers when upset are requested to lie still until picked up—as it is requisite that at least three trains should go over them, to entitle them to the attention of the doctor and assistants.

When a passenger has no money and still wants to go by train, he must stop at whatever station he happens to be at, and earn money—making tea for the stationmaster (who drinks it at all hours of the day and night) and grinding sand for the company (what use they make of it they are not bound to explain).

Two years later, he became the editor and chief contributor for a succession of family magazines, the last of which, *The Rectory Umbrella*, was still appearing after he had become an Oxford don and first printed the opening quatrain of "Jabberwocky."

Thus, at the beginning of his career as a writer, he was writing directly for an audience with which he was intimate and in which he had no literary rival. The average writer, at least today, has a very different experience. When he begins writing, he has no audience except himself; his first audience is likely to be one of rival, as yet unpublished, authors, and his only chance of acquiring an audience of his own is to get published, in little magazines or popular ones; and this audience consists of readers whom he does not know personally.

It seems clear that what, as an imaginative creator, Dodgson valued most was the immediate and intimate response of his audience, and its undivided attention (hence, perhaps, his passion for the theatre). His writings for adults, no less than his children's stories, are for the "family"—Oxford to him was another and larger rectory. Even in the only company with whom he felt so completely at home that his stammer disappeared, the company of little girls, he preferred to see them singly. As he wrote to one mother:

> Would you kindly tell me if I may reckon *your* girls as invitable to tea, or dinner, singly. I know of cases where they are invitable in sets only (like the circulating-library novels), and such friendships I don't think worth going on with. I don't think anyone knows what girl-nature *is*, who has only seen them in the presence of their mothers or sisters.

Many guesses, plausible and implausible, have been made as to the historical origins of the characters and events in the Alice books, but one may be sure that many allusions which were apparent to the Liddell children are now irrecoverable. When he told a story, it was always for a particular child. One of them, not Alice, records:

> One thing that made his stories particularly charming to a child was that he often took his cue from her remarks—a question would set him off on quite a new trail of ideas, so that one felt one had somehow helped to make the story, and it seemed a personal possession.

Very few writers, I believe however much they desire fame for their books, enjoy being a public figure who is recognized on the street by strangers, but Dodgson hated publicity more than most. He refused to allow any picture of himself to appear—"Nothing would be more unpleasant for me than to have my face known to strangers"—and he gave orders that any letters addressed to L. Carroll, Christ Church, Oxford, were to be returned to the sender with the endorsement "not known."

But thanks to Alice Liddell's importunity, and luckily for us, the intimate narrator became a world famous author. As usually happens, with a masterpiece, the initial critical reception of *Alice in Wonderland* was mixed. *The Illustrated London News* and *The Pall Mall Gazette* liked it; *The Spectator*, though generally approving, condemned the Mad Hatter's tea party; *The Atheneum* thought it a "stiff, overwrought story," and *The Illustrated Times*, while conceding that the author possessed a fertile imagination, declared that Alice's adventures "are too extravagantly absurd to produce more diversion than disappointment and irritation."

When, seven years later, *Through the Looking-Glass* appeared, the critics knew, from the enormous public success of its predecessor, that it must be good—though I can think of no more unlikely literary comparison than that of Henry Kingsley, who wrote: "This is the finest thing we have had since *Martin Chuzzlewit*."

And the book's fame has continued to grow. I have always thought one might learn much about the cultural history of a country by going through the speeches made by its public men over a certain period, in legislatures, in law courts and at official banquets, and making a list of the books quoted from without attribution. So far as Great Britain is concerned, I strongly suspect that, for the past fifty years, the two Alice books and *The Hunting of the Snark* have headed it.

How do American readers react? Though nearly all the Americans I know personally loved Lewis Carroll as children, they may not be representative of American taste in general. Certainly, in every American book read by children—from *Huckleberry Finn* to the *Oz* books—which I have come across, nothing could be more remote from their worlds than the world of Alice.

The American child-hero—are there any American child-heroines?—is a Noble Savage, an anarchist and, even when he reflects, predominantly concerned with movement and action. He may do almost anything except sit still. His heroic virtue—that is to say, his superiority to adults—lies in his freedom from conventional ways of thinking and acting: *all* social habits, from manners to creeds, are regarded as false or hypocritical or both. All Emperors are really naked. Alice, surely, must come to the average American as a shock.

To begin with, she is a "lady." When, puzzled by the novelty of Wonderland, she asks herself if she could have changed into some other child, she is quite certain what sort of child she does *not* want to be:

"I'm sure I can't be Mabel, for I know all sorts of things, and she, oh, she knows such a very little. . . . I must be Mabel after all, and I shall have to go and live in that poky little house, and have next to no toys to play with. . . . No, I've made up my mind about it: if I'm Mabel, I'll stay down here."

Among grown-ups, she knows the difference between servants and mistresses:

"He took me for his housemaid," she said to herself as she ran. "How surprised he'll be when he finds out who I am."
"The governess would never think of excusing me lessons for that. If she couldn't remember my name, she'd call me 'Miss' as the servants do."

And when the Red Queen advises her: "Speak in French when you can't think of the English for a thing—turn out your toes as you walk—and remember who you are!"—she knows that the answer to the question, "Who am I?" is really: "I am Alice Liddell, daughter of the Dean of Christ Church."

What is most likely to bewilder an American child, however, is not Alice's class-consciousness, which is easy to miss, but the peculiar relation of children and grown-ups to law and social manners. It is the child-heroine Alice who is invariably reasonable, self-controlled and polite, while all the other inhabitants, human or animal, of Wonderland and the Looking-Glass are unsocial eccentrics—at the mercy of their passions and extremely bad-mannered, like the Queen of Hearts, the Duchess, the Hatter and Humpty Dumpty, or grotesquely incompetent, like the White Queen and the White Knight.

What Alice finds so extraordinary about the people and events in these worlds is the anarchy which she is forever trying to make sense and order out of. In both books, games play an important role. The whole structure of *Alice Through the Looking-Glass* is based on chess, and the Queen of Hearts' favorite pastime is croquet—both of them games which Alice knows how to play. To play a game, it is essential that the players know and obey its rules, and are skillful enough to do the right or reasonable thing at least half the time. Anarchy and incompetence are incompatible with play.

Croquet played with hedgehogs, flamingos and soldiers instead of the conventional balls, mallets and hoops is conceivable, provided that they are willing to imitate the behavior of these inanimate objects, but, in Wonderland, they behave as they choose and the game is impossible to play.

In the Looking-Glass world, the problem is different. It is not, like Wonderland, a place of complete anarchy where everybody says and does whatever comes into his head, but a completely determined world without choice. Tweedledum and Tweedledee, the Lion and the Unicorn, the Red Knight and the White, must fight at regular intervals, irrespective of their feelings. In Wonderland, Alice has to adjust herself to a life without laws; in Looking-

Glass Land, to one governed by laws to which she is unaccustomed. She has to learn, for example, to walk away from a place in order to reach it, or to run fast in order to remain where she is. In Wonderland, she is the only person with self-control; in Looking-Glass Land, the only competent one. But for the way she plays a pawn, one feels that the game of chess would never be completed.

In both worlds, one of the most important and powerful characters is not a person but the English language. Alice, who had hitherto supposed that words were passive objects, discovers that they have a life and will of their own. When she tries to remember poems she has learned, new lines come into her head unbidden and, when she thinks she knows what a word means, it turns out to mean something else.

> "And so these three little sisters—they were learning to draw, you know."
> "What did they draw?"
> "Treacle—from *a treacle well*."
> "But they were in the well."
> "Of course they were: well in." . . .

> "How old did you say you were?"
> "Seven years and six months."
> "Wrong! You never said a word like it!" . . .

> "You take some flour."
> "Where do you pick the flower? In a garden or in the hedges?"
> "Well, is isn't *picked* at all: it's *ground*."
> "How many acres of ground?"

Nothing, surely, could be more remote from the American image of the pioneering, hunting, pre-political hero than this preoccupation with language. It is the concern of the solitary thinker, for language is the mother of thought, and of the politician—in the Greek sense—for speech is the medium by which we disclose ourselves to others. The American hero is neither.

Both of Alice's "dreams" end in a state of developing chaos from which she wakes just in time before they can become nightmares:

> At this the whole pack rose up in the air, and came flying down upon her; she gave a little scream, half of fright and half of anger, and tried to beat them off, and found herself lying on the bank with her head in the lap of her sister.

> Already several of the guests were lying down in the dishes, and the soup ladle was walking up the table towards Alice's chair, and beckoning to her impatiently to get out of its way.
> "I can't stand this any longer!" she cried, as she jumped up and seized

the table-cloth with both hands: one good pull, and plates, dishes, guests and candles came crashing down together in a heap on the floor.

Wonderland and Looking-Glass Land are fun to visit but no places to live in. Even when she is there, Alice can ask herself with some nostalgia "if anything would ever happen in a natural way again," and by "natural" she means the opposite of what Rousseau would mean. She means peaceful civilized society.

There are good books which are only for adults, because their comprehension presupposes adult experiences, but there are no good books which are only for children. A child who enjoys the Alice books will continue to enjoy them when he or she is grown up, though his "reading" of what they mean will probably change. In assessing their value, there are two questions one can ask: first, what insight do they provide as to how the world appears to a child?; and, second, to what extent is the world really like that?

According to Lewis Carroll, what a child desires before anything else is that the world in which he finds himself should make sense. It is not the commands and prohibitions, as such, which adults impose that the child resents, but rather that he cannot perceive any law linking one command to another in a consistent pattern.

The child is told, for example, that he must not do such-and-such, and then sees adults doing precisely that. This occurs especially often in the realm of social manners. In well-bred society, people treat each other with courtesy but, in trying to teach their children to be polite, their method of instruction is often that of a drill sergeant. Without realizing it, adults can be rude to children in ways which, if they were dealing with one of their own kind, would get them knocked down. How many children, when they are silenced with the command, "Speak when you're spoken to!", must have longed to retort as Alice does:

> "But if everybody obeyed that rule, and if you only spoke when you were spoken to, and the other person always waited for *you* to begin, you see that nobody would ever say anything."

It would be an exaggeration to say that children see adults as they really are, but, like servants, they see them at moments when they are not concerned with making a favorable impression.

As everybody knows, Dodgson's Muse was incarnated in a succession of girls between the ages of eight and eleven. Little boys he feared and disliked: they were grubby and noisy and broke things. Most adults he found insensitive. At the age of twenty-four, he wrote in his diary:

> I think that the character of most that I meet is merely refined animal. How few seem to care for the only subjects of real interest in life!

Naturally, most of his "child-friends" came from middle or upper middle class English homes. He mentions having met one American child and the encounter was not a success:

> Lily Alice Godfrey, from New York: aged 8; but talked like a girl of 15 or 16, and declined to be kissed on wishing good-by, on the ground that she "never kissed gentlemen". . . . I fear it is true that there are no children in America.

And the children he understood best were the quiet and imaginative ones. Thus Irene Vanbrugh, who must have been going through a tomboy phase when she met him, says:

> He had a deep love for children, though I am inclined to think not such a great understanding of them. . . . His great delight was to teach me his Game of Logic. Dare I say this made the evening rather long, when the band was playing outside on the parade, and the moon shining on the sea?

The question for an adult reader of Lewis Carroll, however, is not the author's psychological peculiarities, but the validity of his heroine. Is Alice, that is to say, an adequate symbol for what every human being should try to be like?

I am inclined to answer yes. A girl of eleven (or a boy of twelve) who comes from a good home—a home, that is, where she has known both love and discipline and where the life of the mind is taken seriously but not solemnly—can be a most remarkable creature. No longer a baby, she has learned self-control, acquired a sense of her identity and can think logically without ceasing to be imaginative. She does not know, of course, that her sense of identity has been too easily won—the gift of her parents rather than her own doing—and that she is soon going to lose it, first in the *Sturm und Drang* of adolescence and then, when she enters the adult social world, in anxieties over money and status.

But one cannot meet a girl or a boy of this kind without feeling that what she or he is—by luck and momentarily—is what, after many years and countless follies and errors, one would like, in the end, to become.

The New York Times Magazine, 1 July 1962

Strachey's Cry

The Strangled Cry. By John Strachey. Bodley Head, 21s.

I am neither old enough nor young enough to write an objective review of this book. The experiences and reactions of any English-born middle-class intellectual of my generation are so similar to Mr Strachey's that, as I read, I keep stopping to engage in an imaginary dialogue with the author; instead of assessing his book, I find myself trying to rewrite it.

The earliest in date of the articles in this collection are four pieces of reportage about his experiences during the war, as a Warden during the London Blitz, as a passenger on a troop-ship which is torpedoed but manages to limp to port, and as an observer on a bomber sent out to lay mines in the ocean. These, for their clarity and vividness—the reader forgets the narrator because he becomes him—would be remarkable whoever had written them, but one is doubly impressed when one recalls that the author is by profession, not a novelist, but a politician and political philosopher. Primarily concerned as he must be with people in the mass and general ideas, the occupational vice of the politician is a blindness or indifference to the single person and the minor historical detail. It is astounding and heartening to find one who can so successfully switch from the macroscopic to the microscopic view. A politician with the humility to say:

> We don't understand much of what's happening to us, even when it's happening. We simply don't get it. The Man in the modern world, the blind bomber in cloud, the blunt-nosed fish moving through the opaque waters. None of us gets it. No one knows what it's all about. . . .

can be assured of my vote.

Of the pieces in the section entitled "People," one of them ("John Kenneth Galbraith") is not really about the man but a review of his book, *The Affluent Society*, and properly belongs among the books discussed in the first section. Of the others, the most interesting, to me at least, are those on Rathenau and Schacht. Mr Strachey considers it just possible that, had he not been assassinated, Rathenau, whose "immense business experience and splendid mind allowed him to see the mechanics of the economy almost perfectly" and "understood excellently what ought to be done to make the last stage of German capitalism work by progressively modifying its nature," might have enabled the Weimar Republic to meet the shock of the Depression without foundering. As it was, few regretted his death. The German nationalists hated him as an internationally-minded Jewish intellectual, and the German trade union leaders feared him as a big industrialist who spoke of Socialism with patronising contempt. (For the failure of Rathenau and German Labour to come to an understanding, some of the blame was due to Labour.) Rathenau's defect, which cost him his life, was that he had no understanding of the art of political persuasion; as an intellectual, he probably thought it vulgar. (Even if he did, as Mr Strachey claims, have a hero-worship for the blond Aryan, I cannot see that it influenced his political ideas.) The professional politicians who succeeded him, on the other hand, had no understanding of economics and pursued a deflationary policy "exactly calculated to intensify to the uttermost degree the catastrophic consequences of

the world slump. . . ." In view of the appalling crimes committed by the
Nazis, the fact that Hitler came to power with at least the consent of the majority of Germans and, by 1935, had won their enthusiastic support, tempts
us to think of them as a people who must be wicked by nature. It is salutary,
therefore, to be reminded by Mr Strachey that the criminals restored to
them jobs, wages, and security, when the decent democrats "had left them to
starve and rot." He considers that the economic success of the Nazis was due
almost entirely to their willingness to follow the advice of Dr Schacht.
Schacht was not a very nice man, maybe, but to say "The stain which will for
ever discolour his name is that he put his vast abilities at the service of the
Nazis" seems to me too glib a condemnation. Few people in history have
found themselves in his position of being the only man, apparently, who
knows what economic measures to take in order to save his country from
ruin. Suppose I were such a man. The government in power refuses to listen
to me and the chaos grows daily worse. A party, led by persons whom I know
to be crooks, seizes power and asks me to take charge of the economy for
them. What ought my answer to be? If I say No, I condemn my fellow-
countrymen to go on starving: if I say Yes, I shall, however unwillingly, become an accomplice, in whatever crimes the crooks commit. Frankly, I do
not know the answer. No doubt Schacht, who, whatever his faults, was neither a Nazi nor a warmonger, told himself, like many Germans more decent
than he, that the Nazi leaders were too insane to last long and would soon be
overthrown, probably by the Army, and replaced by a respectable regime. I
hesitate to damn him utterly for having guessed wrong. Again I am a little
surprised, when he is describing the war-time use of slave labour by I.G. Far-
ben, that a thinker as clear-headed and just as Mr Strachey should write:

> Such is the end towards which latter-day capitalism, in a dictatorial envi-
> ronment and bereft of all democratic countervailing forces, inevitably
> drives.

Why capitalism? Why inevitably? Under Stalin, Communist Russia had just
as many slaves and treated them no better. Any tyranny, whatever its ideology, has and will do such things, not inevitably, but if it should happen to be
profitable and the moral climate (even dictators can have consciences)
should permit it.

The most important section of the book is, of course, the first from which
it takes its title. In this Mr Strachey examines four examples of what he calls
the literature of reaction, Koestler's *Darkness at Noon*, Orwell's *Nineteen-Eighty-
Four*, Chambers' *Witness*, and Pasternak's *Dr Zhivago*.

The Central European and the American had been for many years active
members of the Communist Party, the Englishman was an independent radical who had been badly wounded in the Spanish Civil War; and their books
are the outcome of their disillusionment with Communism when they dis-

covered what its theories led to in practice. In Orwell's case, I'm sorry Mr Strachey did not select *Homage to Catalonia* instead of *Nineteen-Eighty-Four*; artistically, it is the better book, I believe, and, since it is a direct reportage of how the Communists in Spain actually behaved—to have written and published it when he did was an act of singular moral courage—it cannot be explained away, as an imaginary future world always can, as the product of the author's private neurasthenia. Pasternak's position is quite different. Though he certainly welcomed the Revolution and wanted it to succeed, he was never at any time active politically, but he, alone of the four, had first-hand experience, extending over three-and-a-half decades of Communism in its home country.

As their critic, Mr Strachey has the authority, which most of us lack, of having been all his adult life a practising politician who knows from the inside how policy is made and carried out. He begins by telling us that, in calling these four books reactionary, he does not mean anything pejorative but, on balance, his verdict is, I think, adverse. He feels that they condemn, not merely Marxist or totalitarian politics, but all political activity as such, and by implication, therefore, impugn his own honesty and integrity. How much truth is there in this? Obviously none of them was a madman who fancied that social life in a modern society would be possible without a government of some kind, or that there is no difference between being governed by men like Mr Strachey and men like Himmler, nor, if they were alive, would any of them, I believe, not even Chambers, vote for the extreme Right. On the other hand, all of them regard two beliefs as the deadly enemies of civilisation, the Marxist belief that politics can be a science, and a much older belief, first formulated by Plato, and really inconsistent with the first, that the politician is a kind of artist who moulds society into a good shape as the potter moulds clay. Now, I am convinced that Mr Strachey does not really hold either of these beliefs, but, occasionally he uses language which would suggest to anyone who knew nothing about his career that he did. Politics cannot be a science because, in politics, theory and practice cannot be separated, and the sciences depend upon their separation. The scientist frames a hypothesis and devises an experiment to test it; if the experiment gives a negative result, he knows his hypothesis was wrong and that, however reluctantly, he must abandon it. Only when experiment has confirmed his hypothesis will he begin to consider any practical applications. He can afford to wait for the truth. Since the actual subjects of his experiments have no will of their own, he does not have to take any subjective factor into consideration. The situation of the politician is utterly different. He cannot try out a hypothesis under laboratory conditions, but must immediately apply it to a historical situation and upon human beings who not only have wills and opinions of their own but can also change them. Consequently, no result at any moment can prove beyond doubt that he is mistaken. I hold the theory, let us say, that farmers will be happier and food production increased if agriculture is collectivised. I collectivise it. The farmers are obviously rebellious and food production drops. Does this prove me mistaken? Not necessarily. I can always argue that the failure is due to the malice and stupidity of the farmers and that if I continue with the experiment long enough I shall be proved right. Empirical politics must be kept in bounds by democratic institutions which leave it up to the subjects of the experiment to say whether it shall be tried and to stop if they dislike it because, in politics, there is a distinction, unknown in science, between Truth and Justice. Certain ideas of the Labour Party, for example, may have been true in 1929, but they did not become just until 1945.

The Platonic notion of the politician as a kind of artist has even more disastrous consequences. The poet, painter, or musician works with inanimate material and is totally responsible for the result; every decision, every act is his. The politician who thinks of his activity as analogous must inevitably end up believing that every aspect of human life is a political matter and his concern.

It is against the intrusion of politicians upon matters which are not properly their concern, surely, that Pasternak's polemic is directed. He asserts that in the lives of nearly all human beings, their personal relations, with their lovers, their wives and husbands, their children, their friends, are of immense importance, and that such relations are pre-political. He also asserts that, for those who are fortunate enough to discover a vocation, fidelity to it is also of supreme importance. His hero happens to be a poet, but he could equally well have been a biochemist or a pigeon fancier. In other words, most human beings, including many of the most gifted, are not professional politicians, which is just as well for the latter because, if politics were the primary concern of all, government would be impossible. If Pasternak is "anti-political," it is only because, in the particular society in which he lived, it was the politician who demanded the final word on every subject. Other kinds of professionals have and will make this claim. In thirteenth-century Europe it was the theologian; in the United States at the moment it may be the consultant psychologist to the Public Relations industry.

Mr Strachey's second charge against these books is that they represent a reaction "against five hundred years of rationalism and empiricism; against, in short, the enlightenment." He feels they are dangerously close to those— I wish he had named them—

> who point to the mysteries in order to dissuade us from even attempting to apply reason to society . . . those who have deserted, whether they know it or intend it, and whether their inner motive be weariness, class-prejudice, or simply despair, to the enemies of civilised life.

Again, while I know that Mr Strachey is not a naive nineteenth-century materialist of the Helmholz type, his language is occasionally curiously old-fashioned. He assumes that Christians believe in "the supernatural." Whom has he asked? I have never myself met a Christian who would say that he did. He would say, of course, and most respectable modern scientists would agree with him, that the knowledge of Nature acquirable by the sciences is not exhaustive, that there are important experiences which are comprehensible enough but only to another kind of knowing.

> Is it not possible to conceive of a science which re-embraced, as did the science of the ancient world, at its own level of complexity, everything that we to-day think of as "not science"? If so, it would no doubt, become our aesthetic, our ethic, our religion.

Has Mr Strachey showed this sentence to a professional scientist? The "science" of the ancient world failed to get very far precisely because it was a hodge-podge of empirical observations, poetry, and theology; science only began to have its triumphs when it abandoned the ambition to embrace everything and limited itself to certain kinds of fact and certain methodological procedures. Far from tending towards a unity, it has continued to split up more and more into different sciences.

Mr Strachey is, of course, absolutely right when he says it is high time people of his and my generation gave up wringing their hands over how cruelly Communism deceived them, and turned their attention to the actual social-political problems which now confront England and the United States, some of the most pressing of which are described in Professor Galbraith's *The Affluent Society*. How, for instance, are we to escape from the madness of consumption for consumption's sake which modern technology seems to impose upon us and which, within a few years, may become a problem for Russia too? The Russians may be immune to the American obsession with personal enrichment, but they show every sign of sharing our materialism and our idolatry of production. One political danger in the States—I cannot speak for Great Britain—is the opposite of Russia's; our professional politicians, our Senators and Congressmen, have too little power. It is very difficult for the average citizen in the States not to become politically apathetic because one has the feeling that the people or groups of people with the real power to decide policy cannot be influenced by one's vote. One does not even know their names.

The Senate and Congress make me think of McCarthy and another little bone I have to pick with Mr Strachey and many English labour-liberals when they write about the brief era of that unappetising fellow. Discreditable as it was, I know, having lived through it, that we did not feel we were living under a reign of terror. The atmosphere in Washington was, indeed, deplorable, and in certain limited sectors, cases of gross injustice occurred, but almost without exception the Universities refused to be cowed, and I never met one person during that period who was afraid to say what he thought about anything. To say that McCarthy "did enormous damage to the vigour, freedom, and boldness of American thought and culture" is nonsense. On the other hand, I am sorry to say that what depressed me most at the time was the behaviour of many self-styled liberals. To begin with, their refusal to look at the Hiss case objectively, their willingness to repeat and invent any vileness about Chambers was revolting. For those who, when subpoenaed to testify before Congressional Committees, admitted that they had been Communists but then risked being sent to prison for contempt by refusing to name others, I have the greatest admiration. But I have no sympathy whatsoever with those—and they were the majority—who, taking refuge behind the Fifth Amendment, refused to say what they had been. The general public concluded from their refusal, probably rightly, that they had been Communists; it also concluded, which was certainly false but exactly what McCarthy wanted us to believe, that anyone who had been a Communist or even a fellow-traveller had been engaged in a criminal conspiracy.

If I have spent so much time raising picayune points, it is partly Mr Strachey's fault for writing a book which I so much enjoyed reading. The matter is so interesting and it was obviously written by such a nice man.

P.S.—A political parable. What finally sank McCarthy with the American public was television. Those who watch serials know that the hero is "clean-cut," preferably blond, and that the villain has a heavy beard. When they saw McCarthy and the representatives of the Army on the screen together, they immediately knew what was what.

Encounter, October 1962

Are the English Europeans?*
The Island and the Continent

I am neither an historian nor a politician, neither a scientist nor a philosopher. I am only a poet, and a poet's thinking is known to be misguided, partial, and subjective. Therefore, so that you can judge for yourself what I have to say, it will be useful for me to begin with a few autobiographical details. I come from a middle-class family with intellectual interests. My father was a doctor who had acquired a degree in classical philology before he turned to medicine. My mother had a university diploma at a time when this was rather uncommon for a woman. Both my grandfathers were Anglican clergymen. Sixteen years ago, I became an American citizen, and my perma-

---

* [Retranslated for this edition from Peter Stadelmayer's German translation of Auden's lost original. Auden reused part of his original English text in "England & Europe" (p. 441).]

nent home is New York; I also own a small house near Vienna where I spend my summers. Obviously I remain, despite all this, a true Englishman. I am now fifty-five, which means that at the time of my birth there was still silence in the world and newspapers had no photographs, and that in our present-day Autobahn-Television-Espresso culture I am an old fogey. When I talk to you now about England and Europe, therefore, you should not forget that it is an English middle-class old fogey who is speaking.

Every language has certain untranslatable words and expressions; in German for example "*Schadenfreude*", "*Kitsch*" and "*schöngeistig*". In English—in British English, that is, not in American English—we have the noun "abroad" and the verb "to-go-abroad". In my German dictionary these are defined as "*im Ausland*" and "*ins Ausland gehen*". This is incorrect. When I travel to America or India or Australia, for example, I don't go "abroad" but "overseas". "Abroad" means crossing the Channel, and for every Englishman, the terms "foreign countries" and "Europe" are synonymous. The Englishman may happily travel abroad, he may even prefer to live there rather than in the land of his birth, but he none the less shares the feelings of the late King George VI, who is reported to have said—this cannot be translated—"Abroad is bloody" (roughly, "I don't give a damn about Europe", or "I couldn't care less about Europe"). In any case, for the English, Europe is a different world from England.

If I shut my eyes and say the word *Europe* to myself, the various images which it conjures up have one thing in common: they could not be conjured up by the word *England*. Let me give a few of them as they occur to me, without trying to arrange them in a logical order. Europe is the place:

(1) where the fields are not divided from each other by hedges, the farms are mostly family farms, and the landless farm-hand is a rarity.
(2) where there is a definite social class, the Peasants, conscious of itself as such and often wielding considerable political power.
(3) where very few of the aristocracy take an active part in public and political life.
(4) where the political Liberals and the Socialist Left are anti-clerical, and, for the most part, atheistic.
(5) where the village schoolmaster and the village doctor are usually on the political left.
(6) where shops are open on Sundays and one can get a drink at any hour.
(7) where vegetables are not thoroughly overcooked. I should remark here that English cuisine is not quite so horrible as so many jokes about it make it out to be, but it is *sui generis*. French, Italian, German and Spanish cuisines all differ from each other, but even the most provincial French, Italian, German or Spanish tourist who visits a neighboring

country doesn't spend all his time grumbling about the strangeness, inedibility and the probable unwholesomeness of the food.

(8) where the only comfortable article of furniture is the double-bed.

(9) where hotel bed-rooms are equipped with bidets.

(10) where nothing is wasted. The classical vice of avarice and the miser à la Balzac can still be found.

(11) where outside the big cities the shops never have proper wrapping paper.

(12) where nationals as well as foreigners must carry identification papers and produce them when they register in a hotel.

(13) where in Jurisprudence, codified law plays a much greater role than case law.

(14) where intellectual life has two centres: the Café, exclusively male, where artists of all kinds start "movements" and issue manifestos, and the Salon, presided over by a woman.

(15) where when two educated people meet who do not know the other's language, they talk French.

(16) where if there are any Protestants, they are in the minority. The Protestant countries—Scandinavia, Holland, Prussia, etc.—do not quite belong to Europe. If we consider their inhabitants to be Europeans, then to Europe they are, as the Viennese say, *Tschuschen* [coarse, contemptible outlanders].

Since I am a writer, the word *Europe* conjures up, in addition to such images, certain sacred names. Here are a few of mine: Lichtenberg, Hölderlin, Nietzsche, Nestroy, Rimbaud, Christian Morgenstern, Rilke, Valéry, Kafka, Karl Kraus, Rudolf Kassner. You will notice that, in this list, German names predominate. No Englishman falls in love with Europe as a whole; he falls in love with a particular landscape or city or language. It has been said that nobody ever fell in love with Bulgaria, but I have met a young Englishman who did. Like all lovers, we are prejudiced: one may love French or Italian or Spanish, but one cannot love three equally.

I am one of those—there are not many of us—who fell in love with the German language. I speak it very badly, partly because I have the poet's superstitious fear that the moment when I completely mastered a foreign language I would lose all feeling for my own. I probably also agree completely with Lichtenberg when he says: "To learn to speak a foreign language well, and to speak in company with the real accent of the natives, one must not only have memory and an ear but must also, to some degree, be a bit of a dandy."

Where does my love of the German language originate? Now, when I went down from Oxford in 1928, my parents offered me a year abroad in Europe. For the generation of English intellectuals immediately preceding mine, the only culture that counted was French culture. I was bored with hearing about it, and, therefore, determined that wherever I might go, it would not be to Paris. Where then? Rome? No; Mussolini and fascism made that impossible. Berlin? That was an idea! Why not? I knew no German and hardly any German literature, but, then nobody else I knew did either. Berlin was an unexplored city and might turn out to be fun. I may also have had an unconscious bias in favor of Germany because, when I was a little boy in prep-school during the First World War, if I took an extra slice of bread and margarine, some master was sure to say: "I see, Auden, you want the Huns to win"—thus establishing in my mind an association between Germany and forbidden pleasures. The political instruction of the young is a risky undertaking.

My rather frivolous decision proved to be extraordinarily fortunate, for two reasons. First, as you know, Berlin in the late twenties and until 1933 was culturally a very exciting city. Furthermore, it opened my eyes to the precarious condition of culture in our century. Even the oldest readers of this essay cannot imagine how secure the English middle class still felt in the twenties. Despite the Great War, we could not believe that anything really serious had happened. For example, I never read a newspaper until I went to Berlin. In Berlin, however, I understood for the first time that something irrevocable had happened, that the foundations had been shaken, and that during my lifetime the world would never again be the same secure place it had been in my early childhood.

What I experienced at that time were the final death throes of Europe as I understand that word. To put it briefly, Europe, to me, is, or rather was, the area dominated by a consciousness of the French Revolution, and roughly corresponds geographically to the Napoleonic Empire. It was the product of the French revolutionary thrust and the counter-revolutionary riposte which this provoked. Without the latter, Europe would be a political entity under the political dominance of France, instead of a cultural entity dominated by French culture. Napoleon is balanced by Metternich, and, as cultural centres, Paris by Vienna. Before 1786, there was no Europe, and the Russian Revolution of 1917 heralded its decease.

As for the things I want to discuss in greater detail, I must unfortunately bore the reader with a bit of amateur history.

Before Luther, Calvin and the discovery of the Americas, people in the west thought in terms of Christianity and paganism. The fact that the borders of Christendom happened to coincide more or less with the peninsula that we call Europe did not mean that the people of the Middle Ages thought of themselves as Europeans. They thought in terms of their locality, their feudal lords, and their common beliefs. Consequently England was a part of Christendom in a way that it never became a part of Europe.

The Sixteenth Century is marked by the division of the west into Protestantism and Catholicism, and by the transformation of the feudal dominions into absolute monarchies. The political rivalries and differences in belief were both too great for a sense of Europe like the feudal one to arise.

In order for the peoples of the geographical unit Europe to achieve a common consciousness, and to create the cultural unit that I understand by the word Europe, a new secular gospel and a new secular hero were required. The French provided both: *Liberté, Egalité, Fraternité* was the gospel; Figaro, the low-born barber who through his native wit and natural talent shows himself superior to the blue-blooded Count, was the hero.

England played an important role in the Napoleonic wars because her national security required Napoleon's defeat. However, apart from a few individuals like Burke, she scarcely thought about the ideology of the French revolution, because she had already gone through a revolution of her own. In the year 1786, almost every European country was still ruled by an absolute monarch. In England, however, absolutism had been brought to an end in 1649 with the execution of Charles I. In contrast to the execution of Louis XVI, those who performed it did not regard it as a revolutionary breach with the past. It seemed to them instead a reaffirmation of the medieval idea that the sovereign is not above but is subject to Natural Law. One could say that Charles I had to pay with his life for his ancestor Henry VIII's having executed in 1535 Sir Thomas More who as Lord Chancellor was the Keeper of the King's Conscience. The English revolution that began with the great Civil War of 1642 through 1646 lasted until the exile of James II in 1688, an event known to us as the Glorious Revolution.

The word Revolution here means something different from the downfall of the old and the beginning of the new, as in the French or Russian Revolution; it is a metaphor from astronomy meaning a restoration of proper balance. Under Cromwell's Protectorate, the English discovered that the dangers of arbitrary power are not necessarily removed by the abolition of the crown, that the claims of religious sects to know by divine inspiration what the good life should be, and the consequent right to impose it on the godless, represented as great a threat to freedom as the Divine Right of Kings. The monarchy was therefore restored, but when James II wanted to reign as an absolute monarch he was quickly sent packing, and the Whig landowners imported a dynasty, first from Holland and later, after the death of Queen Anne, from Hanover. Because these kings could not speak English—even Edward VII, who died in 1910, spoke English with a German accent—political power could not be concentrated in the Palace, but was to be found in Parliament and the great country estates. It is a simplification, though not an overly crude one, to say that England was ruled between 1688 and 1914 by the rich—first by the rich landowners, joined later, after the Industrial Revolution, by the bankers and big businessmen.

The destruction of the peasantry in England happened gradually. It started in the Fifteenth Century, when thousands of farmers were dispossessed to turn farmland into sheep-pastures. It progressed with the enclosures of the Eighteenth Century, and the final blow was the invention of machinery, which put an end to cottage industry and forced home workers into the factories.

I said a moment ago that one of the differences between England and Europe that I particularly noticed was that the aristocracy in Europe took little part in public life. It would not be quite correct to claim that it did in England; because "Aristocracy" and "the Aristocrat" are not typically English concepts; we speak instead of the "Gentry" and "the Gentleman". An aristocrat is one through birth and descent, a gentleman through the shaping power of one's environment, through formation and education.

A man from the working class, through luck and talent, can make a fortune. He cannot become a gentleman; his speech betrays his origin. However, he can send his son to Eton and Oxford, and his son will become a gentleman. Maybe the English do not speak of the aristocracy because so few of our titles are older than four hundred years. The rich who ruled England, I scarcely need mention, did not neglect their own interests, but they also established the tradition that expected a gentleman to take an interest, and to participate, in public and political events; in doing so, they developed, as a corrective to the natural egoism of every human being, a sense of obligation toward the general public and the common good.

Another difference that I mentioned was the anti-clerical, even atheistic character of the liberals and the socialist Left in Europe.

A Roman Catholic may justly smile at that curious body, The Church of England, with its vagueness of doctrine and its lack of a central authority, yet, historically, these weaknesses have had certain advantages. If the Archbishops of Canterbury had been able to dogmatise like the Pope about social matters—and you must remember that the Church of England is a State Church and the Archbishop of Canterbury a political appointee—then it would have been the most reactionary body in the State, and the Left in England would now be even more violently anti-clerical than in Europe. The lack of discipline allowed those clergy and laity who had liberal ideas to express and campaign for them. The British Labour Party is the child of the Evangelical Movement, and the first people to bother about the slums and juvenile delinquency were the Anglo-Catholics.

What kinds of Englishmen have had relations to Europe, and for what reasons?

(1) From the Sixteenth to the Eighteenth Century, it was customary for the rich young heir to make the Grand Tour before settling down on his estate; this was part of his Education. In the Nineteenth Century, when they became richer, the middle-class also began to take educational trips through Europe.

(2) After 1815, and mostly to Dieppe, came the bankrupts fleeing from their creditors.

(3) About the same time, English colonies abroad were founded, firstly of those with small independent means who found that their money went further in Europe than at home, and, secondly of artists and bohemians who found the atmosphere and climate congenial to their work and wished to lead a private life far from the eye of Mrs Grundy.

(4) During the latter half of the Nineteenth Century it became quite common for English students to attend some European University or *Conservatoire*, to study some special subject, Medicine, Theology, Music, etc.

(5) Lastly, there came the mountain-climbers, the winter-sportsmen, and the sun-bathers.

During the Eighteenth and Nineteenth Century, England acquired an Empire, which in the Twentieth Century became a Commonwealth of autonomous Dominions. From the start, there were two kinds of colonies: those like Canada, Australia and New Zealand in which the majority of inhabitants were of English origin, and those like India and the African colonies, in which a very small number of Englishmen ruled over a much larger number of foreigners. Most of the English who left England for the first kind wanted to settle there and never return. Those who went into the Indian army or became Indian or colonial administrators, and even those who started business enterprises in India or Africa, intended to return to end their days in England with, if they were lucky, a fortune in their suitcase.

By 1900, there was hardly a middle-class family in England which did not have one or more close relatives employed overseas as tea-planters or Colonial Civil Servants. The majority of these, it is not unfair to say, were not the intellectual members of their families.

One of my uncles wanted to become a military officer, but there wasn't enough money to buy him a post in a good regiment, so the poor man had to become a minister, which didn't appeal to him. He got into trouble over a girl and had to disappear to Australia. For my older brother, studying was difficult and he wanted to be a farmer. Land cost too much in England, so he went to Canada. My other brother, however, *is* an intellectual, who went into the Indian Geological Survey because he was interested in field work. In England, the field work had already been done, so he could only have taught geology at a university.

One will never understand the current debate about England joining the Common Market if one thinks of it as merely a clash between various economic interests. One cannot avoid noticing that the Labour and the Conservative Parties are equally divided on this issue. Beneath the arguments Pro and Con lie passionate prejudices and the eternal feud between the High-Brow and the Low-Brow. I cannot follow the economic arguments and, since I am no longer a British subject, I can take no part in the controversy, but, instinctively, I am Pro. I know Europe at first hand, and as a writer, I cannot conceive of my life without the influence of its literature, art and music.

The Dominions, on the other hand, are for me *tiefste Provinz*, places which have produced almost no art and are inhabited by the kind of person with whom I have least in common, whether it is a matter of our virtues or our faults. Were I to visit one of the Dominions, I would not find that pleasure which is for me one of the greatest joys of travel: to be in a place where no one speaks English and where, in consequence, I am an anonymous individual with no social status and therefore free to associate freely with anyone.

For the Low-Brows—I am thinking of the Low-Brows of my generation and older, for the development of cheap mass travel since the war must have changed the young—for them, the Dominions are inhabited by their relatives and for people like themselves, speaking English, eating English food, wearing English clothes and playing English games, whereas "abroad" is inhabited by immoral strangers—a French novel is synonymous with pornography—and, aside from the mountain-climbers and the winter-sportsmen, an Englishman who goes there often, still worse, decides to live there, is probably up to no good. The Low-Brow, however, draws distinctions between the "abroad" countries. If the Common Market countries were to consist simply of Scandinavia, he would be far less hostile to Britain's entry. Last year I made a sea voyage along the Norwegian coast. My fellow travelers, mostly English, fascinated me because they were representatives of a type I had not met in Europe before. I have the suspicion that the English man-in-the-street still nourishes, though probably unconsciously, strong anti-popery feelings. He may not admit it but, in his heart of hearts, he thinks that Roman Catholics are idolaters, immoral, and physically dirty, that only a Protestant can really be respectable.

England may join the Common Market—and, personally, I hope very much that she does—but that will not make her part of Europe, because Europe no longer exists. The automobile, the aeroplane, television, Espresso bars, etc. are creating a way of life which is the same from San Francisco to Vienna, and if, in due time, the countries behind the Iron Curtain become affluent—and I can see no intrinsic reason why they should not—then, whatever the theoretical political differences between us, life on their side will become indistinguishable from life on ours.

The same goes for High-Brow culture. There are no more distinctive cultural centres. What is Paris? The place where Hegel is still taken seriously. What Vienna? The Karajan city where Wagner is played in complete darkness (Karajan's beautiful hands are of course brightly lit). To-day, every intellectual is at once more isolated and internationalised than his predecessors. One may or may not like this much—I don't think I do: I find the age ill-bred and horribly noisy, but, then, I am a middle-class old fogey and an intellectual snob.

I must not forget that, for most of the population in our countries, life is more agreeable than it has ever been, and I have no choice but to reconcile myself to what I cannot change, and make the best of it. As a poet, I comfort myself with the thought that, so long as different peoples speak different languages, there cannot be such a thing in poetry as an International Style. So long as Germans speak German and I speak English, a genuine dialogue between us is possible; we shall not be simply addressing our mirror images; as Karl Kraus says: "Speech is the mother, not the handmaid, of thought." Let us praise *den lieben Gott*, and thank Him for the Tower of Babel.

"Europäisches Konzert", Bayerischer Rundfunk, 29 October 1962;
Wort und Wahrheit, December 1962

Do You Know Too Much?

A child has not been long in this world before he discovers that there are certain things which his elders, beginning with his parents, have decided that he must know, whether he wants to learn them or not. The subjects of this compulsory education vary, of course, according to the culture into which he has been born and the social status of his family. If he is an Eskimo, for example, he will be taught how to tie knots, but not how to read and write because literacy is not considered essential to the life and prosperity of an adult Eskimo or Eskimo society as a whole.

In considering this compulsory education which every society insists upon, one must never confuse criticism of its contents and methods with criticism of the nature and aims of the society itself. One may disapprove of Sparta as a society, but one must admit that if human beings choose, or are compelled by their historical past, to live as the Spartans did, then what and how they taught their children was, on the whole, effective. So long as any society remains static, so long, that is, as the problems it has to master remain the same, its young are always "well" educated. On the other hand, whenever a society and its circumstances are changing, its educational system is apt to be defective; what, based on past experience, parents and teachers regard as essential and unessential knowledge no longer coincides with what, if they are to function properly as adults in the world as it is, the new generation must know.

Our own educational system, for example has not yet fully adjusted itself to the fact that the demand for unskilled labor has greatly decreased already and will steadily continue to do so, that the demand for specialized knowledge and skill is steadily increasing and that, in most of these specializations, an ability to think quickly and clearly is more important than manual strength or dexterity. In my opinion, the central concern of education at the primary level before specialization begins must therefore be with teaching children how to think. There is no such thing as thinking in abstraction from a medium of thought, of which there are two, verbal speech and the language of numbers. A person like myself, who is only competent in one, discovers that there are large and very important, areas of thought from which he is excluded, and a person who is competent in neither will never think properly at all. Consequently, I believe that, for American children between the ages of six and fourteen, at least three-quarters of their school time should be devoted to the study of the English language—and I mean *language*, not literature, except insofar as literature is a lesson in the use of language—and to the study of mathematics. Though I know it is vain to hope for their resuscitation, I count it a great good fortune that I was compelled to spend so many hours of my childhood in the study of Latin and Greek, not because it taught me to read Classical Literature in the original—in fact, I have forgotten nearly everything I learnt of these tongues—but because the exercise, day after day, of translating into and out of languages so syntactically and rhetorically different from English taught me to understand the nature of my native tongue as no other method, I believe, could have done. (The way in which I was taught mathematics was, alas, atrocious.)

If children are to spend more time on language and mathematics, they will have to spend less time on other subjects. From much of the present school curriculum, one would think that we were still living in an orally transmitted culture before the invention of printing; a great deal of time is wasted, that is to say, in imparting what one might call quiz knowledge, facts which it is unnecessary for anybody to carry in his head because, if he wants to know one, he has only to consult a reference book. It is important, to be sure, to train a child's memory, but there are better methods of doing this, like learning passages of prose and verse by heart, than accumulating random geographical or historical facts. Detailed factual knowledge only becomes important when specialization begins and then it is no educational problem, for whenever someone becomes genuinely interested in a particular subject, be it physics or baseball, he desires to become a scholar in that field. Who, on the other hand, if a classroom subject bored him, will not have forgotten every fact he was taught within a year of leaving school?

The question "What must I know?" is, in early years at least, answered by others. The question "What do I want to know?" can only be answered by myself and never conclusively. I shall continue to ask it and modify my answer until the day I die, for it is a by-product of more important and insoluble questions: "Who am I? Whom do I want to become?"

From the moment we discover what personally interests us, we realize that what others are willing and able to teach us is not identical with what we want to learn, though as a rule, fortunately, they overlap. How great this overlap is depends upon the degree to which our desire to do as we like happens to coincide with the demands and values of the society in which we live. Thus a young man whose greatest desire in life is to become a doctor will have no difficulty in finding teachers who can impart much of the knowledge he requires, because our society regards the existence of doctors as a necessity. On the other hand, if his main concern is the writing of poetry, he will find no educational establishment for the specific purpose of training poets because, though some individual poets become public figures, our society does not regard poetry as a public necessity, does not accord poets a professional status.

In any case, few gifts are more valuable than a flair for finding the right teacher. Some fail to find one from whom they could profit because they imagine no one can teach them anything, some because they are too swayed by fashion and choose their teacher by hearsay, others again because they confuse respect with affection and cannot recognize the one who has most to teach them, because they do not like him personally.

Even when college is behind us and we become solely responsible for what we learn or fail to learn, we are apt to clutter up our minds with knowledge which is irrelevant to our lives, and our motive for doing so is usually a desire for social conformity. We keep imagining we ought to know this or that because those about us know it. Sometimes, it is true, there can be a conflict between duty and interest. I may be bored to tears by political problems but, if I am to do my duty as a citizen, I must learn enough about them to make a rational choice when I vote. But unless conscience can give me unanswerable reasons for learning what bores me, the chances are that it is not my conscience that is speaking. As a rule we should follow the example of Sherlock Holmes who refused to learn about the Copernican system because such knowledge was irrelevant to the life of a detective.

Another reason why we both acquire useless knowledge—and fail to acquire the knowledge which we really need—is, of course, laziness. To be lazy is to do nothing, or rather, since that is impossible, to do nothing in particular. Consider the way in which we read our daily newspaper. For each of us, it probably contains some item of real interest, but how few of us are capable, after we have satisfied our genuine curiosity, of throwing the paper away. We go on reading without real interest or pleasure because we are too lazy to stop.

We may also go on reading for baser reasons. Our pleasure is, on the whole, a reliable guide concerning what each of us, personally, ought to know, but it becomes most unreliable when it is a question of what we ought *not* to know, and the society in which we live does everything it can to discourage us from asking this question seriously. We are prepared to recognize that, while a desire for food or sex is in itself natural and good, and uncontrolled indulgence of either is not, we can hardly tolerate the notion that the same is true of all forms of curiosity from the most vulgar to the most intellectual, if it happens to be our own. (We are easily convinced, of course, that other people should be kept ignorant, but knowledge is always safe with us.) This moral blind spot exists at every social and educational level. The scholar who looks down his nose at the multitude reading their newspaper reports of crimes and personal disasters is proud of having unearthed and edited and published the intimate papers of a dead writer, and his scientific colleague, who thinks much literary curiosity frivolous, sees nothing questionable in his own attempts to discover a nerve gas against which no defense is possible.

The fear with which every human being on earth must now live, of being vaporized without warning, may in the end prove a blessing, for it is compelling us to reexamine certain presuppositions about the nature and purpose of knowledge which for the past three centuries we have taken for granted and which have brought us to this pass. We cannot help seeing, for instance, a problem to which this period was blind, the problem of the relation between knowledge, truth and time. Instead of asking, "What can I discover?", man should always ask, "What ought I to discover next?" We should, that is to say, have devoted our will and intellect to the political problem of international anarchy first and then turned our attention to atomic physics. Nor can we help seeing that the phrase "knowledge for knowledge's sake" is meaningless; man always desires knowledge for a purpose, and the kinds of knowledge an individual or a culture seeks, the ways in which they seek it, betray that purpose.

The original meaning of the verb *to know* referred to a relation between persons. Thus it is said in the Bible, "And Adam knew Eve, his wife," because sexual intercourse is a symbol for personal intimacy, and we still say of a friend, "I know him very well." Knowledge in this sense is mutual; I cannot know anyone well without being equally well-known by him, and, moreover, the better we get to know each other, the better we get to know ourselves. So we behave towards those whom we regard as "brothers." In relation to those we regard as "others," we desire but one thing, to be stronger than they; we must enslave them lest they enslave us.

By the "truth" we now mean the knowledge that gives power; consequently the more we know about them and the less they know about us, the better. Primitive man did not possess our notion of a neuter thing; he supposed the universe to be composed of personal brothers or others, most of them stronger than himself and so responsible for his fortunes and misfortunes. This error kept him reverent; that is to say, he recognized the right of other human beings to exist because he was mistakenly convinced that it was by their permission that he existed.

Today we know better. We know that most of the universe is composed of things about which we can acquire knowledge but which cannot know us, and that this one-sided relation enables us to manipulate them as we wish, but collectively, we have not yet drawn the obvious moral, namely, that if nothing in creation is responsible for our existence then we are responsible for all created things. Most individual scientists, certainly all the best ones, have been and still are contemplatives who rejoice in their discoveries, not for the practical value they may have, but because it is a joy and wonder to know that things are as they are. Unfortunately their innocent indifference to practical values has made them the slaves of that faceless fabulously wealthy Leviathan called Science which has no concern whatever for the right of anything or anyone to exist except its anonymous power that acknowledges no limits, and that has a scarcely disguised contempt for those whom it employs.

Either we shall commit suicide, by bombs or by exhausting essential natural resources, or we shall change our conception of science.

I know it is presumptuous for someone who is not a scientist to suggest what that conception should be, but I shall do so anyway.

I would like to see all scientists accept three presuppositions.

(1) Not only everything that "lives" is holy, but everything that exists, from human beings to electrons. An electron has as much right to exist as we have.

(2) Though it is good that everything exists, the way in which a particular thing exists may be evil or, at least, not as good as it could be.

(3) So far as we know, we are the only created beings who, by their own conscious efforts, can make themselves better or worse, or ask questions about the nature of other beings.

If these presuppositions are accepted, then teleology, which has for a long time been a dirty word, will find its place again in scientific thinking. Is it too fanciful to suppose that it is up to man to enable other created beings to realize goals which are proper to them but which they can only realize with his help, that his authority over nature should be that of a father, not an irresponsible despot?

As our knowledge increases, may we not find that our power and. hence, our duty to educate will extend much further than at present we dream of? What, unknown to itself, does an electron want to become? We don't know and perhaps never shall, but to know that should be the ultimate aim of science.

Esquire, December 1962

Mirror

A Set of Notes

[See "Hic et Ille" in *The Dyer's Hand*, p. 519, and textual notes,
p. 954.]

Vogue, December 1962

England & Europe

(Extracts from a talk on the Bavarian Radio)

If I shut my eyes and say the word *Europe* to myself, the various images which
it conjures up have one thing in common; they could not be conjured up by
the word *England*. Let me give a few of them as they occur to me, without
trying to arrange them in a logical order.

Europe is the place where:

(1) The fields are not divided from each other by hedges, the farms are
mostly family farms, and the landless farm-hand is a rarity.

(2) There is a definite social class, the Peasants, conscious of itself as such
and often wielding considerable political power.

(3) Very few of the aristocracy take an active part in public and political
life.

(4) The Liberal-Socialist Left is anti-clerical, and, for the most part, atheistic.

(5) The village schoolmaster and the village doctor are usually on the political left.

(6) Shops are open on Sundays and one can get a drink at any hour.

(7) The only comfortable article of furniture is the double-bed.

(8) Hotel bed-rooms are equipped with bidets.

(9) Nothing is wasted. The classical vice of avarice and the miser à la Balzac can still be found.

(10) Outside the big cities the shops never have proper wrapping paper.

(11) Nationals as well as foreigners must carry identification papers and
produce them when they register in a hotel.

(12) In Jurisprudence, codified law plays a much greater role than case
law.

(13) Intellectual life has two centres: the Café, exclusively male, where artists of all kinds start "movements" and issue manifestos, and the Salon,
presided over by a woman.

(14) When two educated people meet who do not know the other's language, they talk French.

(15) If there are any Protestants, they are in the minority. The Protestant countries—Scandinavia, Holland, Prussia, etc.—do not *quite* belong to Europe.

★   ★   ★

Since I am a writer, the word *Europe* conjures up, in addition to such images, certain sacred names. Here are a few of mine: Lichtenberg, Hölderlin, Nietzsche, Nestroy, Rimbaud, Christian Morgenstern, Valéry, Kafka, Karl Kraus, Rudolf Kassner.

You will notice that, in this list, German names predominate. No Englishman falls in love with Europe as a whole; he falls in love with a particular landscape or city or language. It has been said that nobody ever fell in love with Bulgaria, but I have met a young Englishman who did. Like all lovers, we are prejudiced: one may love French or Italian or Spanish, but one cannot love three equally.

★   ★   ★

I am one of those—there are not many of us—who fell in love with the German language. When I went down from Oxford in 1928, my parents offered me a year abroad. For the generation of intellectuals immediately preceding mine, the only culture that counted was French culture. I was bored with hearing about it, and, therefore, determined that wherever I might go, it would not be to Paris. Where then? Rome? No; Mussolini and fascism made that impossible. Berlin? That was an idea! Why not? I knew no German and hardly any German literature, but, then nobody else I knew did either. Berlin was an unexplored city and might turn out to be fun. Perhaps, also, I had an unconscious bias in favor of Germany because, when I was a little boy in prep-school during the First World War, if I took an extra slice of bread and margarine, some master was sure to say:—"I see, Auden, you want the Huns to win"—thus establishing in my mind an association between Germany and forbidden pleasures. . . .

★   ★   ★

Europe, to me, is the area dominated by a consciousness of the French Revolution, and roughly corresponds geographically to the Napoleonic Empire. It is the product of the French revolutionary thrust and the counter-revolutionary riposte which this provoked. Without the latter, Europe would be a political entity under the political dominance of France, instead of a cultural entity dominated by French culture. Napoleon is balanced by Metternich, Paris by Vienna. Before 1786, there was no Europe, and the Russian Revolution of 1917 heralded its decease.

★   ★   ★

A Roman Catholic may justly smile at that curious body, The Church of England, with its vagueness of doctrine and its lack of a central authority, yet, historically, these weaknesses have had certain advantages. If the Archbishops of Canterbury had been able to dogmatise like the Pope about social matters—and you must remember that the Church of England is a State Church and the Archbishop of Canterbury a political appointee—then it would have been the most reactionary body in the State, and the Left in England would now be even more violently anti-clerical than in Europe. The lack of discipline allowed those clergy and laity who had liberal ideas to express and campaign for them. The British Labour Party is the child of the Evangelical Movement, and the first people to bother about the slums and the juvenile delinquency were the Anglo-Catholics.

★ ★ ★

When I ask what kinds of Englishmen have had relations to Europe, I find five groups:

(1) From the Sixteenth Century on, it was customary for the rich young heir to make the Grand Tour before settling down on his estate; this was part of his Education. In the Nineteenth Century, when they became richer, the middle-class also began to take educational trips.

(2) After 1815, and mostly to Dieppe, came the bankrupts fleeing from their creditors.

(3) About the same time, English colonies abroad were founded, firstly of those with small independent means who found that their money went further in Europe than at home, and, secondly of artists and bohemians who found the atmosphere and climate congenial to their work and wished to lead a private life far from the eye of Mrs Grundy.

(4) During the latter half of the Nineteenth Century it became quite common for English students to attend some European University or *Conservatoire*, to study some special subject, Theology, Medicine, Music, etc.

(5) Lastly, there came the mountain-climbers, the winter-sportsmen, and the sun-bathers.

★ ★ ★

During the Eighteenth and Nineteenth Century, England acquired an Empire, and, by 1900, there was hardly a middle-class family in England which did not have one or more close relatives employed overseas as farmers, tea-planters, or Colonial Civil Servants. The majority of these, it is not unfair to say, were not the intellectual members of their families.

★ ★ ★

One will never understand the current debate about England joining the Common Market if one thinks of it as merely a clash between various eco-

nomic interests. Beneath the arguments Pro and Con lie passionate prejudices and the eternal feud between the High-Brow and the Low-Brow. I cannot follow the economic arguments and, since I am now an American citizen,
I can take no part in the controversy, but, instinctively, I am Pro. I know Europe at first hand, and as a writer, I cannot conceive of my life without the
influence of its literature, music, and art. The Dominions, on the other hand,
are for me *tiefste Provinz*, places which have produced no art and are inhabited by the kind of person with whom I have least in common.

★   ★   ★

For the Low-Brows—I am thinking of the Low-Brows of my generation and
older, for the development of cheap mass travel since the war must have
changed the young—for them, the Dominions are inhabited by their relatives and for people like themselves, speaking English, eating English food,
wearing English clothes and playing English games, whereas "abroad" is inhabited by immoral strangers—a French novel is synonymous with pornography—and, aside from the mountain-climbers and the winter-sportsmen,
an Englishman who goes there often, still worse, decides to live there, is probably up to no good.

★   ★   ★

The Low-Brow, however, draws distinctions between the "abroad" countries.
If the Common Market countries were to consist simply of Scandinavia, he
would be far less hostile to Britain's entry. I have the suspicion that the English man-in-the-street still nourishes, though probably unconsciously, strong
anti-popery feelings. He may not admit it but, in his heart of hearts, he thinks
that Roman Catholics are idolaters, immoral, and physically dirty, that only a
Protestant can really be respectable.

★   ★   ★

Britain may join the Common Market—and, personally, I hope very much
that she does—but that will not make her part of Europe, because Europe
no longer exists. The automobile, the aeroplane, television, Espresso bars,
etc. are creating a way of life which is the same from San Francisco to Vienna,
and if, in due time, the countries behind the Iron Curtain become affluent—
and I can see no intrinsic reason why they should not—then, whatever the
theoretical political differences between us, life on their side will become
indistinguishable from life on ours.

★   ★   ★

The same unification is taking place in High-Brow culture. There are no
more distinctive cultural centres. What is Paris? The place where Hegel is
taken seriously. What Vienna? The Karajan city where Wagner is played in
complete darkness. To-day, every intellectual is at once more isolated and internationalised than his predecessors. One may not like this much—I don't

think I do: I find the age ill-bred and horribly noisy, but, then, I am a middle-class old fogey and an intellectual snob. As a poet, I comfort myself with the thought that, so long as different peoples speak different languages, there cannot be such a thing in poetry as an International Style. So long as the Germans speak German and I speak English, a genuine dialogue between us is possible; we shall not be simply addressing our mirror images. Let us praise *den lieben Gott*, and thank Him for the Tower of Babel.

Partly published as an untitled contribution to a
symposium, "Going into Europe",
Encounter, January 1963

THE DYER'S HAND

The Dyer's Hand
and Other Essays

———————

[*1962*]

FOR

NEVILL COGHILL

Three grateful memories:
a home full of books,
a childhood spent in country provinces,
a tutor in whom one could confide.

We have Art in order that we may not perish from Truth.

F. W. NIETZSCHE

FOREWORD

It is a sad fact about our culture that a poet can earn much more money writing or talking about his art than he can by practicing it. All the poems I have written were written for love; naturally, when I have written one, I try to market it, but the prospect of a market played no role in its writing.

On the other hand, I have never written a line of criticism except in response to a demand by others for a lecture, an introduction, a review, etc.; though I hope that some love went into their writing, I wrote them because I needed the money. I should like to thank the various publishers, editors, college authorities and, not least, the ladies and gentlemen who voted me into the Chair of Poetry at Oxford University, but for whose generosity and support I should never have been able to pay my bills.

The trouble about writing commissioned criticism is that the relation between form and content is arbitrary; a lecture must take fifty-five minutes to deliver, an introduction must be so and so many thousand, a review so and so many hundred words long. Only rarely do the conditions set down conform exactly with one's thought. Sometimes one feels cramped, forced to omit or oversimplify arguments; more often, all one really has to say could be put down in half the allotted space, and one can only try to pad as inconspicuously as possible.

Moreover, in a number of articles which were not planned as a series but written for diverse occasions, it is inevitable that one will often repeat oneself.

A poem must be a closed system, but there is something, in my opinion, lifeless, even false, about systematic criticism. In going over my critical pieces, I have reduced them, when possible, to sets of notes because, as a reader, I prefer a critic's notebooks to his treatises. The order of the chapters, however, is deliberate, and I would like them to be read in sequence.

W. H. A.

CONTENTS

PART ONE

Prologue

Reading

A book is a mirror: if an ass peers into it you can't expect an
apostle to look out. —G. C. Lichtenberg

One only reads well that which one reads with some quite
personal purpose. It may be to acquire some power. It can
be out of hatred for the author.—Paul Valéry

The interests of a writer and the interests of his readers are never the same
and if, on occasion, they happen to coincide, this is a lucky accident.

In relation to a writer, most readers believe in the Double Standard: they
may be unfaithful to him as often as they like, but he must never, never be
unfaithful to them.

To read is to translate, for no two persons' experiences are the same. A bad
reader is like a bad translator: he interprets literally when he ought to paraphrase and paraphrases when he ought to interpret literally. In learning to
read well, scholarship, valuable as it is, is less important than instinct; some
great scholars have been poor translators.

We often derive much profit from reading a book in a different way from
that which its author intended but only (once childhood is over) if we know
that we are doing so.

As readers, most of us, to some degree, are like those urchins who pencil
mustaches on the faces of girls in advertisements.

One sign that a book has literary value is that it can be read in a number of
different ways. Vice versa, the proof that pornography has no literary value is
that, if one attempts to read it in any other way than as a sexual stimulus, to
read it, say, as a psychological case-history of the author's sexual fantasies,
one is bored to tears.

Though a work of literature can be read in a number of ways, this number is
finite and can be arranged in a hierarchical order; some readings are obviously "truer" than others, some doubtful, some obviously false, and some,
like reading a novel backwards, absurd. That is why, for a desert island, one
would choose a good dictionary rather than the greatest literary masterpiece
imaginable, for, in relation to its readers, a dictionary is absolutely passive
and may legitimately be read in an infinite number of ways.

We cannot read an author for the first time in the same way that we read the
latest book by an established author. In a new author, we tend to see either
only his virtues or only his defects and, even if we do see both, we cannot see

the relation between them. In the case of an established author, if we can still read him at all, we know that we cannot enjoy the virtues we admire in him without tolerating the defects we deplore. Moreover, our judgment of an established author is never simply an aesthetic judgment. In addition to any literary merit it may have, a new book by him has a historic interest for us as the act of a person in whom we have long been interested. He is not only a poet or a novelist; he is also a character in our biography.

A poet cannot read another poet, nor a novelist another novelist, without comparing their work to his own. His judgments as he reads are of this kind: *My God! My Great-Grandfather! My Uncle! My Enemy! My Brother! My imbecile Brother!*

In literature, vulgarity is preferable to nullity, just as grocer's port is preferable to distilled water.

Good taste is much more a matter of discrimination than of exclusion, and when good taste feels compelled to exclude, it is with regret, not with pleasure.

Pleasure is by no means an infallible critical guide, but it is the least fallible.

A child's reading is guided by pleasure, but his pleasure is undifferentiated; he cannot distinguish, for example, between aesthetic pleasure and the pleasures of learning or daydreaming. In adolescence we realize that there are different kinds of pleasure, some of which cannot be enjoyed simultaneously, but we need help from others in defining them. Whether it be a matter of taste in food or taste in literature, the adolescent looks for a mentor in whose authority he can believe. He eats or reads what his mentor recommends and, inevitably, there are occasions when he has to deceive himself a little; he has to pretend that he enjoys olives or *War and Peace* a little more than he actually does. Between the ages of twenty and forty we are engaged in the process of discovering who we are, which involves learning the difference between accidental limitations which it is our duty to outgrow and the necessary limitations of our nature beyond which we cannot trespass with impunity. Few of us can learn this without making mistakes, without trying to become a little more of a universal man than we are permitted to be. It is during this period that a writer can most easily be led astray by another writer or by some ideology. When someone between twenty and forty says, apropos of a work of art, "I know what I like," he is really saying "I have no taste of my own but accept the taste of my cultural milieu," because, between twenty and forty, the surest sign that a man has a genuine taste of his own is that he is uncertain of it. After forty, if we have not lost our authentic selves altogether, pleasure can again become what it was when we were children, the proper guide to what *we* should read.

Though the pleasure which works of art give us must not be confused with other pleasures that we enjoy, it is related to all of them simply by being *our* pleasure and not someone else's. All the judgments, aesthetic or moral, that we pass, however objective we try to make them, are in part a rationalization and in part a corrective discipline of our subjective wishes. So long as a man writes poetry or fiction, his dream of Eden is his own business, but the moment he starts writing literary criticism, honesty demands that he describe it to his readers, so that they may be in the position to judge his judgments. Accordingly, I must now give my answers to a questionnaire I once made up which provides the kind of information I should like to have myself when reading other critics.

EDEN

Landscape

Limestone uplands like the Pennines plus a small region of igneous rocks with at least one extinct volcano. A precipitous and indented sea-coast.

Climate

British.

Ethnic origin of inhabitants

Highly varied as in the United States, but with a slight nordic predominance.

Language

Of mixed origins like English, but highly inflected.

Weights & Measures

Irregular and complicated. No decimal system.

Religion

Roman Catholic in an easygoing Mediterranean sort of way. Lots of local saints.

Size of Capital

Plato's ideal figure, 5004, about right.

Form of Government

Absolute monarchy, elected for life by lot.

Sources of Natural Power

Wind, water, peat, coal. No oil.

Economic activities

Lead mining, coal mining, chemical factories, paper mills, sheep farming, truck farming, greenhouse horticulture.

Means of transport

Horses and horse-drawn vehicles, narrow-gauge railroads, canal barges, balloons. No automobiles or airplanes.

Architecture

State: Baroque. Ecclesiastical: Romanesque or Byzantine. Domestic: Eighteenth Century British or American Colonial.

Domestic Furniture and Equipment

Victorian except for kitchens and bathrooms which are as full of modern gadgets as possible.

Formal Dress

The fashions of Paris in the 1830s and '40s.

Sources of Public Information

Gossip. Technical and learned periodicals but no newspapers.

Public Statues

Confined to famous defunct chefs.

Public Entertainments

Religious Processions, Brass Bands, Opera, Classical Ballet. No movies, radio or television.

If I were to attempt to write down the names of all the poets and novelists for whose work I am really grateful because I know that if I had not read them my life would be poorer, the list would take up pages. But when I try to think of all the critics for whom I am really grateful, I find myself with a list of thirty-four names. Of these, twelve are German and only two French. Does this indicate a conscious bias? It does.

If good literary critics are rarer than good poets or novelists, one reason is the nature of human egoism. A poet or a novelist has to learn to be humble in the face of his subject matter which is life in general. But the subject matter of a critic, before which he has to learn to be humble, is made up of authors, that is to say, of human individuals, and this kind of humility is much more difficult to acquire. It is far easier to say—"Life is more important than anything I can say about it"—than to say—"Mr A's work is more important than anything I can say about it."

There are people who are too intelligent to become authors, but they do not become critics.

Authors can be stupid enough, God knows, but they are not always quite so stupid as a certain kind of critic seems to think. The kind of critic, I mean, to whom, when he condemns a work or a passage, the possibility never occurs that its author may have foreseen exactly what he is going to say.

What is the function of a critic? So far as I am concerned, he can do me one or more of the following services:

(1) Introduce me to authors or works of which I was hitherto unaware.
(2) Convince me that I have undervalued an author or a work because I had not read them carefully enough.
(3) Show me relations between works of different ages and cultures which I could never have seen for myself because I do not know enough and never shall.
(4) Give a "reading" of a work which increases my understanding of it.
(5) Throw light upon the process of artistic "Making."
(6) Throw light upon the relation of art to life, to science, economics, ethics, religion, etc.

The first three of these services demand scholarship. A scholar is not merely someone whose knowledge is extensive; the knowledge must be of value to others. One would not call a man who knew the Manhattan Telephone Directory by heart a scholar, because one cannot imagine circumstances in which he would acquire a pupil. Since scholarship implies a relation between one who knows more and one who knows less, it may be temporary; in relation to the public, every reviewer is, temporarily, a scholar, because he has read the book he is reviewing and the public have not. Though the knowledge a scholar possesses must be potentially valuable, it is not necessary that he recognize its value himself; it is always possible that the pupil to whom he imparts his knowledge has a better sense of its value than he. In general, when reading a scholarly critic, one profits more from his quotations than from his comments.

The last three services demand, not superior knowledge, but superior insight. A critic shows superior insight if the questions he raises are fresh and important, however much one may disagree with his answers to them. Few readers, probably, find themselves able to accept Tolstoi's conclusions in *What Is Art?*, but, once one has read the book, one can never again ignore the questions Tolstoi raises.

The one thing I most emphatically do not ask of a critic is that he tell me what I *ought* to approve of or condemn. I have no objection to his telling me what works and authors he likes and dislikes; indeed, it is useful to know this for, from his expressed preferences about works which I have read, I learn how likely I am to agree or disagree with his verdicts on works which I have not. But let him not dare to lay down the law to me. The responsibility for what I choose to read is mine, and nobody else on earth can do it for me.

The critical opinions of a writer should always be taken with a large grain of salt. For the most part, they are manifestations of his debate with himself as to what he should do next and what he should avoid. Moreover, unlike a scientist, he is usually even more ignorant of what his colleagues are doing than is the general public. A poet over thirty may still be a voracious reader, but it is unlikely that much of what he reads is modern poetry.

Very few of us can truthfully boast that we have never condemned a book or even an author on hearsay, but quite a lot of us that we have never praised one we had not read.

The injunction "Resist not evil but overcome evil with good" may in many spheres of life be impossible to obey literally, but in the sphere of the arts it is common sense. Bad art is always with us, but any given work of art is always bad in a period way; the particular kind of badness it exhibits will pass away to be succeeded by some other kind. It is unnecessary, therefore, to attack it, because it will perish anyway. Had Macaulay never written his review of Robert Montgomery, we would not today be still under the illusion that Montgomery was a great poet. The only sensible procedure for a critic is to keep silent about works which he believes to be bad, while at the same time vigorously campaigning for those which he believes to be good, especially if they are being neglected or underestimated by the public.

Some books are undeservedly forgotten; none are undeservedly remembered.

Some critics argue that it is their moral duty to expose the badness of an author because, unless this is done, he may corrupt other writers. To be sure, a young writer can be led astray, deflected, that is, from his true path, by an older, but he is much more likely to be seduced by a good writer than by a bad one. The more powerful and original a writer, the more dangerous he is to lesser talents who are trying to find themselves. On the other hand, works which were in themselves poor have often proved a stimulus to the imagination and become the indirect cause of good work in others.

You do not educate a person's palate by telling him that what he has been in the habit of eating—watery, overboiled cabbage, let us say—is disgusting, but by persuading him to try a dish of vegetables which have been properly cooked. With some people, it is true, you seem to get quicker results by telling them—"Only vulgar people like overcooked cabbage; the best people like cabbage as the Chinese cook it"—but the results are less likely to be lasting.

If, when a reviewer whose taste I trust condemns a book, I feel a certain relief, this is only because so many books are published that it is a relief to think—"Well, here, at least, is one I do not have to bother about." But had he kept silent, the effect would have been the same.

Attacking bad books is not only a waste of time but also bad for the character. If I find a book really bad, the only interest I can derive from writing about it has to come from myself, from such display of intelligence, wit and malice as I can contrive. One cannot review a bad book without showing off.

There is one evil that concerns literature which should never be passed over in silence but be continually publicly attacked, and that is corruption of the language, for writers cannot invent their own language and are dependent upon the language they inherit so that, if it be corrupt, they must be corrupted. But the critic who concerns himself with this evil must attack it at its source, which is not in works of literature but in the misuse of language by the man-in-the-street, journalists, politicians, etc. Furthermore, he must be able to practice what he preaches. How many critics in England or America today are masters of their native tongue as Karl Kraus was a master of German?

One cannot blame the reviewers themselves. Most of them, probably, would much prefer to review only those books which, whatever their faults, they believe to be worth reading but, if a regular reviewer on one of the big Sunday papers were to obey his inclination, at least one Sunday in three his column would be empty. Again, any conscientious critic who has ever had to review a new volume of poetry in a limited space knows that the only fair thing to do would be to give a series of quotations without comment but, if he did so, his editor would complain that he was not earning his money.

Reviewers may justly be blamed, however, for their habit of labeling and packaging authors. At first critics classified authors as Ancients, that is to say, Greek and Latin authors, and Moderns, that is to say, every post-Classical Author. Then they classified them by eras, the Augustans, the Victorians, etc., and now they classify them by decades, the writers of the '30's, '40's, etc. Very soon, it seems, they will be labeling authors, like automobiles, by the year. Already the decade classification is absurd, for it suggests that authors conveniently stop writing at the age of thirty-five or so.

"Contemporary" is a much abused term. My contemporaries are simply those who are on earth while I am alive, whether they be babies or centenarians.

A writer, or, at least, a poet, is always being asked by people who should know better: "Whom do you write for?" The question is, of course, a silly one, but I can give it a silly answer. Occasionally I come across a book which I feel has been written especially for me and for me only. Like a jealous lover, I don't want anybody else to hear of it. To have a million such readers, unaware of each other's existence, to be read with passion and never talked about, is the daydream, surely, of every author.

Writing

It is the author's aim to say once and emphatically, "He said."—H. D. Thoreau

The art of literature, vocal or written, is to adjust the language so that it embodies what it indicates.
                                        —A. N. Whitehead

All those whose success in life depends neither upon a job which satisfies some specific and unchanging social need, like a farmer's, nor, like a surgeon's, upon some craft which he can be taught by others and improve by practice, but upon "inspiration," the lucky hazard of ideas, live by their wits, a phrase which carries a slightly pejorative meaning. Every "original" genius, be he an artist or a scientist, has something a bit shady about him, like a gambler or a medium.

Literary gatherings, cocktail parties and the like, are a social nightmare because writers have no "shop" to talk. Lawyers and doctors can entertain each other with stories about interesting cases, about experiences, that is to say, related to their professional interests but yet impersonal and outside themselves. Writers have no impersonal professional interests. The literary equivalent of talking shop would be writers reciting their own work at each other, an unpopular procedure for which only very young writers have the nerve.

No poet or novelist wishes he were the only one who ever lived, but most of them wish they were the only one alive, and quite a number fondly believe their wish has been granted.

In theory, the author of a good book should remain anonymous, for it is to his work, not to himself, that admiration is due. In practice, this seems to be impossible. However, the praise and public attention that writers sometimes receive do not seem to be as fatal to them as one might expect. Just as a good man forgets his deed the moment he has done it, a genuine writer forgets a work as soon as he has completed it and starts to think about the next one; if he thinks about his past work at all, he is more likely to remember its faults than its virtues. Fame often makes a writer vain, but seldom makes him proud.

Writers can be guilty of every kind of human conceit but one, the conceit of the social worker: "We are all here on earth to help others; what on earth the others are here for, I don't know."

When a successful author analyzes the reasons for his success, he generally underestimates the talent he was born with, and overestimates his skill in employing it.

Every writer would rather be rich than poor, but no genuine writer cares about popularity as such. He needs approval of his work by others in order to be reassured that the vision of life he believes he has had is a true vision and not a self-delusion, but he can only be reassured by those whose judgment he respects. It would only be necessary for a writer to secure universal popularity if imagination and intelligence were equally distributed among all men.

When some obvious booby tells me he has liked a poem of mine, I feel as if I had picked his pocket.

Writers, poets especially, have an odd relation to the public because their medium, language, is not, like the paint of the painter or the notes of the composer, reserved for their use but is the common property of the linguistic group to which they belong. Lots of people are willing to admit that they don't understand painting or music, but very few indeed who have been to school and learned to read advertisements will admit that they don't understand English. As Karl Kraus said: "The public doesn't understand German, and in Journalese I can't tell them so."

How happy the lot of the mathematician! He is judged solely by his peers, and the standard is so high that no colleague or rival can ever win a reputation he does not deserve. No cashier writes a letter to the press complaining about the incomprehensibility of Modern Mathematics and comparing it unfavorably with the good old days when mathematicians were content to paper irregularly shaped rooms and fill bathtubs without closing the waste pipe.

To say that a work is inspired means that, in the judgment of its author or his readers, it is better than they could reasonably hope it would be, and nothing else.

All works of art are commissioned in the sense that no artist can create one by a simple act of will but must wait until what he believes to be a good idea for a work "comes" to him. Among those works which are failures because their initial conceptions were false or inadequate, the number of self-commissioned works may well be greater than the number commissioned by patrons.

The degree of excitement which a writer feels during the process of composition is as much an indication of the value of the final result as the excitement felt by a worshiper is an indication of the value of his devotions, that is to say, very little indication.

The Oracle claimed to make prophecies and give good advice about the future; it never pretended to be giving poetry readings.

If poems could be created in a trance without the conscious participation of the poet, the writing of poetry would be so boring or even unpleasant an operation that only a substantial reward in money or social prestige could induce a man to be a poet. From the manuscript evidence, it now appears that Coleridge's account of the composition of "Kubla Khan" was a fib.

It is true that, when he is writing a poem, it seems to a poet as if there were two people involved, his conscious self and a Muse whom he has to woo or an Angel with whom he has to wrestle, but, as in an ordinary wooing or wrestling match, his role is as important as Hers. The Muse, like Beatrice in *Much Ado*, is a spirited girl who has as little use for an abject suitor as she has for a vulgar brute. She appreciates chivalry and good manners, but she despises those who will not stand up to her and takes a cruel delight in telling them nonsense and lies which the poor little things obediently write down as "inspired" truth.

> When I was writing the chorus in G Minor, I suddenly dipped my pen into the medicine bottle instead of the ink; I made a blot, and when I dried it with sand (blotting paper had not been invented then) it took the form of a natural, which instantly gave me the idea of the effect which the change from G minor to G major would make, and to this blot all the effect—if any—is due.
>
> (Rossini to Louis Engel)

Such an act of judgment, distinguishing between Chance and Providence, deserves, surely, to be called an inspiration.

To keep his errors down to a minimum, the internal Censor to whom a poet submits his work in progress should be a Censorate. It should include, for instance, a sensitive only child, a practical housewife, a logician, a monk, an irreverent buffoon and even, perhaps, hated by all the others and returning their dislike, a brutal, foul-mouthed drill sergeant who considers all poetry rubbish.

In the course of many centuries a few laborsaving devices have been introduced into the mental kitchen—alcohol, coffee, tobacco, Benzedrine, etc.—but these are very crude, constantly breaking down, and liable to injure the cook. Literary composition in the twentieth century A.D. is pretty much what it was in the twentieth century B.C.; nearly everything has still to be done by hand.

Most people enjoy the sight of their own handwriting as they enjoy the smell of their own farts. Much as I loathe the typewriter, I must admit that it is a help in self-criticism. Typescript is so impersonal and hideous to look at that, if I type out a poem, I immediately see defects which I missed when I looked through it in manuscript. When it comes to a poem by somebody else, the severest test I know of is to write it out in longhand. The physical tedium of doing this ensures that the slightest defect will reveal itself; the hand is constantly looking for an excuse to stop.

Most artists are sincere and most art is bad, though some insincere (sincerely insincere) works can be quite good. (Stravinsky.) Sincerity is like sleep. Normally, one should assume that, of course, one will be sincere, and not give the question a second thought. Most writers, however, suffer occasionally from bouts of insincerity as men do from bouts of insomnia. The remedy in both cases is often quite simple: in the case of the latter, to change one's diet, in the case of the former, to change one's company.

The schoolmasters of literature frown on affectations of style as silly and unhealthy. Instead of frowning, they ought to laugh indulgently. Shakespeare makes fun of the Euphuists in *Love's Labour's Lost* and in *Hamlet*, but he owed them a great deal and he knew it. Nothing, on the face of it, could have been more futile than the attempt of Spenser, Harvey and others to be good little humanists and write English verse in classical meters, yet, but for their folly, many of Campion's most beautiful songs and the choruses in *Samson Agonistes* would never have been written. In literature, as in life, affectation, passionately adopted and loyally persevered in, is one of the chief forms of self-discipline by which mankind has raised itself by its own bootstraps.

A mannered style, that of Gongora or Henry James, for example, is like eccentric clothing: very few writers can carry it off, but one is enchanted by the rare exception who can.

When a reviewer describes a book as "sincere," one knows immediately that it is (a) insincere (insincerely insincere) and (b) badly written. Sincerity in the proper sense of the word, meaning authenticity, is, however, or ought to be, a writer's chief preoccupation. No writer can ever judge exactly how good or bad a work of his may be, but he can always know, not immediately perhaps, but certainly in a short while, whether something he has written is authentic—in his handwriting—or a forgery.

The most painful of all experiences to a poet is to find that a poem of his which he knows to be a forgery has pleased the public and got into the anthologies. For all he knows or cares, the poem may be quite good, but that is not the point; *he* should not have written it.

The work of a young writer—*Werther* is the classic example—is sometimes a therapeutic act. He finds himself obsessed by certain ways of feeling and thinking of which his instinct tells him he must be rid before he can discover his authentic interests and sympathies, and the only way by which he can be rid of them forever is by surrendering to them. Once he has done this, he has developed the necessary antibodies which will make him immune for the

rest of his life. As a rule, the disease is some spiritual malaise of his generation. If so, he may, as Goethe did, find himself in an embarrassing situation.
What he wrote in order to exorcise certain feelings is enthusiastically welcomed by his contemporaries because it expresses just what they feel but,
unlike him, they are perfectly happy to feel in this way; for the moment they
regard him as their spokesman. Time passes. Having gotten the poison out
of his system, the writer turns to his true interests which are not, and never
were, those of his early admirers, who now pursue him with cries of "Traitor!"

The intellect of man is forced to choose
Perfection of the life or of the work. (Yeats.)
This is untrue; perfection is possible in neither. All one can say is that a
writer who, like all men, has his personal weaknesses and limitations, should
be aware of them and try his best to keep them out of his work. For every
writer, there are certain subjects which, because of defects in his character
and his talent, he should never touch.

What makes it difficult for a poet not to tell lies is that, in poetry, all facts and
all beliefs cease to be true or false and become interesting possibilities. The
reader does not have to share the beliefs expressed in a poem in order to
enjoy it. Knowing this, a poet is constantly tempted to make use of an idea or
a belief, not because he believes it to be true, but because he sees it has interesting poetic possibilities. It may not, perhaps, be absolutely necessary
that he *believe* it, but it is certainly necessary that his emotions be deeply involved, and this they can never be unless, as a man, he takes it more seriously
than as a mere poetic convenience.

The integrity of a writer is more threatened by appeals to his social conscience, his political or religious convictions, than by appeals to his cupidity.
It is morally less confusing to be goosed by a traveling salesman than by a
bishop.

Some writers confuse authenticity, which they ought always to aim at, with
originality, which they should never bother about. There is a certain kind of
person who is so dominated by the desire to be loved for himself alone that
he has constantly to test those around him by tiresome behavior; what he
says and does must be admired, not because it is intrinsically admirable, but
because it is *his* remark, *his* act. Does not this explain a good deal of avant-
garde art?

Slavery is so intolerable a condition that the slave can hardly escape delud-
ing himself into thinking that he is choosing to obey his master's commands
when, in fact, he is obliged to. Most slaves of habit suffer from this delusion
and so do some writers, enslaved by an all too "personal" style.

"Let me think: was I the same when I got up this morning? . . . But if I'm
not the same, the next question is 'Who in the world am I?' . . . I'm sure
I'm not Ada . . . for her hair goes in such long ringlets and mine doesn't
go in ringlets at all; and I'm sure I can't be Mabel, for I know all sorts of
things, and she, oh! she knows such a very little! Beside she's she and
I'm I and—oh dear, how puzzling it all is! I'll try if I know all the things
I used to know . . ." Her eyes filled with tears . . . : "I must be Mabel after
all, and I shall have to go and live in that poky little house, and have
next to no toys to play with, and oh!—ever so many lessons to learn! No,
I've made up my mind about it: if I'm Mabel, I'll stay down here!"

(Alice in Wonderland)

At the next peg the Queen turned again and this time she said: "Speak
in French when you can't think of the English for a thing—turn your
toes out as you walk—and remember who you are."

(Through the Looking-Glass)

Most writers, except the supreme masters who transcend all systems of classification are either Alices or Mabels. For example:

Alice	*Mabel*
Montaigne	Pascal
Marvell	Donne
Burns	Shelley
Jane Austen	Dickens
Turgenev	Dostoievski
Valéry	Gide
Virginia Woolf	Joyce
E. M. Forster	Lawrence
Robert Graves	Yeats

"Orthodoxy," said a real Alice of a bishop, "is reticence."

Except when used as historical labels, the terms *classical* and *romantic* are misleading terms for two poetic parties, the Aristocratic and the Democratic,
which have always existed and to one of which every writer belongs, though
he may switch his party allegiance or, on some specific issue, refuse to obey
his Party Whip.

The Aristocratic Principle as regards subject matter:
    No subject matter shall be treated by poets which poetry cannot digest. It
    defends poetry against didacticism and journalism.
The Democratic Principle as regards subject matter:
    No subject matter shall be excluded by poets which poetry is capable of
    digesting. It defends poetry against limited or stale conceptions of what is
    "poetic."

The Aristocratic Principle as regards treatment:
>   No irrelevant aspects of a given subject shall be expressed in a poem which treats it. It defends poetry against barbaric vagueness.

The Democratic Principle as regards treatment:
>   No relevant aspect of a given subject shall remain unexpressed in a poem which treats it. It defends poetry against decadent triviality.

Every work of a writer should be a first step, but this will be a false step unless, whether or not he realize it at the time, it is also a further step. When a writer is dead, one ought to be able to see that his various works, taken together, make one consistent *oeuvre.*

It takes little talent to see clearly what lies under one's nose, a good deal of it to know in which direction to point that organ.

The greatest writer cannot see through a brick wall but, unlike the rest of us, he does not build one.

Only a minor talent can be a perfect gentleman; a major talent is always more than a bit of a cad. Hence the importance of minor writers—as teachers of good manners. Now and again, an exquisite minor work can make a master feel thoroughly ashamed of himself.

The poet is the father of his poem; its mother is a language: one could list poems as race horses are listed—*out of L by P.*

A poet has to woo, not only his own Muse but also Dame Philology, and, for the beginner, the latter is the more important. As a rule, the sign that a beginner has a genuine original talent is that he is more interested in playing with words than in saying something original; his attitude is that of the old lady, quoted by E. M. Forster—"How can I know what I think till I see what I say?" It is only later, when he has wooed and won Dame Philology, that he can give his entire devotion to his Muse.

Rhymes, meters, stanza forms, etc., are like servants. If the master is fair enough to win their affection and firm enough to command their respect, the result is an orderly happy household. If he is too tyrannical, they give notice; if he lacks authority, they become slovenly, impertinent, drunk and dishonest.

The poet who writes "free" verse is like Robinson Crusoe on his desert island: he must do all his cooking, laundry and darning for himself. In a few exceptional cases, this manly independence produces something original and impressive, but more often the result is squalor—dirty sheets on the unmade bed and empty bottles on the unswept floor.

There are some poets, Kipling for example, whose relation to language reminds one of a drill sergeant: the words are taught to wash behind their ears, stand properly at attention and execute complicated maneuvers, but at the cost of never being allowed to think for themselves. There are others, Swinburne, for example, who remind one more of Svengali: under their hypnotic suggestion, an extraordinary performance is put on, not by raw recruits, but by feeble-minded schoolchildren.

Due to the Curse of Babel, poetry is the most provincial of the arts, but today, when civilization is becoming monotonously the same all the world over, one feels inclined to regard this as a blessing rather than a curse: in poetry, at least, there cannot be an "International Style."

My language is the universal whore whom I have to make into a virgin. (Karl Kraus.) It is both the glory and the shame of poetry that its medium is not its private property, that a poet cannot invent his words and that words are products, not of nature, but of a human society which uses them for a thousand different purposes. In modern societies where language is continually being debased and reduced to nonspeech, the poet is in constant danger of having his ear corrupted, a danger to which the painter and the composer, whose media are their private property, are not exposed. On the other hand he is more protected than they from another modern peril, that of solipsist subjectivity; however esoteric a poem may be, the fact that all its words have meanings which can be looked up in a dictionary makes it testify to the existence of other people. Even the language of *Finnegans Wake* was not created by Joyce *ex nihilo*; a purely private verbal world is not possible.

The difference between verse and prose is self-evident, but it is a sheer waste of time to look for a definition of the difference between poetry and prose. Frost's definition of poetry as the untranslatable element in language looks plausible at first sight but, on closer examination, will not quite do. In the first place, even in the most rarefied poetry, there are some elements which are translatable. The sound of the words, their rhythmical relations, and all meanings and association of meanings which depend upon sound, like rhymes and puns, are, of course, untranslatable, but poetry is not, like music, pure sound. Any elements in a poem which are not based on verbal experience are, to some degree, translatable into another tongue, for example, images, similes and metaphors which are drawn from sensory experience. Moreover, because one characteristic that all men, whatever their culture, have in common is uniqueness—every man is a member of a class of one— the unique perspective on the world which every genuine poet has survives translation. If one takes a poem by Goethe and a poem by Hölderlin and makes literal prose cribs of them, every reader will recognize that the two poems were written by two different people. In the second place, if speech can never become music, neither can it ever become algebra. Even in the most "prosy" language, in informative and technical prose, there is a personal element because language is a personal creation. *Ne pas se pencher au dehors* has a different feeling tone from *Nicht hinauslehnen*. A purely poetic language would be unlearnable, a purely prosaic not worth learning.

Valéry bases his definitions of poetry and prose on the difference between the gratuitous and the useful, play and work, and uses as an analogy the difference between dancing and walking. But this will not do either. A commuter may walk to his suburban station every morning, but at the same time he may enjoy the walk for its own sake; the fact that his walk is necessary does not exclude the possibility of its also being a form of play. Vice versa, a dance does not cease to be play if it is also believed to have a useful purpose like promoting a good harvest.

If French poets have been more prone than English to fall into the heresy of thinking that poetry ought to be as much like music as possible, one reason may be that, in traditional French verse, sound effects have always played a much more important role than they have in English verse. The English-speaking peoples have always felt that the difference between poetic speech and the conversational speech of everyday should be kept small, and, whenever English poets have felt that the gap between poetic and ordinary speech was growing too wide, there has been a stylistic revolution to bring them closer again. In English verse, even in Shakespeare's grandest rhetorical passages, the ear is always aware of its relation to everyday speech. A good actor must—alas, today he too seldom does—make the audience hear Shakespeare's lines as verse not prose, but if he tries to make the verse sound like a different language, he will make himself ridiculous.

But French poetry, both in the way it is written and the way it is recited, has emphasized and gloried in the difference between itself and ordinary speech; in French drama, verse and prose *are* different languages. Valéry quotes a contemporary description of Rachel's powers of declamation; in reciting she could and did use a range of two octaves, from F below Middle C to F in alt; an actress who tried to do the same with Shakespeare as Rachel did with Racine would be laughed off the stage.

One can read Shakespeare to oneself without even mentally *hearing* the lines and be very moved; indeed, one may easily find a performance disappointing because almost anyone with an understanding of English verse can speak it better than the average actor and actress. But to read Racine to oneself, even, I fancy, if one is a Frenchman, is like reading the score of an opera when one can hardly play or sing; one can no more get an adequate notion of *Phèdre* without having heard a great performance, than one can of *Tristan und Isolde* if one has never heard a great Isolde like Leider or Flagstad.

(Monsieur St-John Perse tells me that, when it comes to everyday speech, it is French which is the more monotonous and English which has the wider range of vocal inflection.)

I must confess that French classical tragedy strikes me as being opera for the unmusical. When I read the *Hippolytus*, I can recognize, despite all differences, a kinship between the world of Euripides and the world of Shakespeare, but the world of Racine, like the world of opera, seems to be another planet altogether. Euripides' Aphrodite is as concerned with fish and fowl as she is with human beings; Racine's Venus is not only unconcerned with animals, she takes no interest in the Lower Orders. It is impossible to imagine any of Racine's characters sneezing or wanting to go to the bathroom, for in his world there is neither weather nor nature. In consequence, the passions by which his characters are consumed can only exist, as it were, on stage, the creation of the magnificent speech and the grand gestures of the actors and actresses who endow them with flesh and blood. This is also the case in opera, but no speaking voice, however magnificent, can hope to compete, in expressiveness through sound, with a great singing voice backed by an orchestra.

Whenever people talk to me about the weather, I always feel certain that they mean something else. (Oscar Wilde.) The only kind of speech which approximates to the symbolist's poetic ideal is polite tea table conversation, in which the meaning of the banalities uttered depends almost entirely upon vocal inflections.

Owing to its superior power as a mnemonic, verse is superior to prose as a medium for didactic instruction. Those who condemn didacticism must disapprove *a fortiori* of didactic prose; in verse, as the Alka-Seltzer advertisements testify, the didactic message loses half its immodesty. Verse is also certainly the equal of prose as a medium for the lucid exposition of ideas; in skillful hands, the form of the verse can parallel and reinforce the steps of the logic. Indeed, contrary to what most people who have inherited the romantic conception of poetry believe, the danger of argument in verse—Pope's *Essay on Man* is an example—is that the verse may make the ideas *too* clear and distinct, more Cartesian than they really are.

On the other hand, verse is unsuited to controversy, to proving some truth or belief which is not universally accepted, because its formal nature cannot but convey a certain skepticism about its conclusions.

> Thirty days hath September,
> April, June and November

is valid because nobody doubts its truth. Were there, however, a party who passionately denied it, the lines would be powerless to convince him because, formally, it would make no difference if the lines ran:

> Thirty days hath September,
> August, May and December.

Poetry is not magic. In so far as poetry, or any other of the arts, can be said to have an ulterior purpose, it is, by telling the truth, to disenchant and disintoxicate.

"The unacknowledged legislators of the world" describes the secret police, not the poets.

Catharsis is properly effected, not by works of art, but by religious rites. It is also effected, usually improperly, by bullfights, professional football matches, bad movies, military bands and monster rallies at which ten thousand girl guides form themselves into a model of the national flag.

The condition of mankind is, and always has been, so miserable and depraved that, if anyone were to say to the poet: "For God's sake stop singing and do something useful like putting on the kettle or fetching bandages," what just reason could he give for refusing? But nobody says this. The self-appointed unqualified nurse says: "You are to sing the patient a song which will make him believe that I, and I alone, can cure him. If you can't or won't, I shall confiscate your passport and send you to the mines." And the poor patient in his delirium cries: "Please sing me a song which will give me sweet dreams instead of nightmares. If you succeed, I will give you a penthouse in New York or a ranch in Arizona."

PART TWO

The Dyer's Hand

Making, Knowing and Judging*

The art of life, of a poet's life, is, not having anything to do,
to do something. —H. D. Thoreau

Even the greatest of that long line of scholars and poets who have held this chair before me—when I recall the names of some, I am filled with fear and trembling—must have asked themselves: "What *is* a Professor of Poetry? How can Poetry be *professed*?"

I can imagine one possible answer, though unfortunately it is not the right one. I should be feeling less uneasy at this moment than I do, if the duties of the Professor of Poetry were to produce, as occasion should demand, an epithalamium for the nuptials of a Reader in Romance Languages, an elegy on a deceased Canon of Christ Church, a May-day Masque for Somerville or an election ballad for his successor. I should at least be working in the medium to which I am accustomed.

But these are not his duties. His primary duty is to give lectures—which presupposes that he knows something which his audience does not. You have chosen for your new Professor someone who has no more right to the learned garb he is wearing than he would have to a clerical collar. One of his secondary duties is to deliver every other year an oration in Latin. You have chosen a barbarian who cannot write in that tongue and does not know how to pronounce it. Even barbarians have their sense of honor and I must take this public opportunity to say that, for the alien sounds I shall utter at Encaenia, my "affable familiar ghost" has been Mr J. G. Griffith of Jesus.

But it is my primary duty which I must attempt to do this afternoon. If I am in any way to deserve your extraordinary choice for what one of the noblest and most learned of my predecessors so aptly called *The Siege Perilous*, then I must find some topic about which I cannot help knowing something simply because I have written some poems, and, for an inaugural lecture, this topic should be of general and, if possible, central concern to the verbal Art of Numbers.

Many years ago, there appeared in *Punch* a joke which I have heard attributed to the scholar and poet A. E. Housman. The cartoon showed two middle-aged English examiners taking a country stroll in spring. And the caption ran:

> First E. E.   O cuckoo shall I call thee bird
>   Or but a wandering voice?
> Second E. E. State the alternative preferred
>   With reasons for your choice.

*An Inaugural Lecture delivered before the University of Oxford on 11 June 1956.

At first reading this seems to be a satire on examiners. But is it? The moment I try to answer the question, I find myself thinking: "It has an answer and if Wordsworth had put the question to himself instead of to the reader, he would have deleted *bird* as redundant. His inner examiner must have been asleep at the time."

Even if poems were often written in trances, poets would still accept responsibility for them by signing their names and taking the credit. They cannot claim oracular immunity. Admirers of "Kubla Khan," the only documented case of a trance poem which we possess, should not lightly dismiss what Coleridge, who was, after all, a great critic, says in his introductory note:

> The following fragment is here published at the request of a poet of great and deserved celebrity (Lord Byron) and, as far as the Author's own opinions are concerned, rather as a psychological curiosity, than on the grounds of any supposed poetic merits.

It has, of course, extraordinary poetic merits, but Coleridge was not being falsely modest. He saw, I think, as a reader can see, that even the fragment that exists is disjointed and would have had to be worked on if he ever completed the poem, and his critical conscience felt on its honor to admit this.

It seems to me, then, that this might be a possible topic. Anyone who writes poetry ought to have something to say about this critic who is only interested in one author and only concerned with works that do not yet exist. To distinguish him from the critic who is concerned with the already existing works of others, let us call him the Censor.

How does the Censor get his education? How does his attitude towards the literature of the past differ from that of the scholarly critic? If a poet should take to writing criticism, what help to him in that activity are the experiences of his Censor? Is there any truth in Dryden's statement: "Poets themselves are the most proper, though not, I conclude, the only critics"?

In trying to answer these questions, I shall be compelled, from time to time, to give autobiographical illustrations. This is regrettable but unavoidable. I have no other guinea pig.

I

I began writing poetry myself because one Sunday afternoon in March 1922, a friend suggested that I should: the thought had never occurred to me. I scarcely knew any poems—*The English Hymnal,* the Psalms, *Struwwelpeter* and the mnemonic rhymes in *Kennedy's Shorter Latin Primer* are about all I remember—and I took little interest in what is called Imaginative Literature. Most of my reading had been related to a private world of Sacred Objects. Aside from a few stories like George Macdonald's *The Princess and the Goblin* and Jules Verne's *The Child of the Cavern,* the subjects of which touched upon my obsessions, my favorite books bore such titles as *Underground Life, Machinery for Metalliferous Mines, Lead and Zinc Ores of Northumberland and Alston Moor,* and my conscious purpose in reading them had been to gain information about my sacred objects. At the time, therefore, the suggestion that I write poetry seemed like a revelation from heaven for which nothing in my past could account.

Looking back, however, I now realize that I had read the technological prose of my favorite books in a peculiar way. A word like *pyrites,* for example, was for me, not simply an indicative sign; it was the Proper Name of a Sacred Being, so that, when I heard an aunt pronounce it *pirrits,* I was shocked. Her pronunciation was more than wrong, it was ugly. Ignorance was impiety.

It was Edward Lear, I believe,* who said that the true test of imagination is the ability to name a cat, and we are told in the first chapter of Genesis that the Lord brought to unfallen Adam all the creatures that he might name them and whatsoever Adam called every living creature, that was the name thereof, which is to say, its Proper Name. Here Adam plays the role of the Proto-poet, not the Proto-prosewriter. A Proper Name must not only refer, it must refer aptly and this aptness must be publicly recognizable. It is curious to observe, for instance, that when a person has been christened inaptly, he and his friends instinctively call him by some other name. Like a line of poetry, a Proper Name is untranslatable. Language is prosaic to the degree that "It does not matter what particular word is associated with an idea, provided the association once made is permanent." Language is poetic to the degree that it does matter.

> The power of verse [writes Valéry] is derived from an indefinable harmony between what it *says* and what it *is.* Indefinable is essential to the definition. The harmony ought not to be definable; when it can be defined it is imitative harmony and that is not good. The impossibility of defining the relation, together with the impossibility of denying it, constitutes the essence of the poetic line.

The poet is someone, says Mallarmé, who "*de plusieurs vocables refait un mot total,*" and the most poetical of all scholastic disciplines is, surely, Philology, the study of language in abstraction from its uses, so that words become, as it were, little lyrics about themselves.

Since Proper Names in the grammatical sense refer to unique objects, we cannot judge their aptness without personal acquaintance with what they name. To know whether *Old Foss* was an apt name for Lear's cat, we should have had to have known them both. A line of poetry like

> A drop of water in the breaking gulf

is a name for an experience we all know so that we can judge its aptness, and it names, as a Proper Name cannot, relations and actions as well as things.

---

*I was wrong: it was Samuel Butler.

But Shakespeare and Lear are both using language in the same way and, I believe, for the same motive, but into that I shall go later. My present point is that, if my friend's suggestion met with such an unexpected response, the reason may have been that, without knowing it, I had been enjoying the poetic use of language for a long time.

A beginner's efforts cannot be called bad or imitative. They are imaginary. A bad poem has this or that fault which can be pointed out; an imitative poem is a recognizable imitation of this or that poem, this or that poet. But about an imaginary poem no criticism can be made since it is an imitation of poetry-in-general. Never again will a poet feel so inspired, so certain of genius, as he feels in these first days as his pencil flies across the page. Yet something is being learned even now. As he scribbles on he is beginning to get the habit of noticing metrical quantities, to see that any two-syllable word in isolation must be either a *ti-tum*, a *tum-ti* or, occasionally, a *tum-tum*, but that when associated with other words it can sometimes become a *ti-ti*; when he discovers a rhyme he has not thought of before, he stores it away in his memory, a habit which an Italian poet may not need to acquire but which an English poet will find useful.

And, though as yet he can only scribble, he has started reading real poems for pleasure and on purpose. Many things can be said against anthologies, but for an adolescent to whom even the names of most of the poets are unknown, a good one can be an invaluable instructor. I had the extraordinary good fortune to be presented one Christmas with the De la Mare anthology *Come Hither*. This had, for my purposes, two great virtues. Firstly, its good taste. Reading it today, I find very few poems which I should have omitted and none which I should think it bad taste to admire. Secondly, its catholic taste. Given the youthful audience for which it was designed, there were certain kinds of poetry which it did not represent, but within those limits the variety was extraordinary. Particularly valuable was its lack of literary class consciousness, its juxtaposition on terms of equality of unofficial poetry, such as counting-out rhymes, and official poetry such as the odes of Keats. It taught me at the start that poetry does not have to be great or even serious to be good, and that one does not have to be ashamed of moods in which one feels no desire whatsoever to read *The Divine Comedy* and a great desire to read

> When other ladies to the shades go down,
> Still Flavia, Chloris, Celia stay in town.
> These Ghosts of Beauty ling'ring there abide,
> And haunt the places where their Honour died.

Matthew Arnold's notion of Touchstones by which to measure all poems has always struck me as a doubtful one, likely to turn readers into snobs and to ruin talented poets by tempting them to imitate what is beyond their powers.

A poet who wishes to improve himself should certainly keep good company, but for his profit as well as for his comfort the company should not be too far above his station. It is by no means clear that the poetry which influenced Shakespeare's development most fruitfully was the greatest poetry with which he was acquainted. Even for readers, when one thinks of the attention that a great poem demands, there is something frivolous about the notion of spending every day with one. Masterpieces should be kept for High Holidays of the Spirit.

I am not trying to defend the aesthetic heresy that one subject is no more important than any other, or that a poem has no subject or that there is no difference between a great poem and a good one—a heresy which seems to me contrary to human feeling and common sense—but I can understand why it exists. Nothing is worse than a bad poem which was intended to be great.

So a would-be poet begins to learn that poetry is more various than he imagined and that he can like and dislike different poems for different reasons. His Censor, however, has still not yet been born. Before he can give birth to him, he has to pretend to be somebody else; he has to get a literary transference upon some poet in particular.

If poetry were in great public demand so that there were overworked professional poets, I can imagine a system under which an established poet would take on a small number of apprentices who would begin by changing his blotting paper, advance to typing his manuscripts and end up by ghost-writing poems for him which he was too busy to start or finish. The apprentices might really learn something for, knowing that he would get the blame as well as the credit for their work, the Master would be extremely choosy about his apprentices and do his best to teach them all he knew.

In fact, of course, a would-be poet serves his apprenticeship in a library. This has its advantages. Though the Master is deaf and dumb and gives neither instruction nor criticism, the apprentice can choose any Master he likes, living or dead, the Master is available at any hour of the day or night, lessons are all for free, and his passionate admiration of his Master will ensure that he work hard to please him.

To please means to imitate and it is impossible to do a recognizable imitation of a poet without attending to every detail of his diction, rhythms and habits of sensibility. In imitating his Master, the apprentice acquires a Censor, for he learns that, no matter how he finds it, by inspiration, by potluck or after hours of laborious search, there is only one word or rhythm or form that is the *right* one. The right one is still not yet the *real* one, for the apprentice is ventriloquizing, but he has got away from poetry-in-general; he is learning how *a* poem is written. Later in life, incidentally, he will realize how important is the art of imitation, for he will not infrequently be called upon to imitate himself.

My first Master was Thomas Hardy, and I think I was very lucky in my choice. He was a good poet, perhaps a great one, but not *too* good. Much as I loved him, even I could see that his diction was often clumsy and forced and that a lot of his poems were plain bad. This gave me hope where a flaw-less poet might have made me despair. He was modern without being too modern. His world and sensibility were close enough to mine—curiously enough his face bore a striking resemblance to my father's—so that, in imi-tating him, I was being led towards not away from myself, but they were not so close as to obliterate my identity. If I looked through his spectacles, at least I was conscious of a certain eyestrain. Lastly, his metrical variety, his fondness for complicated stanza forms, were an invaluable training in the craft of making. I am also thankful that my first Master did not write in free verse or I might then have been tempted to believe that free verse is easier to write than stricter forms, whereas I now know it is infinitely more difficult.

Presently the curtain rises on a scene rather like the finale to Act II of *Die Meistersinger*. Let us call it The Gathering of the Apprentices. The appren-tices gather together from all over and discover that they are a new genera-tion; somebody shouts the word "modern" and the riot is on. The New Icon-oclastic Poets and Critics are discovered—when I was an undergraduate a critic could still describe Mr T. S. Eliot, O.M., as "a drunken helot"—the po-etry which these new authorities recommend becomes the Canon, that on which they frown is thrown out of the window. There are gods whom it is blasphemy to criticize and devils whose names may not be mentioned with-out execrations. The apprentices have seen a great light while their tutors sit in darkness and the shadow of death.

Really, how do the dons stand it, for I'm sure this scene repeats itself year after year. When I recall the kindness of my tutors, the patience with which they listened, the courtesy with which they hid their boredom, I am over-whelmed by their sheer goodness. I suppose that, having arrived there, they knew that the road of excess can lead to the palace of Wisdom, though it frequently does not.

An apprentice discovers that there is a significant relation between the statement "Today I am nineteen" and the statement "Today is February the twenty-first, 1926." If the discovery goes to his head, it is, nevertheless, a dis-covery he must make, for, until he realizes that all the poems he has read, however different they may be, have one common characteristic—they have all been written—his own writing will never cease to be imitative. He will never know what he himself *can write* until he has a general sense of what *needs to be written*. And this is the one thing his elders cannot teach him, just because they are his elders; he can only learn it from his fellow apprentices with whom he shares one thing in common, youth.

The discovery is not wholly pleasant. If the young speak of the past as a burden it is a joy to throw off, behind their words may often lie a resentment and fright at realizing that the past will not carry them on its back.

The critical statements of the Censor are always polemical advice to his poet, meant, not as objective truths, but as pointers, and in youth which is trying to discover its own identity, the exasperation at not having yet succeeded naturally tends to express itself in violence and exaggeration.

If an undergraduate announces to his tutor one morning that Gertrude Stein is the greatest writer who ever lived or that Shakespeare is no good, he is really only saying something like this: "I don't know what to write yet or how, but yesterday while reading Gertrude Stein, I thought I saw a clue" or "Reading Shakespeare yesterday, I realized that one of the faults in what I write is a tendency to rhetorical bombast."

Fashion and snobbery are also valuable as a defense against literary indigestion. Regardless of their quality, it is always better to read a few books carefully than skim through many, and, short of a personal taste which cannot be formed overnight, snobbery is as good a principle of limitation as any other.

I am eternally grateful, for example, to the musical fashion of my youth which prevented me from listening to Italian Opera until I was over thirty, by which age I was capable of really appreciating a world so beautiful and so challenging to my own cultural heritage.

The apprentices do each other a further mutual service which no older and sounder critic could do. They read each other's manuscripts. At this age a fellow apprentice has two great virtues as a critic. When he reads your poem, he may grossly overestimate it, but if he does, he really believes what he is saying; he never flatters or praises merely to encourage. Secondly, he reads your poem with that passionate attention which grown-up critics only give to masterpieces and grown-up poets only to themselves. When he finds fault, his criticisms are intended to help you to improve. He really wants your poem to be better.

It is just this kind of personal criticism which in later life, when the band of apprentices has dispersed, a writer often finds it so hard to get. The verdicts of reviewers, however just, are seldom of any use to him. Why should they be? A critic's duty is to tell the public what a work is, not tell its author what he should and could have written instead. Yet this is the only kind of criticism from which an author can benefit. Those who could do it for him are generally, like himself, too elsewhere, too busy, too married, too selfish.

We must assume that our apprentice does succeed in becoming a poet, that, sooner or later, a day arrives when his Censor is able to say truthfully and for the first time: "All the words are right, and all are yours."

His thrill at hearing this does not last long, however, for a moment later comes the thought: "Will it ever happen again?" Whatever his future life as a wage-earner, a citizen, a family man may be, to the end of his days his life as a poet will be without anticipation. He will never be able to say: "Tomorrow I will write a poem and, thanks to my training and experience, I already know I shall do a good job." In the eyes of others a man is a poet if he has written one good poem. In his own he is only a poet at the moment when he is making his last revision to a new poem. The moment before, he was still only a potential poet; the moment after, he is a man who has ceased to write poetry, perhaps forever.

II

It is hardly surprising, then, if a young poet seldom does well in his examinations. If he does, then, either he is also a scholar in the making, or he is a very good boy indeed. A medical student knows that he must study anatomy in order to become a doctor, so he has a reason for study. A future scholar has a reason, because he knows more or less what he wants to know. But there is nothing a would-be poet knows he has to know. He is at the mercy of the immediate moment because he has no concrete reason for not yielding to its demands and, for all he knows now, surrendering to his immediate desire may turn out later to have been the best thing he could have done. His immediate desire can even be to attend a lecture. I remember one I attended, delivered by Professor Tolkien. I do not remember a single word he said but at a certain point he recited, and magnificently, a long passage of *Beowulf.* I was spellbound. This poetry, I knew, was going to be my dish. I became willing, therefore, to work at Anglo-Saxon because, unless I did, I should never be able to read this poetry. I learned enough to read it, however sloppily, and Anglo-Saxon and Middle English poetry have been one of my strongest, most lasting influences.

But this was something which neither I nor anybody else could have foreseen. Again, what good angel lured me into Blackwell's one afternoon and, from such a wilderness of volumes, picked out for me the essays of W. P. Ker? No other critic whom I have subsequently read could have granted me the same vision of a kind of literary All Souls Night in which the dead, the living and the unborn writers of every age and in every tongue were seen as engaged upon a common, noble and civilizing task. No other could have so instantaneously aroused in me a fascination with prosody, which I have never lost.

You must not imagine, however, that being a bad boy is all fun. During my three years as an undergraduate, I had a high old time, I made some lifelong friends and I was more unhappy than I have ever been before or since. I might or might not be wasting my time—only the future would show—I was certainly wasting my parents' money. Nor must you think that, because he fails to study, a young poet looks down his nose at all the scholarly investigations going on around him. Unless he is very young indeed, he knows that these lines by Yeats are rather silly.

> Bald heads forgetful of their sins,
> Old, learned, respectable bald heads
> Edit and annotate the lines

That young men, tossing on their beds,
Rhymed out in love's despair
To flatter beauty's ignorant ear.

All shuffle there; all cough in ink;
All wear the carpet with their shoes;
All think what other people think;
All know the man their neighbour knows.
Lord, what would they say
Did their Catullus walk that way?

Ignoring the obvious libel—that all dons are bald and respectable—the sentiments are still nonsense. Edit indeed! Thank God they do. If it had not been for scholars working themselves blind copying and collating manuscripts, how many poems would be unavailable, including those of Catullus, and how many others full of lines that made no sense? Nor has the invention of printing made editors unnecessary. Lucky the poet whose collected works are not full of misprints. Even a young poet knows or very soon will realize that, but for scholars, he would be at the mercy of the literary taste of a past generation, since, once a book has gone out of print and been forgotten, only the scholar with his unselfish courage to read the unreadable will retrieve the rare prize. How much Donne, even, would he have read, had it not been for Professor Grierson? What would he know of Clare or Barnes or Christopher Smart but for Messrs Blunden, Grigson, Force Stead and Bond? Nor is editing all that scholars have already done for him. There is that blessed combination of poet and scholar, the translator. How, for example, without the learning and talent of Sir Arthur Waley, could he have discovered, and without the slightest effort on his part, an entirely new world of poetry, that of the Chinese?

No, what prevents the young poet from academic study is not conceited ingratitude but a Law of mental growth. Except in matters of life and death, temporal or spiritual, questions must not be answered until they have been asked, and at present he has no questions. At present he makes little distinction between a book, a country walk and a kiss. All are equally experiences to store away in his memory. Could he look into a memory, the literary historian would find many members of that species which he calls books, but they are curiously changed from the books he finds in his library. The dates are all different. *In Memoriam* is written before *The Dunciad*, the thirteenth century comes after the sixteenth. He always thought Robert Burton wrote a big book about melancholy. Apparently he only wrote ten pages. He is accustomed to the notion that a book can only be written once. Here some are continually rewritten. In his library books are related to each other in an orderly way by genre or subject. Here the commonest principle of association seems to be by age groups. *Piers Ploughman III* is going about with Kierke-

gaard's *Journals, Piers Ploughman IV* with *The Making of the English Landscape.*
Most puzzling of all, instead of only associating with members of their own
kind, in this extraordinary democracy every species of being knows every
other and the closest friend of a book is rarely another book. *Gulliver's Travels* walks arm in arm with a love affair, a canto of *Il Paradiso* sits with a singularly good dinner, *War and Peace* never leaves the side of a penniless Christmas in a foreign city, the tenth *The Winter's Tale* exchanges greetings with the
first complete recording of *La Favorita.*

Yet this is the world out of which poems are made. In a better and more
sensible poem than "The Scholars" Yeats describes it as a "rag and bone
shop." Let me use the less drab but no less anarchic image of a Mad Hatter's
Tea-Party.

In so reading to stock his memory with images upon which later he may be
able to draw in his own work, there is no critical principle by which a poet
can select his books. The critical judgment "This book is good or bad" implies good or bad at all times, but in relation to a reader's future a book is
good now if its future effect is good, and, since the future is unknown, no
judgment can be made. The safest guide, therefore, is the naïve uncritical
principle of personal liking. A person at least knows one thing about his future, that however different it may be from his present, it will be his. However he may have changed he will still be himself, not somebody else. What
he likes now, therefore, whether an impersonal judgment approve or disapprove, has the best chance of becoming useful to him later.

A poet is all the more willing to be guided by personal liking because he
assumes, I think with reason, that, since he wants to write poetry himself, his
taste may be limited but it will not be so bad as to lead him astray. The
chances are that most of the books he likes are such as a critic would approve
of. Should it come to a quarrel between liking and approving, however, I
think he will always take the side of liking, and he enjoys baiting the critic
with teasers like the problem of the comically bad poem.

> Go, Mary, to the summer house
> And sweep the wooden floor,
> And light the little fire, and wash
> The pretty varnished door;
> For there the London gentleman,
> Who lately lectured here,
> Will smoke a pipe with Jonathan,
> And taste our home-brewed beer.
>
> Go bind the dahlias, that our guest
> May praise their fading dyes;
> But strip of every fading bloom
> The flower that won the prize!
> And take thy father's knife, and prune

> The roses that remain,
> And let the fallen hollyhock
> Peep through the broken pane.
>
> I'll follow in an hour or two;
> Be sure I will not fail
> To bring his flute and spying glass,
> The pipes and bottled ale;
> And that grand music that he made
> About the child in bliss,
> Our guest shall hear it sung and played,
> And feel how grand it is!*

Had this poem appeared last week under the title "Mr Ebenezer Elliott Entertains a Metropolitan Visitor" and been signed by Mr John Betjeman, would it be good? Since it was not written by Mr Betjeman as a comic dramatic monologue but by Mr Elliott himself as a serious lyric, is it bad? What difference do the inverted commas make?

In judging a work of the past, the question of the historical critic—"What was the author of this work trying to do? How far did he succeed in doing it?"—important as he knows it to be, will always interest a poet less than the question—"What does this work suggest to living writers now? Will it help or hinder them in what they are trying to do?"

A few years ago I came across the following lines:

> Wherewith Love to the harts forest he fleeth
> Leaving the enterprise with pain and cry,
> And there him hideth and not appeareth.
> What may I do? When my master feareth,
> But in the field with him to live and die,
> For good is the life ending faithfully.

I found the rhythm of these lines strangely beautiful, they haunted me and I know that they have had an influence upon the rhythm of certain lines of my own.

Of course I know that all the historical evidence suggests that Wyatt was trying to write regular iambics, that the rhythm he was after would have his lines run thus:

> And thére him hídeth and not áppeáreth
>
> What máy I dó? When mý master feáreth
>
> But ín the field with hím to líve and díe
>
> For góod is the lífe ending faíthfully.

---

*Ebenezer Elliott, quoted by Aldous Huxley in *Texts and Pretexts*.

Since they cannot be read this way without sounding monstrous, one must say that Wyatt failed to do what he was trying to do, and a literary historian of the sixteenth century will have to censure him.

Luckily I am spared this duty and can without reservation approve. Between Wyatt and the present day lie four hundred years of prosodic practice and development. Thanks to the work of our predecessors any schoolboy can today write the regular iambics which Wyatt, struggling to escape from the metrical anarchy of the fifteenth and early sixteenth centuries, found so difficult. Our problem in the twentieth century is not how to write iambics but how not to write in them from automatic habit when they are not to our genuine purpose. What for Wyatt was a failure is for us a blessing. Must a work be censored for being beautiful by accident? I suppose it must, but a poet will always have a sneaking regard for luck because he knows the role which it plays in poetic composition. Something unexpected is always turning up, and though he knows that the Censor has to pass it, the memory of the lucky dip is what he treasures.

A young poet may be conceited about his good taste, but he is under no illusions about his ignorance. He is well aware of how much poetry there is that he would like but of which he has never heard, and that there are learned men who have read it. His problem is knowing which learned man to ask, for it is not just more good poetry that he wants to read, but more of the kind he likes. He judges a scholarly or critical book less by the text than by the quotations, and all his life, I think, when he reads a work of criticism, he will find himself trying to guess what taste lies behind the critic's judgment. Like Matthew Arnold I have my Touchstones, but they are for testing critics, not poets. Many of them concern taste in other matters than poetry or even literature, but here are four questions which, could I examine a critic, I should ask him:

"Do you like, and by like I really mean like, not approve of on principle:

(1) Long lists of proper names such as the Old Testament genealogies or the Catalogue of ships in the *Iliad?*
(2) Riddles and all other ways of not calling a spade a spade?
(3) Complicated verse forms of great technical difficulty, such as Englyns, Drott-Kvaetts, Sestinas, even if their content is trivial?
(4) Conscious theatrical exaggeration, pieces of Baroque flattery like Dryden's welcome to the Duchess of Ormond?"

If a critic could truthfully answer "yes" to all four, then I should trust his judgment implicitly on all literary matters.

III

It is not uncommon, it is even usual, for a poet to write reviews, compile anthologies, compose critical introductions. It is one of his main sources of income. He may even find himself lecturing. In such chores he has little to offset his lack of scholarship, but that little he has.

His lazy habit of only reading what he likes will at least have taught him one lesson, that to be worth attacking a book must be worth reading. The greatest critical study of a single figure that I know of, *The Case of Wagner*, is a model of what such an attack should be. Savage as he often is, Nietzsche never allows the reader to forget for one instant that Wagner is an extraordinary genius and that, for all which may be wrong with it, his music is of the highest importance. Indeed it was this book which first taught me to listen to Wagner, about whom I had previously held silly preconceived notions. Another model is D. H. Lawrence's *Studies in Classic American Literature*. I remember my disappointment, when, after reading the essay on Fenimore Cooper which is highly critical, I hurried off to read him. Unfortunately, I did not find Cooper nearly as exciting as Lawrence had made him sound.

The second advantage which a poet possesses is that such satisfactions to the ego as the writing of poetry can provide have been taken care of in his case. I should not expect a poet turned critic to become either a prig, a critic's critic, a romantic novelist or a maniac. By the prig, I mean the critic for whom no actual poem is good enough since the only one that would be is the poem he would like to write himself but cannot. Reading his criticism, one gets the impression that he would rather a poem were bad than good. His twin, the critic's critic, shows no obvious resentment; indeed, on the surface he appears to idolize the poet about whom he is writing; but his critical analysis of his idol's work is so much more complicated and difficult than the work itself as to deprive someone who has not yet read it of all wish to do so. He, too, one suspects, has a secret grievance. He finds it unfortunate and regrettable that before there can be criticism there has to be a poem to criticize. For him a poem is not a work of art by somebody else; it is his own discovered document.

The romantic novelist is a much jollier figure. His happy hunting ground is the field of unanswerable questions, particularly if they concern the private lives of authors. Since the questions to which he devotes his life—he is often an extremely learned gentleman—can never be answered, he is free to indulge his fancies without misgivings. And why shouldn't he? How much duller the Variorum edition of the Shakespeare sonnets would be without him. Jolliest of all is the maniac. The commonest of his kind is the man who believes that poetry is written in cyphers—but there are many other kinds. My favorite is the John Bellenden Ker who set out to prove that English nursery rhymes were originally written in a form of Old Dutch invented by himself.

Whatever his defects, a poet at least thinks a poem more important than anything which can be said about it, he would rather it were good than bad, the last thing he wants is that it should be like one of his own, and his experience as a maker should have taught him to recognize quickly whether a critical question is important, unimportant but real, unreal because unanswerable or just absurd.

He will know, for example, that knowledge of an artist's life, temperament and opinions is unimportant to an understanding of his art, but that a similar knowledge about a critic may be important to an understanding of his judgments. If we knew every detail of Shakespeare's life, our reading of his plays would be little changed, if at all; but how much less interesting *The Lives of the Poets* would be if we knew nothing else about Johnson.

He will know, to take an instance of an unanswerable question, that if the date of the Shakespeare sonnets can ever be fixed, it will not be fixed by poring over Sonnet CVII. His experience as a maker of poems will make him reason something like this: "The feeling expressed here is the not uncommon feeling—All's well with my love and all's well with the world at large. The feeling that all is well with the world at large can be produced in many ways. It *can* be produced by an occasion of public rejoicing, some historical event like the defeat of the Armada or the successful passing of the Queen's climacteric, but it does not have to be. The same feeling can be aroused by a fine day. The figures employed in the lines

> The mortal moon hath her eclipse endured
> And the sad augurs mock their own presage,
> Incertainties now crown themselves assured
> And peace proclaims olives of endless age

come from literature and contain no specific historical reference. They could have been suggested to Shakespeare by some historical event, but he could have written them without one. Further, even if they were so prompted, the date of the event does not have to be contemporary with the occasion celebrated in the sonnet. A present instance of a feeling always recalls past instances and their circumstances, so that it is possible, if the poet chooses, to employ images suggested by the circumstances of a past occasion to describe the present if the feeling is the same. What Shakespeare has written contains no historical clue."

Because of his limited knowledge, a poet would generally be wise, when talking about poetry, to choose either some general subject upon which if his conclusions are true in a few cases, they must be true in most, or some detailed matter which only requires the intensive study of a few works. He may have something sensible to say about woods, even about leaves, but you should never trust him on trees.

Speaking for myself, the questions which interest me most when reading a poem are two. The first is technical: "Here is a verbal contraption. How does it work?" The second is, in the broadest sense, moral: "What kind of a guy inhabits this poem? What is his notion of the good life or the good place? His notion of the Evil One? What does he conceal from the reader? What does he conceal even from himself?"

And you must not be surprised if he should have nothing but platitudes to say; firstly because he will always find it hard to believe that a poem needs expounding, and secondly because he doesn't consider poetry quite that important: any poet, I believe, will echo Miss Marianne Moore's words: "*I, too, dislike it.*"

IV

Away back we left a young poet who had just written his first real poem and was wondering if it would be his last. We must assume that it was not, that he has arrived on the literary scene in the sense that now people pass judgment on his work without having read it. Twenty years have gone by. The table of his Mad Hatter's Tea-Party has gotten much longer and there are thousands of new faces, some charming, some quite horrid. Down at the far end, some of those who used to be so amusing have turned into crashing bores or fallen asleep, a sad change which has often come over later guests after holding forth for a few years. Boredom does not necessarily imply disapproval; I still think Rilke a great poet though I cannot read him any more.

Many of the books which have been most important to him have not been works of poetry or criticism but books which have altered his way of looking at the world and himself, and a lot of these, probably, are what an expert in their field would call "unsound." The expert, no doubt, is right, but it is not for a poet to judge; his duty is to be grateful.

And among the experiences which have influenced his writing, a number may have been experiences of other arts. I know, for example, that through listening to music I have learned much about how to organize a poem, how to obtain variety and contrast through change of tone, tempo and rhythm, though I could not say just how. Man is an analogy-drawing animal; that is his great good fortune. His danger is of treating analogies as identities, of saying, for instance, "Poetry should be as much like music as possible." I suspect that the people who are most likely to say this are the tone-deaf. The more one loves another art, the less likely it is that one will wish to trespass upon its domain.

During these twenty years, one thing has never changed since he wrote his first poem. Every time he writes a new one, the same question occurs to him: "Will it ever happen again," but now he begins to hear his Censor saying: "It must never happen again." Having spent twenty years learning to be himself, he finds that he must now start learning not to be himself. At first he may think this means no more than keeping a sharper look out for obsessive rhythms, tics of expression, privately numinous words, but presently he discovers that the command not to imitate himself can mean something harder than that. It can mean that he should refrain from writing a poem which might turn out to be a good one, and even an admired one. He learns that, if on finishing a poem he is convinced that it is good, the chances are that the poem is a self-imitation. The most hopeful sign that it is not is the feeling of complete uncertainty: "Either this is quite good or it is quite bad, I can't tell." And, of course, it may very well be quite bad. Discovering oneself is a passive process because the self is already there. Time and attention are all that it takes. But changing oneself means changing in one direction rather than another, and towards one goal rather than another. The goal may be unknown but movement is impossible without a hypothesis as to where it lies. It is at this point, therefore, that a poet often begins to take an interest in theories of poetry and even to develop one of his own.

I am always interested in hearing what a poet has to say about the nature of poetry, though I do not take it too seriously. As objective statements his definitions are never accurate, never complete and always one-sided. Not one would stand up under a rigorous analysis. In unkind moments one is almost tempted to think that all they are really saying is: "Read me. Don't read the other fellows." But, taken as critical admonitions addressed by his Censor to the poet himself, there is generally something to be learned from them.

Baudelaire has given us an excellent account of their origin and purpose.

> I pity the poets who are guided solely by instinct; they seem to me incomplete. In the spiritual life of the former there must come a crisis when they would think out their art, discover the obscure laws in consequence of which they have produced, and draw from this study a series of precepts whose divine purpose is infallibility in poetic production.

The evidence, that is to say, upon which the poet bases his conclusions consists of his own experiences in writing and his private judgments upon his own works. Looking back, he sees many occasions on which he took a wrong turning or walked up a blind alley, mistakes which, it seems to him now, he could have avoided, had he been more conscious at the time of the choice he was making. Looking over the poems he has written, he finds that, irrespective of their merits, there are some which he particularly dislikes and some which are his favorites. Of one he may think: "This is full of faults, but it is the kind of poem I ought to write more of"; of another: "This may be all right in itself but it's exactly the sort of thing I must never do again." The principles he formulates, therefore, are intended to guard himself against making unnecessary mistakes and provide him with a guesswork map of the future. They are fallible, of course—like all guesses—the word *infallibility* in Baudelaire's description is a typical poet's fib. But there is a difference between a project which may fail and one which must.

In trying to formulate principles, a poet may have another motive which Baudelaire does not mention, a desire to justify his writing poetry at all, and in recent years this motive seems to have grown stronger. The Rimbaud Myth—the tale of a great poet who ceases writing, not because, like Coleridge, he has nothing more to say, but because he chooses to stop—may not be true, I am pretty sure it is not, but as a myth it haunts the artistic conscience of this century.

Knowing all this, and knowing that you know it, I shall now proceed to make some general statements of my own. I hope they are not nonsense, but I cannot be sure. At least, even as emotive noises, I find them useful to me. The only verifiable facts I can offer in evidence are these.

Some cultures make a social distinction between the sacred and the profane, certain human beings are publicly regarded as numinous, and a clear division is made between certain actions which are regarded as sacred rites of great importance to the well-being of society, and everyday profane behavior. In such cultures, if they are advanced enough to recognize poetry as an art, the poet has a public—even a professional status—and his poetry is either public or esoteric.

There are other cultures, like our own, in which the distinction between the sacred and the profane is not socially recognized. Either the distinction is denied or it is regarded as an individual matter of taste with which society is not and should not be concerned. In such cultures, the poet has an amateur status and his poetry is neither public nor esoteric but intimate. That is to say, he writes neither as a citizen nor as a member of a group of professional adepts, but as a single person to be read by other single persons. Intimate poetry is not necessarily obscure; for someone not in the know, ancient esoteric poetry can be more obscure than the wildest modern. Nor, needless to say, is intimate poetry necessarily inferior to other kinds.

In what follows, the terms Primary and Secondary Imagination are taken, of course, from the thirteenth chapter of *Biographia Literaria*. I have adopted them because, though my description may differ from Coleridge's, I believe we are both trying to describe the same phenomena.

Herewith, then, what I might describe as a literary dogmatic psalm, a kind of private *Quicunque vult.*

The concern of the Primary Imagination, its only concern, is with sacred beings and sacred events. The sacred is that to which it is obliged to respond; the profane is that to which it cannot respond and therefore does not know. The profane is known to other faculties of the mind, but not to the Primary Imagination. A sacred being cannot be anticipated; it must be encountered. On encounter the imagination has no option but to respond. All imaginations do not recognize the same sacred beings or events, but every imagination responds to those it recognizes in the same way. The impression made upon the imagination by any sacred being is of an overwhelming but undefinable importance—an unchangeable quality, an Identity, as Keats said: I-am-that-I-am is what every sacred being seems to say. The impression made by a sacred event is of an overwhelming but undefinable significance. In his book *Witchcraft*, Mr Charles Williams has described it thus:

One is aware that a phenomenon, being wholly itself, is laden with universal meaning. A hand lighting a cigarette is the explanation of everything; a foot stepping from the train is the rock of all existence. . . . Two light dancing steps by a girl appear to be what all the Schoolmen were trying to express . . . but two quiet steps by an old man seem like the very speech of hell. Or the other way round.

The response of the imagination to such a presence or significance is a passion of awe. This awe may vary greatly in intensity and range in tone from joyous wonder to panic dread. A sacred being may be attractive or repulsive—a swan or an octopus—beautiful or ugly—a toothless hag or a fair young child—good or evil—a Beatrice or a Belle Dame Sans Merci—historical fact or fiction—a person met on the road or an image encountered in a story or a dream—it may be noble or something unmentionable in a drawing room, it may be anything it likes on condition, but this condition is absolute, that it arouse awe. The realm of the Primary Imagination is without freedom, sense of time or humor. Whatever determines this response or lack of response lies below consciousness and is of concern to psychology, not art.

Some sacred beings seem to be sacred to all imaginations at all times. The Moon, for example, Fire, Snakes and those four important beings which can only be defined in terms of nonbeing: Darkness, Silence, Nothing, Death. Some, like kings, are only sacred to all within a certain culture; some only to members of a social group—the Latin language among humanists—and some are only sacred to a single imagination. Many of us have sacred landscapes which probably all have much in common, but there will almost certainly be details which are peculiar to each. An imagination can acquire new sacred beings and it can lose old ones to the profane. Sacred beings can be acquired by social contagion but not consciously. One cannot be taught to recognize a sacred being, one has to be converted. As a rule, perhaps, with advancing age sacred events gain in importance over sacred beings.

A sacred being may also be an object of desire but the imagination does not desire it. A desire can be a sacred being but the imagination is without desire. In the presence of the sacred, it is self-forgetful; in its absence the very type of the profane, "The most unpoetical of all God's creatures." A sacred being may also demand to be loved or obeyed, it may reward or punish, but the imagination is unconcerned: a law can be a sacred being, but the imagination does not obey. To the imagination a sacred being is self-sufficient, and like Aristotle's God can have no need of friends.

The Secondary Imagination is of another character and at another mental level. It is active not passive, and its categories are not the sacred and the profane, but the beautiful and ugly. Our dreams are full of sacred beings and events—indeed, they may well contain nothing else, but we cannot distinguish in dreams—or so it seems to me, though I may be wrong—between the beautiful and the ugly. Beauty and ugliness pertain to Form not to Being. The Primary Imagination only recognizes one kind of being, the sacred, but the Secondary Imagination recognizes both beautiful and ugly forms. To the Primary Imagination a sacred being is that which it is. To the Secondary Imagination a beautiful form is as it ought to be, an ugly form as it ought not to be. Observing the beautiful, it has the feeling of satisfaction, pleasure, absence of conflict; observing the ugly, the contrary feelings. It does not desire the beautiful, but an ugly form arouses in it a desire that its ugliness be corrected and made beautiful. It does not worship the beautiful; it approves of it and can give reasons for its approval. The Secondary Imagination has, one might say, a bourgeois nature. It approves of regularity, of spatial symmetry and temporal repetition, of law and order: it disapproves of loose ends, irrelevance and mess.

Lastly, the Secondary Imagination is social and craves agreement with other minds. If I think a form beautiful and you think it ugly, we cannot both help agreeing that one of us must be wrong, whereas if I think something is sacred and you think it is profane, neither of us will dream of arguing the matter.

Both kinds of imagination are essential to the health of the mind. Without the inspiration of sacred awe, its beautiful forms would soon become banal, its rhythms mechanical; without the activity of the Secondary Imagination the passivity of the Primary would be the mind's undoing; sooner or later its sacred beings would possess it, it would come to think of itself as sacred, exclude the outer world as profane and so go mad.

The impulse to create a work of art is felt when, in certain persons, the passive awe provoked by sacred beings or events is transformed into a desire to express that awe in a rite of worship or homage, and to be fit homage, this rite must be beautiful. This rite has no magical or idolatrous intention; nothing is expected in return. Nor is it, in a Christian sense, an act of devotion. If it praises the Creator, it does so indirectly by praising His creatures—among which may be human notions of the Divine Nature. With God as Redeemer, it has, so far as I can see, little if anything to do.

In poetry the rite is verbal; it pays homage by naming. I suspect that the predisposition of a mind towards the poetic medium may have its origin in an error. A nurse, let us suppose, says to a child, "Look at the moon!" The child looks and for him this is a sacred encounter. In his mind the word "moon" is not a name of a sacred object but one of its most important properties and, therefore, numinous. The notion of writing poetry cannot occur to him, of course, until he has realized that names and things are not identical and that there cannot be an intelligible sacred language, but I wonder if, when he has discovered the social nature of language, he would attach such importance to one of its uses, that of naming, if he had not previously made this false identification.

The pure poem, in the French sense of *la poésie pure* would be, I suppose, a celebration of the numinous-in-itself in abstraction from all cases and devoid of any profane reference whatsoever—a sort of *sanctus, sanctus, sanctus.* If it could be written, which is doubtful, it would not necessarily be the best poem.

A poem is a rite; hence its formal and ritualistic character. Its use of language is deliberately and ostentatiously different from talk. Even when it employs the diction and rhythms of conversation, it employs them as a deliberate informality, presupposing the norm with which they are intended to contrast.

The form of a rite must be beautiful, exhibiting, for example, balance, closure and aptness to that which it is the form of. It is over this last quality of aptness that most of our aesthetic quarrels arise, and must arise, whenever our sacred and profane worlds differ.

> To the Eyes of a Miser, a Guinea is far more beautiful than the Sun & a bag worn with the use of Money has more beautiful proportions than a Vine filled with Grapes.

Blake, it will be noticed, does not accuse the Miser of lacking imagination.

The value of a profane thing lies in what it usefully does, the value of a sacred thing lies in what it *is*: a sacred thing may also have a function but it does not have to. The apt name for a profane being, therefore, is the word or words that accurately describe his function—a Mr Smith, a Mr Weaver. The apt name for a sacred being is the word or words which worthily express his importance—Son of Thunder, The Well-Wishing One.

Great changes in artistic style always reflect some alteration in the frontier between the sacred and profane in the imagination of a society. Thus, to take an architectural example, a seventeenth-century monarch had the same function as that of a modern State official—he had to govern. But in designing his palace, the Baroque architect did not aim, as a modern architect aims when designing a government building, at making an office in which the king could govern as easily and efficiently as possible; he was trying to make a home fit for God's earthly representative to inhabit; in so far as he thought at all about what the king would do in it as a ruler, he thought of his ceremonial not his practical actions.

Even today few people find a functionally furnished living room beautiful because, to most of us, a sitting room is not merely a place to sit in; it is also a shrine for father's chair.

Thanks to the social nature of language, a poet can relate any one sacred being or event to any other. The relation may be harmonious, an ironic contrast or a tragic contradiction like the great man, or the beloved, and death; he can relate them to every other concern of the mind, the demands of desire, reason and conscience, and he can bring them into contact and contrast with the profane. Again the consequences can be happy, ironic, tragic and, in relation to the profane, comic. How many poems have been written, for example, upon one of these three themes:

This was sacred but now it is profane. Alas, or thank goodness!
This is sacred but ought it to be?
This is sacred but is that so important?

But it is from the sacred encounters of his imagination that a poet's impulse to write a poem arises. Thanks to the language, he need not name them directly unless he wishes; he can describe one in terms of another and translate those that are private or irrational or socially unacceptable into such as are acceptable to reason and society. Some poems are directly *about* the sacred beings they were written *for*: others are not, and in that case no reader can tell what was the original encounter which provided the impulse for the poem. Nor, probably, can the poet himself. Every poem he writes involves his whole past. Every love poem, for instance, is hung with trophies of lovers gone, and among these may be some very peculiar objects indeed. The lovely lady of the present may number among her predecessors an overshot waterwheel. But the encounter, be it novel or renewed by recollection from the past, must be suffered by a poet before he can write a genuine poem.

Whatever its actual content and overt interest, every poem is rooted in imaginative awe. Poetry can do a hundred and one things, delight, sadden, disturb, amuse, instruct—it may express every possible shade of emotion, and describe every conceivable kind of event, but there is only one thing that all poetry must do; it must praise all it can for being and for happening.

The Virgin & The Dynamo

> There is a square. There is an oblong. The players take the square and place it upon the oblong. They place it very accurately. They make a perfect dwelling-place. The structure is now visible. What was inchoate is here stated. We are not so various or so mean. We have made oblongs and stood them upon squares. This is our triumph. This is our consolation. —Virginia Woolf

The Two Real Worlds

(1) The Natural World of the Dynamo, the world of masses, identical relations and recurrent events, describable, not in words but in terms of numbers, or rather, in algebraic terms. In this world, Freedom is the consciousness of Necessity and Justice the equality of all before natural law. (*Hard cases make bad law.*)

(2) The Historical World of the Virgin, the world of faces, analogical relations and singular events, describable only in terms of speech. In this world, Necessity is the consciousness of Freedom and Justice the love of my neighbor as a unique and irreplaceable being. (*One law for the ox and the ass is oppression.*)

Since all human experience is that of conscious persons, man's realization that the World of the Dynamo exists in which events happen of themselves and cannot be prevented by anybody's art, came later than his realization that the World of the Virgin exists. Freedom is an immediate datum of consciousness; Necessity is not.

The Two Chimerical Worlds

(1) The magical polytheistic nature created by the aesthetic illusion which would regard the world of masses as if it were a world of faces. The aesthetic religion says prayers to the Dynamo.

(2) The mechanized history created by the scientific illusion which would regard the world of faces as if it were a world of masses. The scientific religion treats the Virgin as a statistic. "Scientific" politics is animism stood on its head.

Without Art, we could have no notion of Liberty; without Science no notion of Equality; without either, therefore, no notion of Justice.

Without Art, we should have no notion of the sacred; without Science, we should always worship false gods.

By nature we tend to endow with a face any power which we imagine to be responsible for our lives and behavior; vice versa, we tend to deprive of their faces any persons whom we believe to be at the mercy of our will. In both cases, we are trying to avoid responsibility. In the first case, we wish to say: "I can't help doing what I do; someone else, stronger than I, is making me do it"—in the second: "I can do what I like to N because N is a thing, an *x* with no will of its own."

The pagan gods of nature do not have real faces but rather masks, for a real face expresses a responsibility for itself, and the pagan gods are, by definition, irresponsible. It is permissible, and even right, to endow Nature with a real face, e.g. the face of the Madonna, for by so doing we make nature remind us of our duty towards her, but we may only do this after we have removed the pagan mask from her, seen her as a world of masses and realized that she is not responsible for us.

Vice versa, the saint can employ the algebraic notion of *any* in his relation to others as an expression of the fact that his neighbor is not someone of whom he is personally fond, but anybody who happens to need him; but he can only do this because he has advanced spiritually to the point where he sees nobody as a faceless cypher.

Henry Adams thought that Venus and the Virgin of Chartres were the same persons. Actually, Venus is the Dynamo in disguise, a symbol for an impersonal natural force, and Adams' nostalgic preference for Chartres to Chicago was nothing but aestheticism; he thought the disguise was prettier than the reality, but it was the Dynamo he worshiped, not the Virgin.

Pluralities

Any world is comprised of a plurality of objects and events. Pluralities are of three kinds; crowds, societies and communities.

(1) *A Crowd*

A crowd is comprised of $n > 1$ members whose only relation is arithmetical; they can only be counted. A crowd loves neither itself nor anything other than itself; its existence is chimerical. Of a crowd it may be said, either that it is not real but only apparent, or that it should not be.

(2) *A Society*

A society is comprised of a definite or an optimum number of members, united in a specific manner into a whole with a characteristic mode of behavior which is different from the modes of behavior of its component members in isolation. A society cannot come into being until its component members are present and properly related; add or subtract a member, change their relations, and the society either ceases to exist or is transformed into another society. A society is a system which loves itself; to this self-love, the self-love of its members is totally subordinate. Of a society it may be said that it is more or less efficient in maintaining its existence.

(3) *A Community*

A community is comprised of n members united, to use a definition of Saint Augustine's, by a common love of something other than themselves. Like a crowd and unlike a society, its character is not changed by the addition or subtraction of a member. It exists, neither by chance, like a crowd, nor actually, like a society, but potentially, so that it is possible to conceive of a community in which, at present, $n = 1$. In a community all members are free and equal. If, out of a group of ten persons, nine prefer beef to mutton and one prefers mutton to beef, there is not a single community containing a dissident member; there are two communities, a large one and a small one. To achieve an actual existence, it has to embody itself in a society or societies which can express the love which is its *raison d'être*. A community of music lovers, for example, cannot just sit around loving music like anything, but must form itself into societies like choirs, orchestras, string quartets, etc, and make music. Such an embodiment of a community in a society is an order. Of a community it may be said that its love is more or less good. Such a love presupposes choice, so that, in the natural world of the Dynamo, communities do not exist, only societies which are submembers of the total system of nature, enjoying their self-occurrence. Communities can only exist in the historical world of the Virgin, but they do not necessarily exist there.

Whenever rival communities compete for embodiment in the same society, there is either unfreedom or disorder. In the chimerical case of a society embodying a crowd, there would be a state of total unfreedom and disorder; the traditional term for this chimerical state is Hell. A perfect order, one in which the community united by the best love is embodied in the most self-sustaining society, could be described, as science describes nature, in terms of laws-of, but the description would be irrelevant, the relevant description being, "Here, love is the fulfilling of the law" or "In His Will is our peace"; the traditional term for this ideal order is Paradise. In historical existence where no love is perfect, no society immortal, and no embodiment of the one in the other precise, the obligation to approximate to the ideal is felt as an imperative "Thou shalt."

Man exists as a unity-in-tension of four modes of being: soul, body, mind and spirit.

As soul and body, he is an individual, as mind and spirit a member of a society. Were he only soul and body, his only relation to others would be numerical and a poem would be comprehensible only to its author; were he only mind and spirit, men would only exist collectively as the system Man, and there would be nothing for a poem to be about.

As body and mind, man is a natural creature, as soul and spirit, a historical person. Were he only body and mind, his existence would be one of everlasting recurrence, and only one good poem could exist; were he only soul and spirit, his existence would be one of perpetual novelty, and every new poem would supersede all previous poems, or rather a poem would be superseded before it could be written.

Man's consciousness is a unity-in-tension of three modes of awareness:

(1) A consciousness of the self as self-contained, as embracing all that it is aware of in a unity of experiencing. This mode is undogmatic, amoral and passive; its good is the enjoyment of being, its evil the fear of nonbeing.

(2) A consciousness of beyondness, of an ego standing as a spectator over against both a self and the external world. This mode is dogmatic, amoral, objective. Its good is the perception of true relations, its evil the fear of accidental or false relations.

(3) The ego's consciousness of itself as striving-towards, as desiring to transform the self, to realize its potentialities. This mode is moral and active; its good is not present but propounded, its evil, the present actuality.

Were the first mode absolute, man would inhabit a magical world in which the image of an object, the emotion it aroused and the word signifying it were all identical, a world where past and future, the living and the dead were united. Language in such a world would consist only of proper names which would not be words in the ordinary sense but sacred syllables, and, in the place of the poet, there would be the magician whose task is to discover and utter the truly potent spell which can compel what-is-not to be.

Were the second mode absolute, man would inhabit a world which was a pure system of universals. Language would be an algebra, and there could exist only one poem, of absolute banality, expressing the system.

Were the third mode absolute, man would inhabit a purely arbitrary world, the world of the clown and the actor. In language there would be no relation between word and thing, *love* would rhyme with *indifference*, and all poetry would be nonsense poetry.

Thanks to the first mode of consciousness, every good poem is unique; thanks to the second, a poet can embody his private experiences in a public poem which can be comprehended by others in terms of their private experiences; thanks to the third, both poet and reader desire that this be done.

The subject matter of the scientist is a crowd of natural events at all times; he presupposes that this crowd is not real but apparent, and seeks to discover the true place of events in the system of nature. The subject matter of the poet is a crowd of historical occasions of feeling recollected from the past; he presupposes that this crowd is real but should not be, and seeks to transform it into a community. Both science and art are primarily spiritual activities, whatever practical applications may be derived from their results. Disorder, lack of meaning, are spiritual not physical discomforts, order and sense spiritual not physical satisfactions.

It is impossible, I believe, for any poet, while he is writing a poem, to observe with complete accuracy what is going on, to define with any certainty how much of the final result is due to subconscious activity over which he has no control, and how much is due to conscious artifice. All one can say with certainty is negative. A poem does not compose itself in the poet's mind as a child grows in its mother's womb; *some* degree of conscious participation by the poet is necessary, *some* element of craft is always present. On the other hand, the writing of poetry is not, like carpentry, simply a craft; a carpenter can decide to build a table according to certain specifications and know before he begins that the result will be exactly what he intended, but no poet can know what his poem is going to be like until he has written it. The element of craftsmanship in poetry is obscured by the fact that all men are taught to speak and most to read and write, while very few men are taught to draw or paint or write music. Every poet, however, in addition to the everyday linguistic training he receives, requires a training in the poetic use of language. Even those poets who are most vehemently insistent upon the importance of the Muse and the vanity of conscious calculation must admit that, if they had never read any poetry in their lives, it is unlikely that they would have written any themselves. If, in what follows, I refer to the poet, I include under that both his Muse and his mind, his subconscious and conscious activity.

The subject matter of a poem is comprised of a crowd of recollected occasions of feeling, among which the most important are recollections of encounters with sacred beings or events. This crowd the poet attempts to transform into a community by embodying it in a verbal society. Such a society, like any society in nature, has its own laws; its laws of prosody and syntax are analogous to the laws of physics and chemistry. Every poem must presuppose—sometimes mistakenly—that the history of the language is at an end.

One should say, rather, that a poem is a natural organism, not an inorganic thing. For example, it is rhythmical. The temporal recurrences of rhythm are never identical, as the metrical notation would seem to suggest. Rhythm is to time what symmetry is to space. Seen from a certain distance, the features of a human face seem symmetrically arranged, so that a face with a nose a foot long or a left eye situated two inches away from the nose would appear monstrous. Close up, however, the exact symmetry disappears; the size and position of the features vary slightly from face to face and, indeed, if a face could exist in which the symmetry were mathematically perfect, it would look, not like a face, but like a lifeless mask. So with rhythm. A poem may be described as being written in iambic pentameters, but if every foot in every line were identical, the poem would sound intolerable to the ear. I am sometimes inclined to think that the aversion of many modern poets and their readers to formal verse may be due to their association of regular repetition and formal restrictions with all that is most boring and lifeless in modern life, road drills, time-clock punching, bureaucratic regulations.

It has been said that a poem should not mean but be. This is not quite accurate. In a poem, as distinct from many other kinds of verbal societies, meaning and being are identical. A poem might be called a pseudo-person. Like a person, it is unique and addresses the reader personally. On the other hand, like a natural being and unlike a historical person, it cannot lie. We may be and frequently are mistaken as to the meaning or the value of a poem, but the cause of our mistake lies in our own ignorance or self-deception, not in the poem itself.

The nature of the final poetic order is the outcome of a dialectical struggle between the recollected occasions of feeling and the verbal system. As a society the verbal system is actively coercive upon the occasions it is attempting to embody; what it cannot embody truthfully it excludes. As a potential community the occasions are passively resistant to all claims of the system to embody them which they do not recognize as just; they decline all unjust persuasions. As members of crowds, every occasion competes with every other, demanding inclusion and a dominant position to which they are not necessarily entitled, and every word demands that the system shall modify itself in its case, that a special exception shall be made for it and it only.

In a successful poem, society and community are one order and the system may love itself because the feelings which it embodies are all members of the same community, loving each other and it. A poem may fail in two ways; it may exclude too much (banality), or attempt to embody more than one community at once (disorder).

In writing a poem, the poet can work in two ways. Starting from an intuitive idea of the kind of community he desires to call into being, he may work backwards in search of the system which will most justly incarnate that idea, or, starting with a certain system, he may work forward in search of the community which it is capable of incarnating most truthfully. In practice he nearly always works simultaneously in both directions, modifying his conception of the ultimate nature of the community at the immediate suggestions of the system, and modifying the system in response to his growing intuition of the future needs of the community.

A system cannot be selected completely arbitrarily nor can one say that any given system is absolutely necessary. The poet searches for one which imposes just obligations on the feelings. "Ought" always implies "can" so that a system whose claims cannot be met must be scrapped. But the poet has to beware of accusing the system of injustice when what is at fault is the laxness and self-love of the feelings upon which it is making its demands.

Every poet, consciously or unconsciously, holds the following absolute presuppositions, as the dogmas of his art:

(1) A historical world exists, a world of unique events and unique persons, related by analogy, not identity. The number of events and analogical relations is potentially infinite. The existence of such a world is a good, and every addition to the number of events, persons and relations is an additional good.

(2) The historical world is a fallen world, i.e. though it is good that it exists, the way in which it exists is evil, being full of unfreedom and disorder.

(3) The historical world is a redeemable world. The unfreedom and disorder of the past can be reconciled in the future.

It follows from the first presupposition that the poet's activity in creating a poem is analogous to God's activity in creating man after his own image. It is not an imitation, for were it so, the poet would be able to create like God *ex nihilo*; instead, he requires pre-existing occasions of feeling and a pre-existing language out of which to create. It is analogous in that the poet creates not necessarily according to a law of nature but voluntarily according to provocation.

It is untrue, strictly speaking, to say that a poet should not write poems unless he must; strictly speaking it can only be said that he should not write them unless he can. The phrase is sound in practice, because only in those who can and when they can is the motive genuinely compulsive.

In those who profess a desire to write poetry, yet exhibit an incapacity to do so, it is often the case that their desire is not for creation but for self-perpetuation, that they refuse to accept their own mortality, just as there are parents who desire children, not as new persons analogous to themselves, but to prolong their own existence in time. The sterility of this substitution of identity for analogy is expressed in the myth of Narcissus. When the poet speaks, as he sometimes does, of achieving immortality through his poem, he does not mean that he hopes, like Faust, to live for ever, but that he hopes to rise from the dead. In poetry as in other matters the law holds good that he who would save his life must lose it; unless the poet sacrifices his feelings completely to the poem so that they are no longer his but the poem's, he fails.

It follows from the second presupposition that a poem is a witness to man's knowledge of evil as well as good. It is not the duty of a witness to pass moral judgment on the evidence he has to give, but to give it clearly and accurately; the only crime of which a witness can be guilty is perjury. When we say that poetry is beyond good and evil, we simply mean that a poet can no more change the facts of what he has felt than, in the natural order, parents can change the inherited physical characteristics which they pass on to their children. The judgment good-or-evil applies only to the intentional movements of the will. Of our feelings in a given situation which are the joint product of our intention and the response to the external factors in that situation it can only be said that, given an intention and the response, they are appropriate or inappropriate. Of a recollected feeling it cannot be said that it is appropriate or inappropriate because the historical situation in which it arose no longer exists.

Every poem, therefore, is an attempt to present an analogy to that paradisal state in which Freedom and Law, System and Order are united in harmony. Every good poem is very nearly a Utopia. Again, an analogy, not an imitation; the harmony is possible and verbal only.

It follows from the third presupposition that a poem is beautiful or ugly to the degree that it succeeds or fails in reconciling contradictory feelings in an order of mutual propriety. Every beautiful poem presents an analogy to the forgiveness of sins; an analogy, not an imitation, because it is not evil intentions which are repented of and pardoned but contradictory feelings which the poet surrenders to the poem in which they are reconciled.

The effect of beauty, therefore, is good to the degree that, through its analogies, the goodness of created existence, the historical fall into unfreedom and disorder, and the possibility of regaining paradise through repentance and forgiveness are recognized. Its effect is evil to the degree that beauty is taken, not as analogous to, but as identical with goodness, so that the artist regards himself or is regarded by others as God, the pleasure of beauty taken for the joy of Paradise, and the conclusion drawn that, since all is well in the work of art, all is well in history. But all is not well there.

The Poet & The City

> . . . Being everything, let us admit that is to be something,
> Or give ourselves the benefit of the doubt . . .
> > —William Empson

> There is little or nothing to be remembered written on the subject of getting an honest living. Neither the New Testament nor Poor Richard speaks to our condition. One would never think, from looking at literature, that this question had ever disturbed a solitary individual's musings.
> > —H. D. Thoreau

It is astonishing how many young people of both sexes, when asked what they want to do in life, give neither a sensible answer like "I want to be a lawyer, an innkeeper, a farmer" nor a romantic answer like "I want to be an explorer, a racing motorist, a missionary, President of the United States." A surprisingly large number say "I want to be a writer," and by writing they mean "creative" writing. Even if they say "I want to be a journalist," this is because they are under the illusion that in that profession they will be able to create; even if their genuine desire is to make money, they will select some highly paid subliterary pursuit like Advertising.

Among these would-be writers, the majority have no marked literary gift. This in itself is not surprising; a marked gift for any occupation is not very common. What is surprising is that such a high percentage of those without any marked talent for any profession should think of writing as the solution. One would have expected that a certain number would imagine that they had a talent for medicine or engineering and so on, but this is not the case. In our age, if a young person is untalented, the odds are in favor of his imagining he wants to write. (There are, no doubt, a lot without any talent for acting who dream of becoming film stars but they have at least been endowed by nature with a fairly attractive face and figure.)

In accepting and defending the social institution of slavery, the Greeks were harder-hearted than we but clearer-headed; they knew that labor as such is slavery, and that no man can feel a personal pride in being a laborer. A man can be proud of being a worker—someone, that is, who fabricates enduring objects, but in our society, the process of fabrication has been so rationalized in the interests of speed, economy and quantity that the part played by the individual factory employee has become too small for it to be meaningful to him as work, and practically all workers have been reduced to laborers. It is only natural, therefore, that the arts which cannot be rationalized in this way—the artist still remains personally responsible for what he makes—should fascinate those who, because they have no marked talent, are afraid, with good reason, that all they have to look forward to is a lifetime of meaningless labor. This fascination is not due to the nature of art itself, but to the way in which an artist works; he, and in our age, almost nobody else, is his own master. The idea of being one's own master appeals to most human beings, and this is apt to lead to the fantastic hope that the capacity for artistic creation is universal, something nearly all human beings, by virtue, not of some special talent, but of their humanity, could do if they tried.

Until quite recently a man was proud of not having to earn his own living and ashamed of being obliged to earn it but today, would any man dare describe himself when applying for a passport as *Gentleman*, even if, as a matter of fact, he has independent means and no job? Today, the question "What do you do?" means "How do you earn your living? On my own passport I am described as a "Writer"; this is not embarrassing for me in dealing with the authorities because immigration and customs officials know that some kinds of writers make lots of money. But if a stranger in the train asks me my occupation, I never answer "writer" for fear that he may go on to ask me what I write, and to answer "poetry" would embarrass us both, for we both know that nobody can earn a living simply by writing poetry. (The most satisfactory answer I have discovered, satisfactory because it withers curiosity, is to say *Medieval Historian.*)

Some writers, even some poets, become famous public figures, but writers as such have no social status, in the way that doctors and lawyers, whether famous or obscure, have.

There are two reason for this. Firstly, the so-called Fine Arts have lost the social utility they once had. Since the invention of printing and the spread of literacy, verse no longer has a utility value as a mnemonic, a device by which knowledge and culture were handed on from one generation to the next, and, since the invention of the camera, the draughtsman and painter are no longer needed to provide visual documentation; they have, consequently, become "pure" arts, that is to say, gratuitous activities. Secondly, in a society governed by the values appropriate to Labor (capitalist America may well be more completely governed by these than communist Russia) the gratuitous is no longer regarded—most earlier cultures thought differently—as sacred, because, to Man the Laborer, leisure is not sacred but a respite from laboring, a time for relaxation and the pleasures of consumption. In so far as such a society thinks about the gratuitous at all, it is suspicious of it—artists do not labor, therefore, they are probably parasitic idlers—or, at best, regards it as trivial—to write poetry or paint pictures is a harmless private hobby.

In the purely gratuitous arts, poetry, painting, music, our century has no need, I believe, to be ashamed of its achievements, and in its fabrication of purely utile and functional articles like airplanes, dams, surgical instruments, it surpasses any previous age. But whenever it attempts to combine the gratuitous with the utile, to fabricate something which shall be both functional and beautiful, it fails utterly. No previous age has created anything so hideous as the average modern automobile, lampshade or building, whether domestic or public. What could be more terrifying than a modern office building? It seems to be saying to the white-collar slaves who work in it: "For labor in this age, the human body is much more complicated than it need be: you would do better and be happier if it were simplified."

In the affluent countries today, thanks to the high per capita income, small houses and scarcity of domestic servants, there is one art in which we probably excel all other societies that ever existed, the art of cooking. (It is the one art which Man the Laborer regards as sacred.) If the world population continues to increase at its present rate, this cultural glory will be short-lived, and it may well be that future historians will look nostalgically back to the years 1950–1975 as The Golden Age of Cuisine. It is difficult to imagine a *haute cuisine* based on algae and chemically treated grass.

A poet, painter or musician has to accept the divorce in his art between the gratuitous and the utile as a fact for, if he rebels, he is liable to fall into error.
    Had Tolstoi, when he wrote *What Is Art?*, been content with the proposition, "When the gratuitous and the utile are divorced from each other, there can be no art," one might have disagreed with him, but he would have been difficult to refute. But he was unwilling to say that, if Shakespeare and himself were not artists, there was no modern art. Instead he tried to persuade himself that utility alone, a spiritual utility maybe, but still utility without gratuity, was sufficient to produce art, and this compelled him to be dishonest and praise works which aesthetically he must have despised. The notion of *l'art engagé* and art as propaganda are extensions of this heresy, and when poets fall into it, the cause, I fear, is less their social conscience than their vanity; they are nostalgic for a past when poets had a public status. The opposite heresy is to endow the gratuitous with a magic utility of its own, so that the poet comes to think of himself as the god who creates his subjective universe out of nothing—to him the visible material universe *is* nothing. Mallarmé, who planned to write the sacred book of a new universal religion, and Rilke with his notion of *Gesang ist Dasein*, are heresiarchs of this type. Both

were geniuses but, admire them as one may and must, one's final impression of their work is of something false and unreal. As Erich Heller says of Rilke:

> In the great poetry of the European tradition, the emotions do not interpret; they respond to the interpreted world: in Rilke's mature poetry the emotions do the interpreting and then respond to their own interpretation.

In all societies, educational facilities are limited to those activities and habits of behavior which a particular society considers important. In a culture like that of Wales in the Middle Ages, which regarded poets as socially important, a would-be poet, like a would-be dentist in our own culture, was systematically trained and admitted to the rank of poet only after meeting high professional standards.

In our culture a would-be poet has to educate himself; he may be in the position to go to a first-class school and university, but such places can only contribute to his poetic education by accident, not by design. This has its drawbacks; a good deal of modern poetry, even some of the best, shows just that uncertainty of taste, crankiness and egoism which self-educated people so often exhibit.

A metropolis can be a wonderful place for a mature artist to live in, but, unless his parents are very poor, it is a dangerous place for a would-be artist to grow up in; he is confronted with too much of the best in art too soon. This is like having a liaison with a wise and beautiful woman twenty years older than himself; all too often his fate is that of *Chéri*.

In my daydream College for Bards, the curriculum would be as follows:

(1) In addition to English, at least one ancient language, probably Greek or Hebrew, and two modern languages would be required.

(2) Thousands of lines of poetry in these languages would be learned by heart.

(3) The library would contain no books of literary criticism, and the only critical exercise required of students would be the writing of parodies.

(4) Courses in prosody, rhetoric and comparative philology would be required of all students, and every student would have to select three courses out of courses in mathematics, natural history, geology, meteorology, archaeology, mythology, liturgies, cooking.

(5) Every student would be required to look after a domestic animal and cultivate a garden plot.

A poet has not only to educate himself as a poet, he has also to consider how he is going to earn his living. Ideally, he should have a job which does not in any way involve the manipulation of words. At one time, children training to become rabbis were also taught some skilled manual trade, and if only they knew their child was going to become a poet, the best thing parents could do would be to get him at an early age into some Craft Trades Union. Unfortunately, they cannot know this in advance, and, except in very rare cases, by the time he is twenty-one, the only nonliterary job for which a poet-to-be is qualified is unskilled manual labor. In earning his living, the average poet has to choose between being a translator, a teacher, a literary journalist or a writer of advertising copy and, of these, all but the first can be directly detrimental to his poetry, and even translation does not free him from leading a too exclusively literary life.

There are four aspects of our present *Weltanschauung* which have made an artistic vocation more difficult than it used to be.

(1) *The loss of belief in the eternity of the physical universe.* The possibility of becoming an artist, a maker of things which shall outlast the maker's life, might never have occurred to man, had he not had before his eyes, in contrast to the transitoriness of human life, a universe of things, earth, ocean, sky, sun, moon, stars, etc., which appeared to be everlasting and unchanging.

Physics, geology and biology have now replaced this everlasting universe with a picture of nature as a process in which nothing is now what it was or what it will be. Today, Christian and Atheist alike are eschatologically minded. It is difficult for a modern artist to believe he can make an enduring object when he has no model of endurance to go by; he is more tempted than his predecessors to abandon the search for perfection as a waste of time and be content with sketches and improvisations.

(2) *The loss of belief in the significance and reality of sensory phenomena.* This loss has been progressive since Luther, who denied any intelligible relation between subjective Faith and objective Works, and Descartes, with his doctrine of primary and secondary qualities. Hitherto, the traditional conception of the phenomenal world had been one of sacramental analogies; what the senses perceived was an outward and visible sign of the inward and invisible, but both were believed to be real and valuable. Modern science has destroyed our faith in the naïve observation of our senses: we cannot, it tells us, ever know what the physical universe is *really* like; we can only hold whatever subjective notion is appropriate to the particular human purpose we have in view.

This destroys the traditional conception of art as *mimesis*, for there is no longer a nature "out there" to be truly or falsely imitated; all an artist can be *true* to are his subjective sensations and feelings. The change in attitude is already to be seen in Blake's remark that some people see the sun as a round golden disc the size of a guinea but that he sees it as a host crying Holy, Holy, Holy. What is significant about this is that Blake, like the Newtonians he hated, accepts a division between the physical and the spiritual, but, in opposition to them, regards the material universe as the abode of Satan, and so attaches no value to what his physical eye sees.

(3) *The loss of belief in a norm of human nature which will always require the same kind of man-fabricated world to be at home in.* Until the Industrial Revolution, the way in which men lived changed so slowly that any man, thinking of his great-grandchildren, could imagine them as people living the same kind of life with the same kind of needs and satisfactions as himself. Technology, with its ever-accelerating transformation of man's way of living, has made it impossible for us to imagine what life will be like even twenty years from now.

Further, until recently, men knew and cared little about cultures far removed from their own in time or space; by human nature, they meant the kind of behavior exhibited in their own culture. Anthropology and archaeology have destroyed this provincial notion: we know that human nature is so plastic that it can exhibit varieties of behavior which, in the animal kingdom, could only be exhibited by different species.

The artist, therefore, no longer has any assurance, when he makes something, that even the next generation will find it enjoyable or comprehensible.

He cannot help desiring an immediate success, with all the danger to his integrity which that implies.

Further, the fact that we now have at our disposal the arts of all ages and cultures, has completely changed the meaning of the word tradition. It no longer means a way of working handed down from one generation to the next; a sense of tradition now means a consciousness of the whole of the past as present, yet at the same time as a structured whole the parts of which are related in terms of before and after. Originality no longer means a slight modification in the style of one's immediate predecessors; it means a capacity to find in any work of any date or place a clue to finding one's authentic voice. The burden of choice and selection is put squarely upon the shoulders of each individual poet and it is a heavy one.

(4) *The disappearance of the Public Realm as the sphere of revelatory personal deeds.* To the Greeks the Private Realm was the sphere of life ruled by the necessity of sustaining life, and the Public Realm the sphere of freedom where a man could disclose himself to others. Today, the significance of the terms private and public has been reversed; public life is the necessary impersonal life, the place where a man fulfills his social function, and it is in his private life that he is free to be his personal self.

In consequence the arts, literature in particular, have lost their traditional principal human subject, the man of action, the doer of public deeds.

The advent of the machine has destroyed the direct relation between a man's intention and his deed. If St George meets the dragon face to face and plunges a spear into its heart, he may legitimately say "*I* slew the dragon," but, if he drops a bomb on the dragon from an altitude of twenty thousand feet, though his intention—to slay it—is the same, his act consists in pressing a lever and it is the bomb, not St George, that does the killing.

If, at Pharaoh's command, ten thousand of his subjects toil for five years at draining the fens, this means that Pharaoh commands the personal loyalty of enough persons to see that his orders are carried out; if his army revolts, he is powerless. But if Pharaoh can have the fens drained in six months by a hundred men with bulldozers, the situation is changed. He still needs some authority, enough to persuade a hundred men to man the bulldozers, but that is all: the rest of the work is done by machines which know nothing of loyalty or fear, and if his enemy, Nebuchadnezzar, should get hold of them, they will work just as efficiently at filling up the canals as they have just worked at digging them out. It is now possible to imagine a world in which the only human work on such projects will be done by a mere handful of persons who operate computers.

It is extremely difficult today to use public figures as themes for poetry because the good or evil they do depends less upon their characters and intentions than upon the quantity of impersonal force at their disposal.

Every British or American poet will agree that Winston Churchill is a greater figure than Charles II, but he will also know that he could not write a good poem on Churchill, while Dryden had no difficulty in writing a good poem on Charles. To write a good poem on Churchill, a poet would have to know Winston Churchill intimately, and his poem would be about the man, not about the Prime Minister. All attempts to write about persons or events, however important, to which the poet is not intimately related in a personal way are now doomed to failure. Yeats could write great poetry about the Troubles in Ireland, because most of the protagonists were known to him personally and the places where the events occurred had been familiar to him since childhood.

The true men of action in our time, those who transform the world, are not the politicians and statesmen, but the scientists. Unfortunately poetry cannot celebrate them because their deeds are concerned with things, not persons, and are, therefore, speechless.

When I find myself in the company of scientists, I feel like a shabby curate who has strayed by mistake into a drawing room full of dukes.

The growth in size of societies and the development of mass media of communication have created a social phenomenon which was unknown to the ancient world, that peculiar kind of crowd which Kierkegaard calls The Public.

A public is neither a nation nor a generation, nor a community, nor a society, nor these particular men, for all these are only what they are through the concrete; no single person who belongs to the public makes a real commitment; for some hours of the day, perhaps, he belongs to the public—at moments when he is nothing else, since when he really is what he is, he does not form part of the public. Made up of such individuals at the moments when they are nothing, a public is a kind of gigantic something, an abstract and deserted void which is everything and nothing.

The ancient world knew the phenomenon of the crowd in the sense that Shakespeare uses the word, a visible congregation of a large number of human individuals in a limited physical space, who can, on occasions, be transformed by demagogic oratory into a mob which behaves in a way of which none of its members would be capable by himself, and this phenomenon is known, of course, to us, too. But the public is something else. A student in the subway during the rush hour whose thoughts are concentrated on a mathematical problem or his girl friend is a member of a crowd but not a member of the public. To join the public, it is not necessary for a man to go to some particular spot; he can sit at home, open a newspaper or turn on his TV set.

A man has his distinctive personal scent which his wife, his children and his dog can recognize. A crowd has a generalized stink. The public is odorless.

A mob is active; it smashes, kills and sacrifices itself. The public is passive or, at most, curious. It neither murders nor sacrifices itself; it looks on, or looks away, while the mob beats up a Negro or the police round up Jews for the gas ovens.

The public is the least exclusive of clubs; anybody, rich or poor, educated or unlettered, nice or nasty, can join it: it even tolerates a pseudo revolt against itself, that is, the formation within itself of clique publics.

In a crowd, a passion like rage or terror is highly contagious; each member of a crowd excites all the others, so that passion increases at a geometric rate. But among members of the Public, there is no contact. If two members of the public meet and speak to each other, the function of their words is not to convey meaning or arouse passion but to conceal by noise the silence and solitude of the void in which the Public exists.

Occasionally the Public embodies itself in a crowd and so becomes visible—in the crowd, for example, which collects to watch the wrecking gang demolish the old family mansion, fascinated by yet another proof that physical force is the Prince of this world against whom no love of the heart shall prevail.

Before the phenomenon of the Public appeared in society, there existed naïve art and sophisticated art which were different from each other but only in the way that two brothers are different. The Athenian court may smile at the mechanics' play of Pyramus and Thisbe, but they recognize it as a play. Court poetry and Folk poetry were bound by the common tie that both were made by hand and both were intended to last; the crudest ballad was as custom-built as the most esoteric sonnet. The appearance of the Public and the mass media which cater to it have destroyed naïve popular art. The sophisticated "highbrow" artist survives and can still work as he did a thousand years ago, because his audience is too small to interest the mass media. But the audience of the popular artist is the majority and this the mass media must steal from him if they are not to go bankrupt. Consequently, aside from a few comedians, the only art today is "highbrow." What the mass media offer is not popular art, but entertainment which is intended to be consumed like food, forgotten, and replaced by a new dish. This is bad for everyone; the majority lose all genuine taste of their own, and the minority become cultural snobs.

The two characteristics of art which make it possible for an art historian to divide the history of art into periods, are, firstly, a common style of expression over a certain period and, secondly, a common notion, explicit or implicit, of the hero, the kind of human being who most deserves to be celebrated, remembered and, if possible, imitated. The characteristic style of "Modern" poetry is an intimate tone of voice, the speech of one person addressing one person, not a large audience; whenever a modern poet raises his voice he sounds phony. And its characteristic hero is neither the "Great Man" nor the romantic rebel, both doers of extraordinary deeds, but the man or woman in any walk of life who, despite all the impersonal pressures of modern society, manages to acquire and preserve a face of his own.

Poets are, by the nature of their interests and the nature of artistic fabrication, singularly ill-equipped to understand politics or economics. Their natural interest is in singular individuals and personal relations, while politics and economics are concerned with large numbers of people, hence with the human average (the poet is bored to death by the idea of the Common Man) and with impersonal, to a great extent involuntary, relations. The poet cannot understand the function of money in modern society because for him there is no relation between subjective value and market value; he may be paid ten pounds for a poem which he believes is very good and took him months to write, and a hundred pounds for a piece of journalism which costs him but a day's work. If he is a successful poet—though few poets make enough money to be called successful in the way that a novelist or playwright can—he is a member of the Manchester school and believes in absolute *laisser-faire*; if he is unsuccessful and embittered, he is liable to combine aggressive fantasies about the annihilation of the present order with impractical daydreams of Utopia. Society has always to beware of the Utopias being planned by artists *manqués* over cafeteria tables late at night.

All poets adore explosions, thunderstorms, tornadoes, conflagrations, ruins, scenes of spectacular carnage. The poetic imagination is not at all a desirable quality in a statesman.

In a war or a revolution, a poet may do very well as a guerilla fighter or a spy, but it is unlikely that he will make a good regular soldier, or, in peace time, a conscientious member of a parliamentary committee.

All political theories which, like Plato's, are based on analogies drawn from artistic fabrication are bound, if put into practice, to turn into tyrannies. The whole aim of a poet, or any other kind of artist, is to produce something which is complete and will endure without change. A poetic city would always contain exactly the same number of inhabitants doing exactly the same jobs for ever. Moreover, in the process of arriving at the finished work, the artist has continually to employ violence. A poet writes:

> The mast-high anchor dives through a cleft

changes it to

> The anchor dives through closing paths

changes it again to

> The anchor dives among hayricks

and finally to

> The anchor dives through the floors of a church.

A *cleft* and *closing paths* have been liquidated, and hayricks deported to another stanza.

A society which was really like a good poem, embodying the aesthetic virtues of beauty, order, economy and subordination of detail to the whole, would be a nightmare of horror for, given the historical reality of actual men, such a society could only come into being through selective breeding, extermination of the physically and mentally unfit, absolute obedience to its Director, and a large slave class kept out of sight in cellars.

Vice versa, a poem which was really like a political democracy—examples, unfortunately, exist—would be formless, windy, banal and utterly boring.

There are two kinds of political issues, Party issues and Revolutionary issues. In a party issue, all parties are agreed as to the nature and justice of the social goal to be reached, but differ in their policies for reaching it. The existence of different parties is justified, firstly, because no party can offer irrefutable proof that its policy is the only one which will achieve the commonly desired goal and, secondly, because no social goal can be achieved without some sacrifice of individual or group interest and it is natural for each individual and social group to seek a policy which will keep its sacrifice to a minimum, to hope that, if sacrifices must be made, it would be more just if someone else made them. In a party issue, each party seeks to convince the members of its society, primarily by appealing to their reason; it marshals facts and arguments to convince others that its policy is more likely to achieve the desired goal than that of its opponents. On a party issue it is essential that passions be kept at a low temperature: effective oratory requires, of course, some appeal to the emotions of the audience, but in party politics orators should display the mock-passion of prosecuting and defending attorneys, not really lose their tempers. Outside the Chamber, the rival deputies should be able to dine in each other's houses; fanatics have no place in party politics.

A revolutionary issue is one in which different groups within a society hold different views as to what is just. When this is the case, argument and compromise are out of the question; each group is bound to regard the other as wicked or mad or both. Every revolutionary issue is potentially a *casus belli.* On a revolutionary issue, an orator cannot convince his audience by appealing to their reason; he may convert some of them by awakening and appealing to their conscience, but his principal function, whether he represent the revolutionary or the counterrevolutionary group, is to arouse its passion to the point where it will give all its energies to achieving total victory for itself and total defeat for its opponents. When an issue is revolutionary, fanatics are essential.

Today, there is only one genuine world-wide revolutionary issue, racial equality. The debate between capitalism, socialism and communism is really a party issue, because the goal which all seek is really the same, a goal which is summed up in Brecht's well-known line:

Erst kommt das Fressen, dann kommt die Moral.

i.e. Grub first, then Ethics. In all the technologically advanced countries today, whatever political label they give themselves, their policies have, essentially, the same goal: to guarantee to every member of society, as a psychophysical organism, the right to physical and mental health. The positive symbolic figure of this goal is a naked anonymous baby, the negative symbol, a mass of anonymous concentration camp corpses.

What is so terrifying and immeasurably depressing about most contemporary politics is the refusal—mainly but not, alas, only by the communists—to admit that this is a party issue to be settled by appeal to facts and reason, the insistence that there is a revolutionary issue between us. If an African gives his life for the cause of racial equality, his death is meaningful to him; but what is utterly absurd, is that people should be deprived every day of their liberties and their lives, and that the human race may quite possibly destroy itself over what is really a matter of practical policy like asking whether, given its particular historical circumstances, the health of a community is more or less likely to be secured by Private Practice or by Socialized Medicine.

What is peculiar and novel to our age is that the principal goal of politics in every advanced society is not, strictly speaking, a political one, that is to say, it is not concerned with human beings as persons and citizens but with human bodies, with the precultural, prepolitical human creature. It is, perhaps, inevitable that respect for the liberty of the individual should have so greatly diminished and the authoritarian powers of the State have so greatly increased from what they were fifty years ago, for the main political issue today is concerned not with human liberties but with human necessities. As creatures we are all equally slaves to natural necessity; we are not free to vote how much food, sleep, light and air we need to keep in good health; we all need a certain quantity, and we all need the same quantity.

Every age is one-sided in its political and social preoccupation and in seeking to realize the particular value it esteems most highly, it neglects and even sacrifices other values. The relation of a poet, or any artist, to society and politics is, except in Africa or still backward semifeudal countries, more difficult than it has ever been because, while he cannot but approve of the importance of *every body* getting enough food to eat and enough leisure, this problem has nothing whatever to do with art, which is concerned with *singular persons*, as they are alone and as they are in their personal relations. Since these interests are not the predominant ones in his society—indeed, in so far as it thinks about them at all, it is with suspicion and latent hostility; it secretly or openly thinks that the claim that one is a singular person, or a demand for privacy, is putting on airs, a claim to be superior to other folk— every artist feels himself at odds with modern civilization.

In our age, the mere making of a work of art is itself a political act. So long as artists exist, making what they please and think they ought to make, even if it is not terribly good, even if it appeals to only a handful of people, they remind the Management of something managers need to be reminded of, namely, that the managed are people with faces, not anonymous numbers, that *Homo Laborans* is also *Homo Ludens*.

If a poet meets an illiterate peasant, they may not be able to say much to each other, but if they both meet a public official, they share the same feeling of suspicion; neither will trust one further than he can throw a grand piano. If they enter a government building, both share the same feeling of apprehension; perhaps they will never get out again. Whatever the cultural differences between them, they both sniff in any official world the smell of an unreality in which persons are treated as statistics. The peasant may play cards in the evening while the poet writes verses, but there is one political principle to which they both subscribe, namely, that among the half dozen or so things for which a man of honor should be prepared, if necessary, to die, the right to play, the right to frivolity, is not the least.

PART THREE

The Well of Narcissus

Hic et Ille

A mirror has no heart but plenty of ideas.
—Malcolm de Chazal

A

Every man carries with him through life a mirror, as unique and impossible to get rid of as his shadow.

A parlor game for a wet afternoon—imagining the mirrors of one's friends. A has a huge pier glass, gilded and baroque, B a discreet little pocket mirror in a pigskin case with his initials stamped on the back; whenever one looks at C, he is in the act of throwing his mirror away but, if one looks in his pocket or up his sleeve, one always finds another, like an extra ace.

Most, perhaps all, our mirrors are inaccurate and uncomplimentary, though to varying degrees and in various ways. Some magnify, some diminish, others return lugubrious, comic, derisive, or terrifying images.

But the properties of our own particular mirror are not so important as we sometimes like to think. We shall be judged, not by the kind of mirror found on us, but by the use we have made of it, by our *riposte* to our reflection.

The psychoanalyst says: "Come, my good man, I know what is the matter with you. You have a distorting mirror. No wonder you feel guilty. But cheer up. For a slight consideration I shall be delighted to correct it for you. There! Look! A perfect image. Not a trace of distortion. Now you are one of the elect. That will be five thousand dollars, please."

And immediately come seven devils, and the last state of that man is worse than the first.

The politician, secular or clerical, promises the crowd that, if only they will hand in their private mirrors to him, to be melted down into one large public mirror, the curse of Narcissus will be taken away.

Narcissus does not fall in love with his reflection because it is beautiful, but because it is *his*. If it were his beauty that enthralled him, he would be set free in a few years by its fading.

"After all," sighed Narcissus the hunchback, "on *me* it looks good."

The contemplation of his reflection does not turn Narcissus into Priapus: the spell in which he is trapped is not a desire for himself but the satisfaction of not desiring the nymphs.

"I prefer my pistol to my p . . . ," said Narcissus; "it cannot take aim without my permission"—and took a pot shot at Echo.

Narcissus (drunk): "I shouldn't look at me like that, if I were you. I suppose you think you know who I am. Well, let me tell *you*, my dear, that one of these days you are going to get a very big surprise *indeed*!"

A vain woman comes to realize that vanity is a sin and in order not to succumb to temptation, has all the mirrors removed from her house. Consequently, in a short while she cannot remember how she looks. She remembers that vanity is sinful but she forgets that she is vain.

He who despises himself, nevertheless esteems himself as a self-despiser. (Nietzsche.) A vain person is always vain *about* something. He overestimates the importance of some quality or exaggerates the degree to which he possesses it, but the quality has some real importance and he does possess it to some degree. The fantasy of overestimation or exaggeration makes the vain person comic, but the fact that he cannot be vain about nothing makes his vanity a venial sin, because it is always open to correction by appeal to objective fact.

A proud person, on the other hand, is not proud *of* anything, he *is* proud, he exists proudly. Pride is neither comic nor venial, but the most mortal of all sins because, lacking any basis in concrete particulars, it is both incorrigible and absolute: one cannot be more or less proud, only proud or humble.

Thus, if a painter tries to portray the Seven Deadly Sins, his experience will furnish him readily enough with images symbolic of Gluttony, Lust, Sloth, Anger, Avarice, and Envy, for all these are qualities of a person's relations to others and the world, but no experience can provide an image of Pride, for the relation it qualifies is the subjective relation of a person to himself. In the seventh frame, therefore, the painter can only place, in lieu of a canvas, a mirror.

Le Moi est toujours haïssable. (Pascal.) True enough, but it is equally true that only *le Moi* is lovable in itself, not merely as an object of desire.

B

The absolutely banal—my sense of my own uniqueness. How strange that one should treasure this more than any of the exciting and interesting experiences, emotions, ideas that come and go, leaving it unchanged and unmoved.

The Ego which recalls a previous condition of a now changed Self cannot believe that it, too, has changed. The Ego fancies that it is like Zeus who could assume one bodily appearance after another, now a swan, now a bull, while all the time remaining Zeus. Remembering some wrong or foolish action of the past, the Ego feels shame, as one feels ashamed of having been seen in bad company, at having been associated with a Self whom it regards as responsible for the act. Shame, not guilt: guilt, it fancies, is what the Self should feel.

Every autobiography is concerned with two characters, a Don Quixote, the Ego, and a Sancho Panza, the Self. In one kind of autobiography the Self occupies the stage and narrates, like a Greek Messenger, what the Ego is doing off stage. In another kind it is the Ego who is narrator and the Self who is described without being able to answer back. If the same person were to write his autobiography twice, first in one mode and then in the other, the two accounts would be so different that it would be hard to believe that they referred to the same person. In one he would appear as an obsessed creature, a passionate Knight forever serenading Faith or Beauty, humorless and over-life-size: in the other as coolly detached, full of humor and self-mockery, lacking in a capacity for affection, easily bored and smaller than life-size. As Don Quixote seen by Sancho Panza, he never prays; as Sancho Panza seen by Don Quixote, he never giggles.

An honest self-portrait is extremely rare because a man who has reached the degree of self-consciousness presupposed by the desire to paint his own portrait has almost always also developed an ego-consciousness which paints himself painting himself, and introduces artificial highlights and dramatic shadows.

As an autobiographer, Boswell is almost alone in his honesty.

> I determined, if the Cyprian Fury should seize me, to participate my amorous flame with a genteel girl.

Stendhal would never have dared write such a sentence. He would have said to himself: "Phrases like *Cyprian Fury* and *amorous flame* are clichés; I must put down in plain words exactly what I mean." But he would have been wrong, for the Self thinks in clichés and euphemisms, not in the style of the Code Napoléon.

History is, strictly speaking, the study of questions; the study of answers belongs to anthropology and sociology. To ask a question is to declare war, to make some issue a *casus belli*; history proper is the history of battles, physical, intellectual or spiritual and, the more revolutionary the outcome, the greater the historical interest. Culture is history which has become dormant or extinct, a second nature. A good historian is, of course, both a historian in the strict sense and a sociologist. So far as the life of an individual is concerned, an autobiography probably gives a truer picture of a man's history than even the best biography could have done. But a biographer can perceive what an autobiographer cannot, a man's culture, the influence upon his life of the presuppositions which he takes for granted.

It is possible to imagine oneself as rich when one is poor, as beautiful when ugly, as generous when stingy, etc., but it is impossible to imagine oneself as either more or less imaginative than, in fact, one is. A man whose every thought was commonplace could never know this to be the case.

I cannot help believing that my thoughts and acts are my own, not inherited reflexes and prejudices. The most I can say is: "Father taught me such-and-such and I agree with him." My prejudices must be right because, if I knew them to be wrong, I could no longer hold them.

Subjectively, my experience of life is one of having to make a series of choices between given alternatives and it is this experience of doubt, indecision, temptation, that seems more important and memorable than the actions I take. Further, if I make a choice which I consider the wrong one, I can never believe, however strong the temptation to make it, that it was inevitable, that I could not and should not have made the opposite choice. But when I look at others, I cannot see them making choices; I can only see what they actually do and, if I know them well, it is rarely that I am surprised, that I could not have predicted, given his character and upbringing, how so-and-so would behave.

Compared with myself, that is, other people seem at once less free and stronger in character. No man, however tough he appears to his friends, can help portraying himself in his autobiography as a sensitive plant.

To peek is always an unfriendly act, a theft of knowledge; we all know this and cannot peek without feeling guilty. As compensation we demand that what we discover by peeking shall be surprising. If I peer through the key-hole of a bishop's study and find him saying his prayers, the "idleness" of my curiosity is at once rebuked, but if I catch him making love to the parlor-maid I can persuade myself that my curiosity has really achieved something.

In the same way, the private papers of an author must, if they are to satisfy the public, be twice as unexpected and shocking as his published books.

Private letters, entries in journals, etc., fall into two classes, those in which the writer is in control of his situation—what he writes about is what he chooses to write—and those in which the situation dictates what he writes. The terms personal and impersonal are here ambiguous: the first class is impersonal in so far as the writer is looking at himself in the world as if at a third person, but personal in so far as it is his personal act so to look—the signature to the letter is really his and he is responsible for its contents. Vice versa, the second class is personal in that the writer is identical with what he writes, but impersonal in that it is the situation, not he, which enforces that identity.

The second class are what journalists call "human documents" and should be published, if at all, anonymously.

Rejoice with those that do rejoice. Certainly. But *weep with them that weep*? What good does that do? It is the decent side of us, not our hardness of heart, that is bored and embarrassed at having to listen to the woes of others because, as a rule, we can do nothing to alleviate them. To be curious about suffering which we cannot alleviate—and the sufferings of the dead are all beyond our aid—is *Schadenfreude* and nothing else.

Literary confessors are contemptible, like beggars who exhibit their sores for money, but not so contemptible as the public that buys their books.

One ceases to be a child when one realizes that telling one's trouble does not make it any better. (Cesare Pavese.) Exactly. Not even telling it to oneself. Most of us have known shameful moments when we blubbered, beat the wall with our fists, cursed the power which made us and the world, and wished that we were dead or that someone else was. But at such times, the *I* of the sufferer should have the tact and decency to look the other way.

Our sufferings and weaknesses, in so far as they are personal, *our* sufferings, *our* weaknesses, are of no literary interest whatsoever. They are only interesting in so far as we can see them as typical of the human condition. A suffering, a weakness, which cannot be expressed as an aphorism should not be mentioned.

The same rules apply to self-examination as apply to confession to a priest: *be brief, be blunt, be gone.* Be brief, be blunt, forget. The scrupuland is a nasty specimen.

C

If we were suddenly to become disembodied spirits, a few might behave better than before, but most of us would behave very much worse.

The Body is a born Aristotelian, its guiding principle, the Golden Mean. The most "fleshly" of the sins are not Gluttony and Lust, but Sloth and Cowardice: on the other hand, without a body, we could neither conceive of nor practice the virtue of Prudence.

You taught me language and my profit on't Is, I know how to curse. In the debate between the Body and Soul, if the former could present its own case objectively, it would always win. As it is, it can only protest the Soul's misstatement of its case by subjective acts of rebellion, coughs, belches, constipation, etc., which always put it in the wrong.

All bodies have the same vocabulary of physical symptoms to select from, but the way in which they use it varies from one body to another: in some, the style of bodily behavior is banal, in some highly mannered, in some vague, in some precise, and, occasionally, to his bewilderment, a physician encounters one which is really witty.

Anxiety affects the Body and the Mind in different ways: it makes the former develop compulsions, a concentration on certain actions to the exclusion of others; it makes the latter surrender to daydreaming, a lack of concentration on any thought in particular.

In a state of panic, a man runs round in circles by himself. In a state of joy, he links hands with others and they dance round in a circle together.

In the judgment of my nose, some of my neighbors are bad, but none is my inferior.

The ear tends to be lazy, craves the familiar, and is shocked by the unexpected: the eye, on the other hand, tends to be impatient, craves the novel and is bored by repetition. Thus, the average listener prefers concerts confined to works by old masters and it is only the highbrow who is willing to listen to new works, but the average reader wants the latest book and it is the classics of the past which are left to the highbrow.

Similarly, so long as a child has to be read to or told stories, he insists on the same tale being retold again and again, but, once he has learned to read for himself, he rarely reads the same book twice.

As seen reflected in a mirror, a room or a landscape seems more solidly there in space than when looked at directly. In that purely visual world nothing can be hailed, moved, smashed, or eaten, and it is only the observer himself who, by shifting his position or closing his eyes, can change.

From the height of 10,000 feet, the earth appears to the human eye as it appears to the eye of the camera; that is to say, all history is reduced to nature. This has the salutary effect of making historical evils, like national divisions and political hatreds, seem absurd. I look down from an airplane upon a stretch of land which is obviously continuous. That, across it, marked by a tiny ridge or river or even by no topographical sign whatever, there should run a frontier, and that the human beings living on one side should hate or refuse to trade with or be forbidden to visit those on the other side, is instantaneously revealed to me as ridiculous. Unfortunately, I cannot have this revelation without simultaneously having the illusion that there are no historical values either. From the same height I cannot distinguish between an outcrop of rock and a Gothic cathedral, or between a happy family playing in a backyard and a flock of sheep, so that I am unable to feel any difference between dropping a bomb upon one or the other. If the effect of distance upon the observed and the observer were mutual, so that, as the objects on the ground shrank in size and lost their uniqueness, the observer in the airplane felt himself shrinking and becoming more and more generalized, we should either give up flying as too painful or create a heaven on earth.

Those who accuse the movies of having a deleterious moral effect may well be right but not for the reasons they usually give. It is not what movies are about—gangsters or adultery—which does the damage, but the naturalistic nature of the medium itself which encourages a fantastic conception of time. In all narrative art, the narration of the action takes less time than it would in real life, but in the epic or the drama or the novel, the artistic conventions are so obvious that a confusion of art with life is impossible. Suppose that there is a scene in a play in which a man woos a woman; this may take forty minutes by the clock to play, but the audience will have the sense of having watched a scene which really took, let us say, two hours.

The absolute naturalism of the camera destroys this sense and encourages the audience to imagine that, in real life as on the screen, the process of wooing takes forty minutes.

When he grows impatient, the movie addict does not cry "Hurry!" he cries "Cut!"

A daydream is a meal at which images are eaten. Some of us are gourmets, some gourmands, and a good many take their images precooked out of a can and swallow them down whole, absent-mindedly and with little relish.

Even if it be true that our primary interest is in sexual objects only, and that all our later interests are symbolic transferences, we could never make such a transference if the new objects of interest did not have a real value of their own. If all round hills were suddenly to turn into breasts, all caves into wombs, all towers into phalloi, we should not be pleased or even shocked: we should be bored.

Between the ages of seven and twelve my fantasy life was centered around lead mines and I spent many hours imagining in the minutest detail the Platonic Idea of all lead mines. In planning its Concentrating Mill, I ran into difficulty: I had to choose between two types of a certain machine for separating the slimes. One I found more "beautiful" but the other was, I knew from my reading, the more efficient. My feeling at the time, I remember very clearly, was that I was confronted by a moral choice and that it was my duty to choose the second.

Like all polemical movements, existentialism is one-sided. In their laudable protest against systematic philosophers, like Hegel or Marx, who would reduce all individual existence to general processes, the existentialists' have invented an equally imaginary anthropology from which all elements, like man's physical nature, or his reason, about which general statements can be made, are excluded.

A task for an existentialist theologian: to preach a sermon on the topic *The Sleep of Christ*.

One of the most horrible, yet most important, discoveries of our age has been that, if you really wish to destroy a person and turn him into an automaton, the surest method is not physical torture, in the strict sense, but

simply to keep him awake, i.e. in an existential relation to life without inter-
mission.

All the existentialist descriptions of choice, like Pascal's wager or Kierkegaard's leap, are interesting as dramatic literature, but are they true? When
I look back at the three or four choices in my life which have been decisive,
I find that, at the time I made them, I had very little sense of the seriousness
of what I was doing and only later did I discover that what had then seemed
an unimportant brook was, in fact, a Rubicon.

  For this I am very thankful since, had I been fully aware of the risk I was
taking, I should never have dared take such a step.

  In a reflective and anxious age, it is surely better, pedagogically, to mini-
mize rather than to exaggerate the risks involved in a choice, just as one encourages a boy to swim who is afraid of the water by telling him that nothing
can happen.

D

Under the stress of emotion, animals and children "make" faces, but they do
not have one.

So much countenance and so little face. (Henry James.) Every European visitor to
the United States is struck by the comparative rarity of what he would call a
face, by the frequency of men and women who look like elderly babies. If he
stays in the States for any length of time, he will learn that this cannot be put
down to a lack of sensibility—the American feels the joys and sufferings of
human life as keenly as anybody else. The only plausible explanation I can
find lies in his different attitude to the past. To have a face, in the European
sense of the word, it would seem that one must not only enjoy and suffer but
also desire to preserve the memory of even the most humiliating and unpleasant experiences of the past.

  More than any other people, perhaps, the Americans obey the scriptural
injunction: "Let the dead bury their dead."

When I consider others I can easily believe that their bodies express their
personalities and that the two are inseparable. But it is impossible for me not
to feel that my body is other than I, that I inhabit it like a house, and that my
face is a mask which, with or without my consent, conceals my real nature
from others.

It is impossible consciously to approach a mirror without composing or
"making" a special face, and if we catch sight of our reflection unawares we
rarely recognize ourselves. I cannot read my face in the mirror because I am
already obvious to myself.

The image of myself which I try to create in my own mind in order that I may love myself is very different from the image which I try to create in the minds of others in order that they may love me.

Most faces are asymmetric, i.e. one side is happy, the other sad, one self-confident, the other diffident, etc. By cutting up photographs it is possible to make two very different portraits, one from the two left sides, the other from the two rights. If these be now shown to the subject and to his friends, almost invariably the one which the subject prefers will be the one his friends dislike.

We can imagine loving what we do not love a great deal more easily than we can imagine fearing what we do not fear. I can sympathize with a man who has a passion for collecting stamps, but if he is afraid of mice there is a gulf between us. On the other hand, if he is unafraid of spiders, of which I am terrified, I admire him as superior but I do not feel that he is a stranger. Between friends differences in taste or opinion are irritating in direct proportion to their triviality. If my friend takes up Vedanta, I can accept it, but if he prefers his steak well done, I feel it to be a treachery.

When one talks to another, one is more conscious of him as a listener to the conversation than of oneself. But the moment one writes anything, be it only a note to pass down the table, one is more conscious of oneself as a reader than of the intended recipient.

Hence we cannot be as false in writing as we can in speaking, nor as true. The written word can neither conceal nor reveal so much as the spoken.

Two card players. A is a good loser when, holding good cards, he makes a fatal error, but a bad loser when he is dealt cards with which it is impossible to win. With B it is the other way round; he cheerfully resigns himself to defeat if his hand is poor, but becomes furious if defeat is his own fault.

Almost all of our relationships begin and most of them continue as forms of mutual exploitation, a mental or physical barter, to be terminated when one or both parties run out of goods.

But if the seed of a genuine disinterested love, which is often present, is ever to develop, it is essential that we pretend to ourselves and to others that it is stronger and more developed than it is, that we are less selfish than we are. Hence the social havoc wrought by the paranoid to whom the thought of indifference is so intolerable that he divides others into two classes, those who love him for himself alone and those who hate him for the same reason.

Do a paranoid a favor, like paying his hotel bill in a foreign city when his monthly check has not yet arrived, and he will take this as an expression of personal affection—the thought that you might have done it from a general sense of duty towards a fellow countryman in distress will never occur to him.

So back he comes for more until your patience is exhausted, there is a row, and he departs convinced that you are his personal enemy. In this he is right to the extent that it is difficult not to hate a person who reveals to you so clearly how little you love others.

Two cyclic madmen. In his elated phase, A feels: "I am God. The universe is full of gods. I adore all and am adored by all." B feels: "The universe is only a thing. I am happily free from all bonds of attachment to it." In the corresponding depressed phase, A feels: "I am a devil. The universe is full of devils. I hate all and am hated by all." B feels: "I am only a thing to the universe which takes no interest in me." This difference is reflected in their behavior. When elated A does not wash and even revels in dirt because all things are holy. He runs after women, after whores in particular whom he intends to save through Love. But B in this mood takes a fastidious pride in his physical cleanliness as a mark of his superiority and is chaste for the same reason. When depressed A begins to wash obsessively to cleanse himself from guilt and feels a morbid horror of all sex, B now neglects his appearance because "nobody cares how I look," and tries to be a Don Juan seducer in an attempt to compel life to take an interest in him.

A's God—Zeus-Jehovah: B's God—The Unmoved Mover.

Balaam and His Ass

Am I not thine ass, upon which thou hast ridden ever since
I was thine unto this day?—Numbers: xxii, 30

Friend, I do thee no wrong: didst thou not agree with me
for a penny?—Matthew: xx, 13

I

The relation between Master and Servant is not given by nature or fate but comes into being through an act of conscious volition. Nor is it erotic; an erotic relationship, e.g. between man and wife or parent and child, comes into being in order to satisfy needs which are, in part, given by nature; the needs which are satisfied by a master-servant relationship are purely social and historical. By this definition, a wet nurse is not a servant, a cook may be. Thirdly, it is contractual. A contractual relationship comes into being through the free decision of both parties, a double commitment. The liberty of decision need not be, and indeed very rarely is, equal on both sides, but the weaker party must possess *some* degree of sovereignty. Thus, a slave is not a servant because he has no sovereignty whatsoever; he cannot even say, "I would rather starve than work for you." A contractual relationship not only involves double sovereignty, it is also asymmetric; what the master contributes, e.g. shelter, food and wages, and what the servant contributes, e.g. looking after the master's clothes and house, are qualitatively different and there is no objective standard by which one can decide whether the one is or is not equivalent to the other. A contract, therefore, differs from a law. In law all sovereignty lies with the law or with those who impose it and the individual has no sovereignty. Even in a democracy where sovereignty is said to reside in the people, it is as one of the people that each citizen has a share in that, not as an individual. Further, the relationship of all individuals to a law is symmetric; it commands or prohibits the same thing to all who come under it. Of any law one can ask the aesthetic question, "Is it enforceable?" and the ethical question, "Is it just?" An individual has the aesthetic right to break the law if he is powerful enough to do so with impunity, and it may be his ethical duty to break it if his conscience tells him that the law is unjust. Of a contract, on the other hand, one can only ask the historical question, "Did both parties pledge their word to it?" Its justice or its enforceability are secondary to the historical fact of mutual personal commitment. A contract can only be broken or changed by the mutual consent of both parties. It will be my ethical duty to insist on changing a contract when my conscience tells me it is unfair only if I am in the advantageous position; if I am in the weaker position I have a right to propose a change but no right to insist on one.

When the false oracle has informed Don Quixote that Dulcinea can only be disenchanted if Sancho Panza will receive several thousand lashes, the latter agrees to receive them on condition that he inflict them himself and in his own good time. One night Don Quixote becomes so impatient for the release of his love that he attempts to become the whipper, at which point Sancho Panza knocks his master down.

> DON QUIXOTE. So you would rebel against your lord and master, would you, and dare to raise your hand against the one who feeds you.
> SANCHO. I neither make nor unmake a king, but am simply standing up for myself, for I am my own lord.

Similarly, when Mr Pickwick, on entering the Debtors' Prison, attempts to dismiss Sam Weller because it would be unjust to the latter to expect him to accompany his master, Sam Weller refuses to accept dismissal and arranges to get sent to jail himself.

Lastly, the master-servant relationship is between real persons. Thus we do not call the employees of a factory or a store servants because the factory and the store are corporate, i.e. fictitious, persons.

II

Who is there?
I.
Who is I?
Thou.
And that is the awakening—the Thou and the I.
                                    —Paul Valéry

Man is a creature who is capable of entering into Thou-Thou relationships with God and with his neighbors because he has a Thou-Thou relationship to himself. There are other social animals who have signal codes, e.g. bees have signals for informing each other about the whereabouts and distance of flowers, but only man has a language by means of which he can disclose himself to his neighbor, which he could not do and could not want to do if he did not first possess the capacity and the need to disclose himself to himself. The communication of mere objective fact only requires monologue and for monologue a language is not necessary, only a code. But subjective communication demands dialogue and dialogue demands a real language.

A capacity for self-disclosure implies an equal capacity for self-concealment. Of an animal it is equally true to say that it is incapable of telling us what it *really* feels, and that it is incapable of hiding its feelings. A man can do both. For the animal motto is that of the trolls in Ibsen's *Peer Gynt*—"To thyself be enough"—while the human motto is, "To thyself be true." Peer is perfectly willing, if it is convenient, to swear that the cow he sees is a beautiful young lady, but when the Troll-King suggests an operation which will take away from Peer the power of distinguishing between truth and falsehood so that if he wishes that a cow were a beautiful girl, the cow immediately appears to him as such, Peer revolts.

To present artistically a human personality in its full depth, its inner dialectic, its self-disclosure and self-concealment, through the medium of a single character is almost impossible. The convention of the soliloquy attempts to get around the difficulty but it suffers from the disadvantage of *being* a convention; it presents, that is, what is really a dialogue in the form of a monologue. When Hamlet soliloquizes, we hear a single voice which is supposed to be addressed to himself but, in fact, is heard as addressed to us, the audience, so that we suspect that he is not disclosing to himself what he conceals from others, but only disclosing to us what he thinks it is good we should know, and at the same time concealing from us what he does not choose to tell us.

A dialogue requires two voices, but, if it is the inner dialogue of human personality that is to be expressed artistically, the two characters employed to express it and the relationship between them must be of a special kind. The pair must in certain respects be similar, i.e. they must be of the same sex, and in others, physical and temperamental, polar opposites—identical twins will not do because they inevitably raise the question, "Which is the real one?"— and they must be inseparable, i.e. the relationship between them must be of a kind which is not affected by the passage of time or the fluctuations of mood and passion, and which makes it plausible that wherever one of them is, whatever he is doing, the other should be there too. There is only one relationship which satisfies all these conditions, that between master and personal servant. It might be objected at this point that the Ego-Self relationship is given while the master-servant relationship, as defined above, is contractual. The objection would be valid if man, like all other finite things, had only the proto-history of coming into being and then merely sustaining that being. But man has a real history; having come into being, he has then through his choices to become what he is not yet, and this he cannot do unless he first chooses himself as he is now with all his finite limitations. To reach "the age of consent" means to arrive at the point where the "given" Ego-self relationship is changed into a contractual one. Suicide is a breach of contract.

III

> CRICHTON. There must always be a master and servants in all civilized communities, for it is natural, and whatever is natural is right.
>
> LORD LOAMSHIRE. It's very unnatural for me to stand here and allow you to talk such nonsense.
>
> CRICHTON. Yes, my lord, it is. That is what I have been striving to point out to your lordship.
>
> —J. M. Barrie, *The Admirable Crichton*

Defined abstractly, a master is one who gives orders and a servant is one who obeys orders. This characteristic makes the master-servant relationship peculiarly suitable as an expression of the inner life, so much of which is carried on in imperatives. If a large lady carelessly, but not intentionally, treads on my corn during a subway rush hour, what goes on in my mind can be expressed dramatically as follows:

> SELF (*in whom the physical sensation of pain has become the mental passion of anger*). "Care for my anger! Do something about it!"
>
> COGNITIVE EGO. "You are angry because of the pain caused by this large lady who, carelessly but not intentionally, has trodden on your corn. If you decide to relieve your feelings, you can give her a sharp kick on the ankle without being noticed."
>
> SELF. "Kick her."
>
> SUPER-EGO (*to simplify matters, let us pretend that super-ego and conscience*

are identical, which they are not). "Unintentional wrongs must not be
avenged. Ladies must not be kicked. Control your anger!"

LADY (*noticing what she has done*). "I beg your pardon! I hope I didn't
   hurt you."

SELF. "Kick her!"

SUPER-EGO. "Smile! Say 'Not at all, Madam.'"

VOLITIONAL EGO (*to the appropriate voluntary muscles*).
   either "Kick her!"
   or "Smile! Say 'Not at all, Madam!'"

Of my five "characters," only one, my cognitive ego, really employs the indicative mood. Of the others, my self and my super-ego cannot, either of them, be a servant. Each is a master who is either obeyed or disobeyed. Neither can take orders. My body, on the other hand (or rather its "voluntary muscles"), can do nothing but what it is told; it can never be a master, nor even a servant, only a slave. While my volitional ego is always both, a servant in relation to either my self or my super-ego and a master in relation to my body.

The "demands" of reason are not imperatives because, although it is possible not to listen to them and to forget them, as long as we listen and remember, it is impossible to disobey them, and a true imperative always implies the possibility of either obeying or disobeying. In so far as we listen to reason, we are its slaves, not its servants.

IV

> I care for nobody, no, not I
> And nobody cares for me.
> —"The Miller of Dee"

> But my five wits nor my five senses can
> Dissuade one foolish heart from serving thee,
> Who leaves unswayed the likeness of a man
> Thy proud heart's slave and vassal wretch to be.
> —Shakespeare, Sonnet CXLI

Because of its double role the volitional ego has two wishes which, since the Fall, instead of being dialectically related, have become contradictory opposites. On the one hand it wishes to be free of all demands made upon it by the self or the conscience or the outer world. As Kierkegaard wrote:

> If I had a humble spirit in my service, who, when I asked for a glass of water, brought me the world's costliest wines blended in a chalice, I should dismiss him, in order to teach him that pleasure consists not in what I enjoy, but in having my own way.

When Biron, the hero of *Love's Labour's Lost*, who has hitherto been free of passion, finds himself falling in love, he is annoyed.

> This senior junior, giant dwarf, Dan Cupid,
> Sole emperor and great general
> Of trotting paritors (Oh my little heart)
> And I to be a corporal of his field
> And wear his colours like a tumbler's hoop.

On the other hand, the same ego wishes to be important, to find its existence meaningful, to have a *telos*, and this *telos* it can only find in something or someone outside itself. To have a *telos* is to have something to obey, to be the servant of. Thus all lovers instinctively use the master-servant metaphor.

> MIRANDA.   To be your fellow
>   You may deny me; but I'll be your servant,
>   Whether you will or no.
> FERDINAND.   My Mistress, dearest,
>   And I thus humble ever.
> MIRANDA.   My husband then?
> FERDINAND. Aye, with a heart as willing
>   As bondage e'er of freedom.

And so, with calculation, speaks every seducer.

> BERTRAM. I prithee do not strive against my vows.
>   I was compelled to her, but I love thee
>   By love's own sweet constraint, and will for ever
>   Do thee all rights of service.
> DIANA.   Ay, so you serve us
>   Till we serve you.

To be loved, to be the *telos* of another, can contribute to the ego's sense of importance, provided that it feels that such giving of love is a free act on the part of the other, that the other is not a slave of his or her passion. In practice, unfortunately, if there is an erotic element present as distinct from *philia*, most people find it hard to believe that another's love for them is free and not a compulsion, unless they happen to reciprocate it.

Had man not fallen, the wish of his ego for freedom would be simply a wish not to find its *telos* in a false or inferior good, and its wish for a *telos* simply a longing for the true good, and both wishes would be granted. In his fallen state, he oscillates between a wish for absolute autonomy, to be as God, and a wish for an idol who will take over the whole responsibility for his existence, to be an irresponsible slave. The consequence of indulging the first is a sense of loneliness and lack of meaning; the consequence of indulging the second, a masochistic insistence on being made to suffer. John falls in love with Anne who returns his love, is always faithful and anxious to please. Proud and self-satisfied, he thinks of *my Anne*, presently of *my wife* and finally of *my well-being*. Anne as a real other has ceased to exist for him. He does not suffer in any way that he can put his finger on, nevertheless he begins to feel bored and lonely.

George falls in love with Alice who does not return his love, is unfaithful and treats him badly. To George she remains Alice, cruel but real. He suffers but he is not lonely or bored, for his suffering is the proof that another exists to cause it.

The futility of trying to combine both wishes into one, of trying, that is, to have a *telos*, but to find it within oneself not without, is expressed in the myth of Narcissus. Narcissus falls in love with his reflection; he wishes to become its servant, but instead his reflection insists upon being his slave.

V

Das verfluchte Hier
—Goethe, *Faust*

Goethe's *Faust* is full of great poetry and wise sayings but it is not dramatically exciting; like a variety show, it gives us a succession of scenes interesting in themselves but without a real continuity; one could remove a scene or add a new one without causing any radical change in the play. Further, once the Marguerite episode is over, it is surprising how little Faust himself actually does. Mephisto creates a new situation and Faust tells us what he feels about it. I can well imagine that every actor would like to play Mephisto, who is always entertaining, but the actor who plays Faust has to put up with being ignored whenever Mephisto is on stage. Moreover, from a histrionic point of view, is there ever any reason why Faust should move instead of standing still and just delivering his lines? Is not any movement the actor may think up arbitrary?

These defects are not, of course, due to any lack of dramatic talent in Goethe but to the nature of the Faust myth itself, for the story of Faust is precisely the story of a man who refuses to be anyone and only wishes to become someone else. Once he has summoned Mephisto, the manifestation of possibility without actuality, there is nothing left for Faust to represent but the passive consciousness of possibilities. When the Spirit of Fire appears to Faust, it says:

> *Du gleichst dem Geist, den du begreifst,*
> *Nicht mir*

and in an ideal production, Faust and Mephisto should be played by identical twins.

Near the beginning of the play Faust describes his condition:

> *Zwei Seelen wohnen, ach! in meiner Brust*
> *Die eine will sich von der andern trennen;*

Die eine hält, in derber Liebeslust
Sich an die Welt mit klammernden
Organen; Die andre hebt gewaltsam sich vom Dust
Zu den Gefilden hoher Ahnen.

This has nothing to do, though he may think it has, with the conflict between pleasure and goodness, the kingdom of *this* world and the kingdom of Heaven. Faust's *Welt* is the immediate actual moment, the actual concrete world now, and his *hohe Ahnen* the same world seen by memory and imagination as possible, as what might have been once and may be yet. All value belongs to possibility, the actual here and now is valueless, or rather the value it has is the feeling of discontent it provokes. When Faust signs his contract with Mephisto, the latter says:

Ich will mich hier zu deinem Dienst verbinden,
Auf deinen Wink nicht rasten und nicht ruhn;
Wenn wir uns drüben wieder finden
So sollst du mir das Gleiche tun

to which Faust replies airily:

Das Drüben kann mich wenig kümmern
Schlägst du erst diese Welt zu Trümmern,
Die andre mag danach entstehen

because he does not believe that *Das Drüben,* the exhaustion of all possibilities, can ever be reached—as, indeed, in the play it never is. Faust escapes Mephisto's clutches because he is careful to define the contentment of his last moment in terms of anticipation:

Im Vorgefühl von solchem hohen Glück
Geniess' ich jetzt den höchsten Augenblick.

But, though Faust is not damned, it would be nonsense to say that he is saved. The angels bearing him to Heaven describe him as being in the pupa stage, and to such a condition Judgment has no meaning.

Mephisto describes himself as:

ein Teil des Teils, der Anfangs alles war,
Ein Teil der Finsternis, die sich das Licht gebar

as, that is to say, a manifestation of the rejection of all finiteness, the desire for existence without the limitation of essence. To the spirit that rejects any actuality, the ideal must be the *Abgrund,* the abyss of infinite potentiality, and all creation must be hateful to it. So Valéry's serpent cries out against God:

Il se fit Celui qui dissipe
En conséquences son Principe,
En étoiles son Unité.

Mephisto describes himself as:

ein Teil von jener Kraft,
Die stets das Böse will und stets das Gute schafft,

but it is hard to see what good or evil he does to Faust. Through his agency
or his suggestion, Faust may do a good deal of harm to others, but Faust
himself is completely unaffected by his acts. He passively allows Mephisto to
entertain him and is no more changed in character by these entertainments
than we are by watching the play.

Faust may talk a great deal about the moral dangers of content and sloth,
but the truth is that his discontent is not a discontent with himself but a terror of being bored. What Faust is totally lacking in is a sacramental sense,* a
sense that the finite can be a sign for the infinite, that the secular can be
sanctified; one cannot imagine him saying with George Herbert:

A servant with this clause
Makes drudgery divine;
Who sweeps a room as for Thy laws
Makes that and the action fine.

In this lack Faust is a typical modern figure. In earlier ages men have been
tempted to think that the finite was not a sign for the holy but the holy itself,
and fell therefore into idolatry and magic. The form which the Devil assumed
in such periods, therefore, was always finite; he appeared as the manifestation
of some specific temptation, as a beautiful woman, a bag of gold, etc. In our
age there are no idols in the strict sense because we tire of one so quickly and
take up another that the word cannot apply. Our real, because permanent,
idolatry is an idolatry of possibility. And in such an age the Devil appears in
the form of Mephisto, in the form, that is, of an actor. The point about an
actor is that he has no name of his own, for his name is Legion. One might say
that our age recognized its nature on the day when Henry Irving was knighted.

VI

Voglio far il gentiluomo
E non voglio più servir.
　　　　—Da Ponte, *Don Giovanni*

Dein Werk! O thörige Magd
　　　　—Wagner, *Tristan and Isolde*

The man who refuses to be the servant of any *telos* can only be directly represented, like the Miller of Dee, lyrically. He can sing his rapture of freedom

---

*If Faust holds any theological position, it is pantheist. The pantheist believes that the uni-
verse is numinous *as-a-whole*. But a sacramental sign is always some particular aspect of the finite,
this thing, *this* act, not the finite-in-general, and it is valid for this person, this social group, this
historical epoch, not for humanity-in-general. Pansacramentalism is self-contradictory.

and indifference, but after that there is nothing for him to do but be quiet. In a drama he can only be represented indirectly as a man with a *telos*, indeed a monomania, but of such a kind that it is clear that it is an arbitrary choice; nothing in his nature and circumstances imposes it on him or biases him toward it. Such is Don Giovanni. The *telos* he chooses is to seduce, to "know" every woman in the world. Leporello says of him:

> Non si pica, se sia ricca
> Se sia brutta, se sia bella,
> Purché porti la gonnella

A sensual libertine, like the Duke in *Rigoletto*, cannot see a pretty girl, or a girl who is "his type" without trying to seduce her; but if a plain elderly woman like Donna Elvira passes by, he cries, "My God, what a dragon," and quickly looks away. That is sensuality, and pains should be taken in a production to make it clear why the Duke should have fallen into this particular idolization of the finite rather than another. The Duke must appear to be the kind of man to whom all women will be attracted; he must be extremely good-looking, virile, rich, magnificent, a grand seigneur.

Don Giovanni's pleasure in seducing women is not sensual but arithmetical; his satisfaction lies in adding one more name to his list which is kept for him by Leporello. Everything possible, therefore, should be done to make him as inconspicuous and anonymous in appearance as an FBI agent. If he is made handsome, then his attraction for women is a bias in his choice, and if he is made ugly, then the repulsion he arouses in women is a challenge. He should look so neutral that the audience realizes that, so far as any finite motive is concerned, he might just as well have chosen to collect stamps. The Duke does not need a servant because there is no contradiction involved in sensuality or indeed in any idolatry of the finite. The idol and the idolater between them can say all there is to say. The Duke is the master of his ladies and the slave of his sensuality. Any given form of idolatry of the finite is lacking in contradiction because such idolatry is itself finite. Whenever we find one idol we find others, we find polytheism. We do not have to be told so to know that there are times when the Duke is too tired or too hungry to look at a pretty girl. For Don Giovanni there are no such times, and it is only in conjunction with his servant, as Giovanni-Leporello, that he can be understood.

Don Giovanni is as inconspicuous as a shadow, resolute and fearless in action; Leporello is comically substantial like Falstaff, irresolute and cowardly. When, in his opening aria, Leporello sings the words quoted at the head of this section, the audience laughs because it is obvious that he is lacking in all the qualities of character that a master should have. He is no Figaro. But by the end of the opera, one begins to suspect that the joke is much funnier than one had first thought. Has it not, in fact, been Leporello all along who was really the master and Don Giovanni really his servant? It is Leporello who keeps the list and if he lost it or forgot to keep it up-to-date or walked off with it, Don Giovanni would have no *raison d'être*. It is significant that we never see Don Giovanni look at the list himself or show any pleasure in it; only Leporello does that: Don Giovanni merely reports the latest name to him. Perhaps it should have been Leporello who was carried down alive to hell by the Commendatore, leaving poor worn-out Giovanni to die in peace. Imagine a Leporello who, in real life, is a rabbity-looking, celibate, timid, stupendously learned professor, with the finest collection in the world, of, say, Trilobites, but in every aspect of life outside his field, completely incompetent. Brought up by a stern fundamentalist father (Il Commendatore) he went to college with the intention of training for the ministry, but there he read Darwin and lost his faith. Will not his daydream version of his ideal self be someone very like Don Giovanni?

It is fortunate for our understanding of the myth of Tristan and Isolde that Wagner should have chosen to write an opera about it, for the physical demands made by Wagnerian opera defend us, quite accidentally, from an illusion which we are likely to fall into when reading the medieval legend; the two lovers, for whom nothing is of any value but each other, appear on the stage, not as the handsomest of princes and the most beautiful of princesses, not as Tamino and Pamina, but as a Wagnerian tenor and soprano in all their corseted bulk. When Tamino and Pamina fall mutually in love, we see that the instigating cause is the manly beauty of one and the womanly beauty of the other. Beauty is a finite quality which time will take away; this does not matter in the case of Tamino and Pamina because we know that their romantic passion for each other has only to be temporary, a natural but not serious preliminary to the serious unromantic love of man and wife. But the infinite romantic passion of Tristan and Isolde which has no past and no future outside itself cannot be generated by a finite quality; it can only be generated by finiteness-in-itself against which it protests with an infinite passion of rejection. Like Don Giovanni, Tristan and Isolde are purely mythical figures in that we never meet them in historical existence: we meet promiscuous men like the Duke, but never a man who is absolutely indifferent to the physical qualities of the women he seduces; we meet romantically passionate engaged couples, but never a couple of whom we can say that their romantic passion will not and cannot change into married affection or decline into indifference. Just as we can say that Don Giovanni might have chosen to collect stamps instead of women, so we can say that Tristan and Isolde might have fallen in love with two other people; they are so indifferent to each other as persons with unique bodies and characters that they might just as well—and this is one significance of the love potion—have drawn each other's names out of a hat. A lifelong romantic idolatry of a real person is possible and occurs in life provided that the romance is one-sided, that one party plays the Cruel Fair, e.g. Don José and Carmen. For any finite idolatry is by definition an asymmetric relation: my idol is that which I make responsible for my existence in order that I may have no responsibility for myself; if it turns round and demands responsibility from me it ceases to be an idol. Again, it is fortunate that the operatic medium makes it impossible for Wagner's Tristan and Isolde to consummate their love physically. Wagner may have intended, probably did intend, the love duet in the Second Act to stand for such a physical consummation, but what we actually see are two people singing of how much they desire each other, and consummation remains something that is always about to happen but never does, and this, whatever Wagner intended, is correct: their mutual idolatry is only possible because, while both assert their infinite willingness to give themselves to each other, in practice both play the Cruel Fair and withhold themselves. Were they to yield, they would know something about each other and their relation would change into a one-sided idolatry, a mutual affection or a mutual indifference. They do not yield because their passion is not for each other but for something they hope to obtain by means of each other, Nirvana, the primordial unity that made the mistake of begetting multiplicity, "*der Finsternis die sich das Licht gebar.*"

Just as Don Giovanni is inseparable from his servant Leporello, so Tristan and Isolde appear flanked by Brangaene and Kurvenal. It is Kurvenal's mocking reference to Morold that makes Isolde so angry that she decides to poison Tristan and herself, in consequence of which Tristan and she are brought together; otherwise he would have kept his distance till they landed. It is Brangaene who substitutes the love potion for the death potion so that Tristan and Isolde are committed to each other not by their personal decisions but by an extraneous factor for which they are not responsible. It is Brangaene who tells King Mark about the love potion so that he is willing to forgive the lovers and let them join each other, but tells him too late for his decision to be of any practical help. And it is Kurvenal's leaving of his master to greet Isolde that gives Tristan the opportunity to cause his death by tearing off his bandages. Kurvenal obeys his friend like a slave who has no mind of his own.

> *Dem guten Marke,*
> *dient' ich ihm hold,*
> *wie warst du ihm treuer als Gold!*
> *Musst' ich verrathen*
> *den edlen Herrn,*
> *wie betrogst du ihn da so gern*
> *Dir nicht eigen,*
> *einzig mein*

Tristan tells him, but then points out that Kurvenal has one freedom which he, Tristan, can never have. He is not in love.

> *Nur—was ich leide,*
> *das—kannst du nicht leiden.*

As in the case of Don Giovanni and Leporello, one begins to wonder who are really master and mistress. Imagine a Kurvenal and a Brangaene who in real life are an average respectable lower-middle-class couple (but with more children than is today usual), living in a dingy suburban house. He has a dingy white-collar job and has a hard time making both ends meet. She has no maid and is busy all day washing the diapers of the latest baby, mending the socks of older children, washing up, trying to keep the house decent, etc. She has lost any figure and looks she may once have had; he is going bald and acquiring a middle-aged spread. Their marriage, given their circumstances, is an average one; any romantic passion has long ago faded but, though they often get on each other's nerves, they don't passionately hate each other. A couple, that is, on whom the finite bears down with the fullest possible weight, or provides the fewest of its satisfactions. Now let them concoct their day-dream of the ideal love and the ideal world, and something very like the passion of Tristan and Isolde will appear, and a world in which children, jobs, and food do not exist. His Boss will appear as King Mark, an old disreputable drinking crony of his as Morold, the scandal-mongering neighbors next door as Melot. They cannot, however, keep the sense of reality out of their dream and make everything end happily. They are dreamers but they are sane dreamers, and sanity demands that Tristan and Isolde are doomed.

VII

> The fool will stay
> And let the wise man fly.
> The knave turns fool who runs away,
> The fool, no knave perdy.
> —Shakespeare, *King Lear*

According to Renaissance political theory, the King, as the earthly representative of Divine Justice, is above the law which he imposes on his subjects. For his subjects the law is a universal, but the King who makes the law is an individual who cannot be subject to it, since the creator is superior to his creation—a poet, for instance, cannot be subordinate to his poem. In general, the Middle Ages had thought differently; they held that not even the King could violate Natural Law. In English history, the transition from one view to the other is marked by Henry the Eighth's execution of Sir Thomas More who, as Lord Chancellor, was the voice of Natural Law and the keeper of the King's Conscience. Both periods believed that, in some sense, the King was a divine representative, so that the political question, "Is the King obliged to obey his law?" is really the theological question, "Does God have to obey His own laws?" The answer given seems to me to depend upon what doctrine of God is held, Trinitarian or Unitarian. If the former, then the Middle Ages were right, for it implies that obedience is a meaningful term when applied to God—the co-equal Son obeys the Father. If the latter, then the Renaissance was right, unless the sacramental theory of kingship is abandoned, in which case, of course, the problem does not arise.* An absolute monarch is a representative of the deist God. The Renaissance King, then, is an individual, and the only individual, the superman, who is above the law, not subject to the universal. If he should do wrong, who can tell him so? Only an individual who, like himself, is not subject to the universal because he is as below the universal as the King is above it. The fool is such an individual because, being deficient in reason, subhuman, he has no contact with its demands. The fool is "simple," i.e. he is not a madman. A madman is someone who was once a normal sane man but who, under the stress of emotion, has lost his reason. A fool is born a fool and was never anything else; he is, as we say, "wanting," and whereas a madman is presumed to feel emotions like normal men, indeed to feel them more strongly than the normal man, the fool is presumed to be without emotions. If, therefore, he should happen to utter a truth, it cannot be *his* utterance, for he cannot distinguish between truth and falsehood, and he cannot have a personal motive for uttering what, without his knowing it, happens to be true, since motive implies emotion and the fool is presumed to have none. It can only be the voice of God using him as His mouthpiece. God is as far above the superman-King, whose earthly representative he is, as the King is above ordinary mortals, so that the voice of God is a voice, the only one, which the King must admit that it is his duty to obey. Hence the only individual who can speak to the King with authority, not as a subject, is the fool.

The position of the King's Fool is not an easy one. It is obvious that God uses him as a mouthpiece only occasionally, for most of the time what he says is patently nonsense, the words of a fool. At all moments when he is not divinely inspired but just a fool, he is subhuman, not a subject, but a slave, with no human rights, who may be whipped like an animal if he is a nuisance. On the occasions when he happens to speak the truth, he cannot, being a fool, say, "This time I am not speaking nonsense as I usually do, but the truth"; it rests with the King to admit the difference and, since truth is often unwelcome and hard to admit, it is not surprising that the fool's life should be a rough one.

> FOOL. Prithee, nuncle, keep a schoolmaster that can teach thy fool to lie.
> LEAR. An you lie, sirrah, we'll have you whipped.
> FOOL. I marvel what kin thou and thy daughters are. They'll have me whipped for speaking true; thou'lt have me whipped for lying; and sometimes I am whipped for holding my peace. I had rather be any kind o' thing than a fool; and yet, I would not be thee, nuncle.

---

*Or does it? In recent years we have seen the emergence, and not only in professedly totalitarian countries, of something very like a doctrine of the Divine Rights of States, though the adjective would be indignantly denied by most of its exponents.

It was said above that the cognitive ego never uses the imperative mood, always the indicative or the conditional: it does not say, "Do such-and-such!"; it says, "Such-and-such *is* the case. *If* you want such-and-such a result, you can obtain it by doing as follows. What you want to do, your emotive self can tell you, not I. What you ought to do, your super-ego can tell you, not I." Nor can it compel the volitional ego to listen to it; the choice of listening or refusing to listen lies with the latter.

> Truth's a dog must to kennel; he must be whipped out when Lady the brach may stand by the fire and stink.

We are told that, after Cordelia's departure for France after Lear's first fatal folly, his first "mad" act, the fool started to pine away. After the Third Act, he mysteriously vanishes from the play, and when Lear appears without him, Lear is irremediably mad. At the very end, just before his death, Lear suddenly exclaims "And my poor fool is hanged!" and it is impossible for the audience to know if he is actually referring to the fool or suffering from aphasia and meaning to say Cordelia, whom we know to have been hanged.

The fool, that is, seems to stand for Lear's sense of reality which he rejects. Not for his conscience. The fool never speaks to him, as Kent does, in the name of morality. It was immoral of Lear to make the dowries of his daughters proportionate to their capacity to express their affection for their father, but not necessarily mad because he (and the audience) has no reason to suppose that Cordelia has any less talent for expressing affection than her sisters. Rationally, there is no reason that she should not have surpassed them. Her failure in the competition is due to a moral refusal, not to a lack of talent. Lear's reaction to Cordelia's speech, on the other hand, is not immoral but mad because he knows that, in fact, Cordelia loves him and that Goneril and Regan do not. From that moment on, his sanity is, so to speak, on the periphery of his being instead of at its center, and the dramatic manifestation of this shift is the appearance of the fool who stands outside him as a second figure and is devoted to Cordelia. As long as passion has not totally engulfed him, the fool can appear at his side, laboring "to out jest / His heart-struck injuries." There is still a chance, however faint, that he may realize the facts of his situation and be restored to sanity. Thus when Lear begins to address the furniture as if it were his daughters, the fool remarks:

> I cry you mercy. I took you for a joint-stool.

In other words, there is still an element of theatre in Lear's behavior, as a child will talk to inanimate objects as if they were people, while knowing that, in reality, they are not. But when this chance has passed and Lear has descended into madness past recall, there is nothing for the fool to represent and he must disappear.

Frequently the fool makes play with the words "knave" and "fool." A knave is one who disobeys the imperatives of conscience; a fool is one who cannot hear or understand them. Though the cognitive ego is, morally, a "fool" because conscience speaks not to it but to the volitional ego, yet the imperative of duty can never be in contradiction to the actual facts of the situation, as the imperative of passion can be and frequently is. The Socratic doctrine that to know the good is to will it, that sin is ignorance, is valid if by knowing one means listening to what one knows, and by ignorance, willful ignorance. If that is what one means, then, though not all fools are knaves, all knaves are fools.

> LEAR. Dost thou call me fool, boy?
> FOOL. All thy other titles thou hast given away; that thou wast born with.
> KENT. This is not altogether fool, my lord.
> FOOL. No, faith, lords and great men will not let me. If I had a monopoly on't; they would have part of it.

Ideally, in a stage production, Lear and the fool should be of the same physical type; they should both be athletic mesomorphs. The difference should be in their respective sizes. Lear should be as huge as possible, the fool as tiny.

VIII

> BODY. O who shall me deliver whole
> From bonds of this tyrannic soul?
> Which, stretcht upright, impales me so
> That mine own precipice I go. . . .
> SOUL. What Magick could me thus confine
> Within another's grief to pine?
> Where whatsoever it complain,
> I feel, that cannot feel, the pain . . .
> —Andrew Marvell

> VALENTINE. Belike, boy, then you are in love; for last morning you could not see to wipe my shoes.
> SPEED. True sir; I was in love with my bed. I thank you, you swinged me for my love, which makes me the bolder to chide you for yours.
> —Shakespeare, *Two Gentlemen of Verona*

The Tempest, Shakespeare's last play, is a disquieting work. Like the other three comedies of his late period, *Pericles, Cymbeline* and *The Winter's Tale*, it is concerned with a wrong done, repentance, penance and reconciliation; but, whereas the others all end in a blaze of forgiveness and love—"Pardon's the word to all"—in *The Tempest* both the repentance of the guilty and the pardon of the injured seem more formal than real. Of the former, Alonso is the only one who seems genuinely sorry; the repentance of the rest, both the courtly characters, Antonio and Sebastian, and the low, Trinculo and Stephano, is more the prudent promise of the punished and frightened, "I won't do it again. It doesn't pay," than any change of heart: and Prospero's forgiving is more the contemptuous pardon of a man who knows that he has his enemies completely at his mercy than a heartfelt reconciliation. His attitude to all of them is expressed in his final words to Caliban:

> as you look
> To have my pardon trim it handsomely.

One must admire Prospero because of his talents and his strength; one cannot possibly like him. He has the coldness of someone who has come to the conclusion that human nature is not worth much, that human relations are, at their best, pretty sorry affairs. Even towards the innocent young lovers, Ferdinand and Miranda, and their "brave new world," his attitude is one of mistrust so that he has to preach them a sermon on the dangers of anticipating their marriage vows. One might excuse him if he included himself in his critical skepticism but he never does; it never occurs to him that he, too, might have erred and be in need of pardon. He says of Caliban:

> born devil on whose nature
> Nurture can never stick, on whom my pains,
> Humanely taken, all, all lost, quite lost

but Shakespeare has written Caliban's part in such a way that, while we have to admit that Caliban is both brutal and corrupt, a "lying slave" who can be prevented from doing mischief only "by stripes not kindness," we cannot help feeling that Prospero is largely responsible for his corruption, and that, in the debate between them, Caliban has the best of the argument.

Before Prospero's arrival, Caliban had the island to himself, living there in a state of savage innocence. Prospero attempts to educate him, in return for which Caliban shows him all the qualities of the isle. The experiment is brought to a halt when Caliban tries to rape Miranda, and Prospero abandons any hope of educating him further. He does not, however, sever their relation and turn Caliban back to the forest; he changes its nature and, instead of trying to treat Caliban as a son, makes him a slave whom he rules by fear. This relation is profitable to Prospero:

> as it is
> We cannot miss him. He does make our fire,
> Fetch in our wood, and serve us in offices
> That profit us

but it is hard to see what profit, material or spiritual, Caliban gets out of it. He has lost his savage freedom:

> For I am all the subjects that you have
> Which first was mine own king

and he has lost his savage innocence:

> You taught me language and my profit on't
> Is, I know how to curse

so that he is vulnerable to further corruption when he comes into contact with the civilized vices of Trinculo and Stephano. He is hardly to be blamed, then, if he regards the virtues of civilization with hatred as responsible for his condition:

> Remember
> First to possess his books, for without them
> He's but a sot, as I am.

As a biological organism Man is a natural creature subject to the necessities of nature; as a being with consciousness and will, he is at the same time a historical person with the freedom of the spirit. *The Tempest* seems to me a manichean work, not because it shows the relation of Nature to Spirit as one of conflict and hostility, which in fallen man it is, but because it puts the blame for this upon Nature and makes the Spirit innocent. Such a view is the exact opposite of the view expressed by Dante:

> *Lo naturale è sempre senza errore*
> *ma l'altro puote errar per male obbietto*
> *o per poco o per troppo di vigore.*
>
> (*Purgatorio*, XVII)

The natural can never desire too much or too little because the natural good is the mean—too much and too little are both painful to its natural well-being. The natural, conforming to necessity, cannot imagine possibility. The closest it can come to a relation with the possible is as a vague dream; without Prospero, Ariel can only be known to Caliban as "sounds and sweet airs that give delight and hurt not." The animals cannot fall because the words of the tempter, "Ye shall be as gods," are in the future tense, and the animals have no future tense, for the future tense implies the possibility of doing something that has not been done before, and this they cannot imagine.

Man can never know his "nature" because knowing is itself a spiritual and historical act; his physical sensations are always accompanied by conscious emotions. It is impossible to remember a physical sensation of pleasure or pain, the moment it ceases one cannot recall it, and all one remembers is the emotion of happiness or fear which accompanied it. On the other hand, a sensory stimulus can recall forgotten emotions associated with a previous occurrence of the same stimulus, as when Proust eats the cake.

It is unfortunate that the word "Flesh," set in contrast to "Spirit," is bound to suggest not what the Gospels and St Paul intended it to mean, the whole physical-historical nature of fallen man, but his physical nature alone, a suggestion very welcome to our passion for reproving and improving others instead of examining our own consciences. For, the more "fleshly" a sin is, the more obviously public it is, and the easier to prevent by the application of a purely external discipline. Thus the sin of gluttony exists in acts of gluttony, in eating, drinking, smoking too much, etc. If a man restrains himself from such excess, or is restrained by others, he ceases to be a glutton; the phrase "gluttonous thoughts" apart from gluttonous acts is meaningless.

As Christ's comment on the Seventh Commandment indicates, the sin of lust is already "unfleshly" to the degree that it is possible to have lustful thoughts without lustful deeds, but the former are still "fleshly" in that the thinker cannot avoid knowing what they are; he may insist that his thoughts are not sinful but he cannot pretend that they are not lustful. Further, the relation between thought and act is still direct. The thought is the thought of a specific act. The lustful man cannot be a hypocrite to himself except through a symbolic transformation of his desires into images which are not consciously lustful. But the more "spiritual" the sin, the more indirect is the relationship between thought and act, and the easier it is to conceal the sin from others and oneself. I have only to watch a glutton at the dinner table to see that he is a glutton, but I may know someone for a very long time before I realize that he is an envious man, for there is no act which is in itself envious; there are only acts done in the spirit of envy, and there is often nothing about the acts themselves to show that they are done from envy and not from love. It is always possible, therefore, for the envious man to conceal from himself the fact that he is envious and to believe that he is acting from the highest of motives. While in the case of the purely spiritual sin of pride there is no "fleshly" element of the concrete whatsoever, so that no man, however closely he observes others, however strictly he examines himself, can ever know if they or he are proud; if he finds traces of any of the other six mortal sins, he can infer pride, because pride is fallen "Spirit-in-itself" and the source of all the other sins, but he cannot draw the reverse inference and, because he finds no traces of the other six, say categorically that he, or another, is not proud.

If man's physical nature could speak when his spirit rebukes it for its corruption, it would have every right to say, "Well, who taught me my bad habits?"; as it is, it has only one form of protest, sickness; in the end, all it can do is destroy itself in an attempt to murder its master.

Over against Caliban, the embodiment of the natural, stands the invisible spirit of imagination, Ariel. (In a stage production, Caliban should be as monstrously conspicuous as possible, and, indeed, suggest, as far as decency permits, the phallic. Ariel, on the other hand, except when he assumes a specific disguise at Prospero's order, e.g. when he appears as a harpy, should, ideally, be invisible, a disembodied voice, an ideal which, in these days of microphones and loud-speakers, should be realizable.)

Caliban was once innocent but has been corrupted; his initial love for Prospero has turned into hatred. The terms "innocent" and "corrupt" cannot be applied to Ariel because he is beyond good and evil; he can neither love nor hate, he can only play. It is not sinful of Eve to imagine the possibility of being as a god knowing good and evil: her sin lay in desiring to realize that possibility when she knew it was forbidden her, and her desire did not come from her imagination, for imagination is without desire and is, therefore, incapable of distinguishing between permitted and forbidden possibilities; it only knows that they are imaginatively possible. Similarly, imagination cannot distinguish the possible from the impossible; to it the impossible is a species of the genus possible, not another genus. I can perfectly well imagine that I might be a hundred feet high or a champion heavyweight boxer, and I do myself no harm in so doing, provided I do so playfully, without desire. I shall, however, come to grief if I take the possibility seriously, which I can do in two ways. Desiring to become a heavyweight boxer, I may deceive myself into thinking that the imaginative possibility is a real possibility and waste my life trying to become the boxer I never can become. Or, desiring to become a boxer, but realizing that it is, for me, impossible, I may refuse to relinquish the desire and turn on God and my neighbor in a passion of hatred and rejection because I cannot have what I want. So Richard III, to punish existence for his misfortune in being born a hunchback, decided to become a villain.

Imagination is beyond good *and* evil. Without imagination I remain an innocent animal, unable to become anything but what I already am. In order to become what I should become, therefore, I have to put my imagination to work, and limit its playful activity to imagining those possibilities which, for me, are both permissible and real; if I allow it to be the master and play exactly as it likes, then I shall remain in a dreamlike state of imagining everything I might become, without getting round to ever becoming anything. But, once imagination has done its work for me, to the degree that, with its help, I have become what I should become, imagination has a right to demand its freedom to play without any limitations, for there is no longer any danger that I shall take its play seriously. Hence the relation between Prospero and Ariel is contractual, and, at the end of the drama, Ariel is released.

If *The Tempest* is overpessimistic and manichean, *The Magic Flute* is overoptimistic and pelagian. At the end of the opera a double wedding is celebrated; the representative of the spiritual, Tamino, finds his happiness in Pamina and has attained wisdom while the chorus sing:

> *Es siegte die Stärke und krönet zum Lohn.*
> *Die Schönheit und Weisheit mit ewiger Kron'*

and, at the same time, the representative of the natural, Papageno is rewarded with Papagena, and they sing together:

Erst einen kleinen Papageno
Dann eine kleine Papagena
Dann wieder einen Papageno
Dann wieder eine Papagena

expressing in innocent humility the same attitude which Caliban expresses in guilty defiance when Prospero accuses him of having tried to rape Miranda,

O ho, O ho! Would't had been done.
Thou didst prevent me; I had peopled else
This isle with Calibans.

Tamino obtains his reward because he has had the courage to risk his life undergoing the trials of Fire and Water; Papageno obtains his because he has had the humility to refuse to risk his life even if the refusal will mean that he must remain single. It is as if Caliban, when Prospero offered to adopt him and educate him, had replied: "Thank you very much, but clothes and speech are not for me; It is better I stay in the jungle."

According to *The Magic Flute*, it is possible for nature and spirit to coexist in man harmoniously and without conflict, provided both keep to themselves and do not interfere with each other, and that, further, the natural has the freedom to refuse to be interfered with.

The greatest of spirit-nature pairs and the most orthodox is, of course, Don Quixote–Sancho Panza. Unlike Prospero and Caliban, their relationship is harmonious and happy; unlike Tamino and Papageno, it is dialectical; each affects the other. Further, both they and their relationship are comic; Don Quixote is comically mad, Sancho Panza is comically sane, and each finds the other a lovable figure of fun, an endless source of diversion. It is this omnipresent comedy that makes the book orthodox; present the relationship as tragic and the conclusion is manichean, present either or both of the characters as serious, and the conclusion is pagan or pelagian. The man who takes seriously the command of Christ to take up his cross and follow Him must, if he is serious, see himself as a comic figure, for he is not the Christ, only an ordinary man, yet he believes that the command, "Be ye perfect," is seriously addressed to himself. Worldly "sanity" will say, "I am not Christ, only an ordinary man. For me to think that I can become perfect would be madness. Therefore, the command cannot seriously be addressed to me." The other can only say, "It is madness for me to attempt to obey the command, for it seems impossible; nevertheless, since I believe it is addressed to me, I must believe that it is possible"; in proportion as he takes the command seriously, that is, he will see himself as a comic figure. To take himself seriously would mean that he thought of himself, not as an ordinary man, but as Christ.

For Christ is not a model to be imitated, like Hector, or Aristotle's megalo-psych, but the Way to be followed, If a man thinks that the megalopsych is a desirable model, all he has to do is to read up how the megalopsych behaves and imitate him, e.g. he will be careful, when walking, not to swing his arms.

But the Way cannot be imitated, only followed; a Christian who is faced with a moral problem cannot look up the answer in the Gospels. If someone, for instance, were to let his hair and beard grow till he looked like some popular pious picture of Christ, put on a white linen robe and ride into town on a donkey, we should know at once that he was either a madman or a fake. At first sight Don Quixote's madness seems to be of this kind. He believes that the world of the Romances is the real world and that, to be a knight-errant, all he has to do is imitate the Romances exactly. Like Lear, he cannot distinguish imaginative possibilities from actualities and treats analogies as identities; Lear thinks a stool is his daughter, Don Quixote thinks windmills are giants, but their manias are not really the same. Lear might be said to be suffering from worldly madness. The worldly man goes mad when the actual state of affairs becomes too intolerable for his *amour-propre* to accept; Lear cannot face the fact that he is no longer a man of power or that he has brought his present situation upon himself by his unjust competition. Don Quixote's madness, on the other hand, might be called holy madness, for *amour-propre* has nothing to do with his delusions. If his madness were of Lear's kind, then, in addition to believing that he must imitate the knight-errants of old, he would have endowed himself in his imagination with their gifts, e.g. with the youth and strength of Amadis of Gaul: but he does noth-ing of the kind; he knows that he is past fifty and penniless, nevertheless, he believes he is called to be a knight-errant. The knight-errant sets out to win glory by doing great deeds and to win the love of his lady, and whatever trials and defeats he may suffer on the way, in the end he triumphs. Don Quixote, however, fails totally; he accomplishes nothing, he does not win his lady, and, as if that were not ignominious enough, what he does win is a parody of what a knight-errant is supposed to win, for he does, in fact, become famous and admired—as a madman. If his were a worldly madness, *amour-propre* would demand that he add to his other delusions the delusion of having succeeded, the delusion that the welcome he receives everywhere is due to the fame of his great deeds (a delusion which his audience do everything to encourage), but Don Quixote is perfectly well aware that he has failed to do anything which he set out to do.

At the opposite pole to madness stands philistine realism. Madness says, "Windmills are giants"; philistine realism says, "Windmills are only wind-mills; giants are only giants," and then adds "Windmills really exist because they provide me with flour; giants are imaginary and do not exist because they provide me with nothing." (A student of psychoanalysis who says, "Windmills and giants are only phallic symbols," is both philistine and mad.) Madness confuses analogies with identities, philistine realism refuses to recognize analogies and only admits identities; neither can say, "Windmills are like giants."

At first sight Sancho Panza seems a philistine realist. "I go," he says, "with a great desire to make money"; it may seem to the reader hardly "realistic" of Sancho Panza to believe that he will gain a penny, far less an island governorship, by following Don Quixote, but is not the philistine realist who believes in nothing but material satisfactions precisely the same type to whom it is easiest to sell a nonexistent gold mine?

The sign that Sancho Panza is not a philistine but a "holy" realist is the persistence of his hope of getting something when he has realized that his master is mad. It is as if a man who had been sold a nonexistent gold mine continued to believe in its existence after he had discovered that the seller was a crook. It is clear that, whatever Sancho Panza may say, his motives for following his master are love of his master, and that equally unrealistic of motives, love of adventure for its own sake, a poetic love of fun. Just as Don Quixote wins fame, but fame as a madman, so Sancho Panza actually becomes the Governor of an island, but as a practical joke; as Governor he obtains none of the material rewards which a philistine would hope for, yet he enjoys himself enormously. Sancho Panza is a realist in that it is always the actual world, the immediate moment, which he enjoys, not an imaginary world or an anticipated future, but a "holy" realist in that he enjoys the actual and immediate for its own sake, not for any material satisfactions it provides.

Don Quixote and Sancho Panza are both inveterate quoters: what the Romances are to the one, proverbs are to the other. A Romance is a history, feigned or real. It recounts a series of unique and quite extraordinary events which have, or are purported to have, happened in the past. The source of interest is in the events themselves, not in the literary style in which they are narrated; as long as the reader learns what happened, it is a matter of indifference to him whether the style is imaginative or banal. A proverb has nothing to do with history for it states, or claims to state, a truth which is valid at all times. The context of "A stitch in time saves nine" belongs to the same class as a statement of empirical science like "Bodies attract each other in direct proportion to their masses." The interest of a proverb, therefore, lies not in its content but in the unique way in which that content is expressed; the content is always banal because it is a statement of empirical science, and a scientific statement which was not banal would not be true.

Proverbs belong to the natural world where the Model and imitation of the Model are valid concepts. A proverb tells one exactly what one should do or avoid doing whenever the situation comes up to which it applies: if the situation comes up the proverb applies exactly; if it does not come up, the proverb does not apply at all. Romances, as we have seen, belong to the historical world of the spirit, where the Model is replaced by the Way, and imitation by following. But in man, these two worlds are not separate but dialectically related; the proverb, as an expression of the natural, admits its relation to the historical by its valuation of style; the romance, as an expression of the historical, admits its relation to the natural by its indifference to style.

Don Quixote's lack of illusions about his own powers is a sign that his madness is not worldly but holy, a forsaking of the world, but without Sancho Panza it would not be Christian. For his madness to be Christian, he must have a neighbor, someone other than himself about whom he has no delusions but loves as himself. Without Sancho Panza, Don Quixote would be without neighbors, and the kind of religion implied would be one in which love of God was not only possible without but incompatible with love of one's neighbor.

IX

He that is greatest among you, let him be as the younger;
and he that is chief, as he that doth serve.—Luke: XXII, 26

*Ché per quanti si dice più lì nostro
tanto possiede più di ben ciascuno.*
—Dante, *Purgatorio*, XV

When a lover tells his beloved that she is his mistress and that he desires to be her servant, what he is trying, honestly or hypocritically, to say is something as follows: "As you know, I find you beautiful, an object of desire. I know that for true love such desire is not enough; I must also love you, not as an object of my desire, but as you are in yourself; I must desire your self-fulfillment. I cannot know you as you are nor prove that I desire your self-fulfillment, unless you tell me what you want and allow me to try and give it to you."

The proverb, "No man is a hero to his own valet," does not mean that no valet admires his master, but that a valet knows his master as he really is, admirable or contemptible, because it is a valet's job to supply the wants of his master, and, if you know what somebody wants, you know what he is like. It is possible for a master to have not the faintest inkling of what his servant is really like—unless his servant loves him, it is certain that he never will—but it is impossible for a servant, whether he be friendly, hostile or indifferent, not to know exactly what his master is like, for the latter reveals himself every time he gives an order.

To illustrate the use of the master-servant relationship as a parable of agape, I will take two examples from books which present the parable in a clear, simplified form, *Around the World in Eighty Days* by Jules Verne and the *Jeeves* series by P. G. Wodehouse.

Mr Fogg, as Jules Verne depicts him in his opening chapter, is a kind of stoic saint. He is a bachelor with ample private means and does no work, but he is never idle and has no vices; he plays whist at his club every evening but never more or less than the same number of hands, and, when he wins, he gives the money to charity. He knows all about the world for he is a religious reader of the newspapers, but he takes no part in its affairs; he has no friends and no enemies; he has never been known to show emotion of any kind; he seems to live "outside of any social relation." If "apathy" in the stoic sense is the highest virtue, then Fogg is a saint. His most striking trait, however, is one which seems to have been unknown in Classical times, a ritual mania about the exact time, an idolatry of the clock—his own tells the second, the minute, the hour, the day, the month and the year. He not only does exactly the same thing every day, but at exactly the same moment. Classical authors like Theophrastus have described very accurately most characterological types, but none of them, so far as I know, has described The Punctual Man (the type to which I personally belong), who cannot tell if he is hungry unless he first looks at the clock. It was never said in praise of any Caesar, for instance, that he made whatever was the Roman equivalent for trains run on time. I have heard it suggested that the first punctual people in history were the monks—at their Office hours. It is certain at least that the first serious analysis of the human experience of time was undertaken by St Augustine, and that the notion of punctuality, of action at an exact moment, depends on drawing a distinction between natural and historical time which Christianity encouraged if it did not invent.*

By and large, at least, the ancients thought of time either as oscillating to and fro like a pendulum or as moving round and round like a wheel, and the notion of historical time moving in an irreversible unilateral direction was strange to them. Both oscillation and cyclical movement provide a notion of change, but of change *for-a-time*; this *for-a-time* may be a long time—the pendulum may oscillate or the wheel revolve very slowly—but sooner or later all events reoccur: there is no place for a notion of absolute novelty, of a unique event which occurs once and for all at a particular moment in time. This latter notion cannot be derived from our objective experience of the outside world—all the movements we can see there are either oscillatory or cyclical—but only from our subjective inner experience of time in such phenomena as memory and anticipation.

So long as we think of it objectively, time is Fate or Chance, the factor in our lives for which we are not responsible, and about which we can do nothing; but when we begin to think of it subjectively, we feel responsible for *our* time, and the notion of punctuality arises. In training himself to be superior

---

*The Greek notion of *kairos*, the propitious moment for doing something, contained the seed of the notion of punctuality, but the seed did not flower.

to circumstance, the ancient stoic would discipline his passions because he knew what a threat they could be to the apathy he sought to acquire, but it would not occur to him to discipline his time, because he was unaware that it was his. A modern stoic like Mr Fogg knows that the surest way to discipline passion is to discipline time: decide what you want or ought to do during the day, then always do it at exactly the same moment every day, and passion will give you no trouble.

Mr Fogg has been so successful with himself that he is suffering from *hubris*; he is convinced that nothing can happen to him which he has not foreseen. Others, it is true, are often unreliable, but the moment he finds them so, he severs relations with them. On the morning when the story opens, he has just dismissed his servant for bringing him his shaving water at a temperature of 84° instead of the proper 86° and is looking for a new one. His conception of the just relation between master and servant is that the former must issue orders which are absolutely clear and unchanging—the master has no right to puzzle his servant or surprise him with an order for which he is not prepared—and the latter must carry them out as impersonally and efficiently as a machine—one slip and he is fired. The last thing he looks for in a servant or, for that matter, in anyone else is a personal friend.

On the same morning Passepartout has given notice to Lord Longsferry because he cannot endure to work in a chaotic household where the master is "brought home too frequently on the shoulders of policemen." Himself a sanguine, mercurial character, what he seeks in a master is the very opposite of what he would seek in a friend. He wishes his relation to his master to be formal and impersonal; in a master, therefore, he seeks his opposite, the phlegmatic character. His ideal of the master-servant relation happens, therefore, to coincide with Fogg's, and to the mutual satisfaction of both, he is interviewed and engaged.

But that evening the unforeseen happens, the bet which is to send them both off round the world. It is his *hubris* which tempts Mr Fogg into making the bet; he is so convinced that nothing unforeseen can occur which he cannot control that he cannot allow his club mates to challenge this conviction without taking up the challenge. Further, unknown to him, by a chance accident which he could not possibly have foreseen, a bank robbery has just been committed, and the description of the thief given to the police plus his sudden departure from England have put him under suspicion. Off go Mr Fogg and Passepartout, then, pursued by the detective Fix. In the boat train Passepartout suddenly remembers that in the haste of packing he has left the gas fire burning in his bedroom. Fogg does not utter a word of reproach but merely remarks that it will burn at Passepartout's expense till they return. Mr Fogg is still the stoic with the stoic conception of justice operating as impersonally and inexorably as the laws of nature. It is a fact that it was Passepartout, not he, who forgot to turn off the gas; the hurry caused by his own sudden decision may have made it difficult for Passepartout to remember, but it did not make it impossible: therefore, Passepartout is responsible for his forgetfulness and must pay the price.

Then in India the decisive moment arrives: they run into preparations for the suttee, against her will, of a beautiful young widow, Aouda. For the first time in his life, apparently, Mr Fogg is confronted personally with human injustice and suffering, and a moral choice. If, like the priest and the Levite, he passes by on the other side, he will catch the boat at Calcutta and win his bet with ease; if he attempts to save her, he will miss his boat and run a serious risk of losing his bet. Abandoning his stoic apathy, he chooses the second alternative, and from that moment on his relationship with Passepartout ceases to be impersonal; *philia* is felt by both. Moreover, he discovers that Passepartout has capacities which his normal duties as a servant would never have revealed, but which in this emergency situation are particularly valuable because Mr Fogg himself is without them. But for Passepartout's capacity for improvisation and acting which allow him successfully to substitute himself for the corpse on the funeral pyre, Aouda would never have been saved. Hitherto, Mr Fogg has always believed that there was nothing of importance anyone else could do which he could not do as well or better himself; for the first time in his life he abandons that belief.

Hitherto, Passepartout has thought of his master as an unfeeling automaton, just, but incapable of generosity or self-sacrifice; had he not had this unexpected revelation, he would certainly have betrayed Mr Fogg to Fix, for the detective succeeds in convincing him that his master is a bank robber, and, according to the stoic notion of impersonal justice which Mr Fogg had seemed to exemplify, that would be his duty, but, having seen him act personally, Passepartout refuses to assist impersonal justice.

Later, when the Trans-American express is attacked by Indians, it is Passepartout's athletic ability, a quality irrelevant to a servant's normal duties, which saves the lives of Mr Fogg and Aouda at the risk of his own, for he is captured by the Indians. In such an act the whole contractual master-servant relation is transcended; that one party shall undertake to sacrifice his life for the other cannot be a clause in any contract. The only possible repayment is a similar act, and Mr Fogg lets the relief train go without him, sacrificing what may well be his last chance of winning his bet, and goes back at the risk of his life to rescue Passepartout.

Like Mr Fogg, Bertie Wooster is a bachelor with private means who does no work, but there all the resemblance ceases. Nobody could possibly be less of a stoic than the latter. If he has no vices it is because his desires are too vague and too fleeting for him to settle down to one. Hardly a week passes without Bertie Wooster thinking he has at last met The Girl; for a week he imagines he is her Tristan, but the next week he has forgotten her as completely as Don Giovanni forgets; besides, nothing ever happens. It is nowhere suggested that he owned a watch or that, if he did, he could tell the time by it. By any worldly moral standard he is a footler whose existence is of no importance to anybody. Yet it is Bertie Wooster who has the incomparable Jeeves for his servant. Jeeves could any day find a richer master or a place with less arduous duties, yet it is Bertie Wooster whom he chooses to serve. The lucky Simpleton is a common folk-tale hero; for example, the Third Son who succeeds in the Quest appears, in comparison with his two elder brothers, the least talented, but his ambition to succeed is equal to theirs. He sets out bravely into the unknown, and unexpectedly triumphs. But Bertie Wooster is without any ambition whatsoever and does not lift a finger to help himself, yet he is rewarded with what, for him, is even better than a beautiful Princess, the perfect omniscient nanny who does everything for him and keeps him out of trouble without, however, ever trying, as most nannies will, to educate and improve him.

—I say, Jeeves, a man I met at the club last night told me to put my shirt
    on Privateer for the two o'clock race this afternoon. How about it?
—I should not advocate it, sir. The stable is not sanguine.
—Talking of shirts, have those mauve ones I ordered arrived yet?
—Yes, sir. I sent them back.
—Sent them back?
—Yes, sir. They would not have become you.

The Quest Hero often encounters an old beggar or an animal who offers him advice: if, too proud to imagine that such an apparently inferior creature could have anything to tell him, he ignores the advice, it has fatal consequences; if he is humble enough to listen and obey, then, thanks to their help, he achieves his goal. But, however humble he may be, he still has the dream of becoming a hero; he may be humble enough to take advice from what seem to be his inferiors, but he is convinced that, potentially, he is a superior person, a prince-to-be. Bertie Wooster, on the other hand, not only knows that he is a person of no account, but also never expects to become anything else; till his dying day he will remain, he knows, a footler who requires a nanny; yet, at the same time, he is totally without envy of others who are or may become of some account. He has, in fact, that rarest of virtues, humility, and so he is blessed: it is he and no other who has for his servant the godlike Jeeves.

—All the other great men of the age are simply in the crowd, watching
    you go by.
—Thank you very much, sir. I endeavor to give satisfaction.

So speaks comically—and in what other mode than the comic could it on earth truthfully speak?—the voice of Agape, of Holy Love.

The Guilty Vicarage

I had not known sin, but by the law. —Romans: VII, 7

A Confession

For me, as for many others, the reading of detective stories is an addiction like tobacco or alcohol. The symptoms of this are: firstly, the intensity of the craving—if I have any work to do, I must be careful not to get hold of a detective story for, once I begin one, I cannot work or sleep till I have finished it. Secondly, its specificity—the story must conform to certain formulas (I find it very difficult, for example, to read one that is not set in rural England). And, thirdly, its immediacy. I forget the story as soon as I have finished it, and have no wish to read it again. If, as sometimes happens, I start reading one and find after a few pages that I have read it before, I cannot go on.

Such reactions convince me that, in my case at least, detective stories have nothing to do with works of art. It is possible, however, that an analysis of the detective story, i.e. of the kind of detective story I enjoy, may throw light, not only on its magical function, but also, by contrast, on the function of art.

Definition

The vulgar definition, "a Whodunit," is correct. The basic formula is this: a murder occurs; many are suspected; all but one suspect, who is the murderer, are eliminated; the murderer is arrested or dies.

This definition excludes:

(1) Studies of murderers whose guilt is known, e.g. *Malice Aforethought.* There are borderline cases in which the murderer is known and there are no false suspects, but the proof is lacking, e.g. many of the stories of Freeman Wills Crofts. Most of these are permissible.
(2) Thrillers, spy stories, stories of master crooks, etc., when the identification of the criminal is subordinate to the defeat of his criminal designs.

The interest in the thriller is the ethical and eristic conflict between good and evil, between Us and Them. The interest in the study of a murderer is the observation, by the innocent many, of the sufferings of the guilty one. The interest in the detective story is the dialectic of innocence and guilt.

As in the Aristotelian description of tragedy, there is Concealment (the innocent seem guilty and the guilty seem innocent) and Manifestation (the real guilt is brought to consciousness). There is also peripeteia, in this case not a reversal of fortune but a double reversal from apparent guilt to innocence and from apparent innocence to guilt. The formula may be diagrammed as follows:

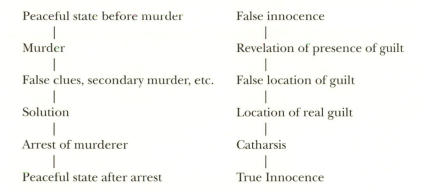

Peaceful state before murder	False innocence
|	|
Murder	Revelation of presence of guilt
|	|
False clues, secondary murder, etc.	False location of guilt
|	|
Solution	Location of real guilt
|	|
Arrest of murderer	Catharsis
|	|
Peaceful state after arrest	True Innocence

In Greek tragedy the audience knows the truth; the actors do not, but discover or bring to pass the inevitable. In modern, e.g. Elizabethan, tragedy the audience knows neither less nor more than the most knowing of the actors. In the detective story the audience does not know the truth at all; one of the actors—the murderer—does; and the detective, of his own free will, discovers and reveals what the murderer, of his own free will, tries to conceal.

Greek tragedy and the detective story have one characteristic in common in which they both differ from modern tragedy, namely, the characters are not changed in or by their actions: in Greek tragedy because their actions are fated, in the detective story because the decisive event, the murder, has already occurred. Time and space therefore are simply the when and where of revealing either what has to happen or what has actually happened. In consequence, the detective story probably should, and usually does, obey the classical unities, whereas modern tragedy, in which the characters develop with time, can only do so by a technical tour de force; and the thriller, like the picaresque novel, even demands frequent changes of time and place.

Why Murder?

There are three classes of crime: (A) offenses against God and one's neighbor or neighbors; (B) offenses against God and society; (C) offenses against God. (All crimes, of course, are offenses against oneself.)

Murder is a member and the only member of Class B. The character common to all crimes in Class A is that it is possible, at least theoretically, either that restitution can be made to the injured party (e.g. stolen goods can be returned), or that the injured party can forgive the criminal (e.g. in the case of rape). Consequently, society as a whole is only indirectly involved; its representatives (the police, etc.) act in the interests of the injured party.

Murder is unique in that it abolishes the party it injures, so that society has to take the place of the victim and on his behalf demand atonement or grant forgiveness; it is the one crime in which society has a direct interest.

Many detective stories begin with a death that appears to be suicide and is later discovered to have been murder. Suicide is a crime belonging to Class C in which neither the criminal's neighbors nor society has any interest, direct or indirect. As long as a death is believed to be suicide, even private curiosity is improper; as soon as it is proved to be murder, public inquiry becomes a duty.

The detective story has five elements—the milieu, the victim, the murderer, the suspects, the detectives.

The Milieu (Human)

The detective story requires:

(1) A closed society so that the possibility of an outside murderer (and hence of the society being totally innocent) is excluded; and a closely related society so that all its members are potentially suspect (*cf.* the thriller, which requires an open society in which any stranger may be a friend or enemy in disguise).

Such conditions are met by: (a) the group of blood relatives (the Christmas dinner in the country house); (b) the closely knit geographical group (the old world village); (c) the occupational group (the theatrical company); (d) the group isolated by the neutral place (the Pullman car).

In this last type the concealment-manifestation formula applies not only to the murder but also to the relations between the members of the group who first appear to be strangers to each other, but are later found to be related.

(2) It must appear to be an innocent society in a state of grace, i.e. a society where there is no need of the law, no contradiction between the aesthetic individual and the ethical universal, and where murder, therefore, is the unheard-of act which precipitates a crisis (for it reveals that some member has fallen and is no longer in a state of grace). The law becomes a reality and for a time all must live in its shadow, till the fallen one is identified. With his arrest, innocence is restored, and the law retires forever.

The characters in a detective story should, therefore, be eccentric (aesthetically interesting individuals) and good (instinctively ethical)—good, that is, either in appearance, later shown to be false, or in reality, first concealed by an appearance of bad.

It is a sound instinct that has made so many detective story writers choose a college as a setting. The ruling passion of the ideal professor is the pursuit of knowledge for its own sake so that he is related to other human beings only indirectly through their common relation to the truth; and those passions, like lust and avarice and envy, which relate individuals directly and may lead to murder are, in his case, ideally excluded. If a murder occurs in a college, therefore, it is a sign that some colleague is not only a bad man but also a bad professor. Further, as the basic premise of academic life is that truth is universal and to be shared with all, the *gnosis* of a concrete crime and the *gnosis* of abstract ideas nicely parallel and parody each other.

(The even more ideal contradiction of a murder in a monastery is excluded by the fact that monks go regularly to confession and, while the murderer might well not confess his crime, the suspects who are innocent of murder but guilty of lesser sins cannot be supposed to conceal them without making the monastery absurd. Incidentally, is it an accident that the detective story has flourished most in predominantly Protestant countries?)

The detective story writer is also wise to choose a society with an elaborate ritual and to describe this in detail. A ritual is a sign of harmony between the aesthetic and the ethical in which body and mind, individual will and general laws, are not in conflict. The murderer uses his knowledge of the ritual to commit the crime and can be caught only by someone who acquires an equal or superior familiarity with it.

The Milieu (Natural)

In the detective story, as in its mirror image, the Quest for the Grail, maps (the ritual of space) and timetables (the ritual of time) are desirable. Nature should reflect its human inhabitants, i.e. it should be the Great Good Place; for the more Eden-like it is, the greater the contradiction of murder. The country is preferable to the town, a well-to-do neighborhood (but not too well-to-do—or there will be a suspicion of ill-gotten gains) better than a slum. The corpse must shock not only because it is a corpse but also because, even for a corpse, it is shockingly out of place, as when a dog makes a mess on a drawing room carpet.

Mr Raymond Chandler has written that he intends to take the body out of the vicarage garden and give the murder back to those who are good at it. If he wishes to write detective stories, i.e. stories where the reader's principal interest is to learn who did it, he could not be more mistaken, for in a society of professional criminals, the only possible motives for desiring to identify the murderer are blackmail or revenge, which both apply to individuals, not to the group as a whole, and can equally well inspire murder. Actually, whatever he may say, I think Mr Chandler is interested in writing, not detective stories, but serious studies of a criminal milieu, the Great Wrong Place, and his powerful but extremely depressing books should be read and judged, not as escape literature, but as works of art.

The Victim

The victim has to try to satisfy two contradictory requirements. He has to involve everyone in suspicion, which requires that he be a bad character; and he has to make everyone feel guilty, which requires that he be a good character. He cannot be a criminal because he could then be dealt with by the law and murder would be unnecessary. (Blackmail is the only exception.) The more general the temptation to murder he arouses, the better; e.g. the desire for freedom is a better motive than money alone or sex alone. On the whole, the best victim is the negative Father or Mother Image.

If there is more than one murder, the subsequent victims should be more innocent than the initial victim, i.e. the murderer should start with a real grievance and, as a consequence of righting it by illegitimate means, be forced to murder against his will where he has no grievances but his own guilt.

The Murderer

Murder is negative creation, and every murderer is therefore the rebel who claims the right to be omnipotent. His pathos is his refusal to suffer. The problem for the writer is to conceal his demonic pride from the other characters and from the reader, since, if a person has this pride, it tends to appear in everything he says and does. To surprise the reader when the identity of the murderer is revealed, yet at the same time to convince him that everything he has previously been told about the murderer is consistent with his being a murderer, is the test of a good detective story.

As to the murderer's end, of the three alternatives—execution, suicide, and madness—the first is preferable; for if he commits suicide he refuses to repent, and if he goes mad he cannot repent, but if he does not repent society cannot forgive. Execution on the other hand, is the act of atonement by which the murderer is forgiven by society. In real life I disapprove of capital punishment, but in a detective story the murderer must have no future.

(*A Suggestion for Mr Chandler:* Among a group of efficient professional killers who murder for strictly professional reasons, there is one to whom, like Leopold and Loeb, murder is an *acte gratuit.* Presently murders begin to occur which have not been commissioned. The group is morally outraged and bewildered; it has to call in the police to detect the amateur murderer, rescue the professionals from a mutual suspicion which threatens to disrupt their organization, and restore their capacity to murder.)

The Suspects

The detective-story society is a society consisting of apparently innocent individuals, i.e. their aesthetic interest as individuals does not conflict with their ethical obligations to the universal. The murder is the act of disruption by which innocence is lost, and the individual and the law become opposed to each other. In the case of the murderer this opposition is completely real (till he is arrested and consents to be punished); in the case of the suspects it is mostly apparent.

But in order for the appearance to exist, there must be some element of reality; e.g. it is unsatisfactory if the suspicion is caused by chance or the murderer's malice alone. The suspects must be guilty of something, because, now that the aesthetic and the ethical are in opposition, if they are completely innocent (obedient to the ethical) they lose their aesthetic interest and the reader will ignore them.

For suspects, the principal causes of guilt are:

(1) the wish or even the intention to murder;

(2) crimes of Class A or vices of Class C (e.g. illicit amours) which the suspect is afraid or ashamed to reveal;

(3) a *hubris* of intellect which tries to solve the crime itself and despises the official police (assertion of the supremacy of the aesthetic over the ethical). If great enough, this *hubris* leads to its subject getting murdered;

(4) a *hubris* of innocence which refuses to cooperate with the investigation;

(5) a lack of faith in another loved suspect, which leads its subject to hide or confuse clues.

The Detective

Completely satisfactory detectives are extremely rare. Indeed, I only know of three: Sherlock Holmes (Conan Doyle), Inspector French (Freeman Wills Crofts), and Father Brown (Chesterton).

The job of the detective is to restore the state of grace in which the aesthetic and the ethical are as one. Since the murderer who caused their disjunction is the aesthetically defiant individual, his opponent, the detective, must be either the official representative of the ethical or the exceptional individual who is himself in a state of grace. If he is the former, he is a professional; if he is the latter, he is an amateur. In either case, the detective must be the total stranger who cannot possibly be involved in the crime; this excludes the local police and should, I think, exclude the detective who is a friend of one of the suspects. The professional detective has the advantage that, since he is not an individual but a representative of the ethical, he does not need a motive for investigating the crime; but for the same reason he has the disadvantage of being unable to overlook the minor ethical violations of the suspects, and therefore it is harder for him to gain their confidence.

Most amateur detectives, on the other hand, are unsatisfactory either because they are priggish supermen, like Lord Peter Wimsey and Philo Vance, who have no motive for being detectives except caprice, or because, like the detectives of the hard-boiled school, they are motivated by avarice or ambition and might just as well be murderers.

The amateur detective genius may have weaknesses to give him aesthetic interest, but they must not be of a kind which outrage ethics. The most satisfactory weaknesses are the solitary oral vices of eating and drinking or childish boasting. In his sexual life, the detective must be either celibate or happily married.

Between the amateur detective and the professional policeman stands the criminal lawyer whose *telos* is, not to discover who is guilty, but to prove that his client is innocent. His ethical justification is that human law is ethically imperfect, i.e. not an absolute manifestation of the universal and divine, and subject to chance aesthetic limitations, e.g. the intelligence or stupidity of individual policemen and juries (in consequence of which an innocent man may sometimes be judged guilty).

To correct this imperfection, the decision is arrived at through an aesthetic combat, i.e. the intellectual gifts of the defense versus those of the prosecution, just as in earlier days doubtful cases were solved by physical combat between the accused and the accuser.

The lawyer-detective (e.g. Joshua Clunk) is never quite satisfactory, therefore, because of his commitment to his client, whom he cannot desert, even if he should really be the guilty party, without ceasing to be a lawyer.

Sherlock Holmes

Holmes is the exceptional individual who is in a state of grace because he is a genius in whom scientific curiosity is raised to the status of a heroic passion. He is erudite but his knowledge is absolutely specialized (e.g. his ignorance of the Copernican system), he is in all matters outside his field as helpless as a child (e.g. his untidiness), and he pays the price for his scientific detachment (his neglect of feeling) by being the victim of melancholia which attacks him whenever he is unoccupied with a case (e.g. his violin playing and cocaine taking).

His motive for being a detective is, positively, a love of the neutral truth (he has no interest in the feelings of the guilty or the innocent), and negatively, a need to escape from his own feelings of melancholy. His attitude towards people and his technique of observation and deduction are those of the chemist or physicist. If he chooses human beings rather than inanimate matter as his material, it is because investigating the inanimate is unheroically easy since it cannot tell lies, which human beings can and do, so that in dealing with them, observation must be twice as sharp and logic twice as rigorous.

Inspector French

His class and culture are those natural to a Scotland Yard inspector. (The old Oxonian Inspector is insufferable.) His motive is love of duty. Holmes detects for his own sake and shows the maximum indifference to all feelings except a negative fear of his own. French detects for the sake of the innocent members of society, and is indifferent only to his own feelings and those of the murderer. (He would much rather stay at home with his wife.) He is exceptional only in his exceptional love of duty which makes him take exceptional pains; he does only what all could do as well if they had the same patient industry (his checking of alibis for tiny flaws which careless hurry had missed). He outwits the murderer, partly because the latter is not quite so painstaking as he, and partly because the murderer must act alone, while he has the help of all the innocent people in the world who are doing their duty, e.g. the postmen, railway clerks, milkmen, etc., who become, accidentally, witnesses to the truth.

Father Brown

Like Holmes, an amateur; yet, like French, not an individual genius. His activities as a detective are an incidental part of his activities as a priest who cares for souls. His prime motive is compassion, of which the guilty are in greater need than the innocent, and he investigates murders, not for his own sake, nor even for the sake of the innocent, but for the sake of the murderer who can save his soul if he will confess and repent. He solves his cases, not by approaching them objectively like a scientist or a policeman, but by subjectively imagining himself to be the murderer, a process which is good not only for the murderer but for Father Brown himself because, as he says, "it gives a man his remorse beforehand."

Holmes and French can only help the murderer as teachers, i.e. they can teach him that murder will out and does not pay. More they cannot do since neither is tempted to murder; Holmes is too gifted, French too well trained in the habit of virtue. Father Brown can go further and help the murderer as an example, i.e. as a man who is also tempted to murder, but is able by faith to resist temptation.

The Reader

The most curious fact about the detective story is that it makes its greatest appeal precisely to those classes of people who are most immune to other forms of daydream literature. The typical detective story addict is a doctor or clergyman or scientist or artist, i.e. a fairly successful professional man with intellectual interests and well-read in his own field, who could never stomach the *Saturday Evening Post* or *True Confessions* or movie magazines or comics. If I ask myself why I cannot enjoy stories about strong silent men and lovely girls who make love in a beautiful landscape and come into millions of dollars, I cannot answer that I have no fantasies of being handsome and loved and rich, because of course I have (though my life is, perhaps, sufficiently fortunate to make me less envious in a naïve way than some). No, I can only say that I am too conscious of the absurdity of such wishes to enjoy seeing them reflected in print.

I can, to some degree, resist yielding to these or similar desires which tempt me, but I cannot prevent myself from having them to resist; and it is the fact that I have them which makes me feel guilty, so that instead of dreaming about indulging my desires, I dream about the removal of the guilt which I feel at their existence. This I still do, and must do, because guilt is a subjective feeling where any further step is only a reduplication—feeling guilty about guilt. I suspect that the typical reader of detective stories is, like myself, a person who suffers from a sense of sin. From the point of view of ethics, desires and acts are good and bad, and I must choose the good and reject the bad, but the I which makes this choice is ethically neutral; it only becomes good or bad in its choice. To have a sense of sin means to feel guilty at there being an ethical choice to make, a guilt which, however "good" I may become, remains unchanged. It is sometimes said that detective stories are read by respectable law-abiding citizens in order to gratify in fantasy the violent or murderous wishes they dare not, or are ashamed to, translate into action. This may be true for the reader of thrillers (which I rarely enjoy), but it is quite false for the reader of detective stories. On the contrary, the magical satisfaction the latter provide (which makes them escape literature, not works of art) is the illusion of being dissociated from the murderer.

The magic formula is an innocence which is discovered to contain guilt; then a suspicion of being the guilty one; and finally a real innocence from which the guilty other has been expelled, a cure effected, not by me or my neighbors, but by the miraculous intervention of a genius from outside who removes guilt by giving knowledge of guilt. (The detective story subscribes, in fact, to the Socratic daydream: "Sin is ignorance.")

If one thinks of a work of art which deals with murder, *Crime and Punishment* for example, its effect on the reader is to compel an identification with the murderer which he would prefer not to recognize. The identification of fantasy is always an attempt to avoid one's own suffering: the identification of art is a sharing in the suffering of another. Kafka's *The Trial* is another instructive example of the difference between a work of art and the detective story. In the latter it is certain that a crime has been committed and, temporarily, uncertain to whom the guilt should be attached; as soon as this is known, the innocence of everyone else is certain. (Should it turn out that after all no crime has been committed, then all would be innocent.) In *The Trial*, on the other hand, it is the guilt that is certain and the crime that is uncertain; the aim of the hero's investigation is not to prove his innocence (which would be impossible for he knows he is guilty), but to discover what, if anything, he has done to make himself guilty. K, the hero, is, in fact, a portrait of the kind of person who reads detective stories for escape.

The fantasy, then, which the detective story addict indulges is the fantasy of being restored to the Garden of Eden, to a state of innocence, where he may know love as love and not as the law. The driving force behind this daydream is the feeling of guilt, the cause of which is unknown to the dreamer. The fantasy of escape is the same, whether one explains the guilt in Christian, Freudian, or any other terms. One's way of trying to face the reality, on the other hand, will, of course, depend very much on one's creed.

The I Without a Self

The joys of this life are not its own, but our dread of ascend-
ing to a higher life: the torments of this life are not its own,
but our self-torment because of that dread. —Franz Kafka

Kafka is a great, perhaps the greatest, master of the pure parable, a literary
genre about which a critic can say very little worth saying. The reader of a
novel, or the spectator at a drama, though novel and drama may also have a
parabolic significance, is confronted by a feigned history, by characters, situations, actions which, though they may be analogous to his own, are not
identical. Watching a performance of *Macbeth*, for example, I see particular
historical persons involved in a tragedy of their own making: I may compare
Macbeth with myself and wonder what I should have done and felt had I
been in his situation, but I remain a spectator, firmly fixed in my own time
and place. But I cannot read a pure parable in this way. Though the hero of
a parable may be given a proper name (often, though, he may just be called
"a certain man" or "K") and a definite historical and geographical setting,
these particulars are irrelevant to the meaning of parable. To find out what,
if anything, a parable means, I have to surrender my objectivity and identify
myself with what I read. The "meaning" of a parable, in fact, is different for
every reader. In consequence there is nothing a critic can do to "explain" it
to others. Thanks to his superior knowledge of artistic and social history, of
language, of human nature even, a good critic can make others see things in
a novel or a play which, but for him, they would never have seen for themselves. But if he tries to interpret a parable, he will only reveal himself. What
he writes will be a description of what the parable has done to him; of what
it may do to others he does not and cannot have any idea.

Sometimes in real life one meets a character and thinks, "This man comes
straight out of Shakespeare or Dickens," but nobody ever met a Kafka character. On the other hand, one can have experiences which one recognizes as
Kafkaesque, while one would never call an experience of one's own Dickensian or Shakespearian. During the war, I had spent a long and tiring day in
the Pentagon. My errand done, I hurried down long corridors eager to get
home, and came to a turnstile with a guard standing beside it. "Where are
you going?" said the guard. "I'm trying to get out," I replied. "You are out,"
he said. For the moment I felt I was K.

In the case of the ordinary novelist or playwright, a knowledge of his personal life and character contributes almost nothing to one's understanding
of his work, but in the case of a writer of parables like Kafka, biographical
information is, I believe, a great help, at least in a negative way, by preventing
one from making false readings. (The "true" readings are always many.)

In the new edition of Max Brod's biography, he describes a novel by a Czech writer, Božena Němcová (1820–1862), called *The Grandmother*. The setting is a village in the Riesengebirge which is dominated by a castle. The villagers speak Czech, the inhabitants of the castle German. The Duchess who owns the Castle is kind and good, but she is often absent on her travels and between her and the peasants are interposed a horde of insolent household servants and selfish, dishonest officials, so that the Duchess has no idea of what is really going on in the village. At last the heroine of the story succeeds in getting past the various barriers to gain a personal audience with the Duchess, to whom she tells the truth, and all ends happily.

What is illuminating about this information is that the castle officials in Němcová are openly presented as being evil, which suggests that those critics who have thought of the inhabitants of Kafka's castle as agents of Divine Grace were mistaken, and that Erich Heller's reading is substantially correct.

> The castle of Kafka's novel is, as it were, the heavily fortified garrison of a company of Gnostic demons, successfully holding an advanced position against the manoeuvres of an impatient soul. I do not know of any conceivable idea of divinity which could justify those interpreters who see in the castle the residence of "divine law and divine grace." Its officers are totally indifferent to good if they are not positively wicked. Neither in their decrees nor in their activities is there discernible any trace of love, mercy, charity or majesty. In their icy detachment they inspire no awe, but fear and revulsion.

Dr Brod also publishes for the first time a rumor which, if true, might have occurred in a Kafka story rather than in his life, namely, that, without his knowledge, Kafka was the father of a son who died in 1921 at the age of seven. The story cannot be verified since the mother was arrested by the Germans in 1944 and never heard of again.

Remarkable as *The Trial* and *The Castle* are, Kafka's finest work, I think, is to be found in the volume *The Great Wall of China*, all of it written during the last six years of his life. The world it portrays is still the world of his earlier books and one cannot call it euphoric, but the tone is lighter. The sense of appalling anguish and despair which make stories like "The Penal Colony" almost unbearable, has gone. Existence may be as difficult and frustrating as ever, but the characters are more humorously resigned to it.

Of a typical story one might say that it takes the formula of the heroic Quest and turns it upside down. In the traditional Quest, the goal—a Princess, the Fountain of Life, etc.—is known to the hero before he starts. This goal is far distant and he usually does not know in advance the way thither nor the dangers which beset it, but there are other beings who know both and give him accurate directions and warnings. Moreover the goal is publicly recognizable as desirable. Everybody would like to achieve it, but it can only be reached by the Predestined Hero. When three brothers attempt the Quest in turn, the first two are found wanting and fail because of their arrogance and self-conceit, while the youngest succeeds, thanks to his humility and kindness of heart. But the youngest, like his two elders, is always perfectly confident that he will succeed.

In a typical Kafka story, on the other hand, the goal is peculiar to the hero himself: he has no competitors. Some beings whom he encounters try to help him, more are obstructive, most are indifferent, and none has the faintest notion of the way. As one of the aphorisms puts it: "There is a goal but no way; what we call the way is mere wavering." Far from being confident of success, the Kafka hero is convinced from the start that he is doomed to fail, as he is also doomed, being who he is, to make prodigious and unending efforts to reach it. Indeed, the mere desire to reach the goal is itself a proof, not that he is one of the Elect, but that he is under a special curse.

Perhaps there is only one cardinal sin: impatience. Because of impatience we were driven out of Paradise, because of impatience we cannot return.

Theoretically, there exists a perfect possibility of happiness: to believe in the indestructible element in oneself and not strive after it.

In all previous versions of the Quest, the hero knows what he ought to do and his one problem is "Can I do it?" Odysseus knows he must not listen to the song of the sirens, a knight in quest of the Sangreal knows he must remain chaste, a detective knows he must distinguish between truth and falsehood. But for K the problem is "What ought I to do?" He is neither tempted, confronted with a choice between good and evil, nor carefree, content with the sheer exhilaration of motion. He is certain that it matters enormously what he does *now*, without knowing at all what that ought to be. If he *guesses* wrong, he must not only suffer the same consequences as if he had *chosen* wrong, but also feel the same responsibility. If the instructions and advice he receives seem to him absurd or contradictory, he cannot interpret this as evidence of malice or guilt in others; it may well be proof of his own.

The traditional Quest Hero has *arete*, either manifest, like Odysseus, or concealed, like the fairy tale hero; in the first case, successful achievement of the Quest adds to his glory, in the second it reveals that the apparent nobody is a glorious hero: to become a hero, in the traditional sense, means acquiring the right, thanks to one's exceptional gifts and deeds, to say *I*. But K is an *I* from the start, and in this fact alone, that he exists, irrespective of any gifts or deeds, lies his guilt.

If the K of *The Trial* were innocent, he would cease to be K and become nameless like the fawn in the wood in *Through the Looking-Glass*. In *The Castle*, K, the letter, wants to become a word, *land-surveyor*, that is to say, to acquire

a self like everybody else but this is precisely what he is not allowed to acquire.

The world of the traditional Quest may be dangerous, but it is open: the
hero can set off in any direction he fancies. But the Kafka world is closed;
though it is almost devoid of sensory properties, it is an intensely physical
world. The objects and faces in it may be vague, but the reader feels himself
hemmed in by their suffocating presence: in no other imaginary world, I
think, is everything so *heavy*. To take a single step exhausts the strength. The
hero feels himself to be a prisoner and tries to escape but perhaps imprisonment is the proper state for which he was created, and freedom would destroy him.

> The more horse you yoke, the quicker everything will go—not the rend-
> ing of the block from its foundation, which is impossible, but the snap-
> ping of the traces and with that the gay and empty journey.

The narrator hero of "The Burrow" for example, is a beast of unspecified
genus, but, presumably, some sort of badger-like animal, except that he is
carnivorous. He lives by himself without a mate and never encounters any
other member of his own species. He also lives in a perpetual state of fear lest
he be pursued and attacked by other animals—"My enemies are countless,"
he says—but we never learn what they may be like and we never actually encounter one. His preoccupation is with the burrow which has been his life-
work. Perhaps, when he first began excavating this, the idea of a burrow-
fortress was more playful than serious, but the bigger and better the burrow
becomes, the more he is tormented by the question: "Is it possible to construct the absolutely impregnable burrow?" This is a torment because he can
never be certain that there is not some further precaution of which he has
not thought. Also the burrow he has spent his life constructing has become
a precious thing which he must defend as much as he would defend himself.

> One of my favorite plans was to isolate the Castle Keep from its sur-
> roundings, that is to say to restrict the thickness of the walls to about my
> own height, and leave a free space of about the same width all around
> the Castle Keep . . . I had always pictured this free space, and not with-
> out reason as the loveliest imaginable haunt. What a joy to lie pressed
> against the rounded outer wall, pull oneself up, let oneself slide down
> again, miss one's footing and find oneself on firm earth, and play all
> these games literally upon the Castle Keep and not inside it; to avoid the
> Castle Keep, to rest one's eyes from it whenever one wanted, to post-
> pone the joy of seeing it until later and yet not have to do without it, but
> literally hold it safe between one's claws. . . .

He begins to wonder if, in order to defend it, it would not be better to
hide in the bushes outside near its hidden entrance and keep watch. He

considers the possibility of enlisting the help of a confederate to share the task of watching, but decides against it.

> . . . would he not demand some counter-service from me; would he not at least want to see the burrow? That in itself, to let anyone freely into my burrow, would be exquisitely painful to me. I built it for myself, not for visitors, and I think I would refuse to admit him. . . . I simply could not admit him, for either I must let him go in first by himself, which is simply unimaginable, or we must both descend at the same time, in which case the advantage I am supposed to derive from him, that of being kept watch over, would be lost. And what trust can I really put in him? . . . It is comparatively easy to trust anyone if you are supervising him or at least can supervise him; perhaps it is possible to trust someone at a distance; but completely to trust someone outside the burrow when you are inside the burrow, that is, in a different world, that, it seems to me, is impossible.

One morning he is awakened by a faint whistling noise which he cannot identify or locate. It might be merely the wind, but it might be some enemy. From now on, he is in the grip of a hysterical anxiety. Does this strange beast, if it is a beast, know of his existence and, if so, what does it know? The story breaks off without a solution. Edwin Muir has suggested that the story would have ended with the appearance of the invisible enemy to whom the hero would succumb. I am doubtful about this. The whole point of the parable seems to be that the reader is never to know if the narrator's subjective fears have any objective justification.

The more we admire Kafka's writings, the more seriously we must reflect upon his final instructions that they should be destroyed. At first one is tempted to see in this request a fantastic spiritual pride, as if he had said to himself: "To be worthy of me, anything I write must be absolutely perfect. But no piece of writing, however excellent, can be perfect. Therefore, let what I have written be destroyed as unworthy of me." But everything which Dr Brod and other friends tell us about Kafka as a person makes nonsense of this explanation.

It seems clear that Kafka did not think of himself as an artist in the traditional sense, that is to say, as a being dedicated to a particular function, whose personal existence is accidental to his artistic productions. If there ever was a man of whom it could be said that he "hungered and thirsted after righteousness," it was Kafka. Perhaps he came to regard what he had written as a personal device he had employed in his search for God. "Writing," he once wrote, "is a form of prayer," and no person whose prayers are genuine, desires them to be overheard by a third party. In another passage, he describes his aim in writing thus:

Somewhat as if one were to hammer together a table with painful and methodical technical efficiency, and simultaneously do nothing at all, and not in such a way that people could say: "Hammering a table together is nothing to him," but rather "Hammering a table together is really hammering a table together to him, but at the same time it is nothing," whereby certainly the hammering would have become still bolder, still surer, still more real, and if you will, still more senseless.

But whatever the reasons, Kafka's reluctance to have his work published should at least make a reader wary of the way in which he himself reads it. Kafka may be one of those writers who are doomed to be read by the wrong public. Those on whom their effect would be most beneficial are repelled and on those whom they most fascinate their effect may be dangerous, even harmful.

I am inclined to believe that one should only read Kafka when one is in a eupeptic state of physical and mental health and, in consequence, tempted to dismiss any scrupulous heart-searching as a morbid fuss. When one is in low spirits, one should probably keep away from him, for, unless introspection is accompanied, as it always was in Kafka, by an equal passion for the good life, it all too easily degenerates into a spineless narcissistic fascination with one's own sin and weakness.

No one who thinks seriously about evil and suffering can avoid entertaining as a possibility the gnostic-manichean notion of the physical world as intrinsically evil, and some of Kafka's sayings come perilously close to accepting it.

There is only a spiritual world; what we call the physical world is the evil in the spiritual one.

The physical world is not an illusion, but only its evil which, however, admittedly constitutes our picture of the physical world.

Kafka's own life and his writings as a whole are proof that he was not a gnostic at heart, for the true gnostic can always be recognized by certain characteristics. He regards himself as a member of a spiritual elite and despises all earthly affections and social obligations. Quite often, he also allows himself an anarchic immorality in his sexual life, on the grounds that, since the body is irredeemable, a moral judgment cannot be applied to its actions.

Neither Kafka, as Dr Brod knew him, nor any of his heroes show a trace of spiritual snobbery nor do they think of the higher life they search for as existing in some other-world sphere: the distinction they draw between *this* world and *the* world does not imply that there are two different worlds, only that our habitual conceptions of reality are not the true conception.

Perhaps, when he wished his writings to be destroyed, Kafka foresaw the nature of too many of his admirers.

PART FOUR

The Shakespearian City

The Globe

Physiological life is of course not "Life." And neither is psychological life. Life is the world. —Ludwig Wittgenstein

It is difficult, perhaps impossible, for us to form a complete picture of life because, for that, we have to reconcile and combine two completely different impressions—that of life as each of us experiences it in his own person, and that of life as we all observe it in others.

When I observe myself, the *I* which observes is unique, but not individual, since it has no characteristics of its own; it has only the power to recognize, compare, judge and choose: the self which it observes is not a unique identity but a succession of various states of feeling or desire. Necessity in my world means two things, the givenness of whatever state of myself is at any moment present, and the obligatory freedom of my ego. Action in my world has a special sense; I act towards my states of being, not towards the stimuli which provoked them; *my* action, in fact, is the giving or withholding of permission to myself to act. It is impossible for me to act in ignorance, for my world is by definition what I know; it is not even possible, strictly speaking, for me to be self-deceived, for if I know I am deceiving myself, I am no longer doing so; I can never believe that I do not know what is good for me. I cannot say that I am fortunate or unfortunate, for these words apply only to my self. Though some states of my self are more interesting to me than others, there are none which are so uninteresting that I can ignore them; even boredom is interesting because it is *my* boredom with which I have to cope. If I try, then, to project my subjective experience of life in dramatic form the play will be of the allegorical morality type like Everyman. The hero will be the volitional ego that chooses, and the other characters, either states of the self, pleasant and unpleasant, good and bad, for or against which the hero's choices are made, or counselors, like reason and conscience, which attempt to influence his choices. The plot can only be a succession of incidents in time—the number I choose to portray is arbitrary—and the passing of time from birth to death the only necessity; all else is free choice.

If now I turn round and, deliberately excluding everything I know about myself, scrutinize other human beings as objectively as I can, as if I were simply a camera and a tape-recorder, I experience a very different world. I do not see states of being but individuals in states, say, of anger, each of them different and caused by different stimuli. I see and hear people, that is to say, acting and speaking in a situation, and the situation, their acts and words are all I know. I never see another choose between two alternative actions, only the action he does take. I cannot, therefore, tell whether he has free will or not; I only know that he is fortunate or unfortunate in his circumstances. I may see him acting in ignorance of facts about his situation which I know, but I can never say for certain that in any given situation he is deceiving himself. Then, while it is impossible for me to be totally uninterested in anything that happens to my self, I can only be interested in others who "catch my attention" by being exceptions to the average, exceptionally powerful, exceptionally beautiful, exceptionally amusing, and my interest or lack of it in what they do and suffer is determined by the old journalistic law that Dog-Bites-Bishop is not news but Bishop-Bites-Dog is.

If I try to present my objective experience in dramatic form, the play will be of the Greek type, the story of an exceptional man or woman who suffers an exceptional fate. The drama will consist, not in the choices he freely makes, but in the actions which the situation obliges him to take.

The pure drama of consciousness and the drama of pure objectivity are alike in that their characters have no secrets; the audience knows all about them that there is to know. One cannot imagine, therefore, writing a book about the characters in Greek tragedy or the characters in the morality plays; they themselves have said all there is to say. The fact that it has been and always will be possible to write books about the characters in Shakespeare's plays, in which different critics arrive at completely different interpretations, indicates that the Elizabethan drama is different from either, being, in fact, an attempt to synthesize both into a new, more complicated type.

Actually, of course, the Elizabethan dramatists knew very little about classical drama and owed very little to it. The closet tragedies of Seneca may have had some influence upon their style of rhetoric, the comedies of Plautus and Terence provided a few comic situations and devices, but Elizabethan drama would be pretty much the same if these authors had never been known at all. Even Ben Jonson, the only "highbrow" among the playwrights, who was strongly influenced by the aesthetic theories of the humanists, owes more to the morality play than he does to Latin Comedy. Take away Everyman, substitute for him as the hero one of the seven deadly sins, set the other six in league to profit from it, and one has the basic pattern of the Jonsonian comedy of humors.

The link between the medieval morality play and the Elizabethan drama is the Chronicle play. If few of the pre-Shakespearian chronicle plays except Marlowe's *Edward II* are now readable, nothing could have been more fortunate for Shakespeare's development as a dramatist than his being compelled for his livelihood—judging by his early poems, his youthful taste was for something much less coarse—to face the problems which the chronicle play poses. The writer of a chronicle play cannot, like the Greek tragedians who had some significant myth as a subject, select his situation; he has to take whatever history offers, those in which a character is a victim of a situation and those in which he creates one. He can have no narrow theory about aesthetic propriety which separates the tragic from the comic, no theory of heroic *arete* which can pick one historical character and reject another. The study of the human individual involved in political action, and of the moral ambiguities in which history abounds, checks any tendency towards a simple moralizing of characters into good and bad, any equating of success and failure with virtue and vice.

The Elizabethan drama inherited from the mystery plays three important and very un-Greek notions.

The Significance of Time

Time in Greek drama is simply the time it takes for the situation of the hero to be revealed, and when this revelation shall take place is decided by the gods, not by men. The plague which sets the action of *Oedipus Rex* in motion could have been sent earlier or postponed. In Elizabethan drama time is what the hero creates with what he does and suffers, the medium through which he realizes his potential character.

The Significance of Choice

In a Greek tragedy everything that could have been otherwise has already happened before the play begins. It is true that sometimes the chorus may warn the hero against a course of action, but it is unthinkable that he should listen to them, for a Greek hero is what he is and cannot change. If Hippolytus had made a sacrifice to Aphrodite, he would have ceased to be Hippolytus. But in an Elizabethan tragedy, in *Othello*, for example, there is no point before he actually murders Desdemona when it would have been impossible for him to control his jealousy, discover the truth, and convert the tragedy into a comedy. Vice versa, there is no point in a comedy like *The Two Gentlemen of Verona* at which a wrong turning could not be taken and the conclusion be tragic.

The Significance of Suffering

To the Greeks, suffering and misfortune are signs of the displeasure of the gods and must therefore be accepted by men as mysteriously just. One of the commonest kinds of suffering is to be compelled to commit crimes, either unwittingly, like the parricide and incest of Oedipus, or at the direct command of a god, like Orestes. These crimes are not what we mean by sins because they are against, not with, the desire of the criminal. But in Shakespeare, suffering and misfortune are not in themselves proofs of Divine displeasure. It is true that they would not occur if man had not fallen into sin, but, precisely because he has, suffering is an inescapable element in life—there is no man who does not suffer—to be accepted, not as just in itself, as a penalty proportionate to the particular sins of the sufferer, but as an occasion for grace or as a process of purgation. Those who try to refuse suffering not only fail to avoid it but are plunged deeper into sin and suffering. Thus, the difference between Shakespeare's tragedies and comedies is not that the characters suffer in the one and not in the other, but that in comedy the suffering leads to self-knowledge, repentance, forgiveness, love, and in tragedy it leads in the opposite direction into self-blindness, defiance, hatred.

The audience at a Greek tragedy are pure spectators, never participants; the sufferings of the hero arouse their pity and fear, but they cannot think, "Something similar might happen to me," for the whole point in a Greek tragedy is that the hero and his tragic fate are exceptional. But all of Shakespeare's tragedies might be called variations on the same tragic myth, the only one which Christianity possesses, the story of the unrepentant thief, and anyone of us is in danger of re-enacting it in his own way. The audience at a tragedy of Shakespeare's, therefore, has to be both a spectator and a participant, for it is both a feigned history and a parable.

Dr Johnson was right, surely, when he said of Shakespeare: "His tragedy seems to be skill, his comedy to be instinct." It seems to me doubtful if a completely satisfactory tragedy is possible within a Christian society which does not believe that there is a necessary relation between suffering and guilt. The dramatist, therefore, is faced with two choices. He can show a noble and innocent character suffering exceptional misfortune, but then the effect will be not tragic but pathetic. Or he can portray a sinner who by his sins—usually the sins have to produce crimes—brings his suffering upon himself. But, then, there is no such thing as a noble sinner, for to sin is precisely to become ignoble. Both Shakespeare and Racine try to solve the problem in the same way, by giving the sinner noble poetry to speak, but both of them must have known in their heart of hearts that this was a conjuring trick. Any journalist could tell the story of Oedipus or Hippolytus and it would be just as tragic as when Sophocles or Euripides tells it. The difference would be only that the journalist is incapable of providing Oedipus and Hippolytus with the noble language which befits their tragedy, while Sophocles and Euripides, being great poets, can.

But let a journalist tell the story of Macbeth or Phèdre and we shall immediately recognize them for what they are, one a police court case, the other a pathological case. The poetry that Shakespeare and Racine have given them is not an outward expression of their noble natures, but a gorgeous robe which hides their nakedness. D. H. Lawrence's poem seems to me not altogether unjust.

> When I read Shakespeare I am struck with wonder
> that such trivial people should muse and thunder
> in such lovely language.

Lear, the old buffer, you wonder his daughters
didn't treat him rougher,
the old chough, the old chuffer.

And Hamlet, how boring, how boring to live with,
so mean and self-conscious, blowing and snoring
his wonderful speeches, full of other folk's whoring!

And Macbeth and his Lady, who should have been choring,
such suburban ambition, so messily goring
old Duncan with daggers!

How boring, how small Shakespeare's people are
Yet the language so lovely! like the dyes from gas-tar.

Comedy, on the other hand, is not only possible within a Christian society, but capable of a much greater breadth and depth than classical comedy. Greater in breadth because classical comedy is based upon the division of mankind into two classes, those who have *arete* and those who do not, and only the second class, fools, shameless rascals, slaves, are fit subjects for comedy. But Christian comedy is based upon the belief that all men are sinners; no one, therefore, whatever his rank or talents, can claim immunity from the comic exposure and, indeed, the more virtuous, in the Greek sense, a man is, the more he realizes that he deserves to be exposed. Greater in depth because, while classical comedy believes that rascals should get the drubbing they deserve, Christian comedy believes that we are forbidden to judge others and that it is our duty to forgive each other. In classical comedy the characters are exposed and punished: when the curtain falls, the audience is laughing and those on stage are in tears. In Christian comedy the characters are exposed and forgiven; when the curtain falls, the audience and the characters are laughing together. Ben Jonson's comedies, unlike Shakespeare's, are classical, not Christian.

If the plays of Shakespeare and Ben Jonson—and Jonson is untypical, anyway—had been lost, we should find in the dramatic literature written between 1590 and 1642, many passages of magnificent poetry, many scenes of exciting theatre, but no play which is satisfactory as a whole; the average Elizabethan play is more like a variety show—a series of scenes, often moving or entertaining enough in themselves, but without essential relation to each other—than like a properly constructed drama in which every character and every word is relevant. For this defect we should probably blame the laxness of Elizabethan stage conventions, which permitted the dramatist to have as many scenes and characters as he liked, and to include tragic and comic scenes, verse and prose, in the same play. Fortunately, Shakespeare's plays have not perished, and we are able to see how greatly, in his case, these conventions contributed towards his achievement. Had the stage conventions of his day been those, for example, of the French classical theatre in the seventeenth century, he could not, given his particular kind of genius and interests, have become the greatest creator of "Feigned Histories" in dramatic form who ever lived. In the preface to *Mrs Warren's Profession*, with his typical mixture of perspicacity and polemical exaggeration, Shaw writes:

> The drama can do little to delight the senses: all the apparent instances to the contrary are instances of the personal fascination of the performers. The drama of pure feeling is no longer in the hands of the playwright: it has been conquered by the musician, after whose enchantment all the verbal arts seem cold and tame. *Romeo and Juliet* with the loveliest Juliet is dry, tedious and rhetorical in comparison with Wagner's *Tristan*, even though Isolde be both fourteen stone and forty, as she often is in Germany. . . . There is, flatly, no future now for any drama without music except the drama of thought. The attempt to produce a genus of opera without music (and this absurdity is what our fashionable theatres have been driving at for a long time past without knowing it) is far less hopeful than my own determination to accept problems as the normal material for drama.*

Every aspect of life is, of course, a problem. The belief Shaw is attacking is the belief that the only problem worth a playwright's attention is love between the sexes, considered in isolation from everything else which men and women think and do. Like all persons engaged in polemic, he accepts the view of Shakespeare held by his opponents, namely, that, as a dramatist, Shakespeare, even when his characters are princes and warriors, was only interested in their "private" emotional life. In actual fact, however, the revolt of Ibsen and Shaw against the conventional nineteenth century drama could very well be described as a return to Shakespeare, as an attempt once again to present human beings in their historical and social setting and not, as playwrights since the Restoration had done, either as wholly private or as embodiments of the social manners of a tiny class. Shakespeare's plays, it is true, are not, in the Shavian sense, "dramas of thought," that is to say, not one of his

---

*Curiously enough, now we have got used to them, what impresses us most about Shaw's plays is their musical quality. He has told us himself that it was from *Don Giovanni* that he learned "How to write seriously without being dull." For all his claims to be just a propagandist, his writing has an effect nearer to that of music than most of those who have claimed to be writing "dramas of feeling." His plays are a joy to watch, not because they purport to deal with social and political problems, but because they are such wonderful displays of conspicuous waste; the conversational energy displayed by his characters is so far in excess of what their situation requires that, if it were to be devoted to practical action, it would wreck the world in five minutes. The Mozart of English letters he is not—the music of the Marble Statue is beyond him—the Rossini, yes. He has all the brio, humor, cruel clarity and virtuosity of that Master of *opera buffa*.

characters is an intellectual: it is true, as Shaw says, that, when stripped of their wonderful diction, the philosophical and moral views expressed by his characters are commonplaces, but the number of people in any generation or society whose thoughts are not commonplace is very small indeed. On the other hand, there is hardly one of his plays which does not provide unending food for thought, if one cares to think about it. *Romeo and Juliet,* for example, is by no means merely a "drama of feeling," a verbal opera about a love affair between two adolescents; it is also, and more importantly, a portrait of a society, charming enough in many ways, but morally inadequate because the only standard of value by which its members regulate and judge their conduct is that of *la bella* or *la brutta figura.* The disaster that overtakes the young lovers is one symptom of what is wrong with Verona, and every citizen, from Prince Escalus down to the starving apothecary, has a share of responsibility for their deaths. Quite aside from their different temperaments and talents, one can see a good reason why Shakespeare does not need to tell the audience his "thoughts," while Shaw is obliged to. Thanks to the conventions and the economics of the Elizabethan theatre, Shakespeare can present his picture of Verona in twenty-four scenes with a cast of thirty speaking roles and a crowd of walk-ons. Shaw has to write for a picture stage framed by a proscenium arch, furnished with sets which admit of few changes of location, and for actors whose salary scale makes a large cast prohibitively expensive. When, therefore, he writes about a social problem such as slum landlords, he is obliged to tell us through an intellectual debate between the few characters in the few locations at his disposal what he cannot present dramatically as evidence from which we could draw the conclusions for ourselves.

As a dramatic historian, Shakespeare was born at just the right time. Later, changes in the conventions and economics of the theatre made it an inadequate medium, and feigned histories became the province of the novelist. Earlier, dramatic history would have been impossible, because the only history which was recognized as such was sacred history. The drama had to become secularized before any adequate treatment of human history was possible. Greek tragedy, like the mystery play, is religious drama. What the hero does himself is subordinate to what the gods make him do. Further, the gods are concerned, not with human society, but with certain exceptional individuals. The hero dies or goes into exile, but his city, as represented by the chorus, remains. The chorus may give him support or warning advice, but they cannot influence his actions and bear no responsibility for them. Only the hero has a biography; the chorus are mere observers. Human history cannot be written except on the presupposition that, whatever part God may play in human affairs, we cannot say of one event, "This is an act of God," of another, "This is a natural event," and of another, "This is a human choice"; we can only record what happens. The allegorical morality plays are con-

cerned with history, but only with subjective history; the social-historical setting of any particular man is deliberately excluded.

We do not know what Shakespeare's personal beliefs were, nor his opinion
on any subject (though most of us privately think we do). All we can notice
is an ambivalence in his feelings towards his characters which is, perhaps,
characteristic of all great dramatists. A dramatist's characters are, normally,
men-of-action, but he himself is a maker, not a doer, concerned, not with
disclosing himself to others in the moment, but with making a work which,
unlike himself, will endure, if possible forever. The dramatist, therefore, admires and envies in his characters their courage and readiness to risk their
lives and souls—qua dramatist, he never risks himself—but, at the same
time, to his detached imagination, all action, however glorious, is vain because the consequence is never what the doer intended. What a man does is
irrevocable for good or ill; what he makes, he can always modify or even destroy. In all great drama, I believe, we can feel the tension of this ambivalent
attitude, torn between reverence and contempt, of the maker towards the
doer. A character for whom his creator felt either absolute reverence or absolute contempt would not, I think, be actable.

The Prince's Dog

> Whoever takes up the sword shall perish by the sword. And
> whoever does not take up the sword (or lets it drop) shall
> perish on the cross. —Simone Weil

It has been observed that critics who write about Shakespeare reveal more
about themselves than about Shakespeare, but perhaps that is the great
value of drama of the Shakespearian kind, namely, that whatever he may see
taking place on stage, its final effect upon each spectator is a self-revelation.

Shakespeare holds the position in our literature of Top Bard, but this deserved priority has one unfortunate consequence; we generally make our
first acquaintance with his plays, not in the theatre, but in the classroom or
study, so that, when we do attend a performance, we have lost that naïve
openness to surprise which is the proper frame of mind in which to witness
any drama. The experience of reading a play and the experience of watching
it performed are never identical, but in the case of *Henry IV* the difference
between the two is particularly great.

At a performance, my immediate reaction is to wonder what Falstaff is
doing in this play at all. At the end of *Richard II*, we were told that the Heir
Apparent has taken up with a dissolute crew of "unrestrained loose companions." What sort of bad company would one expect to find Prince Hal keep-

ing when the curtain rises on *Henry IV*? Surely, one could expect to see him surrounded by daring, rather sinister juvenile delinquents and beautiful gold-digging whores. But whom do we meet in the Boar's Head? A fat, cowardly tosspot, old enough to be his father, two down-at-heel hangers-on, a slatternly hostess and only one whore, who is not in her earliest youth either; all of them seedy, and, by any worldly standards, including those of the criminal classes, all of them *failures*. Surely, one thinks, an Heir Apparent, sowing his wild oats, could have picked himself a more exciting crew than that. As the play proceeds, our surprise is replaced by another kind of puzzle, for the better we come to know Falstaff, the clearer it becomes that the world of historical reality which a Chronicle Play claims to imitate is not a world which he can inhabit.

If it really was Queen Elizabeth who demanded to see Falstaff in a comedy, then she showed herself a very perceptive critic. But even in *The Merry Wives of Windsor*, Falstaff has not and could not have found his true home because Shakespeare was only a poet. For that he was to wait nearly two hundred years till Verdi wrote his last opera. Falstaff is not the only case of a character whose true home is the world of music; others are Tristan, Isolde, and Don Giovanni.*

Though they each call for a different kind of music, Tristan, Don Giovanni, and Falstaff have certain traits in common. They do not belong to the temporal world of change. One cannot imagine any of them as babies, for a Tristan who is not in love, a Don Giovanni who has no name on his list, a Falstaff who is not old and fat, are inconceivable. When Falstaff says, "When I was about their years, Hal, I was not an eagle's talent in the waist; I could have crept into an alderman's thumb-ring"—we take it as a typical Falstaffian fib, but we believe him when he says, "I was born about three in the afternoon, with a white head and something of a round belly."

Time, for Tristan, is a single moment stretched out tighter and tighter until it snaps. Time, for Don Giovanni, is an infinite arithmetical series of unrelated moments which has no beginning and would have no end if Heaven did not intervene and cut it short. For Falstaff, time does not exist, since he belongs to the *opera buffa* world of play and mock action governed not by will or desire, but by innocent wish, a world where no one can suffer because everything he says and does is only a pretense.

Thus, while we must see Tristan die in Isolde's arms and we must see Don Giovanni sink into the earth, because being doomed to die and to go to hell are essential to their beings, we cannot see Falstaff die on stage because, if we did, we should not believe it; we should know that, as at the battle of Shrewsbury, he was only shamming. I am not even quite sure that we believe it when we are told of his death in *Henry V*; I think we accept it, as we accept the

---

*If Verdi's *Macbetto* fails to come off, the main reason is that the proper world for Macbeth is poetry, not song; he won't go into notes.

death of Sherlock Holmes, as his creator's way of saying, "I am getting tired of this character"; we feel sure that, if the public pleads with him strongly enough, Shakespeare will find some way to bring him to life again. The only kind of funeral music we can associate with him is the mock-requiem in the last act of Verdi's opera.

> *Domine fallo casto*
> > *Ma salvagli l'addomine*
> *Domine fallo guasto.*
> > *Ma salvagli l'addomine.*

There are at least two places in the play where the incongruity of the *opera buffa* world with the historical world is too much, even for Shakespeare, and a patently false note is struck. The first occurs when, on the battlefield of Shrewsbury, Falstaff thrusts his sword into Hotspur's corpse. Within his own world, Falstaff could stab a corpse because, there, all battles are mock battles, all corpses straw dummies; but we, the audience, are too conscious that this battle has been a real battle and that this corpse is the real dead body of a brave and noble young man. Pistol could do it, because Pistol is a contemptible character, but Falstaff cannot; that is to say, there is no way in which an actor can play the scene convincingly. So, too, with the surrender of Colevile to Falstaff in the Second Part. In his conversation, first with Colevile and then with Prince John, Falstaff talks exactly as we expect—to him, the whole business is a huge joke. But then he is present during a scene when we are shown that it is no joke at all. How is any actor to behave and speak his lines during the following?

LANCASTER. Is thy name Colevile?
COLEVILE. It is, my lord.
LANCASTER. A famous rebel art thou, Colevile.
FALSTAFF. And a famous true subject took him.
COLEVILE. I am, my lord, but as my betters are,
    That led me hither. Had they been ruled by me,
    You would have won them dearer than you have.
FALSTAFF. I know not how they sold themselves: but thou, like a kind
    fellow, gavest thyself away gratis; and I thank thee for thee.
LANCASTER. Now have you left pursuit?
WESTMORELAND. Retreat is made and execution stayed.
LANCASTER. Send Colevile, with his confederates,
    To York, to present execution.

The Falstaffian frivolity and the headsman's axe cannot so directly confront each other.

Reading *Henry IV*, we can easily give our full attention to the historical-political scenes, but, when watching a performance, attention is distracted by our eagerness to see Falstaff reappear. Short of cutting him out of the play altogether, no producer can prevent him stealing the show. From an actor's point of view, the role of Falstaff has the enormous advantage that he has only to think of one thing—playing to an audience. Since he lives in an eternal present and the historical world does not exist for him, there is no difference for Falstaff between those on stage and those out front, and if the actor were to appear in one scene in Elizabethan costume and in the next in top hat and morning coat, no one would be bewildered. The speech of all the other characters is, like our own, conditioned by two factors, the external situation with its questions, answers, and commands, and the inner need of each character to disclose himself to others. But Falstaff's speech has only one cause, his absolute insistence, at every moment and at all costs, upon disclosing himself. Half his lines could be moved from one speech to another without our noticing, for nearly everything he says is a variant upon one theme—"I am that I am."

Moreover, Shakespeare has so written his part that it cannot be played unsympathetically. A good actor can make us admire Prince Hal, but he cannot hope to make us like him as much as even a second-rate actor will make us like Falstaff. Sober reflection in the study may tell us that Falstaff is not, after all, a very admirable person, but Falstaff on the stage gives us no time for sober reflection. When Hal or the Chief Justice or any others indicate that they are not bewitched by Falstaff, reason might tell us that they are in the right, but we ourselves are already bewitched, so that their disenchantment seems out of place, like the presence of teetotalers at a drunken party.

Suppose, then, that a producer were to cut the Falstaff scenes altogether, what would *Henry IV* become? The middle section of a political trilogy which could be entitled *Looking for the Doctor*.

The body politic of England catches an infection from its family physician. An able but unqualified practitioner throws him out of the sickroom and takes over. The patient's temperature continues to rise. But then, to everybody's amazement, the son of the unqualified practitioner whom, though he has taken his degree, everyone has hitherto believed to be a hopeless invalid, effects a cure. Not only is the patient restored to health but also, at the doctor's orders, takes another body-politic, France, to wife.

The theme of this trilogy is, that is to say, the question: What combination of qualities is needed in the Ruler whose function is the establishment and maintenance of Temporal Justice? According to Shakespeare, the ideal Ruler must satisfy five conditions. (1) He must know what is just and what is unjust. (2) He must himself be just. (3) He must be strong enough to compel those who would like to be unjust to behave justly. (4) He must have the capacity both by nature and by art of making others loyal to his person. (5) He must be the legitimate ruler by whatever standard legitimacy is determined in the society to which he belongs.

Richard II fails to satisfy the first four of these. He does not know what Justice is, for he follows the advice of foolish flatterers. He is himself unjust, for he spends the money he obtains by taxing the Commons and fining the Nobility, not on defending England against her foes, but upon maintaining a lavish and frivolous court, so that, when he really does need money for a patriotic purpose, the war with Ireland, his exchequer is empty and in desperation he commits a gross act of injustice by confiscating Bolingbroke's estates.

It would seem that at one time he had been popular but he has now lost his popularity, partly on account of his actions, but also because he lacks the art of winning hearts. According to his successor, he had made the mistake of being overfamiliar—the ruler should not let himself be seen too often as "human"—and in addition, he is not by nature the athletic, physically brave warrior who is the type most admired by the feudal society he is called upon to rule.

In consequence, Richard II is a weak ruler who cannot keep the great nobles in order or even command the loyalty of his soldiers, and weakness in a ruler is the worst defect of all. A cruel, even an unjust king, who is strong, is preferable to the most saintly weakling because most men will behave unjustly if they discover that they can with impunity; tyranny, the injustice of one, is less unjust than anarchy, the injustice of many.

But there remains the fifth condition: whatever his defects, Richard II is the legitimate King of England. Since all men are mortal, and many men are ambitious, unless there is some impersonal principle by which, when the present ruler dies, the choice of his successor can be decided, there will be a risk of civil war in every generation. It is better to endure the injustice of the legitimate ruler, who will die anyway sooner or later, than allow a usurper to take his place by force.

As a potential ruler, Bolingbroke possesses many of the right qualities. He is a strong man, he knows how to make himself popular, and he would like to be just. We never hear, even from the rebels, of any specific actions of Henry IV which are unjust, only of suspicions which may be just or unjust. But in yielding to the temptation, when the opportunity unexpectedly offers itself, of deposing his lawful sovereign, he commits an act of injustice for which he and his kingdom have to pay a heavy price. Because of it, though he is strong enough to crush rebellion, he is not strong or popular enough to prevent rebellion breaking out.

Once Richard has been murdered, however, the rule of Henry IV is better than any alternative. Though, legally, Mortimer may have a good or better right to the throne, the scene at Bangor between Hotspur, Worcester, Mortimer, and Glendower, convinces us that Henry's victory is a victory for justice since we learn that the rebels have no concern for the interests of the Kingdom, only for their own. Their plan, if they succeed, is to carve up England into three petty states. Henry may wish that Hotspur, not Hal, were his heir, because Hotspur is a brave warrior ready to risk his life in battle against England's foes, while Hal appears to be dissipated and frivolous, but we know better. Hotspur is indeed brave, but that is all. A man who can say

> I'll give thrice so much land
> To any well-deserving friend;
> But in the way of bargain, mark ye me,
> I'll cavil on the ninth part of a hair

is clearly unfitted to be a ruler because his actions are based, not on justice, but on personal whim. Moreover, he is not interested in political power; all he desires is military glory.

Thirdly, there is Prince Hal, Henry V-to-be. To everyone except himself, he seems at first to be another Richard, unjust, lacking in self-control but, unfortunately, the legitimate heir. By the time the curtain falls on *Henry V*, however, he is recognized by all to be the Ideal Ruler. Like his father in his youth, he is brave and personable. In addition, he is a much cleverer politician. While his father was an improviser, he is a master of the art of timing. His first soliloquy reveals him as a person who always sees several steps ahead and has the patience to wait, even though waiting means temporary misunderstanding and unpopularity, until the right moment for action comes; he will never, if he can help it, leave anything to chance. Last but not least, he is blessed by luck. His father had foreseen that internal dissension could only be cured if some common cause could be found which would unite all parties but he was too old and ill, the internal quarrels too violent. But when Hal succeeds as Henry V, most of his enemies are dead or powerless—Cambridge and Scroop have no armies at their back—and his possible right to the throne of France provides the common cause required to unite both the nobles and the commons, and gives him the opportunity, at Agincourt, to show his true mettle.

One of Falstaff's dramatic functions is to be the means by which Hal is revealed to be the Just Ruler, not the dissolute and frivolous young man everybody has thought him; but, so far as the audience is concerned, Falstaff has fulfilled his function by Act III, Scene 2, of the First Part, when the King entrusts Hal with a military command. Up to this point the Falstaff scenes have kept us in suspense. In Act I, Scene 2, we hear Hal promise

> I'll so offend to make offense a skill,
> Redeeming time when men least think I will.

But then we watch the rebellion being prepared while he does nothing but amuse himself with Falstaff, so that we are left wondering whether he meant what he said or was only play-acting. But from the moment he engages in the political action of the play, we have no doubts whatsoever as to his ambition, capacity, and ultimate triumph for, however often henceforward we may see him with Falstaff, it is never at a time when his advice and arms are needed by the State; he visits the Boar's Head in leisure hours when there is nothing serious for him to do.

For those in the play, the decisive moment of revelation is, of course, his first public act as Henry V, his rejection of Falstaff and company. For his subjects who have not, as we have, watched him with Falstaff, it is necessary to allay their fears that, though they already know him to be brave and capable, he may still be unjust and put his personal friendships before the impartial justice which it is his duty as king to maintain. But we, who have watched his private life, have no such fears. We have long known that his first soliloquy meant what it said, that he has never been under any false illusions about Falstaff or anyone else and that when the right moment comes to reject Falstaff, that is to say, when such a rejection will make the maximum political effect, he will do so without hesitation. Even the magnanimity he shows in granting his old companion a life competence, which so impresses those about him, cannot impress us because, knowing Falstaff as they do not, we know what the effect on him of such a rejection must be, that his heart will be "fracted and corroborate" and no life competence can mend that. It is Hal's company he wants, not a pension from the Civil List.

The essential Falstaff is the Falstaff of *The Merry Wives* and Verdi's opera, the comic hero of the world of play, the unkillable self-sufficient immortal whose verdict on existence is

> *Tutto nel mondo è burla. . . .*
> *Tutti gabbàti. Irride*
> *L'un l'altro ogni mortal.*
> *Ma ride ben chi ride*
> *La risata final*

In *Henry IV*, however, something has happened to this immortal which draws him out of his proper world into the historical world of suffering and death. He has become capable of serious emotion. He continues to employ the speech of his comic world:

> I have forsworn his company hourly any time this two-and-twenty years, and yet I am bewitched by the rogue's company. If the rascal have not given me medicines to make me love him, I'll be hanged. It could not be else. I have drunk medicines.

But the emotion so flippantly expressed could equally well be expressed thus:

> If my dear love were but the child of state
> It might for Fortune's bastard be unfathered,
> As subject to Time's love or to Time's hate,

> Weeds among weeds, or flowers with flowers gathered.
> No, it was builded far from accident;
> It suffers not in smiling pomp, nor falls
> Under the blow of thralled discontent,
> Whereto th' inviting time and fashion calls
> It fears not Policy, that heretic
> Which works on leases of short numbered hours,
> But all alone stands hugely politic.

As the play proceeds, we become aware, behind all the fun, of something tragic. Falstaff loves Hal with an absolute devotion. "The lovely bully" is the son he has never had, the youth predestined to the success and worldly glory which he will never enjoy. He believes that his love is returned, that the Prince is indeed his other self, so he is happy, despite old age and poverty. We, however, can see that he is living in a fool's paradise, for the Prince cares no more for him as a person than he would care for the King's Jester. He finds Falstaff amusing but no more. If we could warn Falstaff of what he is too blind to see, we might well say: Beware, before it is too late, of becoming involved with one of those mortals

> That do not do the thing they most do show,
> Who, moving others, are themselves as stone. . . .

Falstaff's story, in fact, is not unlike one of those folk tales in which a mermaid falls in love with a mortal prince: the price she pays for her infatuation is the loss of her immortality without the compensation of temporal happiness.

Let us now suppose, not only that Falstaff takes no part in the play, but is also allowed to sit in the audience as a spectator. How much will he understand of what he sees going on?

He will see a number of Englishmen divided into two parties who finally come to blows. That they should come to blows will in itself be no proof to him that they are enemies because they might, like boxers, have agreed to fight for fun. In Falstaff's world there are two causes of friendship and enmity. My friend may be someone whose appearance and manner I like at this moment, my enemy someone whose appearance and manner I dislike. Thus, he will understand Hotspur's objection to Bolingbroke perfectly well.

> Why, what a candy deal of courtesy
> This fawning greyhound then did proffer me.
> "Look, when his infant fortune came to age,"
> And "gentle Harry Percy" and "kind cousin."
> O the devil take such cozeners.

To Falstaff, "my friend" can also mean he whose wish at this moment coincides with mine, "my enemy" he whose wish contradicts mine. He will see the civil war, therefore, as a clash between Henry and Mortimer who both wish to wear the crown. What will perplex him is any argument as to who has the better right to wear it.

Anger and fear he can understand, because they are immediate emotions, but not nursing a grievance or planning revenge or apprehension, for these presuppose that the future inherits from the past. He will not, therefore, be able to make head or tail of Warwick's speech, "There is a history in all men's lives . . . ," nor any reasons the rebels give for their actions which are based upon anything Bolingbroke did before he became king, nor the reason given by Worcester for concealing the king's peace offer from Hotspur:

> It is impossible, it cannot be
> The King should keep his word in loving us.
> He will suspect us still and find a time
> To punish this offence in other faults.

To *keep his word* is a phrase outside Falstaff's comprehension, for a promise means that at some future moment I might have to refuse to do what I wish, and, in Falstaff's world to wish and to do are synonymous. For the same reason, when, by promising them redress, Prince John tricks the rebels into disbanding their armies and then arrests them, Falstaff will not understand why they and all the audience except himself are shocked.

The first words Shakespeare puts into Falstaff's mouth are, "Now Hal, what time of day is it, lad?" to which the Prince quite rightly replies, "What the devil hast thou to do with the time of day?" In Falstaff's world, every moment is one of infinite possibility when anything can be wished. As a spectator, he will keep hearing the characters use the words *time* and *occasion* in a sense which will stump him.

> What I know
> Is ruminated, plotted, and set down
> And only stays but to behold the face
> Of that occasion that shall bring it on.

> The purpose you undertake is dangerous, the time itself
> unsorted. . . .

> . . . I will resolve to Scotland. There am I
> Till time and vantage crave my company.

Of all the characters in the play, the one he will think he understands best is the least Falstaff-like of them all, Hotspur, for Hotspur, like himself, appears to obey the impulse of the moment and say exactly what he thinks without prudent calculation. Both conceal nothing from others, Falstaff because he has no mask to put on, Hotspur because he has so become his mask that he has no face beneath it. Falstaff says, as it were, "I am I. Whatever I do, however outrageous, is of infinite importance because I do it." Hotspur says:

"I am Hotspur, the fearless, the honest, plain-spoken warrior. If I should ever show fear or tell lies, even white ones, I should cease to exist." If Falstaff belonged to the same world as Hotspur, one could call him a liar, but, in his own eyes, he is perfectly truthful, for, to him, fact is subjective fact, "what I am actually feeling and thinking at this moment." To call him a liar is as ridiculous as if, in a play, a character should say, "I am Napoleon," and a member of the audience should cry, "You're not. You're Sir John Gielgud."

In Ibsen's *Peer Gynt*, there is a remarkable scene in which Peer visits the Troll King. At the entertainment given in his honor, animals dance to hideous noises, but Peer behaves to them with perfect manners as if they were beautiful girls and the music ravishing. After it is over, the Troll King asks him: "Now, frankly, tell me what you saw." Peer replies: "What I saw was impossibly ugly"—and then describes the scene as the audience had seen it. The Troll King who has taken a fancy to him, suggests that Peer would be happier as a troll. All that is needed is a little eye operation, after which he will really see a cow as a beautiful girl. Peer indignantly refuses. He is perfectly willing, he says, to swear that a cow is a girl, but to surrender his humanity so that he can no longer lie, because he cannot distinguish between fact and fiction, that he will never do. By this criterion, neither Falstaff nor Hotspur is quite human, Falstaff because he is pure troll, Hotspur because he is so lacking in imagination that the troll kingdom is invisible to him.

At first, then, Falstaff will believe that Hotspur is one of his own kind, who like himself enjoys putting on an act, but then he will hear Hotspur say words which he cannot comprehend.

> . . . time serves wherein you may redeem
> Your banished honours and restore yourselves
> Into the good thoughts of the world again.

In Falstaff's world, the only value standard is importance, that is to say, all he demands from others is attention, all he fears is being ignored. Whether others applaud or hiss does not matter; what matters is the volume of the hissing or the applause.

Hence, in his soliloquy about honor, his reasoning runs something like this: if the consequence of demanding moral approval from others is dying, it is better to win their disapproval; a dead man has no audience.

Since the Prince is a personal friend, Falstaff is, of course, a King's man who thinks it a shame to be on any side but one, but his loyalty is like that of those who, out of local pride, support one football team rather than another. As a member of the audience, his final comment upon the political action of the play will be the same as he makes from behind the footlights.

> Well, God be thanked for these rebels: they offend none but the virtuous. . . .

A young knave and begging. Is there not employment? Doth not the King lack subjects? Do not the rebels need soldiers?

Once upon a time we were all Falstaffs: then we became social beings with super-egos. Most of us learn to accept this, but there are some in whom the nostalgia for the state of innocent self-importance is so strong that they refuse to accept adult life and responsibilities and seek some means to become again the Falstaffs they once were. The commonest technique adopted is the bottle, and, curiously enough, the male drinker reveals his intention by developing a drinker's belly.

If one visits a bathing beach, one can observe that men and women grow fat in different ways. A fat woman exaggerates her femininity; her breasts and buttocks enlarge till she comes to look like the Venus of Willendorf. A fat man, on the other hand, looks like a cross between a very young child and a pregnant mother. There have been cultures in which obesity in women was considered the ideal of sexual attraction, but in no culture, so far as I know, has a fat man been considered more attractive than a thin one. If my own weight and experience give me any authority, I would say that fatness in the male is the physical expression of a psychological wish to withdraw from sexual competition and, by combining mother and child in his own person, to become emotionally self-sufficient. The Greeks thought of Narcissus as a slender youth but I think they were wrong. I see him as a middle-aged man with a corporation, for, however ashamed he may be of displaying it in public, in private a man with a belly loves it dearly; it may be an unprepossessing child to look at, but he has borne it all by himself.

I do walk here before thee like a sow that hath overwhelmed all her litter but one. . . .

I have a whole school of tongues in this belly of mine, and not a tongue of them all speaks any other word but my name. My womb, my womb undoes me.

Not all fat men are heavy drinkers, but all males who drink heavily become fat.* At the same time, the more they drink, the less they eat. "O monstrous! But one halfpenny worth of bread to this intolerable deal of sack!" exclaims Hal on looking at Falstaff's bill, but he cannot have expected anything else. Drunkards die, not from the liquid alcohol they take so much of, but from their refusal to eat solid food, and anyone who has had to look after a drunk knows that the only way to get enough nourishment into him is to give him liquid or mashed-up foods, for he will reject any dish that needs chewing. Solid food is to the drunkard a symbolic reminder of the loss of the mother's breast and his ejection from Eden.

A plague on sighing and grief. It blows a man up like a bladder. . . .

---

*All the women I have met who drank heavily were lighter and thinner than average.

So Falstaff, and popular idiom identifies the kind of griefs which have this fattening effect—eating humble pie, swallowing insults, etc.

In a recent number of *The Paris Review*, Mr Nicholas Tucci writes:

The death song of the drunkard—it may go on for thirty years—goes more or less like this. "I was born a god, with the whole world in reach of my hands, lie now defeated in the gutter. Come and listen: hear what the world has done to me."

In Vino Veritas is an old saying that has nothing to do with the drunkard's own truth. He has no secrets—that is true—but it is not true that his truth may be found under the skin of his moral reserve or of his sober lies, so that the moment he begins to cross his eyes and pour out his heart, anyone may come in and get his fill of truth. What happens is exactly the opposite. When the drunkard confesses, he makes a careful choice of his pet sins: and these are nonexistent. He may be unable to distinguish a person from a chair, but never an unprofitable lie from a profitable one. How could he see himself as a very insignificant entity in a huge world of others, when he sees nothing but himself spread over the whole universe. "I am alone" is indeed a true cry, but it should not be taken literally.

The drunk is unlovely to look at, intolerable to listen to, and his self-pity is contemptible. Nevertheless, as not merely a worldly failure but also a willful failure, he is a disturbing image for the sober citizen. His refusal to accept the realities of this world, babyish as it may be, compels us to take another look at this world and reflect upon our motives for accepting it. The drunkard's suffering may be self-inflicted, but it is real suffering and reminds us of all the suffering in this world which we prefer not to think about because, from the moment we accepted this world, we acquired our share of responsibility for everything that happens in it.

When we see Falstaff's gross paunch and red face, we are reminded that the body politic of England is not so healthy, either.

> The Commonwealth is sick of its own choice.
> Their over-greedy love hath surfeited. . . .
> Thou (beastly feeder) are so full of him
> That thou provokest thyself to cast him up.
> So, so, thou common dog, didst thou disgorge
> Thy glutton bosom of the royal Richard. . . .
> Then you perceive the body of our kingdom
> How foul it is: what rank diseases grow,
> And with what danger near the heart of it.

It might be expected that we would be revolted at the sight and turn our eyes with relief and admiration to the Hero Prince. But in fact we aren't and we don't. Whenever Falstaff is on stage, we have no eyes for Hal. If Shakespeare did originally write a part for Falstaff in *Henry V*, it would not have taken pressure from the Cobhams to make him cut it out; his own dramatic instinct would have told him that, if Henry was to be shown in his full glory, the presence of Falstaff would diminish it.

Seeking for an explanation of why Falstaff affects us as he does, I find myself compelled to see *Henry IV* as possessing, in addition to its overt meaning, a parabolic significance. Overtly, Falstaff is a Lord of Misrule; parabolically, he is a comic symbol for the supernatural order of Charity as contrasted with the temporal order of Justice symbolized by Henry of Monmouth.

Such readings are only possible with drama which, like Shakespeare's, is secular, concerned directly, not with the relation of man and God, but with the relations between men. Greek tragedy, at least before Euripides, is directly religious, concerned with what the gods do to men rather than what men do to each other: it presents a picture of human events, the causes of which are divine actions. In consequence, a Greek tragedy does not demand that we "read" it in the sense that we speak of "reading" a face. The ways of the gods may be mysterious to human beings but they are not ambiguous.

There can be no secular drama of any depth or importance except in a culture which recognizes that man has an internal history as well as an external; that his actions are partly in response to an objective situation created by his past acts and the acts of others, and partly initiated by his subjective need to re-create, redefine, and rechoose himself. Surprise and revelation are the essence of drama. In Greek tragedy these are supplied by the gods; no mortal can foresee how and when they will act. But the conduct of men has no element of surprise, that is to say, the way in which they react to the surprising events which befall them is exactly what one would expect.

A secular drama presupposes that in all which men say and do there is a gratuitous element which makes their conduct ambiguous and unpredictable. Secular drama, therefore, demands a much more active role from its audience than a Greek tragedy. The audience has to be at one and the same time a witness to what is occurring on stage and a subjective participant who interprets what he sees and hears. And a secular dramatist like Shakespeare who attempts to project the inner history of human beings into objective stage action is faced with problems which Aeschylus and Sophocles were spared, for there are aspects of this inner history which resist and sometimes defy manifestation.

> Humility is represented with difficulty—when it is shown in its ideal moment, the beholder senses the lack of something because he feels that its true ideality does not consist in the fact that it is ideal in the moment but that it is constant. Romantic love can very well be represented in the moment, but conjugal love cannot, because an ideal husband is not one who is such once in his life but one who every day is such. Courage can

very well be concentrated in the moment, but not patience, precisely for the reason that patience strives with time. A king who conquers kingdoms can be represented in the moment, but a cross bearer who every day takes up his cross cannot be represented in art because the point is that he does it every day. (Kierkegaard.)

Let us suppose, then, that a dramatist wishes to show a character acting out of the spirit of charity or agape. At first this looks easy. Agape requires that we love our enemies, do good to those that hate us and forgive those who injure us, and this command is unconditional. Surely, all a dramatist has to do is to show one human being forgiving an enemy.

In *Measure for Measure*, Angelo has wronged Isabella and Mariana, and the facts of the wrong become public. Angelo repents and demands that the just sentence of death be passed on him by the Duke. Isabella and Mariana implore the Duke to show mercy. The Duke yields to their prayers and all ends happily. I agree with Professor Coghill's interpretation of *Measure for Measure* as a parable in which Isabella is an image for the redeemed Christian Soul, perfectly chaste and loving, whose reward is to become the bride of God; but, to my mind, the parable does not quite work because it is impossible to distinguish in dramatic action between the spirit of forgiveness and the act of pardon.

The command to forgive is unconditional: whether my enemy harden his heart or repent and beg forgiveness is irrelevant. If he hardens his heart, he does not care whether I forgive him or not and it would be impertinent of me to say, "I forgive you." If he repents and asks, "Will you forgive me?" the answer, "Yes," should not express a decision on my part but describe a state of feeling which has always existed. On the stage, however, it is impossible to show one person forgiving another, unless the wrongdoer asks for forgiveness, because silence and inaction are undramatic. The Isabella we are shown in earlier scenes of *Measure for Measure* is certainly not in a forgiving spirit—she is in a passion of rage and despair at Angelo's injustice—and dramatically she could not be otherwise, for then there would be no play. Again, on the stage, forgiveness requires manifestation in action, that is to say, the one who forgives must be in a position to do something for the other which, if he were not forgiving, he would not do. This means that my enemy must be at my mercy; but, to the spirit of charity, it is irrelevant whether I am at my enemy's mercy or he at mine. So long as he is at my mercy, forgiveness is indistinguishable from judicial pardon.

The law cannot forgive, for the law has not been wronged, only broken; only persons can be wronged. The law can pardon, but it can only pardon what it has the power to punish. If the lawbreaker is stronger than the legal authorities, they are powerless to do either. The decision to grant or refuse pardon must be governed by prudent calculation—if the wrongdoer is pardoned, he will behave better in the future than if he were punished, etc. But charity is forbidden to calculate in this way: I am required to forgive my enemy whatever the effect on him may be.

One may say that Isabella forgives Angelo and the Duke pardons him. But, on the stage, this distinction is invisible because, there, power, justice and love are all on the same side. Justice is able to pardon what love is commanded to forgive. But to love, it is an accident that the power of temporal justice should be on its side; indeed, the Gospels assure us that, sooner or later, they will find themselves in opposition and that love must suffer at the hands of justice.

In *King Lear*, Shakespeare attempts to show absolute love and goodness, in the person of Cordelia, destroyed by the powers of this world, but the price he pays is that Cordelia, as a dramatic character, is a bore.

If she is not to be a fake, what she says cannot be poetically very impressive nor what she does dramatically very exciting.

> What shall Cordelia speak? Love and be silent.

In a play with twenty-six scenes, Shakespeare allows her to appear in only four, and from a total of over three thousand three hundred lines, he allots to her less than ninety.

Temporal Justice demands the use of force to quell the unjust; it demands prudence, a practical reckoning with time and place; and it demands publicity for its laws and its penalties. But Charity forbids all three—we are not to resist evil, if a man demand our coat we are to give him our cloak also, we are to take no thought for the morrow and, while secretly fasting and giving alms, we are to appear in public as persons who do neither.

A direct manifestation of charity in secular terms is, therefore, impossible. One form of indirect manifestation employed by religious teachers has been through parables in which actions which are ethically immoral are made to stand as a sign for that which transcends ethics. The Gospel parable of the Unjust Steward is one example. These words by a Hasidic Rabbi are another:

> I cannot teach you the ten principles of service but a little child and a thief can show you what they are. From the child you can learn three things:
>
>> He is merry for no particular reason.
>> Never for a moment is he idle.
>> When he wants something, he demands it vigorously.
>
> The thief can instruct you in many things.
>
>> He does his service by night.
>> If he does not finish what he has set out to do in one night, he devotes the next night to it.

He and all those who work for him, love one another.
He risks his life for slight gains.
What he takes has so little value for him that he gives up for a very
    small coin. He endures blows and hardships and it matters noth-
    ing to him.
He likes his trade and would not exchange it for any other.

If a parable of this kind is dramatized, the action must be comic, that is to say, the apparently immoral actions of the hero must not inflict, as in the actual world they would, real suffering upon others.

Thus, Falstaff speaks of himself as if he were always robbing travelers. We see him do this once—incidentally, it is not Falstaff but the Prince who is the instigator—and the sight convinces us that he never has been and never could be a successful highwayman. The money is restolen from him and returned to its proper owners; the only sufferer is Falstaff himself who has been made a fool of. He lives shamelessly on credit, but none of his creditors seems to be in serious trouble as a result. The Hostess may swear that if he does not pay his bill, she will have to pawn her plate and tapestries, but this is shown to be the kind of exaggeration habitual to landladies, for in the next scene they are still there. What, overtly, is dishonesty becomes, parabolically, a sign for a lack of pride, humility which acknowledges its unimportance and dependence upon others.

Then he rejoices in his reputation as a fornicator with whom no woman is safe alone, but the Falstaff on stage is too old to fornicate, and it is impossible to imagine him younger. All we see him do is defend a whore against a bully, set her on his knee and make her cry out of affection and pity. What in the real world is promiscuous lust, the treatment of other persons as objects of sexual greed, becomes in the comic world of play a symbol for the charity that loves all neighbors without distinction.

Living off other people's money and indiscriminate fornication are acts of injustice towards private individuals; Falstaff is also guilty of injustice to others in their public character as citizens. In any war it is not the justice or injustice of either side that decides who is to be the victor but the force each can command. It is therefore the duty of all who believe in the justice of the King's side to supply him with the best soldiers possible. Falstaff makes no attempt to fulfill this duty. Before the battle of Shrewsbury, he first conscripts those who have most money and least will to fight and then allows them to buy their way out, so that he is finally left with a sorry regiment of "discarded unjust serving men, younger sons to younger brothers, revolted tapsters and ostlers trade fallen. . . ." Before the battle of Gaultree Forest, the two most sturdy young men, Mouldy and Bullcalf, offer him money and are let off, and the weakest, Shadow, Feeble and Wart, taken.

From the point of view of society this is unjust, but if the villagers who are subject to conscription were to be asked, as private individuals, whether they would rather be treated justly or as Falstaff treats them, there is no doubt as to their answer. What their betters call just and unjust means nothing to them; all they know is that conscription will tear them away from their homes and livelihoods with a good chance of getting killed or returning maimed "to beg at the town's end." Those whom Falstaff selects are those with least to lose, derelicts without home or livelihood to whom soldiering at least offers a chance of loot. Bullcalf wants to stay with his friends, Mouldy has an old mother to look after, but Feeble is quite ready to go if his friend Wart can go with him.

Falstaff's neglect of the public interest in favor of private concerns is an image for the justice of charity which treats each person, not as a cipher, but as a unique person. The Prince may justly complain:

I never did see such pitiful rascals

but Falstaff's retort speaks for all the insulted and injured of this world:

Tut tut—good enough to toss, food for powder, food for powder. They'll fit a pit as well as better. Tush, man, mortal men, mortal men. . . .

These are Falstaff's only acts: for the rest, he fritters away his time, swigging at the bottle and taking no thought for the morrow. As a parable, both the idleness and the drinking, the surrender to immediacy and the refusal to accept reality, become signs for the Unworldly Man as contrasted with Prince Hal who represents worldliness at its best.

At his best, the worldly man is one who dedicates his life to some public end, politics, science, industry, art, etc. The end is outside himself, but the choice of end is determined by the particular talents with which nature has endowed him, and the proof that he has chosen rightly is worldly success. To dedicate one's life to an end for which one is not endowed is madness, the madness of Don Quixote. Strictly speaking, he does not desire fame for himself, but to achieve something which merits fame. Because his end is worldly, that is, in the public domain—to marry the girl of one's choice, or to become a good parent, are private, not worldly, ends—the personal life and its satisfactions are, for the worldly man, of secondary importance and, should they ever conflict with his vocation, must be sacrificed. The worldly man at his best knows that other persons exist and desires that they should—a statesman has no wish to establish justice among tables and chairs—but if it is necessary to the achievement of his end to treat certain persons as if they were things, then, callously or regretfully, he will. What distinguishes him from the ordinary criminal is that the criminal lacks the imagination to conceive of others as being persons like himself; when he sacrifices others, he feels no guilt because, to the criminal, he is the only person in a world of things. What distinguishes both the worldly man and the criminal from the wicked man is their lack of malice. The wicked man is not worldly, but anti-worldly. His conscious end is nothing less than the destruction of others. He is obsessed by hatred at his knowledge that other persons exist besides himself and cannot rest until he has reduced them all to the status of things.

But it is not always easy to distinguish the worldly man from the criminal or the wicked man by observing their behavior and its results. It can happen, for instance, that, despite his intention, a wicked man does good. Don John in *Much Ado About Nothing* certainly means nothing but harm to Claudio and Hero, yet it is thanks to him that Claudio obtains insight into his own shortcomings and becomes, what previously he was not, a fit husband for Hero. To the outward eye, however different their subjective intentions, both Harry of Monmouth and Iago deceive and destroy. Even in their speech one cannot help noticing a certain resemblance between

> So when this loose behaviour I throw off
> And pay the debt I never promised,
> By how much better than my word I am.
> I'll so offend to make offence a skill
> Redeeming time when men least think I will.

and:

> From when my outward action doth demonstrate
> The native act and figure of my heart
> In compliment extern, 'tis not long after
> But I will wear my heart upon my sleeve
> For daws to peck at. I am not what I am. . . .

and the contrast of both to Sonnet 121:

> No, I am that I am; and they that level
> At my abuses reckon up their own.
> I may be straight though they themselves be bevel.

Falstaff is perfectly willing to tell the world: "I am that I am, a drunken old failure." Hal cannot jeopardize his career by such careless disclosure but must always assume whatever manner is politic at the moment. To the degree that we have worldly ambitions, Falstaff's verdict on the Prince strikes home.

> Thou art essentially mad without seeming so.

Falstaff never really does anything, but he never stops talking, so that the impression he makes on the audience is not of idleness but of infinite energy. He is never tired, never bored, and until he is rejected he radiates happiness as Hal radiates power, and this happiness without apparent cause, this untiring devotion to making others laugh becomes a comic image for a love which is absolutely self-giving.

Laughing and loving have certain properties in common. Laughter is contagious but not, like physical force, irresistible. A man in a passion of any kind cannot be made to laugh; if he laughs, it is a proof that he has already mastered his passion. Laughter is an action only in a special sense. Many kinds of action can cause laughter, but the only kind of action that laughter causes is more laughter; while we laugh, time stops and no other kind of action can be contemplated. In rage or hysteria people sometimes are said to "laugh" but no one can confuse the noises they make with the sound of real laughter. Real laughter is absolutely unaggressive; we cannot wish people or things we find amusing to be other than they are; we do not desire to change them, far less hurt or destroy them. An angry and dangerous mob is rendered harmless by the orator who can succeed in making it laugh. Real laughter is always, as we say, "disarming."

Falstaff makes the same impression on us that the Sinner of Lublin made upon his rabbi.

> In Lublin lived a great sinner. Whenever he went to talk to the rabbi, the rabbi readily consented and conversed with him as if he were a man of integrity and one who was a close friend. Many of the hasidim were annoyed at this and one said to the other: "Is it possible that our rabbi who has only to look once into a man's face to know his life from first to last, to know the very origin of his soul, does not see that this fellow is a sinner? And if he does see it, that he considers him worthy to speak to and associate with." Finally they summoned up courage to go to the rabbi himself with their question. He answered them: "I know all about him as well as you. But you know how I love gaiety and hate dejection. And this man is so great a sinner. Others repent the moment they have sinned, are sorry for a moment, and then return to their folly. But he knows no regrets and no doldrums, and lives in his happiness as in a tower. And it is the radiance of his happiness that overwhelms my heart."

Falstaff's happiness is almost an impregnable tower, but not quite. "I am that I am" is not a complete self-description; he must also add—"The young prince hath misled me. I am the fellow with the great belly, and he is my dog."

The Christian God is not a self-sufficient being like Aristotle's First Cause, but a God who creates a world which he continues to love although it refuses to love him in return. He appears in this world, not as Apollo or Aphrodite might appear, disguised as a man so that no mortal should recognize his divinity, but as a real man who openly claims to be God. And the consequence is inevitable. The highest religious and temporal authorities condemn Him as a blasphemer and a Lord of Misrule, as a Bad Companion for mankind.

Inevitable because, as Richelieu said, "The salvation of States is in this world," and history has not as yet provided us with any evidence that the Prince of this world has changed his character.

Interlude: The Wish Game

Were some fanatic to learn the whole of Proust by heart, word for word, and then try reciting it to an audience in a drawing room after dinner, the chances are, I fancy, that within half an hour most of the audience would have fallen asleep, and their verdict upon *Remembrance of Things Past* would be that it was a boring and incomprehensible story. The difficulty of judging fairly a printed folk tale, still more a collection of tales* that were never intended to be grasped through the eye, is just as great. Our feeling for orally transmitted literature is distorted by the peculiar nature of the only literature of this class that is still alive—for us the spoken tale is the unprintable tale—but it is possible, even in the smoking-room story, to perceive some of the characteristics common to all storytelling. To begin with, both the occasion of the telling and the voice and gestures of the teller are important elements in the effect; the story that has delighted us on one occasion may, in a different context and told by a different speaker, fail utterly to amuse. Then, the ear is much slower in comprehending than the eye, far less avid of novelty, and far more appreciative of rhythmical repetition.

Folk tales have also suffered from certain preconceived ideas on the part of the general public. They are commonly thought of as being either entertainment for children or documents for adult anthropologists and students of comparative religion. Children enjoy them, it is true, but that is no reason why grownups, for whom they were primarily intended, should assume that they are childish. They undoubtedly contain elements drawn from ancient rituals and myths, but a knowledge of such things is no more essential to appreciating them than a knowledge of the reading and personal experience of a modern novelist is essential to enjoying his novels.

A religious rite is a serious matter, an act that must be done in exactly the right way in order to secure supernatural aid, without which the crops will fail and men die. A myth almost always contains playful elements, but it claims to answer a serious question—how did such-and-such come to be?— and to some degree or other demands to be believed. But a tale is to be told only if someone wishes to hear it, and the one question it presupposes is, "How are we to spend a pleasant evening?" As the soldier-narrator of "John-of-the-Bear" says:

---

* *The Borzoi Book of French Folk Tales*, edited by Paul Delarue.

I go through a forest where there is no woods, through a river where
there is no water, through a village where there is no house. I knock at
a door and everybody answers me. The more I tell you, the more I shall
lie to you. I'm not paid to tell you the truth.

"The Doctor and His Pupil" contains a motif common to many folk tales—
that of one character pursuing another through a series of magical metamor-
phoses. The hunted turns into a hare, whereupon the hunter turns into a
dog, whereupon the hare becomes a lark, whereupon the dog becomes an
eagle, and so on. The primal source of this idea is probably a ritual fertility
dance in which the twelve months were symbolically mimed. In such a rite, if
it existed, the symbolical animals would be fixed in number and kind and the
worshipers would know in advance what they were, but a tale that makes use
of the notion can use any beasts, and any number of them it pleases, provided
that the pairs logically match. If the storyteller makes the hunted one a hare,
he cannot make the hunter a donkey; if he wants the hunter to be a donkey,
then he must make the hunted something like a carrot. The pleasure of the
audience is that of suspense, pattern and surprise, so that at each transformation it wonders, "How will the hunted get out of that one?" Similarly, the
motif of the Virgin and the Seven-Headed Dragon in "The Three Dogs and
the Dragon" and "The Miller's Three Sons" may well be derived from the
myth of Perseus and Andromeda, but there is no apparent attempt to relate
these tales to any historical event or person. Questions of religion and history,
however interesting and important, are not the business of the literary critic.
He can only ask the questions he would ask of any work of literature, e.g. what
kind of writing is this, as compared with other kinds? What are its special virtues and its special limitations? Judged by its own intentions, what makes one
tale or one version of a tale better or worse than another?

One characteristic that clearly differentiates the fairy tale from other kinds
of narrative is the nature of the fairy-tale hero. The epic hero is one who,
thanks to his exceptional gifts, is able to perform great deeds of which the
average man is incapable. He is of noble (often divine) descent, stronger,
braver, better looking, more skillful than everybody else. A stranger meeting
him in the street would immediately recognize him as a hero. Some of his
adventures may be sexual, he may marry, but such matters are incidental to
his main object, which is to win immortal fame. Even when he is transformed
into the knight-errant in whose life the ladies play a great role, his honor is
still more important than his love.

Like the epic hero, the fairy story hero performs great and seemingly impossible deeds, but there the resemblance ends. He may be by birth a prince,
but, if so, he is, as it were, a prince of the first generation, for he never possesses, as the epic hero always does, a genealogical tree. More commonly,
however, he is the child of poor parents and starts his life at the very bottom

of the social scale. He is not recognizable as a hero except in the negative sense—that he is the one who to the outward eye appears, of all people, the least likely to succeed. Often he is a child, lacking even the strength and wit of the ordinary adult, and nearly always his relatives and neighbors consider him stupid and lacking in ambition. The virtue by which he succeeds when others fail is the very un-militant virtue of humble good nature. He is the one who stops to share his crust with the old beggar woman or free the trapped beast, thereby securing magical aid, when his proud and impatient rivals pass by and in consequence come to grief. The fairy-story world is purely Calvinist. That is to say, the hero's deeds cannot be called *his*; without magical assistance he would be totally helpless. Officially, he is a lover, not a warrior, who desires glory and treasure only in order that he may deserve the hand of the princess, but no fairy-story character, either in speech or in behavior, shows real erotic feeling. We find neither outright sexual passion nor sentimental *Frauendienst*. Fairy-story "love" is not an emotion but a formal principle, one of the rules by which the story game is played. If the fairy-story hero differs from the epic hero in having no visible *arete*, he differs also from the hero of the modern novel in that he has no hidden qualities that are in time revealed. As a character, he is the same person at the end that he was at the beginning; all that has changed is his status. Nothing that happens to him can be called personally significant in the sense that, thanks to it, his awareness of himself is altered.

Since the characters in a fairy story are either good or bad, benevolent or malevolent—it is rare for a bad character to repent and unknown for a good one to become bad—they cannot be said to be tempted. There are occasions when the hero (or heroine), though warned not to do something—not to pick up a wig or enter a particular room—ignores the warning and gets into trouble, but the prohibited act is never, in itself, immoral. There is only one fairy-tale motif, to my knowledge, that contains an element of inner conflict: the theme of Grimm's "Faithful John" and M. Delarue's "Father Roquelaure." The Prince's loyal servant learns by chance that, in order to save his master, he must do things which will appear to be evil, and that if he explains the reason he will be turned to stone. He does them and—under threat of death or because he cannot bear his master's displeasure—he tells and is turned to stone. The Prince then discovers that to restore his faithful servant he must sacrifice his own child.

In other kinds of fiction, the plot evolves through the clash between fate or chance on the one side and will and desire on the other; the fairy story is peculiar in that the main cause of any event is a wish. A desire is a real and given experience of a human individual in a particular historical context. I am not free to choose what desire I shall feel, nor can I choose the goal that will satisfy it; if the desire is real, it proposes its own satisfaction. When I desire, I know what I want. I am then free to choose either to remain in a state of unsatisfied desire by refusing to assent to its demands or to use my reason and will to satisfy it. A wish, on the other hand, is not given; I am free to wish anything I choose, but the cause of all wishes is the same—that which is should not be. If I say, "I desire to eat," I do not mean, "I desire not to be hungry," for if I were not hungry I should not desire to eat. When a scolded child says to a parent, "I wish you were dead," he does not mean what he actually says; he only means, "I wish I were not what I am, a child being scolded by you," and a hundred other wishes would have done equally well. If the young heir to the fortune of a disagreeable old aunt says, "I wish she were dead," he may really desire her death, but his wish does not express this desire; its real content is, "I wish that my conscience and the law did not, as they do, forbid murder." We can wish anything we choose precisely because all wishes are equally impossible, for all substitute an imaginary present for the real one. A world in which all wishes were magically granted would be a world without desire or will, for every moment of time would be disjunct and there would be no way of distinguishing between animate and inanimate beings, animals and men.

Wishing is not the sole cause of events in the fairy tale but the license it is given prevents the fairy tale from arousing any strong emotions in the audience. This, however, is one of the peculiar pleasures the fairy story affords—that it can take images of beautiful maidens or cannibalistic ogres who, in our dreams, arouse violent emotions of desire or terror, or it can inflict horrible punishments on the wicked (like rolling them downhill in a barrel full of nails) which in real life would be acts of sadism, and make them all *playful.*

A game, of course, must have rules if it is not to be purely arbitrary and meaningless, and the characters in the fairy tale have a "fate" to which even their wishes must submit. They must obey, for instance, the laws of language. We can lie in language, that is to say, manipulate the world as we wish, but the lie must make sense as a grammatical proposition:

> "What are you doing there, good woman?" he asked.
> "I'd like to take some sunshine home, a whole wheelbarrowful, but it's difficult, for as soon as I get it in the shade it vanishes."
> "What do you want a wheelbarrowful of sunshine for?"
> "It's to warm my little boy who is at home half dead from cold."

The other law, so often introduced in the fairy tale, which all must obey is the law of numerical series. The hero who is set three tasks cannot wish them into two or four.

It would be misleading to say that because the fairy tale world is a fantastic one, such literature is "escapist." A work may justly be condemned as escapist only if it claims to portray the real world when in fact its portrait is false. But the fairy story never pretends to be a picture of the real world, and even if its audience were to respond with the feeling, "How I wish we could live in this world instead of the world we have to live in" (and I very much doubt that any audience ever felt this way), it would always know that such a wish was impossible. The kind of enjoyment the fairy tale can provide is similar, I believe, to that provided by the poems of Mallarmé or by abstract painting.

M. Delarue's collection of French folk tales includes versions of several stories that are also to be found in Grimm. A comparison of the one with the other may help to show the qualities we look for in a folk tale and by which we judge it:

The Lost Children — Hansel and Gretel

In their respective openings, the German version is superior both in richness of detail and in dramatic suspense. The French version lacks the conflict between the bad mother and the kind but weak father, and the children do not overhear their conversation, so the drama of the pebbles and the crumbs is lacking. The French children climb a tree, see a white house and a red house, and choose to go to the red house, which, of course, turns out to be the wrong choice, but we never learn what the white house is. This is a violation of one of the laws of storytelling, namely, that everything introduced must be accounted for. In the central part of the story, the French version replaces the witch in her edible house with the Devil and his wife on an ordinary farm, and the children succeed in killing the Devil's wife while he is taking a walk. There is a loss, perhaps, in beauty of imagery but a gain in character interest. In its conclusion, the French version is much superior. In the German version, Hansel and Gretel merely wander through the forest till they come to a river, which they are ferried across by a duck. The presence and nature of the duck are not explained, nor is any reason given why there should be a river between them and their home that they did not have to cross when they set out. But in the French version, the Devil pursues the runaways and his pursuit is punctuated by a ritual verse dialogue between him and those he meets. They all fool him and finally cause him to be drowned in a river that he is told the children have crossed, though in fact they have simply gone home.

The Godchild of the Fairy in the Tower — Rapunzel

In the German version, the witch learns about the Prince from the girl herself, in the French from a talking bitch she has left to keep watch on the girl, a variation that is more interesting and more logical. But the unhappy ending of the French version—the witch turns the girl into a frog and grows a pig's snout on the Prince—seems to me an artistic mistake. In the playful world of the fairy story, all problems, including that of moral justice, must be solved. When a fairy story ends unhappily, we do not feel that we have been told an unpleasant truth; we merely feel that the story has been broken off in the middle.

The Story of Grandmother — Little Red Riding Hood

M. Delarue tells us in his notes that the Grimm story is largely derived from Perrault. The French oral version he prints is infinitely superior to either, and a model of what a folk tale should be:

There was once a woman who had some bread, and she said to her daughter: "You are going to carry a hot loaf and a bottle of milk to your grandmother."

The little girl departed. At the crossroads she met the *bzou*, who said to her: "Where are you going?"

"I'm taking a hot loaf and a bottle of milk to my grandmother."

"What road are you taking," said the *bzou*, "the Needles Road or the Pins Road?"

"The Needles Road," said the little girl.

"Well, I shall take the Pins Road."

The little girl enjoyed herself, picking up needles. Meanwhile the *bzou* arrived at her grandmother's, killed her, put some of her flesh in the pantry and a bottle of her blood on the shelf. The girl arrived and knocked at the door.

"Push the door," said the *bzou*, "it's closed with a wet straw."

"Hello, Grandmother; I'm bringing you a hot loaf and a bottle of milk."

"Put them in the pantry. You eat the meat that's in it and drink a bottle of wine that is on the shelf."

As she ate there was a little cat that said: "A slut is she who eats the flesh and drinks the blood of her grandmother!"

"Undress, my child," said the *bzou*, "and come and sleep beside me."

"Where should I put my apron?"

"Throw it in the fire, my child; you don't need it any more."

And she asked where to put all the other garments, the bodice, the dress, the skirt, and the hose, and the wolf replied: "Throw them into the fire, my child; you will need them no more."

"Oh, Grandmother, how hairy you are!"

"It's to keep me warmer, my child."

"Oh, Grandmother, those long nails you have!"

"It's to scratch me better, my child."

"Oh, Grandmother, those big shoulders you have!"

"All the better to carry kindling from the woods, my child."

"Oh, Grandmother, those big ears you have!"

"All the better to hear with, my child."

"Oh, Grandmother, that big mouth you have!"

"All the better to eat you with, my child!"

"Oh, Grandmother, I need to go outside to relieve myself."

"Do it in the bed, my child."

"No, Grandmother, I want to go outside."

"All right, but don't stay long."

The *bzou* tied a woollen thread to her feet and let her go out, and when the little girl was outside she tied the end of the string to a big plum tree in the yard. The *bzou* got impatient and said: "Are you making cables?"

When he became aware that no one answered him, he jumped out of bed and saw that the little girl had escaped. He followed her, but he arrived at the house just at the moment that she was safely inside.

Brothers & Others

> The possible redemption from the predicament of irreversibility—of being unable to undo what one has done—is the faculty of forgiving. The remedy for unpredictability, for the chaotic uncertainty of the future, is contained in the faculty to make and keep promises. Both faculties depend upon plurality, on the presence and acting of others, for no man can forgive himself and no one can be bound by a promise made only to himself. —Hannah Arendt

The England which Shakespeare presents in *Richard II* and *Henry IV* is a society in which wealth, that is to say, social power, is derived from ownership of land, not from accumulated capital. The only person who is in need of money is the King who must equip troops to defend the country against foreign foes. If, like Richard II, he is an unjust king, he spends the money which should have been spent on defense in maintaining a luxurious and superfluous court. Economically, the country is self-sufficient, and production is for use, not profit. The community-forming bond in this England is either the family tie of common blood which is given by nature or the feudal tie of lord and vassal created by personal oath. Both are commitments to individuals and both are lifelong commitments. But this type of community tie is presented as being ill suited to the needs of England as a functioning society. If England is to function properly as a society, the community based on personal loyalty must be converted into a community united by a common love of impersonal justice, that is to say, of the King's Law which is no respecter of persons. We are given to understand that in Edward III's day, this kind of community already existed, so that the family type of community is seen as a regression. Centuries earlier, a war between Wessex and Mercia, for example, would have been regarded as legitimate as a war between England and

France, but now a conflict between a Percy and a Bolingbroke is regarded as
a civil war, illegitimate because between brothers. It is possible, therefore, to
apply a medical analogy to England and speak of a sick body politic, because
it is as obvious who are aliens and who ought to be brothers as it is obvious
which cells belong to my body and which to the body of another. War, as
such, is not condemned but is still considered, at least for the gentry, a normal and enjoyable occupation like farming. Indeed peace, as such, carries
with it the pejorative associations of idleness and vice.

> Now all the youth of England are on fire
> And silken dalliance in the wardrobe lies.
> Now thrive the Armourers and Honour's thought
> Reigns solely in the breast of every man.
> They sell the pasture now to buy the horse.

The only merchants who appear in *Henry IV* are the "Bacon-fed Knaves and
Fat Chuffs" whom Falstaff robs, and they are presented as contemptible
physical cowards.

In *The Merchant of Venice* and *Othello* Shakespeare depicts a very different
kind of society. Venice does not produce anything itself, either raw materials
or manufactured goods. Its existence depends upon the financial profits
which can be made by international trade,

> . . . the trade and profit of the city
> Consisteth of all nations

that is to say, on buying cheaply here and selling dearly there, and its wealth
lies in its accumulated money capital. Money has ceased to be simply a convenient medium of exchange and has become a form of social power which
can be gained or lost. Such a mercantile society is international and cosmopolitan; it does not distinguish between the brother and the alien other than
on a basis of blood or religion—from the point of view of society, customers
are brothers, trade rivals others. But Venice is not simply a mercantile society; it is also a city inhabited by various communities with different loves—
Gentiles and Jews, for example—who do not regard each other personally as
brothers, but must tolerate each other's existence because both are indispensable to the proper functioning of their society, and this toleration is
enforced by the laws of the Venetian state.

A change in the nature of wealth from landownership to money capital
radically alters the social conception of time. The wealth produced by land
may vary from year to year—there are good harvests and bad—but, in the
long run its average yield may be counted upon. Land, barring dispossession
by an invader or confiscation by the State, is held by a family in perpetuity.
In consequence, the social conception of time in a landowning society is cyclical—the future is expected to be a repetition of the past. But in a mercan-

tile society time is conceived of as unilinear forward movement in which the future is always novel and unpredictable. (The unpredictable event in a landowning society is an Act of God, that is to say, it is not "natural" for an event to be unpredictable.) The merchant is constantly taking risks—if he is lucky, he may make a fortune, if he is unlucky he may lose everything. Since, in a mercantile society, social power is derived from money, the distribution of power within it is constantly changing, which has the effect of weakening reverence for the past; who one's distant ancestors were soon ceases to be of much social importance. The oath of lifelong loyalty is replaced by the contract which binds its signatories to fulfill certain specific promises by a certain specific future date, after which their commitment to each other is over.

The action of *The Merchant of Venice* takes place in two locations, Venice and Belmont, which are so different in character that to produce the play in a manner which will not blur this contrast and yet preserve a unity is very difficult. If the spirit of Belmont is made too predominant, then Antonio and Shylock will seem irrelevant, and vice versa. In *Henry IV*, Shakespeare intrudes Falstaff, who by nature belongs to the world of *opera buffa*, into the historical world of political chronicle with which his existence is incompatible, and thereby, consciously or unconsciously, achieves the effect of calling in question the values of military glory and temporal justice as embodied in Henry of Monmouth. In *The Merchant of Venice* he gives us a similar contrast—the romantic fairy story world of Belmont is incompatible with the historical reality of money-making Venice—but this time what is called in question is the claim of Belmont to be the Great Good Place, the Earthly Paradise. Watching *Henry IV*, we become convinced that our aesthetic sympathy with Falstaff is a profounder vision than our ethical judgment which must side with Hal. Watching *The Merchant of Venice*, on the other hand, we are compelled to acknowledge that the attraction which we naturally feel towards Belmont is highly questionable. On that account, I think *The Merchant of Venice* must be classed among Shakespeare's "Unpleasant Plays."

Omit Antonio and Shylock, and the play becomes a romantic fairy tale like *A Midsummer Night's Dream*. The world of the fairy tale is an unambiguous, unproblematic world in which there is no contradiction between outward appearance and inner reality, a world of being, not becoming. A character may be temporarily disguised—the unlovely animal is really the Prince Charming under a spell, the hideous old witch transforms herself into a lovely young girl to tempt the hero—but this is a mask, not a contradiction: the Prince is *really* handsome, the witch *really* hideous. A fairy story character may sometimes change, but, if so, the change is like a mutation; at one moment he or she is this kind of person, at the next he is transformed into that kind. It is a world in which people are either good or bad by nature; occasionally a bad character repents, but a good character never becomes bad. It is meaningless therefore to ask why a character in a fairy tale acts as he does because his nature will only allow him to act in one way. It is a world in which, ultimately, good fortune is the sign of moral goodness, ill fortune of moral badness. The good are beautiful, rich and speak with felicity, the bad are ugly, poor and speak crudely.

In real life we can distinguish between two kinds of choice, the strategic and the personal. A strategic choice is conditioned by a future goal which is already known to the chooser. I wish to catch a certain train which will be leaving in ten minutes. I can either go by subway or take a taxi. It is the rush hour, so I have to decide which I believe will get me sooner to the station. My choice may turn out to be mistaken, but neither I nor an observer will have any difficulty in understanding the choice I make. But now and again, I take a decision which is based, not on any calculation of its future consequences, for I cannot tell what they will be, but upon my immediate conviction that, whatever the consequences, I must do this now. However well I know myself, I can never understand completely why I take such a decision, and to others it will always seem mysterious. The traditional symbol in Western Literature for this kind of personal choice is the phenomenon of falling-in-love. But in the fairy-tale world, what appear to be the personal choices of the characters are really the strategic choices of the storyteller, for within the tale the future is predestined. We watch Portia's suitors choosing their casket, but we know in advance that Morocco and Arragon cannot choose the right one and that Bassanio cannot choose the wrong one, and we know this, not only from what we know of their characters but also from their ordinal position in a series, for the fairy-tale world is ruled by magical numbers. Lovers are common enough in fairy tales, but love appears as a pattern-forming principle rather than sexual passion as we experience it in the historical world. The fairy tale cannot tolerate intense emotions of any kind, because any intense emotion has tragic possibilities, and even the possibility of tragedy is excluded from the fairy tale. It is possible to imagine the serious passion of Romeo and Juliet having a happy ending instead of a tragic one, but it is impossible to imagine either of them in Oberon's Wood or the Forest of Arden.

The fairy tale is hospitable to black magicians as well as to white; ogres, witches, bogeys are constantly encountered who have their temporary victories but in the end are always vanquished by the good and banished, leaving Arcadia to its unsullied innocent joy where the good live happily ever after. But the malevolence of a wicked character in a fairy tale is a given premise; their victims, that is to say, never bear any responsibility for the malice, have never done the malevolent one an injury. The Devil, by definition malevolent without a cause, is presented in the medieval miracle plays as a fairy-story bogey, never victorious but predestined to be cheated of his prey.

Recent history has made it utterly impossible for the most unsophisticated and ignorant audience to ignore the historical reality of the Jews and think of

them as fairy-story bogeys with huge noses and red wigs. An Elizabethan audience undoubtedly still could—very few of them had seen a Jew—and, if Shakespeare had so wished, he could have made Shylock grotesquely wicked like the
Jew of Malta. The star actors who, from the eighteenth century onwards have
chosen to play the role, have not done so out of a sense of moral duty in order
to combat anti-Semitism, but because their theatrical instinct told them that
the part, played seriously, not comically, offered them great possibilities.

The Merchant of Venice is, among other things, as much a "problem" play as
one by Ibsen or Shaw. The question of the immorality or morality of usury
was a sixteenth century issue on which both the theologians and the secular
authorities were divided. Though the majority of medieval theologians had
condemned usury, there had been, from the beginning, divergence of opinion as to the correct interpretation of Deuteronomy, XXIII, vv. 19–20:

> Thou shalt not lend upon usury to thy brother; usury of money, usury of
> victuals, usury of any thing that is lent upon usury: Unto a stranger thou
> mayest lend upon usury

and Leviticus XXV, vv. 35–37 which proscribe the taking of usury, not only
from a fellow Jew, but also from the stranger living in their midst and under
their protection.

Some Christian theologians had interpreted this to mean that, since the
Christians had replaced the Jews as God's Chosen, they were entitled to
exact usury from non-Christians.*

> Who is your brother? He is your sharer in nature, co-heir in grace, every
> people, which, first, is in the faith, then under the Roman Law. Who,
> then, is the stranger? the foes of God's people. From him, demand usury
> whom you rightly desire to harm, against whom weapons are lawfully
> carried. Upon him usury is legally imposed. Where there is the right of
> war, there also is the right of usury. (St Ambrose.)

Several centuries later, St Bernard of Siena, in a statement of which the sanctity seems as doubtful as the logic, takes St Ambrose's argument even further.

> Temporal goods are given to men for the worship of the true God and
> the Lord of the Universe. When, therefore, the worship of God does not
> exist, as in the case of God's enemies, usury is lawfully exacted, because
> this is not done for the sake of gain, but for the sake of the Faith; and
> the motive is brotherly love, namely, that God's enemies may be weak-
> ened and so return to Him; and further because the goods they have do
> not belong to them, since they are rebels against the true faith; they
> shall therefore devolve upon the Christians.

---

*N.B. For the quotations which follow, I am indebted to Benjamin Nelson's fascinating book
The Idea of Usury, Princeton University Press.

The majority, however, starting from the Gospel command that we are to treat all men, even our enemies, as brothers, held that the Deuteronomic permission was no longer valid, so that under no circumstances was usury permissible. Thus, St Thomas Aquinas, who was also, no doubt, influenced by Aristotle's condemnation of usury, says:

> The Jews were forbidden to take usury from their brethren, i.e. from other Jews. By this we are given to understand that to take usury from any man is simply evil, because we ought to treat every man as our neighbor and brother, especially in the state of the Gospel whereto we are called. They were permitted, however, to take usury from foreigners, not as though it were lawful, but in order to avoid a greater evil, lest to wit, through avarice to which they were prone, according to Isaiah LVI, VII, they should take usury from Jews, who were worshippers of God.

On the Jewish side, talmudic scholars had some interesting interpretations. Rashi held that the Jewish debtor is forbidden to pay interest to a fellow Jew, but he may pay interest to a Gentile. Maimonides, who was anxious to prevent Jews from being tempted into idolatry by associating with Gentiles, held that a Jew might borrow at usury from a Gentile, but should not make loans to one, on the ground that debtors are generally anxious to avoid their creditors, but creditors are obliged to seek the company of debtors.

Had Shakespeare wished to show Shylock the usurer in the most unfavorable light possible, he could have placed him in a medieval agricultural society, where men become debtors through misfortunes, like a bad harvest or sickness for which they are not responsible, but he places him in a mercantile society, where the role played by money is a very different one.

When Antonio says:

> I neither lend nor borrow
> By taking or by giving of excess

he does not mean that, if he goes into partnership with another merchant contributing, say, a thousand ducats to their venture, and their venture makes a profit, he only asks for a thousand ducats back. He is a merchant and the Aristotelian argument that money is barren and cannot breed money, which he advances to Shylock, is invalid in his own case.

This change in the role of money had already been recognized by both Catholic and Protestant theologians. Calvin, for example, had come to the conclusion that the Deuteronomic injunction had been designed to meet a particular political situation which no longer existed.

> The law of Moses is political and does not obligate us beyond what equity and the reason of humanity suggest. There is a difference in the political union, for the situation in which God placed the Jews and

many circumstances permitted them to trade conveniently among themselves without usuries. Our union is entirely different. Therefore I do not feel that usuries are forbidden to us simply, except in so far as they are opposed to equity and charity.

The condemnation of usury by Western Christendom cannot be understood except in relation to the severity of its legal attitude, inherited from Roman Law, towards the defaulting debtor. The pound of flesh story has a basis in historical fact for, according to the Law of the Twelve Tables, a defaulting debtor could be torn to pieces alive. In many medieval contracts the borrower agreed, in the case of default, to pay double the amount of the loan as a forfeit, and imprisonment for debt continued into the nineteenth century. It was possible to consider interest on a loan immoral because the defaulting debtor was regarded as a criminal, that is to say, an exception to the human norm, so that lending was thought of as normally entailing no risk. One motive which led the theologians of the sixteenth century to modify the traditional theories about usury and to regard it as a necessary social evil rather than as a mortal sin was their fear of social revolution and the teachings of the Anabaptists and other radical Utopians. These, starting from the same premise of Universal Brotherhood which had been the traditional ground for condemning usury, drew the conclusion that private property was unchristian, that Christians should share all their goods in common, so that the relation of creditor to debtor would be abolished. Thus, Luther, who at first had accused Catholic theologians of being lax towards the sin of usury, by 1524, was giving this advice to Prince Frederick of Saxony:

> It is highly necessary that the taking of interest should be regulated everywhere, but to abolish it entirely would not be right either, for it can be made just. I do not advise your Grace, however, to support people in their refusal to pay interest or to prevent them from paying it, for it is not a burden laid upon people by a Prince in his law, but it is a common plague that all have taken upon themselves. We must put up with it, therefore, and hold debtors to it and not let them spare themselves and seek a remedy of their own, but put them on a level with everybody else, as love requires.

Shylock is a Jew living in a predominantly Christian society, just as Othello is a Negro living in a predominantly white society. But, unlike Othello, Shylock rejects the Christian community as firmly as it rejects him. Shylock and Antonio are at one in refusing to acknowledge a common brotherhood.

> I will buy with you, sell with you, talk with you, walk with you, and so following, but I will not eat with you, drink with you, nor pray with you.
> (Shylock)

> I am as like
> To spit on thee again, to spurn thee, too.
> If thou wilt lend this money, lend it not
> As to thy friends . . .
> But lend it rather to thine enemy,
> Who if he break, thou mayst with better face
> Exact the penalty. (Antonio)

In addition, unlike Othello, whose profession of arms is socially honorable, Shylock is a professional usurer who, like a prostitute, has a social function but is an outcast from the community. But, in the play, he acts unprofessionally; he refuses to charge Antonio interest and insists upon making their legal relation that of debtor and creditor, a relation acknowledged as legal by all societies. Several critics have pointed to analogies between the trial scene and the medieval *Processus Belial* in which Our Lady defends man against the prosecuting Devil who claims the legal right to man's soul. The Roman doctrine of the Atonement presupposes that the debtor deserves no mercy—Christ may substitute Himself for man, but the debt has to be paid by death on the cross. The Devil is defeated, not because he has no right to demand a penalty, but because he does not know that the penalty has been already suffered. But the differences between Shylock and Belial are as important as their similarities. The comic Devil of the mystery play can appeal to logic, to the letter of the law, but he cannot appeal to the heart or to the imagination, and Shakespeare allows Shylock to do both. In his "Hath not a Jew eyes . . ." speech in Act III, Scene 1, he is permitted to appeal to the sense of human brotherhood, and in the trial scene, he is allowed to argue, with a sly appeal to the fear a merchant class has of radical social revolution:

> You have among you many a purchased slave
> Which, like your asses and your dogs and mules,
> You use in abject and in slavish parts,

which points out that those who preach mercy and brotherhood as universal obligations limit them in practice and are prepared to treat certain classes of human beings as things.

Furthermore, while Belial is malevolent without any cause except love of malevolence for its own sake, Shylock is presented as a particular individual living in a particular kind of society at a particular time in history. Usury, like prostitution, may corrupt the character, but those who borrow upon usury, like those who visit brothels, have their share of responsibility for this corruption and aggravate their guilt by showing contempt for those whose services they make use of.

It is, surely, in order to emphasize this point that, in the trial scene, Shakespeare introduces an element which is not found in *Pecorone* or other versions of the pound-of-flesh-story. After Portia has trapped Shylock through his own insistence upon the letter of the law of Contract, she produces another law by which any alien who conspires against the life of a Venetian citizen forfeits his goods and places his life at the Doge's mercy. Even in the rush of a stage performance, the audience cannot help reflecting that a man as interested in legal subtleties as Shylock, would, surely, have been aware of the existence of this law and that, if by any chance he had overlooked it, the Doge surely would very soon have drawn his attention to it. Shakespeare, it seems to me, was willing to introduce what is an absurd implausibility for the sake of an effect which he could not secure without it: at the last moment when, through his conduct, Shylock has destroyed any sympathy we may have felt for him earlier, we are reminded that, irrespective of his personal character, his status is one of inferiority. A Jew is not regarded, even in law, as a brother.

If the wicked Shylock cannot enter the fairy story world of Belmont, neither can the noble Antonio, though his friend, Bassanio, can. In the fairy story world, the symbol of final peace and concord is marriage, so that, if the story is concerned with the adventures of two friends of the same sex, male or female, it must end with a double wedding. Had he wished, Shakespeare could have followed the *Pecorone* story in which it is Ansaldo, not Gratiano, who marries the equivalent of Nerissa. Instead, he portrays Antonio as a melancholic who is incapable of loving a woman. He deliberately avoids the classical formula of the Perfect Friends by making the relationship unequal. When Salanio says of Antonio's feelings for Bassanio

> I think he only loves the world for him

we believe it, but no one would say that Bassanio's affections are equally exclusive. Bassanio, high-spirited, elegant, pleasure-loving, belongs to the same world as Gratiano and Lorenzo; Antonio does not. When he says:

> I hold the world but as the world, Gratiano,
> A stage, where everyman must play a part,
> And mine a sad one

Gratiano may accuse him of putting on an act, but we believe him, just as it does not seem merely the expression of a noble spirit of self-sacrifice when he tells Bassanio:

> I am a tainted wether of the flock,
> Meetest for death; the weakest kind of fruit
> Drops earliest to the ground, and so let me.

It is well known that love and understanding breed love and understanding.

> The more people on high who comprehend each other, the more there are to love well, and the more love is there, and like a mirror, one giveth back to the other. (*Purgatorio*, XV)

So, with the rise of a mercantile economy in which money breeds money, it became an amusing paradox for poets to use the ignoble activity of usury as a metaphor for love, the most noble of human activities. Thus, in his Sonnets, Shakespeare uses usury as an image for the married love which begets children.

> Profitless usurer, why does thou use
> So great a sum of sums, yet canst not live?
> For having traffic with thyself alone
> Thou of thyself thy sweet self dost deceive.
>
> (Sonnet IV)

> That use is not forbidden usury
> Which happiest those that pay the willing loan,
> That's for thyself, to breed another thee,
> Or ten times happier, be it ten for one.
>
> (VI)

And, even more relevant, perhaps, to Antonio are the lines

> But since she pricked thee out for women's pleasure
> Mine be thy love, and thy love's use their treasure.
>
> (XXXIII)

There is no reason to suppose that Shakespeare had read Dante, but he must have been familiar with the association of usury with sodomy of which Dante speaks in the Ninth Canto of the Inferno.

> It behoves man to gain his bread and to prosper. And because the usurer takes another way, he contemns Nature in herself and her followers, placing elsewhere his hope. . . . And hence the smallest round seals with its mark Sodom and the Cahors. . . .

It can, therefore, hardly be an accident that Shylock the usurer has as his antagonist a man whose emotional life, though his conduct may be chaste, is concentrated upon a member of his own sex.

In any case, the fact that Bassanio's feelings are so much less intense makes Antonio's seem an example of that inordinate affection which theologians have always condemned as a form of idolatry, a putting of the creature before the creator. In the sixteenth century, suretyship, like usury, was a controversial issue. The worldly-wise condemned the standing surety for another on worldly grounds.

> Beware of standing suretyship for thy best friends; he that payeth another man's debts seeketh his own decay: neither borrow money of a neighbour or a friend, but of a stranger. (Lord Burghley)

Suffer not thyself to be wounded for other men's faults, or scourged for other men's offences, which is the surety for another: for thereby, millions of men have been beggared and destroyed. . . . from suretyship as from a manslayer or enchanter, bless thyself. (Sir Walter Raleigh)

And clerics like Luther condemned it on theological grounds.

Of his life and property a man is not certain for a single moment, any more than he is certain of the man for whom he becomes surety. Therefore the man who becomes surety acts unchristian like and deserves what he gets, because he pledges and promises what is not his and not in his power, but in the hands of God alone. . . . These sureties act as though their life and property were their own and were in their power as long as they wished to have it; and this is nothing but the fruit of unbelief. . . . If there were no more of this becoming surety, many a man would have to keep down and be satisfied with a moderate living, who now aspires night and day after high places, relying on borrowing and standing surety.

The last sentence of this passage applies very well to Bassanio. In *Pecorone*, the Lady of Belmonte is a kind of witch and Gianetto gets into financial difficulties because he is the victim of magic, a fate which is never regarded as the victim's fault. But Bassanio had often borrowed money from Antonio before he ever considered wooing Portia and was in debt, not through magic or unforeseeable misfortune, but through his own extravagances,

> 'Tis not unknown to you, Antonio,
> How much I have disabled my estate
> By something showing a more swelling port
> Than my faint means would grant continuance

and we feel that Antonio's continual generosity has encouraged Bassanio in his spendthrift habits. Bassanio seems to be one of those people whose attitude towards money is that of a child; it will somehow always appear by magic when really needed. Though Bassanio is aware of Shylock's malevolence, he makes no serious effort to dissuade Antonio from signing the bond because, thanks to the ever-open purse of his friend, he cannot believe that bankruptcy is a real possibility in life.

Shylock is a miser and Antonio is openhanded with his money; nevertheless, as a merchant, Antonio is equally a member of an acquisitive society. He is trading with Tripoli, the Indies, Mexico, England, and when Salanio imagines himself in Antonio's place, he describes a possible shipwreck thus:

> . . . the rocks
> Scatter all her spices on the stream,
> Enrobe the roaring waters with my silks.

The commodities, that is to say, in which the Venetian merchant deals are
not necessities but luxury goods, the consumption of which is governed not
by physical need but by psychological values like social prestige, so that there
can be no question of a Just Price. Then, as regards his own expenditure,
Antonio is, like Shylock, a sober merchant who practices economic absti-
nence. Both of them avoid the carnal music of this world. Shylock's attitude
towards the Masquers

> Lock up my doors and when you hear the drum
> And the vile squeaking of the wry-necked fife
> Clamber not you up the casement then,
> Let not the sound of shallow foppery enter
> My sober house

finds an echo in Antonio's words a scene later:

> Fie, fie, Gratiano. Where are all the rest?
> 'Tis nine o'clock: our friends all stay for you.
> No masque to-night—the wind is come about.

Neither of them is capable of enjoying the carefree happiness for which
Belmont stands. In a production of the play, a stage director is faced with the
awkward problem of what to do with Antonio in the last act. Shylock, the villain, has been vanquished and will trouble Arcadia no more, but, now that
Bassanio is getting married, Antonio, the real hero of the play, has no further dramatic function. According to the Arden edition, when Alan McKin-
non produced the play at the Garrick theatre in 1905, he had Antonio and
Bassanio hold the stage at the final curtain, but I cannot picture Portia, who
is certainly no Victorian doormat of a wife, allowing her bridegroom to let
her enter the house by herself. If Antonio is not to fade away into a nonentity, then the married couples must enter the lighted house and leave Antonio standing alone on the darkened stage, outside the Eden from which, not
by the choice of others, but by his own nature, he is excluded.

Without the Venice scenes, Belmont would be an Arcadia without any relation to actual times and places, and where, therefore, money and sexual love
have no reality of their own, but are symbolic signs for a community in a state
of grace. But Belmont is related to Venice though their existences are not
really compatible with each other. This incompatibility is brought out in a
fascinating way by the difference between Belmont time and Venice time.
Though we are not told exactly how long the period is before Shylock's loan
must be repaid, we know that it is more than a month. Yet Bassanio goes off
to Belmont immediately, submits immediately on arrival to the test of the
caskets, and has just triumphantly passed it when Antonio's letter arrives to
inform him that Shylock is about to take him to court and claim his pound
of flesh. Belmont, in fact, is like one of those enchanted palaces where time

stands still. But because we are made aware of Venice, the real city, where time is real, Belmont becomes a real society to be judged by the same standards we apply to any other kind of society. Because of Shylock and Antonio, Portia's inherited fortune becomes real money which must have been made in this world, as all fortunes are made, by toil, anxiety, the enduring and inflicting of suffering. Portia we can admire because, having seen her leave her Earthly Paradise to do a good deed in this world (one notices, incidentally, that in this world she appears in disguise), we know that she is aware of her wealth as a moral responsibility, but the other inhabitants of Belmont, Bassanio, Gratiano, Lorenzo and Jessica, for all their beauty and charm, appear as frivolous members of a leisure class, whose carefree life is parasitic upon the labors of others, including usurers. When we learn that Jessica has spent fourscore ducats of her father's money in an evening and bought a monkey with her mother's ring, we cannot take this as a comic punishment for Shylock's sin of avarice; her behavior seems rather an example of the opposite sin of conspicuous waste. Then, with the example in our minds of self-sacrificing love as displayed by Antonio, while we can enjoy the verbal felicity of the love duet between Lorenzo and Jessica, we cannot help noticing that the pairs of lovers they recall, Troilus and Cressida, Aeneas and Dido, Jason and Medea, are none of them examples of self-sacrifice or fidelity. Recalling that the inscription on the leaden casket ran, "Who chooseth me, must give and hazard all he hath," it occurs to us that we have seen two characters do this. Shylock, however unintentionally, did, in fact, hazard all for the sake of destroying the enemy he hated, and Antonio, however unthinkingly he signed the bond, hazarded all to secure the happiness of the friend he loved. Yet it is precisely these two who cannot enter Belmont. Belmont would like to believe that men and women are either good or bad by nature, but Shylock and Antonio remind us that this is an illusion: in the real world, no hatred is totally without justification, no love totally innocent.

As a society, Venice is more efficient and successful than Henry IV's England. Its citizens are better off, more secure and nicer mannered. Politically speaking, therefore, one may say that a mercantile society represents an advance upon a feudal society, as a feudal society represents an advance upon a tribal society. But every step forward brings with it its own dangers and evils for, the more advanced a social organization, the greater the moral demands it makes upon its members and the greater the degree of guilt which they incur if they fail to meet these demands. The members of a society with a primitive self-sufficient economy can think of those outside it as others, not brothers, with a good conscience, because they can get along by themselves. But, first, money and, then, machinery have created a world in which, irrespective of our cultural traditions and our religious or political convictions, we are all mutually dependent. This demands that we accept all other human

beings on earth as brothers, not only in law, but also in our hearts. Our temptation, of course, is to do just the opposite, not to return to tribal loyalties—
that is impossible—but, each of us, to regard everybody else on earth not
even as an enemy, but as a faceless algebraical cipher.

> They laid the coins before the council.
> Kay, the king's steward, wise in economics, said:
> "Good; these cover the years and the miles
> and talk one styles dialects to London and Omsk.
> Traffic can hold now and treasure be held,
> streams are bridged and mountains of ridged space
> tunnelled; gold dances deftly over frontiers.
> The poor have choice of purchase, the rich of rents,
> and events move now in a smoother control
> than the swords of lords or the orisons of nuns.
> Money is the medium of exchange."
>
> Taliessin's look darkened; his hand shook
> while he touched the dragons; he said "We had a good thought.
> Sir, if you made verse, you would doubt symbols.
> I am afraid of the little loosed dragons.
> When the means are autonomous, they are deadly; when words
> escape from verse they hurry to rape souls;
> when sensation slips from intellect, expect the tyrant;
> the brood of carriers levels the good they carry.
> We have taught our images to be free; are ye glad?
> are we glad to have brought convenient heresy to Logres?"
>
> The Archbishop answered the lords;
> his words went up through a slope of calm air:
> "Might may take symbols and folly make treasure,
> and greed bid God, who hides himself for man's pleasure
> by occasion, hide himself essentially: this abides—
> that the everlasting house the soul discovers
> is always another's; we must lose our own ends;
> we must always live in the habitation of our lovers,
> my friend's shelter for me, mine for him.
> This is the way of this world in the day of that other's;
> make yourselves friends by means of the riches of iniquity,
> for the wealth of the self is the health of the self exchanged.
> What saith Heraclitus?—and what is the City's breath?—
> *dying each other's life, living each other's death.*
> Money is a medium of exchange."
>   (Charles Williams, *Taliessin through Logres*)

Interlude: West's Disease

Nathanael West is not, strictly speaking, a novelist; that is to say, he does not attempt an accurate description either of the social scene or of the subjective life of the mind. For his first book, he adopted the dream convention, but neither the incidents nor the language are credible as a transcription of a real dream. For his other three, he adopted the convention of a social narrative; his characters need real food, drink and money, and live in recognizable places like New York or Hollywood, but, taken as feigned history, they are absurd. Newspapers do, certainly, have Miss Lonelyhearts columns; but in real life these are written by sensible, not very sensitive, people who conscientiously give the best advice they can, but do not take the woes of their correspondents home with them from the office, people, in fact, like Betty of whom Mr West's hero says scornfully:

> Her world was not the world and could never include the readers of his column. Her sureness was based on the power to limit experience arbitrarily. Moreover, his confusion was significant, while her order was not.

On Mr West's paper, the column is entrusted to a man the walls of whose room

> were bare except for an ivory Christ that hung opposite the foot of the bed. He had removed the figure from the cross to which it had been fastened and had nailed it to the walls with large spikes. . . . As a boy in his father's church, he had discovered that something stirred in him when he shouted the name of Christ, something secret and enormously powerful. He had played with this thing, but had never allowed it to come alive. He knew now what this thing was—hysteria, a snake whose scales were tiny mirrors in which the dead world takes on a semblance of life, and how dead the world is . . . a world of doorknobs.

It is impossible to believe that such a character would ever apply for a Miss Lonelyhearts job (in the hope, apparently, of using it as a stepping-stone to a gossip column), or that, if by freak chance he did, any editor would hire him.

Again, the occupational vice of the editors one meets is an overestimation of the social and moral value of what a newspaper does. Mr West's editor, Shrike, is a Mephisto who spends all his time exposing to his employees the meaninglessness of journalism:

> Miss Lonelyhearts, my friend, I advise you to give your readers stones. When they ask for bread don't give them crackers as does the Church, and don't, like the State, tell them to eat cake. Explain that man cannot

live by bread alone and give them stones. Teach them to pray each morning: "Give us this day our daily stone."

Such a man, surely, would not be a Feature Editor long.

A writer may concern himself with a very limited area of life and still convince us that he is describing the real world, but one becomes suspicious when, as in West's case, whatever world he claims to be describing, the dream life of a highbrow, lowbrow existence in Hollywood, or the American political scene, all these worlds share the same peculiar traits—no married couples have children, no child has more than one parent, a high percentage of the inhabitants are cripples, and the only kind of personal relation is the sadomasochistic.

There is, too, a curious resemblance among the endings of his four books.

His body broke free of the bard. It took on a life of its own; a life that knew nothing of the poet Balso. Only to death can this release be likened—the mechanics of decay. After death the body takes command; it performs the manual of disintegration with a marvelous certainty. So now, his body performed the evolutions of love with a like sureness. In this activity, Home and Duty, Love and Art were forgotten. . . . His body screamed and shouted as it marched and uncoiled; then with one heaving shout of triumph, it fell back quiet.

He was running to succor them with love. The cripple turned to escape, but he was too slow and Miss Lonelyhearts caught him. . . . The gun inside the package exploded and Miss Lonelyhearts fell, dragging the cripple with him. They both rolled part of the way down stairs.

"I am a clown," he began, "but there are times when even clowns must grow serious. This is such a time. I . . ." Lem got no further. A shot rang out and he fell dead, drilled through the heart by an assassin's bullet.

He was carried through the exit to the back street and lifted into a police car. The siren began to scream and at first he thought he was making the noise himself. He felt his lips with his hands. They were clamped tight. He knew then it was the siren. For some reason this made him laugh and he began to imitate the siren as loud as he could.

An orgasm, two sudden deaths by violence, a surrender to madness, are presented by West as different means for securing the same and desirable end, escape from the conscious Ego and its make-believe. Consciousness, it would seem, does not mean freedom to choose, but freedom to play a fantastic role, an unreality from which a man can only be delivered by some physical or mental explosion outside his voluntary control.

There are many admirable and extremely funny satirical passages in his books, but West is not a satirist. Satire presupposes conscience and reason as the judges between the true and the false, the moral and the immoral, to which it appeals, but for West these faculties are themselves the creators of unreality.

His books should, I think, be classified as Cautionary Tales, parables about a Kingdom of Hell whose ruler is not so much the Father of Lies as the Father of Wishes. Shakespeare gives a glimpse of this hell in *Hamlet*, and Dostoievsky has a lengthy description in *Notes from the Underground*, but they were interested in many hells and heavens. Compared with them, West has the advantages and disadvantages of the specialist who knows everything about one disease and nothing about any other. He was a sophisticated and highly skilled literary craftsman, but what gives all his books such a powerful and disturbing fascination, even *A Cool Million*, which must, I think, be judged a failure, owes nothing to calculation. West's descriptions of Inferno have the authenticity of firsthand experience: he has certainly been there, and the reader has the uncomfortable feeling that his was not a short visit.

All his main characters suffer from the same spiritual disease which, in honor of the man who devoted his life to studying it, we may call West's Disease. This is a disease of consciousness which renders it incapable of converting wishes into desires. A lie is false; what it asserts is not the case. A wish is fantastic; it knows what is the case but refuses to accept it. All wishes, whatever their apparent content, have the same and unvarying meaning: "I refuse to be what I am." A wish, therefore, is either innocent and frivolous, a kind of play, or a serious expression of guilt and despair, a hatred of oneself and every being one holds responsible for oneself.

Our subconscious life is a world ruled by wish but, since it is not a world of action, this is harmless; even nightmare is playful, but it is the task of consciousness to translate wish into desire. If, for whatever reason, self-hatred or self-pity, it fails to do this, it dooms a human being to a peculiar and horrid fate. To begin with, he cannot desire anything, for the present state of the self is the ground of every desire, and that is precisely what the wisher rejects. Nor can he believe anything, for a wish is not a belief; whatever he wishes he cannot help knowing that he could have wished something else. At first he may be content with switching from one wish to another:

> She would get some music on the radio, then lie down on her bed and shut her eyes. She had a large assortment of stories to choose from. After getting herself in the right mood, she would go over them in her mind as though they were a pack of cards, discarding one after another until she found one that suited. On some days she would run through the whole pack without making a choice. When that happened, she would either go down to Fine Street for an ice-cream soda or, if she were broke, thumb over the pack again and force herself to choose.

> While she admitted that her method was too mechanical for the best results and that it was better to slip into a dream naturally, she said that any dream was better than none and beggars couldn't be choosers.

But in time, this ceases to amuse, and the wisher is left with the despair which is the cause of all of them:

> When not keeping house, he sat in the back yard, called the patio by the real estate agent, in a broken down deck chair. In one of the closets he had found a tattered book and he held it in his lap without looking at it. There was a much better view to be had in any direction other than the one he faced. By moving his chair in a quarter circle he could have seen a large part of the canyon twisting down to the city below. He never thought of making this shift. From where he sat, he saw the closed door of the garage and a patch of its shabby, tarpaper roof.

A sufferer from West's Disease is not selfish but absolutely self-centered. A selfish man is one who satisfies his desires at other people's expense; for this reason, he tries to see what others are really like and often sees them extremely accurately in order that he may make use of them. But, to the self-centered man, other people only exist as images either of what he is or of what he is not, his feelings towards them are projections of the pity or the hatred he feels for himself and anything he does to them is really done to himself. Hence the inconsistent and unpredictable behavior of a sufferer from West's Disease: he may kiss your feet one moment and kick you in the jaw the next and, if you were to ask him why, he could not tell you.

In its final stages, the disease reduces itself to a craving for violent physical pain—this craving, unfortunately, can be projected onto others—for only violent pain can put an end to wishing *for* something and produce the real wish of necessity, the cry "Stop!"

All West's books contain cripples. A cripple is unfortunate and his misfortune is both singular and incurable. Hunchbacks, girls without noses, dwarfs, etc., are not sufficiently common in real life to appear as members of an unfortunate class, like the very poor. Each one makes the impression of a unique case. Further, the nature of the misfortune, a physical deformity, makes the victim repellent to the senses of the typical and normal, and there is nothing the cripple or others can do to change his condition. What attitude towards his own body can he have then but hatred? As used by West, the cripple is, I believe, a symbolic projection of the state of wishful self-despair, the state of those who will not accept themselves in order to change themselves into what they would or should become, and justify their refusal by thinking that being what they are is uniquely horrible and uncurable. To look at, Faye Greener is a pretty but not remarkable girl; in the eyes of Faye Greener, she is an exceptionally hideous spirit.

In saying that cripples have this significance in West's writing, I do not mean to say that he was necessarily aware of it. Indeed, I am inclined to think he was not. I suspect that, consciously, he thought pity and compassion were the same thing, but what the behavior of his "tender" characters shows is that all pity is self-pity and that he who pities others is incapable of compassion. Ruthlessly as he exposes his dreamers, he seems to believe that the only alternative to despair is to become a crook. Wishes may be unreal, but at least they are not, like all desires, wicked:

> His friends would go on telling such stories until they were too drunk to talk. They were aware of their childishness, but did not know how else to revenge themselves. At college, and perhaps for a year afterwards, they had believed in Beauty and in personal expression as an absolute end. When they lost this belief, they lost everything. Money and fame meant nothing to them. They were not worldly men.

The use of the word *worldly* is significant. West comes very near to accepting the doctrine of the Marquis de Sade—there are many resemblances between *A Cool Million* and *Justine*—to believing, that is, that the creation is essentially evil and that goodness is contrary to its laws, but his moral sense revolted against Sade's logical conclusion that it was therefore a man's duty to be as evil as possible. All West's "worldly" characters are bad men, most of them grotesquely bad, but here again his artistic instinct seems at times to contradict his conscious intentions. I do not think, for example, that he meant to make Wu Fong, the brothel-keeper, more sympathetic and worthy of respect than, say, Miss Lonelyhearts or Homer Simpson, but that is what he does:

> Wu Fong was a very shrewd man and a student of fashion. He saw that the trend was in the direction of home industry and home talent and when the Hearst papers began their "Buy American" campaign, he decided to get rid of all the foreigners in his employ and turn his establishment into a hundred percentum American place. He engaged Mr Asa Goldstein to redecorate the house and that worthy designed a Pennsylvania Dutch, Old South, Log Cabin Pioneer, Victorian New York, Western Cattle Days, Californian Monterey, Indian and Modern Girl series of interiors. . . .
>
> He was as painstaking as a great artist and in order to be consistent as one he did away with the French cuisine and wines traditional to his business. Instead, he substituted an American kitchen and cellar. When a client visited Lena Haubengruber, it was possible for him to eat roast groundhog and drink Sam Thompson rye. While with Alice Sweethorne, he was served sow belly with grits and bourbon. In Mary Judkins' rooms he received, if he so desired, fried squirrel and corn liquor. In the suite occupied by Patricia Van Riis, lobster and champagne were the

rule. The patrons of Powder River Rose usually ordered mountain oysters and washed them down with forty rod. And so on down the list. . . .

After so many self-centered despairers who cry in their baths or bare their souls in barrooms, a selfish man like this, who takes pride in doing something really well, even if it is running a brothel, seems almost a good man.

There have, no doubt, always been cases of West's Disease, but the chances of infection in a democratic and mechanized society like our own are much greater than in the more static and poorer societies of earlier times.

When, for most people, their work, their company, even their marriages, were determined, not by personal choice or ability, but by the class into which they were born, the individual was less tempted to develop a personal grudge against Fate; his fate was not his own but that of everyone around him.

But the greater the equality of opportunity in a society becomes, the more obvious becomes the inequality of the talent and character among individuals, and the more bitter and personal it must be to fail, particularly for those who have some talent but not enough to win them second or third place.

In societies with fewer opportunities for amusement, it was also easier to tell a mere wish from a real desire. If, in order to hear some music, a man has to wait for six months and then walk twenty miles, it is easy to tell whether the words, "I should like to hear some music," mean what they appear to mean, or merely, "At this moment I should like to forget myself." When all he has to do is press a switch, it is more difficult. He may easily come to believe that wishes can come true. This is the first symptom of West's Disease; the later symptoms are less pleasant, but nobody who has read Nathanael West can say that he wasn't warned.

The Joker in the Pack

Reason is God's gift; but so are the passions. Reason is as guilty as passion. —J. H. Newman

I

Any consideration of the Tragedy of Othello must be primarily occupied, not with its official hero but with its villain. I cannot think of any other play in which only one character performs personal actions—all the *deeds* are Iago's—and all the others without exception only exhibit behavior. In marrying each other, Othello and Desdemona have performed a deed, but this took place before the play begins. Nor can I think of another play in which the villain is so completely triumphant: everything Iago sets out to do, he accomplishes (among his goals, I include his self-destruction). Even Cassio, who survives, is maimed for life.

If *Othello* is a tragedy—and one certainly cannot call it a comedy—it is tragic in a peculiar way. In most tragedies the fall of the hero from glory to misery and death is the work, either of the gods, or of his own freely chosen acts, or, more commonly, a mixture of both. But the fall of Othello is the work of another human being; nothing he says or does originates with himself. In consequence we feel pity for him but no respect; our aesthetic respect is reserved for Iago.

Iago is a wicked man. The wicked man, the stage villain, as a subject of serious dramatic interest does not, so far as I know, appear in the drama of Western Europe before the Elizabethans. In the mystery plays, the wicked characters, like Satan or Herod, are treated comically, but the theme of the triumphant villain cannot be treated comically because the suffering he inflicts is real.

A distinction must be made between the villainous character-figures like Don John in *Much Ado*, Richard III, Edmund in *Lear*, Iachimo in *Cymbeline*—and the merely criminal character-figures like Duke Antonio in *The Tempest*, Angelo in *Measure for Measure*, Macbeth or Claudius in *Hamlet*. The criminal is a person who finds himself in a situation where he is tempted to break the law and succumbs to the temptation: he ought, of course, to have resisted the temptation, but everybody, both on stage and in the audience, must admit that, had they been placed in the same situation, they, too, would have been tempted. The opportunities are exceptional—Prospero, immersed in his books, has left the government of Milan to his brother, Angelo is in a position of absolute authority, Claudius is the Queen's lover, Macbeth is egged on by prophecies and heaven-sent opportunities, but the desire for a dukedom or a crown or a chaste and beautiful girl are desires which all can imagine themselves feeling.

The villain, on the other hand, is shown from the beginning as being a malcontent, a person with a general grudge against life and society. In most cases this is comprehensible because the villain has, in fact, been wronged by Nature or Society: Richard III is a hunchback, Don John and Edmund are bastards. What distinguishes their actions from those of the criminal is that, even when they have something tangible to gain, this is a secondary satisfaction; their primary satisfaction is the infliction of suffering on others, or the exercise of power over others against their will. Richard does not really desire Anne; what he enjoys is successfully wooing a lady whose husband and father-in-law he has killed. Since he has persuaded Gloucester that Edgar is a would-be parricide, Edmund does not need to betray his father to Cornwall and Regan in order to inherit. Don John has nothing personally to gain from ruining the happiness of Claudio and Hero except the pleasure of seeing them unhappy. Iachimo is a doubtful case of villainy. When he and Post-humus make their wager, the latter warns him:

> If she remain unseduced, you not making it appear otherwise, for your ill opinion and th'assault you have made on her chastity you shall an-swer me with your sword.

To the degree that his motive in deceiving Posthumus is simply physical fear of losing his life in a duel, he is a coward, not a villain; he is only a villain to the degree that his motive is the pleasure of making and seeing the innocent suffer. Coleridge's description of Iago's actions as "motiveless malignancy" applies in some degree to all the Shakespearian villains. The adjective *motive-less* means, firstly, that the tangible gains, if any, are clearly not the principal motive and, secondly, that the motive is not the desire for personal revenge upon another for a personal injury. Iago himself proffers two reasons for wishing to injure Othello and Cassio. He tells Roderigo that, in appointing Cassio to be his lieutenant, Othello has treated him unjustly, in which con-versation he talks like the conventional Elizabethan malcontent. In his solil-oquies with himself, he refers to his suspicion that both Othello and Cassio have made him a cuckold, and here he talks like the conventional jealous husband who desires revenge. But there are, I believe, insuperable objec-tions to taking these reasons, as some critics have done, at their face value. If one of Iago's goals is to supplant Cassio in the lieutenancy, one can only say that his plot fails for, when Cassio is cashiered, Othello does not appoint Iago in his place. It is true that, in Act III, Scene 3, when they swear blood-brotherhood in revenge, Othello concludes with the words

> . . . now art thou my lieutenant

to which Iago replies:

> I am your own for ever

but the use of the word *lieutenant* in this context refers, surely, not to a public military rank, but to a private and illegal delegation of authority—the job delegated to Iago is the secret murder of Cassio, and Iago's reply, which is a mocking echo of an earlier line of Othello's, refers to a relation which can never become public. The ambiguity of the word is confirmed by its use in the first line of the scene which immediately follows. Desdemona says

> Do you know, sirrah, where the Lieutenant Cassio lies?

(One should beware of attaching too much significance to Elizabethan ty-pography, but it is worth noting that Othello's lieutenant is in lower case and Desdemona's in upper). As for Iago's jealousy, one cannot believe that a seri-ously jealous man could behave towards his wife as Iago behaves towards Emilia, for the wife of a jealous husband is the first person to suffer. Not only is the relation of Iago and Emilia, as we see it on stage, without emotional tension, but also Emilia openly refers to a rumor of her infidelity as something already disposed of.

> Some such squire it was
> That turned your wit, the seamy side without
> And made you to suspect me with the Moor.

At one point Iago states that, in order to revenge himself on Othello, he will not rest till he is even with him, wife for wife, but, in the play, no attempt at Desdemona's seduction is made. Iago does not make an assault on her virtue himself, he does not encourage Cassio to make one, and he even prevents Roderigo from getting anywhere near her.

Finally, one who seriously desires personal revenge desires to reveal himself. The revenger's greatest satisfaction is to be able to tell his victim to his face—"You thought you were all-powerful and untouchable and could injure me with impunity. Now you see that you were wrong. Perhaps you have forgotten what you did; let me have the pleasure of reminding you."

When at the end of the play, Othello asks Iago in bewilderment why he has thus ensnared his soul and body, if his real motive were revenge for having been cuckolded or unjustly denied promotion, he could have said so, instead of refusing to explain.

In Act II, Scene 1, occur seven lines which, taken in isolation, seem to make Iago a seriously jealous man.

> Now I do love her too,
> Not out of absolute lust (though peradventure
> I stand accountant for as great a sin)
> But partly led to diet my revenge
> For that I do suspect the lusty Moor
> Hath leaped into my seat; the thought whereof
> Doth like a poisonous mineral gnaw my vitals.

But if spoken by an actor with serious passion, these lines are completely at variance with the rest of the play, including Iago's other lines on the same subject.

> And it is thought abroad, that twixt my sheets
> He's done my office: I know not if't be true
> Yet I, for mere suspicion in that kind,
> Will do, as if for surety.

It is not inconceivable, given the speed at which he wrote, that, at some point in the composition of *Othello*, Shakespeare considered making Iago seriously jealous and, like his prototype in Cinthio, a would-be seducer of Desdemona, and that, when he arrived at his final conception of Iago, he overlooked the incompatibility of the *poisonous mineral* and the *wife-for-wife* passages with the rest.

In trying to understand Iago's character one should begin, I believe, by asking why Shakespeare should have gone to the trouble of inventing Roderigo, a character who has no prototype in Cinthio. From a stage director's point of view, Roderigo is a headache. In the first act we learn that Brabantio had forbidden him the house, from which we must conclude that Desdemona had met him and disliked him as much as her father. In the second act, in order that the audience shall know that he has come to Cyprus, Roderigo has to arrive on the same ship as Desdemona, yet she shows no embarrassment in his presence. Indeed, she and everybody else, except Iago, seem unaware of his existence, for Iago is the only person who ever speaks a word to him. Presumably, he has some official position in the army, but we are never told what it is. His entrances and exits are those of a puppet: whenever Iago has company, he obligingly disappears, and whenever Iago is alone and wishes to speak to him, he comes in again immediately.

Moreover, so far as Iago's plot is concerned, there is nothing Roderigo does which Iago could not do better without him. He could easily have found another means, like an anonymous letter, of informing Brabantio of Desdemona's elopement and, for picking a quarrel with a drunken Cassio, he has, on his own admission, other means handy.

> Three lads of Cyprus, noble swelling spirits
> That hold their honour in a wary distance,
> The very elements of this warlike isle
> Have I to-night flustered with flowing cups.

Since Othello has expressly ordered him to kill Cassio, Iago could have murdered him without fear of legal investigation. Instead, he not only chooses as an accomplice a man whom he is cheating and whose suspicions he has constantly to allay, but also a man who is plainly inefficient as a murderer and also holds incriminating evidence against him.

A man who is seriously bent on revenge does not take unnecessary risks nor confide in anyone whom he cannot trust or do without. Emilia is not, as in Cinthio, Iago's willing accomplice, so that, in asking her to steal the handkerchief, Iago is running a risk, but it is a risk he has to take. By involving Roderigo in his plot, he makes discovery and his own ruin almost certain. It is a law of drama that, by the final curtain, all secrets, guilty or innocent, shall have been revealed so that all, on both sides of the footlights, know who did or did not do what, but usually the guilty are exposed either because, like Edmund, they repent and confess or because of events which they could not reasonably have foreseen. Don John could not have foreseen that Dogberry and Verges would overhear Borachio's conversation, nor Iachimo that Pisanio would disobey Posthumus' order to kill Imogen, nor King Claudius the intervention of a ghost.

Had he wished, Shakespeare could easily have contrived a similar kind of exposure for Iago. Instead, by giving Roderigo the role he does, he makes Iago as a plotter someone devoid of ordinary worldly common sense.

One of Shakespeare's intentions was, I believe, to indicate that Iago desires self-destruction as much as he desires the destruction of others but, before elaborating on this, let us consider Iago's treatment of Roderigo, against whom he has no grievance—it is he who is injuring Roderigo—as a clue to his treatment of Othello and Cassio.

When we first see Iago and Roderigo together, the situation is like that in a Ben Jonson comedy—a clever rascal is gulling a rich fool who deserves to be gulled because his desire is no more moral than that of the more intelligent avowed rogue who cheats him out of his money. Were the play a comedy, Roderigo would finally realize that he had been cheated but would not dare appeal to the law because, if the whole truth were made public, he would cut a ridiculous or shameful figure. But, as the play proceeds, it becomes clear that Iago is not simply after Roderigo's money, a rational motive, but that his main game is Roderigo's moral corruption, which is irrational because Roderigo has given him no cause to desire his moral ruin. When the play opens, Roderigo is shown as a spoiled weakling, but no worse. It may be foolish of him to hope to win Desdemona's affection by gifts and to employ a go-between, but his conduct is not in itself immoral. Nor is he, like Cloten in *Cymbeline*, a brute who regards women as mere objects of lust. He is genuinely shocked as well as disappointed when he learns of Desdemona's marriage, but continues to admire her as a woman full of most blessed condition. Left to himself, he would have had a good bawl, and given her up. But Iago will not let him alone. By insisting that Desdemona is seducible and that his real rival is not Othello but Cassio, he brings Roderigo to entertain the idea, originally foreign to him, of becoming a seducer and of helping Iago to ruin Cassio. Iago had had the pleasure of making a timid conventional man become aggressive and criminal. Cassio beats up Roderigo. Again, at this point, had he been left to himself, he would have gone no further, but Iago will not let him alone until he consents to murder Cassio, a deed which is contrary to his nature, for he is not only timid but also incapable of passionate hatred.

> I have no great devotion to the deed:
> And yet he has given me satisfying reasons.
> 'Tis but a man gone.

Why should Iago want to do this to Roderigo? To me, the clue to this and to all Iago's conduct is to be found in Emilia's comment when she picks up the handkerchief.

> My wayward husband hath a hundred times
> Wooed me to steal it . . .
>   what he'll do with it
> Heaven knows, not I,
> I nothing but to please his fantasy.

As his wife, Emilia must know Iago better than anybody else does. She does not know, any more than the others, that he is malevolent, but she does know that her husband is addicted to practical jokes. What Shakespeare gives us in Iago is a portrait of a practical joker of a peculiarly appalling kind, and perhaps the best way of approaching the play is by a general consideration of the Practical Joker.

II

Social relations, as distinct from the brotherhood of a community, are only possible if there is a common social agreement as to which actions or words are to be regarded as serious means to a rational end and which are to be regarded as play, as ends in themselves. In our culture, for example, a policeman must be able to distinguish between a murderous street fight and a boxing match, or a listener between a radio play in which war is declared and a radio news-broadcast announcing a declaration of war.

Social life also presupposes that we may believe what we are told unless we have reason to suppose, either that our informant has a serious motive for deceiving us, or that he is mad and incapable himself of distinguishing between truth and falsehood. If a stranger tries to sell me shares in a gold mine, I shall be a fool if I do not check up on his statements before parting with my money, and if another tells me that he has talked with little men who came out of a flying saucer, I shall assume that he is crazy. But if I ask a stranger the way to the station, I shall assume that his answer is truthful to the best of his knowledge, because I cannot imagine what motive he could have for misdirecting me.

Practical jokes are a demonstration that the distinction between seriousness and play is not a law of nature but a social convention which can be broken, and that a man does not always require a serious motive for deceiving another.

Two men, dressed as city employees, block off a busy street and start digging it up. The traffic cop, motorists and pedestrians assume that this familiar scene has a practical explanation—a water main or an electric cable is being repaired—and make no attempt to use the street. In fact, however, the two diggers are private citizens in disguise who have no business there.

All practical jokes are anti-social acts, but this does not necessarily mean that all practical jokes are immoral. A moral practical joke exposes some flaw in society which is a hindrance to a real community or brotherhood. That it should be possible for two private individuals to dig up a street without being stopped is a just criticism of the impersonal life of a large city where most people are strangers to each other, not brothers; in a village where all the inhabitants know each other personally, the deception would be impossible.

A real community, as distinct from social life, is only possible between persons whose idea of themselves and others is real, not fantastic. There is, therefore, another class of practical jokes which is aimed at particular individuals with the reformatory intent of de-intoxicating them from their illusions. This kind of joke is one of the stock devices of comedy. The deceptions practiced on Falstaff by Mistress Page, Mistress Ford and Dame Quickly, or by Octavian on Baron Ochs are possible because these two gentlemen have a fantastic idea of themselves as lady-charmers; the result of the jokes played upon them is that they are brought to a state of self-knowledge and this brings mutual forgiveness and true brotherhood. Similarly, the mock deaths of Hero and of Hermione are ways of bringing home to Claudio and to Leontes how badly they have behaved and of testing the genuineness of their repentance.

All practical jokes, friendly, harmless or malevolent, involve deception, but not all deceptions are practical jokes. The two men digging up the street, for example, might have been two burglars who wished to recover some swag which they knew to be buried there. But, in that case, having found what they were looking for, they would have departed quietly and never been heard of again, whereas, if they are practical jokers, they must reveal afterwards what they have done or the joke will be lost. The practical joker must not only deceive but also, when he has succeeded, unmask and reveal the truth to his victims. The satisfaction of the practical joker is the look of astonishment on the faces of others when they learn that all the time they were convinced that they were thinking and acting on their own initiative, they were actually the puppets of another's will. Thus, though his jokes may be harmless in themselves and extremely funny, there is something slightly sinister about every practical joker, for they betray him as someone who likes to play God behind the scenes. Unlike the ordinary ambitious man who strives for a dominant position in public and enjoys giving orders and seeing others obey them, the practical joker desires to make others obey him without being aware of his existence until the moment of his theophany when he says: "Behold the God whose puppets you have been and behold, he does not look like a god but is a human being just like yourselves." The success of a practical joker depends upon his accurate estimate of the weaknesses of others, their ignorances, their social reflexes, their unquestioned presuppositions, their obsessive desires, and even the most harmless practical joke is an expression of the joker's contempt for those he deceives.

But, in most cases, behind the joker's contempt for others lies something else, a feeling of self-insufficiency, of a self lacking in authentic feelings and desires of its own. The normal human being may have a fantastic notion of himself, but he believes in it; he thinks he knows who he is and what he wants so that he demands recognition by others of the value he puts upon himself and must inform others of what he desires if they are to satisfy them.

But the self of the practical joker is unrelated to his joke. He manipulates others but, when he finally reveals his identity, his victims learn nothing about his nature, only something about their own; they know how it was possible for them to be deceived but not why he chose to deceive them. The only answer that any practical joker can give to the question: "Why did you do this?" is Iago's: "Demand me nothing. What you know, you know."

In fooling others, it cannot be said that the practical joker satisfies any concrete desire of his nature; he has only demonstrated the weaknesses of others and all he can now do, once he has revealed his existence, is to bow and retire from the stage. He is only related to others, that is, so long as they are unaware of his existence; once they are made aware of it, he cannot fool them again, and the relation is broken off.

The practical joker despises his victims, but at the same time he envies them because their desires, however childish and mistaken, are real to them, whereas he has no desire which he can call his own. His goal, to make game of others, makes his existence absolutely dependent upon theirs; when he is alone, he is a nullity. Iago's self-description, *I am not what I am*, is correct and the negation of the Divine *I am that I am*. If the word motive is given its normal meaning of a positive purpose of the self like sex, money, glory, etc., then the practical joker is without motive. Yet the professional practical joker is certainly driven, like a gambler, to his activity, but the drive is negative, a fear of lacking a concrete self, of being nobody. In any practical joker to whom playing such jokes is a passion, there is always an element of malice, a projection of his self-hatred onto others, and in the ultimate case of the absolute practical joker, this is projected onto all created things. Iago's statement, "I am not what I am," is given its proper explanation in the *Credo* which Boito wrote for him in his libretto for Verdi's opera.

> Credo in un Dio crudel che m'ha creato
> Simile a se, e che nell'ira io nomo.
> Dalla viltà d'un germe o d'un atomo
> Vile son nato,
> Son scellerato
> Perchè son uomo:
> E sento il fango originario in me
> E credo l'uom gioco d'iniqua sorte
> Dal germe della culla
> Al verme dell'avel.

Vien dopo tanto irrision la Morte
E poi? La Morte è il Nulla.

Equally applicable to Iago is Valéry's *"Ébauche d'un Serpent."* The serpent speaks to God the Creator thus

O Vanité! Cause Première
Celui qui règne dans les Cieux
D'une voix qui fut la lumière
Ouvrit l'univers spacieux.
Comme las de son pur spectacle
Dieu lui-même a rompu l'obstacle
De sa parfaite éternité;
Il se fit Celui qui dissipe
En conséquences son Principe,
En étoiles son Unité.

And of himself thus

Je suis Celui qui modifie

the ideal motto, surely, for Iago's coat of arms.

Since the ultimate goal of Iago is nothingness, he must not only destroy others, but himself as well. Once Othello and Desdemona are dead his "occupation's gone."

To convey this to an audience demands of the actor who plays the role the most violent contrast in the way he acts when Iago is with others and the way he acts when he is left alone. With others, he must display every virtuoso trick of dramatic technique for which great actors are praised, perfect control of movement, gesture, expression, diction, melody and timing, and the ability to play every kind of role, for there are as many "honest" Iagos as there are characters with whom he speaks, a Roderigo Iago, a Cassio Iago, an Othello Iago, a Desdemona Iago, etc. When he is alone, on the other hand, the actor must display every technical fault for which bad actors are criticized. He must deprive himself of all stage presence, and he must deliver the lines of his soliloquies in such a way that he makes nonsense of them. His voice must lack expression, his delivery must be atrocious, he must pause where the verse calls for no pauses, accentuate unimportant words, etc.

III

If Iago is so alienated from nature and society that he has no relation to time and place—he could turn up anywhere at any time—his victims are citizens of Shakespeare's Venice. To be of dramatic interest, a character must to some degree be at odds with the society of which he is a member, but his estrangement is normally an estrangement from a specific social situation.

Shakespeare's Venice is a mercantile society, the purpose of which is not military glory but the acquisition of wealth. However, human nature being what it is, like any other society, it has enemies, trade rivals, pirates, etc., against whom it must defend itself, if necessary by force. Since a mercantile society regards warfare as a disagreeable, but unfortunately sometimes unavoidable, activity and not, like a feudal aristocracy, as a form of play, it replaces the old feudal levy by a paid professional army, nonpolitical employees of the State, to whom fighting is their specialized job.

In a professional army, a soldier's military rank is not determined by his social status as a civilian, but by his military efficiency. Unlike the feudal knight who has a civilian home from which he is absent from time to time but to which, between campaigns, he regularly returns, the home of the professional soldier is an army camp and he must go wherever the State sends him. Othello's account of his life as a soldier, passed in exotic landscapes and climates, would have struck Hotspur as unnatural, unchivalrous and no fun.

A professional army has its own experiences and its own code of values which are different from those of civilians. In *Othello*, we are shown two societies, that of the city of Venice proper and that of the Venetian army. The only character who, because he is equally estranged from both, can simulate being equally at home in both, is Iago. With army folk he can play the blunt soldier, but in his first scene with Desdemona upon their arrival in Cyprus, he speaks like a character out of *Love's Labour's Lost.* Cassio's comment

Madam, you may relish him more in the soldier than the scholar

is provoked by envy. Iago has excelled him in the euphuistic flirtatious style of conversation which he considers his forte. Roderigo does not feel at home, either with civilians or with soldiers. He lacks the charm which makes a man a success with the ladies, and the physical courage and heartiness which make a man popular in an army mess. The sympathetic aspect of his character, until Iago destroys it, is a certain humility; he knows that he is a person of no consequence. But for Iago, he would have remained a sort of Bertie Wooster, and one suspects that the notion that Desdemona's heart might be softened by expensive presents was not his own but suggested to him by Iago.

In deceiving Roderigo, Iago has to overcome his consciousness of his inadequacy, to persuade him that he could be what he knows he is not, charming, brave, successful. Consequently, to Roderigo and, I think, to Roderigo only, Iago tells direct lies. The lie may be on a point of fact, as when he tells Roderigo that Othello and Desdemona are not returning to Venice but going to Mauritania, or a lie about the future, for it is obvious that, even if Desdemona is seducible, Roderigo will never be the man. I am inclined to think that the story Iago tells Roderigo about his disappointment over the licutenancy is a deliberate fabrication. One notices, for example, that he contradicts himself. At first he claims that Othello had appointed Cassio in spite of the request of three great ones of the city who had recommended Iago, but then a few lines later, he says

> Preferment goes by letter and affection,
> Not by the old gradation where each second
> Stood heir to the first.

In deceiving Cassio and Othello, on the other hand, Iago has to deal with characters who consciously think well of themselves but are unconsciously insecure. With them, therefore, his tactics are different; what he says to them is always possibly true.

Cassio is a ladies' man, that is to say, a man who feels most at home in feminine company where his looks and good manners make him popular, but is ill at ease in the company of his own sex because he is unsure of his masculinity. In civilian life he would be perfectly happy, but circumstances have made him a soldier and he has been forced by his profession into a society which is predominantly male. Had he been born a generation earlier, he would never have found himself in the army at all, but changes in the technique of warfare demand of soldiers, not only the physical courage and aggressiveness which the warrior has always needed, but also intellectual gifts. The Venetian army now needs mathematicians, experts in the science of gunnery. But in all ages, the typical military mentality is conservative and resents the intellectual expert.

> A fellow
> That never set a squadron in the field
> Nor the division of a battle knows
> More than a spinster . . . mere prattle without practise
> Is all his soldiership

is a criticism which has been heard in every army mess in every war. Like so many people who cannot bear to feel unpopular and therefore repress their knowledge that they are, Cassio becomes quarrelsome when drunk, for alcohol releases his suppressed resentment at not being admired by his comrades in arms and his wish to prove that he is what he is not, as "manly" as they are. It is significant that, when he sobers up, his regret is not that he has behaved badly by his own standards but that he has lost his reputation. The advice which Iago then gives him, to get Desdemona to plead for him with Othello, is good advice in itself, for Desdemona obviously likes him, but it is also exactly the advice a character-type like Cassio will be most willing to listen to, for feminine society is where he feels most at home.

Emilia informs Cassio that, on her own initiative, Desdemona has already spoken on his behalf and that Othello has said he will take the safest occasion by the front to restore him to his post. Hearing this, many men would have been content to leave matters as they were, but Cassio persists; the pleasure of a heart-to-heart talk with a lady about his fascinating self is too tempting.

While he is talking to Desdemona, Othello is seen approaching and she says:

> Stay and hear me speak.

Again, many men would have done so, but Cassio's uneasiness with his own sex, particularly when he is in disgrace, is too strong and he sneaks away, thus providing Iago with his first opportunity to make an insinuation.

Cassio is a ladies' man, not a seducer. With women of his own class, what he enjoys is socialized eroticism; he would be frightened of a serious personal passion. For physical sex he goes to prostitutes and when, unexpectedly, Bianca falls in love with him, like many of his kind, he behaves like a cad and brags of his conquest to others. Though he does not know who the owner of the handkerchief actually is, he certainly knows that Bianca will think that it belongs to another woman, and to ask her to copy it is gratuitous cruelty. His smiles, gestures and remarks about Bianca to Iago are insufferable in themselves; to Othello, who knows that he is talking about a woman, though he is mistaken as to her identity, they are an insult which only Cassio's death can avenge.

In Cinthio nothing is said about the Moor's color or religion, but Shakespeare has made Othello a black Negro who has been baptized.

No doubt there are differences between color prejudice in the twentieth century and color prejudice in the seventeenth and probably few of Shakespeare's audience had ever seen a Negro, but the slave trade was already flourishing and the Elizabethans were certainly no innocents to whom a Negro was simply a comic exotic. Lines like

> . . . an old black ram
> Is tupping your white ewe . . .
> The gross clasps of a lascivious Moor . . .
> What delight shall she have to look on the devil

are evidence that the paranoid fantasies of the white man in which the Negro appears as someone who is at one and the same time less capable of self-control and more sexually potent than himself, fantasies with which, alas, we are only too familiar, already were rampant in Shakespeare's time.

The Venice of both *The Merchant of Venice* and *Othello* is a cosmopolitan society in which there are two kinds of social bond between its members, the bond of economic interest and the bond of personal friendship, which may coincide, run parallel with each other or conflict, and both plays are concerned with an extreme case of conflict.

Venice needs financiers to provide capital and it needs the best general it can hire to defend it; it so happens that the most skillful financier it can find is a Jew and the best general a Negro, neither of whom the majority are willing to accept as a brother.

Though both are regarded as outsiders by the Venetian community, Othello's relation to it differs from Shylock's. In the first place, Shylock rejects the Gentile community as firmly as the Gentile community rejects him; he is just as angry when he hears that Jessica has married Lorenzo as Brabantio is about Desdemona's elopement with Othello. In the second place, while the profession of usurer, however socially useful, is regarded as ignoble, the military profession, even though the goal of a mercantile society is not military glory, is still highly admired and, in addition, for the sedentary civilians who govern the city, it has a romantic exotic glamour which it cannot have in a feudal society in which fighting is a familiar shared experience.

Thus no Venetian would dream of spitting on Othello and, so long as there is no question of his marrying into the family, Brabantio is delighted to entertain the famous general and listen to his stories of military life. In the army, Othello is accustomed to being obeyed and treated with the respect due to his rank and, on his rare visits to the city, he is treated by the white aristocracy as someone important and interesting. Outwardly, nobody treats him as an outsider as they treat Shylock. Consequently, it is easy for him to persuade himself that he is accepted as a brother and when Desdemona accepts him as a husband, he seems to have proof of this.

It is painful to hear him say

> But that I love the gentle Desdemona
> I would not my unhoused free condition
> Put into circumscription or confine
> For the sea's worth

for the condition of the outsider is always unhoused and free. He does not or will not recognize that Brabantio's view of the match

> If such actions may have passage free,
> Bond-slaves and pagans shall our statesmen be

is shared by all his fellow senators, and the arrival of news about the Turkish fleet prevents their saying so because their need of Othello's military skill is too urgent for them to risk offending him.

If one compares *Othello* with the other plays in which Shakespeare treats the subject of male jealousy, *The Winter's Tale* and *Cymbeline*, one notices that Othello's jealousy is of a peculiar kind.

Leontes is a classical case of paranoid sexual jealousy due to repressed homosexual feelings. He has absolutely no evidence that Hermione and Polixenes have committed adultery and his entire court are convinced of their innocence, but he is utterly possessed by his fantasy. As he says to Hermione: "Your actions are my dreams." But, mad as he is, "the twice-nine changes of the Watery Starre" which Polixenes has spent at the Bohemian court, make the act of adultery physically possible so that, once the notion has entered his head, neither Hermione nor Polixenes nor the court can prove that it is false. Hence the appeal to the Oracle.

Posthumus is perfectly sane and is convinced against his will that Imogen has been unfaithful because Iachimo offers him apparently irrefutable evidence that adultery has taken place.

But both the mad Leontes and the sane Posthumus react in the same way; "My wife has been unfaithful; therefore she must be killed and forgotten." That is to say, it is only as husbands that their lives are affected. As king of Bohemia, as a warrior, they function as if nothing has happened.

In *Othello*, thanks to Iago's manipulations, Cassio and Desdemona behave in a way which would make it not altogether unreasonable for Othello to suspect that they were in love with each other, but the time factor rules out the possibility of adultery having been actually committed. Some critics have taken the double time in the play to be merely a dramaturgical device for speeding the action which the audience in the theatre will never notice. I believe, however, that Shakespeare meant the audience to notice it as, in *The Merchant of Venice*, he meant them to notice the discrepancy between Belmont time and Venice time.

If Othello had simply been jealous of the feelings for Cassio he imagined Desdemona to have, he would have been sane enough, guilty at worst of a lack of trust in his wife. But Othello is not merely jealous of feelings which might exist; he demands proof of an act which could not have taken place, and the effect on him of believing in this physical impossibility goes far beyond wishing to kill her: it is not only his wife who has betrayed him but the whole universe; life has become meaningless, his occupation is gone.

This reaction might be expected if Othello and Desdemona were a pair like Romeo and Juliet or Antony and Cleopatra whose love was an all-absorbing Tristan-Isolde kind of passion, but Shakespeare takes care to inform us that it was not.

When Othello asks leave to take Desdemona with him to Cyprus, he stresses the spiritual element in his love.

> I therefore beg it not
> To please the palate of my appetite
> Nor to comply with heat, the young affects
> In me defunct, and proper satisfaction,
> But to be free and bounteous of her mind.

Though the imagery in which he expresses his jealously is sexual—what other kind of images could he use?—Othello's marriage is important to him

less as a sexual relationship than as a symbol of being loved and accepted as
a person, a brother in the Venetian community. The monster in his own
mind too hideous to be shown is the fear he has so far repressed that he is
only valued for his social usefulness to the City. But for his occupation, he
would be treated as a black barbarian.

The overcredulous, overgood-natured character which, as Iago tells us,
Othello had always displayed is a telltale symptom. He had *had* to be overcredulous in order to compensate for his repressed suspicions. Both in his
happiness at the beginning of the play and in his cosmic despair later,
Othello reminds one more of Timon of Athens than of Leontes.

Since what really matters to Othello is that Desdemona should love him as
the person he really is, Iago has only to get him to suspect that she does not,
to release the repressed fears and resentments of a lifetime, and the question
of what she has done or not done is irrelevant.

Iago treats Othello as an analyst treats a patient except that, of course, his
intention is to kill not to cure. Everything he says is designed to bring to
Othello's consciousness what he has already guessed is there. Accordingly,
he has no need to tell lies. Even his speech, "I lay with Cassio lately," can be
a truthful account of something which actually happened: from what we
know of Cassio, he might very well have such a dream as Iago reports. Even
when he has worked Othello up to a degree of passion where he would risk
nothing by telling a direct lie, his answer is equivocal and its interpretation
is left to Othello.

> OTHELLO. What hath he said?
> IAGO. Faith that he did—I know not what he did.
> OTHELLO. But what?
> IAGO. Lie—
> OTHELLO. With her?
> IAGO. With her, on her, what you will.

Nobody can offer Leontes absolute proof that his jealousy is baseless; similarly, as Iago is careful to point out, Othello can have no proof that Desdemona really is the person she seems to be.

Iago makes his first decisive impression when, speaking as a Venetian with
firsthand knowledge of civilian life, he draws attention to Desdemona's hood-
winking of her father.

> IAGO. I would not have your free and noble nature
>   Out of self-bounty be abused, look to't:
>   I know our country disposition well:
>   In Venice they do let God see the pranks
>   They dare not show their husbands; their best conscience
>   Is not to leave undone but keep unknown.

OTHELLO. Dost thou say so?
IAGO. She did deceive her father, marrying you:
        And when she seemed to shake and fear your looks,
        She loved them most.
OTHELLO. And so she did.
IAGO. Why, go to then.
        She that so young could give out such a seeming
        To seal her father's eyes up, close as oak.
        He thought 'twas witchcraft.

And a few lines later, he refers directly to the color difference.

        Not to affect many proposed matches,
        Of her own clime, complexion and degree,
        Whereto we see in all things nature tends,
        Foh! one may smell in such a will most rank,
        Foul disproportion, thoughts unnatural.
        But pardon me: I do not in position
        Distinctly speak of her, though I may fear
        Her will, recoiling to her better judgment
        May fall to match you with her country-forms,
        And happily repent.

Once Othello allows himself to suspect that Desdemona may not be the person she seems, she cannot allay the suspicion by speaking the truth but she can appear to confirm it by telling a lie. Hence the catastrophic effect when she denies having lost the handkerchief.

If Othello cannot trust her, then he can trust nobody and nothing, and precisely what she has done is not important. In the scene where he pretends that the Castle is a brothel of which Emilia is the Madam, he accuses Desdemona, not of adultery with Cassio, but of nameless orgies.

DESDEMONA. Alas, what ignorant sin have I committed?
OTHELLO. Was this fair paper, this most goodly book
        Made to write whore on. What committed?
        Committed. O thou public commoner,
        I should make very forges of my cheeks
        That would to cinders burn up modestly
        Did I but speak thy deeds.

And, as Mr Eliot has pointed out, in his farewell speech his thoughts are not on Desdemona at all but upon his relation to Venice, and he ends by identifying himself with another outsider, the Moslem Turk who beat a Venetian and traduced the state.

Everybody must pity Desdemona, but I cannot bring myself to like her. Her determination to marry Othello—it was she who virtually did the proposing—seems the romantic crush of a silly schoolgirl rather than a mature affection; it is Othello's adventures, so unlike the civilian life she knows, which captivate her rather than Othello as a person. He may not have practiced witchcraft, but, in fact, she is spellbound. And despite all Brabantio's prejudices, her deception of her own father makes an unpleasant impression: Shakespeare does not allow us to forget that the shock of the marriage kills him.

Then, she seems more aware than is agreeable of the honor she has done Othello by becoming his wife. When Iago tells Cassio that "our General's wife is now the General" and, soon afterwards, soliloquizes

> His soul is so infettered to her love
> That she may make, unmake, do what she list
> Even as her appetite shall play the god
> With his weak function

he is, no doubt, exaggerating, but there is much truth in what he says. Before Cassio speaks to her, she has already discussed him with her husband and learned that he is to be reinstated as soon as is opportune. A sensible wife would have told Cassio this and left matters alone. In continuing to badger Othello, she betrays a desire to prove to herself and to Cassio that she can make her husband do as she pleases.

Her lie about the handkerchief is, in itself, a trivial fib but, had she really regarded her husband as her equal, she might have admitted the loss. As it is, she is frightened because she is suddenly confronted with a man whose sensibility and superstitions are alien to her.

Though her relation with Cassio is perfectly innocent, one cannot but share Iago's doubts as to the durability of the marriage. It is worth noting that, in the willow-song scene with Emilia, she speaks with admiration of Ludovico and then turns to the topic of adultery. Of course, she discusses this in general terms and is shocked by Emilia's attitude, but she does discuss the subject and she does listen to what Emilia has to say about husbands and wives. It is as if she had suddenly realized that she had made a *mésalliance* and that the sort of man she ought to have married was someone of her own class and color like Ludovico. Given a few more years of Othello and of Emilia's influence and she might well, one feels, have taken a lover.

IV

And so one comes back to where one started, to Iago, the sole agent in the play. A play, as Shakespeare said, is a mirror held up to nature. This particular mirror bears the date 1604, but, when we look into it, the face that confronts us is our own in the middle of the twentieth century. We hear Iago say the same words and see him do the same things as an Elizabethan audience heard and saw, but what they mean to us cannot be exactly the same. To his

first audience and even, maybe, to his creator, Iago appeared to be just another Machiavellian villain who might exist in real life but with whom one
would never dream of identifying oneself. To us, I think, he is a much more
alarming figure; we cannot hiss at him when he appears as we can hiss at the
villain in a Western movie because none of us can honestly say that he does
not understand how such a wicked person can exist. For is not Iago, the
practical joker, a parabolic figure for the autonomous pursuit of scientific
knowledge through experiment which we all, whether we are scientists or
not, take for granted as natural and right?

As Nietzsche said, experimental science is the last flower of asceticism.
The investigator must discard all his feelings, hopes and fears as a human
person and reduce himself to a disembodied observer of events upon which
he passes no value judgment. Iago is an ascetic. "Love" he says, "is merely a
lust of the blood, and a permission of the will."

The knowledge sought by science is only one kind of knowledge. Another
kind is that implied by the Biblical phrase, "Then Adam knew Eve, his wife,"
and it is this kind I still mean when I say, "I know John Smith very well." I
cannot know in this sense without being known in return. If I know John
Smith well, he must also know me well.

But, in the scientific sense of knowledge, I can only know that which does
not and cannot know me. Feeling unwell, I go to my doctor who examines
me, says "You have Asian flu," and gives me an injection. The Asian virus is as
unaware of my doctor's existence as his victims are of a practical joker.

Further, to-know in the scientific sense means, ultimately, to-have-power-
over. To the degree that human beings are authentic persons, unique and
self-creating, they cannot be scientifically known. But human beings are not
pure persons like angels; they are also biological organisms, almost identical
in their functioning, and, to a greater or lesser degree, they are neurotic,
that is to say, less free than they imagine because of fears and desires of
which they have no personal knowledge but could and ought to have. Hence,
it is always possible to reduce human beings to the status of things which are
completely scientifically knowable and completely controllable.

This can be done by direct action on their bodies with drugs, lobotomies,
deprivation of sleep, etc. The difficulty about this method is that your victims
will know that you are trying to enslave them and, since nobody wishes to be
a slave, they will object, so that it can only be practiced upon minorities like
prisoners and lunatics who are physically incapable of resisting.

The other method is to play on the fears and desires of which you are
aware and they are not until they enslave themselves. In this case, concealment of your real intention is not only possible but essential for, if people
know they are being played upon, they will not believe what you say or do
what you suggest. An advertisement based on snob appeal, for example, can
only succeed with people who are unaware that they are snobs and that their

snobbish feelings are being appealed to and to whom, therefore, your advertisement seems as honest as Iago seems to Othello.

Iago's treatment of Othello conforms to Bacon's definition of scientific enquiry as putting Nature to the Question. If a member of the audience were to interrupt the play and ask him: "What are you doing?" could not Iago answer with a boyish giggle, "Nothing. I'm only trying to find out what Othello is really like"? And we must admit that his experiment is highly successful. By the end of the play he does know the scientific truth about the object to which he has reduced Othello. That is what makes his parting shot, "What you know, you know," so terrifying for, by then, Othello has become a thing, incapable of knowing anything.

And why shouldn't Iago do this? After all, he has certainly acquired knowledge. What makes it impossible for us to condemn him self-righteously is that, in our culture, we have all accepted the notion that the right to know is absolute and unlimited. The gossip column is one side of the medal; the cobalt bomb the other. We are quite prepared to admit that, while food and sex are good in themselves, an uncontrolled pursuit of either is not, but it is difficult for us to believe that intellectual curiosity is a desire like any other, and to realize that correct knowledge and truth are not identical. To apply a categorical imperative to knowing, so that, instead of asking, "What can I know?" we ask, "What, at this moment, am I meant to know?"—to entertain the possibility that the only knowledge which can be true for us is the knowledge we can live up to—that seems to all of us crazy and almost immoral. But, in that case, who are we to say to Iago—"No, you mustn't."

Postscript: Infernal Science

All exact science is dominated by the idea of approximation. (Bertrand Russell.) If so, then infernal science differs from human science in that it lacks the notion of approximation: it believes its laws to be exact.

Ethics does not treat of the world. Ethics must be a condition of the world like logic. (Wittgenstein.) On this God and the Evil One are agreed. It is a purely human illusion to imagine that the laws of the spiritual life are, like our legislation, imposed laws which we can break. We may defy them, either by accident, i.e. out of ignorance, or by choice, but we can no more break them than we can break the laws of human physiology by getting drunk.

The Evil One is not interested in evil, for evil is, by definition, what he believes he already knows. To him, Auschwitz is a banal fact, like the date of the battle of Hastings. He is only interested in good, as that which he has so far failed to understand in terms of his absolute presuppositions; Goodness is his obsession.

The first anthropological axiom of the Evil One is not *All men are evil*, but *All men are the same*; and his second—*Men do not act: they only behave.*

Humanly speaking, to tempt someone means to offer him some inducement to defy his conscience. In that sense, the Evil One cannot be said to tempt us for, to him, conscience is a fiction. Nor can he properly be thought of as trying to make us *do* anything, for he does not believe in the existence of deeds. What to us is a temptation is to him an experiment: he is trying to confirm a hypothesis about human behavior.

One of our greatest spiritual dangers is our fancy that the Evil One takes a personal interest in our perdition. He doesn't care a button about *my* soul, any more than Don Giovanni cared a button about Donna Elvira's body. I am his "one-thousand-and-third-in-Spain."

One can conceive of Heaven having a Telephone Directory, but it would have to be gigantic, for it would include the Proper Name and address of every electron in the Universe. But Hell could not have one, for in Hell, as in prison and the army, its inhabitants are identified not by name but by number. They do not *have* numbers, they *are* numbers.

PART FIVE

Two Bestiaries

D. H. Lawrence

If men were as much men as lizards are lizards.
They'd be worth looking at.

The artist, the man who makes, is less important to mankind, for good or
evil, than the apostle, the man with a message. Without a religion, a philosophy, a code of behavior, call it what you will, men cannot live at all; what they
believe may be absurd or revolting, but they have to believe something. On
the other hand, however much the arts may mean to us, it is possible to imagine our lives without them.

As a human being, every artist holds some set of beliefs or other but, as a
rule, these are not of his own invention; his public knows this and judges his
work without reference to them. We read Dante for his poetry not for his
theology because we have already met the theology elsewhere.

There are a few writers, however, like Blake and D. H. Lawrence, who are
both artists and apostles and this makes a just estimation of their work difficult to arrive at. Readers who find something of value in their message will
attach unique importance to their writings because they cannot find it anywhere else. But this importance may be shortlived; once I have learned his
message, I cease to be interested in a messenger and, should I later come to
think his message false or misleading, I shall remember him with resentment
and distaste. Even if I try to ignore the message and read him again as if he
were only an artist, I shall probably feel disappointed because I cannot recapture the excitement I felt when I first read him.

When I first read Lawrence in the late Twenties, it was his message which
made the greatest impression on me, so that it was his "think" books like
Fantasia of the Unconscious rather than his fiction which I read most avidly. As
for his poetry, when I first tried to read it, I did not like it; despite my admiration for him, it offended my notions of what poetry should be. Today my
notions of what poetry should be are still, in all essentials, what they were
then and hostile to his, yet there are a number of his poems which I have
come to admire enormously. When a poet who holds views about the nature
of poetry which we believe to be false writes a poem we like, we are apt to
think: "This time he has forgotten his theory and is writing according to
ours." But what fascinates me about the poems of Lawrence's which I like is
that I must admit he could never have written them had he held the kind of
views about poetry of which I approve.

Man is a history-making creature who can neither repeat his past nor leave it
behind; at every moment he adds to and thereby modifies everything that
had previously happened to him. Hence the difficulty of finding a single
image which can stand as an adequate symbol for man's kind of existence. If

we think of his ever-open future, then the natural image is of a single pilgrim walking along an unending road into hitherto unexplored country; if we think of his never-forgettable past, then the natural image is of a great crowded city, built in every style of architecture, in which the dead are as active citizens as the living. The only feature common to both images is that both are purposive; a road goes in a certain direction, a city is built to endure and be a home. The animals, who live in the present, have neither cities nor roads and do not miss them; they are at home in the wilderness and at most, if they are social, set up camps for a single generation. But man requires both; the image of a city with no roads leading away from it suggests a prison, the image of a road that starts from nowhere in particular, an animal spoor.

Every man is both a citizen and a pilgrim, but most men are predominantly one or the other and in Lawrence the pilgrim almost obliterated the citizen. It is only natural, therefore, that he should have admired Whitman so much, both for his matter and his manner.

> Whitman's essential message was the Open Road. The leaving of the soul free unto herself, the leaving of his fate to her and to the loom of the open road. . . . The true democracy . . . where all journey down the open road. And where a soul is known at once in its going. Not by its clothes or appearance. Not by its family name. Not even by its reputation. Not by works at all. The soul passing unenhanced, passing on foot, and being no more than itself.

In his introduction to *New Poems*, Lawrence tries to explain the difference between traditional verse and the free verse which Whitman was the first to write.

> The poetry of the beginning and the poetry of the end must have that exquisite finality, perfection which belongs to all that is far off. It is in the realm of all that is perfect . . . the finality and perfection are conveyed in exquisite form: the perfect symmetry, the rhythm which returns upon itself like a dance where the hands link and loosen and link for the supreme moment of the end. . . . But there is another kind of poetry, the poetry of that which is at hand: the immediate present. . . . Life, the ever present, knows no finality, no finished crystallisation. . . . It is obvious that the poetry of the instant present cannot have the same body or the same motions as the poetry of the before and after. It can never submit to the same conditions, it is never finished. . . . Much has been written about free verse. But all that can be said, first and last, is that free verse is, or should be, direct utterance from the instant whole man. It is the soul and body surging at once, nothing left out. . . . It has no finish. It has no satisfying stability. It does not want to get anywhere. It just takes place.

It would be easy to make fun of this passage, to ask Lawrence, for example, to tell us exactly how long an instant is, or how it would be physically possible for the poet to express it in writing before it had become past. But it is obvious that Lawrence is struggling to say something which he believes to be important. Very few statements which poets make about poetry, even when they appear to be quite lucid, are understandable except in their polemic context. To understand them, we need to know what they are directed against, what the poet who made them considered the principal enemies of genuine poetry.

In Lawrence's case, one enemy was the conventional response, the laziness or fear which makes people prefer secondhand experience to the shock of looking and listening for themselves.

> Man fixes some wonderful erection of his own between himself and the wild chaos, and gradually goes bleached and stifled under his parasol. Then comes a poet, enemy of convention, and makes a slit in the umbrella; and lo! the glimpse of chaos is a vision, a window to the sun. But after a while, getting used to the vision, and not liking the genuine draft from chaos, commonplace man daubs a simulacrum of the window that opens into chaos and patches the umbrella with the painted patch of the simulacrum. That is, he gets used to the vision; it is part of his house decoration.

Lawrence's justified dislike of the conventional response leads him into a false identification of the genuine with the novel. The image of the slit in the umbrella is misleading because what you can see through it will always be the same. But a genuine work of art is one in which every generation finds something new. A genuine work of art remains an example of what being genuine means, so that it can stimulate later artists to be genuine in their turn. Stimulate, not compel; if a playwright in the twentieth century chooses to write a play in a pastiche of Shakespearian blank verse, the fault is his, not Shakespeare's. Those who are afraid of firsthand experience would find means of avoiding it if all the art of the past were destroyed.

However, theory aside. Lawrence did care passionately about genuineness of feeling. He wrote little criticism about other poets who were his contemporaries, but, when he did, he was quick to pounce on any phoniness of emotion. About Ralph Hodgson's lines

> The sky was lit,
> The sky was stars all over it,
> I stood, I knew not why

he writes, "No one should say *I knew not why* any more. It is as meaningless as *Yours truly* at the end of a letter," and, after quoting an American poetess

> Why do I think of stairways
> With a rush of hurt surprise?

he remarks, "Heaven knows, my dear, unless you once fell down." Whatever faults his own poetry may have, it never puts on an act. Even when Lawrence talks nonsense, as when he asserts that the moon is made of phosphorous or radium, one is convinced that it is nonsense in which he sincerely believed. This is more than can be said of some poets much greater than he. When Yeats assures me, in a stanza of the utmost magnificence, that after death he wants to become a mechanical bird, I feel that he is telling what my nanny would have called "A story."

The second object of Lawrence's polemic was a doctrine which first became popular in France during the second half of the nineteenth century, the belief that Art is the true religion, that life has no value except as material for a beautiful artistic structure and that, therefore, the artist is the only authentic human being—the rest, rich and poor alike, are canaille. Works of art are the only cities; life itself is a jungle. Lawrence's feelings about this creed were so strong that whenever he detects its influence, as he does in Proust and Joyce, he refuses their work any merit whatsoever. A juster and more temperate statement of his objection has been made by Dr Auerbach:

> When we compare Stendhal's or even Balzac's world with the world of Flaubert or the two Goncourts, the latter seems strangely narrow and petty despite its wealth of impressions. Documents of the kind represented by Flaubert's correspondence and the Goncourt diary are indeed admirable in the purity and incorruptibility of their artistic ethics, the wealth of impressions elaborated in them, and their refinement of sensory culture. At the same time, however, we sense something narrow, something oppressively close in their books. They are full of reality and intellect, but poor in humor and inner poise. The purely literary, even on the highest level of artistic acumen, limits the power of judgment, reduces the wealth of life, and at times distorts the outlook upon the world of phenomena. And while the writers contemptuously avert their attention from the political and economic bustle, consistently value life only as literary subject matter, and remain arrogantly and bitterly aloof from its great practical problems, in order to achieve aesthetic isolation for their work, often at great and daily expense of effort, the practical world nevertheless besets them in a thousand petty ways.
>
> Sometimes there are financial worries, and almost always there is nervous hypotension and a morbid concern with health. . . . What finally emerges, despite all their intellectual and artistic incorruptibility, is a strangely petty impression; that of an upper bourgeois egocentrically concerned over his aesthetic comfort, plagued by a thousand small vex-

ations, nervous, obsessed by a mania—only in this case the mania is called "Literature." (*Mimesis*)

In rejecting the doctrine that life has no value except as raw material for art, Lawrence fell into another error, that of identifying art with life, making with action.

> I offer a bunch of pansies, not a wreath of immortelles. I don't want everlasting flowers and I don't want to offer them to anybody else. A flower passes, and that perhaps is the best of it. . . . Don't nail the pansy down. You won't keep it any better if you do.

Here Lawrence draws a false analogy between the process of artistic creation and the organic growth of living creatures. "Nature hath no goal though she hath law." Organic growth is a cyclical process; it is just as true to say that the oak is a potential acorn as it is to say the acorn is a potential oak. But the process of writing a poem, of making any art object, is not cyclical but a motion in one direction towards a definite end. As Socrates says in Valéry's dialogue *Eupalinos*:

> The tree does not construct its branches and leaves; nor the cock his beak and feathers. But the tree and all its parts, or the cock and all his, are constructed by the principles themselves, which do not exist apart from the constructing. . . . But, in the objects made by man, the principles are separate from the construction, and are, as it were, imposed by a tyrant from without upon the material, to which he imparts them by acts. . . . If a man waves his arm, we distinguish this arm from his gesture, and we conceive between gesture and arm a purely possible relation. But from the point of view of nature, this gesture of the arm and the arm itself cannot be separated.

An artist who ignores this difference between natural growth and human construction will produce the exact opposite of what he intends. He hopes to produce something which will seem as natural as a flower, but the qualities of the natural are exactly what his product will lack. A natural object never appears unfinished; if it is an inorganic object like a stone, it is what it has to be, if an organic object like a flower, what it has to be at this moment. But a similar effect—of being what it has to be—can only be achieved in a work of art by much thought, labor and care. The gesture of a ballet dancer, for example, only looks natural when, through long practice, its execution has become "second nature" to him. That perfect incarnation of life in substance, word in flesh, which in nature is immediate, has in art to be achieved and, in fact, can never be perfectly achieved. In many of Lawrence's poems, the spirit has failed to make itself a fit body to live in, a curious defect in the work of a writer who was so conscious of the value and significance of the body. In his essay on Thomas Hardy, Lawrence made some acute observations about this very problem. Speaking of the antinomy between Law and Love, the Flesh and the Spirit, he says

> The principle of the Law is found strongest in Woman, the principle of Love in Man. In every creature, the mobility, the law of change is found exemplified in the male, the stability, the conservatism in the female.
>
> The very adherence of rhyme and regular rhythm is a concession to the Law, a concession to the body, to the being and requirements of the body. They are an admission of the living positive inertia which is the other half of life, other than the pure will to motion.

This division of Lawrence's is a variant on the division between the City and the Open Road. To the mind of the pilgrim, his journey is a succession of ever-new sights and sounds, but to his heart and legs, it is a rhythmical repetition—tic-toc, left-right—even the poetry of the Open Road must pay that much homage to the City. By his own admission and definition Lawrence's defect as an artist was an exaggerated maleness.

Reading Lawrence's early poems, one is continually struck by the originality of the sensibility and the conventionality of the expressive means. For most immature poets, their chief problem is to learn to forget what they have been taught poets are supposed to feel; too often, as Lawrence says, the young man is afraid of his demon, puts his hand over the demon's mouth and speaks for him. On the other hand, an immature poet, if he has real talent, usually begins to exhibit quite early a distinctive style of his own; however obvious the influence of some older writer may be, there is something original in his manner or, at least, great technical competence. In Lawrence's case, this was not so; he learned quite soon to let his demon speak, but it took him a long time to find the appropriate style for him to speak in. All too often in his early poems, even the best ones, he is content to versify his thoughts; there is no essential relation between what he is saying and the formal structure he imposes upon it.

> Being nothing, I bear the brunt
> Of the nightly heavens overhead, like an immense open eye
> With a cat's distended pupil, that sparkles with little stars
> And with thoughts that flash and crackle in far-off malignancy
> So distant, they cannot touch me, whom nothing mars.

A mere poetaster with nothing to say, would have done something about *whom nothing mars.*

It is interesting to notice that the early poems in which he seems technically most at ease and the form most natural, are those he wrote in dialect,

> I wish tha hadna done it, Tim,
> I do, an' that I do,
> For whenever I look thee i'th' face, I s'll see
> Her face too.

> I wish I could wash 'er off'n thee;
> 'Appen I can, if I try.
> But tha'll ha'e ter promise ter be true ter me
> Till I die.

This sounds like a living woman talking, whereas no woman on earth ever talked like this:

> How did you love him, you who only roused
> His mind until it burnt his heart away!
> 'Twas you who killed him, when you both caroused
> In words and things well said. But the other way
> He never loved you, never with desire
> Touched you to fire.

I suspect that Lawrence's difficulties with formal verse had their origin in his linguistic experiences as a child.

> My father was a working man
> and a collier was he,
> At six in the morning they turned him down
> and they turned him up for tea.

> My mother was a superior soul
> a superior soul was she,
> cut out to play a superior role
> in the god-damn bourgeoisie.

> We children were the in-betweens,
> Little non-descripts were we,
> Indoors we called each other *you*
> outside it was *tha* and *thee*.

In formal poetry, the role played by the language itself is so great that it demands of the poet that he be as intimate with it as with his own flesh and blood and love it with a single-minded passion. A child who has associated standard English with Mother and dialect with Father has ambivalent feelings about both which can hardly fail to cause trouble for him in later life if he should try to write formal poetry. Not that it would have been possible for Lawrence to become a dialect poet like Burns or William Barnes, both of whom lived before public education had made dialect quaint. The language of Burns was a national not a parochial speech, and the peculiar charm of Barnes' poetry is its combination of the simplest emotions with an extremely sophisticated formal technique: Lawrence could never have limited himself to the thoughts and feelings of a Nottinghamshire mining village, and he had neither the taste nor the talent of Barnes for what he scornfully called word games.

Most of Lawrence's finest poems are to be found in the volume *Birds, Beasts, and Flowers*, begun in Tuscany when he was thirty-five and finished three years later in New Mexico. All of them are written in free verse.

The difference between formal and free verse may be likened to the difference between carving and modeling; the formal poet, that is to say, thinks of the poem he is writing as something already latent in the language which he has to reveal, while the free verse poet thinks of language as a plastic passive medium upon which he imposes his artistic conception. One might also say that, in their attitude towards art, the formal verse writer is a catholic, the free verse writer a protestant. And Lawrence was, in every respect, very protestant indeed. As he himself acknowledged, it was through Whitman that he found himself as a poet, found the right idiom of poetic speech for his demon.

On no other English poet, so far as I know, has Whitman had a beneficial influence; he could on Lawrence because, despite certain superficial resemblances, their sensibilities were utterly different. Whitman quite consciously set out to be the Epic Bard of America and created a poetic *persona* for the purpose. He keeps using the first person singular and even his own name, but these stand for a *persona*, not an actual human being, even when he appears to be talking about the most intimate experiences. When he sounds ridiculous, it is usually because the image of an individual obtrudes itself comically upon what is meant to be a statement about a collective experience. *I am large. I contain multitudes* is absurd if one thinks of Whitman himself or any individual; of a corporate person like General Motors it makes perfectly good sense. The more we learn about Whitman the man, the less like his *persona* he looks. On the other hand it is doubtful if a writer ever existed who had less of an artistic *persona* than Lawrence; from his letters and the reminiscences of his friends, it would seem that he wrote for publication in exactly the same way as he spoke in private. (I must confess that I find Lawrence's love poems embarrassing because of their lack of reticence; they make me feel a Peeping Tom.) Then, Whitman looks at life extensively rather than intensively. No detail is dwelt upon for long; it is snapshotted and added as one more item to the vast American catalogue. But Lawrence in his best poems is always concerned intensively with a single subject, a bat, a tortoise, a fig tree, which he broods on until he has exhausted its possibilities.

A sufficient number of years have passed for us to have gotten over both the first overwhelming impact of Lawrence's genius and the subsequent violent reaction when we realized that there were silly and nasty sides to his nature. We can be grateful to him for what he can do for us, without claiming that he can do everything or condemning him because he cannot. As an analyst and portrayer of the forces of hatred and aggression which exist in all human beings and, from time to time, manifest themselves in nearly all human relationships, Lawrence is, probably, the greatest master who ever lived. But that was absolutely all that he knew and understood about human beings; about human affection and human charity, for example, he knew absolutely nothing. The truth is that he detested nearly all human beings if he had to be in close contact with them; his ideas of what a human relationship, between man and man or man and woman, ought to be are pure daydreams because they are not based upon any experience of actual relationships which might be improved or corrected. Whenever, in his novels and short stories, he introduces a character whom he expects the reader to admire, he or she is always an unmitigated humorless bore, but the more he dislikes his characters the more interesting he makes them. And, in his heart of hearts, Lawrence knew this himself. There is a sad passage In *An Autobiographical Sketch*:

> Why is there so little contact between myself and the people I know? The answer, as far as I can see, has something to do with class. As a man from the working class, I feel that the middle class cut off some of my vital vibration when I am with them. I admit them charming and good people often enough, but they just stop some part of me from working.
>
> Then, why don't I live with my own people? Because their vibration is limited in another direction. The working class is narrow in outlook, in prejudice, and narrow in intelligence. This again makes a prison. Yet I find, here in Italy, for example, that I live in a certain contact with the peasants who work the land of this villa. I am not intimate with them, hardly speak to them save to say good-day. And they are not working for me. I am not their padrone. I don't want to live with them in their cottages; that would be a sort of prison. I don't idealise them. I don't expect them to make any millennium here on earth, neither now nor in the future. But I want them to be there, about the place, their lives going along with mine.

For the word *peasants*, one might substitute the words *birds, beasts and flowers*. Lawrence possessed a great capacity for affection and charity, but he could only direct it towards non-human life or peasants whose lives were so uninvolved with his that, so far as he was concerned, they might just as well have been nonhuman. Whenever, in his writings, he forgets about men and women with proper names and describes the anonymous life of stones, waters, forests, animals, flowers, chance traveling companions or passers-by, his bad temper and his dogmatism immediately vanish and he becomes the most enchanting companion imaginable, tender, intelligent, funny and, above all, happy. But the moment any living thing, even a dog, makes demands on him, the rage and preaching return. His poem about "Bibbles," "the walt whitmanesque love-bitch who loved just everybody," is the best poem about a dog ever written, but it makes it clear that Lawrence was no person to be entrusted with the care of a dog.

> All right, my little bitch.
> You learn loyalty rather than loving,
> And I'll protect you.

To which Bibbles might, surely, with justice retort: "O for Chris-sake, mister, go get yourself an Alsatian and leave me alone, can't you."

The poems in *Birds, Beasts, and Flowers* are among Lawrence's longest. He was not a concise writer and he needs room to make his effect. In his poetry he manages to make a virtue out of what in his prose is often a vice, a tendency to verbal repetition. The recurrence of identical or slightly varied phrases helps to give his free verse a structure; the phrases themselves are not particularly striking, but this is as it should be, for their function is to act as stitches.

Like the romantics, Lawrence's starting point in these poems is a personal encounter between himself and some animal or flower but, unlike the romantics, he never confuses the feelings they arouse in him with what he sees and hears and knows about them.

Thus, he accuses Keats, very justly, I think, of being so preoccupied with his own feelings that he cannot really listen to the nightingale. *Thy plaintive anthem fades* deserves Lawrence's comment: *It never was a plaintive anthem—it was Caruso at his jauntiest.*

Lawrence never forgets—indeed this is what he likes most about them—that a plant or an animal has its own kind of existence which is unlike and uncomprehending of man's.

> It is no use my saying to him in an emotional voice:
> "This is your Mother, she laid you when you were an egg"
> He does not even trouble to answer: "Woman, what have I to do
>   with thee?"
> He wearily looks the other way,
> And she even more wearily looks another way still.
> > ("Tortoise Family Connections")

> But watching closer
> That motionless deadly motion,
> That unnatural barrel body, that long ghoul nose . . .
> I left off hailing him.

I had made a mistake, I didn't know him,
This grey, monotonous soul in the water,
This intense individual in shadow,
Fish-alive.
I didn't know his God.

("Fish")

When discussing people or ideas, Lawrence is often turgid and obscure, but when, as in these poems, he is contemplating some object with love, the lucidity of his language matches the intensity of his vision, and he can make the reader *see* what he is saying as very few writers can.

Queer, with your thin wings and your streaming legs,
How you sail like a heron, or a dull clot of air.

("The Mosquito")

Her little loose hands, and sloping Victorian shoulders

("Kangaroo")

There she is, perched on her manger, looking over the boards
    into the day
Like a belle at her window.
And immediately she sees me she blinks, stares, doesn't know me,
    turns her head and ignores me vulgarly with a wooden blank
    on her face.
What do I care for her, the ugly female, standing up there with
    her long tangled sides like an old rug thrown over a fence.
But she puts her nose down shrewdly enough when the knot is
    untied,
And jumps staccato to earth, a sharp, dry jump, still ignoring me,
Pretending to look around the stall
Come on, you crapa! I'm not your servant.
She turns her head away with an obtuse female sort of deafness,
    bête.
And then invariably she crouches her rear and makes water.
That being her way of answer, if I speak to her.—Self-conscious!
Le bestie non parlano, poverine! . . .

Queer it is, suddenly, in the garden
To catch sight of her standing like some huge ghoulish grey bird
    in the air, on the bough of the leaning almond-tree,
Straight as a board on the bough, looking down like some hairy
    horrid God the Father in a William Blake imagination.
Come, down, Crapa, out of that almond tree!

("She-Goat")

In passages like these, Lawrence's writing is so transparent that one forgets him entirely and simply sees what he saw.

Birds, Beasts, and Flowers is the peak of Lawrence's achievement as a poet. There are a number of fine things in the later volumes, but a great deal that is tedious, both in subject matter and form. A writer's doctrines are not the business of a literary critic except in so far as they touch upon questions which concern the art of writing; if a writer makes statements about nonliterary matters, it is not for the literary critic to ask whether they are true or false but he may legitimately question the writer's authority to make them.

The Flauberts and the Goncourts considered social and political questions beneath them; to his credit, Lawrence knew that there are many questions that are more important than Art with an *A*, but it is one thing to know this and another to believe one is in a position to answer them.

In the modern world, a man who earns his living by writing novels and poems is a self-employed worker whose customers are not his neighbors, and this makes him a social oddity. He may work extremely hard, but his manner of life is something between that of a *rentier* and a gypsy, he can live where he likes and know only the people he chooses to know. He has no firsthand knowledge of all those involuntary relationships created by social, economic and political necessity. Very few artists can be *engagé* because life does not engage them: for better or worse, they do not quite belong to the City. And Lawrence, who was self-employed after the age of twenty-six, belonged to it less than most. Some writers have spent their lives in the same place and social milieu; Lawrence kept constantly moving from one place and one country to another. Some have been extroverts who entered fully into whatever society happened to be available; Lawrence's nature made him avoid human contacts as much as possible. Most writers have at least had the experience of parenthood and its responsibilities; this experience was denied Lawrence. It was inevitable, therefore, that when he tried to lay down the law about social and political matters, money, machinery, etc., he could only be negative and moralistic because, since his youth, he had had no firsthand experiences upon which concrete and positive suggestions could have been based. Furthermore, if, like Lawrence, the only aspects of human beings which you care for and value are states of being, timeless moments of passionate intensity, then social and political life, which are essentially historical—without a past and a future, human society is inconceivable—must be, for you, the worthless aspects of human life. You cannot honestly say, "This kind of society is preferable to that," because, for you, society is wholly given over to Satan.

The other defect in many of the later poems is a formal one. It is noticeable that the best are either of some length or rhymed; the short ones in free verse very rarely come off. A poem which contains a number of ideas and feelings can be organized in many different ways, but a poem which makes a single point and is made up of no more than one or two sentences can only be organized verbally; an epigram or an aphorism must be written either in prose or in some strictly measured verse; written in free verse, it will sound like prose arbitrarily chopped up.

> It has always seemed to me that a real thought, not an argument can only exist in verse, or in some poetic form. There is a didactic element about prose thoughts which makes them repellent, slightly bullying, "He who hath wife and children hath given hostages to fortune." There is a point well put: but immediately it irritates by its assertiveness. If it were put into poetry, it would not nag at us so practically. We don't want to be nagged at. (Preface to *Pansies*)

Though I personally love good prose aphorisms, I can see what Lawrence means. If one compares

> *Plus ça change, plus c'est la même chose*

with

> The accursed power that stands on Privilege
> And goes with Women and Champagne and Bridge
> Broke, and Democracy resumed her reign
> That goes with Bridge and Women and Champagne

the first does seem a bit smug and a bit abstract, while, in the second, the language dances and is happy.

> The bourgeois produced the Bolshevist inevitably
> As every half-truth at length produces the contradiction of itself
> In the opposite half-truth

has the worst of both worlds; it lacks the conciseness of the prose and the jollity of the rhymed verse.

The most interesting verses in the last poems of Lawrence belong to a literary genre he had not attempted before, satirical doggerel.

If formal verse can be likened to carving, free verse to modeling, then one might say that doggerel verse is like *objets trouvés*—the piece of driftwood that looks like a witch, the stone that has a profile. The writer of doggerel, as it were, takes any old words, rhythms and rhymes that come into his head, gives them a good shake and then throws them onto the page like dice where, lo and behold, contrary to all probability they make sense, not by law but by chance. Since the words appear to have no will of their own, but to be the puppets of chance, so will the things or persons to which they refer; hence the value of doggerel for a certain kind of satire.

It is a different kind of satire from that written by Dryden and Pope. Their kind presupposes a universe, a city, governed by, or owing allegiance to, certain eternal laws of reason and morality; the purpose of their satire is to demonstrate that the individual or institution they are attacking violates these laws. Consequently, the stricter in form their verse, the more artful their technique, the more effective it is. Satirical doggerel, on the other hand, presupposes no fixed laws. It is the weapon of the outsider, the anarchist rebel, who refuses to accept conventional laws and pieties as binding or worthy of respect. Hence its childish technique, for the child represents the naïve and personal, as yet uncorrupted by education and convention. Satire of the Pope kind says: "The Emperor is wearing a celluloid collar. That simply isn't done." Satiric doggerel cries: "The Emperor is naked."

At this kind of satiric doggerel, Lawrence turned out to be a master.

> And Mr Meade, that old old lily,
> Said: "Gross, coarse, hideous!" and I, like a silly
>
> Thought he meant the faces of the police court officials
> And how right he was, so I signed my initials.
>
> But Tolstoi was a traitor
> To the Russia that needed him most,
> The great bewildered Russia
> So worried by the Holy Ghost;
> He shifted his job onto the peasants
> And landed them all on toast.

Parnassus has many mansions.

Marianne Moore

Why an inordinate interest in animals and athletes? They are subjects for art and exemplars of it, are they not? minding their own business. Pangolins, hornbills, pitchers, catchers, do not pry or prey—or prolong the conversation; do not make us self-conscious; look their best when caring least; although in a Frank Buck documentary, I saw a leopard insult a crocodile (basking on the river bank—head only visible on the bank)—bat the animal on the nose and continue on its way without so much as a look back.

When I first read Lawrence's poetry, I didn't like it much, but I had no difficulty in understanding it. But when in 1935, I first tried to read Marianne Moore's poems, I simply could not make head or tail of them. To begin with,

I could not "hear" the verse. One may have a prejudice against Free Verse as such but, if it is in any way competently written, the ear immediately hears where one line ends and another begins, for each line represents either a speech unit or a thought unit. Accent has always played so important a role in English prosody that no Englishman, even if he has been brought up on the poetry written according to the traditional English prosodic convention in which lines are scanned by accentual feet, iambics, trochees, anapaests, etc., has any difficulty in recognizing as formal and rhythmical a poem, like "Christabel" or "The Wreck of the Deutschland," which is written in an accentual meter. But a syllabic verse, like Miss Moore's, in which accents and feet are ignored and only the number of syllables count, is very difficult for an English ear to grasp. One of our problems with the French alexandrine, for example, is that, whatever we may know intellectually about French prosody, our ear cannot help hearing most alexandrines as anapaestic verse which, in English poetry, we associate with light verse. Try as one may to forget it, *Je le vois, je lui parle; et mon coeur . . . Je m'égare* reminds us of *The Assyrian came down like a wolf on the fold.* But, at least, in listening to Racine all the lines have twelve syllables. Before I had encountered Miss Moore's verse, I was well acquainted with Robert Bridges's syllabic experiments, but he confined his verses to a regular succession of either six-syllable or twelve-syllable lines. A typical poem by Miss Moore, on the other hand, is written in stanzas, containing anything from one up to twenty syllables, not infrequently a word is split up with one or more of its syllables at the end of a line and the rest of them at the beginning of the next, caesuras fall where they may and, as a rule, some of the lines rhyme and some are unrhymed. This, for a long time, I found very difficult. Then, I found her process of thinking very hard to follow. Rimbaud seemed child's play compared with a passage like this:

> they are to me
>   like enchanted Earl Gerald who
>   changes himself into a stag, to
> a great green-eyed cat of
> the mountain. Discommodity makes
>   them invisible; they've dis-
> appeared. The Irish say your trouble is their
> trouble and your
>   joy their joy? I wish
> I could believe it;
> I am troubled, I'm dissatisfied, I'm Irish.

Uncomprehending as I was, I felt attracted by the tone of voice, so I persevered and I am very thankful that I did, for today there are very few poets who give me more pleasure to read. What I did see from the first was that she is a pure "Alice." She has all the Alice qualities, the distaste for noise and excess:

Poets, don't make a fuss;
            the elephant's "crooked trumpet" "doth write";
                        and to a tiger-book I am reading—
                I think you know the one—
            I am under obligation.

                One may be pardoned, yes I know
                one may, for love undying.
                            . . .

    The passion for setting people right is in itself an afflictive disease.
    Distaste which takes no credit to itself is best

the fastidiousness:

    I remember a swan under the willows in Oxford,
        with flamingo-coloured, maple-
            leaflike feet. It reconnoitred like a battle-
        ship. Disbelief and conscious fastidiousness were the staple
            ingredients in its
                disinclination to move. Finally its hardihood was
                    not proof against its
                proclivity to more fully appraise such bits
                    of food as the stream

    bore counter to it; it made away with what I gave it
        to eat. I have seen this swan and
            I have seen you; I have seen ambition without
        understanding in a variety of forms

the love of order and precision:

                    And as
                    MEridian one-two
                one-two gives, each fifteenth second
                    in the same voice, the new
                data—"The time will be" so and so—
                    you realize that "when you
                        hear the signal," you'll be

                hearing Jupiter or jour pater, the day god—
                    the salvaged son of Father Time—
                telling the cannibal Chronos
                    (eater of his proxime
                new-born progeny) that punctuality
                    is not a crime

the astringent ironical sharpness:

> One may be a blameless
> bachelor and it is but a step
> to Congreve.
>
> . . .
>
> She says, "This butterfly,
> this waterfly, this nomad
> that has 'proposed
> to settle on my hand for life'—
> what can one do with it.
> There must have been more time
> in Shakespeare's day
> to sit and watch a play.
> You know so many artists who are fools."
> He says: "You know so many fools
> who are not artists."

Like Lawrence's, many of Miss Moore's best poems are, overtly, at least, about animals. Animals have made their appearance in literature in a number of ways.

(1) The beast fable. In these, the actors have animals' bodies but human consciousness. Sometimes the intention is simply amusing entertainment, but more often it is educative. The fable may be a mythical explanation of how things came to be as they are, and the beast in it may be a folk-culture hero whose qualities of courage or cunning are to be imitated. Or again, though this is a later historical development, the fable may be satirical. What prevents man, individually and collectively, from behaving reasonably and morally is not so much ignorance as a self-blindness induced by some passion or desire. In a satirical beast fable, the beast has the desires of his kind which are different from those which govern man, so that we can view them with detachment and cannot fail to recognize what is good or bad, sensible or foolish behavior. In a beast fable, the descriptions of animal life cannot be realistic, for its basic premise of a self-conscious speaking animal is fantastic. If a human being is introduced into a beast fable, as Mr MacGregor is introduced into *Peter Rabbit*, he appears not as a man but as a God.

(2) The animal simile. This can be expressed in the form:

as an *a* behaves so acted *N*

where *a* is a species of animal with a typical way of behaving and *N* is the proper name of a human individual, mythical or historical, acting in a historical situation. The description of animals in an epic simile is more realistic than it is in the beast fable, but what is described is the behavior considered typical for that animal; everything else about it is irrelevant.

Homer's animal similes are more than merely ways of catching a mood or an impression, more than attempts to place an event in greater relief by stressing external similarities. When Homer has someone go against his enemies "like a lion," we must take him at his word. The warrior and the lion are activated by the same force; on more than one occasion this force is expressly stated to be the *menos*, the forward impulse. The animals of the Homeric similes are not only symbols, but the particular embodiments of universal vital forces. Homer has little regard for anything except the forces in them, and that is the reason why animals are more prominent in the similes than in the narrative itself. By themselves they hold next to no interest for him.

In the clearly defined, the typical forms within which nature has allocated her gifts among the beasts, men find the models for gauging their own responses and emotions; they are the mirror in which man sees himself. The sentence: "Hector is as a lion," besides constituting a comparison, besides focussing the formlessness of human existence against a characteristic type, also signalises a factual connection. (Bruno Snell, *The Discovery of Mind*)

(3) The animal as an allegorical emblem. The significance of an emblem is not, like a simile, self-evident. The artist who uses one must either assume that his audience already knows the symbolic association—it is a legend of the culture to which he belongs—or, if it is his own invention, he must explain it. A Buddhist, for instance, looking at a painting of the Christ Child in which there is a goldfinch, may know enough ornithology to recognize it as a goldfinch and to know that it eats (or used to be thought to eat) thorns, but he cannot possibly understand why the bird is there unless it is explained to him that Christians associate thorns, the goldfinch's supposed diet, with the crown of thorns Christ wore at his crucifixion; the painter has introduced the goldfinch into his picture of the Christ Child to remind the spectator that Christmas, an occasion for rejoicing, is necessarily related to Good Friday, an occasion for mourning.

The painter *may* have represented the bird as naturalistically as possible in order that the spectator shall not mistake it for some other bird, a woodpecker, for instance, which, because it bores holes in trees, is an emblem for Satan who undermines human nature, but correct identification is all that matters; there is no visual resemblance between the emblem and its meaning. In poetry, the mere name would be sufficient.

(4) The romantic encounter of man and beast. In such an encounter, the animal provides an accidental stimulus to the thoughts and emotions of a human individual. As a rule, the characteristics of the animal which make it a stimulus are not those in which it resembles man—as in the epic simile—but those in which it is unlike him. A man whose beloved has died or left him, hears a thrush singing and the song recalls to him an evening when he

and his beloved listened together to another thrush singing. There are two thrushes and one man, but, while the songs of the two thrushes are identical—thrush-life does not change and knows nothing of unhappy love—the man hearing the second is changed from what he was when he heard the first. Since, in these encounters, the nature of the animal itself has little, if anything, to do with the thoughts and emotions he provokes in the human individual, realistic description counts for little. Very few of the famous romantic poems concerned with animals are accurate in their natural history.

(5) Animals as objects of human interest and affection. Animals play an important economic role in the lives of huntsmen and farmers, many people keep them as pets, every major city in our culture has a zoo where exotic animals are on public exhibition, and some people are naturalists who are more interested in animals than in anything else. If an animal lover happens also to be a poet, it is quite possible that he will write poems about the animals he loves and, if he does, he will describe them in the same way that he would describe a friend, that is to say, every detail of the animal's appearance and behavior will interest him. It is almost impossible to make such a description communicable to others except in anthropomorphic terms, so that, in the animal lover's poetry, the order of the Homeric simile is reversed and takes the form:

as n looks or acts so does A

where n is a typical class of human being and A is an individual animal. Its grace and charm are conveyed by likening it to some instance of what makes some human beings admirable; sometimes, too, like Lawrence, the animal lover goes further and contrasts the virtue of a beast with the vices and follies of man.

Overtly, Miss Moore's animal poems are those of a naturalist; the animals she selects are animals she likes—the one exception is the cobra, and the point of the poem is that we, not the cobra, are to be blamed for our subjective fear and dislike—and nearly all of her animals are exotic, to be seen normally only in zoos or photographs by explorers; she has only one poem about a common domestic pet.

Like Lawrence, she has an extraordinary gift for metaphorical comparisons which make the reader see what she has seen. The metaphors may be drawn from other animals and plants. Thus, she describes a tomcat's face:

> the small tuft of fronds
> or katydid-legs above each eye, still numbering the units in each group;
> the shadbones regularly set about the mouth, to droop or rise
> in unison like the porcupine quills—motionless.

. . .

The firs stand in a procession, each with an emerald turkey-foot
   at the top,
reserved as their contours, saying nothing
                              . . .
the lion's ferocious chrysanthemum head

Or the metaphors may be taken from human artifacts.

      pillar body erect
on a three-cornered smooth-working chippendale claw.
                                        ("The Jerboa")

                  the intensively
                  watched eggs coming from
               the shell free it when they are freed,
                  leaving its wasp-nest flaws
                  of white on white and close-
                  laid Ionic chiton-folds
            like the lines in the mane of
            a Parthenon horse
                              ("The Paper Nautilus")

And on occasion, she uses an elaborate reversed epic simile.

            As impassioned Handel—
      meant for a lawyer and a masculine German domestic
      career—clandestinely studied the harpsichord
      and never was known to have fallen in love,
            the unconfiding frigate-bird hides
            in the height and in the majestic
                  display of his art.
                              ("The Frigate Pelican")

But, unlike Lawrence, she likes the human race. For all the evil he does, man
is, for her, a more sacred being than an animal.

            Bedizened or stark
         naked, man, the self, the being we call human, writing—
      master to this world, griffons a dark
         "Like does not like like that is obnoxious"—and writes
               error with four
      r's. Among animals, one has a sense of humour,
         Humour saves a few steps, it saves yours. Unignorant,
            modest and unemotional, and all emotion,
      he has everlasting vigour,
            power to grow

> though there are few creatures who can make one
> breathe faster and make one erecter.

The approach of her poetry is that of a naturalist but, really, their theme is almost always the Good Life. Sometimes, as in the bestiaries, she sees an animal as an emblem—the devilfish, so frightening to look at, because of the care she takes of her eggs becomes an emblem of charity, the camel-sparrow an emblem of justice, the jerboa-rat an emblem of true freedom as contrasted with the false freedom of the conqueror-tyrant—and sometimes, as in the beast fable, the behavior of animals is presented as a moral paradigm. Occasionally, as in "Elephants," the moral is direct, but, as a rule, the reader has to perceive it for himself.

The "Pangolin," written during the war, is a longish poem—nine stanzas of eleven lines each—but it is not until the end of the seventh stanza that a direct likeness between the pangolin and man is drawn:

> in fighting, mechanicked
>   like the pangolin.

On the one hand, the pangolin is an enchanting animal; on the other, it is a great honor to be created a human being. But the one way in which men can physically resemble pangolins is by putting on armor and this should not have to be necessary. The pangolin's armor is an adaptation which secures his survival, for he is an ant-eater; as creatures go, he is unpugnacious and unaggressive. But man wears armor because he is an aggressive creature full of hatred for and fear of his own kind. The moral: men ought to be gentle-natured like pangolins but, if they were, they would cease to look like pangolins, and the pangolin could not be an emblem.

Miss Moore's poems are an example of a kind of art which is not as common as it should be; they delight, not only because they are intelligent, sensitive and beautifully written, but also because they convince the reader that they have been written by someone who is personally good. Questioned about the relation between art and morals, Miss Moore herself has said:

> Must a man be good to write good poems? The villains in Shakespeare are not illiterate, are they? But rectitude *has* a ring that is implicative, I would say. And with *no* integrity, a man is not likely to write the kind of book I read.

PART SIX

Americana

The American Scene

America where there
is the little old ramshackle victoria in the south,
where cigars are smoked on the street in the north;
where there are no proof-readers, no silk-worms, no
digressions;
the wild man's land; grassless linksless, languageless country
in which letters are written
not in Spanish, not in Greek, not in Latin, not in shorthand,
but in plain American which cats and dogs can read!
—Marianne Moore

Two of James' virtues, his self-knowledge, his awareness of just what he could and could not do, and his critical literary sense, his respect for the inalienable right of every subject to its own form and treatment, are nowhere more conspicuous than in *The American Scene.*

Of all possible subjects, travel is the most difficult for an artist, as it is the easiest for a journalist. For the latter, the interesting event is the new, the extraordinary, the comic, the shocking, and all that the peripatetic journalist requires is a flair for being on the spot where and when such events happen—the rest is merely passive typewriter thumping: meaning, relation, importance, are not his quarry. The artist, on the other hand, is deprived of his most treasured liberty, the freedom to invent; successfully to extract importance from historical personal events without ever departing from them, free only to select and never to modify or to add, calls for imagination of a very high order.

Few writers have had less journalistic talent than James, and this is his defect, for the supreme masters have one trait in common with the childish scribbling mass, the vulgar curiosity of a police-court reporter. One can easily imagine Stendhal or Tolstoi or Dostoievski becoming involved in a barroom fight, but James, never. I have read somewhere a story that once, when James was visiting a French friend, the latter's mistress, unobserved, filled his top hat with champagne, but I do not believe it because, try as I will, I simply cannot conceive what James did and said when he put his hat on.

James was, of course, well aware of this limitation; he knew that both his character and circumstances confined his residence to a certain kind of house or hotel, his intimate acquaintance to a certain social class, and that such confinement might be an insuperable obstacle to writing a book of travel in which the author must try to catch the spirit, not of a particular milieu, but of a whole place, a whole social order. Nevertheless, the challenge, perhaps just because it was, for him, so particularly formidable, fascinated James from the first, and *The American Scene* is only the latest, most ambitious and best of a series of topographical writings, beginning in 1870 with sketches of Saratoga and Newport.

Immature as these early American pieces are, they seem to me more satisfactory than the subsequent descriptions of England and Europe, even the charming *A Little Tour in France* (1884). Confronted with the un-American scene, he seems prim and a little amateurish, as if he were a conscientious father writing letters to an intelligent daughter of fourteen; as guidebooks, the European travelogues are incomplete, and as personal impressions, they are timid; the reader is conscious that the traveler must have seen and felt a great deal more than he says, and refrained either from a fear of shocking or from a lack of confidence in his own judgment; but even as a young man, James was unafraid of America as a subject: puzzled often, angry sometimes, yes, but quite certain of what he felt and of his right to say it.

In letters directly and in his novels by implication James makes many criticisms of the English, but he would never have been so outspoken about them as he is, for instance, about the habits of American children of whom he writes in 1870:

> You meet them far into the evening, roaming over the piazzas and corridors of the hotels—the little girls especially—lean, pale, formidable. Occasionally childhood confesses itself, even when maternity resists, and you see at eleven o'clock at night some poor little bedizened precocity collapsed in slumber in a lonely wayside chair.

And again in 1906:

> . . . there were ladies and children all about—though indeed there may have been sometimes *but* the lone breakfasting child to deal with; the little pale, carnivorous, coffee-drinking ogre or ogress, who prowls down in advance of its elders, engages a table—dread vision! and has the "run" of the bill of fare.

All who knew James personally have spoken of the terror he could inspire when enraged, and one of the minor delights of *The American Scene* is that the stranger occasionally gets a glimpse, at a fortunately safe distance, of what these outbursts must have been like—the unhurried implacable advance of the huge offensive periods, the overwhelming alliterative barrage, the annihilating adverbial scorn.

> The freedoms of the young three—who were, by-the-way, not in their earliest bloom either—were thus bandied about in the void of the gorgeous valley without even a consciousness of its shriller, its recording echoes . . . The immodesty was too colossal to be anything but innocence, but the innocence on the other hand, was too colossal to be

anything but inane. And they were alive, the slightly stale three: they talked, they laughed, they sang, they shrieked, they romped, they scaled the pinnacle of publicity and perched on it, flapping their wings; whereby they were shown in possession of many of the movements of life.

Whom were they constructed, such specimens, to talk with or to talk over, or to talk under, and what form of address or of intercourse, what uttered, what intelligible terms of introduction, of persuasion, of menace, what developed, what specific human process of any sort, was it possible to impute to them? What reciprocities did they imply, what presumptions did they, could they, create? What happened, inconceivably, when such Greeks met such Greeks, such faces looked into such faces, and such sounds, in especial, were exchanged with such sounds? What women did they live with, what women, living with them, could yet leave them as they were? What wives, daughters, sisters, did they in fine make credible; and what, in especial, was the speech, what the manners, what the general dietary, what most the monstrous morning meal, of ladies receiving at such hands the law or the license of life?

Just what, one asks with nostalgic awe, would James have said if confronted with the spectacle of a drum-majorette?

In writing *The American Scene*, the "facts" he selected to go on are, even for James, amazingly and, one would have thought, fatally few. Though he seems to have visited Chicago (and not to have "liked" it) he confines his chapters to the East Coast from Boston to Miami. The Far West, the Midwest, the Deep South are totally ignored. This is a pity because the regional differences of the United States are significant, though not, I think, so decisively significant as the professional regionalists insist. Today it would be quite fatal to neglect the states remoter from Europe, not so much as regions in themselves, but because some of the most essential and generally typical American facts, such as the film and automobile industries, the public power projects, the divorce mills, are regionally situated. Still, even in 1906, there were many things west of Massachusetts, the landscape of Arizona, the distinctive atmosphere of San Francisco, to mention only two of them, which would have "amused" "the restless analyst," and in whose amusement his readers would have been very glad to share.*

With the second limitation that James imposed upon himself, however— his decision to reject all second-hand information and sentiment, to stick to those facts, however few, which were felt by him, however mistakenly, to be important, to be unashamedly, defiantly subjective—one can only wholeheartedly agree. In grasping the character of a society, as in judging the character of an individual, no documents, statistics, "objective" measure-

*James originally intended, it appears, to write a second volume dealing with the West and Middle West.

ments can ever compete with the single intuitive glance. Intuition may err, for though its sound judgment is, as Pascal said, only a question of good eyesight, it must be good, for the principles are subtle and numerous, and the omission of one principle leads to error; but documentation which is useless unless it is complete, must err in a field where completeness is impossible. James' eyesight was good, his mind was accurate, and he understood exactly what he was doing; he never confused his observation with his interpretation.

> The fond observer is by his very nature committed everywhere to his impression—which means essentially, I think, that he is foredoomed, in one place as in another, to "put in" a certain quantity of emotion and reflection. The turn his sensibility takes depends of course on what is before him; but when is it not in some manner exposed and alert? If it be anything really of a touchstone, it is more disposed, I hold, to easy bargains than to hard ones; it only wants to be *somehow* interested, and is not without the knowledge that an emotion is after all, at the best or the worst, but an emotion. All of which is a voluminous commentary, I admit, on the modest text that I perhaps made the University Hospital stand for too many things. That establishes at all events my contention—that the living fact, in the United States, *will* stand, other facts not preventing, for almost anything you may ask of it.

> Where, in the United States, the interest, where the pleasure of contemplation is concerned, discretion is the better part of valor and insistence too often a betrayal. It is not so much that the hostile fact crops up as that the friendly fact breaks down. If you have luckily *seen*, you have seen; carry off your prize, in this case, instantly and at any risk. Try it again and you don't, you won't, see.

Yet, if the vision had, necessarily, to be brief, it was neither poor nor vague, and only the most leisurely and luxuriant treatment could do justice to its rich possibilities. In the novels and short stories of the previous decade, James had been evolving a style of metaphorical description of the emotions which is all his own, a kind of modern Gongorism, and in *The American Scene* this imagery, no longer inhibited by the restraining hand of character or the impatient tug of plot, came to its fullest and finest bloom.

Indeed, perhaps the best way to approach this book is as a prose poem of the first order, i.e. to suspend, for the time being, one's own conclusions about America and Americans, and to read on slowly, relishing it sentence by sentence, for it is no more a guidebook than the "Ode to a Nightingale" is an ornithological essay. It is not even necessary to start at the beginning or read with continuity; one can open it at almost any page. I advise, for instance, the reader who finds James' later manner a little hard to get into, to begin by reading the long paragraph about Lee's statue which concludes the chapter on Richmond: this is, admittedly, a purple patch, but there are many others which match it.

James' firsthand experiences were, necessarily, mostly those of a tourist, namely scenic objects, landscapes, buildings, the faces and behavior of strangers, and his own reflections on what these objects stood for. Unlike his modern rival at conveying the sense of Place—D. H. Lawrence—James was no naturalist; one is not convinced that he knew one bird or flower from another. He sees Nature as a city-bred gentleman with a knowledge of the arts, and by accepting this fully, turns it to his advantage in his descriptive conceits.

... the social scene, shabby and sordid, and lost in the scale of space as the quotable line is lost in a dull epic or the needed name in an ageing memory.

The spread of this single great wash of Winter from latitude to latitude struck me in fact as having its analogy in the vast vogue of some infinitely selling novel, one of those happy volumes of which the circulation roars, periodically, from Atlantic to Pacific and from great windy state to state, in the manner as I have heard it vividly put, of a blazing prairie fire; with as little possibility of arrest from "criticism" in the one case as from the bleating of lost sheep in the other.

... the hidden ponds where the season itself seemed to blend as a young bedizened, a slightly melodramatic mother, before taking some guilty flight, hangs over the crib of her sleeping child.

But it is in his treatment of social objects and mental concepts that James reveals most clearly his great and highly original poetic gift. Outside of fairy tales, I know of no book in which things so often and so naturally become persons.

Buildings address James:

Un bon mouvement, therefore: you must make a dash for it, but you'll see I'm worth it.

James addresses buildings:

You overdo it for what you are; you overdo it still more for what you may be; and don't pretend above all, with the object lesson supplied you, close at hand, by the queer case of Newport, don't pretend, we say, not to know what we mean.

Buildings address each other:

Exquisite was what they called you, eh? We'll teach you, then, little sneak, to be exquisite! We'll allow none of that rot round here.

At Farmington, the bullying railroad orders taste and tradition

> off their decent avenue without a fear that they will "stand up" to it.

From Philadelphia the alluring train:

> disvulgarized of passengers, steams away, in disinterested empty form, to some terminus too noble to be marked in *our* poor schedules.

Again, since *The Faerie Queene*, what book has been more hospitable to allegorical figures?
At Mount Vernon:

> the slight, pale, bleeding Past, in a patched homespun suit, stands there taking the thanks of the Bloated Present, having woundedly rescued from thieves and brought to his door the fat, locked pocket book of which that personage appears to be the owner.

At Baltimore the Muse of History descends in a quick white flash to declare that she has found that city "a charming patient."
  In Richmond the Spirit of the South reveals herself for a vivid moment,

> a figure somehow blighted and stricken discomfortably, impossibly seated in an invalid chair, and yet fixing one with strange eyes that were half a defiance and half a deprecation of one's noticing, and much more of one's referring to, an abnormal sign.

In Florida the American Woman is waiting to state her case in the manner of a politician in Thucydides:

> How can I do *all* the grace, all the interest, as I'm expected to? Yes, literally all the interest that isn't the mere interest on the money . . . All I want—that is all I need, for there is perhaps a difference—is, to put it simply, that my parents and my brothers and my male cousins should consent to exist otherwise than occultly, undiscoverably, or, as I suppose you'd call it, irresponsibly.

When the "recent immigrant," to copy the Jamesian nomenclature, compares his own impressions with those of the "restless analyst," he is immediately struck by how little, on the one hand, America has changed in any decisive way—the changes, great as they are, seem but extensions and modifications of a pattern already observable thirty years ago—and, on the other, by the irrevocable and catastrophic alterations in Europe.
  The features of the American scene which most struck the analyst then are those which most strike the immigrant now, whether they be minor details, like the magnificent boots and teeth, the heavy consumption of candy, "the vagueness of separation between apartments, between hall and room, between one room and another, between the one you are in and the one you

are not in," or major matters like the promiscuous gregariousness, the lack, even among the rich, of constituted privacy, the absence of forms for vice no less than for virtue, the "spoiling" of women and their responsibility for the whole of culture, above all the elimination from the scene of the squire and the parson.* It takes the immigrant a little time to discover just why the United States seems so different from any of the countries he resentfully or nostalgically remembers, but the crucial difference is, I think, just this last elimination of "the pervasive Patron" and "the old ecclesiastical arrogance for which, oh! a thousand times, the small substitutes, the mere multiplication of the signs of theological enterprise, in the tradition and on the scale of commercial and industrial enterprise, have no attenuation worth mentioning."

What in fact is missing, what has been consciously rejected, with all that such a rejection implies, is the *romanitas* upon which Europe was founded and which she has not ceased attempting to preserve. This is a point which, at the risk of becoming tedious, must be enlarged upon, since the issue between America and Europe is no longer a choice between social leveling and social distinctions. The leveling is a universal and inexorable fact. Nothing can prevent the liquidation of the European nations or any other nation in the great continents, Asia, Africa, America, the liquidation of the "individual" (in the eighteenth-century liberal meaning of the word) in the collective proletariat, the liquidation of Christendom in the neutral world. From that there is no refuge anywhere. But one's final judgment of Europe and America depends, it seems to me, upon whether one thinks that America (or America as a symbol) is right to reject *romanitas* or that Europe is right in trying to find new forms of it suited to the "democratized" societies of our age.

The fundamental presupposition of *romanitas*, secular or sacred, is that virtue is prior to liberty, i.e. what matters most is that people should think and act rightly; of course it is preferable that they should do so consciously of their own free will, but if they cannot or will not, they must be made to, the majority by the spiritual pressure of education and tradition, the minority by physical coercion, for liberty to act wrongly is not liberty but license. The antagonistic presupposition, which is not peculiar to America and would probably not be accepted by many Americans, but for which this country has come, symbolically, to stand, is that liberty is prior to virtue, i.e. liberty cannot be distinguished from license, for freedom of choice is nei-

---

*The immigrant would like to add one element, the excesses of the climate, which is either much too hot or much too cold or much too wet or much too dry or even, in the case of the California coast, much too mild, a sort of meteorological Back Bay. And then—oh dear!—the *insects*, and the *snakes*, and the *poison ivy* . . . The truth is, Nature never intended human beings to live here, and her hostility, which confined the Indian to a nomad life and forbids the white man to relax his vigilance and will for one instant, must be an important factor in determining the American character.

ther good nor bad but the human prerequisite without which virtue and vice have no meaning. Virtue is, of course, preferable to vice, but to choose vice is preferable to having virtue chosen for one.

To those who make the first presupposition, both State and Church have the same positive moral function; to those who make the second, their functions differ: the function of the State becomes a negative one—to prevent the will of the strong from interfering with the will of the weak, or the wills of the weak with one another, even if the strong should be in the right and the weak in the wrong—and the Church, whether Catholic or Protestant, divorced from the State, becomes a witness, an offered opportunity, a community of *converts*. The real issue has been obscured, for both sides, by the historical struggle for social equality which made liberty seem the virtue—or license the vice—of which equality was the prized or detested precondition. This was natural since, when the struggle began, the most glaring cause of lack of liberty was the privileged position of the few and the unprivileged position of the many, so that a blow struck for equality was, in most cases, at the same time a blow struck for liberty, but the assumed order of priority was false all the same. The possibility that de Tocqueville foresaw from an inspection of America in 1830, has become a dreadful reality in the Europe of 1946, namely, that *romanitas* is perfectly capable of adapting itself to an egalitarian and untraditional society; it can even drop absolute values and replace the priest by the social engineer without violating its essential nature (which is and always was not Christian but Manichean). And it was from America, the first egalitarian society, that it learned how to adapt itself. For instance, it took the technique of mass advertising, eliminated the competitive element and changed the sales object from breakfast foods to political passions; it took the egalitarian substitute for tradition—fashion—and translated it from the putting over of best sellers and evening frocks to the selling of an ever-switching party line; it took the extra-legal vigilantes and put them into official uniforms; it took the inert evil of race prejudice and made it a dynamic evil. An America which does not realize the difference between equality and liberty is in danger, for, start with equality in order to arrive at liberty and the moment you come to a situation where inequality is or seems to you, rightly or wrongly, a stubborn fact, you will come to grief. For instance, the unequal distribution of intellectual gifts is a fact; since they refuse to face it, the institutions of Higher Learning in America cannot decide whether they are to be Liberal Arts Colleges for the exceptional few or vocational schools for the average many, and so fail to do their duty by either. On the other, more sinister, hand, the Southerner, rightly or wrongly, believes that the Negro is his inferior; by putting equality before liberty, he then refuses him the most elementary human liberties, for example, the educational and economic liberties that are the only means by which the Negro could possibly become the equal of the white, so that the latter can never be proven mistaken.

Democratic snobbery or race prejudice is uglier than the old aristocratic snobbery because the included are relatively so many and the excluded relatively so few. The exclusiveness, for instance, of Baron de Charlus is forgivable and even charming. If Charlus will speak to only half a dozen people, it cannot be supposed that the millions suffer severely from being unable to speak to Charlus; his behavior is frankly irrational, a personal act from which, if anyone suffers, it is only himself. The exclusiveness of the American Country Club—I cannot share James' pleasure in that institution—is both inexcusable and vulgar, for, since it purports to be democratic, its exclusion of Jews is a contradiction for which it has to invent dishonest rationalizations.

As the issue between virtue first and liberty first becomes clearer, so does the realization that the cost to any society that accepts the latter is extremely high, and to some may seem prohibitive. One can no longer make the task look easier than it is by pretending, as the liberals of the Enlightenment believed, that men are naturally good. No, it is just as true as it ever was that man is born in sin, that the majority are always, relatively, in the wrong, the minority sometimes, relatively, in the right (everyone, of course, is free at any time to belong to either), and all, before God, absolutely in the wrong, that all of the people some of the time and some of the people most of the time will abuse their liberty and treat it as the license of an escaped slave. But if the principle is accepted, it means accepting this: it means accepting a State that, in comparison to its Roman rival, is dangerously weak (though realizing that, since people will never cease trying to interfere with the liberties of others in pursuing their own, the State can never wither away. Tyranny today, anarchy tomorrow is a Neo-Roman daydream); it means accepting a "Society," in the collective inclusive sense, that is as neutral to values (liberty is not a value but the ground of value) as the "nature" of physics; it means accepting an educational system in which, in spite of the fact that authority is essential to the growth of the individual who is lost without it, the responsibility for recognizing authority is laid on the pupil; it means accepting the impossibility of any "official" or "public" art; and, for the individual, it means accepting the lot of the Wandering Jew, i.e. the loneliness and anxiety of having to choose himself, his faith, his vocation, his tastes. The Margin is a hard taskmaster; it says to the individual: "It's no good your running to me and asking me to make you into someone. You must choose. I won't try to prevent your choice, but I can't and won't help you make it. If you try to put your trust in me, in public opinion, you will become, not someone but no one, a neuter atom of the public."

If one compares Americans with Europeans, one might say, crudely and too tidily, that the mediocre American is possessed by the Present and the mediocre European is possessed by the Past. The task of overcoming mediocrity, that is, of learning to possess instead of being possessed, is thus different in each case, for the American has to make the Present *his* present, and the European the Past *his* past. There are two ways of taking possession of the Present: one is with the help of the Comic or Ironic spirit. Hence the superiority of American (and Yiddish) humor. The other way is to choose a Past, i.e. to go physically or in the spirit to Europe. James' own explanation of his migration—

> To make so much money that you won't, that you don't "mind," don't mind anything—that is absolutely, I think, the main American formula. Thus your making no money—or so little that it passes there for none— and being thereby distinctly reduced to minding, amounts to your being reduced to the knowledge that America is no place for you. . . . The withdrawal of the considerable group of the pecuniarily disqualified seems, for the present, an assured movement; there will always be scattered individuals condemned to mind on a scale beyond any scale of making—

seems to me only partly true; better T. S. Eliot's observation in his essay on James:

> It is the final consummation of an American to become, not an Englishman, but a European—something no born Englishman, no person of European nationality can become.

James wrote a short story, "The Great Good Place," which has been praised by Mr Fadiman and condemned by Mr Matthiessen, in both instances, I think, for the wrong reason, for both take it literally. The former says: "The Place is what our civilization could be. . . . It is a hotel without noise, a club without newspapers. You even have to pay for service." If this were true, then the latter would be quite right to complain, as he does, that it is the vulgar daydream of a rich bourgeois intellectual. I believe, however, that, in his own discreet way, James is writing a religious parable, that is, he is not describing some social Utopia, but a spiritual state which is achievable by the individual now, that the club is a symbol of this state—not its cause, and the money a symbol of the sacrifice and suffering demanded to attain and preserve it. Anyway, the story contains a passage of dialogue which seems relevant to *The American Scene.*

> "Every man must arrive by himself and on his own feet—isn't that so? We're Brothers here for the time as in a great monastery, and we immediately think of each other and recognize each other as such: but we must have first got here as we can, and we meet after long journeys by complicated ways."
> "Where is it?"
> "I shouldn't be surprised if it were much nearer than one ever suspected."

"Nearer 'town,' do you mean?"
"Nearer everything—nearer everyone."

Yes. Nearer everything. Nearer than James himself, perhaps, suspected, to the "hereditary thinness" of the American Margin, to "the packed and hoisted basket" and "the torture rooms of the living idiom," nearer to the unspeakable jukeboxes, the horrible Rockettes and the insane salads, nearer to the anonymous countryside littered with heterogeneous *dreck* and the synonymous cities besotted with electric signs, nearer to radio commercials and congressional oratory and Hollywood Christianity, nearer to all the "democratic" lusts and licenses, without which, perhaps, the analyst and the immigrant alike would never understand by contrast the nature of the Good Place nor desire it with sufficient desperation to stand a chance of arriving.

Postscript: Rome *v.* Monticello

Of course, neither the Roman nor the Liberal presupposition is wholly true, for both represent an abstraction from historical reality.

If we consider human relations purely objectively, in abstraction from the human beings who enter into them, then the moral problem is of right or wrong action and the problem of choice is irrelevant; if we consider human beings purely subjectively, in abstraction from their relations to each other, the moral problem is one of liberty or slavery.

In everyday life we instinctively adopt the Roman position in relation to strangers and the Liberal position in relation to our friends. If a stranger forges my name to a check, I do not ask if he had an unhappy childhood, I call the police; if a friend does the same thing, I ask myself what can be the matter with him and the matter with me, that he should so violate our friendship.

The Roman can show that, at any given time, there is always a class, e.g. children below a certain age, and some individuals, e.g. criminals and lunatics whose inability or refusal to rule themselves makes them a menace to others and whose freedom therefore must be to some degree restrained. The Liberal, on the other hand, can show that a hard and fast division between those who cannot rule themselves and those who can is false. The newborn baby has traces of the capacity to rule itself and the wisest and best man cannot rule himself perfectly. Further, in the wisest ruler there remain traces of selfish passion in his relation to those whom he rules. In so far as he enjoys ruling others—and there always is an element of pleasure in so doing—he must desire that there remain people who cannot rule themselves, that his attempt to educate them to freedom will fail.

Toilet training, for example, would seem at first sight a case in which the Roman position was unassailable; no baby is born in control of his reflexes and no sane adult regards the conditioned control of his reflexes as a mistake or consciously rebels. Yet psychologists have been able to demonstrate that even here, the end of right action cannot be separated from the means of inculcation, that a taste for power, impatience, or even mere ignorance of the right means, can violate the traces of free will already present in the baby with deleterious effects in later life.

The Roman must concede this but then correct the tendency of the Liberal to abandon all conditioning educational techniques in favor of a mixture of rational explanation and learning by trial and error. For example, no free exercise of the human mind is possible until man has learned to exclude the irrelevant distractions of his immediate environment and concentrate on the problem he is attacking, or until he has learned to be truthful, to subordinate his desires to what is the case; it is only when concentration and truthfulness have become second nature to him that he will listen to reason or recognize an error as an error.

In its justifiable reaction against the mechanical learning by rote of, say, mathematical operations, progressive education is tending to carry its distaste for conditioning and authority into a sphere where it is fundamental, and threatening to produce a generation which may not think mechanically but only because it cannot think at all; it has never learned how.

The class distinctions proper to a democratic society are not those of rank or money, still less, as is apt to happen when these are abandoned, of race, but of age. In a democracy it is more, not less, important than in hierarchical and static societies that a distance should be kept between the young and the adult, the adult and the old: it is, I fear, Utopian to hope for them, but what the United States needs are puberty initiation rites and a council of elders.

Red Ribbon on a White Horse

"Mowing hay by hand! Bless their hearts!"
—An American matron in the train
between Bologna and Florence

Reading Miss Yezierska's book* sets me thinking again about that famous and curious statement in the Preamble to the Constitution about the self-evident right of all men to "the pursuit of happiness," for I have read few accounts of such a pursuit so truthful and moving as hers.

*Anzia Yezierska, *Red Ribbon on a White Horse*, Scribner's. 1950.

To be happy means to be free, not from pain or fear, but from care or anxiety. A man is so free when (1) he knows what he desires and (2) what he desires is real and not fantastic. A desire is real when the possibility of satisfaction exists for the individual who entertains it and the existence of such a possibility depends, first, on his present historical and social situation—a desire for a Cadillac which may be real for a prosperous American businessman would be fantastic for a Chinese peasant—and, secondly, on his natural endowment as an individual—for a girl with one eye to desire to be kept by a millionaire would be fantastic, for a girl with two beautiful ones it may not. To say that the satisfaction of a desire is possible does not mean that it is certain but that, if the desire is not satisfied, a definite and meaningful reason can be given. Thus, if the American businessman fails to get the Cadillac he desires and asks himself, "Why?" he can give a sensible answer like, "My wife had to have an emergency operation which took my savings"; but if the Chinese peasant asks, "Why cannot I buy a Cadillac?" there are an infinite number of reasons which can only be summed up in the quite irrational answer, "Because I am I." The businessman suffers disappointment or pain but does not become unhappy; the peasant, unless he dismisses his desire as fantastic, becomes unhappy because to question his lack of satisfaction is to question the value of his existence.

So long as it is a matter of immediate material goods, few sane individuals cherish fantastic desires after the age of puberty, but there are desires for spiritual goods which are much more treacherous, e.g. the desire to find a vocation in life, to have a dedicated history. "What do I want to be? A writer? A chemist? A priest?" Since I am concerned not with any immediate objective good but with pledging the whole of my unknown future in advance, the chances of self-deception are much greater because it will be years before I can be certain whether my choice is real or fantastic. Nor can any outsider make the decision for me; he can only put questions to me which make me more aware of what my decision involves.

Miss Yezierska's book is an account of her efforts to discard fantastic desires and find real ones, both material and spiritual.

She began life in a Polish ghetto, i.e. in the bottom layer of the stratified European heap. In the more advanced countries of Europe, like England, it had become possible for a talented individual to rise a class, a generation, but in Russia, above all for a Jew, it was still quite impossible; if once one had been born in the ghetto, then in the ghetto one would die. For its inhabitants extreme poverty and constant fear of a pogrom were normal, and even so humble a desire as the wish to eat white bread was fantastic. So it had been for centuries until, suddenly, a possibility of escape was opened—immigration to America. What America would provide positively in place of the ghetto remained to be seen, but at least it would be different and any sufferings she might inflict would, at the very least, not be worse.

So Miss Yezierska and her family came and found themselves on the Lower East Side. Here was poverty still but less absolute, exploitation but the possibility of one day becoming an exploiter, racial discrimination but no pogroms. Was their new condition an improvement on their former one? It was hard to be certain. Where poverty is accepted as normal and permanent, the poor develop a certain style of living which extracts the maximum comfort from the minimum materials, but where poverty is held to be temporary or accidental, the preoccupation with escape leaves no time for such amenities; every European visitor to the States, I think, receives the impression that nowhere else in the world is real poverty—admittedly, rarer here than anywhere else—so cheerless, sordid and destitute of all grace.

Moreover, in the "bad old days" of which Miss Yezierska writes—a more lively social conscience and a slackening of the immigrant stream have largely put a stop to it—in no European country, it seems, were the very poor treated with such contempt. In Europe the rich man and the poor man were thought of as being two different kinds of men; the poor man might be an inferior kind but he was a man: but here the poor man was not, as such, a man, but a person in a state of poverty from which, if he were a real man, he would presently extricate himself. The newly arriving poor, to judge from Miss Yezierska's description of the sweatshop, were treated by their predecessors, it seems, like freshmen by upperclassmen, i.e. subjected to a process of "hazing" so as to toughen their character and stiffen their determination to rise to a position of immunity.

For the older generation particularly, who, in any case, had usually immigrated for the sake of their children, not of themselves, the new life often seemed only a little better materially, and spiritually very much worse. The fellowship of suffering lasts only so long as none of the sufferers can escape. Open a door through which many but probably not all can escape one at a time and the neighborly community may disintegrate, all too easily, into a stampeding crowd. Those who had learned how to be happy even in prison and could neither understand nor desire another life stood abandoned, watching the stampede with bewilderment and horror.

Some, like Boruch Shlomoi Mayer, simply wanted to go back:

> To me, America is a worse *Goluth* than Poland. The ukases and pogroms from the Czar, all the killings that could not kill us gave us the strength to live with God. Learning was learning—dearer than gold. . . . But here in New York, the synagogues are in the hands of godless lumps of flesh. A butcher, a grocer, any moneymaker could buy himself into a president of a synagogue. With all that was bad under the Czar, the synagogue was still God's light in time of darkness. Better to die there than to live here. . . .

Others continued to live their old life with uncompromising indifference to the new world. Miss Yezierska's father, for instance, had a vocation, the study of the Torah, which involved his being supported by his wife and children. He had expected them to do so in Plinsk, he expected them to continue doing so in New York. But what they had accepted in Poland as an extra burden, worth bearing for the honor in which a learned and holy man was held by the community, was bound to seem intolerable in America, where not only was a nonearner regarded as an idler but also the possibility for the family of acquiring status existed in proportion to their earning capacity.

His daughter, however, as she later realized, was more like him than either of them at the time could perceive. Had she been less like him, had she simply desired money and a good marriage, there would have been less friction between them but she, too, was seeking for a dedicated life of her own, which in his eyes was impious, for all vocations but one were for men only.

"A woman alone, not a wife and not a mother, has no existence." She, however, wanted a vocation all to herself and thought she had found it in writing. She began, as she tells us, with the hope that "by writing out what I don't know and can't understand, it would stop hurting me." At the same time, of course, she wanted money to satisfy her needs. This is any artist's eternal problem, that he needs money as a man but works for love. Even in the case of the most popular writer, money is not the purpose for which he writes, though popularity may be.

So she begins; she writes a book, *Hungry Hearts*, about the life of a poor immigrant, which is well reviewed but does not sell; then, suddenly, the American Fairy—whether she is a good or wicked fairy, who knows?—waves her wand and she is transported in an instant from Hester Street to Hollywood; from one day to the next, that is, suffering is abolished for her. How does she feel? More unhappy than she has ever been in her life. To have the desires of the poor and be transferred in a twinkling of an eye to a world which can only be real for those who have the desires of the rich is to be plunged into the severest anxiety. The foreshortening of time which is proper to a dream or a fairy story is a nightmare in actual life.

Further, to be called to Hollywood is not like winning a fortune in the Calcutta sweepstakes; money is showered upon one because it is believed that one is a valuable piece of property out of which much larger sums can be made. For a writer this is only bearable if he knows exactly what he wants to write and if what he can write happens to pay off the investors as they expect. Miss Yezierska was too young to be the former and, by snatching her away from Hester Street and the only experiences about which she knew, the film magnates effectively destroyed the possibility that their expensive goose might lay another golden egg. In fact, they gave it such a fright that it stopped laying altogether.

The sudden paralysis or drying up of the creative power occurs to artists everywhere but nowhere, perhaps, more frequently than in America; nowhere else are there so many writers who produced one or two books in their youth and then nothing. I think one reason for this may be the dominance of the competitive spirit in the American ethos. A material good like a washing machine is not a unique good but one example of a kind of good; accordingly one washing machine can be compared with another and judged better or worse. The best, indeed the only, way to stimulate the production of better washing machines is by competition. But a work of art is not a good of a certain kind but a unique good so that, strictly speaking, no work of art is comparable to another. An inferior washing machine is preferable to no washing machine at all, but a work of art is either acceptable, whatever its faults, to the individual who encounters it or unacceptable, whatever its merits. The writer who allows himself to become infected by the competitive spirit proper to the production of material goods so that, instead of trying to write *his* book, he tries to write one which is better than somebody else's book is in danger of trying to write the absolute masterpiece which will eliminate all competition once and for all and, since this task is totally unreal, his creative powers cannot relate to it, and the result is sterility.

In other and more static societies than in the United States an individual derives much of his sense of identity and value from his life-membership in a class—the particular class is not important—from which neither success nor failure, unless very spectacular, can oust him, but, in a society where any status is temporary and any variation in the individual's achievement alters it, his sense of his personal value must depend—unless he is a religious man—largely upon what he achieves: the more successful he is, the nearer he comes to the ideal good of absolute certainty as to his value; the less successful he is, the nearer he comes to the abyss of nonentity.

With the coming of the depression Miss Yezierska ceased to be a solitary failure and became one of millions who could not be called failures, because the positions in which they could succeed or fail no longer existed. It was surely the height of irony that, in a country where the proof of one's importance had been that one was rich and popular, people should suddenly, in order to prove that they were important enough to eat, have to go to elaborate lengths to establish that they were penniless and friendless.

The Arts Project of the W.P.A. was, perhaps, one of the noblest and most absurd undertakings ever attempted by any state. Noble because no other state has ever cared whether its artists as a group lived or died; other governments have hired certain individual artists to glorify their operations and have even granted a small pension from time to time to some artist with fame or influence, but to consider, in a time of general distress, starving artists as artists and not simply as paupers is unique to the Roosevelt administration. Yet absurd, because a state can only function bureaucratically and impersonally—it has to assume that every member of a class is equivalent or comparable to every other member—but every artist, good or bad, is a member of a class of one. You can collect fifty unemployed plumbers, test them to eliminate the unemployable, and set the remainder to work on whatever plumbing jobs you can find, but if you collect fifty unemployed writers, ex-professors, New England spinsters, radicals, Bohemians, etc., there is no test of their abilities which applies fairly to them all and no literary task you can devise which can be properly done by even a minority of them. While only the laziest and most inefficient of your plumbers will let you down, because the jobs you give them are the jobs for which they have been trained and regard as theirs, only the writers with the strictest sense of moral, as distinct from professional, duty will fail to cheat you if, as must almost inevitably be the case, the literary job you offer them is one in which they take no interest, not because writers are intrinsically lazier or more dishonest than plumbers, but because they can see no sense in what you are asking them to do.

It is easy for the accountant to frown on the W.P.A. for its inefficiency and for the artists to sneer at it for its bureaucracy, but the fact remains that, thanks to it, a number of young artists of talent were enabled, at a very critical time in their lives, to get started upon their creative careers. As for the rest, the executive might just as well—and I dare say would have been glad to—have been honest, given them their weekly checks and sent them home, but the legislature which could endure such honesty could exist only in heaven.

Among her companions in poverty and comedy, Miss Yezierska felt once more to some degree that happiness of "belonging" which years before she had felt in Hester Street, though she only realized this after it was over. But belonging to some degree is not enough; one must belong completely or the feeling soon withers. Once again the lack of a common memory of the past and a common anticipation of the future was a fatal barrier, not only for her but for most of her fellows.

> The word "home" raised a smile in us all three,
> And one repeated it, smiling just so
> That all knew what he meant and none would say,
> Between three counties far apart that lay
> We were divided and looked strangely each
> At the other, and we knew we were not friends
> But fellows in a union that ends
> With the necessity for it, as it ought.
>
> (Edward Thomas)

No, the accidental community of suffering was not the clue to happiness and she had to look further.

Miss Yezierska's autobiography is, literally, the story of an early twentieth-century immigrant, but it has a deeper and more general significance today when, figuratively, the immigrant is coming more and more to stand as the symbol for Everyman, as the natural and unconscious community of tradition rapidly disappears from the earth.

Postscript: The Almighty Dollar

Political and technological developments are rapidly obliterating all cultural differences and it is possible that, in a not remote future, it will be impossible to distinguish human beings living on one area of the earth's surface from those living on any other, but our different pasts have not yet been completely erased and cultural differences are still perceptible. The most striking difference between an American and a European is the difference in their attitudes towards money. Every European knows, as a matter of historical fact, that, in Europe, wealth could only be acquired at the expense of other human beings, either by conquering them or by exploiting their labor in factories. Further, even after the Industrial Revolution began, the number of persons who could rise from poverty to wealth was small; the vast majority took it for granted that they would not be much richer nor poorer than their fathers. In consequence, no European associates wealth with personal merit or poverty with personal failure.

To a European, money means power, the freedom to do as he likes, which also means that, consciously or unconsciously, he says: "I want to have as much money as possible myself and others to have as little money as possible."

In the United States, wealth was also acquired by stealing, but the real exploited victim was not a human being but poor Mother Earth and her creatures who were ruthlessly plundered. It is true that the Indians were expropriated or exterminated, but this was not, as it had always been in Europe, a matter of the conqueror seizing the wealth of the conquered, for the Indian had never realized the potential riches of his country. It is also true that, in the Southern states, men lived on the labor of slaves, but slave labor did not make them fortunes; what made slavery in the South all the more inexcusable was that, in addition to being morally wicked, it didn't even pay off handsomely.

Thanks to the natural resources of the country, every American, until quite recently, could reasonably look forward to making more money than his father, so that, if he made less, the fault must be his; he was either lazy or inefficient. What an American values, therefore, is not the possession of money as such, but his power to make it as a proof of his manhood; once he has proved himself by making it, it has served its function and can be lost or given away. In no society in history have rich men given away so large a part of their fortunes. A poor American feels guilty at being poor, but less guilty than an American *rentier* who has inherited wealth but is doing nothing to increase it; what can the latter do but take to drink and psychoanalysis?

In the Fifth Circle on the Mount of Purgatory, I do not think that many Americans will be found among the Avaricious; but I suspect that the Prodigals may be almost an American colony. The great vice of Americans is not materialism but a lack of respect for matter.

Robert Frost

But Islands of the Blessed, bless you son,
I never came upon a blessed one.

If asked who said *Beauty is Truth, Truth Beauty!*, a great many readers would answer "Keats." But Keats said nothing of the sort. It is what he said the Grecian Urn said, his description and criticism of a certain kind of work of art, the kind from which the evils and problems of this life, the "heart high sorrowful and cloyed," are deliberately excluded. The Urn, for example, depicts, among other beautiful sights, the citadel of a hill town; it does not depict warfare, the evil which makes the citadel necessary.

Art arises out of our desire for both beauty and truth and our knowledge that they are not identical. One might say that every poem shows some sign of a rivalry between Ariel and Prospero; in every good poem their relation is more or less happy, but it is never without its tensions. The Grecian Urn states Ariel's position; Prospero's has been equally succinctly stated by Dr Johnson: *The only end of writing is to enable the readers better to enjoy life or better to endure it.*

We want a poem to be beautiful, that is to say, a verbal earthly paradise, a timeless world of pure play, which gives us delight precisely because of its contrast to our historical existence with all its insoluble problems and inescapable suffering; at the same time we want a poem to be true, that is to say, to provide us with some kind of revelation about our life which will show us what life is really like and free us from self-enchantment and deception, and a poet cannot bring us any truth without introducing into his poetry the problematic, the painful, the disorderly, the ugly. Though every poem involves *some* degree of collaboration between Ariel and Prospero, the role of each varies in importance from one poem to another: it is usually possible to say of a poem and, sometimes, of the whole output of a poet, that it is Ariel-dominated or Prospero-dominated.

Hot sun, cool fire, tempered with sweet air,
Black shade, fair nurse, shadow my white hair:
Shine, sun; burn, fire; breathe, air, and ease me;
Black shade, fair nurse, shroud me and please me:
Shadow, my sweet nurse, keep me from burning,
Make not my glad cause, cause for mourning,

Let not my beauty's fire
Inflame unstaid desire,
Nor pierce any bright eye
That wandereth lightly.
                    (George Peele, "Bathsabe's Song")

The road at the top of the rise
Seems to come to an end
And take off into the skies.
So at a distant bend

It seems to go into a wood,
The place of standing still
As long as the trees have stood.
But say what Fancy will,

The mineral drops that explode
To drive my ton of car
Are limited to the road.
They deal with the near and far,

And have almost nothing to do
With the absolute flight and rest
The universal blue
And local green suggest.
                    (Robert Frost, "The Middleness of the Road")

Both poems are written in the first person singular, but the Peele-Bathsabe *I* is very different from the Frost *I*. The first seems anonymous, hardly more than a grammatical form; one cannot imagine meeting Bathsabe at a dinner party. The second *I* names a historical individual in a specific situation—he is driving an automobile in a certain kind of landscape.

Take away what Bathsabe says and she vanishes, for what she says does not seem to be a response to any situation or event. If one asks what her song is about, one cannot give a specific answer, only a vague one:—a beautiful young girl, any beautiful girl, on any sunny morning, half-awake and half-asleep, is reflecting on her beauty with a mixture of self-admiration and pleasing fear, pleasing because she is unaware of any real danger; a girl who was really afraid of a Peeping Tom would sing very differently. If one tries to explain why one likes the song, or any poem of this kind, one finds oneself talking about language, the handling of the rhythm, the pattern of vowels and consonants, the placing of caesuras, epanorthosis, etc.

Frost's poem, on the other hand, is clearly a response to an experience which preceded any words and without which the poem could not have come into being, for the purpose of the poem is to define that experience and draw wisdom from it. Though the beautiful verbal element is not absent—it is a poem, not a passage of informative prose—this is subordinate in importance to the truth of what it says.

If someone suddenly asks me to give him an example of good poetry, it is probably a poem of the Peele sort which will immediately come to my mind: but if I am in a state of emotional excitement, be it joy or grief, and try to think of a poem which is relevant and illuminating to my condition, it is a poem of the Frost sort which I shall be most likely to recall.

Ariel, as Shakespeare has told us, has no passions. That is his glory and his limitation. The earthly paradise is a beautiful place but nothing of serious importance can occur in it.

An anthology selected by Ariel, including only poems like the *Eclogues* of Vergil, *Las Soledades* of Góngora and poets like Campion, Herrick, Mallarmé, would, in the long run, repel us by its narrowness and monotony of feeling: for Ariel's other name is Narcissus.

It can happen that a poem which, when written, was Prospero-dominated, becomes an Ariel poem for later generations. The nursery rhyme *I will sing you One O* may very well originally have been a mnemonic rhyme for teaching sacred lore of the highest importance. The sign that, for us, it has become an Ariel poem is that we have no curiosity about the various persons it refers to: it is as anthropologists not as readers of poetry that we ask who the lily-white boys really were. On the other hand, anything we can learn about the persons whom Dante introduces into *The Divine Comedy*, contributes to our appreciation of his poem.

It is also possible for a poet himself to be mistaken as to the kind of poem he is writing. For example, at first reading, *Lycidas* seems to be by Prospero, for it purports to deal with the most serious matters possible—death, grief, sin, resurrection. But I believe this to be an illusion. On closer inspection, it seems to me that only the robes are Prospero's and that Ariel has dressed up in them for fun, so that it is as irrelevant to ask, "Who is the Pilot of the Galilean Lake?" as it is to ask, "Who is the Pobble who has no toes?" and He who walks the waves is merely an Arcadian shepherd whose name happens to be Christ. If *Lycidas* is read in this way, as if it were a poem by Edward Lear, then it seems to me one of the most beautiful poems in the English language: if, however, it is read as the Prospero poem it apparently claims to be, then it must be condemned, as Dr Johnson condemned it, for being unfeeling and frivolous, since one expects wisdom and revelation and it provides neither.

The Ariel-dominated poet has one great advantage; he can only fail in one way—his poem may be trivial. The worst one can say of one of his poems is that it needn't have been written. But the Prospero-dominated poet can fail in a number of different ways. Of all English poets, Wordsworth is perhaps the one with the least element of Ariel that is compatible with being a poet at all, and so provides the best examples of what happens when Prospero tries to write entirely by himself.

> The Bird and Cage they both were his:
> 'Twas my Son's bird: and neat and trim
> He kept it; many voyages
> This singing bird has gone with him:
> When last he sailed he left the bird behind;
> As it might be, perhaps from bodings in his mind.

Reading such a passage, one exclaims, "The man can't write," which is something that can never be said about Ariel; when Ariel can't write, he doesn't. But Prospero is capable of graver errors than just being ridiculous; since he is trying to say something which is true, if he fails, the result can be worse than trivial. It can be false, compelling the reader to say, not "This poem need not have been written," but "This poem should not have been written."

Both in theory and practice Frost is a Prospero-dominated poet. In the preface to his *Collected Poems*, he writes:

> The sound is the gold in the ore. Then we will have the sound out alone and dispense with the inessential. We do till we make the discovery that the object in writing poetry is to make all poems sound as different as possible from each other, and the resources for that of vowels, consonants, punctuation, syntax, words, sentences, meter are not enough. We need the help of context—meaning—subject matter. . . . And we are back in poetry as merely one more art of having something to say, sound or unsound. Probably better if sound, because deeper and from wider experience. [A poem] begins in delight and ends in wisdom . . . a clarification of life—not necessarily a great clarification such as sects and cults are founded on, but in a momentary stay against confusion.

His poetic style is what I think Professor C. S. Lewis would call Good Drab. The music is always that of the speaking voice, quiet and sensible, and I cannot think of any other modern poet, except Cavafy, who uses language more simply. He rarely employs metaphors, and there is not a word, not a historical or literary reference in the whole of his work which would be strange to an unbookish boy of fifteen. Yet he manages to make this simple kind of speech express a wide variety of emotion and experience.

> Be that as may be, she was in their song.
> Moreover her voice upon their voices crossed
> Had now persisted in the woods so long
> That probably it would never be lost.
> Never again would bird's song be the same.
> And to do that to birds was why she came.

. . .

> I hope if he is where hc sees me now
> He's so far off he can't see what I've come to.
> You *can* come down from everything to nothing.
> All is, if I'd a-known when I was young
> And full of it, that this would be the end,
> It doesn't seem as if I'd had the courage
> To make so free and kick up in folk's faces.
> I might have, but it doesn't seem as if.

The emotions in the first passage are tender, happy, and its reflections of a kind which could only be made by an educated man. The emotions in the second are violent and tragic, and the speaker a woman with no schooling. Yet the diction in both is equally simple. There are a few words the man uses which the woman would not use herself, but none she could not understand; her syntax is a little cruder than his, but only a little. Yet their two voices sound as distinct as they sound authentic.

Frost's poetic speech is the speech of a mature mind, fully awake and in control of itself; it is not the speech of dream or of uncontrollable passion. Except in reported speech, interjections, imperatives and rhetorical interrogatives are rare. This does not mean, of course, that his poems are lacking in feeling; again and again, one is aware of strong, even violent, emotion behind what is actually said, but the saying is reticent, the poetry has, as it were, an auditory chastity. It would be impossible for Frost, even if he wished, to produce an unabashed roar of despair, as Shakespeare's tragic heroes so often can, but the man who wrote the following lines has certainly been acquainted with despair.

> I have stood still and stopped the sound of feet
> When far away an interrupted cry
> Came over houses from another street,
> But not to call me back or say good-bye.
> And further still at an unearthly height
> One luminary clock against the sky
> Proclaimed the time was neither wrong nor right.
> I have been one acquainted with the night.

Every style has its limitations. It would be as impossible to write "*Ebauche d'un Serpent*" in the style of Frost as it would be to write "The Death of the Hired Man" in the style of Valéry. A style, like Frost's which approximates to ordinary speech is necessarily contemporary, the style of a man living in the first half of the twentieth century; it is not well suited, therefore, to subjects from the distant past, in which the difference between then and today is significant, or to mythical subjects which are timeless.

Neither Frost's version of the Job story in *A Masque of Reason* nor his version of the Jonah story in *A Masque of Mercy* seems to me quite to come off; both are a little self-consciously in modern dress.

Nor is such a style well-suited to official public occasions when a poet must speak about and on behalf of the *Civitas Terrenae*. Frost's tone of voice, even in his dramatic pieces, is that of a man talking to himself, thinking aloud and hardly aware of an audience. This manner is, of course, like all manners, calculated, and more sophisticated than most. The calculation is sound when the poems are concerned with personal emotions, but when the subject is one of public affairs or ideas of general interest, it may be a miscalculation. "Build Soil, a Political Pastoral" which Frost composed for the National Party Convention at Columbia University in 1932, was much criticized at the time by the Liberal-Left for being reactionary. Reading it today, one wonders what all their fuss was about, but the fireside-chat I'm-a-plain-fellow manner is still irritating. One finds oneself wishing that Columbia had invited Yeats instead; he might have said the most outrageous things, but he would have put on a good act, and that is what we want from a poet when he speaks to us of what concerns us, not as private persons but as citizens. Perhaps Frost himself felt uneasy, for the last two lines of the poem, and the best, run thus:

> We're too unseparate. And going home
> From company means coming to our senses.

Any poetry which aims at being a clarification of life must be concerned with two questions about which all men, whether they read poetry or not, seek clarification.

(1) *Who am I?* What is the difference between man and all other creatures? What relations are possible between them? What is man's status in the universe? What are the conditions of his existence which he must accept as his fate which no wishing can alter?

(2) *Whom ought I to become?* What are the characteristics of the hero, the authentic man whom everybody should admire and try to become? Vice versa, what are the characteristics of the churl, the unauthentic man whom everybody should try to avoid becoming?

We all seek answers to these questions which shall be universally valid under all circumstances, but the experiences to which we put them are always local both in time and place. What any poet has to say about man's status in nature, for example, depends in part upon the landscape and climate he happens to live in and in part upon the reactions to it of his personal temperament. A poet brought up in the tropics cannot have the same vision as a poet brought up in Hertfordshire and, if they inhabit the same landscape, the chirpy social endomorph will give a different picture of it from that of the melancholic withdrawn ectomorph.

The nature in Frost's poetry is the nature of New England. New England is made of granite, is mountainous, densely wooded, and its soil is poor. It has a long severe winter, a summer that is milder and more pleasant than in most parts of the States, a short and sudden Spring, a slow and theatrically beautiful fall. Since it adjoins the eastern seaboard, it was one of the first areas to be settled but, as soon as the more fertile lands to the West were opened up, it began to lose population. Tourists and city dwellers who can afford a summer home may arrive for the summer, but much land which was once cultivated has gone back to the wild.

One of Frost's favorite images is the image of the abandoned house. In Britain or Europe, a ruin recalls either historical change, political acts like war or enclosure, or, in the case of abandoned mine buildings, a successful past which came to an end, not because nature was too strong, but because she had been robbed of everything she possessed. A ruin in Europe, therefore, tends to arouse reflections about human injustice and greed and the nemesis that overtakes human pride. But in Frost's poetry, a ruin is an image of human heroism, of a defense in the narrow pass against hopeless odds.

> I came an errand one cloud-blowing morning
> To a slab-built, black-paper-covered house
> Of one room and one window and one door,
> The only dwelling in a waste cut over
> A hundred square miles round it in the mountains:
> And that not dwelt in now by men or women.
> (It never had been dwelt in, though, by women.)
> . . .
> Here further up the mountain slope
> Than there was ever any hope,
> My father built, enclosed a spring,
> Strung chains of wall round everything,
> Subdued the growth of earth to grass,
> And brought our various lives to pass.
> A dozen girls and boys we were.
> The mountain seemed to like the stir
> And made of us a little while—
> With always something in her smile.
> To-day she wouldn't know our name.
> (No girl's of course has stayed the same.)
> The mountain pushed us off her knees.
> And now her lap is full of trees.

Thumbing through Frost's *Collected Poems*, I find twenty-one in which the season is winter as compared with five in which it is spring, and in two of

these there is still snow on the ground; I find twenty-seven in which the time
is night and seventeen in which the weather is stormy.

   The commonest human situation in his poetry is of one man, or a man
and wife, alone in a small isolated house in a snowbound forest after dark.

> Where I could think of no thoroughfare,
> Away on the mountain up far too high,
> A blinding headlight shifted glare
> And began to bounce down a granite stair
> Like a star fresh-fallen out of the sky,
> And I away in my opposite wood
> Am touched by that unintimate light
> And made feel less alone than I rightly should,
> For traveler there could do me no good
> Were I in trouble with night tonight.
> . . .
>
> We looked and looked, but after all where are we?
> Do we know any better where we are,
> And how it stands between the night tonight
> And a man with a smokey lantern chimney,
> How different from the way it ever stood?

In "Two Look at Two," nature, as represented by a buck stag and a doe, responds in sympathy to man, as represented by a boy and girl, but the point
of the poem is that this sympathetic response is a miraculous exception. The
normal response is that described in "The Most of It."

> Some morning from the boulder-broken beach
> He would cry out on life that what it wants
> Is not its own love back in copy speech,
> But counter-love, original response.
> And nothing ever came of what he cried
> Unless it was the embodiment that crashed
> In the cliffs talus on the other side,
> And then in the far distant water splashed,
> But after a time allowed for it to swim,
> Instead of proving human when it neared
> And some one else additional to him,
> As a great buck it powerfully appeared . . .

Nature, however, is not to Frost, as she was to Melville, malignant.

> It must be a little more in favor of man,
> Say a fraction of one per cent at least,
> Or our number living wouldn't be steadily more.

She is, rather, the Dura Virum Nutrix who, by her apparent indifference and hostility, even, calls forth all man's powers and courage and makes a real man of him.

Courage is not to be confused with romantic daring. It includes caution and cunning,

> All we who prefer to live
> Have a little whistle we give,
> And flash at the least alarm
> We dive down under the farm

and even financial prudence,

> Better to go down dignified
> With boughten friendship at your side
> Then none at all. Provide, provide!

There have been European poets who have come to similar conclusions about the isolation of the human condition, and nature's indifference to human values, but, compared with an American, they are at a disadvantage in expressing them. Living as they do in a well, even overpopulated, countryside where, thanks to centuries of cultivation, Mother Earth has acquired human features, they are forced to make abstract philosophical statements or use uncommon atypical images, so that what they say seems to be imposed upon them by theory and temperament rather than by facts. An American poet like Frost, on the other hand, can appeal to facts for which any theory must account and which any temperament must admit.

The Frostian man is isolated not only in space but also in time. In Frost's poems the nostalgic note is seldom, if ever, struck. When he writes a poem about childhood like "Wild Grapes," childhood is not seen as a magical Eden which will all too soon, alas, be lost, but as a school in which the first lessons of adult life are learned. The setting of one of his best long poems, "The Generations of Man," is the ancestral home of the Stark family in the town of Bow, New Hampshire. Bow is a rock-strewn township where farming has fallen off and sproutlands flourish since the axe has gone. The Stark family mansion is by now reduced to an old cellar-hole at the side of a by-road. The occasion described in the poem is a gathering together from all over of the Stark descendants, an advertising stunt thought up by the governor of the state. The characters are a boy Stark and a girl Stark, distant cousins, who meet at the cellar-hole and are immediately attracted to each other. Their conversation turns, naturally, to their common ancestors, but, in fact, they know nothing about them. The boy starts inventing stories and doing imaginary imitations of their voices as a way of courtship, making their ancestors hint at marriage and suggest building a new summer home on the site of the old house. The real past, that is to say, is unknown and unreal to them; its role in the poem is to provide a lucky chance for the living to meet.

Like Gray, Frost has written a poem on a deserted graveyard. Gray is concerned with the possible lives of the unknown dead; the past is more imaginatively exciting to him than the present. But Frost does not try to remember anything; what moves him is that death, which is always a present terror, is no longer present here, having moved on like a pioneer.

> It would be easy to be clever
> And tell the stones; men hate to die
> And have stopped dying now for ever.
> I think they would believe the lie.

What he finds valuable in man's temporal existence is the ever-recurrent opportunity of the present moment to make a discovery or a new start.

> One of the lies would make it out that nothing
> Ever presents itself before us twice.
> Where would we be at last if that were so?
> Our very life depends on everything's
> Recurring till we answer from within.
> The thousandth time may prove the charm.

Frost has written a number of pastoral eclogues and, no doubt, has taken a sophisticated pleasure in using what is, by tradition, the most aristocratic and idyllic of all literary forms to depict democratic realities. If the landscape of New England is unarcadian, so is its social life; the leisured class with nothing to do but cultivate its sensibility which the European pastoral presupposes, is simply not there. Of course, as in all societies, social distinctions exist. In New England, Protestants of Anglo-Scotch stock consider themselves a cut above Roman Catholics and those of a Latin race, and the most respectable Protestant denominations are the Congregationalists and the Unitarians. Thus, in "The Ax-Helve," the Yankee farmer is aware of his social condescension in entering the house of his French-Canadian neighbor, Baptiste.

> I shouldn't mind his being overjoyed
> (If overjoyed he was) at having got me
> Where I must judge if what he knew about an ax
> That not everybody else knew was to count
> For nothing in the measure of a neighbor.
> Hard if, though cast away for life with Yankees,
> A Frenchman couldn't get his human rating!

And in "Snow," Mrs Cole passes judgment upon the Evangelical preacher, Meserve.

> I detest the thought of him
> With his ten children under ten years old.
> I hate his wretched little Racker Sect,
> All's ever I heard of it, which isn't much.

Yet in both poems the neighbor triumphs over the snob. The Yankee acknowledges Baptiste's superior skill, and the Coles stay up all night in concern until they hear that Meserve has reached home safely through the storm.

In the Frost pastoral, the place of the traditional worldly-wise, world-weary courtier is taken by the literary city dweller, often a college student who has taken a job for the summer on a farm; the rustics he encounters are neither comic bumpkins nor noble savages.

In "A Hundred Collars," a refined shy college professor meets in a small town hotel bedroom a fat whisky-drinking vulgarian who canvasses the farms around on behalf of a local newspaper. If, in the end, the reader's sympathies go to the vulgarian, the vulgarian is not made aesthetically appealing nor the professor unpleasant. The professor means well—he is a democrat, if not at heart, in principle—but he is the victim of a way of life which has narrowed his human sympathies and interests. The vulgarian is redeemed by his uninhibited friendliness which is perfectly genuine, not a professional salesman's manner. Though vulgar, he is not a go-getter.

> "One would suppose they might not be as glad
> To see you as you are to see them."
>   "Oh,
> Because I want their dollar? I don't want
> Anything they've got. I never dun.
> I'm there, and they can pay me if they like.
> I go nowhere on purpose: I happen by."

In "The Code," a town-bred farmer unwittingly offends one of his hired hands.

> "What is there wrong?"
>   "Something you just now said."
> "What did I say?"
>   "About our taking pains."
> "To cock the hay—because it's going to shower?
> I said that more than half an hour ago.
> I said it to myself as much as you."
> "You didn't know. But James is one big fool.
> He thought you meant to find fault with his work,
>   That's what the average farmer would have meant." . . .
> "He's a fool if that's the way he takes me."

> "Don't let it bother you. You've found out something.
> The hand that knows his business won't be told
> To do work better or faster—those two things. . . ."

The ignorance of the town-bred farmer is made use of, not to blame him, but to praise the quality which, after courage, Frost ranks as the highest of the virtues, the self-respect which comes from taking a pride in something. It may be a pride in one's own skill, the pride of the axe-maker Baptiste, the pride of the Hired Man who dies from a broken heart since old age has taken from him the one accomplishment, building a load of hay, which had hitherto prevented him from feeling utterly worthless, or it may be a pride which, from a worldly point of view, is a folly, the pride of the man who has failed as a farmer, burned his house down for the insurance money, bought a telescope with the proceeds and taken a lowly job as a ticket agent on the railroad. The telescope is not a good one, the man is poor, but he is proud of his telescope and happy.

Every poet is at once a representative of his culture and its critic. Frost has never written satires, but it is not hard to guess what, as an American, he approves and disapproves of in his own countrymen. The average American is a stoic and, contrary to what others are apt to conclude from his free-and-easy friendly manner, reticent, far more reticent than the average Englishman about showing his feelings. He believes in independence because he has to; life is too mobile and circumstances change too fast for him to be supported by any fixed frame of family or social relations. In a crisis he will help his neighbor, whoever he may be, but he will regard someone who is always coming for help as a bad neighbor, and he disapproves of all self-pity and nostalgic regret. All these qualities find their expression in Frost's poetry, but there are other American characteristics which are not to be found there, the absence of which implies disapproval; the belief, for instance, that it should be possible, once the right gimmick has been found, to build the New Jerusalem on earth in half an hour. One might describe Frost as a Tory, provided that one remembers that all American political parties are Whigs.

Hardy, Yeats and Frost have all written epitaphs for themselves.

Hardy
I never cared for life, life cared for me.
And hence I owe it some fidelity. . . .

Yeats
Cast a cold eye
On life and death.
Horseman, pass by.

Frost
> I would have written of me on my stone
> I had a lover's quarrel with the world.

Of the three, Frost, surely, comes off best. Hardy seems to be stating the Pessimist's Case rather than his real feelings. I never cared . . . *Never?* Now, Mr Hardy, really! Yeats' horseman is a stage prop; the passer-by is much more likely to be a motorist. But Frost convinces me that he is telling neither more nor less than the truth about himself. And, when it comes to wisdom, is not having a lover's quarrel with life more worthy of Prospero than not caring or looking coldly?

American Poetry

> The land was ours before we were the land's.
> She was our land more than a hundred years
> Before we were her people. She was ours
> In Massachusetts, in Virginia,
> But we were England's, still colonials,
> Possessing what we still were unpossessed by,
> Possessed by what we now no more possessed.
> Something we were withholding made us weak
> Until we found out that it was ourselves
> We were withholding from our land of living,
> And forthwith found salvation in surrender.
> Such as we were we gave ourselves outright
> (The deed of gift was many deeds of war)
> To the land vaguely realizing westward,
> But still unstoried, artless, unenhanced,
> Such as she was, such as she would become.
>   —Robert Frost

One often hears it said that only in this century have the writers of the United States learned to stand on their own feet and be truly American, that, previously, they were slavish imitators of British literature. Applied to the general reading public and academic circles, this has a certain amount of truth but, so far as the writers themselves are concerned, it is quite false. From Bryant on there is scarcely one American poet whose work, if unsigned, could be mistaken for that of an Englishman. What English poet, for example, in need of emotive place names for a serious poem, would have employed, neither local names nor names famous in history or mythology, but names made up by himself as Poe did in "Ulalume"? Would an English poet have conceived the idea of writing a scientific cosmological prose poem and of prefacing it thus: "I offer this Book of Truths, not in its character of Truth-teller, but for the Beauty that abounds in its Truth, constituting it true. . . . *What I here propound is true:* therefore it cannot die. . . . Nevertheless it is as a Poem only that I wish this work to be judged after I am dead." (Poe, Preface to "Eureka")?

Maud, The Song of Hiawatha and the first edition of *Leaves of Grass* all appeared in the same year, 1855: no two poets could be more unlike each other than Longfellow and Whitman—such diversity is in itself an American phenomenon—yet, when compared with Tennyson, each in his own way shows characteristics of the New World. Tennyson and Longfellow were both highly skillful technicians in conventional forms and both were regarded by their countrymen as the respectable mouthpieces of their age, and yet, how different they are. There is much in Tennyson that Longfellow would never have dared to write, for the peculiar American mixture of Puritan conscience and democratic license can foster in some cases a genteel horror of the coarse for which no Englishman has felt the need. On the other hand Longfellow had a curiosity about the whole of European literature compared with which Tennyson, concerned only with the poetry of his own land and the classical authors on whom he was educated, seems provincial. Even if there had been Red Indians roaming the North of Scotland, unsubjugated and unassimilable, one cannot imagine Tennyson sitting down to write a long poem about them and choosing for it a Finnish meter. Leaving aside all questions of style, there is a difference between Tennyson's "Ode on the Death of the Duke of Wellington" and Whitman's elegy for President Lincoln "When lilacs last in the dooryard bloom'd" which is significant. Tennyson, as one would expect from the title of his poem, mourns for a great public official figure, but it would be very hard to guess from the words of Whitman's poem that the man he is talking of was the head of a State; one would naturally think that he was some close personal friend, a private individual.

To take one more example—two poets, contemporaries, both women, both religious, both introverts preoccupied with renunciation—Christina Rossetti and Emily Dickinson; could anyone imagine either of them in the country of the other? When I try to fancy such translations, the only Americans I can possibly imagine as British are minor poets with a turn for light verse like Lowell and Holmes; and the only British poets who could conceivably have been American are eccentrics like Blake and Hopkins.

Normally, in comparing the poetry of two cultures, the obvious and easiest point at which to start is with a comparison of the peculiar characteristics, grammatical, rhetorical, rhythmical, of their respective languages, for even the most formal and elevated styles of poetry are more conditioned by the spoken tongue, the language really used by the men of that country, than by anything else. In the case of British and American poetry, however, this is the most subtle difference of all and the hardest to define. Any Englishman, with a little effort, can learn to pronounce "the letter *a* in psalm and calm . . . with the sound of *a* in candle," to say *thumb-tacks* instead of *drawing-pins* or twenty-minutes-of-one instead of twenty-minutes-to-one, and discover that, in the Middle West, *bought* rhymes with *hot*, but he will still be as far from speaking American English as his Yankee cousin who comes to England will be from speaking the Queen's. No dramatist in either country who has introduced a character from the other side, has, to my knowledge, been able to make his speech convincing. What the secret of the difference is, I cannot put my finger on; William Carlos Williams, who has thought more than most about this problem, says that "Pace is one of its most important manifestations" and to this one might add another, Pitch. If undefinable, the difference is, however, immediately recognizable by the ear, even in verse where the formal conventions are the same.

> He must have had a father and a mother—
> In fact I've heard him say so—and a dog,
> As a boy should, I venture; and the dog,
> Most likely, was the only man who knew him.
> A dog, for all I know, is what he needs
> As much as anything right here today,
> To counsel him about his disillusions,
> Old aches, and parturitions of what's coming—
> A dog of orders, an emeritus,
> To wag his tail at him when he comes home,
> And then to put his paws up on his knees
> And say, "For God's sake, what's it all about?"
>   (E. A. Robinson, "Ben Jonson Entertains
>   a Man from Stratford")

Whatever this may owe to Browning, the fingering is quite different and un-British. Again, how American in rhythm as well as in sensibility is this stanza by Robert Frost:

> But no, I was out for stars:
> I would not come in.
> I meant not even if asked,
> And I hadn't been.
>
>   ("Come In")

Until quite recently an English writer, like one of any European country, could presuppose two conditions, a nature which was mythologized, humanized, on the whole friendly, and a human society which had become in time, whatever succession of invasions it may have suffered in the past, in race and religion more or less homogeneous and in which most people lived and died in the locality where they were born.

Christianity might have deprived Aphrodite, Apollo, the local genius, of their divinity but as figures for the forces of nature, as a mode of thinking about the creation, they remained valid for poets and their readers alike. Descartes might reduce the nonhuman universe to a mechanism but the feelings of Europeans about the sun and moon, the cycle of the seasons, the local landscape remained unchanged. Wordsworth might discard the mythological terminology but the kind of relation between nature and man which he described was the same personal one. Even when nineteenth-century biology began to trouble men's minds with the thought that the universe might be without moral values, their immediate experience was still of a friendly and lovable nature. Whatever their doubts and convictions about the purpose and significance of the universe as a whole, Tennyson's Lincolnshire or Hardy's Dorset were places where they felt completely at home, landscapes with faces of their own which a human being could recognize and trust.

But in America, neither the size nor the condition nor the climate of the continent encourages such intimacy. It is an unforgettable experience for anyone born on the other side of the Atlantic to take a plane journey by night across the United States. Looking down he will see the lights of some town like a last outpost in a darkness stretching for hours ahead, and realize that, even if there is no longer an actual frontier, this is still a continent only partially settled and developed, where human activity seems a tiny thing in comparison to the magnitude of the earth, and the equality of men not some dogma of politics or jurisprudence but a self-evident fact. He will behold a wild nature, compared with which the landscapes of Salvator Rosa are as cosy as Arcadia and which cannot possibly be thought of in human or personal terms. If Henry Adams could write:

> When Adams was a boy in Boston, the best chemist in the place had probably never heard of Venus except by way of scandal, or of the Virgin except as idolatry. . . . The force of the Virgin was still felt at Lourdes, and seemed to be as potent as X-rays; but in America neither Venus nor Virgin ever had value as force—at most as sentiment. No American had ever been truly afraid of either

the reason for this was not simply that the *Mayflower* carried iconophobic dissenters but also that the nature which Americans, even in New England, had every reason to fear could not possibly be imagined as a mother. A white whale whom man can neither understand nor be understood by, whom only a madman like Gabriel can worship, the only relationship with whom is a combat to the death by which a man's courage and skill are tested and judged, or the great buck who answers the poet's prayer for "someone else additional to him" in "The Most of It" are more apt symbols. Thoreau, who certainly tried his best to become intimate with nature, had to confess

> I walk in nature still alone
>   And know no one,
> Discern no lineament nor feature
>   Of any creature.
> Though all the firmament
>   Is o'er me bent,
> Yet still I miss the grace
> Of an intelligent and kindred face.
> I still must seek the friend
> Who does with nature blend,
> Who is the person in her mask,
> He is the man I ask. . . .

Many poets in the Old World have become disgusted with human civilization but what the earth would be like if the race became extinct they cannot imagine; an American like Robinson Jeffers can quite easily, for he has seen with his own eyes country as yet untouched by history.

In a land which is fully settled, most men must accept their local environment or try to change it by political means; only the exceptionally gifted or adventurous can leave to seek his fortune elsewhere. In America, on the other hand, to move on and make a fresh start somewhere else is still the normal reaction to dissatisfaction or failure. Such social fluidity has important psychological effects. Since movement involves breaking social and personal ties, the habit creates an attitude towards personal relationships in which impermanence is taken for granted.

One could find no better illustration of the difference between the Old and the New World than the respective conclusions of *Oliver Twist* and *Huckleberry Finn*, both the heroes of which are orphans. When Oliver is at last adopted by Mr Brownlow, his fondest dream, to have a home, to be surrounded by familiar friendly faces, to receive an education, is realized. Huck is offered adoption too, significantly by a woman not a man, but refuses because he knows she would try to "civilize" him, and announces his intention to light out by himself for the West; Jim, who has been his "buddy" in a friendship far closer than any enjoyed by Oliver, is left behind like an old shoe, just as in *Moby Dick* Ishmael becomes a blood-brother of Queequeg and then forgets all about him. Naturally the daydream of the lifelong comrade in adventure often appears in American literature:

> Camerado, I give you my hand!
> I give you my love more precious than money,
> I give you myself before preaching or law;

> Will you give me yourself? will you come travel with me?
> Shall we stick by each other as long as we live?
>
> (Whitman, "Song of the Open Road")

but no American seriously expects such a dream to come true.

To be able at any time to break with the past, to move and keep on moving lessens the significance not only of the past but also of the future which is reduced to the immediate future, and minimizes the importance of political action. A European may be a conservative who thinks that the right form of society has been discovered already, or a liberal who believes it is in process of being realized, or a revolutionary who thinks that after long dark ages it can now be realized for the first time, but each of them knows that, by reason or force, he must convince the others that he is right; he may be an optimist about the future or a pessimist. None of these terms applies accurately to an American, for his profoundest feeling towards the future is not that it will be better or worse but that it is unpredictable, that all things, good and bad, will change. No failure is irredeemable, no success a final satisfaction. Democracy is the best form of government, not because men will necessarily lead better or happier lives under it, but because it permits constant experiment; a given experiment may fail but the people have a right to make their own mistakes. America has always been a country of amateurs where the professional, that is to say, the man who claims authority as a member of an élite which knows the law in some field or other, is an object of distrust and resentment.

> Amerika, du hast es besser
> Als unser Kontinent, der alte,
> Hast keine verfallenen Schlösser
> Und keine Basalte

wrote Goethe, by *keine Basalte* meaning, I presume, no violent political revolutions. This is a subject about which, in relation to their own histories, the English and the Americans cherish opposite fictions. Between 1533 and 1688 the English went through a succession of revolutions in which a Church was imposed on them by the engines of the State, one king was executed and another deposed, yet they prefer to forget it and pretend that the social structure of England is the product of organic peaceful growth. The Americans, on the other hand, like to pretend that what was only a successful war of secession was a genuine revolution.

If we apply the term revolution to what happened in North America between 1776 and 1829, it has a special meaning.

Normally, the word describes the process by which man transforms himself from one kind of man, living in one kind of society, with one way of looking at the world, into another kind of man, another society, another conception of life. So it is with the Papal, the Lutheran, the English, and the French revolutions. The American case is different; it is not a question of the Old Man transforming himself into the New, but of the New Man becoming alive to the fact that he is new, that he has been transformed already without his having realized it.

The War of Independence was the first step, the leaving of the paternal roof in order to find out who one is; the second and more important step, the actual discovery, came with Jackson. It was then that it first became clear that, despite similarities of form, representative government in America was not to be an imitation of the English parliamentary system, and that, though the vocabulary of the Constitution may be that of the French Enlightenment, its American meaning is quite distinct. There is indeed an American mentality which is new and unique in the world but it is the product less of conscious political action than of nature, of the new and unique environment of the American continent. Even the most revolutionary feature of the Constitution, the separation of Church and State, was a recognition of a condition which had existed since the first settlements were made by various religious denominations whose control of the secular authority could only be local. From the beginning America had been a pluralist state and pluralism is incompatible with an Established Church. The *Basalte* in American history, the Civil War, might indeed be called Counterrevolution, for it was fought primarily on the issue not of slavery but of unity, that is, not for a freedom but for a limitation on freedom, to ensure that the United States should remain pluralist and not disintegrate into an anarchic heap of fragments. Pluralist and experimental: in place of *verfallenen Schlösser*, America has ghost towns and the relics of New Jerusalems which failed.

The American had not intended to become what he was; he had been made so by emigration and the nature of the American continent. An emigrant never knows what he wants, only what he does not want. A man who comes from a land settled for centuries to a virgin wilderness where he faces problems with which none of his traditions and habits was intended to deal cannot foresee the future but must improvise himself from day to day. It is not surprising, therefore, that the first clear realization of the novelty and importance of the United States should have come not from an American but from outsiders, like Crèvecoeur and de Tocqueville.

In a society whose dominant task is still that of the pioneer—the physical struggle with nature, and a nature, moreover, particularly recalcitrant and violent—the intellectual is not a figure of much importance. Those with intellectual and artistic tastes, finding themselves a despised or at best an ignored minority, are apt in return to despise the society in which they live as vulgar and think nostalgically of more leisured and refined cultures. The situation of the first important American poets—Emerson, Thoreau, Poe— was therefore doubly difficult. As writers, and therefore intellectuals, they were without status with the majority; and, on the other hand, the cultured minority of which they were members looked to England for its literary standards and did not want to think or read about America.

This dependence on English literature was a hindrance to their development in a way which it would not have been had they lived elsewhere. A poet living in England, for instance, might read nothing but French poetry, or he might move to Italy and know only English, without raising any serious barrier between himself and his experiences. Indeed, in Europe, whenever some journalist raises the patriotic demand for an English or French or Dutch literature free from foreign influences, we know him at once to be a base fellow. The wish for an American literature, on the other hand, has nothing to do, really, with politics or national conceit; it is a demand for honesty. All European literature so far has presupposed two things: a nature which is humanized, mythologized, usually friendly, and a human society in which most men stay where they were born and do not move about much. Neither of these presuppositions was valid for America, where nature was virgin, devoid of history, usually hostile; and society was fluid, its groupings always changing as men moved on somewhere else.

The European romantics may praise the charms of wild desert landscape, but they know that for them it is never more than a few hours' walk from a comfortable inn: they may celebrate the joys of solitude but they know that any time they choose they can go back to the family roof or to town and that there their cousins and nephews and nieces and aunts, the club and the salons, will still be going on exactly as they left them. Of real desert, of a loneliness which knows of no enduring relationships to cherish or reject, they have no conception.

The achievement of Emerson and Thoreau was twofold: they wrote of the American kind of nature, and they perceived what qualities were most needed by members of the American kind of society, which was threatened, not by the petrified injustice of any tradition, but by the fluid irresponsibility of crowd opinion. Their work has both the virtues and the vices of the isolated and the protestant: on the one hand it is always genuine and original, it is never superficial; on the other it is a little too cranky, too earnest, too scornful of elegance. Just as in their political thinking Americans are apt to identify the undemocratic with monarchy, so, in their aesthetics, they are apt to identify the falsely conventional with rhyme and meter. The prose of Emerson and Thoreau is superior to their verse, because verse in its formal nature protests against protesting; it demands that to some degree we accept things as they are, not for any rational or moral reason, but simply because they happen to be that way; it implies an element of frivolity in the creation.

Whatever one may feel about Whitman's poetry, one is bound to admit that he was the first clearly to recognize what the conditions were with which any future American poet would have to come to terms.

Plenty of songs had been sung—beautiful, matchless songs—adjusted to other lands than these. . . . the Old World has had the poems of myths, fictions, feudalism, conquest, caste, dynastic wars, and splendid exceptional characters, which have been great; but the New World needs the poems of realities and science and of the democratic average and basic equality. . . . As for native American individuality, the distinctive and ideal type of Western character (as consistent with the operative and even money-making features of United States humanity as chosen knights, gentlemen and warriors were the ideals of the centuries of European feudalism) it has not yet appeared. I have allowed the stress of my poems from beginning to end to bear upon American individuality and assist it—not only because that is a great lesson in Nature, amid all her generalizing laws, but as counterpoise to the levelling tendencies of Democracy.

The last sentence makes it quite clear that by the "average" hero who was to replace the "knight," Whitman did not mean the mediocre, but the individual whose "exceptional character" is not derived from birth, education or occupation, and that he is aware of how difficult it is for such an individual to appear without the encouragement which comes from membership in some elite.

What he does not say, and perhaps did not realize, is that, in a democracy, the status of the poet himself is changed. However fantastic, in the light of present-day realities, his notion may be, every European poet, I believe, still instinctively thinks of himself as a "clerk," a member of a professional brotherhood, with a certain social status irrespective of the number of his readers (in his heart of hearts the audience he desires and expects are those who govern the country), and as taking his place in an unbroken historical succession. In the States, poets have never had or imagined they had such a status, and it is up to each individual poet to justify his existence by offering a unique product. It would be grossly unjust to assert that there are fewer lovers of poetry in the New World than in the Old—in how many places in the latter could a poet demand and receive a substantial sum for reading his work aloud?—but there is a tendency, perhaps, in the former, for audiences to be drawn rather by a name than a poem, and for a poet, on his side, to demand approval for his work not simply because it is good but because it is *his*. To some degree every American poet feels that the whole responsibility for contemporary poetry has fallen upon his shoulders, that he is a literary aristocracy of one. "Tradition," wrote Mr T. S. Eliot in a famous essay, "cannot be inherited, and if you want it you must obtain it by great labour." I do not think that any European critic would have said just this. He would not, of course, deny that every poet must work hard but the suggestion in the first half of the sentence that no sense of tradition is acquired except by conscious effort would seem strange to him.

There are advantages and disadvantages in both attitudes. A British poet can take writing more for granted and so write with a lack of strain and over-earnestness. American poetry has many tones, but the tone of a man talking to a group of his peers is rare; for a "serious" poet to write light verse is frowned on in America and if, when he is asked why he writes poetry, he replies, as any European poet would, "For fun," his audience will be shocked. On the other hand, a British poet is in much greater danger of becoming lazy, or academic, or irresponsible. One comes across passages, even in very fine English poets, which make one think: "Yes, very effective but does he believe what he is saying?": in American poetry such passages are extremely rare. The first thing that strikes a reader about the best American poets is how utterly unlike each other they are. Where else in the world, for example, could one find seven poets of approximately the same generation so different as Ezra Pound, W. C. Williams, Vachel Lindsay, Marianne Moore, Wallace Stevens, E. E. Cummings and Laura Riding? The danger for the American poet is not of writing like everybody else but of crankiness and a parody of his own manner.

Plato, following Damon of Athens, said that when the modes of music change, the walls of the city are shaken. It might be truer to say, perhaps, that a change in the modes gives warning of a shaking of the walls in the near future. The social strains which later break out in political action are first experienced by artists as a feeling that the current modes of expression are no longer capable of dealing with their real concerns. Thus, when one thinks of "modern" painting, music, fiction or poetry, the names which immediately come to mind as its leaders and creators are those of persons who were born roughly between 1870 and 1890 and who began producing their "new" work before the outbreak of World War I in 1914, and in poetry and fiction, at least, American names are prominent.

When a revolutionary break with the past is necessary it is an advantage not to be too closely identified with any one particular literature or any particular cultural group. Americans like Eliot and Pound, for example, could be as curious about French or Italian poetry as about English and could hear poetry of the past, like the verse of Webster, freshly in a way that for an Englishman, trammeled by traditional notions of Elizabethan blank verse, would have been difficult.

Further, as Americans, they were already familiar with the dehumanized nature and the social leveling which a technological civilization was about to make universal and with which the European mentality was unprepared to deal. After his visit to America, de Tocqueville made a remarkable prophecy about the kind of poetry which a democratic society would produce.

> I am persuaded that in the end democracy diverts the imagination from
> all that is external to man and fixes it on man alone. Democratic nations

may amuse themselves for a while with considering the productions of nature, but they are excited in reality only by a survey of themselves. . . . The poets who lived in aristocratic ages have been eminently successful in their delineation of certain incidents in the life of a people or a man; but none of them ever ventured to include within his performances the destinies of mankind, a task which poets writing in democratic ages may attempt. . . .

It may be foreseen in like manner that poets living in democratic times will prefer the delineation of passions and ideas to that of persons and achievements. The language, the dress, and the daily actions of men in democracies are repugnant to conceptions of the ideal. . . . This forces the poet constantly to search below the external surface which is palpable to the senses, in order to read the inner soul; and nothing lends itself more to the delineation of the ideal than the scrutiny of the hidden depths in the immaterial nature of man. . . . The destinies of mankind, man himself taken aloof from his country and his age, and standing in the presence of Nature and of God, with his passions, his doubts, his rare prosperities and inconceivable wretchedness, will become the chief, if not the sole, theme of poetry.

If this be an accurate description of the poetry we call modern, then one might say that America has never known any other kind.

PART SEVEN

The Shield of Perseus

Notes on the Comic

If a man wants to set up as an innkeeper and he does not succeed, it is not comic. If, on the contrary, a girl asks to be allowed to set up as a prostitute and she fails, which sometimes happens, it is comic. —Søren Kierkegaard

A man's character may be inferred from nothing so surely as from the jest he takes in bad part. —G. C. Lichtenberg

General Definition

A contradiction in the relation of the individual or the personal to the universal or the impersonal which does not involve the spectator or hearer in suffering or pity, which in practice means that it must not involve the actor in real suffering.

A situation in which the actor really suffers can only be found comic by children who see only the situation and are unaware of the suffering, as when a child laughs at a hunchback, or by human swine.

A few years ago, there was a rage in New York for telling "Horror Jokes." For example:

A MOTHER (*to her blind daughter*). Now, dear, shut your eyes and count
    twenty. Then open them, and you'll find that you can see.
DAUGHTER (*after counting twenty*). But, Mummy, I still can't see.
MOTHER. April fool!

This has the same relation to the comic as blasphemy has to belief in God, that is to say, it implies a knowledge of what is truly comic.

We sometimes make a witty remark about someone which is also cruel, but we make it behind his back, not to his face, and we hope that nobody will repeat it to him.

When we really hate someone, we cannot find him comic; there are no genuinely funny stories about Hitler.

A sense of humor develops in a society to the degree that its members are simultaneously conscious of being each a unique person and of being all in common subjection to unalterable laws.

Primitive cultures have little sense of humor; firstly, because their sense of human individuality is weak—the tribe is the real unit—and, secondly, because, as animists or polytheists, they have little notion of necessity. To them, events do not occur because they must, but because some god or spirit chooses to make them happen. They recognize a contradiction between the individual and the universal only when it is a tragic contradiction involving exceptional suffering.

In our own society, addicted gamblers who make a religion out of chance are invariably humorless.

Among those whom I like or admire, I can find no common denominator, but among those whom I love, I can: all of them make me laugh.

Some Types of Comic Contradiction

(1) The operation of physical laws upon inorganic objects associated with a human being in such a way that it is they who appear to be acting from personal volition and their owner who appears to be the passive thing.

Example: A man is walking in a storm protected by an umbrella when a sudden gust of wind blows it inside out. This is comic for two reasons:

(a) An umbrella is a mechanism designed by man to function in a particular manner, and its existence and effectiveness as a protection depend upon man's understanding of physical laws. An umbrella turning inside out is funnier than a hat blowing off because an umbrella is made to be opened, to change its shape when its owner wills. It now continues to change its shape, in obedience to the same laws, but against his will.

(b) The activating agent, the wind, is invisible, so the cause of the umbrella turning inside out appears to lie in the umbrella itself. It is not particularly funny if a tile falls and makes a hole in the umbrella, because the cause is visibly natural.

When a film is run backwards, reversing the historical succession of events, the flow of volition is likewise reversed and proceeds from the object to the subject. What was originally the action of a man taking off his coat becomes the action of a coat putting itself on a man.

The same contradiction is the basis of most of the comic effects of the clown. In appearance he is the clumsy man whom inanimate objects conspire against to torment; this in itself is funny to watch, but our profounder amusement is derived from our knowledge that this is only an appearance, that, in reality, the accuracy with which the objects trip him up or hit him on the head is caused by the clown's own skill.

(2) A clash between the laws of the inorganic which has no *telos,* and the behavior of living creatures who have one.

Example: A man walking down the street, with his mind concentrated upon the purpose of his journey, fails to notice a banana skin, slips and falls down. Under the obsession of his goal—it may be a goal of thought—he forgets his subjection to the law of gravity. His goal need not necessarily be a unique and personal one; he may simply be looking for a public lavatory. All that matters is that he should be ignoring the present for the sake of the future. A child learning to walk, or an adult picking his way carefully over an icy surface, are not funny if they fall down, because they are conscious of the present.

Comic Situations in the Relationship Between the Sexes

As a natural creature a human being is born either male or female and endowed with an impersonal tendency to reproduce the human species by mating with any member of the opposite sex who is neither immature nor senile. In this tendency the individuality of any given male or female is subordinate to its general reproductive function. (*Male and female created He them . . . Be fruitful and multiply.*)

As a historical person, every man and woman is a unique individual, capable of entering into a unique relation of love with another person. As a person, the relationship takes precedence over any function it may also have. (*It is not good for man to be alone.*)

The ideal of marriage is a relationship in which both these elements are synthesized; husband and wife are simultaneously involved in relations of physical love and the love of personal friendship.

The synthesis might be easier to achieve if the two elements remained distinct, if the physical, that is, remained as impersonal as it is among the animals, and the personal relation was completely unerotic.

In fact, however, we never experience sexual desire as a blind need which is indifferent to its sexual object; our personal history and our culture introduce a selective element so that, even on the most physical level, some types are more desirable than others. Our sexual desire, as such, is impersonal in that it lacks all consideration for the person who is our type, but personal in that our type is our personal taste, not a blind need.

This contradiction is fertile ground for self-deception. It allows us to persuade ourselves that we value the person of another, when, in fact, we only value her (or him) as a sexual object, and it allows us to endow her with an imaginary personality which has little or no relation to the real one.

From the personal point of view, on the other hand, sexual desire, because of its impersonal and unchanging character, is a comic contradiction. The relation between every pair of lovers is unique, but in bed they can only do what all mammals do.

Comic Travesties

Twelfth Night. The pattern of relationships is as follows:

(1) Viola (Caesario) is wholly in the truth. She knows who she is, she knows that the Duke is a man for whom she feels personal love, and her passionate image of him corresponds to the reality.

(2) The Duke is in the truth in one thing; he knows that he feels a personal affection for Caesario (Viola). This is made easier for him by his

boylike appearance—did he look like a mature man, he would fall into a class, the class of potential rivals in love. The fact that he feels personal affection for the illusory Caesario guarantees the authenticity of his love for the real Viola as a person, since it cannot be an illusion provoked by sexual desire.

His relation to Olivia, on the other hand, is erotic-fantastic in one of two ways, and probably in both: either his image of her does not correspond to her real nature or, if it does correspond, it is fantastic in relation to himself; the kind of wife he really desires is not what he imagines. The fact that, though she makes it clear that she does not return his passion, he still continues to pursue her and by devious strategies, demonstrates that he lacks respect for her as a person.

(3) Olivia has an erotic-fantastic image of Caesario (Viola). Since she is able to transfer her image successfully to Caesario's double, Sebastian, and marry him, we must assume that the image of the kind of husband she desires is real in relation to herself and only accidentally fantastic because Caesario happens to be, not a man, but a woman in disguise.

(4) The illusion of Antonio and Sebastian is not concerned with the erotic relationship, but with the problem of body-soul identity. It is a general law that a human face is the creation of its owner's past and that, since two persons cannot have the same past, no two faces are alike. Identical twins are the exception to this rule. Viola and Sebastian are twins, but not identical twins, for one is female and the other male; dress them both, however, in male or female clothing, and they appear to be identical twins.

It is impossible to produce *Twelfth Night* today in an ordinary theatre since feminine roles are no longer played, as they were in Shakespeare's time, by boys. It is essential to the play that, when Viola appears dressed as a boy, the illusion should be perfect; if it is obvious to the audience that Caesario is really a girl, the play becomes a farce, and a farce in bad taste, for any serious emotion is impossible in a farce, and some of the characters in *Twelfth Night* have serious emotions. A boy whose voice has not yet broken can, when dressed as a girl, produce a perfect illusion of a girl; a young woman, dressed as a boy, can never produce a convincing illusion of a boy.

Der Rosenkavalier and Charley's Aunt. To Baron Lerchenau, the seduction of young chambermaids has become a habit, i.e. what was once a combination of desire and personal choice has become almost an automatic reflex. A costume suggests to him the magic word *chambermaid*, and the word issues the command *Seduce her*. The baron, however, is not quite a farce character; he knows the difference between a pretty girl and an ugly one. The mezzo-soprano who plays Octavian should be good-looking enough to give the illusion of a good-looking young man, when dressed as one. In the third act, when she is dressed as what she really is, a girl, she will be pretty, but her acting the role of a chambermaid must be farcical, and give the impression of a bad actor impersonating a girl, so that only a man as obsessed by habit as the Baron could fail to notice it.

Charley's Aunt is pure farce. The fortune-hunting uncle is not a slave of habit; he really desires to marry a rich widow, but her riches are all he desires; he is totally uninterested in sex or in individuals. He has been told that he is going to meet a rich widow, he sees widow's weeds and this is sufficient to set him in motion. To the audience, therefore, it must be obvious that she is neither female nor elderly, but a young undergraduate pretending, with little success, to be both.

The Lover and the Citizen

Marriage is not only a relation between two individuals; it is also a social institution, involving social emotions concerned with class status and prestige among one's fellows. This is not in itself comic; it only becomes comic if social emotion is the only motive for a marriage, so that the essential motives for marriage, sexual intercourse, procreation and personal affection, are lacking. A familiar comic situation is that of *Don Pasquale*. A rich old man plans to marry a young girl against her will, for she is in love with a young man of her own age; the old man at first looks like succeeding, but in the end he is foiled. For this to be comic, the audience must be convinced that Don Pasquale does not really feel either desire or affection for Norina, that his sole motive is a social one, to be able to boast to other old men that he can win a young wife when they cannot. He wants the prestige of parading her and making others envy him. If he really feels either desire or affection, then he will really suffer when his designs are foiled, and the situation will be either pathetic or satiric. In *Pickwick Papers*, the same situation occurs, only this time it is the female sex which has the social motive. Widow after widow pursues Weller, the widower, not because she wants to be married to him in particular, but because she wants the social status of being a married woman.

The Law of the City and the Law of Justice

Example: Falstaff's speech on Honour (*Henry IV Part I*, Act V, Scene 2).

If the warrior ethic of honor, courage and personal loyalty were believed by an Elizabethan or a modern audience to be the perfect embodiment of justice, the speech would not be sympathetically comic, but a satirical device by which Falstaff was held up to ridicule as a coward. If, on the other hand, the warrior ethic were totally unjust, if there were no occasions on which it was a true expression of moral duty, the speech would be, not comic, but a serious piece of pacifist propaganda. The speech has a sympathetically comic effect for two reasons, the circumstances under which it is uttered, and the character of the speaker.

Were the situation one in which the future of the whole community is at stake, as on the field of Agincourt, the speech would strike an unsympathetic note, but the situation is one of civil war, a struggle for power among the feudal nobility in which the claims of both sides to be the legitimate rulers are fairly equal—Henry IV was once a rebel who deposed his King—and a struggle in which their feudal dependents are compelled to take part and risk their lives without having a real stake in the outcome. Irrespective of the speaker, the speech is a comic criticism of the feudal ethic as typified by Hotspur. Courage is a personal virtue, but military glory for military glory's sake can be a social evil; unreasonable and unjust wars create the paradox that the personal vice of cowardice can become a public virtue.

That it should be Falstaff who utters the speech increases its comic effect. Falstaff has a fantastic conception of himself as a daredevil who plays highwayman, which, if it were true, would require exceptional physical courage. He tries to keep up this illusion, but is always breaking down because of his moral courage which keeps forcing him to admit that he is afraid. Further, though he lacks courage, he exemplifies the other side of the warrior ethic, personal loyalty, as contrasted with Prince Hal's Machiavellian manipulation of others. When Falstaff is rejected by the man to whom he has pledged his whole devotion, his death may truly be called a death for the sake of his wounded honor.

The Banal

The human person is a unique singular, analogous to all other persons, but identical with none. Banality is an illusion of identity for, when people describe their experiences in clichés, it is impossible to distinguish the experience of one from the experience of another.

The cliché user is comic because the illusion of being identical with others is created by his own choice. He is the megalomaniac in reverse. Both have fantastic conceptions of themselves but, whereas the megalomaniac thinks of himself as being somebody else—God, Napoleon, Shakespeare—the banal man thinks of himself as being everybody else, that is to say, nobody in particular.

VERBAL HUMOR

Verbal humor involves a violation in a particular instance of one of the following general principles of language.

(1) Language is a means of denoting things or thoughts by sounds. It is a law of language that any given verbal sound always means the same thing and only that thing.

(2) Words are man-made things which men use, not persons with a will and consciousness of their own. Whether they make sense or nonsense depends upon whether the speaker uses them correctly or incorrectly.

(3) Any two or more objects or events which language seeks to describe

are members, either of separate classes, or of the same class, or of over-lapping classes. If they belong to separate classes, they must be described in different terms, and if they belong to the same class they must be described in the same terms. If, however, their classes overlap, either class can be described metaphorically in terms which describe the other exactly, e.g. it is equally possible to say—the plough swims through the soil—and—the ship ploughs through the waves.

(4) In origin all language is concrete or metaphorical. In order to use language to express abstractions, we have to ignore its original concrete and metaphorical meanings.

The first law is violated by the pun, the exceptional case in which one verbal sound has two meanings.

> When I am dead I hope it may be said:
> His sins were scarlet, but his books were read.

For the pun to be comic, the two meanings must both make sense in the context. If all books were bound in black, the couplet would not be funny.

Words which rhyme, that is to say, words which denote different things but are partially similar in sound, are not necessarily comic. To be comic, the two things they denote must either be so incongruous with each other that one cannot imagine a real situation in which a speaker would need to bring them together, or so irrelevant to each other, that they could only become associated by pure chance. The effect of a comic rhyme is as if the words, on the basis of their auditory friendship, had taken charge of the situation, as if, instead of an event requiring words to describe it, words had the power to create an event. Reading the lines

> There was an Old Man of Whitehaven
> Who danced a quadrille with a raven

one cannot help noticing upon reflection that, had the old gentleman lived in Ceylon, he would have had to dance with a swan; alternatively, had his dancing partner been a mouse, he might have had to reside in Christ Church, Oxford.

The comic rhyme involves both the first two laws of language; the spoonerism only the second. *Example:* a lecturing geologist introduces a lantern slide with the words: "And here, gentlemen, we see a fine example of erotic blacks."

So far as the speaker is concerned he has used the language incorrectly, yet what he says makes verbal sense of a kind. Unlike the pun however, where both meanings are relevant, in the spoonerism the accidental meaning is nonsense in the context. Thus, while the comic nature of the pun should be immediately apparent to the hearer, it should take time before he realizes what the speaker of the spoonerism intended to say. A pun is witty and intended; a spoonerism, like a comic rhyme, is comic and should appear to be involuntary. As with the clown, the speaker appears to be the slave of language, but in reality is its master.

Just as there are people who are really clumsy so there are incompetent poets who are the slaves of the only rhymes they know; the kind of poet caricatured by Shakespeare in the play of *Pyramus and Thisbe.*

> Those lily lips,
> This cherry nose,
> These yellow cowslip cheeks,
> Are gone, are gone,
> Lovers make moan;
> His eyes were green as leeks.
> O Sisters Three,
> Come, come to me
> With hands as pale as milk;
> Lay them in gore,
> Since you have shore
> With shears his thread of silk.

In this case we laugh at the rustic poet, not with him.

One of the most fruitful of witty devices is a violation of the third law, namely, to treat members of overlapping classes as if they were members of the same class. For example, during a period of riots and social unrest when the mob had set fire to hayricks all over the country Sydney Smith wrote to his friend, Mrs Meynell:

> What do you think of all these burnings? and have you heard of the new sort of burnings? Ladies' maids have taken to setting their mistresses on fire. Two dowagers were burned last week, and large rewards are offered. They are inventing little fire-engines for the toilet table, worked with lavender water.

The fourth law, which distinguishes between the occasions when speech is used to describe concrete things and those in which it is used for abstract purposes, provides an opportunity for wit, as in Wilde's epigram:

> Twenty years of romance make a woman look like a ruin, and twenty years of marriage make her look like a public building.

Ruin has become a "dead" metaphor, that is to say, a word which normally can be used as an abstraction, but public building is still a concrete description.

Literary Parody, and Visual Caricature

Literary parody presupposes (a) that every authentic writer has a unique perspective on life and (b) that his literary style accurately expresses that perspective. The trick of the parodist is to take the unique style of the author, *how* he expresses his unique vision, and make it express utter banalities; *what* the parody expresses could be said by anyone. The effect is of a reversal in the relation between the author and his style. Instead of the style being the creation of the man, the man becomes the puppet of the style. It is only possible to caricature an author one admires because, in the case of an author one dislikes, his own work will seem a better parody than one could hope to write oneself.

Example: As we get older we do not get any younger.
Seasons return, and to-day I am fifty-five,
And this time last year I was fifty-four,
And this time next year I shall be sixty-two.
And I cannot say I should like (to speak for myself)
To see my time over again—if you can call it time:
Fidgeting uneasily under a draughty stair,
Or counting sleepless nights in the crowded tube.
(Henry Reed, "Chard Whitlow")

Every face is a present witness to the fact that its owner has a past behind him which might have been otherwise, and a future ahead of him in which some possibilities are more probable than others. To "read" a face means to guess what it might have been and what it still may become. Children, for whom most future possibilities are equally probable, the dead for whom all possibilities have been reduced to zero, and animals who have only one possibility to realize and realize it completely, do not have faces which can be read, but wear inscrutable masks. A caricature of a face admits that its owner has had a past, but denies that he has a future. He has created his features up to a certain point, but now they have taken charge of him so that he can never change; he has become a single possibility completely realized. That is why, when we go to the zoo, the faces of the animals remind one of caricatures of human beings. A caricature doesn't need to be read; it has no future.

We enjoy caricatures of our friends because we do not want to think of their changing, above all, of their dying; we enjoy caricatures of our enemies because we do not want to consider the possibility of their having a change of heart so that we would have to forgive them.

Flyting

Flyting seems to have vanished as a studied literary art and only to survive in the impromptu exchanges of truckdrivers and cabdrivers. The comic effect arises from the contradiction between the insulting nature of what is said which appears to indicate a passionate relation of hostility and aggression, and the calculated skill of verbal invention which indicates that the protagonists are not thinking about each other but about language and their pleasure in employing it inventively. A man who is really passionately angry is speechless and can only express his anger by physical violence. Playful anger is intrinsically comic because, of all emotions, anger is the least compatible with play.

Satire

The object of satire is a person who, though in possession of his moral faculties, transgresses the moral law beyond the normal call of temptation. The lunatic cannot be an object of satire, since he is not morally responsible for his actions, and the wicked man cannot be an object because, while morally responsible, he lacks the normal faculty of conscience. The commonest object of satire is the rogue. The rogue transgresses the moral law at the expense of others, but he is only able to do this because of the vices of his victims; they share in his guilt. The wicked man transgresses the moral law at the expense of others, but his victims are innocent. Thus a black marketeer in sugar can be satirized because the existence of such a black market depends upon the greed of others for sugar, which is a pleasure but not a necessity; a black marketeer in penicillin cannot be satirized because, for the sick, it is a necessity and, if they cannot pay his prices, they will die.

After the rogue, the commonest object of satire is the monomaniac. Most men desire money and are not always too scrupulous in the means by which they obtain it, but this does not make them objects of satire, because their desire is tempered by a number of competing interests. A miser is satirizable because his desire overrides all desires which normal selfishness feels, such as sex or physical comfort.

The Satirical Strategy

There is not only a moral human norm, but also a normal way of transgressing it. At the moment of yielding to temptation, the normal human being has to exercise self-deception and rationalization, for in order to yield he requires the illusion of acting with a good conscience: after he has committed the immoral act, when desire is satisfied, the normal human being realizes the nature of his act and feels guilty. He who is incapable of realizing the nature of his act is mad, and he who, both before, while, and after committing it, is exactly conscious of what he is doing yet feels no guilt, is wicked.

The commonest satirical devices therefore, are two: (1) To present the object of satire *as if* he or she were mad and unaware of what he is doing.

> Now Night descending, the proud scene was o'er,
> But lived in Settle's numbers, one day more.
>
> (Pope)

The writing of poetry which, even in the case of the worst of poets, is a personal and voluntary act, is presented as if it were as impersonal and necessary as the revolution of the earth, and the value of the poems so produced which, even in a bad poet, varies, is presented as invariable and therefore subject to a quantitative measurement like dead matter.

The satiric effect presupposes that the reader knows that in real life Settle was not a certifiable lunatic, for lunacy overwhelms a man against his will: Settle is, as it were, a self-made lunatic.

(2) To present the object of satire as if he or she were wicked and completely conscious of what he is doing without feeling any guilt.

> Although, dear Lord, I am a sinner,
> I have done no major crime;
> Now I'll come to Evening Service
> Whensoever I have time.
> So, Lord, reserve for me a crown,
> And do not let my shares go down.
>
> (John Betjeman)

Again, the satiric effect depends upon our knowing that in real life the lady is not wicked, that, if she were really as truthful with herself as she is presented, she could not go to Church.

Satire flourishes in a homogeneous society where satirist and audience share the same views as to how normal people can be expected to behave, and in times of relative stability and contentment, for satire cannot deal with serious evil and suffering. In an age like our own, it cannot flourish except in intimate circles as an expression of private feuds: in public life the evils and sufferings are so serious that satire seems trivial and the only possible kind of attack is prophetic denunciation.

Don Juan

> *Hört ihr Kindeslieder singen,*
> *Gleich ists euer eigner Scherz;*
> *Seht ihr mich im Takte springen,*
> *Hüpft euch elterlich das Herz.*
> —*Faust*, Part II, Act III

Most of the literary works with which we are acquainted fall into one of two classes, those we have no desire to read a second time—sometimes, we were never able to finish them—and those we are always happy to reread. There are a few, however, which belong to a third class; we do not feel like reading one of them very often but, when we are in the appropriate mood, it is the only work we feel like reading. Nothing else, however good or great, will do instead.

For me, Byron's *Don Juan* is such a work. In trying to analyze why this should be so, I find helpful a distinction which, so far as I have been able to discover, can only be made in the English language, the distinction between saying, "So-and-so or such-and-such is *boring*," and saying, "So-and-so or such-and-such is a *bore*."

In English, I believe, the adjective expresses a subjective judgment; *boring* always means *boring-to-me*. For example, if I am in the company of golf enthusiasts, I find their conversation boring but they find it fascinating. The noun, on the other hand, claims to be an objective, universally valid statement; *X is a bore* is either true or false.

Applied to works of art or to artists, the distinction makes four judgments possible.

(1) Not (or seldom) boring but a bore. *Examples:* The last quartets of Beethoven, the Sistine frescoes of Michelangelo, the novels of Dostoievski.

(2) Sometimes boring but not a bore. Verdi, Degas, Shakespeare.

(3) Not boring and not a bore. Rossini, the drawings of Thurber, P. G. Wodehouse.

(4) Boring and a bore. Works to which one cannot attend. It would be rude to give names.

Perhaps the principle of the distinction can be made clearer by the following definitions:

A. The absolutely boring but absolutely not a bore: the time of day.

B. The absolutely not boring but absolute bore: God.

Don Juan is sometimes boring but pre-eminently an example of a long poem which is not a bore. To enjoy it fully, the reader must be in a mood of distaste for everything which is to any degree a bore, that is, for all forms of passionate attachment, whether to persons, things, actions or beliefs.

This is not a mood in which one can enjoy satire, for satire, however entertaining, has its origin in passion, in anger at what is the case, desire to change what is the case into what ought to be the case, and belief that the change is humanly possible. The *Dunciad*, for example, presupposes that the Goddess of Dullness is a serious enemy of civilization, that it is the duty of all good citizens to rally to the defense of the City against her servants, and that the cause of Common-sense is not hopeless.

In defending his poem against the charge of immorality, Byron said on one occasion: "Don Juan will be known bye-a-bye for what it is intended—a Satire on abuses of the present state of Society": but he was not telling the truth. The poem, of course, contains satirical passages. When Byron attacks Wordsworth, Southey or Wellington, he is certainly hoping to deprive them of readers and admirers and behind his description of the siege of Ismail lies a hope that love of military glory and adulation of the warrior are not incurable defects in human nature but evils against which the conscience of mankind can, in the long run, be persuaded to revolt.

But, as a whole, *Don Juan* is not a satire but a comedy, and Byron knew it, for in a franker mood he wrote to Murray:

I have no plan—I had no plan; but I had or have materials; though if, like Tony Lumpkin, I am to be "snubbed so when I am in spirits," the poem will be naught and the poet turn serious again . . . You are too earnest and eager about a work which was never intended to be serious. Do you suppose that I could have any intention but to giggle and make giggle.

Satire and comedy both make use of the comic contradiction, but their aims are different. Satire would arouse in readers the desire to act so that the contradictions disappear; comedy would persuade them to accept the contradictions with good humor as facts of life against which it is useless to rebel.

> Poor Julia's heart was in an awkward state,
>   She felt it going and resolved to make
> The noblest efforts for herself and mate,
>   For honour's, pride's, religion's, virtue's sake;
> Her resolutions were most truly great;
>   And almost might have made a Tarquin quake;
> She prayed the Virgin Mary for her grace
> As being the best judge in a lady's case.

> She vow'd she never would see Juan more
>   And next day paid a visit to his mother;
> And looked extremely at the opening door,
>   Which by the Virgin's grace, let in another;
> Grateful she was, and yet a little sore—
>   Again it opens—it can be no other.
> 'Tis surely Juan now—No! I'm afraid
> That night the Virgin was no longer prayed.

Julia is presented, neither as a pious hypocrite nor as a slut, but as a young woman, married to an older man she does not like, tempted to commit adultery with an attractive boy. The conflict between her conscience and her desire is perfectly genuine. Byron is not saying that it is silly of Julia to pray because there is no God, or that marriage is an unjust institution which should be abolished in favor of free love. The comedy lies in the fact that the voice of conscience and the voice of desire can both be expressed in the verbal form of a prayer, so that, while Julia's conscience is praying to the Madonna, her heart is praying to Aphrodite. Byron does not pass judgment on this; he simply states that human nature is like that and implies, perhaps, that, in his experience, if Aphrodite has opportunity on her side, the Madonna is seldom victorious, so that, in sexual matters, we ought to be tolerant of human frailty.

Byron's choice of the word *giggle* rather than *laugh* to describe his comic intention deserves consideration.

All comic situations show a contradiction between some general or universal principle and an individual or particular person or event. In the case of the situation at which we giggle, the general principles are two:

(1) The sphere of the sacred and the sphere of the profane are mutually exclusive.

(2) The sacred is that at which we do not laugh.

Now a situation arises in which the profane intrudes upon the sacred but without annulling it. If the sacred were annulled, we should laugh outright, but the sacred is still felt to be present, so that a conflict ensues between the desire to laugh and the feeling that laughter is inappropriate. A person to whom the distinction between the sacred and the profane had no meaning could never giggle.

If we giggle at Julia's prayer, it is because we have been brought up in a culture which makes a distinction between sacred and profane love. Similarly, we miss the comic point if we read the following lines as a satire on Christian dogma.

> as I suffer from the shocks
> Of illness, I grow much more orthodox.
>
> The first attack at once proved the Divinity;
>   (But *that* I never doubted, nor the Devil);
> The next, the Virgin's mystical Virginity;
>   The third, the usual Origin of Evil;
> The fourth at once established the whole Trinity
>   On so uncontrovertible a level,
> That I devoutly wished the three were four
> On purpose to believe so much the more.

If these lines were satirical, they would imply that all people in good health are atheists. But what Byron says is that when people are well, they tend to be frivolous and forget all those questions about the meaning of life which are of sacred importance to everybody, including atheists, and that when they are ill, they can think of nothing else. One could imagine a similar verse by Shelley (if he had had any sense of humor) in which he would say: "The iller I get, the more certain I become that there is no God." Shelley, as a matter of fact, complained that he was powerless "to eradicate from his friend's great mind the delusions of Christianity which in spite of his reason seem perpetually to recur and to lie in ambush for his hours of sickness and distress," and, had Byron lived longer, the prophecy Sir Walter Scott made in 1815 might well have come true.

> I remember saying to him that I really thought that, if he lived a few years longer, he would alter his sentiments. He answered rather sharply. "I suppose you are one of those who prophesy that I will turn Methodist." I replied—"No. I don't expect your conversion to be of such an ordinary kind. I would rather look to see you retreat upon the Catholic faith and distinguish yourself by the austerity of your penances."

The terms "sacred" and "profane" can be used relatively as well as absolutely. Thus, in a culture that puts a spiritual value upon love between the sexes, such a love, however physical, will seem sacred in comparison with physical hunger. When the shipwrecked Juan wakes and sees Haidée bending over him, he sees she is beautiful and is thrilled by her voice, but the first thing he longs for is not her love but a beefsteak.

The sacred can be evil as well as good. In our culture it is considered normal (the normal is always profane) for men to be carnivorous, and vegetarians are looked upon as cranks.

> Although his anatomical construction
>> Bears vegetables in a grumbling way,
> Your laboring people think beyond all question
> Beef, veal, and mutton better for digestion.

Cannibalism, on the other hand, is a crime which is regarded with sacred horror. The survivors from the shipwreck in Canto II are not only starving but also have a craving for meat to which their upbringing has conditioned them. Unfortunately, the only kind of meat available is human. One can imagine a group of men in similar circumstances who would not have become cannibals because they had been brought up in a vegetarian culture and were unaware that human beings could eat meat. The men in Byron's poem pay with their lives for their act, not because it is a sacred crime but for the profane reason that their new diet proves indigestible.

> By night chilled, by day scorched, there one by one
>> They perished until withered to a few,
> But chiefly by a species of self-slaughter
> In washing down Pedrillo with salt water.

It is the silly mistake of drinking salt water, not the sacred crime of consuming a clergyman, that brings retribution.

Most readers will probably agree that the least interesting figure in *Don Juan* is its official hero, and his passivity is all the more surprising when one recalls the legendary monster of depravity after whom he is named. The Don Juan of the myth is not promiscuous by nature but by will; seduction is his vocation. Since the slightest trace of affection will turn a number on his list of victims into a name, his choice of vocation requires the absolute renunciation of love. It is an essential element in the legend, therefore, that Don Juan be, not a sinner out of weakness, but a defiant atheist, the demonic counterimage of the ascetic saint who renounces all personal preference for one neighbor to another in order that he may show Christian charity to all alike.

When he chose the name Don Juan for his hero, Byron was well aware of the associations it would carry for the public, and he was also aware that he himself was believed by many to be the heartless seducer and atheist of the legend. His poem is, among other things, a self-defense. He is saying to his accusers, as it were: "The Don Juan of the legend does not exist. I will show you what the sort of man who gets the reputation for being a Don Juan is really like."

Byron's hero is not even particularly promiscuous. In the course of two years he makes love with five women, a poor showing in comparison with the 1003 Spanish ladies of Leporello's Catalogue aria, or even with Byron's own "200 odd Venetian pieces." Furthermore, he seduces none of them. In three cases he is seduced—by Julia, Catherine, the Duchess of Fitz-Fulk—and in the other two, circumstances outside his control bring him together with Haidée and Dudù, and no persuasion on his part is needed. Then, though he cannot quite play Tristan to her Isolde and commit suicide when he is parted from Haidée, he has been genuinely in love with her.

Far from being a defiant rebel against the laws of God and man, his most conspicuous trait is his gift for social conformity. I cannot understand those critics who have seen in him a kind of Rousseau child of Nature. Wherever chance takes him, to a pirate's lair, a harem in Mohammedan Constantinople, a court in Greek Orthodox Russia, a country house in Protestant England, he immediately adapts himself and is accepted as an agreeable fellow. Had Byron continued the poem as he planned and taken Juan to Italy to be a *cavaliere servante* and to Germany to be a solemn Werther-faced man, one has no doubt that he would have continued to play the roles assigned to him with tact and aplomb. In some respects Juan resembles the Baudelairian dandy but he lacks the air of *insolent* superiority which Baudelaire considered essential to the true dandy; he would never, one feels, say anything outrageous or insulting. Aside from the stylistic impossibility of ending a comic poem on a serious note, it is impossible to imagine Juan, a man without enemies, ending on the guillotine, as apparently Byron was considering doing with him.

When one compares Don Juan with what we know of his creator, he seems to be a daydream of what Byron would have liked to be himself. Physically he is unblemished and one cannot imagine him having to diet to keep his figure; socially, he is always at his ease and his behavior in perfect taste. Had Juan set out for Greece, he would not have had made for himself two Homeric helmets with overtowering plumes nor had engraved on his coat of arms the motto *Crede Don Juan.*

Byron, though very conscious of his rank, never felt fully at ease in the company of his social equals (Shelley was too odd to count). Even when he was the social lion of London, Lord Holland observed:

> It was not from his birth that Lord Byron had taken the station he held in society for, till his talents were known, he was, in spite of his birth, in anything but good society and *but* for his talents would never, perhaps, have been in any better.

And Byron himself confessed to Lady Blessington:

> I am so little fastidious in the selection or rather want of selection of as-
> sociates, that the most stupid men satisfy me as well, nay, perhaps, better
> than the most brilliant. The effort of letting myself down to them costs
> me nothing, though my pride is hurt that they do not seem more sen-
> sible of the condescension.

Juan, though by birth a Spaniard and a Catholic and therefore an outsider
from an Englishman's point of view, is the perfect embodiment of the very
English ideal of succeeding at anything he does without appearing to be
ambitious of success.

Characters which are daydream projections of their authors are seldom
very interesting and, had Byron written *Don Juan* as a straightforward narrative poem in the style of *The Corsair* or *Lara*, it would probably have been
unreadable. Fortunately, he had discovered a genre of poetry which allows
the author to enter the story he is telling. Juan is only a convenience: the real
hero of the poem is Byron himself.

Byron's poetry is the most striking example I know in literary history of the
creative role which poetic form can play. If William Stewart Rose had arrived
in Venice in September 1817 with nothing for him but magnesia and red
tooth powder, Byron would probably today be considered a very minor poet.
He knew Italian well, he had read Casti's *Novelle Galanti* and loved them, but
he did not realize the poetic possibilities of the mock-heroic ottava-rima until
he read Frere's *The Monks and the Giants*.

Take away the poems he wrote in this style and meter, *Beppo, The Vision of
Judgment, Don Juan*, and what is left of lasting value? A few lyrics, though
none of them is as good as the best of Moore's, two adequate satires though
inferior to Dryden or Pope, "Darkness," a fine piece of blank verse marred
by some false sentiment, a few charming occasional pieces, half a dozen stanzas from *Childe Harold*, half a dozen lines from *Cain*, and that is all. Given his
production up till that date, he showed better judgment than his readers
when he wrote to Moore in 1817:

> If I live ten years longer, you will see, however, that all is not over with
> me—I don't mean in literature, for that is nothing: and it may seem odd
> enough to say I do not think it is my vocation.

Soon afterwards, he read Frere: as he had foretold, it was not all over with
him but, as he had not foreseen, his vocation was to be literature. The authentic poet was at last released.

So long as Byron tried to write Poetry with a capital P, to express deep
emotions and profound thoughts, his work deserved that epithet he most
dreaded, una *seccatura*. As a thinker he was, as Goethe perceived, childish,

and he possessed neither the imaginative vision—he could never invent any-thing, only remember—nor the verbal sensibility such poetry demands. Lady Byron, of all people, put her finger on his great defect as a serious poet.

> He is the absolute monarch of words, and uses them as Bonaparte did lives, for conquest without regard to their intrinsic value.

The artistic failure of *Childe Harold* is due in large measure to Byron's disas-trous choice of the Spenserian stanza. At the time, he had only read a few verses of *The Faerie Queene* and when, later, Leigh Hunt tried to make him read the whole of it, one is not surprised to learn that he hated the poem. Nothing could be further removed from Byron's cast of mind than its slow, almost timeless, visionary quality.

His attempts to write satirical heroic couplets were less unsuccessful but, aside from the impossibility of equaling Dryden and Pope in their medium, Byron was really a comedian, not a satirist. Funny things can be said in he-roic couplets, but the heroic couplet as a *form* is not comic, that is to say, it does not itself make what it says funny.

Before *Beppo*, the authentic Byron emerges only in light occasional verse such as "Lines to a Lady who appointed a night in December to meet him in the garden."

> Why should you weep like Lydia Languish
> And fret with self-created anguish
> Or doom the lover you have chosen
> On winter nights to sigh half-frozen;
> In leafless shades to sue for pardon,
> Only because the scene's a garden?
> For gardens seem, by one consent,
> Since Shakespeare set the precedent,
> Since Juliet first declared her passion,
> To form the place of assignation,
> Oh, would some modern muse inspire
> And seat her by a sea-coal fire;
> Or had the bard at Christmas written
> And laid the scene of love in Britain,
> He, surely, in commiseration
> Had changed the place of declaration.
> In Italy I've no objection,
> Warm nights are proper for reflection:
> But here our climate is so rigid
> That love itself is rather frigid:
> Think on our chilly situation,
> And curb this rage for imitation.

In this, a very early poem, one can note already the speed and the use of feminine rhymes which were to become Byron's forte. Feminine rhymes are as possible in a five-foot line as in a four-foot but, at this date, the tune of the Pope couplet was still too much in his ear to allow him to use them. There are only three couplets with feminine rhymes in *English Bards and Scotch Reviewers* and only one in *Hints from Horace*.

Frere was not a great poet, but his perception of the comic possibilities of an *exact* imitation in English of Italian ottava-rima was a stroke of genius. Italian is a polysyllabic language, most of its words end on an unaccented syllable and rhymes are very common. Italian ottava-rima, therefore, is usually hendecasyllabic with feminine rhymes and, because three rhymes can be found without any effort, it became a maid-of-all-work stanza which would fit any subject. An Italian poet could use it for comic or satirical purposes, but he could also be serious and pathetic in it. There is nothing comic, for example, about this stanza from *Gerusalemme Liberata*.

> *Lei nel partir, lei nel tornar del sole*
> *Chiama con voce mesta e prega e plora;*
> *Come usignol cui villan duro invole*
> *Dal nido i figli non pennuti ancora*
> *Che in miserabil canto afflite e sole*
> *Piange le notte, e n'empie, boschi e l'ôra.*
> *Alfin col nuovo dì rinchiude alquanto*
> *I lumi; e il sonno in lor serpe fra il pianto.*

When English poets first copied the stanza, they instinctively shortened the lines to decasyllabics with masculine rhymes.

> All suddenly dismaid, and hartless quite
> He fled abacke and catching hastie holde
> Of a young alder hard behinde him pight,
> It rent, and streight aboute him gan beholde
> What God or Fortune would assist his might.
> But whether God or Fortune made him bold
> It's hard to read; yet hardie will he had
> To overcome, that made him less adrad.

> ("Vergil's Gnat")

The frequent monosyllables, the abruptness of the line endings and the absence of elision completely alter the movement. Further, because of the paucity of rhymes in English, it is almost impossible to write a poem of any length in this stanza without either using banal rhymes or padding the line in order to get a rhyme. If, from Chaucer to Sackville, it was not ottava-rima but rhyme-royal which was the staple vehicle for a long poem, one reason, at least, was that rhyme-royal calls for only one rhyme triplet, not two. So far as I know, the first English poet to combine ottava-rima with the high style was Yeats who, in his later years, wrote many of his finest poems in it. He gets round the rhyming problem by a liberal use of half-rhymes and by ending lines with words which are almost dactyls, so that the rhyming syllable is only lightly accented. For example, in the opening stanza of "Nineteen Hundred and Nineteen," only two of the lines rhyme exactly.

> Many ingenious lovely things are gone
> That seemed sheer miracle to the multitude,
> Protected from the circle of the moon
> That pitches common things about. There stood
> Amid the ornamental bronze and stone
> An ancient image made of olive wood—
> And gone are Phidias' famous ivories
> And all the golden grasshoppers and bees.

Frere was the first fully to realize (though, as W. P. Ker has pointed out, there are anticipations in Gay's "Mr Pope's Welcome from Greece") that the very qualities of the stanza which make it an unsuitable vehicle for serious poetry make it an ideal one for comic verse since in English, unlike Italian, the majority of double or triple rhymes are comic.

Our association of the word *romantic* with the magical and dreamlike is so strong that we are apt to forget that the literary period so classified is also a great age for comic poetry. The comic verse of poets like Canning, Frere, Hood, Praed, Barham, and Lear was a new departure in English poetry, and not least in its exploitation of comic rhyme. Indeed, before them, the only poets I can think of who used it intentionally and frequently were Skelton and Samuel Butler.

The very qualities of English ottava-rima which force a serious poet to resort to banal rhymes and padding are a stimulus to the comic imagination, leading to the discovery of comic rhymes and providing opportunities for the interpolated comment and conversational aside, and Byron developed this deliberate looseness of manner to the full.

> An Arab horse, a stately stag, a barb
>   New broke, a camelopard, a gazelle.
> No—none of these will do—and then their garb!
>   Their veil and petticoat—Alas! to dwell
> Upon such things would very near absorb
>   A canto—then their feet and ankles—well,
> Thank heaven I've got no metaphor quite ready,
> (And so, my sober Muse—come, let's be steady.)

He also exploited to the full the structural advantages of the stanza. As a unit, eight lines give space enough to describe a single event or elaborate on a single idea without having to run on to the next stanza. If, on the other hand, what the poet has to say requires several short sentences, the arrangement of the rhymes allows him to pause at any point he likes without the stanza breaking up into fragments, for his separate statements will always be linked by a rhyme. The stanza divides by rhyme into a group of six lines followed by a coda of two; the poet can either observe this division and use the couplet as an epigrammatic comment on the first part, or he can take seven lines for his theme and use the final one as a punch line.

> Gulbeyaz, for the first time in her days,
>   Was much embarrassed, never having met
> In all her life with aught save prayers and praise;
>   And as she also risked her life to get
> Him whom she meant to tutor in love's ways
>   Into a comfortable tête-à-tête,
> To lose the hour would make her quite a martyr.
> And they had wasted now about a quarter.

> Her form had all the softness of her sex,
>   Her features all the sweetness of the devil,
> When he put on the cherub to perplex
>   Eve, and paved (God knows what) the road to evil;
> The sun himself was scarce more free from specks
>   Than she from aught at which the eye could cavil;
> Yet, somehow, there was something somewhere wanting,
> As if she rather ordered than was granting.

What had been Byron's defect as a serious poet, his lack of reverence for words, was a virtue for the comic poet. Serious poetry requires that the poet treat words as if they were persons, but comic poetry demands that he treat them as things and few, if any, English poets have rivaled Byron's ability to put words through the hoops.

Needless to say, the skill of the comic poet, like that of the lion tamer or the clown, takes hard work to perfect. Byron chose to give others the impression that he dashed off his poetry, like a gentleman, without effort, but the publication of the Variorum edition of *Don Juan* demonstrates that, although he wrote with facility, he took a great deal more pains than he pretended. The editors, with an industrious devotion which is as admirable as it is, to me, incredible, have provided statistical tables. Thus, 87 out of the 172 stanzas in Canto I show revisions in four or more lines, and 123 revisions in the concluding couplet. A few examples will suffice.

Canto I, st. 103.

First draft:

> They are a sort of post-house, where the Fates
> Change horses every hour from night till noon;
> Then spur away with empires and o'er states,
> Leaving no vestige but a bare chronology,
> Except the hopes derived from true theology.

First revision:

> Except the promises derived from true theology.

Final version:

> They are a sort of post-house where the Fates
> Change horses, making history change its tune;
> Then spur away o'er empires and o'er states,
> Leaving at last not much besides chronology
> Excepting the post-obits of theology.

Canto IX, st. 33.

First draft:

> O! ye who build up statues all defiled
> With gore, like Nadir Shah, that costive Sophy,
> Who after leaving Hindostan a wild,
> And leaving Asia scarce a cup of coffee,
> To soothe his woes withal, went mad and was
> Killed because what he swallowed would not pass.

Final version:

> O! ye who build up monuments defiled
> With gore, like Nadir Shah, that costive Sophy
> Who, after leaving Hindostan a wild,
> And scarce to the Mogul a cup of coffee,
> To soothe his woes withal, was slain—the sinner!
> Because he could no more digest his dinner.

Canto XI, st. 60.

First version:

> 'Tis strange the mind should let such phrases quell its
> Chief impulse with a few frail paper pellets.

Second version:

> 'Tis strange the mind, that all celestial Particle,
> Should let itself be put out by an Article.

Final version:

> 'Tis strange the mind, that very fiery Particle,
> Should let itself be snuffed out by an Article.

One should be wary, when comparing an author's various productions, of saying: this piece is an expression of the real man and that piece is not—for nobody, not even the subject himself, can be certain who he is. All we can say is that this piece is the expression of a person who might possibly exist but nobody could possibly exist of whom that piece would be the expression.

There have been poets—Keats is the most striking example—whose letters and poems are so different from each other that they might have been written by two different people, and yet both seem equally authentic. But, with Byron, this is not the case. From the beginning, his letters seem authentic but, before *Beppo*, very little of his poetry; and the more closely his poetic *persona* comes to resemble the epistolary *persona* of his letters to his male friends—his love letters are another matter—the more authentic his poetry seems.

> So Scrope is gone—down diddled—as Doug K writes it, the said Doug being like the man who, when he lost a friend, went down to St James Coffee House and took a new one; "the best of men". Gone to Bruges where he will get tipsy with Dutch beer and shoot himself the first foggy morning.

Reading this letter to Hobhouse, one immediately recognizes its likeness to *Don Juan* and its unlikeness to *Manfred* and one feels that, while the letter and *Don Juan* have been written by someone-in-particular, *Manfred* must have been written, as it were, by a committee.

If one can say that the authentic poet in Byron is Byron the Friend, it is worth asking what are the typical characteristics of friendship. (I am thinking, of course, of friendship between men. To me, as to all men, the nature of friendship between women remains a mystery, which is probably a wise provision of nature. If we ever discovered what women say to each other when we are not there, our male vanity might receive such a shock that the human race would die out.)

The basis of friendship is similarity: it is only possible between persons who regard each other as equals and who have some interests and tastes in common, so that they can share each other's experiences. We can speak of a false friendship but not of an unreciprocated one. In this, friendship differs from sexual love which is based on difference and is all too often unreciprocated. Further, friendship is a nonexclusive, nonpossessive relationship; we can speak of having friends in common, while we cannot speak of having lovers, husbands or wives in common. Between two friends, therefore, there is an indifference towards, even an impatience with, those areas of human experience which they cannot share with each other, religious experiences, for example, which are unsharable with anybody, and feelings of passionate devotion which can be shared, if at all, only with the person for whom they are felt. André Gide was being unduly cynical, perhaps, when he defined a friend as someone with whom one does something disgraceful; it is true, however, that a vice in common can be the ground of a friendship but not a virtue in common. X and Y may be friends *because* they are both drunkards or womanizers but, if they are both sober and chaste, they are friends for some other reason.

The experiences which friends can share range from the grossest to the most subtle and refined, but nearly all of them belong to the category of the Amusing. No lover worries about boring his beloved; if she loves him, she cannot be bored and if she doesn't love him, he is too unhappy to care if she is. But between two friends, their first concern is not to bore each other. If they are persons of heart and imagination, they will take it for granted that the other has beliefs and feelings which he takes seriously and problems of his own which cause him suffering and sorrow, but in conversation they will avoid discussing them or, if they do discuss them, they will avoid the earnest note. One laughs with a friend; one does not weep with him (though one may weep *for* him).

Most poetry is the utterance of a man in some state of passion, love, joy, grief, rage, etc., and no doubt this is as it should be. But no man is perpetually in a passion and those *states* in which he is amused and amusing, detached and irreverent, if less important, are no less human. If there were no poets who, like Byron, express these states, Poetry would lack something.

An authentic and original work nearly always shocks its first readers and Byron's "new manner" was no exception.

> Beppo is just imported but not perused. The greater the levity of Lord Byron's Compositions, the more I imagine him to suffer from the turbid state of his mind.
>
> (Lady Byron)

> Frere particularly observed that the world had now given up the foolish notion that you were to be identified with your sombre heroes, and had acknowledged with what great success and good keeping you had portrayed a grand imaginary being. But the same admiration cannot be bestowed upon, and will not be due to the Rake Juan. . . . All the idle stories about your Venetian life will be more than confirmed.
>
> (Hobhouse)

> Dear *Adorable* Lord Byron, *don't* make a more *coarse* old libertine of yourself. . . . When you don't feel quite up to a spirit of benevolence . . . throw away your pen, my love, and take a little *calomel.*
>
> (Harriette Wilson, who shortly afterwards
offered to come and pimp for him)

> I would rather have the fame of *Childe Harold* for THREE YEARS than an IMMORTALITY of *Don Juan.*
>
> (Teresa Guiccoli)

Some of his friends, among them Hobhouse, admired parts of *Don Juan*, but the only person who seems to have realized how utterly different in kind it was from all Byron's previous work was John Lockhart:

> Stick to Don Juan; it is the only sincere thing you have ever written . . . out of all sight the best of your works; it is by far the most spirited, the most straightforward, the most interesting, and the most poetical . . . the great charm of its style, is that it is not much like the style of any other poem in the world.

Byron was not normally given to praising his own work, but of *Don Juan* he was openly proud:

> Of the fate of the "pome" I am quite uncertain, and do not anticipate much brilliancy from your silence. But I do not care. I am as sure as the Archbishop of Granada that I never wrote better, and I wish you all better taste.

> As to "Don Juan," confess, confess—you dog be candid—that it is the sublime of *that there* sort of writing—it may be bawdy but is it not good English? It may be profligate, but is it not life, is it not the *thing*? Could any man have written it who has not lived in the world?—and tooled in a post-chaise?—in a hackney coach?—in a gondola?—against a wall?—in a court carriage?—In a vis-à-vis?—on a table?—and under it?

There is an element of swank in this description, for the poem is far less bawdy than he makes it sound. Only a small part of the experience upon which Byron drew in writing it was amorous.

What Byron means by life—which explains why he could never appreciate Wordsworth or Keats—is the motion of life, the *passage* of events and thoughts. His visual descriptions of scenery or architecture are not particularly vivid, nor are his portrayal of states of mind particularly profound, but at the description of things in motion or the way in which the mind wanders from one thought to another he is a great master.

Unlike most poets, he must be read very rapidly as if the words were single frames in a movie film; stop on a word or a line and the poetry vanishes—the feeling seems superficial, the rhyme forced, the grammar all over the place—but read at the proper pace, it gives a conviction of watching the real thing which many profounder writers fail to inspire for, though motion is not the only characteristic of life, it is an essential one.

If Byron was sometimes slipshod in his handling of the language, he was a stickler for factual accuracy; "I don't care one lump of sugar," he once wrote, "for my poetry; but for my *costume*, and my *correctness* . . . I will combat lustily," and, on another occasion, "I hate things *all fiction*. . . . There should always be some foundation of fact for the most airy fabric, and pure invention is but the talent of a liar." He was furious when the poem "Pilgrimage to Jerusalem" was attributed to him: "How the devil should I write about *Jerusalem*, never having been yet there?" And he pounced, with justice, on Wordsworth's lines about Greece:

> Rivers, fertile plains, and sounding shores,
> Under a cope of variegated sky.

The rivers are dry half the year, the plains are barren, and the shores as "still" and "tideless" as the Mediterranean can make them; the sky is anything but variegated, being for months and months "darkly, deeply, beautifully blue."

The material of his poems is always drawn from events that actually happened, either to himself or to people he knew, and he took great trouble to get his technical facts, such as sea terms, correct.

When he stopped work on *Don Juan*, he had by no means exhausted his experience. Reading through Professor Marchand's recent biography, one comes across story after story that seems a natural for the poem; Caroline Lamb, for example, surrounded by little girls in white, burning effigies of Byron's pictures and casting into the flames copies of his letters because she could not bear to part with the originals; Byron himself, at Shelley's cremation, getting acutely sunburned, and Teresa preserving a piece of skin when he peeled; Teresa forbidding an amateur performance of *Othello* because she couldn't speak English and wasn't going to have anybody else play Desdemona. And, if Byron's shade is still interested in writing, there are plenty of posthumous incidents. The Greeks stole his lungs as a relic and then lost them; at his funeral, noble carriage after noble carriage lumbered by, all empty, because the aristocracy felt they must show some respect to a fellow-peer but did not dare seem to show approval of his politics or his private life; Fletcher, his valet, started a macaroni factory and failed; Teresa married a French marquis who used to introduce her as "*La Marquise de Boissy, ma femme, ancienne maîtresse de Byron*" and after his death devoted herself to spiritualism, talking with the spirits of both Byron and her first husband. What stanzas they could all provide! How suitable, too, for a *that-there* poet that the room in which his "Memoirs" were burned should now be called the Byron Room, how perfect the scene John Buchan describes of himself and Henry James setting down to examine the archives of Lady Lovelace:

> . . . during a summer weekend, Henry James and I waded through masses of ancient indecency, and duly wrote an opinion. . . . My colleague never turned a hair. His only words for some special vileness were "singular"—"most curious"—"nauseating, perhaps, but how quite inexpressibly significant."

Dingley Dell & The Fleet

To become mature is to recover that sense of seriousness
which one had as a child at play. —F. W. Nietzsche

All characters who are products of the mythopoeic imagination are instantaneously recognizable by the fact that their existence is not defined by their
social and historical context; transfer them to another society or another age
and their characters and behavior will remain unchanged. In consequence,
once they have been created, they cease to be their author's characters and
become the reader's; he can continue their story for himself.

Anna Karenina is not such a character for the reader cannot imagine her
apart from the particular milieu in which Tolstoi places her or the particular
history of her life which he records; Sherlock Holmes, on the other hand, is:
every reader, according to his fancy, can imagine adventures for him which
Conan Doyle forgot, as it were, to tell us.

Tolstoi was a very great novelist, Conan Doyle a very minor one, yet it is the
minor not the major writer who possesses the mythopoeic gift. The mythopoeic imagination is only accidentally related, it would seem, to the talent for
literary expression; in Cervantes' *Don Quixote* they are found together, in Rider
Haggard's *She* literary talent is largely absent. Indeed, few of the writers whom
we call great have created mythical characters. In Shakespeare's plays we find
five, Prospero, Ariel, Caliban, Falstaff and Hamlet, and Hamlet is a myth for
actors only; the proof that, for actors, he is a myth is that all of them without
exception, irrespective of age, build, or even sex, wish to play the part.

After Cervantes, as a writer who combines literary talent and a mythopoeic
imagination, comes Dickens and, of his many mythical creations, Mr Pickwick is one of the most memorable. Though the appeal of mythical characters transcends all highbrow-lowbrow frontiers of taste, it is not unlimited;
every such character is symbolic of some important and perpetual human
concern, but a reader must have experienced this concern, even if he cannot
define it to himself, before the character can appeal to him. Judging by my
own experience, I would say that *Pickwick Papers* is emphatically *not* a book
for children and the reflections which follow are the result of my asking myself: "Why is it that I now read with such delight a book which, when I was
given it to read as a boy, I found so boring, although it apparently contains
nothing which is too 'grown-up' for a twelve-year-old?" The conclusion I
have come to is that the real theme of *Pickwick Papers*—I am not saying Dickens was consciously aware of it and, indeed, I am pretty certain he was not—
is the Fall of Man. It is the story of a man who is innocent, that is to say, who
has not eaten of the Tree of the Knowledge of Good and Evil and is, therefore, living in Eden. He then eats of the Tree, that is to say, he becomes

conscious of the reality of Evil but, instead of falling from innocence into sin—this is what makes him a mythical character—he changes from an innocent child into an innocent adult who no longer lives in an imaginary Eden of his own but in the real and fallen world.

If my conclusion is correct, it explains why *Pickwick Papers* said nothing to me as a boy because, though no boy is innocent, he has no clear notion of innocence, nor does he know that to be no longer innocent, but to wish that one were, is part of the definition of an adult.

However he accounts for it, every adult knows that he lives in a world where, though some are more fortunate than others, no one can escape physical and mental suffering, a world where everybody experiences some degree of contradiction between what he desires to do and what his conscience tells him he ought to do or others will allow him to do. Everybody wishes that this world were not like that, that he could live in a world where desires would conflict neither with each other nor with duties nor with the laws of nature, and a great number of us enjoy imagining what such a world would be like.

Our dream pictures of the Happy Place where suffering and evil are unknown are of two kinds, the Edens and the New Jerusalems. Though it is possible for the same individual to imagine both, it is unlikely that his interest in both will be equal and I suspect that between the Arcadian whose favorite daydream is of Eden, and the Utopian whose favorite daydream is of New Jerusalem there is a characterological gulf as unbridgeable as that between Blake's Prolifics and Devourers.

In their relation to the actual fallen world, the difference between Eden and New Jerusalem is a temporal one. Eden is a past world in which the contradictions of the present world have not yet arisen; New Jerusalem is a future world in which they have at last been resolved. Eden is a place where its inhabitants may do whatever they like to do; the motto over its gate is, "Do what thou wilt is here the Law." New Jerusalem is a place where its inhabitants like to do whatever they ought to do, and its motto is, "In His will is our peace."

In neither place is the moral law felt as an imperative; in Eden because the notion of a universal law is unknown, in New Jerusalem because the law is no longer a law-for, commanding that we do this and abstain from doing that, but a law-of, like the laws of nature, which describes how, in fact, its inhabitants behave.

To be an inhabitant of Eden, it is absolutely required that one be happy and likable; to become an inhabitant of New Jerusalem it is absolutely required that one be happy and good. Eden cannot be entered; its inhabitants are born there. No unhappy or unlikable individual is ever born there and, should one of its inhabitants become unhappy or unlikable, he must leave. Nobody is born in New Jerusalem but, to enter it, one must, either through one's own acts or by Divine Grace, have become good. Nobody ever leaves New Jerusalem, but the evil or the unredeemed are forever excluded.

The psychological difference between the Arcadian dreamer and the Utopian dreamer is that the backward-looking Arcadian knows that his expulsion from Eden is an irrevocable fact and that his dream, therefore, is a wish-dream which cannot become real; in consequence, the actions which led to his expulsion are of no concern to his dream. The forward-looking Utopian, on the other hand, necessarily believes that his New Jerusalem is a dream which ought to be realized so that the actions by which it could be realized are a necessary element in his dream; it must include images, that is to say, not only of New Jerusalem itself but also images of the Day of Judgment.

Consequently, while neither Eden nor New Jerusalem are places where aggression can exist, the Utopian dream permits indulgence in aggressive fantasies in a way that the Arcadian dream does not. Even Hitler, I imagine, would have defined his New Jerusalem as a world where there are no Jews, not as a world where they are being gassed by the million day after day in ovens, but he was a Utopian, so the ovens had to come in.

How any individual envisages Eden is determined by his temperament, personal history and cultural milieu, but to all dream Edens the following axioms, I believe, apply.

(1) Eden is a world of pure being and absolute uniqueness. Change can occur but as an instantaneous transformation, not through a process of becoming. Everyone is incomparable.

(2) The self is satisfied whatever it demands; the ego is approved of whatever it chooses.

(3) There is no distinction between the objective and the subjective. What a person appears to others to be is identical with what he is to himself. His name and his clothes are as much *his* as his body, so that, if he changes them, he turns into someone else.

(4) Space is both safe and free. There are walled gardens but no dungeons, open roads in all directions but no wandering in the wilderness.

(5) Temporal novelty is without anxiety, temporal repetition without boredom.

(6) Whatever the social pattern, each member of society is satisfied according to his conception of his needs. If it is a hierarchical society, all masters are kind and generous, all servants faithful old retainers.

(7) Whatever people do, whether alone or in company, is some kind of play. The only motive for an action is the pleasure it gives the actor, and no deed has a goal or an effect beyond itself.

(8) Three kinds of erotic life are possible, though any particular dream of Eden need contain only one. The polymorphous-perverse promiscuous sexuality of childhood, courting couples whose relation is potential, not actual, and the chastity of natural celibates who are without desire.

(9) Though there can be no suffering or grief, there can be death. If a

death occurs, it is not a cause for sorrow—the dead are not missed—but a social occasion for a lovely funeral.

(10) The Serpent, acquaintance with whom results in immediate expulsion = any serious need or desire.

The four great English experts on Eden are Dickens, Oscar Wilde, Ronald Firbank and P. G. Wodehouse.*

If, in comparing their versions of Eden with those of the Ancient World, I call theirs Christian, I am not, of course, asserting anything about their own beliefs. I only mean that their versions presuppose an anthropology for which Christianity is, historically, responsible. Whether it can exist in a society where the influence of Christianity has never been felt or has been eradicated, I do not know. I suspect that works like *Pickwick Papers, The Importance of Being Earnest, The Flower Beneath the Foot,* and *Blandings Castle* would bewilder a Russian Communist as much as they would have bewildered an Ancient Greek. The Communist would probably say: "It is incredible that anybody should *like* people so silly and useless as Mr Pickwick, Miss Prism, Madame Wetme and Bertie Wooster." The Greek would probably have said: "It is incredible that such people, so plain, middle-aged and untalented, should be *happy*."

When the Greeks pictured Eden, they thought of it as a place which the gods or Chance might permit to exist. In his tenth Pythian Ode, Pindar describes the life of the Hyperboreans.

> Never the Muse is absent
> from their ways: lyres clash and the flutes cry
> and everywhere maiden choruses whirling.
> They bind their hair in golden laurel and take their holiday.
> Neither disease nor bitter old age is mixed
> in their sacred blood; far from labor and battle
> they live; they escape Nemesis
> the overjust.

Or it might exist, like the Islands of the Blessed, as a place of rest and reward for dead heroes. The Greek poets speak of it, not as an imaginary poetic world, but as a distant region of the real world which they have not visited but of which they have heard reports. Pindar's description of the Hyperboreans is related to his definition of the difference between gods and men in the sixth Nemean:

> There is one
> race of men, one race of gods; both have breath
> of life from a single mother. But sundered power

---

* N.B. To my surprise, the only creators of Edens during the last three centuries I can think of, have all been English.

> holds us divided, so that the one is nothing, while for the other the
>   brazen sky is established
> their sure citadel for ever. Yet we have some likeness in great
> intelligence or strength to the immortals,
> though we know not what the day will bring, what course
>   after nightfall
> destiny has written that we must run to the end.

Gods and men do not differ in nature, only in power; the gods are immortal and can do what they like, men are mortal and can never foresee the consequences of their actions. Therefore, the more powerful a man is, the more godlike he becomes. It is possible to conceive of men so gifted by fortune that, like the Hyperboreans, their life would be indistinguishable from that of the gods.

This is a conception natural to a shame-culture in which who a man is is identical with what he does and suffers. The happy man is the fortunate man, and fortune is objectively recognizable; to be fortunate means to be successful, rich, powerful, beautiful, admired. When such a culture imagines Eden, therefore, it automatically excludes the weak and the ungifted, children, old people, poor people, ugly people.

The first significant difference between the conception of man held by a shame-culture and that of a guilt-culture is that a guilt-culture distinguishes between what a man is to other men, the self he manifests in his body, his actions, his words, and what he is to himself, a unique ego which is unchanged by anything he does or suffers. In a shame-culture, there is no real difference between statements in the third person and statements in the first; in a guilt-culture, they are totally distinct. In the statement *Jones is six feet tall*, the predicate qualifies the subject; in the statement *I am six feet tall*, it does not. It qualifies a self which the subject recognizes to be six feet tall; the *I* has no height.

In a shame-culture, the moral judgment a man passes upon himself is identical with that which others pass on him; the virtue or shamefulness of an act lies in the nature of the act itself, irrespective of the doer's personal intention or responsibility. In a guilt-culture, the subject passes moral judgment upon his thoughts and feelings even if they are never realized in action, and upon his acts irrespective of whether others know of them or not, approve of them or not.

In a guilt-culture, therefore, there are a special series of first-person propositions in which the predicate does qualify the subject. For example:

I am innocent/guilty
I am proud/humble
I am penitent/impenitent
I am happy/unhappy.

(I am in a state of pleasure/pain is not, of course, one of them. Pain and pleasure are states of the self, not of the ego.)

If I make any such assertion, it must be true or false, but no person except myself can know which; there is no way in which, from observing me, another can come to any conclusion.

A writer brought up in a Christian society who would describe Eden has, therefore, to cope with a problem which his pagan predecessors were spared. As an artist he can only deal in the manifest and objective—his Eden, like the pagan one, must be a fortunate place where there is no suffering and everybody has a good time—but he has to devise a way of making outward appearances signify subjective states of innocence and happiness to which, in the real world, they are not necessarily related.

If one compares versions of Eden by pagan writers with Christian versions, it is noticeable that the former are beautiful in a serious way and that the latter are for the most part comic, even grotesque; they reserve the serious for descriptions of New Jerusalem.

Suppose a writer wishes to show that every man loves himself, not because of this or that quality he possesses, but simply because he is uniquely he, what can he do? One possible image is that of an exceptionally ugly man—prodigiously fat, let us say—who is nevertheless convinced that he is irresistible to the ladies.

Here the exceptional obesity is an indirect sign for the uniqueness of the subject, and the fantastic vanity—in real life, a man must be reasonably good-looking before he can become vain in this way—an indirect sign for the independence of self-love from any quality of the self. But both signs remain indirect; the ugliest, the most average-looking and the most beautiful human beings all love themselves in the same way.

Suppose he wishes to portray a humble man. The writer can show someone engaging by his own choice—he is perfectly free to refuse—in activities for which he has no talent whatsoever and at which, therefore, he is bound to fail and look ridiculous, and then show him as radiant with self-esteem in his failure as if he had triumphed. Here self-esteem in a situation which in real life would destroy it is an indirect sign for humility; but not a direct sign, for a successful man can be humble too.

Or again, suppose a writer wishes to portray an innocent man. No human being is innocent, but small children are not yet personally guilty. It is possible that they have some knowledge of good and evil, but it is certain they have no innate knowledge of what their parents and society call right and wrong, and apply alike to such diverse matters as toilet habits, social manners, stealing and cruelty.

Compared with a normal adult, a small child is lacking in a sense of honor and a sense of shame. One way, therefore, in which a writer can portray an

innocent man is to show an adult behaving in a way which his society considers outrageous without showing the slightest awareness of public opinion. A
normal adult might wish to behave in the same way and even do so if he were
certain that nobody else would get to hear of his behavior, but fear of social
disapproval will prevent him from behaving so in public. The lack of shame
is an indirect sign of innocence but, once again, not a direct sign, because
lunatics show the same lack of shame.

When the novel opens, Mr Pickwick is middle-aged. In his farewell speech at
the Adelphi, he says that nearly the whole of his previous life had been devoted to business and the pursuit of wealth, but we can no more imagine
what he did during those years than we can imagine what Don Quixote did
before he went mad or what Falstaff was like as a young man. In our minds
Mr Pickwick is born in middle age with independent means; his mental and
physical powers are those of a middle-aged man, his experience of the world
that of a newborn child. The society into which he is born is a commercial
puritanical society in which wealth is honored, poverty despised, and any
detected lapse from the strictest standards of propriety severely punished. In
such a society, Mr Pickwick's circumstances and nature make him a fortunate
individual. He is comfortably off and, aside from a tendency at times to over-
indulge in food and drink, without vices. Sex, for example, is no temptation
to him. One cannot conceive of him either imagining himself romantically
in love with a girl of the lower orders, like Don Quixote, or consorting with
whores, like Falstaff. So far as his experience goes, this world is an Eden
without evil or suffering.

> His sitting-room was the first floor front, his bedroom the second floor
> front; and thus, whether he was sitting at his desk in his parlour or
> standing before the dressing-glass in his dormitory, he had an equal op-
> portunity of contemplating human nature in all the numerous phases it
> exhibits, in that not more populous than popular thoroughfare. His
> landlady, Mrs Bardell—the relict and sole executrix of a deceased cus-
> tom-house officer—was a comely woman of bustling manners and
> agreeable appearance, with a natural genius for cooking, improved by
> study and long practice, into an exquisite talent. There were no chil-
> dren, no servants, no fowls—cleanliness and quiet reigned throughout
> the house; and in it Mr Pickwick's will was law.

His three young friends, Tupman, Snodgrass and Winkle, are equally innocent. Each has a ruling passion, Tupman for the fair sex, Snodgrass for
poetry, and Winkle for sport, but their talents are not very formidable. We
are not given any specimen of Snodgrass's poems, but we may presume that,
at their best, they reach the poetic level of Mrs Leo Hunter's "Ode to an
Expiring Frog."

> Say, have fiends in shape of boys
> With wild halloo and brutal noise
> Hunted thee from marshy joys
> With a dog,
> Expiring frog?

We are shown Winkle at a shoot and learn that the birds are in far less danger than the bystanders. Tupman's age and girth are hardly good qualifications for a Romeo or a Don Juan. Contact with the world cures them of their illusions without embittering them, Eros teaches the two young men that the favors of Apollo and Artemis are not what they desire—Snodgrass marries Emily and becomes a gentleman farmer, Winkle marries Arabella Allen and goes into his father's business—and Tupman comes to acquiesce cheerfully in the prospect of a celibate old age.

The results of Mr Pickwick's scientific researches into the origin of the Hampstead Ponds and the nature of Tittlebats were no more reliable, we may guess, than his archaeology but, as the book progresses, we discover that, if his ability at enquiry is less than he imagines, his capacity to learn is as great. What he learns is not what he set out to learn but is forced upon him by fate and by his decision to go to prison, but his curiosity about life is just as eager at the end of the book as it was at the beginning; what he has been taught is the difference between trivial and important truths.

From time to time, Dickens interrupts his narrative to let Mr Pickwick read or listen to a tale. Some, like the Bagman's story, the story of the goblins who stole a sexton, the anecdote of the tenant and the gloomy ghost, are tall tales about the supernatural, but a surprising number are melodramas about cases of extreme suffering and evil: a broken-down clown beats his devoted wife and dies of D.T.'s; the son of a wicked father breaks his mother's heart, is transported, returns after seventeen years and is only saved from parricide by his father dying before he can strike him; a madman raves sadistically; a man is sent to prison for debt by his father-in-law, his wife and child die, he comes out of prison and devotes the rest of his life to revenge, first refusing to save his enemy's son from drowning and then reducing him to absolute want.

Stories of this kind are not tall; they may be melodramatically written, but everybody knows that similar things happen in real life. Dickens' primary reason for introducing them was, no doubt, that of any writer of a serial—to introduce a novel entertainment for his readers at a point when he feels they would welcome an interruption in the main narrative—but, intentionally or unintentionally, they contribute to our understanding of Mr Pickwick.

Mr Pickwick is almost as fond of hearing horror tales and curious anecdotes as Don Quixote is of reading Courtly Romances, but the Englishman's illusion about the relationship of literature to life is the opposite of the Spaniard's.

To Don Quixote, literature and life are identical; he believes that, when his senses present him with facts which are incompatible with courtly romance, his senses must be deceiving him. To Mr Pickwick, on the other hand, literature and life are separate universes; evil and suffering do not exist in the world he perceives with his senses, only in the world of entertaining fiction.

Don Quixote sets out to be a Knight Errant, to win glory and the hand of his beloved by overthrowing the wicked and unjust and rescuing the innocent and afflicted. When Mr Pickwick and his friends set out for Rochester, they have no such noble ambitions; they are simply looking for the novel and unexpected. Their reason for going to Bath or to Ipswich is that of the tourist—they have never been there.

Don Quixote expects to suffer hardship, wounds and weariness in the good cause, and is inclined to suspect the pleasant, particularly if feminine, as either an illusion or a temptation to make him false to his vocation. The Pickwick Club expects to have nothing but a good time, seeing pretty towns and countrysides, staying in well-stocked inns and making pleasant new acquaintances like the Wardles. However, the first new acquaintance they make in their exploration of Eden is with the serpent, Jingle, of whose real nature they have not the slightest suspicion. When Jingle's elopement with Rachel Wardle opens his eyes, Mr Pickwick turns into a part-time Knight Errant: he assumes that Jingle, the base adventurer, is a unique case and, whenever he comes across his tracks, he conceives it his duty not to rest until he has frustrated his fell designs, but his main purpose in travel is still to tour Eden. Rescuing unsuspecting females from adventurers has not become his vocation.

During his first pursuit of Jingle, Mr Pickwick meets Sam Weller, decides to engage him as a personal servant, and in trying to inform Mrs Bardell of his decision creates the misunderstanding which is to have such unfortunate consequences. Sam Weller is no innocent; he has known what it is like to be destitute and homeless, sleeping under the arches of Waterloo Bridge, and he does not expect this world to be just or its inhabitants noble. He accepts Mr Pickwick's offer, not because he particularly likes him, but because the job promises to be a better one than that of the Boots at an inn.

> I wonder whether I'm meant to be a footman, or a groom, or a gamekeeper or a seedsman? I look like a sort of compo of every one of 'em. Never mind; there's change of air, plenty to see, and little to do; and all this suits my complaint uncommon.

But before the story ends, he is calling Mr Pickwick an angel, and his devotion to his master has grown so great that he insists upon being sent to prison in order to look after him. For Sam Weller had, after all, his own kind of innocence: about the evil in the world he had learned as much as anybody, but his experience had never led him to suspect that a person so innocent of evil as Mr Pickwick could inhabit it.

Mr Pickwick has hardly engaged Sam Weller when the letter arrives from Dodson and Fogg, announcing that Mrs Bardell is suing him for Breach of Promise, and his real education begins.

If, hitherto, he had ever thought about the Law at all, he had assumed that it was what the Law must always claim to be:

(1) Just. Those acts which the Law prohibits and punishes are always unjust; no just or innocent act is ever prohibited or punished.
(2) Efficient. There are no unjust acts or persons that the Law overlooks or allows to go unpunished.
(3) Infallible. Those whom the Law finds guilty are always guilty; no innocent person is ever found guilty.

He has got to learn that none of these claims is fulfilled, and why, in this world, they cannot be fulfilled.

Even were the Law formally perfect, its administration cannot be, because it has to be administered, not by angels or machines, but by human individuals who, like all human beings, vary in intelligence, temperament and moral character: some are clever, some stupid, some kind, some cruel, some scrupulous, some unscrupulous.

Moreover, lawyers are in the morally anomalous position of owing their livelihood and social status to the criminal, the unjust and the ignorant; if all men knew the Law and kept it, there would be no work for lawyers. Doctors also owe their livelihood to an evil, sickness, but at least sickness is a natural evil—men do not desire ill health—but crimes and civil wrongs are acts of human choice, so that the contradiction between the purpose of Law and the personal interest of lawyers is more glaring. And then the complexity of the Law and the nature of the legal process make those who practice law peculiarly liable to a vice which one might call the vice of Imaginary Innocence.

No human being is innocent, but there is a class of innocent human actions called Games.

A game is a closed world of action which has no relation to any other actions of those who play it; the players have no motive for playing the game except the pleasure it gives them, and the outcome of the game has no consequences beyond itself. Strictly speaking, a game in which the players are paid to play, or in which they play for money stakes, ceases to be a game, for money exists outside the closed world of the game. In practice, one may say that a game played for stakes remains a game so long as the sums of money won or lost are felt by the players to be, not real, but token payments, that is to say, what they win or lose has no sensible effect upon their lives after the game is over.

The closed world of the game is one of mock passions, not real ones. Many games are, formally, mock battles, but if any one of the players should feel or display real hostility, he immediately ceases to be a player. Even in boxing and wrestling matches, in which the claim to be called games at all is doubtful, the ritual of shaking hands at the beginning and end asserts that they are not fights between real enemies.

Within the closed world of the game the only human beings are the players; the other inhabitants are things, balls, bats, chessman, cards, etc.

Like the real world, the game world is a world of laws which the players must obey because obedience to them is a necessary condition for entering it. In the game world there is only one crime, cheating, and the penalty for this is exclusion; once a man is known to be a cheat, no other player will play with him.

In a game the pleasure of playing, of exercising skill, takes precedence over the pleasure of winning. If this were not so, if victory were the real goal, a skillful player would prefer to have an unskillful one as his opponent, but only those to whom, like cardsharpers, a game is not a game but a livelihood, prefer this. In the game world the pleasure of victory is the pleasure of *just* winning. The game world, therefore, is an innocent world because the ethical judgment good-or-bad does not apply to it; a good game means a game at the conclusion of which all the players, whether winners or losers, can truthfully say that they have enjoyed themselves, a point which is made by the Little Man's speech after the cricket match between Dingley Dell and Muggleton.

> Sir, while we remember that Muggleton has given birth to a Dumkins and a Podder, let us never forget that Dingley Dell can boast of a Luffey and a Struggles. Every gentleman who hears me, is probably acquainted with the reply made by an individual who—to use an ordinary figure of speech—"hung out" in a tub, to the Emperor Alexander:—"If I were not Diogenes," said he, "I would be Alexander". I can well imagine these gentlemen to say, "If I were not Dumkins, I would be Luffey; If I were not Podder, I would be Struggles."

The vice of Imaginary Innocence consists in regarding an action in the open world of reality as if it were an action in the closed world of the game.

If this world were the worst of all possible worlds, a world where everybody was obliged to do what he dislikes doing and prohibited from doing anything he enjoyed, this vice would be impossible. It is only possible because some people have the good fortune to enjoy doing something which society requires to be done; what, from the point of view of society, is their necessary labor, is, from their own, voluntary play. Men fall into this vice when, because of the pleasure which the exercise of their calling gives them, they forget that what is play for them may for others concern real needs and passions.

Before Mr Pickwick has to suffer in person from this human failing, he has already witnessed a manifestation of it in the party politics of Eatonswill.

Party politics presupposes that it is possible for two people, equally rational and well-meaning, to hold different opinions about a policy and possible for a man to be convinced by argument that his opinion has been mistaken. It also presupposes that, however widely their political opinions may differ, all voters are agreed that the goal of politics is the establishment of a just and smoothly running society. But in Eatonswill the pleasure of party rivalry and debate has become an end in itself to both parties, a closed game world, and the real goal of politics has been forgotten.

> The Blues lost no opportunity of opposing the Buffs and the Buffs lost no opportunity of opposing the Blues. . . . If the Buffs proposed to new skylight the market place, the Blues got up public meetings and denounced the proceeding; if the Blues proposed the erection of an additional pump in the High Street, the Buffs rose as one man and stood aghast at the enormity. There were Blue shops and Buff shops, Blue Inns and Buff Inns; there was a Blue aisle and a Buff aisle in the very church itself.

On such a parochial scale politics as a game is relatively harmless, though on a national scale it is vicious, but there can be no circumstances in which the practice of Law as a game is not vicious. People who are not lawyers never come into court for fun; they come, either because they have been arrested or because they believe they have been wronged and see no other way of redress. Winning or losing their case is never a mock victory or defeat but always a real one; if they lose, they go to prison or suffer social disgrace or are made to pay money.

Rightly or wrongly, it is believed in our culture that, in most criminal and civil trials, the best means of arriving at the ethical judgment guilty-or-not-guilty is through a kind of aesthetic verbal combat between a prosecuting and a defending counsel, to which the judge acts as a referee, and the verdict is given by a jury. To say that a lawyer is a good lawyer, therefore, is an aesthetic not an ethical description; a good lawyer is not one who causes justice to be done, but one who wins his cases, whether his client be innocent or guilty, in the right or in the wrong, and nothing will enhance his reputation for being a good lawyer so much as winning a case against apparently hopeless odds, a state of affairs which is more likely to arise if his client is really guilty than if he is really innocent. As men, Dodson and Fogg are scoundrels but, as lawyers, their decent colleague Mr Perkins has to admit that they are very good.

> Mrs Bardell, supported by Mrs Chappins, was led in and placed in a drooping state at the other end of the seat on which Mr Pickwick sat. . . .

Mrs Saunders then appeared, leading in Master Bardell. At sight of her child, Mrs Bardell started: suddenly recollecting herself, she kissed him in a frantic manner; then relapsing into a state of hysterical imbecility the good lady requested to be informed where she was. In reply to this, Mrs Chappins and Mrs Saunders turned their heads away and wept, while Messrs Dodson and Fogg intreated the plaintiff to compose herself. . . . "Very good notion, that indeed," whispered Perkins to Mr Pickwick. "Capital fellows those Dodson and Fogg; excellent ideas of effect, my dear sir, excellent."

Dodson and Fogg may be scoundrels but they are not wicked men; though they cause undeserved suffering in others, they have no malevolent intent— the suffering they cause gives them no pleasure. To them, their clients are the pieces with which they play the legal game, which they find as enjoyable as it is lucrative. So, too, when Sergeant Buzfuz expresses his detestation of Mr Pickwick's character, or Mr Sumpkins bullies the unfortunate witness Winkle, what their victims feel as real hostility is, in fact, the mock hostility of the player: had they been engaged for the Defense, their abuse would have been directed against Mrs Bardell and Mrs Chappins, and they will have completely forgotten about the whole case by the next morning. The Guild Hall which is a Purgatory to Mr Pickwick is to them what Dingley Dell is to him, an Arcadia.

When he is found guilty, Mr Pickwick takes a vow that he will never pay the damages. In so doing he takes his first step out of Eden into the real world, for to take a vow is to commit one's future, and Eden has no conception of the future for it exists in a timeless present. In Eden, a man always does what he likes to do at the moment, but a man who takes a vow commits himself to doing something in the future which, when the time comes, he may dislike doing. The consequence of Mr Pickwick's vow is that he has to leave his Eden of clean linen and polished silver for a Limbo of dirty crockery and rusty broken toasting forks where, in the eyes of the Law, he is a guilty man, a lawbreaker among other lawbreakers.

The particular class of lawbreakers among whom Mr Pickwick finds himself in The Fleet are debtors. In selecting this class of offender rather than another for him to encounter, one of Dickens' reasons was, of course, that he considered the English laws of his day concerning debt to be monstrously unjust and sending his fictional hero there gave him an opportunity for satirical exposure of a real social abuse. But in a world where money is the universal medium of exchange, the notion of debt has a deep symbolic resonance. Hence the clause in the Lord's Prayer as it appears in the Authorized Version of St Matthew—"Forgive us our debts as we forgive our debtors"— and the parable of the forgiving and unforgiving creditor.

To be in debt means to have taken more from someone than we have given whether the *more* refers to material or to spiritual goods. Since we are not autonomous beings who can create and sustain our lives by ourselves, every human being is in debt to God, to Nature, to parents and neighbors for his existence, and it is against this background of universal human debt that we view the special case of debt and credit between one individual and another. We are born unequal; even if all social inequalities were abolished, there would remain the natural inequalities of talent and inherited tendencies, and circumstance outside our control will always affect both our need to receive and our capacity to give. A rich man, in whatever sense he is rich, can give more than a poor man; a baby and a sick person need more from others than a healthy adult. Debt or credit cannot be measured in quantitative terms; a relation between two persons is just if both take no more than they need and give as much as they can, and unjust if either takes more or gives less than this.

In prison, Mr Pickwick meets three kinds of debtors. There are those like Smangle who are rather thieves than debtors for they have borrowed money with the conscious intention of not paying it back. There are the childish who believe in magic; they intended to return what they borrowed when their luck changed, but had no rational reason to suppose that it would. And there are those like the cobbler who have fallen into debt through circumstances which they could neither foresee nor control.

> An old gentleman that I worked for, down in the country, and died well off, left five thousand pounds behind him, one of which he left to me, 'cause I'd married a humble relation of his. And being surrounded by a great number of nieces and nephews, as well always quarrelling and fighting among themselves for the property, he makes me his executor to divide the rest among 'em as the will provided, and I paid all the legacies. I'd hardly done it when one nevy brings an action to set the will aside. The case comes on, some months afterwards, afore a deaf old gentleman in a back room somewhere down by Paul's Churchyard . . . and arter four counsels had taken a day a piece to buther him regularly, he takes a week or two to consider and then gives his judgment that the testator was not quite right in the head, and I must pay all the money back again, and all the costs. I appealed; the case comes on before three or four very sleepy gentlemen, who had heard it all before in the other court and they very dutifully confirmed the decision of the old gentleman below. After that we went into Chancery, where we are still. My lawyers have had all my thousand pounds long ago; and what between the estate as they call it and the costs, I'm here for ten thousand, and shall stop here till I die, mending shoes.

Yet, in the eyes of the Law, all three classes are equally guilty. This does not mean, however, that all debtors receive the same treatment.

The three chums informed Mr Pickwick in a breath that money was in the Fleet, just what money was out of it; that it would instantly procure him almost anything he desired; and that, supposing he had it, and had no objection to spend it, if he only signified his wish to have a room to himself, he might take possession of one, furnished and fitted to boot, in half an hour's time.

The lot of the penniless debtor, like the Chancery Prisoner, was, in Dickens' time, atrocious, far worse than that of the convicted criminal, for the convict was fed gratis by the State but the debtor was not, so that, if penniless, he must subsist on the charity of his fellow prisoners or die of starvation. On the other hand, for those with a little money and no sense of shame, the Fleet Prison could seem a kind of Eden.

There were many classes of people here, from the laboring man in his fustian jacket, to the broken down spendthrift in his shawl dressing-gown, most appropriately out at elbows; but there was the same air about them all—a listless jail-bird careless swagger, a vagabondish who's afraid sort of bearing which is indescribable in words. . . . "It strikes me, Sam," said Mr Pickwick, "that imprisonment for debt is scarcely any punishment at all." "Think not, sir?," inquired Mr Weller. "You see how these fellows drink and smoke and roar," replied Mr Pickwick, "It's quite impossible that they can mind it much." "Ah, that's just the very thing sir," rejoined Sam, "*they* don't mind it; it's a regular holiday to them—all porter and skittles. It is t'other wuns as gets down over, with this sort of thing: them down-hearted fellers as can't swig away at the beer, nor play at skittles neither: them as would pay as they could, and get's low by being boxed up. I'll tell you wot it is, sir; them as is always a idlin' in public houses it don't damage at all, and them as is always a working wen they can, it damages too much."

His encounter with the world of the Fleet is the end of Mr Pickwick's innocence. When he started out on his adventures, he believed the world to be inhabited only by the well-meaning, the honest and the entertaining; presently he discovered that it also contains malevolent, dishonest and boring inhabitants, but it is only after entering the Fleet that he realizes it contains persons who suffer, and that the division between those who are suffering and those who are not is more significant than the division between the just and the unjust, the innocent and the guilty. He himself, for instance, has been unjustly convicted, but he is in prison by his own choice and, though he does not enjoy the Fleet as much as Dingley Dell, by the standards of comfort within the Fleet, he enjoys the advantages of a king, not because he is morally innocent while Jingle and Trotter are morally guilty, but because he happens to be the richest inmate while they are among the poorest. Then

Mrs Bardell, who through stupidity rather than malice is responsible for the injustice done to him, becomes a fellow prisoner. Mr Pickwick is compelled to realize that he, too, is a debtor, because he has been more fortunate than most people, and that he must discharge his debt by forgiving his enemies and relieving their suffering. In order to do his duty, he has to do in fact what he had been falsely accused of doing, commit a breach of promise by breaking his vow and putting money into the pockets of Dodson and Fogg; for the sake of charity, he has to sacrifice his honor.

His loss of innocence through becoming conscious of the real world has the same consequences for Mr Pickwick as a fictional character as recovering his sanity has for Don Quixote; in becoming ethically serious, both cease to be aesthetically comic, that is to say, interesting to the reader, and they must pass away, Don Quixote by dying, Mr Pickwick by retiring from view.

Both novels are based upon the presupposition that there is a difference between the Law and Grace, the Righteous man and the Holy man: this can only be expressed indirectly by a comic contradiction in which the innocent hero comes into collision with the Law without appearing, in his own eyes, to suffer. The only way in which their authors can compel the reader to interpret this correctly—neither to ignore the sign nor to take it as a direct sign—is, in the end, to take off the comic mask and say: "The Game, the make-believe is over: players and spectators alike must now return to reality. What you have heard was but a tall story."

Postscript: The Frivolous & The Earnest

An aesthetic religion (polytheism) draws no distinction between what is frivolous and what is serious because, for it, all existence is, in the last analysis, meaningless. The whims of the gods and, behind them, the whim of the Fates, are the ultimate arbiters of all that happens. It is immediately frivolous because it is ultimately in despair.

A frivolity which is innocent, because unaware that anything serious exists, can be charming, and a frivolity which, precisely because it is aware of what is serious, refuses to take seriously that which is not serious, can be profound. What is so distasteful about the Homeric gods is that they are well aware of human suffering but refuse to take it seriously. They take the lives of men as frivolously as their own; they meddle with the former for fun, and then get bored.

> When Zeus had brought the Trojans and Hector close to the ships, he left them beside the ships to bear the toil and woe unceasingly, and he himself turned his shining eyes away, gazing afar at the land of the horse-rearing Thracians and the Mysians, who fight in close array, and

the noble Hippomolgoi who live on milk, and the Abioi, most righteous of men.

(Iliad, Book XIII)

They kill us for their sport. If so, no human sportsman would receive one of the gods in his house: they shoot men sitting and out of season.

If Homer had tried reading the *Iliad* to the gods on Olympus, they would either have started to fidget and presently asked if he hadn't got something a little lighter, or, taking it as a comic poem, would have roared with laughter or possibly, even, reacting like ourselves to a tear-jerking movie, have poured pleasing tears.

The songs of Apollo: the lucky improvisations of an amateur.

The only Greek god who does any work is Hephaestus, and he is a lame cuckold.

Render unto Caesar the things that are Caesar's and unto God the things that are God's. Christianity draws a distinction between what is frivolous and what is serious, but allows the former its place. What it condemns is not frivolity but idolatry, that is to say, taking the frivolous seriously.

The past is not to be taken seriously (*Let the dead bury their dead*) nor the future (*Take no thought for the morrow*), only the present instant and that, not for its aesthetic emotional content but for its historic decisiveness. (*Now is the appointed time.*)

Man desires to be free and he desires to feel important. This places him in a dilemma, for the more he emancipates himself from necessity the less important he feels.

That is why so many *actes gratuits* are criminal: a man asserts his freedom by disobeying a law and retains a sense of self-importance because the law he has disobeyed is an important one. Much crime is magic, an attempt to make free with necessity.

An alternative to criminal magic is the innocent game. Games are *actes gratuits* in which the players obey rules chosen by themselves. Games are freer than crimes because the rules of a game are arbitrary and moral laws are not; but they are less important.

The rules of a game give it importance to those who play it by making it difficult, a test of skill. This means, however, that a game can only be important to those who have the particular physical or mental skills which are required to play it, and the gift of such skills is a matter of chance.

To the degree that a vocation or a profession requires some gift, it partakes, for him who is able to practice it, of the nature of a game, however serious the social need it serves. The famous brain surgeon, Dr Cushing, was once consulted by a student as to whether or not he should specialize in surgery: the doctor settled the question for him in the negative by asking; "Do you enjoy the sensation of putting a knife into living flesh?"

To witness an immoral act, like a man beating his wife, makes a spectator angry or unhappy. To witness an untalented act, like a clumsy man wrestling with a window blind or a piece of bad sculpture, makes him laugh.

Life is not a game because one cannot say: "I will live on condition that I have a talent for living." Those who cannot play a game can always be spectators, but no one can hire somebody else to live his life for him while he looks on.

In a game, just losing is almost as satisfying as just winning. But no man ever said with satisfaction, "I almost married the girl I love," or a nation, "We almost won the war." In life the loser's score is always zero.

Nothing can be essentially serious for man except that which is given to all men alike, and that which is commanded of all men alike.

All men alike are given a physical body with physical needs which have to be satisfied if they are to survive, and all men alike are given a will which has the power to make choices. (To say of someone that his will is strong or weak is not like saying that he is tall or short, or even that he is clever or stupid: it is a description of how his will functions, not an assessment of the amount of will power he possesses.)

Corresponding to these gifts are two commands: "In the sweat of thy face shalt thou eat bread," and "Thou shalt love the Lord thy God and thy neighbor as thyself," are both commanded of all men alike.

Thus the only two occupations which are intrinsically serious are the two which do not call for any particular natural gifts, namely, unskilled manual labor and the priesthood (in its ideal aspects as the Apostolate). Any unskilled laborer and any priest is interchangeable with every other. Any old porter can carry my bag, any trumpery priest absolve me of a mortal sin. One cannot say of an unskilled laborer or of a priest that one is better or worse than another; one can only say, in the case of the laborer, that he is employed, in the case of the priest, that he has been ordained.

Of all other occupations, one must say that, in themselves, they are frivolous. They are only serious in so far that they are the means by which those who practice them earn their bread and are not parasites on the labor of others, and to the degree that they permit or encourage the love of God and neighbor.

There is a game called Cops and Robbers, but none called Saints and Sinners.

It is incorrect to say, as the Preamble to the American Constitution says, that all men have a right to the pursuit of happiness. All men have a right to avoid unnecessary pain if they can, and no man has a right to pleasure at the cost of another's pain. But happiness is not a right; it is a duty. To the degree that we are unhappy, we are in sin. (And vice versa.) A duty cannot be pursued because its imperative applies to the present instant, not to some future date.

My duty towards God is to be happy; my duty towards my neighbor is to try my best to give him pleasure and alleviate his pain. No human being can *make* another one happy.

Genius & Apostle

No genius has an *in order that*: the Apostle has absolutely and paradoxically an *in order that*. —Søren Kierkegaard

I

In such theoretical discussions concerning the nature of drama as I have read, it has always seemed to me that insufficient attention was paid to the nature of the actor. What distinguishes a drama from both a game and a rite is that, in a game, the players play themselves and, in a rite, though the participants may *represent* somebody else, a god, for instance, they do not have to *imitate* him, any more than an ambassador to a foreign country has to imitate the sovereign whom he represents. Further, in both a game and a rite, the actions are real actions, or at least, real to the participants—goals are scored, the bull is killed, the bread and wine are transubstantiated—but, in a drama, all actions are mock actions—the actor who plays Banquo is not really murdered, the singer who plays Don Giovanni may himself be a henpecked husband.

No other human activity seems as completely gratuitous as "acting"; games are gratuitous acts, but it can be argued that they have a utile value—they develop the muscles or sharpen the wits of those who play them—but what conceivable purpose could one human being have for imitating another?

The fact that dramatic action is mock action and mimetic art completely gratuitous makes the dramatic picture of human life a peculiar one. In real life, we exist as bodies, social individuals and unique persons simultaneously, so that there can be no human deed or act of personal choice which is without an element of human behavior, what we do from necessity, either the necessities of our physical nature or the habits of our socially acquired "second nature." But on the stage, the kind of human life we see is a life of pure deeds from which every trace of behavior has been eliminated. Consequently, any human activity which cannot be imagined without its element of necessity, cannot be represented on the stage. Actors, for example, can toy with cucumber sandwiches, but they cannot eat a hearty meal because a hearty meal cannot be imagined taking less than three quarters of an hour to consume. Dramatists have been known to expect an actor to write a letter on stage, but it always looks ridiculous; on stage a letter can be read aloud but not written in silence. Nor can an actor do any serious piece of work, for real work cannot be imagined apart from the real time it takes. Only deeds can be divorced from real time. Thus, a man might write in his diary, "I began or I finished work at 9:15," but he would never write "I worked at 9:15"; (as a court witness he might say, "I was working at 9:15"); on the other hand, he might very well write, "At 9:15 I proposed to Julia and she accepted me" because, although his words of proposal and hers of acceptance must have taken a certain length of time to utter, this is irrelevant to the dramatic significance of the event.

Since human life, as the stage can present it, is, firstly, a life of pure action and, secondly, a public life—the actors play to an audience, not to themselves—the characters best-suited to drama are men and women who by fate or choice lead a public existence and whose deeds are of public concern. Worldly ambition, for example, is a more dramatic motive than sexual passion, because worldly ambition can only be realized in public, while sexual passion unless, like that of Antony and Cleopatra, it has political consequences, affects only a handful of persons. Unfortunately for the modern dramatist, during the past century and a half the public realm has been less and less of a realm where human deeds are done, and more and more a realm of mere human behavior. The contemporary dramatist has lost his natural subject.

This process was already far advanced in the nineteenth century and dramatists, like Ibsen, who took their art seriously, were beginning to look for new kinds of heroes. The romantic movement had brought to public notice a new kind of hero, the artist-genius. The public interest taken in figures like Victor Hugo, Dickens and Wagner would have been unthinkable two centuries earlier.

It was inevitable that, sooner or later, a dramatist would ask himself if the artist-genius could be substituted for the traditional man-of-action as a dramatic hero. A sensible dramatist, however, would immediately realize that a direct treatment would be bound to fail. An artist is not a doer of deeds but a maker of things, a worker, and work cannot be represented on stage because it ceases to be work if the time it takes is foreshortened, so that what makes an artist of interest, his art—aside from which he is not an artist but simply a man—will have to take place off stage. Secondly, the audience will have to be convinced that the figure they are told is a genius really is one, not somebody without any talent who says he is a genius. If he is a poet, for example, the poetry of his which the audience hear must be of the first order. But, even if the dramatist is himself a great poet, the only kind of poetry he can write is his own; he cannot make up a special kind of poetry for his hero, unlike his own yet equally great. Lastly, while deeds and character are identical, works and character are not; the relation between who an artist is as a person and what he makes is too vague to discuss. To say that Lesbia's treatment of Catullus and his love for her were the cause of his poetry is a very different thing from saying that Macbeth's ambition and the prophecies of the witches were the cause of Banquo's murder. Had both their characters been different, the poems would, no doubt, have been different, but their characters do not explain why Catullus wrote the actual poems he did, and not an infinite number of others which he might equally well have written but did not.

In order to become an artist, a man must be endowed with an exceptional talent for fabrication or expression, but what makes it possible for him to exercise this talent and for his public to appreciate it is the capacity of all human beings to imagine anything which is the case as being otherwise; every man, for example, can imagine committing a murder or laying down his life for a friend's without actually doing so. Is there, one can picture Ibsen asking himself, perhaps subconsciously, any figure traditionally associated with the stage who could be made to stand for this imaginative faculty? Yes, there is: the actor. Keats' famous description of the poet applies even more accurately to the actor.

> As to the poetic character itself, it is not itself: it has no self—it is everything and nothing. The Sun, the Moon, the sea, and men and women who are creatures of impulse, are poetical and have about them an unchangeable attribute—the poet has none: no identity.

Throughout *Peer Gynt,* one question keeps being asked and answered in various ways, namely, *Who am I? What is my real self?* For the animals, the question does not arise.

> What innocence is in the life of beasts.
> They perform the behest of their great creator.
> They are themselves.

The nearest human approximation to this animal selfhood is the "second nature" a man acquires through heredity and social custom.

> My father thieves,
> His son must steal.
> My father received,
> And so must I.
> We must bear our lot,
> And be ourselves.

So, too, with the drowning cook who gets as far in the Lord's Prayer as *Give us this day our daily bread* and then sinks.

> Amen, lad.
> You were yourself to the end.

Next comes the social "Idiot" in the Greek sense, the individual whose life is as conditioned by one personal overriding interest as the conventional individual's is by social habit. In the first act Peer sees a young peasant cutting off a finger in order to escape conscription; Peer is fascinated and shocked:

> The thought perhaps—the wish to will,
> That I can understand, but really
> To do the deed. Ah me, that beats me.

In the last act he hears a funeral sermon about the same peasant in which the parson says:

> He was a bad citizen, no doubt,
> For Church and State alike, a sterile tree—
> But up there on the rocky mountain side
> Where his work lay, *there* I say he was great
> Because he was himself.

Neither of these human ways of being oneself, however, satisfy Peer. He tells his mother he means to be a King and Emperor, but there is only one kind of empire which nobody else can threaten or conquer, the empire of one's own consciousness, or, as Peer defines it:

> The Gyntian Self—An army that,
> Of wishes, appetites, desires!
> The Gyntian Self—It is a sea
> Of fancies, claims, and aspirations.

But the Peer we see on stage has no appetites or desires in the ordinary sense; he plays at having them. Ibsen solves the problem of presenting a poet dramatically by showing us a man who treats nearly everything he does as a role, whether it be dealing in slaves and idols or being an Eastern Prophet. A poet in real life would have written a drama about slave trading, then another drama about a prophet but, on the stage, play acting stands for making.

The kinship of the poet to the dreamer on the one hand and the madman on the other and his difference from them both is shown by Peer's experiences, first in the kingdom of the trolls and then in the asylum. The kingdom of dreams is ruled by wish or desire; the dreaming ego sees as being the case whatever the self desires to be the case. The ego, that is to say, is the helpless victim of the self; it cannot say, "I'm dreaming." In madness it is the self which is the helpless victim of the ego; a madman says, "I am Napoleon," and his self cannot tell him, "You're a liar." (One of the great difficulties in translating *Peer Gynt* is, I understand, that Norwegian has two words, one for the I *which is conscious* and another for the self *of which it is conscious*, where English has only one. *Myself* can mean either.)

Both the dreamer and the madman are in earnest; neither is capable of play acting. The dreamer is like the moviegoer who writes abusive letters to the actor he has seen playing a villain; the madman is like the actor who believes the same thing about himself, namely, that he is identical with his role.

But the poet pretends for fun; he asserts his freedom by lying—that is to say, by creating worlds which he *knows* are imaginary. When the troll king offers to turn Peer into a real troll by a little eye operation, Peer indignantly refuses. He is perfectly willing, he says, to swear that a cow is a beautiful maiden, but to be reduced to a condition in which he could not tell one from the other—that he will never submit to.

The difference between trolls and men, says the king, is that the Troll Motto is *To Thyself Be Enough*, while the Human Motto is *To Thyself Be True*. The Button-Moulder and the Lean One both have something to say about the latter.

> To be oneself is: to slay oneself.
> But on you that answer is doubtless lost;
> And therefore well say: to stand forth everywhere
> With Master's intention displayed like a sign-board.

> Remember, in two ways a man can be
> Himself—there's a right and wrong side to the jacket.
> You know they have lately discovered in Paris
> A way to take portraits by help of the sun.
> One can either produce a straightforward picture,
> Or else what is known as a negative one.
> In the latter the lights and the shades are reversed.

But suppose there is such a thing as a poetic vocation or, in terms of Ibsen's play, a theatrical vocation; how do their words apply? If a man can be called to be an actor, then the only way he can be "true" to himself is by "acting," that is to say, pretending to be what he is not. The dreamer and the madman are "enough" to themselves because they are unaware that anything exists except their own desires and hallucinations; the poet is "enough" to himself in the sense that, while knowing that others exist, as a poet he does without them. Outside Norway, Peer has no serious relations with others, male or female. On the subject of friendship, Ibsen once wrote to Georg Brandes:

> Friends are a costly luxury, and when one invests one's capital in a mission in life, one cannot afford to have friends. The expensiveness of friendship does not lie in what one does for one's friends, but in what,

out of regard for them, one leaves undone. This means the crushing of many an intellectual germ.

But every poet is also a human being, distinguishable from what he makes, and through Peer's relations to Ase and Solveig, Ibsen is trying to show us, I believe, what kind of person is likely to become a poet—assuming, of course, that he has the necessary talent. According to Ibsen, the predisposing factors in childhood are, first, an isolation from the social group—owing to his father's drunkenness and spendthrift habits, he is looked down on by the neighbors—and second, a playmate who stimulates and shares his imaginative life—a role played by his mother.

> Ay, you must know that my husband, he drank,
> Wasted and trampled our gear under foot.
> And meanwhile at home there sat Peerkin and I—
> The best we could do was to try to forget. . . .
> Some take to brandy, and others to lies;
> And we—why, we took to fairy-tales.

It is not too fanciful, I believe, to think of laboring as a neuter activity, doing as masculine, and making as feminine. All fabrication is an imitation of motherhood and, whenever we have information about the childhood of an artist, it reveals a closer bond with his mother than with his father: in a poet's development, the phrase *The milk of the Word* is not a mere figure of speech.

In their games together, it is the son who takes the initiative and the mother who seems the younger, adoring child. Ase dies and bequeaths to Solveig, the young virgin, the role of being Peer's Muse. If the play were a straight realistic drama, Peer's treatment of Solveig would bear the obvious psychoanalytic explanation—namely, that he suffers from a mother-fixation which forbids any serious sexual relation: he cannot love any women with whom he sleeps. But the play is a parable and, parabolically, the mother-child relationship has, I believe, another significance: it stands for the kind of love that is unaffected by time and remains unchanged by any act of the partners. Many poets, it would seem, do their best work when they are "in love," but the psychological condition of being "in love" is incompatible with a sustained historical relationship like marriage. The poet's Muse must either be dead like Dante's Beatrice, or far away like Peer's Solveig, or keep on being reincarnated in one lady after another. Ase's devotion gives Peer his initial courage to become a poet and live without an identity of his own, Solveig gives him the courage to continue to the end. When at the end of the play he asks her, "Where is the real Peer?"—the human being as distinct from his poetic function—she answers, "In my faith, in my hope, in my love." This is an echo of his own belief. Ibsen leaves in doubt the question whether this faith is justified or not. It may be that, after all, the poet must pay for his vocation by ending in the casting-ladle. But Peer has so far been lucky: "He had women behind him."

The insoluble difficulty about the artist as a dramatic character is that, since his relations with others are either momentary or timeless, he makes any coherent plot impossible. *Peer Gynt* is a fascinating play, but one cannot say its structure is satisfying. Practically the whole of the drama (and nearly all of the best scenes) is a Prologue and an Epilogue: the Prologue shows us how a boy comes to be destined for the vocation of poet rather than a career as a statesman or an engineer, the Epilogue shows us the moral and psychological crisis for a poet in old age when death faces him and he must account for his life. Only in the Fourth Act are we shown, so to speak, the adult poet at work, and in this act the number of scenes and the number of characters introduced are purely arbitrary. Ibsen uses the act as an opportunity to make satirical comments on various aspects of Norwegian life, but Peer himself is only accidentally related to the satire.

II

Two years before *Peer Gynt*, Ibsen wrote *Brand*. Both were composed in Italy, and Ibsen said of them:

> May I not like Christoff in Jacob von Tyboe, point to Brand and Peer Gynt and say—See, the wine cup has done this.

The heroes of these two plays are related to each other by being each other's opposite. To Peer the Devil is a dangerous viper who tempts man to do the irretrievable; to Brand the Devil is Compromise.

Brand is a priest. Ibsen once said that he might equally well have made him a sculptor or a politician, but this is not true. In Rome Ibsen had met and been deeply impressed by a young Norwegian theological student and Kierkegaard enthusiast, Christopher Brunn. At the time Ibsen was very angry with his fellow countrymen for having refused to come to the aid of Denmark when Germany attacked her and annexed Schleswig-Holstein. Brunn had actually fought as a volunteer in the Danish army and he asked Ibsen why, if he had felt as strongly as he professed, he had not done likewise. Ibsen made the answer one would expect—a poet has other tasks to perform—but it is clear that the question made him very uncomfortable and *Brand* was a product of his discomfort.

Whether he had read it for himself or heard of it from Brunn, it seems evident that Ibsen must have been aware of Kierkegaard's essay on the difference between a genius and an apostle. In *Peer Gynt* he deals with the first; in *Brand*, which he wrote first, with the second.

An apostle is a human individual who is called by God to deliver a message to mankind. Oracles and shamans are divine mouthpieces, but they are not apostles. An oracle or a shaman is an accredited public official whose spiritual authority is recognized by all; he does not have to seek out others but sits and waits for them to consult him—Delphi is the navel of the world. He receives a professional training and, in order to qualify, he must exhibit certain talents, such as an ability to enter into a trance state.

An apostle, on the other hand, is called to preach to others a divine message which is new to them, so that he cannot expect others to come looking for him nor expect to have any official spiritual status. While oracle and shaman are, so to speak, radio sets through which at certain moments a god may speak, an apostle is an ordinary human messenger like a man who delivers mail; he cannot wait for certain divinely inspired moments to deliver his message and, if his audience should ask him to show his credentials, he has none.

In the case of any vocation of Genius, a man is called to it by a natural gift with which he is already endowed. A young man, for example, who tells his parents, "I am going to be a sculptor, cost what it may," bases his statement on the conviction that he has been born with a talent for making beautiful, three-dimensional objects. It makes no difference to his decision whether he is a Christian who believes that this talent is a gift of God or an atheist who attributes it to blind Nature or Chance for, even if he is a believer, he knows that he is called by his gift, not by God directly. Since the gift is *his*, to say "I must become a sculptor" and "I want to become one" means the same thing: it is impossible to imagine anyone's saying, "A sculptor is the last thing on earth I want to be, but I feel it is my duty to become one."

An Apostle, on the other hand, is called by God directly. Jehovah says to Abraham: "Go get thee up out of the land"; Christ says to Matthew, the tax-collector; "Follow me!" If one asks, "Why Abraham or Matthew and not two other people?" there is no human answer; one cannot speak of a talent for being an Apostle or of the apostolic temperament. Whatever ultimate spiritual rewards there may be for an Apostle, they are unknowable and unimaginable; all he knows is that he is called upon to forsake everything he has been, to venture into an unknown and probably unpleasant future. Hence it is impossible to imagine the apostolic calling's being echoed by a man's natural desire. Any genuine Apostle must, surely, say, "I would not but, alas, I must." The prospective sculptor can correctly be said to *will* to become a sculptor—that is to say, to submit himself to the study, toil and discipline which becoming a sculptor involves—but an Apostle cannot correctly be said to will anything; he can only say, "Not as I will, but as Thou wilt." It is possible for a man to be deceived about a secular calling—he imagines he has a talent when in fact he has none—but there is an objective test to prove whether his calling is genuine or imaginary: either he produces valuable works or he does not. A great sculptor may die with his works totally unrecognized by the public but, in the long run, the test of his greatness is worldly recognition of his work. But in the case of an Apostle there is no such objective test: he may make a million converts or he may make none, and we are still no nearer knowing whether his vocation was genuine or not. He may give his body to be burned and still we do not know. What makes an apostle a hero in a religious sense is not what he does or fails to do for others, but the constancy of his faith that God has called him to speak in His name.

The message Brand has to deliver is drawn for the most part from Kierkegaard and may be summed up in two passages from Kierkegaard's *Journals*.

> The Christianity of the majority consists roughly of what may be called the two most doubtful extremities of Christianity (or, as the parson says, the two things which must be clung to in life and death), first of all the saying about the little child, that one becomes a Christian as a little child and that of such is the Kingdom of Heaven; the second is the thief on the cross. People live by virtue of the former—in death they reckon upon consoling themselves with the example of the thief.
>
> This is the sum of their Christianity; and, correctly defined, it is a mixture of childishness and crime. . . .

> Most people think that the Christian commandments, "Thou shalt love thy neighbor as thyself, etc." are intentionally oversevere, like putting one's clock ahead to make sure of getting up in the morning.

In some of Brand's speeches, however, there is an emphasis on the human will which is Nietzschean rather than Kierkegaardian.

> A whole shall rise which God shall recognize,
> Man, His greatest creation, His close heir,
> Adam, young and strong.

> It is not
> Martyrdom to die in agony upon a cross
> But to will that you shall die upon a cross.

These are not statements which Kierkegaard would have made. Indeed, he expressly says that there is a great difference between willing a martyrdom which God has willed for you and willing one for yourself before you know whether or not it is required of you, and that to will the second is spiritual pride of an extreme kind.

Brand's prophetic denunciations are directed against three kinds of life, the aesthetic life governed by the mood of the moment, the conventional life of social and religious habit, and the insane life of "The wild of heart in whose broken mind evil seems beautiful," which, presumably, refers to the criminal as well as to the clinically insane.

Ibsen did not, as Shaw might have done, make his play an intellectual debate. Brand has no trouble in demolishing the arguments of his opponents. There is a great deal more to be said for the aesthetic life than a ninny like Ejnar can put forward, and a belief in the value of habit, both in social and religious life, can be and is held by wise good people; it is not confined to cowardly crooks like the Mayor and the Provost. The only antagonist who is in any way his equal is the doctor.

> DOCTOR. . . . I've got to visit a patient.
> BRAND. My mother?
> DOCTOR. Yes . . . You've been to see her already, perhaps?
> BRAND. No.
> DOCTOR. You're a hard man. I've struggled all the way
>   Across the moor, through mist and sleet,
>   Although I know she pays like a pauper.
> BRAND. May God bless your energy and skill.
>   Ease her suffering, if you can. . . .
> DOCTOR. Don't wait for her to send for you.
>   Come now, with me.
> BRAND. Until she sends for me, I know no duty there.
> DOCTOR.   . . . your credit account
>   For strength of will is full, but, priest,
>   Your love account is a white virgin page.

Brand replies with an outburst against the popular use of the word *love* as a veil to cover and excuse weakness, but this does not refute the doctor because the latter, by risking his life to ease the suffering of a dying woman, has proved that he means something quite different by the word. There is, however, no dialectical relation between his position and Brand's because his ethics are those of his profession. Brand has just refused to go and give his dying mother the sacrament because she will not renounce her property. To the Doctor this seems gratuitous cruelty because he can only think about the care of sick souls in terms of the cure of sick bodies. In his world of experience a patient is either in pain or not in pain, and every patient desires to be well. He cannot grasp, because it is outside his professional experience, that, in the soul, a desire may be the sickness itself. Brand's mother clings to her possessions with passionate desire, and to relinquish them will cause her great suffering but, unless she suffers, she can never know true joy. (The analogy to surgery does not hold. The patient must suffer now at the hands of the surgeon in order that he may be free from pain in the future, but he already knows what it means to be free from pain. The sinner does not know what it means to be spiritually happy; he only knows that to give up his sin will be a great suffering.)

In the character of Brand Ibsen shows us an individual of heroic courage who exemplifies in his own life what he preaches and who suffers and dies for what he believes, but, as a religious hero, he won't quite do. Our final impression is of a tragic hero of the conventional kind whose field of action happens to be religion, but whose motives are the same pride and self-will that motivate the tragic heroes of this world.

If, as an apostle, Brand fails to convince us, the fault, I believe, is not due to lack of talent on Ibsen's part, but to his mistaken approach. While, when he came to write *Peer Gynt*, he approached the dramatic portrayal of a genius indirectly, in tackling the portrayal of an apostle, he tried a direct approach and this was bound to fail.

Thus, he gives us a picture of Brand's childhood. Unlike Peer, poor Brand did not have women behind him, and in the end he has to drag Agnes after him. His mother had renounced marriage to the man she loved in order to marry one who was expected to make money. He failed and died, and she had denied all love and happiness both to herself and her son and devoted herself with absolute passion to the acquisition and hoarding of wealth. The relation between mother and son is one of defiant hostility mingled with respect for the other's strength of will and contempt for sentimentality masquerading as love. In preferring damnation to the surrender of all her goods, she shows herself every bit as much a believer in All-or-Nothing as Brand does in refusing to give her the Sacrament unless she renounces her idol. Psychologically, mother and son are alike; the only difference between them is in the God whom each worships.

Such a situation is dramatically interesting and psychologically plausible, but it inevitably makes us suspect Brand's claim to have been called by the True God, since we perceive a personal or hereditary motivation in his thought and conduct. Peer's relation to his mother is a possible psychological background for a certain class of human being, the class of artist-geniuses. But every apostle is a member of a class of one and no psychological background can throw any light on a calling which is initiated by God directly.

It is very difficult to conceive of a successful drama without important personal relations, and of such, the most intense is, naturally, the relation between a man and a woman. The scenes between Brand and Agnes are the most exciting and moving parts of the poem, but their effect is to turn Brand into a self-torturing monster for whose sufferings we can feel pity but no sympathy. Whether one agrees or disagrees with the insistence of the Roman Church that its priests be celibate—The Church Visible, after all, requires administrators, theologians, diplomats, etc., as well as apostles—the apostolic calling, ideally considered, is incompatible with marriage. An apostle *exists* for the sake of others but not as a person, only as a mouthpiece and a witness to the Truth; once they have received the Truth and he has borne his witness, his existence is of no account to others. But a husband and wife are bound by a personal tie, and the demands they make upon each other are based on this. If a husband asks his wife to make this or that sacrifice, he asks her to make it for his sake, and his right to ask comes from their mutual personal love. But when an apostle demands that another make a sacrifice, it cannot be for his sake; he cannot say, "If you love me, please do this," but can only say, "Thus saith the Lord. Your salvation depends upon your doing this."

When Brand first meets Agnes, he is already convinced of his calling and aware that suffering, certainly, and a martyr's death, possibly, will be required of him. His words and his risking of his life to bring consolation to a dying man reveal to her the falseness of her relation to Ejnar. At this point I do not think she is in love with Brand, but she is overwhelmed with admiration for him as a witness to the truth and prepared to fall in love with him if he should show any personal interest in her. He does show a personal interest— he is lonely and longing for personal love—they marry, they are mutually happy and they have a son, Ulf. Then comes disaster. Either they must leave the fjord and his work as the village priest—an act which Brand believes would be a betrayal of his calling—or their child must die. Brand decides that they shall remain, and Ulf does die. One would have thought that the obvious solution was to send his wife and child away to a sunnier climate and remain himself (since he inherited his mother's money, he has the means) but this solution does not seem to have occurred to him. (Of course if it had, the big dramatic scenes which follow could not have been written.) Later, he accuses Agnes of idolatry in not accepting Ulf's death as the will of God and makes her give away all his clothes to a gypsy child. Possibly she is guilty of idolatry and should give the clothes away for the sake of her own soul and, were Brand a stranger, he could tell her so. But he is both the husband whom she loves and the father of her child who took the decision which caused the child's death and so led her into the temptation of idolatry, so that when he tells her:

> You are my wife, and I have the right to demand
> That you shall devote yourself wholly to our calling

the audience feels that he has no such right. This is only the most obvious manifestation of a problem which besets Ibsen throughout the play, namely, the problem of how to make an apostle dramatically interesting. To be dramatically viable, a character must not only act, but also talk about his actions and his feelings and talk a great deal: he must address others as a person—a messenger cannot be a major character on the stage. For dramatic reasons, therefore, Ibsen has to allow Brand to speak in the first person and appear the author of his acts, to say "I will this." But an apostle is a messenger, and he acts not by willing but by submitting to the will of God who cannot appear on the stage. It is inevitable, therefore, that our final impression of Brand is of an idolator who worships not God, but *his* God. It makes no difference if the God he calls his happens to be the true God; so long as he thinks of Him as his, he is as much an idolator as the savage who bows down to a fetish. To me, one of the most fascinating scenes of the play is Brand's final encounter with Ejnar. Ejnar has had some sort of evangelical conversion, believes that he is saved, and is going off to be a missionary in Africa. Brand tells him of Agnes' death, but he shows no sorrow, though he had once loved her.

EJNAR. How was her faith?
BRAND. Unshakable.
EJNAR. In whom?
BRAND. In her God.
EJNAR. Her God cannot save her. She is damned. . . .
BRAND. You dare to pronounce judgment on her and me, poor, sinning fool?
EJNAR. My faith has washed me clean.
BRAND. Hold your tongue.
EJNAR. Hold yours.

Ejnar, is, as it were, a caricature of Brand, but the likeness is cruel.

Though a direct portrayal of an apostle is not possible in art, there exists, though not in drama, one great example of a successful indirect portrayal, Cervantes' *Don Quixote*.

III

The Knight-Errant

The Knight-Errant, whom Don Quixote wishes to become and actually parodies, was an attempt to Christianize the pagan epic hero.

(1) He possesses epic *arete* of good birth, good looks, strength, etc.
(2) This *arete* is put in the service of the Law, to rescue the unfortunate, protect the innocent, and combat the wicked.
(3) His motives are three:
  (a) the desire for glory
  (b) the love of justice
  (c) the love of an individual woman who judges and rewards.
(4) He suffers exceptionally; first, in his adventures and collisions with the lawless; secondly, in his temptations to lawlessness in the form of unchastity; and thirdly, in his exceptionally difficult erotic romance.
(5) In the end he succeeds in this world. Vice is punished and virtue is rewarded by the lady of his heart.

When we first meet Don Quixote he is (a) poor, (b) not a knight, (c) fifty, (d) has nothing to do except hunt and read romances about Knight-Errantry.

Manifestly, he is the opposite of the heroes he admires, i.e. he is lacking in the epic *arete* of birth, looks, strength, etc. His situation, in fact, is aesthetically uninteresting except for one thing: his passion is great enough to make him sell land to buy books. This makes him aesthetically comic. Religiously he is tragic, for he is a hearer not a doer of the word, the weak man guilty in his imagination of Promethean pride. Now suddenly he goes mad, i.e. he sets out to become what he admires. Aesthetically this looks like pride; in fact, religiously, it is a conversion, an act of faith, a taking up of his cross.

The Quixotic Madness and the Tragic Madness

The worldly villain like Macbeth is tempted by an *arete* he possesses to conquer this world of the nature of which he has a shrewd idea. His decisions are the result of a calculation of the probabilities of success, each success increases his madness but in the end he fails and is brought to despair and death. Don Quixote is (a) lacking in *arete*, (b) has a fantastic conception of this world, (c) always meets with failure yet is never discouraged, (d) suffers himself intentionally and makes others suffer only unintentionally.

The Quixotic Madness and the Comic Madness

The comic rogue declares: the world = that which exists to give me money, beauty, etc. I refuse to suffer by being thwarted. He is cured by being forced to suffer through collision with the real world.

Don Quixote declares: The world = that which needs my existence to save it at whatever cost to myself. He comes into collision with the real world but insists upon continuing to suffer. He becomes the Knight of the Doleful Countenance but never despairs.

Don Quixote and Hamlet

Hamlet lacks faith in God and in himself. Consequently he must define his existence in terms of others, e.g. I am the man whose mother married his uncle who murdered his father. He would like to become what the Greek tragic hero is, a creature of situation. Hence his inability to act. for he can only "act," i.e. play at possibilities.

Don Quixote is the antithesis of an actor, being completely incapable of seeing himself in a role. Defining his situation in terms of his own character, he is completely unreflective.

Madness and Faith

To have faith in something or someone means

(a) that the object of faith is not manifest. If it becomes manifest, then faith is no longer required.
(b) the relation of faith between subject and object is unique in every case. Hundreds may believe, but each has to believe by himself.

Don Quixote exemplifies both. (a) He never sees things that aren't there (delusion) but sees them differently, e.g. windmills as giants, sheep as armies, puppets as Moors, etc. (b) He is the only individual who sees them thus.

Faith and Idolatry

The idolater makes things out to be stronger than they really are so that they shall be responsible for him, e.g. he might worship a windmill for its giantlike strength. Don Quixote never expects things to look after him; on the contrary he is always making himself responsible for things and people who have no need of him and regard him as an impertinent old meddler.

Faith and Despair

People are tempted to lose faith (a) when it fails to bring worldly success, (b) when the evidence of their senses and feelings seem against it. Don Quixote (a) is consistently defeated yet persists, (b) between his fits of madness he sees that the windmills are not giants but windmills, etc., yet, instead of despairing, he says, "Those cursed magicians delude me, first drawing me into dangerous adventures by the appearance of things as they really are, and then presently changing the face of things as they please." His supreme test comes when Sancho Panza describes a country wench, whom Don Quixote sees correctly as such, as the beautiful Princess Dulcinea and in spite of his feelings concludes that he is enchanted and that Sancho Panza is right.

Don Quixote and the Knight-Errant

Don Quixote's friends attack the Romances he loves on the grounds that they are historically untrue, and lacking in style.

Don Quixote, on the other hand, without knowing it, by his very failure to imitate his heroes exactly, at once reveals that the Knight-Errant of the Romances is half-pagan, and becomes himself the true Christian Knight.

Epic Dualism

The world of the Romances is a dualistic world where the completely good and innocent fight the completely evil and guilty. The Knight-Errant comes into collision only with those who are outside the Law: giants, heretics, heathens, etc. When he is in one of his spells, Don Quixote, under the illusion that he is showing the righteous anger of the Knight-Errant, comes into collision with the Law, i.e. he attacks innocent clerics and destroys other people's property.

When he is not deluded as to the nature of those he is trying to help, e.g. the convicts or the boy being thrashed, he only succeeds in making things worse and earns enmity, not gratitude.

Frauendienst

Don Quixote affirms all the articles of the Amor religion, namely, that (a) the girl must be noble and beautiful, (b) there must be some barrier, (c) the final goal of the Knight's trials is to be rewarded by having his love reciprocated.

In fact, the girl he calls Dulcinea del Toboso is "a good likely country lass for whom he had formerly had a sort of inclination, though 'tis believed she never heard of it." She is of lower social status, and he is past the age when sexual love means anything to him. Nevertheless, his behavior has all the courage that might be inspired by a great passion.

Again, Don Quixote expects to be tempted to unchastity so that, in the inn when the hunchback maid is trying to reach the carter's bed, he fancies that she is the daughter of the Governor of the Castle, who has fallen in love with him and is trying to seduce him. Bruised and battered as he is, even Don Quixote has to admit that for the moment he has no capacity.

The language is the language of Eros, the romantic idolization of the fair woman, but its real meaning is the Christian agape which loves all equally irrespective of their merit.

Snobbery

The true Knight-Errant has nothing to do with the Lower Orders and must never put himself in an undignified position, e.g. Launcelot is disgraced by riding in a cart. Don Quixote attempts to do likewise but with singular unsuccess. He is constantly having to do with the Lower Orders under the illusion that they are the nobility. His aristocratic refusal to pay, which he adopts out of literary precedence, not personal feeling, never works out—he ends by overpaying. Again the language is the language of the feudal knight, but the behavior is that of the Suffering Servant. This may be compared with the reverse situation in *Moby Dick* when Captain Ahab leaves his cabin boy in his captain's cabin and mounts the lookout like an ordinary seaman: here the behavior is apparently humble, but is in fact the extremity of pride.

This-Worldliness

The Knight-Errant is this-worldly in that he succeeds in arms and in love. Don Quixote professes a similar hope but in fact is not only persistently defeated but also cannot in the end even maintain in combat that Dulcinea is without a rival. Thus, he not only has to suffer the Knight's trials but also must suffer the consciousness of defeat. He is never able to think well of himself. He uses the language of the epic hero, but reveals himself to us as the Knight of Faith whose kingdom is not of this world.

Don Quixote's Death

However many further adventures one may care to invent for Don Quixote—and, as in all cases of a true myth, they are potentially infinite—the conclusion can only be the one which Cervantes gives, namely, that he recovers his senses and dies. Despite the protestations of his friends, who want him to go on providing them with amusement, he must say: "Ne'er look for birds of this year in the nests of the last: I was mad but I am now in my senses: I was once Don Quixote de la Mancha but am now the plain Alonso Quixano, and I hope the sincerity of my words and my repentance may restore me the same esteem you have had for me before."

For, in the last analysis, the saint cannot be presented aesthetically. The ironic vision gives us a Don Quixote who is innocent of every sin but one; and that one sin he can put off only by ceasing to exist as a character in a book, for all such characters are condemned to it, namely, the sin of being at all times and under all circumstances interesting.

Postscript: Christianity & Art

Art is compatible with polytheism and with Christianity, but not with philosophical materialism; Science is compatible with philosophical materialism and with Christianity, but not with polytheism. No artist or scientist, however, can feel comfortable as a Christian; every artist who happens also to be a Christian wishes he could be a polytheist; every scientist in the same position that he could be a philosophical materialist. And with good reason. In a polytheist society, the artists are its theologians; in a materialist society, its theologians are the scientists. To a Christian, unfortunately, both art and science are secular activities, that is to say, small beer.

No artist, qua artist, can understand what is meant by *God is Love* or *Thou shalt love thy neighbor* because he doesn't care whether God and men are loving or unloving; no scientist, qua scientist, can understand what is meant because he doesn't care whether to-be-loving is a matter of choice or a matter of compulsion.

To the imagination, the sacred is self-evident. It is as meaningless to ask whether one believes or disbelieves in Aphrodite or Ares as to ask whether one believes in a character in a novel; one can only say that one finds them true or untrue to life. To believe in Aphrodite and Ares merely means that one believes that the poetic myths about them do justice to the forces of sex and aggression as human beings experience them in nature and their own lives. That is why it is possible for an archaeologist who digs up a statuette of a god or goddess to say with fair certainty what kind of divinity it represents.

Similarly, to the imagination, the godlike or heroic man is self-evident. He does extraordinary deeds that the ordinary man cannot do, or extraordinary things happen to him.

The Incarnation, the coming of Christ in the form of a servant who cannot be recognized by the eye of flesh and blood, but only by the eye of faith, puts an end to all claims of the imagination to be the faculty which decides what is truly sacred and what is profane. A pagan god can appear on earth in disguise but, so long as he wears his disguise, no man is expected to recognize him nor can. But Christ appears looking just like any other man, yet claims that He is the Way, the Truth and the Life, and that no man can come to God the Father except through Him. The contradiction between the profane appearance and the sacred assertion is impassible to the imagination.

It is impossible to represent Christ on the stage. If he is made dramatically interesting, he ceases to be Christ and turns into a Hercules or a Svengali. Nor is it really possible to represent him in the visual arts for, if he were visually recognizable, he would be a god of the pagan kind. The best the painter can do is to paint either the Bambino with the Madonna or the dead Christ on the cross, for every baby and every corpse seems to be both individual and universal, *the* baby, *the* corpse. But neither a baby nor a corpse can say *I am the Way, etc.*

To a Christian, the godlike man is not the hero who does extraordinary deeds, but the holy man, the saint, who does good deeds. But the gospel defines a good deed as one done in secret, hidden, so far as it is possible, even from the doer, and forbids private prayer and fasting in public. This means that art, which by its nature can only deal with what can and should be manifested, cannot portray a saint.

There can no more be a "Christian" art than there can be a Christian science or a Christian diet. There can only be a Christian spirit in which an artist, a scientist, works or does not work. A painting of the Crucifixion is not necessarily more Christian in spirit than a still life, and may very well be less.

I sometimes wonder if there is not something a bit questionable, from a Christian point of view, about all works of art which make overt Christian references. They seem to assert that there is such a thing as a Christian culture, which there cannot be. Culture is one of Caesar's things. One cannot help noticing that the great period of "religious" painting coincided with the period when the Church was a great temporal power.

The only kind of literature which has Gospel authority is the parable, and parables are secular stories with no overt religious reference.

There are many hymns I like as one likes old song hits, because, for me, they have sentimental associations, but the only hymns I find poetically tolerable are either versified dogma or Biblical ballads.

Poems, like many of Donne's and Hopkins', which express a poet's personal feelings of religious devotion or penitence, make me uneasy. It is quite in order that a poet should write a sonnet expressing his devotion to Miss Smith because the poet, Miss Smith, and all his readers know perfectly well that, had he chanced to fall in love with Miss Jones instead, his feelings would be exactly the same. But if he writes a sonnet expressing his devotion to Christ, the important point, surely, is that his devotion is felt for Christ and not for, say, Buddha or Mahomet, and this point cannot be made in poetry; the Proper Name proves nothing. A penitential poem is even more question-able. A poet must intend his poem to be a good one, that is to say, an endur-ing object for other people to admire. Is there not something a little odd, to say the least, about making an admirable public object out of one's feelings of guilt and penitence before God?

A poet who calls himself a Christian cannot but feel uncomfortable when he realizes that the New Testament contains no verse (except in the apocryphal, and gnostic, *Acts of John*), only prose. As Rudolf Kassner has pointed out:

> The difficulty about the God-man for the poet lies in the Word being made Flesh. This means that reason and imagination are one. But does not Poetry, as such, live from there being a gulf between them?
> What gives us so clear a notion of this as metre, verse measures? In the magical-mythical world, metre was sacred, so was the strophe, the line, the words in the line, the letters. The poets were prophets.
> That the God-man did not write down his words himself or show the slightest concern that they should be written down in letters, brings us back to the Word made Flesh.
> Over against the metrical structures of the poets stand the Gospel parables in prose, over against magic a freedom which finds its limits within itself, is itself limit, over against poetic fiction [*Dichtung*], point-ing to and interpreting fact [*Deutung*]. (*Die Geburt Christi*)

I hope there is an answer to this objection, but I don't know what it is.

The imagination is a natural human faculty and therefore retains the same character whatever a man believes. The only difference can be in the way that he interprets its data. At all times and in all places, certain objects, be-ings and events arouse in his imagination a feeling of sacred awe, while other objects, beings and events leave his imagination unmoved. But a Christian cannot say, as a polytheist can: "All before which my imagination feels sacred awe is sacred-in-itself, and all which leaves it unmoved is profane-in-itself." There are two possible interpretations a Christian can make, both of them, I believe, orthodox, but each leaning towards a heresy. Either he can say, lean-ing towards Neoplatonism: "That which arouses in me a feeling of sacred awe is a channel through which, to me as an individual and as a member of a certain culture, the sacred which I cannot perceive directly is revealed to me." Or he can say, leaning towards pantheism: "All objects, beings and events are sacred but, because of my individual and cultural limitations, my imagination can only recognize these ones." Speaking for myself, I would rather, if I must be a heretic, be condemned as a pantheist than as a Neoplatonist.

In our urbanized industrial society, nearly everything we see and hear is so aggressively ugly or emphatically banal that it is difficult for a modern artist, unless he can flee to the depths of the country and never open a newspaper, to prevent his imagination from acquiring a Manichaean cast, from *feeling*, whatever his religious convictions to the contrary, that the physical world is utterly profane or the abode of demons. However sternly he reminds himself that the material universe is the creation of God and found good by Him, his mind is haunted by images of physical disgust, cigarette butts in a half-finished sardine can, a toilet that won't flush, etc.

Still, things might be worse. If an artist can no longer put on sacred airs, he has gained his personal artistic liberty instead. So long as an activity is regarded as being of sacred importance, it is controlled by notions of orthodoxy. When art is sacred, not only are there orthodox subjects which every artist is expected to treat and unorthodox subjects which no artist may treat, but also orthodox styles of treatment which must not be violated. But, once art becomes a secular activity, every artist is free to treat whatever subject excites his imagination, and in any stylistic manner which he feels appropriate.

We cannot have any liberty without license to abuse it. The secularization of art enables the really gifted artist to develop his talents to the full; it also permits those with little or no talent to produce vast quantities of phony or vulgar trash. When one looks into the window of a store which sells devotional art objects, one can't help wishing the iconoclasts had won.

For artists, things may very well get worse and, in large areas of the world, already have.

So long as science regards itself as a secular activity, materialism is not a doctrine but a useful empirical hypothesis. A scientist, qua scientist, does not need, when investigating physical nature, to bother his head with ontological or teleological questions any more than an artist, qua artist, has to bother about what his feelings of sacred awe may ultimately signify.

As soon, however, as materialism comes to be regarded as sacred truth, the distinction between the things of God and the things of Caesar is reabolished. But the world of sacred materialism is very different from the world of sacred polytheism. Under polytheism, everything in life was, ultimately, frivolous, so that the pagan world was a morally tolerant world—far too tolerant, for it tolerated many evils, like slavery and the exposure of infants, which should not be tolerated. It tolerated them, not because it did not know that they were evil, but because it did not believe that the gods were necessarily good. (No Greek, for example, ever defended slavery, as slave owners in the Southern States defended it, on the grounds that their slaves were happier as slaves than they would be as freemen. On the contrary, they argued that the slave must be subhuman because, otherwise, he would have killed himself rather than endure life as a slave.)

But, under religious materialism, everything in life is, ultimately, serious, and therefore subject to moral policing. It will not tolerate what it knows to be evil with a heartless shrug—that is how life is, always has been and always will be—but it will do something which the pagan world never did; it will do what it knows to be evil for a moral purpose, do it deliberately now so that good may come in the future.

Under religious materialism, the artist loses his personal artistic liberty again, but he does not recover his sacred importance, for now it is not artists who collectively decide what is sacred truth, but scientists, or rather the scientific politicians, who are responsible for keeping mankind in the true faith. Under them, an artist becomes a mere technician, an expert in effective expression, who is hired to express effectively what the scientific politician requires to be said.

PART EIGHT

Homage to Igor Stravinsky

Notes on Music and Opera

Opera consists of significant situations in artificially arranged sequence. —Goethe

Singing is near miraculous because it is the mastering of what is otherwise a pure instrument of egotism: the human voice. —Hugo von Hofmannsthal

What is music about? What, as Plato would say, does it imitate? Our experience of Time in its twofold aspect, natural or organic repetition, and historical novelty created by choice. And the full development of music as an art depends upon a recognition that these two aspects are different and that choice, being an experience confined to man, is more significant than repetition. A succession of two musical notes is an act of choice; the first causes the second, not in the scientific sense of making it occur necessarily, but in the historical sense of provoking it, of providing it with a motive for occurring. A successful melody is a self-determined history; it is freely what it intends to be, yet is a meaningful whole, not an arbitrary succession of notes.

Music as an art, i.e. music that has come to a conscious realization of its true nature, is confined to Western civilization alone and only to the last four or five hundred years at that. The music of all other cultures and epochs bears the same relation to Western music that magical verbal formulas bear to the art of poetry. A primitive magic spell may be poetry but it does not know that it is, nor intend to be. So, in all but Western music, history is only implicit; what it thinks it is doing is furnishing verses or movements with a repetitive accompaniment. Only in the West has chant become song.

Lacking a historical consciousness, the Greeks, in their theories of music, tried to relate it to Pure Being, but the becoming implicit in music betrays itself in their theories of harmony in which mathematics becomes numerology and one chord is intrinsically "better" than another.

Western music declared its consciousness of itself when it adopted time signatures, barring and the metronome beat. Without a strictly natural or cyclical time, purified from every trace of historical singularity, as a framework within which to occur, the irreversible historicity of the notes themselves would be impossible.

In primitive proto-music, the percussion instruments which best imitate recurrent rhythms and, being incapable of melody, can least imitate novelty, play the greatest role.

The most exciting rhythms seem unexpected and complex, the most beautiful melodies simple and inevitable.

Music cannot imitate nature: a musical storm always sounds like the wrath of Zeus.

A verbal art like poetry is reflective; it stops to think. Music is immediate, it goes on to become. But both are active, both insist on stopping or going on. The medium of passive reflection is painting, of passive immediacy the cinema, for the visual world is an immediately given world where Fate is mistress and it is impossible to tell the difference between a chosen movement and an involuntary reflex. Freedom of choice lies, not in the world we see, but in our freedom to turn our eyes in this direction, or that, or to close them altogether.

Because music expresses the opposite experience of pure volition and subjectivity (the fact that we cannot shut our ears at will allows music to assert that we cannot *not* choose), film music is not music but a technique for preventing us from using our ears to hear extraneous noises and it is bad film music if we become consciously aware of its existence.

Man's musical imagination seems to be derived almost exclusively from his primary experiences—his direct experience of his own body, its tensions and rhythms, and his direct experience of desiring and choosing—and to have very little to do with the experiences of the outside world brought to him through his senses. The possibility of making music, that is, depends primarily, not upon man's possession of an auditory organ, the ear, but upon his possession of a sound-producing instrument, the vocal cords. If the ear were primary, music would have begun as program pastoral symphonies. In the case of the visual arts, on the other hand, it is a visual organ, the eye, which is primary for, without it, the experiences which stimulate the hand into becoming an expressive instrument could not exist.

The difference is demonstrated by the difference in our sensation of motion in musical space and visual space.

An increase in the tension of the vocal cords is conceived in musical space as a going "up," a relaxation as a going "down." But in visual space it is the bottom of the picture (which is also the foreground) which is felt as the region of greatest pressure and, as the eye rises up the picture, it feels an increasing sense of lightness and freedom.

The association of tension in hearing with up and seeing with down seems to correspond to the difference between our experience of the force of gravity in our own bodies and our experience of it in other bodies. The weight of our own bodies is felt as inherent in us, as a personal wish to fall down, so that rising upward is an effort to overcome the desire for rest in ourselves. But the weight (and proximity) of other objects is felt as weighing down on us; they are "on top" of us and rising means getting away from their restrictive pressure.

All of us have learned to talk, most of us, even, could be taught to speak verse tolerably well, but very few have learned or could ever be taught to sing. In any village twenty people could get together and give a performance of *Hamlet* which, however imperfect, would convey enough of the play's greatness to be worth attending, but if they were to attempt a similar performance of *Don Giovanni*, they would soon discover that there was no question of a good or a bad performance because they could not sing the notes at all. Of an actor, even in a poetic drama, when we say that his performance is good, we mean that he simulates by art, that is, consciously, the way in which the character he is playing would, in real life, behave by nature, that is, unconsciously. But for a singer, as for a ballet dancer, there is no question of simulation, of singing the composer's notes "naturally"; his behavior is unabashedly and triumphantly art from beginning to end. The paradox implicit in all drama, namely, that emotions and situations which in real life would be sad or painful are on the stage a source of pleasure, becomes, in opera, quite explicit. The singer may be playing the role of a deserted bride who is about to kill herself, but we feel quite certain as we listen that not only we, but also she, is having a wonderful time. In a sense, there can be no tragic opera because whatever errors the characters make and whatever they suffer, they are doing exactly what they wish. Hence the feeling that *opera seria* should not employ a contemporary subject, but confine itself to mythical situations, that is, situations which, as human beings, we are all of us necessarily in and must, therefore, accept, however tragic they may be. A contemporary tragic situation like that in Menotti's *The Consul* is too actual, that is, too clearly a situation some people are in and others, including the audience, are not in, for the latter to forget this and see it as a symbol of, say, man's existential estrangement. Consequently the pleasure we and the singers are obviously enjoying strikes the conscience as frivolous.

On the other hand, its pure artifice renders opera the ideal dramatic medium for a tragic myth. I once went in the same week to a performance of *Tristan und Isolde* and a showing of *L'Eternel Retour*, Jean Cocteau's movie version of the same story. During the former, two souls, weighing over two hundred pounds apiece, were transfigured by a transcendent power; in the latter, a handsome boy met a beautiful girl and they had an affair. This loss of value was due not to any lack of skill on Cocteau's part but to the nature of the cinema as a medium. Had he used a fat middle-aged couple the effect would have been ridiculous because the snatches of language which are all the movie permits have not sufficient power to transcend their physical appearance. Yet if the lovers are young and beautiful, the cause of their love looks "natural," a consequence of their beauty, and the whole meaning of the myth is gone.

The man who wrote the Eighth Symphony has a right to rebuke the man who put his rapture of elation, tenderness, and nobility into the mouths of a drunken libertine, a silly peasant girl, and a conventional fine lady, instead of confessing them to himself, glorying in them, and uttering them without motley as the universal inheritance. (Bernard Shaw)

Shaw, and Beethoven, are both wrong, I believe, and Mozart right. Feelings of joy, tenderness and nobility are not confined to "noble" characters but are experienced by everybody, by the most conventional, most stupid, most depraved. It is one of the glories of opera that it can demonstrate this and to the shame of the spoken drama that it cannot. Because we use language in everyday life, our style and vocabulary become identified with our social character as others see us, and in a play, even a verse play, there are narrow limits to the range in speech possible for any character beyond which the playwright cannot go without making the character incredible. But precisely because we do not communicate by singing, a song can be out of place but not out of character; it is just as credible that a stupid person should sing beautifully as that a clever person should do so.

If music in general is an imitation of history, opera in particular is an imitation of human willfulness; it is rooted in the fact that we not only have feelings but insist upon having them at whatever cost to ourselves. Opera, therefore, cannot present character in the novelist's sense of the word, namely, people who are potentially good *and* bad, active *and* passive, for music is immediate actuality and neither potentiality nor passivity can live in its presence. This is something a librettist must never forget. Mozart is a greater composer than Rossini but the Figaro of the *Marriage* is less satisfying, to my mind, than the Figaro of the *Barber* and the fault, is, I think, Da Ponte's. His Figaro is too interesting a character to be completely translatable into music, so that co-present with the Figaro who is singing, one is conscious of a Figaro who is not singing but thinking to himself. The barber of Seville, on the other hand, who is not a person but a musical busybody, goes into song exactly with nothing over.

Again, I find *La Bohème* inferior to *Tosca*, not because its music is inferior, but because the characters, Mimi in particular, are too passive; there is an awkward gap between the resolution with which they sing and the irresolution with which they act.

The quality common to all the great operatic roles, e.g. Don Giovanni, Norma, Lucia, Tristan, Isolde, Brünnhilde, is that each of them is a passionate and willful state of being. In real life they would all be bores, even Don Giovanni.

In recompense for this lack of psychological complexity, however, music can do what words cannot, present the immediate and simultaneous relation of these states to each other. The crowning glory of opera is the big ensemble.

The chorus can play two roles in opera and two only, that of the mob and that of the faithful, sorrowing or rejoicing community. A little of this goes a long way. Opera is not oratorio.

Drama is based on the Mistake. I think someone is my friend when he really is my enemy, that I am free to marry a woman when in fact she is my mother, that this person is a chambermaid when it is a young nobleman in disguise, that this well-dressed young man is rich when he is really a penniless adventurer, or that if I do this such and such a result will follow when in fact it results in something very different. All good drama has two movements, first the making of the mistake, then the discovery that it was a mistake.

In composing his plot, the librettist has to conform to this law but, in comparison to the dramatist, he is more limited in the kinds of mistake he can use. The dramatist, for instance, procures some of his finest effects from showing how people deceive themselves. Self-deception is impossible in opera because music is immediate, not reflective; whatever is sung is the case. At most, self-deception can be suggested by having the orchestral accompaniment at variance with the singer, e.g. the jolly tripping notes which accompany Germont's approach to Violetta's deathbed in *La Traviata*, but unless employed very sparingly such devices cause confusion rather than insight.

Again, while in the spoken drama the discovery of the mistake can be a slow process and often, indeed, the more gradual it is the greater the dramatic interest, in a libretto the drama of recognition must be tropically abrupt, for music cannot exist in an atmosphere of uncertainty; song cannot walk, it can only jump.

On the other hand, the librettist need never bother his head, as the dramatist must, about probability. A credible situation in opera means a situation in which it is credible that someone should sing. A good libretto plot is a melodrama in both the strict and the conventional sense of the word; it offers as many opportunities as possible for the characters to be swept off their feet by placing them in situations which are too tragic or too fantastic for "words." No good opera plot can be sensible for people do not sing when they are feeling sensible.

The theory of "music-drama" presupposes a libretto in which there is not one sensible moment or one sensible remark: this is not only very difficult to manage, though Wagner managed it, but also extremely exhausting on both singers and the audience, neither of whom may relax for an instant.

In a libretto where there are any sensible passages, i.e. conversation not song, the theory becomes absurd. If, for furthering the action, it becomes necessary for one character to say to another "Run upstairs and fetch me a handkerchief," then there is nothing in the words, apart from their rhythm, to make one musical setting more apt than another. Wherever the choice of notes is arbitrary, the only solution is a convention, e.g. *recitativo secco*.

In opera the orchestra is addressed to the singers, not to the audience. An opera-lover will put up with and even enjoy an orchestral interlude on condition that he knows the singers cannot sing just now because they are tired or the scene-shifters are at work, but any use of the orchestra by itself which is not filling in time is, for him, wasting it. Leonora III is a fine piece to listen to in the concert hall, but in the opera house, when it is played between scenes one and two of the second act of *Fidelio*, it becomes twelve minutes of acute boredom.

If the librettist is a practicing poet, the most difficult problem, the place where he is most likely to go astray, is the composition of the verse. Poetry is in its essence an act of reflection, of refusing to be content with the interjections of immediate emotion in order to understand the nature of what is felt. Since music is in essence immediate, it follows that the words of a song cannot be poetry. Here one should draw a distinction between lyric and song proper. A lyric is a poem intended to be chanted. In a chant the music is subordinate to the words which limit the range and tempo of the notes. In song, the notes must be free to be whatever they choose and the words must be able to do what they are told.

The verses of *Ah non credea* in *La Sonnambula*, though of little interest to read, do exactly what they should: suggest to Bellini one of the most beautiful melodies ever written and then leave him completely free to write it. The verses which the librettist writes are not addressed to the public but are really a private letter to the composer. They have their moment of glory, the moment in which they suggest to him a certain melody; once that is over, they are as expendable as infantry to a Chinese general: they must efface themselves and cease to care what happens to them.

There have been several composers, Campion, Hugo Wolf, Benjamin Britten, for example, whose musical imagination has been stimulated by poetry of a high order. The question remains, however, whether the listener hears the sung words as words in a poem, or, as I am inclined to believe, only as sung syllables. A Cambridge psychologist, P. E. Vernon, once performed the experiment of having a Campion song sung with nonsense verses of equivalent syllabic value substituted for the original; only six per cent of his test audience noticed that something was wrong. It is precisely because I believe that, in listening to song (as distinct from chant), we hear, not words, but syllables, that I am not generally in favor of the performances of operas in translation. Wagner or Strauss in English sounds intolerable, and would still sound so if the poetic merits of the translation were greater than those of the original, because the new syllables have no apt relation to the pitch and tempo of the notes with which they are associated. The poetic value of the words may provoke a composer's imagination, but it is their syllabic values which determine the kind of vocal line he writes. In song, poetry is expendable, syllables are not.

"History," said Stephen Dedalus, "is the nightmare from which I must awake." The rapidity of historical change and the apparent powerlessness of the individual to affect Collective History has led in literature to a retreat from history. Instead of tracing the history of an individual who is born, grows old and dies, many modern novelists and short story writers, beginning with Poe, have devoted their attention to timeless passionate moments in a life, to states of being. It seems to me that, in some modern music, I can detect the same trend, a trend towards composing a static kind of music in which there is no marked difference between its beginning, its middle and its end, a music which sounds remarkably like primitive proto-music. It is not for me to criticize a composer who writes such music. One can say, however, that he will never be able to write an opera. But, probably, he won't want to.

The golden age of opera, from Mozart to Verdi, coincided with the golden age of liberal humanism, of unquestioning belief in freedom and progress. If good operas are rarer today, this may be because, not only have we learned that we are less free than nineteenth-century humanism imagined, but also have become less certain that freedom is an unequivocal blessing, that the free are necessarily the good. To say that operas are more difficult to write does not mean that they are impossible. That would only follow if we should cease to believe in free will and personality altogether. Every high C accurately struck demolishes the theory that we are the irresponsible puppets of fate or chance.

Cav & Pag

If a perfume manufacturer were to adopt the "naturalistic"
aesthetic, what kind of scents would he bottle? —Paul Valéry

While we all know that every moment of life is a living moment, it is impossible for us not to feel that some moments are more lively than others, that certain experiences are clues to the meaning and essential structures of the whole flux of experience in a way that others are not. This selection is, in part, imposed by experience itself—certain events overwhelm us with their importance without our knowing why—and in part is due to a predisposition on our side, by personal temperament and by social tradition, to be open to some kinds of events and closed to others. Dante's encounter with Beatrice, for example, was *given* him, but he would probably not have received or

interpreted the revelation in exactly the way that he did if the love poetry of
Provence had never been written. On the other hand, many people before
Wordsworth must have experienced feelings about Nature similar to his, but
they had dismissed them as not very relevant.

Every artist holds, usually in common with his contemporaries, certain
presuppositions about the real *Nature* concealed behind or within the stream
of phenomena, to which it is his artistic duty to be true, and it is these which
condition the kind of art he produces as distinct from its quality.

Suppose that a dramatist believes that the most interesting and significant
characteristic of man is his power to choose between right and wrong, his
responsibility for his actions; then, out of the infinite number of characters
and situations that life offers him, he will select situations in which the temptation to choose wrong is at its greatest and the actual consequences incurred by the choice are most serious, and he will select characters who are
most free to choose, least in the position to blame their choice afterwards on
circumstances or other people.

At most periods in history he could find both of these most easily among
the lives of the rich and powerful, and least among the lives of the poor. A
king can commit a murder without fear of punishment by human law; a poor
man cannot, so that, if the poor man refrains from committing one, we feel
that the law, not he, is largely responsible. A king who steals a country is
more interesting dramatically than a starving peasant who steals a loaf, firstly
because the country is so much bigger, and secondly because the king is not
driven, like the peasant, by an impersonal natural need outside his control,
but by a personal ambition which he could restrain.

For many centuries the dramatic role of the poor was to provide comic
relief, to be shown, that is, in situations and with emotions similar to those of
their betters but with this difference: that, in their case, the outcome was not
tragic suffering. Needless to say, no dramatist ever believed that in real life
the poor did not suffer but, if the dramatic function of suffering is to indicate moral guilt, then the relatively innocent cannot be shown on the stage
as suffering. The comic similarity of their passions is a criticism of the great,
a reminder that the king, too, is but a man, and the difference in destiny a
reminder that the poor who, within their narrower captivity, commit the same
crimes, are, by comparison, innocent.

Such a view might be termed the traditional view of Western culture
against which naturalism was one form of revolt. As a literary movement,
nineteenth-century naturalism was a corollary of nineteenth-century science, in particular of its biology. The evidence of Evolution, the discovery of
some of the laws of genetics, for example, had shown that man was much
more deeply embedded in the necessities of the natural order than he had
imagined, and many began to believe that it was only a matter of time before

the whole of man's existence, including his historical personality, would be found to be phenomena explicable in terms of the laws of science.

If the most significant characteristic of man is the complex of biological needs he shares with all members of his species, then the best lives for the writer to observe are those in which the role of natural necessity is clearest, namely, the lives of the very poor.

The difficulty for the naturalistic writer is that he cannot hold consistently to his principles without ceasing to be an artist and becoming a statistician, for an artist is by definition interested in uniqueness. There can no more be an art about the common man than there can be a medicine about the uncommon man. To think of another as common is to be indifferent to his personal fate; to the degree that one loves or hates another, one is conscious of his or her uniqueness. All the characters in literature with universal appeal, those that seem to reveal every man to himself, are in character and situation very uncommon indeed. A writer who is committed to a naturalist doctrine is driven by his need as an artist to be interesting to find a substitute for the tragic situation in the pathetic, situations of fantastic undeserved misfortune, and a substitute for the morally responsible hero in the pathological case.

The role of impersonal necessity, the necessities of nature or the necessities of the social order in its totality upon the human person can be presented in fiction, in epic poetry and, better still, in the movies, because these media can verbally describe or visually picture that nature and that order; but in drama, where they are forced to remain offstage—there can be no dramatic equivalent to Hardy's description of Egdon Heath in *The Return of the Native*—this is very difficult. And in opera it is impossible, firstly, because music is in its essence dynamic, an expression of will and self-affirmation and, secondly, because opera, like ballet, is a virtuoso art; whatever his role, an actor who sings is more an uncommon man, more a master of his fate, even as a self-destroyer, than an actor who speaks. Passivity or collapse of the will cannot be expressed in song; if, for example, a tenor really sings the word "*Piango*" he does not cry, a fact of which some tenors, alas, are only too aware. It is significant as a warning sign that the concluding line of *Cavalleria Rusticana*, "*Hanno ammazzato compare Turiddu*" and the concluding line of *Pagliacci*, "*La commedia è finita*" are spoken, not sung.

In practice, the theory of *verismo*, as applied to opera, meant substituting, in place of the heroic aristocratic setting of the traditional *opera seria*, various exotic settings, social and geographic. Instead of gods and princes, it gives us courtesans (*La Traviata, Manon*), gypsies and bullfighters (*Carmen*), a diva (*Tosca*), Bohemian artists (*La Bohème*), the Far East (*Madama Butterfly*), etc., social types and situations every bit as unfamiliar to the average operagoer as those of Olympus or Versailles.

Giovanni Verga was no doctrinaire naturalist. He wrote about the Sicilian peasants because he had grown up among them, knew them intimately, loved them and therefore could see them as unique beings. The original short story *Cavalleria Rusticana* which appeared in *Vita dei Campi* (1880) differs in several important respects from the dramatized version which Verga wrote four years later and upon which the libretto is based. In the short story the hero Turiddu is the relatively innocent victim of his poverty and his good looks. Santuzza is not the abused defenseless creature we know from the opera but a rich man's daughter who knows very well how to look after herself. Turiddu serenades her but he has no chance of marrying her since he has no money and though she likes him, she does not lose her head. Her betrayal to Alfio of Turiddu's affair with Lola is therefore much more malicious and unsympathetic than it is in the opera. Finally, the reason that Turiddu gives Alfio for insisting upon a fight to the death is not Santuzza's future—he has completely forgotten her—but the future of his penniless old mother.

Santuzza's seduction and pregnancy, Turiddu's brutal rejection of her, her curse upon him, his final remorse were all added by Verga when he had to build up Santuzza into a big and sympathetic role for Duse. As a subject for a short libretto, it is excellent. The situation is strong, self-contained and immediately clear; it provides roles for a convenient number and range of voices; and the emotions involved are both singable emotions and easy to contrast musically. The psychology is straightforward enough for song but not silly: how right it is, for instance, that Turiddu should reproach Santuzza for having let him seduce her—"*Pentirsi è vano dopo l'offesa*." Thanks to the swiftness with which music can express a change in feeling, even Turiddu's sudden switch of attitude from contempt to remorse becomes much more plausible in the opera than it seems in the spoken drama. Targioni-Tozzetti and Menasci quite rightly stuck pretty closely to Verga's story, their chief addition being the lines in which Turiddu begs Lucia to accept Santuzza as a daughter. But, having at their disposal as librettists what a dramatist no longer has, a chorus, they took full advantage of it. The choral episodes, the chorus of spring, the mule-driving song, the Easter hymn, the drinking song take up more than a quarter of the score. It might have been expected that, particularly in so short a work, to keep postponing and interrupting the action so much would be fatal; but, in fact, if one asks what was the chief contribution of the librettists towards giving the work the peculiar impact and popularity it has, I think one must say it was precisely these episodes. Thanks to them, the action of the protagonists, their personal tragedy, is seen against an immense background, the recurrent death and rebirth of nature, the liturgical celebration of the once-and-for-all death and resurrection of the redeemer of man, the age-old social rites of the poor, so that their local history takes on a ritual significance; Turiddu's death is, as it were, a ritual sacrifice in atonement for the sins of the whole community. One of the most moving moments in the opera, for example—and nothing could be less *verismo*—occurs when Santuzza, the excommunicated girl who believes that she is damned, is translated out of her situation and starts singing out over the chorus, like Deborah the Prophetess, "*Inneggiamo il Signor non è morto!*"

If the interplay of rite and personal action which is the secret of *Cavalleria Rusticana* is not a typical concern of the *verismo* school, the libretto interest of *Pagliacci* is even less naturalistic, for the subject is the psychological conundrum—"Who is the real me? Who is the real you?" This is presented through three contradictions. Firstly, the contradiction between the artist who creates his work out of real joys and sufferings and his audience whom it amuses, who enjoy through it imaginary joys and sufferings which are probably quite different from those of its creator. Secondly, the contradiction between the actors who do not feel the emotions they are portraying and the audience who do, at least imaginatively. And, lastly, the contradiction between the actors as professionals who have to portray imaginary feelings and the actors as men and women who have real feelings of their own. We are all actors; we frequently have to hide our real feelings for others and, alone with ourselves, we are constantly the victims of self-deception. We can never be certain that we know what is going on in the hearts of others, though we usually overestimate our knowledge—both the shock of discovering an infidelity and the tortures of jealousy are due to this. On the other hand, we are too certain that nobody else sees the real us.

In the Prologue, Tonio, speaking on behalf of Leoncavallo and then of the cast, reminds the audience that the artist and the actor are men. When we reach the play within the play all the contradictions are going simultaneously. Nedda is half-actress, half-woman, for she is expressing her real feelings in an imaginary situation; she is in love but not with Beppe who is playing Harlequin. Beppe is pure actor; as a man he is not in love with anybody. Tonio and Canio are themselves, for their real feelings and the situation correspond, to the greater amusement of the audience for it makes them *act* so convincingly. Finally there is Nedda's lover Silvio, the member of the audience who has got into the act, though as yet invisibly. When Nedda as Columbine recites to Harlequin the line written for her, "*A stanotte—e per sempre tua sarò!*" Canio as Pagliaccio is tortured because he has heard her use, speaking as herself, these identical words to the lover he has not seen. One has only to imagine what the opera would be like if, with the same situation between the characters, the *Commedia* were omitted, to see how much the interest of the opera depends on the question of Illusion and Reality, a problem which is supposed only to concern idealists.

About the music of these two operas, I can, of course, only speak as a layman. The first thing that strikes me on hearing them is the extraordinary strength and vitality of the Italian operatic tradition. Since 1800 Italian opera had already produced four fertile geniuses, Bellini, Rossini, Donizetti and

Verdi, yet there was still enough left to allow, not only the lesser but still formidable figure of Puccini, but also the talents of Ponchielli, Giordano, Mascagni and Leoncavallo to create original and successful works. Today, indeed—it may have seemed different in the nineties—we are more conscious
in the works of these later composers of the continuity of the tradition than
of any revolutionary novelty. We do not emerge from the house, after hearing *Cavalleria* or *Pagliacci* for the first time, saying to ourselves, "What a
strange new kind of opera!" No, before the first ten bars are over, we are
thinking: "Ah, another Italian opera. How jolly!"

Comparing one with the other (a rather silly but inevitable habit), Leoncavallo strikes me as much more technically adroit. One of the strange things
about Mascagni is the almost old-fashioned simplicity of his musical means;
he writes as if he were scarcely aware of even the middle Verdi. There are
dull passages in *Cavalleria Rusticana*, e.g. the music of the mule-driving song,
but, in the dramatic passages, the very primitive awkwardness of the music
seems to go *with* the characters and give them a conviction which Leoncavallo fails to give to his down-at-heel actors. For instance, when I listen to
Turiddu rejecting Santuzza in the duet, "*No, no! Turiddu, rimani*" I can believe that I am listening to a village Don Giovanni, but when I listen to Silvio
making love to Nedda in the duet, "*Decidi, il mio destin*," I know that I am listening to a baritone. As a listener, then, I prefer Mascagni; if I were a singer,
I daresay my preference would be reversed.

In making their way round the world, *Cav & Pag* have had two great advantages: they are relatively cheap to produce and the vocal writing is effective but does not make excessive demands so that they are enjoyable even
when performed by provincial touring companies, whereas works like *La
Gioconda* or *Fedora* are intolerable without great stars. Take, for example, the
famous aria "*Vesti la giubba*": if the singer is in good voice, he has a fine opportunity to put it through its paces; if his voice is going, he can always throw
away the notes and just bellow, a procedure which some audiences seem to
prefer.

All the various artistic battle cries, Classicism, Romanticism, Naturalism,
Surrealism, The-language-really-used-by-men, The-music-of-the-future, etc.,
are of interest to art historians because of the practical help which, however
absurd they may seem as theories, they have been to artists in discovering
how to create the kind of works which were proper to their powers. As listeners, readers and spectators, we should take them all with a strong dose of salt,
remembering that a work of art is not *about* this or that kind of life; it *has* life,
drawn, certainly, from human experience but transmuted, as a tree trans-
mutes water and sunlight into treehood, into its own unique being. Every
encounter with a work of art is a personal encounter; what it *says* is not information but a revelation of itself which is simultaneously a revelation of ourselves. We may dislike any particular work we encounter or prefer another to

it but, to the degree that our dislike or our preference is genuine, we admit its genuineness as a work of art. The only real negative judgment—it may be ourselves, not the works, that are at fault—is indifference. As Rossini put it: "All kinds of music are good except the boring kind."

Translating Opera Libretti

(Written in collaboration with Chester Kallman)

> SILVA. The cup's prepared, and so rejoice;
> And more, I'll let thee have thy choice.
> (*He proudly presents him a dagger*
> *and a cup of poison*)
> —from an old translation of *Ernani*

To discover just how arrogant and stupid reviewers can be, one must write something in collaboration with another writer. In a literary collaboration, if it is to be successful, the partners to it must surrender the selves they would be if they were writing separately and become one new author; though, obviously, any given passage must be written by one of them, the censor-critic who decides what will or will not do is this corporate personality. Reviewers think they know better, that they can tell who wrote what; I can only say that, in the case of our collaborations, their guesses as to which parts were actually written by Mr Kallman and which my myself have been, at a conservative estimate, seventy-five per cent wrong.

Ten years ago, if anybody had prophesied that we would one day find ourselves translating libretti, we would have thought him crazy. We had always been fanatic advocates of the tradition upheld by British and American opera houses of giving opera in its original tongue as against the European tradition of translation. If people want to know what is going on, we said, let them buy a libretto with an English crib and read it before coming to the opera house; even if they know Italian and German well, they should still do this because, in a performance, one rarely hears more than one word in ten. As regards performances in opera houses, we still feel pretty much the same way, but televised opera for mass audiences is another matter. Whether the TV audience could ever be persuaded to tolerate operas in foreign languages is doubtful, not only because mass audiences are lazy but also because, on a television set, every syllable can be heard so that the irritation caused by failing to understand what is said is greater than in an opera house. (And then, of course, the big broadcasting companies are willing to pay handsomely for translations and we saw no reason why, if a translation *was* going to be made, we shouldn't get the money.) Once we started, we felt our aesthetic prejudices weakening for a reason which is not perhaps a valid one since it is purely selfish: we found ourselves completely fascinated by the task.

The three libretti we have translated together so far are Da Ponte's libretto for *Don Giovanni*, Schikaneder-and-Giesecke's libretto for *Die Zauberflöte* and Brecht's text for the song-ballet *Die sieben Todsünden* with music by Kurt Weill. Each has its special problems. *Don Giovanni* is in Italian, with sung recitatives and, stylistically, an *opera giocosa; Die Zauberflöte* is in German, written as a series of numbers with spoken dialogue in between and, stylistically, an *opera magica. Die sieben Todsünden* is not a traditional opera in which, as Mozart said, "poetry absolutely has to be the obedient daughter of music," but, like all the Brecht-Weill collaborations, a work in which the words are at least as important as the music, and its language is that of contemporary speech and full of popular idiom.

In comparison with the ordinary translator, the translator of a libretto is much more strictly bound in some respects and much freer in others. Since the music is so infinitely more important than the text, the translator must start with the premise that his translation must demand no change of musical intervals or rhythms in order to fit it. This law is absolute for arias and ensembles; in recitative, occasions may arise when the dropping or addition of a note is justified, but they are very rare. The translator of a libretto, therefore, has to produce a version which is rhythmically identical, not with the verse prosody of the original as it would be spoken, but with the musical prosody as it is sung. The difficulty in achieving this lies in the fact that musical prosody is both quantitative, like Greek and Latin verse, and accentual like English and German. In a quantitative prosody, syllables are either long or short and one long syllable is regarded as being equal in length to two short syllables; in an accentual prosody like our own, the length of the syllables is ignored—metrically, they are regarded as all being equal in length— and the distinction is between accented and unaccented syllables. This means that the rhythmical value of the trisyllabic feet and the dissyllabic feet are the reverse in a quantitative prosody from what they are in an accentual. Thus

> A quantitative dactyl or anapaest is in 4/4 or 2/4 time. (March time.)
> A quantitative trochee or iamb is in 3/4 or 6/8 time. (Waltz time.)
> An accentual dactyl or anapaest is in waltz time.
> An accentual trochee or iamb is in march time.

But in music both quantity and accent count:

> A 2/4 bar made up of a half note followed by two quarter notes is, quantitatively, a dactyl but, accentually, a bacchic.
> A musical triplet ♫ is, quantitatively, a tribrach but, accentually, a dactyl.

To add to the translators' troubles, the felt tempo of the spoken word and of musical notes is utterly different. If, timing myself with a stop watch, I recite, first the most rapid piece of verse I can think of—The Nightmare Song from *Iolanthe*, let us say—and then the slowest verse I can think of—Tennyson's *Tears, idle tears*—I find that the proportional difference between the time taken in each case to recite the same number of syllables is, at most, 2–1, and much of this difference is attributable, not to the change in speed of uttering the syllables but to the pauses in speaking which I make at the caesuras in the slow piece. Further, the two tempi at which I speak them both lie in what is in music the faster half of the tempo range. The tempo which in speaking verse is felt to be an adagio is felt in music as an allegretto. The consequence of this difference is that, when a composer sets verses to a slow tempo, verse dactyls and anapaests turn into molossoi, its trochees and iambs into spondees. The line *Now thank we all our God* is iambic when spoken but spondaic when sung.

This means that it is not enough for the translator to read the verses of the libretto, scan them, and produce a prosodic copy in English for, when he then matches his copy against the score, he will often find that the musical distortion of the spoken rhythm which sounded possible in the original tongue sounds impossible in English. This is particularly liable to happen when translating from Italian because, even when speaking, an Italian has a far greater license in prolonging or shortening the length of his syllables than an Englishman.

Two Examples

(1) In Leporello's aria at the beginning of *Don Giovanni* occurs the line *Ma mi par che venga gente* (But it seems to me that people are coming).

To begin with, we decided that Leporello must say something else. He is on guard outside the house where Don Giovanni is raping or trying to rape Donna Anna. Da Ponte's line suggests that a crowd of strangers are about to come on stage; actually, it will only be Don Giovanni pursued by Donna Anna and some time will elapse before the Commendatore enters. Our first attempt was

> What was that? There's trouble brewing.

Spoken, *che venga gente* and *there's trouble brewing* sound more or less metrically equivalent, but the phrase is set to three eighth notes and two quarter notes, so that *gente* which, when spoken, is a trochee becomes a spondee. But *brewing*, because of the lack of consonants between the syllables, sounds distorted as a spondee, so we had to revise the line to

> What was that? We're in for trouble.

(2) When Tamino approaches the doors of Sarastro's temple, a bodiless voice cries *Zurück!*, strongly accentuating the second syllable. This looks easy to translate literally by *Go Back!* and, were the tempo a slow one, it could be. Unfortunately, the tempo indication is *allegro assai* and at that

speed, the two English monosyllables sound like a nonsense disyllable *ge-BACK*. Another solution had to be found; ours was *Beware!*

Sometimes the translator is forced to depart from the original text because of differences in the sound and association between the original and its exact English equivalent. Take, for example, the simple pair, *Ja* and *Nein*, *Si* and *No*, *Yes* and *No*. In the Leporello-Giovanni duet *Eh, via buffone* which is sung *allegro assai*, Leporello's two stanzas are built around the use of *no* in the first and *si* in the second.

> *Ed io non burlo, ma voglio andar.*
> *No, no, padrone, v'andar vi dico.*
> *No! No! No!*
> *No, no, no, no, no, no, no, no, no, no, no.*
> *Non vo' restar, si!*
> *Si! Si! Si!*
> *Si, si, si, si, si, si, si, si, si, si!*

In English as in Italian, one can sing rapidly no, no, no, no . . . but one cannot sing yes, yes, yes, yes . . . The opening lines of Tamino's first aria run

> *Dies Etwas kann ich zwar nicht nennen,*
> *Doch fühl ich's hier wie Feuer brennen;*
> *Soll die Empfindung Liebe sein?*
> *Ja, Ja,*
> *Die Liebe ist's allein.*

The tempo this time is moderate so that it is physically possible to sing *Yes, Yes*, but Yes-Yes in our culture has a comic or at least unromantic association with impatience or boredom. Similarly, one cannot translate *Komm, Komm* which occurs in one of the choruses in the same opera as *Come, Come*, without making the audience laugh.

Another problem is that feminine rhymes which are the commonest kind in Italian and frequent in German, are not only much rarer in English, but most of the ones that do exist are comic rhymes. It is possible for a competent versifier to copy the original rhyme scheme but often at the cost of making the English sound like Gilbert and Sullivan. On rare occasions such as Leporello's Catalogue aria, the tendency of double rhymes to be funnier in English than in Italian can be an advantage but, in any tender or solemn scene, it is better to have no rhyme at all than a ridiculous one. The marble statue rebukes Don Giovanni in the churchyard scene with the couplet

> *Ribalde, audace,*
> *Lascia'l morti in pace.*

Here any rhyme in English will sound absurd.

Then, languages differ not only in their verbal forms, but also in their rhetorical traditions, so that what sounds perfectly natural in one language, can, when literally translated, sound embarrassing in another. All Italian libretti are full of polysyllabic interjections; such as *Traditore! Scelerato! Sconsigliato! Sciugurato! Sventurato!* etc., and these sound effective, even at moments of high emotion. But in the English language, aside from the fact that most of our interjections are one or two syllables long, they are seldom, if ever, used in serious situations and are mostly employed in slanging matches between schoolboys or taxicab drivers. In serious situations we tend, I think, to make declarative statements; instead of shouting *Traditore!* (Vile seducer!) to shout *You betrayed me!*

Now and again the translator may feel that a change is necessary, not because the habits of two languages are different but because what the librettist wrote sounds too damn silly in any language. When Donna Anna, Donna Elvira, and Don Ottavio arrive at Don Giovanni's party in the finale of Act I, Donna Elvira sings

> *Bisogn' aver corraggio,*
> *O cari' amici miei.*

which is perfectly sensible, but Don Ottavio's reply is not.

> *L'amica dice bene!*
> *Corragio' aver conviene.*

that is to say:

> Our lady friend says wisely;
> Some courage would do nicely.

Nor in the finale to *Die Zauberflöte* when the Spirits see Pamina approaching distraught, can one allow them to say, as they do in German:

> Where is she, then?
> She is out of her senses.

With such alterations, no musician or musicologist is likely to quarrel. A more controversial matter is syllabification, for some purists consider the original syllabification and slurs to be as sacrosanct as the notes themselves. We believe, however, that there are occasions, at least in libretti written before 1850, when changes in syllabification are justifiable. In the days of Mozart and Rossini, the speed at which operas were expected to be turned out made any studied collaboration between librettist and composer impossible. The librettists produced his verses and the composer set them as best he could; he might ask for an extra aria but not for detailed revisions. The insistence shown by Verdi in his later years, by Wagner and by Strauss upon having a text which exactly matched their musical ideas was unknown. Mozart frequently spreads a syllable over two or more notes, and not in coloratura runs only. In many cases, his reason for doing so was, we believe, quite simple:

his musical idea contained more notes than the verse he had been given contained syllables—just as, when he has not been given enough lines for his music, he repeats them.

Now it so happens that in English, on account of its vowels and its many monosyllabic words, there are fewer syllables which sing well and are intelligible when spread over several notes than there are in either Italian or German; English is, intrinsically, a more staccato tongue. The first stanza of the duet between Papageno and Pamina runs thus:

> *Bei Männern welche Liebe fühlen*
> *Fehlt auch ein gutes Herze nicht.*
> *Die süssen Triebe mitzufühlen*
> *Ist dann des Weihes erste Pflicht.*

The rhythm is iambic, that is to say in 4/4 time. But Mozart has set it to a tune in 6/8 time so, to make the words fit, he spreads each accented syllable over two notes linked by a slur. It is, of course, not difficult to write an English iambic quatrain.

> When Love his dart has deep implanted,
> The hero's heart grows kind and tame.
> And by his passion soon enchanted,
> The nymph receives the ardent flame.

But, to our ears, this sounded wrong somehow; they kept demanding an anapaestic quatrain which would give one syllable to every note of the melody.

> When Love in his bosom desire has implanted,
> The heart of the hero grows gentle and tame.
> And soon by his passion enkindled, enchanted,
> The nymph receives the impetuous flame.

This, of course, involves doing away with the slurs in the score, and some purists may object. One can only ask singers to sing both iambic and anapaestic versions several times without prejudice and then ask themselves which, in English, sounds the more Mozartian.

All such details which demand the translator's attention are part of the more general and important problem of finding the right literary style for any given opera. The kind of diction suitable to an *opera seria*, for example, is unsuitable in an *opera buffa*, nor can a supernatural character like the Queen of the Night use the speech of a courtesan like Violetta. In deciding upon a style for a particular opera, the translator has to trust his intuition and his knowledge of the literature, both in the original tongue and in his own, of the period in which the opera is supposed to be set. While he must obviously avoid solecisms, the literary traditions of any two languages are so different that a puristic exactness is often neither necessary nor even desirable; it does not follow that the best equivalent for the Italian spoken and written in 1790 is the English spoken in that year.

Scene Five of *Don Giovanni* shows the peasants dancing. Zerlina sings:

> *Giovinette, che fate, all'amore, che fate, all'amore,*
> *Non lasciate, che passi l'età,*
> > *Che passi l'età,*
> > *Che passi l'età.*
> *Se nel seno vi bulica il core, bulica il core,*
> *Il rimedio vedetelo quà.*
> *Che piacer, che piacer, che sarà.*

Given the character of the music, it seemed to us that the natural English equivalent was not something late-eighteenth-century like Da Ponte's Italian, but Elizabethan pastoral.

> Pretty maid with your graces adorning the dew-spangled morning,
> The red rose and the white fade away,
> > Both wither away,
> > All fade in a day.
> Of your pride and unkindness relenting, to kisses consenting,
> All the pains of your shepherd allay.
> As the cuckoo flies over the may.

A different kind of stylistic problem is presented by the Brecht-Weill ballet *Die sieben Todsünden* which is set in a contemporary but mythical America. A contemporary American diction is called for, but it must not be too specifically so or the mythical element will disappear. Thus, while the translation must not contain words which are only used in British English—*Haus* must be translated as *home* not as *house*—it would be wrong, although the family are said to live in Louisiana, to translate the German into the speech of American Southerners.

In one chorus the family list various delicious foods.

> *Hörnchen! Schnitzel! Spargel! Hühnchen!*
> *Und die kleinen gelben Honigküchen*

that is:

> Muffins! Cutlets! Asparagus! Chickens!
> And those little yellow honey-buns!

Though Americans do eat all of these, they do not make a characteristic list of what Americans, particularly from the South, would think of with the greatest greedy longing. Accordingly, we changed the list to:

> Crabmeat! Porkchops! Sweet-corn! Chicken!
> And those golden biscuits spread with honey!

The images and metaphors characteristic of one culture and language are not always as effective in another. Thus, a literal translation of one of the verses sung by Anna in *Lust* would go:

> And she shows her little white backside,
> Worth more than a little factory,
> Shows it gratis to starers and corner-boys,
> To the profane look of the world.

The most powerful line in this verse is the second, but, in American English, "a little factory" makes no impact. Some other comparison must be thought of:

> Now she shows off her white little fanny,
> Worth twice a little Texas motel,
> And for nothing the poolroom can stare at Annie
> As though she'd nothing to sell.

Translating Arias

An aria very rarely contains information which it is essential for the audience to know in order to understand the action and which must, therefore, be translated literally; all that a translation of an aria must do is convey the emotion or conflict of emotions which it expresses. At the same time, the arias in an opera are as a rule its high points musically, so that it is in them that the quality of the translation matters most. So far as an original librettist is concerned, all that matters is that his verses should inspire the composer to write beautiful music, but the translator is in a different position. The music is already there, and it is his duty to make his verses as worthy of it as he can.

Before Wagner and Verdi in his middle years, no composer worried much about the libretto; he took what he was given and did the best he could with it. This was possible because a satisfactory convention had been established as to the styles and forms in which libretti should be written which any competent versifier could master. This meant, however, that, while a composer could be assured of getting a settable text, one libretto was remarkably like another; all originality and interest had to come from the music. Today, it is idle to pretend that we can listen to a Mozart opera with the ears of his contemporaries, as if we had never heard the operas of Wagner, the late Verdi and Strauss in which the libretto plays an important role. In listening to a Mozart opera, we cannot help noticing when the text is banal or silly, or becoming impatient when a line is repeated over and over again. Having the beautiful music in his ears, a modern translator must feel it his duty to make his version as worthy of it as he can.

(1) *Don Ottavio's first aria*

> *Dalla sua pace*
> *La mia depende,*
> *Quelch'al lei piace*
> *Vita mi rende,*
> *Quel che l'incresce*
> *Morte mi da.*
> *S'ella sospira*
> *Sospir' anchio,*
> *E mia quell'ira*
> *Que pianto è mio,*
> *E non ho bene*
> *S'ella non l'ha.*

(Upon her peace / my peace depends / what pleases her / grants me life / and what saddens her / gives me death. If she sighs / I also sigh / mine is her anger / and her grief is mine / I have no joy / if she has none.)

When one compares English poetry with Italian or that of any Romance language, one sees that English poetic speech is more concrete in its expressions; an English poet writing a love lyric tends to express his feelings in terms of imagery and metaphors drawn from nature, rather than stating them directly. Further, English and Italian notions of what it is proper for an amorous male to say and do are different. To an English sensibility, Ottavio's exclusive concentration upon himself—she mustn't be unhappy because it makes him unhappy—is a bit distasteful. Lastly, Da Ponte's lyric contains only a single idea repeated over and over again with but slight variations, but Mozart has given his second stanza a completely different musical treatment. Accordingly we tried to write a lyric which should be (a) more concrete in diction, (b) make Ottavio think more about Donna Anna than himself and (c) less repetitive.

> Shine, Lights of Heaven,
> Guardians immortal,
> Shine on my true love,
> Waking or sleeping,
> Sun, moon and starlight,
> Comfort her woe.
>
> O nimble breezes,
> O stately waters,
> Obey a lover,
> Proclaim her beauty
> And sing her praises
> Where'er you go.

                    (*da capo*)
                    When grief beclouds her,
                    I walk in shadow,
                    My thoughts are with her,
                    Waking or sleeping;
                    Sun, moon and starlight,
                    Comfort her woe.

(2) *Pamina's Aria in Die Zauberflöte, Act II*

> *Ach, ich fuhl's, es ist verschwunden*
> *Ewig hin, mein ganzes Glück, der Liebe Glück.*
> *Nimmer kommt ihr, Wonne-stunden*
> *Meinem Herzen mehr zurück.*
> *Sieh, Tamino*
> *Diese Tränen fliessen, Trauter, dir allein, dir allein.*
> *Fühlst du nicht der Liebe Sehnen, Liebe Sehnen,*
> *So wird Ruhe im Tode sein,*
> *Fühlst du nicht der Liebe Sehnen,*
> *Fühlst du nicht der Liebe Sehnen,*
> *So wird Ruhe im Tode sein,*
> *Im Tode sein.*

(Ah, I feel it / it has vanished / for ever away / the joy of love. Never will you come / hours of wonder / back to my heart / See, Tamino / these tears flowing, beloved, for you alone / If you do not feel the sighs of love / then there will be peace in death.)

The aria contains a number of high notes, long runs and phrases which repeat like an echo. Any English version, therefore, must provide open vowels for the high notes and runs, and phrases which can sound like echoes. There is a certain kind of English poetry which is based upon the repetition of a word or words in slightly different context, for instance, Donne's "The Expiation."

> Go, go, and if that word hath not quite killed thee,
> Ease me with death by bidding me go too,
> Or, if it have, let my word work on me
> And a just office on a murderer do;
> Except it be too late to kill me so,
> Being double dead, going and bidding go.

Given Pamina's situation it seemed to us that we might make use of this style and build our lyric round the words *silent* and *grief.*

> Hearts may break though grief be silent,
> True hearts make their love their lives,

Silence love with ended lives;
Love that dies in one false lover
Kills the heart where love survives.

O Tamino, see the silence
Of my tears betray my grief,
Faithful grief.
If you flee my love in silence,
In faithless silence,
Let my sorrow die with me.
If you can betray Pamina,
If you love me not, Tamino,
Let my sorrow die with me
And silent be.

(3) *Donna Anna's last aria in Don Giovanni*

This consists of an orchestral recitative, a cavatina and a cabaletta.

RECIT.   *Crudele? Ah no, mia bene. Troppo mi spiace
allontanarti un ben che lungamente la nostra
alma desia . . . Ma, il mondo . . . O Dio! . . . Abbastanza
per te mi parla amore. Non sedur la constanza
del sensibil mio core!*

CAVATINA.   *Non mi dir, bell'idol mio,
Che son to crudel con te;
Tu ben sai quant'io t'amai,
Tu conosci la mia fè,
Tu conosci la mia fè.
Calma, calm'il tuo tormento,
Se di duol non vuoi ch'io mora,
Non vuoi ch'io mora
Non mi dir, bell'idol mio,
Che son io crudel con te;
Calma, calm'il, etc. . . .*

CABALETTA.   *Forsè, forsè un giorn'il cielo
Sentirà pietà di mè.*

(Cruel? O no, my dear. Too much it grieves me to withhold from you a
joy that for a long time our soul desires. But, the world . . . O God! Do
not weaken the constancy of my suffering heart. Sufficiently for you
Love speaks to me.)

Do not tell me, my dearest dear,
That I am cruel to you;

> You know well how much I love you,
> You know my fidelity,
> Calm your torment
> If you do not wish me to die of grief.
> Perhaps, one day, Heaven will take pity on me.

The aria is one of the most beautiful which Mozart ever wrote, but the words are of an appalling banality and make Donna Anna very unsympathetic, now leading poor Don Ottavio on, now repulsing him. We felt, therefore, that we must forget the original text entirely and write something quite new. In a coloratura aria of this kind, it is wise to start with translating or reinventing the cabaletta which, like a cadenza, is written to provide the singer with the opportunity to display her vocal virtuosity in runs and range of pitch. This means that, whatever lines one writes, the key syllables must contain long open vowels, preferably ā, ēī and ǣ. Accordingly, the first line of the aria we composed was the last, after taking a hint from the *cielo* in the preceding line.

> On my dark His light shall break.

We then wrote a line to precede it and complete the cabaletta:

> God will surely wipe away thy tears, my daughter,
> On thy (my) dark His light shall break.

These lines suggested the idea that they might be some kind of message from Heaven, so that some lines, at least, of the cavatina would be concerned with where the message was coming from. We then remembered that, in the graveyard scene which immediately precedes it, Don Giovanni mentions that it is a cloudless night with a full moon, and that the supper scene which immediately follows it opens with the Don's hired musicians playing suitable supper music. These two facts suggested two ideas: (a) that Donna Anna might be gazing at the full moon, from which, so to speak, the message of her cabaletta would emanate and (b) effective use might be made of the Neoplatonic contrast between the music of the spheres which her "spiritual" ear catches from the moon and the carnal music of this world as represented by the supper music. The stage direction in the piano score we were using says *A darkened chamber*, but there seems to be nothing about the action which makes this necessary. Why shouldn't the chamber have an uncurtained open window through which the moon could be seen? Accordingly, we changed the stage direction and wrote the aria as follows:

RECIT. Disdain you? Hear me, my dearest! None can foretell what the rising sun may bring, a day of sorrow or a day of rejoicing. But, hear me! Remember, when the jealous misgivings of a lover beset you, all the stars shall fall down ere I forget you!

CAVATINA. Let yonder moon, chaste eye of heaven
    Cool desire and calm your soul;
    May the bright stars their patience lend you
    As their constellations roll,
    Turn, turn, turn about the Pole.
    Far, too far they seem from our dying,
    Cold we call them to our sighing;
    We, too, proud, too evil-minded,
    By sin are blinded.
    See, how bright the moon shines yonder,
    Silent witness to all our wrong:
    Ah! but hearken! O blessed wonder!
    Out of silence comes a music,
    And I can hear her song.
CABALETTA. "God will surely, surely, wipe away thy tears, my
      daughter,
    On thy dark His light shall break.
    God is watching thee, hath not forgotten thee,
    On thy dark His light shall break."
    God will heed me, sustain me, console me.
    On my dark His light shall break.

Anyone who attempts to translate from one tongue into another will know moods of despair when he feels he is wasting his time upon an impossible task but, irrespective of success or failure, the mere attempt can teach a writer much about his own language which he would find it hard to learn elsewhere. Nothing else can more naturally correct our tendency to take our own language for granted. Translating compels us to notice its idiosyncrasies and limitations, it makes us more attentive to the sound of what we write and, at the same time, if we are inclined to fall into it, will cure us of the heresy that poetry is a kind of music in which the relations of vowels and consonants have an absolute value, irrespective of the meaning of the words.

Music in Shakespeare

Musick to heare, why hear'st thou musick sadly,
Sweets with sweets warre not, joy delights in joy:
Why lov'st thou that which thou receav'st not gladly,
Or else receav'st with pleasure thine annoy?

Professor Wilson Knight and others have pointed out the important part played in Shakespeare's poetry by images related to music, showing, for instance, how music occupies the place in the cluster of good symbols which is held in the bad cluster by the symbol of the Storm.

His fondness for musical images does not, of course, necessarily indicate that Shakespeare himself was musical—some very good poets have been musically tone deaf. Any poet of the period who used a musical imagery would have attached the same associations to it, for they were part of the current Renaissance theory of the nature of music and its effects.

Anyone at the time, if asked, "What is music?" would have given the answer stated by Lorenzo to Jessica in the last scene of *The Merchant of Venice*. Mr James Hutton in an admirable article in the *English Miscellany* on "Some English Poems in praise of Music" has traced the history of this theory from Pythagoras to Ficino and shown the origin of most of Lorenzo's images. The theory may be summarized thus:

(1) Music is unique among the arts for it is the only art practiced in Heaven and by the unfallen creatures. Conversely, one of the most obvious characteristics of Hell is its discordant din.

(2) Human reason is able to infer that this heavenly music exists because it can recognize mathematical proportions. But the human ear cannot hear it, either because of man's Fall or simply because the ear is a bodily organ subject to change and death. What Campanella calls the *molino vivo* of the self drowns out the celestial sounds. In certain exceptional states of ecstasy, however, certain individuals have heard it.

(3) Man-made music, though inferior to the music which cannot be heard, is a good for, in its mortal way, it recalls or imitates the Divine order. In consequence, it has great powers. It can tame irrational and savage beasts, it can cure lunatics, it can relieve sorrow. A dislike of music is a sign of a perverse will that defiantly refuses to submit to the general harmony.

(4) Not all music, however, is good. There is a bad kind of music which corrupts and weakens. "The Devil rides a fiddlestick." Good is commonly associated with old music, bad with new.

Nobody today, I imagine, holds such a theory, i.e. nobody now thinks that the aesthetics of music have anything to do with the science of acoustics. What theory of painting, one wonders, would have developed if Pythagoras had owned a spectroscope and learned that color relations can also be expressed in mathematical proportions.

But if he has never heard of the theory, there are many things in Shakespeare which the playgoer will miss. For example, the dramatic effect of the recognition scene in *Pericles*.

PERICLES. But what music?
HELICANUS. My lord, I hear none.
PERICLES. None! The music of the spheres! List, my Marina!
LYSIMACHUS. It is not good to cross him: give him way.

PERICLES. Rarest sounds! Do ye not hear?
HELICANUS. My Lord, I hear.

(Act V, Scene 1)

or even such a simple little joke as this from *Othello*:

CLOWN. If you have any music that may not be heard, to't again;
    but, as they say, to hear music the general does not greatly care.
1ST MUS. We have none such, sir.

(Act III, Scene 1)

Music is not only an art with its own laws and values; it is also a social fact. Composing, performing, listening to music are things which human beings do under certain circumstances just as they fight and make love. Moreover, in the Elizabethan age, music was regarded as an important social fact. A knowledge of music, an ability to read a madrigal part were expected of an educated person, and the extraordinary output of airs and madrigals between 1588 and 1620 testifies to both the quantity and quality of the music making that must have gone on. When Bottom says, "I have a reasonable good ear in music: let's have the tongs and the bones," it is not so much an expression of taste as a revelation of class, like dropping one's aitches; and when Benedick says, "Well, a horn for my money when all's done," he is being deliberately *épatant*.

Whether he personally cared for music or not, any dramatist of the period could hardly have failed to notice the part played by music in human life, to observe, for instance, that the kind of music a person likes or dislikes, the kind of way in which he listens to it, the sort of occasion on which he wants to hear or make it, are revealing about his character.

A dramatist of a later age might notice the same facts, but it would be difficult for him to make dramatic use of them unless he were to write a play specifically about musicians.

But the dramatic conventions of the Elizabethan stage permitted and encouraged the introduction of songs and instrumental music into the spoken drama. Audiences liked to hear them, and the dramatist was expected to provide them. The average playgoer, no doubt, simply wanted a pretty song as part of the entertainment and did not bother about its dramatic relevance to the play as a whole. But a dramatist who took his art seriously had to say, either, "Musical numbers in a spoken play are irrelevant episodes and I refuse to put them in just to please the public," or, "I must conceive my play in such a manner that musical numbers, vocal or instrumental, can occur in it, not as episodes, but as essential elements in its structure."

If Shakespeare took this second line, it should be possible, on examining the occasions where he makes use of music, to find answers to the following questions:

(1) Why is this piece of music placed just where it is and not somewhere else?

(2) In the case of a song, why are the mood and the words of this song what they are? Why this song instead of another?

(3) Why is it this character who sings and not another? Does the song reveal something about this character which could not be revealed as well in any other way?

(4) What effect does this music have upon those who listen to it? Is it possible to say that, had the music been omitted, the behavior of the characters or the feelings of the audience would be different from what they are?

II

When we now speak of music as an art, we mean that the elements of tone and rhythm are used to create a structure of sounds which are to be listened to for their own sake. If it be asked what such music is "about," I do not think it too controversial to say that it presents a virtual image of our experience of living as temporal, with its double aspect of recurrence and becoming. To "get" such an image, the listener must for the time being banish from his mind all immediate desires and practical concerns and only think what he hears.

But rhythm and tone can also be used to achieve non-musical ends. For example, any form of physical movement, whether in work or play, which involves accurate repetition is made easier by sounded rhythmical beats, and the psychological effect of singing, whether in unison or in harmony, upon a group is one of reducing the sense of diversity and strengthening the sense of unity so that, on all occasions where such a unity of feeling is desired or desirable, music has an important function.

> If the true concord of well-tuned sounds
> By unions married do offend thine ear,
> They do but sweetly chide thee, who confounds
> In singleness the parts that thou shouldst bear.
> Mark how one string, sweet husband to another,
> Strikes each in each by mutual ordering;
> Resembling sire and child and happy mother,
> Who all in one, one pleasing note do sing;
> Whose speechless song, being many, seeming one,
> Sings this to thee, "Thou single wilt prove none."
>
> (Sonnet VIII)

The oddest example of music with an extramusical purpose is the lullaby. The immediate effect of the rocking rhythm and the melody is to fix the baby's attention upon an ordered pattern so that it forgets the distractions of arbitrary noises, but its final intention is to make the baby fall asleep, that is to say, to hear nothing at all.

Sounds, instrumental or vocal, which are used for social purposes, may of course have a musical value as well but this is usually secondary to their function. If one takes, say, a sea-shanty out of its proper context and listens to it on the gramophone as one might listen to a *lied* by Schubert, one is very soon bored. The beauty of sound which it may have been felt to possess when accompanied by the sensation of muscular movement and visual images of sea and sky cannot survive without them.

The great peculiarity of music as an art is that the sounds which comprise its medium can be produced in two ways, by playing on specially constructed instruments and by using the human vocal cords in a special way. Men use their vocal cords for speech, that is, to communicate with each other, but also, under certain conditions, a man may feel, as we say, "like singing." This impulse has little, if anything, to do with communication or with other people. Under the pressure of a certain mood, a man may feel the need to express that mood to himself by using his vocal cords in an exceptional way. If he should sing some actual song he has learned, he chooses it for its general fitness to his mood, not for its unique qualities.

None of the other arts seem suited to this immediate self-expression. A few poets may compose verses in their bath—I have never heard of anyone trying to paint in his bath—but almost everyone, at some time or other, has sung in his bath.

In no other art can one see so clearly a distinction, even a rivalry, between the desire for pattern and the desire for personal utterance, as is disclosed by the difference between instrumental and vocal music. I think I can see an analogous distinction in painting. To me, vocal music plays the part in music that the human nude plays in painting. In both there is an essential erotic element which is always in danger of being corrupted for sexual ends but need not be and, without this element of the erotic which the human voice and the nude have contributed, both arts would be a little lifeless.

In music it is from instruments that rhythmical and tonal precision and musical structure are mostly derived so that, without them, the voice would have remained tied to impromptu and personal expression. Singers, unchastened by the orchestral discipline, would soon lose interest in singing and wish only to show off their voices. On the other hand, the music of a dumb race who had invented instruments would be precise but dull, for the players would not know what it means to strive after expression, to make their instruments "sing." The kind of effect they would make is the kind we condemn in a pianist when we say: "He just plays the notes."

Lastly, because we do not have the voluntary control over our ears that we have over our eyes, and because musical sounds do not denote meanings like words or represent objects like lines and colors, it is far harder to know what a person means, harder even for himself to know, when he says, "I like this piece of music," than when he says, "I like this book or this picture." At one extreme there is the professional musician who not only thinks clearly and completely what he hears but also recognizes the means by which the composer causes him so to think. This does not mean that he can judge music any better than one without his technical knowledge who has trained himself to listen and is familiar with music of all kinds. His technical knowledge is an added pleasure, perhaps, but it is not itself a musical experience. At the other extreme is the student who keeps the radio playing while he studies because he finds that a background of sound makes it easier for him to concentrate on his work. In his case the music is serving the contradictory function of preventing him from listening to anything, either to itself or to the noises in the street.

Between these two extremes, there is a way of listening which has been well described by Susanne Langer.

> There is a twilight zone of musical enjoyment when tonal appreciation is woven into daydreaming. To the entirely uninitiated hearer it may be an aid in finding expressive forms at all, to extemporise an accompanying romance and let the music express feelings accounted for by its scenes. But to the competent it is a pitfall, because it obscures the full vital import of the music, noting only what comes handy for a purpose, and noting only what expresses attitudes and emotions the listener was familiar with before. It bars everything new and really interesting in a world, since what does not fit the *petit roman* is passed over, and what does fit is the dreamer's own. Above all it leads attention, not only to the music, but away from it—via the music to something else that is essentially an indulgence. One may spend a whole evening in this sort of dream and carry nothing away from it, no musical insight, no new feeling, and actually nothing heard. (*Feeling and Form*, Chap. X)

It is this kind of listening, surely, which is implied by the Duke in *Twelfth Night*, "If music be the food of love, play on," and by Cleopatra, "Give me some music—music, moody food / Of us that trade in love," and which provoked that great music-lover, Bernard Shaw, to the remark, "Music is the brandy of the damned."

III

Shakespeare uses instrumental music for two purposes: on socially appropriate occasions, to represent the voice of this world, of collective rejoicing as in a dance, or of mourning as in a dead march and, unexpectedly, as an auditory image of a supernatural or magical world. In the last case the music generally carries the stage direction, "Solemn."

It may be directly the voice of Heaven, the music of the spheres heard by Pericles, the music under the earth heard by Antony's soldiers, the music which accompanies Queen Katharine's vision, or it may be commanded, either by spirits of the intermediate world like Oberon or Ariel, or by wise men like Prospero and the physicians in *King Lear* and *Pericles*, to exert a magical influence on human beings. When doctors order music, it is, of course, made by human musicians, and to the healthy it may even sound "rough and woeful," but in the ears of the patient, mad Lear or unconscious Thaisa, it seems a platonic imitation of the unheard celestial music and has a curative effect.

"Solemn" music is generally played off stage. It comes, that is, from an invisible source which makes it impossible for those on stage to express a *voluntary* reaction to it. Either they cannot hear it or it has effects upon them which they cannot control. Thus, in Act II, Scene 1 of *The Tempest*, it is an indication of their villainy, the lack of music in their souls, that Antonio and Sebastian are not affected by the sleeping-spell music when Alonso and the others are, an indication which is forthwith confirmed when they use the opportunity so created to plan Alonso's murder.

On some occasions, e.g. in the vision of Posthumus (*Cymbeline*, Act V, Scene 4), Shakespeare has lines spoken against an instrumental musical background. The effect of this is to depersonalize the speaker, for the sound of the music blots out the individual timbre of his voice. What he says to music seems not *his* statement but a message, a statement that has to be made.

Antony and Cleopatra (Act IV, Scene 3) is a good example of the dramatic skill with which Shakespeare places a supernatural musical announcement. In the first scene of the act we have had a glimpse of the cold, calculating Octavius refusing Antony's old-fashioned challenge to personal combat and deciding to give battle next day. To Octavius, chivalry is one aspect of a childish lack of self-control and "Poor Antony" is his contemptuous comment on his opponent. Whereupon we are shown Antony talking to his friends in a wrought-up state of self-dramatization and self-pity:

> Give me thy hand,
> Thou hast been rightly honest; so hast thou;
> Thou—and thou—and thou; you have serv'd me well. . . .
> Perchance to-morrow
> You'll serve another master. I look on you
> As one that takes his leave. Mine honest friends,
> I turn you not away; but like a master
> Married to your good service, stay till death:
> Tend me to-night two hours, I ask no more,
> And the gods yield you for't.

We already know that Enobarbus, who is present, has decided to desert Antony. Now follows the scene with the common soldiers in which supernatural music announces that

> the god Hercules whom Antony lov'd
> Now leaves him.

The effect of this is to make us see the human characters, Octavius, Antony, Cleopatra, Enobarbus, as agents of powers greater than they. Their personalities and actions, moral or immoral, carry out the purposes of these powers but cannot change them. Octavius' self-confidence and Antony's sense of doom are justified though they do not know why.

But in the ensuing five scenes it appears that they were both mistaken, for it is Antony who wins the battle. Neither Octavius nor Antony have heard the music, but we, the audience, have, and our knowledge that Antony must lose in the end gives a pathos to his temporary triumph which would be lacking if the invisible music were cut.

Of the instances of mundane or carnal instrumental music in the plays, the most interesting are those in which it is, as it were, the wrong kind of magic Those who like it and call for it use it to strengthen their illusions about themselves.

So Timon uses it when he gives his great banquet. Music stands for the imaginary world Timon is trying to live in, where everybody loves everybody and he stands at the center as the source of this universal love.

TIMON. Music, make their welcome!
FIRST LORD. You see, my lord, how ample y'are beloved.
(Timon of Athens, Act I, Scene 2)

One of his guests is the professional sneerer, Apemantus, whose conceit is that he is the only one who sees the world as it really is, as the absolutely unmusical place where nobody loves anybody but himself. "Nay," says Timon to him, "an you begin to rail on society once, I am sworn not to give regard to you. Farewell, and come with better music."

But Timon is never to hear music again after this scene.

Neither Timon nor Apemantus have music in their souls but, while Apemantus is shamelessly proud of this, Timon wants desperately to believe that he has music in his soul, and the discovery that he has not destroys him.

To Falstaff, music, like sack, is an aid to sustaining the illusion of living in an Eden of childlike innocence where nothing serious can happen. Unlike Timon, who does not love others as much as he likes to think, Falstaff himself really is loving. His chief illusion is that Prince Hal loves him as much as he loves Prince Hal and that Prince Hal is an innocent child like himself.

Shakespeare reserves the use of a musical background for the scene between Falstaff, Doll, Poinz, and Hal (Henry IV, Part II, Act II, Scene 4). While the music lasts, Time will stand still for Falstaff. He will not grow older, he will not have to pay his debts, Prince Hal will remain his dream-son and boon companion. But the music is interrupted by the realities of time with the arrival of Peto. Hal feels ashamed.

> By heaven, Poinz, I feel me much to blame
> So idly to profane the present time. . . .
> Give me my sword and cloak. Falstaff, good-night!

Falstaff only feels disappointed:

> Now comes in the sweetest morsel of the night, and we must hence, and
> leave it unpick'd.

In Prince Hal's life this moment is the turning point; from now on he will
become the responsible ruler. Falstaff will not change because he is incapable of change but, at this moment, though he is unaware of it, the most important thing in his life, his friendship with Hal, ceases with the words
"Good-night." When they meet again, the first words Falstaff will hear are—
"I know thee not, old man."

Since music, the virtual image of time, takes actual time to perform, listening to music can be a waste of time, especially for those, like kings, whose
primary concern should be with the unheard music of justice.

> Ha! Ha! keep time! How sour sweet music is
> When time is broke and no proportion kept!
> So is it in the music of men's lives.
> And here have I the daintiness of ear
> To check time broke in a disordered string;
> But, for the concord of my time and state,
> Had not an ear to hear my true time broke.
>
> (*Richard II*, Act V, Scene 5)

IV

We find two kinds of songs in Shakespeare's plays, the called-for and the
impromptu, and they serve different dramatic purposes.

A called-for song is a song which is sung by one character at the request of
another who wishes to hear music, so that action and speech are halted until
the song is over. Nobody is asked to sing unless it is believed that he can sing
well and, little as we may know about the music which was actually used in
performances of Shakespeare, we may safely assume from the contemporary
songs which we do possess that they must have made demands which only a
good voice and a good musician could satisfy.

On the stage, this means that the character called upon to sing ceases to
be himself and becomes a performer; the audience is not interested in him
but in the quality of his singing. The songs, it must be remembered, are interludes embedded in a play written in verse or prose which is spoken; they
are not arias in an opera where the dramatic medium is itself song, so that
we forget that the singers are performers just as we forget that the actor
speaking blank verse is an actor.

An Elizabethan theatrical company, giving plays in which such songs occur, would have to engage at least one person for his musical rather than his histrionic talents. If they had not been needed to sing, the dramatic action in *Much Ado, As You Like It* and *Twelfth Night* could have got along quite well without Balthazar, Amiens and the Clown.

Yet, minor character though the singer may be, he has a character as a professional musician and, when he gets the chance, Shakespeare draws our attention to it. He notices the mock or polite modesty of the singer who is certain of his talents.

> DON PEDRO. Come, Balthazar, we'll hear that song again.
> BALTHAZAR. O good my lord, tax not so bad a voice
> To slander music any more than once.
> DON PEDRO. It is the witness still of excellency
> To put a strange face on his own perfection.

He marks the annoyance of the professional who must sing for another's pleasure whether he feels like it or not.

> JAQUES. More, I prithee, more.
> AMIENS. My voice is ragged: I know I cannot please you.
> JAQUES. I do not desire you to please me: I desire you to sing. Will you sing?
> AMIENS. More at your request than to please myself.

In the dialogue between Peter and the musicians in *Romeo and Juliet*, Act IV, Scene 4, he contrasts the lives and motives of ill-paid musicians with that of their rich patrons. The musicians have been hired by the Capulets to play at Juliet's marriage to Paris. Their lives mean nothing to the Capulets; they are things which make music: the lives of the Capulets mean nothing to the musicians; they are things which pay money. The musicians arrive only to learn that Juliet is believed to be dead and the wedding is off. Juliet's life means nothing to them, but her death means a lot; they will not get paid. Whether either the Capulets or the musicians actually like music is left in doubt. Music is something you have to have at a wedding; music is something you have to play if that is your job. With a felicitous irony Shakespeare introduces a quotation from Richard Edwardes' poem, "In Commendation of Musick."

> PETER.   *When griping grief the heart doth wound*
> *And doleful dumps the mind oppress*
> *Then music with her silver sound—*
> Why "silver sound"? Why "music with her silver sound"?
> What say you, Simon Catling?
> 1ST MUS. Marry, sir, because silver hath a sweet sound.
> PETER. Pretty! What say you, Hugh Rebeck?
> 2ND MUS. I say, "silver sound," because musicians sound for silver.
> (*Romeo and Juliet*, Act IV, Scene 5)

The powers the poet attributes to music are exaggerated. It cannot remove the grief of losing a daughter or the pangs of an empty belly.

Since action must cease while a called-for song is heard, such a song, if it is not to be an irrelevant interlude, must be placed at a point where the characters have both a motive for wanting one and leisure to hear it. Consequently we find few called-for songs in the tragedies, where the steady advance of the hero to his doom must not be interrupted, or in the historical plays in which the characters are men of action with no leisure.

Further, it is rare that a character listens to a song for its own sake since, when someone listens to music properly, he forgets himself and others which, on the stage, means that he forgets all about the play. Indeed, I can only think of one case where it seems certain that a character listens to a song as a song should be listened to, instead of as a stimulus to a *petit roman* of his own, and that is in *Henry VIII*, Act III, Scene 1, when Katharine listens to *Orpheus with his lute*. The Queen knows that the King wants to divorce her and that pressure will be brought upon her to acquiesce. But she believes that it is her religious duty to refuse, whatever the consequences. For the moment there is nothing she can do but wait. And her circumstances are too serious and painful to allow her to pass the time daydreaming:

> Take thy lute, wench; my soul grows sad with troubles;
> Sing and disperse them, if thou canst; leave working.

The words of the song which follows are not about any human feelings, pleasant or unpleasant, which might have some bearing on her situation. The song, like Edwardes' poem, is an *encomium musicae*. Music cannot, of course, cure grief, as the song claims, but in so far that she is able to attend to it and nothing else, she can forget her situation while the music lasts.

An interesting contrast to this is provided by a scene which at first seems very similar, Act IV, Scene 1 of *Measure for Measure*. Here, too, we have an unhappy woman listening to a song. But Mariana, unlike Katharine, is not trying to forget her unhappiness; she is indulging it. Being the deserted lady has become a role. The words of the song, *Take, O take, those lips away*, mirrors her situation exactly, and her apology to the Duke when he surprises her gives her away.

> I cry you mercy, sir; and well could wish
> You had not found me here so musical:
> Let me excuse me, and believe me so—
> My mirth it much displeased, but pleas'd my woe.

In his reply, the Duke, as is fitting in this, the most puritanical of Shakespeare's plays, states the puritanical case against the heard music of this world.

> 'Tis good; though music oft hath such a charm
> To make bad good, and good provoke to harm.

Were the Duke to extend this reply, one can be sure that he would speak of the unheard music of Justice.

On two occasions Shakespeare shows us music being used with conscious evil intent. In *The Two Gentlemen of Verona*, Proteus, who has been false to his friend, forsworn his vows to his girl and is cheating Thurio, serenades Silvia while his forsaken Julia listens. On his side, there is no question here of self-deception through music. Proteus knows exactly what he is doing. Through music which is itself beautiful and good, he hopes to do evil, to seduce Silvia.

Proteus is a weak character, not a wicked one. He is ashamed of what he is doing and, just as he knows the difference between good and evil in conduct, he knows the difference between music well and badly played.

HOST. How do you, man? the music likes you not?
JULIA. You mistake; the musician likes me not.
HOST. Why, my pretty youth?
JULIA. He plays false, father.
HOST. How? Out of tune on the strings?
JULIA. Not so; but yet so false that he grieves my very heart-strings . . .
HOST. I perceive you delight not in music.
JULIA. Not a whit, when it jars so.
HOST. Hark, what a fine change is in the music!
JULIA. Ay, that change is the spite.
HOST. You would have them always play but one thing?
JULIA. I would always have one play but one thing.
                                    (*Two Gentlemen of Verona*, Act IV, Scene 2)

The second occasion is in *Cymbeline*, when Cloten serenades Imogen. Cloten is a lost soul without conscience or shame. He is shown, therefore, as someone who does not know one note from another. He has been told that music acts on women as an erotic stimulus, and wishes for the most erotic music that money can buy:

First a very excellent, good, conceited thing; after, a wonderful sweet air, with admirable rich words to it, and then let her consider.

For, except as an erotic stimulus, music is, for him, worthless:

If this penetrate, I will consider your music the better; if it do not, it is a vice in her ears which horse-hairs and calves' guts, nor the voice of the unpaved eunuch to boot can never amend.
                                    (*Cymbeline*, Act II, Scene 3)

V

The called-for songs in *Much Ado About Nothing*, *As You Like It* and *Twelfth Night* illustrate Shakespeare's skill in making what might have been beautiful irrelevancies contribute to the dramatic structure.

Much Ado About Nothing

Act II, Scene 3.
SONG: Sigh no more, ladies.
AUDIENCE: Don Petro, Claudio, and Benedick (in hiding).

In the two preceding scenes we have learned of two plots, Don Pedro's plot to make Benedick fall in love with Beatrice, and Don John's plot to make Claudio believe that Hero, his wife-to-be, is unchaste. Since this is a comedy, we, the audience, know that all will come right in the end, that Beatrice and Benedick, Don Pedro and Hero will get happily married.

The two plots of which we have just learned, therefore, arouse two different kinds of suspense. If the plot against Benedick succeeds, we are one step nearer the goal; if the plot against Claudio succeeds, we are one step back.

At this point, between their planning and their execution, action is suspended, and we and the characters are made to listen to a song.

The scene opens with Benedick laughing at the thought of the lovesick Claudio and congratulating himself on being heart-whole, and he expresses their contrasted states in musical imagery.

> I have known him when there was no music in him, but the drum and the fife; and now had he rather hear the tabor and the pipe. . . . Is it not strange that sheeps' guts should hale souls out of men's bodies?—Well, a horn for my money when all's done.

We, of course, know that Benedick is not as heart-whole as he is trying to pretend. Beatrice and Benedick resist each other because, being both proud and intelligent, they do not wish to be the helpless slaves of emotion or, worse, to become what they have often observed in others, the victims of an imaginary passion. Yet whatever he may say against music, Benedick does not go away, but stays and listens.

Claudio, for his part, wishes to hear music because he is in a dreamy, lovesick state, and one can guess that his *petit roman* as he listens will be of himself as the ever-faithful swain, so that he will not notice that the mood and words of the song are in complete contrast to his daydream. For the song is actually about the irresponsibility of men and the folly of women taking them seriously, and recommends as an antidote good humor and common sense. If one imagines these sentiments being the expression of a character, the only character they suit is Beatrice.

> She is never sad but when she sleeps; and not even sad then; for I have heard my daughter say, she hath often dream'd of happiness and waked herself with laughing. She cannot endure hear tell of a husband. Leonato by no means: she mocks all her wooers out of suit.

I do not think it too far-fetched to imagine that the song arouses in Benedick's mind an image of Beatrice, the tenderness of which alarms him. The violence of his comment when the song is over is suspicious:

> I pray God, his bad voice bode no mischief! I had as lief have heard the night-raven, come what plague could have come after it.

And, of course, there *is* mischief brewing. Almost immediately he overhears the planned conversation of Claudio and Don Pedro, and it has its intended effect. The song may not have compelled his capitulation, but it has certainly softened him up.

More mischief comes to Claudio who, two scenes later, shows himself all too willing to believe Don John's slander before he has been shown even false evidence, and declares that, if it should prove true, he will shame Hero in public. Had his love for Hero been all he imagined it to be, he would have laughed in Don John's face and believed Hero's assertion of her innocence, despite apparent evidence to the contrary, as immediately as her cousin does. He falls into the trap set for him because as yet he is less a lover than a man in love with love. Hero is as yet more an image in his own mind than a real person, and such images are susceptible to every suggestion.

For Claudio, the song marks the moment when his pleasant illusions about himself as a lover are at their highest. Before he can really listen to music he must be cured of imaginary listening, and the cure lies through the disharmonious experiences of passion and guilt.

As You Like It

Act II, Scene 5.
SONG: Under the Greenwood Tree.
AUDIENCE: Jaques.

We have heard of Jaques before, but this is the first time we see him, and now we have been introduced to all the characters. We know that, unknown to each other, the three groups—Adam, Orlando; Rosalind, Celia, Touchstone; and the Duke's court—are about to meet. The stage is set for the interpersonal drama to begin.

Of Jaques we have been told that he is a man who is always in a state of critical negation, at odds with the world, ever prompt to strike a discordant note, a man, in fact, with no music in his soul. Yet, when we actually meet him, we find him listening with pleasure to a merry song. No wonder the Duke is surprised when he hears of it:

> If he, compact of jars, grows musical,
> We shall have shortly discord in the spheres.

The first two stanzas of the song are in praise of the pastoral life, an echo of the sentiments expressed earlier by the Duke:

> Hath not old custom made this life more sweet
> Than that of painted pomp? Are not these woods
> More free from peril than the envious court?

The refrain is a summons, *Come Hither*, which we know is being answered. But the characters are not gathering here because they wish to, but because they are all exiles and refugees. In praising the Simple Life, the Duke is a bit of a humbug, since he was compelled by force to take to it.

Jaques' extemporary verse which he speaks, not sings, satirizes the mood of the song.

> If it so pass
> That any man turn ass,
> Leaving his wealth and ease,
> A stubborn will to please,
> Ducdamé, ducdamé, ducdamé:
> Here shall he see
> Gross fools as he,
> An if he will come to me.

At the end of the play, however, Jaques is the only character who chooses to leave his wealth and ease—it is the critic of the pastoral sentiment who remains in the cave. But he does not do this his stubborn will to please, for the hint is given that he will go further and embrace the religious life. In Neoplatonic terms he is the most musical of them all for he is the only one whom the carnal music of this world cannot satisfy, because he desires to hear the unheard music of the spheres.

Act II, Scene 7.
SONG: Blow, blow, thou winter wind.
AUDIENCE: The Court, Orlando, Adam.

Orlando has just shown himself willing to risk his life for his faithful servant, Adam. Adam, old as he is, has given up everything to follow his master. Both were expecting hostility but have met instead with friendly kindness.

The Duke, confronted with someone who has suffered an injustice similar to his own, drops his pro-pastoral humbug and admits that, for him, exile to the forest of Arden is a suffering.

The song to which they now listen is about suffering, but about the one kind of suffering which none of those present has had to endure, ingratitude from a friend. The behavior of their brothers to the Duke and Orlando has been bad, but it cannot be called ingratitude, since neither Duke Frederick nor Oliver ever feigned friendship with them.

The effect of the song upon them, therefore, is a cheering one. Life may be hard, injustice may seem to triumph in the world, the future may be dark and uncertain, but personal loyalty and generosity exist and make such evils bearable.

Twelfth Night

I have always found the atmosphere of *Twelfth Night* a bit whiffy. I get the impression that Shakespeare wrote the play at a time when he was in no mood for comedy, but in a mood of puritanical aversion to all those pleasing illusions which men cherish and by which they lead their lives. The comic convention in which the play is set prevents him from giving direct expression to this mood, but the mood keeps disturbing, even spoiling, the comic feeling. One has a sense, and nowhere more strongly than in the songs, of there being inverted commas around the "fun." There is a kind of comedy, *A Midsummer Night's Dream* and *The Importance of Being Earnest* are good examples, which take place in Eden, the place of pure play where suffering is unknown. In Eden, Love means the "Fancy engendered in the eye." The heart has no place there, for it is a world ruled by wish not by will. In *A Midsummer Night's Dream* it does not really matter who marries whom in the end, provided that the adventures of the lovers form a beautiful pattern; and Titania's fancy for Bottom is not a serious illusion in contrast to reality, but an episode in a dream.

To introduce will and real feeling into Eden turns it into an ugly place, for its native inhabitants cannot tell the difference between play and earnest and in the presence of the earnest they appear frivolous in the bad sense. The trouble, to my mind, about *Twelfth Night* is that Viola and Antonio are strangers to the world which all the other characters inhabit. Viola's love for the Duke and Antonio's love for Sebastian are much too strong and real.

Against their reality, the Duke, who up till the moment of recognition has thought himself in love with Olivia, drops her like a hot potato and falls in love with Viola on the spot, and Sebastian, who accepts Olivia's proposal of marriage within two minutes of meeting her for the first time, appear contemptible, and it is impossible to believe that either will make a good husband. They give the impression of simply having abandoned one dream for another.

Taken by themselves, the songs in this play are among the most beautiful Shakespeare wrote and, read in an anthology, we hear them as the voice of Eden, as "pure" poetry. But in the contexts in which Shakespeare places them, they sound shocking.

Act II, Scene 3
SONG: O mistress mine, where are you roaming?
AUDIENCE: Sir Toby Belch, Sir Andrew Aguecheek.

Taken playfully, such lines as

> What's to come is still unsure:
> In delay there lies no plenty;

> Then come kiss me, sweet-and-twenty.
> Youth's a stuff will not endure

are charming enough, but suppose one asks, "For what kind of person would these lines be an expression of their true feelings?" True love certainly does not plead its cause by telling the beloved that love is transitory; and no young man, trying to seduce a girl, would mention her age. He takes her youth and his own for granted. Taken seriously, these lines are the voice of elderly lust, afraid of its own death. Shakespeare forces this awareness on our consciousness by making the audience to the song a couple of seedy old drunks.

Act II, Scene 4.

SONG: Come away, come away, death.

AUDIENCE: The Duke, Viola, courtiers.

Outside the pastures of Eden, no true lover talks of being slain by a fair, cruel maid, or weeps over his own grave. In real life, such reflections are the day-dreams of self-love which is never faithful to others.

Again, Shakespeare has so placed the song as to make it seem an expression of the Duke's real character. Beside him sits the disguised Viola, for whom the Duke is not a playful fancy but a serious passion. It would be painful enough for her if the man she loved really loved another, but it is much worse to be made to see that he only loves himself, and it is this insight which at this point Viola has to endure. In the dialogue about the difference between man's love and woman's which follows on the song, Viola is, I think, being anything but playful when she says:

> We men say more, swear more; but, indeed,
> Our vows are more than will; for still we prove
> Much in our vows, but little in our love.

VI

The impromptu singer stops speaking and breaks into song, not because anyone else has asked him to sing or is listening, but to relieve his feelings in a way that speech cannot do or to help him in some action. An impromptu song is not art but a form of personal behavior. It reveals, as the called-for song cannot, something about the singer. On the stage, therefore, it is generally desirable that a character who breaks into impromptu song should not have a good voice. No producer, for example, would seek to engage Madame Callas for the part of Ophelia, because the beauty of her voice would distract the audience's attention from the real dramatic point which is that Ophelia's songs are to the highest degree *not* called-for. We are meant to be horrified both by what she sings and by the fact that she sings at all. The other characters are affected but not in the way that people are affected by music. The

King is terrified, Laertes so outraged that he becomes willing to use dirty means to avenge his sister.

Generally, of course, the revelation made by an impromptu song is comic or pathetic rather than shocking. Thus the Gravedigger's song in *Hamlet* is, firstly, a labor song which helps to make the operation of digging go more smoothly and, secondly, an expression of the *galgenhumor* which suits his particular mystery.

Singing is one of Autolycus' occupations, so he may be allowed a good voice, but *When daffodils begin to peer* is an impromptu song. He sings as he walks because it makes walking more rhythmical and less tiring, and he sings to keep up his spirits. His is a tough life, with hunger and the gallows never very far away, and he needs all the courage he can muster.

One of the commonest and most deplorable effects of alcohol is its encouragement of the impromptu singer. It is not the least tribute one could pay to Shakespeare when one says that he manages to extract interest from this most trivial and boring of phenomena.

When Silence gets drunk in Shallow's orchard, the maximum pathos is got out of the scene. We know Silence is an old, timid, sad, poor, nice man, and we cannot believe that, even when he was young, he was ever a gay dog; yet, when he is drunk, it is of women, wine, and chivalry that he sings. Further, the drunker he gets, the feebler becomes his memory. The first time he sings, he manages to recall six lines, by the fifth time, he can only remember one:

> And Robin Hood, Scarlet, and John.

We are shown, not only the effect of alcohol on the imagination of a timid man, but also its effect on the brain of an old one.

Just as the called-for song can be used with conscious ill-intent, so the impromptu song can be feigned to counterfeit good fellowship.

The characters assembled on Pompey's galley at Misenum who sing *Come, thou monarch of the Vine*, are anything but pathetic; they are the lords of the world. The occasion is a feast to celebrate a reconciliation, but not one of them trusts the others an inch, and all would betray each other without scruple if it seemed to their advantage.

Pompey has indeed refused Menas' suggestion to murder his guests, but wishes that Menas had done it without telling him. The fact that Lepidus gets stinking and boasts of his power, reveals his inferiority to the others, and it is pretty clear that the Machiavellian Octavius is not quite as tight as he pretends.

Again, when Iago incites Cassio to drink and starts singing

> And let the can clink it

we know him to be cold sober, for one cannot imagine any mood of Iago's which he would express by singing. What he sings is pseudo-impromptu. He pretends to be expressing his mood, to be Cassio's buddy, but a buddy is something we know he could never be to anyone.

VII

Ariel's songs in *The Tempest* cannot be classified as either called-for or im-promptu, and this is one reason why the part is so hard to cast. A producer casting Balthazar needs a good professional singer; for Stephano, a come-dian who can make as raucous and unmusical a noise as possible. Neither is too difficult to find. But for Ariel he needs not only a boy with an unbroken voice but also one with a voice far above the standard required for the two pages who are to sing *It was a lover and his lass*.

For Ariel is neither a singer, that is to say, a human being whose vocal gifts provide him with a social function, nor a nonmusical person who in certain moods feels like singing. Ariel *is* song; when he is truly himself, he sings. The effect when he speaks is similar to that of *recitativo secco* in opera, which we listen to because we have to understand the action, though our real interest in the characters is only aroused when they start to sing. Yet Ariel is not an alien visitor from the world of opera who has wandered into a spoken drama by mistake. He cannot express any human feelings because he has none. The kind of voice he requires is exactly the kind that opera does not want, a voice which is as lacking in the personal and the erotic and as like an instru-ment as possible.

If Ariel's voice is peculiar, so is the effect that his songs have on others. Ferdinand listens to him in a very different way from that in which the Duke listens to *Come away, come away, death*, or Mariana to *Take, O take those lips away*. The effect on them was not to change them but to confirm the mood they were already in. The effect on Ferdinand of *Come unto these yellow sands* and *Full fathom five*, is more like the effect of instrumental music on Thaisa: direct, positive, magical.

Suppose Ariel, disguised as a musician, had approached Ferdinand as he sat on a bank, "weeping against the king my father's wrack," and offered to sing for him; Ferdinand would probably have replied, "Go away, this is no time for music"; he might possibly have asked for something beautiful and sad; he certainly would not have asked for *Come unto these yellow sands*.

As it is, the song comes to him as an utter surprise, and its effect is not to feed or please his grief, not to encourage him to sit brooding, but to allay his passion, so that he gets to his feet and follows the music. The song opens his present to expectation at a moment when he is in danger of closing it to all but recollection.

The second song is, formally, a dirge, and, since it refers to his father, seems more relevant to Ferdinand's situation than the first. But it has noth-ing to do with any emotions which a son might feel at his father's grave. As Ferdinand says, "This is no mortal business." It is a magic spell, the effect of which is, not to lessen his feeling of loss, but to change his attitude towards his grief from one of rebellion—"How could this bereavement happen to me?"—to one of awe and reverent acceptance. As long as a man refuses to accept whatever he suffers as given, without pretending he can understand why, the past from which it came into being is an obsession which makes him deny any value to the present. Thanks to the music, Ferdinand is able to accept the past, symbolized by his father, as past, and at once there stands before him his future, Miranda.

The Tempest is full of music of all kinds, yet it is not one of the plays in which, in a symbolic sense, harmony and concord finally triumph over dissonant disorder. The three romantic comedies which precede it, *Pericles, Cymbeline,* and *The Winter's Tale,* and which deal with similar themes, injustice, plots, separation, all end in a blaze of joy—the wrongers repent, the wronged forgive, the earthly music is a true reflection of the heavenly. *The Tempest* ends much more sourly. The only wrongdoer who expresses genuine repentance is Alonso; and what a world of difference there is between Cymbeline's "Pardon's the word to all," and Prospero's

> For you, most wicked sir, whom to call brother
> Would even infect my mouth, I do forgive
> Thy rankest fault—all of them; and require
> My dukedom of thee, which perforce I know
> Thou must restore.

Justice has triumphed over injustice, not because it is more harmonious, but because it commands superior force; one might even say because it is louder.

The wedding masque is peculiar and disturbing. Ferdinand and Miranda, who seem as virginal and innocent as any fairy story lovers, are first treated to a moral lecture on the danger of anticipating their marriage vows, and the theme of the masque itself is a plot by Venus to get them to do so. The masque is not allowed to finish, but is broken off suddenly by Prospero, who mutters of another plot, "that foul conspiracy of the beast Caliban and his confederates against my life." As an entertainment for a wedding couple, the masque can scarcely be said to have been a success.

Prospero is more like the Duke in *Measure for Measure* than any other Shakespearian character. The victory of Justice which he brings about seems rather a duty than a source of joy to himself.

> I'll bring you to your ship and so to Naples
> Where I have hope to see the nuptials
> Of these our dear-beloved solemnis'd
> And thence retire me to my Milan, where
> Every third thought shall be my grave.

The tone is not that of a man who, putting behind him the vanities of mundane music, would meditate like Queen Katharine "upon that celestial harmony I go to," but rather of one who longs for a place where silence shall be all.

APPENDICES

Creweian Orations

One of the duties of the Professor of Poetry at Oxford is to deliver on alternate years the Creweian Oration that commemorates benefactors to the university; on other years, the duty is performed by the Public Orator. The oration is delivered at Encaenia, the ceremony held in June on the Wednesday in the week after Trinity Term, at which honorary degrees are awarded. Until Roy Fuller became Professor in 1968, the Professor of Poetry delivered the oration in Latin; until 1971 the Public Orator did the same. Auden wrote his three orations in English; John G. Griffith, Tutor in Classics at Jesus College (later Professor and Public Orator), translated them into witty and allusive Latin prose interspersed with a few lines of Latin verse.

Griffith had performed the same service for Auden's friend Cecil Day-Lewis, who had preceded him in the Professorship. Griffith wrote in his own 1975 Creweian Oration: "In those years when it was the turn of the Professor of Poetry to give this speech, it was fascinating to observe the very different approaches of scholar-poets such as Day-Lewis and Wystan Auden to the problems of selecting and arranging the material, much of it quite unpoetic, with an eye to the demands of translation into Latin and to the needs of rhetoric in declaiming the final version. Thus the trouble spent on latinizing what was provided had some justification" (quoted in his *Oratiunculae Oxonienses Selectae*, 1985, p. iv).

Auden recited the Latin text at Encaenia, and joked to friends that he wondered whether Griffith might have given him absurdities and improprieties to speak which he could not understand. The Latin and English texts were printed on facing pages of pamphlets made available at the ceremony, and the English texts are reprinted below, followed by brief annotations. The Latin texts, but not the English, were also printed in the weekly *Oxford University Gazette.*

Auden makes several allusions refer to the procedures of Encaenia: in addition to the Creweian Oration, as many as nine honorary degrees are presented in the course of a single hour, and the event, which starts at noon, is followed by a luncheon at All Souls.

Auden wrote to Robert Graves, his successor as Professor, on 6 March 1961 about the structure of the lectures:

Many thanks for your letter of Feb 28th and the wire. Though you won't have to do the Creweian Oration this year—lucky you to get only two of them!—in case you don't know the conventional structure, it is as follows:

(1) Public events. (Royal visits, important changes of University policy, controversional issues like roads, etc.)

(2) Benefactions. The Registry keeps clippings of all of these, so you won't have any problem about collecting the information.

(3) Obits. Difficult when one is not a resident. You will probably have to ask someone in Oxford to keep a record and clippings for you.

(4) Retiring dons and new dons.

(5) Peroration consisting of fulsome flattery of the Vice-Chancellor.

As no doubt you know, you raise your cap at any mention of the Deity, semi-divine personages, i.e. the Queen, the Chancellor, the Vice-Chancellor, the Proctors,—and the dead.

I was the first ever to use Church Latin pronunciation and I shall be flattered if you did the same. After all, Church Latin is the only living Latin and besides, one can speak it much faster than the official Oxford dialect.

I am a pretty good bellower myself, but you will be Mr Gladstone if you can make yourself heard without aid.

I have not been able to learn what pronunciation Graves (who wrote his own Latin texts) used in his orations.

ORATIO CREWEIANA MCMLVI

Arrived but lately from a far shore, your orator must crave indulgence for deficiencies which his oration must of necessity exhibit. Distance may lend enchantment; it cannot give knowledge. Those felicitous allusions to family matters—a motor accident or a domestic animal—which have so often enlivened the speeches of his predecessors are denied him. Oxford has never courted vulgar publicity, and only at intervals does news of her doings reach those of her children who dwell *in partibus infidelium*. For some years, however, a menacing vehicular roar has been audible even on the other side of the Atlantic, and, lately, rising above it, the sounds of conflict, shrill battle-cries, and the clash of polemical pens have reached my ears and inflamed my passions. Biased, no doubt, by a nostalgic love for certain meadows, I profess myself willing to die for a tunnel.

There are occasions, too, when what Oxford does not court she cannot avoid. Never before, perhaps, in her long history, have the eyes and ears of the world been so turned in her direction as during the recent visit, after inspecting Harwell, of Messrs Bulganin and Krushchev.

You who were present know the facts: I only know what I could read in the Italian Press which has an unabashed passion for romantic fiction. Its account was strange indeed. It spoke of busts and pictures magically displaced; it hinted darkly at some startling welcome awaiting the distinguished statesmen in Christ Church, had not you, Mr Vice-Chancellor, by luck or foresight, diverted their steps in time; it claimed that the undergraduates had discovered in the lament of a darkie beside the Sewanee River an esoteric and prophetic meaning. It added, I am glad to say, that the guests maintained their composure admirably. Blessed is that City where *Homo Desipiens* dwells, for there neither bigotry nor hate shall enter! Blessed is that City where the irreverence and levity of youth are the custodians of its custodians!

Those with the power as well as the desire to give have, as in previous years, remembered us again, in affection and in faith.

I am sure you would have me first offer thanks to our Chancellor who has most kindly presented us with six eighteenth-century chairs for the use of honorands at degree ceremonies. As one would expect of a man who is both a scholar and a statesman, his gift combines good taste with common sense. Henceforth, distinguished strangers invited to Oxford to receive their honours need have no fear that, on arriving in this seat of learning, they will find no worthy seats.

That you, my Lord, beset by so many demands of greater immediacy, should find time to preside over this ceremony makes what is always a happy occasion an important one, and encourages your orator, making his maiden speech, by the hope that your presence today may be for him an auspicious omen.

Next I would speak of the moving donation by Mr and Mrs Henry Rissik Marshall to the Ashmolean Museum. Mr Marshall has given his entire collection of Old Worcester china and Mrs Marshall a valuable collection of glass and silver wine-labels in memory of their only child, Lieutenant William Somerville Marshall of the Scots Guards, who was killed in action during the last war. May the timeless beauty of these many things ever remind us of the greater glory of that quick and single sacrifice.

Theirs is not the only gift from which the Ashmolean has benefited. From two private donors, Mr A. D. Passmore and Mr H. E. Stapleton, it has received coins, British from the one, Indian from the other, and, thanks to the generosity of Prof. E.S.G. Robinson, the Pilgrim Trust, the Coulthurst Trust, and the National Art-Collections Fund, it is now in the position to purchase more of these small but lovely and instructive objects. Thanks again to the last of these bodies, those of us who derive a greater pleasure from painting will be able to enjoy some more pictures, among them an early drawing by Antoine Watteau and a panel painting of St Mark by Giovanni Antonio da Pesaro.

An American and a Canadian have enriched our libraries. To the Bodleian Mr James M. Osborn of Yale has given a precious manuscript, the life of Thomas Wythorne by his own hand, before whom, it is said, no Englishman ever wrote about himself; and a bequest by the late Professor Samuel Benjamin Slack of McGill will be greatly appreciated by users of the Taylorian Modern Language Library.

The Foundations, those great incorporated Princes, have displayed their customary munificence. Nuffield College is to complete its buildings and, by the liberality of the Ford Foundation, to acquire a Fellow in Comparative Politics, a subject which, even in our ignorance, we know concerns us all.

The same fortunate College has also received a grant from the Leverhulme Trust for a Fellowship in Industrial Relations. None but a disembodied and sullen humanist could envy the wealth of encouragement given the Science—or is it the Art?—of Medicine by the Lasker, Rockefeller, and Nuffield Foundations, the Lady Tata Memorial Trust, and the National Council to Combat Blindness. Who will not rejoice to learn, for example, that researches are to go forward upon tubercular meningitis, leukaemia, and cataract, nor pray that such efforts be crowned with success and a prevention or cure for these dread diseases found at last? Is it not also an excellent thing that, thanks to the Nuffield Provincial Hospitals Trust, our Social Medicine Unit is to get more equipment?

Nor have the other sciences been forgotten. Imperial Chemical Industries have remembered plant morphology and phototoxicity, and Monsanto Chemicals Physics; the B. P. Training Company has turned its thoughts to Geochemistry; the Rockefeller Foundation and Arthur Guinness & Co. are concerned for the future of X-ray Crystallography and Microbiological Chemistry respectively; the Pressed Steel Company continues to honour its late chairman by believing in Research; the Elmgrant Trustees are resolved that a gifted graduate from North America shall be privileged to study Agricultural Economics in our more temperate climate; Major H. W. Hall has earned the double gratitude of the Sciences and the Humanities by contributing towards the purchase of an optical spectrograph—a very expensive instrument it would seem—for use in the research laboratory for Archaeology and the History of Art. I do not know what kind of behaviour or whose is studied by the "Behavioural Sciences"—the words have a slightly sinister ring—but the Ford Foundation is going to encourage them. The Radcliffe Trustees have also aided scientists in general by a grant to the Radcliffe Science Library, especially acceptable now, when technical books cost so much.

Out of the estate of the late Mr Martin Wronker will come endowments for prizes in Medicine and Law. The prizewinners, if all else fails, will no doubt be able to write detective stories.

Two items remain which I must mention, one because I understand it, the other because I do not.

On its fiftieth anniversary, past and present members of the School of Forestry have subscribed to endow a prize. This I can understand. As a famous poem has it,

> Poems are made by fools like me,
> But only God can make a tree.

Who in these unsettled days would not love to study such harmless and sedentary lives? But there are also men, it seems, who recoil at nothing. The late Sir Arthur Pickard-Cambridge has left a considerable sum to the Arachnological Library. Like the heroine of another poem, at the mere thought of those dreadful creatures I am frightened away.

To each and all of these benefactors our lasting thanks.*

Each new year must ever bring its new litany of loss, nor, though it be a tribute to the excellence of her teaching, is it a consolation to know that, when Oxford mourns, she seldom mourns alone.

To the moving and knowledgeable tributes which the Chancellor has already paid two famous men, the Rt Hon. Leopold Charles Amery and Sir Dougal Orme Malcolm, it would be impertinent for me to add.

The Church has suffered greatly, with us, through the deaths of the Archbishop of York, the Rt Hon. and Most Rev. Cyril Garbett and the Rt Rev. Gerald Allen, Canon of Christ Church and former Bishop of Dorchester: like the Apostles, both served much of their ministry on foot.

Peterborough and with her the Merchant Taylors' School and Winchester College mourn the loss of the Rt Rev. Spencer Leeson; he did much to discover and encourage suitable candidates for Holy Orders.

With the passing of Sir Cyril Norwood, St John's has lost a former President, Bristol, Harrow, and Marlborough a former headmaster; all will remember with gratitude the strength and flexibility of his character, neither avid of novelty nor afraid of change.

Two distinguished agriculturalists are gone from us—Mr Charles Orwin and the president of the University Plough Club, Major G. D. Amery—and two figures famous in museum circles, Mr Sherwood Taylor, a man of vast and curious learning, and Mr Edward Leeds, long-time keeper of the Ashmolean.

The sad list continues. All Souls has lost Professor Leslie Brierly, Professor Alfred Radcliffe-Brown, and Mr Lionel Curtis; Balliol, Professor F. W. Thomas, an eminent Sanscritist, who died at the age of eighty-nine; St Catherine's Society its former Censor, Mr James Baker; Magdalen, Sir Arthur Tansley and Mr Sydney Plant.

Some deserve remembrance for their writings and discoveries, some for their influence upon the lives of others. Among the second I should like to mention Mr G. R. Brewis and Mr Giles Alington.

For thirty-two years Mr Brewis was Senior Tutor of St Edmund Hall; he lives in the affectionate memories of colleagues and generations of undergraduates. Mr Alington of University College died at an early age. It is never easy for two cultures to understand each other and never harder than when they share a common tongue. Great Britain and the United States owe as great a debt to Mr Alington for his patient and unobtrusive labours to replace prejudice and suspicion by tolerance and good humour as they owe to any who have enriched our Western civilization with more tangible monuments.

Latest but not least on the roll of the departed comes the name of Sir Max Beerbohm, equally beloved, as was Zuleika, his incomparable heroine, by our Established Mother and her dissenting Sister, and, so long as civil literature is read, immortal.

---

*This Oration includes those benefactions accepted on or before 26 June 1956.

Time brings us other and less bitter news. We are happy to congratulate the recipients of Her Majesty's Birthday honours; we rejoice in the Viscountcy conferred upon Lord Cherwell in recognition of his great abilities and of the advances in physics made by others under his wise direction; we are sorry that he ceases to be Professor after 37 years, and wish him many years of joy in his retirement. The choice of his successor has happily proved a simple one, and we welcome Sir Francis Simon, a leading authority on Low Temperature research in his place.

We are delighted that Harry Champion, Professor of Forestry, and Mr Basil Blackwell, most enlightened of booksellers, have become knights. The Bodleian Library itself is hardly more world-famous than that rival reading room in its vicinity where the student may consult the shelves and even smoke.

Among the six professors leaving us is Sir John Beazley who has put so many thousands of pots to the question and learned their inmost secrets. While enjoying his retirement we hope he remembers how much we should enjoy a reprint of his opuscula, especially *Herodotus at the Zoo.*

Exeter says a regretful farewell to its Rector, Mr E. A. Barber, while Keble welcomes a new Warden, the Rev. Eric Abbott, and the University Press Mr J.G.N. Brown as their London Publisher and Manager in succession to Mr Geoffrey Cumberlege. This year there will be no less than fifteen new Professors. Time forbids me to mention them all and I must confine myself to the new Chairs. Out of the North comes the learned flame of Professor Ian Richmond to enlighten us in the Archaeology of the Roman Empire; and the Chair of the History of Art is now occupied, I am delighted to see, by my friend and former colleague, Professor Edgar Wind. Those of you who have had the good fortune to hear him will have discovered that he is not only a prodigy of learning but also a virtuoso without rival of the lecturing art.

And now it is towards you, Mr Vice-Chancellor, that the thoughts of all here present are turned. We are happy to hear of the degree conferred upon you by the University of Pennsylvania while celebrating the two-hundred-and-fiftieth anniversary of the birth of Benjamin Franklin. How logical of Pennsylvania—to commemorate one wise man by honouring another!

I can but speak of you, alas, by hearsay, but, in this place where all tongues are quick and many sharp, what is said is soon heard. With one accord they tell of a man, learned without ostentation, dignified without pomp, humane and shrewd in all his dealings; they speak of him as a strong swimmer whom no current of controversy shall deflect nor tempestuous committee engulf. They wish you where you are, and they wish you well.

Auden delivered his first Creweian Oration on 20 June 1956. The opening paragraph alludes to the dispute over a proposal (later abandoned) to build a road through Christ Church Meadow.

The third paragraph alludes to the visit on 21 April 1956 by Soviet Premier Nikolai Bulganin and First Secretary Nikita Khrushchev to the Atomic Energy Establishment at Harwell and then to Oxford. At the Town Hall they were greeted by cheerfully raucous and insulting town-and-gown crowds (the pubs had closed for the afternoon shortly before), and a poster declared "Stalin for Prof". As they visited the Sheldonian, the crowds cheered and booed, and sang the Volga Boatmen's Song, but the visitors reacted with gestures of delighted satisfaction, like politicians on an election tour. Auden cites a report in the "Italian Press"; this was either an account derived from an editorial in the *Oxford Magazine*, 26 April 1956, or perhaps that editorial itself, misattributed by Auden to the Italian Press. The magazine reported of the Soviet visitors' arrival at the Hall of New College:

> Here the portrait of Bishop Waynflete [Founder of the College] was seen to be obscured by a Soviet poster of early post-war period . . . it featured, in the foreground and very large, Stalin. Above him floated, disembodied so to speak and somewhat smaller, Lenin. To Stalin's immediate right were Malenkov and Zhdanov, to his immediate left Beria and Molotov. Further back it was possible to descry the two principal Soviet visitors of the day.
>
> The Vice-Chancellor appeared to be surprised by this innovation in the décor, which the visitors inspected with much interest. . . . Turning, the Vice-Chancellor observed that a bust of himself at the other end of the hall (another example of the work of the bourgeois formalist rootless cosmopolitan Epstein) had been reversed on its pedestal, and now faced the wall. This seemed to make the score even, and the visitors took the point.

The magazine further reported that a visit to Christ Church was cancelled due to "the stifling embraces of the crowds in St Aldate's"; a thunderflash firework had earlier been set off at the foot of the steps leading to New College Hall. Auden's allusion to the Sewanee River seems to be a confusion between two songs by Stephen Foster. The *Oxford Magazine* editorial reported that the visitors, facing the crowds on Broad Street outside the Clarendon Building, "can hardly have failed to hear the ably-executed chant of undergraduate lament, 'Poor old Joe.'" Auden was recalling Foster's song "Old Folks at Home" ("Way down upon de Swanee ribber. . . . Oh! darkeys how my heart grows weary"), but the undergraduates apparently sang the refrain of another song by Foster, "Old Black Joe" ("Gone are the days when my heart was young and gay"), the refrain of which was originally not "Poor old Joe" but "Old Black Joe". (The undergraduates were alluding to Stalin, popularly known in Britain as "Uncle Joe".) *Desipiens* means witless.

The Vice-Chancellor of the University was Alic Halford Smith; the Chancellor was the Earl of Halifax.

ORATIO CREWEIANA MCMLVIII

Paraphrase

Since last Encaenia, Mr Vice-Chancellor, Oxford has been little in the news, and that, in itself, is good news. Much, of course, has happened elsewhere. The Polar regions have been added to the worries of insomniac Statesmen; the pyrotechnic arts have developed new subtleties; human artifacts have gate-crashed the august assembly of the Heavenly Bodies and, for a brief while, a tiny Dog-Star gazed down with animal incomprehension upon our sorry and conceited sphere. As one of our Oxford poets has written:

Luna hominum. . . .

Remote from, but not indifferent to these striking events, our academic life has remained what has come to be considered normal—the students many, the rooms few, the teachers overworked, underpaid, and harried by the demands of an insatiable Fisc. But the State, that modern Pharaoh, is still, it seems, not content. It would have us increase our enrolment yet further and at the same time is resolved to reduce its subventions. "Your labours", it cries, "shall be more, your moolah less!"

Let Pharaoh, however, beware lest, one fine morning, this seat of learning present a picture with which seats of industry are already familiar. The tutor's oak sported, the lecturer's dais vacant, pickets around Bodley, and hapless Youth condemned to sloth or folly, uninstructed, unexamined, unprogged, un-degreed. The decision, Mr Vice-Chancellor, rests with you: you have but to issue the call, and out we shall loyally come.

But let us turn to more cheerful matters. In the last few weeks we have been honoured by a flying visit from H.R.H. Prince Philip, Duke of Edinburgh, who so graciously descended on us for the official opening of Nuffield College and to present a charter of incorporation to St Edmund Hall. It is not these colleges only but the entire University who will rejoice at these acts of kindness from His Royal Highness, whose intelligent and untiring concern for the problems of teaching and learning have put this nation in his debt.

We still have many friends, as willing as ever to offer tangible proofs of their affection.

The sins of the Headington quarrymen, visited upon our fabric from generation to generation with cumulative severity, have brought us to the point where we must confess that we have no power of ourselves to help ourselves. And how nobly and generously from every quarter and from all sorts and conditions of men has our cry for help been heeded! The total sum required is enormous and we still have some way to go, but we are in sight of success. Conspicuous among the multitude of donors who have come to our rescue are the Pilgrim Trust, the Rhodes Trustees, the Dulverton Trust, and the Ford Foundation. In expressing our gratitude to them, let it not be thought that we are unmindful of all the others, in particular of individual graduates, some of whom may have made their contributions at great personal sacrifice.

Oscar Wilde observed that twenty years of romance make a woman look like a ruin and twenty years of marriage make her look like a public building. Thanks to our friends, we can now with confidence foresee the day when the raddled old harridan whom we have all so passionately loved will be rehabilitated and transformed into a respectable spouse whom we shall probably take for granted.

Other problems beset us. How are we to win the Battle of the Bulge? How are we to do our duty by the country in training the scientists so urgently needed? Thanks to a princely gift from the Mullard Company there are now plans in an advanced state for a new college in which half the undergraduates are to be either scientists, mathematicians, or engineers. The remainder are presumably to be allowed to study other subjects, but one will be curious to learn whether any will have the nerve.

Other friends, old and new, continue to support us in one or other of the multifarious branches of science, all of which it is the function of a university to study.*

Thanks to the generosity of Mr Isaac Wolfson, the importance of Metallurgy has at last been recognized with the dignity of an academic Chair. And high time too! But for this study where should we be? Still slaying each other with sticks and stones. Seriously though, this is a well-timed gift, for the first skyscraper soon to arise in the new "Keble Triangle" will be that devoted to Metallurgy. When the practitioners of that study are established on the tenth story, we shall at last know the truth about the "brazen heaven" the ancients spoke of. Furthermore the first occupant of this new Chair will be Mr William Hume-Rothery, a man of high distinction in this field, to whom we offer congratulations and all good wishes.

Research Fellowships in Physics will be maintained by the English Electric Co., Metropolitan Vickers Ltd, and the British Thomson-Houston Company, while Messrs Albright and Wilson will assist a research chemist. Time precludes the Latinization of the names of all those in whose debt we stand; those concerned with acetylene, organo-metallic compounds, and geochemistry are recorded in a footnote. On behalf of the Engineers, however, I name here the British Non-Ferrous Metals Research Association to thank them for a grant towards the further study of metals, the MacFarlane Engineering Company for two generators, and Associated Electrical Industries for some valuable micro-wave and other electrical apparatus.

Man may be the Lord of the Earth, but he would starve if it were not for the humble vegetable, and even the most impassioned carnivore among us will feel grateful to the Leverhulme Trust for fostering the study of environment and plant growth and to Messrs Fisons Ltd. for their concern with soil-plant relations, and also towards the Forestry Commission for its contribution towards the purchase of a Beckman spectrophotometer.

Man is mortal, but that is no reason why he should die earlier and in greater pain than his knowledge could prevent. The Nuffield Foundation, ever solicitous in such matters, is furthering the attack on that particularly cruel and stubborn disease, disseminated arterio-sclerosis, while Mr Curtis

---

*It has not been possible to include references to benefactions accepted after Gazette No. 2965 of 8 May 1958.

Cannon and the Trustees of the estate of Mrs Lucy Wood are encouraging the cause of Social Medicine and Medicine generally.

Merchandizing, we are happy to say, is no longer regarded as an occupation suitable only for metics. The Nuffield Foundation has made a donation for statistical research on the distributive trades, and the Institute of Transport has decided to establish a Readership and at least two Research Fellowships for the disinterested study of transport problems. A munificent gift, but one cannot help wondering whether the choice of location for such a study is altogether wise; to believe that a man can live for any length of time in this city and retain a disinterested attitude towards transport is, surely, to overestimate the powers of the human will.

Alas, in a fallen world science provides more opportunities for sin than cures, and we must still rely largely upon that ancient remedy, the Law. The University has long been in need of a Law Library and benefactors have now come forward to help us to erect one. The Rockefeller Foundation and the Calouste Gulbenkian Foundation are willing to contribute handsome sums, the one for the building itself, the other for lecture-room accommodation, on condition that we are able to raise the rest of the money required in the course of the next two years.

Indeed no University can maintain a high intellectual standard for long unless its museums and libraries are more than adequate. The Bodleian Library has the Trustees of the International Law Fund to thank for a grant with which to purchase law books, the late Miss E.D.M. Winters for a bequest to be used at the discretion of the Curators, Messrs Lionel and Philip Robinson for the personal papers of Sir Thomas Phillips, Mr Esmond de Beer for assisting in the enlargement of its John Locke collection, Mr Bertram Shuttleworth for a number of books by Richard Brinsley Sheridan, Mr Stephen Murray and Mrs Rosalind Toynbee for the letters and papers of the late Professor Gilbert Murray, a gift which will touch the hearts of all Oxonians as well as delight their minds. The binding needs of the Grenfell and Hunt papyrological library have been relieved by the kindness of Mrs A. S. Hunt.

I next mention a somewhat romantic gift—a collection of old scientific instruments donated to the Museum of the History of Science by Mr J. A. Billmeir. It includes fifty astrolabes, nocturnals, armillary spheres, and a fifteenth-century brass equatorium of the utmost rarity. If some wealthy eccentric should see fit to endow a Chair of Astrology, the professor on his appointment will find the apparatus awaiting him.

Thoughtful donors have also enriched the Ashmolean Museum. With the help of the National Arts Collection it has acquired another picture, the Dead Christ supported by Two Angels painted by Roderigo de Osana the Younger, and an exceptionally fine Roman engraved glass bowl. Mr H. E. Stapleton of St John's College and the E.S.G. Robinson Fund have added to its store of Greek and Asiatic coins; Sir Herbert Ingram, not content with his great generosity in the past, has considerately provided money for the upkeep of his collection; the late Principal of Brasenose College, H. M. Last, has left the Museum many valuable offprints and pamphlets, while Mrs J. M. Hanbury has presented a collection of rare gold and enamel snuff-boxes in memory of her son, John Mackenzie Hanbury of Pembroke College, killed in action early in the last war, a gift which to receive is an honour beyond speech.

Universities are generally thought of as receivers rather than as dispensers of charity, but the late Mrs Ellen ffennell knew better, for she has bequeathed a very substantial sum to facilitate the development of the University's activities on the Wytham Estate. To her and all who have remembered us, our heartfelt thanks.

In paying homage on behalf of the University to those members who have died during the year, your orator is only too conscious at every name he utters that, for someone in this audience, he is speaking of a personal friend. He can but ask you to supply from your own memories and affections all that is lacking in the frigid brevity of an official tribute.

Though the last years of his life were spent elsewhere, neither Trinity College nor the University have ever forgotten Monsignor Ronald Knox or thought of him with anything but pride and joy. Dazzlingly gifted, he triumphed at everything to which he set his hand, were it a satire, an epigram, translating the Bible, or preaching to a Girl's School. But the primary impression he made on those who met him, whatever their religious beliefs, was not so much, I think, of a gifted man as of a holy one.

The sudden death of Viscount Cherwell, ascetic, dandy, and V.I.P., was felt in more exalted and mundane circles than ours, but not more keenly. Many may have disagreed with his political views but none ever doubted his integrity in holding them or failed to recognize how much the University owed to him for his enthusiasm in promoting the study of the physical sciences. The senior members of Christ Church will long remember his devotion to that College, and its undergraduates his unfailing courtesy to the young, however tiresome and brash.

Another figure well known in the world was the former Montague Burton Professor of International Relations, Sir Alfred Zimmern. In the many posts he held and as one of the inspirers of Chatham House he devoted his life to the cause of comity between the nations and through all the disasters of this century resolutely maintained his faith in liberal principles.

Those in Oxford who study Chemistry and those everywhere who appreciate the beauties of Worcester china will regret the passing of C. W. Dyson Perrins.

Among Classical scholars our losses have been particularly severe. The long familiar figure of Cyril Bailey is no more with us. He was one of the last, perhaps, of that long line of humanists to whom the Classics were not merely the fascinating creations of a vanished civilization, but rather an inspiration to a decent way of life. One of Hitler's most valuable gifts to us was Paul Jacobsthal, and we can legitimately take pride in the fact that it was in his exile at Christ Church that he was able to write his great works on Early Celtic Art and on Greek Pins. St John's College, Brasenose, and Roman Studies have lost H. M. Last, as meticulous a scholar as he was an accurate shot. The memory of H. L. Drake will linger for a long time in Pembroke College as one who was selflessly devoted to its affairs and ever hospitable to its guests: his passionate concern for the quality of its port was a trait as admirable as it is rare.

T. D. Weldon will be missed in philosophical circles and in Magdalen, where he was a leader of the Young Turks who were responsible for raising the scholastic status of that College to its present eminence.

Two Modern Historians are gone from us: Dr Cecilia Ady, formerly of St Hugh's, and Richard Pares of All Souls. Dr Ady was distinguished alike for her studies of Italy in the Middle Ages and the Renaissance and for devout but unbigoted loyalty to the Anglican Church. Richard Pares, who died at a relatively early age after years of illness bravely borne, impressed us all by the formidable acumen of his intellect and his singular grace of person and he will be greatly missed.

Two renowned and revered Jurists are dead: R. W. Lee, the Rhodes Professor of Roman-Dutch Law, and Francis de Zulueta, Regius Professor of Civil Law. Professor Lee was as famous as a teacher as he was as a scholar; Professor de Zulueta combined the precise erudition of a true Oxford don with the pride and passion of a Spanish grandee.

Among the philologists of his time none was better known or more loved than Sir William Craigie, and by Icelandic fishermen no less than by those who shared his interest in the Teutonic languages.

His former students will not soon forget how much they owe in their comprehension of French literature to the rigour of textual examination and the originality of critical judgement displayed by the late Marshall Foch Professor, Gustave Rudler.

Jesus College mourns the loss of D. L. Chapman, who for many years both as a teacher and as an investigator into the theory of detonation showed himself a man absorbed in the pursuit of truth to the utter exclusion of all self-interest.

Finally both the Bodleian Library and the University Press have cause for sadness, the former on account of Strickland Gibson whose knowledge of bindings and of Oxford antiquities was unrivalled, the latter because of W. H. Wheeler who maintained its great tradition as a printer of Bibles and Prayer Books and who was largely responsible for those delightful and instructive annuals, the University Almanack and University Pocket Diary.

The number of those leaving and joining us this year is small but select.

The Warden of New College will shortly lay down his office: his personal charm went with a characteristic vigour with which he handled both College and University business as well as the duties of Vice-Chancellor. Two years ago I paid my tribute to him as Vice-Chancellor, and refrain from adding to what I said then; his achievements are his own commendation. In his place the College has selected Sir William Hayter, Her Majesty's Ambassador to Moscow; we welcome him very warmly on his return to his old College where not so long ago two heads of the State to which he has been accredited were received with a certain undergraduate hilarity.

Since he will be absent from Oxford when he officially leaves us, I am sure you would have me take this occasion to mention Canon Hodgson who will be retiring from the Regius Chair of Divinity at the end of next Term. Famous and admired on two continents as a theologian, his learning is matched by a courtesy of manner and charity of spirit for which those who serve the Queen of the Sciences have not always been celebrated. To our good wishes I have no doubt that the shade of Nestorius is at this moment adding his own, found innocent at last, thanks to the researches of Canon Hodgson, of the Nestorian heresy.

Professor Alfred Ewart is retiring from the Chair of Romance Languages. His absence will be felt not only by his pupils but also in the many Committees to which his goodwill and common sense have contributed so much. His place will be taken by Mr T. V. Reid, whom we are as happy to acquire as Manchester University must be sorry to lose.

A fitting tribute to another Fellow of Trinity, our revered Public Orator, Mr T. F. Higham, could only be written and delivered by himself. To him Latin has ever been, not the dead language once spoken by a severely practical people, but of all living tongues the one most sacred to the Muses. For many years he has made every public occasion at which he assisted a literary event with his curious wit and felicity of phrase, but today, alas, he must endure the ordeal of hearing his valediction spoken by one who, like the Pythian Priestess in her trance, utters he knows not what. We wish him many leisured and happy years to come and hope that he may continue to add new finds to his singular and exquisitely beautiful collection of objects made from sea-shells.

For our consolation and his, Providence and Worcester College have begotten an Elisha upon whom his mantle may becomingly fall, Mr A. N. Bryan-Brown.

Future historians of the University may well refer to the years 1930–58 as the Veale Era. For it was Sir Douglas Veale who with his knowing brain and skilful fingers took apart the rusty, creaking, ramshackle eighteenth-century administrative engine which he inherited when he assumed the office of Registrar and rebuilt it into the smoothly running high-powered contemporary dynamo which he now hands over to his fortunate successor, Sir Folliott Sandford.

H.M. the Queen has recently conferred Knighthoods upon Keith Grahame Feiling, formerly Chichele Professor of Modern History, and Thomas

Armstrong, formerly organist at Christ Church and Choragus of the University; we congratulate them both upon an honour which they so well merit.

And now it is with the liveliest pleasure that we conclude this survey of the past year with a word of thanks to you, Mr Vice-Chancellor. The character we look for in all who hold your high office is synonymous with the name you bear and how shall I better express our sense of good fortune than by saying that this identity seems providential? Whatever problems beset you, we know that you will dispose of them with the dexterity of a Cricketer. Future Vice-Chancellors shall bless your name as that of the man who, by shortening their period of tenure, reduced the risk of their developing ulcers. Long may you continue to teach the Senators on both sides of the Atlantic the wisdom of which they so sorely stand in need. And please, we implore you, provide us soon with more corpses: our appetite for blood is insatiable. Which reminds me that we are hungry in a more literal sense and the cooks of All Souls must be fuming. Dixi: vale et valete.

Auden delivered this, his second Creweian Oration, on 25 June 1958. The opening paragraph alludes to Laika, the dog sent into orbit in November 1957 in a Soviet space satellite in which she soon died. The words "*Luna hominum*" in the English text refer to verses in the Latin text, evidently written by Griffith:

> Luna hominum quae facta manu complecteris orbem
>   circuitu duplici tribus horis,
> scire volunt utrique Canes, caelestia signa,
>   cur surrexeris alta caninum
> pondus in astra ferens. summo mortalibus olim
>   de caelo praesaga futuri
> mittebant portenta dei; nunc sidera mundo
>   quid fatum paret ipsa timebunt.

In rough translation: "Moon-satellite made by hand of man, you who encircle the earth with your double orbit in three hours, each of the two Dogs, heavenly constellations both, wants to know why you have risen up on high carrying to the stars the weight of a dog. It was once the case that the gods sent from high heaven portents that bespoke the future for mortals. But now the stars themselves will go in fear of what fate has in store for the firmament."

The Vice-Chancellor was J. C. Masterman who had recently published a detective novel, hence Auden's plea for "more corpses". The Vice-Chancellor's term of office was reduced in 1957 from three years to two.

ORATIO CREWEIANA MDCCCCLX

Abstract

So many names, so few minutes, demand of your orator this year a Tacitean brevity hard to realize in a polysyllabic tongue.

The face of our Ancient Mother has long been in need of extensive plastic surgery; and now, as the traceries of scaffolding, pneumatic drills, and cranes which everywhere surround us testify, she has found the means, thanks to her many loyal admirers, to pay for the operation.

We have grown civil enough to have a Representative of the Women's Colleges, we have laicized the Regius Chair of Hebrew, and modified our entrance requirements with regard to Latin. Those who regret this last decision must lay the blame where it properly belongs—not on the scientists but on those sixteenth-century humanists who so foully murdered what might to this day have remained a lively and international language. Candidates are to be tested in their command of English. As Professor of Poetry, may I express the hope that they will be required to show some understanding of English metres: too many now with us have ears of tin.

Then, as the whole world knows, we have elected a new Chancellor, to whom it is now my privilege to address a word of congratulation and welcome. For you, Sir, who hold the highest office under the Crown, to have condescended to become a mere University Chancellor must seem a small matter, but it is a signal honour for us. We shall, we hope, ask little of you save that, when more urgent duties permit, you will grace our gatherings with your presence, robed gorgeously and looking the imposing statesman that you are.

The yearly list of our benefactors is as extensive as the catalogue of ships in the *Iliad*. Had I the talent to invent and you the patience to listen, they should each be graced by an appropriate Homeric epithet; lacking both, we must endure a bare and bleak recital.

There are, however, four items which I must single out for mention, two because of their public interest, and two because of their especial local appeal.

Mr Mellon has given to the Bodleian Library what has been described as the most munificent single gift it has yet received, a large collection of MSS. and books from the library of John Locke. Rumours are already circulating as to the exciting secrets which this collection contains, and we shall wait eagerly for their disclosure.

Many people who live in or near Oxford have dreamed for years of a University Theatre and auditorium, and at last this dream has come true. Contributions have already been received from Colora Printing Inks Ltd and from Associated Television Ltd, for which all lovers of the drama will thank them, whenever they visit the Playhouse in its renovated form.

The late Lord Cherwell, the late Sir Francis Simon, and the late Mr G. A. Kolkhorst had each a circle of friends who will be delighted to learn that their names are not to be forgotten by later generations of Oxonians. Funds have been raised to provide for an annual Cherwell-Simon Memorial Lecture on some aspect of Physics, and Mr Kolkhorst himself has bequeathed the necessary means for an Exhibition in Spanish which is to be named after him.

I must from now on confine myself to brief mentions. Let me cite the lines of Manilius, on the rendering of Greek star-names into Latin:

> Not all can be translated;
> Better record them by the names we know.

You have heard fourteen speeches of presentation already during this ceremony; I have twice that number of benefactors alone outstanding. Forgive me therefore for having had them set out below in English; twenty are of primarily scientific interest, and eight more nearly concern the Fine Arts. Let us not forget, in thanking these generous donors, that each one of them has made possible either some valuable piece of research or some lasting aesthetic satisfaction.

The list runs:

The B. P. Trading Co.
Boake Roberts & Co.
The Dartington Hall Trustees
The Development Commissioners
The Du Pont Corporation
European Research Associates
Ferranti Ltd.
General Electric Corporation of New York
The Gulbenkian Foundation
Messrs Lawrence, Scott, and Electromotors, Ltd.
The National Foundation for Muscular Dystrophy
The Nuffield Foundation
Messrs C. Pfizer Ltd.
The Rockefeller Foundation
The Royal Society
Smith, Kline, and French Laboratories, Ltd.
Squibb Research Institute
United Cerebral Palsy Research and Educational Foundation,
    Incorporated
The University of Birmingham
The Wellcome Trustees.

We also gratefully remember:

The American Trust Fund for Oxford University
The late H. M. Bannister
Dr E. S. de Beer
Mrs C. J. Conway
The Jowett Copyright Trustees
The late Miss K. M. Kemp

The National Arts Collection Fund
Mr E.S.G. Robinson.

And talking of benefactors, since this is my third and last appearance as his dummy, I wish publicly to thank my kindly ventriloquist, Mr John Griffith, but for whose selfless industry and mastery of Latin Prose you would never have gotten so much as a squeak out of me.

I turn to more solemn themes. Of the unhappily large number of our members who have died during the last year the name best known to the public was that of our late Chancellor, Lord Halifax, whose services to his Country, to his Church, and to his University are matters of history. The England in which he was born and bred is fast disappearing, but it will go ill with us if we should ever come to consider the patrician virtues of honour, dignity, and courtesy out-of-date and undemocratic.

We have lost two men, both at an untimely age, of exceptional intellectual stature. During the post-war years Professor Austin exerted an influence on philosophical circles in Oxford comparable to that of Professor Wittgenstein in Cambridge during the thirties. There are good philosophers still living, but those who knew Professor Austin best declare that his loss is irreparable, for there is work which will never now be done because only he could have done it. A mathematician can only be judged by his peers, and Professor Whitehead's own field, topology, is one of the purest in all the chaste domain of numbers, but his colleagues are as unanimous in their praise of his professional achievements as his friends are agreed as to the charm and vivacity of his personal character.

Some scholars earn recognition in the world at large. Every amateur student of political theory and international law will have noted with regret the passing of Sir Ernest Barker, every amateur archaeologist be grieved that Sir Leonard Woolley, the excavator of Carchemish, has ended his exciting career, every amateur historian be sorry that there will be no more books by Mr G. M. Young, the distinguished historian of the Victorian Age.

There are others who, though less well known to the general public, are especially dear to us because some College or branch of this University was especially dear to them. Some were known for their wit, some for their endearing eccentricities, some for their goodness; some understood the young; some could keep accounts or steer committees: to all Oxford was the centre of their lives.

Thus Worcester will long remember Cyril Wilkinson, Merton Ernest Brudenhall Walter Gill, Wadham its former Warden, John Stenning, Christ Church Michael Foster and Robert Schofield, Reader in Soil Science, and the Clarendon Press the former Secretary to its Delegates, Mr Robert William Chapman. Neither must I omit Charles Neville Ward-Perkins, who, though he died young, had proved himself as effective in the affairs of his

College as in debates in Congregation. We also mourn Miss Agnes Ramsey and Miss Christina Burrows, a keen champion of women's education.

In this hard world, Professors of Poetry are granted neither security of tenure nor retirement with pension, so that it is with some degree of envy that I turn to the names of those who are leaving us this year with the second and those who succeed them with the first.

Of E. R. Dodds, the retiring Regius Professor of Greek, I shall not pretend to speak impartially. I believe him to be a scholar of the first rank because those with the authority to judge all tell me so, but I know him to be the wisest human being whom it has ever been my privilege to meet, and had I a trumpet, the whole world should know that we are saying farewell to a great man. To his successor Mr Lloyd-Jones, we extend a warm welcome. May his days in the Chair be long and fruitful, and may what he has to teach us about his primary concern, the nature of Tragedy, never be learned at first hand.

Professor Liddell is vacating the Waynflete Chair of Physiology, to be followed by Sir Lindor Brown, an authority on the peripheral nervous system.

Professor H. H. Plaskett will cease after twenty-eight years to observe the stars from the Savilian Chair of Astronomy, and D. E. Blackwell will keep official watch in his stead.

Professor H. J. Davis, the Swift scholar, is retiring as Reader in Textual Criticism and Miss Alice Walker, a lady of impressive erudition, will succeed him. After many years of service, Mr J. K. Bostock will hand over the exposition of the German tongue in all its intricacies to Mr Peter Ganz.

Criminology must be a less exciting and more exacting discipline than I had imagined; otherwise it would not be deemed worthy of a University Readership. Be that as it may, if Virtue still wishes in the future to understand Vice, she will be sitting at the feet of Mr N. D. Walker and no longer at the feet of Mr M. Grünhut.

Only 4 years ago I welcomed the Rev. Eric Abbott as Warden of Keble. He has already been summoned to the Deanery of Westminster, but the College has been fortunate in his successor, Dr Austen Farrer, a philosopher-theologian of high distinction.

Lastly, we congratulate the Hon. Charles Ritchie Russell, Q.C., on his elevation to the Bench and welcome as the new Counsel to the University, Sir Edward Milner Holland, of Hertford College.

As the text of this speech goes to press, the retirement of the Principal of Brasenose is announced, who for 38 years has energetically promoted the well-being of the College.

To the departing our thanks, to the arriving our greetings; to both our good will.

It is always a cause for rejoicing when the work of one of our members receives the honour of a Royal recognition. Her Majesty has graciously conferred an O.M. upon Sir Charles Hinshelwood, Dr Lee's Professor of Chemistry, a G.C.B. upon Sir Roger Makins, diplomat and Fellow of All Souls, a K.B. upon the Keeper of the Ashmolean, Sir Karl Parker, and also upon Professor John Goronwy Edwards, Honorary Fellow of Jesus College and Director of the Institute of Historical Research, and a C.B.E. upon the well-known composer, Edmund Rubbra.

And now, Mr Vice-Chancellor, it is only left for me, on behalf of the University, to express our gratitude to you for the skill with which you have guided our destinies during the past two years and to congratulate you upon your restoration to health. To shepherd a flock most of whom are either anarchists or scrupulists of procedure was never an easy task, and now that our academic pasture has been converted into a hideous and raucous conurbation, it must be enough to kill the strongest. I cannot but wonder if you, as you watch these proceedings for the last time as Vice-Chancellor, are not saying to yourself as I, making my last Creweian Oration, am saying: "Well, it has been great fun, but, thanks be to the gods, I shall never, never, never have to do it again."

Auden delivered his final Creweian Oration on 22 June 1960. The third paragraph refers to recent decisions by Congregation: the women's colleges had been elevated from the status of societies to that of full colleges; the Regius Professorship of Hebrew, formerly open only to those in Anglican orders (through being tied to a Canonry at Christ Church) was opened to any candidate; scientists, but not arts students, were permitted to substitute an entrance examination in a modern language for one in Greek or Latin.

Harold Macmillan had recently been elected Chancellor of the University.

In the Latin text a footnote gives the source of the quotation from Manilius as "*Astronomica* iii. 41–42."

Auden as Anthologist and Editor

In 1957 Auden, Marianne Moore, and Stephen Spender were the judges for the first Publication Award given by the Poetry Center of the 92nd Street YM-YWHA, New York, in conjunction with Harper & Brothers. The judges chose Ted Hughes's *The Hawk in the Rain* from 287 typescripts, and Harper published the book in the United States. (It was published in Britain by Faber & Faber.) The three judges seem to have worked separately; Auden wrote to Spender from Italy on 1 February 1957:

> Just a line to give my judgements on the Y.M.H.A. Poetry Centre competition. I thought the entries pretty crummy on the whole.
>   Despite a certain overviolence of style I thought
>   Ted Hughes, *The Hawk in the Rain*
> by far the best.
>   After and a long way after him, I put
>   (2) Pat [P. J.] Kavanagh. *Poems*
>   (3) Christopher Levenson. *In Transit*
>   (4) James Harrison. *Catchment Area.*
>   What are your views.

THE YALE SERIES OF YOUNGER POETS

Auden selected, edited, and introduced volumes 45 through 55 in this annual series published by the Yale University Press; his choices were published each year from 1947 through 1959, except in 1950 and 1955, when he found no suitable manuscripts. The earlier years of his editorship are described in *Prose I*, pp. 459–60, and *Prose II*, pp. 622–24.

Further details of Auden's editorship from 1956 through 1959 may be found in the notes to the introductions to the books he selected in those three years, James Wright's *The Green Wall* (1957, p. 39), John Hollander's *A Crackling of Thorns* (1958, p. 113), and William Dickey's *Of the Festivity* (1959, p. 179).

On 1 April 1956, a few months before Auden chose James Wright's collection, he sent a postcard to Eugene Davidson at the Yale University Press: "I have heard of one applicant who might be possible, Mr Robert Mezey who will probably send his stuff too late." As Auden anticipated, Mezey's manuscript reached the press after the deadline and was returned unread.

When Auden wrote to Davidson on 15 August 1958 enclosing his foreword for William Dickey's collection, he ended his note: "As you will see from my remarks, I have decided that it is time you got a younger and fresher editor for the Yale Younger Poets. Twelve years is a long time." His successor as editor was Dudley Fitts.

THE READERS' SUBSCRIPTION

The Readers' Subscription was a book club intended for a better-educated audience than that of the Literary Guild and the Book-of-the-Month Club. Auden and his co-editors Jacques Barzun and Lionel Trilling were associated with the club from its beginnings in 1951 until they severed relations with it early in 1959 and founded a second club, The Mid-Century Book Society. (A book club is a subscription service of a kind introduced early in the twentieth century; each month, the "club", which is open to any paying customer, ships to its members one or two books chosen by a board of editors and sold at reduced prices; members receive a monthly bulletin announcing the next selection, which is then sent to them with an invoice unless they return a form indicating that they do not want it.)

The history of The Readers' Subscription and its monthly magazine, the *Griffin*, is told in *Prose III*, pp. 631–33. As reported there, the three coeditors resigned from the club on 1 January 1959, and the last number of the *Griffin* that contained their work was the one dated February 1959. The editors resigned after Barzun and Trilling at last acknowledged that (as Auden had warned them) the founder and owner of the club, Gilman Kraft, a former student of Barzun and Trilling at Columbia, had systematically cooked the books in order to underpay the editors. The editors seem to have allowed their reviews to appear in the magazine after they resigned in order to avoid an interruption that might hinder the sale of the club and reduce their chances of receiving final payments from Kraft; those payments never arrived. The club was bought by the publisher Arthur Rosenthal, who continued to issue the *Griffin* in the same format as before, until adopting a more modern design later in 1959. Under Rosenthal's ownership, the reviews were written by well-known authors and academics, including some of Barzun and Trilling's colleagues at Columbia. The club and the *Griffin* survived, with a few further changes of ownership, until 2008.

Auden's final review for the *Griffin*, "Two Apollonians", had not appeared when the editors resigned, and it appeared instead in the August 1959 number of the *Mid-Century*, the monthly magazine of The Mid-Century Book Society, under the title "The Creation of Music and Poetry" (p. 190).

In addition to the pieces published under the editors' names, the *Griffin* twice included brief comments, probably written by Barzun but signed with the initials of all three editors, about a book that was offered to subscribers but not formally reviewed in the magazine. The first, in the January 1956 number, was a note on *Finnegans Wake*, "Jameschoice for January"; the second, in October 1958, was an untitled note on a translation of Schopenhauer's *The World as Will and Invention*.

THE MID-CENTURY BOOK SOCIETY

After resigning from The Readers' Subscription on 1 January 1959, Auden, Jacques Barzun, and Lionel Trilling quickly organized a second book club to be managed by

Sol Stein, another former student of Barzun and Trilling, who gave himself the title
Executive Vice-President and found a deep-pocketed owner (and President) for the
club in Arnold Bernhard, a successful investment counselor with a commitment to
general education.

The club was announced in an unsigned article in the *New York Times*, 1 April 1959,
"New Book Society Established Here". The last two paragraphs read:

> Mr Auden asked yesterday, in discussing the new club, "Is it inappropriate for a
> poet to comment on price?" His own reply was:
>   "Poets and professors and all those whose love of books exceeds their love of
> automobiles will welcome a chance to save in excess of 50 per cent on their book
> purchases."

Auden probably never said anything of the kind. The newspaper story mostly reproduced a press release sent out on 30 March 1959 by Stein, who reported to Auden,
Barzun, and Trilling that he had invented or modified some of their comments (Barzun papers, Columbia University Library). Auden's supposed reply was quoted again
by Stein in an editorial note in the first number of the *Mid-Century*, which was dated
July 1959, and referred to by Stein in his editorial notes in later numbers.

The editors met at the club's New York office every two weeks; alternate meetings
were devoted to choosing a few titles for closer consideration from galley proofs of
forthcoming books that had been submitted by publishers, and to making their final
selection and assigning reviews among themselves. Barzun and Trilling made the
choices when Auden was away in Europe, although he was kept informed of their
decisions.

In addition to writing reviews Auden also selected at least one poem for publication
in the *Mid-Century*, "Raceway" by Lewis Turco, which appeared in the October 1959
number. He probably also suggested the appearance of Christopher Smart's "My Cat
Jeoffrey" in the November 1959 number, where it followed Trilling's review of T. S.
Eliot's recording of *Old Possum's Book of Practical Cats*. Others who occasionally wrote
for the magazine included John Simon, Sol Stein, and, as "guest reviewers", Leslie
Fiedler and Irving Kristol. John Simon worked for the club as Director of Member
Service and associate editor; Auden later wrote a blurb for Simon's first book (see p.
894).

Probably early in 1961 Stein proposed to Barzun and Trilling that they join him in
founding a publishing firm separate from The Mid-Century Book Society, from which
Stein would take the lion's share of profits while Barzun and Trilling, serving as editors, would receive token amounts. Barzun and Trilling refused, but kept the door
open for other arrangements through which they would act as a paid editorial board,
with Auden acting as a paid consultant. Nothing came of this, and Auden only learned
about the project at a meeting of the Mid-Century board, when Stein said that Barzun
and Trilling had proposed a publishing venture that excluded Auden (although in
fact it was Stein who proposed the venture and who planned to exclude Auden).
Barzun wrote a long letter to Auden explaining the facts; Auden replied on 1 April
1961 that he had never been "in the slightest degree suspicious of you or Lionel—I
know you both to be men of honor and that's that. One of Sol's least attractive habits
is that whenever he is questioned about anything, he always tries to put the responsi-

bility on others. Since he saw fit to assert that you and Lionel had agreed to exclude me from the publishing venture, I was bound to ask you the straight question to which, of course, I already knew the answer."

While Stein was working on his plans to start a publishing house, the club's finances began to fall apart. At one point Arnold Bernhard provided emergency help and offered to have one of his assistants at his investment counseling firm supervise the finances of the club. Sol Stein assured Bernhard that this was unnecessary, but Bernhard remained distressed by the Society's financial troubles and considered a sale of his interest to a group of "underwriters"; this plan collapsed, apparently, when the leader of the group changed his mind and withdrew. In the summer of 1961, as the crisis deepened, an arrangement was proposed (apparently by Stein) that would reduce the equity of each member of the editoral board from ten to two-and-one-half percent, a proposal to which Auden seems to have objected.

Auden wrote to Trilling on 8 July: "Have received the news about Mid-Century. It is rather a shock isn't it. What I don't understand is why, quite apart from [illegible name] reneging, our financial situation has been allowed to get so bad." On 16 September 1961 Auden wrote to his friend Orlan Fox, "*Entre nous* (Top Secret!), the Mid-Century Book Society turns out, as I long suspected but no one would believe me, to be on the verge of bankruptcy. But maybe we shall just survive" (Berg Collection). One visible sign of the club's parlous finances was the physical appearance of the November 1961 number of the *Mid-Century*, which was not typeset in the conventional way but reproduced from printer's copy created on a typewriter that produced proportionally spaced text. Bernhard seems to have decided at some point to take direct control, a plan that the editors welcomed, and Stein was forced out early in 1962. He was replaced by Steven Frimmer.

Despite these changes, the club's expenses continued to increase beyond Bernhard's willingness to pay, and he finally devised a plan that would summarily dismiss the editorial board and turn the club into a simple merchandizing operation. Barzun and Trilling regarded this plan as a violation of their contract, and told Auden they preferred to resign, but in October 1962, before they could take further action, the club suffered a total financial collapse. The forty-fifth and last number of the *Mid-Century* was dated October 1962. In a letter to Barzun on 28 November 1962 Auden asked in passing, "Does Mid-Century still exist?" The three editors formally resigned as of 31 December 1962. The club returned briefly to life, offering erotica and other supposedly popular books together with bad customer service, before it dissolved entirely. Sol Stein went on to found the publishing house of Stein & Day.

During the last months of the club's active existence, Auden wrote a review of Albert Camus' *The Plague*, but it was returned to him when the *Mid-Century* ceased publication. The typescript seems to have disappeared.

In November 1959, after the club had been operating for half a year, the three editors appeared on a television discussion program, *Open End; see p. 874*). In December 1959 each of the three editors prepared a separate memorandum on the club's methods and intentions, for use by each other and the club's management. Auden's memorandum, which Stein sent to Barzun and Trilling on 22 December 1959, appears below, reproduced from his typescript in the Barzun papers in the Columbia University Library. I have regularized the layout and omitted rows of stars between many of the sections.

SOME REFLECTIONS ON THE MID-CENTURY BOOK SOCIETY

Definition of M-C-B-S

An organisation for supplying such Americans as want them with NEW
BOOKS.

Def. of Book

A BOOK is a piece of writing—it can be one page long or one thousand
pages—which is unconsumable. Everything else is READING MATTER, either
entertaining (e.g. Detective Stories) or informative (articles on Current Affairs), mentally consumable goods as soups are physically consumable goods.
Like good soups, good Reading Matter is useful and valuable but it should
not be our concern.

How to recognise a book

A BOOK is a piece of writing which one does not read but is read by. Since
one is always changing, it reads one differently every time. That is why one
cannot consume it. (A special case, Reference books, Cook books, etc. Again
one doesn't read them, but they are unconsumable because one's need to
consult them from time to time is a permanent need.)

Generally speaking, a Book strikes one on first acquaintance as being *either*
DIFFICULT & FORBIDDING *or* FRIVOLOUS & CHILDISH. High-brows have to
beware of their earnestness.

Def. of New

A NEW book is a book one has not read before. The date of publication is
irrelevant.

M-C's Competitors

Our real rivals, I believe, are *not* the other book-clubs but paper-back series like Anchor Books, the Harper series, Penguins etc. Our competitive
task is to spot books before they do.

Our Task

It is the task of the editors to discover, and of the management to make the
arrangements to procure twenty-four such New Books per annum. The
chances of twenty-four being published in the U.S.A. in any current year are
infinitesimal. If we live in the present, as I fear we have been doing, that is to
say, content to inspect the current catalogues of U.S. publishers and make
the best selection we can from them, at least half our selections will be Reading Matter not Books. Every time this happens, we have failed our members
AND WE ARE CONSCIOUS OF HAVING FAILED THEM.

We cannot possibly hope for 100% success, but I should like to see our
conscious failures reduced to 25%.

I see two ways of improving our standard of performance. Both of them, I am only too well aware, put a far greater burden upon Management than they do upon the editors.

(1) The discovery of books, previously published, which either through chance or snobberies, social and academic, have been neglected or ignored. Each of the editors, I am sure, could cite a number. For example, I think of two, published around 1940, of first-rate importance and virtually unknown: Charles Cochrane's *Christianity and Classical Culture* and Rosenstock-Huessy's *Out of Revolution*. Such books can be a headache for Management because some publisher may have to be persuaded to reprint them.

(2) The discovery of books published abroad but for which no American publication has yet been contemplated. Between them, the Editors have sufficient command of French, German and Italian, to be able at least to recognise a book in these tongues, and, again, I am sure, each of them knows of several at this moment. For example here are two from my own list: *Sens Plastique* by Malcolm de Chazal and *Grenzen der Physiognomik* by Max Picard.

Again, too, another headache for Management who must persuade some American publisher to get such books properly translated and publish them.

Planning

Management cannot possibly be expected to tackle the problems which forgotten or untranslated books raise unless given plenty of time, and alternative choices, so that, if one negotiation breaks down, hope remains elsewhere.

It seems to me that, at our editorial meetings, we should try to plan our tentative choices much further ahead than we are doing at present. I say tentative because it should always be possible to advance or postpone the use of a selection if need arises. But I shall only feel completely happy about our selections when we reach the point, which we probably never shall, when we know that we do not have to make more than half our selections from current American lists unless we really want to.

Being attached to a University, both Jacques and Lionel have the periodical room of a good library near at hand, which I have not, but they are both very busy men who must snatch moments when they can to glance through periodicals and catalogues, and such moments may often occur at times when libraries are shut.

Would it be possible for Management to provide each of us with certain key foreign periodicals, e.g. *The Times Literary Supplement, N.R.F.* and *Merkur?* I know that it would be an immense help to me.

A note on our American choices

Editors are mortal and cannot escape their limitations of taste and interest. Even so, I think, in our selection of current books, we are making our task more difficult than we need by being even more *literary* in our choices than we are by temperament. There are some kinds of book—books on Natural History or Animal Behaviour, to give only one example—which we seem to ignore. Yet, do we not all find such books fascinating? Cook-books are another field.

Educative goal of Mid-Century

To turn our members, not into high-brows, but into intellectual dandies.

Definition of an Intellectual Dandy

(1) Is a member of a class of one. No dandy is like another dandy.

The high-brow, on the other hand, is a cell in a minority social group, which like all societies, has its conventions and tabus. It may be only a Little Social Beast, but a Social Beast it is. A Social Beast undergoes historical change—it is possible for a historian to write a history of high-brow taste, but its cells have no history—the high-brows at any given point in time are subject-matter not for the historian but for the anthropologist. Once you have met a few highbrows, you can safely predict the tastes of the next one (even what you will get if he asks you to dinner). You know who are the U-authors whom he will admire (even if you mention a book by one of them which he hasn't read) and who are the non-U authors whom he will condemn without having read them. A high-brow is as easy to shock as a Baptist Minister: an intellectual Dandy is unshockable.

(2) A Dandy is neither a conformist nor a rebel, for both attitudes presuppose a concern for Public Opinion, and the Dandy has no such concern, It makes no difference to him if a million people agree with him or none.

(3) The most embarrassing fate which can befall a dandy, and it is not an uncommon one, is to discover that he has created a fashion. He is embarrassed, not because others agree with him, but because they agree, not as individuals, but as cells in the Social Beast.

(4) The Dandy, however, is not a self-sufficient solipsist who has no relations with others. He knows that it is only through other persons who are unique and therefore, not himself, that he can become himself. He knows that, at any given moment and in any given field, there are persons with greater authority than he to whom he must listen, but he chooses his authorities at first not second hand, and his authorities have to prove themselves by performance. The Dandy with literary interests is highly suspicious of all literary critics (even L.T., J.B., and W.H.A.).

(5) The more passionate a dandy's concern for a matter, the more frivolously he speaks about it to others.

M-C Advertising

Someone—I think it was Sol [Stein]—said at our last meeting that our problem is how to appeal to the person who would never dream of joining a

Book-Club. We are in the paradoxical position of being a Book Society, i.e. a Literary Social Beast, to satisfy persons who want to be individuals, not cells. All advertising I have ever seen is based on the presupposition that unique persons do not exist, only social beings with socially conditioned and predictable desires. I must confess that I do not myself see how a method of advertising can be devised which speaks to its audience not collectively but one-by-one, but it makes a nice challenge to an advertiser. Certainly no previous experience of his will be the slightest help. The only advice I can give him is: "Be modest. Keep your voice low. Remember that you are selling books, not authors. Be brief, be ABSOLUTELY HONEST. NEVER EXAGGERATE. Be witty, if you can, but remember that nothing is more awful than a bad joke."

W. H. A.

POETRY PILOT

As guest poetry editor of the 1 March 1959 number of this monthly magazine of the Academy of American Poets, Auden chose six poems for inclusion: "Eve" (Auden's title for a widely printed extract from the alliterative poem "Death and Life"; the extract begins "Shee was brighter of her blee . . ."); Bartholomew Griffin, "Faire is my love"; Walter de la Mare, "Reflections"; Lord Herbert of Cherbury, "Sonnet" ("Innumerable Beauties, thou white haire"); Richard Lovelace, "La Bella Bona Roba"; and Robert Frost, "The Silken Tent".

THE LOOKING GLASS LIBRARY

Auden, Phyllis McGinley, and Edmund Wilson were advisory editors of this series of children's books published from 1959 to 1961; it seems to have been initiated by Clelia Carroll and proposed as a series to various publishers in the summer of 1959. Random House and The Mid-Century Book Society were among those who offered to publish it, but Random House offered the best terms. This produced some embarrassment for Auden, who was on the board of both the proposed series and the Mid-Century, but this was smoothed over when the Book Society distributed some of the later volumes.

In the official organization of the Library, Jason Epstein was editor; Clelia Carroll was managing editor; and Edward Gorey was art director. Though distributed by Random House, the series was nominally published by the firm of Epstein & Carroll. Twenty-eight titles appeared; the ones by George Macdonald and perhaps a few others were presumably recommended by Auden:

1   E. Nesbit, *Five Children and It* (1959)
2   Andrew Lang, *The Blue Fairy Book* (1959)
3   George Macdonald, *The Princess and the Goblin* (1959)
4   Rex Warner, *Men and Gods* (1959)
5   Ernest Thompson Seton, *Wild Animals I Have Known* (1959)
6   Lucretia P. Hale, *The Peterkin Papers* (1959)
7   Edward Lear, *A Book of Nonsense* (1959)

8   *The Looking Glass Book of Verse*, edited by Janet Adam Smith (1959)
9   *The Haunted Looking Glass*, ghost stories chosen and illustrated by Edward
     Gorey (1959)
10   Sir Arthur Conan Doyle, *The Lost World* (1959)
11   E. Nesbit, *The Phoenix and the Carpet* (1960)
12   George Macdonald, *The Princess and Curdie* (1960)
13   Andrew Lang, *The Red Fairy Book* (1960)
14   *The Looking Glass Book of Stories*, edited by Hart Day Leavitt (1960)
15   Howard Pyle, *Otto of the Silver Hand* (1960)
16   L. Frank Baum, *The Wizard of Oz & The Land of Oz* (1960)
17   Charlotte M. Yonge, *Countess Kate* (1960)
18   E. Nesbit, *The Story of the Amulet* (1960)
19   Henry Williamson, *Tarka the Otter* (1960)
20   Andrew Lang, *The Green Fairy Book* (1960)
21   H. G. Wells, *The War of the Worlds* (1960)
22   Frank Richard Stockton, *Buccaneers and Pirates of Our Coasts* (1960)
23   Richard Hughes, *The Spider's Palace, and Other Stories* (1960)
24   E. Nesbit, *The Book of Dragons* (1961)
25   Anthony Hope, *The Prisoner of Zenda* (1961)
26   Sir Arthur Conan Doyle, *The Hound of the Baskervilles* (1961)
27   Mrs Molesworth, *The Tapestry Room: A Child's Romance* (1961)
28   *The Comic Looking Glass*, edited by Hart Day Leavitt (1961)

Edward Gorey's *The Bug Book* (1959) was an unnumbered volume first issued as a
Christmas card by the series, then published in a small hardcover edition.

The Viking Book of Aphorisms

The origins of this book are unknown. Auden's coeditor Louis Kronenberger was a
critic and essayist whom Auden perhaps met in literary circles in New York when Kronenberger was working as drama critic for *Time* from 1938 through 1961. Kronenberger was also the editor of the Great Letters series for which Auden was commissioned to prepare a selected letters of Sydney Smith (which became his *Selected
Writings of Sydney Smith*).

Auden had been collecting quotations and aphorisms on paper cards for many
years; Kronenberger seems to have done the same. After contracting with the Viking
Press to prepare this book, they worked separately on their own collections. Auden
seems to have translated some of the French and German entries, and translated or
retranslated some of the Italian ones. For example, his translations from Cesare Pavese differ from those in the edition he reviewed in 1961; see p. 378.

Some of the items by Karl Kraus derive from an unpublished translation of Kraus's
aphorisms made in 1941 by Albert Bloch; a few pages exist of Bloch's typescript with
additions and changes in Auden's hand, probably made around 1961; these match
some of the items in the anthology (typescript in a private collection); Leo Lensing
referred to Auden's changes to this translation in a review in *TLS*, 21 December 2001.

The two editors combined and organized their notes in a marathon session in Kronenberger's house in Boston, probably in the spring of 1961. The design of the book

seems to have been worked out between the authors and the publisher; they agreed that the authors of the aphorisms would be identified by last name only in the main text, but by full names in the index; women authors, however, would be identified with full names in both the main text and index, and initials would be used when two or more male authors had the same last name. Some further exceptions were made, for example both Henry James and William James were identified by their full names; the two Samuel Butlers were distinguished as Samuel Butler (I) and Samuel Butler (II). V. V. Rozanov's name was misspelled Rozinov throughout.

A letter to Auden from Pascal Covici at the Viking Press, 14 May 1962, refers to "Your book of *Aphorisms of the Western World*", which may have been the title under which the book was conceived. Covici at that point wanted to change the title to something more vivid, perhaps *A Mirror for Man*, but the sales and promotion staff at Viking insisted on a simple factual title, and Covici suggested the final title sometime during the late spring.

Kronenberger read proofs of the book probably in June 1962, and Viking sent Auden only galleys with queries that Kronenberger had been unable to answer. Auden asked for a full set of proofs, which were sent in August. The book was published 26 November 1962. Faber & Faber published a British edition as *The Faber Book of Aphorisms* in 1964.

In 1965 the Viking Press made plans to prepare a paperback edition of the book and wrote Auden and Kronenberger to ask their approval for the inclusion of an index of key words; this "Informal Key-Word Index", prepared by Edwin Kennebeck, an editor at Viking, duly appeared in the new edition. Viking also asked Auden and Kronenberger to suggest changes for the book that would not require repagination; Auden seems not to have sent such a list to Viking, but he sent to Faber a list of additional items that is first mentioned in Faber's production files on 11 February 1965; Faber's production manager Donald Bland refers to it in a internal memorandum as "the enclosed large list of corrections". Faber and Viking agreed that these could not be incorporated without taking the prohibitively costly step of resetting the entire book, and Auden's list has been lost. Probably most or all appeared in his commonplace book *A Certain World* (1970).

No one noticed that at least one aphorism, a sentence by Lichtenberg about motives, occurs twice in slightly different translations (on pp. 147 and 332).

Auden's copy of the first edition, marked with his notes and corrections, is in the Harry Ransom Center at the University of Texas at Austin.

Public Lectures

Auden's most notable lectures from 1956 through 1960 were the three annual lectures he delivered in each year of his five-year term as Professor of Poetry. This professorship normally required him to give one lecture in each of the three Oxford terms, but Auden asked for a change in this schedule so that he could remain in New York during the winter. The *Guardian* reported on 17 October 1956: "The Professor of Poetry at Oxford, Mr W. H. Auden was given permission by Congregation yesterday to give three lectures during the summer term of each year, instead of one lecture in each of the three university terms. The senior proctor, Mr B. G. Mitchell, explained that difficulties with the Home Office and the American immigration authorities made it practically impossible for Professor Auden to live in England for the whole academic year and comply with the existing regulations." After his inaugural, he delivered all his lectures during Trinty term, except in his last year, when he delivered his two lectures during Michelmas. (He gave only two lectures in his last year because in his first year he had given four, including his inaugural.)

The titles of Auden's lectures, as announced in the *Oxford University Gazette*, were as follows. Most of his lectures appeared in modified form in *The Dyer's Hand*.

Making, Knowing and Judging. 11 June 1956. (See p. 477.)
Robert Frost. 6 May 1957. (See p. 689.)
D. H. Lawrence. 13 May 1957. (See p. 647.)
The Dramatic Use of Music in Shakespeare's Plays. 20 May 1957. (See p. 807.)
Byron's Don Juan. 12 May 1958. (See p. 725.)
The Quest Hero. 19 May 1958. (See p. 360.)
Dingley Dell and the Fleet: Reflections on *Pickwick Papers*. 16 May 1958. (See p. 741.)
Marianne Moore. 4 May 1959. (See p. 660.)
Translating Opera Libretti. 11 May 1959. (See p. 795.)
The Fallen City: Some Reflections on Shakespeare's Henry IV. 25 May 1959. (See "The Prince's Dog", p. 580.)
The Hero in Modern Poetry. 2 May 1960. (For other lectures with this title, see p. 862 below.)
The Alienated City, I: Reflections on *The Merchant of Venice*. 9 May 1960. (See "Brothers & Others", p. 605.)
The Alienated City, II: Reflections on *Othello*. 16 May 1960. (See "The Joker in the Pack", p. 624.)
The Genius and the Apostle: A Problem of Poetic Presentation. 24 October 1960. (See p. 759.)
Mainly Valedictory. 31 October 1960. (Perhaps partly included among the aphoristic sections of *The Dyer's Hand*.)

In addition to the lectures described below, Auden was reported to have given a few other lectures of which few details survive.

Auden gave three lectures in Ursula Niebuhr's "Religion 26" class at Barnard College, 17 and 29 February and 9 March 1956. The *Barnard Bulletin* reported on 16 February that his first lecture would be about "poetry as 'the affirmation of personal being and personal becoming'" and that his remaining lectures would (both?) be titled "An Analysis of Religion in Contemporary Society and Culture".

On 27 January 1958, at the Washington [D.C.] School of Psychiatry, Auden gave the opening lecture, titled "A History-Making Animal", in a series with the general title "Character in Literature and Psychoanalysis"; the *Washington Post*, the next day, reported on Auden's answers to two questions after the talk, and summarized the talk itself: "Auden said there is a common bond between psychoanalysis and poetry in that both regard the life of the mind as historical and unique, not susceptible to [being] studied by quantitative methods" (the word in square brackets emends the newspaper's nonsensical "study cannot be").

In January through March 1958, Auden delivered six lectures at Princeton University to the Christian Gauss Seminars in Criticimsm.

ADDRESS FOR THE NATIONAL BOOK AWARD, 1956

Auden received the National Book Award for poetry from the National Book Committee at a ceremony in New York on 7 February 1956. His acceptance speech was distributed as a mimeographed press release headed "Address of W. H. Auden | National Book Award | New York City." A copy in the Emory University Library has eleven revisions that are clearly authorial (they include the addition of "The Demon Lover or" and "Romeo or") but are pencilled in by an unknown hand; I have incorporated these in the text below. A brief excerpt appeared in *Publishers Weekly*, 18 February 1956, in a report that seems to have been based on the speech as Auden delivered it and has a few minor errors and other variations from the mimeographed text. Auden mentions the fiction and nonfiction winners of the award, who were John O'Hara and Herbert Kubly.

In an award, as in any piece of good fortune, there is an element of luck of which the recipient cannot but be humbly aware. That your choice for poetry should have fallen upon me is, of course, as gratifying personally as it is surprising, but it is as a representative of all who practice what has become, in the eyes of most, a somewhat old-fashioned craft rather than as a successful candidate that I now speak, and it is for the recognition you have given to our Muse rather than for the honor you have paid one of her servants that I would thank you.

That I should be standing here at all gives the lie to an essay of G. K. Chesterton's which began, "Now Barabbas was a publisher." Winners along with me are a writer of fiction and a writer of non-fiction who are, I haven't the slightest doubt, valuable property—but what, in the name of profit, dear foolish publishers, sweet unworldly booksellers, am I doing here, out of whom you know as well as I you will never earn enough to pay the wages of one incompetent typist. I can only suppose that something inside you whispers that poetry has some value when common sense and your accountants tell you that it has none, and I shall devote the rest of my remarks to saying why I think you are right.

The poet is perhaps the only person who can truthfully say, and with full knowledge of what he is saying, that he would rather have been born in an earlier age—very much earlier—an age, I'm afraid, in which publishers and booksellers did not yet exist—an age when the statement "The real man speaks in poetry" seemed as self-evident as the statement "Men really speak in prose" seems today.

The real meant "sacred" or "numinous." A real person was not a personality but someone playing a sacred role, apart from which he or she might be nobody. A real act was some sacred rite by the re-enactment of which the universe and human life were sustained in being and reborn. The individual, the particular, the novel, the secular was of no account. Particularity existed but only as the particulars of a rite; thus it was important that Hercules should have neither more nor less than twelve labors; and that iambics should be used for curses and satire.

In such an age and culture, the poet has no problem of subject matter— the sacred occasions are public and shared by all—no problems of communication, and, in addition, is a highly honored and well-rewarded social figure.

The concern of the poet in 1956 A.D. is still the same as it was in 1956 B.C. That is to say, he is *not* interested in personalities or psychology or progress or news—the diametrical opposite of poetry is the daily newspaper. What moves him to write are his encounters with the sacred or numinous, in nature, in human beings and nothing else. By the sacred, I do not, of course, mean only the good. The Demon Lover or La belle Dame sans Merci is as sacred as Romeo or Beatrice. The sacred can arouse terror and despair as well as awe and wonder or joy and gratitude. Nor is the sacred confined to the romantically mysterious fairy lands forlorn. Indeed every set of verses, whatever their subject, are by their formal nature a hymn to Natural Law and a gesture of astonishment at that greatest of mysteries, the order of the universe. No one and nothing becomes sacred, and hence a poetic subject, by their own efforts; it is rather the sacred that chooses them as agents through which to manifest itself. Similarly, the poet cannot feel its presence by wishing to. To say that good poetry must be inspired means, not that poems are a sort of automatic writing enticing us to work, but that the stimulus to a good poem is given the poet—he cannot simply think one up.

The essential difficulty for the poet in the present age is not that he has some peculiar experiences which others do not have. No, all of us, readers and non-readers alike, are in the same boat. We all have experiences of the sacred, but fewer and fewer of them are public, so that the present-day reader of poetry has to translate a poem into his own experiences before he can understand it. Readers in earlier times did not.

Before people complain about the obscurity of modern poetry, they should, I think, first ask themselves how many profound experiences they themselves have really shared with another person.

One further point. I am inclined to think that the rhythmical character of poetry is, in a technological civilization, an obstacle. Rhythm involves repetition and today I fear that the notion of repetition is associated in most people's minds with all that is most boring and lifeless, punching time clocks, road drills, etc.

But enough—I'm getting boring myself. For your award, ladies and gentlemen, my thanks: for the dollars I shall never bring you, my apologies.

A Sermon in St Giles' Cathedral, Edinburgh

Auden delivered a sermon in St Giles' Cathedral, Edinburgh, on 24 February 1957. The report below appeared on 25 February in the *Scotsman*, and an almost identical report appeared in the *Glasgow Herald*.

Professor W. H. Auden, who is to give a public lecture on "The Detective Story" in Edinburgh this afternoon and his inaugural address as president of the Associated Societies of Edinburgh University this evening, arrived by air on Saturday night and preached at the university service in St Giles' Cathedral last night.

Taking as his text verses 15–17 of the 16th chapter of St Matthew's Gospel, Professor Auden, in the course of his sermon, considered the question of whether there was any manifest, important difference between pre-Christian literature, and that created under Christian influences, "I believe there can be no such thing as Christian literature," he said, "any more than there can be a Christian science or a Christian political theory. To a Christian a painting of the Crucifixion is no more sacred than a still life."

To say that literature or any other lay activity was secular was not to condemn it, but to say that it was an aspect of that humanity which Christ assumed in order to redeem it.

Professor Auden was critical of poems expressing personal devotion to Christ as distinct from verses written for liturgical uses. "A young man," he said, "writes a sonnet expressing his feelings of love for a young lady. This is quite in order, because he and she both know that it is accidental to the feelings that it is this girl who arouses them and not another. Indeed, poets have been known to address sonnets to one lady while intending them for another.

"A man who writes a sonnet," he continued, "expressing his feelings of devotion for Christ can, like the lover, only express what he feels. But surely the important point here is the uniqueness of the relation that his feelings are concerned with Christ and not, say, Dionysus or Buddha. But this distinction cannot be made in poetry.

"Even more problematical is the penitential poem like some of Donne's best sonnets. A poem is a work of art which must be beautiful and arouse admiration. It cannot be made without talent and without calculation. Is there not something rather odd about using one's feelings of guilt and repentance before God as the occasion for the calculated production of an admirable object? I do not say that such poetry should not be written—I myself would miss a lot of it—but I do think there is a problem."

The difference between the pagan and the Christian writer, Professor Auden said, was that the pagan could give a direct religious interpretation to what he imagined and the Christian could not. Fortune and misfortune were to the pagan the proof of divine favour and disfavour, so that, from observing cases of fortune and misfortune, it was possible to discover what the gods required of man. But Christ put an end to such interpretations. "God sends His rain alike on the just and the unjust. We are not to worship Fate or Chance, but believe in God's Providence without pretending we can understand it."

A number of questions arising from his sermon were answered by Professor Auden at an informal gathering of university students and staff in the chaplaincy centre, New North Church, after the service. The chaplain to the university, the Rev. James C. Blackie, who had conducted the service in St Giles', presided at the gathering.

The Hero in Modern Poetry

Auden used this title for various lectures that he delivered during the 1950s; for earlier examples, see *Prose II*, pp. 659–62. He again delivered a lecture under this title as the nineteenth W. P. Ker Memorial Lecture at Glasgow University on 5 May 1958. *The Times* reported the event on 6 May:

The mere action of writing poetry in modern world conditions was a deed, however small in itself, that deserved to be honoured by all men of good will, said Professor W. H. Auden, of the Chair of Poetry at Oxford University, when he delivered to-day at Glasgow University the W. P. Ker Lecture for 1958.

Lecturing on "The hero in modern poetry," he described all art as a curious mixture of doing and making, but, after illustrating his theme mainly from works by W. B. Yeats, Robert Frost, D. H. Lawrence, and T. S. Eliot—four modern poets "all either old or dead"—suggested that the public life offered by the modern world was no longer a sphere in which the deed of tradition was possible.

Scientists, psychologists, and physicists were the true men of significant deeds in the modern age. Their discoveries, however, were not translatable in personal speech but intelligible only to scientists within the discipline, and the scientific deed was not therefore a public deed.

The four poets Professor Auden discussed within the framework of his lecture were modern in that they wrote of conditions which had not greatly changed in the past half-century. What they sensed about the world in writing their poetry was now obvious to the man in the street, and all four seemed to agree that the contemporary hero as a human individual was the person who succeeded both in becoming for a moment himself and in resisting the immense pressures of society to make him a unit in a crowd.

Professor Auden said it was not surprising in a technological age, in which decisions were taken not by persons but by officials, that the unique and personal aspects of art received much attention. The fact that it was not possible to-day to manifest oneself, as the romantic hero did, by an act of revolt created enormous difficulties for the poet in expressing his feelings in which all might share.

This made understandable the reason for so many poets seeking refuge in the magic world of childhood and also for the customary accusation that modern poetry was obscure in meaning and uneasy in style. There was much truth in all that, but there was also cause for thankfulness that any poetry was being written at all in an age when the application of science, itself a highly valuable form of knowledge, was causing such change in the conditions of life.

Every poem written to-day was at least a deed, a blow struck against all those who deliberately kept human beings down or reduced them to a sub-personal level in which they could be scientifically controlled. Such deeds, small though they were, deserved the honour of all men of good will.

A similar report appeared in the *Glasgow Herald*, also on 6 May 1958:

The nineteenth W. P. Ker lecture, on "The Hero in Modern Poetry," was delivered at Glasgow University yesterday by W. H. Auden: an occasion distinguished both by the character of the lecturer, now Professor of Poetry at Oxford, and by subject.

Poetry and poets have a share in the Ker lectures, proportionate perhaps with their place in the general body of literature, which must give such addresses scarcity-value. Beyond this, and his own poetic reputation, Professor Auden's title must have roused the curiosity of many who may have doubted whether poetry or heroes have any place in the modern world.

Professor Auden expounded this paradox, which was at the centre of his address, with particular reference to four poets, Yeats, Robert Frost, D. H. Lawrence, and T. S. Eliot. All, he said, were "either old or dead"; but all four were in a true sense poets of the modern world, who either dealt directly with the problems that have overtaken contemporary society, or prophetically foresaw them. What they were concerned with had not especially changed in the past fifty years; "the public life of the modern world is no longer a sphere in which the traditional Deed is possible."

In this technological world, in which decisions are taken, not by persons but by officials, Professor Auden pointed to the scientists as the "true men of significant deeds"; their discoveries had the nature of individual acts, and they were personally responsible for them. But though they could communicate with each other, it was generally impossible to translate their language for anyone outside their discipline; however important, their acts were not public deeds.

Nor, Professor Auden found, were politics much more accessible as matter for poetry. He has himself made political utterance among the chief contents of his verse, but he did not refer to his own work. He modestly owned Yeats as the sole exception, "the only modern poet I can think of who has been able to write great poetry about contemporary political events"; and Yeats, he suggested, was a special case, having had the good fortune to be "born in a small country of much hatred, where exciting and tragic events took place on a parochial scale."

In this age dominated by science ("a highly valuable form of knowledge," Professor Auden allowed) the poet had such difficulties to face that it must be a matter for gratitude that any poems were being written at all, and allowances should be made for poets who took refuge in "the magic world of childhood" or in the private world of obscurity. Nevertheless, poets had a function still, and here Professor Auden approached the resolution of his paradox.

The contemporary hero is commonly represented as "a person who succeeds in becoming for a moment himself," and not a unit in the crowd. Poetry itself—partaking of the nature of all art, "a curious mixture of doing and making"—emerges as an act that may conceivably be called heroic: "Every poem written to-day is at least a deed, a blow at all those who deliberately keep human beings in subjection or reduce them to a sub-personal level in which they can be scientifically controlled."

Even when dealing with minutiae (of which Professor Auden concluded by giving two notable contemporary examples from America, by E. E. Cummings and Marianne Moore) the poet delivers this blow. Consequently, it may be concluded (though Professor Auden did not put it in so many words) the hero in modern poetry is chiefly the poet himself.

Auden again used the title "The Hero in Modern Poetry" for his penultimate Oxford lecture on poetry, 2 May 1960.

The Pattern and the Way

At the 1958 Venice Biennale Auden gave the opening speech at a "Round Table" discussion titled "Tradition and Innovation". A mimeographed text, probably distributed in advance, has a cover page on which the title is followed by: "Opening Speech to be delivered at the Inaugural Session of the Round Table discussions to be held in Venice under the sponsorship of the Cini Foundation and the Congress for Cultural Freedom in collaboration with the Contemporary Music Festival of the Biennale | Venice, From September 16 to September 23, 1958". Auden gave a copy of the mimeographed text to Robert Craft on 18 September 1958.

The title of his speech was either the title on the cover page, "The Pattern and the Way" (which I have used here) or the title at the top of the first page of text, "The Model and the Way". The mimeographed text, reprinted below with minor emendations, seems to be Auden's notes for a talk that would necessarily have been more fluid in organization.

THE PATTERN AND THE WAY

[Title on first page of text: The Model and the Way]

Modern Art

Around 1800 a change began to take place in all the arts which makes "modern" art distinguishable from that of all previous periods. The main characteristics of this change are:—

1. The disappearance of a common style. Each artist makes in his own way as if he were the only artist alive. In some cases, he may model his way of making upon some style of the past, even the remote past, but this is his personal idiosyncratic choice.
2. The disappearance of the artist as the mouthpiece of the Public Muses, and his replacement by the isolated Genius who is recognised because what he makes is extraordinary or shocking. The Genius can have fame among those who know nothing of his works.
3. The enormously increased value attached to an artist's originality, and the corresponding severer condemnation of "imitation".
4. The disappearance of "folk" art and its replacement by Mass Entertainment. Whatever the differences between "folk" art and "court" art, both were made to endure; the productions of Mass Entertainment, on the other hand, are designed to be consumed as fast as they appear.

Three Aspects of Man

1. *Man the Laborer*

As a biological organism, every man is an anonymous example of his species, subject as every other, to the laws of nature and the temporal cycle of generation.

All animals "labor" to some degree in order to survive, but the pre-eminently laboring animal (excepting bees and ants?) is man. Life for him means laboring to produce what he consumes in order to be able to continue to produce.

For man the laborer, only the present point on the biological cycle is real—it may be pleasant or painful—but it has no intrinsic value.

Man the laborer does not perform acts of his own, he exhibits human behaviour, the purpose of which is biological survival and propagation.

It is possible for a man to survive by himself alone on a desert island. If we speak of man as a social animal, we only mean that co-operation in labor assists the survival of the species. As a laborer, that is, man requires the company of others, not as people, but as bodies, as another set of muscles or a member of the opposite sex.

2. *Man the Maker*

As a conscious individual, man is aware, as other animals are not, that he must die. Out of this awareness arises the desire to transcend the natural cycle of birth and death by making a human world of things which do not die but endure.

The things he makes are of two kinds: use-objects which future generations can continue to use for some particular purpose, and art-objects which future generations can continue to enjoy for their own sake. Many things which he makes are, of course, at once use-objects and art-objects.

Since man the maker is not concerned with his own survival but with the survival of what he makes, his definition of time is: that which must not be wasted. He does not labor, nor does he act; he works.

Man the maker is only indirectly [related] to others through the things he makes. As far as he himself is concerned, the best condition for work is solitude.

3. *Man the Person*

As a self-conscious person who can say "I", man is aware that his life and death are uniquely his, that an identical being has never existed before and will never exist again. Out of this awareness arises the desire to disclose who he is to others and be recognised by them as a unique being.

As a person, man neither labors nor works; he acts, and the purpose of his action is to make himself known.

Since he can only act in the present, the present moment is of unique importance, but this present moment is not the real present of the biological cycle but the valuable historical instant which gives him the opportunity to realise himself through his act.

Man the maker desires permanence for his works; man the person desires immortality for his memory. This means that his act must be immediately recognised for, if it is not, there is nothing left to remember.

Personal action, unlike behaviour or fabrication, is impossible except in the public presence of others.

The Relation of These Three Aspects to Tradition

1. *Tradition and Behaviour*

In man, purely instinctive behaviour is confined to the biological processes inside his body. Everything he must do in order to survive, he must learn from others.

In any human society, the "right" survival behaviour includes the practical: how to use one's limbs and how to eat; the social: how to co-operate with others; and the religious: what must and must not be done to please the gods upon whose favour human survival is believed to depend.

Since survival means simply life, without any qualifications like good or evil, the mere fact that a society has survived for some time gives its tradition of behaviour authority. Cultural habits of behaviour, therefore, are more dominated by tradition than any other human sphere and the last to break down.

2. *Tradition and Making*

Two elements can enter into making; craft, and art or thought. Though a talent for craftsmanship may be greater in some individuals than in others, a craft is learned, not given at birth. Art, the element of thought, which makes a new thing, cannot, on the other hand, be traditionally acquired.

In the fabrication of use-objects, like tools, art only enters into the invention of a new or a better object of its kind. Once the original model of a use-object has been made, it only requires craftsmanship to reproduce it.

An art-object requires both craft and art throughout the process of fabrication, for no art-object is identical with another.

Traditional theory recognised, at least in the case of poetry, that there was a distinction between craft and art, but this difference was expressed by saying that the artist was a craftsman who was inspired in his making by the Muses; the element of art in his work was not recognised as being due to him. Why, we shall discuss later.

3. Tradition and Action

Man can be taught how to behave, and certain individuals can be taught crafts of skill in making, but no person can be taught to act, for, if this were possible, then his action could be done by somebody else. All a person can learn from the actions of others is that action is humanly possible. There can be no tradition of action, only a number of examples, each of them unique.

The Traditional Subjects of the Arts

In the case of both the verbal and the visual arts (I must leave it to others to say what is comparable in music), one can say what a given work is *about* just as one can say what a given tool is *for.*

Traditionally, what inspired the craftsman so that he became an artist was his theme, and the themes which were thought capable of so inspiring him were:

1. The nature and ways of the gods
2. The actions of heroes, the word "hero" being itself a definition of a man capable of self-revelatory action.

So long as these views prevailed, there existed a certain style common to all the artists of a given historical period, and when a change in style occurred it was the result, not of the decision of individual artists to break with tradition and do something new, but of a change of attitude towards the divine and the heroic in the community to which the artists belonged.

The Modern Age

The three characteristics of the last one hundred and fifty years which have had the greatest effect on its arts, seem to me to be:

1. The loss of belief in the eternity of the natural universe and in the objective truth of sensory experience.
2. The loss of belief in a norm of human nature by which all individuals at all times are to be measured.

3. The radical shift in both the meaning and the value attached to the words *public* and *private*.

Art and Eternity

Until the modern age, the man who desired to make an enduring thing which should outlast his own life, had before his eyes, as a model: a universe, earth, ocean, sky, sun, moon and stars which were everlasting and unchanging. Human generations might come and go, but the model was always there.

Physics, geology, and biology have destroyed this picture and replaced it by a picture of nature as a process in which nothing is what it was or what it will be. Further, science now tells us that we cannot hope to know what the universe is "really like". We can only hold subjective notions determined by the structure of the human mind and its particular purpose for inquiry.

This destroys the traditional theory of art as mimesis, for there is no longer a permanent and real nature "out there" to be a model for the artist to imitate. The "nature" the artist is left with is reduced to the subjective feelings and sensations of the human mind.

Art and Human Nature

Until modern times, the way in which any given human society lived changed so slowly that a man, thinking of his grandchildren, could reasonably believe that they would be persons with the same kinds of wants and satisfactions as himself. But in a technological society like our own, we can no longer imagine what life will be like twenty years from now.

Then, until modern times, men knew and cared little about cultures unlike their own. By human nature they meant the kind of behaviour exhibited by their own culture.

Now anthropology and archaeology have destroyed this naive self-confidence. We know that human nature is so plastic that it can exhibit varieties of behaviour which, in the animal world, could only be exhibited by different species.

This knowledge has cut away the basic premise of all tradition, whether in the arts or in any other human sphere, namely that there is only one way of being fully human. The human nature the artist is left with as "real" is therefore not even the thoughts, feelings and sensations of the human mind, but what goes on in *his* mind.

Art, the Public and the Private Life

To the Greeks, Private Life meant the life of the household which existed by natural necessity, for the relation between its members, whether master or slave, parent or child. It arose out of the natural need to produce in order to survive and to propagate the race. The household was the place where all labor was performed (and also the place where things could be made). The Private Life, therefore, could know nothing of freedom, but must be governed either by force or tradition. Public Life meant the life led by free and equal citizens when the necessities of life had been taken care of and it was possible, in consequence, for a man to be a person and act freely as himself, winning glory or shame. It was for the Public Realm, also, that all major works of art were made.

Since Public Life was the only place where inspiring deeds could be done, the subject-matter of poets and dramatists was taken from it. The characters in the *Oresteia* or *Oedipus Rex* may be members of a family, but these plays are not domestic dramas. What the characters do and suffer is significant only because they are persons who appear in public.

But today, it is only the house-wife who labors, and the artist who works, at home. Everyone else goes out into public places to earn their living, so that public life has come to mean the life governed by necessity where a man is not himself but a wage-earner, a functionary, and the terms *Personal Life* and *Private Life* have become synonymous.

For the Greeks, public life was reserved for a superior minority of the population; those who took part in it were therefore few enough to all know each other personally. To us public life has become the vast anonymous realm which everybody is compelled to enter unless he has "private means". Consequently, we have a term *The Public* which the Greeks lacked and which has been well-defined by Kierkegaard.

> A public is neither a nation, nor a generation nor a community nor a society, nor these particular men, for all these are only what they are through the concrete; no single person who belongs to the public makes a real commitment- for some hours of the day, perhaps, he belongs to the public—at moments when he is nothing else, since when he really is what he is, he does not form part of the public.

The Public is, one might say, our equivalent for the Slavery of the Ancient World. It is for the Public that the products of Mass Entertainment are designed and, since the public has neither an identity of its own nor a memory, works of art of any kind, that is, enduring, unique things, are incomprehensible to it.

The modern poet—I must confine myself to the art I know best—is in a quandary. Like his predecessors, his imagination can only respond to the personal deed and, like his predecessors, his audience can only consist of persons.

There are persons in the modern world who correspond to the heroes of the past in that their deeds are both their own and, in the original sense of the word, political, for they profoundly affect the history of the community—and these are the great scientific discoverers.

Unfortunately, poetry cannot celebrate them, as it could Achilles, because their deeds are not translatable into personal speech. Anybody can understand what King Lear did, and Shakespeare can tell us what he thought and felt about himself, but what a scientist does or thinks is only intelligible to his colleagues. Further, though his deed is personal, it is not done in the personal domain but in the impersonal domain of nature.

The only place where the modern poet can find personal actions of a kind that he is capable of dealing with is private life which, in practice, means the lives of himself and his acquaintances, and it is only in private life that he can find his audience, large or small.

Art and Action

A work of art is, as we have seen, something made by craft and created with art. Art, as distinct from craft has a certain affinity, overlooked by classical theory, with action.

As a work of craft, a poem is like a table or a tool and unlike an action, in that it does not occur at a moment but is there at hand; Achilles can only kill Hector once, but the Iliad can always be re-read. But, as a creation of art, a poem is unlike a table and like an action, in that it is unique—every poem is the only one of its kind—and discloses its author as an action discloses its agent. The plays of Shakespeare could not have been written by Ben Jonson and vice versa. There remains, of course, a great difference; the person King Lear is identical with what he does and suffers; the person Shakespeare is not identical with any or all of his plays. We can judge Lear as a person; we can only judge Shakespeare as a poet.

It is not surprising, however—every aspect of the modern world drives him to it—if the modern artist should come to think of his work as a kind—even maybe, the only kind now possible—of personal deed, and of himself, not as a maker of enduring objects, but as a heroic creator of a unique universe.

To the degree that this is so, the works of art of the past are for him not traditional models, but inspiring examples, and the examples which mean most to one artist may mean nothing to another.

CHRISTIANITY AND THE ARTS

Under this general title, Auden delivered two lectures at Northwestern University, 28–29 January 1959. Both were reported in the *Daily Northwestern* on the following day. *The Things That Are Caesar's.* The newspaper's summary was written by Cricket Stanton:

> W. H. Auden told an overflow crowd at Tech auditorium last night that there was no "such thing as Christian art" in the traditionally accepted sense. . . .
>
> Maintaining that Christian art cannot be developed or recognized by the mere use of Christian symbols, Auden cited a painting of Van Gogh as an instance of really Christian art.
>
> He referred to a vivid painting of a lightning-struck tree as "painting anguish without painting the historic garden of Gethsemane."

Parables, Auden continued, make up a great part of the New Testament, but they are on the surface secular stories with no reference to theology.

Quoting the Biblical text, "He that hath ears to hear, let him hear," Auden stressed the importance of "Christian reading." It is necessary, Auden said, to interpret what the artist has shown in a Christian manner and in a framework of Christian thought. He pointed out that the early fathers of the Church found just reading the scriptures was inadequate in spite of their theological content.

Auden defined some characteristics of all works of art, whatever their date:

• Works of art are artificial, man-made objects, and when man chooses to use natural materials in his work, he must kill them first. Nature does not qualify as a work of art.

Thus, a living tree cannot be part of a work of art until it has been cut down and made into dead wood. Or, Auden continued, "living thoughts" must be transformed into letters and soundwaves to be incorporated into a work of art.

• Art is distinct from craftsmanship, and a work of art has a unique value. The original creation is a work of art, according to Auden, while copies of it are merely displays of craftsmanship.

• A work of art may be recognized as such without knowing its meaning as intended by the artist. We can, Auden said, appreciate art from different cultures and different eras though they are quite foreign to our own.

Dingley Dell and the Fleet. The second lecture was summarized by Cricket Stanton and Mark Haggard:

W. H. Auden drew on Charles Dickens' *Pickwick Papers* last night in Tech auditorium to illustrate certain Christian concepts in literature.

The real meaning of *Pickwick Papers*, as Auden defined it, lies not in its being categorized as a children's novel, but in a theme that Dickens might not have been aware of: fall from innocence.

According to Auden's interpretation, Pickwick was the epitome of the "innocent" man, one who was not even aware of evil, but who subsequently discovers it.

Pickwick, in this interpretation, was living in an Eden which Auden characterized as a place of original innocence, "where contradictions have not yet arisen, where universals are lacking, and the prerequisites for entrance are to be born happy and likable."

The characteristics of Pickwick's Eden are several:

• There is no distinction, between the objective and the subjective view. Man appears to others just as he appears to himself.

• The only impulse for an action is pleasure; no action has a goal beyond performance.

• The only "serpent" is any serious need or desire that would upset Eden's equilibrium.

Because of Pickwick's state of "innocence" in his personal Eden, Auden points out that Pickwick is at first actually playing in a kind of "closed world of a game" where "mock passions" are indulged in. And, as far as Pickwick is concerned, the "good game is one which all the players enjoy."

Subsequent developments in the story cast Pickwick into a lawsuit and Fleet

Street prison, where he loses his original innocence and finds that reality is not played like a game.

Auden explained that Pickwick learns the law and does not find the unjust guilty and the innocent unguilty. "Pickwick's innocence is lost as he recognizes the evils inherent in the English court systems and debtors' prisons."

While Dickens is known to have wished Fleet prison and the attendant evils abolished, Auden hinted that Pickwick's "fall from innocence" may not have been Dickens' original meaning for the story.

This would be in accordance with Auden's remarks in the first lecture. Wednesday night, when he postulated that the author's intentions might not be a central condition for producing a meaningful work.

Auden also explored the idea of a "debtor" and "creditor" in philosophical terms. The question is not one that "can be answered quantitatively," Auden maintained. Justice is satisfied when one "gets what he needs and gives what he can."

Thus, though Pickwick went to prison of his own volition and not because he could not pay what was demanded of him, Auden indicated that Pickwick eventually realizes that he is a debtor because "he is more fortunate than most."

Auden contrasted Pickwick's "innocence" with that of Don Quixote, Cervantes' knight-errant. Though Quixote set out to win honor and the trappings of the knightly tradition, expecting suffering, and Pickwick eschewed ambition and moral causes, expecting a good time, their fates may have been parallel.

Pickwick, Auden pointed out, cannot be restored to his original innocence, and Quixote renounces knight-errantry with the astute and applicable observation that "in last year's nest, there are no birds this year."

Or, as Auden concluded, "take off the comic mask; the game is over."

Auden on the Air

This appendix lists Auden's radio and television talks, readings, and discussions. Other broadcasts almost certainly occurred but have left no trace.

Auden recorded a talk on Dostoyevsky for a series of talks under the general title "What Dostoyevsky Means to Me", broadcast by Radio Liberation, 9 February 1956. A transcript and further notes appear below.

Auden appeared briefly on the CBS Television quiz program *Strike It Rich*, probably on or before 5 March 1956, to appeal for funds for Dorothy Day's Catholic Worker shelter on the Bowery in New York. He had received wide publicity for having given $250 to Dorothy Day so that she could pay a fine that had been imposed on her for not having made required repairs to the shelter. He insisted on saying that one of Dorothy Day's merits was that she helped the "undeserving poor", a term that made CBS uncomfortable. In a letter to Phyllis McGinley, 6 March 1956, Auden wrote: "Thank you so much for your very sweet note. You know how it is: when St Joseph gives an order, what's the use of arguing? How I agree with you about the Undeserving Poor! Our temptation, of course, is to be snooty about Social Welfare, as if unromantic S.W. were not also doing le Bon Dieu's work." (Syracuse University)

The BBC TV series *Panorama* broadcast on 13 February 1956 a program "Professor of Poetry at Oxford" that included a filmed interview with Auden in New York.

The NBC Television series *Frontiers of Faith* broadcast on 11 March 1956 an interview with Auden by Dr Stanley Hopper, with readings (by Auden?) of some poems.

Auden was interviewed, and read some poems, on the NBC Television program *Home*, 27 March 1956; no further details are known.

The panel of guests on the BBC TV series *The Brains Trust*, 17 June 1956, comprised Auden, Oliver Franks, Solly Zuckerman, and David Daiches. Asked for an example of last words that posterity might cherish, Auden offered "I've never done this before" (reported in *Manchester Guardian*, 18 June 1956).

The BBC Third Programme broadcast a recording of Auden's Oxford inaugural lecture, "Making, Knowing and Judging", 29 September 1956. A transcript is in the BBC Written Archives Centre (see p. 949).

A discussion of Henry James by Auden, R. P. Blackmur, and G. Stanley Koehler, recorded at Amherst, Mass., 18 February 1956, was broadcast in a radio series *As Others Read Us: American Fiction Abroad*, by stations in the National Association of Educational Broadcasters starting late in 1956. This was the second in a series of eight broadcasts prepared by the Literary Society of the University of Massachusetts; a tape recording and transcript are in the library of the University of Massachusetts at Amherst.

A sermon that Auden delivered at Edinburgh University was broadcast by the BBC Scottish Service, 10 March 1957.

Auden, J. Bronowski, and the Very Rev. F. W. Dillistone participated in a discussion, "How Should We Use Our New [Liverpool] Cathedral?" in the BBC TV series *Meeting Point*, 26 May 1957.

The CBS Television series *Camera Three*, devoted to cultural and intellectual themes, broadcast two programs on Auden on 2 and 9 March 1958. The first, "The Secret Agent", had actors reading Auden's poems, and he did not appear; in the second, "The Search for the Hero", he discussed "The Shield of Achilles" and "In Memory of W. B. Yeats" with James Macandrew. Videotape copies of a kinescope recording of the broadcast are intermittently available from commercial rental services.

The BBC Third Programme broadcast Auden's Oxford lecture "Byron's *Don Juan*", 14 May 1958. A transcript is the BBC Written Archives Centre (see p. 971).

Auden and Norman Dello Joio held a recorded, scripted discussion under the title "Realism in Opera" during a *Texaco Metropolitan Opera Broadcast* of *Cavalleria Rusticana*, on CBS Radio, 3 January 1959. A mimeographed transcript is in the Metropolitan Opera archives; a similar transcript, in the Berg Collection, is apparently based on a preliminary version of the recorded discussion, and has Auden's pencilled notes on changes to be made when part of the discussion was re-recorded prior to the broadcast.

Auden read "Homage to Clio" and talked with Anne Fremantle on the CBS Television religious series *Look Up and Live*, 1 March 1959; the broadcast was the first of a series of four, titled "This Bent World", on the problems of Christianity today. (The actress Siobhán McKenna appeared separately in the same broadcast.)

Auden, Jacques Barzun, and Lionel Trilling held an unscripted discussion under the title "Culture in Conflict" on the program *Open End*, WNTA television, New York, 8 November 2000; the program was moderated by David Suskind. This broadcast, which seems to have resulted from the publicity the three had received for their editorship of The Mid-Century Book Society (see p. 849), was the object of much derision; accounts of it include an anonymous review in *Variety*, 4 November 1959, and Kenneth Tynan's review in *Observer*, 17 January 1960 (reprinted in his *Curtains* [1966]). Barzun recalls the event in his foreword to *A Company of Readers: Uncollected Writings of W. H. Auden, Jacques Barzun, and Lionel Trilling from The Reader's Subscription and Mid-Century Book Clubs*, ed. Arthur Krystal (2001).

Auden was interviewed by Philip Burton on the BBC TV series *Monitor*, 24 April 1960; a transcript is in the BBC Written Archives Centre and was partly printed in the *Listener*, 5 May 1960.

Auden and the Rev. Sidney Lanier discussed poetry and religion on the CBS Television Network series *Look Up and Live*, 22 January 1961. A videotape is in the Museum of Television and Radio in New York.

Auden's talk on Ronald Firbank, titled "An Amateur World", was broadcast on the BBC Third Programme, 29 April 1961. The talk was published in *The Listener* (p. 335).

Auden, Chester Kallman, and Hans Werner Henze discussed their opera *Elegy for Young Lovers* in the BBC Third Programme, 13 July 1961. A transcript is in the BBC Written Archives Centre.

Malcolm Muggeridge spoke with Auden, Stephen Spender, Christopher Isherwood, and Cyril Connolly on his Granada Television series *Appointment with . . .* , 23 March 1962. A transcript is in the archives of Granada Television, and a slightly edited version appears in *Muggeridge, Ancient & Modern* (1981).

Auden recorded a series of three talks on Robert Graves for the BBC Third Programme; these were broadcast as "W. H. Auden on Robert Graves", 15, 22, and 26 March 1962. Transcripts and further notes appear below.

A CBC Radio broadcast, "Igor Stravinsky: Inventor of Music", 13 June 1962, included comments by Auden, Kallman, and others.

"Ein Engländer sieht Europa", a talk written in English and translated into German by Peter Stadelmayer (probably with corrections by Auden), was broadcast by the Bayerischer Rundfunk's First Program in its series *"Europäisches Konzert"*, 29 October 1962. The talk was published in *Wort und Wahrheit*, December 1962, as "Sind die Engländer Europäer?", and a retranslation in English appears in this edition (p. 428; notes on p. 935).

On the BBC Television series *Bookstand*, 31 October 1962, Auden was interviewed by A. Alvarez.

Auden and Romney Brent discussed the Strauss-Hofmannsthal collaboration in a scripted discussion during the interval of a Metropolitan Opera radio broadcast of *Der Rosenkavalier*, 22 December 1962. The opera was broadcast in the Texaco-Metropolitan Opera Radio Network and syndicated on many American radio stations; the interval discussions in each performance were given a series title, *Opera News on the Air*. Recordings are in the Metropolitan Opera archives and the New York Public Library.

Auden read a selection of his poems on the BBC Third Programme, 24 December 1962; a transcript is in the BBC Written Archives Centre.

On the NBC television series *The Merv Griffin Show*, 24 December 1962, Auden read some verse and was interviewed by Griffin. In the preceding segment of the broadcast a few dozen children were given Christmas presents, which they continued to unwrap while Auden was speaking. Griffin describes the event in *Merv: An Autobiography*, by Griffin with Peter Barsocchini (1980).

A BROADCAST TO THE SOVIET UNION ON DOSTOEVSKY

Radio Liberation (renamed Radio Liberty in 1959) was an organizaton founded in 1951 that in 1953 began transmitting propaganda to the Soviet Union in seventeen languages. It was based in Munich, with a New York office, and purported to present the voice of Soviet émigrés. It was ostensibly supported by an organization called the American Committee for Liberation from Bolshevism, which was secretly funded by the Central Intelligence Agency. Late in 1955, to commemorate the seventy-fifth anniversary of Dostoyevsky's death on 9 February 1956, the New York office began preparing a series of broadcast statements by American and émigré writers; the general title was "What Dostoyevsky Means to Me". Auden was one of forty-five writers and artists who made statements for the series; among them were his friends Lionel Trilling and V. S. Yanovsky. An account of the series, with texts by some of the participants (not Auden) appears in Gene Sosin, *Sparks of Liberty: An Insider's Memoir of Radio Liberty* (1999).

Gene Sosin of Radio Liberty recorded Auden's talk in his New York apartment, probably late in 1955; a photograph was circulated of Auden sitting before a microphone labeled "Radio Liberation". When the talk was broadcast from Munich, the first two sentences were in Auden's voice, after which a spoken Russian translation faded in and continued to the end, with Auden's voice again heard near the end, speaking part of the sentence that begins "The moment anybody is". A recording of this broadcast version of the talk is the Radio Liberty archives at the Hoover Institution, Stanford University.

The original transcript by Radio Liberty is lost, but a copy is in the BBC Written Archives Centre; a further copy of this was evidently the basis of a text published as a news story in the *Manchester Guardian*, 17 February 1956, headed "W. H. Auden on Dostoyevsky". The text below is based on the transcript at the BBC, but incorporates what may be an editorial emendation made by the newspaper: in the fifth paragraph, where the transcript has "depths of the soul . . ., the alternating", the newspaper replaces the ellipses with "nobody has so spoken about". The newspaper text also corrects Auden's grammar and omits his opening sentence. Excerpts from Auden's and another broadcast in the series were quoted in "Dostoevski at Home", *Newsweek*, 13 February 1956.

The transcript in the BBC Written Archives Centre is headed "Radio Liberation | Dostoevsky Show | W. H. Auden speaks on the 75th Anniversary of Dostoevsky's Death | (Feb. 9, 1881–Feb. 9, 1956)". The square brackets below represent typed diagonals in the original. The paragraphing below is editorial; the transcript has a single-sentence first sentence followed by two long paragraphs, broken at the foot of the first page.

This is W. H. Auden speaking over Radiostation Osvobozhdenie [Liberation] on the 75th anniversary of Dostoevsky's death.

I am really the last person on earth to be talking about Dostoevsky. In the first place, I myself [am] a poet and I find it very difficult to read fiction. In the second place, I was born and brought up in England and I can think of no literary tradition that is so different as the Russian tradition and the English tradition. The English tradition of fiction is much more kind of genteel and polite. My own natural taste in fiction is for writers like Jane Austen or the Alice books of Lewis Carroll. I like books about my betters, people who are nice-looking, who are richer than I am, who have nicer food and are cleverer.

Now, obviously this Dostoevsky does not write about those sort of people, nor is Dostoevsky reticent in the English tradition. I think it is a very interesting difference between Dickens, who I understand both influenced Dostoevsky and whom Dostoevsky liked very much, and Dostoevsky. A Dickens character, whoever he may be, whatever class he comes from, whether he is a scoundrel, whether he is a virtuous character, is completely himself—you might almost say that no Dickens character has a conscience, because there is no contrast between what he is and what he thinks he ought to be. Now, [in] Dostoevsky always the characters are intensely aware of the difference, between what they think they ought to be and what they actually are and do.

Now I don't believe that I would ever have been able to read Dostoevsky at all, if he weren't very funny. After all, Dostoevsky is not, in the English sense of the word, a gentleman. He doesn't write about gentlemen. None of his characters are nice-looking, you don't feel they wash much, and then, they don't even enjoy their food, and oh, how they *talk* about the soul. Furthermore they are all worldly failures and know that they are worldly failures.

Yet, I have to say yes (I don't like this) but here obviously is one of the greatest geniuses—the writer—who ever lived. What he shows you are the depths of the soul; nobody has so spoken about the alternating love of and terror of freedom that every human being feels. When one reads such a wonderful book as, shall we say, *Notes from Underground*, one understands for the first time *really* profoundly why people become Fascists.

The importance ultimately of Dostoevsky does seem to me to be a moral importance, in that the people who need to read him are people who are successful, in this world, whether they are successful intellectuals, whether they are successful managers of businesses, whether they are successful politicians. The moment anybody is, then we all try and think, "Well, things are fine as they are, what we are doing is good," and then comes Dostoevsky screaming, "No, it is not good enough." Society could not *exist* if everybody were like Dostoevsky or his characters. But no society can ever be decent that forgets the kind of criticism Dostoevsky offers us.

THREE BROADCASTS ON ROBERT GRAVES

This series of three broadcast talks for the BBC was recorded by the producer D. G. Bridson in Auden's house in Austria in September 1961 and broadcast in the Third Programme on 15, 22, and 26 March 1962. The text survives in transcripts made by the BBC shortly before the broadcasts. The transcripts are each titled "W. H. Auden on Robert Graves: The first [*or* second *or* last] of three programmes in which W. H. Auden discusses and reads the poetry of Robert Graves."

Except where Auden quotes two different versions of Graves's poems, I have included only the titles (in square brackets) of the complete poems by Graves that he read aloud. Where Auden quotes excerpts from a poem I have appended the title in square brackets. I have made some trivial corrections to the otherwise apparently accurate transcripts, but I have not corrected Auden's abridged quotations from Grave's prose.

In the second lecture, in the paragraph that begins "Among Graves's contemporaries" I have omitted "to" in the phrase "utterly opposed to". In the third lecture, in the paragraph that begins "I would hazard" I have emended "horrors and" to "horrors of", and in the paragraph that begins "Horace is not" the second sentence makes no grammatical sense though the meaning is more or less clear; "size and" could well be an error for "size of".

W. H. AUDEN ON ROBERT GRAVES

I

If I read in the *Radio Times* that Mr Smith is going to give a talk on the poetry of Mr Jones, it is unlikely that I shall feel tempted to listen. The only conditions that might induce me to turn on my wireless set are: firstly, that I have read little or none of Mr Jones, and secondly, that I have sufficient respect for Mr Smith's taste to believe that he would not talk about a poet who's not worth reading. Even then, if I do listen, I shall pay very little attention to Mr

Smith's own remarks and concentrate upon his quotations. And I hope in listening to these talks on the poetry of Robert Graves you will do the same.

Ten years ago I should have felt less superfluous than I do now. I first came across Mr Graves's poetry when I was a schoolboy in the volumes of *Georgian Poetry*, and ever since he has been one of very few poets whose volumes I have always bought the moment they appeared. There were, no doubt, many others who did the same. But until recently Graves was not a public figure in the way that, for instance, Yeats and Eliot were. His poetry would crop up in private conversation between individuals who had discovered it for themselves. But his name was not bandied about at cocktail parties to show that the speaker was au courant—nor was his work made the subject of critical articles or Ph.D. theses. But now this has changed.

["From the Embassy"]

So wrote Mr Graves a few years ago, and it is already out of date. The photographers have reached his front door. When one looks at Mr Graves's bibliography one is astonished (if one is as lazy as I am, a bit depressed) by the variety of his talents and his incredible industry. He has written long historical novels, short stories, autobiography, biblical criticisms, anthropological and sociological studies, translations from Latin, German, Greek, French and Spanish.

Admirable as all of these are, I shall confine myself to poetry. One may remark, however, that whether he is right or wrong in the very sharp division he makes between the themes proper to poetry and those proper to prose, it is a view which is easier for someone to take who has the rare good fortune to possess equal talents in both media. A writer who can only write prose or only write poetry must either renounce all hope of dealing with a wide range of experience or attempt, again rightly or wrongly, to extend the domain of the medium he commands.

Theory or no theory, Graves himself writes short poems. Here, for example are two picked more or less at random—a fairly early one and a fairly late one.

["Outlaws" and "Through Nightmare"]

After hearing these, I think one can guess why the kind of critic who selects his poet according to the opportunity his work provides for displaying his own brilliant ingenuity, steers clear of Mr Graves. There are, it is true, some poems of his which benefit from a gloss, but this he has provided himself in *The White Goddess* about which I shall have a few words to say later. But the majority of his poems, like these two, are self-contained in reference. Graves happens to be a very learned man: he's not a descendant of the great historian Von Ranke for nothing. He does not demand scholarship of his readers; the diction of his poems is simple; the reader seldom has to consult a dictionary; their syntax is unambiguous, and their subject matter experiences with which everyone is familiar, and in which everyone is interested: dreams, love, nature, the morality of a personal life, and so forth.

Robert Frost has said that the difference between prose and poetry is that the former is translatable and the latter is not. Though personally I think this is only a half-truth—I prefer Nietzsche's remark, "It is neither the better nor the worst in a work which is translatable"—still, it is a very important half-truth.

Among the arts, poetry is unique in two respects: its medium, speech, is not reserved for poets, as paint is only used by painters, as musical notes by composers, but is the creation of a whole society which uses words for a thousand different purposes. And then, poetry is a local, even a parochial art. One can only read poetry which is written in a language one happens to know, and one can only fully understand poetry written in one's own tongue. There can never really be an international poetic style.

There are, however, as anyone who has studied the poetry of this century will know—though it is not only a modern phenomenon, I believe—there *are* poets who have tried to incorporate into their native poetry tradition, as much as they can from the poetic tradition of other languages. Graves is one of the few English poets of our time whose work shows no influences other than English—none, for example, of the French Symbolists.

So far as English poetry is concerned, it is interesting to observe he has ignored the fashionable taste of the metaphysical. I should guess that his personal taste in English poetry is pretty much today what it was when he began writing—though of course age is less indulgent than youth. He has always liked nursery rhymes, ballads, Skelton, the Caroline poets like Rochester and Lovelace, romantic poets like Blake, Coleridge and Christina Rosetti, and he has never liked Virgil, Milton, Dryden or Pope.

In his poetic technique he is what one may call a traditionalist rather than a revolutionary; in the way, that is, that in music would call Mozart a traditionalist and Beethoven a revolutionary. This does not mean, of course, that the traditionalist is less original than the revolutionary. It only means that he accepts the conventions and uses them in a personal way, while the revolutionary tries to create new conventions.

Graves, for example, has never, like so many of his contemporaries, experimented with free verse or sprung rhythm or unusual metres of any kind, nor tried to find new patterns of poetic organisation. In reading a poet I am always interested to note what he does *not* write about—what subjects he considers unsuitable for poetry. Graves, for example, has nothing to say in poetry about public life, politics, the world situation, and so forth.

This does not mean, of course, that he is an anarchist who denies any significance to public events. He could not have written his historical novels if he were. He would hold, I am sure, that a poet like other citizens must pay his taxes and in time of crisis perform whatever duty is required of him, but without undue hope or passion, for the public world has been irredeemable since it became a masculine province. And in our age, no writer, least of all a poet, can have a public function; his realm is that of the intimate life. I can imagine circumstances in which Mr Graves might become a guerilla fighter, but I cannot see him writing pamphlets for any cause.

Here is a poem which seems to me to indicate his attitude towards politics:

["The Cuirassiers of the Frontier"]

Another interesting question is the judgement of a poet about his own work. Almost all poets, I think, have published poems which later they came to dislike or be ashamed of. From its author's point of view, a poem can fail in various ways. The initial conception may be all right, but the expression is defective, clumsy, imprecise, ill-proportioned. In this case, it is possible to correct these thoughts by careful revision. Much more embarrassing are those poems which one realises one should never have tried to write. It does not necessarily follow that such a poem is bad itself, and it may even have success with the public. Only the poet knows that *he* should not have written it. It is lacking somehow in personal authenticity: the handwriting, as it were, is not his.

We could only discover what a poet's private opinions are if he publishes successive *Collected Poems* which are the same time selective. This Graves has done repeatedly, and to compare one with the other is revealing. His first *Collected Poems* were published in 1926, his latest this year. When I look to see how many poems in the first volume he has retained, some interesting facts emerge. Of the poems he wrote between 1914 and 1920 he rejects altogether those he wrote on the subject of the War—and little less than half of the rest.

Then between 1920 and 1923, he had in his opinion a good period, for he has reprinted more than half of them. But then, in the following three years, he evidently feels he was erring from his true path: for of the forty-three poems from that period printed in the first collection he has rejected all but four.

The special devil—I don't know his name—whose task it is to lead all poets astray adapts his temptations to the individual case. Graves has told us himself about his own temptations:

> But you know, I know, and you know I know
>   My principal curse;
> Shame at the mounting dues I have come to owe
>   A devil of verse,
> Who caught me young, inexperienced and uncouth,
>   Prompting me how
> To evade the clumsiness of truth—
>   Which I do now.
>
>   ["To Calliope"]

Graves was born (the term is inaccurate but convenient) with a natural talent for writing verse. Ask him to write a poem on any subject, and in ten minutes he will turn out something competent and musical. This is a very valuable gift, but a dangerous one, for the poet who possesses it can all too easily forsake the truth for verbal display. Personally, I object to verbal virtuosity less than Graves does, provided that the poet is honest about what he is doing, and does not pretend to be offering us wisdom, or does not deceive us into believing he does. Graves does allow a place for virtuosity, but only in comic poetry. Actually, I suspect that we differ only in our notion of the comic. To me, for instance, Milton's "Lycidas" is a marvellous nonsense poem which I could learn, to use as a touchstone of Graves, by heart not by rote, as I can learn the poems of Edward Lear.

But here, as an illustration of Graves's virtuosity—here is a parody of a guidebook instruction. Here is a poem called "Welcome to the Caves of Arta":

["Welcome to the Caves of Arta"]

His other temptation has been the tendency of the romantic imagination to regard the extraordinary and remote as being more "poetic" (in quotes), more numinous than everyday events, dreams as truer than waking life. Of some of his earlier poems, one might say—to adopt a saying of Puccini's about the music of Gluck—"Puzzano di poesia":

> The lost, the freakish, the unspelt
> Drew me; for simple sights I had no eye.
> And did I swear allegiance then
> To wildness, not (as I thought) to truth—
> Become a virtuoso, and this also,
> Later, of simple sights, when tiring
> Of unicorn and upas?

["The Ages of Oath"]

In overcoming both of these temptations—to verbal display and to romantic indulgence—the personal accounts and poetic example of Laura Riding is obviously of immense value. Successful as he has been in disciplining his imagination and his style, on occasions (admittedly they are rare) he seems to me to indulge his feelings at the expense of objective fact. Here, for example, is a recent poem, "Turn of the Moon":

["Turn of the Moon"]

I find this a beautiful poem and at the first reading I was completely carried away. But on repeating it to myself, the question obtruded: "But are rainfall and drought really caused by the moon? What would a meteorologist say?"

Graves believes, as most poets do, that a good poem is a gift from the Muse and cannot be created by an act of will and conscious calculation.

> Call the man a liar who says I wrote
> All that I wrote for love, for love of art.
> > ["A Plea to Boys and Girls"]

But the young must not misinterpret this, and think that everything that comes into their head is inspiration and that conscious or critical revision is unnecessary—even wicked. If young poets should *believe* that Graves believes this, a look at his own revisions will disillusion them. Here are two poems—first, as they were originally printed, and then as they now appear in the last volume of his *Collected Poems*:

"One Hard Look"—first version:

> Small gnats that fly
> In hot July
> And lodge in sleeping ears,
> Can rouse therein
> A trumpet's din
> With Day of Judgment fears.
>
> Small mice at night
> Can wake more fright
> Than lions at midday.
> An urchin small
> Torments us all
> Who tread his prickly way.
>
> A straw will crack
> The camel's back,
> To die we need but sip,
> So little sand
> As fills the hand
> Can stop a steaming ship.
>
> One smile relieves
> A heart that grieves
> Though deadly sad it be,
> And one hard look
> Can close the book
> That lovers love to see.

"One Hard Look"—second version:

> Small gnats that fly
> In hot July
> And lodge in sleeping ears,

Can rouse therein
A trumpet's din
With Day of Judgment fears.

Small mice at night
Can wake more fright
Than lions at midday;
A straw will crack
The camel's back;
There is no easier way.

One smile relieves
A heart that grieves
Though deadly sad it be,
And one hard look
Can close the book
That lovers love to see.

"The Sea Horse"—first version:

Tenderly confine your secret love
(For one who never pledged you less than love)
To this indomitable hippocamp,
Child of your element, coiled a-ramp,
Having ridden out worse elements than you know of:
Make much of your despair, and shed
Salt tears to bathe his taciturn dry head.

"The Sea Horse"—second version:

Since now in every public place
Lurk phantoms who assume your walk and face,
You cannot yet have utterly abjured me
Nor stifled the insistent roar of the sea.

Do as I do: confide your unquiet love
(For one who never owed you less than love)
To this indomitable hippocamp,
Child of your element, coiled a-ramp,
Having ridden out worse elements than you know of;
Under his horny ribs a blood-red stain
Portends renewal of our pain.
Sweetheart, make much of him and shed
Tears on his taciturn dry head.

That is what I call craftsmanship.

II

The main theme of poetry Graves has written is properly the relations of Man and Woman rather than those of man and man as the Apollonian classicist would have it. This statement implies that most of the good poems will probably be love poems in the strict sense. But to be properly understood the reader must know something of Graves's views about what the proper relationship between Man and Woman should be. I have no time to give anything but the sketchiest account of them: nor have I the erudition. And I can only recommend that you read *The White Goddess, The Greek Myths* and *Watch the North Wind Rise* for yourselves. Not only because they are fascinating reading but also for the light they throw on Graves's own poetry. Indeed, during the whole of this talk I'm going to take the part rather of an anthologist than anything else, and let Graves speak for himself.

According to Graves, the original deity of the Mediterranean was the Mother Goddess, worshipped under her three aspects: as Virgin, Queen Mother, and Crone. The social organisation that went with this belief was a matriarchy with a ritual killing of the Queen's male consort or consorts. Then came a time, I think at the beginning of the Iron Age, when the cult of the Mother Goddess was replaced by the cult of the masculine Sun God and matriarchal society replaced by patriarchal, in which women were relegated to an inferior status. This change, in Graves's opinion, was the real fall—the point in which humanity took the wrong turning. Wisdom and numinous power belonged to Woman. Man by himself has only brute force. So that the moment he loses his reverence and awe for Woman, he becomes greedy, vulgar and destructive. It is not only poetry that suffers but every sphere of life.

The sacredness Graves accords to Woman is not however simply a moral value. He is far from believing that women are saints. On the contrary his awe includes terror. The Goddess who gives life also brings death. The White Goddess (I quote) "is the flower-goddess Olwen or Blodeuwedd; but she is also Blodeuwedd the Owl, lamp-eyed, hooting dismally with her foul nest in the hollow of a dead tree, or Circe the pitiless falcon, or Lamia with her flickering tongue, or the snarling-chopped Sow-goddess, or the mare-headed Rhiannon who feeds on raw flesh".

Now here is a poem based on Graves's reconstruction of her original cult. But as a gloss to it, let me first read another passage.

> In Europe there were at first no male Gods contemporary with the Goddess to challenge her prestige or power. But she had a lover who was alternatively the beneficent serpent of wisdom and the beneficent star of life—her son. The son was incarnate in the male daemons in the various totem societies ruled by her who assisted in the erotic dances held in her honour. The serpent incarnate in the sacred serpents which were the ghosts of the dead, sent the winds. The son who was also called

Lucifer, or Phosporous, bringer of light (because as the Evening Star he led in the light of the Moon), was reborn every year, grew up as the year advanced, destroyed the serpent and won the Goddess's love. Her love destroyed him, but from her ashes was born another serpent, which, at Easter laid the red egg which she ate, so that the son was reborn to her as a child once more. There are as yet, no fathers. For the serpent is no more the father of the star son than the star son is of the serpent: they are twins. And here we are returned to the single poetic theme. The poet identifies himself with the star son. His hated rival is the serpent. Only if he is writing as a satirist does he play the serpent. The triple Muse is woman in her divine character—the poet's enchantress, the only theme of his songs. (*The White Goddess*, pp. 320–21)

And now the poem—it is called "To Juan at the Winter Solstice".

["To Juan at the Winter Solstice"]

The Goddess bestows favours as she chooses, and she withdraws them when she chooses. Here is a poem about her in her aspect as the Goddess of Death. The title: "Dethronement".

["Dethronement"]

The Goddess rules not only over men, but also over all living things. Here is a poem about her in her role as Mother Nature or Dame Kind. "Rhea":

["Rhea"]

The Sun God who replaced her is a God of Thunder and War. And the consequences of his cult are a glorification of war and the wasteful, ruthless, irreverent exploitation of Nature, of which Graves speaks in another poem, "The Destroyer".

["The Destroyer"]

In the Arts, when the feminine Muse is deposed in favour of the masculine Apollo, the consequence is imitative and academic art, hence for example this poem, "Apollo of the Physiologists".

["Apollo of the Physiologists"]

However, because the Sun God has no sacred power of his own—only brute force—in the end he dooms himself; for as soon as his worshippers have acquired, through technique, enough force of their own they cease to believe in him. He becomes Blake's Old Nobodaddy and by the end of the Nineteenth Century Nietzsche can confidently write his obituary. Since I believe that poets are the best judges of their own works, I must apologise for now using as an illustration a poem which Graves has omitted from his Collected Poems. It is called "The Twelve Days of Christmas."

["The Twelve Days of Christmas"]

Among Graves's contemporaries there's another writer who has also asserted that the main theme of literature is the relation between man and woman: D. H. Lawrence. But that is the only point upon which they agree. Lawrence was a worshipper of the masculine deity, either as the Sun God or as the dark Dionysus. He believed that the male should dominate the female for she can only take life from him. Like Graves's *bête noire*, Milton, he subscribes to the doctrine "He for God only, she for God in him". To this, of course, Graves is utterly opposed, and nothing could be more different from Lawrence's exaltation of the phallus than this poem "Down Wanton, Down!".

["Down, Wanton, Down!"]

The only concession that Graves is willing to make to male vanity is that he allows the writing of poetry is normally a masculine activity. Woman, he says, is not a poet. "She is either a Muse or she is nothing. A woman who concerns herself with poetry should, I believe, either be a silent Muse and inspire the poets by her womanly presence, or she should be the Muse in the complete sense. She should be in turn Arianrhod, Blodeuwedd and the Old Sow of Maenawr Penardd, and should write about each of these capacities with antique authority. She should be the visible Moon, impartial, loving, cruel, wise."

It is not necessary to agree on every point of Graves's mythology to appreciate the excellence of his love lyrics,—in which genre of poetry I think one can say without hesitation that no English poet of this century has excelled him. His only possible rival is Thomas Hardy, and most of Hardy's best-loved poems are elegies. Yeats wrote many beautiful love poems, but no single one of them seems to me to do equal justice to all elements of love. In his earlier poems "love expressed" seems too disembodied and up in the clouds—passion in a world where nobody catches cold or goes to the bathroom. His later poems on the other hand—he goes to the opposite extreme, and seems to be almost exclusively concerned with the physical element in love. In the first lot he is more Petrarch than Petrarch, and in the second he is a merry old rake. But Graves always manages to pay equal homage in his poems both to physical desire and to personal affection. He has enumerated the various one-sided heresies about sex in a poem, "Cry Faugh!"

["Cry Faugh!"]

To show the variety of lovers' moods which he can express, here is an anxious one, "The Straw".

["The Straw"]

And here is a sad one, "Lament for Pasiphaë".

["Lament for Pasiphaë"]

And here is one I have chosen because it is personally one of my favourites. It is called "A Dialogue on the Headland".

["A Dialogue on the Headland"]

Indeed the only mood which I find missing in Mr Graves's poems, though he admits that it always will occur when the beloved is a real incarnation of the Goddess, is the Catullian mode "*Odi et amo*".

And here in conclusion are two observations of a lighter nature about the feminine character. The first is called "Beauty in Trouble".

["Beauty in Trouble"]

And the second, "A Slice of Wedding Cake".

["A Slice of Wedding Cake"]

Well—these poems—what critical comments can one make except "Thank you"?

III

Graves has written no poems in praise of heroic individuals. But taken as a whole, his poetry, like that of every serious poet, expresses by implication his notion of the hero. That is to say, of the kind of man whom everyone should try to be. And of his opposite—the churl—the kind of man who no one ought to be.

Although the male figure who appears in his poems is usually the poet in love, this does not mean that Graves believes as some of the Romantics did, the poet is superior to all other folks—the only true hero—a view which is generally accompanied by the belief that the poetic genius is the exception to which the ordinary laws of morality do not apply. He would certainly not agree with Yeats' lines, "The intellect of man is forced to choose / Perfection of the life or of the work". On the contrary, he has always stressed the intimate relation between Art and Ethics. The poet, in fact, has to be more careful than other people because he leads a life of continual self-exposure.

A scientist, for example, might in his human relations be vicious, cowardly, dishonest without affecting his work in the laboratory, but any flaw in a poet's character will betray itself in his poems. I think that on the whole I agree with Graves—with this proviso: that some personal defects are more fatal to poetry than others. It is obvious for example that a man who is dishonest with himself about what he feels will never write good poetry. It is not so clear what effect it will have on his writing if he is avaricious or gluttonous. Moreover, it is impossible surely to deny that there have been artists whose personal lives were far from admirable, whose art compels admiration even when one can detect their flawed character in it. I think, for example, of the music of Wagner.

Graves's conception of the good life is a marriage between what are conventionally called Romantic and Classical attitudes. "The true poet" he has written, "is not to be identified with the *Romantic* poet".

Romantic, a useful word while it covered the re-introduction into Western Europe, via the writers of the romances, of a mystical reverence for woman, has become tainted by indiscriminate use. The typical romantic poet of the nineteenth century was physically degenerate or ailing, addicted to drugs and melancholia, critically unbalanced, and a true poet only in his fatalistic regard for the Goddess as the mistress who commanded his destiny.

The classical poet, however gifted and industrious, fails to pass the test because he claims to be the Goddess's master. She is his mistress only in the derogatory sense of one who lives in coquettish ease under his protection. Now, what application has this to the lives of everybody, whether they happen to write poetry or not?

Everybody who lives in a technological civilisation (and in the West we have lived in one for a century and a half), is in constant danger of ceasing to be himself—ceasing to be even a member of a certain nation, class, or profession and becoming an anonymous unit of the public.

The public, as Kierkegaard said, is an abstraction since it is composed of people at moments when they are not themselves. This can happen to any of us—rich or poor, vicious or virtuous—if we relax our vigilance. The way in which the public exists has been well described by another poet whom Graves admires—E. E. Cummings:

> pity this busy monster manunkind,
>
> not. Progress is a comfortable disease:
> your victim (death and life safely beyond)
>
> plays with the bigness of his littleness
> —electrons deify one razorblade
> into a mountainrange; lenses extend
>
> unwish through curving wherewhen till unwish
> returns on its unself.
>   A world of made
> is not a world of born-pity poor flesh
>
> and trees; poor stars and stones, but never this
> fine specimen of hypermagical
>
> ultraomnipotence. We doctors know
>
> a hopeless case if—listen: there's a hell
> of a good universe next door; let's go

The Romantic mistake was to identify the public with the bourgeoisie. The bourgeoisie and the public share, it is true, one characteristic. They both lack reverence for the magical mysterious. But that is all they do share. The bourgeoisie has a sense of order, even if it be an uninspired one. It believes that there are things which should be done, and things which should not be done,—even its moral views are one-sided or distorted. The public, on the other hand, is totally chaotic: it has no conventions of behaviour in which it believes, but is moved by the fashion of the moment.

To the Romantic, therefore, the hero, the authentic Man, was the rebel against all order—one who like Baudelaire's Dandy, cultivates his hysteria with delight and terror. Graves shares the romantic belief only in his insistence upon the importance of the irrational. Dreams are an essential element in life, and we must be grateful even for nightmares. He's written a poem indeed, called "Gratitude for a Nightmare".

["Gratitude for a Nightmare"]

And also like the Romantics, Graves believes that authenticity can no longer be achieved through accepting the life of any group; one's true path is to-day necessarily a solitary one. As he expresses in a poem "The Cloak":

["The Cloak"]

Nor are there any printed guides any more to what one's true path should be. Tradition is no longer trustworthy. Hence this poem "No More Ghosts".

["No More Ghosts"]

The ordinary man no less than the poet has to learn to fly crooked like the cabbage-white. There is a poem by Graves called "Flying Crooked".

["Flying Crooked"]

But (and here Graves is at one with the Classicists) the search for authenticity is also a search for an authentic order and morality. A sense of mystery and commonsense are not incompatible but complementary. As Graves pointed out in quite an early poem about Alice in Wonderland, "Alice":

["Alice"]

I would hazard a guess that what first made Graves conscious of the dramatic fallacy was his experience as a soldier in the First World War. A man who has experienced the horrors of absolute disorder on a mass scale, is unlikely ever again to seek a solution for his personal problems in personal excesses. Having known public madness he knows the value of personal sanity, and he suggests this in the only poem of his about the war, I think, called "Recalling War":

["Recalling War"]

Graves like the classicists believes very strongly in the value of the Golden Mean. Though unlike them he regards it as a gift of the Goddess, for all Gods are Gods of some kind of excess or other. Here is one poem of his in celebration of the Mean: "Ogres and Pygmies".

["Ogres and Pygmies"]

Horace is not, I imagine, a poet of whom Graves approves. The size and the difference between their Muses—Horace's unpassionate and easy-going: Graves's passionate and puritanical. But they have a common dislike of crankiness and theatrical gestures. If, as a poet of common sense, Graves is the more convincing advocate of the two it is because one feels that he has had to fight to achieve it. One doubts, perhaps unjustly, that Horace ever suffered from nightmares or from a passion so violent that it threatened to destroy him. But Horace would have admired, and approved of, I think, Graves's description of a climate of thought.

["The Climate of Thought"]

And like any good bourgeois, Graves dislikes laziness and untidiness. A man should work to earn his living, support his wife and children and pay his debts. Those who don't will be haunted by unwelcome visitors like the Lollocks.

["Lollocks"]

As I said at the beginning of my first talk, I have a fear that I may be wasting my time, telling you things which you know already, especially since Graves has now become a public figure. I do not know whether for his sake to be glad or sorry about this. One always is glad of course when a poet one has long admired gains wide recognition, publicity at least means greater sale. But public fame has its dangers, not, if one has Graves's years and strength of character, for the poet himself,—but for his public. He becomes—with his consent or without it—responsible for a fashion, and though some fashions are better than others, there is an element of falsehood in them all. Moreover, the more original and forceful his poetical personality, the greater his potential threat to the integrity of the others. Yet, instead of being inspired by his example to follow their own paths, they take him as a model, whose manner of writing and literary tastes they blindly copy. If a poet is good, one should surrender completely to his poems. One should always be wary about his poetic theories and critical judgements. Especially about his negative ones. No good poet, once he has grown up, I believe, has ever admired a poem which was bad, but all good poets have, in their own interest, had to reject certain kinds of poems—even if to others they are good.

As to what is a good poem or a bad one, perhaps in the long run all one can say is what Rossini said about musical compositions—"All kinds are good except the boring kind." Graves has said something of this in another way.

["A Plea to Boys and Girls"]

Well, the test is sound enough: a good poem is the one you find that you can learn by heart. But for God's sake—I beg your pardon—for the Goddess's sake, do not let Mr Graves or Mr Eliot, or me or anyone else on earth tell you what you ought to learn by heart. But go your own way as Graves has gone his, so that when the time comes, this valedictory poem could apply to you.

["Leaving the Rest Unsaid"]

Endorsements and Citations

Auden was one of 168 writers, artists, composers, philosophers, scientists, and "heads of cultural institutions" who were invited to John F. Kennedy's inauguration as president on 20 January 1961. About eighty accepted, and, after the event, wrote brief inscriptions in a manuscript book for presentation to Kennedy. Auden's read: "The honor of an invitation to your Inaugural was as thrilling as it was surprising. You have, assuredly, captured the heart of one poet" (quoted by Douglass Cater in "The Kennedy Look in the Arts", *Horizon*, September 1961).

ENDORSEMENTS

The back cover of Chester Kallman's first book of poems, *Storm at Castelfranco*, published by the Grove Press in 1956, has an unsigned four-paragraph description of the book, the third paragraph of which was obviously written by Auden:

It is useless to try to classify poets as if they were brands of soup. Every poet, if he is any good, is unique, even if—as Mr Kallman does not—he announces himself an "-ist" of some sort or other. After reading a poet, however, one can guess, though only in a very rough and general way, what he considers the nature of poetry and of its composition to be. Thus, after reading Mr Kallman's poems, one can feel pretty sure that he would subscribe to the opinion of Paul Valéry that a poet is someone whose imagination is stimulated by arbitrary restrictions (they are not really arbitrary, of course, but they appear so), and agree with the Greeks that a poet, whatever else he may be besides, is first and foremost a "maker." The reader who cares to look for them will be enchanted by subtle and unobtrusive feats of technical skill, and even the most casual reader cannot fail to notice the remarkable rhythmical variety of this book, Mr Kallman's first published collection. It is a pleasure to read a poet who can write both in a complex, "dense" style and in a light one, yet remain himself in both.

The dust jacket of Paul Goodman's novel *The Empire City*, published by the Bobbs-Merrill Company in 1959, includes excerpts from a lost longer statement by Auden:

He has fantastic scenes, but they are not silly; he has "frank" scenes but no one in their right mind could call them obscene. . . . Mr Goodman, like all real novelists, is, at bottom, a moralist. What really interests him are the various ways in which human beings living in a modern metropolis gain, keep or lose their integrity and sense of selfhood.

A note about the Looking-Glass Library (see p. 855) in the *Griffin*, October 1959, says of Rex Warner's *Men and Gods*: "According to W. H. Auden, these are the best modern versions in the English language."

William F. Lynch, S.J., was the editor of the quarterly *Thought* for which Auden wrote three essays in the early 1950s; for his book *Christ and Apollo: The Dimensions of the Religious Imagination*, published by Sheed & Ward in 1960, Auden wrote a long endorsement that appeared on the dust jacket and in the publisher's newsletter, *Sheed & Ward's Own Trumpet*, Fall 1960. Correspondence in the publisher's archives at Notre Dame University indicates that Auden wrote this at some time before February 1960:

Surprisingly little work of value has been done on the aesthetic implications of Christian theology, about such questions, for example as—Is there a kind of imagination which can be recognised and defined as Christian? Is it possible for an artist who is a perfectly orthodox Christian in his conscious beliefs to exhibit a heretical imagination in his art, or for one who is not a Christian believer to produce works of art which are aesthetically orthodox?

In my opinion, Father Lynch belongs, with Dr Auerbach and Rudolf Kassner, to the very small group indeed of critics who have something really illuminating to say on such matters.

An excerpt appeared in a Sheed & Ward advertisement in the *New York Times Book Review*, 15 October 1960.

The dust jacket of Ruthven Todd's collection of poems, *Garland for the Winter Solstice*, published by J. M. Dent in 1961, includes a statement by Auden, which he sent to the publisher on 16 November 1960; the typescript and letter are in the University of Michigan Library. The same statement appears on the dust jacket of the American edition published by Little, Brown in 1962. Auden had been friendly with Todd since the 1930s. The statement reads:

I always think of Mr Ruthven Todd as a Nineteenth Century Country Clergyman who has mysteriously managed to get born and to survive in this hectic age. He is that contemporary oddity, a poet who actually seems to be happy. He enjoys writing and he writes about things he enjoys, quietly, honestly, without fuss. As a "nature" poet, he is almost the only one today who is a real naturalist and can tell one bird or flower from another—his erudition in these matters makes me very jealous. It is pleasant, too, in reading a selection from twenty-five years' work, to find a poet who has grown steadily better, more himself, with each succeeding year.

An advertisement for books by William Carlos Williams, in *Encounter*, January 1962, included a statement by Auden:

William Carlos Williams happens to be an important figure in contemporary American poetry. But that is beside the point. Nobody wants to read a writer because he is important: we want to read one who will give us joy. Dr Williams is one of those rare and lucky poets whose work has got steadily better and richer as they went on writing, so that the poems of his old age are his best. In my opinion, "Asphodel, That Greeny Flower" is one of the most beautiful love poems in the language.

A typescript in the New Directions archives has the earlier name of Williams's poem, "Work in Progress", instead of the later name, "Asphodel, That Greeny Flower".

The dust jacket of John Simon's *Acid Test*, published by Stein & Day in 1963, has a statement by Auden: "As a critic Mr John Simon is lucid, learned, witty and, even when he is most savage, just and in good taste." John Simon had worked with Auden at The Mid-Century Book Society (see p. 849). Auden sent the comment to Simon (omitting "he") in a letter postmarked 17 November 1962 but perhaps written earlier (the letter is on the letterhead of a Chicago hotel, but the envelope is postmarked New York): "Hope it will do as a blurb. Actually, I think, you are sometimes too kind, e.g. to Mr Albee" (Argosy Book Store, New York).

CITATIONS

The American Academy of Arts and Letters and the National Institute of Arts and Letters holds an annual Ceremonial in New York at which the winners of prizes and awards are announced. Members of the Academy and Institute write brief anonymous citations for the Institute's Arts and Letters awards; these are printed in the Academy and Institute's annual *Proceedings*. For the Academy and Institute's Ceremonial on 22 May 1957, Auden wrote two of the tributes in the category of Literature:

To James Baldwin, born in New York, for the excellent directness of his prose style and for the combination of objectivity and passion with which he approaches his subject matter.

To Henry Russell Hitchcock, born in Boston, Massachusetts, for his great erudition, sound taste and humor, and for the contribution he has made to our understanding of Victorian Architecture.

These printed versions are slightly altered from the nonauthorial typescript in the Academy and Institute's archives. A third tribute in the same typescript was not used at the Ceremonial:

[To] Stanley Kunitz for his lyrical gift, his spiritual vision, and the conscientiousness with which he has worked at and developed his craft.

For the 1959 Ceremonial Auden wrote a longer tribute that he hoped would be presented to Lincoln Kirstein, but it was never used. His typescript is in the Academy and Institute's archives:

Mr Lincoln Kirstein

It is admirable when a man of great fortune, believing that the arts are a good thing, allots a portion of his surplus wealth to their encouragement, but it is even more laudable when a man cares so passionately about the arts that he is prepared to devote all his time and all his money, not to the furtherance of the arts in general, but to making it possible for the particular kind of work which he admires to come into being.

Mr Lincoln Kirstein is such a man. He has never been, by Texan standards, rich, but whatever he has had, he has spent, with a single-minded devotion, upon commissioning works of art and ensuring their adequate performance.

As a young man, in the early years of the Depression, he founded the literary magazine *Hound & Horn*, in which many writers and critics now famous first appeared; later, he was one of the group responsible for The Museum of Modern Art, and his unotrusive personal patronage of painters has never ceased; lastly, it was Mr Kirstein who, by bringing the great choreographer, George Balanchine, to this country and commissioning the best living composers to write ballet scores for him, is responsible for the creation of what is, almost certainly, the finest ballet company, both by artistic and technical standards, in the world.

Mr Kirstein is one of the very few persons of whom it may be said that, though not themselves artists, without them the history of the arts during the last twenty-five years would have been different and poorer.

W.H.A.

An Addendum to Prose III

In addition to the citations that Auden wrote for the 1954 Ceremonial of the American Academy and National Institute, reprinted in *Prose III*, p. 674, Auden wrote a citation to David Jones that was not used at the Ceremonial and never published:

To David Jones for his beautiful epic poem *The Anathemata*, distinguished alike for its technical skill in the handling of the contemporary idiom and its profound and learned reverence for the traditions of Western Culture.

Public Letters Signed by Auden and Others

This appendix lists letters to the press and other documents signed by Auden but not written by him.

A Statement on Racial Discrimination

In December 1959, the British organization Christian Action released a statement on racial discrimination, signed by twenty-eight British writers including Auden. Christian Action was a politically activist organization founded in 1946 by L. John Collins, later Canon of St Paul's, with an office in London. The text below is from the report in *The Times*, 24 December 1959, which described the statement as a "Christmas declaration":

> Our declaration is a simple one. It is, in essence, that the future of mankind must never be distorted by the cruel irrelevance of racial discrimination. It is of the nature of the Ten Commandments, the Magna Carta, and the Bill of Rights, which should carry their authority wherever human beings live together. We believe that man is born free and that it is his inalienable right to be treated as an equal by his brothers.
>
> Religion and science alike repudiate racial discrimination. The Unesco report of 1951 contains this clause on the concept of colour: "None of the scientific evidence of the past 150 years provides any biological reason for limiting the principle of equality as applied to race."
>
> As writers, we can express ourselves truthfully only in a society where justice predominates over passion and the quality of a man's mind and character is put before the colour of his skin. We look with horror on the injustice, violence and cruelty, no matter how provoked, which we see directed to-day in all parts of the world against coloured people. We believe this evil to be a relic of barbarism, and akin to the race-hatred of Hitler's maniacal reign, and as human beings we here rededicate ourselves to the fight against it.

The signers included Auden, Phyllis Bottome, Joseph Braddock, Richard Church, B. H. Liddell Hart, L. P. Hartley, Jacquetta Hawkes, Julian Huxley, H. Montgomery Hyde, Pamela Hansford Johnson, Storm Jameson, Doris Lessing, Louis MacNeice, Somerset Maugham, Daphne du Maurier, Roger Manvell, Iris Murdoch, John Osborne, J. B. Priestley, Herbert Read, C. P. Snow, and Colin Wilson. Similar reports, quoting only part of the statement, appeared in the *Guardian*, 22 December 1959, and the *Bookseller*, 2 January 1960.

A Birthday Greeting to P. G. Wodehouse

An eightieth-birthday greeting to Wodehouse was published as an advertisement by his American publisher, Simon & Schuster, in the *New York Times*, 14 October 1931.

The advertisement was headed "Happy Birthday, Mr Wodehouse", and was signed by eighty writers. The advertisement is quoted in Barry Phelps, *P. G. Wodehouse: Man and Myth* (1992).

ROOKS NEST, HEREFORDSHIRE

Rooks Nest (sometimes spelled Rook's Nest), Herefordshire, was threatened with development in 1960, but received a reprieve from the Ministry of Housing and Local Development in 1961. Local protests against the redevelopment were endorsed by a letter in the *Guardian*, 24 December 1960, headed "Rook's Nest" but with the spelling "Rooks Nest" in the letter itself:

> Sir,—Rooks Nest, in Hertfordshire, with the old parish church fields, approximately 200 acres of unspoiled upland countryside with beautiful views, is threatened under compulsory purchase orders by Stevenage Development Corporation for acquisition for building.
>
> It is our hope that this country will be allowed to remain as it is, rural farmland, not only because it is one of the last remaining beauty spots within 30 miles of London but because it is the Forster country of *Howards End*, which it is felt by literate people the world over should be preserved in its original setting as one of our great literary landmarks.—Yours &c.,
>
> W. H. AUDEN, JOHN BETJEMAN, ARTHUR BRYANT,
> DAVID CECIL, JOHN G. MURRAY, HAROLD NICOLSON,
> MAX REINHARDT, C. V. WEDGWOOD, V. SACKVILLE-WEST.

A news item in *The Times*, 28 December 1960, under the headline "Authors Fear Threat to 'Forster Country'", reported that "novelists and poets have expressed to *The Times* their alarm about the future of Rook's Nest". The news item quoted part of the letter (in a slightly different text) and paraphrased the rest.

Translations

Auden collaborated on two prose translations during the period covered by this volume.

ITALIAN JOURNEY, BY JOHANN WILHELM VON GOETHE

This translation by Auden and his friend Elizabeth Mayer, with whom he had been close since 1939 and the addressee of his "New Year Letter", was the longest of his prose translations. The project seems to have taken shape early in 1960; Elizabeth Mayer apparently sent Auden a draft of a partial translation during the summer of that year. He wrote to her on 7 July 1960 (Berg Collection):

> Got here a week ago to find the parcel which I have now read through. It will be great fun to work on. I wish the Old Boy, though, wouldn't talk *quite* so much about Art. He's much better on geology.

On 8 August 1960 he responded to a further part of the translation:

> Many thanks for your letter, the Sicily section and the new book.
> *Sicily* is wonderful but the geological terms *are* going to be a head-ache, e.g. what are *pyrite* hills? Pyrites I know, but one never speaks of pyrites hills. As soon as I have gotten myself a German text, I am going to copy out all the geological sentences and send them to my brother John for elucidation.

Auden wrote to Christopher Isherwood on 24 Feburary 1961 that he had finished the translation and was starting on the introduction. Meanwhile, he continued to re-vise Elizabeth Mayer's version, and sent her a final list of corrections in two parts, on 13 and 18 April. Extensive manuscript drafts of the translation, in Auden's and Eliza-beth Mayer's hands, are in the Berg Collection of the New York Public Library.

On 18 September 1961 Auden complained to Elizabeth Mayer that the publishers had not yet sent proofs. The proofs were finally sent in May 1962 when Auden was in Austria, and were read only by Elizabeth Mayer.

For an account of the introduction, see the notes to p. 324.

The book was published by Cassell in a sumptuous edition on 12 November 1962; some copies were issued the same year in the United States by Pantheon.

ON POETRY, BY ST-JOHN PERSE

"Poésie" was the title of St-John Perse's acceptance speech for the Nobel Prize in Lit-erature, delivered in French on 10 December 1960. Auden's translation seems to have been distributed to the press by the Swedish Academy around the same time, in a form that has not been traced and that does not survive as a typescript or similar document in the Swedish Academy's archives. The translation was first printed in the *Washington Post*, 22 January 1961 (Perse lived in Washington); then in pamphlet form by the Bollingen Foundation, which published it for private distribution on 20 October 1961. It was later reprinted in a regularly published book, *Two Addresses*, together with "Dante", translated by Robert Fitzgerald; the book was issued by Pantheon for the Bollingen Foundation in 1966. Auden refers to the circumstances of this translation in "Dag Hammarskjöld" (p. 354).

Auden's translation opens: "On behalf of Poetry I have accepted the honour which has here been paid to Her, an honour which I shall now hasten to restore to Her." This slightly exaggerates the personification in the French original: "J'ai accepté pour la Poésie l'hommage qui lui est ici rendu, et que j'ai hâte de lui restituer." The English version of Perse's speech made available in later years by the Swedish Academy is more literal than Auden's.

Lost and Unwritten Work

Notes in the archives of Auden's agents, Curtis Brown Ltd, suggest that in 1959 he was planning to compile an anthology of children's fiction for the Looking Glass Library (see p. 855). This may have been a confused report based on his membership in the advisory board or it may have been a project that was completed by someone else.

Auden and Stephen Spender, sitting at different desks in the same room, wrote each other's obituaries for *The Times* early in July 1962. These obituaries, which would have appeared anonymously, were replaced in the newspaper's files by obituaries written by others in later years, and the printed obituaries of each seem to contain nothing by the other.

Auden was apparently scheduled to review Karl Kerényi's *Heroes of the Greeks* for the *Mid-Century* in the autumn of 1961, but the book was sent by sea and arrived too late. Auden's review of Albert Camus' *The Plague* was returned to him, and then disappeared, when the *Mid-Century* ceased publication in October 1962.

TEXTUAL NOTES

Essays and Reviews

1956–1962

A few of Auden's essays that were published in 1956 were written earlier and appear in *Prose III*; these include his untitled essay in *Modern Canterbury Pilgrims* and his introduction to *The Faber Book of Modern American Verse*. A few prose pieces associated with Auden and Chester Kallman's version of *The Magic Flute* (1956) may be found in the volume of this edition titled *Libretti*. These include the translators' preface and notes to their version; a newspaper piece, "Putting It in English", by Auden, also published in 1956; and a reply to a reviewer, "The Magic Flute: Auden-Kallman v. Cross", by Auden and Kallman, published in 1958. A few similar prose pieces associated with Auden and Kallman's libretto *Elegy for Young Lovers* (1961) may also be found in *Libretti*; these include their "Genesis of a Libretto" and their synopsis of the opera.

At the End of the Quest, Victory

Page 3.

Auden had reviewed the first volume of Tolkien's trilogy for the *New York Times Book Review*, 31 October 1954 (*Prose III*, p. 489); the second volume in the trilogy was reviewed by Donald Barr. Auden probably lobbied to review this final volume.

In the third sentence the italicization of "seems" makes no sense, but is unquestionably present in the original. Some text seems to have been omitted preceding the paragraph that begins "Evil, that is".

Tolkien's notes to himself about this review appear in *Letters of J. R. R. Tolkien*, ed. by Humphrey Carpenter (1981), pp. 238–44.

An Appreciation of the Lyric Verse of Walter de la Mare

Page 6.

Probably another piece that Auden urged on the editors of the *New York Times Book Review*. He wrote a similar appreciation of de la Mare for the *Observer* after de la Mare's death later the same year (p. 34) and his selection of de la Mare's verse was published in 1963 (p. 396).

I have emended "jejeune" to "jejune". As always, Auden omits the punctuation from de la Mare's title *Behold, This Dreamer!*

Stimulating Scholarship

Page 8.

The *Griffin*, the monthly circular of The Readers' Subscription book club, offered both new and older books to its members; Lewis's volume in the Oxford History of English Literature was published in October 1954.

The magazine seems to have been proofread only casually, and, here and else-where, I have lightly corrected its punctuation and spelling more or less in the way that any competent editor would have done at the time.

HIC ET ILLE

Page 12.
    See the textual notes to *The Dyer's Hand* (p. 954).

INTRODUCTION TO *Selected Writings of Sydney Smith*

Page 13.
    Around 1950 Auden was commissioned to prepare a selection of letters by Syd-ney Smith for the Great Letters Series, edited by Louis Kronenberger, published in New York by Farrar, Straus and Young. The first volume in the series was Lionel Trilling's selection of Keats's letters. Early volumes in the series listed titles in prep-aration, including Auden's selection, and an early version of Auden's introduction was published in 1950 as "Portrait of a Whig" (*Prose III*, p. 273). The selection of letters never appeared, and the book transformed itself into an edition of *Selected Writings*, with a rewritten introduction. The title of the book appears on the title page as *Selected Writings of Sydney Smith*; it appears on the dust jacket as *The Selected Writings of Sydney Smith*.
    Auden prepared his selection probably late in 1955 or early 1956, taking its con-tents from *The Works of the Rev. Sydney Smith* (1859), *A Memoir of the Rev. Sydney Smith*, by his daughter, Lady Holland (1855), *The Life and Times of Sydney Smith* by Stuart J. Reid (1885), and *Letters of Sydney Smith*, ed. by Nowell C. Smith (1953). He probably finished the introduction in March or April 1956. His agents, Curtis Brown, sent it to the publisher on 17 April 1956.
    The publisher sent Auden the page proofs of the book on 13 July 1956; he cabled back corrections on 19 July. The book was published by Farrar, Straus and Cudahy on 19 November 1956. A British edition, arranged by Auden's agents, was pub-lished by Faber & Faber in 1957 after the book was turned down by Secker & War-burg.
    Auden compiled the quotations that appeared under the heading "Sydney Smith" on the rear flap of the dust jacket:

    "He is a very clever fellow, but he will never be a bishop."— *George III.*
    "A more profligate parson I never met."—*George IV.*
    "The loudest wit I e'er was deafened with."—*Lord Byron.*
    "I sat next to Sydney Smith, who was delightful . . . I don't remember a more agreeable party."—*Benjamin Disraeli.*
    "The ancient and amusing defender of our faith."—*Daniel O'Connell.*
    "I think it the most argumentative, logical, ingenious, and by far the wittiest per-formance I ever met with."—*Richard Brinsley Sheridan* (on the Peter Plymley Letters).
    "Sydney at breakfast made me actually cry with laughing. I was obliged to start up from the table."—*Thomas Moore.*
    "My noble-hearted husband."—*Mrs Sydney Smith.*

"To a dissenter like myself . . . there was something very painful in the tone always taken by Sydney Smith about Church matters."—*Harriet Martineau.*

"A fellow of infinite fun (if not much humour) and of a fine digestion and some sense."—*Thomas Carlyle.*

"I wish you would tell Mr Sydney Smith that of all the men I ever heard of and never saw, I have the greatest curiosity to see . . . and to know him."—*Charles Dickens.*

"Now I shall be able to do something for Sydney Smith."—*Lord Grey* (on becoming Prime Minister).

"He was the first in the literary circles of London to assert the value of Modern Painters."—*John Ruskin.*

"He drew such a ludicrous caricature . . . that Sir James Mackintosh rolled on the floor in fits of laughter."—*Lord John Russell.*

"The only wit on record, whom brilliant social success had done nothing to spoil or harden."—*Henry Fothergill Chorley.*

"The Smith of Smiths."—*Lord Macaulay.*

A secretarial typescript of the list of quotations in the Manuscripts Division of the New York Public Library includes three that did not appear on the printed dust jacket; the first follows the quotation from Byron, the second and third follow the one from Dickens:

"After dinner, he spoke to me for some time very kindly."—*W. E. Gladstone.*

"What a hideous, odd-looking man Sydney Smith is! with a mouth like an oyster and three double chins."—*Mrs Brookfield.*

"His faun-like face is a sort of promise of a good thing when he does but open his lips."—*Henry Crabb Robinson.*

In the list of characteristics of liberalism (p. 21) "enforced" is my updating of the obsolete spelling "inforced". In the paragraph that begins "There is a certain type" (p. 22), in the sentence that begins "Laws prohibiting" I have placed a comma before, instead of after, "which". The quotation that begins "What is Whiggery" is from Yeats's "The Seven Sages".

Under the title "Sydney Smith" the introduction was reprinted in the *Griffin*, October 1956; the *Griffin* text makes a few minor errors and omits section III. The complete essay was reprinted in *Forewords and Afterwords* (1973) as "Portrait of a Whig" with trivial editorial changes (including "enforced" for "inforced").

INTRODUCTION TO *The Descent of the Dove*

Page 25.

This project seems to have originated in a plan for a larger collection of Charles Williams's books in a single volume. Auden wrote to J.R.R. Tolkien on 14 June 1955 that he was editing "a sort of Omnibus Williams for an American publisher" (*Prose III*, p. 699). At some point later in 1955 or early in 1956, the plan was reduced to a single paperback reprint of *The Descent of the Dove*, to be published by Meridian Books as one of the first titles in its series of Living Age Books. Auden's introduction was probably written early in 1956, and the book was published on 20 August 1956.

The introduction first appeared in *Christian Century*, 2 May 1956, as "Charles Williams: A Review Article", a heading that contradicts an editorial note which identifies the essay as the introduction to a forthcoming reprint of *The Descent of the Dove*. The magazine text may have been taken from a carbon copy of Auden's typescript; it is more lightly and erratically punctuated and capitalized than the version in the book. I have taken the text in this edition from the book, but I have restored from the magazine a sentence not present in the book, "Thus Williams in *The Descent of the Dove*." (p. 29) and have removed some commas that do not appear in the magazine text and which are unlikely to have been authorial.

Among the differences between the two texts is a paragraph break in the magazine text (followed in this edition) before "In describing the state of damnation" (p. 27). Also in the magazine text, the paragraph that begins "The doctrine" has "but a few" instead of "however, a few"; in the paragraph that begins "It is a pity" the magazine has "Second" for "Secondly"; and in the paragraph that begins "Thus Williams" the magazine has dashes instead of commas preceding the two lists of issues and leaders (but commas instead of dashes after the lists). Also following the *Christian Century* text, in the paragraph that begins "Charles Williams was a devout member" (p. 28) I have changed "body of the Anglican" to "body the Anglican" ("of" was presumably added by an inattentive editor).

WISDOM, WIT, MUSIC

Page 30.

Jacques Barzun was one of Auden's coeditors at The Readers' Subscription book club (see Appendix II). The quotations in the review are accurate except for some minor silent omissions. I have corrected some spelling and capitalization.

MAKING, KNOWING AND JUDGING

Page 34.

See the textual notes to *The Dyer's Hand* (p. 948).

WALTER DE LA MARE

Page 34.

Walter de la Mare died on 22 June 1956. Auden was a moderately frequent contributor to the *Observer*'s book pages and perhaps offered to write this tribute while in Oxford at the time of his inaugural address as Professor of Poetry. The selection mentioned near the end of the piece is *Selected Poems*, chosen by R. N. Green-Armytage (1954).

As always, Auden omitted the punctuation from de la Mare's title *Behold, This Dreamer!*

AN EYE FOR MYSTERY

Page 37.

The American edition of *Harper's Bazaar* published essays and poems in addition to articles about fashion; Auden was a frequent contributor. I cannot find the source of the quotations in the paragraph that begins "As never before".

Auden seems to have quoted "Stars" from memory, and I have let his misrecollections stand; "rudd-eyed" for "rudd-red" may, however, have been a compositor's misreading of Auden's hand.

FOREWORD TO *The Green Wall*

Page 39.

Auden wrote to Wright on 2 July 1956 (letter in the University of Minnesota Library):

I expect that the Yale University Press have already informed you that you are the Yale Younger Poet for next year. They forgot to send me your address so I must send it via them.

May I take this opportunity of saying how impressed I am by your work: it is the best manuscript, I think, that I have read since I started being the judge for this series.

It is, however, considerably too long, from a commercial point of view— And even from yours, I believe you will make a better impression upon your reader by giving them less. I hope you will forgive me for suggesting the following cuts which do not imply that I do not like the poems. If you have any alternatives you would prefer, of course make them instead, but the number of pages lost must be about the same. . . .

The next page lists seventeen poems that might be omitted.

Auden wrote to Eugene Davidson at the Yale University Press on 24 July 1956, "The Mss are on their way home. I haven't had an answer yet from Mr Wright who I wrote to care of the Press since there isn't an address on the envelope." Auden probably wrote his foreword around August 1956. The book was published on 17 April 1957.

THE GREAT CAPTAINS

Page 44.

For Auden's connection with *Encounter* see *Prose III*, p. 757. The novel by Bryher (Annie Winnifred Ellerman) alluded to in the opening paragraph is *Roman Wall* (1954). Medrawt is another name for Mordred.

D. H. LAWRENCE AS A CRITIC

Page 48.

Auden's quotations silently abridge and alter the originals. I have made only very minor corrections in order to undo nonsense (for example, in the long quotation that begins "whereas in Shakespeare" I have corrected "and lesser" to "the lesser").

DOSTOEVKSY IN SIBERIA

Page 53.

Auden's quotations are typically approximate. In the quotation that begins "After dinner" (p. 55) I have restored the name Aristov, which was reduced in the magazine's text to the single letter "A", probably because a typist or compositor could not make sense of Auden's hand. In the paragraph fragment that begins "Of the other" (p. 56) "the major Commandant, tyrannical" should probably be emended by the omission of "Commandant", as it is the major, not the commandant, to whom Auden's description applies.

The magazine's text has an additional, and apparently unauthorial, line break before the paragraph that begins "Over against" (p. 56).

CONCRETE AND FASTIDIOUS

Page 57.

Nothing by Auden appeared in the *New Statesman & Nation* between the time he left Britain in 1939 and the beginning of his term as Oxford Professor of Poetry in June 1956, when the magazine printed his poem "The History of Science". I have emended "Patolles" to "Parolles".

SQUARES AND OBLONGS

Page 63.

An earlier set of aphorisms and notes with the same title was published in 1948 (*Prose II*, p. 339). The editor of the book, Ruth Nanda Anshen, was a philosopher and a tireless organizer of multivolume collections of books and essays under such general titles as "World Perspectives", "Perspectives in Humanism", and others of the same kind. *Language: An Enquiry Into Its Meaning and Function* was volume VII in her "Science of Culture Series", published by Harper & Brothers on 2 October 1957. It was conceived as an affirmation of what the dust-jacket describes as "the mystery, the miracle, and the magic of language", a counter-argument to the prevailing philosophical treatment of language as morally neutral.

Auden adapted and rewrote some of these notes and aphorisms for "The Virgin & The Dynamo" in *The Dyer's Hand* (p. 497).

The line breaks in the printed text probably represent rows of stars in Auden's lost typescript.

THE WISH GAME

Page 66.

See the textual notes to *The Dyer's Hand* (p. 961).

GUY BURGESS

Page 67.

Stephen Spender's letter, in the *Sunday Times*, 13 January 1957, read as follows:

Sir,—In his book *Guy Burgess, a Portrait with Background*, Mr Driberg writes that Burgess would have gone to stay with Professor W. H. Auden in Ischia, but for the fact that my wife, Natasha Spender, failed to deliver a telephone message to the Professor.

This statement has been taken up by several of the reviewers, and I now feel it should be replied to. It is untrue, both in the fact, and its implications. My wife did deliver the message. Professor Auden said he did not wish either to speak to him or see him.

If Mr Driberg had bothered to inquire either of my wife or myself, he could have ascertained all this. Actually, Burgess telephoned twice, and on the second occasion, spoke with me and again said he was anxious to get in touch with Professor Auden, who, by this time, was no longer staying with us.

The only point of Burgess's statement to Driberg could be to imply that Professor Auden would have been delighted to have Burgess staying with him in Ischia. It is evident that this implication is false. It seems curious that the Vice-Chairman of the Labour Party should publish a statement which is not only untrue but could be damaging to Professor Auden.

STEPHEN SPENDER
London, S.W.1.

Auden wrote to Spender on 14 January 1957: "I enclose a copy of a letter I am sending to the Sunday Times, modifying your account for the reasons which I state. What a bore it all is." The typescript copy that Auden sent to Spender matches the printed text except for paragraphing and punctuation, and the closing "I am Sir, | Your obedient servant".

THE VOLTAIRE OF MUSIC

Page 67.

Time and Tide was a weekly news magazine edited by Lady Rhondda; its politics turned from militant feminism in the 1920s to an antisocialist position in the 1950s when she saw personal freedoms threatened by socialism. Auden's first contribution (other than a brief letter to the editor in 1937 about the joint authorship of *Letters from Iceland*) was a poem that appeared in December 1956. This review was his only other contribution.

A GREAT HATER

Page 71.

Auden's quotations slightly modify the originals. This edition of *Diary of a Writer* was a one-volume reissue of the two-volume edition published in 1949.

A GRECIAN EYE

Page 74.

Trypanis was professor of Byzantine and Modern Greek at Oxford, where Auden probably met him in 1956.

JUST HOW I FEEL

Page 77.

The two books under review were published in 1947; The Readers' Subscription perhaps chose them because its offering of C. S. Lewis's volume in the same series (p. 8) had been a commercial success.

The *Griffin*'s text is infested with errors that I have corrected silently. These begin in the first paragraph with "works on scholarships" (for "works of scholarship"), and continue through one that Auden perhaps rejoiced to find, "*The King is Quair*" (for "*The Kingis Quair*"). In the paragraph fragment that begins "However, I found" the compositor mistook Auden's mistyped word "excekkent" (for "excellent") as a quotation and placed it in quotation marks.

In the paragraph that begins "Poor old Lydgate", the phrase "dramas, lyrics, ballads" perhaps needs an "and". In the paragraph that begins "Again, Accepted Opinion" I have emended "Fifteen Century" to "Fifteenth Century", although Auden could well have written "XV Century".

Sydney Smith: The Kind-Hearted Wit

Page 82.

This piece, probably adapted by Auden from his introduction to *Selected Writings of Sydney Smith* (p. 13), was the third in a *Sunday Times* series of six weekly essays under the heading "Great Writers Rediscovered". The first two in the series were E. M. Forster on Elizabeth Gaskell and Joyce Cary on Surtees; the last three were Raymond Mortimer on Anatole France, Edith Sitwell on Gordon Bottomley and Ralph Hodgson, and Lord David Cecil on Gosse. The series was revived a few months later, with further essays including Stephen Spender on Clough and William Empson on Fielding.

The verse quotation is from Yeats's "The Seven Sages".

West's Disease

Page 88.

See the textual notes to *The Dyer's Hand* (p. 963).

Straw Without Bricks

Page 88.

In the quoted phrase after the first set-off quotation, the printed text has the obviously mistaken "lovéd me not" where Auden perhaps wrote from memory "lov'd me not"; I have restored Housman's text.

Seventh Heavens

Page 92.

In the transcriptions of Sanskrit words the *Observer*'s compositor accurately supplied the dots below three of the letters.

Crying Spoils the Appearance

Page 95.

A secretarial typescript, dated 11 June 1957, was prepared by the *New Yorker* from Auden's lost manuscript and is now in the Manuscripts Division of the New York

Public Library. The printed version varies only in paragraphing and in minor improvements in phrasing. In the closing paragraph Auden refers to a review he wrote in 1942 (*Prose II*, p. 161).

PREFACE TO *Nulla Vogliamo dal Sogno*

Page 99.

Nino D'Ambra was a lawyer and historian who lived near Auden's summer home in Ischia. He pestered Auden to write this preface, probably when Auden was in Italy in July and August 1957. The book was published in Milan by Casa Editrice G. Intelisano in December 1957. In the book, Auden's preface is headed "Prefazione" and appears in English and Italian texts. Auden is identified beneath his name as "(Premio Acc. dei Lincei per la poesia 1957)".

COMMENTARY ON THE POETRY AND TRAGEDY OF *Romeo and Juliet*

Page 100.

The Laurel Shakespeare was one of a number of series of cheap paperback editions of the plays and poems that began to appear in the 1950s. The general editor of the Laurel series was Francis Fergusson; *Romeo and Juliet* was the third volume to appear and was published by Dell on 29 April 1958. The title of Auden's "Commentary", like that of the "Commentary" in each of the other volumes, was chosen by the general editor. Auden perhaps wrote the piece in the summer of 1957; in a notebook in the Berg Collection, fragments of a rough draft immediately follow the draft of his preface to *Nulla Vogliamo dal Sogno*.

FOREWORD TO *A Crackling of Thorns*

Page 113.

On 2 August 1957 Auden wrote to Eugene Davidson at the Yale University Press: "This is just to tell you that I have chosen for the next Yale Younger Poet Mr John Hollander of 20 Prescott Street, Cambridge 38, Mass. I am sorry I have been so long about it, but I have been completely immersed in translating *Don Giovanni*." On the same day, Auden wrote to Hollander (Yale University Library):

I am happy to be able to tell you that your volume of poems, *Confidences*, has been chosen for publication in the Yale Younger poets series.

Herewith a few trivial suggestions: if you don't agree, please ignore them.

(1) I find the title for the Glaucon songs, *Glaucon in Connecticut*, a little Laforguish-Eliotish. How about just calling them *Five Songs for Glaucon?*

(2) The same criticism applies to the epigraphs to *Late August on the Lido* and *By the Sea*, and to the Quine quotation you put before the section *For Certain Others*. If I were you, I should omit them. (The Buber quote before *The Fable of the Bears in Winter* is quite another matter and should certainly be there.)

(3) *Susanna's Song*, stanza 2, line 8, and stanza 3, line 1. Are you *sure* you want to say *mastic* trees? Is such an unfamiliar vegetable essential to Susanna's situation? You may say, and with justice, that I'm a fine person to raise such an objection. I raise it precisely because I am overfascinated by odd words.

Hollander took Auden's suggestion in item (1), but omitted "Five" from the suggested title; from item (2) he accepted the first and third suggestions, but retained the epigraph to "By the Sea"; he ignored item (3).

The printed text treats each paragraph of the foreword as a separate block of text, each separated from the next by a line space, and with no indentation in the first line. Auden almost certainly expected the text to be paragraphed normally, but a typist or compositor misunderstood his intentions. He also may have used one or more line spaces to break the foreword into sections, and a typist or compositor may have mistakenly applied the same style of break to the entire text.

Auden probably wrote his foreword in August 1957. The book was published on 21 May 1958.

TALENT, GENIUS, AND UNHAPPINESS

Page 118.

A secretarial typescript, dated 16 September 1957, was prepared by the *New Yorker* from Auden's lost manuscript and is now in the Manuscripts Division of the New York Public Library. The printed text differs from the typescript by adding some explanatory phrases that more precisely identify Sainte-Beuve's views, by slightly reducing Auden's paragraphing, and by regularizing spellings such as "Slavophil" (in the printed text "Slavophile"). In the typescript the third sentence from the end lists "the Legion of Honor" after "the Academy".

THE GREAT DIVIDE

Page 129.

In the second sentence of the paragraph that begins "Goethe spent his life" (p. 130) I have emended "which is just" to "which are just". Auden's quotations omit and alter a few words in Heller's text.

"A MENTAL PRINCE"

Page 132.

The title is Blake's description of himself. In the second paragraph the *Observer* has "Scholfield", which may have been Auden's misrecollection of Blake's "Schofield", which was one of Blake's many misspellings of Scofield.

A response to Auden's piece by Kathleen Raine, in the form of a letter to the editor, appeared on 24 November 1957. Raine, a friendly acquaintance of Auden, was a champion of the visionary Blake. She wrote in part:

Sir,—Professor Auden, following an established precedent by which it is permissible to write upon Blake without having read or understood the great bulk of his writings, makes the amazing assertion that Blake accepted the reality of the Newtonian universe. So far as Professor Auden is concerned, Blake has written in vain the many hundreds of lines that are devoted to refuting the philosophy of Locke and Newton, upon sound philosophical grounds derived from his careful study of Berkeley, Plato, Plotinus, the *Hermetica*, and other works of traditional philosophy.

Normal philosophy has at all times distinguished between the phenomena, and substantial realities. Blake objected that Newton and Locke formed "Accident into Substance" and imputed to natural phenomena a status that no serious philosopher, from Plato to Aquinas, has been prepared to accord them. Professor Whitehead points to Descartes as the originator of this fallacy, using arguments that Blake had already employed, in full force, against Locke and Newton. "The independence ascribed to bodily substances," he wrote, caused them "to degenerate into a mechanism entirely valueless."

If, instead of wishing that Blake had wasted his time at the age of fifty upon a piece of buffoonery (a continuation of *An Island in the Moon*) Professor Auden would take the trouble to read what Blake did write in his mature years upon mature topics, he might be surprised by the strength of the argument he presents against the heresy of Western European thought—the "sickness of Albion," which is, according to Blake, precisely the worship of phenomena. Blake's view that "Nature is a Vision of the Science of the Elohim," and "natural cause only seems," needs no apology, for it is philosophically normal, traditional, and orthodox.

Perhaps I have not quite understood the precise meaning of Professor Auden's somewhat schoolboyish adjective "dotty," under which he includes Blake, Rimbaud and Rilke, three poets who seem to have no other attribute in common. (Had he said Blake, Yeats and Joyce, one might have understood him, for these three are at least similar in many respects.). . . .

May I also point out that while Blake did criticise Homer, Shakespeare, Dante and Milton on specific points, these were the poets whom he most loved and admired. Milton he chose as the type of the Inspired Man; on his deathbed he was illustrating Dante and he learnt Italian in order to read him; and he compares Achilles with Aeneas as a superior work of imaginative creation.

Auden's reply appeared on 1 December 1957:

Sir,—Of course I did not mean to suggest that Blake was a Newtonian; I know as well as Miss Raine that he spent his life attacking, and with great acuity, mechanistic conceptions of the Universe. But what his attack fails to do is save the Appearances, so that the Appearances are left to the mechanists, for, if you make an absolute gulf, as Blake sometimes does, between Vision and the visible, the visionary can make no criticism about theories of the visible. "I assert for My Self that I do not behold the outward Creation & that to me it is hindrance & not Action; it is as the dirt upon my feet. No part of Me," surrendered too much to the enemy. Again, in his just objection to the theory of the mind as a *tabula rasa* and the conclusion that genius can be taught, Blake goes to the extreme of saying that "Imagination has nothing to do with Memory," a separation which hands over education to the Behaviourists.

I am not sufficiently acquainted with Miss Raine's own position to know exactly what she means by "the heresy of Western European thought." If she means that the "worship of phenomena" is an error which is likely to occur only as a deviation from an orthodoxy which holds that the material phenomenal world is real and good, because God-created, and to be taken seriously—that, for example, the sun which is "a round disk of fire somewhat like a Guinea" is the real outward and visible sign of "an Innumerable company of the Heavenly host crying Holy!"—I agree with her. But if she means that it is a heresy of the West, as compared with the East, to take the phenomenal world seriously, then we must agree, politely, to differ.

From a Christian point of view, the materialist is a heretic, but so is the Blake who wrote: "Thinking as I do that the Creator of this World is a very Cruel Being, & being a Worshipper of Christ, I cannot help saying: 'the Son, O how unlike the Father!' First God Almighty comes with a Thump on the Head. Then Jesus Christ comes with a balm to heal it."

If I have to choose, I prefer buffoonery to pretentiousness. *An Island in the Moon* is a crude juvenile work, but I can read it, whereas I simply cannot get through *The Four Zoas.* I would have liked to see Blake in his maturity explore in a connected piece the satirical vein which appears so admirably in his epigrams.

I am sorry that, to Miss Raine, the adjective *dotty* sounds schoolboyish. I used it, in preference to words like *cranky* or *eccentric*, because, for me, it has an affectionate overtone which they lack.

To the list of such artists that I gave, Yeats and Joyce certainly belong as well. In one way or another, all reject the phenomenal world.

I never said that Blake did not admire Shakespeare personally. There is evidence, however, that he thought his public influence a danger. One clause of Blake's translation of Doctor Thornton's Tory translation of the Lord's Prayer runs thus: "Lead us not to read the Bible, but let our Bible be Virgil & Shakespeare."

New York.   W. H. AUDEN.

MUSIC IN SHAKESPEARE: ITS DRAMATIC USE IN HIS PLAYS

Page 135.
    See the textual notes to *The Dyer's Hand* (p. 976).

PREFACE TO *Jean Sans Terre*

Page 135.

The translations of Goll's poems in this book were made by twenty writers, including Louise Bogan, Paul Goodman, Galway Kinnell, W. S. Merwin, Kenneth Patchen, Kenneth Rexroth, William Jay Smith, and William Carlos Williams; the book also includes critical essays by Louise Bogan, Clark Mills, Jules Romains, and Allen Tate, and drawings by Eugene Berman, Marc Chagall, and Salvador Dalí. No general editor is named. The book, which was published by Thomas Yoseloff on 14 November 1958, was a greatly expanded version of an edition published by the Grabhorn Press, San Francisco, in 1944, with the same title, but without Auden's preface.

In the third paragraph I have inserted "like each other's than" in order to correct an eyeskip by a typist or compositor.

The printed text may have reduced Auden's capitalization; in the sixth paragraph, for example, he perhaps originally wrote "Heavenly City" and "Universal City of Reason", not "Heavenly city" and "universal city of Reason".

A JOLLY MAGPIE

Page 137.

An undated secretarial typescript, prepared by the *New Yorker*, is now in the Manuscripts Division of the New York Public Library. The printed text adds the name of the publisher at the end of the first sentence, makes minor stylistic changes, and slightly reduces capitalization and paragraphing.

Confidential (mentioned in the opening paragraph) was a popular American magazine, begun in 1952, that specialized in innuendo about the sex lives of Hollywood stars. In 1957, shortly before Auden wrote this review, its editor was tried, under vast publicity, for criminal libel.

REFLECTIONS UPON READING WERNER JAEGER'S *Paideia*

Page 145.

The English translations of the three volumes of *Paideia* were published in 1939, 1943, and 1944. I have slightly regularized punctuation and spelling.

THE LIFE OF A THAT-THERE POET

Page 153.

Auden's typescript is in the *New Yorker* archives in the Manuscripts Division of the New York Public Library; it was probably written around December 1957 and was apparently set in type on 8 January 1958. The parenthetical description of the book as a "twenty-dollar venture" was added by the magazine, which also reduced Auden's paragraphing and made some minor stylistic changes.

The quotation in the opening paragraph is misremembered from Yeats's "The Death of Synge". The paragraph that begins "If William Stewart Rose" (p. 162) alludes to the story that it was Rose who brought to Byron in September 1817 a copy of John Hookham Frere's mock-heroic poem commonly known as *The Monks and the Giants*.

Auden used parts of this essay in his Oxford lecture, "*Don Juan*" and in the printed version of the lecture in *The Dyer's Hand* (p. 725).

The Kitchen of Life

Page 166.

This book was published in 1954. An expanded version of this review became the introduction to the British edition of *The Art of Eating*, published in 1963 (see *Prose V*); the introduction was reprinted, again with the title "The Kitchen of Life", in *Forewords and Afterwords* (1973). I have corrected a few misspellings. In the paragraph that begins "The portrait which" (p. 169) I have removed a nonsensical question mark and asterisk after "frightens her", which perhaps represent a compositor's attempt to reproduce an inkspot in the manuscript. Auden's quotations omit or alter a few words and slightly modify punctuation.

In the paragraph that begins "One grows older" (p. 167) non-British readers may wish to know that Dead Man's Leg is a rolled-up suet pudding with jam; in the paragraph fragment that begins "In the reverse" (p. 170) Cold Shape is a molded gelatin or pudding. In the quotation that begins "I know a large" (p. 171) Canfield is a variety of solitaire or patience.

The Sacred Cold

Page 173.

The New Statesman and Nation became *The New Statesman* in 1957. The airplanes mentioned in the final paragraph are named after Arctic explorers. Auden's quotations are approximate.

A Song of Life's Power to Renew

Page 177.

Auden met Alexis Leger (St-John Perse) in the 1940s and wrote the first version of "Nature, History and Poetry" as an *hommage* to him (*Prose III*, p. 161). Auden's anticipation of Perse's Nobel Prize was fulfilled in 1960. The title of this piece was almost certainly written by an editor. Auden's quotations are approximate.

Foreword to *Of the Festivity*

Page 179.

Auden sent this foreword to Arthur Davidson at the Yale University Press on 15 August 1958:

Herewith my foreword to Mr Dickey's volume which I am sending you by registered sea-mail.

As you will see from my remarks, I have decided it is time you got a younger and fresher editor for the Yale Younger Poets. Twelve years is a long time.

Auden forgot that there were two years (1950 and 1955), not one, when none of the submissions seemed good enough.

Dickey's book was published on 20 May 1959.

Thinking What We Are Doing

Page 184.

Auden wrote this review for the *Griffin*; then, when Stephen Spender invited him to review the book for *Encounter*, Auden replied on 6 October 1958:

I have already done a long review (not bad, I think) of the Arendt book for *The Griffin*, our little mag for The Readers Subscription Club. Since no one sees this except the subscribers, it could be re-printed in Encounter, if you liked. Let me know if you do want it. I [shall] tell them to send you a copy by air-mail.

The piece appeared in *Encounter* as a review of the edition published in Britain by the Cambridge University Press at 36s.

Auden probably read proof of the *Encounter* version and made one substantive change that I have incorporated into this edition. In the first paragraph under "Action" (p. 187) the final sentence in the *Encounter* text replaces this sentence in the *Griffin* text: "For human action, as distinct from human behaviour, speech is essential, the means by which the person identifies who he is, what he is doing, has done, and intends to do."

The paragraph that follows this sentence, which begins "Labor is recurrent", is in *Encounter* divided into two (probably by an editor) with the second paragraph beginning "The three principal" ("principal" is misspelled "principle" in both texts). The paragraph that begins "Our own modern" (p. 189) is similarly divided into two in *Encounter*, with the second paragraph beginning "So long as these". The *Encounter* text also anglicizes spelling, and in the third paragraph corrects "has seemed" to "have seemed".

In the paragraph that begins "Miss Arendt is not" (p. 184) I have added a comma between "what we are doing" and "which". In the paragraph that begins "Labor is recurrent" (p. 187) I have emended "will effect" to "will affect".

The Creation of Music and Poetry

Page 190.

Auden wrote this essay, originally titled "Two Apollonians", for the *Griffin* after The Readers' Subscription made arrangements with the publishers to offer the two books as a dual selection. (The original title is noted in the archives of the book club in the Columbia University Library.) During the confusion that accompanied the sale of the club and the resignation of the editors, the books were not offered to subscribers and Auden's essay therefore did not appear in the *Griffin*. It was printed a few months later in the second number of the monthly circular of the successor book club, The Mid-Century Book Society; the printed title may not be authorial. For the history of these two book clubs, see Appendix II.

An editorial headnote in the *Mid-Century* reads: "This essay, published here for the first time, explores the views of a poet and a composer. . . . The quotations are taken from two books published earlier this year, *Conversations with Stravinsky* [*sic*, omitting *Igor*] edited by Robert Craft . . . and Valéry's *The Art of Poetry* . . . (These books are *not* offerings of the Society.)"

In the fourth quotation from the end, the point of Stravinsky's joke is that his *Pulcinella* was based on music mistakenly attributed to Pergolesi.

The Co-Inherence

Page 197.

Auden's only contribution to the *National Review*, a right-wing political weekly edited by William F. Buckley, Jr. Auden later told friends that he had never seen the magazine and knew nothing about it. Buckley, about whom Auden knew nothing, invited him to write about Charles Williams, which he readily did. When the issue with Auden's review arrived and he saw its political content, he reportedly told Buckley that he, Buckley, had been "naughty" not to have told him about the magazine's politics when inviting him to contribute.

In the paragraph fragment that begins "But it is" (p. 199) the ellipsis perhaps reflects Auden's erratic typing of two full stops instead of one. Auden's quotations slightly modify punctuation and italicization.

The Greek Self

Page 201.

The book, which Auden mistitled in the second paragraph *The Discovery of Mind* (corrected here), was published in 1953. "Was ist der Mensch?" was the subject of the annual conference of the Internationale Hochschulwochen des Österreich-ischen College, in Alpbach-Tirol, August 1953.

The Readers' Subscription offered this book as a dual selection with Kathleen Freeman's *Ancilla to the Pre-Socratic Philosophers*. Auden's essay was followed by three pages of excerpts (perhaps chosen by Jacques Barzun) headed "Some Sayings of the Pre-Socratic Philosophers".

I have slightly rationalized some erratic punctuation. Auden's quotations silently abridge the original.

Calm Even in the Catastrophe

Page 209.

This piece prompted the New York Graphic Society to commission Auden to se-lect the paintings for *Van Gogh: A Self-Portrait* (p. 281).

The *Mid-Century* text, published as a review of the edition issued by the New York

Graphic Society at $50, is a heavily cut version of the text in *Encounter*. It omits the paragraph that begins "The Theo letters are followed"; in the quotation after the paragraph fragment that begins "Furthermore, though" (p. 211) it omits the opening paragraph of the quotation (the sentences before and after the line of French); in the quotation that begins "As far as I know", it omits everything from "All academic" to "a peasant woman"; in the paragraph that begins "Where he differs" (p. 212) it omits from "On the contrary" through the quotation, omits the "and" after the quotation, and starts a new sentence with "How opposed"; in the paragraph that begins "When he talks" it omits everything after "but in fact" and then omits the remaining paragraphs and quotations, resuming with the paragraph that begins "Van Gogh had very little fun".

In the quotation that begins "People still talk" (p. 213) I have corrected Auden's (or a typist's) misreading of "*capelots*" for "*capelets*".

John Betjeman's Poetic Universe

Page 216.

Auden's contribution to the first number of the *Mid-Century*. This number also reprinted "Agee on Films" (*Prose II*, p. 239) under the title "Agee on the Movies", in place of a review of the collection *Agee on Film*. Betjeman's book and recording were the first offering of the club, in May 1959, and a brief excerpt from Auden's review appeared in advertisements for the club that month; Agee's book was the offering for June 1959.

Auden and Betjeman met as undergraduates. Auden wrote an introduction to his own earlier selection of Betjeman's poems, *Slick But Not Streamlined* (*Prose II*, p. 303), published in 1947; the essay "Topographical Verse," which Auden quotes in this review, was apparently written for that volume.

The Private Life of a Public Man

Page 221.

Auden's quotations are approximate; for example, in "Under Ben Bulben", he omits "the" in "beaten into the clay". I have corrected a typist's or compositor's misreadings of Yeats's titles.

Miss Marianne Moore, Bless Her!

Page 226.

Auden's list of Alices and Mabels may be compared to the one he prepared in 1954 (*Prose III*, p. 487). His quotations are close to the originals.

The Fallen City: Some Reflections on Shakespeare's *Henry IV*

Page 230.

See the textual notes to "The Prince's Dog" in *The Dyer's Hand* (p. 960).

Foreword: Brand *versus* Peer

Page 230.

Auden had been interested in *Peer Gynt* since at least the 1930s, and adapted its final tableau for the final scene of Ransom and his mother in *The Ascent of F6* in 1936. How this foreword to Michael Meyer's translation of *Brand* came to be written is unknown; possibly it emerged from a suggestion by Auden's friend Jason Epstein (later his editor at Random House), who edited the Anchor Books series of paperbacks in which this was the first of a series of translations of Ibsen. The book was published by Doubleday in the Anchor Books series on 8 July 1960.

Auden reused parts of this essay in "Genius & Apostle" in *The Dyer's Hand* (p. 759).

Foreword to *Times Three*

Page 241.

Auden seems to have been acquainted with Phyllis McGinley since at least the mid-1950s, perhaps earlier.

I have restored the first two sentences from Auden's typescript (Syracuse University Library); they were evidently cut by the same editor who changed two other passages the originals of which I have restored. At the start of the paragraph fragment immediately after the first quotation, the editor changed "Without knowing their author, I can" to "Without knowing who wrote them, I could"; and in the paragraph that begins "In contrast" (p. 243) the editor changed "above" to "on page ix". I have left some slight misquotations uncorrected.

The book was published by the Viking Press on 23 September 1960; a British edition was published by Secker & Warburg in 1961.

The Magician from Mississippi

Page 247.

Auden's review appeared in the same number of the *Mid-Century* with the item that follows it in this edition, "A Children's Anthology", the two pieces being separated by a review by Lionel Trilling. In the quotation that begins "'But you can'" (p. 250) Auden's review represents by four asterisks the word that Faulkner represented by a blank space.

A Children's Anthology

Page 251.

This was the first children's book offered by The Mid-Century Book Society; Auden's review was followed by the book's table of contents. The "two Taylor pieces" were "Greedy Richard" by Jane Taylor and "The Watchfulness of Papa" by Jane and Anne Taylor; "John Gilpin" was the ballad by William Cowper. The book is the same anonymous collection published by Gollancz in Britain as *The Golden Treasury of Stories for Boys and Girls* (1959).

Apologies to the Iroquois

Page 252.

Auden and Wilson met within weeks of Auden's arrival in New York in 1939 and maintained a warm but slightly formal friendship. Auden's quotations are approximate.

An Unclassical Classic

Page 259.

Graves took every opportunity to attack Auden for (in Graves's view) having plagiarized the poems of Laura Riding; Auden invariably praised Graves in print. During the late 1950s and early 1960s Auden also wrote "A Poet of Honor" (p. 342) and a series of three BBC broadcasts on Graves (p. 877).

The Queen Is Never Bored

Page 266.

Auden mailed his typescript to the *New Yorker* on 1 February 1960, with a two-sentence cover letter: "Here is my piece on Queen Mary. Rather long, I fear." The typescript, with his corrections, is now in the Manuscripts Division of the New York Public Library. The magazine reduced Auden's paragraphing and made minor changes in wording and punctuation. Auden slightly miscopied and abridged his quotations.

In the final paragraph, "New Ebor and Cantuar" are the Bishop of New York and the Archbishop of Canterbury.

Foreword to *Van Gogh: A Self-Portrait*

Page 281.

The New York Graphic Society invited Auden to select the letters for this volume after he had reviewed the full three-volume edition (p. 209) The publisher approached him through The Mid-Century Book Society; Auden wrote to Sol Stein at the Society on 18 September 1959: "I would be perfectly prepared to make a selection from the Van Gogh letters, provided they don't want editorial comment, which is quite unnecessary and for which I am not a competent expert" (Columbia University Library).

The publisher reported to The Mid-Century Book Society on 2 May 1960 that the book had "recently" been finished, so Auden perhaps made his selection in April 1960.

The publisher's acknowledgements describe the book as "a selected condensation by W. H. Auden of *The Complete Letters of Vincent Van Gogh*, published in 1958 by the New York Graphic Society in three volumes. . . . Finally, the New York Graphic Society is also most grateful to W. H. Auden for his thoughtful selection of the material for this book from among some 750 entries of the entire correspondence." The book was published on 5 September 1960; a British edition was published by Thames & Hudson in 1961.

Statement by W. H. Auden on Cultural Freedom

Page 282.

The Congress for Cultural Freedom was one of many organizations with similar names organized by left-wing anticommunist intellectuals with funds that were ultimately and secretly derived from the United States Central Intelligence Agency and, to a much lesser extent, British intelligence services. Auden's friend Nicolas Nabokov was one of the most active organizers of these groups; Stephen Spender was coeditor of its most widely circulated publication, *Encounter.* Auden seems never to have been told the source of the Congress's funding, but he probably made a shrewd guess.

The magazine in which this item appeared was published from the Paris office of the Congress and included mostly puff pieces and organizational news.

Greatness Finding Itself

Page 283.

Auden reprinted this piece in *Forewords and Afterwords* (1973) with no change other than the restoration of a missing quotation mark (also added here) at the close of the question asked in the Generativity crisis (p. 284). Auden's inconsistent capitalization seems to be at least partly deliberate.

K

Page 289.

See the textual notes to "The I Without a Self" in *The Dyer's Hand* (p. 959).

Introduction to *The Complete Poems of Cavafy*

Page 290.

Auden seems to have written this introduction at the request of the translator Rae Dalven whom he had known for some years through New York literary circles; he had earlier reviewed, probably at her request, an anthology she edited of modern Greek poetry (*Prose III*, p. 188).

The book was published by Harcourt, Brace & World on 12 April 1961; the Hogarth Press published a British edition later the same year. Auden's introduction also appeared in the *Atlantic,* April 1961, as "The Poems of C. P. Cafavy", with, in the first paragraph, R. M. Dawkins's initials expanded by an editor to Richard McGillivray. The introduction was also reprinted without change in *Forewords and Afterwords* (1973) as "C. P. Cavafy".

Auden had met R. M. Dawkins at Oxford.

Two Ways of Poetry

Page 298.

Copies of Hill's book sold in the United States had dustjackets identifying the distributor as Dufour Editions, but the publisher named on and in the book itself was the British publisher, André Deutsch, who was also identified as the publisher in the headnote to Auden's review.

The Problem of Nowness

Page 303.

In the third sentence a comma after "poetry" might be helpful. A more alert magazine editor would have replaced many of Auden's colons with semi-colons. Auden's quotations slightly alter the originals.

Three Memoranda on the New Arden Shakespeare

Page 307.

Auden's note was followed by similar notes by Jacques Barzun and Lionel Trilling. A copy of Auden's typescript among Barzun's papers in the Columbia University Library has his original title: "Proper Plumage for the Swan" (preceded by a deleted "The"). The typescript has handwritten additions that seem to be authorial although they are not in Auden's hand; for example, at the end of the section that begins "Shakespeare's work", the sentence that begins "It is never sufficient" is written in. Probably these additions were copied from Auden's handwritten additions in his top copy.

The magazine's text presents Auden's piece as a series of ordinary paragraphs, ignoring the division in the typescript into separate sections (some with more than one paragraph) divided by rows of stars. This edition restores Auden's divisions, but, as in most similar pieces, omits the rows of stars.

A Public Art

Page 309.

The occasion for this piece was the announcement of the forthcoming Glyndebourne première of *Elegy for Young Lovers*. Auden's other contributions to this British monthly were a response in 1952 to objections by Ronald Duncan to an essay on music that Auden had printed elsewhere (*Prose III*, p. 731) and a piece about his and Kallman's later libretto, *Love's Labour's Lost*, in 1973.

Il Faut Payer

Page 312.

Auden probably wrote this review in mid-December 1960. Sol Stein wrote to Auden, Barzun, and Trilling on 21 December that the piece was "quite a bit longer than the 1500 words we had agreed on as the outside limit" and proposed cutting some of the details of the plot, a plan evidently accepted by one or more editors.

A copy of Auden's typescript in the same file in the Barzun papers at the Columbia University Library makes it possible to restore the material cut by Stein. The restored material includes the following: the third of the five opening quotations (the one that begins "He began"); in the paragraph fragment after the quotations, the sentence that begins "Smart young debs"; and at the end of the paragraph that begins "As seen through" (p. 313) the closing sentence and quotation. The printed text moves the sentence that begins "As a family" to the start of the paragraph that begins "The first Tietjens" and omits the paragraph that begins "Christopher's father". The printed text omits the quotation that begins "It was the most damnable" (p. 315). In the paragraph that begins "Christopher first meets" (p. 316) the printed text omits the sentence that begins "Later they go".

In the paragraph that begins "It is impossible" (p. 317) the printed text reduces the second and third sentences to "I have said nothing about such an important character in the novel as Mark Tietjens, a kind of Phineas Fogg dandy, or Marie Louise, his French mistress, or Ford's fascinating technique of presentation." (Phineas is Auden's slip for Phileas.)

Auden's quotations silently alter and abridge the originals.

The Poet as Professor

Page 317.

An occasional piece, written and published at the time of the election (won by Robert Graves) for Auden's successor as Professor of Poetry at Oxford.

Two Cultural Monuments

Page 320.

I have neither regularized Auden's shifts between "*Phèdre*" and "*Phaedre*" nor corrected minor slips in the quotations.

Introduction to *Italian Journey*

Page 324.

For an account of the translation, see Appendix VII (p. 898). Auden began writing the introduction late in February 1961. The book was published by Cassell on 12 November 1962.

The *Encounter* text of the introduction appeared a few weeks (at most) before the book was published; the magazine's version, titled "On Goethe: For a New Translation", is signed by Auden alone, surely reflecting its true authorship. The introduction in the book is signed by both Auden and Elizabeth Mayer.

I have followed the text in the book except where I have incorporated some apparently last-minute changes that occur in the *Encounter* text, which may have been typeset from a proof of the book. Thus, in the third paragraph, the book has "his *Italian Journey*" where *Encounter* (followed by this edition) omits "his". In the paragraph that begins "The first crisis" (p. 327) *Encounter* (followed here) corrects a minor historical error: near the end of the paragraph the book version reads: "the young Grand Duke of Weimar was passing through in his coach and invited Goethe to go with him". In the paragraph that begins "Those first eleven" (p. 328) the book version begins "These first eleven". In the paragraph that begins "Lastly, an artistic"

(p. 331), in the sentence that begins "One of the reasons", the book version reads "that one feels that much". In the paragraph that begins "Even in the first" (p. 332) the book version sets the final sentence as a separate paragraph. In the paragraph that begins "We have seen", the book reads "not all Goethe's but chiefly Moritz's". The *Encounter* version also varies in minor typographic details.

The *Encounter* text was reproduced in *Forewords and Afterwords* (1973) under the title "Italian Journey", and with further corrections to the account of Goethe's departure from Weimar. In the paragraph that begins "The first crisis", the book revises "but he did not go" to "and he was making plans to go"; in the following sentence, Auden ends the sentence after "to join him" and, in place of the original final part of the sentence adds a new sentence: "A day or two later Goethe did so."

THE CASE IS CURIOUS

Page 333.

Auden wrote more extensively about detective stories in 1946, in "The Guilty Vicarage" (*Prose II*, p. 261); revised in *The Dyer's Hand* (p. 556). One sentence in *The Dyer's Hand* version of "The Guilty Vicarage", the sentence that begins "In real life" (p. 560), is adapted from item (3) in the list of questions on p. 334.

On the page following Auden's review in the *Mid-Century* Barzun contributed "An Answer to Mr Auden's Questions":

> Since *The Delights of Detection* grew out of repeated conversations between Mr Auden and me, his three direct questions form a kind of summary of his principles and deserve, not to say require, an answer.
>
> 1. I agree, of course that detection differs from chess problems and crossword puzzles. For one thing, detection involves issues of life and death, and for another it leads us to view the material world in a very special way, as I try to show in the introduction to my book.
>
> 2. Here I disagree: a good theft, or even the threat of one, can provide the stuff for great detective stories; just think of "The Purloined Letter" and "The Red-Headed League."
>
> 3. Once again we part company: in real life I approve of capital punishment; in fiction, unless the murderer has been especially heartless, I like him to clap a pellet into his determined mouth or drive his expensive car over a cliff.
>
>   —J.B.

RONALD FIRBANK AND AN AMATEUR WORLD

Page 335.

The BBC broadcast Auden's talk on 29 April 1961 after recording it in New York perhaps a few weeks earlier. The talk as broadcast was perhaps slightly cut from the lost original.

The text printed in the *Listener* derives from a transcript made by the BBC from the broadcast recording and corrected by an unknown hand. I have not corrected Auden's epidemic misquotations, some drastically abridged without notice, some apparently written from memory, some improved over the original (Auden adds "the" before "Ludwig of Bavaria"). I have, however, corrected misplaced quotation marks and misspelled proper names that were misheard or misremembered by the typist. I have set off as a separate quotation the miscellany of quotations that begins "'I think I am going in'"; the *Listener* runs in the first of these quotations and the introductory sentence. The set-off quotation from *The Flower beneath the Foot* that begins "invitations to meet" is in the printed version run-in with the text as if it were Auden's prose, not Firbank's. In the paragraph that begins "Only those" (p. 338) the printed text begins a new sentence with "because a spectator". At the end of the one-sentence paragraph fragment that begins "Even the jilted" (p. 339) I have replaced an exclamation mark with a colon.

A Poet of Honor

Page 342.

Auden mailed this piece to Sol Stein at The Mid-Century Book Society on 12 May 1961. It is another of Auden's essays and broadcasts in praise of Graves; see also "An Unclassical Classic" (p. 259), and his three BBC broadcasts on Graves (p. 877). The piece was reprinted in a special issue of *Shenandoah* (a literary quarterly published at the University of Virginia) "by permission of The Mid-Century Book Society, Inc." In the paragraph that begins "A comparison" (p. 345) the *Shenandoah* text, followed here, corrects the quotation from Graves's "A Plea to Girls and Boys" from "by heart not by rote" to "by heart not rote" (both versions lack Graves's comma after "heart").

Auden wrote to Stephen Spender on 13 April 1961:

Have just written a piece about Graves' *Collected Poems*. How good they are, but I do hope that, now he is in fashion, les jeunes won't swallow his literary opinions whole. Incidentally for a poet who is so insistent upon TRUTH, he mustn't, as he does in a beautiful poem, *Turn of the Moon*, tell a meteorological lie and assert that she controls drought and rainfall.

After the opening paragraph, after the quotation, "the first two lines are out of date" refers to Grave's widely publicized election as Professor of Poetry at Oxford, Auden's successor in the chair, in February 1961.

The Alienated City: Reflections on *Othello*

Page 347.

See the textual notes to "The Joker in the Pack" in *The Dyer's Hand* (p. 963).

A Marriage of True Minds

Page 348.

This was the only review Auden wrote for the *Times Literary Supplement*, although he printed a few poems in its pages, contributed a signed essay to a special number on American literature in 1954 (*Prose III*, p. 481), and gave permission for it to print one of his T. S. Eliot Memorial Lectures (*Secondary Worlds*) in 1967. The *TLS* version of this review, like all other reviews in the paper, was unsigned.

The piece seems to have been written in late July or early August 1961. Auden wrote to Lionel Trilling on 3 August: "I have just written a leader for the T.L.S. on the Strauss-Hoffmannsthal correspondence." He wrote to Elizabeth Mayer on 18 September: "Did I tell you that I have done a leader for the T.L.S. about the Strauss-Hoffmannsthal Letters? What surprised me, having always heard that S was so nasty, is how well he comes out of the correspondence, while H makes rather a poor show-ing—so touchy, so humorless, so full of self-praise" (Berg Collection).

The signed, shorter version of the review that appeared in the *Mid-Century* ap-peared as a review of the American edition, which had been retitled *A Working Friend-ship: The Correspondence between Richard Strauss and Hugo von Hoffmannsthal*, published by Random House at $10. Auden seems to have lobbied for its American publica-tion, which Random House undertook when The Mid-Century Book Society pro-posed to distribute it to its subscribers. Auden also supplied the title for The Ameri-can edition in a letter to Sol Stein at The Mid-Century Book Society, 4 September 1961: "The Strauss-Hoffmannsthal correspondence. As you know, I dislike fancy ti-tles: *A Working Friendship* is the least misleading I can think of." Auden reported to Stein on 18 September that Jason Epstein at Random House was in correspondence with the British publisher, and "I hope very much indeed that Jacques and Lionel will agree with my judgment of them" [the letters] (Columbia University Library).

I have followed the *TLS* text because it contains much material omitted in the *Mid-Century* version, but the relation between the two versions is unclear. It seems possible that the *Mid-Century* version was set from a heavily cut carbon copy of the typescript that Auden had given to the *TLS* and, although much shorter, may more closely reflect Auden's wording and paragraphing than does the *TLS* version. Some minor differences may be the result of editorial style, as when the *Mid-Century* re-places the *TLS* reading "First World War" (probably the reading of Auden's type-script) with "World War I".

In the second sentence the *TLS* version, "as Octavian", is expanded in the *Mid-Century* to "as, in *Rosenkavalier*, Octavian". In the second paragraph, in the sentence that begins "It is fortunate", the *TLS* readings "one is sorry for" and "brain" are re-placed in the *Mid-Century* with "one has to pity" and "brains"; in the sentence that follows, the *Mid-Century* adds "for example," after "Whitehead" and replaces ""one surmises," with "I suspect" (with the comma omitted). In the third paragraph, the *Mid-Century* omits "kept" immediately before the quotation.

The *Mid-Century* version combines into a single opening paragraph the first three paragraphs of the *TLS* version; in the *TLS* the second paragraph began with "Sometimes, however" and the third with "One rather suspects".

In the paragraph that begins "In their collaboration", the *Mid-Century* cuts every-thing from "In practice" and runs in, without a break, the paragraph that follows (which begins "As in a marriage"). The *Mid-Century* also cuts everything from "A composer like Wagner" through the end of the paragraph that begins "That Wag-ners are rare". In the paragraph fragment that begins "And in the second place" (p. 351) the *Mid-Century* omits "dramatic" from "dramatic flaw".

In the paragraph that begins "Again like marriage" (p. 351) the *TLS* reading "established about how" is changed in the *Mid-Century* to "established as to how".

The *Mid-Century* combines this paragraph with the following two (up to "incomprehensible texts"). In the paragraph that begins "A librettist is always" the *Mid-Century* omits the sentence that begins "Very sensibly" and runs in the paragraph that follows. In the paragraph that begins (in the *TLS*) "A librettist is at a further" the *Mid-Century* changes "is not what the librettist" to "are not what the librettist".

The *Mid-Century* omits everything from "To begin with" through "what Philistia thinks?" In the final paragraph the *Mid-Century* changes "a document so fascinating and so important" to "a document of such importance".

In the first paragraph the quotation "with the necessity" is from Edward Thomas's "'Home'".

Auden reprinted the essay in *Forewords and Afterwords* (1973), omitting the final paragraph (which begins "The translators"). The text used was the *Mid-Century* version, not the longer *TLS* version, solely because, when I compiled the printer's copy for that book at Auden's request, I chose the more legible of the two printed texts (the *TLS* used a smaller typeface), and had not yet noticed that the *Mid-Century* text was shorter and perhaps inferior.

Dag Hammarskjöld

Page 354.

Hammarskjöld, who was secretary-general of the United Nations, died in an airplane crash on 18 September 1961 in the midst of the crisis over Katanga. Shortly after the Congo gained its independence from Belgium in 1960 the province of Katanga seceded, with the support of many Belgians who had remained in the country. The United Nations Security Council called for an end to the secession and the withdrawal of foreign forces, and Hammarskjöld died while conducting negotiations for an end to the fighting that had developed between UN forces and Katangan forces. Auden alludes to the presence of Belgians in the Katangan army and to the widespread sense that Katanga was a puppet of Belgian and other colonial interests, including the Federation of Rhodesia and Nyasaland, of which Roy Welensky was prime minister. Welensky denounced Hammarskjöld for taking action against Katanga; Nikita Khrushchev denounced him for not taking forceful enough action against it.

The other selfless person to whom Auden alludes at the end of the piece may perhaps have been Charles Williams.

With Leif Sjöberg, Auden translated Hammarskjöld's *Markings*, published in 1964 (see *Prose V*).

The Untruth about Beethoven

Page 356.

This was Auden's only contribution to the *Spectator* between 1939 and 1971; the paper was the mostly conservative weekly counterweight to the mostly liberal *New Statesman*, to which Auden contributed far more often. Auden's tone suggests that he had not asked to review this book, and the reason he was asked to do so remains obscure.

In the paragraph that begins "The publication of letters" (p. 359) Auden may have written a hyphen or vergule between the two names "Rolfe Corvo", referring to Frederick Rolfe, who called himself Baron Corvo.

THE QUEST HERO

Page 360.

This essay is almost certainly a slightly modified version of a lecture with the same title that Auden delivered as Professor of Poetry at Oxford on 19 May 1958; he also gave a lecture with this title at the 92nd Street YM-YWHA, New York, 30 October 1958. The *Texas Quarterly*, begun in 1958, published works of general interest mostly by well-known writers, academics, and scientists. Its first editor, Harry H. Ransom, probably asked Auden for a contribution.

In the paragraph that begins "To take a man" (p. 365) I have amended "motive for understanding" to "motive for undertaking", and in the paragraph that begins "The Elves, the Wizards" (p. 368) I have emended "the One the Valas, to whom" (probably a misreading of Auden's typescript) to "the One, the Valar to whom".

A UNIVERSAL ECCENTRIC

Page 374.

The Christmas number of the *Mid-Century* preceded the December number in which appeared Auden's "The Conscience of an Artist" (p. 378).

In Auden's lost typescript, the final paragraph of the printed text occurred before the paragraph that begins "I should be failing". Sol Stein, the executive vice-president of The Mid-Century Book Society, who also put together the monthly magazine, proposed in a memo in October 1961 (presumably shortly after the essay was written) that the paragraph should be moved in order to make the desirability of the book more evident; it is unclear whether Auden actively approved, but it is unlikely that he objected.

THE CONSCIENCE OF AN ARTIST

Page 378.

In his letter to Sol Stein at The Mid-Century Book Society on 4 September 1961 (see also p. 927) Auden wrote: "Though not wildly enthusiastic about the *Pavese*, I think I could do a fair descriptive review. Again, I should need another copy, having left mine in England, and an indication as to the length it should be. With the various changes in the Mag, I no longer know how alternates are to be treated." (This refers to the book-club practice of designating some titles as main selections and some as "alternate selections" that subscribers might choose if they did not wish to take the main selection.)

In the list of books translated by Pavese, "*Alice B. Toklas*" is Gertrude Stein's *Autobiography of Alice B. Toklas*.

In the paragraph fragment that begins "So far as I know" (p. 380) I have added a

comma after "sophisticated regions". Auden's quotations silently abridge the originals.

Books of the Year . . . from W. H. Auden

Page 382.

One of a number of contributions by well-known writers to the newspaper's annual year-end gathering of such lists.

The poetry that was still in manuscript was probably Chester Kallman's second
book, *Absent and Present*, published in 1963.

The *Scientific American* article, which appeared in August 1961 and was written by
Conrad Limbaugh, was titled "Cleaning Symbiosis", not "Cleaning Shrimps"; it describes shrimp and fish that clean other, larger fish. The article concludes: "From
the standpoint of the philosophy of biology, the extent of cleaning behavior in the
ocean emphasizes the role of co-operation in nature as opposed to the tooth-and-
claw struggle for existence."

The Chemical Life

Page 382.

R. C. Zaehner, "Mr Ginsberg" (Allen Ginsberg), and Daniel Breslaw were among
the authors excerpted in the book under review. Zaehner, unlike the others, regarded his experience with peyote as meaningless. "Lexington" was the Federal
hospital for narcotic addicts at Lexington, Kentucky.

Anger

Page 385.

Auden's was the seventh in a series of essays, "The Seven Deadly Sins", written for
the *Sunday Times*. The other contributors were Angus Wilson on envy, Edith Sitwell
on pride, Cyril Connolly on covetousness, Patrick Leigh Fermor on gluttony, Evelyn
Waugh on sloth, and Christopher Sykes on lust. The series was first proposed
around 1957 by Ian Fleming when he was Foreign Manager at the *Sunday Times*.
The idea was revived late in 1961 by another editor, Leonard Russell, who substituted Auden for Malcolm Muggeridge, whom Fleming had suggested as the writer
on anger. The series was published in book form by Sunday Times Publications on
29 October 1962, and reprinted in an American edition by William Morrow the
following month, with a "Special Foreword" by Fleming.

I have followed the text in the book version, which adds a few passages to the
Sunday Times text and omits one. Auden probably revised the book version in proof,
although some of the added material may have been in his original typescript but
omitted from the newspaper in order to save space. In the second paragraph, the
book version adds the two final sentences, beginning "No animal". In the paragraph that begins "Simone Weil" (p. 388) the book version omits the closing sentence found in the newspaper text: "One-and-one-tenth of an eye for an eye is our
idea of justice."

Auden probably rewrote the paragraph that begins "The transferability-of-suffering" (p. 388), in response to criticism. In the newspaper text, the middle phrases of the first sentence read "and there is so little evidence that the threat of punishment is an effective deterrent to crime, or that its infliction has a reformatory effect,". The second sentence of the paragraph is added in the book version.

In the paragraph that begins "Righteous anger" (p. 388) the newspaper has "there have been no just peaces". In the paragraph that begins "Such a picture" (p. 389) the newspaper has "the Devil and the damned". In the paragraph that begins "If God created" the book version adds the quotation from Wittgenstein.

I have omitted the four subheads evidently introduced by the newspaper and retained in the book version.

FOREWORD TO *The Viking Book of Aphorisms*

Page 390.

For the history of this collection, see Appendix II (p. 856). The book was published 26 November 1962; Faber & Faber published a British edition in 1964.

A MARIANNE MOORE READER

Page 392.

Auden earlier wrote about Marianne Moore in the *Mid-Century* in the Fall 1959 number (p. 226). The "serious misquotation" mentioned in the final paragraph occurs in the essay "Humility, Concentration, and Gusto" in the course of a quotation from Auden; see *Prose III*, p. 614.

THE POET AND THE CITY

Page 395.

See the textual notes to "The Poet & The City" in *The Dyer's Hand* (p. 952).

INTRODUCTION TO *A Choice of de la Mare's Verse*

Page 396.

Auden and his British publisher Faber & Faber seem to have agreed late in 1961 or early in 1962 to publish this paperback selection. Auden provided a list of contents some time before 22 February 1962, when Richard de la Mare (Walter's son), an editor at Faber, suggested to him that the title of the selection should match T. S. Eliot's earlier *A Choice of Kipling's Verse*, and that the specimen pages (which he enclosed with his letter) reflected a design that would allow the inclusion of all the poems on Auden's list. He also asked Auden when his introduction could be expected. Auden sent it on 27 March 1962 with a letter apologizing for the delay ("an avalanche of chores suddenly descended on me which I could not neglect").

Richard de la Mare told Auden he was delighted with the introduction and asked again whether Auden approved of the specimen pages. Auden replied on 16 April 1962 (Faber archives):

As to the specimen pages, I like the type very much, but I do hope when they actually set the book, they won't split the fifth stanza of *The Children of Stare*. Aside from the ugly look, it distorts the reading of a poem. In printing lyric poetry one simply cannot, as in printing prose, standardise the number of lines to a page.

Meanwhile Alan Pringle, another editor at Faber, read Auden's introduction and found many faults with it. It was agreed at Faber that the most tactful way to ask for changes was to have T. S. Eliot present the suggestions as his own, which he did in a long letter to Auden on 8 May. The following paragraphs list those of Eliot's objections to which Auden responded in a letter quoted below.

Eliot first objected to Auden's opening observation that de la Mare was widely known in England "though not, I fear, in the United States", a statement, Eliot said, more suitable to a book to be published in America. The purpose of a preface, Eliot wrote, was to "commend, as well as to interpret, an author to new readers", and the fact that de la Mare was not well-known in America did not commend him to English readers. Eliot was also doubtful about the second paragraph in which Auden wrote that de la Mare's inspiration sprang from the Pre-Raphaelites: Eliot's and especially Pound's early poetry stemmed from the Pre-Raphaelites, Eliot agreed, but from Rossetti and Swinburne, not from William Morris, the only Pre-Raphaelite named by Auden. Eliot asked that the two opening paragraphs be omitted, and Auden evidently agreed.

Eliot then objected to Auden's distinction between Ariel and Prospero (which Auden retained).

Eliot disputed Auden's statement that de la Mare had been influenced by the French *symbolistes* (a claim that Auden removed); "Nobody was before T.S.E., and nobody has been since." Eliot also wondered whether de la Mare could have been, as Auden wrote, influenced by Hardy.

Eliot proceeded to object to Auden's general statements about children's verse, and hoped he would focus on de la Mare's poetry for children, not on children's poetry in general.

Eliot then wrote that he did not agree that the English climate is as kindly as Auden said, although this was a widely believed fiction.

Auden had written that de la Mare's poetry was "preserved from gentility"; Eliot wrote that the word "gentility" is offensive in the way that the phrase "a sensible woman" is offensive.

Auden had closed by writing that de la Mare is "never a bore", to which Eliot responded: "O God! O Montreal!"

Auden responded on 10 May 1962:

(1) As you say, the first two paragraphs are unsatisfactory. The problem is this. However well, on paper, he may sell, I consider a poet neglected if he is not being read by those under 35 when I think he should be. If I am correct in believing that the younger generation do not read de

la Mare, what is their preconceived notion of his poems which prevents them? Is it not that they think his style "out-of-date"? In a preface which is meant to "commend" an author, should one not mention possible objections before showing that they are unjust?

As for the Pre-Raphaelite influence, it was certainly obvious in early Pound (though not to me, in early Eliot) and it put me off. One reason why Hardy's poetry appealed to me so much as a boy was that, though metrically influenced by Swinburne, the sensibility was so unswinburnian. As to the particular Pre-Raphaelites who influenced de la Mare, I should have guessed them to be Christina R. (not D.G.) whom I mention and William Morris, but not Swinburne. But you may know better.

I may, of course, be quite wrong in attributing a certain similarity in the way both Hardy and he construct their more complicated stanzas to the former's example, but I am sure that a "mature" poet can still pick up hints from another poet on such formal matters.

(2) Ariel-Prospero. Yes, too fancy, I suppose. But I find the distinction useful and I prefer mythological descriptions to abstract ones.

(3) Les symbolistes. Touché. That comes of living in the U.S. where at least one poet in three believes his tradition is French.

(3) [*Auden misnumbers this first item on his second page*] Children's verse. Is it a wrong approach to begin with the general desiderata and then show how a particular poet satisfies them?

(4) Having now lived in a variety of climates, I grow more and more nostalgic for the British one, maybe because I have never suffered from bronchial trouble, perpetual sunshine makes me depressed and temperatures over 75°F reduce me to a mindless jelly. My one complaint about it is that it makes me very lazy.

(5) "Gentility" is an offensive word and was meant to be. What I was trying to say was that a "counterfeit" de la Mare poem would be genteel. A counterfeit Eliot poem would be something else (and, alas, there are quite a number of them about). However the sentence must obviously be rephrased.

(6) "never a bore". Is that a dreadful thing to say? I can think of poems, and even poets, that are quite good but, unfortunately, a bore, and so, I'm sure, can you.

I have no copy of the piece, so could you send it me with the offending passages scored with red pencil and I will see what I can do.

Eliot responded on 7 June thanking Auden for his comments but asking that the whole piece be slanted differently; he proposed that he and Auden discuss the matter when Auden came to England that month. Auden and Eliot did not meet in England, but on 15 August 1962 Auden wrote: "Herewith a revised de la Mare introduction which, I hope, meets your objections." (Auden had dated his letter from Austria "Maria Himmelfahrt", the Feast of the Assumption of the Blessed Virgin Mary. Eliot's new secretary acknowledged the letter with a note addressed to "Frau Himmelfahrt".) Eliot replied on 8 September that everyone at Faber was happy with the new version.

Auden's quotations are slightly inexact, but I have corrected only the second to last sentence in the opening quotation where Auden had "Mr Taroone" for "Miss Taroone". As always, Auden omits the punctuation from de la Mare's title *Behold, This Dreamer!*

The book was published 17 May 1963. Auden included the introduction, without change, in *Forewords and Afterwords* (1973), as "Walter de la Mare".

Today's Poet

Page 404.

One of Auden's occasional contributions to *Mademoiselle*, a young women's magazine which interspersed fashion news with essays and poems. For an earlier contribution, see *Prose III*, p. 164.

A Disturbing Novelist

Page 405.

The first of two reviews by Auden in the same number of the *Mid-Century*.

"The Geste Says this and the Man Who Was on the Field . . ."

Page 408.

The second of two reviews by Auden in the same number of the *Mid-Century*. Auden reviewed Jones's *Anathemata* in *Encounter*, February 1954 (*Prose III*, p. 407). Auden or the compositor found Jones's eccentrically laid-out text difficult to transcribe, and I have made some trivial corrections to layout and capitalization.

The Justice of Dame Kind

Page 412.

The Midsummer 1962 number of the *Mid-Century* appeared between the July and August numbers. This was Auden's last contribution; the magazine lasted three more numbers before the book club folded.

Auden reprinted this essay without change in *Forewords and Afterwords* (1973).

Today's "Wonder-World" Needs Alice

Page 414.

The title was supplied by the editors of the Magazine section of the *New York Times*. All articles in the Magazine section were divided for the sake of typographic clarity into separate parts; I have retained a few of these breaks that may have been authorial. Some of the newspaper's run-in quotations have been reset as set-off quotations. I have removed the first word from the erroneous title *Alice Through the Looking-Glass* (p. 418).

Auden reprinted the piece as "Lewis Carroll" in *Forewords and Afterwords* (1973); the text used there was reproduced from an anthology, *Aspects of Alice*, edited by Robert Phillips (1971), in which the same substitutions of set-off for run-in quotations had been made that are also made in this edition. The newspaper's section breaks survived into the anthology but were removed for *Forewords and Afterwords*.

STRACHEY'S CRY

Page 422.

Auden perhaps met John Strachey (1901–63) during the 1930s when Strachey worked with the publisher Victor Gollancz in organizing the Left Book Club. Strachey was a Labour M.P. from 1945 until his death. A listing of his papers (still in private hands) mentions a correspondence with Auden about this review, but the letters have not been found.

ARE THE ENGLISH EUROPEANS?

Page 428.

This was originally a broadcast talk for the Bayerische Rundfunk in its series "Europäisches Konzert". Auden wrote the talk in English; it was translated by Peter Stadelmeyer into German with the title "Ein Engländer sieht Europa". Auden recorded the German text on 16 October 1962, and it was broadcast on 29 October 1962. A carbon-copy typescript made by the radio station of the German text (now in the Berg Collection) has minor revisions in Auden's hand.

The text in *Wort und Wahrheit*, from which the text in this edition was translated, appears below. It has further minor changes from the broadcast version, including some that transform the text from a broadcast talk (in which a few phrases are addressed to listeners in the second-person plural) into a printed essay.

Auden's revisions in the typescript of the German broadcast text seem largely intended to correct readings in which Stadelmayer's German erred through false cognates (words in one language that look similar to, but have different meanings from, words in another language) and through overly exact translations of Auden's prose. For example, in the opening paragraph, Auden changed "Selbstverständlich bleibe ich trotzdem ein echter Engländer" to "Trotzdem bleibe ich selbstverständlich ein lauter[er] Engländer" (Auden probably wrote "true", in the sense of "thorough" or "unalloyed"). In the second paragraph Auden changed "Das ist unkorrekt" to "Das ist falsch" ("unkorrekt" in this context is a false cognate of "incorrect"). In the paragraph that begins "I said a moment ago" (p. 433) Auden changed "ein Gentleman durch die prägende Kraft der Umwelt und durch Erziehung" to "ein Gentleman durch Bildung und Erziehung" ("Bildung" conveys in a single word a meaning that requires a whole phrase in English).

In the paragraph that begins "A Roman Catholic" (p. 433) Auden changed "das Kind der Evangelischen Bewegung" to "das Kind der Nonconformismus" ("Evangelical" has different meanings in German and English) and changed "die sich mit den Problemen der Volksbildung und der Jugendkriminalität beschäftigten" to "die sich Slums und Halb-Starken gekümmert hatten" (a change only partly made in the printed text). For an earlier statement of the same thoughts about English religion and social justice, see the introduction to *Selected Writings of Sydney Smith* (p. 20).

In the paragraph that begins "For the Low-Brows" (p. 435) Auden changed "englische Spiele spielten" to "englischen Sport betrieben" (to give the correct equivalent of "games"). He changed the final sentence from "So lassen Sie uns denn lieben Gott für den Babylonischen Turm loben und ihm danken" to "Preisen wir, also, den lieben Gott und ihm danken für den Babylonischen Turm" (an ungrammatical construction, corrected in the printed text).

In the same typescript of the German broadcast text, a change marked by an unknown hand seem to have obscured Auden's original meaning. In the first sentence, Stadelmeyer first wrote "weder Wissenschaftler noch Philosoph"; the unknown hand changed "Wissenschaftler" to "Wirtschaftler", which was changed again in the printed German text to "Wirtschaftsmann"; this change may have been a mistaken one, because the original "Wissenschaftler" was probably a translation of Auden's word "scientist".

The printed German text may perhaps have been further revised by Auden in proof.

In this English retranslation from the printed text, made with the generous help of Barbara Thimm, I have adjusted some paragraph breaks to correspond with those in the typescript of the broadcast. The German printed text follows.

SIND DIE ENGLÄNDER EUROPÄER?
Die Insel und der Kontinent

Ich bin weder Historiker noch Politiker, weder Wirtschaftsmann noch Philosoph. Ich bin nur ein Dichter, und wie bekannt, sind die Gedanken eines Dichters leicht verkehrt, einseitig, subjektiv. Damit man sich aber ein Urteil bilden kann über das, was ich sage, ist es also nur recht und billig, wenn ich mit ein paar autobiographischen Einzelheiten beginne. Ich entstamme einer Mittelstandsfamilie mit geistigen Interessen. Mein Vater war ein Arzt, der ein abgeschlossenes Studium der Altphilologie hinter sich hatte, ehe er sich der Medizin zuwandte. Meine Mutter besaß ein Universitätsdiplom zu einer Zeit, in der so etwas für eine Frau ziemlich ausgefallen war. Meine beiden Großväter waren Geistliche der englischen Hochkirche. Vor sechzehn Jahren wurde ich amerikanischer Staatsbürger, und mein ständiger Wohnsitz ist New York. Außerdem besitze ich ein Häuschen bei Wien, in dem ich meine Sommer verbringe. Trotzdem bleibe ich selbstverständlich ein lauterer Engländer. Ich bin jetzt 55 Jahre alt, und damit ist gesagt, daß es zur Zeit meiner Geburt in der Welt noch etwas gab, was man mit „Stille" bezeichnet, die Zeitungen noch keine Bilder hatten und daß ich in unserer heutigen Autobahn-Fernseh-Espresso-Kultur bereits ein alter Rauschebart bin. Wenn ich also jetzt über England und Europa spreche, dann sollte man nicht vergessen, daß da ein mittelständischer englischer Rauschebart spricht.

Es gibt in jeder Sprache gewisse Wörter und Ausdrücke, die unübersetzbar sind, im Deutschen zum Beispiel die Wörter „Schadenfreude", „Kitsch" und „schöngeistig". Im Englischen—das heißt im britischen Englisch, nicht im amerikanischen— gibt es das Substantiv „abroad" und das Verbum „to go abroad". Dafür steht in meinem deutschen Wörterbuch „im Ausland" und „ins Ausland gehen". Das ist falsch. Wenn ich beispielsweise nach Amerika oder Indien oder Australien reise, begebe ich mich nicht ins Ausland, sondern nach Übersee. Ins Ausland gehen bedeutet, daß man den Kanal überquert, und für jeden Engländer sind die Wörter „Ausland" und „Europa" identisch. Der Engländer mag gern ins Ausland reisen, ja er mag es sogar vorziehen, dort und nicht in seinem Geburtsland Wohnsitz zu nehmen, oder er mag die Gefühle des verstorbenen Königs Georg VI. teilen, der gesagt haben soll—was wiederum nicht übersetzbar ist—: „Abroad is bloody" (ungefähr: Ich pfeife auf Europa, oder: Europa ist mir egal)—auf jeden Fall aber ist für den Engländer Europa eine andere Welt als England.

Schließe ich die Augen und sage ich mir das Wort „Europa" vor, dann haben die verschiedenen Vorstellungen, die dieses Wort heraufbeschwört, alle eins gemeinsam: keine könnte durch das Wort „England" hervorgerufen werden. Ich werde jetzt einige davon nennen, so wie sie mir in den Sinn kommen und ohne mich um eine logische Reihenfolge zu bemühen. Europa ist der Ort,

1. wo die Felder nicht durch Hecken unterteilt sind, die Gehöfte zum größten Teil in Familienbesitz sind und der besitzlose Landarbeiter eine Seltenheit ist;

2. wo es eine bestimmte soziale Schicht gibt, die Bauern, die sich als solche bestimmte Schicht fühlen und häufig eine beachtliche politische Macht darstellen;

3. wo nur sehr wenige Angehörige der Aristokratie aktiv am öffentlichen politischen Leben teilnehmen;

4. wo die politisch Liberalen und die sozialistische Linke antiklerikal und meist atheistisch sind;

5. wo der Dorfschullehrer und der Landarzt meist politisch links orientiert sind;

6. wo am Sonntag die Läden aufhaben und zu jeder Stunde des Tages alkoholische Getränke ausgeschenkt werden;

7. wo die Gemüse beim Kochen nicht völlig ausgelaugt werden. Man möge mir an dieser Stelle die Bemerkung erlauben, daß die englische Küche nicht ganz so schauderhaft ist, wie man aus den vielen darauf abzielenden Witzen schließen könnte; aber sie ist eine Sache für sich. Die französische, italienische, deutsche und spanische Küche unterscheiden sich voneinander, aber auch der provinziellste französische, italienische, deutsche oder spanische Tourist, der ein Nachbarland besucht, verbringt nicht seine ganze Zeit damit, über die Eigenartigkeit, Ungenießbarkeit und die vermutliche Unbekömmlichkeit des Essens zu schimpfen;

8. wo das einzig behagliche Möbelstück das Doppelbett ist;

9. wo die Badezimmer in den Hotels mit Bidets ausgestattet sind;

10. wo nichts vergeudet wird, wo man noch heute das klassische Laster des Geizes und den Geizhals à la Balzac finden kann;

11. wo es nur in den Läden der Großstädte richtiges Einwickelpapier gibt;

12. wo Einheimische wie Ausländer einen Ausweis mit sich führen und bei der Anmeldung in einem Hotel vorweisen müssen;

13. wo in der Rechtswissenschaft Gesetzbücher eine größere Rolle spielen als durch Rechtsprechung erfolgte Urteile;

14. wo das geistige Leben zwei Zentren hat: ein ausschließlich männliches, das Cafe, in dem Künstler aller Art Bewegungen gründen und Manifeste erlassen, und den Salon, den eine Frau beherrscht;

15. wo zwei gebildete Menschen, von denen keiner die Sprache des anderen spricht, sich französisch unterhalten;

16. wo die Protestanten, wenn überhaupt vorhanden, in der Minderheit sind.

Die protestantischen Länder—Skandinavien, Holland, Preußen—gehören eigentlich nicht ganz zu Europa. Zählen wir ihre Einwohner zu den Europäern, dann sind sie, nun sagen wir es einmal auf wienerisch, Tschuschen.

Da ich Schriftsteller bin, beschwört das Wort Europa natürlich außer diesen Vorstellungen auch noch eine Anzahl erlauchter Namen herauf. Hier einige, die mir einfallen: Lichtenberg, Hölderlin, Nietzsche, Nestroy, Rimbaud, Christian Morgenstern, Rilke, Valéry, Kafka, Karl Kraus, Rudolf Kassner. Sicher ist auffallend, daß in dieser Liste die deutschen Namen überwiegen. Kein Engländer verliebt sich in Europa als Ganzes, er verliebt sich in eine bestimmte Landschaft oder Stadt oder Sprache Europas. Es ist behauptet worden, niemand könne sich jemals in Bulgarien verlieben; ich aber kenne einen jungen Engländer, der es tat. Wie alle Verliebten sind wir parteiisch. Wir können Französisch, Italienisch oder Spanisch lieben, aber nie alle drei gleich stark. Ich gehöre zu denen—es sind unserer nicht viele—, die sich in die deutsche Sprache verliebten. Ich spreche sie sehr schlecht, teilweise deshalb, weil ich die abergläubische Furcht des Dichters habe, ich könnte, sobald ich einmal eine fremde Zunge vollkommen beherrsche, das Gefühl für meine eigene Sprache verlieren. Auch stimme ich wohl Lichtenberg ganz und gar zu, wenn er sagt: „Um eine fremde Sprache recht gut sprechen zu lernen und wirklich in Gesellschaft mit dem eigentlichen Akzent des Volkes zu sprechen, muß man nicht allein Gedächtnis und Ohr haben, sondern auch in gewissem Grad ein kleiner Geck sein."

Woher stammt meine Liebe zur deutschen Sprache? Nun, als ich 1928 Oxford verließ, boten mir meine Eltern an, ein Jahr in Europa zu studieren. Für die Generation englischer Intellektueller, die der meinen unmittelbar voranging, gab es nur eine europäische Kultur von Rang, und das war die französische. Das Gerede über die Franzosen langweilte mich, und so war ich fest entschlossen, auf keinen Fall nach Paris zu gehen. Wohin also dann? Rom? Nein, das machten Mussolini und der Faschismus unmöglich. Berlin? Das war eine Idee! Weshalb nicht? Ich konnte kein Deutsch und kannte kaum etwas von der deutschen Literatur, aber so ging es schließlich all meinen Bekannten. Berlin war eine unerforschte Hauptstadt, die sich vielleicht als amüsant herausstellen konnte. Vielleicht war ich auch unbewußt für Deutschland eingenommen, denn wenn ich als kleiner Junge während des ersten Weltkrieges im Internat mir ein Extra-Butterbrot nahm, sagte mit Gewißheit jedesmal einer der Lehrer: „Auden, ich merke, du willst die Hunnen gewinnen lassen!" Und damit setzte sich bei mir die Vorstellung fest, es bestehe eine Verbindung zwischen Deutschland und verbotenen Freuden. Die politische Unterweisung der Jugend ist ein riskantes Unternehmen.

Meine so frivol getroffene Wahl erwies sich aus zwei Gründen als außerordentlich glücklich. Zunächst einmal war Berlin, wie bekannt, in den späten zwanziger Jahren und bis 1933 kulturell eine sehr aufregende Stadt. Außerdem öffnete es mir die Augen für die prekäre Situation der Kultur in unserem Jahrhundert. Auch die ältesten Leser dieses Artikels können sich nicht vorstellen, wie sicher sich der englische Mittelstand in den zwanziger Jahren noch fühlte. Trotz des ersten Weltkrieges konnten wir nicht glauben, daß etwas wirklich Ernstes geschehen war. Ich las beispielsweise, ehe ich nach Berlin ging, nie die Zeitung. In Berlin jedoch begriff ich zum erstenmal, daß etwas Unwiderrufliches geschehen war, daß die Grundfesten wankten und daß die Welt zu meinen Lebzeiten nie wieder der sichere Ort sein würde, der sie in meiner frühen Kindheit gewesen.

Was ich damals erlebte, waren die letzten Todeszuckungen jenes Europa, das ich unter diesem Wort verstehe. Kurz und gut, Europa ist oder war vielmehr, glaube ich, das Gebiet, in dem das Gedankengut der Französischen Revolution immer wach war und das geographisch mehr oder weniger mit dem Napoleonischen Reich übereinstimmte. Es war das Ergebnis des revolutionären Stoßes Frankreichs und des konterrevolutionären Gegenstoßes, den dieser Stoß herausforderte. Ohne den Gegenstoß wäre Europa eine politische Einheit unter französischer Herrschaft statt eines Raumes unter dem Einfluß französischer Kultur. Napoleon wird durch Metternich aufgewogen und, was die Kulturzentren anbelangt, Paris durch Wien. Vor 1786 gab es kein Europa, und die Russische Revolution von 1917 bezeichnete sein Ende.

Um das, was ich meine, etwas näher zu erläutern, muß ich den Leser leider mit ein wenig Amateurgeschichte langweilen. Vor Luther, Calvin und der Entdeckung der beiden Amerika dachten die westlichen Menschen in Begriffen von Christentum und Heidentum. Daß die Grenzen der Christenheit zufälligerweise ungefähr mit der Halbinsel zusammenfielen, die wir häufig Europa nennen, bedeutet nicht, daß die Menschen des Mittelalters sich für Europäer hielten. Sie dachten in Begriffen ihrer allernächsten Umgebung, ihres Oberlehensherrn und ihres gemeinsamen Glaubens. Somit war England auf eine Weise ein Teil der Christenheit, wie es nie ein Teil Europas wurde.

Das 16. Jahrhundert ist durch die Spaltung des Westens in Protestantismus und Katholizismus gekennzeichnet sowie durch die Zusammenfassung feudaler Herrschaftsgebiete in absolutistische Reiche. Weil sowohl die politischen Rivalitäten wie die Glaubensdifferenzen zu groß waren, konnte ein feudales Europa-Bewußtsein nicht aufkommen. Um den Menschen des geographischen Europa ein gemeinsames Bewußtsein zu geben und somit die kulturelle Einheit zu schaffen, die ich unter dem Wort Europa verstehe, bedurfte es eines neuen säkularen Evangeliums und eines neuen säkularen Helden. Die Franzosen lieferten beides: Liberté, Egalité, Fraternité war das Evangelium; Figaro, der Barbier niederer Herkunft, der sich durch seinen Mutterwitz und seine natürliche Begabung dem blaublütigen Grafen überlegen zeigt, wurde der Held.

England spielte in den napoleonischen Kriegen eine bedeutende Rolle, weil seine nationale Sicherheit Napoleons Niederlage erforderte. Es befaßte sich aber, abgesehen von wenigen einzelnen wie Burke, kaum mit der Ideologie der Französischen Revolution, denn es hatte eine eigene Revolution bereits hinter sich. Im Jahre 1786 wurde fast jedes europäische Land noch immer von einem absolutistischen Herrscher regiert, in England jedoch hatte der Absolutismus 1649 mit der Enthauptung Karls I. sein Ende gefunden. Dieser Akt wurde, im Gegensatz zur Enthauptung Ludwigs XVI., von den dafür Verantwortlichen nicht als ein revolutionärer Bruch mit der Vergangenheit empfunden. Er erschien ihnen vielmehr als eine neuerliche Bekräftigung der mittelalterlichen Idee, daß der Herrscher dem Naturrecht Untertan ist und nicht darübersteht. Man könnte sagen, Karl I. habe dafür büßen müssen, daß sein Vorfahre Heinrich VIII. anno 1535 Sir Thomas More enthaupten ließ, der als Lordkanzler Hüter des königlichen Gewissens war. Die englische Revolution, die mit dem Großen Bürgerkrieg 1642 bis 1646 ihren Anfang nahm, dauerte bis zur Vertreibung Jakobs II. im Jahre 1688 an, einem Ereignis, das uns als die Glorreiche Revolution bekannt ist.

Das Wort Revolution bedeutet hier etwas anderes als das Umstürzen des Alten und Beginn des Neuen, wie bei der Französischen oder der Russischen Revolution. Es ist eine aus der Astronomie entlehnte Metapher und bedeutet: Wiederherstellung des Gleichgewichts. Unter Cromwells Protektorat entdeckten die Engländer, daß die Gefahr willkürlicher Macht nicht unbedingt durch die Abschaffung der Krone behoben wird; denn der Anspruch der Heiligen von eigenen Gnaden, kraft göttlicher Eingebung zu wissen, was das rechte Leben sei, und das Recht zu besitzen, diese ihre Vorstellungen den Gottlosen aufzuzwingen, konnte eine ebenso große Bedrohung der Freiheit darstellen wie das Gottesgnadentum der Könige. Die Monarchie wurde also wieder eingesetzt, doch als Jakob II. als absolutistischer Herrscher regieren wollte, setzte man ihn eilig ab, und die Whig-Grundbesitzer importierten eine Dynastie, zuerst aus Holland und später, nach dem Tod der Königin Anna, aus Hannover. Weil diese Könige nicht Englisch konnten—selbst Eduard VII., der 1910 starb, sprach Englisch mit deutschem Akzent—, konnte die politische Macht sich nicht am Hofe konzentrieren, sondern war beim Parlament und auf den großen Landsitzen zu finden.

Es ist eine Vereinfachung, wiewohl keine allzu grobe, wenn man sagt, daß England zwischen 1688 und 1914 von den Reichen regiert wurde—zunächst von den reichen Grundbesitzern, zu denen sich später, nach der industriellen Revolution, die Bankiers und die großen Geschäftsleute gesellten. Die Vernichtung des Bauernstandes in England vollzog sich allmählich. Sie begann im 15. Jahrhundert, als Tausende von Bauern enteignet wurden, damit man aus dem Ackerland Schafweiden gewann; sie nahm ihren Fortgang mit den Einfriedungen des 18. Jahrhunderts, und der letzte Schlag war die Erfindung der Maschinen, die aller Heimarbeit ein Ende bereiteten und die Heimarbeiter in die Fabriken zwangen.

Ich sagte bereits vorhin, daß zu den Unterschieden zwischen England und Europa, die mir besonders auffielen, auch der gehört, daß in Europa die Aristokratie wenig Anteil am öffentlichen Leben nahm. Es wäre nicht ganz korrekt, zu behaupten, sie habe es in England getan; denn *Aristokratie* und *Aristokrat* sind keine typisch englischen Begriffe; wir sprechen statt dessen von der *Gentry* und dem *Gentleman*. Ein Aristokrat ist man durch Geburt und Abstammung, ein Gentleman durch die prägende Kraft der Umwelt, durch Bildung und Erziehung. Ein Mann aus der Arbeiterklasse kann es durch Glück und Talent zu einem Vermögen bringen; ein Gentleman kann er nicht werden, seine Sprache wird seine Herkunft verraten. Er kann aber seinen Sohn nach Eton und Oxford schicken, und sein Sohn wird ein Gentleman werden. Vielleicht sprechen die Engländer deshalb nicht von der Aristokratie, weil nur sehr wenige unserer Adelstitel älter als vierhundert Jahre sind. Die Reichen, die England regierten, vernachlässigten, was ich wohl kaum erwähnen muß, die eigenen Interessen nicht, begründeten jedoch auch die Tradition, der zufolge man von einem Gentleman Interesse und Teilnahme am öffentlichen und politischen Geschehen erwartet; und indem sie dies taten, entwickelten sie als Korrektiv zum natürlichen Egoismus jedes Menschen ein Gefühl der Verpflichtung gegenüber der Allgemeinheit und dem Gemeinwohl.

Ein weiterer Unterschied, den ich erwähnte, war der antiklerikale, ja atheistische Charakter der liberalen und der sozialistischen Linken in Europa. Der Katholik mag lächeln über jene seltsame Institution der anglikanischen Kirche mit ihrer vagen Doktrin und ihrer nicht vorhandenen zentralen Autorität—doch, historisch gesehen, hatte sie durchaus ihre großen Vorzüge. Hätten die Erzbischöfe von Canterbury, wie die Päpste, in sozialen Angelegenheiten dekretieren können—man muß bedenken, daß die anglikanische Kirche eine Staatskirche ist und der Erzbischof von Canterbury auf Vorschlag der Politiker ernannt wird—, dann wäre die Kirche die reaktionärste Körperschaft des Staates gewesen und die Linke in England womöglich noch antiklerikaler als in Europa. Der Mangel an Gehorsamspflicht ermöglichte es den Klerikern und Laien, die liberale Ideen hatten, diese zu äußern und für sie einzutreten. Die britische Labour-Partei ist das Kind des Nonkonformismus, und die ersten Leute, die sich mit den Problemen der Slums und der Halbstarken beschäftigten, waren die Anglo-Katholiken.

Welcherlei Engländer hatten schließlich Beziehungen zu Europa und aus welchen Gründen?

1. Vom 16. bis zum 18. Jahrhundert war es Sitte, daß die reichen jungen Erben eine große Europareise machten, ehe sie sich auf ihren Besitzungen etablierten; das gehörte zu ihrer Erziehung. Im 19. Jahrhundert, als der Mittelstand reicher wurde, wurde es auch in dieser Schicht üblich, daß man eine Bildungsreise durch Europa unternahm.

2. Nach 1815 flohen Bankrotteure, die ihren Gläubigern entrinnen wollten, nach Europa, insbesondere nach Dieppe.

3. Etwa um die gleiche Zeit beginnen sich in Europa englische Kolonien zu bilden, die aus zwei Sorten Menschen bestehen: solchen mit kleinen privaten Einkünften, die herausgefunden hatten, daß sie in Europa mit ihrem Geld größere Sprünge machen konnten als zu Hause, und Künstlern und Bohemiens, die fanden, daß das Klima und das Milieu ihrer Arbeit förderlich waren, und die ein Privatleben fern der Zensur heimischen Muckertums führen wollten.

4. Gegen Ende des 19. Jahrhunderts wurde es unter der studierenden englischen Jugend Usus, an irgendeiner europäischen Universität oder Hochschule ein ganz bestimmtes Fach zu studieren: Medizin, Theologie, Musik usw.

5. Als letzte kamen die Bergsteiger, die Wintersportler und die Sonnenbader.

Während des 18. und 19. Jahrhunderts erwarb sich England ein überseeisches Reich, aus dem im 20. Jahrhundert ein Commonwealth autonomer Dominions wurde. Von Anfang an gab es zwei Arten von Kolonien: jene, in denen die Mehrzahl der Einwohner englischer Herkunft waren, wie Kanada, Australien und Neuseeland, und jene, in denen eine sehr kleine Zahl von Engländern eine sehr große Zahl Fremder regierte, wie Indien und die afrikanischen Kolonien. Von den Engländern, die England verließen, um sich in die erstgenannten Kolonien zu begeben, wollten die meisten sich dort niederlassen, um nie mehr zurückzukehren. Diejenigen, die in die indische Armee, den indischen oder kolonialen Verwaltungsdienst eintraten, und selbst die, die in Indien oder Afrika Geschäftsunternehmen gründeten, hatten vor, zurückzukehren und ihre Tage in England zu beschließen—wenn sie Glück hatten, mit einem Vermögen in der Tasche.

Um das Jahr 1900 gab es in fast jeder Mittelstandsfamilie einen oder mehrere Angehörige, die entweder ausgewandert waren oder einen Kolonialberuf in Übersee hatten. Von fast allen Auswanderern und von der Mehrzahl der Verwaltungsbeamten und Teepflanzer darf man sagen, daß sie nicht zu den Intellektuellen ihrer Familien gehörten. Einer meiner Onkel wollte Offizier werden; weil aber nicht genug Geld vorhanden war, um ihn in ein gutes Regiment zu bringen, mußte der arme Kerl den Beruf eines Geistlichen ergreifen, wozu ihm die Berufung fehlte. Er geriet in Schwierigkeiten wegen eines Mädchens und mußte nach Australien verschwinden. Meinem ältesten Bruder fiel das Studieren schwer, er wollte Landwirt werden. In England war Grund und Boden zu teuer, deshalb ging er nach Kanada. Mein anderer Bruder *ist* ein Intellektueller, trat jedoch in den indischen geologischen Vermessungsdienst, weil er sich für die praktische Arbeit interessierte. In England war die praktische Arbeit nämlich bereits getan, so daß er nur noch an irgendeiner Universität hätte Geologie lehren können.

Man wird in Europa die derzeitige Debatte in England wegen des Beitritts zum Gemeinsamen Markt nie verstehen, wenn man sie nur unter dem Aspekt unterschiedlicher wirtschaftlicher Interessen sieht. Sicher hat man bemerkt, daß die Labour-Partei und die Konservative Partei in dieser Frage gleichermaßen gespalten sind. Jeglichem Pro und Kontra liegen leidenschaftliche, emotionelle Vorurteile zugrunde und auch die uralte Fehde zwischen den High-Brows und den Low-Brows. Ich kann den wirtschaftlichen Argumenten nicht folgen, und weil ich kein britischer Bürger mehr bin, kann ich an der Kontroverse nicht teilnehmen. Instinktiv bin ich jedoch für den Gemeinsamen Markt. Ich kenne Europa aus eigener Anschauung, und als Schriftsteller könnte ich mir mein Leben ohne die europäische Literatur, Kunst und Musik nicht vorstellen.

Die Dominions hingegen sind für mich *tiefste Provinz*, Orte, die fast keinerlei Kunst hervorgebracht haben und von jener Art Menschen bewohnt werden, mit denen ich am wenigsten gemeinsam habe, ob es sich nun um unsere Tugenden oder unsere Laster handelt. Würde ich eine dieser Provinzen besuchen, so käme ich nicht in den Genuß dessen, was für mich zu den größten Freuden einer Reise gehört—an einem Ort zu sein, wo man kein Englisch spricht und wo ich infolgedessen ein anonymes Individuum ohne sozialen Status und damit frei bin, nach Gutdünken mit jedermann zu verkehren.

Für den Low-Brow—ich spreche jetzt von den Low-Brows meines Jahrgangs und der älteren, denn dank der billigen Massenreisen nach Europa seit dem Krieg sind die jungen sicherlich ganz anders—, für die Low-Brows also waren die Dominions von ihren Verwandten und ihresgleichen bevölkert, von Leuten, die Englisch sprachen, englisches Essen aßen, englische Kleider trugen und englischen Sport betrieben. „Europa" hingegen war für sie von unmoralischen Fremden bevölkert—ein französischer Roman war gleichbedeutend mit Pornographie—, und jeder Engländer, Bergsteiger und Wintersportler ausgenommen, der häufig ins Ausland reiste oder dort dauernden Wohnsitz nahm, führte vermutlich nichts Gutes im Schilde. Der Low-Brow unterscheidet jedoch zwischen den einzelnen europäischen Ländern.

Wären die europäischen Partner des Gemeinsamen Marktes die skandinavischen Länder, dann stünde der Low-Brow dem Gedanken eines Beitritts Englands weit weniger feindselig gegenüber. Im vergangenen Jahr machte ich eine Seereise die norwegische Küste entlang. Meine Mitreisenden, meist Engländer, faszinierten mich, denn sie waren Vertreter eines Typs, dem ich nie zuvor in Europa begegnet war. Ich habe den Verdacht, daß der Durchschnittsengländer noch immer, wenn auch vermutlich unbewußt, ziemlich starke antipapistische Gefühle hegt. Wenn er es auch vor sich selber nicht eingestehen mag, so hält er doch in der Tiefe seines Herzens die Katholiken für Götzenanbeter, für unmoralisch und für Menschen, die sich nicht waschen, und er glaubt, daß nur ein Protestant wirklich respektabel sein kann.

Vielleicht tritt England dem Gemeinsamen Markt bei—und ich hoffe sehr, daß es das tut—, aber dadurch wird es nicht ein Teil Europas werden, denn es gibt kein Europa mehr. Das Automobil, das Flugzeug, das Fernsehen usw. schaffen eine internationale Lebensweise, die von San Franzisko bis Wien die gleiche ist. Und wenn die Länder hinter dem Eisernen Vorhang zu Wohlstand gelangen—und ich sehe keinen essentiellen Grund, weshalb ihnen das im Lauf der Zeit nicht gelingen sollte—, dann wird das Leben in diesen Ländern, wie immer die theoretischen politischen Unterschiede sein mögen, vom Leben auf unserer Seite nicht mehr zu unterscheiden sein.

Das gleiche gilt für die High-Brow-Kultur. Es gibt keine Kulturzentren mehr, die sich in ihrer Eigenart deutlich voneinander unterscheiden. Was ist Paris? Ein Ort, an dem man Hegel noch ernst nimmt. Was ist Wien? Die Karajan-Stadt, wo Wagner in völliger Dunkelheit gespielt wird (selbstverständlich sind Karajans schöne Hände gut beleuchtet). Heutzutage ist jeder Intellektuelle gleichzeitig isolierter und internationalisierter als seine Vorgänger. Das mag einem gefallen oder nicht—ich glaube, mir gefällt es nicht. Ich finde, es ist eine unmanierliche und abscheulich laute Zeit, aber ich bin ja ein mittelständischer Rauschebart und ein intellektueller Snob.

Ich darf nicht vergessen, daß das Leben für die Mehrzahl der Menschen in unseren Ländern angenehmer ist, als es früher war, und im übrigen muß ich mich in das schikken, was ich nicht ändern kann, und das Beste daraus machen. Als Dichter tröstet mich überdies der Gedanke, daß in der Dichtung ein internationaler Stil so lange unmöglich ist, als die verschiedenen Völker verschiedene Sprachen sprechen. Solange man in Deutschland deutsch spricht und ich englisch spreche, ist ein echtes Zwiegespräch möglich, sprechen wir nicht nur jeder das Spiegelbild des anderen an; denn wie Karl Kraus sagt: „Die Sprache ist die Mutter, nicht die Magd des Gedankens." Preisen wir daher den lieben Gott, und danken wir ihm für den Babylonischen Turmbau!

Do You Know Too Much?

Page 436.

Esquire was at this time a men's magazine that published serious essays and fiction. Auden's piece may have been commissioned by Gene Lichtenstein, an *Esquire* editor who sublet Auden's New York apartment in 1958 (the same year when the magazine published his poem "The More Loving One") but who left the magazine before Auden's piece appeared.

Correspondence between the magazine and Auden's agents, Curtis Brown Ltd., indicates that the manuscript title was "What Ought We To Know?" (Cf. the question "What ought I to do?" in *The Dyer's Hand*, p. 567.) The copyright registration for the essay lists the title as "What We Ought To Know", probably a typist's misreading of the original, but possibly a title devised but abandoned by the magazine.

In the paragraph that begins "Another reason" (p. 438) the dashes were probably added by an editor.

Mirror: A Set of Notes

Page 441.

See the textual notes to "Hic et Ille" in *The Dyer's Hand* (p. 954).

ENGLAND & EUROPE

Page 441.

The talk referred to in the subtitle was the German version of "Are the English Europeans?" (p. 428). In preparing this piece Auden seems to have retyped and slightly changed some sections of his (now lost) original English text of the broadcast.

The title, heading, and text are from Auden's typescript, formerly in the *Encounter* archives. The magazine did not print the full text, but instead used excerpts from it as an untitled contribution, headed "W. H. Auden", to "Symposium: Going into Europe", a series that appeared in three numbers of *Encounter*, December 1962, January and February 1963. Auden's contribution was the first of those in the January number.

The text published in *Encounter* omits the sections that begin "Europe, to me", "A Roman Catholic", and "During the Eighteenth"; these are heavily deleted in the typescript by an unknown hand. The *Encounter* text also eliminates the stars that divide the sections, leaving only paragraph breaks between most sections and an additional line space before "When I ask" and "Britain may join". *Encounter* makes a single paragraph of the sentence "Europe is the place" and the list of fifteen items that follow it. It also treats as a single unbroken paragraph the two sections that begin "For the Low-Brows" and "The Low-Brow, however".

In the second to last sentence the typescript, retaining the second-person address of the original broadcast, has "So long as you, Ladies and Gentlemen, speak German"; an unknown hand replaced this with "So long as the Germans speak German", the reading printed in *Encounter* and followed here.

One notable difference between the versions Auden prepared for German and British audiences is the omission of Rilke from the British version of his list of sacred names.

The Dyer's Hand

The Dyer's Hand was Auden's only book of prose that he devised as a single cohesive work about disparate subjects. It was made up partly of newly written notes and essays, partly of older essays and reviews newly revised and reorganized to suit its setting in a larger whole. His other prose books were *The Enchafèd Flood* (1951) and *Secondary Worlds* (1969), both based on series of lectures; *A Certain World* (1970), a common-place book made up largely of quotations from other writers; and *Forewords and Afterwords* (1973), made up entirely of essays he had previously published.

Auden had begun planning a volume of essays in the late 1940s but seems not to have got beyond tentative lists of titles, such as the list reproduced in *Prose III*, p. 698. Probably in the early 1950s Auden's secretary Alan Ansen made for his own use tran-scripts of some essays that Auden may perhaps have been considering for use in the book. These mostly untitled transcripts, copied from otherwise lost manuscripts or typescripts, include unpublished versions of the introductions to *Poets of the English Language* (in the form of a single essay), "Notes on the Comic", "The Ironic Hero", "Nature, History and Poetry," "Hic et Ille", "Some Reflections on Opera as a Me-dium," and "The Guilty Vicarage". Auden had separately preserved some of this mate-rial and a few fragments first appeared in *The Dyer's Hand*.

During the years of Auden's Oxford professorship of poetry he seems to have in-tended to make use of his lectures in a large book of prose. He gave his final Oxford lecture in October 1960, and began planning the book in earnest shortly afterward.

At this time, the only list he had of his published essays and reviews was one (now lost) prepared by Alan Ansen, apparently in the early 1950s. Probably after Auden's return from Austria in the autumn of 1961 he asked Orlan Fox, a young friend who sometimes worked as his secretary, to visit the New York Public Library to copy some of the essays on Ansen's list. Fox copied one essay by hand before discovering that the library had a photocopying service. Most or all of the older items in the book seem to have been based on the texts that Fox photocopied. Auden wrote to his old Oxford tutor Nevill Coghill on 6 December 1961: "I am preparing a volume of my critical prose—it looks like being a monster tome—and I want your permission to dedicate it to you" (Berg Collection).

Monroe K. Spears, a professor at the University of the South, was at this time writ-ing his critical study of Auden's work, *The Poetry of W. H. Auden: The Disenchanted Island* (1963), and was in correspondence with Auden, who came to respect Spears's indus-try and intelligence. In Auden's response on 19 February 1962 to Spears's first letter to him, Auden reported:

> I have just sent to the publishers the collection of such critical essays of mine as I wish to preserve. It contains, among other things, my answers to a questionnaire I invented on the topic *What is your dream of Eden?* (Eden, *not* New Jerusalem) because I think anyone who writes criticism and so makes judgements is in honor bound to give the public this information.

The poet or novelist doesn't need to, because it is implicit in his work, but it might amuse you to know, so I enclose it.

In a later letter, on 21 July 1962, Auden sent Spears a typescript table of contents of the book, with some titles marked with a single asterisk to indicate "unpublished lectures" and some with two asterisks indicating "substantially new material". He marked as unpublished lectures "Brothers & Others", "D. H. Lawrence", "Marianne Moore", "Robert Frost", "Don Juan", "Dingley Dell & The Fleet", and "Translating Opera Libretti". (He also marked "The Poet & The City" in the same way, but deleted the asterisk.) He marked as substantially new material "Reading", "Writing", "The Globe", "Postscript: Infernal Science", "Postscript: Rome v. Monticello", "Postscript: The Almighty Dollar", "Postscript: The Frivolous & The Earnest", and "Postscript: Christianity & Art".

The titles in the typescript list that Auden sent to Spears differ slightly from those in the finished book; "The I Without a Self" is titled in Auden's typescript list "K" (its title in its magazine publication); the "Postscripts" in the book are abbreviated "P.S."; "The Almighty Dollar" lacks the initial "Postscript:"; "American Poetry" is listed as "Modern American Poetry"; "The Frivolous & The Earnest" lacks the initial "Postscript:"; "Postscript: Christianity & Art" is titled "Art & Christianity"; and "Notes on Music and Opera" is titled "Notes on Opera". Auden added a few parenthetical notes for Spears's benefit: "(Aphorisms)" appears next to the items that are made up of brief sections, except for "The Poet & The City" which is labeled "(Art & Society)", and "The Globe" which is labeled "(notes on the nature of S's drama)".

The book was probably finished early in 1962 and was published by Random House on 27 November 1962.

Auden's editor at Random House, Jason Epstein, remarked more than once that he did not presume to edit Auden's prose, and he seems to have done little more with the typescript than pass it on to a copyeditor, who seems to have been equally reluctant to correct obvious mistakes. The published book is notably inconsistent in its typographic treatment of quotations, lists, and other features. I have made a few minor typographical adjustments to the most flagrant inconsistencies but I have not tried to alter the miscellaneous flavor of the book.

Auden noticed a few errors before the book was officially published and sent a list of three to Nevill Coghill on 8 November 1962: in "The Poet & The City", in the last sentence of the second to last section (p. 516), he corrected "anonymous members" to "anonymous numbers"; in "Marianne Moore", near the end of the first paragraph (p. 661) he corrected "*Je m'égaré*" to "*Je m'égare*"; and in "Translating Opera Libretti", in the extract that begins "When Love in his bosom" (p. 800) he corrected "enkindled, exchanged," to "enkindled, enchanted".

Some weeks after the book appeared, Monroe K. Spears wrote about it to Auden, noting his annoyance at the relatively few reviews that the book had received. Auden replied on 6 January 1963:

Am so glad you like *The Dyer's Hand* which, as no doubt you have observed, contains all the autobiography I am willing to make public. As to reviews, I am one of the victims of the [New York] newspaper strike. It had the lead review in the Sunday Book Section of The New York Times, but, of course, this couldn't appear.

Auden included with this letter a list of sixteen corrections to the text, all of which (except for corrections to a few obvious typographical mistakes) are mentioned in the notes to the separate sections; this list includes the three that Auden sent to Coghill earlier.

Spears responded by sending Auden on 7 March 1963 a further list of corrections, many of them fixing obvious typographical slips that I have silently corrected in the present text. Three are worth noting: In "Brothers & Others", in the paragraph fragment that begins "The majority, however" (p. 610), Spears noted that the text had a nonsensical comma between "Gospel" and "command". In "Dingley Dell & The Fleet", in the last item in the list of axioms about Eden (p. 744), Spears suggested replacing the dash in "expulsion—any serious" with an equals sign, a suggestion I have followed here. And in "Genius & Apostle", in the paragraph that begins "Ibsen did not" (p. 768), Spears suggested changing "can and is" to "can be and is"; although Auden's usage is perhaps acceptable as conversational style, an attentive copyeditor would have corrected it, and I have therefore done so here.

In a copy inscribed to Chester Kallman (now in the Harry Ransom Center at the University of Texas at Austin) Auden marked many of the same changes that he sent to Spears and that he added to a later paperback edition. A few further changes that never appeared in print are incorporated in this edition and noted below.

Auden expected his British publisher Faber & Faber to issue the book with the same text that Random House had published, but Faber panicked at the size of the book and after much in-house discussion sought advice outside the firm on whether to publish the book as written. Stuart Hampshire suggested dividing the book into two volumes, with some omissions, and this proposal seems to have been transmitted to Auden. His response has not survived, but Faber dropped its plans to reduce the book and published a lithographic reprint of the American edition on 19 April 1963.

Random House issued a paperback edition of the book in the Vintage Books series in February 1968; this incorporated some corrections evidently supplied by Auden and some made independently by the publisher. All that were not merely obvious typographical corrections, or that were not noted in the preceding paragraphs, are described below. Further corrections were made at my suggestion in later posthumous printings when the paperback was reissued in the Vintage International series in 1989. The first of these printings mistakenly added "Selected by Edward Mendelson" to the title page, apparently because the same attribution had appeared, more or less correctly, on the title page of Auden's *Forewords and Afterwords* (1973).

In the chapter titles I have retained Auden's use of the ampersand and his capitalization of "The" in the middle of a title, as in "The Virgin & The Dynamo", "The Poet & The City", "Dingley Dell & The Fleet", and "Postscript: The Frivolous & The Earnest". The ampersands and capitalized "The" also appear in the typescript table of contents that Auden sent to Monroe K. Spears (with the exception, perhaps accidental, of the typescript table's "The Frivolous and the Earnest").

READING

Page 457.

    Much of this was newly written for *The Dyer's Hand* or adapted from Auden's lectures. The questionnaire on Eden, and the explanatory paragraph that precedes it, are based on "Qui è l'uom' felice", first published in 1955 (*Prose III*, p. 569), and printed as part I, "Prelude", of a magazine article, "The Poet and the City", published in 1962, while *The Dyer's Hand* was already in the process of publication (see notes to p. 505).

For the 1968 paperback reprint (followed here) Auden added "narrow-gauge railroads" to the list of means of transport in his Eden (p. 460). He had written "narrow-gauge railways" in his 1963 list of corrections for Monroe K. Spears and in the copy he gave to Chester Kallman, now in the Harry Ransom Center at Texas, but he had written "railroads" (not "railways") in the manuscript version of the questionnaire that he had sent Spears earlier.

I have corrected Lichtenberg's initials in the first epigraph from "C. G." to "G. C." In the questionnaire on Eden, I have not corrected the size of Plato's ideal city from 5004 to 5040 because the mistaken figure occurs in the manuscript that Auden sent to Monroe K. Spears (see p. 946); however, Auden had earlier got it right in his review of Werner Jaeger's *Paideia* (p. 151)

WRITING

Page 464.

Some of this material is adapted from earlier essays. The list of Alices and Mabels modifies one that first appeared in "Holding the Mirror Up to History" in 1954 (*Prose III*, p. 487), and again in "Miss Marianne Moore, Bless Her!" in 1959 (p. 227). Some of the material that follows the list derives from the 1957 essay "Squares and Oblongs" (p. 63), and some material near the end derives from the earlier essay also titled "Squares and Oblongs" from *Poets at Work*, 1948 (*Prose II*, p. 339).

In the section that begins "In theory" (p. 464) Auden corrected "receives does not seem" to "receive do not seem" in his 1963 list of corrections for Monroe K. Spears and in the 1968 paperback.

MAKING, KNOWING AND JUDGING

Page 477.

This was Auden's inaugural lecture as Professor of Poetry at Oxford, delivered in the Sheldonian on 11 June 1956.

The predecessor referred to in the fourth paragraph was W. P. Ker, who said of his professorship in his inaugural lecture, "this is the Siege Perilous" (*The Art of Poetry* [1923], p. 9). The friend who suggested that Auden should write poetry was Robert Medley, later a painter and one of Auden's collaborators in the Group Theatre. In the paragraph that begins "The romantic novelist" (p. 489) John Bellenden Ker (corrected from Auden's Bellendon) was an English botanist who, after an illness, wrote *An Essay on the Archaeology of Popular English Phrases and Nursery Rhymes* (1834).

In the paragraph that begins "Presently the curtain" (p. 482), the phrase "when I was an undergraduate a critic could still describe Mr T. S. Eliot. O.M., as 'a drunken helot'", repeats and misdates a misrecollection by Ezra Pound in a widely quoted essay in the *Egoist*, 1917. No critic called Eliot a drunken helot; Arthur

Waugh, reviewing the *Catholic Anthology* in 1916, had condemned "The Love Song of J. Alfred Prufrock" without naming Eliot, then offered "a hint of warning" by recalling that in ancient feasts "a drunken slave" was displayed to the sons of the household to discourage them from following him into drunken folly.

Auden's lecture exists in a number of slightly different forms. The earliest surviving text is the typescript (top copy in the first third, carbon copy in the rest) from which he delivered the lecture; this was prepared by a typist, but has additions and corrections in Auden's hand and three inserted pages typed by Auden, which add brief passages that were too long to write legibly on the original. This typescript, titled "Making, Knowing & Judging", is now in the library of Exeter College, Oxford; Auden gave it to his old tutor Nevill Coghill who presented it to the college. The typed additional pages include Auden's two references to W. P. Ker: the allusion to one of his "predecessors" in the fourth paragraph and the three sentences about Ker in the paragraph that begins "But this was something" (p. 484). Further notes on this typescript appear below.

The text of the corrected typescript closely corresponds to a transcript (now in the BBC Written Archives Centre) prepared with moderate accuracy by a BBC typist from a recording made while Auden delivered the lecture. The recording seems to have been transcribed shortly before a shortened version of it was broadcast in the BBC Third Programme, 29 September 1956. The transcript reflects many trivial changes in the text, some of them probably improvised while Auden was speaking. In the paragraph that begins "Many years ago" (p. 477) the transcribed text omits the attribution to A. E. Housman; the quotation from Mallarmé (p. 479) appears in English instead of French as "who from syllables recomposes a total word." The transcript includes corrections, in unknown hands, of minor errors by the typist.

A long excerpt from the lecture, evidently based on a copy of Auden's orginal typescript that lacked the corrections he marked in the Exeter College copy, appeared in the *Sunday Times*, 17 June 1956, with acknowledgement to the Oxford University Press. In the *Sunday Times* excerpt the list of early readings in the first paragraph of section I begins with *Hymns Ancient & Modern*; this was the original reading in the Exeter College typescript, corrected in Auden's hand in that typescript, but not in the one used by the *Sunday Times*, to *The English Hymnal*.

The lost typescript that Auden gave to the Oxford University Press for publication as a pamphlet was perhaps the same typescript used by the *Sunday Times*. If so, Auden either visited the Press and added corrections to the typescript after the *Sunday Times* had used it, or he made his corrections in proof. Most but not all the changes that he had marked in the Exeter College typescript from which he delivered the lecture found their way into the pamphlet text, which was published on 24 August 1956. The notes below report the changes that Auden wrote into the typescript from which he delivered the lecture but that he seems to have forgotten when revising the text for the pamphlet. The title at the head of the text in the pamphlet edition has a comma after "Knowing", but the title on the title page does not. The Press was probably responsible for the expansion of the ampersand to "and" in Auden's title.

The pamphlet text was the basis of the revised version that appeared in *The Dyer's Hand*. It was also the basis of a heavily abridged and unauthoritative version published as "Making and Judging Poetry" in the *Atlantic*, January 1957.

The differences between the pamphlet and *The Dyer's Hand* are mostly slight; I have not noted minor changes in punctuation and spelling. The pamphlet includes many footnotes omitted from the book. In the fourth paragraph the pamphlet's footnote to "of my predecessors" reads "Professor W. P. Ker". In the quotation from Coleridge (p. 478) the pamphlet has square brackets, not parentheses, around "Lord Byron". Near the end of the paragraph that begins "It seems to me" the pamphlet has "already existing work" (not "works").

In the introductory section, at the end of the opening paragraph Auden's typescript has "possibly" written in after "How can Poetry"; the absence of the word in the printed texts may be an error. In the paragraph that begins "It was Edward Lear", the pamphlet's footnote to "once it has been made permanent" reads "George Boule, *An Investigation of the Laws of Thought.*" The pamphlet's footnote to the quotation from Valéry immediately below reads "*Tel Quel,* ii." And its footnote to the quotation from Mallarmé in the following sentence reads "*Divagations,* Crise de Vers." In the following paragraph, the pamphlet's footnote to the quotation "A drop of water" reads "*Comedy of Errors,* II. 2."

In the paragraph that begins "And, though as yet" (p. 480), in his typescript Auden revised "equality of unofficial poetry, such as counting-out rhymes, and official poetry, such as the odes of Keats" to "equality of the unofficial, like counting-out rhymes, and the official[,] like the odes of Keats"; this change does not occur in the printed texts, possibly through an oversight. The pamphlet's footnote to the quotation "When other ladies" reads "Alexander Pope, *Epigram.*"

In the last words of the paragraph that begins "My first Master" (p. 481) the pamphlet lacks "now" in "whereas I now know". The first sentence of the paragraph that begins "Presently the curtain rises" continues in the pamphlet "*Die Meistersinger,* the setting of which in my own memories is geographically close to this afternoon." In the paragraph that begins "Really, how do the dons" the pamphlet has "the kindness of our tutors" (not "my") and "having got there" (not "having arrived there"). At the end of the paragraph, Auden's typescript underlines "can" in "can lead" and inserts "so" before "frequently"; the absence of these changes in the printed texts may have been an oversight.

At the end of the next paragraph, "An apprentice discovers", the pamphlet has "in common, they are all contemporaries" (not "in common, youth"). In the paragraph that begins "It is just this kind" the pamphlet has "band of apprentices have" (not "has"), and has "A critic is dealing with a published work, not a manuscript. His job is to tell the public what that work" (not "A critic's duty is to tell the public what a work").

In Part II, the pamphlet's footnote to Yeats's poem (p. 485) reads "*The Scholars.*" In the typescript (followed here) the text of the poem correctly reads "love's despair", but this is altered in Auden's hand to "their despair", an error that survived in all printed texts. And in the second sentence after the poem the pamphlet has "Edit indeed! Thank God", where *The Dyer's Hand* replaces the exclamation mark by a semicolon (I have restored the pamphlet's reading, which seems required by the uppercase letter that follows it). At the end of this long paragraph, after "Chinese?" the pamphlet (following a handwritten addition to Auden's typescript, confirmed by the BBC transcript) has: "And then, however different they may be in other ways, poets and scholars have one thing in common. They are not gentlemen. The U is that which both, being non-U, with passion worship." In the paragraph that begins "No, what prevents" the pamphlet capitalizes "Thirteenth Century" and "Sixteenth".

In Part III, in the paragraph that begins "His lazy habit" (p. 489) the pamphlet has in the first sentence "must first be worth". The paragraph that begins "Speaking for myself" (p. 490) is one of Auden's typed additions to his typescript.

In Part IV, near the end of the paragraph that begins "During these twenty" (p. 491) the pamphlet has "the theory of poetry" (not "theories"). In the pamphlet the footnote to the quotation from Baudelaire (p. 492) reads "*L'Art Romantique.*" In the paragraph fragment that follows the quotation the pamphlet has "They are as fallible, of course, as all guesses—the word". Near the end of the same sentence the pamphlet has "is a typical" where *The Dyer's Hand* has "is typical"; the omitted article may have been lost in a misreading of Auden's correction to the sentence on a preceding line.

In the paragraph that begins "There are other cultures" (p. 493) the pamphlet three times has "private" where *The Dyer's Hand* substitutes "intimate" and, in the last sentence in the paragraph, the pamphlet has "worse than" instead of "inferior to". In the paragraph that begins "A sacred being" the pamphlet's footnote to the quotation "'The most unpoetical'" reads "Keats, letter to Charles Woodhouse."

In the paragraph that begins "The Secondary Imagination", the pamphlet has "the beautiful and the ugly" and in a later sentence has "it has feelings of satisfaction" not "it has the feeling of satisfaction". In the third sentence, a dash might be helpful after "nothing else". In the paragraph that begins "Lastly the Secondary" (one of Auden's typed additions to his typescript) the pamphlet has "we both cannot" (not "we cannot both"). The footnote in the pamphlet to the quotation from Blake (p. 496) reads "Letter to the Rev. Dr Trusler."

In the paragraph fragment that begins "But it is from the" (p. 497) the pamphlet has "Thanks to language" (not "to the language"). In the sentence that begins "Every love poem" (the pamphlet has "love-poem") has "among these there may" (the book omits "there"). In the final sentence (final only in the book version) the pamphlet has "being as for happening" (not "and for").

Immediately after the final paragraph of the book version, the pamphlet has an additional paragraph followed by the text of Thomas Hardy's "Afterwards". Auden's paragraph reads:

In illustration of what I have been saying and as an epilogue to this lecture, I will recite a famous poem. I have chosen it because I like it, because I approve of it, because it is so plainly a rite of homage to sacred objects which are neither gods nor objects of desire, and because, but for the man who wrote it, I should not now be here.

The poem is identified in a footnote that reads, "Thomas Hardy, *Afterwards.*"

The epigraph was added in *The Dyer's Hand*, as were two footnotes, one to the title and the other to "It was Edward Lear" (p. 479).

THE VIRGIN & THE DYNAMO

Page 497.

Parts of this section derive from two earlier sets of notes and aphorisms: "Squares and Oblongs" (p. 63) and "Nature, History and Poetry" (*Prose III*, p. 226), first published in *Thought*, September 1950. *Thought* was a learned Roman Catholic quarterly published by Fordham University. "Nature, History and Poetry" was the first of Auden's three essays in the magazine; the other two were "Balaam and the Ass" (1954), revised in *The Dyer's Hand* as "Balaam and His Ass" (p. 528), and "Notes on the Comic" (1952), revised in *The Dyer's Hand* under the same title (p. 715). Some sections, including those on the real and chimerical worlds and the aestheticism of Henry Adams, derive from an unpublished version of "Nature, History and Poetry" that survives in a typed transcript made by Alan Ansen, probably in the early 1950s, from a lost manuscript or typescript (Berg Collection).

Under the heading "The Two Real Worlds", in item (2) *The Dyer's Hand* capitalizes "World" in the phrase "In this World"; this seems to be a mistake, as Auden capitalizes "World" elsewhere in the essay only in proper-noun phrases such as "World of the Dynamo", not in phrases such as "in this world".

Under the subheading "The Two Chimerical Worlds" the two paragraphs that begin "Without Art" are in *The Dyer's Hand* indented the same distance from the left margin as the numbered items immediately above them; this seems mistaken, so I have moved these paragraphs back to the left margin as a slightly better alternative. Auden may perhaps have intended the two paragraphs to appear as a separate section preceded by a line space.

Under the heading "Pluralities", the paragraph that begins "Whenever rival communities" (p. 499) has in *The Dyer's Hand* the same indentation as the paragraph immediately above it, and therefore appears to be the second paragraph that falls under the subheading "A Community". I have let this formatting stand, but it is at least possible that Auden did not think of this paragraph as part of subsection headed "A Community", and the paragraph should therefore not have been indented.

Near the start of the paragraph that begins "It follows from the second" (p. 504) I have removed a comma after "presupposition".

In his copy of the version of "Nature, History and Poetry" printed in *Thought* Auden corrected the closing paragraph by inserting "as" before "identical"; I have applied the same correction here. I have left unchanged his inconsistent capitalization of "Paradise".

Following Auden's practice elsewhere in the book I have italicized the algebraic symbols n and x where the original text prints them in roman.

Auden learned to type in an era when many typewriters lacked a numeral 1 and most typists represented the numeral 1 with a lower-case letter l; Auden, however, typically used an upper-case I instead. The early printings of *The Dyer's Hand* mistakenly followed him in using an uppercase I for 1 in the arithmetical expressions on p. 499, but these were corrected in the posthumous paperback reprint issued in 1989.

The Poet & The City

Page 505.

An essay with almost the same title ("The Poet and the City") and much of the same content appeared in *Massachusetts Review*, Spring 1962. A note on the first page reads: "This essay was presented on February 28, 1962, as the inaugural lecture in the celebration of the 125th anniversary of Mt Holyoke College." The text was probably taken from a copy of the typescript of *The Dyer's Hand*. The opening section and the text from "A poet writes" through "out of sight in cellars" (p. 514) are excerpted and adapted from the earlier of Auden's two essays titled "Squares and Oblongs", from *Poets at Work*, 1948 (*Prose II*, p. 339).

The magazine's version is divided into three parts, preceded by the same two epigraphs found in *The Dyer's Hand*. "I. Prelude" comprises the questionnaire on Eden (and its introductory paragraph) that became part of "Reading" in *The Dyer's Hand* (p. 459); the texts are almost identical except for Auden's British spellings ("aeroplanes") in the magazine version. The magazine, like the first edition of the book, omits "narrow-gauge railroads" from "Means of transport", and has the same error of 5004 (for 5040) citizens in Plato's ideal city.

Part II closely matches "The Poet & The City" in *The Dyer's Hand* except for minor differences (not noted here) in verb tenses, conjunctions, spelling, and punctuation. The magazine has three stars between the separate sections where the book has only a line space. I have followed the magazine in capitalizing "Fine Arts" in the paragraph that begins "Some writers" (p. 506). In the paragraph that begins "Had Tolstoi" (p. 507) the magazine has "and of art as propaganda . . . into it, then the cause" where the book omits "of" and "then". In the paragraph that begins "In our culture" (p. 508) the magazine has "persons" for "people" in the last sentence (the book's "people" may be an editor's alteration). In the paragraph that begins "In my daydream college", in item (4) the magazine has "select three out of an offering of courses" where the book has "select three courses out of courses".

In the paragraph that begins "In a crowd" (p. 512) the magazine has "between members" for "among members". The magazine places the section that begins "Occasionally the Public" after the section that begins "Before the phenomenon", not before. The magazine treats as a separate section the two final sentences of the section that begins "Before the phenomenon", so that the magazine has a sequence of three sections that begin "Before the phenomenon", "Occasionally the Public", and "What the mass media offer", where the book has two sections, beginning "Occasionally the Public" and "Before the phenomenon".

In the paragraph that begins "All political theories" (p. 514) the book adds "whole" before "aim of a poet". In the section that begins "There are two kinds", in the first sentence the magazine has "issue" not "issues", and, later in the paragraph, "their sacrifice" not "its sacrifice".

In the paragraph that begins "Every age" (p. 516) the magazine in the first sentence has "to neglect and even sacrifice" for "it neglects and even sacrifices". I have followed the magazine in treating the italicized "*every body*" as two words not one (the separate word "body" takes up the theme of the preceding paragraph, and the combined form was probably an editor's mistaken regularization). In the same sentence the magazine has "relaxation" not "leisure". In the final sentence, the magazine has "in so far as society thinks" (not "in so far as it thinks") and, perhaps in changes made by an editor, tries to disentangle the syntax of the end of the sentence as follows: "in his society—indeed . . . hostility (it secretly . . . singular person—or a demand for privacy—is putting . . . other folk)—every artist . . .". The book's punctuation of the end of the sentence is obviously defective, and for this edition I have replaced the book's semicolon after "his society" with a dash, and have replaced the book's dash after "hostility" with a semicolon.

The magazine's text has a final part, "III: Postscript. Christianity & Art". This differs only slightly from the similarly titled section included elsewhere in *The Dyer's Hand* (p. 775); for details see the notes on that section.

In the first sentences of the paragraph that begins "This destroys the traditional" (p. 509) I have removed the italicization of "art" (although possibly Auden intended to italicize the entire phrase "art as mimesis").

In the group of paragraphs that begin with "In a crowd" (p. 512) I have left unchanged Auden's inconsistent capitalization of "the Public". In the section that begins "In our age" (p. 516), in the last sentence, "numbers" is a correction for "members"; Auden made the change in his 1963 list of corrections for Monroe K. Spears and in the 1968 paperback edition.

In the section that begins "All political theories" (p. 514) the quotations are from Dylan Thomas's manuscript of "The Ballad of the Long-Legged Bait", a page of which was reproduced at the front of Auden's essay "Squares and Oblongs" in *Poets at Work*, 1948 (*Prose II*, p. 339).

HIC ET ILLE

Page 519.

Some of the contents are similar to an essay published in a French translation in *Preuves*, May 1952, "De Droite et de Gauche" (*Prose III*, p. 323).

The text in *The Dyer's Hand* is revised from a piece also titled "Hic et Ille" that appeared in *Encounter*, April 1956. The *Encounter* text has stars between sections where the book has line spaces. I have restored some capitalization from the *Encounter* version. The following notes compare the book version with the 1956 *Encounter* text.

The book adds the epigraph. In part A, in the third section, which begins "The psychoanalyst", the magazine has "£666", not "five thousand dollars". In the section that begins *"He who despises"* (p. 520) *Encounter* has "phantasy" not "fantasy" (the change was probably made by an editor).

In part B, in the section that begins "Every autobiography" (p. 521) *Encounter* has "Ego who is the narrator" where the book drops "the"; at the end of that section, the book inverts *Encounter*'s apparently mistaken inversion of "prays" and "giggles". In part B the book version adds the section that begins "History is" (p. 521) and all the sections from *"Rejoice with"* to the end of part B (pp. 522–23).

In part C, in the section that begins "The ear tends" (p. 524) *Encounter* has "by the old masters" for "by old masters" and, in the second paragraph, "the old tale" for "the same tale". In the section that begins "As seen reflected" *Encounter* has "than they look themselves" for "than when looked at directly". In the section that begins "Those who accuse" the magazine has "phantastic" for "fantastic"; the book drops "take" in "than it would take in real life".

In the section that begins "Between the ages" (p. 525) *Encounter* has "phantasy" not "fantasy". In the section that begins "Like all polemical" *Encounter* has "all historical existence to nature" for "all individual existence to general processes". In the section that begins "All the existentialist" (p. 526) in the first paragraph *Encounter* has "and it was only later I discovered" for "and only later did I discover".

In part D *Encounter* begins with a section that corresponds to part of a paragraph in the book's "Notes on the Comic" (p. 723):

Since he is the only one who has a real history, man is the only creature who has a face. Every face is a present witness to the fact that its owner has a past behind him which might have been otherwise, and a future ahead of him in which some possibilities are more probable than others.

To "read" a face is to guess at what might have been and what may still be. The noblest face reveals potential evil overcome, the vilest potential good suppressed.

Children, for whom most future possibilities are equally probable, and the dead for whom all possibilities have been reduced to zero, do not have faces but, like animals, wear inscrutable masks.

Later in part D, between the section that begins "*So much countenance*" and the section that begins "When I consider" (p. 526), *Encounter* has an additional section that corresponds to the second part of the same paragraph in "Notes on the Comic":

A caricature of a face admits that its owner has a past but denies him a future. He has created his features up to a point but now they have taken charge of him so that he can never change. A mask is inscrutable—it cannot be read: a caricature is obvious—it does not need to be read.

We enjoy equally caricatures of our friends and of our enemies: of our friends because we cannot bear the thought of their dying, of our enemies because the thought that they might become lovable is unwelcome.

The *Encounter* version concludes with two sections that appear elsewhere in *The Dyer's Hand*:

The fellowship of suffering lasts only so long as none of the sufferers can escape. Open a door through which many, but not all, can escape one at a time, and the community of prisoners all too easily disintegrates into a stampeding crowd.

The crowd collects to watch the wrecking-gang demolish the old mansion, fascinated by yet another proof that physical force is the Prince of this world against whom no love of the heart shall prevail.

The first of these appears in "Red Ribbon on a White Horse", in the paragraph that begins "For the older generation" (p. 684); the second, in slightly modified form, appears in "The Poet & The City", in the paragraph that begins "Occasionally the Public" (p. 512).

The text in *The Dyer's Hand* also appeared in the American edition of *Vogue*, December 1962, under the title "Mirror: A Set of Notes"; an editorial note says that the piece "comes from his new book *The Dyer's Hand*". Except for slight typographical differences, the *Vogue* text, including the epigraph, matches that of *The Dyer's Hand*,

and was probably set from a late set of proofs of the book. In the section that begins "From the height" (p. 524) the *Vogue* text has an apparently erroneous section break before the sentence that begins "That, across it". The editorial director of *Vogue* was Alexander Liberman, who was friendly with Auden. As the editorial note reported, this was Auden's fourth essay for the American edition of the magazine.

In part B, in the section that begins "*Rejoice with those*", I have amended the text in the book and in *Vogue* by italicizing the whole phrase "*weep with them that weep*", where both texts italicize only the first "*weep*". At the very end of the essay, the colon in the closing paragraph should be read as a semicolon; Auden almost invariably reversed the common usage of these two marks.

BALAAM AND HIS ASS

Page 528.

This is a revised version of "Balaam and the Ass: The Master-Servant Relationship in Literature", from *Thought*, Summer 1954, reprinted in *Encounter*, July 1954 (*Prose III*, p. 444). Auden's other essays in *Thought* that he revised for *The Dyer's Hand* are "The Virgin & The Dynamo" (p. 497) and "Notes on the Comic" (p. 715).

For a detailed account of the 1954 versions of this essay, see *Prose III*, pp. 760–63. The version in *The Dyer's Hand* seems to be based on a typescript made from the version in *Thought*, but it also has a few corrections from the *Encounter* version. Possibly Auden had a copy of the *Thought* version that he had marked with corrections when it first appeared and used this as the basis for the version in *The Dyer's Hand*.

The *Encounter* version has no epigraph immediately below the title; the *Thought* version has an epigraph from Numbers XXII, 32–33 and the first five words of 34, in the Douay translation favored by the Roman Catholic Church (*Thought* was published by Fordham University, a Roman Catholic institution). The first epigraph in *The Dyer's Hand* substitutes a new epigraph for the one in *Thought*. In both 1954 texts the epigraph from Matthew is the epigraph to part I only, not to the whole essay.

In section I, in the first sentence, the 1954 texts have "and Servant is agnatic, not cognatic; that is to say, it is not given by nature"; and the second sentence begins "Secondly, it is not erotic". Later in the same paragraph, the 1954 texts have "it is as a member of the people that he has a share", revised in *The Dyer's Hand* to "it is as one of the people that each citizen has a share".

In section II, in the paragraph that begins "To present artistically" the 1954 texts have "get round the difficulty" where *The Dyer's Hand* has "around", probably a change made by a copyeditor. Later in the same paragraph, the 1954 texts have "and it is impossible not to suspect", revised in *The Dyer's Hand* to "so that we suspect".

In section V, in the opening paragraph, the 1954 texts have "any reason why he", clarified in *The Dyer's Hand* to "any reason why Faust". In the paragraph fragment that begins "as, that is to say" (p. 535), "ideal must be" and "and all creation" are corrections (based on the 1954 texts) for "idea must be" and "and will creation". In the paragraph that begins "In this lack" (p. 536) the *Thought* text has "is always finite", where *Encounter* and *The Dyer's Hand* have "was always finite".

In section VI, I have emended minor misspellings in the epigraphs and quotations. In the paragraph that begins "Don Giovanni is as inconspicuous" (p. 537) *Thought* has after "*raison d'être*" a redundant "for existing" which is omitted in *Encounter* and *The Dyer's Hand*. In the paragraph that begins "Just as Don Giovanni" (p.

539) the 1954 texts have "mocking references" and "make", corrected in *The Dyer's Hand* to "mocking reference" and "makes". In the paragraph that begins "As in the case" (p. 540), the first two phrases of the sentence that begins "His Boss" are reduced from the confusing 1954 versions: "His Boss and her husband will appear as King Mark, an old beau of hers (to him), and an old disreputable drinking crony of his (to her) as Morold" (which seems to mean: in the eyes of the husband, his Boss will appear as King Mark and an old beau of the wife will appear as Morold; while in the eyes of the wife, her husband will appear as King Mark and an old crony of her husband will appear as Morold).

In section VII, in the paragraph fragment that begins "It was said above" (p. 542) the 1954 reading "conscience" is revised in *The Dyer's Hand* to "super-ego". In the paragraph that begins "The fool, that is" the 1954 texts have "Rationally, there is no reason why", revised in *The Dyer's Hand* to "Rationally, there is no reason that".

In section VIII, in the first sentence of the paragraph that begins "As Christ's comment" (p. 546) I have restored "Seventh Commandment" from the *Encounter* text in place of the single word "commandment" that *The Dyer's Hand* reproduces from the text in *Thought*. As explained in *Prose III*, p. 762, Auden probably wrote "Seventh Commandment", but the editor of the Roman Catholic magazine *Thought* removed "Seventh" because the commandment against adultery has a different number in the Catholic and Protestant traditions, and the editor preferred to remove rather than replace the number written by Auden. In the sentence that begins "But the more 'spiritual'" the 1954 reading "relation between" is changed in *The Dyer's Hand* to "relationship between". In the sentence that begins "While in the case" I have restored "mortal sins" from *Encounter* for the *Thought* reading "capital sins", another change made by the editor of the magazine in order to conform to Roman Catholic terminology.

In the paragraph that begins "Caliban was once" (p. 547) the 1954 texts have "was not sinful of Eve", revised in *The Dyer's Hand* to "is not sinful of Eve". I have followed the *Encounter* text in breaking a paragraph before "Imagination is beyond good *and* evil"; in the 1954 texts that same opening sentence continues (after a comma) "but it is only with the help of imagination that I can become good *or* evil", and the omission of that phrase in *The Dyer's Hand* may have been an error by a typist or compositor. In the sentence that begins "In order to become" the 1954 texts have "to work, to limit its playful activities, to imagining"; the second comma in this is intrusive, and *The Dyer's Hand* clears up the confusion by revising to "to work, and limit its playful activity to imagining".

In the paragraph that begins "But the Way" (p. 549), in the sentence that begins "If his madness", the 1954 texts have "endowed himself in his imagination with all their gifts", mistakenly altered in *The Dyer's Hand* to "endowed himself in their imagination with their gifts"; I have restored "his" in order to correct an obvious error, but not "all", as the omission seems plausible as a revision.

In the paragraph that begins "Don Quixote and Sancho Panza are both" (p. 550), *The Dyer's Hand* inserts "quite" before "extraordinary".

In the paragraph that begins "Don Quixote's lack" (p. 551) the 1954 texts have, after "a forsaking of the world", the incomplete phrase "to follow," (probably an error for something like "to follow the example of Christ,"). *The Dyer's Hand* omits the phrase.

In section IX, in the paragraph that begins "To illustrate" (p. 551) *The Dyer's Hand* reduces the 1954 phrase "from books which are not great works of art but for that very reason present" to "from books which present". In the paragraph that begins "Mr Fogg, as Jules Verne" I have corrected "it" to "he" in "who cannot tell if he is hungry unless it first looks", because Auden or an editor seems to have revised incompletely the 1954 version's "which cannot tell if it is hungry unless it first looks". In the penultimate sentence of the same paragraph I have restored the capitalized "Office" from the 1954 text.

In the first sentence of the paragraph that begins "Like Mr Fogg" (p. 554) *The Dyer's Hand* inserts "the" in "there all the resemblance".

THE GUILTY VICARAGE

Page 556.

This is a revised version of an essay written around January 1946 and printed in *Harper's Magazine*, May 1948 (*Prose II*, p. 261). See the notes to *Prose II* for the early textual history of the piece.

The text in *The Dyer's Hand* omits the 1948 subtitle ("Notes on the Detective Story, by an Addict"), adds the epigraph, and reduces some italicization used for emphasis in the 1948 text. In the chart in the second section the book mistakenly omits the item "Murder". A copyeditor presumably replaced the psychoanalytically tinged word "phantasy" throughout the 1948 text with the more neutral "fantasy". *The Dyer's Hand* version also omits three section breaks found in the 1948 text. I have restored one of these, before the paragraph that begins "The detective story has five" (p. 558). The others may have been omitted deliberately, perhaps because Auden or his typist thought the breaks had been introduced by an editor at *Harper's* (although they also occur in an early typescript). These omitted breaks occur before the sentence "It is sometimes said" (p. 564) and the paragraph that begins "The fantasy, then, which" (p. 564).

In the section "Why Murder?" in the paragraph that begins "Murder is a member" (p. 557), *The Dyer's Hand* omits the italicized first word in the 1948 version's "*directly*, its representatives". In the second paragraph of the section "The Milieu (Natural)" *The Dyer's Hand* inserts "the" in "give the murder back to those", possibly mistakenly. In the section "The Murderer", at the end of the paragraph that begins "As to the murderer's" (p. 560), *The Dyer's Hand* adds the sentence that begins "In real life", which Auden adapted from "The Case is Curious" (p. 334). At the end of the closing "Suggestion for Mr Chandler" (p. 560), "organization, and restore their capacity to murder" is a correction in *The Dyer's Hand* for the 1948 reading "organization and to injure their capacity to murder". In the section "The Suspects" (p. 561), item (2) omits the closing parenthesis from 1948: "(see *Why Murder?*)".

In the section "The Detective", in the first sentence of the second paragraph, I have restored from 1948 the second "the" in the opening phrase "The job of the detective". In the paragraph that begins "Most amateur detectives" (p. 561), *The Dyer's Hand* replaces the noun "failures" in the 1948 text with the adjective "unsatisfactory". In the last paragraph of the section, which begins "The lawyer-detective" (p. 562), the phrase "because of his commitment to his client" replaces the longer 1948 version, "because his interest in the truth or in all the innocent is subordinate to his interest in his client". In the opening sentence of the section headed "Inspector French" the 1948 text, "culture are the natural ones for a Scotland Yard", is revised in *The Dyer's Hand* to "culture are those natural to a Scotland Yard".

In the section "The Reader" (p. 563), in the last sentence of the first paragraph, *The Dyer's Hand* omits "and evil" after "absurdity" in the 1948 text. In the second paragraph *The Dyer's Hand* omits "my" from the 1948 text "guilty about my guilt". In the same paragraph, after "remains unchanged" the 1948 version has a sentence which provides *The Dyer's Hand* text with its epigraph: "As St Paul says: 'Except I had known the law, I had not known sin.'" In the paragraph that begins "If one thinks" (p. 564) *The Dyer's Hand* omits "compelled" from the 1948 version "identification of art is a compelled sharing in the suffering"

Auden made one further correction and one further revision to the text in *The Dyer's Hand*. In the section "Definition" (p. 556) the first edition of the book has the error "ethical and characteristic" for "ethical and eristic"; Auden noted the correction in the list he sent to Monroe K. Spears in 1963, and it was made in the 1968 paperback edition. In the third paragraph of the section headed "Why Murder?" (p. 557) the first edition (following the 1948 text) has "demand restitution"; Auden revised this to "demand atonement" in the list of corrections that he sent to Monroe K. Spears in 1963 and in the 1968 paperback edition.

Malice Aforethought was a 1931 novel by Francis Iles; the Philo Vance stories were by S. S. Van Dine; Joshua Clunk was the detective in novels by H. C. Bailey.

The I Without A Self

Page 565.

Reprinted with revisions from "K", in the *Mid-Century*, Fall 1960, where it was a review of *The Great Wall of China*, by Franz Kafka (Schocken, $4.50; first published 1946) and *Franz Kafka: A Biography*, by Max Brod (Schocken, $4.50; revised edition published 1960, original edition 1947). The *Dyer's Hand* version adds the epigraph and revises the text as follows.

In the first sentence *The Dyer's Hand* adds "pure"; in the second sentence *The Dyer's Hand* replaces "is confronted by characters" with "though novel . . . history, by characters". Later in the paragraph *The Dyer's Hand* adds "pure" in "cannot read a pure parable", and replaces "meaning of the parable" with "meaning of parable".

In the paragraph that begins "In the new edition" (p. 566) the *Mid-Century* has "Brod's well-known biography". The paragraph that begins "Remarkable as" replaces these three paragraphs in the *Mid-Century*:

The function of a critic who did not have the privilege of knowing Kafka is reduced to the very humble one of simple description of his works for the benefit of those who have not yet read them.

The material collected in *The Great Wall of China* was all written during the last six years of his life. It consists of a number of short stories, varying in length from seventy pages to half a page, and two series of remarkable aphorisms, "He" and "Reflections on Sin, Pain, Hope and the True Way."

In my opinion this volume contains his finest work. The world he portrays is still the world of his earlier books and one cannot call it euphoric, but the tone is lighter. The sense of appalling anguish and despair which make stories like "The Penal Colony" almost unbearable has gone. (For those who like horror stories, however, there is a grim enough little parable of two and a half pages, "The Knock on the Manor Gate.") Existence may be as difficult and frustrating as ever, but the characters are more humorously resigned to it. Aside from their intrinsic merit, the aphorisms are an indispensable guide to what Kafka thought he was up to.

The Dyer's Hand adds the three paragraphs from "In all previous versions" (p. 567) through the end of the paragraph that begins "If the K of *The Trial*". In the paragraph that begins "The narrator hero of 'The Burrow' for example, is a beast" (p. 568), the *Mid-Century* opens with "To give some idea of what these later stories are like, I must content myself with describing one, 'The Burrow.' The narrator hero is a beast".

In the paragraph fragment that begins "One morning" (p. 569) *The Dyer's Hand* replaces "woken" with "awakened" and replaces "Edwin Muir in his introduction suggests" with "Edwin Muir has suggested". In the paragraph that begins "No one who thinks" (p. 570) *The Dyer's Hand* replaces "perilously near" with "perilously close". In the penultimate paragraph *The Dyer's Hand* replaces "heroes shows" with "heroes show" and replaces "otherworldly" with "other-world".

The *Dyer's Hand* version also makes minor changes in punctuation and minor mistakes (corrected here) in quotations from Kafka that were correct in the magazine. In the paragraph fragment that begins "One morning" (p. 569) I have appended a question mark to the fourth sentence.

THE GLOBE

Page 573.

In the paragraph that begins "The link between" (p. 574) all editions read "youthful taste was something"; Auden inserted "for" after "was" in the list of corrections that he sent to Monroe K. Spears in 1963.

Near the end of the paragraph headed "The Significance of Time" (p. 575) I have changed "medium in which" to "medium through which", following a correction marked by Auden in Geoffrey Gorer's copy.

In the final sentence, the first edition had "character for which"; Auden's 1963 list of corrections sent to Monroe K. Spears and the 1968 paperback edition correct this to "character for whom".

THE PRINCE'S DOG

Page 580.

Based on Auden's Oxford lecture, "The Fallen City: Some Reflections on Shakespeare's *Henry IV*", delivered on 25 May 1959, published in *Encounter*, November 1959, under the same title and subtitle as the lecture. I have made some minor corrections in the quotations.

Auden made only a few revisions when preparing the text for *The Dyer's Hand*. The book adds the epigraph. In the paragraph that begins "At a performance" (p.

580) *Encounter* has "Surely, one would" where the book has "Surely, one could". In the paragraph that begins "Time, for Tristan" (p. 581) the magazine has, in the last sentence, "everything they say and do"; possibly the change in *The Dyer's Hand* to "everything he says and does" was made by an editor. In the next paragraph, which begins "Thus, while we must", the magazine similarly has "their being" which may have been changed by an editor to "their beings" for *The Dyer's Hand*.

In the paragraph that begins "Moreover, Shakespeare" (p. 583) the magazine has "or anybody else" where the book has "or any others". In the paragraph that begins "For those in the play" (p. 586) the book adds "false" in "under any false illusions". In the paragraph that begins "Not all fat men" (p. 590) the magazine has "anyone who has had to look after a drunkard", which is shortened in *The Dyer's Hand* to "anyone who had to look after a drunk"; I have restored the magazine's "has".

In the paragraph that begins "Such readings" (p. 592) the magazine has "rather than with what men"; the book omits "with". In the paragraph that begins "Temporal Justice" (p. 594) the magazine has "the use of power"; the book replaces "power" with "force". In the paragraph that begins "Thus, Falstaff" (p. 595) the magazine has "but that is shown", which is revised in the book to "but this is shown". In the paragraph that begins "These are Falstaff's" (p. 596) the book, perhaps through an editorial error, adds "a" in "As a parable". In the paragraph that begins "Laughing and loving" (p. 598) I have restored the magazine's "we do not desire to change them" where the book has "we do not desire them to change them" (perhaps a trace of an abandoned intention to revise the phrase to "we do not desire them to change"). In the final paragraph, I have restored the magazine's "disguised as a man" where the book omits "a".

In the paragraph that begins "In a recent number" (p. 591) Nicholas Tucci is a slip for Niccolo Tucci, whose "To Be and Not to Be: Notes on Drunkenness" appeared in the *Paris Review*, Summer 1958; Auden's quotation simplifies the punctuation.

In the paragraph that begins "Hence, in his" (p. 589) Auden corrected "the consequences" to "the consequence" in the list of changes that he sent to Monroe K. Spears and in the 1968 paperback edition. In the quotation from Tucci (p. 591) Auden similarly corrected "significant" to "insignificant".

The "words by a Hasidic Rabbi" (p. 594) are adapted from Martin Buber's *Ten Rungs: Hasidic Sayings* (1947), and the story of the Sinner of Lublin (p. 598) is taken from Buber's *Tales of the Hasidim: The Early Masters* (1947).

Interlude: The Wish Game

Page 599.

Reprinted with changes from "The Wish Game", Auden's review in the *New Yorker*, 16 March 1957, of *The Borzoi Book of French Folk Tales*, selected and edited by Paul Delarue, translated from the French by Austin E. Fife (Knopf, $5).

A secretarial typescript, dated 26 November 1956, was prepared by the *New Yorker* from Auden's lost manuscript and is now in the Manuscripts Division of the New York Public Library. The printed text cleans up minor awkwardnesses in phrasing. Under the heading "'The Godchild of the Fairy in the Tower'" (p. 603), in the first sentence the *New Yorker* mistakenly emends the typescript's "in the French form" to "in the French form, from" instead of (as in *The Dyer's Hand*) "in the French from".

Auden's revisions of the *New Yorker* text for *The Dyer's Hand* are mostly stylistic. In the second paragraph he changed "that" to "why" in "no reason why grownups". At the end of the paragraph that begins "A religious rite" (p. 599) the magazine had "'John-of-the-Bear', one of the stories in *The Borzoi Book of Folk Tales*, edited by Paul Delarue, says". Similarly, immediately after the quotation from that story, the magazine had "another of the stories in the book," after "The Doctor and His Pupil,". In the paragraph that begins "Wishing is not" (p. 602), the magazine has "That, however . . . ogres that . . . that in real life"; the book changes the three instances of "that" to "This", "who", and "which". In the paragraph that begins "A game, of course," the book corrects the magazine by omitting "and" before "manipulate the world". In the paragraph that begins "The other law" the magazine has "that they must", which the book revises to "which all must". In the description of "The Lost Children", the book revises the magazine's "nor is the reason there should . . . cross before" to "nor is any reason given why there should . . . cross when they set out."

The Dyer's Hand omits from the *New Yorker* text an additional passage that occurs at the end:

I wish I could say nice things about the translation of this book, but it shows defects that I cannot pass over in silence. I have not seen the French text, but when I read, "A *coal miner* whose hovel of branches stood in the wood," I cannot but think that he was really a charcoal burner. However a prince may be addressed in French, in English he is Your Highness, not Your Excellency. A proofreader should have caught "Let's transform ourselves, you into a pear tree, and I into an old woman." And no one, even though he is translating from a foreign tongue, should write such sentences as these:

He, seeing her fright, reassured her by explaining to her that he could become a man when he chose, either day or night.

At the end of a moment when the club was well entertained at their expense, and seeing them almost at the end of their strength: "Wretches!" he said.

As they were passing near a house where a man was busy heating his oven, having in his hand a long iron fork, the knight stopped.

Or else one asks a man whom one wants to separate from his wife in order to deceive him the easier to supply some undefined object having a strange name, and the man receives from a fairy a wand that permits him to cause beings to stick together in postures that are sometimes improper, and he brings in the chain thus formed, which he calls by the name he has been told.

The illustrations, if not remarkable, are in good taste, and that, in books of this kind, is as rare as it is praiseworthy.

I cannot guess what Auden had in mind when he wrote that a proofreader should have caught "Let's transform ourselves, you into a pear tree and I into an old woman", as the sentence is not obviously wrong (unless he thought it obvious that "into a pear tree" should have been "into a pear on a pear tree"). Auden may have objected to a version of the sentence that appeared only in the proof copy that he perhaps was sent for review, as the published book does not have the version that Auden quotes, but instead has the last phrase as "you into a pear on a pear tree and I into an old woman who wants to knock it down".

BROTHERS & OTHERS

Page 605.

Based on Auden's Oxford lecture, "The Alienated City, I: Reflections on *The Merchant of Venice*", delivered on 9 May 1960.

In the paragraph that begins "Recent history" (p. 608) "Jew of Malta" perhaps should not be italicized, as Auden is referring to the character, not the play.

In the paragraph that begins "As a society, Venice" (p. 617), in the copy he gave to Kallman, now in the Harry Ransom Center at Texas, Auden corrected "the social organization" to "a social organization".

INTERLUDE: WEST'S DISEASE

Page 619.

Reprinted with minor changes from the *Griffin*, May 1957, where it was titled "West's Disease" and was a review of *The Complete Works of Nathanael West* (Farrar, Straus and Cudahy, $5).

In the first paragraph the magazine has "sensible but not very" where the book has "sensible, not very". The paragraphing in the book differs slightly from that of the magazine.

THE JOKER IN THE PACK

Page 624.

Based on Auden's Oxford lecture, "The Alienated City, II: Reflections on *Othello*", delivered 16 May 1960, and on the text of the lecture published in *Encounter*, August 1961, as "The Alienated City: Reflections on Othello". The book version, in addition to changing the title, omits the subtitle of the magazine version and adds the epigraph.

In section I, in the opening paragraph, I have omitted the dash added in the book version between "accomplishes" and "(among". In the paragraph that begins "A distinction" (p. 625) the magazine has "the villain-figures like", changed in the book to "the villainous character—figures like". In the paragraph that begins "The villain" the magazine has "this grudge is comprehensible" where the book omits the redundant "grudge"; the magazine has "persuaded his father" and "Edmund has no need to betray Gloucester", which the book changes to "persuaded Glouces-ter" and "Edmund does not need to betray his father".

In the paragraph fragment that begins "To the degree" (p. 626), in the first sen-tence the magazine has "Iachimo's motive" and "simply a fear", which the book changes to "his motive" and "simply physical fear", and the book adds "in a duel". The magazine has "all Shakespeare's" for the book's "all the Shakespearian"; the book adds "clearly" in "are clearly not the principal", "with himself" in "his solilo-quies with himself", and adds "who desires revenge". In the first quotation in the same paragraph fragment, Auden (probably quoting from memory) inverted "art thou" so the line reads "now thou art my lieutenant" (misprinted "thou are" in *The Dyer's Hand*).

In the paragraph that begins "Since Othello" (p. 628) the magazine has "mur-derer and a man who holds", changed in the book to "murderer and also holds".

In section II, in the paragraph that begins "Social life" (p. 630), the magazine has "I should be a fool if I did not"; the book adds "little" to "little men". In the para-graph that begins "Two men" the book adds "and" in "and pedestrians". In the paragraph that begins "To convey this" (p. 633) the book changes "violent contrast between" to "violent contrast in".

In section III, in the paragraph that begins "This reaction" (p. 638) the magazine has "all-absorbing passion like that of Tristan and Isolde, but". In the paragraph fragment that begins "Though the imagery" the magazine has "fear he has sup-pressed", changed in the book to "fear he has so far repressed". In the paragraph that begins "Though her relation" (p. 641), the final sentence is identical in both the magazine and book versions, but the second "and", after "influence", should perhaps be replaced with a comma.

The book adds the section heading "IV" above the paragraph that begins "And so one comes" (p. 641), where the magazine has only a break; and in the same paragraph the magazine has "1961", which the book revises to "the middle of the twentieth century".

The book version also makes minor changes in number and tense.

POSTSCRIPT: INFERNAL SCIENCE

Page 643.

The aphorisms in this section were either newly written for *The Dyer's Hand* or extracted from notebooks and printed for the first time.

D. H. LAWRENCE

Page 647.

Based on Auden's Oxford lecture, "D. H. Lawrence", delivered on 13 May 1957. Auden's quotations slightly alter the originals.

In the fourth paragraph I have corrected "*Fantasia on*" to "*Fantasia of*". In the paragraph that begins "However, theory" (p. 649) the full stop after "aside" is plau-sible enough to retain, but should perhaps be changed to a comma; at my perhaps overzealous suggestion, this change was made in posthumous paperback printings of *The Dyer's Hand*.

MARIANNE MOORE

Page 660.

Partly based on Auden's Oxford lecture, "Marianne Moore", delivered on 4 May 1959. In preparation for the lecture, Auden had made his own tape recordings of Marianne Moore reading her poems, which he replayed during the lecture itself; at one point, she was heard asking "Am I loud enough, Wystan?" (information from John Fuller).

Auden quotes from the versions of Marianne Moore's poems that were in print at the time of his lecture but later revised. I have corrected only some minor typographical confusions.

THE AMERICAN SCENE

Page 671.

Based on the introduction Auden wrote in 1946 for a new edition of *The American Scene*, by Henry James; for details of the 1946 text, see *Prose II*, p. 538. The version in *The Dyer's Hand* was taken from an accurate reprint of the 1946 text in an anthology, *American Critical Essays: Twentieth Century*, selected by Harold Beaver (1959).

In the quotation that begins "The freedoms of the young three" (p. 672), *The Dyer's Hand* mistakenly corrects "shelter" to "shrill", which I have emended to James's word "shriller". I have made other minor corrections to quotations, as described in the notes to *Prose II*.

In revising the 1946 text for *The Dyer's Hand* Auden added the epigraph and made other cuts and changes as follows.

In the paragraph that begins "When the 'recent immigrant'" (p. 676) the phrase that follows the final dash in *The Dyer's Hand* replaces a longer passage in the 1946 text:

and by the irrevocable catastrophic alterations in Europe, on the other— what recognizable identity is there between the confident glittering hostess of those days and the bruised, beggared, debased, dead-beat harridan of ours? For has not what James called *The Margin* "by which the total of American life, huge as it already appears, is still so surrounded as to represent for the mind's eye on a general view but a scant central flotilla huddled as for very fear of the fathomless depth of water, the too formidable future" become the contemporary ambience of Europe, with this difference, that, while its vague and vast fluidity still, on the whole, continues to affect the observer on this side of the Atlantic as being, if not positively friendly, at least neutral, to the observer on the other side it looms with the extreme of menace, charged with every foreboding of worse disasters to come?

In the long paragraph that begins "To those who make" (p. 678), in the sentence that begins "This was natural" *The Dyer's Hand* omits "the" from "cause of the lack". After the parenthesis that ends "but Manichaen)" the 1946 text has a comma followed by "which it reveals in its democratic form by its persecution of dissident minorities".

In the paragraph that begins "As the issue" (p. 679), the 1946 version has a footnote after "the 'nature' of physics": "Is not the aesthetic effect of Rockefeller Center due to the *completeness* with which, in its handling of material and its design as a public building, this double neutrality of 'Nature' and 'Society' is accepted?"

Preceding the paragraph that begins "If one compares" (p. 679), the 1946 text has an additional paragraph:

> Poets living in democratic times will prefer the delineation of passions and ideas to that of persons and achievements. . . . The destinies of mankind, man himself taken aloof from his country and his age and standing in the presence of Nature and God, with his passions, his doubts, his rare prosperities and inconceivable wretchedness, will become the chief, if not the sole, theme of poetry. . . . I do not fear that the poetry of democratic nations will prove insipid or that it will fly too near the ground. I rather apprehend that it will be forever losing itself in the clouds and that it will range at last to purely imaginary regions. I fear that the productions of democratic poets may often be surcharged with immense and incoherent imagery, with exaggerated descriptions and strange creations; and that the fantastic beings of their brain may sometimes make us regret the world of reality.

In the paragraph that begins "If one compares" the 1946 text has, after "with Europeans," "those, that is, who grew up before the ruin of Europe,". Later in the paragraph, after "Yiddish) humor" the 1946 text has an additional sentence: "Compared with *The New Yorker*, how insufferably stuffy and provincial the comic papers of all other countries, even France, appear, and, politically and religiously, how incorrigibly shallow and naïve."

Preceding the section that begins "James wrote a short story" (p. 680) the 1946 text has an additional paragraph fragment followed by three additional paragraphs:

> It is from American critics like James and Eliot that we Europeans have learned to understand our social and literary traditions in a way we could never have learned by ourselves, for they, with natural ease, look at our past, as it is extremely difficult for us to look, with contemporary eyes. Eliot's criticism of Milton, for example, may be unjustified, but only an American could have made it in such a way that it deserves serious consideration from lovers of Milton; an Englishman might have criticized him, but it would have been for some personal reason, like annoying his father.

> It is harder for an American than it is for a European to become a good writer, but if he succeeds, he contributes something unique; he sees something and says it in a way that no one before him has said it. Think of the important American writers of the past—Poe, Emerson, Hawthorne, Mel-

ville, Whitman, Emily Dickinson, Henry Adams, Henry James—or of any group of contemporary American poets—Eliot, Frost, Marianne Moore, Cummings, Wallace Stevens, Laura Riding—could any European country (except, possibly, Germany) produce writers who in subject matter, temperament, language, are so utterly unlike one another or anybody else? (Blake and Hopkins are the only English poets I can think of who might have been Americans.) Further, without mentioning names, is there any country where discipleship is attended by such disastrously banal results, in contrast to Europe where apprenticeship is the normal and fruitful state for the beginner?

The great danger for the young American writer is impatience. A wise uncle would advise him thus: "Publish nothing before you are thirty but study, absorb, experiment. Take at least three years over every book. Be very careful about your health and lead a life as regular as a commuter's. Above all, do not write your autobiography, for your childhood is literally the whole of your capital."

The great danger for the European writer on the other hand is, or rather was, indolence. (For the present and future, as the novels of Kafka testify, his situation is probably to be the "American" one.) It was easier for him to write fairly well, but much harder to write as well as he possibly could, because he was a cultural *rentier*. His problem was how to possess the Past, to do which he had to choose a present, and he was always tempted to think that rebellion against the Past was such a choice, which it was not, for the rebel is a mirror image of the conformist. He had in fact to become by art what the American writer is by nature, *isolated*, and perhaps the only advice as to how to achieve this that *his* wise uncle could have given was: "Get out, or get drunk, or get ill."

The text in *The Dyer's Hand* also has many minor copyediting changes to spelling and punctuation.

POSTSCRIPT: ROME *v.* MONTICELLO

Page 681.

These notes, which continue the argument about *romanitas* in "The American Scene", seem to have been newly written for *The Dyer's Hand.*

RED RIBBON ON A WHITE HORSE

Page 682.

Based on the introduction written for the 1950 first edition of Anzia Yezierska's book. For the elaborate prepublication history of the 1950 version of the text, see *Prose III*, p. 719.

The edited version of the 1950 introduction printed in *Prose III* (p. 177) restores many passages that had been cut at Yezierska's request from Auden's typescript. The version printed in *The Dyer's Hand* closely matches the shorter version published in 1950.

The Dyer's Hand adds the epigraph to the essay and the footnote to the opening sentence. In the first paragraph *The Dyer's Hand* revises "as truthful" to "so truthful". In the second paragraph, *The Dyer's Hand* revises "he has a sensible answer, say:" to "he can give a sensible answer, like,".

In the paragraph that begins "Moreover, in the" (p. 684) *The Dyer's Hand* revises "such a total disregard of their human rights" to "such contempt". In the paragraph that begins "So she begins" (p. 685) *The Dyer's Hand* drops "a" from "or a wicked"; I have emended "waves her hand" to the 1950 reading "waves her wand". In the paragraph that begins "The sudden paralysis" *The Dyer's Hand* revises "the reason for this is" to "one reason for this may be"; later in the paragraph, after "book is in danger", *The Dyer's Hand* omits a phrase between commas, "because of the unreality of such an attempt".

In the paragraph that begins "The Arts Project" (p. 686) *The Dyer's Hand* revises "Noblest because" to "Noble because" and, at the end of the paragraph, revises "in what you ask" to "in what you are asking". Here and throughout *The Dyer's Hand* inserts "the" before "W.P.A."

In the paragraph that begins "Among her companions" (p. 687) *The Dyer's Hand* revises "though she realized it only after she had left" to "though only she [*sic*] realized this after it was over"; I have moved "only" after "she", although Auden conceivably intended to place it after "this".

The Dyer's Hand adds the attribution to Edward Thomas (from his poem "Home"). In the paragraph fragment that begins "No, the accidental" *The Dyer's Hand* revises "she must look" to "she had to look"; in the 1950 text this sentence ends with a semicolon, followed by: "where she went and what she found the reader can learn for himself." The closing phrase of the essay reads in the 1950 text "for the natural . . . tradition is rapidly disappearing", revised in *The Dyer's Hand* to "as the natural . . . tradition rapidly disappears".

In the opening sentence I have left uncorrected, as many copyeditors did over the years, Auden's misattribution to the Preamble to the Constitution of a phrase from the Declaration of Independence; it was corrected by the publisher in the 1968 paperback edition.

In the paragraph that begins "It is easy" (p. 687) *The Dyer's Hand* has "might just as well have been honest—and I dare say would have been glad to—given them". This seems like a typist's or compositor's error in which "have been honest" has been misplaced, and I have restored the reading of the 1950 version, which places it after the second dash and adds a comma after "honest".

Postscript: The Almighty Dollar

Page 688.

This section seems to have been newly written for *The Dyer's Hand*, although the final sentence paraphrases a sentence from "Transplanted Englishman Views U.S.", written in 1953: "When Europeans call Americans materialistic, what they ought to say is that Americans don't respect matter enough" (*Prose III*, p. 374, and a similar remark from a broadcast, p. 382).

ROBERT FROST

Page 689.

Based on Auden's Oxford lecture, "Robert Frost", delivered on 6 May 1957. A corrected typescript of the first section, up to the quotation that begins "We're too unseparate" (p. 694), is in the Berg Collection, as is a notebook with early drafts.

In the paragraph fragment that begins "She is, rather" (p. 697) "Dura Virum Nutrix" (stern nurse of men) is the motto of the Sedbergh School, the culture of which fascinated Auden during the 1920s.

AMERICAN POETRY

Page 701.

A revised and expanded version of Auden's introduction to his anthology *The Faber Book of Modern American Verse*, published in 1956 (*Prose III*, p. 506); for a history of the anthology itself, see *Prose III*, p. 634. I have made some minor emendations, partly on the basis of the text of the version of the text that appeared in the *Anchor Review* in 1955, as one of two essays under the title "The Anglo-American Difference: Two Views" (the other view was written by David Daiches).

The text in *The Dyer's Hand* is based on that of the introduction to the anthology. *The Dyer's Hand* adds the epigraph and makes some minor stylistic changes from the version printed in 1956. In the paragraph that begins "Normally, in" (p. 702) *The Dyer's Hand* corrects the allusion from the "King's" to the "Queen's" English. In the same paragraph the quotation that begins "the letter" is from Marianne Moore's "England", where it immediately follows the lines quoted in the epigraph to "The American Scene" (p. 671).

In the paragraph that begins "To be able" (p. 706), immediately before the quotation from Goethe, the 1956 text has an additional sentence: "(In the field with which we are here concerned, one symptom of this is that curious American phenomenon, the class in 'Creative Writing'.)" After the closing words of this paragraph ("genuine revolution"), *The Dyer's Hand* inserts new material that extends to the words "meaning is quite distinct" in the middle of the paragraph that begins "The War of Independence" (p. 707). In the 1956 text there is no break after "genuine revolution" and the paragraph continues to the end of the paragraph that (in *The Dyer's Hand*) begins "The War of Independence". However, at the point where *The Dyer's Hand* inserts this new material, the 1956 text has a footnote: "1829, though bloodless, was a more revolutionary year than 1776."

The Dyer's Hand adds the five paragraphs from "The American had not" (p. 707) through the end of the paragraph that begins "The achievement of" (p. 708).

In the paragraph fragment that begins "The last sentence" (p. 709) *The Dyer's Hand* corrects "average here" to "average hero". In the paragraph that begins "There are advantages" (p. 710) *The Dyer's Hand* compresses the first half of a sentence that reads in the 1956 text: "American poetry has many tones, a man talking to himself or one intimate friend, a prophet crying in the wilderness, but the easygoing tone of a man talking to a group of his peers is rare;". In the middle of the paragraph, after "will be shocked", the 1956 text has a parenthetical sentence that alludes to the Kenyon College school of poets influenced by John Crowe Ransom: "(In this Cambridge-on-the-Cam is perhaps a few leagues nearer Gambier, Ohio than is Oxford-on-Thames.)" At the end of the paragraph, after "his own manner", the 1956 text has a footnote:

The undeniable appearance in the States during the last fifteen years or so of a certain literary conformity, of a proper and authorized way to write poetry is a new and disquieting symptom, which I cannot pretend to be able to explain fully. The role of the American college as a patron of poets has been discussed a good deal both here and in England. Those who criticize it, often with some reason, fail to suggest a better alternative. It would be nice if the colleges could ask no more from the poets in return for their keep than occasional pieces, a Commencement Day masque or an elegy on a deceased trustee; if that is too much to ask, then the poets themselves should at least demand that they give academic courses in the literature of the dead and refuse to have anything to do with modern literature or courses in writing. There has been a vast output of critical studies in contemporary poetry, some of them first rate, but I do not think that, as a rule, a poet should read or write them.

In the paragraph that begins "Plato, following" (p. 710) the phrase "following Damon of Athens" is added in *The Dyer's Hand.*

At the end of the essay, after a break the 1956 text adds the following paragraphs that refer to the original anthology:

Exigencies of space have compelled me to draw a line which is necessarily arbitrary, excluding all poets born after 1923. This does not mean, of course, that I think no one under thirty worthy of inclusion.

Two obvious omissions will be noted. If the decisive factors in determining the sensibility of a poet belong to the first twenty years of his life, then Mr T. S. Eliot is an American poet whatever his citizenship. I have, however, with his consent, left him out of this collection because, since its primary purpose is to give the English reader a broad picture of American poetry, the space that could be gained for less familiar work by omitting one whose work is as well known in England as his seemed to justify such a course. The second omission, at her insistence and to my regret, is Miss Laura Riding.

In the paragraph that begins "This dependence" (p. 708) I have restored a comma after "nothing to do" and have restored some other minor punctuation on the basis of the 1956 texts.

NOTES ON THE COMIC

Page 715.

This is a largely rewritten version of an essay with the same title that Auden published in *Thought*, Spring 1952 (*Prose III*, p. 307). Auden's other essays in *Thought* that he revised for *The Dyer's Hand* are "The Virgin & The Dynamo" (p. 497) and "Balaam and His Ass" (p. 528).

Auden so extensively revised the 1952 essay when preparing *The Dyer's Hand* that a detailed collation would be impractical. Much material from the 1952 version is omitted; much is newly added. *The Dyer's Hand* adds the two epigraphs and expands the opening section, "General Definition". It drops a section in the *Thought* version headed "The Hierarchy of Universals". It adds the part-heading "Verbal Humor" and much of the material up to the heading "Literary Parody, and Visual Caricature". *The Dyer's Hand* drops the entire Part II of the *Thought* version, headed "Falstaff, or the Comic Presentation of the State of Grace", and transfers much of its material to "The Prince's Dog".

In the paragraph that begins "Words which rhyme" (p. 721) the joke at the end alludes to the informal name of Christ Church, "the House". In the paragraph that begins "The comic rhyme" "erotic blacks" is a spoonerism for "erratic blocks".

Don Juan

Page 725.

Based on Auden's Oxford lecture, "Byron's Don Juan", delivered on 12 May 1958. Some material in this essay appears in different form in "The Life of a That-There Poet" (p. 153); some parts are rewritten from sections of an essay published only in a French translation in *Preuves*, May 1952, "De Droite et de Gauche" (*Prose III*, p. 741).

The BBC broadcast Auden's lecture in the Third Programme two days after he delivered it; an unreliable transcript is in the BBC Written Archives Centre. When revising the lecture for *The Dyer's Hand* Auden omitted a few passages that duplicated material in "Notes on the Comic". He also dropped a few passages of explanation that perhaps seemed redundant in print; for example, in the paragraph that begins "Most readers" (p. 729), after "seduction is his vocation" the lecture continues, after a comma, "as in others it might be medicine or poetry. For him all women, beautiful or ugly, young or old, were equal. And the sole difference between them is their position in an arithmetical sequence. Alice is 674, Jane is 675."

In the paragraph that begins "His attempts" (p. 732) the second word is an emendation for "attempt". Near the end of the paragraph that begins "When he stopped" (p. 740), the printed texts have "after his death maîtresse devoted herself"; Auden deleted the unnecessary "maîtresse" in the marked copy now at Texas.

For the reference to William Stewart Rose in the paragraph that begins "Byron's poetry is the most" (p. 731), see the notes to "The Life of a That-There Poet" (p. 915).

Dingley Dell & The Fleet

Page 741.

Based on Auden's Oxford lecture, "Dingley Dell and the Fleet: Reflections on *Pickwick Papers*", delivered on 26 May 1958.

In the list of attributes of Eden, I have adopted Monroe K. Spears's suggestion (in a letter to Auden) that in item (10) the printed text's dash after "expulsion" should instead be an equals sign. I have corrected some minor errors in quotations (probably errors by a typist) and a few obvious printer's errors.

In the first sentence of the final paragraph the phrase "with the law" is an addition that Auden noted in the list of corrections that he sent to Monroe K. Spears. The phrase was also added to the 1968 paperback reprint, but, in adding it, the compositor mistakenly omitted the remainder of the sentence ("without appearing, in his own eyes, to suffer"). The omitted phrase was restored in the 1989 paperback edition.

Postscript: The Frivolous & The Earnest

Page 756.

A few sentences of this newly written section express the same thoughts that appear in different form in various earlier essays, especially "The Things Which are Caesar's", published in *Theology* in 1950 (*Prose III*, p. 196).

In the second to last section, the mistaken attribution to the Preamble to the Constitution of a phrase from the Declaration of Independence was corrected in a posthumous 1989 reprint, but the mistake was Auden's so I have let it stand. See also the notes to "Red Ribbon on a White Horse" (p. 968).

Genius & Apostle

Page 759.

Based on Auden's penultimate Oxford lecture, "The Genius and the Apostle: A Problem of Poetic Presentation", delivered on 24 October 1960. Auden wrote to Orlan Fox on 5 September 1960: "Must return to my last Oxford lectures. *What* a relief it will be when they are done" (Berg Collection).

Sections I and II of this essay are partly newly written, partly expanded and rearranged from Auden's foreword to a translation of Ibsen's *Brand*, published in 1960 ("Foreword: Brand *versus* Peer", p. 230). Section III is excerpted, with minor changes in wording, from the essay "The Ironic Hero", published in 1949.

In section I, the paragraphs from "The kinship of the poet" through "In their games" (pp. 762–64) are adapted and expanded from the similar paragraphs in the foreword to *Brand* (pp. 233–35).

In section II, the paragraphs from "In the case of any" through the penultimate sentence of the paragraph that follows (p. 766) are adapted from the corresponding material in the foreword (p. 231). The paragraphs from "Thus, he gives" through the end of section II (pp. 769–71) are adapted and rearranged from the paragraphs in the foreword from "It is very difficult to conceive" through "Ejnar is, as it were" (pp. 235–37).

In section III (pp. 771–75), taking material from "The Ironic Hero", Auden reused the sections from "The Knight Errant" to the end, omitting the section headed "Sancho Panza and Don Quixote" and the two final sentences (see *Prose II*, pp. 380–84). In addition to minor grammatical changes, *The Dyer's Hand* makes the following revisions.

In the 1949 text the opening sentence, before the list, ends "epic hero, i.e. the Knight Errant" and item (a) lacks the opening "He".

In the paragraph that begins "The worldly villain" *The Dyer's Hand* replaces the original opening "The tragic hero" with "The worldly villain like Macbeth", alters "whose nature he knows" to "of the nature of which he has a shrewd idea", omits "and" before "each success", and, after "his madness", replaces the 1949 parenthesis "(e.g. Iago)" with "but in the end he fails and is brought to despair and death."

In the paragraph that begins "To have faith in something", in item (a) *The Dyer's Hand* replaces "the latter" with "the object of faith".

In the paragraph that begins "The world of the Romances" the opening of the sentence that begins "When he is in one of his spells, Don Quixote," replaces the 1949 version, "Don Quixote when in one of his spells,".

Two revisions to this essay were noted in Auden's list of changes that he sent to Monroe K. Spears and were made in the 1968 paperback edition: in the paragraph that begins "In their games" (p. 764) "courage to be a poet" was revised to "courage to become a poet"; and in the paragraph that begins "In the character of Brand" (p. 769) "his motives" is corrected to "whose motives".

In the paragraph that begins "The worldly villain" (p. 772) I have removed a stray open parenthesis before "Don Quixote is".

POSTSCRIPT: CHRISTIANITY & ART

Page 775.

Most of this material seems to have been newly written for *The Dyer's Hand*. The section was first published as part III ("Postscript. Christianity & Art") of "The Poet & The City", *Massachusetts Review*, Spring 1962; see the notes to "The Poet & The City" (p. 952) for further details.

In the opening sentence, I have followed the *Massachusetts Review* in capitalizing "Science", and in the section that begins "The only kind" (p. 776) I have followed the magazine in capitalizing "Gospel". At the end of the paragraph that begins "The Incarnation" (p. 776) the magazine has the error "impossible" for "impassible". In the quotation from Kassner (p. 777) the magazine has "Word made Flesh" for "Word being made Flesh" and "What else could give us" for "What gives us"; the book moves the identification of the source from the sentence that precedes the quotation ("pointed out in *Die Geburt Christi*") to the end of the quotation; in the quotation itself, following the style in the magazine, I have replaced two sets of parentheses with square brackets.

In the paragraph that begins "The imagination" (p. 777) the magazine has "only recognize these", changed in the book to "only recognize these ones". In the paragraph that begins "As soon, however" (p. 778), in the first sentence the magazine has "abolished", changed in the book to "reabolished".

NOTES ON MUSIC AND OPERA

Page 783.

A revised version, with cuts and additions, of the essay "Some Reflections on Music and Opera", published in *Partisan Review* in January–February 1952 (*Prose III*, p. 296). See the notes to this essay in *Prose III* for details of its complicated history.

The version in *The Dyer's Hand* adds the two epigraphs. In the first section, the two sentences "Our experience of Time" through "than repetition" replace the

1952 version's one-word sentence "Choice." In the section that begins "Lacking a historical" the 1952 version has "the Greek theories of music", revised in *The Dyer's Hand* to "the Greeks, in their theories of music,".

The section that begins "The difference (p. 784) in the 1952 version opens "This difference"; in the third paragraph of this section, *The Dyer's Hand* omits "in" from "and in seeing with down" and twice replaces "an experience" with "our experience". In the section that begins "If music in general" (p. 786), at the end of the first paragraph, *The Dyer's Hand* corrects "maniacal busybody" to "musical busybody". In the section that begins "In opera the orchestra" (p. 788) *The Dyer's Hand* revises "where it is played" to "when it is played". *The Dyer's Hand* omits a section that in 1952 followed the one that begins "In opera the orchestra"; see *Prose III*, p. 301.

In the paragraph that begins "If the librettist" (p. 788) *The Dyer's Hand* omits a sentence that in 1952 followed "do what they are told": "Much as I admire Hofmannsthal's libretto for *Rosenkavalier,* it is, I think, too near real poetry. The Marschallin's monologue in Act I, for instance, is so full of interesting detail that the voice line is hampered in trying to follow everything." In the next sentence, after "*La Somnambula*", *The Dyer's Hand* omits "on the other hand".

In the section that begins "There have been" (p. 788) *The Dyer's Hand* changes "I am violently hostile to" to "I am not generally in favor of". (Auden began translating libretti into English after he had written the original version.) The next sentence begins in the 1952 text "Wagner in Italian or Verdi in English", revised in *The Dyer's Hand* to "Wagner or Strauss in English".

The section that begins "'History,' said Stephen Dedalus" (slightly misquoting the rest of the sentence) is added in *The Dyer's Hand.* In the final sentence, *The Dyer's Hand* omits "utterly" before "demolishes".

In the paragraph that begins "All of us have" (p. 785), in the sentence that begins "The paradox", I have added a comma after "source of pleasure".

In P. E. Vernon's experiment (p. 788), published in the *Musical Times*, 1 March 1929, the "nonsense verses" used ordinary English words in nonsensical phrases. Auden evidently learned of the experiment from Jacques Barzun, who cited Vernon's article (but not this detail) in his *Berlioz and the Romantic Century* (1950), which Auden read and reviewed (*Prose III*, p. 193).

CAV & PAG

Page 789.

Slightly revised from an essay Auden wrote for the libretto booklet that accompanied the RCA Victor Records recording of *Cavalleria Rusticana* and *I Pagliacci*, released in 1953 (*Prose III*, p. 358). I cannot explain the curiously stiff style of this piece, which is unlike anything else in Auden's later prose. He may deliberately have written the piece in a style that an editor at the record company required for libretto booklets.

The Dyer's Hand adds the epigraph, slightly revises verb number and tenses, and omits the translations of Italian phrases provided in 1953, presumably by the record company. In the first paragraph *The Dyer's Hand* revises, in the first sentence, "structure" to "structures"; in the second sentence revises "in part the result of" to "in part due to"; and in the third sentence adds "in" before "exactly". In the paragraph that begins "Suppose that a dramatist" (p. 790) *The Dyer's Hand* revises "really free" to "most free", omits "who are" before "least in", and revises "others" to "other people".

In the paragraph that begins "At most periods" the 1953 version has "if he commits one, we feel he must be mad and therefore not responsible, and if he refrains we feel", revised in the book to "if the poor man refrains from committing one, we feel". In the paragraph that begins "Santuzza's seduction" (p. 792), in the sentence that begins "Thanks to them", *The Dyer's Hand* corrects "rhythmical significance" to "ritual significance". In the paragraph that begins "If the interplay" (p. 793), in the sentence that begins "Firstly", I have restored the 1953 version "through it", which *The Dyer's Hand* mistakenly alters to "through its". In the sentence that begins "We are all actors" *The Dyer's Hand* removes "with others" from before "to hide our real feelings" and inserts "for others" after it.

In the paragraph that begins "In the Prologue" (p. 793) *The Dyer's Hand* reverses the 1953 order of the words "*sarò tua*" but both readings occur in texts of the opera. In the sentence that follows, *The Dyer's Hand* inserts "speaking" before "as herself". In the paragraph that begins "About the music" *The Dyer's Hand* omits, after "new kind of opera!" these additional sentences in the same fictional quotation: "How shall I classify it? I've got it. *Verismo*."

In the paragraph that begins "Comparing one" (p. 794), *The Dyer's Hand* inserts "e.g." after "*Rusticana*" and reduces "song, and the drinking song seem to me pretty *imaginary*. Yet, in the dramatic" to "song, but, in the dramatic".

Before the opening sentence of the paragraph that begins "All the various" (p. 794) the 1953 text has a sentence omitted in the book: "The idea of *verismo* may have meant a lot to Mascagni and Leoncavallo; I don't know." In the final paragraph *The Dyer's Hand* revises "we, not the work," to "ourselves, not the works,"

At the end of the paragraph that begins "In the Prologue" (p. 793) both printed versions italicize the last word, "idealists". I suspect that Auden may have written a horizontal line after this paragraph to indicate a break in the text, and a typist or compositor misinterpreted it as an italicization of the word that chanced to be above it. I have removed the italicization but have not inserted an (entirely speculative) additional break.

TRANSLATING OPERA LIBRETTI

Page 795.

Based on Auden's Oxford lecture, with the same title, delivered on 11 May 1959. Auden's attribution of coauthorship to Chester Kallman may have been a courtesy on Auden's part, but some of the thinking behind the piece probably derived from Auden's talks with Kallman about their translations. I have corrected some minor typographical errors, and, in the first word of the concluding paragraph, have emended "Any one" to "Anyone".

In the paragraph that begins "Nor in the finale" (p. 799) the quoted lines occur in the scene that precedes the finale.

Music in Shakespeare

Page 807.

Based on Auden's Oxford lecture "The Dramatic Use of Music in Shakespeare's Plays", delivered on 20 May 1957, and on the text of the lecture published in *Encounter*, December 1957, as "Music in Shakespeare: Its Dramatic Use in His Plays".

In revising the text in *Encounter* for the book, Auden added the epigraph and dropped the subtitle. In addition to the changes noted below, the book has minor changes in spelling and in the numbers and tenses of verbs.

After the paragraph that begins "Nobody today" (p. 808) the magazine has an additional paragraph:

Indeed, for us there is something comic about Milton's lines

> the fair music that all creatures made
> To their great Lord, whose love their motion swayed
> In perfect Diapason

with its suggestion that, in the music of Paradise, the only musical interval is the octave.

The paragraph that begins "Whether he" (p. 809) begins in the magazine "Whether he cared for music itself or not,". In the list in the paragraph that begins "If Shakespeare took" (p. 810), in item (3), I have restored the magazine's "about this character" where the book has "about his character". In the same item, the magazine's "so well" was probably changed by an editor to the book's "as well".

In the paragraph that begins "In no other art" (p. 811) the magazine ends the second sentence, "in painting, though it may sound rather far-fetched."

In the paragraph that begins "We find two types of song" (p. 815), the magazine's version reads in full: "We find two types of song in Shakespeare's plays, the called-for song and the impromptu song." In the next paragraph the magazine begins "A called-for song is one which" and has "wishes to hear some music, and, while it lasts, all action and speech are halted" (the book adds "until the song is over"). In the remainder of the paragraph, the magazine has "in contemporary performances of Shakespeare's plays" (reduced by the book to "in performances of Shakespeare"). In the next paragraph, the magazine begins "On the stage, this means that the character so asked ceases"; the next sentence begins in the magazine "We are thinking, of course, of songs introduced into a play written in verse or prose which is spoken, not of arias in an opera", and continues "itself song, and we forget that the singers are performers as we forget".

The paragraph that begins "An Elizabethan theatrical" (p. 816) in the magazine has "songs occurred, would therefore have to hire at least one person as a singer rather than as an actor". The following paragraph, which begins "Yet, minor character" has in the magazine "character which is peculiar to those who practise his mystery", revised in the book to "character as a professional musician"; in the next sentence the magazine lacks "who is" before "certain of his talents".

The paragraph fragment that begins "In the dialogue between Peter" (p. 816) is, in the magazine, a paragraph that begins "And in the scene between Peter"; the

magazine has "musicians and their rich", where the book replaces "and" with "with
that of". Later in the paragraph the magazine has "have at weddings; music is something you have to make if", changed in the book to "have at a wedding; music is
something you have to play if".

In Section V the book formats the subheadings inconsistently; Auden seems to
have had no preference, so I have followed the formatting that the book uses in the
latter part of the section.

The paragraph that begins "More mischief" (p. 820) begins in the magazine
"Worse mischief", and has "as her sister does" (corrected to "cousin" in the book).

The paragraph that begins "Jacques' extemporary verse" (p. 821) is preceded in
the book by a narrow break which may have been inserted by a compositor in order
to make two facing pages have equal lengths. The break does not occur in the
magazine, and I have omitted it.

In the paragraph that begins "Against their reality" (p. 822) the magazine has
"but then" before "drops her". In the paragraph that begins "Outside the pastures"
(p. 823) the magazine begins "Again, outside the pastures"; and the following paragraph begins in the magazine "And again, Shakespeare", not "Again, Shakespeare".

In the paragraph that begins "The impromptu singer" (p. 823) the magazine
begins the paragraph with two additional sentences written for the lecture hall: "So
much for the called-for song. Let us now consider the impromptu." In the paragraph that begins "Generally, of course" the magazine has "is first a work-song,
which", revised in the book to "is, firstly, a labor song which".

In the paragraph fragment that begins "We are shown" (p. 824) the magazine has
"affect on the brain" for the book's "effect on the brain".

INDEX OF TITLES AND
BOOKS REVIEWED

This index includes titles of each of the works printed or described in this edition and the titles and authors of the books Auden reviewed.

Titles of Auden's works that were originally published (or intended to be published) as separate books or pamphlets are printed in LARGE AND SMALL CAPITALS. Titles of books and other works that Auden edited or reviewed are in *italics*. Titles of Auden's essays and reviews are all printed in roman type, as are the names of authors of books reviewed, the names of persons who were the subjects of his essays, and the names of his coauthors.